W9-AZF-166

DOUGLAS F. GREER
SAN JOSE STATE UNIVERSITY

Business, Government, and Society

THIRD EDITION

Macmillan Publishing Company
New York

Collier Macmillan Canada, Inc.
Toronto

Maxwell Macmillan International
New York • Oxford • Singapore • Sydney

To Kathy, Den, Peg, Chris, and John
(in chronological order of their influence)

Editor: Jill Lectka
Production Supervisor: John Travis
Production Manager: Sandra Moore
Text Designer: Anne Flanagan
Cover Designer: Cathleen Norz
Cover photograph © Westlight, Inc.
This book is set in Times Roman by Compset, Inc. and printed and
bound by Halliday. The cover was printed by Lehigh Press.

Copyright © 1993 by Macmillan Publishing Company, a division of
Macmillan, Inc.

Printed in the United States of America

All rights reserved. No part of this book may be reproduced or transmitted in any form or by any means, electronic or mechanical, including photocopying, recording, or any information storage and retrieval
system, without permission in writing from the publisher.

Earlier editions copyright © 1983 by Douglas F. Greer. Copyright
© 1987 by Macmillan Publishing Company.

Macmillan Publishing Company
866 Third Avenue, New York, New York 10022

Macmillan Publishing Company is part of the Maxwell Communication
Group of Companies.

Maxwell Macmillan Canada, Inc.
1200 Eglinton Avenue East
Suite 200
Don Mills, Ontario M3C 3N1

Library of Congress Cataloging in Publication Data
Greer, Douglas F.
   Business, government, and society / Douglas F. Greer.—3rd ed.
     p.   cm.
   Includes indexes.
   ISBN 0-02-347150-6
   1. Industry and state—United States.   2. Trade regulation—United
States.
IN PROCESS   92-434
                                                                CIP

Printing: 1 2 3 4 5 6 7 8   Year: 3 4 5 6 7 8 9 0 1 2

Preface

The march of events compels revision of any book on public policy that aspires to freshness. Such is true here. Countless instances of update in this third edition of *Business, Government, and Society* make it as current as possible. Its new topics include the following: Marketable permits for SO_2 abatement from power plants under the Clean Air Act of 1990; the revival of antitrust enforcement after President Reagan's departure from Washington; incentive regulation of electric power companies; price cap regulation in long-distance telecommunications; state deregulation of local telecommunications; the Civil Rights Act of 1991; deregulation and then reregulation of cable television; Japanese purchases of U.S. companies; relaxation of the Foreign Corrupt Practices Act; new competition in electric power from PURPA qualified facilities and independent producers; the FCC's new rules on TV syndication rights; the Supreme Court's reconsideration of the Robinson-Patman Act in *Texaco* v. *Hasbrouck*; Nintendo's brush with some renewed enforcement of the resale price maintenance law; continued consolidation and concentration in airlines under deregulation; the price fixing case involving elite universities; the FDA's efforts to speed up new drug approvals; and the adoption of airbags to meet passive restraint regulations in auto safety. Apart from policy changes, this third edition contains new statistics on the annual emissions of air pollutants, income differentials between men and women, farm subsidies, and many other issues.

No new chapters have been added. No old chapters have been dropped. Hence the basic format of previous editions remains intact, mainly because that format has been popular with professors and students.

Although the original format endures, a number of substantial revisions have been incorporated. These include the following:

- Expanded discussion of imperative versus teleological value judgments.
- A new approach to explaining the market's ideal operation and its problems.
- Expanded discussions of Ramsey prices and cross subsidies.
- Extended treatment of energy conservation as a new topic.
- Strategic trade policy as a major qualification to considerations of comparative advantage.
- Expanded discussion of the auto industry, import protection, and America's strength in the world economy.

This renewal offers another opportunity to thank all those who had a hand in making the first two editions of this book successful. Now my debts extend to a wider circle. I would like to thank Chris Colburn for his feedback during the development of the third edition and Carson Bays, George S. Cole, Louis Esposito, Bruce W.

Marion, William Nichols, and Eleanor C. Snellings for their valuable advice. John W. Wilson can be credited with assistance of various sorts, including space in his suite of offices close to the action in Washington, D.C. while I was on leave from the university during the 1991–1992 academic year. Several people at Macmillan likewise deserve thanks—John Travis, Jill Lectka, and the copyeditor, Shirley Covington of Jonesborough, Tennessee. I am especially grateful to my wife Lill for her editorial and typing skills.

D.F.G.

Brief Contents

Detailed Contents

PART I

Introduction and Overview

Chapter 1

Introduction: Functions and Values

The importance of the government-business relationship to the American people cannot be overestimated. Government and business are the key institutions of the nation; how they interact is of profound significance to all Americans.
— Arthur Selwyn Miller

R andomly pick any day in the life of the *Wall Street Journal*. What do you find? A parade of reports from the government and business front. Let's take the issue of March 21, 1991, for instance. The Supreme Court ruled that employers could not bar women of childbearing age from risky jobs because of potential harm to fetuses. The Justice Department rebuffed a proposal by a group of elite private universities that would have settled the department's investigation into allegations that the universities had violated the antitrust laws by collusively determining their tuitions. Eastern Airlines pleaded guilty and agreed to pay a $3.5 million fine for falsifying its maintenance records in violation of Federal Aviation Administration safety regulations. The National Highway Traffic Safety Administration revealed plans for a new rule that would require light trucks and vans to be equipped with automatic seat belts or air bags. A letter to the editor complained that the Federal Trade Commission had moved too slowly in a deceptive advertising case involving Kraft General Foods Corporation. All this on a typical day.

The purpose of this book is to give you a broad understanding of government policies toward business and their impact on society. Such an understanding will bring some order to the apparent chaos of government intervention. It will convert any newspaper clippings you might collect into something more than overgrown confetti.

The three main characters in this tale are business, government, and society. *Business* includes colossal corporations and small proprietorships. It encompasses manufacturing, mining, transportation, and everything in between. Business is conducted in markets, which comprise the central nervous system of our economy and which are the real focus of government intervention. *Government* spans federal, state, and local levels. It includes commissions, agencies, courts, and committees as well as the more familiar congresses, senates, and presidents. *Soci-*

ety of course includes those in business and government, but the term is meant to cover all of us taken together—consumers, students, employees, children, authors, whoever.

Ideally, business pursues its own self-interest by providing products and services that best satisfy the preferences of those in society, something that benefits both society and business. Profit is the incentive, the honey of this harmony. But profit can also be made in "antisocial" ways, so if for some reason business fails to meet the expectations of society, society may then call on government to straighten things out. Ideally, government responds with policies that best serve society's interests, again measured by private personal preferences. Unfortunately, government is likewise capable of failure, just as a would-be rescuer might throw a heavy life ring to a drowning man, inadvertently clubbing the poor fellow senseless. Stated differently, we attempt (1) to *explore* this interesting triangle of business, government, and society; (2) to *organize* the diverse relationships linking the triangle; (3) to *analyze* how business and government function; and (4) to *evaluate* how fully business and government satisfy the preferences and expectations of society.

Among the numerous specific issues that we address along the way, the following are apt to be of greatest interest. Why do just a few firms dominate some of our markets, such as those for autos, beer, telephone service, and aluminum? What are the effects of such dominance for profits, innovation, and efficiency? What policies attempt to check the power of big firms? What does government hope to accomplish with measures like truth-in-lending, grade rating, and product standardization? What is false advertising? What have been the costs and benefits of auto safety regulation and environmental protection policy? Are we running out of oil and natural gas? How has government regulated energy? What purposes do patents serve? Should we protect the auto, steel, electronics, and apparel in-dustries from foreign imports? What is the trend in radio and TV regulation? What will its impact be on the upcoming communications revolution?

Of course, not everything can be said all at once, so in these first four chapters comprising Part I we begin at the beginning. This chapter sets out some basic *definitions,* outlines the main *functions* that society calls on business and government to perform, and surveys the *values* that society uses in evaluating both business and government. In brief, the purpose of this chapter is to specify our preferences as a society, to delineate what is good and bad. By inference, we also indicate what problems arise when either business or government fails to satisfy those preferences.

On the business side, our focus is actually on markets rather than on business as such, because markets are the institutions through which businesses serve society's interests. Accordingly, we apply this chapter's findings to Chapter 2, which explains what is good and bad about markets. On the good side, markets can "regulate" businesses for society's great benefit, and the first object of Chapter 2 is to explain why such private free enterprise regulation is generally superior to government intervention. The second object is to show why markets are occasionally deficient. In Chapter 3 we shift attention to the government, detailing government's good and bad aspects. Finally, to conclude Part I, Chapter 4 surveys the main ideologies that help determine the mix of private free enterprise and government intervention that we actually experience in the United States. It also sketches the history of government intervention from our country's birth to the present.

Stated differently the purpose of these first chapters is threefold:

1. To explain the *problems* needing attention, such as monopoly power and hazardous pollution.
2. To specify potential policy *solutions* (including doing nothing) and to establish criteria,

3

such as benefit-cost analysis, for *choosing* among alternative solutions.

3. To survey the *feasibility* of implementing the various policy options by gaining an appreciation of *political ideologies and historical context.*

Lest you get irritated by all the theory you encounter at the outset, the importance of finding theoretical models that match problems with proper solutions can be illustrated by a poignant example of two competing theories. By far the most disturbing problem in seventeenth-century Monte Lupo, Italy, was the plague. On the one side were public health officials who correctly theorized from empirical study that the spread of the disease could be checked by enforcing a policy of quarantine and segregation on the populace. On the other side were the town's religious leaders who believed that the plague was a scourge sent by God to punish the people. Following this theory, they urged that everyone be brought together in massive religious processions and rituals to atone for their sins. Unfortunately, this second solution was implemented, partly because of political feasibilities. The people themselves preferred processions to quarantine regulations.[1]

I. Basic Definitions

Simply put, a **market** is an organized process by which buyers and sellers exchange goods and services for money. Notice that every market has two sides to it—a demand side (made up of buyers) and a supply side (made up of sellers). Notice also that markets can be local, regional, national, or international in scope. When the exchange alternatives of either buyers or sellers are geographically limited—as is true of barbering and cement manufacturing, for example—then exchange and competition are correspondingly limited in geographic scope. Strictly speaking, the word *industry* denotes a much broader con-

cept than the word *market* because an industry can include numerous local or regional markets. When we speak of the construction industry, we usually refer to something more than local business. In practice, however, *market* and *industry* are often used synonymously, without careful distinction—a practice we too follow when precision is not required.

Most generally, **government** is the process within a group for making and enforcing decisions that affect human behavior. Public government can claim a monopoly on the legitimate use of physical force or coercion within a given territory. Indeed, some scholars place particular emphasis on this matter of force:

> Legitimate force is the thread that runs through the inputs and outputs of the political system, giving it its special quality and salience and its coherence as a system. The inputs into the political system are all in some way related to claims for the employment of legitimate compulsion, whether these are demands for war or for recreational facilities. The outputs of the political system are also all in some way related to legitimate physical compulsion, however remote the relationship may be.[2]

The market and the government are institutions. An *institution* may be defined as selected elements of a scheme of values mobilized and coordinated to accomplish a particular purpose or function.[3] Accordingly, this definition implies that markets and governments have two principal aspects—a *value* aspect and a *functional* aspect.

II. The Functional Aspect

A. Markets

With respect to function, we rely on markets to cope with the fundamental problem of scarcity, which is what economics is all about. Scarcity would be no problem if wants were severely curtailed. Scarcity would be no problem if our productive capabilities knew no bounds. But, alas, neither of these conditions hold. We have neither limited wants nor unlimited resources. Quite the contrary, Americans are among the most prosperous people who have ever lived; yet we still want more goods and services—more than our limited resources of land, capital, labor, energy, and time can produce. Proof of this statement is easy: Markets, prices, wages, and all the other trappings of our economy would not exist save for scarcity.

To be more specific about the function of markets, crucial decisions must be made and the preferences of society must be accounted for in making those decisions. The *input function* of markets is to account for those preferences and signal scarcity's constraints. That is to say, buyers' and sellers' preferences are articulated and communicated through myriad markets by actions of paying and receiving. The *output function* of markets is to provide answers to the four basic questions that scarcity forces upon us:

1. *What goods and services shall we produce and in what amounts?* At first glance the answer may seem simple and obvious. We need such basics as food, clothing, and shelter. But even in this context our limitations impose trade-offs. Shall it be more "Twinkies" and less "Granola"; more apartments and fewer single-family dwellings; more sweaters and fewer jackets? What combination of goods is most desirable?

2. *How are goods and services to be produced?* Many different methods of production are possible for most goods. Cigars, for instance, can be made by man as well as by machine. What mixture of the two will it be? Should coal be mined by strip or underground methods? In short, what combination of resource commitments is most efficient?

3. *Who shall get and consume the goods and services we produce?* There are two aspects to this question. One aspect relates to income distribution—what share of our total national income should each household receive? The

other aspect relates to rationing of specific goods. Not enough gasoline can be produced for all drivers to get as much as they would like. Hence some form of rationing is required.

4. *How shall we maintain flexibility for changes over time?* No condition of scarcity is static, ironclad, or unchanging. Advances in technology and better educational attainments continually expand our productive capabilities. Consumer tastes also alter. Thus we are confronted with questions of change. Shall we convert to nuclear power, electric autos, and digital TVs? Decisions of acceptance and rejection must continually be made. Flexibility allows us to probe new opportunities as they arise.

By and large we entrust these decisions to the *market,* to millions of consumers, workers, employers, land owners, investors, and proprietors, each pursuing self-interest in the market place. *The function of markets is to coordinate and control this decentralized decision-making process, which answers these four crucial questions.*

B. The Government

Government, too, is an answer machine, one that dabbles, and in some countries even dominates, in deciding these economic questions of what, how, who, and what's new. Speaking more broadly to include the political system generally, the governmental process likewise has input functions and output functions.[4] The *input functions* include (1) preference articulation by means of citizens' letters, interest groups, referenda, and the like, (2) preference aggregation, mainly through party platforms, congressional compromises, coalitions, and broadly based interest groups like agriculture, and (3) political communication through governmental and independent media, mainly the press, radio, and TV. The *output functions* are, most broadly, (1) rule making or legislating, (2) rule application or law enforce-

---

Table 1–1
The Main Institutional Functions

Functions of the Market System	*Functions of the Government System*
Input Functions: 1. Preference articulation 2. Economic communication	*Input Functions:* 1. Preference articulation 2. Preference aggregation 3. Political communication
Output Functions: 1. Decide *what* to produce 2. Decide *how* to produce 3. Decide *who* gets the goodies 4. Decide *what's new*	*Output Functions:* 1. Rule making (legislative) 2. Rule application (executive) 3. Rule adjudication (judicial)

---

ment, and (3) rule adjudication in the judicial branch of government. Table 1–1 summarizes for both markets and government.

The main economic powers delegated to the U.S. federal government, as enumerated in Article 1, Section 8 of the Constitution, are the following:

- To lay and collect Taxes, Duties, Imports and Excises, to pay the Debts and provide for the common Defence and the general Welfare. . . .
- To borrow Money. . . .
- To regulate Commerce with foreign Nations and among the several States. . . .
- To coin Money, regulate the value thereof . . . and fix the Standard of Weights and Measures. . . .
- To establish Post Offices and Post Roads;
- To promote the progress of Science and useful Arts, by securing for limited Times to Authors and Inventors the exclusive Right to their respective Writing and Discoveries. . . .

The most important of these clauses for our purpose is the so-called commerce clause, which grants power "To regulate Commerce . . . among the several States. . . ." This plus the other clauses permits extensive government participation in deciding the economic questions of what,

how, who, and what's new, thereby nosing into the market's domain. Not mentioned among the four basic questions concerning scarcity is an economic area where the market formerly held free reign but now most definitely is the province of the federal government for good or ill—namely, maintenance of aggregate economic stability.

III. The Value Aspect

As far as values are concerned, our society generally believes that, at their best, markets tend to perform their functions of coordination and control very nicely.[5] That is to say, the market system accords well with many of our society's values by (1) typically providing fairly good answers to the four basic economic questions, and (2) arriving at these answers in an appealing way. Exactly what these answers are and exactly how the market system goes about arriving at them are discussed in the next chapter. Right now we need to explain which values we refer to and thereby specify what is meant here by "good" and "appealing." We also need to note that such favorable assessments of the market system imply rather unfavorable scores for the government in these matters. Two chief reasons for looking warily upon the government system are apparent from our previous discussion: (1) Government decision making entails preference aggregation to arrive at generally applicable policies—such as all cars must have safety belts—something that may brutalize individual preferences. (2) Lurking beneath practically all government policy is that unsavory element of coercion.

In the present context, **values** are simply generalized concepts of the desirable. They are objectives, ends, or aims that guide our attitudes and actions. Among the most generalized concepts of the desirable are such notions as "welfare and happiness," "freedom," "justice," and "equality." These may be called **ultimate** values because they reign supreme in the minds of most men and women.

Although these are truly noble aims, they are also too vague and too ill-defined to provide a basis for specific institutional arrangements and policy decisions; so, for purposes of actual application, they can be translated into more specific concepts—like "full employment" and "allocation efficiency"—which may be called **proximate** values. Table 1–2 presents a summary list of proximate values that are relevant here, together with the ultimate values from which they derive. Allocation efficiency, full employment, clean environment, and health and safety, for example, are several proximate values that convey the spirit of "welfare and happiness." The list is intended to be more illustrative than exhaustive, so only a brief discussion of it is warranted.

Table 1–2
Some Proximate Values and the Ultimate Values from Which They Derive

Ultimate Values	*Proximate Values*
Freedom	Free choice in consumption and occupation Free entry and investment Limited government intervention Free political parties National security
Equality	Diffusion of economic and political power Equal bargaining power for buyers/sellers Equal opportunity Limited income inequality
Justice and fairness	Prohibition of unfair practices Fair labor standards Honesty Full disclosure Fair return on fair value
Welfare and happiness	Allocation and technical efficiency Full employment Price stability Health and safety Clean environment
Progress	Rising real income Technological advancement Productivity improvement

Freedom. Proximate values reflecting freedom include such notions as "free choice in consumption and occupation," and "free entry and investment." They imply active, unhampered participation in the economic decision-making process by all of us. The market furthers these objectives because the market affords free expression to individual choice in deciding answers to the key economic questions outlined earlier—what, how, who, and what's new? Unfettered individual choice is possible *only* under favorable circumstances, however. For if markets are burdened with barriers to entry, monopoly power, price fixing, or similar restraints of trade—imposed *either* by government *or* by private groups—then this freedom is sharply curtailed. Although the government has often imposed these and other restraints (usually under the influence and for the benefit of special interest groups), most people in our society favor "limited government intervention" and "free political parties," both of which inhibit centralized command and coercion. Thus, to the extent government intervention is properly called for, most would probably agree that it should be for purposes of *preventing* private restraints of trade rather than for *imposing* official restraints.

Equality. When one person's freedom encroaches upon another person's freedom, some criterion is needed to resolve the conflict. In our society the ideal criterion is "equality" or "equity."[6] This usually means that everybody's preferences and aspirations are weighted equally, as in the political cliché: one man, one vote. In economics, the notion that each individual's dollar counts the same as anyone else's dollar reflects a similar sentiment. Among the more important proximate values stemming from equality are "a wide diffusion of economic and political power," "equal bargaining power on both sides of an exchange transaction," "equal opportunity, regardless of race, religion, sex, or national origin," and "*limited in*equality in the distribution of income." Under favorable conditions, the market

system can further these objectives as well as those associated with freedom.

Justice and Fairness. The market is often given high marks for justice and fairness because, under ideal circumstances, it generates answers to the key economic questions that are not arbitrary, despotic, or peremptory answers. Adam Smith's metaphorical "invisible hand" eloquently illustrates this deduction. Unfortunately, real-world circumstances often fall short of the ideal, so that free pursuit of profits in the marketplace may not always yield fair or just results. As Vernon Mund has written, "Profit can be made not only by producing more and better goods but also by using inferior materials, by artificially restricting supply to secure monopoly profits, by misleading and deceiving consumers, and by exploiting labor."[7] Thus, to account for these sad possibilities and to introduce several forms of market regulation that are discussed in later chapters, we have listed "full disclosure," "honesty," and "prohibition of unfair practices" among the proximate values of Table 1–2.

Welfare, Happiness, and Progress. The foregoing discussion of freedom, equality, justice, and fairness helps to explain our earlier statement that the market system arrives at answers to the key economic questions in a *particularly appealing way,* but it remains to be demonstrated that the answers themselves are *fairly good answers*. In other words, as far as markets are concerned, the foregoing values relate more to the decision-making process than to the decisions made—to *means* rather than to *ends*. So, what about ends? Fortunately for us, the answers provided by the market system (again under favorable circumstances) comport fairly well with our society's concepts of welfare, happiness, and progress. As already indicated, a thorough exploration of these answers is deferred until later chapters when we can elaborate on the meaning of the phrases "favorable circumstances" and "ideal conditions" that we have used interchangeably. Nevertheless, for a prelude, we can note briefly that the market system is generally efficient and flexible. Thus, markets answer the question "what will be produced" by allocating labor and material resources to the production of goods and services yielding the greatest social satisfaction. And with respect to the question of how goods are produced, markets encourage the use of low-cost production techniques that consume the least amount of scarce resources possible for a given bundle of output. Finally, flexibility: The market is generally receptive to good new ideas and new resource capabilities so that, with each passing year, we can produce more and better goods with less and less time, effort, and waste; all of which implies progress. As regards "clean environment" and "health and safety," which are also mentioned as proximate values in Table 1–2, the market alone has not performed very well in the past. The reason for this failure is discussed later.

Although these ultimate and proximate values are widely shared and vigorously advocated by most people in our society (why else would they pop up so conspicuously in most political speeches?), they are also sources of conflict, frustration, and disappointment simply because they are not always consistent with each other. Among the more obvious examples of inconsistency, consider the following:

1. "Health and safety" may be furthered by requiring seat belts and air bags in every auto, but this requirement interferes with "free choice in consumption."
2. Measures designed to procure a "clean environment," such as banning the use of sulfur-laden coal, may seriously diminish what we can achieve in the way of "rising real income."
3. Enforcement of "honesty" and the "prohibition of unfair practices" in the marketing of products may conflict with many people's concepts of "limited government intervention."
4. Patents may be deemed the best means of encouraging "technological progress," but each

patent confers monopolistic privileges that run counter to both "free entry" and "diffusion of economic power."
5. For a conflict between efficiency and equity, see the Appendix to this chapter.

Lest the picture painted by these examples look too bleak, we hasten to add that in many instances there may not be inconsistencies among values, and in other instances the inconsistencies may be so mild that they are amenable to compromise. Still, as just suggested, inconsistencies do exist and are often sharp, which helps to explain several important facts of political and economic life.

First, for various reasons (including material self-interest, educational background, emotional empathy, and social position) each individual gives differing *weights* and *definitions* to these values. It is the particular weight and definition that guides each person's judgment of conflicts among values, precluding the possibility of unanimous agreement on almost anything.

Second, several economic philosophies or schools of thought have evolved that differ primarily in terms of the weights they apply to these values and the definitions they give to them. Thus, for example, conservatives generally believe that freedom is superior to equality and fairness. They prefer less government intervention—even at the expense of more private monopoly power, greater consumer deception, and aggravated income inequalities. In contrast, liberals often stress equality and fairness over freedom, and their list of preferences is consequently quite different from that of conservatives.

Third, people's definitions and weights are by no means static or immutable. They obviously change with time and events. Indeed, economic policy formulation has been described as "a trial and error process of self-correcting value judgments."[8] Nothing is absolute or final, especially in this field. *Knowledge* and *policy* have within them and between them certain irreconcilable inconsistencies. They are both undergoing continuous review and revision, and opinions about both are strongly influenced by values.

IV. Ethics: Goals and Imperatives

Table 1–2 makes no distinction between moral and nonmoral values such as "justice" and "progressiveness." Likewise, it makes no distinction between ethical criteria based on achieving some ultimate goal, such as "efficiency," and ethical criteria based on moral imperatives such as "honesty." Yet a full understanding of how policies can be judged "right" and "wrong" rests on just such distinctions.

Moral philosophers inform us that there are two ethical standards for evaluating policies as outlined in Table 1–3.[9] One type is teleological, from the Greek word *telos,* or "end." A **teleological standard** judges the rightness or wrongness of acts, rules, and policies by the end results or ultimate nonmoral consequences they produce. Such ends might be the satisfaction of consumer preferences, the maximization of gross national product, or the speed of technological change.[10] Teleological standards are typically concerned with ends that are *continuously* variable, subject to *balancing,* and offer opportunities of *comparison.* An important example drawn from economics is "cost-benefit" analysis, which purports to satisfy society's preferences by (1) casting all the relevant effects of alternative policies into dollar terms, (2) comparing the costs and benefits, and (3) recommending the policy that, on balance, yields the greatest benefit less cost. A more general teleological rule is this: "An act *ought to be done* if and only if it or the rule under which it falls produces, will probably produce, or is intended to produce *a greater balance of good over evil* than any available alternative."[11]

In contrast, a nonteleological or **imperative standard** holds that actions or rules are morally right or wrong in and of themselves, regardless of their consequences or end effects. Thus a rule such as "Thou shalt not commit murder, no matter what," would be an imperative rule. "You should never lie," is another. Notice that such rules have a flavor of finality, have discrete "yes-no" qualities that cannot be quantified, have no reference to balancing good and bad consequences, and have an air of absoluteness.

To illustrate the two views, suppose that the government has the resources to build one of two dams, Dam A or Dam B, but not both. Suppose, further, that a benefit-cost analysis reveals net benefits of $3 billion for A and $2 billion for B. A teleological economist would say that A "ought to be built" because of the nice comparative consequences. Suppose, however, that either A or B

Table 1–3
A Comparison of Characteristics of Ethical Criteria

Teleological Ethics	*Imperative Ethics*
1. Some nonmoral end is served, e.g., satisfaction of consumer preferences	1. Rightness or wrongness intrinsic to the deed, e.g., honesty for its own sake
2. Continuous variables involved, e.g., dollar benefits and costs	2. Discrete prescriptions, e.g., do not kill
3. Balance or adding up involved	3. No balance, categorical imperative
4. Comparisons of policies to find which is "better"	4. Absolute, policies judged "right" or "wrong" independently

would completely wipe out three species of mammals. An environmentalist adopting an imperative standard might say "we should build *neither* A or B" because it is "immoral" to commit "genocide" against other species. Our teleological economist might at this point try to meet the protest of our nonteleological environmentalist by first apologizing for leaving the endangered animals out of account and then reckoning the monetary value of the lost species at $2.5 billion, based on a survey of how much people would be willing to pay to protect these three classes of creatures from oblivion. Once the $2.5 billion is deducted from the $3 billion and $2 billion of net benefits in the original analysis, the teleological economist might now admit that Dam B was indeed damnable but still insist that A was desirable because of the remaining net positive benefit of $0.5 billion. Would this persuade the environmentalist? No, not if the "no genocide against species" is truly a moral imperative to the environmentalist, something warranting even the risk of jail, or worse, in its defense.

You must thus be put on notice that most economists and perhaps the bulk of businessmen as well tend to rely on teleological ethics. If a potent chemical quickens the maturity of chickens, increasing productivity and reducing the consumers' cost of broilers by $500 million per year, it does not much matter that, statistically or randomly, ten people will die excruciating deaths from the chemical each year, given that those deaths can be "valued" at, say, $1 million each, for a total of $10 million, which cannot outweigh the $500 million. Or what about theft or fraud? According to prominent economist Roland McKean, they are wrong not for any intrinsic reason but because of their teleologic cost savings: "Honesty can save extra burglar alarms, time clocks, monitoring devices, legal actions, hours spent checking up on each other's statements, time wasted when appointments and promises are broken, energy and good humor squandered on bitterness and reprisal, and

gains from trades that would otherwise not take place."[12] Or, furthermore, what about punishment for criminal acts? Gary Becker, an equally prominent economist, argues that imprisonment not only reduces possible sources of crime, it also prevents inmates from producing and earning. Penalizing very productive people (those who earn high salaries) in this way thus detracts substantially from the GNP. Becker therefore proposes fines and freedom instead of incarceration for such people because of society's alleged net benefit.[13] But this teleological view completely ignores any ethical standard that proper retribution is "right" regardless of the consequences.

Although I am an economist, I am by no means a strict teleologist. I believe that a blend of teleological and imperative standards is both possible and desirable, especially when trying to comprehend and assess policy. The fact that imperative standards tend to be *discrete* and teleological standards tend to be *continuous* offers an opportunity for such blending because these characteristics permit teleological optimization *subject* to imperative constraints.[14] Thus, for example, one could devise a system of electric power generation that maximized society's net benefit, subject to the constraint that no more nuclear plants be built if most everyone came to consider "nukes" morally odious. Or we might have a policy that businessmen could promote their products all they want to, as long as they did not engage in false advertising. Oddly enough, economists theorize constantly about optimizing various things (e.g., profits) subject to constraints (e.g., technology), yet many seem blind to the possibility and necessity of blending teleological and imperative ethics in this fashion.[15] In short, the end does *not* always justify the means, even though the end we generally propound is the laudable one of satisfying people's preferences. After all, those preferences appear to include many ethical notions of an imperative nature.

To take but one example just alluded to, the Endangered Species Act has an imperative thrust. During 1990–1991 a controversy raged over the northern spotted owl (a species whose continued existence depends on vast expanses of ancient forest that the timber industry wants to cut down). Approximately 14,000 logging jobs were at stake. Scientific experts recommended that logging be reduced by about 50 percent. However, Bush administration officials thought the endangered species law was "too tough," so it proposed that the harvest be trimmed only 20 percent. Imperative-minded environmentalists then protested, claiming that the law was not being properly enforced.

Summary

Markets and government are our nation's key institutions. Problems arise when either of these institutions fails to live up to what society expects of them. Excessively priced and unsafe products, for instance, would not satisfy the preferences of those in society, signaling a problem. Likewise, outrageously costly and coercive government intervention, even if aimed at remedying market deficiencies, would be less than desirable. Problems of both kinds are the concern of this book.

We have taken a few first steps in assessing government policies toward business. We have defined business markets, government, and society. Table 1–1 has listed the ways in which markets and government serve society. We find that the basic function of both is, in two words, *decision making*. Markets are called on for private, decentralized, individualized, capitalistic decision making. Government is called on for collective, official decision making. The input functions of both thus include preference articulation and communication, but the government side also includes preference aggregation because government decisions are collective. The output, or substantive function, of markets is to coordinate and control private decision making in finding answers to the basic questions scarcity imposes on us—what, how, who, and what's new. The output functions of government are, most broadly, rule making, rule application, and rule adjudication. Less broadly and most importantly for our purposes, the government is authorized by the Constitution to "regulate commerce" and thereby to influence what, how, who, and what's new.

We shall be evaluating these institutions in two main ways: (1) *how* they go about making their decisions, a question of *means,* and (2) *how good* are the results, a question of *ends.* Such evaluation necessarily entails the application of ethical criteria or value judgments, some of which are *moral* value judgments. In this connection one must distinguish between *teleological standards,* which focus on the nonmoral outcomes or results of acts or rules, and *imperative standards,* which hold that certain acts or rules are right or wrong in themselves, regardless of the economic or other consequences. Both types of standards may be found in the government's formulation and execution of policy. Both types of standards are employed by scholars and other folks to evaluate those policies. Hence, both will be encountered often on our journey.

Questions and Exercises for Chapter 1

1. Explain how market and government differ by referring to their definitions. Next explain how they are similar by referring to the definition of institution.
2. Compare market and government in terms of the functions they perform for society.
3. Society tends to judge both market and government by the same criteria, those outlined in Table 1–2. Why? Could it be that in the end their functions are often quite similar?

4. For each question raised by scarcity, select one or two proximate values you think are particularly pertinent and then explain your choice.
5. It is stated that freedom, equality, and justice (or fairness) relate to *means,* whereas welfare, happiness, and progress concern *ends*. Demonstrate this by comparing one of the values in the first group (e.g., equality) with one of the values in the second group (e.g., progress), using the proximate values of each to bolster your answer.
6. Compare teleological and imperative ethics.
7. Would you consider the following to be governed by teleological or imperative standards? (a) Equal opportunity in employment. (b) The use of animals for experimenting on the toxicity of new cosmetics and drugs. (c) Government funding of research and development in electronics. (d) The commercial sale of Native American artifacts taken from old burial grounds. (e) Restrictions on the number of dolphins that can be killed while tuna fishing.
8. Explain why wanting efficiency is a value judgment.

Appendix to Chapter 1

The following exchange of views is excerpted from the *Wall Street Journal:*

Editorial Page Article "In Hugo's Path, a Man-Made Disaster," (September 27, 1989):

> In the wake of the devastation wrought by Hurricane Hugo in Charleston, stories of a different sort of "hardship" have appeared.
>
> For days now, tens of thousands of people have been without power. Food, fresh water, gasoline and other commodities are in short supply. Not surprisingly—to economists at least—prices of certain commodities rose to alleviate the imbalance between individuals' desires and local availability. Bags of ice that normally sold for $1 were being sold for $10. A post-hurricane chain saw was in the $600 range, plywood was available at $200 a sheet.
>
> To many, price gouging is unconscionable, especially when someone else profits at your expense. Indeed, on Saturday (two days after Hugo

hit), emergency legislation was passed making the charging of higher prices post-Hugo than pre-Hugo a crime, punishable by a fine of up to $200 and/or a 30-day jail term. Give the politicians credit for being politically astute. Give them all an F in economics.

> Government-mandated restrictions on price levels will slow the cleanup effort as much as another Hugo. High prices are the free market's mechanism for ensuring that economic resources flow to their most highly valued uses. On the demand side, high prices guarantee that scarce goods are allocated to those buyers who place the highest value on them. . . .
>
> For fast, efficient reaction to problems caused by natural disaster, the price system can't be beat.

David N. Laband
Associate Professor of Economics
Clemson University[16]

Letter to the Editor (October 19, 1989):

> Economist David N. Laband's September 27 editorial-page article, "In Hugo's Path, a Man-Made Disaster," decries the control of price gouging, swiftly ordered by South Carolina's governor after Hurricane Hugo. According to Mr. Laband, "screaming" for price controls occurs when income redistribution "threatens to hit home." To be sure, the threat has hit home down here.
>
> Yet in Mr. Laband's rehash of free-market logic, human greed and self-interest are the only permissible psychological reactions. Allowing uncontrolled prices for necessities would indeed shorten the lines at stores, as he contends. But not because resources are going to their most efficient use, leaving scarce goods "allocated to those buyers who place the highest value on them." Rather, lines would diminish because at higher prices many victims could not afford necessities such as food and medical supplies.
>
> It is inhumane to imply that a poor, unemployed woman cannot receive immediate relief for her family at fair prices because she does not have as much to protect as a rich family. Moreover, essential relief supplies such as ice must be distributed throughout the population because of potential health problems from spoiled food and possible outbreak of disease. Such spillover ef-

fects give the state a right to intervene in the marketplace and temporarily coordinate allocation of resources. . . .

South Carolina deserves an A for its quick and timely relief efforts. Mr. Laband, meanwhile, gets an A for his rote recital of economic-efficiency arguments. Give him an F for his failure to understand the ethics of economic equity.

Signed by 25 students
of Douglas Woodward's
Honors Economics Class,
University of South Carolina[17]

Notes

1. Carlo M. Cipolla, *Faith, Reason, and the Plague in Seventeenth Century Tuscany* (Ithaca, NY: Cornell University Press, 1979).

2. Gabriel A. Almond and James S. Colman, eds., *The Politics of the Developing Areas* (Princeton, NJ: Princeton University Press, 1960), p. 7.

3. Talcott Parsons and Neil Smelser, *Economy and Society* (New York: Free Press, 1965), p. 102.

4. Almond and Colman, *Politics of Developing Areas,* pp. 17–58.

5. For more extensive discussions of values see Donald S. Watson, *Economic Policy, Business and Government* (Boston: Houghton Mifflin, 1960), pp. 24–25; Scott Gordon, *Welfare, Justice, and Freedom* (New York: Columbia University Press, 1980); and Allen Buchanan, *Ethics, Efficiency, and the Market* (Totowa, NJ: Rowman & Allanheld, 1985).

6. Robert A. Dahl and Charles E. Lindblom, *Politics, Economics, and Welfare* (New York: Harper & Row, 1963), p. 41.

7. Vernon A. Mund, *Government and Business,* 4th ed. (New York: Harper & Row, 1965), p. 24.

8. H. H. Liebhafsky's entire book *American Government and Business* (New York: Wiley, 1971) is devoted to this theme, but see especially Chapters 1, 2, 6 and 8. See also Marc R. Tool, *Essays in Social Value Theory: A Neoinstitutionalist Contribution* (Armonk, NY: M. E. Sharpe, 1986).

9. William K. Frankena, *Ethics* (Englewood Cliffs, NJ: Prentice-Hall, 1963); Charles Fried, *Right and Wrong* (Cambridge, MA: Harvard University Press, 1978).

10. Such ends cannot be "morally" desirable in and of themselves because the teleological standard would then be circular.

11. Frankena, *Ethics,* p. 13.

12. Roland N. McKean, "Collective Choice," in *Social Responsibility and the Business Predicament,* ed. James W. McKie (Washington, DC: Brookings Institution, 1974), p. 121.

13. Gary S. Becker, "Crime and Punishment: An Economic Approach," *Journal of Political Economy* (March/April 1968): 169–217.

14. Duncan MacRae, Jr. and James A. Wilde, *Policy Analysis for Public Decisions* (North Scituate, MA: Duxbury Press, 1979), p. 54. This approach is also implied by G. Warren Nutter, "On Economism," *Journal of Law & Economics* (October 1979): 263–268. For an especially good elaboration see Amitai Etzioni, *The Moral Dimension: Toward a New Economics* (New York: Free Press, 1988).

15. Some economists are so glued to teleological thinking that they fail to realize their ethical judgments. Can you find the contradiction in the following? "This book makes no moral assumptions and is strictly utilitarian in its approach to legal institutions." Gordon Tullock, *The Logic of the Law* (New York: Basic Books, 1971), p. vi.

16. *Wall Street Journal,* editorial page, 27 September 1989.

17. *Wall Street Journal,* editorial page, 19 October 1989.

Chapter 2

The Market:
Ideal and Real

Every man hath a good and bad angel attending on him in particular, all his long life.
— *Robert Burton*

Having sketched the place markets occupy in our economy and having noted the value judgments we use to assess markets, we are now ready for a more detailed analysis. An outline of this chapter follows its aims:

1. To specify *ideal results* for the questions raised by scarcity—What? How? Who? and What's new?
2. To identify the *ideal conditions* that must hold for free markets to achieve one of those ideals—static efficiency.
3. To explain *how markets work* under these ideal conditions.
4. To identify *real world problems* with markets, problems that might justify government intervention.

I will assume (in later chapters as well as in this one) that you are familiar with demand elasticities and production costs. Hence, only a refresher on these points appears in an appendix to this chapter if you feel that you need it.

The main principle applied in what follows may be called *two-question logic*. A general statement of the two questions is easy:

Question 1: What are the *benefits* of doing something?

Question 2: What are the *costs* of doing it?

The logic, which relates to teleological ethics, compares answers:

If the answer to Question 1 is *greater* than the answer to Question 2, *do it*.

If the answer to Question 1 is *less* than the answer to Question 2, *don't do it*.

Application of two-question logic as we go along may seem complicated because the specific benefits and costs involved vary and so do the people asking the questions. For example, a price is a "benefit" to a seller because it reflects added revenue when sales occur, but that price is a "cost" to a buyer who must pay it to obtain the goods. To society as a whole, which is comprised of both buyers and sellers, price is neither a benefit nor a cost. For another example, society's "benefits" will sometimes take the form of reduced "costs," as when the "benefits" of eliminating 10 million tons of SO_2 pollution are the reduced "costs" of the damages otherwise caused by the pollution—for example, fewer dead trees, fish, and people. Still, complications aside, two-question logic is indispensable to understanding the market in its ideal and real states.

I. Ideal Answers to the Basic Economic Questions

Economic theory has ideal answers to the basic questions of what, how, who, and what's new. These ideal answers are used to evaluate the day-to-day performance of the market and the government, which together share the task of giving answers. To the extent that real-world markets and governments give answers to these questions that approach the ideal answers, we can say these institutions perform well for society. Hence, coverage of the ideal answers is critical. We start with static efficiency, which is theory's ideal answer to the what and how questions taken together. We then tackle who and what's new.

A. Static Efficiency (What and How)

What should be produced in what amounts? How should these goods and services be produced? Using our scarce resources one way as opposed to another always entails benefits and costs. **Static efficiency,** the ideal here, is achieved when

we *maximize* the *net* benefit from the use of our resources, subtracting the total costs from the total benefits.

This statement of static efficiency refers to total dollar benefits and costs. Alternatively, this ideal can be stated in dollars per unit (e.g., per pizza produced) by the use of two-question logic. As long as the *marginal social benefit* (MSB) of using our resources in some way (e.g., producing pizzas) is greater than the *marginal social cost* (MSC), we should expand that production. Marginal social benefit is the added total benefit to society of an added unit. Marginal social cost is the added total cost of the added unit. As long as the added total benefit exceeds the added total cost, society's net benefit is rising. Once MSB equals MSC that net benefit is maximized, so MSB = MSC is an alternative statement of static efficiency. Producing units beyond the point of MSB = MSC reduces net benefit.

Figure 2–1 illustrates static efficiency. In each of the three panels the vertical axis represents dollars per unit (e.g., dollar benefit per pizza produced), and units of quantity are depicted horizontally. The curves representing marginal social benefit (MSB) and marginal social cost (MSC) are identical in each panel. All that varies across the panels is the level of output and, consequently, the benefits and costs associated with those different outputs. Static efficiency requires (1) production efficiency and (2) allocation efficiency. **Production efficiency** requires that the cost of producing any given amount be as low as possible. This is assumed for Figure 2–1 because all MSC curves are as low as possible. **Allocation efficiency** requires that the quantity produced be just right to maximize the total net benefit (given production efficiency).

Panel (b) of Figure 2–1 depicts static efficiency in two ways—first by a comparison of total benefits and costs and second by a comparison of the marginal benefits and costs. Total benefit of output Q_0 is the area under the MSB curve out to Q_0, namely, area N + C. Total cost is the

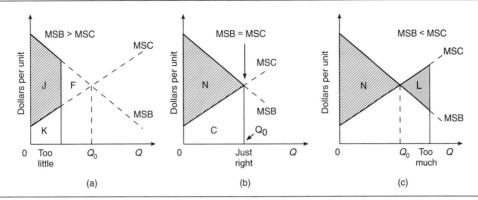

Figure 2–1
Static Efficiency (b), Flanked by Cases of Inefficiency: Too Little (a) and Too Much (c)

area under the MSC curve labeled C. Hence, total net benefit in this case is $(N+C) - C$, which is area N. This net is the largest total net benefit possible under the circumstances, and its attainment corresponds to the level of output that equates MSB and MSC, a result that would be obtained by applying two-question logic unit by unit.

Panel (a) of Figure 2–1 illustrates that outputs below Q_0 are not efficient because they are too little. Total benefit in panel (a) is area $J + K$, whereas total cost amounts to area K. Net benefit is therefore $(J + K) - K$, or simply J. This net benefit J is much less than it could be—that is, less than area N of panel (b). The amount of shortfall, or forgone net benefit, is shown by area F. (That is to say, $J + F = N$). Notice also that MSB is greater than MSC in this case.

Panel (c), in contrast, shows that outputs greater than Q_0 are not efficient because they are too much. As output expands beyond Q_0 in panel (c), MSB falls below MSC. Beyond Q_0, resources are being wasted on outputs that at the margin are not valued enough to warrant the effort (just as any resources devoted to the production of garlic-flavored mouthwash would be wasted resources). The loss for each unit beyond Q_0 is indicated by the amount by which MSB is less than

MSC in each case. The total net loss depicted for the output beyond Q_0 in panel (c) is area L. Hence, the total net benefit of panel (c) could be $N - L$, where N is the total net benefit up to output Q_0 as before. Because $(N - L)$ is less than N, the results of panel (c) are inferior to those of panel (b).

In short, panel (b) of Figure 2–1 depicts static efficiency because (1) the costs in MSC are as low as possible and (2) output Q_0 yields the greatest net benefit (N) with MSB = MSC. That is to say, static efficiency requires both production efficiency and allocation efficiency. In simple English, production efficiency requires that we produce as much of each desirable good or service as we can, given the production of other desirable goods and services. Allocation efficiency requires that we produce the goods and services people want most.

Another way of expressing static efficiency, a way that stresses the human experiences behind these welfare results, is called **Pareto optimality** (after its formulator, Vilfredo Pareto). This is *a situation in which no one can be made better off without making someone else worse off.* Conversely, we are *not* at Pareto optimality if Al's welfare can be improved at no loss to anyone else—Barb, Carl, Doris, whoever.

Figure 2–2 illustrates Pareto optimality for a simple society comprised of only Al and Barb. Vertical movements represent improvements in Al's welfare (e.g., more steak dinners and trousers for him). Horizontal movements depict improvements in Barb's welfare (e.g., more quiche dinners and dresses for her). The collection of points like Z and Y sloping downward are all points of Pareto optimality. Once a point like Z is reached, Barb cannot be made better off without reducing Al's welfare, and conversely Al could not be made better off without hurting Barb. Any point inside the boundary, like X, is not Pareto optimal because from there the welfare of either of these individuals could be improved with no loss to the other. Indeed, from X a movement toward Y would improve the welfare of *both* Al and Barb simultaneously. At X allo-

cation efficiency would be absent (as, say, too much food is being produced and too little apparel). Also, production could be inefficient at X (as, say, wheat is being grown in Florida and oranges in North Dakota). Being the same as static efficiency, Pareto optimality requires the achievement of both allocation efficiency and production efficiency.[1]

B. Equity (Who?)

Equity is the ideal regarding the question of who gets the goods and services. Theorists have not yet devised a sweeping definition of equity that wins a consensus of approval. Unlike efficiency, equity grapples directly with issues of distribution. Difficulties arise partly because of difficulties in making interpersonal comparisons of well-being. For example, taking from the rich to give to the poor in hopes of improving society's overall happiness assumes that the resulting anguish of the rich is outweighed by the greater comfort of the poor, an assumption that cannot be proven or disproven. If we abandon teleological considerations such as this for more imperative value judgments concerning the "rights" of the poor, we move no closer to a consensus.

Still, some limited notions of equity receive widespread support.[2] We favor equal opportunity in employment, housing, consumer credit, and other respects. Although equal opportunity is not the same as equal results, it promotes equity. We also tend to oppose redistributions of income or wealth that take from the poor and give to the rich—Robin Hood in reverse.

Figure 2–2 illustrates another notion of equity and demonstrates differences in equity and efficiency. Generally, our society dislikes enormous disparities between the rich and the poor, so it favors government policies that reduce the degree of inequality that free markets yield. Such policies may create some inefficiencies but be supported for their achievements in equity. Notice in Figure 2–2 that point Z is a point of static

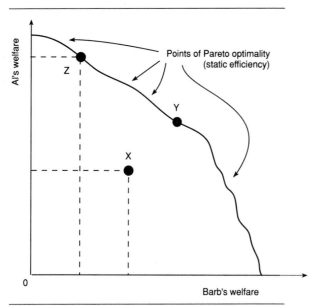

Figure 2–2
Pareto Optimal Points and Considerations of Equity:
Z is efficient but not equitable
X is equitable but not efficient
Y is both efficient and equitable.

efficiency (Pareto optimality), but it could be considered inequitable. At Z, Al enjoys immense wealth while Barb languishes in poverty. In contrast, point X is not efficient, but it represents greater equity between Al and Barb. If society wishes, it may prefer an outcome like X to one like Z. It would sacrifice efficiency in moving from Z to X, but value judgment priorities or imperatives might justify the change. (Y could be considered both efficient and equitable and thereby preferable to both Z and X. But Y might not be attainable for some practical reason.)

Figure 2–2 alerts us to other equity issues as well. Note *first* that Al and Barb are the only creatures taken into account in Figure 2–2. No consideration is given to northern spotted owls, blue whales, or other species that might be obliterated by human economic activities. Only human interests are of concern to efficiency. Nonhumans receive protection from pain or extinction by the efficiency criterion only insofar as humans include such protection in the calculation of their own (human) welfare. Is that equitable?

Notice *second* that Al and Barb are presently alive. They are not members of some future generation. Future generations are frequently affected by our present actions, as illustrated by the global warming that results from combustion of fossil fuels. But static efficiency ignores the interests of future generations to a degree that some people in the present generation might consider inequitable. They might say we are burning oil resources too fast, for instance.

C. Dynamic Efficiency (What's New?)

Future generations are not completely ignored by economic theorists or by present and past generations. A theoretical ideal for efficiency over time encompasses the interests of future generations to some degree. That is **dynamic efficiency.** An allocation of resources to future time periods is dynamically efficient if it maximizes the present value of the total net benefits that could be received from all possible ways of allocating those resources over those future time periods.[3] Total net benefits are once again maximized. But these net benefits occur in future years as well as in the present one. Because future dollars are not the same as present dollars (at least not to the present generation), future net benefits in 2010 dollars are not the same as those in 1998 dollars or today's dollars (even apart from inflation). Hence, all future net benefits are discounted into "present values" before they are added together for a calculation of dynamic efficiency.

Dynamic efficiency defies easy diagramming. It can be vaguely understood, however, by imagining a sequence of triangular total net benefits, such as the one shown alone in panel (b) of Figure 2–1, a sequence like the frames in a strip of motion picture film. Mentally discount each triangle in the sequence, discounting ever more heavily as the imagined net benefits appear later in time. Then sum these discounted net benefits. The allocation over time that yields the greatest present value of net benefits is dynamically efficient.

The purely theoretical nature of this concept needs emphasis. Its practical application suffers severe impossibilities. For example, no one knows what interest rate should be used for discounting. Indeed, it can be argued that for some purposes under some conditions the interest rate should be zero, implying no discounting of future generation benefits whatever.[4] Moreover, no one knows how to handle the huge uncertainties that the future hides.

The concept of dynamic efficiency is useful, though, for demonstrating that the future consequences of today's actions can be momentous. Energy policy cannot ignore conservation. Environmental policy cannot look only to present-day impacts of CFCs, nuclear wastes, or other materials that could mangle the well-being of future centuries. Today's investments in research and development will bring amazing future technological changes. And so on.

In short, dynamic efficiency is a crude way to imagine, at least in principle, an ideal for the what's new question. If nothing else, its acknowledgment points to a further limitation of static efficiency. For many purposes, static efficiency is much too tightly bound to the present, to this year and maybe the next, to be useful even in theory.

II. The Conditions for Markets to Achieve Static Efficiency

Limited though it may be, the ideal of static efficiency carries tremendous weight in Washington because it provides the foundation for benefit-cost analysis, which guides much governmental decision making. It also gives economists great influence.

In particular, economists find the concept of static efficiency useful for assessing the performance of markets. Under certain ideal conditions, the free market will in theory obtain static efficiency. Those conditions include the following:

1. *An absence of external benefits.* A market's buyers always act on their own marginal private benefits (MPB), such as the benefits you receive from eating a pizza. Absent external benefits, your marginal *private* benefits match the marginal *social* benefits associated with your purchase (i.e., MPB = MSB). However, private benefits fall short of social benefits when there are external benefits. You benefit when you buy a car with safe brakes, and you also benefit others by reducing the chances that you will run into them. Hence, MPB plus any external benefits equals MSB, and MPB < MSB when there are external benefits.

2. *An absence of external costs.* A market's sellers always act on their own marginal private costs (MPC), such as the cost your favorite pizza parlor bears to make you a pizza. With zero ex-

ternal costs, these marginal *private* costs will equal the marginal *social* costs associated with this sale (i.e., MPC = MSC). With pollution, however, there will be external costs. Airplanes create noise pollution. The CFCs from semiconductor manufacturing destroy the ozone layer of the upper atmosphere, which protects us from solar radiation. And so on. In these cases of external costs, MPC < MSC because MSC is then MPC plus any external costs.

3. *Pure competition.* Pure competition requires a very large number of buyers and sellers such that none of them acting individually can affect the market's price. A standardized product is also a must, which means that sellers offer identical products, each closely substitutable for the others (e.g., Farmer Smith's Grade A eggs are the same as Farmer Brown's). Finally, easy entry and exit are needed for pure competition. Under these several conditions, sellers have no power over price, so price will match their marginal private costs (P = MPC), including a normal profit.

4. *Full information.* All buyers must be fully informed about prices, product qualities, health effects, and so forth of their purchases. Ignorance throws buyers off. They buy more or less than they would had they full knowledge. They may pay more in price than they should. Meeting this condition of full information assures that buyers will not be ripped off. Specifically, each buyer's marginal private benefit must equal the price (i.e., MPB = P).

5. *No public goods or common property resources.* Public goods benefit everyone within their range, so excluding people from them is either impossible or too expensive. Classic examples include national defense and abatement of air pollution. As explained later, the market cannot cope with public goods chiefly because of the "free rider" problem. Common property resources are a variant of this theme because they are resources open to use by anyone without restriction. Examples are ocean fishing or the air before the days of environmental protection.

Table 2–1

Summary of the Conditions Necessary for the Market to Achieve Static Efficiency

MSB = MPB   (No external benefits)
      MPB = P   (Full information)
          P = MPC   (Pure competition)
             MPC = MSC   (No external costs)

MSB   =   MSC $\left(\begin{array}{l}\text{All the above plus strictly}\\ \textit{private}\text{ goods and properties}\end{array}\right)$

Source: Where MSB = marginal social benefit
              MPB = marginal private benefit
                P = market price
             MPC = marginal private costs
              MSC = marginal social costs

Because anyone can use common property resources, they tend to be wastefully overused. Absent public goods or common property resources, marginal social benefit can equal marginal social costs: MSB = MSC. Strictly private goods and private properties meet this requirement.[5]

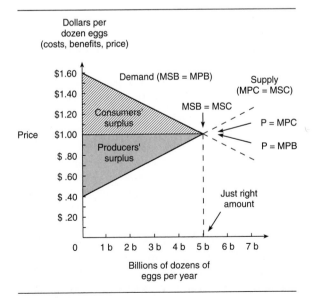

Figure 2–3

Conditions Necessary for the Market to Achieve Static Efficiency

These five conditions are summarized in Table 2–1. Notice the stairstep linkage between the lines. The MPB in the first line drops to the MPB in the second line, and so on. Notice also that in the end MSB = MSC if all the conditions are met. Each condition is thus a necessary but not sufficient condition for the market to achieve static efficiency. All must be met simultaneously.

These conditions come more alive in Figure 2–3, where the familiar demand and supply curves of economics textbooks are shown (hypothetically) together with specifications that meet the conditions of Table 2–1. With all the conditions met, 5 billion dozen eggs would achieve static efficiency. Price is $1.00 per dozen. Total *net benefit* is the combination of consumers' surplus and producers' surplus (which are defined shortly). And given MSB = MSC, this net is optimal.

III. How the Market Achieves Static Efficiency under Ideal Conditions

A quick understanding of how the market achieves static efficiency under ideal conditions may be achieved by consulting Figure 2–2 again. Steps toward static efficiency (Pareto optimality) would occur if *both* Al and Barb were made better off simultaneously, as in a movement from

point X toward point Y. The market, by definition and everyday action, entails *voluntary exchange*. And whenever voluntary exchange takes
place, the people involved in the exchange are becoming better off, improving their welfare. Otherwise, they would not engage in the exchange.
For example, when you buy a hamburger at
McDonald's, you feel better off with the hamburger than with your money, and McDonald's is
glad to have your money instead of the hamburger. (This is not, in other words, the world of
the Godfather, where people are given offers
they cannot refuse because of the bloody consequences of refusal.)

Given ideal circumstances, these perceptions of improvement by market participants are
genuine social improvements. That is to say, the
parties are fully informed, so their gains are real.
Moreover, there are no external costs from the
exchange that adversely affect innocent bystand-
ers. And so on. Under ideal circumstances,
therefore, the market—with its countless voluntary exchanges creating benefits—will achieve
static efficiency.

Figure 2–3 and two-question logic tell the
same story differently. Consumers will buy additional dozens of eggs as long as the marginal
private benefit (MPB) they experience from the
eggs exceeds the price they have to pay for them.
The MPB, which is represented by the demand
curve in Figure 2–3, shows answers to the first
question in the consumers' two-question logic
(benefit per unit?). Price, which is $1.00 in Figure
2–3, represents the answer to their second question (costs?). As long as the benefits of buying
(MPB) exceed the costs ($1), consumers con-
tinue to buy. The difference in these answers
(MPB − $1) generates **consumers' surplus,** which
is *the difference between what they would be
willing to pay and what they actually pay.* The
buying continues out to 5 billion dozen eggs in
Figure 2–3. More than that would have MPB
falling below price, which would violate two-
question logic.

On the supply side, producers will sell additional dozens of eggs as long as the price they
receive (their benefit) exceeds their cost of production (marginal private costs, MPC). Each
dozen passing this test generates some surplus
for the producers (in the form of profits or scarcity rents). **Producers' surplus** *is the difference between the total dollar amount producers receive
and the amount they must give up to cover their
costs.* Producers' surplus for each unit is positive
out to 5 billion dozen eggs. More than that would
fail their two-question logic because costs, MPC,
would rise above the revenue that price
represents.

Both consumers and producers act strictly in
their own self-interest, according to their own
benefits and costs, perceiving net benefits (surpluses) on every dozen eggs out to 5 million. Under ideal circumstances, this results in static
efficiency in egg production. With MSB = MPB,
MPB = P, P = MPC, and MPC = MSC, the
overall result is MSB = MSC. Together the *combined consumer and producer surpluses comprise the maximum net benefits for society*
because society is made up of both consumers
and producers.

Strictly speaking, the ideal conditions must
be achieved in *all* markets for Pareto optimality
to prevail, not just those for eggs or for bacon
and eggs. According to the theory of *second
best,* we cannot be sure that welfare will be improved if we take steps to achieve these ideal
conditions in just one market, such as eggs, or
even in most markets, while the conditions remain unmet in some markets.[6] This problem reduces the usefulness of the static efficiency
concept for public policy. The most that any policy can truthfully claim, given the theory of second best, in some partial, or local, improvement
in static efficiency. This may or may not mean an
overall improvement. Fortunately, the theory of
second best does not completely ruin the usefulness of the static efficiency concept in identifying
problems with real-world markets, which is our

next task. Likewise, the theory of second best does not undermine other criteria besides efficiency that may motivate policy. Equity, for instance, remains intact, as does an appreciation for dynamic conditions.

Summary

Under certain circumstances, then, the market system is a wonderful social machine for coping with scarcity. It is attractive in both means and ends. Under ideal circumstances, its decentralized decision-making process, its efficient performance, and its achievements in other respects further most of the value judgments outlined earlier. Unfortunately, the purely competitive model that comprises part of the theoretical ideal is quite unrealistic (e.g., countless sellers) and is in some respects even undesirable (e.g., standardized products), so we cannot and should not slavishly pursue its formula. Still, it provides a foundation for notions of "workable competition," which we encounter later. And the ideal of static efficiency provides a basis for benefit-cost analysis, which much public policy relies on.

IV. Problems with Real Markets

If you believe that problems make life interesting, then you should find Table 2–2 and the ensuing discussion thoroughly engrossing. For outside the economic paradise just explored there is a crowd of instances when real-world free enterprise markets do not live up to the expectations or preferences of society. Among the market system's many past feats are the following: Faulty baby cribs that killed over 100 babies per year; a 40 percent increase in the price of steel following the merger of 170 steel companies; enough pollution to cause a river to catch fire; a concentration of wealth such that one-half of 1 percent of the population owned 30 percent;

parts fraud for an estimated one out of every two TV set repairs.

The importance of these shortcomings and countless others is obvious. They may justify or explain government intervention.

Before probing Table 2–2's particulars, notice that the first two broad categories, "Imperfections" and "Failures," assume acceptance of static efficiency as the chief ethical criterion to be concerned about. The direction of deviation from marginal-social-benefit-equals-marginal-social-cost is indicated in each instance by MSB > MSC (for *under*allocations of resources) and by MSB < MSC (for *over*allocations of resources). Such designations are not appropriate for the last two broad categories because they concern problems arising outside the static efficiency context. Whereas the first two categories refer to free-market equilibriums that are undesirable, the last two are not really concerned with static equilibriums at all. "Dynamic Incapacities" includes problems encountered in moving from one equilibrium to another, such as the difficulties people may face in rapidly converting from a world of cheap energy to a world of expensive energy. "Ethical Criteria Other Than Efficiency" is distinguished by giving due recognition to the fact that free market results may not conform to society's notions of morality or fairness or equity. Thus, for instance, the free market may be superefficient in providing liquor, sex, gambling, and cocaine, but such efficiency would be (and has been) rejected by moral outrage. The differences in these broad categories are clarified by filtration through more detailed discussion.

A. Imperfections

1. MONOPOLY POWER
Three assumptions of the purely competitive model preclude the possibility of monopoly power—a large number of relatively small sellers, easy entry, and standardized products. These give firms

Table 2–2
Problems with Private Free Enterprise Markets
(MSB = Marginal Social Benefit, MSC = Marginal Social Cost, MPB = Marginal
Private Benefit, MPC = Marginal Private Cost, P = Price)

A. Imperfections
  1. Monopoly power: MSB > MSC (because P > MPC)
    a. Artificially attained (e.g., mergers, cartels)
    b. Natural monopoly (e.g., public utilities)
  2. Information inadequacies
    a. Errors of commission MSB < MSC (because MPB < P)
    b. Errors of omission MSB > MSC (because MPB > P)
B. Market Failures
  1. Externalities
    a. External benefits MSB > MSC (because MSB > MPB)
    b. External costs MSB < MSC (because MPC < MSC)
  2. Public goods MSB > MSC
    a. People excludable, but zero marginal cost (highways)
    b. Nonexcludables (national defense, administration of laws)
  3. Common property resources MSB < MSC
C. Dynamic Incapacities
  1. Micro instability and transition immobilities
  2. Macro instability
  3. Growth: short-run protection and promotion for long-run gain
D. Ethical Criteria Other Than Efficiency
  1. Equity
    a. Income distribution
    b. Equal opportunity
    c. Resource conservation
  2. Merit goods: education, health, safety
  3. Demerit goods: liquor, tobacco, hazardous products
  4. Miscellaneous political and social goals

perfectly elastic demand curves. They are "price takers," not "price makers." Though Farmer Brown may fit this mold, IBM, GM, Procter & Gamble, DuPont, and the other giant firms that account for the bulk of our industrial output do not. Most of these enterprises are oligopolists, operating in industries dominated by just a few sellers, industries also protected by barriers to entry and providing differentiated, not standardized, products. These several characteristics bestow monopoly power of various degrees. And at the noncompetitive extreme, full-fledged monopoly prevails, with just one seller, blockaded entry, and a product that can be considered perfectly differentiated owing to an absence of close substitutes.

The static insufficiency created by pure monopoly is sketched in Figure 2–4. Monopoly raises price and reduces output in comparison with the purely competitive case shown in Figure 2–3. Price rises from $1.00 to $1.20 when output falls from 5 billion dozen to 3.4 billion dozen. This happens because the monopolist sees the entire marketwide demand curve. It's the only firm in the market. The answer, for each output, to the first question in the firm's two-question

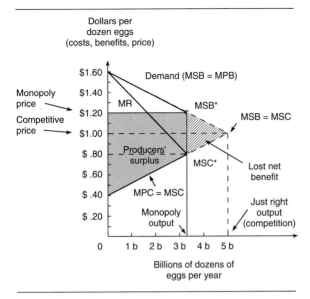

Figure 2–4
Monopoly Price and Quantity with Net Benefit Loss

logic to maximize profit is given by the marginal revenue curve (MR), which is the change of total revenue that results from added units of sale. The MR lies below the demand curve because price falls with added units of sale. Comparing MR to MPC, which answers the second question, the monopolist expands production out to 3.4 billion units but no further. The resulting producer's surplus of the dotted area is greater than before in Figure 2–3.

The lack of static efficiency can be seen two ways in Figure 2–4. First, at 3.4 billion units, marginal social benefit (MSB*) is greater than marginal social cost (MSC*). More precisely, MSB* = \$1.20 and MSC* = \$.80, so MSB* > MSC*. Second, the shaded triangular area to the right of 3.4 billion units shows the lost net benefit caused by monopoly, a situation similar to panel (a) in Figure 2–1.

Table 2–2 distinguishes between artificially attained monopoly power and natural monopoly. Sources of artificial monopoly power include

mergers, cartelization, predatory practices, and other factors of human creation. In contrast, natural monopoly stems from technical imperatives or basic conditions, such as economies of scale, which make a single firm the lowest-cost means of supply. Examples include local telephone service, water supply, and electricity.

The customary policy for dealing with artificial monopolies or cartels in antitrust legislation aimed at maintaining competition. Monopolies may be broken up into a number of firms. Cartels may be banned. Anticompetitive mergers can be dissolved. And so on. The typical policy approach to natural monopoly is quite different. Single-firm dominance is endorsed and even encouraged in the belief that any attempt to enforce competition would be futile (because monopoly is inevitable) and even stupid (given that numerous firms would mean high-cost production or shoddy service). Good performance, though not necessarily static efficiency, is then sought through direct regulation of performance by public utility commissions or, less frequently, by outright public ownership and operation.

2. INFORMATION INADEQUACIES

The second broad category of market imperfections itemized in Table 2–2—information inadequacies—honors the fact that real-world buyers are often led astray by ignorance, misjudgment, and sundry other deviations. This is particularly true of household consumers as opposed to professional business and government buyers who tend to be experienced, well-informed experts. Thus, for instance, consumer ineptitude emerges from studies of the correlation between price level and brand quality. For a given product, low quality should sell only at a low price and high quality should sell at a high price, yielding a correlation coefficient near +1 if consumers really know what they are doing. But observed correlations are on average always much closer to zero than to one, and the range across products includes a substantial number of goods with *negative* correlations.[7]

Of course, we could not reasonably expect consumers to invest the necessary time, effort, and expense to become *perfectly* informed. Furthermore, private enterprise does supply some information by way of advertising and buyer's guides like *Consumer Reports*. But the very nature of the commodity in question—information—is such that imperfections prevent its optimal provision by free markets. One problem is that sellers of information may face the same problem as the little boy who climbs and shakes the apple tree but gets few of the fallen apples because his buddies on the ground run off with the loot before he can get down. This is "inappropriability," and it often applies to information because information may be spread by means outside the control of the information's original producer—for example, piracy by word of mouth. When private producers of information are not rewarded in just proportion to the social value of their effort, they expend less effort than is socially optimal. A second and more striking problem arises because buyers of information cannot be truly *well informed* about the information they want to buy. If they were, they would not need to buy the information.[8] In other words, sellers of information cannot let potential buyers meticulously examine their product prior to sale lest they thereby give it away free. Buyers of information therefore do not know the value of the product they seek (information) until after they buy it.

Advertising is often informative, but the purpose of advertising is not to inform. Its purpose is to persuade, so it is informative only to the extent the informative approach persuades, which is true mainly of ads for producers' goods, not consumers' goods. Indeed, it can be shown that advertising is *least* informative where it is *most* intense, and these conditions correspond to products about which consumers are inherently *least* informed—drugs, beer, soft drinks, prepared foods, cosmetics, detergents, and the like.[9] Still worse, advertisers frequently have an incentive to mislead, misrepresent, and even lie, behaviors

that cannot be said to contribute to consumer competence.

Later, two directions of consumer error are detailed. *Errors of commission* occur when buyers make purchases on the basis of excessively favorable prepurchase assessments. The favoritism then leads to more spending than accuracy would entail and a consequent *over*allocation of resources to the favored brand or product. Conversely, *errors of omission* arise when buyers buy *less* than they would with full knowledge. The misallocation here would obviously be an *under*allocation. (See Table 2–2.)

B. Market Failures

Market failures occur when in one sense or another markets fail to exist. Free enterprise markets for clean air, clean water, national defense, criminal justice, and other highly desirable goods and services cannot be expected to flourish in the absence of some form of government intervention. Without viable markets, society's benefits and costs have no private decentralized place of registration and realization. Stated differently, a world of pure competition all around would not be sufficient to attain Pareto optimality. Much more would be required—an absence of externalities, public goods, and common property resources.

1. EXTERNALITIES

When Jones and Smith engage in free and voluntary exchange, they weigh only the benefits and costs they themselves experience. They do not take into account any benefits bestowed or costs imposed on third parties, say, Wong and the rest of us. Yet such "external" benefits and costs often arise, and the market's failure to account for them leads to free market misallocations of too little in the case of external benefits and too much in the case of external costs.

External Benefits.   Your planting of a flower garden in your front yard benefits your neighbors as well as yourself. An airline's installation of engine silencers for the benefit of its passengers also benefits groundlings near airports.

When benefits extend beyond buyers as in these instances, the price buyers are willing to pay is not a good index of the social value of the purchased good. Price is an underestimate of the value. Figure 2–5 indicates the implications by showing two demand curves, one reflecting only the benefits buyers alone perceive, D_1, the other, D_2, reflecting *all* of society's benefits, external benefits as well. More technically, D_1 includes only marginal *private* benefit, MPB, whereas D_2, represents marginal *social* benefit, MSB, the difference being external benefit. The free market solution is output Q_1, which emerges from the intersection of D_1 (or MPB) and supply (MSC). The optimal solution, however, would be output Q_2, where D_2 and supply meet and where MSB = MSC. Most simply stated, the problem is one of too little production in light of society's true preferences. There is no market registering these preferences and rewarding producers for greater

deeds done, so with the free market's Q_1, MSB at J exceeds MSC at K, or MSB > MSC. To hint at policy solutions, a subsidy equaling the external benefit would lower price to P_2 and thereby lead to optimal output Q_2.

External Costs. External costs are imposed on society and are *not* borne by producers or consumers in the course of production and consumption. Pollution provides the classic example of an external cost; pollution imposes costs of avoidance (air conditioning, moving out of town), of repair (painting, medical treatment), and of raw damage (death, ugly air) that are not paid for out of the pockets of polluters. Acting in their own best interests, market participants equate price with their own *private* marginal cost. But when external costs are recognized and added to these private costs, the result is MSB < MSC.

Figure 2–6 illustrates this problem with two supply curves—S_1, which reflects only *private* costs (and is therefore also labeled MPC), and S_2,

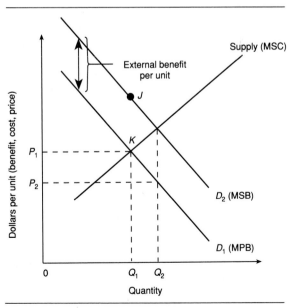

Figure 2–5
External Benefit and Underallocation

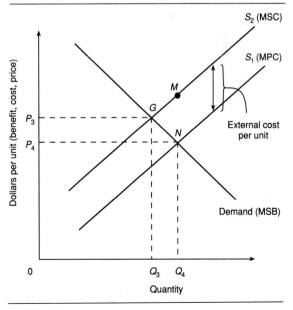

Figure 2–6
External Cost and Overallocation

which includes both private and external costs for all costs to society (MSC). A free competitive market would produce Q_4, as that is the result associated with P = MPC, or MSB = MPC. But this is too much. At Q_4, the marginal social cost M exceeds marginal social benefit N. Resources should be shifted out of this market into others until Q_3 is achieved and MSB = MSC at G, but the free market system fails to comply because these external costs are not imposed on producers here.

Whereas subsidies might be an appropriate policy to encourage added output in cases of external benefit, taxes might discourage the output of products laced with external costs. A per-unit tax matching external costs—the vertical difference between S_1 and S_2 in Figure 2–6—would raise costs of production to the point of reflecting all of society's costs, moving the market to output Q_3 and price P_3.

2. PUBLIC GOODS

There are various definitions of *public goods,* and there are three elements common to most definitions: (1) Their production and consumption usually coincide, so they cannot be inventoried. (2) One individual's consumption does not subtract from any other individual's consumption. And (3) additional consumers can partake of these goods at no additional social cost or near zero cost.[10] With marginal social costs of consumption approaching zero, the nature of the free market failure leaps to mind. *Any* positive price charged for these goods, as would be necessary to reward free market suppliers, would exceed marginal cost. The resulting P > MC, or more generally MSB > MSC, would then lead to the free market's underallocation of resources to these goods.

Excludable Public Goods. Two subcategories of public goods may be usefully distinguished.[11] The first may be called *excludables.* These public goods are illustrated by highways and bridges as long as congestion is no problem. In the absence of congestion, these are public goods because, once the highway or bridge is available, it costs nothing to have an additional trip or crossing. People can in principle be excluded from the use of highways and bridges by the judicious construction of limited entry points, and fares can be collected with toll booths; thus the name *excludable* public goods. But such restrictions are usually not imposed because they are costly.

Nonexcludable Public Goods. The second subcategory, the one of greatest interest to us, includes public goods like national defense, antitrust law enforcement, and clean air. Exclusion of individuals from their consumption is impossible even in principle, because we consume these goods *collectively.* If you wish, you may consume more apple cider, a private good, than I do. Indeed, the more for you the less for me, once cider output is given for the season. But whatever the level of national defense—say $300 billion worth in planes, tanks, ships, soldiers, and so on—we each and every one consume that amount precisely because that is a pure *collective* good.

A main problem with free market provision of these goods is the "free rider." Imagine the invention of an auto pollution control device that would provide the collective good of clean air in your city if almost all auto owners paid the modest $400 necessary to get it. Would you and everyone else scurry to garages and gas stations for its installation? Probably not. In fact, such a pollution control package was offered some years ago and its sales fizzled. Two possibilities deflate your motivation: (1) the possibility that even though you do not buy the device almost everyone else does, in which case you are a "free rider," getting clean air without paying a dime, or (2) the possibility that you pay your $400 for clean air but hardly anyone else does, in which case you have lost $400.

This, then, is what distinguishes these nonexcludable public goods from ordinary goods in the free market setting. With an ordinary good, you get it if you pay; you don't get it if you don't pay. Choice is individualized. Amounts may vary with taste and fortune among separate souls. Paying and receiving correspond closely. With a public good, however, you may get it even if you don't pay, and you may not get it even if you do pay. Free markets tend to be stunted under such conditions.

3. COMMON PROPERTY RESOURCES

Closely related to the foregoing are common property resources, such as fisheries, the radio spectrum, deep-ocean minerals, and at one time oil. These resources tend to be abused or used up too rapidly with competitive exploitation because the private costs of those using them fall short of the full social costs. With excessive haste in milking these resources, MSB is less than MSC.

A fisherman, for example, will face costs for fuel, labor, seaworthy capital equipment, and so on. He will also impose costs on others, however, because additions to his catch reduce the fish available to other fishermen, causing them to spend more time, effort, and energy for any given number of fish they may successfully net. The same, of course, applies to each fisherman. This communal working at cross-purposes is a form of external cost, which when not taken into account leads to an error in the direction of overallocation or, in this case, overfishing.

One corrective in many such cases is government's improved definition of property rights. Other approaches include quota systems, severance taxes, and government stewardship through public ownership. For international problems, like the recovery of mineral-bearing nodules from the ocean floor, treaties are needed.

C. Dynamic Incapacities

To this point we have merely sorted out desirable and undesirable equilibrium solutions, using Pareto optimality as a sieve. But situations of disequilibrium are equally important. Indeed, disequilibrium is the normal state of the world, and some economists claim a greater concern for the attendant dynamic problems than for the comparative static problems of previous pages.

1. MICRO INSTABILITY AND TRANSITION IMMOBILITIES

Substantial shifts of a market's supply and demand curves—due to cyclical swings, the vagaries of the weather, and other contingencies—can cause rocky instability. During the first decades of this century, for instance, prior to federal intervention in agriculture, farm incomes in some regions varied hundreds of percentage points from one year to the next.[12] Serious instability has also plagued petroleum markets at various times, as nature has alternately hidden and disclosed her black gold and as OPEC countries have occasionally withheld supplies. Such instabilities can lead to inefficiencies as producers and consumers try to hedge their bets in rather costly ways. Moreover, the instability itself may be judged rattling, injurious to national defense, and even downright painful for some in society, spawning government programs like price supports, commodity agreements, and insurance reserves.

Disequilibrium in particular markets may also accompany marked changes from one equilibrium to another. An obvious problem in this connection might be the *delay* society experiences in realizing the added welfare a new equilibrium will bring. As Peter Steiner has written, "If resources respond to market signals surely but slowly, the market process may prove an expensive way to achieve resource shifts."[13] Likewise, the burdens of shifting may press particularly hard on certain members of society. The move from Q_4 to Q_3 in Figure 2–6, for instance, benefits society as a whole but may hurt the paper makers, steelworkers, and others whose relocation out of polluting industries is necessitated by the transition. Indeed, failure to meet this problem may create strong political opposition to solving the external cost problem. More generally, such transitional disruptions are referred to as *frictional unemployment,* and government has sought to alleviate the welfare strain with unemployment compensation, job training, and payments to transform industries hard hit by import competition.

2. MACRO INSTABILITY

The Great Depression uncorked an era of fervent social concern for macroeconomic disequilibriums. Depression and recession are undesirable because they frustrate the employment and income aspirations of many people. Inflation has been an even more bruising bane of late. Rapid inflation drastically reshuffles people's real incomes; some keep up and others, especially those on fixed incomes, fall behind. It also creates speculators who dabble in otherwise worthless games of buy and sell. It shrinks savings, disrupts corporate finance, and undermines long-term projects.

The total dollar losses society suffers from macro instabilities could exceed its losses from market imperfections and failures. Thus, policy efforts abound in this realm, though this book focuses most diligently on micro issues.

3. GROWTH: SHORT-RUN PROTECTION AND PROMOTION FOR LONG-RUN GAIN

In the week these words were first written Congress passed a $20 billion subsidy program to promote the development of synthetic fuels (oil distilled from tar sands, oil shale, and coal), the Supreme Court ruled that patents could apply to manmade organisms created from recombinant DNA technology, and *Business Week* published a special issue bemoaning the U.S. economy's languid growth and urging a massive effort by business, government, and labor to achieve the "Reindustrialization of America." Each of these developments illustrates society's deep-seated concern for long-run achievement, for growth, for research and development, and for freedom from foreign dependency. Moreover, these events illustrate society's doubt that the free-market system can always perform satisfactorily on these scores. Thus, society willingly accepts some short-run sacrifices to offer inducements—such as the seventeen-year grant of patent monopoly—in hopes of building brighter futures. The exchange may often look no better than the few beans Jack-in-the-Beanstalk got for his mother's cow, but then we all know what happened to lucky Jack in the end.

For energy especially, it may be argued that there are immense external benefits from technological progress, benefits such as strengthened national defense, general economic prosperity, and improved foreign trade balances. Because private firms are unable to appropriate such benefits, their bland free-market inducements may occasionally need to be sweetened with government honey.[14]

D. Ethical Criteria Other Than Efficiency

The last broad category of Table 2–2 acknowledges that free-market solutions may be rejected on value judgment grounds. The efficient satisfaction of given individual preferences is an attractive ethical criterion, but there are other ethical criteria that decisively influence policy. After all, it is not a Statue of Efficiency that graces New York harbor. And A. Lincoln, W. Shakespeare, F. Nightingale, and M. L. King are not revered for their furtherance of Pareto optimality. It will become apparent that many of these other criteria rest on nonteleological imperatives.

1. EQUITY

Two ethical criteria guide assessments of equity. *Horizontal equity* holds that equals should be treated equally. A main difficulty lies in delineating and measuring the relevant characteristics that define equals. Should two families with the same income be taxed equally even though the source of one family's income is inherited property and the other's is manual labor? Should the water pollution of two agricultural enterprises be reduced by equal percentages even though one is a small dairy farm and the other is a gigantic corporate chain of beef lots? Despite the difficulties, it should be clear that horizontal equity was the main force behind such legislation as the Equal Pay Act of 1963, the Civil Rights Act of 1964, and the Equal Employment Opportunity Act of 1972.

Vertical equity, the second standard, holds that unequals should be treated unequally. Once again problems of definition preclude clear applications, but this notion guides decisions concerning two particular unequals who have been with us since ancient times—the rich and the poor. Sympathy for the poor instructs that we should not reward the rich with pennies taken from the poor, that the chief cost burden of a government program should not fall on the poor, and that if price differentials are to be permitted they should favor the poor rather than the rich. We later encounter many specifics engendered by this sympathy.

Less ancient are questions of equity between generations. For most of history, living mankind seems to have been rather nonchalant about the plight of subsequent generations. The tacit assumption of each generation appears to have been that progress presides, that those who follow would certainly have fatter times. Lately, however, this assumption has been called into question. Future generations may not appreciate our shoddy storage of millions of tons of toxic wastes. They may not have the magic technology we assume they will have to get along comfortably without oil. In short, our market system has no way of registering the willingness of future generations to pay us for the preservation of their options. And some present generation commentators argue that we should not blithely and selfishly eliminate those options. They call for intergenerational equity or fairness, which when translated into policy comes out looking a lot like conservation.[15]

2 & 3. MERIT AND DEMERIT GOODS

Several ethical criteria hostile to the ethic of consumer preference satisfaction can be captured in the concept of "merit goods" and its opposite, "demerit goods." As Duncan MacRae and James Wilde say, "These concepts refer to goods that are judged to be good or bad for consumers, *regardless* of the consumers' preferences."[16] Education, fuel-efficient cars, motorcycle helmets, and retirement insurance are examples of merit goods. Government provision of such goods, or regulation or subsidy to encourage market provision, assumes that consumers may not freely or wisely buy goods or services whose main benefits are realized in the long run rather than the short run. Conversely, some goods and services may be judged particularly attractive in short-term seductiveness but harmful in their long-term consequences, warranting a bad reputation and the tag "demerit good." Cigarettes, liquor, narcotics, gambling, snake-oil medicines, and easy-to-open poison containers might be among these. Official discouragement of these goods might be partly based on external costs, as is illustrated by the fact that liquor is a major cause of highway fatalities. But it is also based on paternalistic judgments that ignore some people's preferences.

Stated a bit more technically, intervention on grounds of merit and demerit goods tramples on the ethic of consumer sovereignty, which is part of Pareto optimality. **Consumer sovereignty** asserts that people's preferences are somehow given and unchanging, that those preferences ought to be fully respected, and that the market is efficient because it forces producers to satisfy those sacred preferences as well as possible within the bounds of scarcity. Thus, support for merit and demerit measures is usually based on some theory that consumers are not really sovereign, that their interests would be better served by nonmarket means. One of the most famous of these theories is propounded by John Kenneth Galbraith. He argues that consumers' tastes are *not* innately given. Rather, their tastes are manipulated by producers through advertising, style variation, and other means of persuasion.[17] Galbraith thus replaces consumer sovereignty with producer sovereignty, which does not necessarily serve the consumer interest. Just how accurate Galbraith's theory is is uncertain. When polled, a vast majority of people claim that advertising causes them to buy things they don't really need or can't afford.[18] The econometric evidence, however, is mixed.[19] In any event, dismissal of Galbraith would not dismiss the problem, because there are other, more sophisticated theories of similar thrust.[20] All this obviously overlaps with our previous discussion of information problems.

Closely related to merit and demerit goods are areas where policy is brought into play largely on *moral* grounds, where the consumer's or producer's material welfare is not so much at issue (as in the preceding), but his or her behavior is, in itself, judged to be right or wrong. Gladiatorial contests, pornography, painful slaughter of animals, extermination of species like the bald eagle and great blue whale, abortion—each of these fires strong moral indignation among millions in our society. And each of these therefore provoke policies of discouragement. It might be possible to fit these offenses into some standard economic shortcoming. Pornography establishments, for instance, allegedly have adverse effects on surrounding areas or external costs—that is, deteriorating property values, higher crime rates, and depressed neighborhood conditions.[21] But this is stretching economics a bit too far and needlessly so. Economics cannot explain everything.[22] Furthermore, its teleological ethics must occasionally give way to imperative ethics, at least in my opinion.[23]

4. MISCELLANEOUS POLITICAL AND SOCIAL GOALS

Finally, the goodness and badness of the free-market system is often judged by a variety of criteria that do not easily fit into any of the foregoing categories. Mention of a few of these miscellaneous goals to be cited later will give you the basic idea.

Let's start with decentralization of economic power. To sing the praises of the market, pure competition in particular, solely in the key of static efficiency seriously limits one's repertoire. As will become apparent in Part II, a main purpose of the antitrust laws is not static efficiency but, rather, decentralization of power and the maintenance of competition.

> The greatest common denominator in antitrust decisions is a commitment to smallness and decentralization as ways of discouraging the concentration of discretionary authority.[24]

> The grounds for the policy include not only dislike of restriction of output and of one-sided bargaining power but also desire to prevent excessive concentration of wealth and power, desire to keep open the channels of opportunity, and concern lest monopolistic controls of business lead to political oligarchy.[25]

By the same token, there appears to be a soft spot in the heart of many Americans for small business. In social character, in charitable contributions to community, and in furtherance of independence and self-reliance, small business is often thought to be worthy of society's special support and attention. Such sentiments have found policy expression in the Small Business Administration's assistance programs, in the Robinson-Patman Act's prohibition of price discrimination injurious to competitors, and in favorable treatment under federal environmental, safety, and health regulations.

Other miscellaneous ethical standards that appear later are honesty and fairness. False advertising, unfair competition, and payola are the focus of policies, at least partly it seems, because they reflect behavior of scandalous repute.

Summary

Economic theory identifies ideal answers to the key questions raised by scarcity—what, how, who, and what's new? Static efficiency, or Pareto optimality, is theory's ideal for what and how. Static efficiency is achieved when we maximize the net benefit from our resources (in the current period). This requires allocation efficiency for the what question and production efficiency for the how question. Allocation efficiency is achieved by outputs that equalize marginal social benefit and marginal social cost (MSB = MSC). This assures that we produce what people want most. Production efficiency requires that the marginal social costs be as low as possible in a technical sense for any given level of output. This allows us to produce as much of each desirable good as possible in light of the production of other desirable goods.

Simultaneous achievement of both allocation and production efficiency yields Pareto optimality—a situation in which no one can be made better off without making someone else worse off (see Figure 2–2).

Theory has no clear, single notion of equity for the who question, but we tend to dislike extreme inequality or redistributions that take from the poor and give to the rich. Broader considerations would pay heed to the plight of nonhumans and future generations.

Dynamic efficiency is the ideal answer for what's new. This, in theory, is an allocation of resources over time that maximizes the present value of the total net benefits that could be received from all possible alternative allocations. This in practice is impossible to estimate. Still, the notion is useful for alerting us to the importance of dynamic considerations and for indicating the limits of static efficiency.

The conditions necessary for the market to achieve static efficiency include the following:

1. An absence of external benefits (MSB = MPB)
2. An absence of external costs (MSC = MPC)
3. Pure competition (P = MPC)
4. Full information (P = MPB)
5. No public goods or common property resources

Markets operate on the private benefits and costs perceived by buyers and sellers, all of whom apply two-question logic to maximize their welfare. When social benefits and costs match these private benefits and costs, and when the other ideal conditions hold, these market forces lead to optimal results.

Unfortunately, free markets frequently come up short. As outlined in Table 2–2, they may suffer imperfections, failures, dynamic incapacities, and ethical inadequacies unrelated to efficiency. Imperfections and failures produce equilibriums that deviate from *Pareto optimal* efficiency. A market's deviation in the direction of underallocation of resources, or not enough, is symbolized by MSB > MSC. Deviation in the direction of overallocation, or too much, is reflected by MSB < MSC. In either case, correction gives society benefits that exceed the costs of change.

Dynamic incapacities arise from jarring instabilities, painfully prolonged disequilibriums, transition traumas, and gaps between short-run forces and long-run fortunes. Macroeconomic problems of inflation and unemployment are particularly important because of the massive costs they impose on society. Microeconomic problems of this type fit the micro focus of this book a bit better, so they receive greater attention.

Finally, government interference in the marketplace is often based on ethical criteria that cannot be calibrated in benefit-cost accounting. Equity, fairness, honesty, morality, and decentralization are among these criteria. Your value judgments determine whether or not you agree that considerations of this kind should guide government policy. As for myself, be warned that I am an economist, one of a breed that tends to be uncomfortable analyzing virtues and vices other than those measured in dollar benefits and costs. Still, I shall try to overcome my discomfort because the world is not ruled by economists (luckily so, perhaps).

Questions and Exercises for Chapter 2

1. Why can it be said that static efficiency is related to teleological ethics instead of imperative ethics?
2. Explain static efficiency, using two-question logic

from society's point of view. Figure 2–1 may help here.

3. Achievements regarding both the what and how questions lie behind static efficiency. What are they?
4. Explain Pareto optimality in your own words with the aid of a diagram.
5. We may not want to do everything that fits the static efficiency standard because of limitations in that standard. What are those limitations? (Hint: There may be other, more important, conflicting standards.)
6. What conditions must be met in order for the free market to achieve static efficiency?
7. Using two-question logic for buyers and sellers, briefly explain how the market achieves static efficiency under ideal circumstances.
8. Which of the problems mentioned in Table 2–2 pertain to the scarcity question, "What should be produced in what amounts?" (Apply this question to the other key questions: how, who, what's new.)
9. Why are market imperfections and failures alike? Why are they different?
10. What are the adverse effects of monopoly?
11. Define external benefits and explain their consequences for static efficiency.
12. Define external costs and explain their consequences for static efficiency.
13. The text claims that most if not all problems in segment D of Table 2–2 are problems when judged by nonteleological imperatives. Explain.

Appendix to Chapter 2: Demand and Revenues, Costs and Supply

A. Demand and Revenues

Under conditions of pure competition (large numbers of buyers and sellers, easy entry, and standardized product), the demand curve facing each individual firm is perfectly elastic with respect to price. This is a supremely important statement, yet its specific content is meaningless without an understanding of two of its key terms—demand and elasticity. In the very broad

sense, **demand** refers to the quantity of product that would be purchased at various possible prices during some given period, holding all determinants of demand other than product price constant. Specifically, demand can refer (1) to the demand *of an individual buyer,* (2) to the demand *of all buyers* in the market taken together, or (3) to the demand *facing an individual seller* in the market. Generally speaking, the purchases of a single buyer are only a function of product price, income, tastes, prices of substitute goods (for example, coffee for tea or vice versa), prices for complements (for example, coffee and donuts), and expectations. Similarly, since total market demand is simply the summation of all the demands of the individual buyers in the market, total market demand is a function of the same variables that determine individual demand (price, incomes, tastes, prices of related goods, and expectations), plus one additional factor—the number of buyers in the market.

Figure 2–7 illustrates several **marketwide** demand curves. According to the conventional law of demand, each demand curve must have a neg-

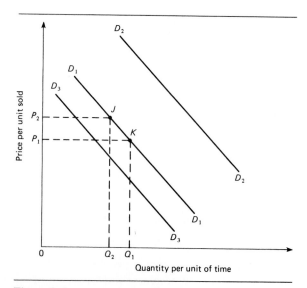

Figure 2–7
Examples of Marketwide Product Demand

ative slope because price and quantity are inversely related. Thus, on curve D_1D_1, an increase in the price of the product from P_1 to P_2 causes quantity demanded to drop from Q_1 to Q_2, resulting in a movement along the demand curve from point K to point J. Such movements along the demand curve, under the impetus of price changes, should not be confused with *shifts* of demand, which are caused by changes in variables *other* than the product's price. An increase in income, for instance, is likely to shift demand outward from D_1D_1 to D_2D_2. Conversely, a reduction of income is likely to shift demand down from D_1D_1 to D_3D_3, resulting in fewer purchases than before at each possible price.

Later, it will be important to know just *how responsive* demand is to variations in price. To measure such responsiveness, economists rely on the **elasticity** of demand in relation to price, which is defined as follows:

$$\text{price elasticity of demand} = \frac{\text{percentage change in quantity demanded}}{\text{percentage change in price}}$$

Strictly speaking, the negative slope of demand always yields a negative elasticity, but the negative sign is usually suppressed for simplification. When the percentage change in quantity demanded exceeds the percentage change in price for some given price change, quantity demand is highly responsive to price and the elasticity ratio will be greater than 1, or elastic. Conversely, if the percentage change in quantity demanded is less than the percentage change in price, demand is relatively *un*responsive to price variations and the elasticity will be less than 1, or inelastic.

Although marketwide demand tends to be inversely related to price, this may not be the same view of demand held by the typical *individual firm* selling in the market, unless, of course, there is only one firm in the market (a monopolist). In the case of pure competition, the product is standardized, and each seller is so small rela-

tive to the total market that it views its demand as in Figure 2–8—a horizontal line running parallel to the quantity axis and intersecting the vertical axis at the going market price.

There are numerous profit-maximizing rules of thumb (for example, "never give a sucker an even break"). The formal economic principle is, in essence, *equalize marginal revenue and marginal cost*. Because demand determines marginal revenue, we discuss the revenue portion of the formula first, postponing consideration of marginal cost until the next section. **Marginal revenue** *is the change in total revenue attributable to the sale of one more unit of output*. Indeed, "incremental revenue" might be a better name for it. Because price and quantity are always the two basic components of demand, and because total revenue is always price *times* quantity sold, there is a very intimate relationship between demand and marginal revenue. In the purely competitive case, the firm's total revenue rises directly with quantity sold at a constant rate of increase because, according to the firm's demand curve, price is constant over the firm's range of product sales. In other words, the additional sale of one unit of output always adds to total revenue an

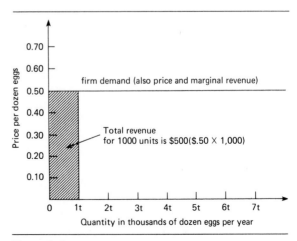

Figure 2–8
Demand of a Perfectly Competitive Seller

amount that *just equals the price*. Hence, price and marginal revenue are equal when, as shown in Figure 2–8, the demand curve of the firm is perfectly elastic. Using that figure's data, an additional sale of one dozen eggs adds $0.50 to the firm's total revenue, regardless of whether it is the first dozen sold or the 3000th dozen sold. Hence, marginal revenue is $0.50.

B. Costs and Supply

Marginal cost, the second portion of the profit maximizing rule of thumb, may be defined as *the addition to total costs due to the additional production of one unit of output*. What are total costs? In the short run, total costs are made up of two components—total fixed costs and total variable costs. The short run, as already mentioned, is a period short enough for certain factors of production—such as land, buildings, and equipment—to be immobile. Those immobile factors generate **total fixed costs**—such as rent, debt repayments, and property taxes—that *in terms of total costs* do not vary with output. In terms of *cost per unit* of output, or average fixed cost, however, these costs actually decline with greater output because average fixed cost is the total fixed cost (a constant) divided by the number of units produced. Thus, as output rises these fixed costs are spread over a larger and larger number of units.

Total variable costs, on the other hand, *are those costs associated with variable factors of production,* such as labor, raw materials, and purchased parts. In terms of *total* costs these costs *always* rise with greater amounts of output, but in terms of *per unit*, or average costs, these may fall, remain unchanged, or rise, depending on the prices and productivity of these variable factors as they are variously applied to the fixed factors. Average, or per-unit, variable cost is the total variable cost at some given level of output divided by the number of units in that quantity of output. Thus, functionally speaking, if total variable cost rises less rapidly than quantity does,

per-unit variable cost will fall; if total variable cost rises one for one with quantity at a constant rate, per-unit variable cost will be constant; and if the total rises more rapidly than the quantity, per-unit variable cost will rise.

Figure 2–9 depicts this family of cost curves on a per-unit, or average, basis according to conventional forms. ATC indicates short-run average total cost, and AVC indicates short-run average variable cost. Average fixed cost, AFC, constitutes the difference between ATC and AVC. When ATC is falling, marginal cost, MC, will be below ATC. Once ATC begins to rise, however, MC exceeds ATC. If the P = MR (price equals marginal revenue) line represents the individual firm's demand curve for a prevailing price of OA, profit maximization is achieved by producing OH units of output because, at that level of output, marginal cost just equals marginal revenue at point K. Bearing in mind that total profits are simply total revenue less total cost, the profit-maximizing firm adds to its output so long as the added revenue thereby obtained, MR, exceeds the added cost thereby

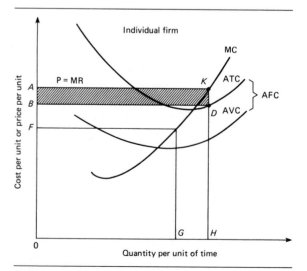

Figure 2–9
Shortrun Cost Curves of the Firm Together with Perfectly Competitive Demand

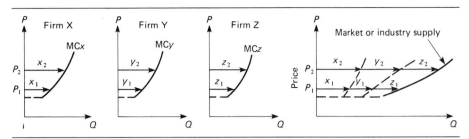

Figure 2–10
Horizontal Summation of Firm Supply Curves for Industry Supply

incurred, MC. This is true of all output levels up to *OH*. However, once the added cost of added output, MC, exceeds the added revenue obtained, MR, total profits begin to fall. Hence, the astute firm will not produce an output greater than *OH*. At output *OH*, total economic profit is the shaded rectangle *BAKD,* which is the economic profit per unit, *KD,* times the number of units produced *AK*. This is called **economic profit** or **excess profit** because the average total cost *includes* a "normal" profit for the investors that is just sufficiently large, say 9 percent per year, to pay the cost of capital. Provision of this normal profit rate discourages the investors from withdrawing their capital in the long run and investing it elsewhere.

At price *OF* there would be neither excess profit nor normal profit; there would be a loss. Still, in the short run, the firm would continue to produce an amount *OG*, which would again equate marginal revenue (now *OF*) with marginal cost. The firm thus minimizes its losses. Only if price were to drop so low that the firm could not recover its variable cost (AVC) on each unit would it minimize loss by closing down. The firm should *never* lose in total dollars more than its total fixed cost.

Two major conclusions emerge from this analysis. First, since price equals marginal revenue for the perfectly competitive firm, the MR = MC profit rule of thumb causes price to equal marginal cost and fulfills the optimal welfare requirement. Second, the supply curve for the firm

is identical to its marginal cost curve above the AVC curve. Over the range of possible prices, the quantity offered for sale by the firm may be read from the MC curve. It follows, then, that marketwide short-run supply under pure competition is determined by simply adding up the short-run supplies of all individual firms in the market at each possible price, as is illustrated in Figure 2–10.

It is the interaction of this supply with marketwide demand that yields market price under pure competition. See Figure 2–3.

Notes

1. For more on static efficiency or Pareto optimality, see any good intermediate microeconomic theory test—for example, Edwin Mansfield's *Microeconomics: Theory and Applications* (New York: Norton, 1970). For an extensive discussion of the limitations of these concepts, see Warren J. Samuels, "Welfare Economics, Power, and Property," in *Law and Economics,* ed. W. J. Samuels and A. A. Schmid (Boston: Martinus Nijhoff Publishing, 1981), pp. 9–51.

2. A. K. Sen, *On Economic Inequality* (New York: Oxford University Press (Clarendon Press), 1973); A. B. Atkinson, *The Economics of Inequality,* 2nd ed. (New York: Oxford University Press (Clarendon Press), 1983).

3. Tom Tietenberg, *Environmental and Natural Resource Economics* (Glenview, IL: Scott, Foresman, 1988).

4. Talbot Page, *Conservation and Economic Efficiency* (Baltimore: Johns Hopkins University Press, 1979). See also Robert C. Lind et al., *Discounting for Time and Risk in Energy Policy* (Baltimore: Johns Hopkins University Press, 1983).

5. This specific approach and Table 2–1 are inspired by Nicholas Mercuro and Timothy P. Ryan, *Law, Economics, and Public Policy* (Greenwich, CT: JAI Press, 1984).

6. R. G. Lipsey and Kelvin Lancaster, "The General

Theory of Second Best," *Review of Economic Studies* 24, no. 1 (1956): 11–32.

7. Alfred R. Oxenfeldt, "Consumer Knowledge: Its Measurement and Extent," *Review of Economics and Statistics* (October 1950): 300–315; R. T. Morris and C. S. Bronson, "The Chaos of Competition Indicated by Consumer Reports," *Journal of Marketing* (July 1969): 26–34; Monroe P. Friedman, "Quality and Price Considerations in Rational Decision Making," *Journal of Consumer Affairs* (Summer 1967): 13–23; Peter C. Riesz, "Price-Quality Correlations for Packaged Food Products," *Journal of Consumer Affairs* (Winter 1979): 236–247.

8. Kenneth Arrow, "Economic Welfare and the Allocation of Resources for Invention," in *The Rate and Direction of Inventive Activity: Economic and Social Factors* (New York: National Bureau of Economic Research, 1962).

9. Douglas F. Greer, *Industrial Organization and Public Policy,* 2nd ed. (New York: Macmillan, 1984), pp. 54–73.

10. Paul A. Samuelson, "The Pure Theory of Public Expenditure," *Review of Economics and Statistics* (November 1954): 386–389; James M. Buchanan, *The Demand and Supply of Public Goods* (Chicago: Rand McNally, 1968).

11. For a good discussion see Duncan MacRae, Jr., and James A. Wilde, *Policy Analysis for Public Decisions* (North Scituate, MA: Duxbury Press, 1979), pp. 179–186.

12. Dale E. Hathaway, *Government and Agriculture: Economic Policy in a Democratic Society* (New York: Macmillan, 1963), pp. 45–46.

13. Peter O. Steiner, "The Public Sector and the Public Interest," in *Public Expenditures and Policy Analysis* ed. Haveman and Margolis (Chicago: Rand McNally, 1977), pp. 36–37.

14. John E. Tilton, *U.S. Energy R & D Policy* (Washington, DC: Resources for the Future, 1974), pp. 22–66.

15. Talbot Page, *Conservation and Economic Efficiency* (Baltimore: Johns Hopkins University Press, 1977), especially chapters 8 and 9; Herman E. Daly, *Steady-State Economics* (San Francisco: Freeman, 1977).

16. MacRae and Wilde, *Policy Analysis,* p. 188.

17. John Kenneth Galbraith, *The New Industrial State* (Boston: Houghton Mifflin, 1967), pp. 198–210.

18. R. A. Bauer and S. A. Greyser, *Advertising in America: The Consumer View* (Cambridge: Division of Research, Graduate School of Business Administration, Harvard University, 1968), p. 71.

19. William S. Comanor and Thomas A. Wilson, *Advertising and Market Power* (Cambridge, MA: Harvard University Press, 1974), pp. 64–92; Ronald P. Wilder, "Advertising and Inter-Industry Competition: Testing a Galbraithian Hypothesis," *Journal of Industrial Economics* (March 1974): 215–226; Henry G. Grabowski, "The Effects of Advertising on the Interindustry Distribution of Demand," *NBER Explorations in Economic Research* (Winter 1976): 21–75.

20. Herbert Gintis, "Consumer Behavior and the Concept of Sovereignty: Explanations of Social Decay," *American Economic Review* (May 1972): 267–278; A. Dixit and V. Norman, "Advertising and Welfare," *Bell Journal of Economics* (Spring 1978): 1–17; Robert A. Pollak, "Endogenous Tastes in Demand and Welfare Analysis," *American Economic Review* (May 1978): 374–379. Steven E. Rhoads is especially good on consumer sovereignty: *The Economist's View of the World* (Cambridge, England: Cambridge University Press, 1985).

21. William Toner, *Regulating Sex Businesses* (Chicago: American Society of Planning Officials, 1977).

22. Tibor Scitovsky, "The Place of Economic Welfare in Human Welfare," *Quarterly Review of Economics and Business* (Autumn 1973): 7–19.

23. Amitai Etzioni, *The Moral Dimension* (New York: Free Press, 1988).

24. Donald Dewey, "The New Learning: One Man's View," in *Industrial Concentration: The New Learning,* ed. H. J. Goldschmid, H. M. Mann, and J. F. Weston (Boston: Little, Brown, 1974), p. 13.

25. Corwin Edwards, *Maintaining Competition* (New York: McGraw-Hill, 1949), p. 9. See also Hans Thorelli, *The Federal Antitrust Policy* (Baltimore: Johns Hopkins University Press, 1955), pp. 570–571; Richard Hofstadter, "What Happened to the Antitrust Movement?" in *The Business Establishment* ed. E. F. Cheit (New York: Wiley, 1964), pp. 113–151; and Robert Pitofsky, "The Political Content of Antitrust," *University of Pennsylvania Law Review* (April 1979): 1051–1081.

26. Michael Klass and Leonard Weiss, *Study on Federal Regulation,* vol. IV, "Framework for Regulation," U.S. Senate, Committee on Governmental Affairs (December 1979), pp. xi–xii.

Chapter 3
Government Policy: Ideal and Real

People often appear to think of government as some sort of half-drugged servant: if one can only get him to act, he will of course do exactly what one has in mind. Without exception though . . . there are numerous inherent shortcomings.
— *Roland McKean*

We have seen that the wardrobe of the free-market system is generally a fine one for society to wear. But we have also found a long laundry list of stains that society might ask government to clean up, namely, imperfections, failures, dynamic difficulties, and miscellaneous ethical boltches.

Our format for discussing the role of government in this chapter follows our earlier format for markets. In broad division, it first presents the good news, with a look at government under ideal circumstances. Next comes the bad news, with a catalogue of government's real-world shortcomings. Our discussion of the ideal state is further divided into two parts—one for political *process,* the other for political *performance*—a division that corresponds to the two questions of *how* and *how well* the market works. Similarly, there is a convenient correspondence for our discussion of government's real-world shortcomings because those bedevilments may be labeled imperfections, failures, dynamic problems, and miscellaneous ethical stumbles. Without embroidery, we cover the following:

I. IDEAL GOVERNMENT
  A. Political processes or "How" (preference articulation, preference aggregation, etc.)
  B. Political performance or "How well"
    1. Allocation efficiency (benefit-cost)
    2. Dynamic welfare (stability, growth)
    3. Equity and other desirables (bliss)
II. REAL GOVERNMENT
  A. Imperfections (misallocation)
  B. Failures (misallocation)
  C. Dynamic difficulties (delays, etc.)
  D. Other ethical shortcomings (e.g., inequity)

The discussion presumes that the major ethical criteria previously applied to markets—static efficiency and economic equity in particular—are also the appropriate ethical criteria to apply to government. Be warned that many people would disagree with that presumption. Goodness and badness in markets are fairly widely agreed on, thanks to the idea of Pareto optimality. But goodness and badness in government are nowhere nearly as well-defined. Even if we ignore the anarchists and the totalitarians, we confront a spectrum of alternative ethical criteria.[1] It could thus be argued that government should not be gauged by Pareto efficiency or related yardsticks.

Our present course can be defended on several grounds, however. First, the application of economic criteria seems reasonable insofar as we are concerned with government's intervention in economic matters. In such other matters as treason, kidnapping, and blackmail, we may readily grant that economic ethics have no place. But our primary concerns are instances when government attempts to rescue us from the market's deficiencies. Second, the Pareto ethic generally offers a fairly clear, concise, and consistent criterion. Can the same qualities be attributed to such slippery notions as "justice" or "self-realization"? Probably not. Third, it must be stressed that we do not follow the Pareto ethic with pathological rigidity. Our discussion gives equal time to dynamic considerations and other ethical convictions. Thus, for example, we acknowledge that society may wish to promote small businesses even at some loss in allocation efficiency.

All of this is to say that, once again, the satisfaction of personal preferences is taken as the chief barometer of achievement. Still, satisfaction of personal preferences does not always correspond to society's pursuit of the general welfare, so several qualifications are accepted.

I. Government at Its Best

A. Political Processes (How?)

The political methods and procedural steps taken to reach government policies can be as important as the policies themselves. An athlete can lose gracefully if the game is played fairly. So, too, citizens who happen to come out on the short end of a government decision tend to accept their lot more readily if they believe the political proceedings were on the level. In essence, the procedures should fit the many qualities connoting goodness in government—democracy, impartiality, clarity, consistency, and so on.

Table 3–1 partitions the procedural steps into four parts (with loose correspondence to the political functions outlined in Chapter 1). The steps are fairly self-evident—problem recognition, policy formulation, policy application, and private sector compliance.

1. PROBLEM RECOGNITION AND PREFERENCE ARTICULATION

Accurate articulation of citizens' preferences is crucial. Aside from the obvious ideal of one person—one vote, several further conditions fos-

---

Table 3–1
Ideal Governmental Procedures

---

1. Problem Recognition: Preference Articulation
    a. One person—one vote
    b. Full participation by society's members
    c. Full information on problem
    d. Full employment to ease burden of change
2. Policy Formulation (Aggregation and Legislation)
    a. Preference aggregation through ideal voting rules and representation
    b. Selection of proper focus for policy: structure, conduct, or performance
    c. Selection of proper instrument for policy (e.g., tax, subsidy, direct regulation, etc.)
3. Policy Application (Executive Enforcement and Judicial Review)
    a. Impartial application, consistency
    b. Efficient and expeditious application
    c. Minimum interference with private decision making
    d. Penalty fits the crime
4. Private Sector Compliance
    a. Clear knowledge of behavior required
    b. Appropriate incentives to comply
    c. Dependable and automatic compliance
    d. Low-cost means for private party compliance

---

ter accuracy. *Full participation* would require. that everyone affected by any policy be heard from. In some cases this is obviously not possible or practical. We cannot reliably hear from future generations or the insane. We do not jump at the slightest suggestions of children or criminals. Yet the basic idea is unexceptionable. Nearly everyone should have a vote and use it when his or her fate is affected.

Full information would require that all these participants be completely knowledgeable about the policy options—the benefits, the costs, the short-run implications, and the long-run consequences. This requirement too is difficult to meet, given the horrendous complexities and large number of policies posed by our modern world. Indeed, even experts cannot tell us precisely where taxes will bite or the degree of calamity caused by cholesterol in our food.

Implicit in the market ideal of Pareto efficiency was an assumption of full employment. In an ideal political context, *full employment* would permit voters to judge policies solely on intrinsic merit, without worry or hope about their jobs.[2] Thus, when voting for or against a 10¢ deposit on soda pop containers, each person should decide on the basis of allocative benefits (reduced litter, lower container costs) and allocative costs (inconvenience, higher costs of deposit procedures). If bottle plant workers vote against the measure solely from fright of job loss, the ideal calculation would be upset, at least as it relates to Pareto efficiency.

2. POLICY FORMULATION: AGGREGATION AND LEGISLATION

Voting Rules. Majority rule seems as sacred as mom and apple pie. Yet it cannot, in general, be accepted as the ideal voting rule because it gives the majority an opportunity to tyrannize the minority.

To illustrate, imagine a ballot proposition that, if passed, would provide 330 days of clean air per year instead of the present 300. Notice the public good here: *Everyone* would get 30 additional clean days regardless of their personal preferences. Assume further that this change would cost $15 per person per year, or $0.50 for each additional day of clean air. Those voting in favor of the measure would think this a good deal. Indeed, many on the yes side would willingly pay for *more* additional clean days at $0.50 each, or pay *more* than $15 for the 30 specified on the ballot. Conversely, those voting against the proposition would not value clean air as highly. They would feel that $15 was too high a price to pay for 30 additional clean days, or they would feel that they should get more than 30 days for that kind of money. The implication is that majority rule will make one of these groups worse off. If the proposition passes, the naysayers will sulk. If it fails, the yea-sayers suffer. Yet the Pareto ideal is to make some better off *without* making anyone else worse off.

Another way of stating this is that, under majority rule, the median voter—that is, the middle one that swings the outcome off 50–50 dead center—is the voter of greatest consequence, and in a narrow race, the only voter whose preferences are most nearly satisfied. The power of the median voter is observed in the tendency of presidential candidates to snuggle close to the middle of the road, to abandon extreme positions of either the left or right. Moreover, as Anthony Downs observes, competition over the median turf "forces both [political] parties to be much less than perfectly clear about what they stand for."[3]

The *ideal* for dealing with allocation improvements such as public goods or externalities is thus *unanimous rule* rather than majority rule. If in fact a Pareto improvement is possible from a change, then it should also be possible to specify the change in a ballot proposition that could gain unanimous consent. To continue our example of clean air, the 30 additional days of benefit could not be varied to suit individual preferences because they are a public good, but the cost of

$15 per head might be individually variable. Those fervently desiring greater cleanliness would still support the proposition if their cost were raised to $40, say, or whatever would more closely approach their willingness to pay. Conversely, opponents could be converted into supporters by amendments *lowering* their cost burden to levels just less than their willingness to pay. With support all around, unanimity emerges.

This endorsement of unanimity is admittedly utopian. The problems of practicality are gargantuan. How can we learn each individual's preference for a proposition when it is in his or her interest to "free ride," to keep that preference hidden or understated, given the public good nature of the decision? How can we be sure that no egocentric nitwit will take the opportunity to play last holdout just to gain notoriety? In reality, few if any decisions would ever be made under a rule of unanimity.[4]

Moreover, unanimity can claim perfection *only* when applied to policies improving *static efficiency*. Policies that deliberately redistribute income to achieve some greater degree of *equality* cannot be decided under unanimous procedures for the simple reason that they necessarily hurt some people while helping others. A unanimous rule would be hopeless in such instances. Thus, it has been argued that truly ideal procedures would require different voting rules for different types of policies: a unanimous rule for efficiency improvements and a majority rule for equity adjustments.[5] Theoretical problems remain, and this dichotomy does not wash away the practical difficulties, but we momentarily postpone further allusions to reality.

The Focus of Policy. As Figure 3–1 shows, markets have three main elements that may be the focus of public policy—structure, conduct, and performance. Market *structure* sets the environment in which sellers operate. Among the most important variables of structure are the number of sellers and their size distribution, product differentiation (determined partly by ad-

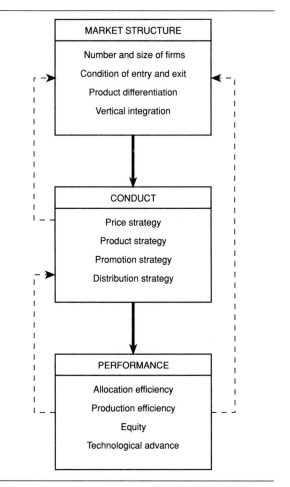

Figure 3–1
Elements of Market Operation and Policy Focus

vertising and promotion), and the condition of entry (which is affected by patents, licensing, and product differentiation, among other things). The word *conduct* denotes behavior and strategy by firms in the market, so the several items listed under conduct in Figure 3–1 reflect action, not static condition. Finally, *performance* relates to achievements as determined by such variables as efficiency, technological advance, and product quality.

The solid arrows in the center of Figure 3–1 indicate traditional theory's causal flow, running from structure to conduct to performance. For example, the number and size of firms in structure influence the price conduct of firms. If there are many firms (pure competition), each firm is a price taker, perceiving demand as perfectly horizontal (see Figure 2–8). If there is one firm (pure monopoly), the firm sees the marketwide demand curve and thereby has enough control to raise price (see Figure 2–4). In turn, these variations in conduct determine performance. Pure competition can yield static efficiency in contrast to monopoly's inefficiency.

The dashed lines of Figure 3–1 represent causal flows running in the opposite direction from the traditional model. They, too, will occasionally attract our attention.

Given structure, conduct, and performance, government has some range of choice when selecting its focus for policy. Moreover, the choice can be important. By analogy, if a car's sputter comes from a dirty fuel line, it does little good to focus repairs on the tires or upholstery.

Table 3–2 illustrates the principle of proper focus by outlining the most fitting targets of policies designed to remedy the market imperfections listed at the top of Table 2–2 in the last chapter. Policies countering "artificial" blemishes in competition would best be directed toward structure and conduct rather than performance, because good performance would tend to follow automatically if structure and conduct were made workably competitive. Antimonopoly law could deconcentrate monopolized markets, and merger law could prevent anticompetitive combinations. Preservation of rivalous conduct could be furthered by prohibitions on restrictive practices like price fixing and tying. It is important to note that structure and conduct would also be the

Table 3–2
Basic Government Policies Concerning Markets

Policy Type	Structure	Conduct	Performance
Maintenance of competition with antitrust	1. Monopoly law 2. Merger laws	1. Price-fixing law 2. Price discrimination law 3. Exclusive dealing law 4. Tying law	
Public utility regulation of natural monopolies		1. Price regulation in telephone, electricity, and gas 2. Abandonment of service and extension of service	1. Profit regulation 2. Service requirements 3. Safety 4. Innovation regulation
Information improvement	1. Disclosure of information, truth-in-lending law 2. Grading and standardization, general weights and measures 3. Trademark and copyright protection	1. False advertising 2. Deceptive practices	

proper focus if the intent of policy were to maintain competition as an end in itself, regardless of the consequences for performance.

Where technological imperatives spawn "natural" monopolies, the best strategy would probably be acceptance of monopoly structure but regulation of conduct and performance—surveillance of price patterns, product quality, and profit level in particular. Such regulation is a difficult and distorting exercise, one that occasions much more intervention in the daily affairs of business than competition policy. At the same time, regulation may be judged superior to outright government ownership, a still more meddlesome policy option for handling the problem of monopoly. Thus, an array of the alternatives from least to most intrusive reads: competition, regulation, then government ownership.

Imperfections of ignorance and misinformation could also be treated with performance regulation, in which case government would have to specify product standards, check assembly-line compliance, levy penalties for noncompliance, and in various other ways get quite nosey. As suggested in Table 3–2, however, the alternatives of disclosing information (a structural approach) and curbing misleading claims (a conduct approach) are generally superior in efficacy and efficiency. These approaches leave buyers greater leeway; they do not choke off the consumers' range of choice; and they entail scant bureaucracy.

Selection of Policy Instruments. A corollary to the foregoing is that excellence in government requires selection of the best instrument to do the job at hand. Appreciation of this platitude hinges on explanations of "best" and "instrument."

Policy instruments are means rather than ends. They are usually the guts of legislation. They are what government actually does on a daily basis. Instruments are also as varied as cooking utensils. The main ones are mentioned in Table 3–3 together with the problems they are best suited for, not necessarily those they are ac-

Table 3–3
Policy Instruments and Problems Addressed

Problem	Policy Instrument
Monopoly power & restraint of trade	Antitrust
Natural monopoly	Public utility regulation
Information inadequacies	Information disclosure
	Prohibitions on misrepresentation
	Trademark rights
External benefits	Subsidy
External costs	Regulatory prohibitions, taxes, fees
Public goods	Public provision or subsidy
Common property resources	Regulation, public ownership
Instabilities	Loans, insurance
Transition immobilities	Temporary payments, job retraining
Macroeconomic instability	Monetary and fiscal policies
Growth and promotion	Tax exemptions, public works, patents
Equity	Transfer payments
Merit goods	Subsidy, information provision
Demerit goods	Taxes, prohibitions
Safety	Regulation, information disclosure

tually employed against.[6] For two reasons the table conceals the still greater variety that will be encountered throughout the book. First, each instrument mentioned covers a vast territory. Take subsidies, for instance. They can take the form of direct subsidies, such as grants of money and land, or indirect subsidies, such as tax exemptions, loan guarantees, or stockpile purchases. Second, many policy instruments are not mentioned in Table 3–3 because they are rarely appropriate for anything. These include (1) direct price controls outside the public utility context, (2) licensing and other forms of entry constraint, and (3) tariffs and quotas.

As for what is best in an instrument, there are many criteria by which to judge. Among the most obvious are speed of effect and sufficiency. In *speed,* which is the time passing from implementation to effect, brevity is usually best. Quickness is especially important in policies treating instability.

The *sufficiency,* or strength of an instrument, is best when neither too potent nor too weak to achieve the intended result. Thus, ideally, an effluent tax on a polluting industry should be just high enough to curtail pollution until marginal social benefit matches marginal social cost; not so high as to close the industry down completely, nor so low as to barely make a dent in the degree of environmental damage. In other aspects of policy, strength depends on breadth of coverage, intensity of surveillance, and severity of remedies. But mention of these elements moves us beyond issues of policy formulation into issues of policy application and compliance.

3 & 4. POLICY APPLICATION AND COMPLIANCE

With ample notice, the Food and Drug Administration banned DES, a synthetic hormone used to spur growth in cattle and a known carcinogen (cause of cancer), after November 1, 1979. Confident of quick compliance, the FDA shortly thereafter discontinued monitoring meat for DES contamination. But six months later it was discovered that compliance was spotty, that as many as 10 percent of the country's cattlemen failed to heed the government's order.[7]

Ideally, policy application and compliance would conform to the features mentioned in the last half of Table 3–1. Those features are largely self-evident, fulfilling the spirit of such qualities as impartiality, consistency, efficiency, clarity, dependability, and unobtrusiveness. You will no-

tice that achievement of these qualities depends on more than bureaucratic procedures, company compliance efforts, and the like. It also depends on achievements made earlier in the policy process, namely, good diagnosis of the nature of the problem, registration of society's preferences, wise choice of policy instrument, and so on. Fantastic feats at the later stages cannot be expected without building on solid foundations.

B. Political Performance (How Well?)

Ideal processes are desirable in themselves, but the best proof of the pudding is, as they say, in the eating. Thus we come to government performance as it is measured by (1) benefit-cost analysis, (2) dynamic welfare, and (3) miscellaneous ethical convictions.

1. BENEFIT-COST ANALYSIS (FOR OPTIMAL ALLOCATIONS)

From July 1979 to April 1980 federal regulations specified that during the winter, temperatures in most commercial and industrial buildings could be no more than 65 degrees and during the summer no less than 78 degrees. This was an energy conservation measure, the main benefit of which was the saving of about 40.5 million barrels of oil, or $810 million, assuming a price of $20 per barrel. There were costs, however. In addition to the costs of keeping energy bureaucrats employed, substantial costs were borne by businesses when the productivity of their workers fell. In the winter, typists complained that their cold fingers hit more wrong keys than usual, and telephone assembly-line workers said the cold robbed them of dexterity. In the summer, accounts receivable clerks were delayed when papers kept sticking to their elbows and reports of general sluggishness were heard throughout the land.[8] Whether the total monetary cost of these adversities exceeded the $810 million benefit is unknown, but if it did, the wisdom of the policy could be questioned.

To the extent static efficiency (i.e., Pareto

optimality) is accepted as the standard by which to judge government performance, *excellence would require that policies be implemented or expanded only when the added social benefits of the change exceeded the added social costs, up to the point where costs equal benefits.* The similarity between this standard and that emerging from ideal markets, as pictured in Figure 2–1, is no accident. The idea is that if government is going to pick up where markets leave off, then ideally it should simulate the ideal results of the market. Satisfaction of personal preferences is the target. Resources are the ammunition.

Stated technically, the **benefit** of a policy change is *the maximum amount people who gain would be willing to pay* to have resources used in the way the policy entails. The **cost** of a policy change is *the minimum amount people who make sacrifices must receive to be fully compensated* when the resources are not used in other ways.[9] This follows the logic of the ideal marketplace, where demand is maximum willingness to pay and supply is minimum willingness to receive. Stated numerically, government's grade rating of tires might cost $50 million per year (for tires destroyed in tests, test equipment, salaries of test personnel, and other resources). But if consumers of tires would be willing to pay $75 million per year for this information (as measured by their savings from better purchase accuracy and from lower tire prices due to greater competition), then the program would be a good one. Efficiency would improve.

Figure 3–2 illustrates the benefits and costs from antitrust action that converts a monopoly industry into a competitive industry. Constant unit costs are assumed for simplicity. Under monopoly, price is P_1 and quantity is Q_1. Under competition, price is P_2 and quantity is Q_2. Thus, the relevant benefits and costs derive from the increased output from Q_1 to Q_2 and the reduced price from P_1 to P_2. The total benefit from change matches the area under the demand curve, which is Q_1ABQ_2, because that is the amount folks are

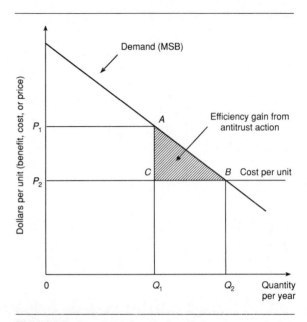

Figure 3–2
Benefits and Costs from Antitrust Action

willing to pay for the added output. The total cost of producing the added output, or the minimum suppliers must receive, is the area under the cost-per-unit curve, Q_1CBQ_2, because that is the cost per unit times the number of additional units. Not pictured are the costs of lawyers' time in prosecuting the case, court costs, and the like, but let's assume that these legal costs are small enough to be ignored. Then the benefit less cost is the difference between these areas, that is, the shaded triangle ABC. In equation form, with Δ indicating "change in":

$$\frac{\Delta \text{ Net}}{\text{benefit}} = \text{Social benefit} - \text{Social cost}$$
$$ABC = Q_1ABQ_2 \qquad - Q_1CBQ_2$$

It must be stressed that this is only the *efficiency gain* associated with the *reallocation of resources* from elsewhere to here and the associated jump in quantity from Q_1 to Q_2. Consumers also gain from the reduced price on all the units purchased prior to the antitrust action, ranging over O to Q_1. This total savings is area P_2P_1AC, which is the price difference times quantity. But this is not counted in the foregoing calculation because it represents a *transfer* of money from the sellers to the buyers, or a possible improvement in *equity* rather than an improvement in *efficiency*. The seller's revenue before the action is OP_1AQ_1, part of which, rectangle P_2P_1AC, is excess profit. The seller's revenue for this quantity after change is OP_2CQ_1. The difference, P_2P_1AC, is transferred from the producer's pocket to the consumer's. Indeed, as is explained shortly, it would be best at this point if equity considerations were kept out of the story by assuming that the consumer-gainers actually paid producer-losers to compensate them for the loss of P_2P_1AC. Then there would be no redistribution effect at all. And triangle ABC still represents the resulting Pareto-efficiency improvement.

Figure 3–3 illustrates the benefits and costs associated with a tax on pollution, when the tax rate just equals the external costs of the pollution. In this case, the direction of reallocation is opposite to that just discussed, namely a decrease in output and an increase in price rather than an increase in output and a decrease in price. Thus the benefits in this case are best thought of as *cost reductions,* particularly a reduction in the external cost caused by pollution, and these benefits still reflect willingness to pay, particularly the willingness of those wanting to reduce the level of pollution. Similarly, the costs in this case are best thought of as *benefit reductions* because reduced output and higher prices mean that benefits are forgone. Consumers, producers, and employees bear the cost.

The pretax, free-market result is an equilibrium at N, with price P_1 and quantity Q_1. After the tax, which corresponds to KJ per unit and MN per unit, the market moves to point K as the cost of the tax is added to the marginal private cost, MPC. The total *benefit* from the change is

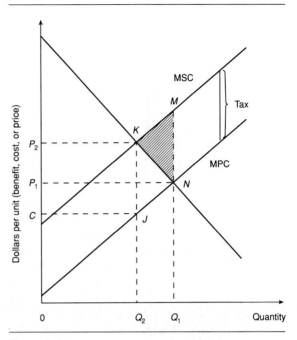

Figure 3–3
Benefits and Costs from Pollution Tax

the area Q_1MKQ_2, because that is the reduced social cost of moving from Q_1 to Q_2, counting both reduced private costs of Q_1NJQ_2 and reduced external costs of $NMKJ$. Conversely, the total *cost* (i.e., forgone benefit) associated with the change is the area under the demand curve over the $Q_1 - Q_2$ range, or Q_1NKQ_2. Thus, the net benefit from the tax is the shaded area KMN. Algebraically, this change reads:

$$\begin{matrix} \Delta \text{ Net} \\ \text{benefit} \end{matrix} = \Delta \text{ Social benefit} - \Delta \text{ Social cost}$$
$$KMN = Q_1MKQ_2 \qquad - Q_1NKQ_2$$

Notice that reallocation beyond this point to quantities less than Q_2 would not be optimal because the cost of further reductions in Q, as read off the demand curve, exceed the benefits, as read off the MSC curve. Notice, too, that efficiency does not necessarily imply elimination of the pollution, only its abatement.

By these lights, ideal performance in government requires more than mere adherence to the benefit-cost technique; it also requires perfection of the technique. To attain such perfection numerous conditions must be met, perfect knowledge and distributional neutrality being the most important.

Perfect knowledge requires that all the relevant benefits and costs must be identified and measured in dollar values. This is anything but simple. Almost every change in policy has myriad benefits and costs that ideally need identification and measurement. When people's lives are at stake, as they are in safety and environmental issues, they must be counted and evaluated. When species are threatened, they must be monetarily weighed. When market prices are used to estimate wage costs, the value of crop outputs, and the many other tangible items entering the analysis, those market prices must accurately reflect marginal social benefits and marginal social costs. All externalities raised by policy action must also be accounted for as when, for instance, government dams kill fish or add salinity to river water.

Distribution neutrality requires that no adverse changes in the distribution of well-being occur when the benefit-cost criterion is applied. This condition could easily be met (a) if those people experiencing the benefits were exactly the same as those bearing the costs, or (b) if each dollar of benefit to gainers could always be given the same equity or distributional weight as a dollar of cost to losers. Inconveniently, however, those who gain and those who lose are usually not the same. What is more, it is doubtful that we can justifiably give equal weight to all the dollars involved. Thus, blind pursuit of the benefit-cost criterion, with nothing more, might make the rich richer and the poor poorer if those who gain are typically rich and those who lose are typically poor.

The ideal of distribution neutrality therefore requires that the gainers of reallocation policies always compensate the losers, as suggested a moment ago in our example of monopoly. In all cases in which benefits actually exceed costs, gainers *should be able* to pay losers and still come out ahead. The ideal of requiring that such payments *actually be made* assures that income *inequality will at least not grow worse*. It also corresponds to the market ethic of voluntary exchange, which implies no rip-offs. Finally, it dovetails with our earlier observation that unanimous blessing is best for efficiency improvements.[10]

2. DYNAMIC WELFARE (STABILITY AND GROWTH)

When issues of static resource allocation are at stake, Pareto optimality provides a standard of excellence by which to judge government performance because that is a widely accepted ideal for evaluating market performance. In other areas of economic concern, such as stability and growth, there is no clear consensus on what constitutes good market performance, so there is likewise no clear consensus on what constitutes good governmental performance. To be sure, there are some vague notions that gain wide enough acceptance to drive any Gallup Poll of popularity through the roof, notions like full employment and price stability. But the closer one gets to concrete yardsticks, such as 3.5 percent unemployment and 5 percent annual growth in real GNP per capita, the smaller the group one can find in support of those yardsticks.

Rather than waffle our way through every aspect of dynamic behavior with this message, we can focus on growth to illustrate the point. In times past, economic growth was universally applauded as glorious, so the ideal standard was something like: "the more, the better."[11] As the founder of economics, Adam Smith, wrote in 1776:

> It is in the progressive state, while the society is advancing to the further acquisition, rather than when it has acquired its full complement of riches, that the conditions of the labouring poor, of the

great body of the people, seems to be the happiest and most comfortable. It is hard in the stationary, and miserable in the declining state.[12]

In 1960 a good text on government and business asked, "Who would question the desirability of economic growth?"[13]

Conformity of convictions has now crumbled, however. A growing number of doubters is questioning the *possibility* and the *desirability* of vigorous economic growth. In questioning desirability, the issue of main interest here, skeptics claim that growth does not really improve the subjective satisfaction of individuals,[14] that it produces bad by-products of air pollution, water degradation, toxic waste, and disruptive congestion, which will eventually make matters worse,[15] and that much growth has been based on a rate of resource extraction—especially of nonrenewables like oil and natural gas—too rapid to be either wise for ourselves or comforting to future generations.[16] Although these awesome considerations are probably not yet serious enough to warrant a complete halt to growth, some portion of potential growth might prudently be sacrificed to preserve the environment and nonrenewable resources.[17]

To the extent that there are no precisely defined welfare criteria for evaluating solutions to dynamic problems, we are forced to rely on rather crude value judgments as to what is good and bad. Thus more stability may be better than less, but freedom and flexibility in economic change require *some* instability. Speedy adoption of new technologies may be desirable, but too much speed would probably be disruptively costly. And so on. The role of rough value judgments is even more important in assessing government performance in the area of equity, our next topic.

3. EQUITY AND OTHER DESIRABLES

The top 20 percent of American families enjoy approximately 45 percent of the country's income while the lowest 20 percent account for about 5 percent (after adjustment for means-tested noncash transfers to the poor, such as medical care and housing).[18] Is this the ideal or best result government should achieve in income distribution, or equity? No one knows. Economists cannot demonstrate that one distribution is better than another. Indeed, if anything, economists have demonstrated the *impossibility* of attaining a democratically determined consensus on what the ideal should be.[19] The puzzle remains a puzzle mainly because of the nature of the problem: Changes in distribution create gainers and losers. In judging such changes, value judgments play a particularly dominant role.

A brief review of the debate between egalitarians and nonegalitarians unearths the ethical judgments. Let's take *teleological* arguments first—that is, those favoring or opposing redistributions on grounds that the *end result* is good or bad. The classic teleological argument favoring redistribution is utilitarianism. Comparing the mental and emotional states of the rich and the poor, a utilitarian would argue that $1,000 means less to a family with $200,000 annual income than it does to a family with $10,000 annual income. Therefore, if government were to take $1,000 from the rich and give it to the poor, the relatively small loss of utility by the rich would be more than offset by the relatively large gain of utility by the poor.[20] The implication is one of greater good for a greater number. In contrast, a *non*egalitarian argument of the same teleological stripe would maintain that *in*equality has desirable consequences. Poverty builds character. Wealth encourages risk taking and investment that bolsters economic growth, benefiting everyone. Moreover, it may be argued that the prospect of earning one's way up the ladder provides incentive to work hard, to use one's talents to the fullest, and so on.[21]

Nonteleological theories argue in favor of ethical convictions that are said to be good or bad in themselves. An egalitarian might argue, for instance, that people in an affluent society have a *right* to some minimum level of sustenance or, failing that, a *right* to minimum levels of certain goods and services like health care and education, provision of which should not hinge on income level alone.[22] While this line of argument stresses some equalization of *realized welfare,* related lines urge the attainment of equal *opportunity* as a basic right—equal opportunity in employment and education in particular. *Non*-egalitarian theories of the nonteleological type are also possible and even popular in some circles. Rather than be concerned with the rights of the underprivileged, these theories, as you might well expect, are especially concerned about protecting or furthering the rights of the privileged. One of the most widely cited of these theories is that of Robert Nozick, who argues that *process* is all important, that as long as people attain their riches through "just" acquisition, they have an absolute *right* to every penny so acquired, regardless of any consequences for the poor. Basically, you originally acquire something "justly" if you take something that belongs to nobody, without thereby lessening the lot of others. Subsequently, voluntary exchange, gifts, and inheritance are also just.[23] The intriguing implications of this theory may be appreciated by imagining what the world would be like if Christopher Columbus and his heirs could have claimed America as their property for all time. A related argument, propounded by Irving Kristol, holds that compulsory redistributions seriously compromise liberty, the greatest of all blessings.[24]

Given the circumstances, one might wonder whether there is widespread agreement about anything even remotely related to this issue. Yet the following standards seem acceptable to most folks:

1. Substantial protection of equal *opportunity* in employment seems desirable and defensible to prevent discrimination based on race, religion, and sex.
2. Compulsory redistribution of income can be justified for the aged, infirm, disabled, and truly destitute to assure their subsistence if not opulence.
3. To the extent the wealthy gain their riches by questionable means, such as fraud and artificial monopolization, their rights to retention of the treasure may be questioned.
4. Taking from the needy to benefit the affluent is unambiguously frowned on.

Performance standards are also nebulous in still other areas of ethical conviction—such as safety, health, competition for its own sake, preservation of small business, and so on. Some people, economists especially, like to think that most if not all these other goals should meet benefit-cost criterion. This book, too, occasionally speaks of the benefits and costs of, say, safety regulation and environmental protection. However, benefit-cost cannot always carry this burden. As we shall see, it has serious weaknesses in practical application and ethical conviction, the last of which is explained by Steven Kelman:

> Since the costs of injury are borne by its victims, while its benefits are reaped by its perpetrators, simple cost-benefit calculations may be less important than more abstract conceptions of justice, fairness and human dignity. We would not condone a rape even if it could be demonstrated that the rapist derived enormous pleasure from his actions, while the victim suffered in only small ways. Behind the conception of "rights" is the notion that some concept of justice, fairness, and human dignity demands that individuals ought to be able to perform certain acts, despite the harm to others, and ought to be protected against certain acts, despite the loss this causes to the would-be perpetrators. Thus we undertake no cost-benefit analysis of the effects of freedom of speech or trial by jury before allowing them to continue.[25]

To the extent this view is adopted, little of precision can be said of ideal goals. Goals must emerge from a social stew of various value judgments, stirred and blended by political processes. What *can* be said is that, *once a goal is set, it should be achieved efficiently.* Assume for instance, that society, without knowing the precise benefits, deems it desirable to have no more than 80 decibels of noise reaching the eardrums of manufacturing workers. Assume further that this objective can be achieved in only one of two ways: (1) modifications to machinery, including extensive noise insulation, or (2) workers' wearing hearing protectors that are inconvenient but not too uncomfortable. If the cost of method (1) is $3 billion annually and the cost of method (2) is $0.5 billion annually, then the latter method should be adopted.[26] It would be *cost-effective.* It would be using the fewest resources to achieve the stated goal.

If you are not nodding off at this point, you will notice that cost-effectiveness is a first cousin of benefit-cost. Under benefit-cost, *both* the dollar benefits and the dollar costs are known and variable. Under cost-effectiveness, either the benefits are fixed in physical standards and the dollar costs are variable (as in the noise example), or the dollar costs are fixed and the hard-to-measure benefits are variable. It should be obvious that cost-effectiveness is a handy way of assessing ideal performance in instances where ethics *other* than allocation efficiency are being served. Nonteleological ethics tend to set minimums, which in turn fix goals or budgets.

Summary

The ideal of having consensus ideals for every governmental occasion eludes us. All of us have our own notions of utopia, and the overlap among these notions is limited. Nevertheless, there is enough overlap to venture the assertion that, ideally, the governmental decision-making *process* should be as democratic as possible, with fairly full participation, abundant knowledge, and minimum potential for minority injury.

The focus of policies should be fitting. The choice of instruments should be adroit. And the steps of application and compliance should abide by the guidelines of Table 3–1. Overlapping ideals concerning government *performance* include the satisfaction of benefit-cost criterion when allocation efficiency is the objective and cost-effectiveness when ethical convictions fix a beneficial nonmonetary goal or when budget constraints freeze the costs. Additional ideals, such as equity and stability, also prevail, but nothing that can claim precision.

All in all, it can be argued that collective and deliberative decision making by government is often superior to individual and impulsive decision making by markets. Government can be more rational and efficient, as well as more equitable.[27]

II. Real Government

One does not have to look far to find flaws in markets. Imagining ideal government remedies is equally easy. There is a temptation to conclude, then, that government *should* always intervene. But the temptation should be stoutly resisted. Government too is flawed, and its intervention may make a bad situation worse.

Before we explore those flaws, which are itemized in Table 3–4, it must be stressed that jumping to conclusions by an opposite chain of reasoning must also be resisted.[28] When government botches the job a bit, it does not necessarily follow that markets would do better. They might do worse. Waste in the military, for instance, is a perennial problem, but turning national defense over to the free market would prove disastrous. Thus, the main implication of what follows is not that government ought to be pushed into the nearest abyss but, rather, that society must choose between two faulty mechanisms—markets and government. Care is required to choose the least imperfect in each instance of need.

Table 3–4
Government Shortcomings

A. Imperfections Like Those of Markets (Misallocation)
   1. Monopoly power (no competition or bankruptcy for government)
   2. Voter ignorance and nonparticipation
   3. Official ignorance
B. Failures (Misallocations from Gaps in Benefit-Cost)
   1. Special interest effects
   2. External costs in government
   3. Bundle purchases by electorate
   4. Uniform treatment of diverse situations
C. Dynamic Problems (Delay and Myopia)
   1. Delays and inaction
   2. Short-run cost, long-run benefit: inaction
   3. Short-run benefit, long-run cost: overaction
D. Other Ethical Criteria
   1. Distributional inequity
   2. National defense

Overall, some mix of the two seems best, depending on the situation.

A. Imperfections Mimicking Those of Markets

1. MONOPOLY POWER

First, and most obviously, government is by nature a monopolist. It is not goaded by competition to be lean, productive, or competent, although public-spiritedness among government employees may provide some measure of these qualities. Moreover, government does not face bankruptcy, the means by which costly failure is ended in private enterprise. Government often never knows when to quit.

Take old Sanford, for example, a horse whose tale is told by Professor Almarin Phillips of the University of Pennsylvania:

> Not long ago, my wife and I had occasion to wander through New Market, a restored section of Philadelphia. There, harnessed to a renovated, four-wheeled Studebaker carriage, was a well-

aged bay horse. Neatly lettered on the side of the carriage was "P.U.C. 3714." For a regulated price of $10, old Sanford, as the horse was called, takes passengers for a regulated ride of one-half hour.

> Shortly after our ride with old Sanford, I had occasion to talk with Commissioner Helen O'Bannon of the Pennsylvania Public Utility Commission. "Why," I asked, after explaining the delights of travel with old Sanford, "is that business regulated?" Commissioner O'Bannon, a reform-oriented member of the commission, replied, "You know as well as I do. It started before there were automobiles in the taxi service, and no one has seriously pressed for deregulation."[29]

2. VOTER IGNORANCE AND NONPARTICIPATION

There are public good aspects (e.g., free-rider problems) in the political process. Citizens tend to feel like grains of sand, believing that great efforts on their part to become informed and to participate actively will in the end make very little difference. They might "pay" and "not get" or "get" and "not pay." Indeed, we would surely go daft if each of us were to become intently concerned about all the problems that plague us— energy shortages, water pollution, inflation, auto safety, drug abuse, traffic congestion, abortion, trashy television programs, health care for the elderly, nuclear power, student cheating, excess population growth, Arab-Israeli conflicts, business fraud, tax reform, Cambodian relief . . . blah, blah, blah (the list alone would take at least a day to write).

This is not to say that people are generally apathetic. They are *selectively* apathetic. Each person seems to have a subjective list of priorities, with a few items at the top that get most of the worry and commitment. Individuals' lists differ, and most change with time. This explains why at any one moment excitement over any one issue varies across the populace, and why the aggregate rankings of concern vary from year to year. In 1912, monopoly was a very hot topic. In 1970, environmental protection reached a peak of popularity.

Knowledge and participation are thus less than perfect. And the consequences, like 50 percent of the electorate not voting, are sometimes astounding. A survey of 805 adults was recently taken to mark the two hundredth anniversary of the Supreme Court. It found that most of those persons surveyed could not name a single member of the Supreme Court, and most did not even know how many justices the court has.[30]

3. OFFICIAL IGNORANCE OR ERROR

Should the Interstate Commerce Commission impose elaborately expensive regulations on the railroads to assure that several dozen small towns get rail service? Should the government try to regulate the manufacturing techniques of tens of thousands of plants to curb pollution when an effluent tax would do the job better?

These real-life queries illustrate government imperfections that arise at least in part from official ignorance. They relate to ill-advised instrument selection and policy focus. The problem of official ignorance also prevents proper benefit-cost calculations. For example, at the time of its passage, the Clean Air Act of 1990 had estimated costs of abatement ranging from $19 billion annually (according to the act's supporters) to $104 billion annually (according to its opponents). A respected nonpartisan group, Resources for the Future (RFF) estimated an intermediate cost of $30 billion to $35 billion. Although plausible, even this estimate could not be considered rock solid. When asked how these figures were determined, Paul Portney of RFF said, "It's sort of a gut feeling."[31] When presented with uncertainty and ignorance such as this, officials must often act on their intuition.

Most startling was President Ronald Reagan's reliance on astrology. In 1988, several White House sources revealed that President Reagan made some executive decisions based on advice his wife Nancy received from a California astrologer.[32]

Of course, these failings are not necessarily

government's fault. Knowledge eludes even the best professors. The point is that limitations in ken must be appreciated.

B. Failures (Gaps in Benefit-Cost)

1. SPECIAL INTEREST EFFECTS

Preference articulation and aggregation in the real world are heavily influenced by a few thousand interest groups. These bands are typically formed by parties sharing some common, everyday economic interest. The Association of American Railroads, American Pharmaceutical Association, American Petroleum Institute, AFL-CIO, American Bar Association, United Auto Workers, and American Medical Association are examples. There are also "cause groups," which spring up around specific issues. Some of these are the Environmental Defense Fund, Energy Action, Consumer Federation of America, and Action for Children's Television. It is in these interest groups that we find the most participation and knowledge.

Much public policy furthers *neither* economic efficiency *nor* greater equality, and a major explanation for this failure lies in special interest politics. When the benefits of a policy are concentrated among a relatively few, and the costs are diffusely spread by little bits throughout society, then the special interests that benefit have the advantage of being able to muster particularly well-organized, vociferous support in favor of passage, while selective apathy silences the many who bear the cost. Thus, for years economists have pointed out that quota and tariff protection against steel and sugar imports is inefficient, that restrictive licensing of barbers, taxis, and countless other services is anticompetitive and costly to consumers, that cartelization of the milk industry is not in the public interest, and so on. Yet all these policies and more like them abound because special interest groups exploit the mismatch between concentrated benefits and diffuse costs. Setting the message in concrete, a 1980 study by the Federal Trade Commission staff estimated that import restrictions on five products alone cost U.S. consumers $2 billion annually but that the benefits to the industries were at most $281 million. The products studied were color television sets, textiles, citizens' band radios, shoes, and sugar.[33]

When a policy change carries an opposite distribution of benefits and costs, with benefits diffused and costs concentrated, the problem is reversed. Then the cost side typically has the more powerful interest group representation, raising the hurdles against change. This seems to explain why *de*regulation is usually more difficult to attain than original regulation when that regulation serves narrow economic interests such as trucking, agriculture, or banking. It also seems to explain why measures in the broad public interest—safety, antitrust, environmental protection, and equal opportunity—are taken only as a result of severe crisis. Calamity tends to elevate issues to the top of people's selective apathy lists, thereby precipitating the formation of cause organizations, intensifying public outcries, and provoking political support. Thus, action in cases of diffuse benefit and concentrated cost is by no means impossible, but it tends to be timorous and halting.[34] The history of environmental protection policy, for instance, dates from the last century. But nothing was really accomplished until a string of tragedies incited action in the early 1970s.[35]

Apart from lobbying and letter writing, the main way special interest groups gain influence is by contributing money to election campaigns. Although the evidence is mixed, the best and most recent studies find that corporate campaign contributions sway congressional voting in a pro-business direction.[36]

2. EXTERNAL COSTS IN GOVERNMENT

When it comes to external costs, government is sometimes the problem, not the solution. Within the standard framework, government is often a major polluter. Aside from such obvious offenses as municipal government failure to treat raw sewage, government defiles the environment with military bases, power plants, dams, irrigation projects, and canals. Indeed, the federal government has been accused of being the single greatest source of water pollution in the western United States.[37]

Another form of external cost occurs when one government agency pursues a policy that contradicts the policy of another agency. This might be called internal-external cost, or incoherent-inconsistency. Whatever it is called, it is less than ideal, shrinking the likelihood of optimal allocations. Table 3–5 outlines several examples.

3. BUNDLE PURCHASES BY THE ELECTORATE

Ideally, citizens should be able to express their opinions on each governmental decision separately, much the same way they are able to make marginal adjustments in the marketplace, spending a little more here and a little less there. But such is not the case. The political process works in bundles, which are imprecise. As James Gwartney and Richard Stroup explain, voters are usually forced to act through a legislator or president who represents a bundle of political goods and tax prices:

> The voter either gets the bundle of political goods offered by candidate A or the bundle offered by candidate B. Often, neither of these bundles of political goods represents what a specific consumer (voter) would like to have. The political consumer does not have the freedom to "shop around" buying some goods from any of several suppliers. He is forced to accept the bundle favored by the majority coalition.[38]

Moreover, most government services are financed from general funds, so citizens and their representatives are not presented proposals that directly link government service with the tax to finance it. This use of general fund financing can create fiscal illusions on the part of voters that

---

Table 3–5
Examples of Government Externalities or Contradictory Policies, Circa 1980

On the one hand . . .	*. . . on the other*
The National Highway Traffic Safety Administration mandates weight-adding safety equipment for cars.	The Transportation Department insists on lighter vehicles to conserve gasoline.
The Justice Department offers guidance to companies on complying with the Foreign Corrupt Practices Act.	The Securities and Exchange Commission will not promise immunity from prosecution for practices Justice might permit.
The Environmental Protection Agency restricts use of pesticides.	The Agriculture Department promotes pesticides for agricultural and forestry uses.
The Energy Department tries to keep down rail rates for hauling coal, to encourage plant conversions.	The Transportation Department tries to keep coal rates high to bolster ailing railroads.
The Occupational Health and Safety Administration wants guard rails along beef-killing operations to prevent worker falls.	The Agriculture Department says the guard rails are unsanitary because carcasses touch them.

---

they are under- or overtaxed, leading to an over- or underexpansion of government operations.[39]

**4.   UNIFORM TREATMENT OF
       DIVERSE SITUATIONS**

A corollary of the bundle problem is uniformity. The uniformity is partly due to a striving for equal treatment but much more to the need for administrative simplicity. Thus, the cars in tiny Paradise, California, must meet the same pollution standards as those in smoggy Los Angeles; wealthy people with salaries exceeding $100,000 must belong to Social Security just like low-paid toothpick packers; prohibitions against price discrimination face Bruce's Juices with the same force as Campbell's Soup Company; the minimum wage law treats janitors and journeyman pipefitters alike; all wheat farmers get the same level of price support regardless of their size, cost per bushel, or location; no swimming pool slide may slip beneath the standards of the Consumer Product Safety Commission; and so

on. As George Stigler quipped, "We ought to call him Uncle Same."[40]

C. Dynamic Problems (Delay and Myopia)

1.   DELAYS AND INACTION

To some extent, delay is inevitable and even desirable in government actions. ("Haste makes . . .") There is a difference, however, between delay occasioned by prudent consideration and delay deriving from dalliance, inertia, confusion, inability, and laziness. There are no benefits from such delay and the economic and human costs can be staggering.

Evidence of undue delay in the federal regulatory process is rampant.[41] A Senate committee's questionnaire survey of about a thousand lawyers who practice regularly before federal commissions revealed that, in their opinion, undue delay was by far the most important deficiency of federal regulation. Administrative law judges, who are key personnel inside regulatory agencies, were also surveyed by the committee. Sixty-seven percent of the judges ranked undue delay as one of the top three problems of regulation. In still another survey, 96 percent of the Federal Trade Commission's attorneys admitted that cases were not "handled in a timely fashion."

What is the basis for these opinions? Figure 3–4 gives you some idea. The chart derives from data on six regulatory agencies collected by the Administrative Conference of the United States. The data concerned cases that were actually referred to an administrative law judge for a hearing and that were concluded in 1975. Cases successfully terminated without hearing were thus excluded. As indicated, the regulatory process is less than swift. From beginning to end, licensing proceedings averaged more than 19 months' duration, ratemaking cases typically took 21 months, and enforcement actions were strung out over three years.

It should be recognized that these statistics concern fairly *routine* matters. When new regu-

lations pass Congress, implementation must start afresh, with calendar consumption indicated by the fact that it took six years—from initial legislation to ultimate specification—to get safety regulations for mechanical hazards like sharp edges and sharp points in children's toys. Indeed, it took a citizens' lawsuit against the government to pry the regulations loose.[42]

2. SHORT-RUN COST, LONG-RUN BENEFIT: INACTION

Voters and their political representatives tend to be shortsighted. The priorities on voters' selective apathy lists seem heavily influenced by immediacy. And elected officials seem to have time horizons limited to the next election. Therefore, government policies with high *short-run costs* as compared to amply off-setting *future benefits* tend to be unduly slighted, leading to inaction. The instincts of the political process are, in short, not generally geared to squirrelling away nuts against hard winters.

Gwartney and Stroup point out that this

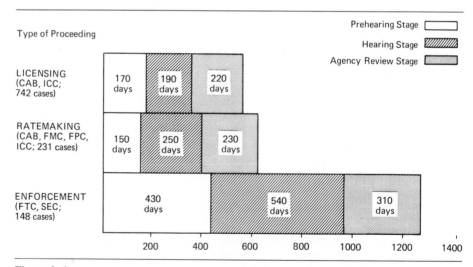

Figure 3–4
Days Elapsed in Formal, on the Record Regulatory Proceedings (1975)

Source: U.S. Senate, Committee on Governmental Affairs, *Study on Federal Regulation,* Vol. IV, "Delay in the Regulatory Process," (July 1977), p. 6.

helps to explain why public action in areas such as safety, energy, trade balance, environmental protection, and inflation is crisis-oriented—with little more than lip service being paid to problems until eleventh-hour efforts are spent. "Given the public sector bias against proposals with current costs but future benefits that are difficult to identify, the crisis phenomenon is understandable."[43]

Table 3–6
Examples of Federal Government Crises that Emerged During the "Hands-off" Years of the Reagan Administration

SAVINGS AND LOAN INDUSTRY COLLAPSE
Problem: A deregulated industry that couldn't survive open competition, fraud, and stonewalling of reform by congressional and administration officials.
Cost to taxpayers: $300 billion.

PENTAGON PROCUREMENT SCANDAL
Problem: Defense contractors took advantage of an incestuous system. Revolving door profited insiders and outsiders; lawmakers wanted to feather their nests.
Cost to taxpayers: At least several billion dollars.

FARM CREDIT SYSTEM BAILOUT
Problem: No congressional oversight, reckless lending policies.
Cost to taxpayers: $4.6 billion in losses and $690 million to reinvigorate the farmer-owned farm lending cooperatives.

HOUSING AND URBAN DEVELOPMENT SCANDALS
Problem: Waste and abuse in HUD management, fraud and profiteering in private construction and administration of HUD-backed programs, lax congressional controls on programs themselves.
Cost to taxpayers: $4 billion, possibly $6 billion to $8 billion.

NUCLEAR WEAPONS PLANT CLEANUP
Problem: Three decades of carelessness, underestimated radiation risk, and secrecy that prevented public oversight and debate.
Cost to taxpayers: $130 billion to $150 billion.

Source: Newsweek, August 14, 1989, p. 20.

The Reagan Administration had a particularly strong hands-off attitude. Coupled with a lack of congressional oversight and some of the problems already identified, this led to a number of crisis situations within government itself, as suggested by Table 3–6.

3. SHORT-RUN BENEFIT, LONG-RUN COST: ACTION

When benefits are concentrated in the near term and costs are concentrated in the distant term, shortsightedness has the opposite effect—namely, hasty or excessive action. This deficiency is especially evident in the area of macroeconomic stability. The benefits of reduced unemployment and spritely prosperity can be obtained in the short run by expansive government policies like deficit spending and rapid growth of the money supply. But the long-run cost of these policies is inflation. Stabilizing policies that were not really stabilizing in the long run preceded the presidential elections of 1964, 1968, 1972, and 1976.

D. Other Ethical Criteria

It should by now be apparent that in practice government rarely bases its actions on careful benefit-cost analysis, that distribution neutrality in allocation decisions is never honored, that unanimity is never the voting rule, and that most of the other ideals based on economic criteria are rarely pursued. Apparently, real politics and sound economics seldom seem to match. To some unknown extent this is perhaps as it should be, for simple benefit-cost must sometimes give way to other ethical considerations. As noted earlier, rights alone may often justify government regulation.

A related but different tack is that of Duncan MacRae, who argues that the economic ethic of preference satisfaction is often at odds with human welfare. To the extent this is true, and to the extent welfare is really what counts, it is wrong to criticize government for departing from the ethic of benefit-cost preference satisfaction. In defending his position, MacRae points out that policies not conforming to existing preferences may in the end *change* those preferences for the better. Moreover, the general welfare might well be served if government considers the interests of persons affected but *not* represented in official chambers—that is, children, future generations, disfranchised minorities, resident aliens, and foreigners.[44]

By these lights it may be comforting to know that empirical analyses of congressional voting behavior find ideology and noneconomic ethics playing a major role.[45] Economic interests alone are by no means the guide. Yet, we must be wary in condoning departures from preference satisfaction. Enlarging one's rights often shrinks another's. And not every regulation can be justified by rights. As for laws altering preferences, laws often fail to change society for the better, as Prohibition dramatically demonstrated. And some

laws may even change society for the worse, as illustrated by the Jim Crow laws enforcing racial segregation.[46]

When it comes to business regulation, most of government's deficiencies in this realm of ethics arise from conflicts and inconsistencies when one ethic is served at the inadvertent cost of another. For example, the Robinson-Patman Act serves a notion of fairness to small business but probably at the expense of maintaining competition. For another example, environmental regulations further the amenity rights of people, but as Table 3–7 shows, they do so at the expense of distributional equity. Through higher commodity prices, higher taxes, and other such effects, people in low income classes pay a substantially higher portion of their income for environmental improvement than do those in high income brackets, a distribution of burden that runs contrary to estimates of who gains greatest benefit.

A final problem with other ethical criteria

Table 3–7
Per-Family Pollution Control Costs as a Percentage of Income (Average by Income Class)

		Air Pollution		
Income Class	*Grand Total (percentage)*	*Industry & Government (percentage)*	*Automobile (percentage)*	*Water Pollution[a] (percentage)*
Less than $3,000	12.4	3.4	4.8	4.2
$ 3,000– 3,999	9.1	2.4	3.6	3.1
$ 4,000– 5,999	7.9	2.1	3.0	2.8
$ 6,000– 7,999	6.9	1.9	2.5	2.5
$ 8,000– 9,999	6.2	1.7	2.2	2.3
$10,000–11,999	5.8	1.6	2.0	2.2
$12,000–14,999	5.4	1.6	1.8	2.0
$15,000–19,999	5.0	1.4	1.6	2.0
$20,000–24,999	4.6	1.4	1.3	1.9
$25,000–plus	3.4	1.1	0.7	1.6

[a]Best practical technology standard excluding runoff.

Source: Leonard P. Gianessi and Henry M. Peskin, "The Distribution of the Costs of Federal Water Pollution Control Policy," *Land Economics* (February 1980), pp. 99–100.

arises when government misleads the public by using high moral principles to justify policies that serve narrow special interests. The adopt-a-horse program of the Bureau of Land Management (BLM) is an example. It was ostensibly set up to put wild horses in the hands of caring owners while protecting federal lands from overgrazing, but a General Accounting Office (GAO) investigation has found quite the opposite on both points. From 1985 through 1988 at least 4,000 wild horses were sold for slaughter, many suffering cruel mistreatment in the process. More than 8,000 others that were given away free met the same fate. The GAO study found little evidence that the wild horses, which were never very numerous, had been overgrazing federal lands in the first place. After the horses were removed, government officials allowed ranchers to expand the number of cattle they had grazing on BLM lands. By 1990, cattle outnumbered wild horses on BLM land 4.1 million to 42,000. Hence, the adopt-a-horse program has been run largely to satisfy ranchers who graze cattle on the land while, for public relations purposes, it has been promoted as a project of lofty moral achievement.[47]

A Qualifying Reminder. It may be argued that in some respects and in some instances, government's flaws may be a source of strength instead of weakness. If the state always moved swiftly and reflected every personal whim precisely, our society, as George Stigler says, "would become the victim of every fad in morals and every popular fallacy in philosophy."[48] If the state could overcome its proclivity toward uniformity of treatment, adapting all laws to minute individual circumstances, the result might well be capricious control, immense uncertainty, and inequitable favoritism. If government always gave up easily, shedding its often annoying persistence, the United States might never have won World War II or put a man on the moon. These reflections merely underscore a point made earlier. Wisdom would have us relying on markets in some respects and government in others. Par-

adise is not to be found in either alone. Thus, in the chapters remaining we explore blends and mixes, old ones actually observed and new ones wishfully sought.

Summary

This chapter ticks off characteristics of government in the ideal and real, using individual preferences as the main measuring rod. The political *process* requires (1) problem recognition through preference articulation, (2) policy formulation, entailing preference aggregation and legislation, (3) policy application, and (4) private sector compliance. Model attributes for each of these steps are outlined in Table 3–1. Among the most important are full participation, full information, and full employment in the first stage, plus proper selections of voting rules, policy focuses, and policy instruments in the second stage. The last stages are deftly handled if qualities like impartiality, consistency, efficiency, unobtrusiveness, clarity, and dependability are achieved.

As for results, ideal performance in static efficiency would square with benefit-cost: policies committing resources only when the added social benefits exceed the added social costs up to the point at which costs equal benefits. Such, theoretically, is the golden rule of remedies for market imperfections and failures. Widely accepted performance ideals for other policy objectives simply do not exist. Indeed, it has been argued that democratic determination of a clear, concise ideal criterion for equity is impossible. Thus, we are left with such vague guides as minimum sustenance for the poor, maintenance of competition for its own sake, and product safety where hazards are particularly sneaky and dangerous.

When actual government is examined under the admittedly dim light of these ideals, we find blemishes abounding. As suggested in Table 3–4, government perpetuates misallocations of too much and too little owing to imperfections and failures. Monopoly and freedom from bankruptcy foster misguided persistence and inefficiency. Ignorance among voters and officials invites dead-end journeys. Special interest effects tip the balance of power in favor of those experiencing concentrated benefits or costs. Externalities of various kinds produce benefit-cost mismatches. And lumpiness in the electoral process and in the treatment of diverse individual circumstances often leads to crude, sometimes heavy-handed outcomes.

Delay and myopia create dynamic problems. Although some delay is good, undue delay is not. Lacking in benefits, its costs are huge. Myopia gives disproportionate weight to current as compared to future costs and benefits. When the costs are immediate and the benefits far off (as when we try to stop smoking), there is a tendency to postpone or even abandon action. A reverse sequence stimulates the opposite tendency of inducing action when abstinence is best (much as the costs of late-night revelry appear only the next morning).

Finally, despite the ill-defined nature of ethical criteria other than allocation efficiency, deficiencies are discernible by such lights. Inconsistencies crop up when progress in one direction, like safety, entails regress in another, like equity.

Taking this and Chapter 2 together, we find defects in both markets and government. Society has no perfect servant. Tasks must nevertheless be assigned. The trick is to find what's right for the lazy butler and what's right for the awkward maid.

Questions and Exercises for Chapter 3

1. Compare and contrast the following particular matchups of ideal and real government:
   a. Full participation in procedure (ideal) *versus* voter ignorance and selective apathy (real).
   b. Efficient and expeditious instrument application (ideal) *versus* delays and inaction (real).
   c. Cost-benefit performance (ideal) *versus* special interest effects and official ignorance (real).
   d. Cost-benefit performance (ideal) *versus* short-run/long-run benefit-cost (real)
   e. Minimum interference with private decision making (ideal) *versus* government as a monopolist (real).
   f. Equity performance (ideal) *versus* special interest effects and distributional inequity in Table 3–7 (real).
2. Use your knowledge of benefit-cost as illustrated in Figure 3–3 (which cured the problem of Figure 2–6) to do a similar analysis curing the "external benefit" problem of Figure 2–5 with a subsidy.
3. Some pundits say that government performance should not be governed by Pareto (efficiency) criterion. Argue for and against this in light of this chapter's findings.
4. Briefly define cost effectiveness and explain why this approach may be preferred over benefit-cost analysis.
5. Curbing monopoly power may further goals of efficient allocation and equity. Use a diagram to explain these effects.

Notes

1. John H. Hallowell, *The Moral Foundation of Democracy* (Chicago: University of Chicago Press, 1954); John Rawls, *A Theory of Justice* (Cambridge, MA: Harvard University Press, 1971); Robert Nozick, *Anarchy, State, and Utopia* (New York: Basic Books, 1974); Mark A. Lutz and Kenneth Lux, *The Challenge of Humanistic Economics* (Menlo Park, CA: Benjamin/Cummings, 1979); H. H. Liebhafsky, *American Government and Business* (New York: Wiley, 1971), pp. 18–39, 565–571.
2. D. T. Savage, M. Burke, J. D. Coupe, T. D. Duchesneau, D. F. Wihry, and J. A. Wilson, *Economics of Environmental Improvement* (Boston: Houghton Mifflin, 1974) pp. 130–132.
3. A. Downs, *An Economic Theory of Democracy* (New York: Harper & Row, 1957), p. 136.
4. James M. Buchanan, *The Demand and Supply of Public Goods* (Chicago: Rand McNally, 1968), pp. 94–95.
5. Dennis C. Mueller, *Public Choice* (Cambridge, England: Cambridge University Press, 1979), pp. 223–225, 263–270.
6. For an alternative typology, see Robert G. Harris and James M. Carmen, "Public Regulation of Marketing Activity: Part II: Regulatory Responses to Market Failures," *Journal of Macromarketing* (Spring 1984): 41–52.
7. *Wall Street Journal*, 15 July 1980, p. 48.

8. *Wall Street Journal,* 11 March 1980, p. 48.

9. This so-called compensating variation is the most widely prescribed concept of benefit and cost. E. J. Mishan, *Economics for Social Decisions: Elements of Cost-Benefit Analysis* (New York: Praeger, 1973), pp. 14–15. But there are serious problems with this and substitute concepts on theoretical and practical levels. A good summary is by A. Myrick Freeman III, *The Benefits of Environmental Improvement* (Baltimore: Johns Hopkins University Press, 1979), pp. 33–61. In the end Freeman takes a leap of faith (p. 59), believing it "better to use the data at hand . . . than to forgo the opportunity to shed perhaps a little light on a policy issue because the data were not perfect."

10. In practice, most economists follow the "Kaldor criterion," which says that a policy should be accepted if those who gain *could* fully compensate those who lose. It does not require *actual* payment. But of course this criterion is merely one of *potential* Pareto improvement, not actual. I think potentials are nice but not ideal. Nicholas Kaldor, "Welfare Propositions of Economics and Interpersonal Comparisons of Utility," *Economic Journal,* vol. 49: 549–552; Alan T. Peacock and Charles K. Rowley, *Welfare Economics: A Liberal Restatement* (London: M. Robertson, 1975).

11. Technically, this is not quite right. A theoretically attractive limit to growth based on free-market operation can be derived by assuming that people prefer present consumption over future consumption as measured by the rate of interest they must be paid to forgo present consumption in anticipation of greater future consumption. This interest rate may then guide both saving and investment activity, which investment then generates growth. But this classical formulation ignores many problems also affecting the question of optimal growth, such as the optimal rate of natural resource extraction and the optimal rate of population change. So to my knowledge no clear consensus on a precise optimum currently exists among economists.

12. Adam Smith, *Wealth of Nations,* Book I, Chap. VIII, Cannan edition (Modern Library), p. 81.

13. Donald S. Watson, *Economic Policy: Business and Government* (Boston: Houghton Mifflin, 1960), pp. 470–471.

14. Tibor Scitovsky, *The Joyless Economy* (New York: Oxford University Press, 1976), pp. 133–145; Staffan B. Linder, *The Harried Leisure Class* (New York: Columbia University Press, 1970); Fred Hirsch, *The Social Limits to Growth* (Cambridge, MA: Harvard University Press, 1978).

15. E. J. Mishan, *The Economic Growth Debate* (London: Allen & Unwin, 1977); Allen Schaniberg, *The Environment from Surplus to Scarcity* (New York: Oxford University Press, 1980).

16. Herman E. Daly, *Steady-State Economics: The Economics of Biophysical Equilibrium and Moral Growth* (San Francisco: Freeman, 1977). See also the papers by P. R. Ehrlich, A. H. Ehrlich, J. P. Holdren, and Georgescu-Roegen in *Economics, Ecology, Ethics,* ed. H. E. Daly (San Francisco: Freeman, 1980).

17. Talbot Page, *Conservation and Economic Efficiency* (Baltimore: Johns Hopkins University Press, 1977), pp. 143–207.

18. U.S. Department of Commerce, *Statistical Abstract of the United States 1990,* p. 449.

19. The classic proof is that of Kenneth Arrow, *Social Choice and Individual Values* (New York: Wiley, 1951). There have since been attempts to show possibility, but they suffer various deficiencies. For a review see *Public Choice,* Mueller, pp. 184–206.

20. Jeremy Bentham originated the argument more than a century ago. A modern, sophisticated version is that of J. C. Harsanyi, *Rational Behavior and Bargaining Equilibrium in Games and Social Situations* (Cambridge, England: Cambridge University Press, 1977).

21. Irving Kristol, "Thoughts on Equality and Egalitarianism," in *Income Redistribution,* ed. C. D. Campbell (Washington, DC: American Enterprise Institute, 1977), pp. 35–42. See also Richard Sennett, "Our Hearts Belong to Daddy" *New York Review of Books* (May 1, 1980), pp. 32–35.

22. Arthur M. Okun, "Further Thoughts on Equality and Efficiency," in Campbell *Income Distribution,* p. 28. See also the papers by Lester Thurow and Charles Fried in *Markets and Morals,* ed. G. Dworkin, G. Berment, and P. G. Brown (Washington, DC: Hemisphere Publishing, 1977).

23. Robert Nozick, *Anarchy, State, and Utopia* (New York: Basic Books, 1974).

24. Irving Kristol, "What Is Social Justice?" *Wall Street Journal,* 12 August, 1976.

25. Steven Kelman, "Regulation that Works," *The New Republic* (November 25, 1978), p. 19. See also Kelman, "Cost-Benefit Analysis: An Ethical Critique," *Regulation* (Jan/Feb 1981): 33–40; and Norman E. Bowie (ed.), *Ethical Issues in Government* (Philadelphia: Temple University Press, 1981).

26. John F. Morrall III, "Exposure to Occupational Noise," in *Benefit-Cost Analyses of Social Regulation,* ed. J. C. Miller III and B. Yandle (Washington, DC: American Enterprise Institute, 1979), pp. 33–58.

27. Amitai Etzioni, *The Moral Dimension: Toward a New Economics* (New York: Free Press, 1988), pp. 185–198.

28. The list in Table 3–4 draws mainly from George J. Stigler, "The Government of the Economy" in *Economics: Readings, Issues, and Cases,* 3rd ed., ed. E. Mansfield (New York: Norton, 1980), pp. 35–48; J. D. Gwartney and R. Stroup, *Microeconomics: Private and Public Choice,* 2nd ed. (New York: Academic Press, 1979), pp. 439–451; and Charles Wolf, Jr., "A Theory of Nonmarket Failure: Framework for Implementation Analysis," *Journal of Law & Economics* (April 1979): 107–139.

29. Almarin Phillips, "Regulation and Its Alternatives" in *Regulating Business: The Search for an Optimum* (San Francisco: Institute for Contemporary Studies, 1978), p. 159.

30. *San Jose Mercury News,* 19 February 1990, p. 4A.

31. *Newsweek,* 12 February 1990, p. 21.

32. *San Jose Mercury News,* 3 May 1988, p. 1A.

33. *Wall Street Journal,* 25 July 1980.

34. James Q. Wilson, "The Politics of Regulation," in *Social Responsibility and the Business Predicament,* ed. J. W. McKie (Washington, DC: Brookings Institution, 1974), pp. 143–146; John E. Sinclair, *Interest Groups in America* (Morristown, NJ: General Learning Press, 1976), pp. 46–47.

35. John Esposito, *Vanishing Air: The Report on Air Pollution* (New York: Grossman, 1970); David Zwick and Mary Benstock, *Water Wasteland* (New York: Grossman, 1971); John C. Whitaker, *Striking a Balance: Environment and Natural Resources Policy in the Nixon-Ford Years* (Washington, DC: American Enterprise Institute, 1976).

36. Al Wilhite and Chris Paul, "Corporate Campaign Contributions and Legislative Voting," *Quarterly Review of Economics and Business* (Autumn 1989): 73–85; Thomas Stratmann, "What Do Campaign Contributions Buy?", *Southern Economic Journal* (January 1991): 606–619.

37. Richard L. Berkman and W. Kip Viscusi, *Damning the West* (New York: Grossman, 1973).

38. Gwartney and Stroup, *Microeconomics,* p. 445.

39. Mueller, *Public Choice,* p. 90.

40. Stigler, "Government of the Economy," p. 38.

41. The following samples come from U.S. Congress, Senate, Committee on Governmental Affairs, *Study on Federal Regulation,* Vol. IV, "Delay in the Regulatory Process" (July 1977), pp. 1–25.

42. Ibid., pp. 17–19.

43. Gwartney and Stroup, *Microeconomics,* p. 447.

44. Duncan MacRae, Jr., *The Social Function of Social Science* (New Haven, CT: Yale University Press, 1976), pp. 186–202.

45. James B. Kau and Paul H. Rubin, *Congressmen, Constituents, and Contributors* (Boston: Martinus Nijhoff, 1982); Joseph P. Kalt and Mark A. Zupan, "Capture and Ideology in the Economic Theory of Politics," *American Economic Review* (June 1984): 279–300.

46. C. Van Woodward, *The Strange Career of Jim Crow,* 2nd ed. (New York: Oxford University Press, 1966).

47. General Accounting Office, *Range land Management: Improvements Needed in Federal Wild Horse Program,* GAO/RCED–90–110 (August 1990).

48. Stigler, *Public Choice,* p. 38.

Chapter 4

Philosophical and Historical Background

History is philosophy learned from examples.
— *Dionysius of Halicarnassus*

Ponder the public debate on some current economic policy. What arguments stir Congress and the press? Are words like "freedom," "fairness," and "justice" bandied about? Are historical lessons cited and precedents invoked? More than likely they are. Hence, the purpose of this chapter is to provide this background.

We begin with economic philosophies. The full ideological spectrum ranges from right to left with positions that can be labeled libertarian, conservative, moderate, liberal, and socialist. Libertarians advocate completely free markets, with virtually no government intervention whatever. Socialists advocate the extreme opposite—pervasive government intervention even to the point of doing away with private property. Neither of these extremes has much of a following in the United States, so we may ignore them. Most of the interesting action occurs on the conservative-moderate-liberal portion of the spectrum. Here we find our leading politicians, economists, journalists, and businesspeople. For convenience and clarity we focus solely on conservatives and liberals. Moderates span the range in between, so it will be easy for you to fill in the center by imagining blends of these two schools of thought.

These philosophies—conservative and liberal—differ in their value judgments, their views of capitalism, their assessments of government, and their mental outlooks. In turn, these differences decisively influence judgments on economic policy. So, after surveying philosophical positions, we indicate where people of each persuasion stand on several major policy issues like antitrust and product safety. One sweeping generalization that emerges is easy to state at the outset: Conservatives typically place tremendous faith in free-market capitalism, stressing its good points and downplaying its bad points. Their view of government runs in reverse. That is, government's flaws get close attention while its virtues tend to be neglected. Liberals hold contrary views. On the whole they tend to be more skeptical of markets and more favorable toward government intervention than conservatives are.

The last half of this chapter recounts historical foundations built over the past century. Two sweeping conclusions emerge from this backward glance. First, there is a general trend toward ever greater government intervention in the United States economy. Whereas laissez-faire (from the French "allow to do") characterized the economy ten decades ago, government regulation, supervision, subsidization, taxation, and intercession tattoo today's economy. Second, this tide toward greater government involvement did not swell steadily with time. Rather, it grew with alternating periods of spurt and pause, vacillating between eras of liberalism and conservatism.

I. Major Economic Philosophies

English economist Joan Robinson once said that an ideology is like an elephant—you cannot precisely define an elephant, but you know one when you see one. Thus, conservative and liberal positions cannot be delineated with perfect clarity. Moreover, summarization imparts to each a misleading stiffness. Many conservatives would disagree with any statement purporting to describe the representative conservative position on a particular issue. The same could be said of liberals. Even the use of these labels meets criticism. Many conservatives prefer to be called liberals because this designation stems from the Latin word meaning "free," and conservatives elevate freedom to the very highest priority among value judgments. Conservatives also claim classical liberalism of the eighteenth and nineteenth centuries as their chief ideological heritage, so they lament "the corruption of the term liberalism" and register their "reluctance to surrender the term to proponents of measures that would destroy liberty."[1] Liberals counter by contending that modern conservatives cannot commandeer the vocabulary of liberalism without committing

the "Great Train Robbery of American intellectual history."[2]

Risky as the attempt may be, a summary of these philosophies is nevertheless quite pertinent.[3]

A. Conservative Beliefs

The Nature of Mankind.   Anchoring the conservative economic philosophy is a particular view of human nature, concisely captured in the name *Homo economicus,* or economic man. All men (and women) are believed to be (1) inherently materialistic, that is, filled with substantial wants, desires, and preferences for goods and services, and (2) completely rational in pursuing their own self-interest. The main implication of these notions is individualism. Satisfaction of individual wants is or should be the main objective of any social order, and individuals themselves are the best judges of the worth of those wants and the means of fulfilling them.

Value Judgments.   As measured by their own words, conservatives stress freedom. Any conflict with other value judgments, such as equality, security, or fairness, is usually resolved in favor of freedom. Its prominence is conveyed by Milton Friedman, a leading spokesman for conservatives and a Nobel laureate in economics, who writes, "As [conservatives], we take freedom of the individual, or perhaps the family, as our ultimate goal in judging social arrangements."[4]

When it comes to defining freedom, conservatives usually mean freedom from government. Friedrich A. Hayek's book *Road to Serfdom* indicates this by its title and by its main theses: (1) that government intervention in the economy heralds socialism, (2) that freedom and democracy cannot exist under socialism, and (3) that therefore the trend toward government intervention should be abruptly reversed.[5]

Conservatives' precepts on equality follow from their views on freedom and human nature. The significant equality is equality of opportunity or equality of economic liberty, not equality in income or wealth or any other economic result. Men should be equal in their *right* to hold property and their *right* to enter contracts. But pressing equality much beyond this tramples freedom. Each individual must experience the consequences of his own behavior. As Clinton Rossiter puts it, "The drunkard belonged in the ditch, the lazy man in the poorhouse, the dullard in the shack, the hard-working man in the cottage, the hard-working and talented man in the mansion."[6]

Regard for Markets. Conservatives have great faith in the beneficence of free markets. How can the individualistic and materialistic instincts of man be controlled and coordinated to avoid chaos, to serve the maximum satisfaction of society? "By the market or price system," they answer. According to a best-selling conservative book:

> Adam Smith's flash of genius was his recognition that the prices that emerged from voluntary transactions between buyers and sellers—for short, the free market—could coordinate the activity of millions of people each seeking his own interest, in such a way as to make everyone better off. It was a startling idea then, and it remains one today, that economic order can emerge as the unintended consequence of the actions of many people, each seeking his own interest.
>
> The price system works so well, so efficiently, that we are not aware of it most of the time.[7]

Most conservatives are careful to qualify their faith by specifying that *competitive* markets, not just any markets, are the ones required, because competition provides *alternatives* for consumers and employees (and for merchants and employers as well). There is, then, freedom to choose. No one is pushed into deals. Competition protects consumers and employees from coercion. Henry Simons may have said it best over thirty years ago: *"The great enemy of democracy is monopoly, in all its forms."*[8]

None of the free market's trappings cause conservatives to flinch in their faith. Advertising, for instance, is praised by many conservatives as an unmitigated blessing, informing consumers rather than persuading them, gently guiding consumers to their best buys rather than manipulating them.[9] Thus, consumer sovereignty and rationality reign supreme. The free market is said to register consumer preferences with commendable accuracy.

Regard for Government. If the free market is conservatives' delight, government is their despair. Their mention of government is often coupled with allusions of despotism or tyranny. To quote Friedman again:

> Fundamentally, there are only two ways of coordinating the economic activities of millions. One is central direction involving the use of coercion—the technique of the army and of the modern totalitarian state. The other is voluntary cooperation of individuals—the technique of the market place.[10]

Government not only endangers individual freedom; its efforts rarely improve economic conditions. Rather, its efforts, however well intended, usually make matters worse. Minimum wage laws throw people out of work. Monetary policy destabilizes the economy. Drug regulation on the whole creates more costs than benefits. And so on. Thus, conservatives' distaste for government rests on more than moral or ethical sensitivities. It rests on perceived impracticalities.

Accordingly, conservatives' ideal constitution for government action is short. "That government is best which governs least," could be their motto. Even so, they are not anarchists. They prescribe government action for the following:

1. Prevention of coercion or violence by individuals.
2. Provision for defense from foreign attack.
3. Enforcement of property rights and legal contracts.
4. Regulation of the monetary system in a conservative manner.

5. Provision of certain public goods like highways, sewers, and city parks.
6. Assurance of some minimal degree of security and care for cripples, the mentally retarded, orphans, and the elderly.[11]

Beyond these matters, conservatives are divided. Some condone government intervention to assuage external costs like pollution (as long as the benefits exceed the costs), while others seem to believe that the free market is so efficient that external costs do not distort market results very seriously at all.[12] Some endorse and others oppose safety regulation. Perhaps the most curious area of disagreement concerns antitrust and public utility regulation. Conservatives of yesteryear, sticking to the logic that only competitive markets produce the glories of freedom, efficiency, fairness, and so forth, argued for (1) vigorous antitrust policies to combat private restraints of trade and artificial monopoly, plus (2) government regulation or ownership of natural monopoly.[13] More recently, however, conservatives have become anti-antitrust,[14] and they tend to doubt that public utility regulation or state ownership of natural monopolies is either necessary or wise.[15]

Explaining this switch to accommodation and approval of big business is not easy, but there seem to be three main reasons.[16] First, conservatives now make the empirical judgment that monopoly power is rare or nonexistent, so there is in their view no "real" problem at all. Despite oligopolistic and monopolistic dominance of many major U.S. industries (telephones, airlines, drugs, soft drinks, detergents, and so forth), conservatives find competition everywhere—in interindustry rivalry, in dynamic change over time, in the fragility of cartels, in low barriers to entry, in countervailing power, and in international trade. Second, in instances in which monopoly power cannot be dismissed as illusory, modern conservatives claim to find a great deal of goodness in big business—efficiency and pro-

gressiveness, in particular. Indeed, many conservatives set freedom, decentralization, and other individualistic goals aside at this point to argue that the main aim of antitrust should be economic efficiency. This leads to the result that *non*conservatives are now the main defenders of antitrust on grounds of liberty.[17] Finally, to the extent conservatives admit that monopoly *does* exist and *is* undesirable, many still do not brook. Here they face a choice between two evils—government and big business—and many of them choose big business as the lesser of the two. This choice is not surprising, given conservatives' strong skepticism of officialdom.

Frame of Mind. Among many conservatives, defense of laissez-faire capitalism and steadfast opposition to government intervention border on the dogmatic. Conservatives of the past have contended that theirs is the only philosophy conforming to the "laws" of nature, religion, economics, sociology, and morality.[18] Social Darwinism was one such conservative doctrine (advocating "survival of the fittest," economically and socially, as absolutely essential).[19] Most modern conservatives have dropped references to religion, natural science, and Truth with a capital "T", but they often argue that their position is free of value judgments. Some strain to bolster their authority with favorable interpretations of anthropological evidence, and still others seek to explain every aspect of life in terms of economic rationality.[20] In these several ways and others, conservatives, especially those on the extreme right, evince doctrinaire inclinations.

Extent of Popularity. Conservatives constitute a *very* strong and influential segment of our society. The affinity of businessmen for the conservative position is widely known and readily understandable, an affinity that is affirmed through advertising campaigns touting the benefits of free-enterprise capitalism, through substantial financial support for conservative political candidates, and through extensive lobbying to erode government controls. In politics, there are numerous prominent standard bearers for the conservative cause—Jesse Helms, Orrin Hatch, Jack Kemp, Strom Thurmond, and Ronald Reagan, to name just a few. Among academics, Milton Friedman is undoubtedly the most widely known conservative, what with his best-selling books, his *Newsweek* column, and his frequent appearances on TV. In addition, the departments of economics and business at several major universities could be considered bastions of conservative thought—the University of Chicago and UCLA in particular. Conservatism, in short, is quite popular.

B. Liberal Philosophy

Frame of Mind. The liberal's philosophy cannot be characterized as clearly as can the conservative's, in part because liberals seem to be less philosophical. In general, however, liberalism stands for positive and active government intervention in economic affairs but not to the extent advocated by socialists (or communists). Words often associated with the liberal stance are welfare state, mixed capitalism, progressivism, regulated capitalism, and reformism.

One particularly distinguishing characteristic of liberals is their pragmatism. Whereas many conservatives often follow their ideologies dogmatically, liberals display flexibility. That is to say, liberals usually measure ideas and policies by the cogency with which they address problems and by the results obtained. Their thinking is *ad hoc;* their method, trial and error. During the Great Depression, for instance, Franklin D. Roosevelt was willing to try *anything that might work* to lift the country out of its misery. "Above all," he snorted, "try something." In the early days of the New Deal, this included a suspension of the antitrust laws and sweeping cartelization of industry under the National Recovery Administration. Later, after failure with that tack, he tried the opposite by reinstating the antitrust laws and pressing their enforcement with greater vigor than America had seen before or since.[21] More recent times have witnessed extensive *de*regulation in energy, finance, transportation, and communication, all spearheaded by such liberals as Jimmy Carter and Ted Kennedy, despite the liberal origins of those regulations in the first place. In legal circles, pragmatism also goes by names like "instrumentalism" and "sociological jurisprudence."

The Nature of Humankind. Liberals reject *Homo economicus* for his unrealistically cold and calculating manner. Their view of humankind makes room for needs, for cooperation, and for fallibility. To quote John Maynard Keynes:

> The world is *not* so governed from above that private and social interest always coincide. It is *not* a correct deduction from the Principles of Economics that enlightened self-interest always operates in the public interest. Nor is it true that self-interest generally *is* enlightened; more often individuals acting separately to promote their own ends are too ignorant or too weak to attain even these. Experience does *not* show that individuals, when they make up a social unit, are always less clear-sighted than when they act separately.[22]

Moreover, liberals are less eager than most conservatives to use materialistic human pleasure as the measure of all things. Liberals therefore seem more willing to grant rights of painless slaughter to animals even though such may be "uneconomic," and to extend rights of preservation to trees even though the benefits to a human minority may not exceed the costs to the majority.

Value Judgments. Liberals ardently defend freedom, even the freedom to do foolish things. But they define freedom as Nobel laureate Paul Samuelson does, to permit substantial government intervention:

> I must raise some questions about the notion that absence of government means increase in "freedom." Is freedom simply a quantifiable magnitude, as much [conservative] discussion seems to

presume? Traffic lights coerce me and limit my freedom. Yet in the midst of a traffic jam on the unopen road, was I really "free" before there were lights? And has the algebraic total of freedom, for me or the representative motorist or the group as a whole, been increased or decreased by the introduction of well-engineered stop lights? Stop lights, you know, are also go lights.[23]

To liberals, freedom thus includes freedom from oppressively long work hours, stock fraud, stifling pollution, and seriously hazardous products. Similarly, liberals more readily accept government intervention to further equality than do conservatives.

Regard for Market.   Like conservatives, liberals hold the free market (and private property) in high regard. They admire its potentials for efficiency, fairness, flexibility, prosperity, and progress. Even so, liberals readily find market flaws—the imperfections, failures, and ethical deficiencies outlined two chapters ago. Liberal politicians recognize these flaws not so much from the theories of economists or the polemics of leftist ideologues but from real-world observation and historical experience as illuminated by their value judgments. Thus, if the market system generates unemployment of 25 percent, something is wrong. If it produces cars that unnecessarily kill and maim, something is wrong. If it fosters false advertising, something is wrong. And since the market system is neither sacred nor shielded by categorical rights, liberals are quite willing to tinker with possible governmental remedies.

Regard for Government.   As liberals see it, government can *strengthen* the operation of market forces when they produce desirable results. Antitrust and consumer information policies, both of which improve market structures, illustrate this approach. In addition, government can *modify* market forces or *overturn* them when the results are deemed undesirable. Direct regulation of auto safety and provision of sewage treatment exemplify this approach. Underlying ei-

ther approach are two liberal tenets regarding government.

> The first is that in a capitalist democracy it is possible to separate political affairs from the dominance of economic power, and that the actions of the government can thus be made to reflect the interest of the people.
> The second is that the government has expanded its role in the economy in the last few decades in order to fulfill those needs of society that the private sector could not or would not. The thrust for growth in the public sector thus emanates from the demands of a general population living in a changing social and economic climate.[24]

Many liberals seem to think government can do anything. Still, most liberals have developed, especially in recent years, an appreciation for government's blemishes. Their attitude is reflected in Winston Churchill's remark that democracy appears to be the worst form of government until one considers the alternatives. Balance is best; experimentation, permissible. "Dogmatic absolutes being thus ruled out," Paul Samuelson explains, "democratic society is left in the position of pragmatically attempting to choose among partial evils so as to preserve as much as possible of human liberties and freedoms."[25]

Extent of Popularity.   Given current tendencies of many people to drift to the right, statements concerning liberalism's popularity may be imminently perishable. Assuming a broad definition, however, this camp has a wide following. Even the conservative business community often displays more than a tincture of liberalism. A 1980 Conference Board survey found that the 300 executives it polled accepted the underlying need for "virtually every" federal regulatory program then on the books. Their complaints did not attack principle but, rather castigated execution: "The regulatory system as a whole is poorly managed and marred by jurisdictional overlaps and conflicts, duplicative or overly detailed reporting requirements, and lengthy delays in setting standards and issuing rules and permits."[26]

II. Specific Policy Positions

What emerges from the foregoing may seem paradoxical. In ultimate *objective,* both philosophies profess a deep concern for the interests and welfare of the people. Neither philosophy, except perhaps in its most extreme variations, openly advocates harsh treatment of some folks to pry loose benefits for others. What, then, separates them? Mainly two things it seems. The first is different *definitions* of what comprises "interest" and "welfare." In the conservatives' ideal world, for instance, the "freedom" of the disadvantaged outweighs their poverty, or loss to fraud, or other injury. The second is different institutional *mechanics*. To conservatives, only capitalist, free-enterprise markets register people's preferences accurately, and any argument to the contrary must bear a heavy burden of proof that the market blunders. To liberals, capitalistic markets are usually the best template for reflecting people's preferences, but democratic government can likewise be responsive, so there is ample room for tampering to improve or supplant the market.

When these differences in the abstract are reduced to differences in the concrete, we find an array of varied positions on specific policies. Table 4–1 puts these in a nutshell at some risk of misrepresentation by oversimplification. Once again it must be stressed that a continuum bridges these schools of thought. Clustering tends to draw caricatures. Still, as items 1 and 4 of Table 4–1 suggest, modern conservatives take the monopoly problem lightly (for reasons mentioned earlier), while liberals staunchly support antitrust enforcement where competition is deemed possible and advocate public utility regulation where natural monopoly prevails.

Multinational corporations (MNCs) like IBM, Exxon, GE, and Coca Cola, span the globe, dominating foreign markets to a degree that often matches or exceeds their dominance at home. They therefore occupy a branch of the monopoly problem and generate divergent reactions among philosophical schools. Conservatives look favorably upon MNCs, arguing that they promote efficient allocations of the world's resources; benefit poor nations with transfers of technology and capital; stimulate U. S. exports; and develop the export potentials of backward areas. Liberals appreciate these pluses to some degree, but they are also skeptical. They argue that MNCs can use their power and international flexibility to undermine the national interests of the United States and other countries, especially others of weak and less-developed stature. Among the tricks MNCs have up their sleeves, "transfer" pricing, cartelization, bribery, and extraction of "unfair" terms in technology agreements are the most frequently denounced. Accordingly, liberals tend to support a code of ethics for MNCs, with surveillance and some degree of enforcement.

As for protecting consumers from unsafe products, conservatives argue that the free market shields consumers by keeping hazardous mistakes "on a small scale" and by allowing consumers to "experiment for themselves, decide what features they like and what features they do not like."[27] Government should keep out of the marketplace because, "If it is appropriate for the government to protect us from using dangerous bicycles and cap guns, the logic calls for prohibiting still more dangerous activities such as hang-gliding, motorcycling, and skiing."[28] Information disclosures are tolerated to a limited degree: "Insofar as the government has information not generally available about the merits or demerits of the items we ingest or activities we engage in, let it give us the information. But let it leave us free to choose what chances we want to take with our own lives."[29] The conservative's faith in the market extends to working conditions, where the "most reliable and effective protection for most workers is provided by the existence of many employers" competing for the employee's services.[30] Even policies that conservatives admit may "have had a favorable effect on conditions

Table 4–1
Some Comparisons Between Economic Philosophies on Major Policy Issues

Issues	Conservative	Liberal
1. Monopoly and Restraint of Trade	1. No serious problem—should relax antitrust laws	1. Serious problem: enforce and maybe strengthen antitrust laws
2. Multinational Corporations	2. MNCs beneficial; no policy	2. Surveillance and moderate control justified
3. Consumer Fraud, Misrepresentation	3. Competition protects consumers; little need for policy	3. Information disclosure plus ban on fraud
4. Public Utility Regulation	4. Remove or reduce all such regulation	4. Appropriate for natural monopoly situations
5. Energy Shortage	5. Abandon all government intervention	5. Tax excess profits and subsidize new resource development
6. Inflation	6. Fixed and limited rate of money supply expansion	6. Money restraint plus limited wage-price control or procompetition policy
7. Product Safety	7. Information disclosure alone	7. Product regulation and information disclosure
8. Labor Safety	8. Liability law and competition protect workers	8. Some regulation needed, especially for health, workmen's compensation, and child labor
9. Environmental Protection	9. Limited tax inducements at most	9. Tax inducements plus regulation and subsidy
10. Agriculture	10. Free market	10. Some say free market; others, price or income supports

of work . . . like workmen's compensation and child labor laws," are needless policies because their achievements would have been attained by the market anyway, given that they "simply embodied in law practices that had already become common in the private market, perhaps extending them somewhat to fringe areas."[31] To stem pollution, some conservatives concede a need for emission taxes, but only cautiously and reluctantly, urging that the "imperfect market may, af-

ter all, do as well or better than the imperfect government."[32]

Liberals disagree. They sanction direct regulation, taxation, information disclosure, and related policies to correct the market's imperfections and failures. Moreover, they applaud most of the results:

Many of the protections instituted by these programs have been so successful that the security they provide is taken for granted: pasteurization, meat and poultry inspection, control of patent medicines are among the classical examples of success. Also, we rarely acknowledge the excellent Federal performance in such areas as aviation safety or drug testing requirements or highway safety. CPSC Commissioner Pittle has recently outlined some of the benefits from those and similar programs which include: a 40 per cent reduction in ingestions of poisons by children over a 4-year period, due to safety packaging requirements; a decrease of 45 per cent in the number of crib deaths, since the safety standards for cribs became effective in 1974; the saving of some 28,000 lives between 1966 and 1974 as well as a substantial reduction in serious injuries, because of Federal motor vehicle safety regulations; and what appears to be a complete elimination of flame-burn injuries involved in children's sleepwear, as a result of Government standards for that clothing.[33]

Liberals admit that the government can occasionally go too far in these areas, but they trust the democratic process to correct large errors, as happened when Congress and the FDA bowed to public demands that saccharin, a popular but carcinogenic artificial sweetener, not be banned.

On the energy front, conservatives blame past problems on erroneous, ill-conceived, and unjustified government policy, price controls in particular. The conservatives' favored approach is, in this light, no mystery. Liberals, on the other hand, point an accusing finger at OPEC and other lumps of monopoly power.[34]

On inflation, conservatives call for strict money supply constraint and balanced federal budgets. Liberals likewise recognize the importance of monetary and fiscal stringency, but their knees tend to weaken when given the opportunity to put their monetary-fiscal policies where their collective mouth is because they fear that stringency alone would produce terrible side effects on employment. Many liberals thus advocate a multipronged attack in which the monetary-fiscal prong is flanked by one or more complementary policies—such as temporary wage-price control, a tax-based income policy, or sweeping procompetition policies for labor and business—to achieve less inflation without markedly augmenting unemployment.

Finally, among politicians, different positions in farm policy arise mainly from geography, not philosophy, with many conservative southerners and midwesterners betraying their ideology by backing government aid to agriculture. Speaking very generally, however, liberals have been the chief architects of crop insurance, price supports, income subsidies, and related farm supports, whereas conservatives have criticized such policies.

III. Historical Roots

A. The Sweeping View

However tantalizing or compelling philosophical arguments may be, they serve mainly as stage props, adding color to the unfolding drama of economic, political, and social history. Contributing to policies more greatly than ideological tracts are wars, depressions, financial panics, technological revolutions, and sundry other events. What makes no sense philosophically or economically often makes good sense historically.

A two-word summary of the steps government intervention has taken would be "ever more." In *level of authority* the march of policy in any area usually began at the local or state level and then proceeded to the national and occasionally even the international level. Public utility regulation, for instance, started in Colonial times with local controls over inns, ferries, roads, and bridges; advanced during the late nineteenth and early twentieth centuries to surveillance of railroads, grain elevators, and other businesses "affected with a public interest," only to wind up with federal public utility regulation of interstate dealings in transportation, communications, and energy. Environmental protection policy followed a similar course. Local ordinances concerning sewage treatment, garbage disposal, and trash burning came first. State authorities eventually added their clout, as most notably illustrated by California's early steps during the 1950s and 1960s to limit automobile pollution. Finally, federal environmental intervention blossomed prodigiously in the early 1970s.

History's expanding government interference is also indicated by *scope by industrial coverage*. Starting in the republic's earliest times with controls or franchises for harbors, ports, canals, highways, and bridges, government's attention thereafter broadened to encompass railroading, drug manufacturing, food processing, banking, agriculture, barbering, undertaking, physician's services, plumbing, and telecommunications. Controls over electric utilities, radio broadcasters, truckers, oil producers, oystermen, retailers, wholesalers, jobbers, distillers, insurers, stock brokers, and chiropractors followed. Spread has progressed within old agencies, such as the Texas Railroad Commission's branching out to regulate oil and gas production. Furthermore, the spread for any one problem, such as product safety, often ripples outward from a few items to so many that new government agencies have to be created to police them all. Federal product safety regulation began with foods, drugs, and cosmetics (FDA, 1906, 1938); stretched to flammable fabrics and toxic substances (FTC, 1954, and FDA, 1960); then reached autos, motorcycles, and related equipment (NHTSA, 1966); swamped boats (Coast Guard, 1971); and finally culminated with coverage of virtually every other consumer product on the market (CPSC, 1972). Indeed, an important hallmark of much recent regulation—environmental protection, equal employment opportunity, and job safety as well as product safety—has been its ubiquitous compass.

As for *types or tools of intervention,* U. S. history begins with (1) protective measures such as tariffs, patents, and exclusive franchises; progresses to (2)subsidies and land grants to encourage agricultural settlement, railroad expansion, agricultural education, and other pioneering endeavors; introduces (3) public utility regulation during the last century; moves shortly thereafter into (4) antitrust policy with the Sherman Act of 1890; branches into (5) conservation under the prodding of Theodore Roosevelt; takes up (6) product safety and job safety, beginning in limited areas like food and drugs for consumers and mining for workers; unveils (7) prohibitions against unfair practices and misrepresentation with the FTC Act of 1914 and Wheeler-Lea Act of 1938; presses (8) bank and finance supervision beginning with the Federal Reserve Act of 1913, the Federal Home Loan Bank Act of 1932, and the Securities Act of 1933; undertakes (9) product labeling and information disclosure; covers (10) oil production control; introduces (11) equal opportunity in employment, housing, and consumer credit; steps into (12) regulation for environmental protection; and so on.

This sweep toward "ever more" is best appreciated when quantified. Figure 4–1 depicts the expansion in raw numbers of federal regulatory agencies. At the outset, in 1900, only six regulatory agencies graced the federal bureaucracy. By the end of 1989, nearly sixty agencies could be counted, a ten-fold increase. Decades of particularly rapid multiplication, as indicated by the white segments in Figure 4–1 showing agency additions, were 1910 to 1919, 1930 to 1939, 1960 to 1969, and 1970 to 1979. Other decades were sleepy by comparison.

Alternatively, Figure 4–2 depicts the mushrooming growth of federal intervention by showing the number of major regulatory laws passed by Congress during each decade of this century. Of the two subcategories of legislation specified, *economic legislation* refers to laws governing price policies, mergers, monopolization, imports, finance, agriculture, transportation, and the like. *Social legislation,* on the other hand, refers to forms of business regulation that are designed to

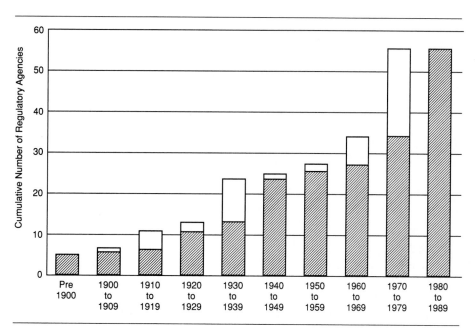

Figure 4–1
A Historical Perspective on Federal Agency Growth

Source: Center for the Study of American Business, *Directory of Federal Regulatory Agencies* (St. Louis: Washington University, 1980 edition), p. 2, and author's estimate.

improve social conditions, such as to gain clean air and water, safety of consumers and workers, equal employment opportunity, and highway beautification. Looking first at the combined total, we again see a ten-fold multiplication—from ten items of legislation to well over a hundred—punctuated by the same decades of especially feverish activity: the 1910s, 1930s, 1960s, and 1970s. Looking next at each subcategory, we see that during most of this century the total was divided fairly evenly between economic and social legislation. But during the 1960s and 1970s social legislation outstripped economic legislation by a mile.

Overall, the end result of this growth may be seen in a few cost statistics. First, there are the costs the government incurs to administer its many regulatory activities. In 1990, these were roughly $9 billion at the federal level. Second,

there are the compliance costs borne by businesses and consumers—for example, the costs of auto safety equipment or pollution abatement personnel plus the costs of paper work. These compliance costs are impossible to estimate accurately. But they probably lie somewhere in the range between $90 billion and $200 billion annually.[35] These are large numbers, yet compared to the GNP they fall on either side of 3 percent of the GNP, which seems less awesome. Moreover, do not forget that regulation generates considerable benefits as well as costs.[36]

B. 1877–1920: Concentration and Progressivism

It all started, at least its modern headwaters started, a little over 100 years ago. Depression haunted the 1870s. The 1880s then brought

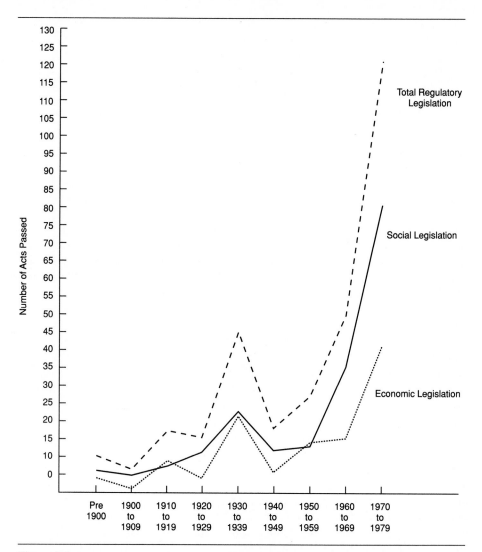

Figure 4–2

A Decade-by-Decade Comparison of Major Regulatory Legislation

Source: Center for the Study of American Business, Directory of Federal Regulatory
Agencies (St. Louis: Washington University, 1980 edition), p. 5.

prosperity, but they also brought giantism to
commerce:

> During the Eighties huge corporations kept rising
> like so many portents of a Europeanized future.

In the decade after the depression more than five
thousand firms were wrought into giant combines,
virtually all of which were pushing toward monopolies in their fields. At the end of the decade
United States Senator John Sherman, whose ba-

sic friendliness to business could not be questioned, spoke the worry of a good many of his countrymen. "If we are unable or unwilling [to take action against the trusts]," Sherman told the Senate, "there will soon be a trust for every production and a master to fix the price of every necessity of life."[37]

Action was taken, timorous and ineffectual action at first, but action that set the pattern for government control up to this day. In 1877 the U. S. Supreme Court ruled in *Munn* v. *Illinois* that the Illinois legislature legally could fix the maximum price charged for warehousing grain. "When private property is devoted to a public use, it is subject to public regulation," concluded the Court. Before *Munn,* state regulatory power was limited to cases of franchise or pure monopoly. *Munn* introduced the public's right to regulate private business that is merely "affected with a public interest."[38]

Moreover, *Munn* served as precedent when Congress established the Interstate Commerce Commission (ICC) in 1887 to regulate the railroads. The immensity and importance of the railroads to the economy of that time cannot be grasped today without imagining some kind of momentous collective movement among our modern airline, truck, bus, and railroad enterprises. Although some historians and economists have argued that the railroads themselves were the main impetus behind the ICC's establishment, urging regulation in hopes that it would officially enforce protective cartelization in railroading, such does not seem to have been the case. Agitation for regulation came mainly from disgruntled shippers—farmers in the south and midwest who had successfully pressed for such regulation at the state level prior to 1887, and east coast merchants and manufacturers who felt that railroad rates were structured to their disadvantage, fostering the low-cost penetration of competing products from inland rivals. In particular, "reform agitation in New York during the 1870s was the most important factor leading to the Act of

1887."[39] The fact that long-haul rates were frequently lower than short-haul rates was especially irritating to many shippers, so the Act of 1887 declared that rates must be "reasonable." More sweeping federal action came three years later in 1890 with the Sherman Antitrust Act, which outlawed restraints of trade and monopolization.

These several events turned out to be no more than a few rays of light in the dawning of a new age, the full blaze of sun being much delayed. First, the Supreme Court thereafter retreated from the *Munn* doctrine to strike down abundant regulatory legislation by evoking "due process" and "freedom of contract."[40] The most famous (or infamous) of these cases was *Lochner* v. *New York* (1905), which killed a New York law limiting bakery workers to a ten-hour work day and a sixty-hour work week.[41] The law had been based on extensive research disclosing that many bakers sweated through "more than one hundred hours per week" in hot bakeshops that were "damp, fetid, and devoid of proper ventilation and light," some with ceilings so low the bakers were forced to "work in a stooped position."[42] Second, the Interstate Commerce Commission wallowed in failure for at least twenty years. The reasons for this failure are now no mystery:

> Federal regulation on such a large scale was new to the country; procedures had to be worked out and legal precedents developed. . . . More important was the strong opposition after 1890 of the railroads and the attitude of the courts, which appeared to have little sympathy with the purpose of the act. Of sixteen decisions on rate cases appealed to the Supreme Court for enforcement between 1887 and 1905, fifteen were decided in favor of the carriers and but one sustained in part for the commission.[43]

Finally and similarly, early enforcement of the Sherman Act was handicapped by a lack of adequate administrative funding and by a Supreme Court wedded to the belief that "manufacturing is not commerce." Thus in *United States v. E. C. Knight Company* (1895), the Court ruled that the Sherman Act could not be used against the American Sugar Refining Company, which through merger had garnered control of about 90 percent of the U. S. sugar industry.[44]

The ambivalence of government policy toward business in those days is underscored by the fact that government, especially state government, not only failed to control and constrain monopolistic combinations; it actually took steps that encouraged combinations. These developments were part of the far-reaching social changes occurring in what has been dubbed the "associational movement" of the late nineteenth century. An economic and social order made up of many contending interest groups or collectives was at that time rapidly replacing the relatively atomistic, independent, individualistic, and pioneering disorder that prevailed in pre–Civil War America. Lawrence Friedman delineates four broad classes of economic associations—one each for industrial enterprises, labor, professionals or small businessmen, and farmers—as follows: "first, 'trusts' and other associations of industrial firms, loosely or tightly organized, including trade associations; second, labor unions; third, associations of occupations and small businesses (for example, retail druggists' associations, the master barbers, bar associations); fourth, farmers' organizations, including the state granges, the American Society of Equity, and farmers' co-operatives."[45] Economically and politically, labor unions and farm organizations were then the weakest of the lot. They languished under financial privation, unwieldy numbers of potential members, and government hostility. Illustrative of the hostility, early application of the Sherman Act was aimed mainly at crushing labor unions instead of business monopolies, and in 1887 President Cleveland blocked a congressional appropriation of $10,000 to aid drought-stricken farmers in buying new grain seed with a declaration that "though the people support the Government, the Government should not support the people."[46]

In contrast, changes in the law were assisting the associational movement among industrial enterprises and professional groups. Throughout most of the 1800s, corporate forms of business were severely curtailed by the states, which then, as now, held the power to grant certificates of incorporation. Corporations were typically limited by their certificates to very narrowly defined activities, such as providing railroad transportation between two points. Their capitalization was often tightly capped. Their life spans were relatively brief. And they could not own stock in other corporations. These shackles stunted corporate size and frustrated combinations except insofar as businessmen could devise evasions, one such evasion being the "trust." The first trust was the Standard Oil Trust, founded in 1882 when shareholders of fifty oil refineries surrendered their stock for trust certificates. (Hence, the word *trust* came to mean monopoly.) Despite evasions, perpetuation of certificate restrictions would certainly have crimped today's *Fortune 500*. "But," as Roger Sherman writes, "states abandoned many of these restrictions when they began to compete with each other to raise revenue by granting [lax] corporate charters in the 1890s. . . . The modern business corporation with its wide range of rights and powers was born during this period."[47] We might amend this to read *big* corporation, for it was this newly granted leniency that facilitated a massive merger movement from 1897 to 1903, a movement that converted approximately seventy-one important oligopolistic or near-competitive industries into near monopolies dominated by such firms as U. S. Steel, U. S. Gypsum, Du Pont, American Tobacco, International Paper, International Harvester, American Can, and National Biscuit.

State legal developments of the day were equally friendly to occupational licensure, which ostensibly protects the public from unscrupulous, incompetent, and dangerous professionals but which also entails some degree of officially sanctioned cartelization. Licensing usually grants economic control to a governing board made up of the occupation's practitioners. This board determines or heavily influences the criteria for licensing candidates (exams, apprenticeships, and such) to the exclusion of all unlicensed practitioners. And the board also promulgates codes of "proper" pricing, advertising, and professional conduct, all with at least one eye fixed on economic self-interest. The associational movement provided the seedbed, and occupational licensing won many successes that still linger in state laws:

> By 1910 in Wisconsin, for example, doctors, veterinarians, pharmacists, midwives, nurses, embalmers, and barbers had all achieved some form of licensing. Wisconsin had experimented, too, with plumbers' licensing; many states regulated this occupation. Other "professions" were licensed in scattered jurisdictions. Some of these trades were soon to extend their licensing statutes throughout the land.[48]

Thus it was that, up until about 1910, the philosophical temperament of government was, on balance, decidedly conservative—largely laissez faire with probusiness leanings. But reform was afoot. Among the first reformers were the Populists, whose party platform of 1892 emphasized that "the powers of government should be expanded . . . to the end that oppression, injustice, and poverty shall eventually cease in the land." Aside from farm relief, rights for women, an income tax, an expanded currency, and various election reform measures, the Populists wanted to strengthen the moribund Interstate Commerce Act of 1887 and the Sherman Antitrust Act of 1890 to the point of effectively regulating or dissolving monopolies. Though influential to the point of seeing many of their proposals eventually adopted, the Populists never gained federal power. Led by eccentrics like "Sockless" Jerry Simpson, who "easily left the impression of a howl from the backwoods," and supported

mainly by ignorant farmers and beggarly paupers, the Populist Party never won wide acceptance among the middle classes. It was, in short, a party of irresponsible and rabid failures.

Beginning in about 1900, however, reform began to acquire respectability. It was boosted (1) by the inadvertent presidency of Theodore Roosevelt, who was openly curt toward big-business men, (2) by the insolent attitude and crude conduct of enterprising robber barons, who could be so insensitive as to say things like, "The public be damned" (W. H. Vanderbilt), and (3) by the sensational revelations of the muckrakers, whose popular investigative journalism for respectable magazines and newspapers exposed many sordid business (and government) practices, from food adulteration to oil monopolization to union corruption. The Progressives spearheading the movement represented mainly *middle-class* views. "On one side Progressives feared the power of the plutocracy, on the other the poverty and restlessness of the masses."[49] Their remedies to calm the needy on the bottom came mainly from state legislatures:

> In the years following 1900 an impressive body of legislation was passed dealing with workmen's compensation, the labor of women and children, hours of work, minimum wages for women, and old-age pensions. Even when much allowance is made for spottiness in administration and enforcement, and for the toll that judicial decisions took of them, the net effect of these laws in remedying the crassest abuses of industrialism was very considerable.[50]

The Progressives' solutions for the plutocratic topside were sharply debated during the presidential election of 1912 when two Progressive candidates dominated the scene. On the one hand, Theodore Roosevelt, running for a third term after a four-year vacation from the presidency, propounded a policy of New Nationalism. "Combinations in industry," Roosevelt declared, "are the result of an imperative economic law."

Accordingly, he would allow concentration and monopolization to proceed unchecked *but closely regulate* the resulting behemoths in the "public interest," presumably much as the ICC regulated the railroads following the improvements brought by the Hepburn Act of 1906. On the other hand, Woodrow Wilson advocated New Freedom, insisting that widespread monopoly was not inevitable, that competition could be and should be restored by deconcentration plus tariff cuts, that moreover *competition should be continuously maintained by revitalized antitrust policy*. Of the two methods of controlling monopoly power, Wilson's was actually the more conservative because it entailed much less government intervention.

Wilson won. The Federal Reserve Act followed in 1913 to staunch the "money trust." Tariffs were cut substantially in the same year. Shortly thereafter in 1914 the Federal Trade Commission was established to "prevent . . . unfair methods of competition in commerce." And one month later Congress passed the Clayton Antitrust Act, which among other things (1) strengthened the remedies open to private parties under the Sherman Act, (2) prohibited certain anticompetitive business practices like predatory pricing, and (3) outlawed anticompetitive mergers achieved by stock acquisition. These several measures emerged despite the fact that in 1911, just before their passage, enforcement of the Sherman Act had reached a pinnacle of sorts with the Supreme Court's dissolution of two of the most notorious trusts of the day—the Standard Oil Company and the American Tobacco Company.

Although at the national level the regulatory approach was rejected in favor of the competitive approach, state governments were busy establishing commission regulation over such public utilities as gas, light, power, and telephone companies. Led by the actions of New York and Wisconsin in 1907, more than two-thirds of the states had regulatory commissions by 1920.

C. 1921–1959: Crash, Collectivization, and Security

The Roaring '20s were actually very quiet from the perspective of this chronicle. The conservative administrations of Harding, Coolidge, and Hoover presided over a temporary prosperity with a friendly, accommodating attitude toward business. Then between 1929 and 1933 the economy fell apart. The GNP plunged from $104 billion to $56 billion. Wholesale and consumer prices tumbled by one-third and one-fourth, respectively. Industrial production sank by one-half. And unemployment soared to nearly 25 percent of the workforce.

The disaster pulled Franklin Roosevelt into office and sparked a massive explosion of government activity symbolized by a startling accumulation of official acronyms—RFC, NIRA, AAA, WPA, CCC, FDIC, SEC, TVA, FCC, NLRB, and others. The intent was security and recovery.[51]

Four major forms of intervention emerged, setting enduring precedents. The first may be called *passive cartelization*, under which the government suspended the antitrust laws and to various degrees encouraged economic groups to cooperate, coordinate, and rationalize their behavior. Under the National Recovery Administration (NRA), for instance, industries were urged to draft "codes of fair competition" that set minimum prices, prescribed terms of sale, controlled output, regulated working conditions, and the like. By June 7, 1934, some 459 codes covering over 90 percent of the eligible industries had been approved. But the biggest firms in each industry dominated the game, oligopolistic industries took advantage of consumers, and competitive industries remained competitive, spreading disillusion. The NRA was finally throttled by the Supreme Court for being unconstitutional, and after March 1938 antitrust was revived for most industries with intense vigor under Assistant Attorney General Thurman Arnold. Still, vestiges of passive cartelization survived for groups that were considered disadvantaged or weak as compared to their economic counterparts, the idea being one of protection through counterorganization. Thus, for example, labor unions were promoted by the National Labor Relations Act of 1935, which gave unions the right to organize free from employer pressures. Similarly, the Agricultural Marketing Agreement Act of 1938 permitted collective conduct in milk and fruit production. Small wholesale and retail traders were granted different but related exemptions from competition with passage of the Robinson-Patman Act (1938) and the Miller-Tydings Act (1937).

Second, *active cartelization* also blossomed. Whereas passive cartelization entailed little more than government approval, active cartelization entailed exclusive government participation, enforcement, and regulation—setting prices, curtailing outputs, restricting entry, allocating territories, and the like. The alleged intent in most cases was once again to prevent "destructive competition" or to gain a "fair balance of power" between buyers and sellers. These regulations were therefore often welcomed by those affected. Examples include (1) trucking regulation under an expanded ICC, (2) agriculture price supports under the Agricultural Adjustment Act and subsequent farm legislation, (3) airline regulation under the Civil Aeronautics Board, (4) radio spectrum management under the Federal Communications Commission, (5) shipping protection and subsidization under the Federal Maritime Commission, and (6) coal cartelization under the National Bituminous Coal Commission.[52] It is interesting that the New Deal's cartelization efforts, both active and passive, descended from Teddy Roosevelt's rejected New Nationalism.

Government *insurance* provided a third major avenue toward security. The term *insurance* is used loosely here to indicate no more than the presence of contributory payments of some kind, as opposed to pure handouts, plus protection against losses. Still with us from the New Deal is insurance against the loss of income from unemployment (state unemployment compensation systems), against depositor losses in bank failures (FDIC), against dependency from disability and old age (Social Security), and against crop loss (Federal Crop Insurance Corporation).

Finally, *subsidies* flowed. Although certainly not new, government subsidies took several novel twists during the Depression and they climbed to new heights. Among indirect aids to business, Roosevelt increased public works spending to an annual rate 100 percent above Hoover's level. The TVA became the most famous New Deal project. More directly, the Reconstruction Finance Corporation (RFC) was established in 1932. Offering direct loans to such diverse businesses as railroads, banks, and insurance companies, it kept many from going under. The Rural Electrification Administration (REA) made low-cost loans to cooperative associations to build and operate electric facilities in the hinterlands. And through other agencies direct subsidies supported everything from leaf raking to the arts to the airlines.

However much these various New Deal dealings may have contributed to the security of their beneficiaries, they did not bring economic recovery. World War II can be credited with that feat. After recovery, government intervention entered a period of consolidation and conservative calm, as indicated earlier in Figures 4–1 and 4–2. The Employment Act of 1946 created the Council of Economic Advisors and endorsed federal activism in aggregate economic affairs. The Celler-Kefauver Act (1950) bolstered antitrust in the area of mergers. And the Small Business Administration (SBA) was established in 1953. But little more that is worthy of note transpired in the way of policy innovation.

What is worthy of note is that most of the New Deal's innovations endured in one shape or another well into the 1950s and beyond. Now, long after the fearsome shadow of the Great

Depression has passed, the government's telephone directory still lists the CCC, TVA, SEC, REA, OASI, and many others. The Reconstruction Finance Corporation died in 1953 but largely for reasons of scandalous mismanagement rather than obsolescence. And, indeed, as this is written, pressure is building to reinstate the RFC or something like it to lend businesses massive transfusions of capital for the "reindustrialization" of America.

D. 1960–1979: The Era of Social Regulation

In *economic* regulation, the 1960s and 1970s brought no abrupt departures from the heritage of earlier years. The period's major economic regulatory legislation amounted to little more than a broadening, deepening, and refining of old policies and agencies.

Take mergers for example. The basic policy had been set in 1914 and 1950. The Bank Merger Act of 1960 modified its application to banks, and the Antitrust Improvement Act of 1976 introduced merger notification procedures. Simultaneously, the courts were busy building a body of case law interpreting the old acts.

The only areas of significant change in economic regulation came about in (1) consumer information improvement, such as the Fair Packaging and Labeling Act and the Truth-in-Lending Act; (2) matters arising from technological change, such as the Communications Satellite Act; (3) a spell of peacetime wage and price control; and (4) efforts to revitalize rather than merely regulate America's railroads. Few new agencies in the old commission mold were established.

The period's brightest fireworks were provided by burgeoning *social* regulation (albeit having an economic impact). Table 4–2 outlines this chronology, dividing the legislation three ways—consumer health and safety, job safety and work conditions, and environment *cum* energy. Many factors prompted this striking expansion. Sobering crises erupted—contaminating the air, burning ghettos, crippling babies, and killing motorists. Popular books, such as Rachel Carson's *Silent Spring* and Ralph Nader's *Unsafe at Any Speed,* broadcast the sad news. Well-organized interest groups sprang up and perked up, representing consumers, workers, environmentalists, and disadvantaged minorities. All was not well.

From this atmosphere, social regulatory policies and agencies multiplied apace. Compared to economic policies and agencies, their novelty lay not so much in their essentials as in their emphasis and profusion. First, the new agencies were given especially wide scopes of industrial coverage. Whereas oldsters like the ICC, FDA, and FCC attended to at most a few industries, the Environmental Protection Agency (EPA), Equal Employment Opportunity Commission (EEOC), Consumer Product Safety Commission (CPSC), and Occupational Safety and Health Administration (OSHA) were given jurisdictions spanning nearly the entire length and width of the private sector. An important consequence of this far-ranging characteristic is that it lessens the degree to which the regulated industries can extract favoritism from the agencies. The older agencies have often been accused of being "captured" by their wards.

Second, this broader coverage has typically been accompanied by a narrower material focus as compared to older agencies. The veteran agencies have often been concerned with the totality of business operations of their charges—pricing, product quality, entry, plant location, service offerings, and so on. In contrast, the newcomers restrict their attention to, say, employment practices (EEOC), or design safety (CPSC), or polluting practices (EPA). As Murry Wiedenbaum observes, "This restriction prevents the agency from developing too close a concern with the overall well-being of any company or industry. Rather, it can result in a total lack of concern over the effects of its specific actions on a company or industry."[53]

There is, finally, a trend toward increasing

Table 4–2
Chronology of Major Social Regulatory Legislation, 1960–1979

Year	Legislation	Agency to Which Law Applies
Consumer Safety and Health		
1962	Drug Amendments of 1962	Food and Drug Administration
1966	Highway Safety Act	National Highway Traffic Safety Administration
1966	Federal Hazardous Substances Act	Food and Drug Administration
1970	Poison Prevention Packaging Act	Consumer Product Safety Commission
1972	Consumer Product Safety Act	Consumer Product Safety Commission
1974	Mobile Home Construction and Safety Standards Act	Housing and Urban Development
1974	Hazardous Material Transportation Act	Federal Highway Administration Materials Transportation Bureau
1976	Medical Devices Amendments	Food and Drug Administration
Job Safety and Work Conditions		
1963	Equal Pay Act	Equal Employment Opportunity Commission
1964	Civil Rights Act	Equal Employment Opportunity Commission
1969	Coal Mine Health and Safety Act	Mine Safety and Health Administration
1970	Occupation Safety and Health Act	Occupational Safety and Health Administration
1972	Equal Employment Opportunity Act	Equal Employment Opportunity Commission
1977	Mine Safety and Health Amendments	Mine Safety and Health Administration
1978	Pregnancy Discrimination Act	Equal Employment Opportunity Commission
Environment and Energy		
1970	National Environmental Improvement Act	Council on Environmental Quality
1970	Clean Air Act Amendments	Environmental Protection Agency
1972	Water Pollution Control Act Amendments	Environmental Protection Agency
1973	Endangered Species Act	Fish and Wildlife Service
1974	Federal Energy Act	Economic Regulatory Administration
1976	Toxic Substances Control Act	Environmental Protection Agency
1977	Dept. of Energy Reorganization Act	Economic Regulatory Administration
1977	Clean Air Act Amendments	Environmental Protection Agency
1977	Surface Mining Control and Reclamation Act	Department of Interior

Source: Ronald J. Penoyer, *Directory of Federal Regulatory Agencies* (St. Louis: Center for the Study of American Business, Washington University, 1980), pp. 83–98.

regulation by line operating departments and bureaus in the executive branch of the government as well as by independent commissions patterned after the ICC, CAB, and FTC. Examples include the Occupational Safety and Health Administration, housed in the Department of Labor; the Materials Transportation Bureau, which strives to assure the safe transportation of hazardous substances (their containers, mode of shipment, etc.) and which is located in the Department of Transportation. This recognition of line offices is not meant to slight the new independent agencies—EPA, CPSC, EEOC, CFTC, and NCUA.

E. 1980–Present: Retreat and Recovery

History is supposed to repeat itself, and it appears to comply in the case at hand. The 1980s followed the example of the 1890s, 1920s, and 1950s. The 1980s brought a retreat of the intense government tinkering that characterized the 1960s and 1970s. The retreat began when the Carter Administration, prodded by CAB chairman Alfred E. Kahn, took steps to deregulate the airlines in 1978. Backed by Congress, the deregulation movement spread to railroads, trucking, energy, banking, and communications. However appropriate the active cartelization of the 1930s might have been for fighting the Great Depression, it was no longer appropriate to the inflationary conditions of the 1970s. Thus, the deregulation launched by the Carter camp was confined largely to economic regulations, where there was little economic justification for regulation in the first place, areas that would be governed by competition in the absence of intervention. In telephone communications, for instance, deregulation first hit equipment manufacturing and long-distance transmission, not basic, local phone service.

Under the avidly conservative ideology of President Ronald Reagan, the retreat in economic regulation quickened and spread. For example, the Reagan Administration engineered the most dramatic retrenchment of federal antitrust enforcement in the twentieth century. From 1981 through 1988, strictures against horizontal mergers were substantially relaxed, monopolization cases dwindled toward zero, and nonprice vertical restraints of trade were completely ignored.[54] Moreover, the Reagan Administration achieved massive cutbacks in social regulation as well, a fact supported by one simple statistic: The number of people employed as federal regulators declined 15 percent during Reagan's first term.[55]

It is important to recognize here that Reagan and his people did not seek regulatory *reform;* they sought regulatory *relief.* They did not want to improve the quality of regulation; they wanted to erase as much of it as possible. When campaigning for the presidency Reagan exclaimed, "There are tens of thousands of . . . regulations I would like to see eliminated." He followed up on that.[56]

Among the factors contributing to the deregulation movement of the 1980s, the most interesting was a reversal of the historic pattern: private crisis—government response. The government, in the eyes of many Americans, had created some crises of its own, thereby becoming the problem, not the solution. Energy shortages provoked by low price ceilings and costly transportation inefficiencies resulting from regulatory entry barriers and route restrictions—these and other difficulties attracted attention to the government's failings. Aiding the cause were muckraking books, some even from Ralph Nader's shop, such as *Interstate Commerce Omission* and *The Monopoly Makers.*[57]

Then history repeated itself. After George Bush won the presidency, the regulatory pendulum swung from the conservative right toward the moderate center. Within its first eighteen months, the Bush Administration had among other things (1) increased antitrust scrutiny of business mergers, (2) drawn up rules to make light trucks and minivans safer, (3) pushed OSHA to reduce workplace asphyxiations and mutilations, and (4) initiated major advances in air pollution control with passage of the Clean Air Act of 1990. According to *Business Week,* "Bush has replaced antigovernment crusaders with nonideological problem-solvers."[58] According to the antigovernment crusaders who were replaced, this revival of regulation was deplorable. James Miller, who served Reagan as chairman of the FTC and head of OMB, complained in 1990 that "Bush has just lost control. The system has broken down."[59]

Encouraging revival of regulation were several crises that, to a large degree, could be blamed on the deregulation of the 1980s. There were, for example, smelly scandals involving the savings and loan industry and the FDA's supervision of generic drugs.[60] Moreover, there was considerable support for revived federal regulation among business people. "This," as an executive of Lever Brothers Corporation admitted,"is an anomaly. Normally, we would shout and fight."[61] Why the business support? One reason was that during the 1980s state governments moved in to fill the void left by the federal government's retreat. Because state regulations varied from state to state, business compliance grew severely complicated. Hence, business supported federal reregulation in hope of restoring nationwide uniformity and thereby curbing their costs of compliance. The areas especially affected by this phenomenon were hazardous waste treatment, automotive emissions, and other environmental issues.

Summary

It should now be clear that current public policies toward business are woven from philosophical and historical threads as well as the largely theoretical fibers discussed in the first three chapters. Oversimplifying the rich range of economic philosophies, we have fabricated conservative and liberal flags.

Conservatives have the greatest faith in capitalist, free-enterprise markets and the least regard for government intervention. This combination of positions derives largely from conservatives' beliefs that (1) human nature corresponds closely to that of *Homo economicus,* an acquisitive, rational, knowledgeable creature who almost always acts wisely in self-interest; (2) freedom should reign supreme, without more than minor compromise for such other ends as equity, fairness, safety, and security; and (3) government ineptitude transforms even the best of intentions into bad results.

In contrast, liberals have greater faith in government than do conservatives, advocating mixed capitalism or the welfare state. To liberals, (1) humans display vulnerabilities and needs uncharacteristic of *Homo economicus;* (2) freedom should be honored but defined in a way to include freedom from the market's worst offenses and tempered to allow much equality; and (3) market imperfections and failures should be taken very seriously, to the point of attempting pragmatic policy remedies.

The history of government intervention in many ways traces a seesaw battle between liberals and conservatives, with liberals winning more often than not over the long pull. Periods of particularly rapid growth in officialdom—the 1910s, 1930s, 1960s, and 1970s—were fertilized by the appearance of what many people believed were awesome developments, namely, the combination movement at the turn of the century, the Great Depression, the outbreak of racial strife, and so on. Periods of relatively conservative consolidation or retrenchment followed these spurts but never to the extent of large-scale dismantlement (at least not until recently). The overall result is that government has become mountainous by any measure—number of agencies, size of regulatory budgets, proportion of people employed in government, private cost of compliance, and so on.

The 1980s and 1990s provide an especially interesting chapter for future chronicles. Staunch laissez-faire Reaganites tried to eliminate much, if not most, of the eocnomic and social regulation developed during earlier decades. They slashed budgets, reduced the ranks of officialdom, refused to enforce long-standing rules, and promoted legislation curbing federal controls. In contrast, Bush's regulators appear moderate. They are "problem solvers, not agenda setters," according to an analyst at the conservative American Enterprise Institute. The change reflects what another observer calls Mr. Bush's "limited-government rather than no-government" philosophy.[62] It now seems clear that history's inertia will prevent a return to the days when government was content just to deliver the mail, set a tariff, issue currency, distribute public lands, and fight the Native Americans.

Questions and Exercises for Chapter 4

1. Briefly compare and contrast Conservative and Liberal philosophies in three of the following areas: (a) value judgments, (b) view of human nature, (c) frame of mind, (d) regard for market/government.
2. Is it possible to be Conservative on some issues but Liberal on others? Explain your yes or no. (Table 4–1 may help here.)
3. Outline the spread of government along dimensions of level, scope, and instrument.
4. Compare and contrast the "populist" and "progressive" movements.
5. The association movement involved four groups, two of which were most successful. Identify them, then explain how and why they were particularly successful.
6. Identify and briefly describe the four main forms of government intervention prompted by the Great Depression.
7. Compare New Nationalism and New Freedom. What aspects of the New Deal relate to each?
8. How does "social" regulation differ from "economic" regulation in (a) historical trend, (b) subject matter, and (c) industrial scope?
9. To what extent does history influence the popularity of philosophies? To what extent do philosophies shape history? (The 1930s and 1980s are particularly pertinent here.)

Notes

1. Milton Friedman, *Capitalism and Freedom* (Chicago: University of Chicago Press, 1962), p. 6.

2. Clinton Rossiter, *Conservatism in America* (New York: Vintage Books, 1962), pp. 128–131; Mark A. Lutz and Kenneth Lux, *The Challenge of Humanistic Economics* (Menlo Park, CA: Benjamin/Cummings Publishing, 1979), pp. 27–29.

3. For other surveys see Robert B. Carson, *Microeconomic Issues Today, Alternative Approaches* (New York: St. Martin's Press, 1980); Benjamin Ward, *The Ideal Worlds of Economics* (New York: Basic Books, 1979); Donald S. Watson, *Economic Policy: Business and Government* (Boston: Houghton Mifflin, 1960), Chapters 2, 3, and 4; Rossiter, *Conservatism in America*, Chapter 1; and Conrad P. Waligorski, *The Political Theory of Conservative Economists* (Lawrence: University Press of Kansas, 1990).

4. Friedman, *Capitalism and Freedom*, p. 12.

5. Friedrich A. Hayek, *The Road to Serfdom* (Chicago: University of Chicago Press, 1944). Alternatively, freedom is defined as the availability of choice, and conservatives assume that individuals always prefer a choice to a lack of choice. Gordon Tullock, *The Logic of the Law* (New York: Basic Books, 1971). The problem with this is that people often prefer a lack of choice and call on the government to implement restrictions of such "freedom." Would you favor giving people the choice of driving on the left or right hand side of the street, whichever they fancy, whenever they travel?

6. Rossiter, *Conservatism in America*, p. 132.

7. Milton Friedman and Rose Friedman, *Free to Choose* (New York: Harcourt Brace Jovanovich, 1980), pp. 13–14.

8. Henry C. Simons, *Economic Policy for a Free Society* (Chicago: University of Chicago Press, 1948), p. 43 (emphasis in original).

9. Dean A. Worcester, Jr., *Welfare Gains from Advertising: The Problem of Regulation* (Washington, DC: American Enterprise Institute, 1978).

10. Friedman, *Capitalism and Freedom*, p. 13.

11. Ibid., pp. 22–36; Friedman and Friedman, *Free to Choose*, pp. 27–33; Simons, *Economic Policy*, pp. 40–77.

12. Ronald Coase, "The Problem of Social Cost," *Journal of Law and Economics* (October 1969): 1–44. This position has since come under withering attack from nonconservatives. See, e.g., H. H. Liebhafsky, "The Problem of Social Cost—An Alternative Approach," *Natural Resources Journal* (1973): 615–76; S. Todd Lowry, "Bargain and Contract Theory in Law and Economics," in *The Chicago School of Political Economy*, ed. W. J. Samuels (East Lansing: Michigan State University Graduate School of Business Administration, Division of Research, 1976), pp. 215–36; Mark Kelman, "Consumption Theory, Production Theory, and Ideology in the Coase Theorem," *Southern California Law Review* (March 1979): 669–98.

13. Simons, *Economic Policy*, pp. 40–62, 81–83, 107–120; George J. Stigler, "The Case Against Big Business," *Fortune* (May 1952): 123–127; Stigler, "Mergers and Preventive Antitrust Policy," *University of Pennsylvania Law Review* (November 1955): 176–184.

14. For recent Stigler see *Report of Nixon's Task Force on Productivity and Competition* (February 18, 1969), reprinted in *The Journal of Reprints for Antitrust Law and Economics* (Winter 1969): 827–881. Robert H. Bork, *The Antitrust Paradox: A Policy at War with Itself* (New York: Basic Books, 1978), and M. L. Greenhut and

Bruce Benson, *American Antitrust Laws in Theory and in Practice* (Brookfield, VT: Avebury, 1989).

15. Friedman, *Free to Choose*, p. 28; Harold Demsetz, "Why Regulate Utilities?" *Journal of Law and Economics* (April 1968): 55–66.

16. Friedman, *Free to Choose*, pp. 119–132; John S. McGee, *In Defense of Industrial Concentration* (New York: Praeger, 1971); Yale Brozen, ed., *The Competitive Economy* (Morrison, NJ: General Learning Press, 1975); Robert H. Bork and Ward S. Bowman, Jr., "The Crisis in Antitrust," *Columbia Law Review* (March 1965): 363–375.

17. Harlan M. Blake and William K. Jones, "In Defense of Antitrust," *Columbia Law Review* (March 1965): 377–399; Robert Pitofsky, "The Political Content of Antitrust," *University of Pennsylvania Law Review* (April 1979): 1051–1081.

18. Eric F. Goldman, *Rendevous with Destiny* (New York: Vintage Books, 1956) Chapter 5.

19. Richard Hofstadter, *Social Darwinism in American Thought* (Boston: Beacon Press, 1955).

20. Eirik Furubotn and Svetozar Pejovich, (eds.) *The Economics of Property Rights* (Cambridge, MA: Ballinger, 1974); Gary Becker, Elizabeth Landes, and Robert Michael, "An Economic Analysis of Marital Instability," *Journal of Political Economy* (December 1977): 1141–87; William M. Landes, "An Economic Study of U. S. Aircraft Hijacking, 1961–1976," *Journal of Law and Economics* (April 1978): 1–31; Richard A. Posner, "A Theory of Primitive Society, With Special Reference to Law," *Journal of Law and Economics* (April 1980): 1–53. For a critical analysis of the first of these see A. A. Schmid in *Chicago School;* and for an interesting contrast to the last item read Calvin Martin, *Keepers of the Game* (Berkeley: University of California Press, 1978).

21. E. W. Hawley, *The New Deal and the Problem of Monopoly* (Princeton, N.J.: Princeton University Press, 1966).

22. John M. Keynes, "The End of Laissez-Faire," in *Essays in Persuasion* (New York: Norton, 1963), p. 312. (emphasis in original) For more on rationality see Amitai Etzioni, *The Moral Dimension: Toward a New Economics* (New York: Free Press, 1988), especially pp. 136–150.

23. Paul Samuelson, "Personal Freedoms and Economic Freedoms in the Mixed Economy," in *The Business Establishment,* ed. E. F. Cheit (New York: Wiley, 1964), pp. 218–219. For elaboration see Karl Polayni, *The Great Transformation* (Boston: Beacon Press, 1957), pp. 249–258. See also the articles by Thomas C. Schelling and Albert O. Hirschman in *American Economic Review* (May 1984): 1–11, 89–96, and Amartya Sen, "Individual Freedom as a Social Commitment," *New York Review of Books,* June 14, 1990, pp. 49–54.

24. Richard Romano and Melvin Leiman, *Views on Capitalism,* 2nd ed. (Beverly Hills, CA: Glencoe Press, 1975), p. 142.

25. Samuelson, p. 224.

26. *Business Week,* June 30, 1980, p. 67.

27. Milton Friedman and Rose Friedman, *Free to Choose,* p. 212.

28. Ibid., p. 227.

29. Ibid., p. 227.

30. Ibid., p. 246.

31. Ibid., p. 243.

32. Ibid., p. 218.

33. Michael W. Klass and Leonard W. Weiss, *Study on Federal Regulation* Vol. VI, *Framework for Regulation,* U.S. Senate, Committee on Governmental Affairs (1978), p. 34.

34. Robert Stobaugh and Daniel Yergin, eds. *Energy Future* (New York: Random House, 1979).

35. John E. Schwartz, "The Hidden Truth About Regulation," *Challenge* (Nov./Dec. 1983): 54–56; *Washington Post National Weekly Edition,* October 10–16, 1988, p. 33; Robert W. Hahn and John A. Hird, "The Costs and Benefits of Regulation," *The Yale Journal on Regulation* (Winter 1991): 233–278.

36. *Ibid.*

37. Eric F. Goldman, *Rendezvous with Destiny* (New York: Vintage Books, 1956), p. 28.

38. *Munn* v. *Illinois,* 94 U.S. 113 (1877).

39. Albro Martin, "The Troubled Subject of Railroad Regulation in the Gilded Age—A Reappraisal," *Journal of American History* (September 1974): 339–371.

40. Arthur S. Miller, *The Supreme Court and American Capitalism* (New York: Free Press, 1968), pp. 50–62.

41. *Lochner* v. *New York,* 198 U.S. 45 (1905).

42. Quoted by Lawrence M. Friedman, "Freedom of Contract and Occupational Licensing 1890–1910: A Legal and Social Study," *California Law Review* (May 1965): 490.

43. Harold U. Faulkner, *The Decline of Laissez-Faire, 1897–1917* (New York: Harper Torchbooks, 1968), pp. 187–188.

44. *United States* v. *E.C. Knight Company* 156 U.S. 1 (1895).

45. Friedman, "Freedom of Contract," pp. 503–504.

46. Goldman, *Rendezvous with Destiny,* p. 33.

47. Roger Sherman, *Antitrust Policies and Issues* (Reading, MA: Addison-Wesley, 1978), p. 3.

48. Friedman, "Freedom of Contract," p. 510.

49. Richard Hofstadter, *The Age of Reform* (New York: Vintage Books, 1955), p. 238.

50. Ibid., p. 242.

51. For a brief account see Jonathan Hughes, "Roots of Regulation: The New Deal," *Regulatory Change in an Atmosphere of Crisis,* ed. G. M. Walton (New York: Academic Press, 1979), pp. 31–55.

52. For a detailed treatment on all these efforts see E. W. Hawley, *The New Deal and the Problem of Monopoly* (Princeton, NJ: Princeton University Press, 1966), Chaps. 10–14.

53. Murray Weidenbaum, *The Costs of Government Regulation of Business,* Study for the Subcommittee on Economic Growth and Stabilization of the Joint Economic Committee, U. S. Congress (1978), p. 10.

54. William E. Kovacic, "The Sherman Antitrust Act and the World: Comment," *Antitrust Law Journal* (59, no. 1, 1990): 125–126.

55. *Business Week,* June 26, 1989, p. 58.

56. Jonathan Lash, Katherine Gillman, and David Sheridan, *A Season of Spoils* (New York: Pantheon Books, 1984), pp. 19–29.

57. Robert Fellmeth, *The Interstate Commerce Omission* (New York: Grossman, 1970); Mark J. Green, ed., *The Monopoly Makers* (New York: Grossman, 1973).

58. *Business Week,* June 26, 1989, p. 58. See also *Wall Street Journal,* 27 November 1989, pp. A1, A5.

59. *Newsweek,* May 7, 1990, p. 24.

60. *Wall Street Journal,* 13 September 1989, pp. A1, A10.

61. *New York Times,* 24 February 1991, p. E6.

62. *Wall Street Journal,* 27 November 1989, p. A1.

PART II

Antitrust Policy

Chapter 5

Introduction to Antitrust Policy

The public interest is best protected from the evils of monopoly and price control by the maintenance of competition.
— *Chief Justice Stone*

The antitrust laws of the United States are in many ways unique. No other country can boast of a bigger body of law for monopolies and restrictive business practices. No other area of U. S. policy toward business can be considered more basic. As James McKie once remarked, "Perhaps the simplest kind of government intervention in the economic system is to ensure that the private system itself will work satisfactorily, by preserving effectively competitive markets. It is a Deistic kind of intervention: it sets the rules and conditions for the game, and then lets the system run itself."[1]

This chapter first specifies the problems addressed by antitrust policy. Second, the aims of antitrust policy receive attention. Third, an outline of the statutory laws is given, followed by a description of the agencies that enforce them. Finally, exceptions are explored. Ensuing chapters review specific antitrust policies in detail.

1. The Problems

Previous chapters explained why competition is desirable. But those explanations were sketchy. Elaboration is now in order, organized around the three main elements of any market—structure, conduct, and performance. Reduced to barest essentials, the problem is one of market power—its mere attainment or possession (as reflected in structure), its exercise (as revealed in anticompetitive conduct), and its consequences (as measured by performance).

A. Structure

The ill effects of monopoly power, or more generally, market power, have long been recognized. Aristotle tells of a Sicilian who monopolized the iron trade, thereby profiting 100 percent.[2] Grassroots sentiment against monopoly power is based on more, however. It is based on a distrust of *power itself,* power that can be measured by such structural conditions as market concentration, barriers to entry, product differentiation, and firm diversification.

1. MARKET CONCENTRATION

The president of Western Auto Supply Company, Joseph Grissom, acknowledged the power bestowed by large market share when he said, "I would rather have 50 percent of one market than 10 percent of five markets. That way we can influence the market rather than react to it."[3]

Percentages above 50 would look even better to Mr. Grissom. They attracted the organizers and promoters of some of America's largest firms. Table 5–1 gives examples by reporting data on the merger history of ten major U. S. companies that ascended to dominance during the years 1895–1904, a period of feverish merger activity. These ten firms accounted for the disappearance of 577 formerly independent companies, thereby gaining single-firm market shares ranging from 65 percent in the case of U. S. Steel and Otis Elevator to 90 percent in the case of American Tobacco. The *market share of the leading firm* is thus one method of measuring market concentration, a method occasionally disclosing dominance.

Aside from public utilities and merchants in one-horse towns, leading-firm market shares of the size in Table 5–1 are now relatively rare, thanks in part to antitrust policy. Many of our most familiar leading firms hold market shares well below those of Table 5–1: General Motors in autos, 35 percent (counting imports); Anheuser-Busch in beer, 44 percent; Kellogg in cereals, 45 percent; Coca-Cola in soft drinks, 40 percent; Alcoa in aluminum, 32 percent; Procter & Gamble in detergents, 50 percent. Still, market power prevails in these markets and others like them because of the collective power of just a few firms. This power may be measured by the market share held by several leading firms taken together, the **concentration ratio**. The *four-firm* concentration ratio is the one most widely cited because it is the form traditionally used by the

Table 5–1
Selected Major Mergers Causing High Concentrations 1895–1904

Company (or Combine)	Number of Firms Disappearing	Rough Estimate of Market Controlled (%)
U.S. Steel	170	65
U.S. Gypsum	29	80
American Tobacco	162	90
American Smelting & Refining	12	85
DuPont de Nemours	65	85
Diamond Match	38	85
American Can	64	65–75
International Harvester	4	70
National Biscuit (Nabisco)	27	70
Otis Elevator	6	65

Source: Ralph L. Nelson, *Merger Movements in American Industry 1895–1956* (Princeton, N.J.: Princeton University Press, 1959), pp. 161–62.

U. S. Census Bureau. It is the collective shares of the top four firms in a market. Table 5–2 shows examples.

Herfindahl-Hirschman Indexes (or H-Indexes) may be used instead of the concentration ratio. Instead of measuring market concentration by the sum of the shares of the four leading firms, the H-index squares the shares of all firms and then adds them. For example, the H-index for a market of five firms with shares of 35 percent, 25 percent, 20 percent, 15 percent, and 5 percent would be:

$$35^2 + 25^2 + 20^2 + 15^2 + 5^2$$
$$= 1225 + 625 + 400 + 225 + 25 = 2,500$$

The squaring of market shares gives especially large weight to the largest market shares. This may yield a better reflection of anticompetitive impact than leaving the market shares unsquared. Summing the shares of all firms instead of just the top four also makes the H-index more comprehensive than the four-firm concentration ratio. The H-index is thus fancier than the concentration ratio. Still, the two are highly correlated, as suggested by the H-indexes in Table 5–2.

The numbers in Table 5–2 roughly indicate the general pattern of concentration—that is, four-firm concentration above 80 or below 20 is relatively rare. The vast bulk of markets could be called oligopolies, with four-firm ratios ranging from 80 on the tight end to 20 on the loose end.

The causes of high as opposed to low concentration vary greatly, but for present purposes only two broad categories of causes need to be acknowledged—those that are "natural" or economically warranted, and those that are "artificial" or deliberately contrived. Among *natural* causes we find (1) large economies of scale relative to the extent of the market, (2) unusually scarce resource inputs, and (3) early or late stages in the industry's life cycle. Antitrust policy cannot be very concerned with high concentration produced and perpetuated by these factors because the concentration would be thrust on the leading firms, it would be necessary to achieving efficiency, or it would be difficult if not impossible to dissolve. Among *artificial* causes of concentration we find (1) mergers of otherwise competing firms, as illustrated by the examples of Table 5–1, (2) restrictive business practices

---

Table 5–2
Concentration Ratios and H-Indexes of Selected Industries, 1982

Industry	Four-Firm Ratio	H-Index
Household refrigerators	94	2,745
Aircraft engines	72	1,778
Tires and inner tubes	66	1,591
Glass containers	50	966
Metal office furniture	45	900
Macaroni and spaghetti	42	646
Copper rolling and drawing	35	503
Frozen fruits and vegetables	27	306
Sawmills and planing mills	17	113

Source: U.S. Bureau of the Census, *1982 Census of Manufacturers, Concentration Ratios in Manufacturing.* MC 82–S–7 (Washington, DC, 1986).

like predatory pricing, and (3) product differentiation. It is these kinds of causes that antitrust policy might counter. Indeed, these possibilities explain a crucial assumption underlying any antitrust policy aimed at maintaining competitively structured markets, namely, the assumption that for most markets a monopolistically high level of concentration is not technically inevitable, not economically justifiable, and not indelible.

This distinction between concentration that is natural and artificial, warranted and unwarranted, is very important. Many critics of antitrust defend large aggregations of power by contending that *all* concentration derives from efficiency or some related blessing.[4] Whether or not this is true, however, depends on the empirical evidence. And the best evidence available discloses that, indeed, *some* instances of high concentration *are* warranted by economies of scale, *but only some.* Efficiency in automobile production, for example, apparently requires that a firm's output reach at least 1 million cars per year or thereabouts.[5] This amounts to roughly 10 percent of annual U. S. auto sales, implying that the industry would have room for no more than about ten efficient oligopolistic firms. Other highly concentrated industries evincing substantial economies of scale relative to total sales are turbogenerators and refrigerators. The question has been studied intensely for many more industries than these, however, and the appropriate generalization to draw is that these are not typical of industry as a whole. To quote the conclusion of a leading study in this regard: "National market seller concentration appears in most industries to be much higher than it needs to be for leading firms to take advantage of all but slight residual multiplant scale economies."[6]

A similar conclusion holds for other natural factors that may warrant high concentration, like scarce inputs and industry life cycles. Scarce inputs favor fewness only in rare instances, such as molybdenum mining (with its unique ore deposits). Life-cycle effects, which are more frequent, may occur in industries that follow a history of distinct phases—that is, birth, growth, maturity, and decline. At birth, an entire industry may well be made up of a sole innovator, one protected from rivals by secret knowhow or key patents (which grant monopoly rights for seventeen years). Xerox was such an innovator. With growth and maturity, imitators may then invade the new field, reducing concentration with their competition. Finally, in the event obsolescence and decline set in with old age, high concentration may return as survivors dwindle. The accuracy of this scenario varies from industry to industry, however. Many industries, like autos, defy the pattern with competitive births and oligopolistic adolescences.[7] All in all, then, *some* instances of especially lofty concentration are warranted on these natural grounds, but like economies of scale they too fall short of giving a generalized accounting.

2. BARRIERS TO ENTRY

Any factor that inhibits new entry into an unusually profitable market may be called a *barrier to entry.* Like high concentration, high barriers to entry may be either natural or artificial, bestowing power on established firms in either case.

As with concentration, economies of scale may pose a *natural barrier.* Figure 5–1 illustrates this possibility. Long-run cost per unit, *LRUC,* falls with ever greater scales of operation up to an output level *MES,* which indicates minimum efficient scale. Assume that this long-run unit cost curve confronts established firms and would-be entrants alike. Assume further that *DD'* is industry demand. Then if two existing firms share industry demand equally, each firm would view its demand as d_2, which is half of *DD'* at each possible price. Since d_2 lies above *LRUC* over a considerable range, each of the two firms could produce and sell at a profit. However, a potential entrant would not have such a favorable situation. If it is assumed that demand would be split evenly three ways in the event of a third firm's

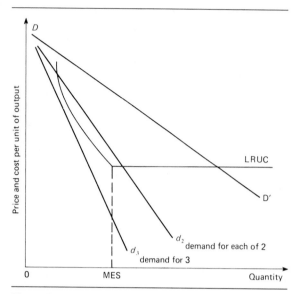

Figure 5–1
Economies of Scale Acting as a Barrier to the Entry
of a Third Firm

entry (a very optimistic assumption for a new entrant to make), each firm's demand would then
become d_3, which is one-third of DD' at each
possible price. But given d_3, there is *no* plant
scale that yields a profit to the entrant. There is
no point at which *LRUC* falls below d_3. The result: no third firm entry because existing firms
will have already built efficient plants, and the
added output of an entrant's efficient plant would
be so large relative to industry demand that, after
entry, product price would fall below the entrant's cost per unit.

If the capital costs of building a minimum efficient scale of operations are substantial, $2 bil-
lion, say, those costs could likewise pose a
natural barrier to all but the wealthiest potential
entrants. Another possibility is that the unit-cost
curve of potential entrants lies above the unit-
cost curve of established firms at all possible levels of output, thereby likewise impeding entry.

Many of the most potent *artificial,* or *man-
made, barriers* are erected by government policy.

Patents, for instance, grant exclusive rights lasting seventeen years, rights that may or may not
be important, depending on the significance of
the inventions concerned. Although they are artificial barriers, patents are beneficial to the extent they stimulate technological progress. They
therefore may be warranted barriers. Unfortunately, patents may also be used to build unwarranted barriers. Exclusive cross-licensing,
aggressive acquisition, blocking out, and fraudulent attainment are a few of the anticompetitive
manipulations associated with patents. Occupational licensing is another official barrier that
may be abused. More directly within the reach of
businessmen, vertical integration may pose a
barrier.

This does not exhaust the list of artificial barriers. But most of those remaining are discussed
as matters of conduct rather than of structure.

3. PRODUCT DIFFERENTIATION

Product differentiation is a source of market
power when it gives sellers power over price.
That power may stem from many genuine, objective nonprice elements—such as flavor, durability, and convenience of location in retailing. A
Mercedes-Benz is thus really worth more than a
Hyundai. On the other hand, that power may be
grounded on spurious, subjective influences—
such as exhortative advertising or frivolous designer labels. Thus, all brands of liquid chlorine
bleach are essentially identical (5.25 percent sodium hypochlorite plus 94.75 percent water), as
are all brands of aspirin (5 grains of $C_9H_8O_4$), yet
the heavily advertised brands of these products
sell at premium prices and account for more sales
volume than unadvertised, private-label brands.

ReaLemon brand reconstituted lemon juice,
for example, captured 90 percent of its market
during the 1950s and 1960s by virtue of strong
brand allegiance. A measure of that trademark's
power was disclosed in 1962 when Borden paid
$12.4 million to acquire ReaLemon, an amount
four times greater than the book value of the
company's assets at the time.[8]

4. DIVERSIFICATION

Most of the largest corporations span many markets: (1) diversifying backward or forward into different stages of their production process to become *vertically integrated*, (2), diversifying into widely differing fields—such as meat packing, aerospace, and steel—to become *conglomerates*, and (3) spreading operations and subsidiaries hither and yon internationally to become *multinationals*.

Take the prominent corporations listed in Table 5–3, for instance. Each is associated in the popular mind with some relatively narrow activity, such as photographic equipment (Kodak), oil (Mobil), or computers (IBM). Yet, in fact, each engages in a vast array of enterprises scattered over the globe. Typical of the big oil companies is Exxon, with vertically integrated operations in petroleum mining, transportation, refining, and marketing; with 73 percent of its total revenues coming from foreign sources; and with conglomerated activities in uranium and chemicals. Then there is General Motors, with numerous auto parts subsidiaries; with large plants in Europe and Latin America; plus substantial activities in locomotives, trucks, buses, consumer finance, aerospace, and other fields. Philip Morris controls Miller Brewing and General Foods. More than half of IBM's revenues originate overseas. And so on.

Table 5–3
Some of America's Largest Industrial Firms, 1990

Rank	Company	Main Line of Business	Sales (Billions)
1	General Motors	Motor vehicles	$126,017
2	Exxon	Oil and gasoline	105,885
3	Ford Motor	Motor vehicles	98,274
4	IBM	Computers	69,018
5	Mobil	Oil and gasoline	58,770
6	General Electric	Electronics and TV	58,414
7	Philip Morris	Tobacco, beer, food	44,323
8	Texaco	Oil and gasoline	41,235
9	DuPont	Chemicals	39,839
10	Chevron	Oil and gasoline	39,262
11	Chrysler	Motor vehicles	30,868
13	Boeing	Aircraft	27,595
14	Procter & Gamble	Detergents, groceries	24,376
20	Eastman Kodak	Photo supplies, film	19,075
22	Xerox	Copiers	18,382
23	Pepsico	Food and beverages	17,803
28	RJR Nabisco	Tobacco, groceries	13,879
32	International Paper	Paper	12,960

Source: Fortune, April 22, 1991, p. 286.

The powers conferred by diversification are difficult to measure and subject to dispute. But one thing is certain: Diversification boosts absolute firm size and this size in turn contributes to *aggregate concentration,* which is the total economic activity, very broadly defined, accounted for by the leading firms. It is estimated, for instance, that in 1985 the 200 largest manufacturing corporations accounted for over 60 percent of all manufacturing assets, up from 47 percent in 1950. The asset holdings of the largest 200 corporations in other broad fields in 1974 were as follows: finance, insurance, and real estate, 47.8 percent; services, 33.5 percent; wholesale and re-

tail trade, 30.9 percent; and transportation, communication, and public utilities, 86.8 percent.[9]

Figure 5–2 gives a historical profile of aggregate concentration, one primarily concerned with manufacturing. Different measures of size, different definitions of scope, and different notions of how many firms constitute a "few" obviously affect the picture. But, generally speaking, aggregate concentration has risen.[10]

5.   **OTHER STRUCTURAL FEATURES**
Instances where one or more of the foregoing variables reaches lofty heights may portend ominous results for competition. But the ultimate

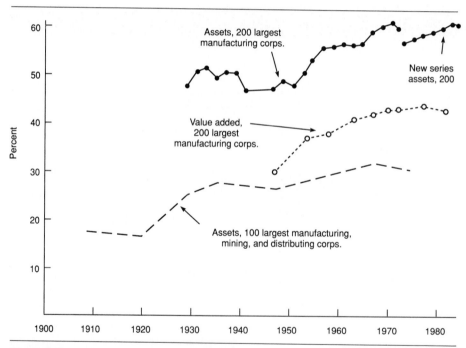

Figure 5–2
Long-Term Trends in Aggregate Concentration

Sources: Federal Trade Commission Staff, *Economic Report on Corporate Mergers* (1969), p. 173; Lawrence J. White, "What has been Happening to Aggregate Concentration in the United States?" *Journal of Industrial Economics,* (March 1981), p. 225; Bureau of the Census, 1982 *Census of Manufacturers: Concentration Ratios in Manufacturing,* MC82-5-7 (Washington D.C., 1986), p. 3; Robert J. Stonebraker, "Turnover and Mobility among the 100 Largest Firms: An Update," *American Economic Review* (December 1979), pp. 968–973; *1986 Statistical Abstract,* p. 534.

consequences for competitive conduct and performance often depend heavily on other, more subtle structural conditions. An industry having, say, only three large firms may nevertheless be quite competitive (or rivalrous) if sales go in very large and infrequently negotiated lots, if technological change moves briskly, and if price elasticity of demand is quite high. Lumpy sales and high price elasticity raise the pay offs gained from price cutting. Rapid technological change adds turmoil to any market by upsetting collusive understandings, by aggravating uncertainty, and by stimulating competition in innovation and invention. Accordingly, an important qualification is in order. High concentration (or high entry barriers and so forth) may or may not pose a problem worthy of antitrust attention, depending on the circumstances.

B. Conduct

Anticompetitive conduct falls into two broad classes: (1) *collusive actions,* wherein rivals act jointly to achieve monopolistic aims, and (2) *individual exclusionary policies* that bolster a firm's power vis-à-vis existing or potential rivals. The first is generally inclusive; the second, exclusive.

1. COLLUSIVE ACTIONS

Collusion may be *implicit,* in which case rivals act uniformly through tacit "understanding" and "conscious parallelism," usually aided by price leadership. It may also be *explicit,* in which case rivals enter into an express cartel agreement to fix prices, to allocate sales territories, or to curb competition in some other way. Implicit collusion is possible only when structural conditions are especially accommodating, that is, when concentration is quite high, entry is at least partially impeded, sales are not particularly lumpy, and the like. Explicit collusion has a much broader range. It may serve as a substitute for implicit collusion when structural conditions are tightly oligopolistic but not quite right for tacit agreement. On the other hand, explicit cartelization

may also arise under structural conditions that would ordinarily produce quite vigorous competition. Most commonly, though, cartel conduct appears to occur somewhere between these two extremes in moderately to tightly knit oligopolistic markets. For example, a sample of thirty-five explicit price-fixing agreements came from markets with an average four-firm concentration ratio of 77 percent, which is well above the average for all manufacturing but nowhere near 100 percent.[11] In a different sample of 606 cases of price fixing, the median number of firms actively involved was eight, which gives a rough idea of the median number of firms in cartelized markets. By contrast, the median number of firms in manufacturing markets generally is about eighteen.[12]

When it is effective, implicit and explicit collusion leads to higher prices. Certainly the most dramatic demonstration of this result is provided by the Organization of Petroleum Exporting Countries (OPEC), which is a cartel comprised of thirteen of the world's leading oil producers. Beginning with a quadrupling of price in late 1973 and continuing with subsequent price hikes ranging from 5 to 60 percent, OPEC had a colossal impact on the world economy during the 1970s and early 1980s. More generally, several dozen statistical studies have shown that market concentration and price level are positively associated. A study of grocery retailing, for instance, indicated that the price of a "standard" grocery basket of goods was 5.3 percent higher when local four-firm concentration was 70 as compared to 40.[13] Other products and services yielding similar evidence include gasoline retailing, life insurance, air travel, business loans, newspaper advertising space, cement, and drug retailing.[14]

2. EXCLUSIONARY PRACTICES

Exclusionary practices may be collusively contrived, as is true of collective boycotts and exclusive cross-licensing of patents. More commonly, though, individual firms wield exclusionary weapons. *Predatory pricing* is one such weapon. A relatively large, "deep-pocketed" firm aggressively cuts prices below cost for purposes of imposing losses on smaller existing rivals, or threatening financial injury to potential rivals, thereby driving them from the market or softening them up for eventual merger. After so garnering market power, the predator can raise prices in hope of recovering battle losses. Two of the most notorious monopolies built in the days of the robber barons—Standard Oil of New Jersey and American Tobacco—were found guilty of such predatory behavior.[15]

Price discrimination occurs when the seller sets different prices relative to costs to different buyers. Such discrimination can be anticompetitive when used systematically by a powerful firm. But it can also be procompetitive, as when a small firm shades prices, catch as catch can, to stimulate sales during a slump.

Under *tying arrangements,* a seller gives buyers access to one line of the seller's goods only if the buyer purchases others as well. A tying arrangement exists, for instance, when a manufacturer of canning machines requires that his canning-machine customers also buy their cans from him. If the seller has monopoly power over the tying good, machines in this example, he might with this method extract greater monopoly profits than otherwise, and he may lessen competition in the market for the tied good.[16]

A practice related to tying is *exclusive dealing,* which occurs when a seller prohibits his buyers from buying goods from the seller's rivals. For instance, an auto manufacturer might require that its franchised dealers carry only its line of products, shunning rivals' offerings. When used by a relatively small or fledgling manufacturer, exclusive dealing can be procompetitive to the extent it fires the interests and efforts of the manufacturer's retailers or protects the manufacturer's good will. In the hands of a dominant manufacturer with strong brand image, however, the practice can heighten entry barriers.[17]

C. Performance

1. PROFIT

As suggested earlier, structure and conduct may affect many aspects of performance—for example, profit level, technical efficiency, and technological progress. Of these, none has been more thoroughly studied than *profit level,* which when excessively high tends to reflect poor performance in allocation efficiency (because, as shown earlier in Figure 2–4, price is then above marginal cost) and poor performance in income equity (to the extent relatively rich owners collect the excess profits at the expense of relatively poor consumers). More than 100 statistical studies have tested the relationship between profit level and various measures of market power, and most have found a positive relationship, suggesting that monopolistic and oligopolistic structures generally do have adverse consequences for performance in this respect.[18]

Figures 5–3(a) and 5–3(b) illustrate these results for *concentration.* Such positive associations as these have been found for several different measures of profit, for many different measures of concentration, and for substantially different periods. Moreover, the positive relationship holds for broad interindustry samples (including all manufacturing industries), narrow interindustry samples (limited to producer goods, for instance), and in*tra*industry samples across diverse geographic markets (such as those in banking and grocery retailing). The positive relationship also emerges from data gathered from every corner of the world.

It is now fairly well established that the *market share* of a firm also has a positive impact on profit, and substantially so. By one estimate, pretax return on investment rises about 5 percentage points for every 10 percentage-point increase in market share.[19] Many factors contribute to this relationship—among them, the market power and/or efficiency associated with greater market share.[20]

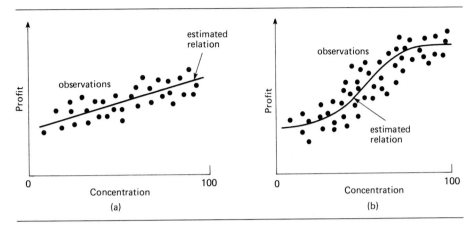

Figure 5–3
Positive Relationships Between Profit and Concentration

Interindustry variances in *entry barriers* have been estimated by variances in economies of scale, capital requirements, advertising intensity, and the risk faced by small firms occupying market fringes.[21] When tested, these measures tend to reveal a positive association between the height of entry barriers and profit. Table 5–4 gives numerical values for advertising (which doubles as a measure of product differentiation) from a study of food manufacturing firms, a study that also found an effect from concentration similar to that depicted in Figure 5–3(b). For any given level of concentration, profit is 4.4 percentage points higher when advertising as a percentage of sales is 5 percent as compared to 1 percent (e.g., 10.7 − 6.3 = 4.4 from the top line). Such a strong positive effect is limited to products for which advertising is particularly potent in image building, namely, relatively low-priced convenience goods with hidden qualities—for example, prepared foods, soda pop, detergent, beer, cigarettes, and drugs. For other products (and services) advertising can be procompetitive.[22]

2. PRODUCTION EFFICIENCY
On the face of it, one might expect to find a positive association between production efficiency

(i.e., productivity) and market power because market power is often grounded on genuine economies of scale. To some extent this is probably true. But there are also reasons to expect that a lack of competition leads to lassitude, inertia, delay, and other adverse effects on productivity that have come to be called *X-inefficiency*.[23] Several examples of competitive impact come from cartel case studies. A study of price fixing in the

Table 5–4
Profit Rates of Food Manufacturing Firms Associated with Levels of Industry Concentration and Advertising to Sales Ratios

Four-Firm Concentration	*Advertising to Sales Ratio (percentages)*				
	1.0	*2.0*	*3.0*	*4.0*	*5.0*
40	6.3	7.4	8.5	9.6	10.7
50	9.3	10.4	11.5	12.6	13.7
60	11.0	12.1	13.2	14.3	15.4
70	11.5	12.6	13.7	14.8	15.9

Source: William H. Kelly, *On the Influence of Market Structure on the Profit Performance of Food Manufacturing Companies* (Federal Trade Commission, 1969), p. 7.

gymnasium seating, rock salt, and structural steel industries found cost increases of 10 to 23 percent due to competition's strangulation.[24] After a massive study of cartel records, Corwin Edwards concluded that available evidence "indicates that the characteristic purposes of cartels point away from efficiency and that their activities tend to diminish efficiency."[25]

Intermarket statistical assessments of X-inefficiency are difficult to devise, but the few so far completed indicate that X-inefficiency is positively associated with market power. One of the most interesting of these compared costs of electricity production in two separate sets of cities—those with electric utility *monopolies* and those with direct competition between *two firms* (of which there were 49 cities). The study found "that average cost is reduced, at the mean, by 10.75 percent because of competition. This reflects a quantitative value of the presence of X-efficiency gained through competition."[26]

3.   PROGRESSIVENESS
Technological progress entails three steps—invention, innovation, and diffusion. Invention is the first realization and crude proof that something will work. Innovation is the first commercial application of the invention. And diffusion is the spread of its adoption. Performance at each step has been measured various ways, permitting tests of the influence of *firm size* generally and *market concentration* in particular. In both respects there appear to be *some* benefits to bigness, but those benefits are usually exhausted well before reaching the aggregate sizes of the top 100 or market concentration ratios in the 70s.[27]

For example, the most recent large-scale study of these issues was conducted by Zoltan Acs and David Audretsch using 1982 data on 4,476 innovations in 247 industries.[28] Regarding *firm size,* they found that small firms (defined as those with fewer than 500 employees) were remarkably more innovative than large firms were

(those with more than 500 employees). In particular, the average innovation rate for small firms was about 43 percent higher than that for large firms. Regarding concentration, they found higher concentration to be *negatively* associated with innovation activity to a significant degree. Because small firms are especially innovative in these data, it is interesting that Acs and Audretsch also found a negative association between high market concentration and two measures of small-firm innovative activity—(1) the number of small-firm innovations per industry and (2) the share of total industry innovations accounted for by small firms. Overall, Acs and Audretsch conclude that their results are "unequivocal"—"industry innovation tends to decrease as the level of concentration rises."[29]

Summary

The path leading to antitrust policy is thus lit by a vast array of candles from economic theory and evidence. Some parts of the path are better illuminated than others, but the general direction is clear. According to the foregoing evidence, it may be presumed that antitrust policy is both *desirable* and *necessary*. First, it is *desirable* because competition is usually desirable. Competitive structure, conduct, and performance typically serve the public interest by gratifying many, if not most, of the value judgments specified in Chapter 1. Moreover, antitrust policy is not hopelessly at odds with economies of scale or with technological progress. Second, antitrust policy is *necessary* because the desired degree of competition is not self-sustaining, not automatically occurring. In its absence, mergers among competitors would be much more common, cartels would flourish, and the use of various exclusionary practices would proliferate simply because businesses tend to profit by them.[30]

Notice that desirability and necessity are the *key* presumptions underlying antitrust policy.

Critics of antitrust law typically attack one or both. The most vocal critics are conservatives who argue that antitrust policy should be largely abolished. When questioning its *desirability,* they argue that bigness is best for achieving efficiency or technological progress. On efficiency, for instance, Yale Brozen speaks bluntly:

> . . . concentration benefits the nation by increasing the accumulated experience and learning in large firms where these factors can increase productivity.[31]

Those questioning the *necessity* of antitrust policy see intense competition occurring naturally everywhere without any governmental umpiring. They see this in dynamic innovation, in easy entry, and in other ways. According to Harold Demsetz, for example:

> There is ample evidence that competition *is* robust. There is a constant search for new ways to acquire the business of customers. When a new product is developed, imitators are rarely far behind.[32]

Even cartels are no problem because competition spontaneously crushes them. To quote Robert Bork:

> They are fragile. Changing market conditions and the temptation to "cheat" to pick up profitable business frequently break down almost all cartels.[33]

Some critics go so far as to say that *anything* businesses might do is beneficial to society. Monopolies merely signal that customers occasionally "prefer" monopoly. A cartel agreement is "explicit evidence of an attempt [by businesses] to increase efficiency."[34]

Still, these seem to be minority views. A recent survey of economists found only 15 percent who "generally disagreed" with the statement that "Antitrust laws should be used vigorously to reduce monopoly power from its current level."[35]

II. The Aims of Antitrust Policy

Antitrust policy may serve a variety of ends, enough of a variety to spark controversy over what ends should be chosen.[36] For our purposes, four possible aims may be considered—(1) the maintenance of competition as an end in itself, (2) the prohibition of unfair business conduct, (3) the achievement of desirable economic performance, efficiency in particular, and (4) the containment of absolute business size.[37]

(1) The Maintenance of Competition. As Carl Kaysen and Donald Turner remark, "Competition as an end in itself draws its justification from the desirability of limiting business power."[38] This is largely a structural goal, whose earmarks would include such features as fairly free entry, an ample number of alternative sellers and buyers in markets, and no more than moderate concentration. Conduct could also be covered, with hard prohibitions against cartelization. It is important to note that these are standards for *workable competition,* not pure competition. The requirements for pure competition are so extremely unrealistic, given the natural deviations mentioned previously, as to be poor guides to policy. Thus, workable competition is a less precise but more realistic derivative.

Although business power is thus most typically reckoned in economic features, it may also carry political and social implications because political and social power are often grounded on economic power. Senator Kefauver gave expression to this view many years ago when in defense of his antimerger act he argued: "Through monopolistic mergers the people are losing power to direct their own economic welfare. When they lose the power to direct their economic welfare they also lose the means to direct their political future."[39]

(2) Fair Conduct. The foregoing relates primarily to the *mere possession* of market power, not to its *exercise.* In contrast, aims of fair conduct relate more to the way business power is used rather than its mere presence. Should sellers be allowed to engage in tying and exclusive dealing? Should large buyers get their supplies more cheaply than small buyers merely because of bargaining power? Also, what about group boycotts and aggregated rebates? Antitrust policy could attempt to lay down certain standards of fair business conduct that would curtail these kinds of practices without necessarily attacking the economic power that makes them onerous.

(3) Desirable Economic Performance. Because market structure and conduct affect economic performance, antitrust policy could be concerned with structure and conduct *only* insofar as they clearly produce poor performance, while overlooking any concentrations of power or unfair practices that had no discernible effect on performance or promised potential improvements therein. Advocates of this aim typically ignore performance as it relates to progressiveness, macro stability, or income equity. Rather, they advocate static efficiency as the sole aim for antitrust policy.[40]

(4) Limiting Big Business. Given the substantial contributions that product and geographic diversification can make to business size, antitrust policy could serve a goal of limiting absolute firm size (apart from any aim of limiting power in particular markets). For political and social reasons many Americans, Thomas Jefferson among them, have seen danger in gargantuan aggregations of power. An outsized conglomerate may, for instance, "gain favors regarding taxes, import competition, government contracts, and other amenities which will give it an advantage over its rivals."[41] Conversely, small independent businesses may be encouraged and protected under this aim if we consider them to be exemplars of good citizenship.

These four objectives being the main possibilities, what are the actualities? Which of these aims is the target of U. S. antitrust policy as revealed in the pronouncements and actions of our legislatures, enforcement agencies, and courts? There is no clearcut answer. All four have played a part, depending on time, circumstance, and source. But, at least until recently, the first two, maintenance of competition and fair conduct, seem to have dominated. To cite some authorities:

- "If there has been any persistent policy and approach, it has been that of protecting competitive opportunities and competitive processes by preventing unfair, unreasonable, or coercive conduct. . . ."[42]
- "The rationale of antitrust is essentially a desire to provide legal checks to restrain economic power and is not a pursuit of efficiency as such."[43]
- "[The Antitrust Division of the U. S. Justice Department has a] core mission—to preserve competitive markets. . . ."[44]

These aims remain alive in the latest congressional debates and court opinions, but the aim of economic efficiency has recently been gaining a larger share of attention. Hence, a mix of aims presently prevails, a mix that draws from structure, conduct, and performance.

Some commentators have argued that to the contrary, the *sole* aim of antitrust law was originally and now should be static efficiency.[45] This position has been challenged on several grounds, however. First, the historical record does not support the notion that static efficiency riled the original legislators. Indeed, the Sherman Act was passed well before economists had developed the meaning of efficiency as we know it. Efficiencies from scale economies were appreciated at the time, but antitrust law cannot provide those efficiencies.[46] Second, and aside from original intent, one may question whether static efficiency *should* be the sole aim of antitrust policy. Skeptics question the practicality, clarity, accuracy, and general wisdom of such an approach.[47]

You may wonder whether this dispute poses any hopeless dilemmas. As we have seen, empirical evidence demonstrates that success at maintaining competition will likely bear fruits of efficiency, not to mention such other fruits of good performance as spirited progressiveness and equitable income distribution. Yet there is some substance to the debate because those advocating the efficiency approach question the evidence linking competition with good results. They favor giving greater latitude to big business. And the rising frequency of court judgments partially adopting the efficiency approach has led to decisions with distinctive earmarks.

III. Outline of the Antitrust Laws

A. Statutes

The objective of maintaining free and fair competition may be found in the language of the antitrust statutes themselves. Very briefly, the laws have five main divisions as follows:

1. *Collusion.* Under Section 1 of the Sherman Act, it is illegal to enter into a contract, combination, or conspiracy in restraint of trade. This forbids cartelization to fix prices or allocate territories and bans collective boycotts.
2. *Monopolization.* Under Section 2 of the Sherman Act, it is illegal to monopolize, to attempt to monopolize, or to combine or conspire to monopolize trade. (Despite the word *monopolize,* market shares of less than 100 percent may be in violation.)
3. *Exclusionary Practices.* The Clayton Act, in Section 2 (as amended by the Robinson-Patman Act) and Section 3, prohibits price discrimination, exclusive dealing, tying, and related practices when the effect may substantially lessen competition.
4. *Mergers.* Section 7 of the Clayton Act (as amended by the Celler-Kefauver Act) bans mergers that may substantially lessen competition.

5. *Unfair or deceptive practices.* The Federal Trade Commission Act makes it illegal to use unfair or deceptive practices (regardless of their impact or competition).

Because anticompetitive effects need not be shown to establish the illegality of deceptive practices, our discussion of those practices is postponed until Part III. As for the rest, it should be noted that the statutes make no special references to performance considerations. Cartel participants cannot defend themselves by claiming that their conspiracy fosters static efficiency. Anticompetitive mergers are not excused by the statutes if they yield production efficiencies.

B. Remedies

Violations of the Sherman Act may be greeted by either criminal or civil proceedings. If **criminal,** the proceedings may establish guilt by jury trial, wherein the violation must be shown by proof beyond a reasonable doubt, or by the defendant's plea of guilty. The remedies in such cases may be *fines* or *imprisonment* or both. Criminal proceedings may be settled without trial, however, in which case the out-of-court settlement is called a *nolo contendere* plea (I do not wish to contend). Although technically speaking nolo contendere pleas are not admissions of guilt, they too can result in rather severe penalties. Given the severity of the consequences of criminal proceedings and given the stiff standards of proof they require, such proceedings are usually confined to violations of Section 1 of the Sherman Act. Section 2 typically prompts civil actions, as is always true of the other statutes.

Civil proceedings may be awakened by any of the offenses mentioned. They may likewise result in trials, but the vast majority of civil proceedings are terminated by *consent decrees*— that is, negotiated settlements subject to court approval. The remedies accompanying civil offenses are supposed to be corrective, not punitive, as in criminal proceedings. Civil remedies are therefore less dramatic than fines and imprisonment, but they are often no less serious to guilty parties. These remedies include injunction, divestiture, and treble damages. An *injunction,* or cease-and-desist order, typically prohibits an antitrust violator from some specified future conduct. For instance, mergers may be banned for ten years or tying may be proscribed indefinitely. If *divestiture* is ordered, the defendant must sell off a part of its business, or dissolve into a number of separate independent entities. Such structural surgery is, for obvious reasons, limited to violations of the monopolization and merger statutes. Last, *treble damages* may be extracted from violators by *private* parties who feel injured by the violators' antitrust offenses, provided those private parties can successfully sue for such damages. These treble damage actions are almost wholly confined to transgressions involving cartelization and exclusionary practices. Private plaintiffs have the dual burden of proving *both* violations and damages. If a violation has been previously proven by trial verdict or guilty plea in a government case, the first half of a private plaintiff's burden is generally satisfied. That is, *prima facie* proof of wrongdoing has been established. But if the government settles its case with a consent decree or nolo contendere, the private plaintiff's burden remains whole and heavy. Thus, for purposes of evading private treble damage suits, defendants in government suits often like to settle those suits without trial. Private plaintiffs may still file suit in any event, and they may sue even when there is no official action at all.

IV. Enforcement

A. Introduction

Federal government enforcement is shared by the Antitrust Division of the Department of Justice and the Federal Trade Commission. (A large number of states also have their own antitrust laws, which are enforced by state attorneys general.) Private enforcement, instigated by offended enterprises or consumers, is generally conducted by private lawyers in the "antitrust bar," now numbering 10,000 or so in membership. These lawyers also spend a great deal of their valuable time and talent (often billed at well over $200 per hour) *defending* those on the receiving end of government and private actions.

Table 5–5 gives some rough, historical idea of the extent and focus of official enforcement activity by reporting the number of antitrust cases and number of specific allegations in those cases from the origins of the Antitrust Division and the FTC up through 1982. The operations of the two agencies overlap substantially. The main reason for this overlap is that the Antitrust Division and the FTC have concurrent jurisdiction to enforce the Clayton Act and its amendments. The Sherman Act is, technically speaking, the sole province of the Antitrust Division, whereas the Federal Trade Commission Act is enforceable only by the FTC. Overlap occurs in these areas also, however, because the FTC can reach violations of the Sherman Act through actions brought under the broad language of the FTC Act. That is, the "unfair methods of competition" condemned by the FTC Act have been interpreted by the courts to include those things running afoul of the Sherman Act. The result is that, in practice, overlap prevails except in two main respects. For one, only the Antitrust Division can press criminal charges. For another, only the FTC enforces the FTC Act and the Robinson-Patman amendment to the Clayton Act. Faced with concurrent jurisdiction in other antitrust areas, the Department of Justice and the FTC exchange notifications and clearances to assure that they do not duplicate their efforts on specific cases. This exchange seems to have worked well.

There are no such clearances between private plaintiffs and the official agencies, but pri-

Table 5–5
Number of Antitrust Violations Alleged up to 1982, Antitrust Division of Department of Justice and Federal Trade Commission

Violation Charged	Antitrust Division (1890–1982)	Federal Trade Commission (1915–1982)
Horizontal Price Fixing	1,411	317
Boycott	262	125
Monopolization	423	74
Merger	323	279
Resale Price Maintenance	42	256
Tying	96	99
Exclusive Dealing	156	170
Price Discrimination[a]	129	159
Labor	127	13
Patents	176	10
Other	451	326
Total Cases[b]	2,219[b]	1,320[b]

[a]Excludes Robinson-Patman cases except those charging predatory price discrimination.

[b]Total cases are less than total allegations because of multiple allegations per case.

Source: Richard A. Posner, "A Statistical Study of Antitrust Enforcement," *Journal of Law & Economics* (October 1970), pp. 398, 408; Joseph C. Gallo and Steven C. Bush, "A Statistical Study of Federal Antitrust Enforcement for the Period 1963–1982," (mimeo 1983).

vate actions by nature tend to march to the beat of different drummers. When it comes to proving violations, aggrieved private parties readily allow and even encourage the government to bear the expense. Private plaintiffs can then concentrate their resources on treble damage suits, riding the wakes of government victories. When the government does not act, private parties are entirely on their own. Budget boundaries and bureaucratic judgments keep the government from bearing the expense in many instances, leaving ample room for private action. Over the past thirty years, private suits have outnumbered government suits substantially. The 1950s witnessed about 300 private suits per year. The pace then quickened to reach over 1,000 such suits per year during the late 1970s and the early 1980s. It then fell to 600 cases per year thereafter.[43]

Public and private divergence extends to subject matter, too. The vast majority of these private cases are not concerned with structural matters such as monopolization and merger but rather with conduct abuses such as price discrimination and exclusive dealing.

Subsequent chapters reveal that relatively few of the thousands of cases ever brought, public or private, are real blockbusters. Relatively few set legal precedents. Relatively few send businessmen to jail. Relatively few result in the wholesale restructuring of industries.

B. The Antitrust Division of the Department of Justice

Where do the Antitrust Division's cases begin? Usually with staff lawyers, somewhere in the lower portion of the organization structure given in Figure 5–4. The lawyers supervising the division are political appointees rather than career bureaucrats, and although they have final approval on which cases will be brought, they rarely initiate cases.

An investigation usually springs from the complaints of citizens, of businessmen, of other government agencies, or from reports in the business press. From there, the investigation may progress to rather formal stages, including the use of a grand jury in criminal proceedings. Most investigations never go beyond preliminary probings, but for those that do, a draft complaint is drawn up, a supporting report is written, and nu-

---

Thumbnail Sketch 1: Antitrust Division, U.S. Department of Justice

---

Established: 1903

Purpose: To administer and enforce antitrust and related laws.

Legislative Authority: Sherman Act of 1890; Clayton Act of 1914; Celler-Kefauver Act of 1950; Hart-Scott-Rodino Antitrust Improvement Act of 1976; various statutory provisions that require government regulatory agencies to consider preservation of competition.

Regulatory Activity: Investigates possible violations, conducts grand jury proceedings for criminal cases, prepares and argues cases in federal courts, pursues appeals, and negotiates and enforces final judgments.

Organization: The agency is a part of the Department of Justice and is headed by an Assistant Attorney General. Major subdivisions include General Litigation Section, Regulated Industries Section, and Economic Analysis Division.

Budget: 1991 appropriation, $54 million.

Staff: 1991 positions, 623.

---

merous consultations are held among division personnel. Upon approval of the Assistant Attorney General for Antitrust, the case is then filed in one of our ninety federal district courts for trial or settlement sanction. From there on, the federal courts become the instrument through which the Department of Justice must work. The decision of the district court may be appealed by either plaintiff or defendant to the appropriate circuit court of appeals (there are eleven of them). Eventually, the case may be appealed to a third and final level, the Supreme Court, which may or may not grant a hearing, depending on whether at least four of the nine members of that august body want to review the case. (Acceptance is called granting *certiorari*.)

The ultimate test of a division lawyer's work-product is how well it stands up in court. In this context, a star government lawyer prosecutes adroitly:

> He conceives of his practice of law as an active and combative occupation rather than as a calling that at times resembles academic scholarship in the thoroughness of its research and its concern with clarity and distinctions. And antitrust law attracts him not because of its close connection with economic theory but because its cases are exciting cases, with important consequences and with powerful men for opponents.[49]

To some extent, this picture of legal professionalism is tainted by occasional accusations of impropriety, or worse, corruption at high levels. Whether there is a large or small number of such accusations is a judgment call. According to one authority on the division's operations, Suzanne Weaver, the number is so small as to cause her to wonder why the division has been corrupted so little. "Part of the answer," she says, "seems to be found in the nature of antitrust work: division personnel rarely work alone on a matter of any size, and they must frequently provide extensive written justification of their actions. Part probably comes from the fact of competition: for every businessman who is enraged by having to

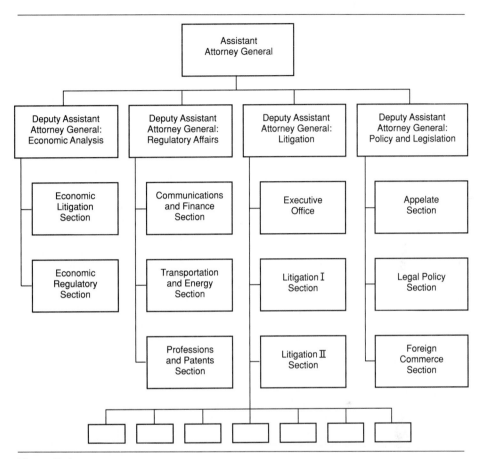

Figure 5–4
Antitrust Division Organization Chart

defend himself against an antitrust prosecution, there is another who is absolutely delighted to see him suffering."[50]

Although good market performance is not the express aim of antitrust policy, such performance is by no means irrelevant. We therefore should heed Leonard Weiss's benefit-cost analysis of the Antitrust Division's work. Drawing on empirical evidence of the extent to which prices are elevated by various anticompetitive practices, and making certain assumptions about the probabilities of successfully prosecuting cases against those practices, Weiss estimated the eq-

uity and efficiency gains bestowed on consumers from the division's enforcement efforts during 1968–1970. Table 5–6 presents the monetary values of these estimates. The equity or distribution gains substantially outshine the allocation efficiency gains in each instance by the very nature of the arithmetic. As pictured earlier in Figure 3–2 (on page 46), the income distribution gains represent the value of consumer price reductions, area P_1ACP_2, whereas the value of improved allocation efficiency is limited to the area ABC. Notice also that these benefits in Table 5–6 are expressed in terms of thousands of dollars per

Table 5–6
Estimated Benefits Per Lawyer Year of Antitrust Division, 1969

Type of Case	Distribution Gain Per Lawyer-Year ($ thousands)	Allocation Efficiency Gain Per Lawyer-Year ($ thousands)
Criminal Collusion	900	46
Civil Collusion	46,700	1,398
Monopolization	13,700	958
Horizontal Merger	17,700	355
Exclusionary Practices	2,800	14
Regulation-Practices[a]	52,800	2,640

[a]Cases in which the division argues for competition before regulatory agencies.

Source: Leonard W. Weiss, "An Analysis of the Allocation of Antitrust Division Resources," in J. A. Dalton and S. Levin (eds.), *The Antitrust Dilemma* (Lexington, MA: Lexington Books, 1974), pp. 50, 53.

Thumbnail Sketch 2: Federal Trade Commission

Established: 1914

Purpose: To maintain vigorous, free, fair and nondeceptive competition in the market place.

Legislative Authority: Federal Trade Commission Act of 1914; Clayton Act of 1914; Export Trade Act of 1918; Robinson-Patman Act of 1936; Product Labeling Acts of 1940, 1951, 1958, and 1966; Truth-in-Lending Act of 1969; Fair Credit Acts of 1970 and 1974; Magnuson-Moss Warranty—FTC Improvement Act of 1975.

Regulatory Activity: The FTC has authority to prevent through cease-and-desist orders and other means: (1) general trade restraints such as price fixing; (2) activities that tend to lessen competition such as mergers, tying, price discrimination; (3) false or deceptive advertising; (4) untruthful labeling of textile and fur products; (5) other unfair or deceptive practices.

Organization: A five-member, independent commission with quasi-judicial, quasi-executive, and quasi-legislative power, supported by bureaus for competition, consumer protection, and economics.

Budget: 1991 appropriation, $77 million.

Staff: 1991 positions, 919.

lawyer-year. To compare these benefits with costs, Weiss estimated the government's cost of a lawyer-year to have been $32 thousand, a cost well below all but one of the benefit figures. Furthermore, if estimated private defense costs are added to the government's costs, $192 thousand becomes the figure for comparison. And this cost also amounts to no more than a mere fraction of the estimated benefit in all but two instances—allocation efficiency in criminal collusion and exclusionary practices. Thus, it appears that for the most part antitrust policy gives good value for the money when measured solely (and perhaps inappropriately) by economic criteria.[51]

C. The Federal Trade Commission

Housed in a quaint triangular building on Pennsylvania Avenue in Washington, the Federal Trade Commission is headed by a panel of five commissioners, each appointed to seven-year terms by the president and approved by the Senate. A supporting staff includes over 900 others—administrative law judges, lawyers, economists, and so on—scattered about in the groups diagrammed in Figure 5–5 (and in regional offices throughout the United States). The commission's work is divided into two main areas under the Bureau of Competition and the Bureau of Consumer Protection. The first is of interest here because it is responsible for antitrust matters. The second is responsible for deceptive advertising and related matters that we take up later. Lawyers dominate both these branches, so economic input is supplied by the Bureau of Economics, a separate but coequal branch staffed with economists.

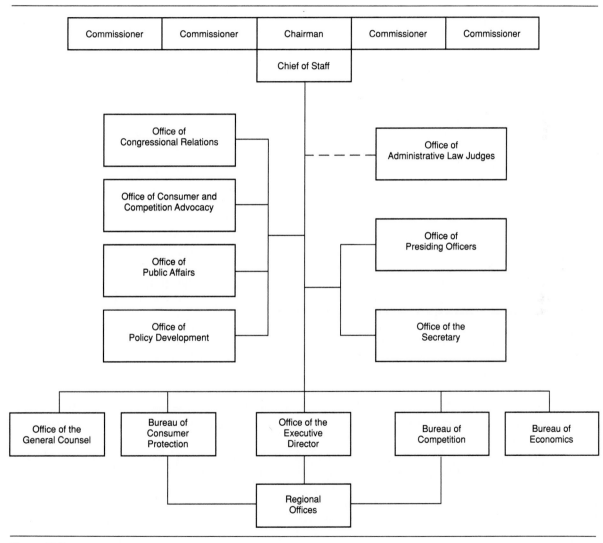

Figure 5–5
Organization of the Federal Trade Commission

Unlike the Justice Department, which files its cases in federal district courts, almost all formal FTC proceedings are initiated by an administrative complaint issued to one or more respondents, who are then tried before an administrative law judge if the case is not settled by consent. Although an integral part of the commission, these judges maintain an appropriate degree of independence so they can serve as impartial triers of facts, following procedures and setting standards of proof similar to those found in district court civil trials. Either the respondents or the FTC staff attorneys may seek alteration of the administrative law judge's opinion by appeal to the commission itself. The FTC then reviews the case, scrutinizing the issues, exhibits, and trial record. If the FTC's decision satisfies the respondent, it then becomes final. Disgruntled respondents may appeal FTC decisions to federal appellate courts, including (eventually or directly, depending on the circumstances) the Supreme Court.

The procedures of the FTC differ from Antitrust Division procedures in other ways as well. The FTC's inability to bring criminal actions accounts for many of these further differences. The chief remedy relied on by the FTC, for instance, is simply a "cease-and-desist" order, which if disobeyed can elicit daily fines of up to $10,000. This is supplemented by an occasional divestiture order in structural cases. Another major difference, is that under the Magnuson-Moss Act of 1975 the commission may bring federal or state civil actions to obtain redress for consumers or businesses injured by certain violations of the FTC Act. The Magnuson-Moss Act also provides the FTC with authority to formulate "trade regulation rules," which can be much like legislation, carrying the force of law and setting standards for entire industries. Trade regulation rules are employed primarily to combat deceptive practices rather than antitrust trespasses, however, so our treatment of them is postponed.

Summary and Recent Trends

There are three main parties in the antitrust process—the Congress (which writes the statutes), the courts (which judge the cases), and the enforcement agencies (which press the cases). The importance of the latter may be seen in the fact that under President Reagan enforcement was significantly relaxed in all areas except collusive price fixing. The average annual number of civil cases filed by the Department of Justice under Reagan was 13, compared to 30 under President Carter and 48 under Presidents Nixon and Ford.[52] Enforcement activity at the Federal Trade Commission fell by 57 percent when measured by the annual number of complaints issued during 1981–1988 compared to 1972–1980.[53] Moreover, Reagan's appointees to the enforcement agencies frequently spoke as if they were anti-antitrust. This prompted an American Bar Association Task Force of prominent antitrust experts to recommend that the "non-enforcement rhetoric end."[54] And the lack of enforcement activity prompted the Congress to cut the budgets of the agencies. Between 1980 and 1989, for instance, the number of attorneys staffing the Antitrust Division of the Department of Justice plunged from 409 to 237.

Conservative ideology produced the lull in policy. But President Bush's moderate, pragmatic approach brought revival. As this is written, Bush's trustbusters are initiating more cases, blocking more mergers, and hiring more enforcement personnel. "Moreover," as the *Washington Post* says, "Justice Department officials have taken pains to publicly and explicitly reject the free-market theories of the [conservative] Chicago School that informed the Reagan era policy."[55]

D. Private Suits

Table 5–7 offers a statistical summary of the primary violations alleged in a sample of 2,350 pri-

Table 5–7
Primary Violations, Alleged in Private Antitrust
Complaints, 1973–1983 (Five Federal Districts)

Violation Alleged[a]	Percentage of Cases
Horizontal Price Fixing	21.0
Refusal to Deal	16.0
Tying or Exclusive Dealing	12.8
Price Discrimination	6.7
Dealer Termination	5.9
"Restraint of Trade"	5.7
Monopolization	4.9
Vertical Price Fixing	4.7
Predatory Pricing	4.1
Merger	3.5
Other	18.2

Note: Excludes sampled cases with "no information."

Source: Steven C. Salop and Lawrence J. White, "Private Antitrust Litigation: An Introduction and Framework," in *Private Antitrust Litigation,* edited by Lawrence J. White (Cambridge, MA: MIT Press, 1988), p. 6.

vate antitrust cases filed in five federal district courts during the period 1973–1983. Notice first that private and government cases are alike in that horizontal price fixing is far and away the practice most frequently attacked in both. Notice second, however, that beyond this similarity there is in the private cases a strong emphasis on what may be called conduct abuses. This contrasts to the ample attention paid to structural matters by the government agencies, as shown earlier in Table 5–5. Whereas mergers and monopolization account for about 25 percent of all government allegations, they account for no more than about 8 percent of private allegations. Conversely, allegations of tying, exclusive dealing, refusal to deal, dealer termination, and price discrimination show up much more prominently in private as compared to government cases.

There are many reasons for this difference. First, the time and expense of merger and monopolization cases loom very large, leaving few outside the government to pick up the tab as a plaintiff. Second, damages are especially difficult to prove in these instances. Third, many private plaintiffs use the antitrust laws as a handy weapon to gain leverage in business disputes, and claims of conduct abuse seem to serve this purpose best (especially when the defendant lacks the market power to raise even slight structural suspicions). Finally, the possibilities of collecting treble damages give hungry private plaintiffs an enticing incentive. Damage claims of $100 million after trebling are common.

Given the many private suits filed each year, it is fortunate for the courts that very few mature into trial combat. Almost 20 percent of all private cases end in dismissal. Nearly 70 percent more are otherwise settled prior to trial. Whether most of these many abandonments are due to the plaintiffs' lack of resources or to a lack of merit in their allegations is unknown, but it is probably a mix of both. The typical plaintiff is financially small, both absolutely and relative to the defendant. Moreover, suits actually ending in trial are usually decided in favor of the defendants.[56]

To the extent private cases are meritorious, they contribute *positively* to the overall enforcement effort. Suits under well-established parts of the law stimulate compliance. Private suits may also lead to new and much-needed law, thereby complementing official efforts. On the other hand, private cases can contribute *negatively*. Those built on skimpy factual foundations merely congest the courts. Those that are poorly argued, or framed in such a way as to distort the issues, may end up setting undesirable precedents. Whether the pluses of private cases exceed the minuses is a matter of judgment. In any event, the official agencies still spearhead the formulation and refinement of mainstream policy.

V. Exemptions from Antitrust

Since passage of the Sherman Act in 1890, exemptions from antitrust law have accumulated like attic junk. Some of the most important of them guard export cartels, labor unions, agricultural cooperatives, and regulated industries from the reaches of the law.

The first of these was the 1918 Webb-Pomerene Act exemption of export cartels. Export associations organized under the act can fix prices on their foreign sales, allocate foreign territories, operate a single sales agency, and act in other ways that would clearly violate Section 1 of the Sherman Act. Only a few constraints apply: (1) Webb cartels must register with the Federal Trade Commission, supplying such information as the FTC may require. (2) They cannot restrain trade within the United States or artificially influence domestic prices. (3) They cannot coerce domestic competitors who wish to export independently. The intent of the exemption was to assist American exporters, especially small enterprises, by allowing coordinated marketing efforts, larger and more efficient scales of merchandising, volume buying of transportation services, and the like. Yet despite the apparent advantages the loophole allows, few exporters have exploited it. In 1965, for instance, only 29 active export cartels were registered with the FTC, and these accounted for a piddling 4.2 percent ot total U. S. exports.[57] Although the record of the Webb Act is thus weak, industry spokesmen intermittently urge an expansion of the exemption to include services as well as commodities and to permit collaborations on transfers of technology.[58]

Exemptions for agricultural organizations are granted by a number of federal statutes. The Capper-Volstead Act of 1922, for instance, allows farmers, ranchers, and dairymen to collectively process and market their products (subject to certain conditions) so long as they do not "unduly" enhance the prices of those products. The theory is that, independently, farmers cannot market their yields efficiently or match the bargaining power of buyers, but collectively they can achieve these aims without attaining the power to restrain trade. (Actually many do restrain trade; milk coops especially.)

The rationale of equal bargaining power also motivated labor union immunity. Attempts by workers to secure higher wages and better working conditions were especially encouraged by the National Labor Relations Act of 1935. Unions forfeit their exemption, however, when they conspire with businesses to bolster a price-fixing agreement or drive nonunion enterprises from the field.[59] Likewise, an association of business proprietors cannot assume the disguise of a labor union in hope of escaping the Sherman Act by subterfuge.[60]

Certainly the most pervasive exemptions relate to regulated industries. No one-sentence summary can capture the scope of these exemptions, for they are as various as the regulated industries themselves—insurance, electric power, ocean shipping, communications, and so on. One way or another, however, permissiveness often prevails, resulting in price-fixing rings, anticompetitive mergers, entry restrictions, and other restraints. Regulation of economic results may check the otherwise bad implications. Moreover, in recent years the deregulation movement has stripped some industries of their most comfortable immunities, exposing them to the cold winds of competition. Details on these developments occupy us in subsequent chapters.[61] Other areas in which exemptions have been relaxed or abandoned include business practices in learned professions like architecture and in professional team sports.[62]

Summary

The central problem addressed by antitrust policy is market power. Our review of economic evidence—as manifested in market structure, conduct, and performance—reveals the desirability and necessity of such a policy. In regard to *desirability,* competitive market structure, conduct, and performance typically serve society's interests. They imply decentralized decision making, fair dealing, efficiency, equity, progress, and general prosperity. Moreover, many if not most deviations from workable competition are achieved by artificial as opposed to natural means. In other words, attempts to maintain competition are not hopelessly at odds with economies of scale, and they do not undermine technological progress.

In regard to *necessity,* antitrust law appears to be necessary in light of the fact that competition can be suppressed or crippled. Competition is not automatic or inevitable, at least not to the degree that seems desirable. In the absence of antitrust law, businesses usually have the incentive to monopolize, cartelize, or otherwise restrain trade.

The specific aims any antitrust policy might adopt include four main options: (1) maintenance of competition as an end in itself (or as a means to political-social decentralization), (2) prescription of fair conduct, (3) good market performance, and (4) absolute limitations on corporate size. Legislative, judicial, and scholarly tradition support selection of the first two options for U. S. policy, although traces of support may be found for all four. Greater use of goal (3) has been urged by conservatives. They recently acquired power and would like to see the relaxation of much antitrust law, so they argue for the exclusive acceptance of goal (3) in a narrow form, namely, static efficiency.

In essence, the antitrust laws prohibit restraints of trade, monopolization, and unfair methods of competition plus mergers and various restrictive practices when they may lessen competition. Structure and conduct share the focus. Performance may indirectly benefit but only presumptively. The remedies backing up these pro-visions fall into five main classes: fines and imprisonment for criminal violations, plus injunctions, divestitures, and treble damages under civil actions. These remedies may be reached either by trial or negotiated settlements. The latter are more common in practice than the former, and in government suits go by the names nolo contendere and consent decree.

Enforcement suits may be initiated by the Antitrust Division of the Department of Justice, the Federal Trade Commission, or private plaintiffs, only the first of which can press criminal proceedings. The official agencies enjoy concurrent jurisdiction, but continuing coordination between them eliminates duplication on specific cases. Case selection entails much sorting, sifting, and deliberation. As intended, most cases emerging from the agencies stand up well under trial test. The cases remaining tend to be innovative probes searching the boundaries of law and economics. Private suits cannot, on the whole, qualify for such flattery. But they offer occasional surprises, and certainly amount to more than just trash.

When the underlying assumptions of antitrust law do not hold, when ambivalence in our commitment to competition leads to permissiveness, and when interest groups succeed in securing escape, exemptions prevail. Some immunities have been removed, but they remain in place for export cartels, agricultural cooperatives, labor unions, and regulated industries.

Questions and Exercises for Chapter 5

1. Distinguish between natural and artificial causes of concentration and barriers to entry. Why is this distinction important to antitrust policy?
2. It is possible to have fairly low concentration in every specific market, yet at the same time have firms that are huge in absolute size. Explain why.
3. Explain the difference between "collusive" and "exclusionary" conduct, using of examples.

4. What is the relationship between competition (in structure and conduct) and performance as measured by profits, production efficiency, and technical progress?

5. What kinds of empirical evidence or theoretical argument would cast doubt on the wisdom of antitrust policy?

6. Why is structure the focus of much antitrust policy (i.e., that concerning monopolization and merger)?

7. Use structure, conduct, and performance to explain several possible goals of antitrust policy.

8. What is Congress's contribution to antitrust policy?

9. How do the Department of Justice and the Federal Trade Commission differ in their powers, procedures, and remedies?

10. Quantity but not quality characterize private antitrust suits. True or false? Why?

11. Discuss antitrust exemptions in light of (a) the assumptions underlying antitrust policy, (b) the goals of antitrust policy, and (c) special interest politics.

Notes

1. James W. McKie, "Government Intervention in the Economy of the United States," in *Government Intervention in the Developed Economy,* ed. Peter Maunder (New York: Praeger 1979), p. 74.

2. Ernest Barker, ed., *The Politics of Aristotle* (New York: Oxford University Press, 1962), p. 31.

3. *Business Week,* October 9, 1978, p. 143.

4. John S. McGee, *In Defense of Industrial Concentration* (New York: Praeger, 1971); Sam Peltzman, "The Gains and Losses from Industrial Concentration," *Journal of Law & Economics* (October 1977): 229–263.

5. Lawrence White, *The Automobile Industry Since 1945* (Cambridge, MA: Harvard University Press, 1971), Chap. 4.

6. F. M. Scherer, A. Beckenstein, E. Kaufer, and R. D. Murphy, *The Economics of Multi-Plant Operation* (Cambridge, MA: Harvard University Press, 1975), p. 339. See also Joe Bain, *Barriers to New Competition* (Cambridge, Harvard University Press, 1965), Leonard W. Weiss, "Optimal Plant Size and the Extent of Suboptimal Capacity," in Masson and Qualls, eds., *Essays on Industrial Organization* (Cambridge, MA: Ballinger, 1976), pp. 123–141, F. M. Scherer, "The Causes and Consequences of Rising Industrial Concentration," *Journal of Law & Economics* (April 1979): 191–208; and H. P. Marvel, "Foreign Trade and Domestic Competition," *Economic Inquiry* (January 1980): 114–115.

7. William G. Shepherd, *The Treatment of Market Power* (New York: Columbia University Press, 1975), pp. 51–53.

8. For details see Richard Schmalensee, "On the Use of Economic Models in Antitrust: The *RealLemon* Case," *University of Pennsylvania Law Review* (April, 1979): 994–1050.

9. U. S. Senate, Committee on the Judiciary, Subcommittee on Antitrust, Monopoly and Business Rights, *Mergers and Economic Concentration,* Hearings, Part 1 (1979), pp. 89–92.

10. For contrary views see statements by Weston and Schwartzman, *Mergers and Economic Concentration, ibid,* pp. 536–614.

11. George A. Hay and Daniel Kelley, "An Empirical Survey of Price-Fixing Conspiracies," *Journal of Law and Economics* (April 1974): 13–38.

12. A. G. Fraas and D. F. Greer, "Market Structure and Price Collusion: An Empirical Analysis," *Journal of Industrial Economics* (September 1977): 21–44.

13. B. W. Marion, W. F. Mueller, R. W. Cotteril, F. E. Geithman, and J. R. Schmelzer, *The Profit and Price Performance of Leading Food Chains 1970–74,* Joint Economic Committee, U. S. Congress, 95th Congress, 1st Session (1977), p. 66.

14. For a partial survey see Leonard W. Weiss, ed., *Concentration and Price* (Cambridge, MA: MIT Press, 1989).

15. *United States* v. *Standard Oil Company of New Jersey,* 221 U. S. 1 (1911); *United States* v. *American Tobacco Company,* 221 U. S. 106 (1911).

16. Michael D. Whinston, "Tying, Foreclosure, and Exclusion," *American Economic Review* (September 1990): 837–859.

17. Richard Caves, *American Industry: Structure, Conduct, Performance* (Englewood Cliffs, NJ: Prentice-Hall, 1977), 4th ed., p. 96; and William S. Comanor and H. E. Frech III "The Competitive Effects of Vertical Agreements," *American Economic Review* (June 1985): 539–546.

18. For surveys see Leonard W. Weiss, "The Concentration-Profits Relationship," in *Industrial Concentration: The New Learning,* ed. H. Goldschmid, M. Mann, and F. Weston (Boston: Little, Brown, 1974), pp. 196–200; Stephen A. Rhoades, "Structure-Performance Studies in Banking: A Summary and Evaluation," Staff Economic Studies, No. 92 (Board of Governors of the Federal Reserve System, 1977); F. M. Scherer and David Ross, *Industrial Market Structure and Economic Performance,* 3rd ed. (Boston: Houghton Mifflin, 1990), pp. 411–448.

19. R. D. Buzzell, B. T. Gale, and R. G. M. Sultan, "Market Share—A Key to Profitability," *Harvard Business Review* (January/February 1975): 97–106.

20. R. E. Caves and T. A. Pugel, *Intraindustry Differences in Conduct and Performance* (New York: New York University, Graduate School of Business Monograph Series in Financial Economics, 1980); L. Amato and R. P. Wilder, "The Effects of Firm Size on Profit Rates in U. S. Manufacturing," *Southern Economic Journal* (July 1985):

181–190; S. A. Rhoades, "Market Share as a Source of Market Power: Implications and Some Evidence," *Journal of Economics and Business* (vol. 37, 1985): 343–363.

21. R. E. Caves, J. Khalilzadeh-Shirazi, and M. E. Porter, "Scale Economies in Statistical Analyses of Market Power," *Review of Economics and Statistics* (May 1975): 133–140; William S. Comanor and Thomas A. Wilson, "Advertising, Market Structure, and Performance," *Review of Economics and Statistics* (November 1967): 423–40; Dale Orr, "An Index of Entry Barriers and its Application to the Structure Performance Relationship," *Journal of Industrial Economics* (September 1974): 39–49; and Robert J. Stonebraker, "Corporate Profits and the Risk of Entry," *Review of Economics and Statistics* (February 1976): 33–39.

22. D. F. Greer, *Industrial Organization and Public Policy* (New York: Macmillan, 1984), pp. 357–365.

23. W. S. Comanor and H. Leibenstein, "Allocative Efficiency, X-Efficiency and the Measurement of Welfare Losses," *Economica* (August 1969): 304.

24. W. Bruce Erickson, "Price Fixing Conspiracies: Their Long-term Impact," *Journal of Industrial Economics* (March 1976): 189–202.

25. Corwin D. Edwards, *Economic and Political Aspects of International Cartels*, U. S. Senate, Subcommittee on War Mobilization of the Committee on Military Affairs, 78th Congress, Second Session (1944), p. 40.

26. Walter J. Primeaux, "An Assessment of X-Efficiency Gained Through Competition," *Review of Economics and Statistics* (February 1977): 105–08. See also R. Stevenson, "X-Inefficiency and Interfirm Rivalry," *Land Economics* (February 1982): 52–65; and J. L. Stevens, "Bank Market Concentration and Costs," *Business Economics* (May 1983): 36–44.

27. For surveys see Scherer and Ross, *Industrial Market Structure*, pp. 613–685; M. I. Kamien and N. L. Schwartz, "Market Structure and Innovation: A Survey," *Journal of Economic Literature* (March 1975): 1–37; E. Mansfield, J. Rapoport, A. Romeo, E. Villani, S. Wagner, and F. Husic, *The Production and Application of New Industrial Technology* (New York: Norton, 1977), pp. 1–20.

28. Zoltan J. Acs and David B. Audretsch, *Innovation and Small Firms* (Cambridge, MA: MIT Press, 1990); Acs and Audretsch, "Innovation, Market Structure, and Firm Size," *Review of Economics and Statistics* (November 1987): 567–574.

29. Zoltan J. Acs and David B. Audretsch, "Innovation in Large and Small Firms: An Empirical Analysis," *American Economic Review* (September 1988): 688. See also K. Paritt, M. Robson, and I. Townsend, "The Size Distribution of Innovating Firms in the UK: 1947–1983" *Journal of Industrial Economics* (March 1987): 297–316.

30. Without an antitrust policy, the United Kingdom experienced widespread cartelization. According to one estimate, 50 to 60 percent of U.K. manufacturing experienced restraints of trade in 1956. Roger Clarke, *Industrial Economics* (Oxford, England: Basil Blackwell, 1985), pp. 242–243.

31. Yale Brozen, *Concentration, Mergers, and Public Policy* (New York: Macmillan, 1982), pp. 82, 382.

32. Harold Demsetz, "The Trust Behind Antitrust," in *Industrial Concentration and the Market System,* ed. by Eleanor Fox and J. T. Halverson (Section on Antitrust Law, American Bar Association, 1979), pp. 81–161. (Emphasis in original.)

33. Robert Bork, "Antitrust and the Theory of Concentrated Markets," *Industrial Concentration and the Market System, ibid.,* p. 85.

34. D. T. Armentano, *Antitrust and Monopoly* (New York: Wiley, 1982), pp. 43, 137.

35. J. R. Kearl et al., "A Confusion of Economists?," *American Economic Review* (May 1979): 30. For an interesting critique of the conservative view see Walter Adams and James W. Brock, *Antitrust Economics on Trial* (Princeton NJ: Princeton University Press, 1991).

36. See, for example, R. H. Bork, W. S. Bowman, Jr., H. M. Blake, and W. K. Jones, "The Goals of Antitrust: A Dialogue on Policy," *Columbia Law Review* (March 1965): 363–443.

37. Carl Kaysen and Donald F. Turner, *Antitrust Policy* (Cambridge, MA: Harvard University Press, 1959), pp. 11–22.

38. Ibid., p. 14.

39. Quoted by Robert Pitofsky, "The Political Content of Antitrust," *University of Pennsylvania Law Review* (April 1979): 1063.

40. Robert Bork, "Legislative Intent and the Policy of the Sherman Act," *Journal of Law and Economics (October 1966): 7–48.*

41. Kenneth G. Elzinga, "The Goals of Antitrust: Other Than Competition and Efficiency, What Else Counts?" *University of Pennsylvania Law Review* (June 1977): 1198.

42. Kaysen and Turner, *Antitrust Policy,* p. 18.

43. A. D. Neale, *The Antitrust Laws of the U.S.A.* (Cambridge, England: Cambridge University Press, 1962), p. 487.

44. ABA Antitrust Law Section, Task Force on the Antitrust Division of the U.S. Department of Justice, "Report," *Antitrust Law Journal* (vol. 58, no. 3, 1989): 746.

45. Bork, "Legislative Intent. . . ," *op. cit.*; Richard A. Posner, *Antitrust Law: An Economic Perspective* (Chicago: University of Chicago Press, 1976).

46. In fact, the Sherman Act was passed over the strenuous objections of prominent economists who thought that all big businesses were forged from such efficiencies. F. M. Scherer, "The Posnerian Harvest: Separating Wheat from Chaff," *Yale Law Review* (April 1977): 974–984; William L. Baldwin, *Antitrust and the Changing Corporation* (Durham, NC: Duke University Press, 1961), pp. 3–39; Richard Hofstadter, "What Happened to the Antitrust Movement" in *The Business Establishment,* ed. E. F. Cheit (New York: Wiley, 1964), pp. 113–151.

47. Scherer and Ross, *Industrial Market Structure;* Lawrence A. Sullivan, *Handbook of the Law of Antitrust* (St. Paul, MN: West Publishing, 1977), pp. 2–8; Roger Sherman, *Antitrust Policies and Issues* (Reading, MA: Addison-Wesley, 1978), pp. 25–26; Walter Adams, "The Case for Structural Tests," in *Public Policy Toward Mergers,* ed. F. Weston and S. Peltzman (Pacific Palisades, CA:

Goodyear, 1969), pp. 13–26; Richard Schmalensee, "Antitrust and the New Industrial Economics," *American Economic Review* (May 1982): 24–28; Joseph Brodley, "The Goals of Antitrust—Pretrial Hearing No. 1," *Antitrust Bulletin* (Winter 1983): 823–838; Keith Leffler, "Toward a Reasonable Rule of Reason," *Journal of Law & Economics* (May 1985): 381–386; D. Swann, D. P. O'Brien, W. P. J. Maunder, and W. S. Howe, *Competition in British Industry* (London: George Allen & Unwin, 1974), pp. 92–133; the articles by E. Fox, L. Sullivan, F. M. Scherer, and J. Brodley in the November 1987 issue of the *New York University Law Review;* A. A. Fisher and R. H. Lande, "Efficiency Considerations in Merger Enforcement," *California Law Review* (December 1983): 1580–1696; and P. A. Geroski and A. Jacquemin, "Dominant Firms and Their Alleged Decline," *International Journal of Industrial Organization* (March 1984): 19–21.

48. Terry Calvani and Michael L. Sibarium, "Antitrust Today: Maturity or Decline," *Antitrust Bulletin* (Spring 1990): 177.

49. Suzanne Weaver, *Decision to Prosecute: Organization and Public Policy in the Antitrust Division* (Cambridge, MA: MIT Press, 1977), p. 52.

50. Suzanne Weaver, "Antitrust Division of the Department of Justice," in *The Politics of Regulation,* ed. J. Q. Wilson (New York: Basic Books, 1980), p. 149.

51. This is not to say, however, that the division's cases are selected to maximize the extent to which the benefits exceed the costs. Extensive study of this question led John Siegfried to conclude that "economic variables have little influence on the Antitrust Division." Siegfried, "The Determinants of Antitrust Activity," *Journal of Law & Economics* (October 1975): 573.

52. U.S. General Accounting Office, "Changes in Antitrust Enforcement Policies and Activities of the Justice Department," *BNA Antitrust and Trade Regulation Report,* special supplement, vol. 51, no. 1495, December 13, 1990, p. S-33.

53. ABA Report on the Federal Trade Commission, *Antitrust Law Journal* (vol. 58, no. 1, 1989): 147.

54. ABA Antitrust Law Section Task Force on the Antitrust Division, "Report," *Antitrust Law Journal* (vol. 58, no. 3, 1989): 745.

55. Steven Mufson, "Taking the Sherman Act Out of Mothballs," *Washington Post, National Weekly Edition* (25 June–1 July, 1990), p. 20. See also *Business Week,* June 25, 1990, pp. 64–67.

56. Steven C. Salop and Lawrence J. White, "Private Antitrust Litigation: Introduction and Framework," in *Private Antitrust Litigation,* ed. L. J. White (Cambridge, MA: MIT Press, 1988), pp. 10–11. See also Jeffrey M. Perloff and Daniel L. Rubinfeld, "Settlements in Private Antitrust Litigation," *ibid,* pp. 149–184.

57. Federal Trade Commission, *Economic Report on Webb-Pomerene Associations: A 50 Year Review* (Washington, DC, 1967), pp. 23, 45. See also David A. Larson, "An Economic Analysis of the Webb-Pomerene Act," *Journal of Law & Economics* (October 1970): 461–500.

58. U. S. Senate, Subcommittee on Foreign Commerce and Tourism, *Export Expansion Act of 1971, Hearings,* 92nd Cong., 2nd Sess. (1972).

59. *Allen Bradley Co.* v. *Local 3, IBEW,* 325 U. S. 797 (1945); *UMW* v. *Pennington,* 381 U. S. 657 (1965).

60. *Los Angeles Meat & Provision Drivers Union* v. *U. S.,* 371 U. S. 94 (1962).

61. Almarin Phillips, ed., *Promoting Competition in Regulated Markets* (Washington, DC: Brookings Institution, 1975).

62. Roger G. Noll, "Major League Team Sports," in *The Structure of American Industry,* ed. Walter Adams (New York: Macmillan, 1977), pp. 365–400.

Chapter 6

Antitrust Policy: Collusive Restraints of Trade

Between 1969 and 1973 I saw the retail price of a loaf of bread in Phoenix go from 35¢ to 69¢. At least 15% of that increase could be traced to our conspiracy. There's no question that price-fixing is a cost factor for the consumer.
— *Confession of Donald Phillips, former vice-president of Baird's Bread Company*

T he most venerable words in antitrust law make up Section 1 of the Sherman Act (1890), which states that:

> Every contract, combination . . . or conspiracy, in restraint of trade or commerce among the several States, or with foreign nations, is hereby declared to be illegal.

The problem with this is that it cannot mean what it says. If *every* agreement that restrained trade in some way were illegal, then commerce would shrivel to death. Long-term supply contracts, for instance, impose restraints on buyers and sellers. Another problem with Section 1 is its brevity. Its simple language hides potent barbs. Extensive judicial interpretation must therefore be made. The statute's words resemble land mines set to explode when tripped by specific cases.

This chapter surveys the battle field of Section 1 cases in three steps. First, we must distinguish between several possible rules of legal analysis, per se rules and rules of reason in particular. Second, clear-cut cases like direct price fixing receive attention. Consideration of gray areas like "conscious parallelism" and trade association "information activities" comes next. One class of Section 1 cases we cannot cover concerns collective boycotts, which are essentially illegal per se.

I. Rules and Remedies

A. Rules of Analysis

Many business agreements whose purpose is not to restrain trade may nevertheless include some incidental or ancillary restraints. Sam's Bakery, for instance, may be sold to Joe under a contract that prohibits Sam from starting a new bakery within two miles of the old one for five years. Such a covenant not to compete enables Joe to get what he is paying for—a bakery with established goodwill. Early judicial interpretations of the Sherman Act held that such incidental re-

115

straints escaped condemnation. The courts recognized that Congress was after bigger game, namely, "all concerted arrangements which are adopted for the purpose of reducing competition, or which, regardless of purpose, have a significant tendency to reduce competition."[1] The key question, then, is whether an arrangement has the *purpose* or *effect* of seriously damaging competition. In turn, this question may be answered through application of one of two subsidiary rules, a *per se rule* or *rule of reason.*

If conduct is governed by a *per se rule,* prosecuting authorities need do no more to establish violation than prove that the offending conduct actually occurred. Direct price-fixing qualifies for this kind of treatment, so proof by such evidence as minutes of competitors' meetings or exchange of letters would be enough. No inquiry into the rationale of the conspirators, or the economic condition of the industry, or the impact on price level, or other considerations need be made. By contrast, a *rule of reason* entails a more open-ended analysis, one in which circumstances, consequences, and motives play a big part. As the Supreme Court puts it:

> There are, thus, two complementary categories of antitrust analysis. In the first category are agreements whose nature and effect are so plainly anticompetitive that no elaborate study of the industry is needed to establish their illegality—they are "illegal per se"—in the second category are agreements whose competitive effect can only be evaluated by analyzing the facts peculiar to the business, the history of the restraint, and the reasons why it was imposed.[2]

Aside from direct price fixing, conduct subject to per se analysis includes collusion to restrain output, to divide market territories, or to allocate customers. Monopolizing, merging, tying, and exclusive dealing are, on the other hand, governed by the rule of reason.

It is important to note that the rule of reason is usually applied under U. S. law only to determine whether, on balance, *competition is lessened,* not whether on balance some act is *generally good or bad.* Continuing the foregoing quotation on the Supreme Court's comparison of per se and rule of reason analysis:

> In either event, the purpose of the analysis is to form a judgment about the competitive significance of the restraint; it is not to decide whether a policy favoring competition is in the public interest, or in the interest of the members of an industry. Subject to exceptions defined by statute, that policy decision has been made by the Congress.[3]

The United States's antitrust policy could be broadened. Reasonableness could be determined by comparing the costs of lessened competition with *any* alleged social benefits, in which case we would then have what F. M. Scherer calls an *expanded rule of reason.*[4] Such an approach is used by the British, whose law bans price-fixing agreements unless participants can prove that such an agreement is necessary to the provision of some specific social benefit, which benefit outweighs the detriments of restriction. Eight such potential benefits, or "gateways" to cartelization, are mentioned in English law, including (a) the protection of customers or their property against physical injury, (b) the prevention of serious and persistent adverse effects on employment in an industrialized area, and (c) the prevention of stunted export sales.[5]

Although collusive restraints are typically treated by the per se rule in the United States, there are a few instances in which expanded rules of reason have crept into the law. In particular, the Supreme Court has tackled a few unusual cases in which it has allowed defendants to present evidence that the collusive restraint in question was absolutely necessary to achieve some significant efficiency or some new product. In *Broadcast Music, Inc.* v. *Columbia Broadcasting System* (1979) the court refused to find the use of "blanket licenses" by the major associations of music copyright owners to be illegal price fixing per se. Blanket licenses are used by radio stations and others who play music for profit. Radio stations can pay blanket royalties to an association representing numerous songwriters, singers, and other artists rather than negotiate royalties with every artist individually, something that would be much more costly than the association approach.[6] In *NCAA* v. *Board of Regents of the University of Oklahoma* (1984) the court allowed consideration of the argument that universities had to act collectively to arrange television broadcasts of college football games. The court rejected the argument, thereby forcing individualized deals. But the fact that the defendants were allowed to make the argument is notable because it ran counter to the strict per se approach.[7]

Apart from these rare exceptions, the Supreme Court rejects the rule of reason for price fixing. It did so most resoundingly in its judgment of *National Society of Professional Engineers* v. *U.S.* (1978).[8] The Society's Code of Ethics prohibited construction engineers from bidding competitively when offering their services, such as designing bridges and office buildings. This restrained engineers from submitting "any form of price information to a prospective customer which would enable that customer to make a price comparison on engineering services." The Society admitted the restraint but defended it by arguing that competitive bidding would lead to shoddy engineering workmanship, endangering "public health, safety, and welfare." Rejecting the opportunity to weigh the detriments of the restraint against its alleged advantages, the Supreme Court wrote:

> The Sherman Act reflects a legislative judgment that ultimately competition will not only produce lower prices, but also better goods and services. . . . Even assuming occasional exceptions to the presumed consequences of competition, the statutory policy precludes inquiry into the question of whether competition is good or bad.[9]

The reasons the court prefers a per se approach when dealing with blatant restraints of trade can be briefly explained. The benefits of such a rule in reduced legal expenses, reduced business uncertainty, and reduced court confusion exceed the costs of an occasional error in enforcement. As Justice Black explained it over twenty years ago, "The principle of *per se* unreasonableness . . . avoids the necessity for an incredibly complicated and prolonged economic investigation into the entire history of the industry involved, as well as related industries, in an effort to determine at large whether a particular restraint has been unreasonable—an inquiry so often wholly fruitless when undertaken."[10]

B. Remedies

This rigourous, per se standard of illegality might lead you to think that businessmen strenuously shun conspiracies for fear of being caught. Alas, life is not so simple. Well over 1,000 civil and criminal prosecutions have been brought under Section 1 and many more will surely follow. During the 1980s the Justice Department launched about sixty criminal cases a year, some of them against the nation's most prominent business enterprises. In 1980, *Fortune* magazine canvassed the 1,043 companies that appeared at some point on its lists of the 800 largest corporations during the 1970s in order to compile a catalog of instances in which those corporations were successfully prosecuted for serious violations of federal law during that decade. Five improprieties were surveyed—bribery, criminal fraud, illegal political contributions, tax evasion, and criminal antitrust violations (essentially price fixing). The startling results disclosed that, 117, or 11 percent of these corporations proved to be seriously delinquent at least once during the 1970s, and many of them were multiple offenders. In all, 163 separate offenses were tabulated, and the lion's share of these, 98, were antitrust violations.[11] Table 6–1 gives a glimpse of some of the guilty.

What is more, some industries distinguish themselves with repeated delinquency. Begin-

Table 6–1
Major Companies Running Afoul of Sherman Act, Section 1, During the 1970s

Company	Offense and Date of Settlement
Allied Chemical	1974—Fixing prices of dyes. Pleaded nolo contendere.
Bethlehem Steel	1973–74—Two cases of fixing prices of steel reinforcing bars. Company and one employee pleaded nolo; another convicted after trial.
Combustion Engineering	1973—Fixing prices of chromite sand. Company and executive pleaded nolo.
Dean Foods	1977—Price fixing of dairy products. Nolo pleas by company and executive.
DuPont	1974—Fixing prices of dyes. Nolo plea.
FMC	1976—Fixing prices of persulfates. Company and executive pleaded nolo.
Flintkote	1973—Fixing prices of gypsum board. Company, chairman, and president pleaded nolo.
Gulf Oil	1978—Fixing uranium prices. Pleaded guilty.
ITT	1972—ITT Continental Baking subsidiary charged with fixing prices of bread. Nolo plea.
International Paper	1974—Fixing prices of paper labels. Company and two executives pleaded nolo. 1976—Fixing prices of folding cartons. Company and four executives pleaded nolo. 1978—Fixing prices of corrugated containers. Nolo plea. Fined $617,000.
Purolator	1978—Bid rigging and allocation of markets for security services. Nolo plea.
R. J. Reynolds Industries	1979—Fixing prices of ocean shipping. Nolo plea. Fined $1 million.
Rockwell International	1978—Fixing prices of gas meters. Pleaded guilty.

Source: Irwin Ross, "How Lawless Are Big Companies?," *Fortune* (December 1, 1980), pp. 59–61.

ning with the *Trenton Potteries* case of 1927, for instance, members of the bathroom pottery industry have been caught and found guilty of price fixing three times (a rather unsanitary record). The latest conspiracy came to light when Internal Revenue Service agents stumbled onto three tape recordings of price-fixing meetings stashed in the abandoned desk of a man they were investigating for income tax evasion. Estimates of impact indicate that prices were lifted roughly 7 percent on

$1 billion worth of business. "Price fixing rather than competition has been a way of life in the industry," commented an industry official who testified as a key government witness.[12]

A major contributor to the problem of widespread and repeated offenses has been the prevalence of kid-glove penalties. Until recently, criminal violations were merely misdemeanors; fines could be measured in peanuts ($50,000 at most); suspended sentences were fashionable;

jailings were rare and brief; and many civil cases were brought. In short, crime paid. Donald Phillips, the confessed price-fixer we quoted at the outset, put it this way: "When you're doing $30 million a year and stand to gain $3 million by fixing prices, a $30,000 fine doesn't mean much."[13]

A trend toward stiffer penalties has developed, however. The Sherman Act was amended to make criminal violation a potential *felony,* punishable by as many as three years in prison, with fines as high as $250,000 for individuals and $1 million for corporations. Thus, for stark comparison, we may observe that from 1890 to 1970 only 19 people actually went to jail for pure antitrust violations for a total of 28 months. Yet during the 1980s more than 250 people received jail sentences for a total exceeding 960 months. Maximums are still rarely imposed, but the law may no longer be taken lightly. (In the early 1980s a convicted company sought to avoid its fine by making a charitable donation—$1,475,000 to the University of Nebraska to endow a professorship in *business ethics*. The court's reaction? Thumbs down.)

Liability for treble damages adds still further punch. Fines in the plumbing fixture case totaled only $752,500. The treble damages, however, were reckoned at $210 million, of which $28 million was actually paid as a result of out-of-court settlements with victimized plaintiffs.[14]

II. Varieties of Violation: Direct Agreements

A. Introduction

Given a punitive per se rule, the key remaining question is *what* constitutes price fixing or collusive restraint. Businessmen have demonstrated skill when it comes to colluding. Their artistry may be divided into two categories: (1) cases with clear evidence of anticompetitive collusion, and (2) cases offering no more than circumstan-

tial evidence. This section covers the first category. Section III handles the second.

For sheer simplicity of obvious evidence, no collusive technique tops the *single sales agency,* whereby producers refuse to sell directly to their customers and instead sell through a common central agency that sets the price for all participants. Equally obvious would be a short, written *contract* specifying minimum prices. Only a bit more complicated is the *market allocation* approach, whereby each cartel member is assigned exclusive access to certain geographic areas or customers.

The classic *Addyston Pipe & Steel* case of 1899 provides a good example of this last tactic. Six manufacturers of cast iron pipe, including Addyston, entered into an agreement that, among other things, assigned certain southern and central United States cities to individual members of the cartel. These "reserved cities" were the exclusive province of the designated member. The price at which pipe was sold in each reserved city was determined jointly by members of the cartel, the member to whom the business was assigned paying a fixed bonus into the cartel's profit-sharing pool. To give the appearance of continued competition, other members submitted fictitious bids to customers in reserved cities, fictitious because these bids were always at prices higher than those charged by the designated member.[15]

More sensational cases of express collusion come from the oil, electrical equipment, paper, and uranium industries.

B. Dancing Partners in Oil

One of the Justice Department's most celebrated victories was *U. S.* v. *Socony-Vacuum* (now called Mobil) in 1940. The defendants were major integrated oil companies accounting for 83 percent of all gasoline sales in the Midwestern states. They instituted a "dancing partner" program in the Midwest, under which each major company agreed to buy the "surplus" gasoline of some particular independent refinery. "Surplus" was gasoline that could not be disposed of except at "distressed" prices. The independents were small and lacked spacious storage facilities. They consequently sold their "surpluses" at whatever discounted price they could get.

The defendant majors were not accused of direct price fixing. The essence of the accusation was that removal of excess supply from the market *indirectly* propped up the price. The defendants argued that their activities did not constitute price fixing. They were even so bold as to argue before the Supreme Court that their innocence was confirmed by their buying most heavily when prices were *falling* and lightly when prices were *rising*. But this is exactly the way an indirect method of price support should work. The Court was not fooled:

> In this [oil] case, the result was to place a floor under the market—a floor which served the function of increasing the stability and firmness of market prices. . . . Under the Sherman Act a combination formed for the purpose and with the effect of raising, depressing, fixing, pegging, or stabilizing the price of a commodity in interstate or foreign commerce is illegal *per se*.[16]

C. The Electrical Equipment Cases

The electric equipment cases are to American price fixing what Watergate is to American political corruption.[17] The collusion began some time in the 1920s or 1930s. At first it was a rather casual adjunct to the industry's trade association activities, involving just a few products. By the 1950s, however, conspiracy had spread to every corner of the trade. Table 6–2 gives some idea of the scope of the price fixing and of the structure of the markets involved. Roughly $7 billion of business was involved. The products ranged from $2.00 insulators to multimillion dollar turbine generators. The average number of firms participating in each market was 6.6. Several of the larger participants—such as General Electric and Westinghouse—operated and conspired in many

of the markets. Smaller firms—like Moloney Electric and Wagner—were more specialized. In all, 29 firms and 44 individuals were indicted during 1960 for criminal conspiracies in 20 separate product lines.

Table 6–2 gives the impression that high concentration and a paucity of firms might have permitted *tacit* collusion in four or five of these markets. But conditions not revealed in the table provided substantial competitive pull, thereby inducing explicit collusion. First, many of these products were not standardized but custom made and differentiable. Various collusive steps were taken to standardize product quality, especially in the early years. Second, many items of equipment were sold in big chunks, which amplified the incentive to cut prices to gain business. Even within given product lines, large orders received larger discounts off "book" price than did small orders. A third factor was the volatility of the business cycle in the electrical apparatus field. These goods are durable capital equipment and experience fluctuations in demand far beyond those encountered by most other industries. Slack demand seems to have caused much price cutting, even when the conspiracies were in high gear. Finally, technological change was fairly brisk during the decades involved.

Collusive procedures and experiences varied from product to product, from sealed-bid sales to off-the-shelf transactions, and from higher to lower levels of management. One common thread, however, was the atmosphere of skullduggery surrounding all the conspiracies. Code names, pay-phone communications, plain envelope mailings, destruction of evidence, clandestine meetings in out-of-the-way places, faked expense account records, and secret market allocations all entered the plot. Perhaps the most sensational technique devised was the "phases of the moon" system developed for sealed-bid switchgear sales:

> This system was intended to fix automatically the price each conspirator would quote, with a rotation of the low price among competitors to create

Table 6–2
Extent and Coverage of the Electrical Equipment Price-Fixing Conspiracies

Product	Annual (1959) Dollar Sales ($ millions)	Number of Firms Indicted	Share of Market (percentage)
Turbine generators	$400[a]	3 (6)[a]	95 (100)
Industrial control equipment	262[a]	9*	75[a]
Power transformers	210	6	100
Power switchgear assemblies	125	5 (8)[a]	100
Circuit breakers	75	5	100
Power switching equipment	35[a]	8 (15)[a]	90–95[a]
Condensers	32	7	75–85
Distribution transformers	220	8	96
Low-voltage distribution equip.	200[a]	6 (10)[a]	95[a]
Meters	71	3	100
Insulators	28	8	100
Power capacitors	24	6	100
Instrumental transformers	16[a]	3 (4)[a]	95[a]
Network transformers	15	6	90
Low-voltage power circuit breakers	9	3 (5)[a]	100
Isolated phase bus	7.6	4	100
Navy and marine switchgear	7	3	80
Open-fuse cutouts	6	8	75
Bushings	6	4	100
Lightning arresters	16	7	100

[a]Includes companies named as co-conspirators but not indicted.

Source: Adapted from *Corporations on Trial: The Electrical Cases* by Clarence C. Walton and Frederick W. Cleveland, Jr., © 1964 by Wadsworth Publishing Company, Inc., Belmont, California 94002. Reprinted by permission of the publisher.

the illusion of random competition. The contemplated range of bid prices was modest. According to the "moon sheet," which was in effect from December 5, 1958 through April 10, 1959, position would be rotated among the five major competitors every two weeks.[18]

Despite all the shenanigans, it is not clear that the conspirators were able to raise or stabilize prices appreciably in all product lines. Double-crossing was fairly commonplace. A "white sale"

drove prices down to 60 percent of book in 1955. Many participants made self-serving claims that their efforts failed.[19] On the other hand, a federal trial judge was persuaded by the evidence that prices of turbine generators would have been 21 percent lower had it not been for the conspiracy. In addition, much evidence indicates a substantial price impact in several sectors of the trade plus some indirect overall effect via stabilization of market shares.[20] In any event, economic consequences were relevant only to the treble damage suits, which yielded $400 million or thereabouts. The government's criminal suits were settled under the per se rule, with seven executives serving brief stints in the slammer and with fines totaling $1,954,000, the bulk of which was paid by the companies.

D. The Paper Products Cases

During the mid-1970s, two paper product workers, disgruntled by job loss and paltry severance pay, spilled the beans on their former employers.[21] They gave the Justice Department evidence of price fixing in paper labels (the kind that go on food cans) and consumer bags (like those for cookies). One thing led to another, and further investigation revealed conspiracies in three other paper product fields—folding cartons (such as those for breakfast cereal and cake mix), corrugated containers and sheets (large cardboard boxes), and fine paper (like these pages). In fact, the folding carton case began unfolding when a witness in the paper label case testified: "Hell, I used to work for the folding carton division, and they do the same thing over there." The overall result was a series of criminal, civil, and treble damage cases during the late 1970s that rivaled the electrical equipment cases in scope, scale, and sensationalism.

In one segment of the industry, competing manufacturers actually met to set prices, but the most common mode of operation in these cases took a rough form of customer allocation. When a paper products customer sought offers from the colluding suppliers, each potential supplier telephoned the company that previously held the business to find out how much that company was bidding. Knowing that bid price, these other potential suppliers would come in with *higher* bids. Thus, in effect, paper product customers were unwittingly wedded to their traditional suppliers, and no supplier could increase its market share at a rival's expense through price cutting.

Taking all these cases together, fines and damages exceeded $500 million. The vast bulk of

this money came from the folding carton and corrugated container segments, enveloping the biggest cases of the lot. In folding cartons, for instance, twenty-three companies and fifty individuals were indicted. All but one of the defendant companies and two of the accused individuals elected to plead *nolo contendere*. As it turned out, the timing of these pleas could not have been worse, for they occurred shortly after Congress had stiffened the penalties for antitrust violations. Donald Baker, then head of the Justice Department's Antitrust Division, took the opportunity to argue before the judge that an example should be set, that pocket-change fines would not be enough under the new law. Although the judge shied away from imposing maximum penalties, he nevertheless responded to the situation by sentencing fourteen people to jail terms. One of the highest-ranking business executives ever to serve time was caught in this group—R. Harper Brown, then president of Container Corporation, who ended up with fifteen days in prison plus nine months' probation and twelve hours per week in penitent good works.

E. The Uranium Cartel or "Club"

In the fall of 1975, Westinghouse Corporation, one of the largest suppliers of nuclear reactors for generating electricity, stunned the business world by defaulting on commitments to deliver approximately eighty million pounds of uranium yellowcake, the raw material of nuclear fuel fabrication.[22] The reason for defaulting was simple: Westinghouse would have lost roughly $2 billion if it had honored its contracts, a loss caused by an enormous increase in the price of yellowcake. Westinghouse was merely a middleman in this market, buying yellowcake from mining and milling companies, then selling it to electric utilities. When the miners' price for yellowcake was $6 to $10 a pound during 1971–1974, Westinghouse committed itself to supply twenty-seven electric utilities at prices averaging $10 a pound. But the supply was for *future* delivery, and Westinghouse unwisely did not buy for the future while it sold.

When the future arrived, Westinghouse's buying price was skyrocketing—first to $14 in late 1974, then to $26 in August 1975 just before the default. Shortly thereafter in 1976 the price escalated further to $41 a pound for a 600 percent increase in just thirty months.

In August 1976, the drama heightened. Secret memos and letters were stolen from the files of Mary Kathleen Uranium Company in Australia and made public through a bit of trickery. They revealed incriminating details of an international uranium producers' cartel, or "the Club" as members called it. Starting in 1972, the Club included every major yellowcake producer in the free world outside the United States and was surreptitiously aided by the governments of the principal producing countries—Canada, South Africa, France, and Australia. The United States market was excluded at the time because U. S. policy prevented the importation of yellowcake. United States prices nevertheless followed world prices fairly closely because of certain links between the domestic and world markets. The link receiving greatest U. S. attention was the cartel participation of Gulf Minerals Limited, a Canadian subsidiary of the Gulf Oil Corporation.

Moreover, circumstantial evidence indicated the existence of some collusion among U. S. producers in the U. S. market.

The Club divided the international uranium market, established minimum prices, set terms and conditions, rigged bidding procedures, and laid plans to eliminate middlemen like Westinghouse. Details were worked out in a series of meetings in Paris, Cannes, Sydney, and elsewhere. Market quotas, such as those illustrated in Table 6–3 were modified from time to time to reflect changes in each participant's productive capacity, especially that of Australia.

The cartel probably cannot be blamed for all of the mid-1970's leap in yellowcake price because other factors also contributed. Still, precise estimates of the cartel's influence are hampered by the fact that the most revealing evidence of the cartel's activities remains hidden outside the United States. International collusive acts adversely affecting U. S. trade and commerce are subject to prosecution under the Sherman Act but only insofar as these acts are perpetrated by private parties rather than foreign governments and only insofar as U. S. enforcement officials and courts can gain access to evi-

Table 6–3
The Uranium Club's Market Quotas as Decided March, 1974, for Deliveries Through 1983 (in Percentages)

	Period of Reference		
Cartel Participants	*1972–1977*	*1978–1980*	*1981–1983*
Canadian producers	37.30%	21.86%	26.87%
South African producers	26.40	18.30	14.77
French producers	24.20	18.38	22.39
Australian producers	7.60	27.81	24.57
Rio Tinto Zinc	4.50	13.65	11.40

Note: Except for Rio Tinto Zinc, with subsidiaries, affiliates, or joint ventures in every one of the participating countries, the quotas were set by country. Allocations within individual countries were achieved by subcartels, such as NUFCOR of South Africa.

Source: J. H. Taylor and M. D. Yokell, *Yellowcake: The International Uranium Cartel* (New York: Pergamon Press, 1979), p. 81.

dence that all too often is sequestered abroad (sometimes at the insistence of foreign governments).[23] Foreign cartel activities in quinine, radios, watches, and other products have thus been attacked under Section 1 along with uranium. But much information on the Club remains abroad.

The Justice Department filed misdemeanor charges against Gulf Oil, to which Gulf pleaded *nolo contendere*.[24] In more rousing action, Westinghouse sued Gulf and twenty-eight other foreign and domestic yellowcake suppliers for billions of dollars in damages. In turn, Gulf countersued, accusing Westinghouse of conspiring to monopolize the nuclear reactor market. Legally and economically, the cases were very complex. About forty law firms, including a nice sample of the nation's most prestigious, entered the arena (so many that presiding trial judge Prentice Marshall called this "The Lawyers' Full-Employment Case"). A full-scale battle was avoided when in 1981 out-of-court settlements gave Westinghouse hundreds of millions in damages.

F. Damages and Illinois Brick

Left unmentioned in the foregoing tally of whopping damages is a question that has sparked burning controversy: *Who may sue for damages?* Is it only those who purchase *directly* from colluders, such as the cereal manufacturers who bought folding cartons to package cornflakes? What if those direct purchasers merely pass on the higher prices they pay with higher prices charged to their buyers, such as grocery retailers? And what if, in turn, some or all of those higher costs are passed further on to ultimate cornflake consumers like you and me? Can we as downstream buyers sue for damages, too?

In 1977 the Supreme Court handed down a key opinion on this issue—*Illinois Brick Co.* v. *Illinois*, which involved downstream plaintiffs suing members of a cartel.[25] The court held that *only direct purchasers* can sue to collect illegal overcharges, even when those overcharges have been passed on to subsequent downstream buyers. The court reached this conclusion for essentially three reasons. *First, unfair multiplication.* In an earlier case, *Hanover Shoe, Inc.* v. *United Shoe Machinery Corp.*, the court ruled that an antitrust violator may not defend itself from the damage claims of direct buyers by arguing that those buyers had passed on the overcharges.[26] Having thus given direct buyers a crack at the treble damages, even when the single damages had been passed on, the court in *Illinois Brick* said that downstream buyers could not also sue because such suits would subject violators to unfair risks of multiple treble damage liability. *Second, simplicity.* The court stressed the complexity of attempting to deal with pass-through issues, so to keep things simple it would ignore the claims of downstream buyers. *Finally, deterrence.* The court felt that the deterrent effect of treble damage liability would be maximized by giving rights of action to direct purchasers only, whether or not those direct purchasers were in fact injured.

The immense debate touched off by *Illinois Brick* spilled into Congress, where legislation overturning the decision has been repeatedly introduced but to date never passed. A feeling for the difficulties in reaching a satisfactory resolution may be gained by asking yourself where you would stand on the ticklish issues. You probably agree that violators should not be subject to multiple liability, not in light of the ruinous damages that might result, but should direct purchasers who pass on overcharges be given great windfalls while those truly damaged cannot recoup? Simplicity in court proceedings also has its attractions, but why can't that be compromised out of fairness to final consumers? Can we count on direct purchasers to pursue aggressively their damage opportunities, thereby providing deterrence, when those purchasers may be vulnerably dependent on their offending and perhaps revengeful suppliers for continued prosperity? Why not simply overturn *Hanover* and allow pass-through as a defense?[27]

III. Gray Areas and Circumstantial Evidence

A. Introduction

Express agreements are without doubt per se illegal. But what if firms behave uniformly, like a well-rehearsed chorus line, without generating evidence of meetings, phone calls, or other concrete communications? What if rivals do no more than *tacitly* agree, perhaps through price leadership?

Such "conscious parallelism" frequently occurs when market conditions are particularly conducive to a meeting of minds—that is, very few firms, very high concentration, standardized product, inelastic demand, slow growth, and smoothly flowing small-lot sales. Under these conditions, each firm can readily appreciate that price competition will lessen profit rather than increase it. (An Appendix to this chapter gives the reasons for this.) All firms may therefore avoid price competition, all acting uniformly yet independently. Legal treatment of such conduct is ticklish but important.

A related problem arises when firms exchange information on prices, costs, or other factors. The anticompetitive results just hypothesized were largely based on each firm's *certainty* about the acts of rivals and an inability to discount secretly. Stated conversely, *un*certainty can often contribute to competition. Thus, interfirm exchanges of information may heighten knowledge, lessen uncertainty, and thereby facilitate collusion even in the absence of any express agreement about how to act on the knowledge. Trade associations pose particular problems in this connection.

Our heightened knowledge of the law in these areas is best gained by discussing trade associations first and conscious parallelism second, followed by two related topics—basing-point pricing and professional associations.

B. Trade Associations

Competitors are free to take active part in trade associations. Because education is a prime purpose of trade associations, it is quite common for them to collect and disseminate information on a wide variety of subjects, prices included. Moreover, trade association meetings are conducive to talk of prices. As a former assistant manager for a textile firm once said: "I don't know what people would do at a trade association meeting if not discuss prices. They aren't going to talk just about labor contracts and new technology."[28] Fortunately for the consumer, trade association cover cannot immunize outright conspiracies from prosecution. In truth, approximately 30 percent of all cases brought by the government involve trade associations.

Still, the information activities of trade associations do pose problems for drawing the legal line between what does and what does not constitute price fixing. On the one hand, it can be argued that enhanced knowledge on the part of industry members lessens market imperfections, thereby fostering more effective competition. On the other hand, too much knowledge may inhibit price competition.

Illegal information activities are illustrated by the *American Column and Lumber* case of 1921.[29] The hardwood flooring trade association required each of 365 participants to submit six reports to its secretary: (1) a daily report of all actual sales; (2) a daily shipping report, with exact copies of the invoices; (3) a monthly production report; (4) a monthly stock report; (5) current price lists; and (6) inspection reports. In turn, the trade association secretary supplied detailed reports to the firms from this information. The exchange was supplemented by monthly meetings where, among other things, speakers urged cartel-like cooperation with exhortations such as, "If there is *no increase in production,* particularly in oak, there is going to be good business," and "*No man is safe in increasing production.*" The Supreme Court decided this was "not the conduct of competitors."

In subsequent cases the court has frowned on trade association programs involving elaborate standardization of the conditions surrounding sales, reports of future prices, and requirements that members must adhere to their reported prices. An especially important case concerning exchanges of information was *U. S.* v. *Container Corp. of America.* (1969).[30] Although not exactly a trade association case, this case broke new ground because its analysis looked at conduct *and* structure together, rather than conduct alone, to determine the legality of an information exchange program. Moreover, this combination analysis took the court about as far as it could go in condemning such exchanges.

The conduct at issue in *Container,* whose defendants were eighteen of fifty-one manufacturers of corrugated containers in the Southeast, was on its face seemingly innocuous:

> All that was present was a request by each defendant of its competitor for information as to the most recent price charged or quoted, whenever it needed such information and whenever it was not available from another source. Each defendant on receiving that request usually furnished the data with the expectation that it would be furnished reciprocal information when it wanted it.

These exchanges were infrequent and irregular. Moreover, sellers were free to deviate from their quotes, and those receiving quotes often undercut the informant's prices. Nevertheless, the court's majority found a violation, stressing the oligopolistic market *structure,* which apparently solidified this conduct into noticeable if minor adverse *effects:*

> The corrugated container industry is dominated by relatively few sellers. The product is fungible and the competition for sales is price. The demand is inelastic, as buyers place orders only for immediate, short-run needs. The exchange of price data tends toward price uniformity. For a lower price does not mean a larger share of the available business but a sharing of existing business at a lower return. Stabilizing prices as well as raising them is within the ban of Section 1 of the Sherman Act . . .

Three dissenters to the *Container* opinion voiced opposite structural views. They emphasized the large number of sellers (fifty-one) and the ease of entry (possible with an investment of only $50,000 to $75,000). The structural analysis of the majority may therefore be questioned. Still, it is significant that the court was of one mind on the importance of using structural conditions to gauge the competitive consequences of information exchange.

From this and earlier cases it may be concluded that price information exchanges appear to be lawful only when the industry's structure is rather competitive and "when they limit price reports to past transactions, preserve the anonymity of individual traders, make data available to buyers as well as sellers, and permit departure from prices that are filed."[31]

C. Conscious Parallelism

How have the courts handled this problem? Does mere conscious parallelism fall within the meaning of "contract, combination, or conspiracy," as specified by the Sherman Act? The simplified answer that we must limit ourselves to here is of two parts. First, *in and of itself,* conscious parallelism is not illegal. It does not provide conclusive circumstantial evidence of conspiracy. (No more than everyone's living is proof of a conspiracy to breathe, as Lawrence Sullivan said.[32]) The Supreme Court's clearest statement to this effect is found in the *Theatre Enterprises* case of 1954:

> This Court has never held that proof of parallel business behavior conclusively establishes agree-

ment or, phrased differently, that such behavior itself constitutes a Sherman Act offense . . . "conscious parallelism" has not yet read conspiracy out of the Sherman Act entirely.[33]

Second, and on the other hand, consciously parallel behavior may well indicate an unlawful conspiracy or agreement *when viewed in conjunction with additional facts.* These additional facts, or "plus factors," may be subdivided into two categories:

1. Additional independent evidence of a more formal agreement, as illustrated by the following:
   a. Elaborate exchanges of information, such as those encountered in trade association cases.
   b. Simultaneous and substantial price increases (coupled with output reductions) unexplained by any increase in cost.
   c. Unnatural product standardization or false denials of interfirm quality differences.
   d. Identical sealed bidding on nonstandard items (for example, large turbine generators).
   e. Basing-point pricing systems, whereby all sellers quote identical delivered prices to any given buyer despite substantial transportation costs and widely differing delivery distances.
2. Additional independent evidence that the conduct is restrictive or *exclusionary,* such as:
   a. Parallel buying up of scarce raw materials that are not, in fact, used.
   b. Parallel and predatory price cutting.
   c. Cross-licensing of patents.[34]

Appreciation of the "parallelism plus" doctrine may be gained by contrasting two cases—*U.S.* v. *C-O Two Fire Equipment Co.* and *U. S.* v. *Pevely Dairy Co.* Violation was found in the first but not the second:

> In the *C-O Two* case, four competing manufacturers of fire extinguishers had regularly communicated with each other, had engaged in a meticulous program of product standardization, raised prices at a time of industry surplus, made identical bids on public contracts, used substantially identical licensing agreements with distributors . . . and carefully policed these agreements. On this evidence a finding of conspiracy was warranted. . . . In *Pevely,* the product [milk] was identical due to natural causes and health requirements applicable to processing. Defendants also had substantially identical cost structures because each paid the same government-controlled price for raw milk and the same wages which resulted from bargaining with the same union. In this context, the court concluded, identity of prices was well-nigh inevitable, and as consistent with the assumption that defendants had not reached a consensual accord as with the conclusion that they had.[36]

These clouded references to product standardization should not be taken to indicate that such agreements are always illegal. As we shall see later, some standardization, such as uniform bed sizes, is procompetitive and efficient. It is merely the case that standardization can under certain circumstances also aid price collusion.

D. Basing-Point Pricing as Conscious Parallelism

One item on the list of plus factors deserves special elaboration because of its complexity and its propagation of a whole family of cases—namely, basing-point pricing. A simple example of this is the old "Pittsburgh Plus" single basing-point system of the steel industry. Until 1924 all steel producers, regardless of their mill locations, quoted prices as if they were shipping from Pittsburgh. A steel company located in Gray, Indiana, when quoting a price to a buyer located in nearby Chicago, would add to the factory price the railroad freight cost from Pittsburgh to Chicago, rather than the slight freight cost from Gary to Chicago. The excess transportation charge pinned on the buyer was called "phantom freight."

Conversely, if the Gary plant was quoting a price to a buyer in New York, it would add to the factory price the freight cost from Pittsburgh to New York, rather than the larger and truer freight cost from Gary to New York. This undercharging of New York buyers meant that the seller had to "absorb freight." The mills located at the base, in Pittsburgh, neither charged phantom freight nor absorbed freight on *any sale*. Their transport charges matched their transport costs. But sellers at all other locations dealt shamelessly in fictitious transport figures. When they were located closer to the buyer than the Pittsburgh mills, they quoted phantom freight. When they were located farther from the buyer than the Pittsburgh mills, they absorbed freight.

The system is illustrated in Figure 6–1, where horizontal distance represents geographic distance (with Chicago, Pittsburgh, and New York located west to east) and vertical distance represents seller's cost—manufacturing cost first (which does not differ with location) and trans-

portation cost second (which goes up with distance travelled). Thus, the transportation cost of mill M_1 shipping to buyer B_1 is zero, but to buyer B_2 it is yx and to buyer B_3 it is vz. Under the Pittsburgh Plus system, the double shafted line emanating from Pittsburgh would be the delivered price line for *all* sellers. Price x would be quoted to buyer B_2 by M_2 and M_3 as well as M_1, even though the transport costs of M_2 and M_3 would be quite different, as indicated by the single solid and broken lines, respectively. Delivered price to buyer B_1 would be u. To buyer B_3 it would be z. When M_2 charges buyer B_2 price x, it is charging phantom freight equal to xy. When M_2 charges buyer B_3 price z, it must absorb the wz portion of total freight cost wv.

The Pittsburgh Plus system achieved one important result. As a given *buyer* saw it, *all sellers* were quoting exactly the same price. This did not mean that all buyers were quoted the same price, because buyers close to the base saw low identical quotes and buyers distant from the base saw

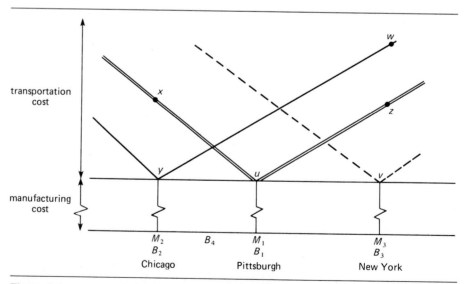

Figure 6–1
The Pittsburgh Plus Basing-point System

high identical quotes. Yet each buyer saw but one price. The single base system of Pittsburgh Plus was abandoned under pressure from the FTC in 1924. Yet this uniform result still held after the steel industry converted to a *multiple* basing-point system by introducing Gary and Birmingham as additional bases. The base closest to the buyer then provided the key to all quotes.

Why would the sellers want to quote identical prices to each buyer? To facilitate collusion and effective price leadership. These systems simplify the pricing of colluding firms. They nullify any interfirm cost advantages attributable to geographic location. They enable the leader to lead with ease from the base. They permit price discrimination as when in Figure 6–1 seller M_2 charges a high price x to low-cost buyer B_2 while charging a low price of u to high-cost buyer B_1. They have also been attacked on these grounds as indicative or supportive of restrictive agreements.[37]

Attacks against basing-point pricing in steel, cement, and corn oil were carried out in the late 1940s with the aid of evidence indicating artificially contrived support.[38] The circulation of uniform railroad rate books, the policing of shipments to prevent destination diversion or truck hauling, the creation of fictitious rail rates to places not served by railroads, the complete absence of f.o.b. pricing—all these and other facets of the systems revealed that they were not innocently natural competitive developments but conspiracies. Moreover, the products involved—steel, cement, and corn syrup—indicated that such systems are especially pertinent to homogeneous, bulky commodities with relatively high transportation costs. In steel, for instance, transportation averages 10 percent of buyers' total cost.

Official attention to basing-point pricing was rekindled during the late 1970s when the plywood industry was challenged for a scheme that was simultaneously simple and complex.[39] Prior to 1963 all construction plywood was produced from Douglas fir in the Pacific Northwest. The South had abundant yellow pine timber, but the peculiar resins and pitch of yellow pine prevented its bonding into a durable sandwich board. Development of a new glue solved this problem, giving birth to a Southern pine plywood industry. This Southern branch grew prodigiously from one producer in 1963 to twenty-five in 1973, nurtured in part by freight cost advantages vis-à-vis the Northwest industry. Southern plywood could be delivered in Chicago, for example, at half the transport cost of Northwestern plywood, a potential saving of 10 percent to plywood purchasers off their total delivered price. Yet the full potential of this saving was not realized by buyers because the Southern mills priced their plywood as if it had been shipped from a fictitious base mill in Portland, Oregon, discounting slightly to make Southern pine plywood a bit more attractive in price. Georgia-Pacific initiated the system when it expanded beyond the Northwest into the South but declined to offer f.o.b. mill prices at its Southern mills for buyers desirous of providing their own transportation (although G-P did offer f.o.b. prices from its Northwest mills). Subsequent Southern producers, even those without Northwest mills, followed Georgia-Pacific's lead, to the financial disappointment of Southern and Eastern plywood purchasers. Complexities arose, however, because the system was not, strictly speaking, a Portland-base-price-plus-freight system. Moreover, plywood prices vary sharply with variations in construction demand and vary somewhat between producers, giving the appearance of some competition. After trial the Federal Trade Commission concluded that the industry's pricing system illegally restrained price competition and maintained an undue amount of phantom freight for Southern producers. This opinion was reversed on appeal, but the case illustrates that basing-point pricing is more than just a fossil of ancient enforcement.[40]

E. The Professions

The late 1970s saw a flurry of activity in applying Section 1 of the Sherman Act to professional societies—producing cases bearing a hybrid relationship to those concerning trade associations, conscious parallelism, and direct price fixing. The story best begins with one Lewis H. Goldfarb, a government attorney, and his wife Ruth. While arranging to buy a house in Virginia, this young couple discovered that all lawyers charged no less than 1 percent of the price of the house for a routine title search, the fee being derived from a "recommended" minimum fee schedule promulgated by the Fairfax County Bar Association and enforced by the Virginia State Bar. The Goldfarbs sued under Section 1. The defendant bar associations argued that, among other things, lawyers were different from other folks, that they were members of a "learned profession" dedicated to the public's service rather than to profit's call, not in trade or commerce at all, and therefore exempt from the Sherman Act. Unconvinced, the trial court decided against the bar associations.

At this point we are treated to an intriguing spectacle. Defense counsel advised the bars not to appeal, urging them to cut their losses and settle quietly. But the lawyers being sued by a lawyer did not take their lawyer's advice and appealed anyway. When the case reached the lawyers on the Supreme Court, they found for lawyer Goldfarb. They found the fee schedule to be "a fixed, rigid price floor" rather than an advisory aid to attorneys. Furthermore, as for the "learned profession" exemption, they could not "find support for the proposition that Congress intended any such sweeping exclusion." In a bit of obvious understatement, Chief Justice Burger noted that the practice of law had a "business aspect" and "plays an important part in commercial intercourse."[41]

The Goldfarbs inspired the FTC and Justice Department to act against "learned professions"

generally even before the Supreme Court ruled on *Goldfarb*. During the summer of 1972, for instance, the American Institute of Certified Public Accountants, the American Institute of Architects, the American Society of Civil Engineers, and the American Society of Mechanical Engineers all agreed under Justice Department prodding to abandon their antibidding strictures. Subsequently, the Federal Trade Commission obtained consent decrees from a number of medical groups that prohibited practices construed as price fixing. These include the American College of Radiology, the American Academy of Orthopedic Surgeons, and the American College of Obstetricians and Gynecologists.[42] When challenged by recalcitrant learned professions, the authorities did not cave in and won, as illustrated by *U. S.* v. *National Society of Professional Engineers,* which carried the high court in 1978 (and which we mentioned earlier when discussing per se rules).[43]

Furthermore, professional society restraints other than price fixing have come under official and private attack. A common restraint on competition has been the prohibition of price advertising or *all* advertising. Lee Benham demonstrated the anticompetitive effect of such restrictions when in the early 1960s he compared the retail prices of eyeglasses in states that legally restricted optometrists' advertising and retail prices in states that had few or no restrictions on advertising. Comparing the most and least restrictive states, he found average prices of $37.48 and $17.98, respectively, a 100 percent difference.[44] Similarly, John Cady analyzed state restrictions on pharmacists' price advertising. Comparing the retail prices of ten representative prescription drugs across states, he found that prohibitions of price advertising *raised* prices an average of 4.3%.[45] The FTC has moved against such restrictions by optometrists, pharmacists, doctors, dentists, and lawyers but not always with complete success. There are intervening complexities, such as the fact that many such restrictions are *expressly* imposed by state laws rather than merely suggested or permitted, immunizing them to some degree from federal attack.[46] In *Bates* v. *State Bar of Arizona* (1977) for instance, the U. S. Supreme Court held that the Sherman Act could not nullify a ban on advertising by lawyers because that ban had been expressly commanded by state authorities.[47]

Even so, such restraints may be shattered by other means, and the *Bates* majority broke the advertising ban for violating the Constitution's first amendment. Free speech includes commercial speech, apparently. And we now see lawyers pitching on TV right along with the brewers and soapers. More substantive results have come in dramatic reductions in legal fees for many routine services. In Phoenix, for instance, where *Bates* originated, the going rate for an uncontested divorce went from $350 before *Bates* to between $150 and $200 after *Bates*. And legal name changes in Manhattan dropped from $150 to $75.[48]

In 1990, fifty-seven private universities came under intense investigation by the Justice Department for the way they set tuitions and awarded financial aid. Included in the inquiry were such elite schools as Harvard, Princeton, Cornell, Yale, and the rest of the Ivy League. Regarding tuition Christopher Daly wrote the following:

> A key piece of evidence may be a memo written at Wesleyan University in the spring of 1988, when students were upset about a pending tuition hike. To calm protests and put the increase in context, Wesleyan released a confidential memo, written well before other schools also announced increased rates. The unsigned document . . . predicted forthcoming tuition rates at six elite colleges within one percentage point.[49]

Regarding financial aid, so-called Overlap meetings had been held since the 1950s. At the meetings, school officials collectively reviewed the financial information of prospective students who had been accepted at more than one university. As a result, financial aid offers from these overlap universities tended to be remarkably uniform for any one student.

The universities defended themselves against the resulting suit by pointing to their nonprofit status. Yet, in the end, all but one settled out of court, promising improved future behavior (the one exception being MIT).

IV. Assessment

Almost all U. S. economists and antitrust practitioners—conservative and liberal alike—support our vigorous policy against collusive restraints of trade. During the early years of the conservative Reagan Administration, cases against conspirators more than doubled (due mainly to many dozens that arose in just one industry—highway construction). At the same time, antitrust actions in all other areas fell roughly 75 percent. Substantial economic evidence indicates the wisdom of attacking conspiracies, for it shows that antitrust enforcement in this area has desirable effects. Using data on price-cost margins for 288 firms in 1970, Robert Feinberg found that those indicted in previous years had price-cost margins 2 percent lower than those not indicted.[50] A more elaborate study by Choi and Philippatos produced similar findings.[51] It seems, then, that antitrust action against colluders does have a deterrent effect. Indictments instill more competition into pricing.

Summary

All court trials and government hearings are stenographically recorded and transcribed. In 1980 it was revealed that five companies performing these services had been rigging bids for government contracts for nearly twenty years, covering more than $30 million worth in business. Guilty pleas and fines were extracted from the conspirators.[52]

Thus, price fixing goes on almost daily, even under the government's nose, by businesses that could not be better informed about the law. The heart of the law in this context is Section 1 of the Sherman Act which prohibits "contract, combination, or conspiracy in restraint of trade." This language gains potency through application of a per se rule, wherein motives, economic conditions, and the like are of no account. Violation is established merely by proof that the offending conduct actually occurred, in particular, explicit price fixing, market allocation, bid rigging, or collective boycott. Clear-cut offenses may now be punished by harsh criminal remedies. In addition, civil proceedings raise liability for single damages to the government and treble damages to private parties. Although more ominous penalties now threaten the guilty than before, the population of offenders has apparently not diminished much.

Despite the per se rule, there are some gray areas where shadows of uncertainty complicate matters. In regard to price fixing, trade association information exchange programs pose particular problems. Information exchanges can invigorate or deflate competition, depending on their characteristics and surrounding circumstances. Those with restrictive elements, such as prenotification of price changes, or those housed in tight-knit oligopolistic structures stand exposed to official attack. Conscious parallelism creates related difficulties because behavioral uniformity may or may not indicate illegal conspiracy. A rule has emerged, however. Conscious parallelism *alone* escapes. Conscious parallelism that is coupled with *additional evidence* of collusion does not escape. The plus factors include elaborate basing-point pricing, exchanges of information, artificial standardization of product, and predatory pricing.

An area that represents a hybrid of the factors is restraints on professional societies. Protected for many years by appearances of state sanction and questions of commercial definition, the learned professions have experienced an upheaval from application of the Sherman Act. Strictures on pricing conduct and advertising in particular have been loosened or destroyed, bringing greater competition into the lives of doctors, dentists, pharmacists, lawyers, optometrists, engineers, and accountants.

Questions and Exercises for Chapter 6

1. It can be argued that explicit price fixing arises most commonly when structural conditions are neither so uncompetitive as to allow tacit collusion nor so intensely competitive as to preclude collusion altogether. Why? (Hint: focus on the *need* to collude to achieve join profit maximization and the *ability* to collude at all.)
2. Compare *Socony-Vacuum* and the electrical equipment conspiracies in facts, issues, and outcomes.
3. What evidence would you need to prosecute a case of illegal collusion? What evidence would you *not* need?
4. Are criminal penalties appropriate to per se offenses? Would they be appropriate to rule of reason offenses?
5. Would identical bids verify collusion? Would nonidentical bids disprove collusion?
6. How would you resolve the problem of pass-through damages?
7. Why can basing-point pricing be considered a plus factor in moving parallelism across the line of illegality?
8. What was the importance of *Goldfarb?*
9. How would you defend the electrical equipment cartel under a rule of reason?

Appendix to Chapter 6: Oligopolistic Interdependence

The incentive (and ability) to collude instead of compete is most easily seen as it relates to one structural variable—market share (and its corollary, concentration). Whereas a purely competitive firm and a monopolist each face one demand curve (shown earlier in Figures 2–4 and 2–8), an oligopolist may see two demand curves, as shown in Figure 6–2. The oligopolist firm might perceive either one or portions of both of these demand curves, depending on what assumptions it makes concerning its rivals' behavior. If the firm assumes that its rivals will follow any price change it makes up or down from P_0, which is the going price, then it will consider the followship demand, FF', the applicable demand curve. In contrast, the nonfollowship demand curve, NN', is based on the assumption that rivals in the market do *not* follow the price changes of the firm depicted but instead leave their prices unchanged at P_0. The elasticity of FF' is much lower than the elasticity of NN' at point S because the followship in FF' leaves mar-

ket share for this firm unchanged. The added sales from a price cut or lost sales from a price increase along FF' derive solely from sale variations at marketwide level. In contrast, price changes that are *not* followed cause *shifts* of customers among firms as well as marketwide sales variations—a shift away from rivals toward this firm if price is cut below P_0 or a shift toward rivals away from this firm price is raised above P_0. Hence NN' is more elastic than FF'.

Structure, as measured primarily by market share, enters the story by affecting two things—(1) the extent to which these two demand curves diverge, and (2) the assumption the firm actually makes about followship and nonfollowship (that is, the "visibility" of the curves). Regarding point (1) a firm with a very large market share confronts curves that are fairly close. For example, an unfollowed price cut by a firm already having 90 percent of the market would gain very little added sales from rivals (reflected in S toward N') as compared to the marketwide added sales (reflected in S toward F'). Small firms, in contrast, can experience wide swings in sales due to shifts in share as compared to marketwide developments, so NN' for them diverges substantially from FF' and is highly elastic. Regarding point (2), visibility, large firms tend to see FF' more clearly than NN', whereas small firms see NN' more clearly than large firms do. A price cut by a large firm is, for example, more noticeable among its rivals and more likely to be actually followed than a price cut by a small firm.

In short, firms with large market shares tend to see inelastic demand curves (like FF'), whereas firms with small shares tend to see elastic demand curves (like NN'). A middle-sized firm might see a mix—SN for price increases and SF' for price decreases—thereby producing a kinked demand curve. Because elasticities are crucial to what happens to total revenue (and therefore profit) in the event of a price change, these diverse views influence price behavior. A price *decrease* increases total revenue if elastic-

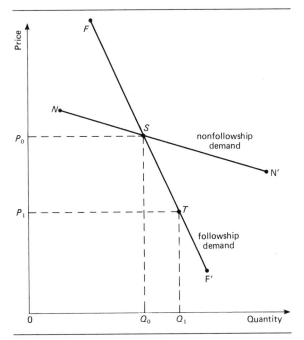

Figure 6–2
Oligopolistic Interdependence and the Incentive to Collude

ity is high (greater than 1) but decreases total revenue if elasticity is low (less than 1).

Visually compare total revenue OP_0SQ_0 with total revenue OP_1TQ_1 on the inelastic followship demand of Figure 6–2 to fully appreciate this. Conversely, a price *increase* decreases total revenue if elasticity is high but increases total revenue if elasticity is low. Thus, a market comprised of only large firms (i.e., tight oligopoly) will have members who shun price decreases and who appreciate the profitability of collusive price increases because they tend to see demand curves like FF'. Each firm foresees the probability that if it cuts price, its rivals will also cut prices to preserve market shares. Each firm then foresees that price cuts will not yield greater profits through relatively greater quantity sales. Rather, each anticipates lower profits from the lower revenues associated with lower prices on fairly constant sales.

On the other hand, a market comprised entirely of relatively small firms will have members who are enticed to cut price and who are hesitant to raise price. Markets of mixed, small and large composition may include those who are trying to collude plus a lot of "cheaters" who try to probe their elastic nonfollowship demand curves with price cuts below cartel-imposed levels. Secrecy may encourage price cutting because it curbs followship.

The influence of other structural features may be analyzed in similar fashion. If, for instance, sales are lumpy, as they are for airplanes and pipeline steel, price shading is encouraged because a small cut can create enormous sales. If overall market demand is highly elastic, the FF' curve will likewise be elastic, and collusion will be difficult as even large firms will be drawn into price competition.

Notes

1. Lawrence A. Sullivan, *Handbook of the Law of Antitrust* (St. Paul, MN: West Publishing, 1977), p. 166.

2. *National Society of Professional Engineers* v. *U. S.* 434 U. S. 679, at 692 (1978).

3. Ibid.

4. F. M. Scherer, *Industrial Market Structure and Economic Performance,* 2nd ed. (Chicago: Rand McNally, 1980), p. 502.

5. Corwin D. Edwards, *Cartelization in Western Europe* (Washington, DC: U. S. Department of State, 1964), pp. 37–38.

6. *Broadcast Music, Inc.* v. *Columbia Broadcasting System, Inc.,* 441 U. S. 1 (1979).

7. *NCAA* v. *Board of Regents of the University of Oklahoma,* 468 U. S. 85 (1984). For further discussion of this and related cases, see Donald L. Beschle, "What, Never? Well, Hardly Ever," *Hastings Law Journal* (March 1987): 471–515.

8. 434 U. S. 679 (1978).

9. Ibid., p. 695. On the other hand, the court softened its line a bit in a recent, rather unique private case involving the collective representation of copyright holders in what is called "blanket licensing." *Broadcast Music, Inc.* v. *Columbia Broadcasting System, Inc.,* 441 U. S. 1 (1979).

10. *Northern Pacific Railway* v. *U. S.,* 356 U. S. 1, 5 (1958).

11. Others of note: 28 cases of kickbacks, bribery, or illegal rebates, 21 instances of illegal political contributions, and 11 cases of fraud. Only domestic cases were included; "the list would have been longer had it included foreign bribes and kickbacks." *Fortune* (December 1, 1980), p. 57.

12. See *Washington Post,* 6 June 1971; and *Fortune,* December 1969.

13. *Business Week,* June 2, 1975, p. 48.

14. For more on penalties see K. G. Elzinga and W. Breit, *The Antitrust Penalties: A Study in Law and Economics* (New Haven, CT: Yale University Press, 1976).

15. *Addyston Pipe and Steel Company* v. *U. S.,* 175 U. S. 211 (1899).

16. *U. S.* v. *Socony-Vacuum Oil Co.,* 310 U. S. 150 (1940).

17. This section draws from R. G. M. Sultan, *Pricing in the Electrical Oligopoly, Vol. 1* (Cambridge, MA: Harvard University Press, 1974); C. C. Walton and F. W. Cleveland, Jr., *Corporations on Trial: The Electrical Cases* (Belmont, CA: Wadsworth, 1964); and R. A. Smith, *Corporations in Crisis* (Garden City, NY: Anchor Books, 1966), Chapters 5 and 6.

18. Sultan, *Pricing in Electrical Oligopoly,* p. 39.

19. *Ibid.,* Sultan is the industry's best defender.

20. *Ibid.,* p. 85, 210, 273; D. F. Lean, J. D. Ogur, and R. P. Rogers, *Competition and Collusion in Electrical Equipment Markets,* Staff Report, Federal Trade Commission (July 1982).

21. For an interesting account of the folding carton offenses see J. Sonnenfeld and P. L. Lawrence, *Harvard Business Review* (July–Aug. 1978): 145–157. See also *Forbes* (June 25, 1979): 33–36.

22. For details see June H. Taylor and Michael D.

Yokell, *Yellowcake: The International Uranium Cartel* (New York: Pergamon, 1979), Geoffrey Rothwell, "Market Coordination by the Uranium Oxide Industry," *Antitrust Bulletin* (Spring 1980): 233–268, and U. S. Congress, House, Subcommittee on Oversight and Investigations of the Committee on Interstate and Foreign Commerce, *International Uranium Cartel,* Hearings Vols. 1 and 2, 95th Congress, 1st Sess. (1977).

23. Leading cases in this regard include *American Banana Co.* v. *United Fruit Co.,* 213 U. S. 347 (1909); *U. S.* v. *Pacific & Arctic Ry. & Nav. Co.,* 228 U. S. 87 (1913); and *U. S.* v. *Sisal Sales Corp.,* 274 U. S. 268 (1927).

24. *Wall Street Journal,* 5 June 1978, p. 2.

25. *Illinois Brick Co.* v. *Illinois* 431 U. S. 720 (1977).

26. *Hanover Shoe, Inc.* v. *United Shoe Machinery Corp.,* 382 U. S. 481 (1968).

27. For the answers of others see Robert G. Harris and Lawrence A. Sullivan, "Passing on the Monopoly Overcharge: A Comprehensive Policy Analysis," *University of Pennsylvania Law Review* (December 1979): 269–360 and the references therein; U. S. Senate, Committee on the Judiciary, *Antitrust Enforcement Act of 1979, S. 300,* Hearings, 96th Congress, 1st Sess. (1979); plus G. J. Werden and Marius Schwartz, "*Illinois Brick* and the Deterrence of Antitrust Violations," Antitrust Division EPO Discussion Paper (July 1983).

28. *Business Week,* June 2, 1975, p. 48.

29. *American Column and Lumber Co. et al.* v. *United States,* 257 U. S. 377 (1921).

30. *United States* v. *Container Corp. of America et al.,* 393 U. S. 333 (1969). For a related case see *United States* v. *United States Gypsum Co. et al.,* 438 U. S. 422 (1978).

31. Clair Wilcox, *Public Policies Toward Business,* 3rd ed. (Homewood, IL: Irwin, 1966), p. 129.

32. Sullivan, *Handbook,* p. 315.

33. *Theatre Enterprises, Inc.* v. *Paramount Film Distributing Corp.,* 346 U. S. 537 (1954).

34. D. F. Turner, "The Definition of Agreement Under the Sherman Act: Conscious Parallelism and Refusals to Deal," *Harvard Law Review* (February 1962), pp. 655–706; and R. A. Posner, *Antitrust Law, An Economic Perspective* (Chicago: University of Chicago Press, 1976), pp. 62–70.

35. *C-O Two Fire Equip. Co.* v. *United States,* 197 F. 2d 489 (9th Cir.) cert. denied 344 U. S. 892 (1952); *Pevely Dairy Co.* v. *United States,* 178 F. 2d 363 (8th Cir.), cert. denied 339 U. S. 492 (1950).

36. Sullivan, *Handbook,* p. 318.

37. D. D. Haddock theorizes that basing-point pricing is the result of innocent competition, not collusion. "Basing-Point Pricing: Competitive vs. Collusive Theories," *American Economic Review* (June 1982): 289–306. However, his theory is refuted by the historical record. The Pittsburgh Plus system was collusively established to curb price competition. See W. T. Hogan, *Economic History of the Iron and Steel Industry of the United States* (Lexington, MA: Lexington Books, 1971), pp. 1095–1101. Also, until the Supreme Court relaxed its standards of proof in

FTC vs. *Cement Institute* (1948), the FTC successfully challenged a number of basing-point systems by proving the presence of collusive agreements. See Alan M. Anderson, "Conscious Parallelism in the Use of Delivered Pricing Systems," *Cornell Law Review* (vol. 66, 1981): 1202.

38. *Corn Products Refining Company* v. *Federal Trade Commission,* 324 U. S. 726 (1945); *FTC* v. *Cement Institute,* 333 U. S. 683 (1948); *Triangle Conduit and Cable Co.* v. *FTC,* 168 F. 2d 175 (7th Cir. 1948). In *Cement* price uniformity was strikingly illustrated when each of eleven companies, bidding for a 6,000 barrel government order in 1936, submitted sealed bids of $3.286854 per barrel.

39. For details see Samuel M. Loescher, "Economic Collusion, Civil Conspiracy, and Treble Damage Deterrents: The Sherman Act Breakthrough with Southern Plywood," *The Quarterly Review of Economics and Business* (Winter 1980): 6–35.

40. *Boise Cascade Corp.* v. *Federal Trade Commission,* 637 F. 2d 573 (9th Cir. 1980).

41. *Lewis H. Goldfarb* v. *Virginia State Bar et al.,* 421 U. S. 773 (1975).

42. The groups did not set prices directly but used an indirect formula called a "relative value scale." The scale specified comparative values in nonmonetary units, such as operation X was 2.5 times operation Y. These values, however, were convertible into dollar amounts by application of a "dollar conversion factor."

43. *National Society of Professional Engineers* v. *U. S.* 435 U. S. 679 (1978).

44. Lee Benham, "The Effect of Advertising on the Price of Eyeglasses," *Journal of Law & Economics* (October 1972): 337–352.

45. John F. Cady, "An Estimate of the Price Effects of Restrictions on Drug Price Advertising," *Economic Inquiry* (December 1976): 493–510.

46. The key case here is *Parker* v. *Brown,* 317 U. S. 341 (1943). For discussion see S. Paul Posner, "The Proper Relationship Between State Regulation and the Federal Antitrust Laws," 49 *New York University Law Review* (1974): 693–739; J. H. Young and A. F. Troy, "Federal Trade Commission Preemption of State Regulation: A Reevaluation," 12 *Suffolk University Law Review* (1978): 1248–1281.

47. *Bates* v. *State Bar of Arizona,* 433 U. S. 350 (1977). But see also *Cantor* v. *Detroit Edison Co.,* 428 U. S. 579 (1976).

48. *Wall Street Journal* (18 October 1978), p. 1. See also *Wall Street Journal* (31 July 1980), pp. 1, 9. The ambivalence of government policy should be obvious here. On the one hand we have the FTC and Justice Department attempting to instill the healthy upheavals of competition, while on the other hand we have states curbing competition through their "regulation" of professions. Over 1,500 state licensing boards provide more or less protective umbrellas for dog trainers, landscapers, doctors, funeral directors, and so on indefinitely. See Kenneth J. Meier, *Regulation: Politics, Bureaucracy, and Economics* (New York: St. Martin's Press, 1985), pp. 175–201.

49. Christopher Daly, "The College Tuition Caper,"

Washington Post, National Weekly Edition (April 16–22, 1990), pp. 9–10.

50. Robert M. Feinberg, "Antitrust Enforcement and Subsequent Price Behavior," *Review of Economics and Statistics* (November 1980): 609–612.

51. D. Choi and G. C. Philippatos, "Financial Con-

sequences of Antitrust Enforcement," *Review of Economics and Statistics* (August 1983): 501–506. See also M. K. Block, F. C. Nold, and J. G. Sidak, "The Deterrent Effect of Antitrust Enforcement," *Journal of Political Economy* (June 1981): 429–445.

52. *Wall Street Journal,* 9 June 1980, p. 16.

Chapter 7

Monopolization: Power and Intent

Every day in our lives monopoly takes its toll.
— *Senator Estes Kefauver*

P ractically everything about monopolization is big. The cases are big. The stakes are big. And chapters written about it are big.

We begin by exploring the wording of the Sherman Act and its rule of reason interpretation. Next we trace the history of monopolization law through three eras: (1) 1890–1940, the era of dastardly deeds, (2) 1945–1970, the era of *Alcoa,* and (3) 1970 to the present, an era of refinement and retreat.

I. The Sherman Act: Section 2

A. The Rule of Reason

Section 2 of the Sherman Act declares:

> Every person who shall monopolize, or attempt to monopolize, or combine or conspire with any other person or persons, to monopolize any part of the trade or commerce among the several States, or with foreign nations, shall be deemed guilty of a felony.

Although Section 2 covers those who "combine or conspire" to monopolize, it is primarily concerned with the activities and structural conditions of single firms. Having said that, we have not said it all. Why the word *monopolize?* Why not *monopoly?* What is the test of monopolization? How large a market share is required? What is meant by a "part of trade or commerce"?

A simple summary of answers to these questions might seem feasible. The Sherman Act is, after all, over 100 years old, and several hundred cases have been brought by the Justice Department under Section 2. Most issues, it would seem, should be settled now. Unfortunately, they are not. Judicial personnel, economic knowledge, political philosophies, and business practices change over time, much as fashion changes. Even more significant, the wording of the statute is vague enough to invoke extensive judgment, opinion, and even hunch.

A Sherman Act Section 2 violation is not as clear-cut as shoplifting or murder. Pricefixing is similar to these crimes in that, under Section 1, it is a per se offense. Just as one can be caught in the act of shoplifting, so a group of competitors can be caught in a smoke-filled room conspiring to raise their prices. But monopolizers cannot be caught in the act. They are never really caught at all. They are accused and judged by a "rule of reason." The result is drawn-out deliberations. Trials lasting many years are not unheard of, and in one case more than 1,200 witnesses testified.

The crime of monopolization cannot be established without proof of two factors: (1) substantial market power, and (2) intent. As Justice William Douglas wrote in the *Grinnell* case, the offense of monopoly "has two elements: (1) the possession of monopoly power in the relevant market and (2) willful acquisition or maintenance of that power . . ."[1] Reason is exercised to establish both elements. In appraising monopoly **power,** the courts have considered barriers to entry of various kinds. Profits, too, have come under review. The one index of monopoly power consistently receiving greatest attention, however, is the market share of the accused. Indeed, although the Supreme Court has defined monopoly power as "the power to control prices or exclude competition," it has acted as if the "existence of such power ordinarily may be inferred from the predominant share of the market." (*Grinnell* again.) In this interpretation, reason must be called upon to answer two key questions: What is the relevant market? What market share is sufficient to establish unlawful power?

B. Market Definition: Power Question 1

Section 2 refers to "any part of trade or commerce," a phrase now taken to mean "relevant market." Unfortunately, markets do not have bright-line boundaries as do nations or conti-

nents. Their borders are often more like rubber, susceptible to compression or expansion by the forces of argument and evidence. This quality is perhaps best appreciated by considering some of the many factors that influence market determination.[2]

1.   PRODUCT MARKET
The product itself is one issue.

a. *The physical characteristics of products:* Blade razors and electric razors may constitute different markets despite their similar end uses.

b. *Distinct customers or end uses of products:* Money is money, but commercial banks and finance companies may occupy different loan markets because finance company loans, in contrast to bank loans, tend to go to relatively high-risk borrowers for such purposes as debt consolidation.

c. *Cross-elasticity of demand:* If price changes for books have no impact on the demand for phonograph records, and vice versa, books and records cannot be considered close substitutes in the eyes of consumers.

d. *The absolute level of product prices, apart from consideration of cross-elasticities:* First-run motion picture theaters might comprise a separate market because they command a substantial price premium relative to subsequent-run theaters.

e. *Unique production facilities or supply elasticities:* Aluminum ingots made from scrap might be excluded from the market for aluminum ingots made from bauxite, because scrap has a low price elasticity of supply.

f. *Industry recognition or firm behavior:* The scope of trade association membership, the nature of a firm's internal organization, the rivalries revealed in competitors' advertising, and the classifications used to record and report economic data may be helpful in delineating market boundaries.

2. GEOGRAPHIC MARKET

Some of the foregoing may guide delineation of geographic markets (as when price levels vary markedly from spot to spot), but the following more typically signal regional range.[3]

a. *Transportation costs:* If high relative to product value, transportation costs tend to limit geographic scope.

b. *Legal barriers:* Tariffs and quotas may exclude foreign competition. Likewise, states may impose legal restrictions inhibiting full-fledged interstate competition.

c. *Product differentiation:* Localized product differentiation may cause a narrower geographic scope than otherwise.

The diversity of judgments the relevant market has provoked may be illustrated by two contrasting cases.

In *Du Pont* (1956) a majority of the Supreme Court defined the market broadly to include *all* flexible packaging materials (cellophane, foil, pliofilm, polyethylene, and so on) instead of merely cellophane, which Du Pont dominated.[4] The decisive argument for the court's majority was cross-elasticity of demand, as may be seen from the following opinion:

> If a slight decrease in the price of cellophane causes a considerable number of customers of other flexible wrappings to switch to cellophane, it would be an indication that a high cross-elasticity of demand exists between them; that the products compete in the same market. The court below held that the "great sensitivity of customers in the flexible packaging markets to price or quality changes" prevented Du Pont from possessing monopoly control over price. . . . We conclude that cellophane's interchangeability with other materials mentioned suffices to make it a part of this flexible packaging material market.[5]

Although Du Pont produced 75 percent of all cellophane sold in the United States, this amounted to only 14 percent of all "flexible packaging." Hence, the broad definition made a big difference, and Du Pont won acquittal.

Three dissenting justices had doubts. They felt that cellophane was unique. Cellophane's price, in particular, had been two to seven times higher than that of many comparable materials between 1924 and 1950. Yet during this period "cellophane enjoyed phenomenal growth," *more* growth than could be expected "if close substitutes were available at from one seventh to one half cellophane's price." Furthermore, they thought cross-elasticity was low, not high. The price of cellophane fell substantially whereas other prices remained unchanged. Indeed, "during the period 1933–1946 the prices for glassine and waxed paper actually increased in the face of a 21% decline in the price of cellophane." If substantial "shifts of business" due to "price sensitivity" had in fact occurred, producers of these rival materials would have had to follow cellophane's price down lest they lose sales.[6]

Ten years later, in the *Grinnell* case a majority of the Court spoke as the minority did in *Du Pont*. They defined the market narrowly to include only "accredited central station protective services" (whereby a client's property is wired for burglaries and fires, signals of which are then sent electronically to a continuously manned central station accredited by insurance underwriters). Other means of property protection were excluded from the relevant market for various reasons:

> Watchmen service is far more costly and less reliable. Systems that set off an audible alarm at the site of a fire or burglary are cheaper but often less reliable. They may be inoperable without anyone's knowing it . . . Proprietary systems that a customer purchases and operates are available, but they can be used only by a very large business or by government. . . . And, as noted, insurance companies generally allow a greater reduction in premiums for accredited central station service than for other types of protection.[7]

Because Grinnell had 87 percent of the market as defined, the court could not let it off the hook like an undersized trout. Grinnell suffered some dismemberment.

C. Market Share: Power Question 2

The cases cited indicate that a market share of 14 percent does not amount to illegal monopoly but 87 percent does. What about the area in between? What market share makes an illegal monopoly? In two major cases, the Supreme Court ruled that 64 percent of the farm machinery industry and 50 percent of the steel industry did not amount to monopoly. An influential appeals court judge, Learned Hand, once expressed the opinion that, although any percentage over 90 "is enough to constitute a monopoly; it is doubtful whether sixty or sixty-four per cent would be enough; and certainly thirty-three per cent is not."[8] For these several reasons, the consensus seems to hold that market shares below 60 percent lie snugly beneath the court's reach. And even 70 or 75 percent may manage to escape its grasp.

Notice, this means that *relative* size, not absolute size, is the focus. Famous firms, huge in absolute size (like General Motors and Mobil Oil), may elude attack because their market shares are less than awesome, their markets being also huge. On the other hand, unknown firms, rather small in absolute size (like Griffith Amusement Company and Grinnell Corporation), may be challenged because they are giants relative to their markets.

D. Intent

Actually, there is even more uncertainty than the foregoing figures suggest. The issue of **intent** is also important. Generally speaking, there is a trade-off between the market share and the degree of intent the prosecuting attorneys must prove to win a guilty verdict. A clear-cut case of 95 percent market share would now probably run afoul of the law with little proof of intent. Conversely, intent would gain importance when a market share of less than 60 percent was involved.

Indeed, it will be recalled that Section 2 forbids mere *attempts* to monopolize as well as monopolization itself. Although the scope of this offense is somewhat unclear, it seems safe to say that the requirements for proving a charge of attempt are now much more rigorous with respect to intent than they are in cases of pure monopolization. Traditionally, proof of an attempt to monopolize requires two elements: (1) a *specific intent* to monopolize and (2) a *dangerous probability of success*.[9] The requirement of specific intent—such as would be shown by clearly anticompetitive acts like blatant predatory pricing, coercive refusals to deal, sabotage, and gross misrepresentation—arises because in this context the monopolization is not actually achieved. Without indications of specific intent, a court could not be sure that monopolization was what the defendant had in mind. Moving beyond attempts to situations where monopoly has been achieved, only "general" intent need be proved because any specific intent is then largely manifest in the end result.[10]

Use of the word *monopolize* in the Sherman Act (rather than *monopoly*) implies that simple possession of a large market share is not itself frowned on, at least not enough to earn a conviction. An illegality requires more: some positive drive, some purposeful behavior, some intent to seize and exert power in the market. Only a moment's reflection reveals the wisdom of this policy. What of the innovator whose creativity establishes a whole new industry, occupied at first by his firm only? What of the last surviving firm in a dying industry? What of the superefficient firm that underprices everyone else through genuine economies of scale or some natural advantages of location? What of a large market share gained purely by competitive skill? To pounce on these monopolies would have to be regarded as cruel (since they are actually innocent), stupid (since it would be punishing good performance), and irrational (since no efficient structural remedy, such as dissolution, could ensue). Thus, a finding of intent to monopolize is essential, even though it may not be easy.

In Section 2 cases, a monopolist's intent is not determined by subjecting its executives to lie detector tests or psychoanalysis. Intent emerges from the firm's particular acts or its general course of action. With this statement, we come to the point at which, for pedagogical purposes, three more or less distinctive eras of Section 2 interpretation may be distinguished, depending on what the courts have required of plaintiffs to prove intent.

- *1890–1940:* In the early days, the Supreme Court usually held that an offensive degree of intent could be established only with evidence of abusive acts. This could be called the era of leniency because "well-behaved" monopolists with as much as 90 percent of the market were welcomed if not cherished.
- *1945–1970:* The *Alcoa* case of 1945 set a very stringent standard, excusing monopolists only when power was thrust upon them, as if by accident. Little was needed to show offensive intent because "no monopolist monopolizes unconscious of what he is doing."[11]
- *1970–Present:* Most recently the pendulum has swung back toward leniency. A string of lower court decisions gives monopolists spacious room for aggressive, if not abusive, conduct. Still, this era's record is mixed because the Supreme Court has not spoken clearly.

We take up each era successively.

II. The Early Days: 1890–1940

A. An Overview

Before *Alcoa,* the Supreme Court usually held that an offensive degree of intent could be estab-

lished only with evidence of abusive, predatory, or criminal acts. The types of conduct that qualified included the following: (1) predatory pricing, that is, cutting prices below costs on certain products or in certain regions and subsidizing the resulting losses with profits made elsewhere; (2) predatory promotional spending or predatory pricing on "fighting brands" or "bogus independent" firms or on new facilities or new products; (3) physical violence to competitors, their customers, or their products; (4) exaction of special advantages from suppliers, such as railroad rebates; (5) misuse of patents, copyrights, or trademarks; and (6) preclusion of competitive opportunities by refusals to sell, exclusive dealing arrangements, or anticompetitive tie-in sales.

For the most part, this list of predatory tactics is derived from the major early cases listed in Table 7–1. The first five cases mentioned there ended in convictions. The last five ended in acquittals. Notice from the center column that the market shares of the convicted monopolizers are not markedly greater than those of the acquitted firms, although in the latter group there are two with only 50 percent of industry sales. The big difference lies in the next column, where a "Yes" indicates that obviously predatory tactics were used by the defendant and a "No" indicates a fairly clean slate in this regard. With but one exception, those guilty of dirty tricks were also found guilty of monopolizing. Conversely, the "good" trusts managed to get off. The obvious implication must be qualified by the possibility that changes in court personnel could have made some difference, as suggested perhaps by the dates of the decisions in the last column. Another qualification that lessens the strength of the argument is the exclusion of several railroad cases from consideration. Between 1904 and 1922, the Supreme Court decided against three railroad combinations that did not employ predatory practices to gain substantial market shares.[12] Even so, we can buttress the message of Table 7–1 by consulting the court's opinions.

Table 7–1
Major Section 2 Cases, 1911–1927

	Industry	Percentage of the Industry	Predatory Tactics Present?	Date of Final Judgment
I. Unlawful monopolies				
Standard Oil of N. J.	Petroleum	85–90	Yes	1911
American Tobacco Co.	Tobacco products	76–97	Yes	1911
E. I. Du Pont	Explosives	64–100	Yes	1911
Eastman Kodak Co.	Photo equipment	75–80	Yes	1915
Corn Products Refining Co.	Glucose	53	Yes	1916
II. Cases of acquittal				
United Shoe Machinery Co.	Shoe machinery	90	No	1917
American Can Co.	Packers' cans	50	Yes	1916
Quaker Oats Co.	Rolled oats cereal	75	No	1916
U. S. Steel Corp.	Steel	50	No	1920
International Harvester Co.	Harvesters	64	No	1927

Source: Milton Handler, *Trade Regulation*, 3rd ed. (New York: Foundation Press, 1960), pp. 378–379.

B. Standard Oil of New Jersey (1911)

Standard Oil (now Exxon) was the most notorious monopoly of its time. First organized in Ohio in 1870, by 1872 it had acquired all but a few of the three dozen refineries in Cleveland. Additionally, it had garnered complete control of the pipelines running from oil fields to refineries in Cleveland, Pittsburgh, Philadelphia, New York, and New Jersey. Further transportation advantages were gained from the railroads through preferential rates and large rebates. From this strategic footing, Standard Oil was able to force competitors to join the combination or be driven out of business. As a result, the combine grew to control 90 percent of the petroleum industry, a dominance that produced enormous profits. Under legal attack from authorities in Ohio, the company was reorganized in 1899 as Standard Oil of New Jersey, a holding company. The new combine continued to exact preferential treatment from railroads and to cut crude oil supplies to competing refiners. Business espionage,

local price warfare, and the operation of bogus independents were also Standard tactics. As the Supreme Court said, "The pathway of the combination . . . is strewn with the wrecks resulting from crushing out, without regard to law, the individual rights of others."[13]

In writing the Supreme Court's opinion, Chief Justice White emphasized intent, contrasting the tainted history of Standard Oil with what he called "normal methods of industrial development." Thus, by implication, the court acknowledged that power alone was not enough, that monopoly in the concrete was condoned absent the willful drive. In applying this interpretation of Section 2 to the facts of Standard Oil, White said that the combine's merging and acquiring alone gave rise to a *"prima facie* presumption of intent." He went on, however, to state that this *prima facie* presumption was "made conclusive" by considering the rapacious conduct of the New Jersey corporation.

In sum, White gave birth to an infantile form of the rule of reason as we know it today. He found himself "irresistibly driven to the conclusion that the very genius for commercial development and organization which it would seem was manifested from the beginning soon begot an intent and purpose to exclude others . . . by acts and dealings wholly inconsistent with . . . normal methods." Given its context, White's rule of reason came to mean that a monopolist would not be forced to walk the plank unless he had *behaved unreasonably*.

Dissolution of the combine followed, yielding thirty-four separate companies. Historically, these offspring tended to be regionally and vertically specialized—for example, Standard Oil of California (now Chevron), Standard Oil of Ohio (Sohio), Standard Oil of New York (Mobil), Standard Oil of Indiana (American), and Standard Oil of New Jersey (Exxon).[14] With time, they spread into each other's territory to compete.

C. American Tobacco (1911)

The story in tobacco is similar to that in oil except that advertising and promotion were big weapons.[15] The story centers on James Duke, whose power play started in cigarettes, then spread to other branches of the trade. By 1885 Duke had secured 11 to 18 percent of total cigarette sales for his company through an arduous promotional effort. He then escalated ad and promotional outlays to nearly 20 percent of sales, thereby forcing a five-firm merger in 1889 and acquiring 80 percent control of all cigarette sales. His American Tobacco Company grew still further until he held 93 percent of the market in 1899. Coincident with this final gathering of power, cigarette ad expense as a percentage of sales fell to 11 percent in 1894, then to 0.5 percent in 1899. And cigarette profits swelled to 56 percent of sales in 1899.

With these stupendous profits, Duke was able to launch massive predatory campaigns to capture other tobacco markets, which were at the time bigger than that of cigarettes. One measure of this effort is the American Tobacco Company's annual advertising and selling cost as a percentage of sales at crest levels in the target markets—28.9 percent for plug and twist, 24.4 percent for smoking tobacco, 31.7 percent for fine-cut chewing, and 49.9 percent for cigars. Duke even went so far as to introduce deliberately unprofitable "fighting brands," one of which was appropriately called "Battle Ax." Losses ensued; mergers followed; and after the entire industry (except for cigars) was under American's thumb, advertising receded substantially to such relatively peaceful neighborhoods as 4 and 10 percent of sales.

Just before the Supreme Court's ruling against American in 1911, the combine controlled the following shares: smoking tobacco, 76.2 percent; chewing tobacco, 84.4 percent; cigarettes 86.1 percent; snuff, 96.5 percent; cigars 14.4 percent. Stressing the crude behavior of the combine, the court found American's acts unreasonable. Dissolution ensued, creating oligopoly in place of monopoly.[16] Competition improved, but not markedly.

D. United States Steel (1920)

A chain of mergers occurred around the turn of the century, eliminating the independence of 170 steel companies and culminating in the formation of U. S. Steel Corporation in 1901. When formed, this behemoth accounted for 66 percent of all American steel production. Its market power is evident in the fact that U. S. Steel's capitalization was double the market value of the stock of its constituent companies. Still, the corporation's market share dwindled a bit by 1911 when, flush with success in *Standard Oil* and *American Tobacco*, the Justice Department filed suit. Its share fell further, and in 1920 U. S. Steel won acquittal.

In acquitting United States Steel, the Court held that the corporation's 50 percent market share (at the time of the case) did not amount to excessive power, and even if it had amounted to excessive power, the corporation had not abused it: "It resorted to none of the brutalities or tyrannies that the cases illustrate of other combinations." The corporation "did not oppress or coerce its competitors . . . it did not undersell its competitors in some localities by reducing its prices there below those maintained elsewhere, or require its customers to enter into contracts limiting their purchases or restricting them in resale prices; it did not obtain customers by secret rebates . . . there was no evidence that it attempted to crush its competitors or drive them out of the market." In short: "The corporation is undoubtedly of impressive size. . . . But the law does not make mere size an offense, or the existence of unexerted power an offense. It, we repeat, requires overt acts."[17] U. S. Steel was indeed a combination formed by *merger,* but merger was not then considered evidence of intent even though it is obviously an overt act.

Allowing monopoly by merger was no oversight, for in a stinging dissent Justice Day reminds the majority that the Sherman Act expressly bans "combinations" and goes on to argue that the "contention must be rejected that the [U. S. Steel] combination was an inevitable evolution of industrial tendencies compelling union of endeavor." Nevertheless, the view that abusive overt acts were required to prove intent prevailed in this and other opinions of the day.

III. The ALCOA Era: 1945–1970

A. An Overview

Although the *U. S. Steel* interpretation may not have gutted Section 2, it certainly bloodied it a bit. Section 2 lay incapacitated until 1945, when the *Alcoa* decision brought recuperation.[18] In essence, *Alcoa* lengthened the list of intent indications beyond predatory and abusive tactics. According to *Alcoa,* unlawful intent can almost be assumed unless the defendant is a "passive beneficiary" of monopoly power or has had monopoly power "thrust upon" him. To *any* extent

the monopolist reaches out to grasp or strives actively to hold his dominant position, he cannot claim that he has no unlawful intent. This hard line is softened by other language in the opinion that exempts monopoly gained by "superior skill, foresight and industry." Subsequent cases changed the wording to permit monopoly grounded on "a superior product, business acumen or historic accident."[19] But the *Alcoa* interpretation remained intact for nearly three decades.

B. Alcoa (1945)

The Aluminum Company of America provides many interesting economic lessons as well as legal lessons.[20] For more than half a century it dominated all four stages of the United States aluminum industry: (1) bauxite ore mining, (2) conversion of bauxite into aluminum oxide, or alumina, (3) electrolytic reduction of alumina into aluminum ingots, and (4) fabrication of aluminum products, such as cable, foil, pots and pans, sheets, and extrusions. Alcoa's dominance derived mainly from various barriers to entry.

Patents. Until 1886, the processes for extracting pure aluminum were so difficult and costly that it was a precious metal like gold or platinum. In that year, just after graduating from Oberlin College, Charles Hall discovered the electrolytic reduction of alumina into aluminum. His discovery was later duplicated by C. S. Bradley. Alcoa acquired the rights to both patents and thereby excluded potential entrants legally until 1909.

Resources Controlled. Resource limitations also barred entry. Alcoa integrated backward into bauxite mining and electric power, the two key resources for producing aluminum. Although these resources were too plentiful to be fully preempted by a single firm, Alcoa vigorously acquired, developed, and built the lowest-cost sources of each.

Economies of Scale. As if all that were not enough, economies of scale constituted an additional barrier. Of the several stages of the production process, the second stage—conversion of bauxite into alumina—yielded the greatest efficiencies from increased size. Until 1938 there was only *one* alumina plant in the entire United States. The unit costs of a 500,000-ton per year plant embodying 1940 technology were 10 to 20% below the unit costs of a 100,000-ton plant. And it was not until 1942 that United States consumption of alumina topped 500,000 tons. The dire implications for entry into alumina production during that era should be obvious.

Economies were not nearly so pronounced for reduction and fabrication (there being four smelting plants in the United States during the 1930s and a goodly number of fabricators). Nonetheless, the barriers associated with alumina spilled over into these other stages because Alcoa was *vertically integrated*. However efficient a producer of ingot or fabricated products might be, he was ultimately dependent on Alcoa for his raw materials and simultaneously competing with Alcoa as a seller. This puts independents in a precarious position. Alcoa could control the independents' costs *and* selling price. Were Alcoa unkind enough to raise its price of ingot and lower its price of foil, say, the foil fabricators would be in a bind. The price squeeze would pinch the margin between their costs and selling price. Just such squeezes were alleged in 1926 and 1927, when Alcoa reduced the margin between ingot and certain types of aluminum sheet from $0.16 a pound to $0.07 a pound and then kept it there until 1932. Two independent rollers of sheet initiated an antitrust suit that was settled out of court.

The Antitrust Suit. The government lost its antitrust suit at the district court level in 1941 after a three-year trial. The district judge relied heavily on the *U. S. Steel* case of 1920. He felt that mere size, unaccompanied by dastardly deeds, did not violate Section 2. The Supreme Court could not hear the Justice Department's appeal because four court justices disqualified themselves on grounds of prior participation in the case, leaving less than a quorum. However, the New York Circuit Court of Appeals was designated court of last resort for the case. That panel, acting under Judge Learned Hand, decided against Alcoa, thereby reversing the lower court and boldly overturning precedent.[21]

On the question of market power, the circuit court determined that Alcoa controlled over 90 percent of primary aluminum sales in the United States, the other 10 percent being accounted for by imports.[22] "That percentage," Hand said, "is enough to constitute a monopoly." On the issue of intent, the court *rejected* the notion that evil acts must be in evidence. Lacking substantial judicial precedent for this position, the court looked to congressional intent:

> [Congress] did not condone "good trusts" and condemn "bad" ones; it forbade all. Moreover, in so doing it was not necessarily actuated by economic motives alone. It is possible, because of its indirect social or moral effect, to prefer a system of small producers . . . to one in which the great mass of those engaged must accept the direction of a few.

By this interpretation a monopolist could escape only if its monopoly had been "thrust upon it," only if "superior skill, foresight and industry" were the basis for its success. Was this true of Alcoa? The court thought not, emphasizing conditions of entry:

> It would completely misconstrue "Alcoa's" position in 1940 to hold that it was the passive beneficiary of a monopoly. . . . This increase and this continued undisturbed control did not fall undesigned into "Alcoa's" lap. . . . There were at least one or two abortive attempts to enter the industry, but "Alcoa" effectively anticipated and forestalled all competition . . . [by] doubling and redoubling its capacity before others entered the field.

Assistance to Entrants. Today, partly as a result of this decision, Alcoa accounts for less than one-third of all United States aluminum ingot capacity. The government did not bring this about by breaking Alcoa into fragments. Instead, it encouraged new entry into the industry. Shortly after World War II, the government's war plants were sold at bargain-basement prices to Reynolds and Kaiser (two former fabricators). This move alone reduced Alcoa's market share to 50 percent. Later, during the Cold and Korean Wars of the 1950s, the government aided the entry of Anaconda, Harvey, and Ormet. These firms were the beneficiaries of rapid amortization certificates, government-guaranteed construction loans, long-term contracts to supply the government's stockpile of aluminum, and cut-rate government electricity. Changing economic conditions also helped. The demand for aluminum in the United States increased 3000% after 1940 and 1000 percent after 1950. As a consequence, economies of scale shrank to the point at which an alumina plant of minimum efficient scale would account for only about 8 percent of total United States capacity, and an ingot plant of minimum efficient scale would account for only about 3 percent. These developments enabled still further entry.

An interesting assessment of these events was given in 1984 by a prominent Alcoa executive who had been involved in the case. When asked if the case had been in the interest of society, he said, "Definitely. Definitely." He thought that "in the end," it was also in the interest of Alcoa because the new competition improved Alcoa's performance.[23]

C. United Shoe Machinery (1953)

The case of *U. S.* v. *United Shoe Machinery* was tried in 1953, was decided against United Shoe, and was affirmed per curiam by the Supreme Court in 1954.[24] United was found to supply somewhere between 75 and 85 percent of the machines used in boot and shoe manufacturing. Moreover, it was the only machinery producer

offering a full line of equipment. United had many sources of market power, but the following are especially noteworthy:

1. Like Alcoa, United held patents covering the fundamentals of shoe machinery manufacture at the turn of the century. These basic patents had long expired by the 1950s. Still, at the time of the suit, United held 2,675 patents, some of which it had acquired and some of which impeded entry.
2. A logical strategy for a new entrant would have been to start with one or two machine types and then branch out into a more complete line. Indeed, this was the approach of United's major rival, Compo, which specialized in cementing machines. United's answer to the challenge, however, was a discriminatory price policy that fixed a lower rate of return when competition was of major significance and a higher rate of return when competition was weak or nonexistent.
3. United never sold its machines; it only leased them. This policy precluded competition from a secondhand market.
4. Furthermore, the terms of the leases restricted entry into new machinery production. Ten years was the duration of the standard lease. If a lessee wished to return a machine before the end of the ten-year term, he paid a penalty that tapered down from a substantial amount in the early years to a small amount in the later years. If he was returning the machine for replacement, he paid a lower penalty if he took another United machine than if he switched to a rival manufacturer's machine. Moreover, service was tied in. No separate charges were made for repairs and maintenance, with the result that a newly entering firm had to build a service organization as well as manufacturing and marketing capabilities.

On the basis of these facts, the court ruled against United, saying that the "defendant has, and exercises, such overwhelming strength in the shoe machinery market that it controls that market." What is more, "this strength excludes some potential, and limits some actual, competition." Regarding intent, the court conceded that "United's power does not rest on predatory practices." However, United's lease-only system, its restrictive lease clauses, its price discrimination, and its acquisition of patents

> are not practices which can be properly described as the inevitable consequences of ability, natural forces, or law. They represent something more. . . . They are contracts, arrangements, and policies which, instead of encouraging competition based on pure merit, further the dominance of a particular firm. In this sense they are *unnatural* barriers [italics added].

The court ordered United to sell as well as lease its machines, to modify the terms of its leases, and to divest itself of some assets.

Among other cases of the *Alcoa* era, *Grinnell* (1966) is notable for saying that monopolization based on "superior product, business acumen, or historic accident" would not be illegal. Grinnell Corp. did not pass the test.[25]

V. 1970–Present: Revision and Retreat

The *Alcoa* era sputtered to an end during the 1970s and early 1980s. Cases against two giant firms that seemed vulnerable under *Alcoa* standards—IBM and Kodak—were won by the defendants. I say "sputtered to an end," however, for three reasons. First, the Supreme Court did not explicitly decide to make the change; the court has not ruled on a major monopolization case for quite some time. Second, two giant firms, Xerox and AT&T, each had trouble with Section 2 of the Sherman Act, trouble serious enough to indicate that Section 2 remains alive. Finally, Section 2's vitality is revealed in a minor case decided by the Supreme Court in 1985, *Aspen Skiing Company.*

Let's begin discussion of this final era with a glance at Xerox and AT&T. That is followed by details on Kodak, IBM, and Aspen Skiing.

A. Xerox and AT&T

In 1973 the FTC charged Xerox with monopolizing the copier industry, alleging that Xerox controlled 95 percent of the plain-paper copier business and 86 percent of the total market for office copiers. The allegations of offensive conduct paralleled those of *United Shoe Machinery.* That is, Xerox's licensing, pricing, and patent policies were said to exclude competition artificially. Xerox responded by negotiating a settlement in 1975, one that provided for (1) licensing patents on reasonable royalties, (2) supplying know-how to competitors, (3) modifying price policies, and (4) selling as well as leasing copy machines. The consent decree may have helped the entry of Savin, IBM, and others—entries that jolted the industry with new competition.[26]

The American Telephone & Telegraph case was launched by the Justice Department in 1974. Admitting that AT&T's monopoly of most telephone service could be justified by natural economies of scale, the Justice Department claimed that AT&T should not be allowed to extend that monopoly power into contiguous fields where economies were significantly less consequential—equipment manufacturing in particular. The government sought to split AT&T into portions representing regulated natural monopoly activities and *non*regulated, potentially competitive activities. Such a split would prevent AT&T from using its monopoly power in regulated markets to subsidize its operation in unregulated markets, hurting competition in the latter. The suit was settled in early 1982 by a consent decree that caused AT&T to shed its regulated regional phone service companies, leaving a unit comprised of AT&T Long Lines, Bell Laboratories, and Western Electric. Complete review of the case is reserved for Chapter 16.[27]

B. Greater Leniency with Kodak and IBM

To set the scene for Kodak and IBM it may be noted that, despite *Alcoa, United Shoe,* and the other cases of the 1945–1970 era, some uncertainty remained about what kind of conduct proved intent. The uncertainty stemmed from the difficulty of trying to curb monopoly without at the same time squashing business incentive. Indeed, the uncertainty could be seen in the *Alcoa* opinion itself. Tension separates two of Judge Hand's statements: (1) Congress "did not condone 'good trusts' and condemn 'bad' ones; it forbade all;" and yet (2) "The successful competitor, having been urged to compete, must not be turned upon when he wins." This tension, a circuit court complained, "makes the cryptic *Alcoa* opinion a litigant's wishing well, into which, it sometimes seems, one may peer and find nearly anything he wishes."[28]

In 1979, the lower courts began issuing a series of opinions in the *Kodak* and *IBM* cases that stressed the second position. These lower courts exonerated Kodak and IBM of monopolization in major private suits. They found that many allegedly exclusionary practices merely reflected these firms' "superior product, business acumen," or "skill, foresight, and industry"—not the willful maintenance of monopoly power. As one commentator put it, these cases give a monopolist "greater freedom to fight off its competitors." And in so doing, "they invite comparison with the earliest Section 2 cases," which required "overt acts" for proof of intent.[29] Topping things off, a major U.S. government case against IBM was withdrawn in 1982.

We first cover the private suits against Kodak and IBM, then the big *U. S.* v. *IBM* case.

1. KODAK (1979)

Kodak lords it over the photography industry, dominating the manufacture of still cameras, film, and paper used to print color pictures. During the late 1960s and early 1970s its shares

of these markets ranged from 64 to 94 percent. In photofinishing, however, it held about 10 percent.

Berkey is primarily a photofinisher, but between 1966 and 1978 it competed with Kodak in still cameras. Disappointed with its lack of success in still cameras, Berkey sued Kodak for monopolizing the camera and film markets. A jury favored Berkey, but the circuit court of appeals reversed, and the Supreme Court let the reversal stand.[30]

Berkey's claims concerning Kodak's massive dominance were never questioned. As the court put it, "If a finding of monopoly power were all that were necessary to complete a violation of Section 2, our task in this case would be considerably lightened." Berkey's claims concerning intent were severely questioned, however. These claims centered on Kodak's introduction in 1972 of its 110 compact camera *system*. The *system* needs stress because it was more than just a new camera; it included entirely new film (Kodacolor II), film format, and photofinishing. Berkey challenged the introduction of the 110 system, using essentially three arguments:

> *First,* that because Kodak set *de facto* standards for the photography industry, it had a special duty to refrain from surprise innovations and was required to make adequate predisclosure to enable rivals to stay competitive with it; *second,* that the introduction of Kodacolor II as part of the 110 system was not technically necessary for the new camera and was instead a use of Kodak's monopoly power in film to gain a competitive advantage in cameras; and *finally,* that limiting Kodacolor II to the 110 format unlawfully foreclosed competition by other manufacturers in existing formats.[31]

Although rejecting Berkey's arguments the circuit court explicitly rejected *Alcoa's* "thrust upon" standard. Kodak, the court said, may "compete aggressively," even to the point of using its *combined* film and camera capabilities to bolster its faltering camera sales. An integrated business does not "offend the Sherman Act whenever one of its departments benefits from association with a division possessing a monopoly in its own market."[32]

2.   CALCOMP (1979)[33]

In 1969 and 1970 IBM began to suffer substantial competition from new "plug compatible" peripherals manufacturers, or PCMs. By May 1971 the PCMs had 14.5 percent of IBM's disk-drive market and 13.7 percent of its tape-drive market. Moreover, these shares would have been about 20 percent by 1976 had IBM not done something. But IBM did do something. On May 27, 1971, it introduced long-term leases coupled with price reductions of 20 to 35 percent on equipment vulnerable to such competition.

Within the year following, PCM equipment orders were off 44 percent from the previous year, despite deep defensive price cuts by the PCM companies. They lost money for the next two years. For its part, IBM made up its lost revenues by increasing prices in other product lines—central processing units, card equipment, and maintenance services—just two months after the May reductions. These increases varied from 4 to 8 percent on equipment, and some maintenance charges rose 25 percent.

This and related episodes sparked a rash of PCM suits charging IBM with monopolization of peripherals markets.[34] CalComp's suit was typical, and all of CalComp's allegations of IBM wrongdoing were rejected by the circuit court. *First,* IBM's price cuts on peripherals were allegedly predatory, but this claim was rejected because CalComp failed to prove that IBM's prices were below cost. *Second,* CalComp argued that IBM's recoupment with price increases on other products was an unlawful use of IBM's power in the mainframe market. This claim also lost its wheels, however, because *complete* recoupment had not been shown and because rising costs may have justified those price increases (suspicious timing notwithstanding). In language reminiscent of *U. S. Steel,* the court concluded that IBM's conduct was not "*unreasonably* restrictive of competition."

SUMMARY

Kodak and *CalComp* thus offer cover for a monopolist's hard competition. *Berkey's* instructions seem especially solid. Monopolists may innovate significantly improved products without disclosure of trade secrets or provision of other aids to rivals. Monopolists need not restrain their research and development efforts. Furthermore, diversified monopolists may exploit benefits of association among their various divisions insofar as those benefits are based on "more efficient production, greater ability to develop complementary products, reduced transaction costs," and so forth: (*not* including coercive acts like tying).

The clear teaching from *CalComp* is that a monopolist may fend off rivals with price cuts so long as its prices remain profitable—that is, remain above average total cost. Beyond this, *CalComp's* lessons become muddled and even questionable. In particular, the Ninth Circuit Court gave its opinion on a very important issue that was not presented in the facts of *CalComp* when it said that *even deeper* price reductions "down to the point of marginal cost [or average variable cost] are consistent with competition on the merits." This position has since been rejected by the Ninth Circuit Court and other courts of appeal.[35] Because the Supreme Court has not yet spoken clearly on this issue, however, the question of just how deep a monopolist may innocently reduce its prices remains open. This question is important, much debated, and therefore deserving of an Appendix to this chapter.

In any event, *Berkey* and *CalComp* paved the way for Reagan's Assistant Attorney General Baxter, who withdrew the government's big case against IBM even though it had been prosecuted for thirteen years under four presidents before Reagan and was just months away from a district court opinion. This withdrawal was historic.

3. IBM (DISMISSED 1982)[36]

As shown in Figure 7–1, a computer system has numerous components. Unisys, IBM, and the other big companies are called **systems suppliers,** for they produce and market a full line of hardware equipment together with software programs and services to run their systems. A second sector is made up of **plug-compatible** or **peripherals** manufacturers. They produce printers, tape drives, disk drives and other individual items of peripheral equipment that can be plugged into the central system. Third, there is a host of service bureaus, consulting groups, programmers, and leasing firms that deal primarily in services rather than manufacturing. They are often lumped together as **software houses.** Finally, the newest segment of the industry sells **minicomputers.** Responsibility for development of these devices rests not with the huge systems suppliers but with smaller firms like Data General, Hewlett-Packard, and Apple.

IBM's Market Share. Before Baxter, the Justice Department contended that the market should be defined narrowly to include general purpose computers and peripheral products com-

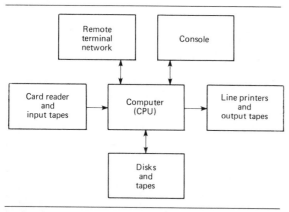

Figure 7–1
Overview of a Computer System

patible with IBM equipment—systems suppliers, essentially. By this reckoning, IBM's annual market share ranged between 68 and 75 percent over the period 1964–1972.[37]

In contrast, IBM argued that the market should include practically everything having to do with computers. Inclusion of all electronic data processing businesses reduced IBM's market share to 33 percent.

IBM's Intent. IBM contended that, even if the 68 to 75 percent figures were accurate, its power derived from superior skill, foresight, and industry. But the historical record is far from clear on this point.

From 1924 IBM has supplied a broad line of business machines. Its early forte was punch card tabulating equipment. In 1935, IBM had under lease 85.7 percent of all tabulating machines, 86.1 percent of all sorting machines, and 82 percent of all punch card installations then used in the United States. IBM did not fully appreciate the computer's potential until 1951, when one of IBM's best customers, the U. S. Census Bureau, accepted delivery of the world's first commercial computer from Univac, a division of Remington Rand (now Unisys). At the time, IBM held 90 percent of the punch card tabulating machine market, and Remington Rand accounted for the remaining 10 percent. Hence, IBM viewed Univac I as a threat to its existence.

Shortly after IBM entered the computer field (delivering its first machine in 1953), two other business machine manufacturers joined IBM and Remington Rand—National Cash Register (NCR) and Burroughs. As it turned out, prior business-machine experience was a crucial determinant of success in computers. IBM's big advantage lay in its accumulation of tabulating machine customers who had vast amounts of data already coded on punch cards, plus a natural interest in any means of rapidly processing them. IBM catered to this group by designing its computers to read their cards. IBM had more than just good contacts, it had a good reputation; and during 1956, "IBM shipped 85.2 percent of the value of new systems, and Remington Rand only 9.7 percent—approximately the same relative shares as then existing in the tabulating machine market."[38]

IBM's "lag-behind-then-recover-quickly" pattern of behavior became commonplace thereafter. Remington Rand and RCA were the first to introduce transistorized computers. Philco introduced the first large-scale solid-state system. Data General was the first with medium-scale integration and complete semiconductor memories. Honeywell and Burroughs were the most innovative with operating systems and compilers. General Electric developed time sharing. And so on. Attempted entry often motivated these efforts. What is more, these efforts nibbled away much of IBM's early market share, but IBM always managed a rebound by duplication. By contrast, many of these innovators have left the industry.

Specific Charges.   On intent, the Justice Department levied a number of specific charges. It alleged that IBM tried to maintain control and to inhibit entry deliberately through a wide variety of questionable marketing, financial, and technical maneuvers. These included the following:

> "Bundling," whereby IBM quoted a *single* price for hardware, software, and related support. (IBM unbundled in 1970.)
>
> "Fighting machines," whereby IBM introduced selected computers with inordinately low prices in those sectors of the industry where its competitors appeared to be on the verge of success.
>
> "Paper machines," whereby IBM tried to dissuade computer users from acquiring or leasing Control Data's 6600 (an advanced, truly remarkable machine) by announcing that IBM would soon have a comparable and perhaps even superior product, when in fact IBM had no such thing.

After reviewing the evidence amassed against IBM, Assistant Attorney General Baxter was not convinced, so he withdrew the suit in January 1982. He said that several of the acts attributed to IBM "may have occurred." But he said the most persuasive instances took place outside the market covered by the lawsuit. He did not think IBM had committed any "serious business improprieties," so the case was "without merit" and the government's chances of winning were "only one in ten thousand."[39]

Several days later Judge Edelstein, who had presided over six years of trial only to be denied the chance to decide the case, was quoted as saying that Mr. Baxter suffered from "myopia and misunderstanding of the antitrust laws and this case specifically." "Even one with a prodigious intellect," Edelstein said, "couldn't be expected to come up with a reasoned evaluation" of the case in the four or five months Mr. Baxter spent studying it.[40]

C. Aspen Skiing Company vs. Aspen Highlands Skiing (1985)

The Reagan Administration not only dropped the government's IBM case; it initiated no monopolization cases of its own. During the preceding 1970–1980 period, an average of five such cases were filed each year. The adverse IBM decision and an inactive Justice Department made it seem as if Section 2 was dying as it approached its one-hundredth birthday. However, a private suit decided by the Supreme Court in 1985 let everyone know that Section 2 was still alive—*Aspen Skiing Company* vs. *Aspen Highlands Skiing*.[41]

Aspen Skiing Company (Ski Company) was found to have monopolized the market for downhill skiing services in Aspen, Colorado—a market that it had previously shared with a much smaller rival, Aspen Highlands Skiing Company (Highlands). Ski Company drove Highlands to the brink of bankruptcy in a rather unique way. Of four major mountain ski facilities in Aspen, Colorado, Ski Company owned three and Highlands owned one. For many years the two companies had an arrangement whereby skiers could purchase six-day tickets usable each day at any of the four facilities. It was a package deal for the economic convenience of vacationing skiers who wanted to try a variety of slopes during their stay. The six-day tickets were quite popular, and the two companies divided the revenues according to statistics on actual usage of the several slopes. Before the 1977–1978 ski season, Ski Company, the dominant firm with three of the four facilities, tried to force the smaller Highlands to accept a much lower percentage of the revenues than Highlands would have been awarded by actual usage. Highlands refused to bow, so Ski Company took the offense. Ski Company stopped selling the all-Aspen six-day tickets and instead sold six-day tickets featuring only its own three ski slopes. It also took added actions that made it extremely difficult for Highlands to market its own multiarea package to replace the previous all-Aspen pass. Highlands' market share fell sharply thereafter. A trial jury found in favor of the injured Highlands and against the dominant Ski Company.

On appeal, the Supreme Court upheld the jury's verdict, saying that although a firm with monopoly power has no general obligation to engage in a joint marketing program with a smaller competitor, the absence of an unqualified duty to cooperate does not mean that the dominant firm can do anything it pleases. In language reminiscent of *Grinnell,* the Supreme Court unanimously concluded that Ski Company's surge of power at Highlands' expense did not reflect "only a superior product, a well-run business, or luck" but, rather, it reflected "practices which tend to exclude or restrict competition." Moreover, there were no "valid business reasons" for Ski Company to discontinue the all-Aspen tickets.

In short, the structural approach grounded on *Alcoa* now seems forsaken. This is so despite *Aspen Ski,* because the facts of Aspen Ski were unusual and the Supreme Court's opinion in that case did nothing to restore the *Alcoa* era. Thus, illegal monopolization will apparently not be found without proof of *palpably anticompetitive conduct,* a conduct approach reminiscent of *U. S. Steel.* The structural approach of *Alcoa* could be faulted for possibly punishing some meritorious winners of the competitive battle, thereby casting a wet blanket on incentives.[42] On the other hand, the conduct approach of *Berkey,*

Table 7–2
Summary of Conduct Indicating Intent to Monopolize (Illustrative Cases in Parentheses)

1890–1940 Early Days	1. Predatory pricing and advertising (Standard Oil and American Tobacco)
	2. Bogus firms and fighting brands (Standard Oil and American Tobacco)
	3. Secret rebates from suppliers (Standard Oil)
1945–1970 Alcoa Era	4. Mergers to achieve power (Grinnell)
	5. Preclusive acquisition of key inputs (Alcoa)
	6. Acquisition of patents (United Shoe)
	7. Restrictive licensing (United Shoe)
	8. Bundling or tying (United Shoe, IBM)
	9. Deep price cutting (Grinnell, United Shoe, IBM)
Refinement and Retreat	10. Paper machines (IBM)
	11. Systems exploitation (Kodak, IBM)
	12. Preclusive product design (IBM, Kodak)

CalComp, and the Reagan Administration might yield more artificial monopoly power than is desirable.

Table 7–2 sketches the resulting history. In the early days, dastardly deeds indicated intent. During the *Alcoa* era a large dominant firm could not do the same things as a smaller rival—for example, aggressively gain control of key inputs, accumulate acquired patents, restrictively license instead of sell goods, engage in tying, or vary price sharply depending on competitive conditions (even if pricing above cost). Although "normal" or "reasonable" for a small firm, such tactics could not be used by a dominant firm to maintain dominance—that is, drive smaller rivals from the field. Most recently, since 1970, several new tactics have been questioned but found permissible—for example, IBM's paper machines and preclusive product designs. Moreover, several things found unacceptable during the *Alcoa* era now seem to be excused as nothing more than hard competition. Just how far the law has retreated remains unclear.

Summary

The Sherman Act outlaws monopolization. Establishing a violation requires proof of two elements: (1) substantial market power, and (2) intent. Reason, estimation, and hunch make appraisal of these elements uncertain. Hence, we find very big cases in this area. Just about everything is considered except the rainfall in Indianapolis.

When attempting to examine market power, the courts consider profits and barriers to entry of various kinds. The item receiving greatest attention, however, is market share. Broad definitions of the market tend to favor defendants; narrow definitions favor the prosecutors. Which way the court will turn in any particular case is often unpredictable. Once a market definition is established, percentage points become all important. The consensus is that a market share well below 60 percent lies beneath the reach of the law (unless abusive practices are present), whereas shares above 80 percent make Justice Department attorneys look good in court.

On the issue of intent, interpretations may be divided into three periods. (1) Before *Alcoa* in 1945, intent could be demonstrated only by evidence of predatory, exclusionary, or unfair acts. The rule of reason essentially meant condemnation of unreasonable behavior. (2) After *Alcoa* and until recently, intent could be demonstrated by evidence that a dominant firm's actions were not "honestly industrial," not "passive," not reflective of "superior skill," "superior product," "business acumen," or "historic accident." This reading of Section 2 left monopolists room to maneuver, but not much. (3) The period since about 1970 reveals conflicting strains and ambiguity. Contributing to the muddle is a basic tension in the law as inherited from *Alcoa,* a tension created by a willingness to condone monopoly (pure and simple) and a simultaneous desire to condemn monopolization (tainted and crude).

Thus, the early portion of the current period saw efforts to confirm and even extend *Alcoa*. Big cases were brought against Xerox, AT&T, and IBM. Most recently, however, these rumblings have been silenced. *Xerox and AT&T* were settled by stringent consent decrees. But more important, we have seen a substantial movement away from *Alcoa* toward *U. S. Steel. Kodak* and *CalComp* led the way. Baxter's withdrawal of *IBM* capped the trend. Whether these developments take us too far in condoning monopolization is a much-debated question. *Aspen Skiing* indicates that Section 2 of the Sherman Act is still alive, though.

Questions and Exercises for Chapter 7

1. Why is it necessary to define the relevant market in a monopolization case? What factors are considered for a definition?

2. Why is intent necessary for a Section 2 violation? What is the economic rationale for requiring evidence of intent?

3. Why do *Standard Oil* and *U. S. Steel,* taken together, seem to define an "era of dastardly deeds"?

4. Compare and contrast the facts of *Alcoa* and *IBM.* Which of the following would be easiest to argue: (1) both guilty, (2) both innocent, (3) Alcoa guilty/IBM innocent, or (4) Alcoa innocent/IBM guilty? Explain your choice.

5. Do the exercise called for in (4) above comparing *United Shoe* and *CalComp.*

6. Why are *Du Pont* and *Grinnell* contrasting cases on market definition?

7. Why does *Aspen Skiing* signal that Section 2 of the Sherman Act is still alive?

8. Compare and contrast the AVC and ATC rules that are discussed in the Appendix.

Appendix to Chapter 7: An AVC Rule versus an ATC Rule

In stating that a monopolist's price may fall to marginal or average variable cost, the Ninth Circuit Court in *CalComp* adopted what has

come to be called the Areeda-Turner Rule, after its main advocates, Professors Areeda and Turner.[43] We call it the AVC rule because it is most pertinent in its average variable cost form. The AVC rule would permit monopolists to cut price down to average variable costs but no further. As shown in Figure 7–2, which shows two cost configurations depending on technology, the AVC curves mark the threshold. Price-quantity combinations below the AVC lines (below the gray areas) would be illegal; price-quantity combinations anywhere above the AVC lines would be legal. The main justification for such a standard is short-run allocative efficiency. That is to say, AVC approximates marginal cost (MC), and static welfare economics theorizes that prices equal to marginal cost are allocatively efficient. Proponents of the AVC rule also claim it is simple and practical to employ.

Criticisms of the AVC rule have been diverse and numerous.[44] Its service to allocative efficiency and its alleged ease of application have both been questioned. Moreover, the use of short-run data to detect long-run strategic behavior has been challenged as illogical. Of greatest

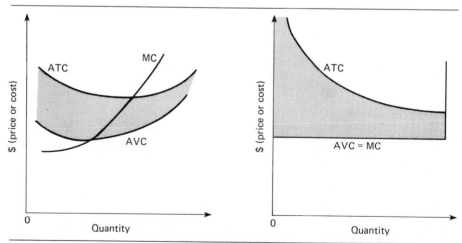

Figure 7–2
Cost Curves for Comparison of AVC and ATC Rules

interest to us, however, is a criticism that is easily appreciated: Namely, the AVC rule produces a defendant's paradise, a monopolist's heaven. Notice from Figure 7–2 that *any* price below average *total* cost (ATC) generates losses. If price falls below ATC *and* AVC, then the losses are so great that in the short run the firm would normally shut down to minimize its losses.[45] If price falls below ATC but is above AVC so as to be in the gray area, the firm will not shut down immediately, but eventually it will. Thus, a monopolist with abundant financial reserves could, under the AVC rule, drive less financially secure but equally efficient rivals from the market without fear of prosecution merely by pricing *below ATC* and *above AVC*. The requirement of a deep financial pocket does not detract from the point. Monopolists are often if not usually well heeled. The point is that the AVC rule is inaccurate. Under it, wolves are mistaken for sheep. Given this bias, the AVC rule fails to maintain competition (whatever its merits in short-run allocative efficiency). Its full-fledged adoption could well push us back to pre-*Standard Oil,* not to mention pre-*Alcoa.*

What is a better rule? Together with numerous others, I advocate a two-part standard keyed to average *total* cost, or the ATC rule.[46] That is, culpable monopolistic conduct would be shown by (1) pricing below average total cost, plus (2) substantial evidence of predatory intent. The call for explicit evidence of intent is necessary because prices fall below ATC all the time for wholly innocent reasons (e.g., drastically flagging sales, short-term promotions, spoiling perishables, and so forth). Pricing below AVC as well as ATC would be one possible indicator of intent because such very deep pricing cannot be minimize loss. Other indicators include (a) documents revealing long-term business plans of injurious price-cutting activity, (b) bribing distributors to refuse service to victims, (c) building immense new capacity in a market that is clearly not large enough to use fully that capacity at a profitable price, and (d) extremely sharp escalation of advertising outlays for a prolonged period.

In terms of Figure 7–2, pricing in the gray area may or may not be predatory, so indicators of intent are needed to sort out the wolves from the sheep, the anticompetitive from the procompetitive. Really deep price cutting, below AVC, is itself indicative of intent.

As of 1990, the ATC rule had been adopted in seven circuits. The clearest statement of the rule comes from the Eleventh Circuit Court of Appeals in *McGahee v. Northern Propane Gas Company* (1988).[47] Regarding the Areeda and Turner AVC rule, the court said, "It is like the Venus de Milo; it is much admired and often discussed, but rarely embraced." The court's formulation of the ATC rule had three parts, as follows:

1. If a defendant's prices were above average total cost "then there is no predatory pricing and thus no circumstantial evidence of predatory intent."
2. Prices below average total cost but above average variable cost provide circumstantial evidence of predation, but a plaintiff must have other evidence reflecting predatory intent.
3. If a defendant's prices were below average variable cost, the circumstantial evidence is strong enough to create a rebuttable presumption of predatory intent.

Notes

1. *U. S.* v. *Grinnell Corporation,* 384 U. S. 563 (1966).

2. For an overview see Alvin M. Stein and Barry J. Brett, "Market Definition and Market Power In Antitrust Cases—An Empirical Primer on When, Why and How," *New York Law School Law Review* 24 (1979): 639–676.

3. George Hay, John C. Hilke, and Philip B. Nelson, "Geographic Market Definition in an International Context," *Chicago–Kent Law Review* (vol. 64, no. 3; 1989): 711–739.

4. *U. S.* v. *E. I. duPont de Nemours Company,* 351 U. S. 377 (1956).

5. Ibid.

6. For an economic critique see, G. W. Stocking and W. F. Mueller, "The Cellophane Case and the New Competition," *American Economic Review* (March 1955): 29–63.

7. *U. S.* v. *Grinnell Corporation et al.*, 384 U. S. 563 (1966).

8. *U. S.* v. *Aluminum Company of America*, 148 F.2d 416 (1945), 424.

9. Lawrence Sullivan, *Handbook of the Law of Antitrust* (St. Paul, Minn.: West Publishing Co., 1977), pp. 134–140.

10. The "dangerous probability" requirement has stirred controversy of late because some lower courts have recently held that near monopoly or a high probability of actual monopolization are necessary to a finding of dangerous probability. See especially *U. S.* v. *Empire Gas Co.* 537 F.2d 296 (8th Cir. 1976), *cert. denied*, 429 U. S. 1122 (1977).

11. *U. S.* v. *Aluminum Company of America*, 148 F.2d 416 (1945).

12. Northern Securities Co. (1904), Union Pacific (1912), and Southern Pacific (1922).

13. *Standard Oil Company of New Jersey* v. *U. S.*, 221 U. S. 1 (1911). John McGee has argued that Standard's predatory pricing was less than alleged, even nonexistent, "Predatory Price Cutting: The Standard Oil (N. J.) Case," *Journal of Law & Economics* (October 1958): 137–169. But his account has been questioned by F. M. Scherer, *Industrial Market Structure and Economic Performance* (Chicago: Rand McNally, 1970), pp. 274–276.

14. Others included Atlantic Refining, Conoco, Marathon, Std. of Kentucky, Std. of Louisiana, and Std. of Nebraska.

15. For a summary see D. F. Greer, "Some Case History Evidence on the Advertising-Concentration Relationship," *Antitrust Bulletin* (Summer 1975), pp. 311–315.

16. *U. S.* v. *American Tobacco Co.*, 221 U. S. 106 (1911).

17. *U. S.* v. *United States Steel Corporation*, 251 U. S. 417 (1920).

18. *U. S.* v. *Aluminum Company of America*, 148 F.2d 416 (2d Cir. 1945).

19. *U. S.* v. *Grinnell Corp.*, 384 U. S. 563 (1966).

20. Primary sources for this section are L. W. Weiss, *Economics and American Industry* (New York: Wiley, 1961), Chapter 5; Merton J. Peck, *Competition in the Aluminum Industry: 1945–1958* (Cambridge, MA: Harvard University Press, 1961).

21. *U. S.* v. *Aluminum Company of America*, 148 F.2d 416 (1945).

22. A debate over market definition centered on the question of whether scrap aluminum should be excluded or included in the market along with primary aluminum. Judge Hand's exclusion of scrap has been vindicated. See Robert E. Martin, "Monopoly Power and the Recycling of Raw Materials," *Journal of Industrial Economics* (June 1982): 405–419.

23. George David Smith, *From Monopoly to Competition* (Cambridge, England: Cambridge University Press, 1988), p. 214.

24. *U. S.* v. *United Shoe Machinery Corp.*, 110 F. Supp. 295 (D. Mass. 1953), aff'd per curiam, 347 U. S. 521 (1954). See also Carl Kaysen, *United States* v. *United Shoe Machinery Corporation* (Cambridge, MA: Harvard University Press, 1956).

25. *U. S.* v. *Grinnell Corporation*, 384 U. S. 563 (1966). The case apparently stimulated competition substantially. See Don E. Waldman, *Antitrust Action and Market Structure* (Lexington, MA: Lexington Books, 1978), pp. 49–57.

26. Don E. Waldman, "Economic Benefits in the *IBM, AT&T,* and *Xerox* cases: Government Antitrust in the 70's," *Antitrust Law and Economics Review* (No. 2, 1980): 75–92.

27. *Wall Street Journal,* 11 January 1982, pp. 1, 4; 12 January 1982, p. 3; 21 January 1982, pp. 1, 21.

28. *Berkey Photo* v. *Eastman Kodak Co.*, 603 F.2d 263 (2d Cir. 1979).

29. John A. Maher, "Draining the ALCOA 'Wishing Well,' the Section 2 Conduct Requirement after *Kodak* and *CalComp*," *Fordham Law Review* (December 1979): 294–295.

30. *Berkey Photo, Inc.* v. *Eastman Kodak Company* 603 F.2d 263 (2d Cir. 1979), cert. denied 444 U. S. 1093 (1980).

31. Maher, "Draining ALCOA Wishing Well," pp. 312–313 (emphasis added).

32. Many major innovations like miniature cameras and cartridge-loading cannot be credited to Kodak. Indeed, diffusion of these innovations was delayed for decades because of Kodak's film monopoly. James W. Brock, "Structural Monopoly, Technical Performance, and Predatory Innovation," *American Business Law Journal* (Fall 1983): 291–306.

33. *California Computer Products, Inc. et al.* v. *International Business Machines*, 613 F.2d 727 (9th Cir. 1979).

34. *Telex Corp.* v. *IBM*, 510 F.2d 894 (10 Cir. 1975), *Memorex Corp.* v. *IBM*, 636 F.2d 1188 (9th Cir. 1980), *Transamerica Computer Co.* v. *IBM*, 481 F. Supp. 965 (1979).

35. Page I. Austin, "Predatory Pricing Law Since *Matsushita*," *Antitrust Law Journal* (vol. 58, no. 3, 1989): 895–911.

36. *U. S.* v. *International Business Machines Corp.*, 69 CIV 200, So. Dist. of N. Y.

37. For brief discussion see Leonard W. Weiss, "The Structure-Conduct-Performance Paradigm and Antitrust," *University of Pennsylvania Law Review* (April 1979): 1124–1130.

38. Gerald Brock, *The U. S. Computer Industry: A Study of Market Power* (Cambridge, MA: Ballinger, 1975), p. 13.

39. *Wall Street Journal,* 11 January 1982, pp. 1, 6; 26 January 1982, p. 10.

40. *Wall Street Journal,* 26 January 1982, p. 10. For the debate among economists see F. M. Fisher et al.,

Folded, Spindled, and Mutilated (Cambridge, MA: MIT Press, 1983); Russell Pittman, "Predatory Investment: U. S. vs. IBM," *International Journal of Industrial Organization* (December 1984): 341–365; Lee Preston, "Predatory Marketing," in *Regulation of Marketing and the Public Interest,* ed. F. E. Balderson et al., (New York: Pergamon Press, 1981), pp. 81–112; Alan McAdams, "The Computer Industry," in *The Structure of American Industry,* 6th ed., ed. Walter Adams (New York: Macmillan, 1982); and Richard T. DeLamarter, *Big Blue: IBM's Use and Abuse of Power* (New York: Dodd, Mead, 1986). By the way, although IBM won a withdrawal, new entrants (like Tandem, Hitachi, and Amdahl) and new products (like laptops, workstations, and minis) have given IBM new competition. See *Business Week,* October 16, 1989, pp. 75–86.

41. *Aspen Skiing Company* v. *Aspen Highlands Skiing Corporation,* 472 U. S. 585 (1985).

42. Defenders of the structural approach point out, however, that power meritoriously gained cannot justify an award of perpetual power. Patents, for instance, last only 17 years.

43. Phillip Areeda and Donald F. Turner, "Predatory Pricing and Related Practices under Section 2 of the Sherman Act," 88 *Harvard Law Review* (1975): 697–733. See also Areeda and Turner, *Antitrust Law* (Boston: Little, Brown, 1978), Vol. III, pp. 148–194.

44. F. M. Scherer, "Predatory Pricing and the Sherman Act: A Comment," 89 *Harvard Law Review* 869 (1976); Oliver Williamson, "Predatory Pricing: A Strategic and Welfare Analysis," 87 *Yale Law Journal* 284 (1977); William J. Baumol, "Quasi-Permanence of Price Reductions: A Policy for Prevention of Predatory Pricing," 89 *Yale Law Journal* 1 (1979); Paul L. Joskow and Alvin K. Klevorick, "A Framework for Analyzing Predatory Pricing Policy," 89 *Yale Law Journal* 213 (1979); and Roland H. Koller II, "When Is Pricing Predatory?" *Antitrust Bulletin* (Summer 1979): 283–306. For a good review see Joseph F. Brodley and George A. Hay, "Predatory Pricing: Competing Economic Theories and the Evolution of Legal Standards," *Cornell Law Review,* 66 (April 1981): 738–803.

45. The most a firm should ever lose (if it is loss minimizing) is its total fixed cost. Prices not covering average variable cost by, say, one dollar per unit lead to loss equal to all fixed cost *plus* $1 for every unit produced and sold.

46. D. F. Greer, "A Critique of Areeda and Turner's Standard for Predatory Practices," *Antitrust Bulletin* (Summer 1979): 233–261; Richard A. Posner, *Antitrust Law: An Economic Perspective* (Chicago: University of Chicago Press, 1976), pp. 184–195; National Commission to Review Antitrust Laws and Procedures, *Report to the President and Attorney General* (Washington DC, January, 1979), 149–151; Maher, "Draining ALCOA Wishing Well." The courts are moving in this direction. See James D. Hurwitz and William E. Kovacic, "Judicial Analysis of Predation: The Emerging Trends," *Vanderbilt Law Review* (vol. 35, 1982): pp. 63–157.

47. *McGahee* v. *Northern Propane Gas Company,* 858 F.2d 14 87 (11th Cir. 1988).

Chapter 8
Merger Policy

The game of picking up companies is open to everybody. All you have to do is have indefatigable drive, a desire to perpetuate yourself or your family in control of an industry, or an unabsorbed appetite for corporate power.
— *Meshulam Riklis*
(who parlayed $25,000 into a $755 million empire fittingly called Rapid-American, Inc.)

Each decade has its distinguishing characteristics. The 1980s witnessed a spate of mergers—more than 2,000 occurring each year, totaling more than $50 billion annually. The year 1986 broke all records with 4,446 mergers and acquisitions worth about $205.8 billion.[1]

Yet there is a paradox here. In 1950 Congress passed the Celler-Kefauver Act, which became one of the most stringent laws governing mergers in the world. Vigorous enforcement during the act's first twenty-seven years resulted in 437 merger complaints, challenging 1,406 acquisitions with combined assets exceeding $40 billion.[2] It seems that the 1980s may have nullified these antitrust achievements of the 1960s and 1970s.

This chapter explores this paradox and related matters. We begin with a brief description of various types of mergers and proceed to a historical review of merger activity. An outline of the causes of mergers comes next, followed by a rundown of policy developments under the Celler-Kefauver Act.

I. Background

A. Merger Types

The union of two or more direct competitors is called a **horizontal** merger. The combining companies operate in the same market, as illustrated in Figure 8–1. Bethlehem Steel's acquisition of the Youngstown Sheet and Tube Company in 1957 is an example. A **vertical** merger links companies that operate at different stages of the production-distribution process. This too is illustrated in Figure 8–1, and Bethlehem would provide an example of this type were it to acquire Ford Motors, a big buyer of steel. Broadly speaking, **conglomerate** mergers are all those that are neither horizontal nor vertical. This conglomerate definition covers a lot of ground, however, so the category may be subdivided into three classes: (1) **product extension,** involving produc-

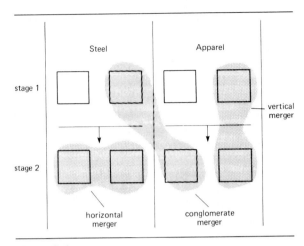

Figure 8–1
Types of Mergers

ers of two different but related products, such as bleach and detergent; (2) **market extension,** involving firms producing the same product but occupying different geographic markets—for example, dairies in two distant towns; and (3) **pure conglomerate,** involving firms with nothing at all in common, as would be true of a retail grocer and a furniture manufacturer.

B. Some History

Figure 8–2 shows why it is customary to speak of four major merger movements in American history. (No single source of data spans the entire century, so Nelson, Thorpe, FTC, and M&A designate separate sources.) The first movement occurred around the turn of the century. In the

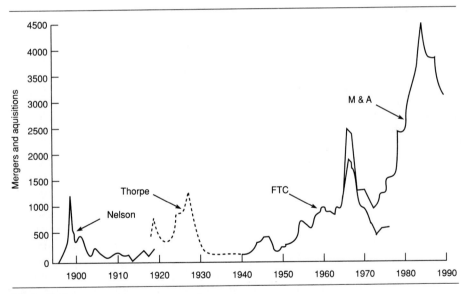

Figure 8–2
Annual Number of Mergers and Acquisitions: Nelson Series, Thorpe Series, FTC "Broad" Series, and *M&A* "Domestic" Series

Source: Devra L. Golbe and Lawrence J. White, "Mergers and Acquisitions in the US Economy: An Aggregate and Historical Overview," *Mergers and Acquisitions,* edited by A. J. Auerbach (Chicago: University of Chicago Press, 1988), p. 37; and *Mergers and Acquisitions* (March/April 1990), p. 95.

seven years from 1897 to 1903, 2,864 mergers were recorded in mining and manufacturing. Measured against our current and more recently set records, this number may not seem like much. However, when measured against the economy of 1900 and the resulting market concentration, this first great wave was awesome. The number of mergers *per dollar of real GNP* was much greater at the turn of the century than during the 1980s, almost five times greater in 1898 than 1988.[3] Horizontal mergers dominated the scene. Moreover, simultaneous *multiple* mergers, which are now very rare, were an everyday affair. Mergers involving at least five firms accounted for 75 percent of firm disappearances during this period.[4] This turn-of-the-century merger boom produced such giant companies as U. S. Steel, U. S. Gypsum, Du Pont, American Tobacco, International Paper, American Sugar Refining, American Can, Pittsburgh Plate Glass, and National Biscuit.

The second major merger wave arose during the Roaring Twenties. From 1925 through 1930, 5,382 mergers were recorded for manufacturing and mining. During the peak year of 1929, ownership shares moved at the feverish pace of more than four mergers per business day. This second movement exceeded the first not only in numbers tallied but also in variety of merger types. Horizontal mergers were again popular, but vertical, market-extension, and product-extension mergers were also in vogue. It was during this second period that General Foods Corporation put together a string of product-extension acquisitions that became the first big food conglomerate. Its acquisitions included Maxwell House Coffee, Jello, Sanka, Birds Eye, and Swans Down Cake Flour. Unlike the first merger movement, countless mergers in these years were in sectors other than manufacturing and mining. At least 2,750 utilities, 1,060 banks, and 10,520 retail stores were swallowed up by acquisition during the 1920s.[5]

After two decades of nothing more than a meager ripple in the late 1940s, momentum began to build once again in the mid-1950s. Thereafter, the movement swelled incredibly. From 1960 through 1970, the Federal Trade Commission recorded 25,598 mergers. Slightly more than half of these were in manufacturing and mining. The total value of manufacturing and mining assets acquired over this period exceeded $65 billion. This sector's peak year was 1968, when 2,407 firms amounting to more than $13.3 billion were acquired. Putting the matter in relative terms and using an averaging process, we can deduce that, over the period from 1953 to 1968, approximately 21 percent of all manufacturing and mining assets were acquired.[6]

After a lull in the mid-1970s, the pace quickened again in the 1980s, as shown in Figure 8–2. Many of the most spectacular recent acquisitions have been made by oil companies, whose financial coffers grew fat during the oil shortages of the 1970s. Other interesting acquisitions include many that occurred in 1988. Philip Morris's purchase of Kraft for $12.9 billion and Kodak's acquisition of Sterling Drug for $5.1 billion illustrate those events. In many respects, this most recent merger movement appears to be the greatest of all time.

As for merger types, these latest waves have been quite different from those of yesteryear. Horizontal mergers have become much less numerous than have conglomerate mergers. As we see shortly, much of this trend away from horizontals and toward conglomerates, especially toward pure conglomerates, was due partly to public policy. The enforcement agencies cracked down rather hard on horizontal mergers, whereas they generally ignored conglomerates.

II. Reasons for Merger

When counting the reasons for merger, one can get by with only ten fingers but just barely. In simplest terms, corporate marriage is a matter of finding a price that buyers are willing to pay and sellers are willing to accept. Going beyond this truism, however, we encounter complexities. Some motives are constant in the sense that they explain a fairly steady stream of mergers year in and year out. Other motives are more cyclical, a characteristic that helps to explain why merger activity heats up and cools down over time. In other words, there are two interrelated issues—underlying cause and timing.

A. Timing of Mergers

Let us consider timing first. Several researchers have found a high positive correlation between the number of mergers per year and the general business cycle.[7] Merger frequency tends to rise and fall as the average level of stock market prices rises and falls.

Exactly why this correlation exists is not entirely clear. Experts speculate that owners of firms expecting eventually to sell out may feel that they can get the best deal when stock prices are generally high. Conversely, from the buyers' point of view, the basic problem is raising enough cash and securities to make an attractive offer. Hence, acquiring firms may find funds for acquisitions easier and cheaper to come by when stock prices are high.

B. Underlying Causes of Mergers

Underlying causes of mergers involve as much intuitive understanding as timing does. Sellers and buyers may see things differently while benefiting mutually.[8] *Sellers* have several reasons for wanting to seek out a buyer. First, and most obvious, is the "failing firm" problem. As every used car owner knows, poor performance may prompt a sale. In the case of business enterprises, failure is measured in terms of declining revenues, recurring losses, and even bankruptcy. Although failure may be an important motive for the sale of many small firms, it could be no more than a very minor motive for most sales of large firms.[9]

A second class of seller's motives relates to individually or family owned firms that are typically small. Merger may be the easiest means for an aging owner-manager to cash in on a lifetime's effort and perpetuate the business after retirement. Again, however, these seem to be minor factors, mere droplets in the tidal waves of time past.

The motives of *buyers* are more important. They are the ones who typically initiate deals. Moreover, the prices buyers pay to former owners typically exceed the book value of the purchased firms' assets and the market value of the former owner's stock holdings. This excess, or premium, averaged around 40 percent in the late 1980s, which means that premiums of 50 percent and more were common. For example, Kodak paid $89.25 per share to acquire Sterling Drug, which just before the bidding was priced at $54.75—hence, a 63 percent premium. Bridgestone paid a premium of 78 percent to acquire Firestone's stock in 1988.[10] Indeed, buyers may be so aggressive that they occasionally pull a raid, or takeover, in which case they succeed in buying a firm whose management opposes the acquisition. The buyers' motives we cover include monopoly power, risk spreading, efficiency, speculation, and sheer growth.

1. MONOPOLY POWER

U. S. Steel was apparently worth more than the sum of its 170 parts. Before merger in 1901, the total value of the tangible property of the separate firms stood at roughly $700 million. After merger, U. S. Steel estimated its value at close to $1,400 million. Why the enormous difference? Market power. After merger, U. S. Steel produced two-thirds of all United States semifinished steel and similar percentages of all rails, tin plate, rods, and other products. The consequences for the price of pig iron are pictured in Figure 8–3, which shows two price trend lines, one deflated by the wholesale price index, the other not. The discontinuous price jump of about 50 percent in 1901 coincides with the formation of U. S. Steel. This may lead the astute reader to suspect a substantial rise in annual profit rates

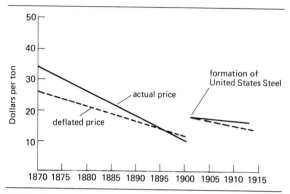

Figure 8–3
Pig Iron Price Trend, Before and After U. S. Steel

Source: Parsons and Ray, "The United States Steel Consolidation: The Creation of Market Control." *Journal of Law and Economics* (April 1975), p. 186.

also, and you would be correct. Hence, market power may motivate merger.

Xidex Corporation is a more recent example. During the 1970s, it acquired two competitors in microfilm. The first acquisition increased its market share from 46 percent to 55 percent; the second from 61 percent to 70 percent. As a result of these mergers, Xidex's prices jumped first by 11 percent then by an additional 23 percent.[11]

An analysis of six airline mergers occurring during 1986–1987 yields equally interesting results.[12] Those results vary depending on whether the reduction in competitors through merger occurred on an airline route involving a hub city. (Dallas is a hub for American Airlines. Chicago is one for United. An airline concentrates its flights to a given region through a hub, flying people in, and then flying them out to their ultimate destinations after most of the passengers have changed planes.) In percentage terms, the price effect of losing a competitor to merger ranged "from 2 percent to 32 percent with no hub effects, and up to 55 percent when hub effects come into play."[13] Corroborating these statistics, an airline executive explained the torrent of airline mergers during the 1980s by saying, "Car-

riers are trying to achieve the market dominance that will give them better control over their prices."[14]

Just how many horizontal mergers are motivated by market power is difficult to estimate, partly because U.S. law discourages them. In Britain, where the law is relatively lenient, 27 percent of the respondents in a survey of 380 firms said that achievement of market dominance was the single most important reason for their merger (and this sample included some nonhorizontal mergers).[15] Hence, market power can be an important motive for horizontal mergers.

Whether market power can motivate *vertical* and *conglomerate* mergers as well as horizontal mergers is a much debated question. These other forms of merger produce no immediate or obvious increases in market share for the consolidated firm. Nor do they promise added *market concentration.* Hence, theories and empirical tests of possible adverse competitive effects of these mergers must attack the question indirectly.

The major potentially anticompetitive effects of vertical mergers are (1) *foreclosure,* wherein nonintegrated businesses at one level of the production-distribution chain are foreclosed from dealing with suppliers or buyers at other levels because those other suppliers or buyers are owned by vertically integrated rivals, and (2) strengthened *barriers to entry,* which may arise from the foreclosure of potential entrants and the enlarged capital cost requirements associated with multilevel entry.[16] U. S. Steel provides an example of the barrier effect because the main source of its market power was its aggressive vertical acquisition of most iron ore supplies in North America. Charles Schwab, a prominent steel executive of the day, explained the consequences of U. S. Steel's 75 percent ore control while testifying in 1911:

Mr. Schwab. I do not believe there will be any great development in iron and steel by new companies, but rather development by the companies now in business.

Mr. Chairman. Now, explain that to us.

Mr. Schwab. For the reason that the possibility of a new company getting at a sufficiently large supply of raw materials would make it exceedingly difficult if not impossible.[17]

As for conglomerate mergers, the greater size and diversity they gain improves the possibility of *reciprocity.* This is a policy of "I buy from you if you buy from me," and it may tend to foreclose rivals from affected markets. Conglomerate mergers may also eliminate *potential* competitors. In either event, profits might follow from the added power implied. Substantiation or refutation of these and other possible effects is difficult in particular cases and in general. However, several researchers have found that the market shares of firms acquired by conglomerates do not usually grow after acquisition. They say this shows an absence of adverse competitive effect, implying that most conglomerate mergers could not be motivated by quests for market power.[18]

2. RISK SPREADING THROUGH DIVERSIFICATION

Suppose you want to get two dozen eggs delivered to your grandmother. Suppose further that she lives in the woods, and the only available delivery service relies on brave but clumsy six-year-old girls attired in red. Experience shows that stumbles over roots and stones make successful egg delivery by any one girl a 50:50 proposition (even apart from the danger of wolves). Your problem then is this: If you want at least *some* of your two dozen eggs to get through, what delivery arrangements should you make? Placing the entire shipment in the hands of one girl means a 0.5 probability that *none* will arrive. However, if you give one dozen to one girl and one dozen to another, there is only one chance in four that no eggs will be delivered because that is the probability of both girls' falling down. Similarly, the split shipment offers one chance in four

that all eggs will arrive safely. Two times in every four, one dozen will be broken and one dozen will get through. This example was developed by Roger Sherman to demonstrate the power of diversification in reducing risks. He also demonstrated that still further diversification yields further risk reduction: "The best thing to do is to send 24 girls, each with one egg. The chance that no egg will arrive is then infinitesimally small, and it becomes very probable that about 12 eggs will arrive safely."[19] The obvious moral (don't put all your eggs in one basket) may motivate many vertical and conglomerate mergers.

Diversification, however, is not always favorable; nor is merger the only means of achieving diversification. The conditions required for a positive effect for an acquiring firm are more limited than this simple example suggests.[20] In particular, the variances of the components of a combination must be independent of each other. (The independence of several delivery girls would be severely compromised if they all held hands and thereby tripped over each other.) Failure to meet the conditions necessary for risk reduction may explain why researchers have been unable to find any risk reduction among conglomerate mergers generally.[21] Indeed, mergers often augment risk rather than reduce it.

3. ECONOMIC EFFICIENCY

The larger size that mergers bring to combinations may yield lower costs of various kinds. These efficiencies may be divided into two broad groups—pecuniary economies and technical economies **Pecuniary economies** are monetary savings derived from buying inputs more cheaply. Pecuniary gains thus include such things as larger volume discounts for the bulk purchase of raw materials or advertising space, lower interest rates on borrowed capital, and greater negotiating strength vis-à-vis labor, tax assessors, and others. In contrast, **technical economies** of scale are genuine cost savings. They imply fewer real inputs for a given level of output. Their primary sources are (1) greater specialization of equipment and operators, (2) high-speed automation, (3) scaled-up equipment, and (4) in the case of vertical mergers, a refined coordination of effort between several stages of the production process.

Well, then, do mergers produce such economies? The general answer is "yes" and "no." It is "yes" if we look only at the justifications businessmen most frequently offer the public for their mergers. It is "no" if we look at the evidence assembled and assessed by most economists studying the question. As Dennis Mueller puts it, the empirical literature draws a surprisingly consistent picture: "Whatever the stated or unstated goals of managers are, the mergers they have consummated have on average not generated extra profits for the acquiring firms, have not resulted in increased economic efficiency."[22] Thus, although *some* mergers yield economies, they usually do not. (See the Appendix to this chapter for elaboration on this point.)

4.   SPECULATIVE AND FINANCIAL MOTIVES

Several influences may raise the price of an acquiring company's stock after a merger or series of mergers, even *without* any increment in market power, or economies of scale, or reduced risk, or changes of the real assets under the combined control of the merging companies. Such stock price increases stem from speculation and often feed further speculation.

They may stem from the mere *expectation* of real changes, as would be the case if investors expected a merger to capture as much market power as U. S. Steel acquired. Indeed, around the turn of the century many merger promoters exploited the expectations of investors by arranging mergers that had little chance of achieving real monopoly power while exaggerating monopoly power's prospects, planting rumors, and pointing to U. S. Steel's success. Once expectations were running wild and the deal was closed, promoters would hasten to sell the stock they had obtained as a promotion fee to unsus-

pecting investor-speculators. These unfortunate folks often "took a bath."[23]

Tax considerations also fit this category. The interest cost of any new debt used to finance corporate acquisitions is tax deductible. Moreover, changes in the tax law in 1981 spurred the merger movement of the 1980s. After 1981, new owners could take huge accelerated depreciation write-offs, and do so on the basis of asset values set by the acquisition price of the merger. This meant that new owners could get more tax breaks out of a given corporation than its old owners, something that would foster acquisitions.[24]

5.   GROWTH AND PERSONAL AGGRANDIZEMENT

This survey would not be complete without mention of sheer growth and personal aggrandizement as motives. Just how important they are is impossible to say. The Napoleonic aspirations of acquisitive business leaders cannot be captured by statistics, except insofar as statistics may disprove the importance of other motives, such as economies of scale. You are free to judge for yourself. You may draw on your knowledge of human nature and your reading of whatever biographical material you may wish to look into. Three typical examples are the following:

- Harold Geneen led ITT in the acquisition of more than 250 companies. A close colleague of his once said, "Three things should be written on Hal Geneen's tombstone—earnings per share, 15% growth per year, and size."[25]
- Charles G. Bluhdorn, who guided Gulf & Western Industries through more than 80 acquisitions in eleven years, had this to say about his company and himself: "No mountain is high enough for us, nothing is impossible. The sky is the limit. . . . I came to this country without a penny, and built a company with 100,000 employees. This is what America is all about . . . to be able to do what I've done is a matter of pride to me and to the country."[26]
- The largest takeover of all time, that of RJR Nabisco for $25 billion in 1989, precipitated a

huge clash of egos. It was "a grudge match be-tween a bunch of infants."[27]

To summarize, the motives for merger are many and varied. No one explanation clearly surpasses all others. At any one time, there is a diversity of inducements.

III. Antitrust Merger Policy

Antitrust law governing most mergers has a structural focus and is designed to curb market power in the early stages (to nip it in the bud before it fully blossoms). As stated in its preamble, the purpose of the Clayton Act of 1914 was "to arrest the creation of trusts, conspiracies and monopolies *in their incipiency and before consummation*." Section 7 of the Clayton Act prohibited potentially anticompetitive mergers—but it had enormous loopholes that were not plugged until 1950 with passage of the Celler-Kefauver Amendment. The amended statute outlaws mergers

> where in any line of commerce in any section of the country, the effect of such acquisition may be substantially to lessen competition, or tend to create a monopoly.

The law is enforced by the Justice Department and the Federal Trade Commission. Although hundreds of cases have been decided under the law, we review only a few of the more important ones. Before we do, a brief outline of what to look for may be helpful:

1. The phrase "in any line of commerce" refers to product markets. Major factors affecting the courts' definition of relevant product markets include (a) the product's physical characteristics and uses, (b) unique production facilities, (c) distinct customers, (d) cross-elasticity of demand with substitutes, and (e) the absolute price level of possible substitutes.

2. The phrase "in any section of the country" refers to particular geographic markets. Major factors affecting the courts' definition of relevant geographic markets include (a) the costs of transportation, (b) legal restrictions on geographic scope, (c) the extent to which local demand is met by outside supply (e.g., little in from outside), and (d) the extent to which local production is shipped to other areas (e.g., little out from inside).[28]

3. The phrase "may be . . . to lessen competition" reflects the importance of *probable* adverse effect. In this regard, the factors considered by the courts differ somewhat, depending on whether the merger at issue is horizontal, vertical, or conglomerate. Factors for (a) *horizontal mergers* include the market shares and ranks of the merging firms; concentration in the market; *trends* in market shares and concentration; ease of entry; and the elimination of a strong, competitively vigorous independent firm. Factors considered for (b) *vertical mergers*, where foreclosure and entry barriers are the potentially adverse effects, include the market shares of the merging firms (each at their respective levels in the production-distribution process); and the trend toward vertical integration in the industry. Factors considered for (c) *conglomerate mergers* include the elimination of a prime potential entrant and the danger of reciprocal buying.

IV. Horizontal Mergers: Early Cases

THE BETHLEHEM-YOUNGSTOWN CASE (1958)

Bethlehem Steel's acquisition of Youngstown Sheet & Tube in 1957 was the first large merger challenged under the Celler-Kefauver Act.[29] The firms ranked second and sixth nationally among steel producers. Their combined ingot capacity amounted to 21 percent of total industry capacity. The number one firm, U. S. Steel, had a 30 percent share at the time, so this merger would have boosted the share of U. S. Steel and Bethlehem taken together from 45 to 51 percent. In the court's opinion, "This would add substantially to concentration in an already highly concentrated industry and reduce unduly the already limited number of integrated steel companies."

Bethlehem's defense for acquiring Youngstown Sheet & Tube was that the national market was not the relevant geographic market for steel products. Its attorneys urged acceptance of three separate markets within the United States—eastern, midcontinental, and western. Since all Youngstown's plants were located in the midcontinent area, whereas all of Bethlehem's plants were either eastern or western, the defense went on to argue that the high costs of steel transportation prevented head-on competition between the merging firms. Moreover, they claimed that the acquisition would bring Bethlehem into the Chicago area, where it could then compete more effectively with U. S. Steel, the dominant force in that area.

The court rejected these arguments. It said that even though Bethlehem did not have ingot capacity in the midcontinent area, Bethlehem's annual shipments of more than 2 million tons into the area indicated direct competition with Youngstown. Furthermore, the court said that market delineation "must be made on the basis of where *potentially* they could make sales." In other words, Bethlehem was surely capable of entering the Chicago market by internal expansion instead of by acquisition. As for the argument that the combined companies could better compete with U. S. Steel, the same faulty logic could justify successive mergers until just two or three firms were left in the industry, a situation that could hardly be considered competitive. Thus, the merger was enjoined. The benefits of the court's denial were realized for all to see a few years later when Bethlehem *did* build a massive steel plant thirty miles east of Chicago.

THE BROWN SHOE CASE (1962)

Failure to appeal the *Bethlehem* case allowed *Brown Shoe* to become the first case to reach the Supreme Court under the Celler-Kefauver Act.[30] In 1955, the date of this merger, Brown was the fourth largest manufacturer of shoes in the United States, accounting for about 4 percent of total shoe production. Brown was also a big shoe retailer, owning or controlling over 1,230 retail shops. The mate in Brown's merger was Kinney, which likewise engaged in shoe manufacturing and retailing. Retailing was Kinney's *forte,* however; it was at the time the nation's largest "independent" retail shoe chain, with over 400 stores in more than 270 cities and about 1.2 percent of all retail shoe sales by dollar volume. The case thus had vertical as well as horizontal aspects. Here we take up the horizontal aspects at retail level.

The Supreme Court decided that relevant product lines could be drawn to distinguish men's, women's, and children's shoes. Defendant Brown wanted still narrower delineations such as "medium-priced" and "low-priced" shoes, but the court did not agree. As for geographic markets at retail level, the court decided on "cities with a population exceeding 10,000 and their environs in which both Brown and Kinney retailed shoes." By this definition, the market shares of the merging companies were enough to arouse the court's disapproval. For example, the combined share of Brown and Kinney sales of women's shoes exceeded 20 percent in 32 cities. And in children's shoes, their combined share exceeded 20 percent in 31 cities. In addition to raw shares, *trends* caught the court's attention: "We cannot avoid the mandate of Congress that tendencies toward concentration in industry are to be curbed in their incipiency, particularly when those tendencies are being accelerated through giant steps striding across a hundred cities at a time. In the light of the trends in this industry we agree with the Government and the court below that this is an appropriate place at which to call a halt."

THE VON'S CASE (1966)

The Von's case is to horizontal mergers what the Sixth Commandment is to homicide.[31] The acquisition was denied, although neither firm involved was really very big and by usual standards the market was not highly concentrated. Von's ranked third among retail grocery store chains in the Los Angeles area when in 1960 it acquired Shopping Bag Food Stores, which ranked sixth. Their market shares were, respectively, 4.3 and 3.2 percent. Hence, their combined sales amounted to 7.5 percent. This would have boosted the four-firm concentration ratio in the Los Angeles market from 24.4 percent before merger to 28.8 percent after. Moreover, eight-firm and twelve-firm concentration had been on the rise before merger.

These facts might have been moderately damning. But Justice Black chose to neglect them when writing the Supreme Court's majority opinion. He stessed other factors, as follows:

> The number of owners operating a single store in the Los Angeles retail grocery market decreased from 5,365 in 1950 to 3,818 in 1961. By 1963, three years after merger, the number of single store owners had dropped still further to 3,590.

Black thus defined concentration in terms of the *number* of independent firms. He went on to state that "the basic purpose of the 1950 Celler-Kefauver Bill was to prevent economic concentration in the American economy by keeping a large number of small competitors in business." By this reasoning, a divestiture order was unavoidable.

However laudable these sentiments might have been, we may question as a matter of economics whether the massive demise of mom-and-pop grocery stores in Los Angeles was due to mergers like the one denied. Divestiture of Shopping Bag did not resurrect them. They fell by the wayside for reasons of economies of scale, cheap automobile transportation to shopping centers, and the like. Thus, the court seems to have set a stringent legal standard while deferring to a moderate standard of economic proficiency.

THE GENERAL DYNAMICS CASE (1974)

With *Von's* the law reached a peak of stringency against horizontal mergers. Since then greater leniency has been shown. In grocery retailing, for instance, the enforcement agencies have given the green light to three substantial horizontal mergers by large companies—Lucky, Allied, and A&P.

The *General Dynamics* case of 1974 stands out as a turning point in this shift toward leniency.[32] The product was coal. Through its subsidiary coal company (Materials Service Corporation), General Dynamics acquired a controlling interest in United Electric Coal. The government challenged the merger because, according to Justice Department definitions, this merger gave General Dynamics a 12.4 percent share of a broad midwestern coal market and a 23.2 percent share of a narrower Illinois submarket, shares that would easily violate the *Von's* standard.

General Dynamics successfully defended itself by arguing that rule of reason considerations should be taken into account. It claimed that the government's share figures for the acquired firm, United Electric, were biased upward by being based on current sales. The true measure of United's position, it was argued, was not current sales but coal *reserves* that would feed production in the near future, or better yet *uncommitted reserves* (i.e., reserves not yet already sold by long-term contracts). By this alternative measure, United's stature in the market shrank considerably because it was very short of reserves, especially the uncommitted kind. The Supreme Court sided with General Dynamics, finding its method of assessment more meaningful:

> A . . . significant indicator of a [coal] company's power effectively to compete with other companies lies in the state of a company's uncommitted reserves of recoverable coal. A company with relatively large supplies of coal which are not already under contract to a customer will have a more

important influence upon competition in the contemporaneous negotiation of supply contracts than a firm with small reserves, even though the latter may presently produce a greater tonnage of coal . . .

Thus, with this case, the Court said it would not follow the rigid formulas of the 1960s.

V. Horizontal Mergers: Recent Developments

THE GUIDELINES (1982, 1992)

Horizontal mergers remain one area in which the antitrust laws retain some potency. Still, the trend started by *General Dynamics* in 1974 continued into the 1980s. Among the many big horizontal mergers recently completed that probably would not pass muster under the old standards were Chevron and Gulf Oil, Texaco and Getty Oil, Bank of America and Security Pacific, plus a joint venture between General Motors and Toyota. (Some of these approvals required modest divestiture or other conditions.)

The current situation is best summarized by the "Merger Guidelines" promulgated by the Department of Justice and the FTC in 1982 and 1992 to alert the business world about the kinds of mergers that would likely be challenged. These guidelines relaxed the rules considerably. In so doing, the guidelines incorporated four new twists.

First, they measure structural impact by Herfindahl-Hirschman indexes (or H-indexes) instead of by concentration ratios. The H-index simply transforms market share data into a form that many economists find useful. Market shares are squared, so that, for example, a share of 10 percent becomes 100, a share of 2 percent becomes 4, and their combination of 12 percent becomes 144. Moreover, instead of measuring market concentration by the sum of the shares of the four leading firms, the H-index of concentration *squares* the shares of *all* firms and then adds

them. For example, the H-index for a market of five firms with shares of 35 percent, 25 percent, 20 percent, 15 percent, and 5 percent, would be:

$$35^2 + 25^2 + 20^2 + 15^2 + 5^2$$
$$= 1225 + 625 + 400 + 225 + 25 = 2500$$

Squaring market shares gives especially large weight to large market shares, so it may be a better reflection of anticompetitive impact than market shares plain and simple. The new guidelines permit horizontal mergers in markets having a post-merger H-index of 1000 or less, pose a warning in the 1000 to 1800 range, and threaten serious trouble for any substantial merger in markets with H-indexes greater than 1800. (In particular, the threshold change in H is 100 in the 1000 to 1800 range and 50 over 1800. Very roughly, an H of 1000 corresponds to four-firm concentration ratios in the range of 45 to 55.)

The *second* twist in the guidelines is that they incorporate consideration of factors other than market shares and concentration when deciding whether to challenge particular mergers. That is to say, competition may be either less or more intense than is suggested by a given level of concentration. It may be *less* intense if, for example, barriers to entry are particularly high or if extensive joint venture activity inhibits competitive independence. Conversely, competition may be *more* intense if (1) there is *rapid technological change* to stifle collusive understandings and disrupt stodgy strategies, or (2) there is *rapid industry growth,* which creates market turbulence and reduces incentives to collude, or (3) especially *easy entry* to provide potential competition. Consideration of these and related factors allows the authorities to approve mergers that look bad by H-indexes alone.

Third, in defining the relevant market, the guidelines refer to traditional earmarks such as "differences between products in customary usage, design, physical composition and other technical characteristics," but they go further. They rely more on economic theory. The "market" is to be defined ever more broadly as long as a hypothetical 5 percent price hike for the product would drive a "significant percent" of buyers to purchase substitute products.

Fourth, the guidelines say that the enforcement agencies will permit otherwise illegal mergers if those mergers are likely to result in substantial *cost-reducing efficiencies.*[33] This is a controversial change. Statute law grants no explicit exemptions for cost-saving mergers. Moreover, this change is predicated on the assumption that efficiency is the sole aim of antitrust, an assumption that many officials and economists question.[34] Finally, controversy is still further kindled by a lack of empirical support. Prices tend to rise with anticompetitive mergers, causing large adverse transfers from buyers to sellers.[35] And mergers seldom create efficiencies (as shown in the Appendix to this chapter).

What has enforcement been like under the guidelines? Table 8–1 suggests the answer. Noti-

fications to the authorities by merging firms rose substantially from 1978 to 1989, reflecting the merger mania of the 1980s. However, the number of official investigations initiated by the Justice Department did not rise, and the number of challenges filed fell substantially. The result was a significant drop in the percentage of investigations that produced challenges. So merger enforcement by the Department of Justice dropped sharply during the 1980s. The record of the FTC shows less decline, partly because the Department of Justice turned an increasing volume of cases over to the FTC for enforcement. Still, the combined record of these agencies during the Reagan years was one of leniency.

Analysis of 156 proposed mergers that the Department of Justice investigated between 1982 and 1987 reveals the nature of the leniency. Of the 156 investigated mergers, 103 adversely affected market concentration to the point of exceeding the guidelines' standards. Yet no chal-

Table 8–1
Department of Justice Merger Enforcement: 1978–1989

Year	Premerger Notifications	Investigations Initiated	Cases Filed	Cases Filed as Percentage of Investigations
1978	147	20	7	50.0%
1979	859	101	11	10.9
1980	824	56	10	17.9
1981	993	67	4	6.0
1982	1,204	55	8	14.5
1983	1,101	62	4	6.5
1984	1,339	79	5	6.3
1985	1,604	106	7	6.6
1986	1,949	85	6	7.1
1987	2,533	89	6	6.7
1988	2,747	56	6	10.7
1989	2,883	64	5	7.8

Source: "Special Supplement, General Accounting Office Report on Changes in Antitrust Enforcement Policies," *Antitrust and Trade Regulation Report,* December 13, 1990, p. 5–37.

lenge was issued in 58 of these 103 cases. The Department of Justice felt that mitigating circumstances made these 58 mergers less worrisome than they appeared. The mitigating circumstance most frequently cited was, by a huge margin, *ease of entry* into the market being concentrated by the merger.[36] The department has said that it judges entry to be easy if a 5 to 10 percent increase in market price would likely induce new entry within two years.

The idea that ease of entry can excuse an otherwise illegal merger has been endorsed by the courts. The Second Circuit Court of Appeals lead the way in *United States* v. *Waste Management, Inc.* in 1984.[37] The merger at issue in that case joined two trash hauling companies with a combined market share of 48.8 percent. This crossed the concentration threshold of the guidelines. The court, however, found the entry exception to fit, saying that "individuals operating out of their homes can acquire trucks and some containers and compete successfully with any other company."

There are serious problems with an exemption based on the ease of entry, as indicated by the frequency of its application. First, although there is some agreement among economists on what factors one ought to consider in judging ease of entry, "there is much less agreement about how to assess those factors, and even less about how to combine them into an overall measure of the difficulty of entry."[38] There is, in short, no Herfindahl-Hirschman index for entry. Second, the measure used by the Justice Department (i.e., entrant response to a price increase) has not been supported in the empirical literature. There is no solid evidence that high prices typically induce entry.[39] Entrants appear to base their behavior on the prices they expect will prevail *after* entry, and those prices need not have any correspondence to prices *before* entry. Finally, the condition of entry into a market is not determined solely by exogenous elements such as economies of scale or market growth. Firms

can *create* substantial barriers through strategic behavior, such as advertising intensely, engaging in exclusive dealing, proliferating new brands, or granting loyalty rebates to customers.[40] Hence, a merger policy that allows large increases in concentration on the presumption that entry is easy may, in the end, be elevating firms to a position so high that they can make entry difficult after they merge. The easy entry would then vanish after the merger that was permitted by the easy entry.[41]

COCA-COLA AND DR. PEPPER (1986, 1990)

The most interesting case to be tried under the guidelines arose from Coca-Cola's attempt to acquire Dr. Pepper in 1986, an attempt that followed close on the heels of Pepsi Cola's proposed acquisition of the 7-Up Company. These four companies compete in the production and sale of flavoring concentrates used in the manufacture of carbonated soft drinks. The concentrate is sold to local bottlers, some of whom are owned by the concentrate producers but most of whom are independent. These local bottlers add carbonated water and sweetener to the concentrates, bottle and can the beverage, and then distribute it to retail outlets and vending machines. These "bottled" sales account for about 75 percent of all sales of carbonated soft drinks. The remaining 25 percent come from "fountain" consumption at restaurants, sports arenas, and other such outlets. Many local bottlers service these fountain outlets as well as those selling bottled soft drinks.

The Federal Trade Commission challenged these mergers. Pepsi dropped its bid for 7-Up abruptly, but Coca-Cola persisted in its pursuit of Dr. Pepper. The FTC won a preliminary injunction against the Coca-Cola/Dr. Pepper combination after a small-scale trial in Federal District Court in 1986. And although Dr. Pepper thereafter withdrew its consent to be acquired, the FTC continued its case against Coca-Cola with a full-scale trial before an administrative law judge, whose opinion of 1990 likewise opposed the merger.[42]

In its defense Coca-Cola argued for an extremely broad definition of the product market— that is, all potable beverages, including milk, coffee, tea, beer, tap water, and fruit juices as well as carbonated soft drinks. Coca-Cola contended that all beverages quench thirst and that the "human stomach can consume only a finite amount of liquid in any given period of time." Although not false, these physical truisms had little economic meaning. The federal court and administrative law judge rejected them, the latter saying:

> The all potables market is not one which can be looked to with any confidence in an analysis of the probably competitive consequences of the proposed acquisition, for . . . this record reveals that products which are not soft drinks have little impact on the day-to-day competitive activities of a firm like Coca-Cola which does not consider the prices of other beverages when it sets its concentrated prices or, when acting as a bottler, its finished product prices.

The federal court found a national carbonated soft drink market, and by that definition the market shares involved in the two proposed mergers were Coca-Cola 37.4 percent, Dr. Pepper 4.6 percent, Pepsi Cola 28.9 percent, and 7-Up 5.7 percent. Allowing the mergers would have given Coke a share of 42.0 percent and Pepsi one of 34.6 percent—a combined total of 76.6 percent in the hands of the top two firms. The FTC's administrative law judge defined the market a little more narrowly to include only branded concentrates, thereby excluding generic and private-label soft drinks. By this definition, Coca-Cola's acquisition of Dr. Pepper would have increased the H-index 443 points to 3572. This would have shattered the guideline's thresholds.

Arguing that its intense competition with Pepsi would not be lessened by the merger, Coca-Cola claimed that this immense increase in concentration would not substantially lessen competition in the market, however it might be defined. Brushing aside Coca-Cola's contention, all the judges found the shares involved to be presumptively illegal. Quoting the Supreme Court, Federal Judge Gerhard Gesell wrote that "a merger which produces a firm controlling an undue percentage share of the relevant market, and results in a significant increase in the concentration of firms in that market, is so inherently likely to lessen competition substantially that it must be enjoined in the absence of evidence clearly showing that the merger is not likely to have such anticompetitive effects."

Apart from its argument about intense competition, Coca-Cola tried to declaw these large market shares by also arguing that entry into the industry was easy. Once again, however, Coca-Cola's case lacked evidence. A key barrier facing any potential entrant is the tight grip by which Coke and Pepsi hold their bottlers through flavor restrictions. Operating under flavor restrictions, bottlers committed to Coca-Cola's flavors cannot carry competing flavors produced by rival concentrate companies. The same applies to Pepsi bottlers. The impact of the resulting exclusivity was illustrated when 7-Up tried to enter the cola segment of the market in 1982 with Like, which distinguished itself from other cola-flavored soft drinks available at that time by being caffeine-free. Although Like's introduction was funded by Philip Morris (a marketing powerhouse that owns Marlboro, Miller Lite, and many other famous brands), Like never gained sufficient acceptance among bottlers to be offered to more than 50 percent of the consuming public. Apart from Like's problems with flavor restrictions, Coca-Cola and Pepsi responded to Like's introduction by launching caffeine-free colas of their own and marketing them aggressively.

Thus, in the end, Coca-Cola lost on all points. Its merger had to be abandoned.

The *Coca-Cola* case signalled that horizontal merger enforcement was not completely dead during the Reagan years. Still, all merger policy bordered on the comatose. It took the Bush Administration to change that:

> The single most striking development in merger law [since Reagan's departure] has been the rejuvenation of the enforcement agencies under new leadership. The FTC and Antitrust Division are acting like law enforcement agencies once again. Their staffs are aggressive, morale is high, . . . and a lot of transactions are being subjected to threats of injunction.[43]

VI. Vertical Mergers

Short of monopoly, the critical issue in nearly all vertical merger cases is "foreclosure." Before merger, numerous suppliers can compete for each independent user's purchases. After merger, supplier and user are linked by ownership. Products then typically flow between the merged firms as far as is practicable, and the sales opportunities of other suppliers diminish. If the vertical linkage is trivial, as would be true of a farmer owning a roadside vegetable stand, competition is not affected. If, on the other hand, the foreclosure covers a wide portion of the total market, there may be anticompetitive consequences. Here, too, history shows a shift toward leniency in recent years.

THE BROWN SHOE CASE (1962): VERTICAL ASPECTS[44]

Before Brown Shoe's acquisition of Kinney in 1955, Brown had acquired a large number of retail shops. Thus, Kinney was just one in a series of vertical mergers by Brown. In effect, then, Brown was attempting to accumulate captive retail distributors who would buy heavily from Brown's manufacturing arm.

On these vertical aspects the Supreme Court stressed several points. First, since Kinney was the largest independent retail chain, the court felt that in this industry "no merger between a manufacturer and an independent retailer could in-

volve a larger potential market foreclosure." Second, the evidence showed that Brown would use the acquisition "to force Brown shoes into Kinney stores." Third, there was a *trend* toward vertical integration in the industry, a trend in which the acquiring manufacturers had "become increasingly important sources of supply for their acquired outlets," and the "necessary corollary of these trends is the foreclosure of independent manufacturers from markets otherwise open to them." The court thus ordered divestiture.

THE CEMENT CASES (1961–1967)

Approximately three-fourths of all cement is used to produce ready-mixed concrete (cement premixed with sand or other aggregate). Prior to 1960 there was virtually no integration between the cement and ready-mixed concrete industries. By 1966, however, after an outbreak of merger activity, at least 40 ready-mix concrete companies had been acquired by leading cement companies, and several large producers of ready-mixed concrete had begun to make cement. The Federal Trade Commission issued a series of complaints, directed its staff to make an industry-wide investigation, and in January 1967 issued a policy statement challenging vertical mergers in the industry, all of which reduced acquisition activity appreciably.[45]

VERTICAL MERGER GUIDELINES (1982, 1992)

The current status of vertical mergers is now muddled by a lack of recent cases. It's clear, however, that the trend is toward greater tolerance. The Guidelines say that vertical mergers are unlikely to be challenged unless a combination of factors makes the foreclosure effect particularly odious. Among these factors are (1) very high concentration in either the upstream or downstream market, that is, an H-index greater than 1800, and (2) very little capacity that is not already vertically integrated between the two markets. Thus the law here still has some bite, but very few deal-makers need to fear a challenge.

VII. Conglomerate Mergers

The record-breaking merger statistics of the 1960s and 1980s show that the law has been almost inconsequential when it comes to conglomerate acquisitions. Officials are reluctant to apply curbs except where mergers clearly affect *particular markets*. And conglomerate mergers rarely have direct effects on particular markets.

Challenges to **product-extension** and **market-extension** conglomerates can be based on arguments of *potential competition*. Absent its acquisition of the leading bleach company, for instance, a major detergent manufacturer might have entered the bleach market by itself through internal expansion (*de novo*), or by "toehold" acquisition of a small bleach producer, thereby increasing the number of competitors in the bleach market or lessening concentration. Even in the absence of any intended *de novo* entry or toehold acquisition, potential competition might still be worth preserving. The *Procter & Gamble* case reviewed subsequently gives an example.

Pure conglomerates are less likely to affect specific markets. If the merging parties are truly dominant firms (IBM and GM, say), that too might be vulnerable. But these instances are so rare as to leave pure conglomerates essentially untouchable.

THE PROCTER GAMBLE CASE (1967)[46]
Procter & Gamble's 1958 acquisition of Clorox Chemical Co. could be considered a product extension merger. Among other things, Procter was the dominant producer of soaps and detergents, accounting for 54.4 percent of all packaged detergent sales. Clorox, on the other hand, was the nation's leading manufacturer of household liquid bleach, with approximately 48.8 percent of total sales at the time. As these statistics suggest, the markets for detergents and bleach were both highly concentrated. The Supreme Court decided that the merger was illegal, but not wholly or even mainly because of these market shares.

Anticompetitive effects were found in several respects. First, and most obviously, Procter was a prime prospective entrant into the bleach industry. Thus, "the merger would seriously diminish potential competition by eliminating Procter as a potential entrant." Indeed, before the acquisition, "Procter was in the course of diversifying into product lines related to its basic detergent-soap-cleanser business," and liquid bleach was a distinct possibility because it is used with detergent.

Second, the court expressed concern that the merger would confer anticompetitive advantages in the realm of marketing. Although all liquid bleach is chemically identical (5.25 percent sodium hypochlorite and 94.75 percent water), it is nevertheless highly differentiated. Clorox spent more than 12 percent of its sales revenues on advertising, and priced its bleach at a premium relative to unadvertised brands. For its part, Procter was the nation's leading advertiser (and still is).

The court therefore felt that Procter would unduly strengthen Clorox against other firms in the bleach market by extending to Clorox the same volume discounts on advertising that it received from the advertising media. Moreover, "retailers might be induced to give Clorox preferred shelf space since it would be manufactured by Procter, which also produced a number of other products marketed by retailers." In sum, "the substitution of the powerful acquiring firm for the smaller, but already dominant, firm may substantially reduce the competitive structure of the industry by raising entry barriers and dissuading the smaller firms from aggressively competing."

THE ITT-GRINNELL CASE (1970)[47]
This case is of interest because the Justice Department tried to argue that a finding of specific anticompetitive effect in specific product and geographic markets was *not* required for illegality. It argued instead that, in the wake of a "trend

among large diversified industrial firms to acquire other large corporations," it could be concluded that "anticompetitive consequences will
appear in numerous though *undesignated* individual 'lines of commerce.' "

The merger at issue was ITT's acquisition
of Grinnell, a large manufacturer of automatic
sprinkler devices and related products. Since
ITT had been a major participant in the conglomerate merger mania, and since Grinnell was big,
this was a good case to test the theory that adding to *aggregate concentration* was alone offensive under the law. But the District Court did not
agree, and the Justice Department lost:

> The Court's short answer to this claim . . . is that
> the legislative history, the statute itself and the
> controlling decisional law all make it clear beyond
> a peradventure of a doubt that in a Section 7 case
> the alleged anticompetitive effects of a merger
> must be examined in the context of *specific prod-
> uct and geographic markets;* and the determina-
> tion of such markets is a necessary predicate to a
> determination of whether there has been a sub-
> stantial lessening of competition within an area of
> effective competition.

The District Court opinion was not reviewed by
the Supreme Court because the case was settled
by consent decree prior to appeal.[48] Thus, we
have bumped into the outer limit of the law. Because this limit is limited, conglomerate mergers
proceed apace.

The guidelines for conglomerates reflect this
limitation. They merely suggest possible challenges in which main potential entrants are
eliminated.

VIII. Remedies and Notification

Judicial statements of legality tell only part of the
story. *Remedies* are equally important. For if illegal mergers are allowed to stand, they might as
well be declared legal. The record on this score
is blemished because total divestiture to achieve

premerger status is not always achieved. The
data for 1951 to 1977 prove the point:

> Total divestiture was accomplished in 53 per cent
> of the completed cases brought by the antitrust
> agencies. The assets divested represented only 44
> per cent of the total assets challenged in all com-
> plaints. On the other hand, no divestiture was
> achieved in 7 per cent of the completed cases. . . .
> The remaining cases either were dismissed (13 per
> cent) or achieved only partial divestiture (27 per
> cent).[49]

Even when divestiture is achieved, there
may be little remedial improvement if, as is all
too common, the divested assets create a nonvi-
able firm or are absorbed by a rival.[50]

One of the main reasons divestiture is reluctantly and imperfectly imposed is that it is difficult to unscramble the eggs once they are
scrambled. Less scrambling occurs when the antitrust agencies are given advance notice of mergers, for then preliminary injunctions can be
obtained preventing the merger's consummation
until after completion of legal review. This, in
fact, was the purpose of the premerger notification provisions of the Hart-Scott-Rodino Act of
1976. Specifically, the Antitrust Division of the
Department of Justice and the Federal Trade
Commission must receive thirty days notice of
acquisitions if one of the parties to the transaction has sales or assets of $100 million or more
and the other party has sales or assets of $10 mil-
lion or more.[51]

Summary

History reveals an annual stream of mergers that
occasionally swells to a flood. Around the turn of
the century thousands of multifirm horizontal
mergers transformed many manufacturing and
mining industries into tight-knit oligopolies and
near monopolies. A second major movement
during the late 1920s brought further horizontal
couplings and introduced extensive vertical and

conglomerate activity as well. During the 1960s, 25,598 mergers were recorded, involving scores of billions of dollars in assets. Most recently, the 1980s witnessed what appears to have been the most frenzied merger movement of all time. (So far the 1990s are quieter.)

Generally speaking, merger frequency tends to rise and fall as the average level of stock market prices rises and falls. Thus, the timing of mergers is influenced by financial considerations. In addition, there are several basic underlying stimulants to merger, all of which have played some role in the past, none of which has clearly dominated the scene: (1) The pursuit of market power is most clearly associated with horizontal mergers. The first merger movement provides the best examples of this—including the U. S. Steel merger of 1901. (2) A desire to diversify and thereby reduce risk motivates some conglomerate mergers. Although some mergers may further this goal, most apparently do not. (3) Businessmen like to justify their mergers with claims of efficiency or economies of scale. Such claims may occasionally be valid, but the available evidence indicates that they are overly optimistic (if that is the right word). (4) Speculation and tax considerations have contributed substantially to some mergers. (5) We cannot rule out growth and personal aggrandizement, although these factors are difficult to quantify.

As for policy, these recent surges have been possible chiefly because conglomerate mergers are almost untouchable under current law. The competitive effects of conglomerates elude structural measurement even when they are adverse, and the law bans only those mergers that may "substantially lessen competition" in some product and geographic market. Application of this standard led to a hard line against horizontal mergers during the 1960s, as illustrated by the *Brown Shoe* and *Von's* cases. The *General Dynamics* case relaxed matters in the 1970s with considerations of the rule of reason. The most recent interpretations grant further relaxation. "Official Guidelines" indicate the pattern. They

(1) menace horizontal mergers when the H-index is in the 1000 to 1800 range and thwart them only above 1800; (2) flexibly allow for other factors like barriers to entry; (3) define the market somewhat differently than before; and (4) permit otherwise illegal mergers in the event of substantial efficiencies.

Vertical merger policy has taken a similar course. Tight at first, it too has been relaxed.

Questions and Exercises for Chapter 8

1. Identify by dates and main features the four major merger waves in American history.
2. Why have conglomerate mergers become the main type?
3. Compare and contrast monopoly power and risk spreading as possible merger motives. Which is most likely for horizontal mergers? For conglomerates? Why?
4. What were the main indicators of "may be . . . to lessen competition" used by the court in horizontal cases *Brown Shoe* and *Von's?* Is the court consistent?
5. Discuss *General Dynamics* in facts, decision, and significance.
6. What are the distinctive features of the "Merger Guidelines"?
7. What are advantages and disadvantages of considering entry conditions when assessing the competitive effects of horizontal merger?
8. During the 1960s, it is doubtful that the Coca-Cola/Dr. Pepper and Pepsi/7-Up mergers would have been attempted. Why?
9. Use the cement cases to explain what is meant by foreclosure.
10. Are conglomerate mergers completely free from challenge? If not, which conglomerate mergers seem most vulnerable?

Appendix to Chapter 8

Some economists argue that mergers and acquisitions are almost always socially desirable because they generate efficiencies. The main argument of these economists is that mergers and acquisitions comprise a market for corporate control. This market is said to foster efficiencies because well-managed firms seek to acquire control of target firms in order to replace inept managements or force existing managements to maximize profits. In short, good managers supposedly oust bad managers through acquisitions.[52]

Economists defending mergers in this manner cite two main items of evidence to support their argument: (1) Acquisitions always entail hefty gains for the target firms' shareholders, who receive a premium over the market value of their firm; (2) it also appears, though less certainly, that the acquiring company's shareholders break even, on average, with their share prices, neither rising nor falling in response to bidding announcements.[53] These two findings suggest to some economists that mergers are generally profitable, and by implication that they are profitable because of the efficiencies they create. As Richard Caves summarizes this view, "A bundle for the target's shareholders plus zero for the bidder's still sums to a bundle, supporting the conclusion that mergers create value and accordingly are economically efficient."[54]

Although some acquisitions yield efficiencies, the bulk of the evidence is strongly against this as an important explanation for the vast majority. The contrary evidence may be divided into three categories depending on timing: (1) "event" evidence from the time of the acquisition; (2) "premerger" evidence from before the event; and (3) "postmerger" evidence from after the event.

The findings for changes in share price during the bidding referred to previously come from *event* evidence. Although that evidence may seem to support the efficiencies hypothesis, it does so only very weakly. For example, the premiums paid to shareholders of the target firm do not depend on prospective efficiencies because

they are paid even when, as often happens, there are no intended changes in the target firm at all. And without changes, there can be no efficiencies. Because the payment of premiums does not hinge on the prospect of efficiencies, it offers no proof of efficiencies. Leveraged management buy-outs are the clearest examples. In such instances, which have become very common (e.g., Dan River, Inc., Macy's, and Safeway), top *existing* managers borrow heavily to buy ownership control of their firm and then take it private, saving their jobs.[55] The premiums paid for such control match those of takeover acquisitions. "Greenmail" is another contrary example. In greenmail cases, premiums are paid to buy out raiders who own minority stakes and merely threaten takeovers.

Regarding the other main finding mentioned previously—that of no change in share prices for stockholders of the acquiring firms, on average—the efficiency interpretation of that evidence may also be questioned. The event studies producing this finding are usually based on the "efficient stock market" hypothesis (the idea that stock prices reflect all available information at any moment). This hypothesis has suffered numerous setbacks, especially since the stock market crash of October 1987.[56] Moreover, any negative influences on the acquiring firms' share prices are likely to be obscured by the very large size of the typical acquirer relative to its target and by the upward trend in share price that is common for the acquirer's stock just before bidding occurs.[57] Hence, the "event" finding of a breakeven for the typical buyer's owners may be a mirage.

The *premerger* evidence centers on the premerger conditions of the acquiring firms and target firms. If the efficiency hypothesis were correct, the superior management capabilities of the acquiring firms would presumably result in exceptionally high premerger profits for acquiring firms, and the inferior performance hypothesized for the target firms would presumably lead to poor premerger performance for the target firms. The evidence is somewhat mixed on both points, but it generally runs against the efficiency hypothesis. Acquiring companies tend to be bigger than average and may be growing at especially brisk paces, but in general they do not have exceptionally good managements as measured by profitability.[58] As for target companies, two massive studies of more than 800 acquisitions in manufacturing and banking during the 1960s and 1970s reveal that target firms typically are *not* poor performers before their acquisition.[59] Indeed, those in manufacturing had especially high profits before acquisition. Hence, the bulk of the premerger evidence disrespects the theory that mergers purge the economy of bad managers to create efficiencies.

The *postmerger* evidence is, by its nature, most compelling. And it comes in several forms—real effects, profitability changes, shifts in market share, and stock market evaluations. *Real effects* are measured by changes in productivity, in personnel staffing, and the like. Data for real effects are difficult to compile, so studies of this sort are scarce. Those available reveal some positive results and some negative results, but on the whole there appear to be no systematic gains in efficiency.[61] Indeed, optimistic claims of efficiency at the time of merger have all too often proved to be embarrassing later.[61] Postmerger corporate *changes in profitability* have been much more thoroughly studied. They provide little support for the view that mergers raise relative profitability. The great weight of evidence shows on average a zero or negative impact.[62] Observed *shifts in the market shares* of acquired companies corroborate these findings on profitability. If acquired firms became more efficient as a result of merger, their market shares would presumably rise as they became more competitive. On the contrary, however, evidence shows market shares to be unaffected or falling after takeover.[63] Finally, the *stock market's evaluation* of the acquiring firm typically deteriorates during the months and years following takeover, some-

thing quite different from the stock market's evaluation during the event, when share prices of the acquiring firm appear to remain unaffected. Share prices of acquiring firms tend to fall in the postmerger world, apparently reflecting the adverse profit and market share trends. F. M. Scherer puts the long-term share price evidence in a nutshell:

> When the time frame has been extended to one to three years after the event, acquiring firms are found to experience *negative* abnormal returns. In the seven one-year studies surveyed by Jensen and Ruback (1983), the abnormal returns averaged -5.5 percent; over the three-year post-takeover period examined by Magenheim and Mueller (1987), the abnormal returns were -16 percent by the most conservative measurement technique.[64]

Overall, the postmerger evidence is therefore not favorable to the efficiency hypothesis. The single most telling summary statistic in this regard is the estimate of Ravenscraft and Scherer that approximately one out of every three acquisitions of the 1960s and 1970s turned out so badly that the acquired assets were eventually sold off, as Mobil Oil Company divested itself of Montgomery Ward after a decade of disappointment and Coca-Cola rid itself of Columbia Pictures after a string of box-office bombs like *Ishtar.*[65]

In sum, virtually all the best evidence available stacks up against the notion that the market for corporate control breeds efficiency. It creates larger firms, but size and efficiency do not necessarily correspond. After surveying the thousands of divestitures of the late 1980s, Donald Povejsil, former executive of Westinghouse, said, "Most of the classical justifications of large size have proved to be of minimal value, or counter-productive, or fallacious."[66] Acquisitions undoubtedly yield efficiencies in certain cases, but as a general rule they do not.

Where, then, do the acquisition premiums come from? There are several explanations.

They come partly from losses experienced by the bondholders of the acquiring companies. They come partly from a grossly mistaken optimism, or hubris, among the acquiring firms' managers.[67] Perhaps the best explanation relies on the likelihood that the demand for a firm's stock is typically downward sloping, just like the demand for apples or other goods. Daily stock market activity occurs at the margin, involving relatively few ownership shares, thereby generating the observed price for marginal exchanges. In contrast, bids for control of 50 percent or more of a company's stock must aim at a place well up the demand curve, at a much higher price, because of the much larger number of ownership shares involved in a bid for control.[68]

Notes

1. *Mergers and Acquisitions* (March/April 1990): 95.
2. Willard F. Mueller, *The Celler-Kefauver Act: The First 27 Years,* U.S. House of Representatives, Committee on the Judiciary, Subcommittee on Monopolies and Commercial Law (Nov. 7, 1979), pp. 7–8.
3. Devra L. Golbe and Lawrence J. White, "Mergers and Acquisitions in the U.S. Economy: An Aggregate and Historical Overview," in *Mergers and Acquisitions,* ed. Alan J. Auerbach (Chicago: University of Chicago Press, 1988), pp. 25–47.
4. Ralph L. Nelson, *Merger Movements in American Industry, 1895–1956* (Princeton, NJ: Princeton University Press, 1959), p. 29.
5. Jesse W. Markham, "Survey of the Evidence and Findings on Mergers," in *Business Concentration and Price Policy* (Princeton, NJ: Princeton University Press, 1955), pp. 168–169.
6. Federal Trade Commission, *Economic Report on Corporate Mergers* (Washington, DC, 1969), p. 666.
7. Nelson, *Merger Movements,* pp. 106–26; Markham, "Survey of Evidence and Findings," pp. 146–154; and Willard Mueller, testimony in *Economic Concentration,* Hearings before the Senate Subcommittee on Antitrust and Monopoly, Part 2 (1965), p. 506.
8. For an excellent discussion of causes see Peter O. Steiner, *Mergers: Motives, Effects, Policies* (Ann Arbor: University of Michigan Press, 1975), especially Chapter 2.
9. Stanley E. Boyle, "Pre-Merger Growth and Profit Characteristics of Large Conglomerate Mergers in the United States: 1948–1968," *St. Johns Law Review* (Spring 1970, Special Edition): 160–161. See also Robert L. Conn, "The Failing Firm/Industry Doctrines in Conglomerate Mergers," *Journal of Industrial Economics* (March 1976): 181–187.
10. *Business Week,* April 4, 1988, pp. 28–29; May 30, 1988, pp. 82–83.
11. The associated gain in monopoly profit was in each case sufficient to recoup the cost of the acquisition in just two years. David M. Barton and Roger Sherman, "The Price and Profit Effects of Horizontal Merger: A Case Study," *Journal of Industrial Economics* (December 1984): 165–177.
12. Steven A. Morrison and Clifford Winston, "Enhancing the Performance of the Deregulated Air Transportation System," *Brookings Papers on Economic Activity: Microeconomics 1989* (Washington, DC: Brookings Institution, 1989), pp. 61–112. Included were American Airlines and Air California plus Delta and Western Airlines.
13. Ibid., p. 73. Other researchers have had similar results. Gloria Hurdle and her associates found fare increases of 12 to 33 percent if two carriers merged to form a monopoly, and increases of 4 to 12 percent for a merger creating duopoly. Gloria Hurdle et al., "Concentration, Potential Entry, and Performance in the Airline Industry," U.S. Department of Justice Antitrust Division Economic Analysis Discussion Paper, 1988.
14. *Wall Street Journal,* 17 September 1986, p. 35. Another nice quotation comes from *Forbes* regarding hat tycoon Irving Joel (October 17, 1988, p. 108):
[He] has bought up the brand names that account for an estimated 70% of the $75 million quality western and dress hat market in the U.S. "If you play Monopoly," says Joel of his acquisition strategy, "the idea is to own all the properties on the board."
15. Gerald D. Newbould, *Management and Merger Activity* (Liverpool, England: Guthstead Ltd., 1970), pp. 138–139.
16. Willard F. Mueller, "Public Policy Toward Vertical Mergers," in *Public Policy Toward Mergers,* ed. F. Weston and S. Peltzman (Pacific Palisades, CA: Goodyear, 1969), pp. 150–166.
17. Donald O. Parsons and Edward J. Ray, "The United States Steel Consolidation: The Creation of Market Control," *Journal of Law and Economics* (April 1975): 198.
18. L. G. Goldberg, "Conglomerate Mergers and Concentration Ratios," *Review of Economics and Statistics* (August 1974): 303–309; S. E. Boyle and P. W. Jaynes, *Economic Report on Conglomerate Merger Performance* (Washington, DC: Federal Trade Commission, 1972), pp. 82–83. On the other hand, see John T. Scott, "Purposive Diversification as a Motive for Merger," *International Journal of Industrial Organization* (March 1989): 35–47.
19. Roger Sherman, *The Economics of Industry* (Boston: Little, Brown, 1974), p. 105.
20. H. Bierman, Jr. and J. L. Thomas, "A Note on Mergers and Risk," *Antitrust Bulletin* (Fall 1974): 523–529. Also, the risk reduction benefits managers, not owners. Yakov Amihud and Baruch Lev, "Risk Reduction as a Managerial Motive for Conglomerate Mergers," *Bell Journal of Economics* (Autumn 1981): 605–617.
21. B. Lev and G. Mandelker, "The Microeconomic

Consequences of Corporate Mergers," *Journal of Business* (January 1972): 85–104; Samuel R. Reid, *The New Industrial Order* (New York: McGraw-Hill, 1976), pp. 94–98; R. W. Melicher and D. F. Rush, "The Performance of Conglomerate Firms: Recent Risk and Return Experience," *Journal of Finance* (May 1973): 381–388; C. W. L. Hill, "Conglomerate Performance Over the Economic Cycle," *Journal of Industrial Economics* (December 1983): 197–211.

22. Dennis C. Mueller, "The Effects of Conglomerate Mergers," *Journal of Banking and Finance,* 1 (December 1977): 315–344. In addition to Mueller's citations see G. Meeks, *Disappointing Marriage: A Study of the Gains from Mergers* (Cambridge, UK: Cambridge University Press, 1977); D. W. Colenutt and P. P. O'Donnell, "The Consistency of Monopolies and Mergers Commission Merger Reports," *Antitrust Bulletin* (Spring 1978): 51–82; Alan A. Fisher and Robert H. Lande, "Efficiency Considerations in Merger Enforcement," *California Law Review* (December 1983): 1580–1697; David J. Ravenscraft and F. M. Scherer, *Mergers, Sell-Offs, and Economic Efficiency* (Washington, DC: Brookings Institution, (1987); and Alan Hughes, "The Impact of Merger," in *Mergers & Merger Policy,* ed. J. A. Fairburn and J. A. Kay (Oxford, England: Oxford University Press, 1989), pp. 30–98.

23. Shaw Livermore, "The Success of Industrial Mergers," *Quarterly Journal of Economics* (November 1935): 68–96.

24. Alan J. Auerbach and David Reishus, "The Impact of Taxation on Mergers and Acquisitions," in *Mergers and Acquisitions,* ed. A. J. Auerbach (Chicago: University of Chicago Press, 1988), pp. 69–88.

25. Spoken by Richard H. Griebel, a former ITT executive and president of Lehigh Valley Industries, *Business Week,* May 9, 1970, p. 61. For more on Geneen see Anthony Sampson, *The Sovereign State of ITT* (New York: Fawcett Crest Paperback, 1974).

26. *Business Week,* July 5, 1969, p. 34. For more solid evidence favoring growth, see Alan R. Beckenstein, "Merger Activity and Merger Theories: An Empirical Investigation," *Antitrust Bulletin* (Spring 1979): 105–128.

27. Joe Queenan, "The RJR Nabisco Slugfest," *Wall Street Journal,* 11 January 1990, p. A12. See also Bryan Burrough and John Helyar, *Barbarians at the Gate* (New York: Harper & Row, 1990). For a broader discussion, see Stephen A. Rhoades, *Power, Empire Building and Mergers* (Lexington, MA: Lexington Books, 1983).

28. K. G. Elzinga and T. F. Hogarty, "The Problem of Geographic Market Delineation of Antimerger Suits," *Antitrust Bulletin* (Spring 1973): 45–81. See also Ira Horowitz, "Market Definition in Antitrust Analysis: A Regression Based Approach," *Southern Economic Journal* (July 1981): 1–16. For the "Guidelines" approach, see Gregory J. Werden, "Market Delineation under the Merger Guidelines," Department of Justice, Antitrust Division, Economic Analysis Group, Working Paper EAG 92-1, January 2, 1992.

29. *United States* v. *Bethlehem Steel Corp.,* 168 F. Supp. 576 (1958).

30. *Brown Shoe Company* v. *United States,* 370 U. S. 294 (1962).

31. *United States* v. *Von's Grocery Co.,* 384 U. S. 270 (1966).

32. *United States* v. *General Dynamics Corp.* 415 (U. S.) 486 (1974).

33. Oliver E. Williamson, "Economies as an Antitrust Defense: The Welfare Tradeoffs," *American Economic Review* (March 1968): 18–36.

34. A. A. Fisher, F. I. Johnson, and R. H. Lande, "Mergers, Market Power, and Property Rights," Bureau of Economics Working Paper No. 130, Federal Trade Commission (1985), pp. 9–10.

35. David B. Audretsch, "An Evaluation of Horizontal Merger Enforcement," in *Industrial Organization, Antitrust, and Public Policy,* ed. J. V. Craven (Boston: Kluwer-Nijhoff, 1983), pp. 69–88.

36. "Special Supplement, General Accounting Office Report on Changes in Antitrust Enforcement Policies," *Antitrust & Trade Regulation Report,* December 13, 1990, pp. 5–40.

37. *United States* v. *Waste Management, Inc.,* 743 F. 2d 976 (2d Cir. 1984). See also *United States* v. *Baker Hughes, Inc.,* 908 F. 2d 981 (D.C. Cir. 1990) and *United States* v. *Syufy Enterprises,* 903 F. 2d 659 (9th Cir. 1990).

38. Richard Schmalensee, "Ease of Entry: Has the Concept Been Applied Too Readily?", *Antitrust Law Journal* (vol. 56, no. 1, 1987): 44.

39. Andrew S. Joskow, Gregory J. Werden, and Richard L. Johnson, "Entry, Exit, and Performance in Airline Markets," Department of Justice, Economic Analysis Group Paper, EAG 90-10, December 31, 1990; S. A. Morrison and Clifford Winston, "The Dynamics of Airline Pricing and Competition," *American Economic Review* (May 1990): 389–393.

40. Robert Smiley, "Empirical Evidence on Strategic Entry Deterence," *International Journal of Industrial Organization* (no. 2, 1988): 167–180.

41. J. D. Gribbin and M. A. Utton, "The Treatment of Dominant Firms in the U.K. Competition Legislation," in *Mainstreams in Industrial Organization,* Vol. II, ed. H. W. de Jong and W. G. Shepherd (Dordrecht: Kluwer Academic Publishers, 1986), pp. 243–272; Daniel Shapiro and R. S. Khemani, "The Determinants of Entry and Exit Reconsidered," *International Journal of Industrial Organization* (March 1987): 15–26; William F. Chappell, M. S. Kimenyi, and Walter J. Mayer, "A Poisson Probability Model of Entry and Market Structure," *Southern Economic Journal* (April 1990): 918–927.

42. The opinions are *F.T.C.* v. *Coca-Cola Co.,* 641 F. Supp. 1128 (1986); *In the Matter of The Coca-Cola Company,* Federal Trade Commission, initial decision, November 30, 1990. For a good summary see Lawrence J. White "Application of the Merger Guidelines: The Proposed Merger of Coca-Cola and Dr. Pepper," in *The Antitrust Revolution,* ed. I. E. Kwoka, Jr., and L. J. White (Glenview, IL: Scott, Foresman, 1989), pp. 80–98.

43. Malcolm R. Pfunder, "Developments in Merger

Law and Enforcement 1989–90," *Antitrust Law Journal* (vol. 59, no. 2, 1990): 319–337.

44. *Brown Shoe Company* v. *United States,* 370 U. S. 294 (1962).

45. Federal Trade Commission, *Economic Report on Mergers and Vertical Integration in the Cement Industry* (Washington, DC: 1966); Enforcement Policy with Respect to Vertical Mergers in the Cement Industry, January 1967, in Commerce Clearing House, 1971 *Trade Regulation Reports,* #4520. For more on this and other vertical cases, see Oliver Hart and Jean Tirole, "Vertical Integration and Market Foreclosure," *Brookings Papers on Economic Activity* (Microeconomics 1990), pp. 205–276.

46. *Federal Trade Commission* v. *Procter & Gamble Co.,* 386 U. S. 568 (1967).

47. *United States* v. *International Telephone and Telegraph Corp.,* 324 F. Supp. 19 (D. Conn. 1970).

48. For a similar district court opinion see *United States* v. *Northwest Industries,* 301 F. Supp. 1066 (N.D.Ill. 1969) at 1096.

49. W. Mueller, *The Celler-Kefauver Act,* p. 89. This excludes banking cases.

50. For further discussion see Kenneth G. Elzinga, "The Antimerger Law: Pyrrhic Victories?" *Journal of Law and Economics* (April 1969): 43–78.

51. Actually, the rules are much more complex than this. See T. W. Brunner, T. G. Krattenmaker, R. A. Skitol, and A. A. Webster, *Mergers in the New Antitrust Era* (Washington, DC: Bureau of National Affairs, 1985), pp. 151–170.

52. Henry G. Manne, "Mergers and the Market for Corporate Control," *Journal of Political Economy* (April 1965): 110–120; *Economic Report of the President,* 1985, Chapter 6, pp. 187–202.

53. For a survey of the evidence, see Michael C. Jensen and Richard S. Ruback, "The Market for Corporate Control: The Scientific Evidence," *Journal of Financial Economics* (vol. 11, 1983): 5–50.

54. Richard E. Caves, "Mergers, Takeovers, and Economic Efficiency," *International Journal of Industrial Organization* (March 1989): 153.

55. *Wall Street Journal,* 29 December 1983, p. 1; Anne B. Fisher, "Oops! My Company," *Fortune,* July 23, 1984, p. 18.

56. Douglas K. Pearce, "Challenges to the Concept of Stock Market Efficiency," *Economic Review of the Federal Reserve Bank of Kansas City* (September/October, 1987): 16–33; Colin Camerar, "Bubbles and Fads in Asset Prices," *Journal of Economic Surveys* (vol. 3, no. 1, 1989: 3–41; Gary Hector, "What Makes Stock Prices Move?", *Fortune,* October 10, 1988, pp. 69–76; *Business Week,* February 22, 1988, pp. 140–142; Robert J. Shiller, "Fashions, Fads, and Bubbles in Financial Markets," in *Knights, Raiders, and Targets,* ed. J. Coffe (New York: Oxford University Press, 1987).

57. Dennis C. Mueller, "United States Antitrust: At the Crossroads," in *Mainstreams in Industrial Organization,* ed. H. W. de Jong and W. G. Shepherd (Dordrecht: Martinus Nijhoff Publishers, 1986), pp. 215–241.

58. Dennis C. Mueller, *Determinants and Effects;* G. Meeks, *Disappointing Marriage: A Study of the Gains from Mergers* (Cambridge, UK: Cambridge University Press, 1977); Alan Hughes, "The Impact of Merger: A Survey of Empirical Evidence for the UK," in *Mergers and Merger Policy,* ed. James A. Fairburn and John A Kay (Oxford: Oxford University Press, 1989), pp. 68–69. Australian acquirers have been exceptionally profitable premerger, but this distinction is tarnished by their exceptionally bad post-merger performance. F. M. McDougall and David K. Round, *The Effects of Mergers & Takeovers in Australia, 1970–1981* (Melbourne: Information Australia for the Australian Institute of Management, 1986).

59. Ravenscraft and Scherer, *Mergers, Sell-Offs, and Economic Efficiency;* Stephen A. Rhoades, "The Operating Performance of Acquired Firms in Banking," in *Issues After a Century of Federal Competition Policy,* ed. R. L. Wills, J. A. Caswell, and J. D. Culbertson (Lexington, MA: Lexington Books, 1987), pp. 280–290. See also Hughes, "Impact of Merger," p. 66.

60. Hughes, "Impact of Merger," pp. 74–75. The most favorable study is Frank R. Lichtenberg and David Siegel, "Productivity Changes in Ownership of Manufacturing Plants," *Brookings Papers on Economic Activity* (No. 3, 1987), pp. 643–683.

61. For example, when RJR acquired Nabisco Brands, it claimed that Nabisco's cookie and cracker business would yield "enormous synergies" when blended with Del Monte, its fresh fruits and canned foods subsidiary. But after three years and numerous corporate reorganizations Nabisco and Del Monte were finally split apart when RJR concluded they were in very different businesses, marching at "entirely different tempos." *Wall Street Journal,* 12 May 1980, p. 12. Even more embarrassing are cases in which bankruptcy follows closely after merger (e.g., Penn-Central). For a survey, see A. A. Fisher and R. H. Lande, "Efficiency Considerations in Merger Enforcement," *California Law Review* (December 1983): 1580–1696.

62. Hughes, "Impact of Merger"; Ravenscraft and Scherer, *Merger, Sell-Offs, and Economic Efficiency;* and Rhoades, "Operating Performance."

63. Lawrence G. Goldberg, "The Effect of Conglomerate Mergers on Competition," *Journal of Law and Economics* (April 1973): 137–158; Dennis C. Mueller, "Mergers and Market Share," *Review of Economics and Statistics* (May 1985): 259–267.

64. F. M. Scherer, "Corporate Takeovers: The Efficiency Arguments," *Journal of Economic Perspectives* (Winter 1988): 71.

65. Ravenscraft and Scherer, *Mergers, Sell-Offs, and Economic Efficiency,* pp. 159–191.

66. Walter Kiechel III, "Corporate Strategy for the 1990s," *Fortune,* February 29, 1988, p. 34.

67. Richard Roll, "The Hubris Hypothesis of Corporate Takeovers," *Journal of Business* (April 1986): 197–216.

68. For elaboration, see Hughes, "Impact of Merger," pp. 94–95.

Chapter 9

Price Discrimination: The Robinson-Patman Act

That the Robinson-Patman Act . . . is the most controversial of our antitrust laws may be the understatement of the century.
— *Frederick Rowe*

There are many things in life that can be either good or bad simultaneously, depending on the circumstances—wealth and wine, to name just two. The same applies to price discrimination. Under some circumstances, it may increase competition. At times it may lessen competition. This good/bad dichotomy makes public policy in this area a delicate exercise. Indeed, public policy itself can be procompetitive or anticompetitive.

This chapter reviews and assesses price discrimination policy. The statute law in this area began in 1914 with Section 2 of the Clayton Act. This was amended by the Robinson-Patman Act of 1936. Now, more than a thousand enforcement actions later, we confront a large body of case law that requires summary consideration. The controversy sparked by this policy also receives attention. Before considering legal matters, however, we should explore a simple economic definition of price discrimination.

I. Economic Definition

Price discrimination occurs whenever a seller sells the same commodity or service at more than one price. Moreover, even if the sale items are not exactly the same, economic theory says that price discrimination occurs if the seller sells very similar products at different price/cost ratios. For instance, IBM used to rent two disk-drive systems that differed only slightly in cost and model number (the 2314 and 2319) but immensely in price ($1,455 a month versus $1,000). The broad definition includes cases in which costs differ and identical prices are charged, and cases involving high prices on low-cost sales coupled with low prices on high-cost sales.

Three conditions are essential for price discrimination: (1) The seller must have some *market power.* A purely competitive firm does not have sufficient control over price to engage in discrimination. (2) The seller must confront buyers who have *differing price elasticities of de-*

mand. These elasticity differences among classes of buyers may be due to differences in income level, differences in "needs," differences in the availability of substitutes, differences in use of the product, and so on. Without different elasticities, buyers would not willingly pay different prices. (3) These various buyer elements must be kept *separate*. Without separation, low-price customers could resell their purchases to the high-price customers, subverting the seller's ability to identify and segregate the different demands.

Figure 9–1 illustrates these points with a conventional economic model of price discrimination. The negatively sloped demand curves indicate monopoly power. Differences in their angles of descent and intercepts indicate differing elasticities of demand at each possible price, with the result that buyers in market X have the relatively more elastic demand. Average total cost (ATC) per unit is the same in both markets because the product is basically the same. Moreover, ATC is assumed to be constant. This means that ATC and marginal cost (MC) are identical. Following the conventional profit-maximizing formula of MR = MC, we find that P_x and Q_x are the optimal combination in market X, whereas P_y

and Q are the optimal combination in market Y. Shading indicates excess profits. Notice that price in the relatively elastic market, P_x, is substantially below price in the relatively inelastic market, P_y. Indeed, nothing would be sold in market X at price P_y. Notice also that if these markets could not be kept separate, their demands, their elasticities, and of course their buyers, too, would blend, leaving only one market for the seller instead of two.

Moving from this general economic model to legal matters requires that three observations be borne in mind. First, the law covers price discrimination that occurs within a given market as well as that which occurs across markets. Indeed, intramarket discrimination between buyers may be said to be its primary concern. Second, the law is concerned with discrimination only insofar as it may injure competition or competitors. Price discrimination itself is not condemned, so *countless* instances of price discrimination go untouched by the law (as when you get a better deal on a new car than your neighbor does). Third, the law addresses mere price differences rather than price/cost differences. The one exception to this legal quirk is the "cost justi-

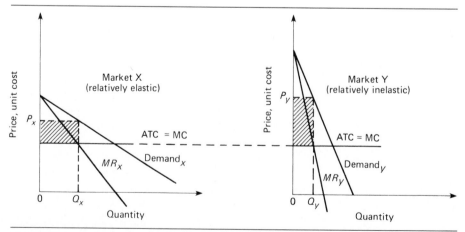

Figure 9–1
Price Discrimination in Theory

fication" defense, something that is explained shortly.

II. Price Discrimination Law

The Clayton Act's original Section 2 outlawed only flagrantly predatory price discrimination. Its limited scope, plus several loopholes, yielded few prosecutions. While this law lay idle, chain stores revolutionized grocery, drug, and department store merchandising. Small, single-shop, mom-and-pop stores suffered and, during the Great Depression, began dropping like blighted apples. The outcries of their owners caused the Federal Trade Commission to study and report. Although the FTC's report found much virtue in chain stores, it also found that "a most substantial part of the chains' ability to undersell independents" could be attributed to the chains' ability to buy goods from manufacturers more cheaply than independents could. The chains' oligopsony buying power forced manufacturers to discriminate in favor of chains. Moreover, their large size enabled chains to buy directly from manufacturers, thereby sidestepping independent brokers, wholesalers, jobbers, and other middlemen as well as to undersell independent retailers. So Congress went to bat for small business. In the words of Congressman Patman, mid-1935:

> The day of the independent merchant is gone unless something is done and done quickly. He cannot possibly survive under that system. So we have reached the crossroad; we must either turn the food . . . business of this country . . . over to a few corporate chains, or we have got to pass laws that will give the people, who built this country in time of peace and who saved it in time of war, an opportunity to exist.[1]

In short, the purpose of the Robinson-Patman Act of 1936 went well beyond the traditional antitrust purpose of maintaining competition. It injected two new objectives: *protection* of small business and maintenance of *fair* or equitable price relationships between buyers who compete with each other as sellers.

A. Subsection 1(a) of Robinson-Patman

The aims of protection and equity lurk beneath the tortured language of all six main subsections in the act, especially 2(a). Subsection 2(a) prohibits a seller from charging *different prices to different purchasers* of "goods of like grade and quality" when the effect "may be substantially"

1. "to lessen competition or tend to create a monopoly in any line of commerce," or
2. "to injure, destroy, or prevent competition with any person" (or company)
   a. "who either grants or"
   b. "knowingly receives" the benefit of the discrimination, or
   c. "with customers of either of them."

Thus, there are two definitions of **illegal competitive effect:** (1) a *broad* definition that refers to substantial lessening of competition in the *market as a whole,* and (2) a *narrow* definition that refers to injury to *particular competitors.* The broad definition reflects the traditional antitrust aim of maintaining competition, and its language matches that applying to mergers. In contrast, it is the narrow definition that reflects the aims of protection, equity, and fairness.

Either of these two forms of competitive damage may occur in

1. the seller's market, which is called **primary level injury**
2. the buyers' market, which is called **secondary level injury**
3. the market containing customers of the buyers, which is called **tertiary level injury.**

If, for example, a manufacturer cuts price to one wholesaler but not to others, it might damage competition among manufacturers (primary level), or among wholesalers (secondary level), or among retailers who buy from the wholesalers (tertiary level). If it were a matter of direct sales to retailers, then retailers would be the buyers of the discriminating seller, and they would then be considered secondary level. If this sounds confusing, take heart. You are not alone, as indicated by itemization of the first common criticism of the act.

Common Criticism 1: The act is "a roughly hewn, unfinished block of legislative phraseology," a "masterpiece of obscurity," a source of "crystal clear confusion."[2]

Compounding the confusion, several types of price discrimination have been found to be injurious to competition: (1) volume or quantity discounts, (2) territorial price discrimination, (3) functional discounts, and (4) catch-as-catch-can price discrimination. These are outlined in Table 9–1, together with indications of the level at which they are said to damage competition and the specified breadths of injury typically used in the past by the FTC and appellate courts when enforcing the statute. The dashes in the table identify combinations of level and type that are rarely attacked under the law. These blank combinations are eligible for illegality, but the authorities tend to ignore them. The bottom row of Table 9–1 shows the defenses discriminators of

each type occasionally use to fend off FTC attorneys. These defenses—cost and good faith—are explicitly recognized by the Robinson-Patman Act:

- *Cost defense:* "nothing herein . . . shall prevent differentials which make only due allowance for differences in the cost of manufacture, sale, or delivery resulting from [differing methods of sale or delivery]."
- *Good faith defense,* Subsection 2(b): "nothing herein . . . shall prevent a seller rebutting the prima-facie case . . . by showing that his lower price . . . was made in good faith to meet an equally low price of a competitor."

Often, these defenses offer relatively little protection in practice. The cost defense has fallen into disuse because the FTC and appellate courts have been rather stingy in allowing its application. They require elaborate proofs and reject justifications based on reallocations of overhead costs.

The defense of meeting competition in good faith is much more useful. It allows a low price to match competition. This defense has been expanded to allow low prices that obtain new customers as well as retain old ones and that unwittingly or unknowingly beat a rival's prices.[3]

Table 9–1

Summary Outline of Injury Definition Applied, Given the Basic Types of Discrimination Found to Be Illegal and Market Level of Reference

	Type of Price Discrimination			
Level of Injury	*Volume or Quantity Discounts*	*Territorial Price Discrimination*	*Functional Discounts*	*Catch-as-Catch-Can Pricing*
Primary level	Broad or narrow	Broad or narrow	—	Narrow
Secondary level	Narrow	Narrow	Narrow	Narrow
Tertiary level	—	—	Narrow	—
Main line of possible defense	Cost	Good faith	Cost or good faith	Good faith

Still, critics of the Robinson-Patman Act favor further liberalization of the good faith defense as well as the cost defense.

Common Criticism 2: By amendment or reinterpretation, the defenses open to discriminators ought to be liberalized.

Before delving further into the case law concerning the act, we note two major anomalies in its language. First, despite its origins, the statute's fire is focused not on the power or conduct of oligopsonistic *buyers* but on the conduct of *sellers*. As Corwin Edwards observed:

> The avowed purpose of the Congress was to use the law of price discrimination to curb the buying power of chain stores and other large buyers. However, the means to be employed consisted primarily in forbidding sellers, the presumed victims of that buying power, from granting the concessions that were exacted from them. . . . If the statute was an effort to protect competition from the pressure of powerful buyers on weak sellers, it was anomalous to provide that protection primarily by action against weak sellers who succumbed to the pressure. Such a process bears some resemblance to an effort to stamp out mugging by making it an offense to permit oneself to be mugged.[4]

A second notable quirk concerns the statute's definition of price discrimination. Price differences unjustified by cost differences are "discriminatory," but cost differences unaccompanied by price differences are not. In other words, the economic definition of discrimination—differing price/cost ratios, even if prices are identical—is rejected by the statute in favor of a definition that hinges almost entirely on price differences alone. The consequences of this approach are illustrated by the *Binney & Smith* case. Binney & Smith, Co. was found by the FTC to have sold school supplies at a uniform price to both jobbers, who are middlemen, and large retail chains. This price uniformity, though obviously injurious to jobbers, was not questioned by the FTC.[5]

Common Criticism 3: Even accepting the act's purposes as proper, the statute is ill-conceived. Indeed, many proponents of protection and fairness are disappointed with it.

Before discussing the types of discrimination listed in Table 9–1, we should first specify the kinds of evidence that indicate "broad" or "narrow" injury, the two designations comprising the body of Table 9–1. **Broad (or market-wide) injury** to competition is indicated by substantial reductions in the number of competitors in the market, elevated barriers to entry, a lack of competitive behavior in pricing, or foreclosure of substantial parts of the market to existing competitors. **Narrow (or competitor) injury** is indicated by simple price differences among customers, or a price difference coupled with diversion of business from the disadvantaged buyer toward the favored buyer, or diversions away from a nondiscriminating seller toward a discriminating seller. Injuries embraced by this narrow definition are clearly more personal than those embraced by the broad definition. That is, the discrimination appears to cripple a *single* firm or particular *class* of firms. Obviously, the broad definition coincides more nearly with a purely economic definition of competition, whereas the narrow definition coincides with some notions of fairness.

A quick glance at Table 9–1 reveals that narrow evidence of injury has been more commonly used by the FTC, especially when judging injury at secondary and tertiary levels. At primary level, broad injury has been found only in cases concerning volume or quantity discounts and territorial price discrimination.[6]

Volume and Quantity Discounts. Quantity discounts are based on the amount purchased in a *single* transaction, with large quantities lowering price. Volume discounts are based on *cumulative* purchases, involving numerous transactions, during some stated period of time, such as one year. Of the two, volume discounts are least likely to be cost-justifiable and more anticompetitive in the broad sense. For these reasons, the FTC has attacked volume discounts much more vigorously than it has quantity discounts. At primary level, volume discounts can heighten barriers to entry or foreclose small sellers from substantial segments of the market.[7] An Appendix to this chapter illustrates this.

Although such discounts may have genuine anticompetitive effects at the primary (sellers') level, very few cases have actually been argued on these grounds. The rarity may be due to a dearth of situations causing broad injury at that level. Then again, it may also be a consequence of the fact that, under the act, volume and quantity discounts are more easily prosecuted on grounds of narrow injury at the secondary or buyer level. Recall that a major purpose of the act was to make such prosecutions as these easier.

The classic case here is *Morton Salt,* decided by the Supreme Court in 1948. Morton sold its table salt at $1.60 a case in less-than-carload lots, at $1.50 a case for carload lots, and at still lower prices of $1.40 and $1.35 for annual volumes exceeding 5,000 and 50,000 cases, respectively. In defense of these prices, Morton claimed that they were equally available to all, that salt was just one tiny item in grocers' inventories, and that therefore competitive injury could not arise. Rejecting these arguments the court concluded as follows:

> The legislative history of the Robinson-Patman Act makes it abundantly clear that Congress considered it to be an evil that a large buyer could secure a competitive advantage over a small buyer solely because of the large buyer's quantity purchasing ability. . . . Here the Commission found what would appear to be obvious, that the competitive opportunities of certain merchants were injured when they had to pay [Morton] substantially more for their goods than their competitors had to pay. . . . That [Morton's] quantity discounts did result in price differentials between competing purchasers sufficient to influence their resale price of salt was shown by the evidence. . . . Congress intended to protect a merchant from competitive injury attributable to

discriminatory prices on any or all goods sold in interstate commerce, whether the particular goods constituted a major or minor portion of his stock. . . . [In] enacting the Robinson-Patman Act Congress was especially concerned with protecting small business.[8]

This narrow, numerical interpretation of injury was later carried to such extremes that during the 1950s the FTC inferred injury despite evidence that "the beneficiaries of the discrimination were small and weak," and despite "unanimous statements by the disfavored customers that they were not injured."[9] Since then, this hard line has softened, but a fairly stringent interpretation of secondary line injury still prevails.

Critics of this policy argue that although individual *competitors* may suffer, *competition* may not. Such discrimination in favor of large buyers is said to "introduce flexibility into the distributive system, helping to compress traditional markups, and prevent or disrupt a rigid stratification of functions." Moreover, a large buyer "which does indeed make possible cost savings on the part of its suppliers may yet, in facing impure markets, have to coerce suppliers into giving it the concessions which its greater efficiency justifies."[10] In short, price discrimination may increase price flexibility and rivalry at primary and secondary levels; it may also contribute to efficiency. Even so, enhanced competition is not automatic. Price concessions are not always passed on to the consumers or spread throughout the market. Moreover, loss of even a few competitors diminishes competition when there are only a few to begin with. The ultimate effect depends heavily on the circumstances. Hence controversy will continue.[11]

Territorial Price Discrimination. This type of discrimination takes two forms: (1) selective geographic price cutting and (2) fictional freight charges imposed under basing-point pricing systems. The former has produced many illegal primary line injuries, whereas the latter has been charged with injuring competition at the secondary level. As indicated in Table 9–1, neither can be defended by cost justifications. Because geographic price cutting includes predatory pricing, several primary line cases of this sort cast a good light on the Robinson-Patman Act. In fact, they give the FTC its finest hours of enforcement.[12] These cases contain poignant examples of genuine broad injury to competition; they also contain striking evidence of predatory intent. Some excerpts from business correspondence follow:

> "So by continuing our efforts and putting a crimp into him wherever possible, we may ultimately curb this competition if we should not succeed in eliminating it entirely."

> "Don't try to follow me. If you do, we will put you out of business."

The latter message was no idle threat; ensuing below-cost prices ultimately throttled the smaller competitor.[13]

Still, geographic price discrimination may also be procompetitive. It may be used for promotional purposes; for entering new geographic markets; or for further penetrating established markets to spread overhead costs. When used for these laudable purposes, it is usually less systematic than the sharpshooting associated with predation. Nevertheless, procompetitive territorial pricing has occasionally been attacked by the FTC. In the *Page Dairy* case, for instance, the FTC myopically went after a firm whose unsystematic price discrimination was actually undermining its competitors' efforts at cartelization.[14]

The line between geographic price cutting that is predatory or destructive of competition and that which promotes or expands competition is difficult to draw. "But," according to the critics, "one thing is certain: it cannot be drawn merely at the point where a price reduction diverts trade from a competitor."[15]

Common Criticism 4: As interpreted, the law stifles genuine price competition, thereby raising and stiffening price levels.

Returning to the bright side of the coin, the FTC put the Robinson-Patman Act to good use in attacking collusive basing-point price systems in the *Corn Products Refining* case of 1945 and others.[16] As we have seen, basing-point systems are price-fixing mechanisms, but the FTC's initial assault was based on narrow secondary line injury under Subsection 2(a). (Later, in *Cement Institute*, a restraint of trade approach was applied.)[17] The defendant in *Corn Products* produced glucose in Chicago and Kansas City plants but maintained Chicago as a single basing point. Thus, both plants sold only at delivered prices computed as if all shipments originated in Chicago. Kansas City candy manufacturers who bought glucose from the Kansas City plant were charged phantom freight, as if the sweetening had come all the way from Chicago. After hearing the case on appeal, the Supreme Court accepted the FTC's finding that the candy manufacturers located in Kansas City competed with those in Chicago. The court also bought the idea that, though small, the price differentials on glucose would affect the candy makers' cost and final prices. The cost differences were said to be "enough to divert business from one manufacturer to another." Consequently, narrow competitive injury was adjudged at the secondary or buyer level (between candy manufacturers), and the price system was banned.

Functional Discounts. As indicated by Table 9–1, primary level injury is not usually associated with functional discounts, but findings of narrow injury at secondary and tertiary levels have been frequent. By definition, functional discounts are determined not by amounts purchased or buyer location but by the functional characteristics of buyers. Functions in the traditional distribution network are well known: Producers sell to wholesalers, who sell at a higher price to jobbers, who in turn sell at a higher price to retailers, who finally sell at a still higher price to consumers. Other functional differences may be based on other buyer classifications, such as government versus private.

The problem of illegal price discrimination arises when folks of different functions compete.

Most commonly, traditional channels get jumbled, as when resale competition crops up between resellers in different classifications, or when a producer sells at various levels in the distribution network to someone's disadvantage. In other words, discrimination between buyers who are *not* in competition with each other is *not* a violation. The FTC has never ruled against a functional discount per se; somebody down the line must be disadvantaged relative to his competitors.

For example, a problem arises when a buyer performs a dual role, say wholesaling *and* retailing, in which case the buyer may get a large wholesaler's discount that gives him a competitive advantage when reselling as a retailer but not when reselling as a wholesaler. This was the issue in a major private case, *Texaco, Inc.* v. *Hasbrouck*, which was decided by the Supreme Court in 1990.[18] Texaco sold gasoline in Spokane (1) directly to retailers like Ricky Hasbrouck, who was one of twelve plaintiffs, and also (2) to a couple of wholesalers who doubled as retailers. The wholesaler/retailers got huge wholesale discounts off the price Texaco charged to Hasbrouck and the other plaintiffs. As a result, the retailers who received their gasoline from the wholesalers (even independent stations) were able to charge motorists prices that were below the prices charged by Hasbrouck and the other retailers who got no discounts from Texaco. After bringing suit, Hasbrouck argued that these wholesale discounts were illegal because they placed his station and the others buying directly at a competitive disadvantage at the retail level. Texaco defended itself by contending that its different prices were legal because they applied to buyers of different functions and because the same prices were available to all buyers at each particular distributional level. Texaco felt it should not have to be responsible for its customers' pricing decisions in their subsequent sales. It argued, in effect, that a functional discount should be legal as long as the favored buy-

ers actually perform different functions. Finally, Texaco argued that competitive injury had not been proven and that a *Morton Salt* inference would not do in this case.

The Supreme Court ruled against Texaco. It said that legitimate functional discounts could be illegal under certain circumstances, especially when the retail and wholesale functions were "scrambled" for some buyers. Moreover, the court said that *Morton Salt* is alive, that injury can sometimes be inferred from the circumstances rather than rigorously proven.

Critics of this decision and others like it contend that compliance with the Robinson-Patman Act in these instances often raises a serious inconsistency. Compliance implies that the producer must control the prices at which his independent middlemen resell. But such control involves the producer in "resale price maintenance," or vertical price fixing, which is generally illegal under Section 1 of the Sherman Act.[19]

Common Criticism 5: Compliance with the price discrimination law in this and other respects is inconsistent with other antitrust policies.

Catch-as-Catch-Can Discrimination. This kind of discrimination is a miscellaneous category, best explained by illustration. In four cases brought during the 1940s, the FTC found that competition among manufacturers of rubber stamps had been injured by price discrimination. This was a highly competitive market, with seventy manufacturers in New York City alone. The companies chastised were very small, ten to twenty employees being typical. Moreover, they charged whatever prices were necessary "to get the business." That is, concessions varied from one customer to another in catch-as-catch-can fashion: "Moss's price for a one-line stamp, two inches long, varied from 4 cents to 15 cents, and for a oneline stamp three inches long, from 4 cents to 30 cents . . . [and so on]."[20] The FTC found primary line injury on grounds that this practice diverted trade *to* the discriminator *from* his competitors. Since price concessions typically have the effect of diverting business, "the principle adopted in these cases means that *any* discrimination large enough to serve as an effective inducement to buy is unlawful in the absence of one of the statutory justifications [cost or good faith]."[21]

Need we say that this policy was injurious to competition? The effects of this brand of policy emerged from an extensive study conducted by Corwin Edwards on the effects of decisions in eighty-three pre-1957 cases of all kinds (so far as these effects could be ascertained by interviews with the businessmen involved): "There is a consensus of opinion among both buyers and sellers that the result has been to diminish the flexibility of prices."[22] Edwards found no clear tendency for prices to rise or fall as a result of early Robinson-Patman enforcement. Adjustments in all directions were observed. However, the interviews "strongly" indicated stickier and less flexible prices. Fortunately, the FTC seems to have responded to this criticism, for it has not prosecuted any cases like those in rubber stamps since the mid-1960s.

Another form of miscellaneous price discrimination that may be procompetitive is "under-the-table" discounting by oligopolists:

Oligopolists may be unwilling to chance price reduction unless . . . they can make them secretly and selectively; they may similarly be unwilling to attempt promotional pricing except in a selective fashion. To require open, nondiscriminatory pricing may therefore deprive oligopoly markets of their only sources of price flexibility and rivalry.[23]

Although critics of the law have accused the FTC of discouraging such under-the-table discrimination, the charge cannot be verified by specific cases of the last several decades.

An Overview. Critical analyses of the Robinson-Patman Act suggest that procompetitive discriminations may be distinguished from anticompetitive discriminations by whether they are unsystematic or systematic and whether they are perpetrated by firms with small or large market shares. *Systematic, large-firm discriminations tend to be anticompetitive whereas unsystematic, small-firm discriminations tend to be competitive.* But there are exceptions.

The criticism may give the added impression that enforcement zealous enough to crush many small-firm discriminations must have also stamped out large-firm discriminations altogether. But this inference would be fallacious. Discrimination can take many forms not reached by the law. A powerful seller may favor particular buyers by making uniform price reductions on that part of his product line most important to those particular buyers. Moreover, a powerful seller can sometimes refuse to sell to those he disfavors. Similarly, a powerful buyer, deprived of discriminatory price concessions, can nevertheless obtain substantial advantages in acquiring goods:

It can (a) take a seller's entire output at a low price; (b) obtain low prices from sellers who are meeting some other seller's lawful competition; (c) buy goods cheaply abroad; (d) obtain low prices upon goods so differentiated from what bears higher prices that the prohibition of the law is inapplicable; (e) obtain goods of premium quality without paying a premium price; (f) buy large amounts under long-term contract when prices are usually low; or (g) produce goods for itself.[24]

For these many reasons, chain stores have thrived despite the law.[25] The shrewd reader may think up other avenues of evasion. Brokerage payments and preferential promotional services or allowances cannot be among them, however. Discrimination via these routes is foreclosed by Subsections 2(c), (d), and (e) of the Robinson-Patman Act, each of which warrants a few words.

B. Subsections 2(c), (d), and (e)

As may be seen from Table 9–2, these portions of the Robinson-Patman Act are *not* simple ex-

Table 9–2
Comparative Outline of Subsections 2(a), (c), (d), (e), and (f), of the Robinson-Patman Act

Subsection	(1) Competitive Injury Required?	(2) Cost Defense Available?	(3) Good Faith Defense Available?	(4) Violator is Buyer or Seller?
2(a) General	Yes	Yes	Yes	Seller
2(c) Brokerage	No	No	No	Both
2(d) Promotional pay	No	No	Yes	Seller
2(e) Services	No	No	Yes	Seller
2(f) Buyer inducement	Buyer liability for knowingly inducing violation of one of the above			

tensions of Subsection 2(a) governing sellers' price differences. Whereas some kind of probable competitive injury must be shown under 2(a), such is not the case for (c), (d), and (e). Furthermore, whereas 2(a) discriminators may defend themselves by cost justifications or demonstrations of meeting competition in good faith, those running afoul of Subsections 2(c), (d), and (e) may not, except for (d) and (e) with respect to good faith. In other words, these additional provisions of the act specify what could be considered per se violations.

Subsection 2(c), the **brokerage provision,** outlaws payment or receipt of brokerage fees that cross the sales transaction from seller to buyer. It also prohibits any compensation in lieu of brokerage. Brokers (whose job it is to match up buyers and sellers without ever taking title to the goods) are quite active in the grocery game plus a few other distributive trades. Subsection 2(c) was aimed primarily at a practice in the food industry by which chain stores large enough to buy direct, without benefit of brokers, got price reductions equivalent to the brokerage fees that sellers would have otherwise paid. In practice, however, this provision outlawed *all* brokerage commissions, large or small, except those paid to a truly independent broker. At times, 2(c)'s rigorous application has harpooned marketing arrangements that helped small concerns. In the *Biddle* case,

for instance, Biddle sold market-information services to 2,400 grocery buyers—placing their orders with sellers, collecting brokerage from sellers, and then passing some brokerage on to the buyers in the form of reduced information fees.[26] This practice was declared illegal, however, as were others equally beneficial to small independents.[27] The courts held that "The seller may not pay the buyer brokerage on the latter's purchases for his own account" (period). The Supreme Court's *Broch* opinion of 1960 has since introduced a modicum of flexibility into brokerage cases, but a modicum is not a magnum.[28]

Subsection 2(d) makes it unlawful for a seller to make any **payment to a buyer** in consideration of the buyer's promotion of the seller's goods, unless similar payments are made available on "proportionately equal terms" to *all* competing buyers. Subsection 2(e) makes it unlawful for the seller himself to **provide promotional services** to or through a buyer unless he provides opportunity for such services on "proportionally equal terms" to *all* other competing buyers.

For example, if Revlon were to provide Bullock's and Sears with in-store demonstrators of Revlon cosmetics, or if they *paid* these large retailers to conduct these demonstrations, then Revlon would have to make equal-proportionate opportunities of some kind open to all retailers who compete with Bullock's and Sears in cosmetics. You may ask proportionate to what? And in what way? Does that mean that Revlon must circulate a midget giving one-shot fifteen-minute demonstrations among independent corner drug stores for every fully developed model it sets up in Sears for a weekend visit?

The FTC and the courts have chopped through a thick jungle of questions such as these during the past forty years. And, to guide the ordinary, time-pressed businessman through the treacherous path so cleared, the FTC has kindly drawn up a long "Guide for Advertising Allowances and other Merchandising Payments and Services" that attempts to clarify the case law for laymen. Among other things, it states that a seller's burden under the law is heavier than mere selection of the appropriate allowances or services. He must (1) know which customers compete with each other, (2) notify each competing buyer that these aids are available, and (3) police the destination of any payments to make sure they are properly spent.[29] Although the general economic effect of these regulations is unclear, a multitude of small merchants seems to support them on grounds of fairness and equity. Interviews with apparel merchants, after intensive FTC activity concerning 2(d), turned up the following typical response: "It cleaned up the problem of individually negotiated advertising allowances which was inherently unfair to the small guy."[30] Although most economists do not ridicule such sentiments, they tend to be skeptical, even cynical.

Common Criticism 6: Subsections 2(c), (d), and (e) should not pose per se violations. Discriminations of any kind should be subjected to tests of competitive injury and be allowed liberal cost and good faith defenses.

C. Subsection 2(f), Buyer Inducement

Subsection 2(f) makes it unlawful for any buyer "knowingly to induce or receive a discrimination in price which is prohibited by this Section."

Here Congress finally addressed the problem it was really most worked up about—the big buyer who pressures his suppliers for discriminatory concessions. However, this subsection has been used more sparingly than a spare tire because the Supreme Court has made it difficult for the FTC to apply. The FTC's attorneys have the burden of proving (1) that an illegally injurious discrimination occurred, (2) that it was not cost justified, and (3) that the buyer *knew* it was not cost justified.

D. Declining Robinson-Patman Enforcement

On the one side we have seen corrective action appropriate to antitrust policy. On the other side we have seen official applications of dubious merit—attacks on harmless trade practices, protective interventions where injury was slight, and even anticompetitive proceedings. The controversy between those seeing Dr. Jekyll and those seeing Mr. Hyde reached a particularly high pitch during the late 1960s and early 1970s. Two task forces on antitrust policy appointed by two successive presidents (Johnson and Nixon), plus a blue-ribbon committee appointed by the American Bar Association, severely criticized the act and the FTC's enforcement of it. Later President Ford's people in the Justice Department proposed radical modifications in the statute. Central to this and similar proposals is abolition of the narrow-injury test, but some critics have urged *complete abolition* of the Robinson-Patman Act. In response to these developments, Congress held three sets of hearings, but no new legislation came of them, primarily because small-business trade associations mobilized to thwart reform.[31] Small business merchants seem to revere the current law with religious fervor, despite the fact that it has often been used to their disadvantage. "Please don't let the Robinson-Patman Act die," they plead. "All small businesses need it to survive."[32] Admittedly, the act's principal achievements lie in the realms of protection and fairness (though not necessarily fairness to consumers).

For its part, the FTC seems to have responded to the criticism by drastically altering its enforcement policies. In 1963 the FTC issued 219 complaints and 250 orders under the act. For the year ending June 30, 1975, the FTC issued only two complaints and three orders. During the mid-1980s, the FTC issued no complaints. Of late, the FTC's most notable action was taken in late 1988 against six of the nation's largest book publishers (including Macmillan). They allegedly violated the law by selling books at lower prices to major bookstore chains, such as Waldenbooks, and at higher prices to independent stores.[33] Given the sharp drop in official Robinson-Patman activity, a former FTC commissioner said it best: "Robinson-Patman is being slowly anesthetized."[34]

Aside from official enforcement, private suits are also possible and quite common. A private treble damage suit, *Utah Pie Co.* v. *Continental Baking Co.,* was the fuse that ignited much of the recent debate.[35] The Utah Pie Company, a small Salt Lake City purveyor of frozen pies, sued three formidable pie opponents—Continental, Carnation, and Pet—for injuriously cutting prices below cost in Salt Lake City while maintaining prices elsewhere. In 1967, the Supreme Court held that the three national firms had violated Subsection 2(a) despite the fact that Utah Pie had enjoyed the largest share of the local market and had maintained profits throughout the price war. According to one critic, the Supreme Court used subsection 2(a) "to strike directly at price competition itself."[36]

Summary

The Robinson-Patman Act has been called the Magna Carta of small business. Others have named it Typhoid Mary. Ever since it amended Section 2 of the Clayton Act in 1936, it has stirred controversy. Perhaps *any* law governing price discrimination would be controversial. Price discrimination always entails a high price somewhere and a low price somewhere else. Those who see evil in price discrimination tend to see the high price more readily than the low price. Those who see goodness in price discrimination seem to have reverse viewing capabilities. In addition to viewer attitudes, circumstances make a difference.

In any event, the Robinson-Patman Act outlaws price differences when the effect may be broad or narrow competitive injury at any one of three levels—primary, secondary, or tertiary—unless the difference can be defended on grounds of cost justification or good faith price mimicry. Four major classes of price discrimination have been found to violate these standards at least occasionally: (1) volume or quantity discounts, (2) territorial discrimination, (3) functional discounts, and (4) catch-as-catch-can pricing. The first two are particularly prone to true anticompetitive effects, and a number of these cases cast the FTC in good light. On the other hand, attacks against all four have produced instances of ill-advised enforcement.

Subsections 2(c), (d), and (e) prohibit any discrimination that takes the form of brokerage payments, discounts in lieu of brokerage, payments for promotion or other services, and direct provision of promotion or other service. These are generally per se prohibitions because potential competitive injury need not be shown, and for the most part these practices cannot be defended on grounds of cost or good faith. Finally, Subsection 2(f) addresses the problem that Congress was most concerned about, for it bans knowing inducement or receipt of an unlawfully discriminatory price. Despite the efforts of Congress and the FTC, the act has apparently not stemmed the advance of chain stores. Chains have found ways around the law. In addition, the FTC has recently eased up on the act's enforcement, at least in terms of formal proceedings and orders.

Still, the law remains on the books and the Supreme Court reluctantly respects it. As the court said in 1983:

> The Robinson-Patman Act has been widely criticized, both for its effects and for the policies that it seeks to promote. Although Congress is well aware of these criticisms, the Act has remained in effect for almost half a century. And it certainly is not for [this Court] to indulge in the business of policy making in the field of antitrust legislation.[37]

Questions and Exercises for Chapter 9

1. Why was the Robinson-Patman Act passed? How does it differ from other antitrust legislation?
2. Compare and contrast narrow and broad injury? Which corresponds most closely with traditional antitrust policy?
3. How are the economic and R-P Act definitions of price discrimination alike? How do they differ?
4. Has the growth of chain stores been stifled by the law? Explain.
5. Why is it easier to prosecute quantity discount violations at secondary level than at primary level?
6. Compare and contrast territorial and functional discounts in (a) definition, (b) level of likely anticompetitive effect, and (c) lines of defense.
7. Why has the FTC stopped attacking catch-as-catch-can discrimination? Is this good or bad?

Appendix to Chapter 9: Volume Discounts as Barriers to Entry

Figure 9–2 illustrates a volume discount structure. Buyers purchasing 1 to 200 units per month pay $8.00 per unit. Buyers purchasing 201 to 400 units per month pay $7.00 per unit on *all* units (even units 1 to 200). Volumes in the 401 to 600 range yield per unit price of $6.00. And volumes in excess of 600 lower the price to $5.00 per unit.

If this were the price structure of a dominant established supplier, it could pose a barrier to entry to smaller but equally efficient potential suppliers. Suppose, for example, that a small potential supplier does not have the capacity to supply a big buyer with all his requirements of 500 units per month. Indeed, because of uncertainty, this big buyer may not want to buy all his 500 units per month from the newcomer even if the newcomer has the capacity. The buyer might prefer instead to purchase small trial quantities or to build ties with two suppliers, the old and the new. What price would the potential supplier have to charge to get this big buyer to buy 200 units from him? Would it be the going price the buyer pays to the established supplier, namely, $6.00 per unit, as shown in Figure 9–2? No. It would have to be a substantially lower price than $6.00. Why? Because the buyer's purchase of 200 units from the potential supplier would drop the buyer's purchases from the established supplier below 400 units to 300 (500 − 200 = 300), thereby causing the buyer to lose part of his discount from the established supplier. Price on the 300 units from the established supplier jumps from $6.00 to $7.00, costing the buyer $300. Hence, the price the potential supplier charges must be low enough to compensate the buyer for this loss. Otherwise, he won't make the sale. The potential supplier's price must be $4.50 per unit. This is derived by noting that, at a price of $6.00, the 200 units would cost the buyer $1,200. From this, the potential supplier must subtract the $300 the buyer loses in dollar discounts, leaving the potential supplier with $900 revenue on 200 units, which amounts to $4.50 per unit (900/200). The shaded areas in Figure 9–2 indicate the buyer's lost discount and the potential supplier's price reduction below $6.00 per unit.

Of course, the potential seller could charge $6.00 if he sold no more than 100 units to the buyer, because such lesser volumes would not cause the buyer to lose his $6.00 price from the established seller. Small buyers may also be

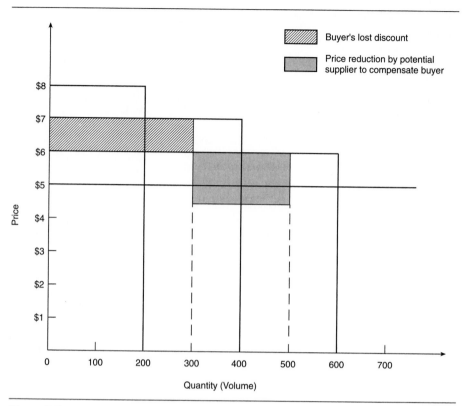

Figure 9–2
Volume Discount Structure

available. But the competitive implications of these possibilities are limited:

> Foreclosed from selling to the larger customers, the smaller supplier may be prevented from ever growing to a size sufficient to enable him to compete for this business. Potential competition may thus be suppressed by the volume-discount structure.[38]

Notes

1. Hearings Before the House Committee on the Judiciary on *Bills to Amend the Clayton Act,* 74th Congress First Session (1935), pp. 5–6. For more historical background see Thomas W. Ross, "Winners and Losers under the Robinson-Patman Act." *Journal of Law & Economics* (October 1984): 243–271.

2. "Eine Kleine Juristische Schlummergeschichte," *Harvard Law Review* (March 1966): 922.

3. *United States* v. *United States Gypsum Co.,* 438 U. S. 422 (1978); *Great Atlantic & Pacific Tea Co.* v. *Federal Trade Commission,* 440 U. S. 69 (1979). See also Richard A. Whiting, "R-P: May It Rest in Peace," *Antitrust Bulletin* (Fall 1986): 709–732.

4. Corwin D. Edwards, *The Price Discrimination Law* (Washington, DC: Brookings Institute, 1959), p. 63.

5. Edwards, *Price Discriminations,* p. 311. See also *In the Matter of Bird and Son,* 25 FTC 548 (1937).

6. R. C. Brooks, Jr., Testimony, *Small Business and the Robinson-Patman Act,* Hearings before the Special Subcommittee on Small Business and the Robinson-Patman Act of the Select Committee on Small Business, U. S. Congress, House, 91st Congress, Second Session (1970), Vol. 2, p. 657.

7. R. C. Brooks, Jr., "Volume Discounts as Barriers

to Entry and Access," *Journal of Political Economy* (February 1961): 65.

8. *Federal Trade Commission* v. *Morton Salt Co.,* 334 U. S. 37 (1948).

9. Edwards, *Price Discrimination,* p. 533, referring to Standard Motor Products (Docket No. 5721), and Moog Industries (Docket No. 5723).

10. J. B. Dirlam and A. E. Kahn, *Fair Competition* (Ithaca, NY: Cornell University Press, 1954), pp. 204–205.

11. Ibid., Chapters 7 and 8. See also L. S. Keyes, "Price Discrimination in Law and Economics," *Southern Economic Journal* (April 1961): 320–328.

12. *E. B. Muller & Co.* v. *FTC,* 142 F.2d 511 (6th Cir. 1944); *Maryland Baking Co.* v. *FTC,* 243 F.2d 716 (4th Cir. 1957); *Forster Mfg. Co.* v. *FTC,* 335 F.2d 47 (1st Cir. 1964). Among private cases see *Volasco Prods. Co.* v. *Lloyd A. Fry Roofing Co.,* 346 F.2d 661 (6th Cir. 1965); *Moore* v. *Mead's Fine Bread Co.,* 348 U.S. 115 (1954); and *Continental Baking Co.* v. *Old Homestead Bread Co.,* 476 F.2d 97 (10th Cir. 1973).

13. *Forster Manufacturing Co.,* v. *FTC.*

14. Edwards, *Price Discrimination,* pp. 443–444. For a related example, see William K. Jones, Testimony, *Small Business and the Robinson-Patman Act,* Hearings before Special Subcommittee on Small Business of the Select Committee on Small Business, House, 91st Congress, First Session (1969), Vol. 1, p. 109.

15. Philip Elman, "The Robinson-Patman Act and Antitrust Policy: A Time for Reappraisal," *Washington Law Review,* vol. 42 (1966): 13.

16. *Corn Products Refining Company* v. *FTC,* 324 U. S. 726 (1945).

17. *FTC* v. *Cement Institute,* 333 U. S. 683 (1948).

18. *Texaco Inc.* v. *Hasbrouck,* 110 S.Ct. 2535 (1990); *Hasbrouck* v. *Texaco Inc.,* 842 F.2d 1034 (9th Cir. 1988). For previous cases see *FTC* v. *Standard Oil Co.,* 355 U. S. 396 (1958) and 340 U. S. 231 (1951); *Mueller Co.* v. *FTC,* 323 F.2d 44 (7th Cir., 1963).

19. Edwards, *Price Discrimination,* p. 312.

20. Ibid., p. 479.

21. Ibid., p. 482 (emphasis added).

22. Ibid., p. 630.

23. Dirlam and Kahn, *Fair Competition,* p. 204.

24. Corwin D. Edwards, "Control of the Single Firm: Its Place in Antitrust Policy," *Law & Contemporary Problems* (Summer 1965): 477.

25. Stanley C. Hollander and Mary Jane Sheffet, "The Robinson-Patman Act: Boon or Bane for Retailers?", *Antitrust Bulletin* (Fall 1986): 759–795.

26. *Biddle Purchasing Co.* v. *FTC,* 96 F.2d 687 (1938).

27. See, e.g., *Quality Bakers* v. *FTC,* 114 F.2d 393 (1940); and *Southgate Brokerage Co.* v. *FTC,* 150 F.2d 607 (1945).

28. *FTC* v. *Henry Broch & Co.,* 363 U.S. 166 (1960).

29. P. Areeda, *Antitrust Analysis* (Boston: Little, Brown, 1974), pp. 951–960.

30. *Recent Efforts to Amend or Repeal the Robinson-Patman Act,* Part 1, Hearings before the Ad Hoc Subcommittee on Antitrust . . . and Related Matters of the Committee on Small Business, U. S. Congress, House, 94th Congress, First Session (1975), pp. 282–312.

31. *Recent Efforts to Amend or Repeal . . . ,* Parts 1, 2, and 3; *Small Business and the Robinson-Patman Act,* 3 volumes; *Price Discrimination Legislation—1969,* Hearings before the Subcommittee on Antitrust and Monopoly of the Committee on the Judiciary, U.S. Senate, 91st Congress First Session (1969).

32. *Recent Efforts to Amend or Repeal . . . ,* Part 3, p. 207.

33. *Wall Street Journal,* 23 December, 1988, p. B6.

34. "Robinson-Patman Is Not Dead—Merely Dormant," address by Paul Rand Dixon, May 21, 1975 (mimeo).

35. *Utah Pie Co.* v. *Continental Baking Co.,* 386 U.S. 685 (1967).

36. W. S. Bowman, "Restraint of Trade by the Supreme Court: The Utah Pie Case," *Yale Law Journal* (November 1967): 70.

37. *Jefferson County Pharmaceutical Association, Inc.,* v. *Abbott Laboratories,* 460 U.S. 150 (1983), at 170.

38. Robert C. Brooks, Jr., "Volume Discounts as Barriers to Entry and Access," *Journal of Political Economy* (February 1961): 65. See also Karin Wagner, "Competition and Productivity: A Study of the Metal Can Industry in Britain, Germany, and the United States," *Journal of Industrial Economics* (September 1980): 32.

Chapter 10

Vertical Market Restrictions

The sensitive focal points of the competitive general market system are, as the name implies, in marketing by individual enterprises and in the buying choices of their customers.
— E. T. Grether

As we have seen, the lion's share of antitrust law addresses horizontal restraints and monopolization. Now we explore the lamb's share—antitrust concerning vertical restraints. Tying, exclusive dealing, territorial restrictions, and resale price maintenance fit this description because they operate between sellers and buyers. In order of their treatment in this chapter:

1. *Tying* occurs when the seller allows the buyer to buy one line of the seller's goods *only* if the buyer also buys other goods, as would be true if Kodak tied film developing to its film.
2. *Exclusive dealing* binds a buyer (usually a retailer) to make *all* his purchases of a given line of goods from a particular seller (usually a manufacturer). This differs from tying in that it may cover a considerable range of goods, and it limits buyers to a single source of supply. This would be true, for instance, if an appliance store agreed with General Electric to carry only G.E. appliances.
3. *Territorial restrictions* give distributors exclusive territories or assigned locations. Thus Coca-Cola might assign Boston to one bottler, Providence to another bottler, and still other areas to other bottlers, prohibiting each bottler from raiding the territories of others.
4. *Resale price maintenance* occurs when manufacturers or other suppliers set the prices that their distributors may charge. Were Ford to insist that its auto dealers stick to the suggested retail prices given on window stickers, it would be practicing resale price maintenance.

Businessmen offer various justifications for these practices, and some justifications are good enough that public interests are served as well as private business interests. Such goodness depends on the structural circumstances, however. When *small firms* in highly *competitive markets* engage in these practices, the results may tilt toward *goodness*. On the other hand, when used

Table 10–1
Outline of Vertical Restraints

Restrictive Practice	Potential Anticompetitive Effect	Main Statute Law	Judicial Rule Applied
1. Tying	Exclusionary	Clayton, Sec. 3 and Sherman, Sec. 1	Mixed: per se, rule of reason
2. Exclusive dealing	Exclusionary	Clayton, Sec. 3	Rule of reason
3. Territorial restrictions	Collusive	Sherman, Sec. 1	Rule of reason
4. Resale price maintenance	Collusive	Sherman, Sec. 1	Per se rule

by *large firms* in *oligopolistic settings,* these vertical restraints tend to be *anticompetitive.*

Table 10–1 summarizes these potential competitive problems with simple labels. Tying and exclusive dealing tend to be *exclusionary* because they discourage new entry or handicap small rivals. Territorial restraints and resale price maintenance are said to be *collusive* because they may have cartel-like consequences. They may promote oligopolistic interdependence, thereby aiding tacit or explicit price collusion. Table 10–1 also indicates the main statutory laws and judicial rules governing these practices. Thus, Table 10–1 outlines this chapter.

Esoteric though these restraints and policies may seem, their importance has grown immensely with the growth of franchising. Beginning with auto dealerships, soft drink bottlers, and gasoline service stations many decades ago, franchising has now spread to fast food, real estate, hotels, convenience stores, rental services, and even suntan parlors. Total franchise sales were a whopping $640 billion in 1988. Franchise establishments number over 500,000.[1] Surveys of franchise companies reveal their heavy use of various forms of exclusive dealing, tying, and territorial allocations.[2] Moreover, the case law in these areas carries many familiar names from franchising–Dunkin Donuts and Coca-Cola to name just two. Still, more than franchising alone

is involved. Nearly all forms of distribution are affected by policies in these areas, even direct sales to some extent.

I. Tying

A. Business Justifications for Tying

The sale of one item is often tied to the sale of another with innocuous purpose and effect—multigame season tickets for instance. An understanding of policy is therefore best grounded on an understanding of some of the main purposes served by tying.

Economies and Conveniences. Shirts sold with buttons, autos with tires, and pencils with erasers illustrate combinations more efficiently manufactured and distributed together than apart. These ties are so close that we think of each as being one product, the parts of which come in fixed proportions, such as nine buttons to a shirt. Since consumers would probably have to pay more for the privilege of buying separate parts, these ties are economically "natural."

Goodwill. A franchisor of fast food might require that his franchisees purchase their chickens, cooking equipment, and packaging materials from the franchisor, thereby tying these materials to use of a trade name. In this way the franchisor could assure standardization of quality (not necessarily high quality) among his many franchisees. Without such assurance, one fast-food outlet might exploit the general reputation of the trade name by offering poor quality while charging rich prices.

Price Discrimination.[3] A machine's consumption of materials, such as paper, ink, staples, or film, may, like a meter, measure intensity of use. Thus, when meters are impractical, easily tampered with, or prohibitively expensive, manufacturers of machines may try to sell or lease their machines at a low rate and tie in the sale of materials priced well above cost. In this way, customers with intense demands would pay more than marginal users. Moreover, profits would be greater than those obtained without such price discrimination, especially if the producer has monopoly power in the machine's market. Notice that this tie-in may merely *exploit* more fully some already existing monopoly power. It does not necessarily entail an *extension* of market power into the tied good's market. For example, even in the absence of antitrust policy, Xerox could not monopolize the paper industry if it tied copy paper to its machines because very little paper is used for that specific purpose.

However laudable these several justifications may be, they do not necessarily justify a lenient policy on tying. When economies are present, the lower costs could be reflected in a lower price for the combination product as compared to the constituent parts. When goodwill is an issue, quality specifications and surveillance may substitute for forced ties. And when price discrimination is at stake, untying would reduce monopoly profits, but buyers would not feel hurt.[4]

B. Adverse Competitive Effects

To some, a major problem with tying is that it can be anticompetitive. It can raise barriers to entry in the market of the tied good or seriously disadvantage smaller tied-good competitors. Both effects are exclusionary, but neither effect necessarily occurs. It depends on the circumstances. If a firm has a monopoly in the tying good, and the tying and tied goods are complements used in varying proportions, such as bread and butter, the problem is particularly pernicious. William Baldwin and David McFarland explain:

> Assume that a seller with a complete monopoly on bread ties sales of his brand of butter to the bread, where butter was formerly sold in a perfectly competitive market. If there is no use for butter except to spread on bread, the tie-in will lead to a complete monopoly in the butter market. In any event, the bread monopolist will achieve some degree of monopoly power in the butter market.[5]

A different but more concrete example is offered by Kodak, which a while back tied film processing (developing) to its sale of film. When tied, Kodak enjoyed a 90 percent share of the amateur film and film-processing industry. As a result of a 1954 antitrust consent decree, however, Kodak severed the tie, licensed its processing technology to new entrants, and agreed to substantial divestiture of its processing facilities. A flood of new entry followed, which combined with the divestiture to cause Kodak's processing market share to tumble 55 percentage points in just five years. With entry, prices of film processing fell substantially. Although Kodak retained its near monopoly on film, and even raised prices on film, it appears that the newfound competition in processing benefitted shutterbugs.[6]

C. The Law on Tying

Section 1 of the Sherman Act covers tying, but the most explicit prohibition is found in Section 3 of the Clayton Act, which bans tie-in sales "where the effect . . . may be to substantially lessen competition or tend to create a monopoly." Judicial interpretation of these acts approaches a per se rule. Ties are, in the Supreme Court's opinion, "*unreasonable in and of themselves* whenever a party has sufficient economic power with respect to the tying product to appreciably restrain free competition in the market for the tied product and a 'not insubstantial' amount of interstate commerce is affected."[7] This statement discloses, however, certain *rule of reason* elements, particularly for judgments about "sufficient economic power." Thus, it is best to summarize by saying that violations will be found when the answers to *all* the following questions are "yes":

1. Are two products (or services) involved?
2. Does the seller possess sufficient economic power in the market of the tying product?
3. Is there substantial commerce in the tied goods?
4. Are defenses of reasonableness absent?

Of these questions, the first and third rarely raise thorny problems. The first is needed merely to prevent single products, like shirts with buttons, from being considered two products. The third is easily answered because "substantial commerce" seems to mean to the court anything over a million dollars worth of business.

As regards "sufficient economic power" in the tying good, question (2), the Supreme Court has found a variety of conditions providing yes answers: (a) a large market share or "market dominance" in the tying good, (b) patents, copyrights, or trademarks for the tying good, (c) high barriers to entry in the tying-good market, and (4) uniqueness or "special desirability" of the tying good.

For example, a landmark case in patents is *International Salt* of 1947.[8] International had a limited patent monopoly over salt dispensing machines used in food processing. Users of the machines had to buy their salt from International or find other machines. International argued that preservation of goodwill required the tie-in, that only its own salt was of sufficient purity to provide top-quality dispensing. The Supreme Court rejected this assertion, observing that no evidence had been presented to show "that the ma-chine is allergic to salt of equal quality produced by anyone except International." Moreover, the presence of the patents caused the court to dispense some salty per se references, such as, "It is unreasonable, per se, to foreclose competitors from any substantial market."

Requisite power based on copyrights and uniqueness is illustrated by *U. S.* v. *Loew's, Inc.*, (1962), which involved "block booking." When selling motion pictures to television stations, Loew's had "conditioned the license or sale of one or more feature films upon the acceptance by the station of a package or block containing one or more unwanted or inferior films." Put bluntly, the practice could tie *Gone With the Wind* and *Getting Gertie's Garter*. On the question of economic power, the Supreme Court decided that each film "was in itself a unique product"; that feature films "were not fungible"; that "since each defendant by reason of its copyright had a 'monopolistic' position as to each tying product, 'sufficient economic power' to impose an appreciable restraint on free competition in the tied product was present."[9] On this precedent the distributors of *Star Wars* had to back down when caught tying a mediocre film to that big money-maker.

When potent patents, copyrights, or trademarks do not conveniently show tying-good power, the courts can get bogged down in matters that plague monopolization cases. What is the relevant market? What market share constitutes market power? In the *Times-Picayune* case, the court defined the relevant tying-good market as all newspaper advertising in New Orleans, a definition that let the defendant off the hook.[10] In the Supreme Court's recent case *Jefferson Parish Hospital District* v. *Hyde,* it was found that a 30 percent share of the tying-good market was not enough to establish tying-good power.[11]

Finally, the fourth question concerning reasonable defenses has on rare occasions been answered in favor of defendants. The defendant in *U. S.* v. *Jerrold Electronics,* for instance, was an early 1950s pioneer in the development of community television antenna systems. Rather than sell separately its bits and pieces of equipment and technical services, Jerrold sold only on a full systems basis, including services for layout, installation, and maintenance as well as equipment. There was no question that Jerrold had hefty market power in the tying good—equipment—given its 75 percent market share. Nor was there any question of substantial business in the tied services. Nevertheless, Jerrold successfully defended its tying with proof that the industry was at the time very young, that these antenna systems were extremely delicate, and that full control through tying was required to build customer confidence in the industry and preserve Jerrold's reputation. In short, this was a goodwill defense in an infant industry context. The court agreed but granted only a *temporary* waiver, because these special conditions would evaporate with the passage of time—the industry maturing and the equipment toughening.[12]

In sum, tying is virtually a per se violation when there is power in the tying good. Still, in the absence of patents or such, rule of reason judgment enters the determination of power. Indeed, the Department of Justice issued "Vertical Restraints Guidelines" in January 1985, which say that "tying will *not* be challenged if the party imposing the tie has a market share of *thirty percent or less* in the market for the tying product," unless it can be positively proven that the tying "unreasonably restrains competition" in the tied-good market.[13]

Certain rule of reason defenses grant further freedom even though they are rarely acceptable. Hence, the law here is a mixture of per se and rule of reason elements, with the rule of reason elements gaining ever greater ground over time.

II. Exclusive Dealing

Under an exclusive dealing agreement, the buyer obtains the seller's product on condition that he will not deal in the products of the seller's rivals. The buyer, say a sugar wholesaler, agrees to secure his total requirements of sugar from one supplier, say Amstar.

A. Business Justifications for Exclusive Dealing

From the supplier's point of view, exclusive dealing assures that distributors will devote their undivided energy to the supplier's products, something particularly important when personal sales, repair service, and promotion are required. Moreover, exclusive dealers often represent the manufacturer's interests more religiously. In 1974, for instance, Amstar stopped selling its sugar through general sugar brokers who served as agents for more than one sugar refiner. The stated reason for this action was that these general brokers acted with such "customer orientation" toward *their* buyers that "they at times acted more nearly as purchasing agents" for their buyers than as sales agents for Amstar, causing Amstar lost profits. Thereafter, Amstar sold only through exclusive dealing "direct brokers," who carried only Amstar sugar, and through its own sales force.[14]

From the buyer's or distributor's point of view, there are a number of reasons for accepting exclusive dealing:

- Supplies may be more certain and steady, especially in times of shortage.
- Specialization entails lower inventories than would be required with several brands of the same product.
- If exclusive dealing is rejected, the buyer may no longer be a buyer (that is, the seller forces acceptance).
- Acceptance may be conceded in exchange for a commitment from the seller that protects the buyer-dealer from the competition of other buyer-dealers handling the same brand (for example, territorial assignments or limits on the number of dealerships in an area).

Recognizing that exclusive dealing offers advantages for buyers as well as sellers, the Supreme Court has been more lenient toward exclusive dealing as compared to tying.

B. Adverse Competitive Effects

Exclusive dealing may foreclose new entrants or small suppliers from main distribution channels, especially when used singly or collectively by dominant manufacturers or franchisors. Anticompetitive effects may ensue:

> Once a large or dominant supplier in a market obtains for his exclusive use a correspondingly large share of available outlets on a lower level of distribution, he has probably imposed prohibitive cost disadvantages on existing or potential rivals, since they are likely to have to create new outlets in order to participate in the market. The same is true where a group of suppliers collectively (if not collusively) obtain exclusive obligations from dealers—and thus produce an aggregate foreclosure.[15]

A recent example comes from the market for industrial gases (e.g., oxygen, nitrogen, and acetylene). That market has two segments: (1) a *bulk* segment, in which producers of industrial gas sell directly to large customers like U. S. Steel, and (2) a *small-lot* segment, in which producers sell to independent distributors who in turn sell to welding supply stores serving small customers like construction companies. During the 1960s, the dominant established producers, such as Union Carbide and Airco, encountered growing competition at the gas-manufacturing level because of changing technology and fresh entrants. This new competition spread rapidly in the bulk segment of the industry. Union Carbide and Airco consequently experienced fizzling sales and profit margins in their dealings with direct buyers. However, the new competition did not reach small-lot sales because Union Carbide and Airco were able to foreclose that segment of the market. A combination of exclusive dealing and tying kept the new rivals away from small-lot distributors:

> Union Carbide and Airco both responded to the changed market conditions by strengthening and formalizing the ties between manufacturer and distributor. Both companies imposed formal contractual requirements that all gases used by a distributor must be purchased from the franchizing manufacturers. In addition, informal but implicit ties between the sale of gases and the sale of welding equipment were imposed [because of the strong market power these firms enjoyed in welding equipment].[16]

Action by the FTC finally ended these practices in 1979.

The power behind the anticompetitive use of exclusive dealing is often a popular brand name. During the 1980s, Pillsbury Company tried to maintain market share for its Häagen-Dazs ice cream by imposing exclusive dealing on its distributors. This hurt the sales of Ben & Jerry's Ice Cream, so Ben and Jerry sued Häagen-Dazs and launched a public relations campaign that produced some clever bumper stickers: "What's the Doughboy afraid of?" and "Häagen, your Dazs are numbered."[17] In the beer industry, Anheuser-Busch discourages its wholesale distributors from carrying rivals' brands, especially in major metropolitan areas where A-B has huge market shares and its distributors can boast of immense marketing clout. Dennis Long, former president of A-B, said their intent in this strategy was to deprive rivals: "We discourage them [our distributors] from carrying other brands. We want to keep the advantage of size in-house."[18]

C. The Law on Exclusive Dealing

Section 3 of the Clayton Act covers exclusive dealing as well as tying, for it bans sales or leases conditioned on an "agreement or understanding that the lessee or purchaser . . . shall not use or deal in the [goods or wares] of a competitor" of the seller or lessor, where the effect "may be to substantially lessen competition." According to the Supreme Court's interpretation of Section 3, exclusive dealing is not per se illegal. Hence, the court has considered economic conditions and purposes when determining illegalities. Two main factors are the seller's market share and the prevalence of the practice among all sellers.[19]

In 1985, the Antitrust Division of the Justice Department stated its position in its "Vertical Restraints Guidelines." According to those guidelines, "Uses of vertical restraints by firms with small market shares, those restraints operating in unconcentrated markets, and those that do not cover a substantial percentage of the sales or capacity in the secondary (foreclosed) market, are unlikely to effectively facilitate collusion or to foreclose competitors from the market."

How small a market share? How unconcentrated? How extensive the coverage? The answers are spelled out in a multistep process of review, as shown in Figure 10–1. Under step one, structural conditions are reviewed. If the firm imposing the restraint has less than 10 percent of its market, *or* if any of three other structural thresholds are favorably met, then the restraint will be permitted. If on the other hand, *all* structural thresholds are violated, step two commences. This second step considers the condition of entry in the affected markets. If entry is thought to be easy, then again the restraint is permitted. Finally, if the structural tests of step one and the entry tests of step two make the restraint look bad, it may still escape challenge if further study can find some way to excuse it.

On the whole, these guidelines seem quite lenient. For example, if three manufacturers with 19 percent market shares and five dealers with 15

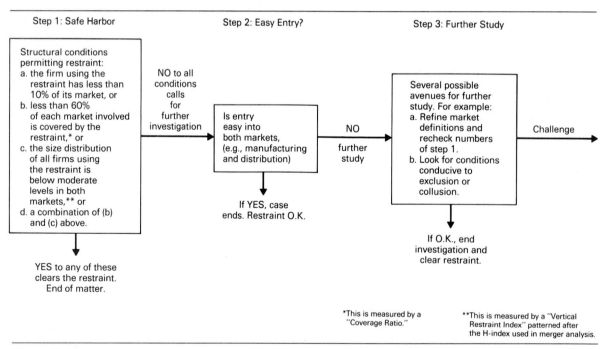

Figure 10–1

Diagram of Vertical Restraint Guidelines for Exclusive Dealing and Territorial Restraints

Source: U. S. Department of Justice, "Vertical Restraints Guidelines" January 23, 1985.

percent market shares were engaged in vertical restraints, they would be safe from challenge according to the "safe harbor" structural standards of step one. As regards easy entry—step two—it appears that the exclusive dealing arrangements in industrial gases would have been allowed by the guidelines' standard even though substantial economic evidence indicates that those restraints were anticompetitive. Indeed, the leniency of the guidelines is suggested by the fact that all fifty state attorneys general have banded together to issue conflicting, more stringent guidelines of their own.

Thus, exclusive dealing is governed by a rule of reason which in some versions could be considered rather lenient. Moreover, difficulties of detection can occasionally offer further freedom for the practice. It need not be written into contracts. Manufacturers can reach *tacit* understandings with their distributors, understandings enforced by the manufacturers' refusals to deal. Although *collective* refusals to deal (boycotts) are essentially per se illegal, the courts have a long-standing tradition of recognizing the right of a manufacturer or other supplier to choose his distributors. Thus, dominant firms have been able to impose exclusive dealing by using refusal to sell as their cat's paw.[20]

III. Territorial Restrictions

The Justice Department's "Guidelines" on exclusive dealing also apply to vertical territorial restrictions. These come in many forms—exclusive territories, areas of "prime responsibility," exclusive franchising, and limited outlet franchising among them. The basic result of all such restraints is the same, however—more or less restrictive allocations of territories to the distributors or franchisees of a given brand, limiting intrabrand competition. If such restrictions were devised *horizontally* among distributors and franchisees, they would obviously be per se violations of Sherman Section 1. If *vertically* imposed

by manufacturers and franchisors, Sherman Section 1 is still the only applicable statute, but these restraints are not so obviously dangerous as to warrant per se treatment.

A. Business Justifications for Territorial Restrictions

Broadly stated, the main business justification for territorial restrictions is that they promote *inter*brand competition even though they may stifle *intra*brand competition. If, for example, the maker of Sylvania TV sets allocated territories among its distributors, these distributors could not compete against each other, but they could channel their competitive efforts toward outselling RCA, Zenith, and Sony. There are a number of reasons why this might be so:

1. Distributors or franchisees may have to make considerable investments in their enterprise for facilities, advertising, inventory and so on. If the brand promoted is weak, the high risks facing distributors can be lessened by territorial protection. This would then aid in attracting new outlets.
2. For products needing full service retailing, such as demonstration, service, and credit, territorial isolation protects distributors who provide these costly services from the raids of price discounters who do not provide such services.
3. Territorial isolation may aid quality maintenance if it facilitates the tracing and recall of faulty products and removes incentives one outlet may have for exploiting through adulteration the good reputation built up by other outlets of the same brand.

It should be noted that these justifications are most valid in instances where the manufacturer or franchisor is in a weak position vis-à-vis his rival manufacturers or franchisors. Moreover, these justifications are enfeebled by the fact that in many instances less restrictive means of attaining the same ends are available.[21] Still, these rationales cannot be dismissed.

B. Adverse Competitive Effects

The potentially adverse competitive consequences of territorial restrictions are fairly obvious—cartel-like restraint, especially at distributor level where intrabrand competition is shackled. The greater the concentration at manufacturer or franchisor level, the more serious the problem. If, for instance, Chevrolet happened to capture 90 percent of all U. S. auto sales, intrabrand competition among Chevy dealers would be the main form of competition remaining in the industry. And restraints on this competition could prove costly to consumers.

Even where concentration is relatively low, interbrand competition might be muted by strong product differentiation. Consumers loyal to their preferred brand would then probably benefit substantially by vigorous intrabrand competition. Intrabrand competition in soft drinks has been curbed since Coke, Pepsi, and the other major syrup manufacturers allocated exclusive territories among their bottlers. And in 1973 FTC economists estimated that removal of these territorial restrictions would save drinkers of soda pop approximately $250 million a year.[22] (Congress prevented removal, however, when it later passed legislation specifically exempting the soda pop industry. Intense industry lobbying paid off.)

The problem for wise policy in this area now becomes clear. Territorial restrictions blunt *intrabrand* competition, but they may foster *interbrand* competition.

C. The Law on Territorial Restrictions

Given the ambiguous character of this practice, it is not surprising that a rule of reason now applies in assessing its legality. What is a bit surprising is that such a rule emerged under Section 1 of the Sherman Act, a section notorious for its per se interpretations.

The Supreme Court first fully confronted vertical territorial restraints in *United States* v. *White Motors* (1963).[23] White was a relatively small manufacturer of trucks that had assigned territories to its distributors and dealers. Recognizing that White might thereby be better able to compete with giants like GMC, the Supreme Court held that a rule of reason should apply and remanded the case for lower court trial. Four years later in *Schwinn* the Supreme Court waffled a bit by judging a portion of Schwinn's plan under a per se rule and the rest under a rule of reason.[24] The ensuing confusion was cleared up in 1977 with *Continental TV* v. *GTE Sylvania,* which confirmed the rule of reason approach.[25]

The facts of *Sylvania* were simple: Suffering from lagging TV set sales, Sylvania shifted its marketing strategy in the early 1960s to a program that included greater selectivity in choosing retailers. These franchised retailers were bound by contract not to sell except from locations approved by Sylvania. The strategy encouraged retailers to promote Sylvania sets more aggressively than before, thereby boosting Sylvania's market share from about 2 percent in 1962 to 5 percent in 1965. A fracas erupted, however, between Sylvania and one of its main San Francisco retailers, Continental TV, who fought Sylvania with a treble damage suit claiming the restrictions on dealer locations were illegal under the *Schwinn* decision.

On hearing the case, the Supreme Court abandoned the per se portion of *Schwinn,* sided with Sylvania, and came out four-square for a rule of reason. Such was necessary, the court held, to balance the harm of lessened intrabrand competition with the benefits of heightened interbrand competition:

> Vertical restrictions reduce intrabrand competition by limiting the number of sellers of a particular product competing for the business of a given group of buyers . . . [But . . .]
> Vertical restrictions promote interbrand competition by allowing the manufacturer to achieve

certain efficiencies in the distribution of his products. These "redeeming virtues" are implicit in every decision sustaining vertical restrictions under the rule of reason.

The court felt that the facts favored Sylvania. Now, in light of what was said previously, we can conclude that the harm of lessened intrabrand competition is more likely to outweigh the benefit of heightened interbrand competition (1) the greater the market power of the manufacturer, (2) the greater the overall market concentration, (3) the stronger the tethers of product differentiation, (4) the older and richer the manufacturer in question, and (5) the more tightly drawn the constraint. As already suggested, several of these factors are found in the 1985 Justice Department guidelines summarized in Figure 10–1.

IV. Resale Price Maintenance

Resale price maintenance, in pure form, is *vertical* price fixing. A manufacturer specifies to its downstream wholesalers or retailers the minimum prices they may charge when reselling to their customers. A toaster manufacturer, for instance, might require its retailers to price its toasters at $35 or more. To assure adherence to such resale prices, manufacturers typically must discipline mavericks by cutting off their supplies, delaying their shipments, or threatening some other penalty.

What makes resale price maintenance especially interesting is the heated controversy that has surrounded it for decades. This is reflected in its roller-coaster legal history—being illegal in the U. S. from 1911 to the 1930s, legal from the 1930s to roughly 1975, and then illegal again since 1975. Controversy is also reflected in sharply divided opinions. During the Reagan Administration, those who were supposed to prosecute offenders (the Department of Justice and the FTC) wanted to legalize resale price

maintenance at least partially and they refused to file cases. Conversely, Congress and the courts persisted in their opposition, thankful that private antitrust suits could make up for the lack of official enforcement. The acute controversy might seem overly dramatic to sideline spectators like you. After all, when resale price maintenance was legal, it never covered more than about 4 to 10 percent of all retail sales in the U. S. Still, the potential is immense. It covered 30 to 40 percent of all retail sales in Britain when previously legal there. Its use has also been heavily concentrated on relatively few products for which it can be immensely important—drugs and medicines, cosmetics and perfumes, small electrical appliances, and alcoholic beverages.[26]

A. Business Rationale for Resale Price Maintenance and Anticompetitive Effects

Although many manufacturers apparently like to engage in resale price maintenance, it is not altogether clear why they like it. Casual reasoning would lead us to expect that once a manufacturer has set his own price, his interests would best be served by having the lowest price possible charged to final consumers, because that would maximize sales given the manufacturer's price. An efficient, competitive distribution system, earning the minimum distribution markup possible, would then seem most desirable. And resale price maintenance would not encourage distributor competition, efficiency, or markup minimization. Still, there are a few explanations deserving mention, because they help us assess whether a per se rule might be justifiable.[27]

First, it may be that the manufacturer is responding to the blandishments of his retailers who use the manufacturer's resale price maintenance as a means of maintaining a retailer cartel. The manufacturer is not initiating the program, and the program is actually *horizontal* price fixing at retail level enforced by the manufacturer, not vertical price fixing. A rule preventing this seems quite acceptable. While passing this judgment, we should acknowledge that retailers need not engage in full-fledged cartelization to find comfort in resale price maintenance (RPM). In particular, it tends to shield small retailers from the price competition of larger, more efficient merchants. Numerous empirical studies have shown that prices of many commodities tend to be higher with RPM than without; that these elevated prices preserve *in*efficiency; and that discount retailing is hampered.[28] Thus, if society wished to nurture small businesses for the sake of furthering some populist value judgments, resale price maintenance might win acceptance. But such value judgments seem to be losing favor of late.

Second, resale price maintenance may be used to facilitate a cartel at manufacturers' level. The practice cements vertical relationships and aids cartel discipline by readily disclosing cheaters and double-crossers. This too would actually be horizontal price fixing, unworthy of being saved by legalizing resale price maintenance.

Third, it is often argued that some manufacturers want the retail price of their wares to be kept high because consumers equate a high price with high quality. In the absence of the support resale price maintenance offers, prices would fall, pulling down with them the brand's quality image. This justification is weak, however, because there is another way the same result could be attained. If a manufacturer wants a high retail price for his product, he can simply jack up his own price. When downstream distributors pay the manufacturer more, they will in turn charge more. Still, if manufacturers cannot control retail prices, the retailers can cut their prices *below cost*. They might engage in "loss-leader" selling, discounting a few familiar brands drastically to attract customers whose purchases of other goods might more than compensate for the loss. Thus, some manufacturers claim that resale price maintenance protects their products from loss-leader degradation.

Fourth, resale price maintenance may serve the interests of both manufacturers and resellers simultaneously if *both* have some monopoly power. The reasoning is complex, and it entails some of the "quality" elements of the foregoing, but it makes sense of numerous cases that would otherwise be inexplicable. Resale price maintenance is said to grow out of "mutual dependence between two insecure partial monopolists" at different levels—production and distribution—where "the existence of the monopoly power of each depends in some significant degree upon the monopoly power of the other."[29] When producers of prominent brands engage in resale price maintenance and are selective in their choice of distributors, the power of selected distributors is enhanced by the reduced intrabrand competition, by the limited retail availability of the product, and by the quality image that may result. Conversely, retailers reward the price-maintaining producers by stocking their brands in preference to others, by steering consumers toward their brands, and by boosting the producer's quality image. Levi's jeans, Florsheim shoes, and Russell Stover candies provide examples.[30]

Finally, some products, such as appliances, may be most effectively promoted through the provision of retailer services—such as demonstrations, fittings, bridal registers for wedding gifts, and repairs. Resale price maintenance may thus operate to protect retailers who offer these services from the poaching of discounters who do not offer these services. Full-Service Sam would not last long if the customers he convinces to buy go down the street to consummate their purchases with Cut-Rate Carl. So, the argument goes, Sam must be protected.[31]

B. The Law on Resale Price Maintenance

Under Section 1 of the Sherman Act, resale price maintenance is now regarded illegal per se. In light of the full-service dealer rationale just noted, however, a per se rule may seem too crude and too destructive of a laudable business practice (as compared with a rule of reason). Still, it can be argued in defense of the per se rule that these laudable ends can be reached by other, less restrictive means. A manufacturer, for instance, can require his retailers to provide certain services as a condition for continuing as his retailers. Even when such alternatives are limited, the present per se rule offers manufacturers much room to maneuver, enough room to achieve some degree of resale price maintenance. In other words, there is a large loophole in the law, a hole punched by what may be called the legal rights of unilateral refusal to sell.

To the extent resale price maintenance is *totally and completely a unilateral* undertaking on the part of an *individual manufacturer,* it is *not* considered a restraint of trade. Resale price maintenance meets this legally unilateral standard if the manufacturer does *nothing more* than announce his desire that resale prices be maintained at or above some specified level and then refuses to sell to those who defy that desire. Anything beyond this unilateral program may invite prosecution. Anything that smacks of multilateral agreement stands exposed. Retailers cannot agree to adhere to the suggested prices. Rebellious retailers cut off from supplies cannot be reinstated through an understanding with the manufacturer that they will not shade prices again. Indeed, manufacturers best comply with unilateralism if, when they sever ties with a discounter, they do not mention the grounds for the divorce. Still, the manufacturer can engage in resale price maintenance through unilateral refusal to deal. This avenue to legality stems from a tradition of business practice—that is, enterprises have a wide-ranging right to choose those with whom they will do business, including the right of refusal to sell.

Beyond such unilateralism, however, resale price maintenance is per se illegal. Civil suits have confronted such firms as Pendleton Woolen Mills, Lenox Company (producers of fine china), and Levi Strauss, the last of which ended up paying more than $12 million in damages. Although

the Reagan Administration did not prosecute in this area, the Bush Administration revived the law. In 1991, for instance, the FTC attacked Nintendo Company, the leader in home video games. Its suit was settled when Nintendo agreed to redress its bad deeds by providing up to $25 million in coupons to some 9 million customers nationwide who were allegedly injured by Nintendo's resale price maintenance.[32]

The saga of per se illegality begins with *Dr. Miles Medical Co.* v. *John D. Park and Sons Co.* in 1911.[33] The Dr. Miles company manufactured proprietary medicines and sought to prescribe the resale prices of both its wholesalers and retailers. Wholesaler Park and Sons refused to enter a resale contract with Dr. Miles and undermined the program by cutting prices on Dr. Miles drugs it obtained from other wholesalers. Dr. Miles sued but without success because the Supreme Court decided that a manufacturer parts with control once he parts with the goods. "Where commodities have passed into the channels of trade and have been sold by complainant to dealers at prices satisfactory to complainant, the public is entitled to whatever advantage may be derived from competition in the subsequent traffic."

A lengthy interlude of legality occurred when, during the Great Depression, many states responded to the urgings of retailers by enacting so-called fair trade laws, which made resale price maintenance permissible. Notice that it was *retailers,* not manufacturers, who lobbied most vehemently, suggesting that retailers are shielded from competition when resale price maintenance is effective. This period of legality ended, however, in 1975 with passage of the Consumer Goods Pricing Act of 1975. This act removed these exemptions, thereby limiting legal fair trade pricing to the unilateral actions just discussed.

As regards this unilateralism—simple announcement plus cutoffs—the leading precedent is *U. S.* v. *Colgate,* decided only eight years after *Dr. Miles.*[34] Colgate practiced resale price maintenance, disciplining maverick dealers with refusals to sell. But the court was favorably impressed by Colgate's circumspection: "In the absence of any purpose to create or maintain a monopoly" a firm is free "to exercise his own independent discretion as to parties with whom he will deal; and of course, he may announce in advance the circumstances under which he will refuse to sell."

In 1983, in *Russell Stover Candies,* it was found that dealer acquiescence in a manufacturer's suggested resale price policy was well within the protection of *Colgate.*[35] As one commentator put it:

> *Russell Stover* shows that a manufacturer may suggest resale prices, preticket his goods, terminate price-cutters, effectively prevent dealers who wish to cut price from doing so out of fear of termination, and succeed in having 97.4% of his products retailed at or above their designated resale price—all while remaining within the safe harbor of *Colgate.*[36]

The currently controlling cases are *Monsanto Co.* v. *Spray-Rite* (1984) and *Business Electronics Corp.* v. *Sharp Electronics Corp.* (1988), both of which strongly affirm the *Colgate* doctrine.[37] In *Monsanto* the Supreme Court said that a manufacturer would be permitted to terminate price cutters even if "that termination came about 'in response to' complaints" from distributors hurt by the maverick. Such complaints "arise in the normal course of business and do not indicate illegal concerted action." Thus, a manufacturer may announce a policy of resale price maintenance and enforce it. The manufacturer should *act unilaterally* though by (1) not requiring the express agreement of its distributors, and (2) not referring to distributor complaints even if acting in response to those complaints. Furthermore, the manufacturer should *avoid coercion,* (1) not harassing distributors into compliance, and (2) not terminating mavericks only to reinstate them once they agree to adhere to suggested resale prices.[38]

To conclude, the *Colgate* loophole takes the teeth out of the per se rule against resale price maintenance. The critical question for legality has become whether manufacturers conspire with some retailers to eliminate others. Through winks and nods plus unilateralism, a manufacturer can conspire with its cooperating retailers to set resale prices fairly easily. "Only the stupidest manufacturers will get caught with specific agreements on prices," says Diane Wood, University of Chicago law professor.[39]

Summary

Tying, exclusive dealing, territorial restrictions, and resale price maintenance constitute vertical restrictions. Tying is the sale of two or more products contractually bound. Exclusive dealing prevents a buyer-distributor from dealing in more than one brand of a given line of wares. Territorial restrictions insulate distributors from intrabrand competition, and resale price maintenance is vertical price fixing. Policies concerning these practices have gained importance with the remarkable growth of franchising.

Tying may gain efficiencies, preserve business good will through the preservation of quality, or aid price discrimination. Tying may also be used to leverage monopoly power from the tying good's market into the tied good's market, and therein lies the rub. It can be exclusionary. Under Section 1 of the Sherman Act and Section 3 of the Clayton Act, tying is judged illegal if (1) there really are two products involved; (2) the seller possesses sufficient economic power in the tying good; (3) there is substantial commerce in the tied good; and (4) no defenses of reasonableness afford themselves. Although laced with rule of reason potential, these criteria boil down to a per se rule in some instances, such as tie ins to patented products.

Exclusive dealing is also potentially exclusionary and also covered by Clayton Section 3.

Nevertheless, given the possible benefits of this practice for distributors and ultimate consumers as well as instigating manufacturers, it is appropriate that a rule of reason prevail. The two main factors determining its legality are the seller's market share and the prevalence of the practice. If either or both are quite large, the exclusionary effect will be magnified and, with it, the likelihood of illegality.

Territorial restraints and resale price maintenance curb intrabrand competition among distributors, thereby inviting scrutiny under Section 1 of the Sherman Act. A main business justification for both is that they nourish incentives for vigorous, full-service retailing and wholesaling. Such incentives may foster interbrand competition if used by the weak against the strong. On the other hand, both practices have anticompetitive potentials. Territorial restraints are therefore susceptable to challenge if used by a dominant firm or if used by most firms in a tight-knit oligopoly with high concentration. Resale price maintenance is at present illegal. But it has been legal in the past, and there are pressures to make it legal again.

Regardless of the law, many vertical restraints escape through the use of tacit arrangements that are cemented by an ample freedom of choice in the selection of distributors and franchises. This "out" is especially noteworthy for resale price maintenance, where the *Colgate* doctrine has held sway since 1919. It has recently been reinforced by the Supreme Court's decisions in *Monsanto* and *Sharp*.

Questions and Exercises for Chapter 10

1. After specifying the several reasons why tying may be in the interests of businesses using it, explain which of these are in the social interest and which are not.
2. Why can it be said that tying is neither per se illegal nor rule of reason but mixed?
3. Is policy toward tying so tight that socially laudable uses of it are prevented? Explain.
4. Why are exclusive dealing and tying alike? Why are they different?
5. Given the similarities between tying and exclusive dealing, are policies toward them consistent? Explain.
6. When is resale price maintenance in the public interest and when is it not?
7. Resale price maintenance is said to be per se illegal, but in the real world it is commonplace. Why?
8. Does the ruling in *Continental TV* v. *GTE Sylvania* make economic sense? Explain your yes or no.
9. When is exclusive dealing in the public interest and when is it not?
10. What is the *Colgate* doctrine? What are its history and implications?
11. Why can the "Guidelines" of Figure 10–1 apply to both exclusive dealing and territorial restrictions?

Notes

1. U. S. Department of Commerce, *Franchising in the Economy 1986–1988* (Washington, DC: 1988).
2. Donald N. Thompson, *Franchise Operations and Antitrust* (Lexington, MA: Heath Lexington Books, 1971), pp. 45–52.
3. M. L. Burstein, "A Theory of Full-Line Forcing," *Northwestern University Law Review* (March-April 1960): 62–95; Arthur Lewbel, "Bundling of Substitutes or Complements," *International Journal of Industrial Organization* (March 1985): 101–107.
4. James M. Ferguson, "Tying Arrangements and Reciprocity: An Economic Analysis," *Law and Contemporary Problems* (Summer 1965): 553–565.
5. W. L. Baldwin and David McFarland, "Tying Arrangements in Law and Economics," *Antitrust Bulletin* (September-October 1963); 769. See also Jean Tirole, *The Theory of Industrial Organization* (Cambridge, MA: MIT Press, 1988), pp. 333–336; and Michael D. Whinston, "Tying, Foreclosure, and Exclusion," *American Economic Review* (September 1990): 837–859.
6. Don E. Waldman, *Antitrust Action and Market Structure* (Lexington, MA: Lexington Books, 1978), pp. 143–150. Tying's anticompetitive effect need not be limited to exclusion. It may, for instance, aid cartel discipline. See F. J. Cummins and W. E. Ruhter, "The *Northern Pacific Case*," *Journal of Law and Economics* (October 1979): 329–350. Cases like these undermine the position of Bork and others who argue that tying is never anticompetitive. See Louis Kaplow "Extension of Monopoly Power Through Leverage" *Columbia Law Review* (vol. 85, 1985): 515–556.

7. *Northern Pacific Railroad Co.* v. *United States,* 356 U. S. 1 (1958). Emphasis added.

8. *International Salt Co.* v. *U. S.,* 332 U. S. 392 (1947).

9. *U. S.* v. *Loew's Inc.,* 371 U. S. 38 (1962).

10. *Times-Picayune Publishing Co.* v. *U. S.,* 354 U. S. 594 (1953). This definition was erroneous, however. See J. Dirlam and A. E. Kahn, *Fair Competition: The Law and Economics of Antitrust Policy* (Ithaca, NY: Cornell University Press, 1954), pp. 106–108.

11. *Jefferson Parish Hospital District No. 2* v. *Hyde,* 104 S. Ct. 1551 (1984).

12. *U. S.* v. *Jerrold Electronics,* 187 F. Supp. 545 (E.D. Pa. 1960), affirmed per curiam 365 U. S. 567 (1961). For another successful use of the goodwill defense, see *Dehydrating Process Co.* v. *A. O. Smith Corp.,* 292 F. 2d 653 (1st Cir. 1961).

13. U. S. Department of Justice, Antitrust Division, "Vertical Restraints Guidelines" (January 23, 1985), p. 41. (emphasis added)

14. *Fuchs Sugar and Syrups, Inc. et al.* v. *Amstar Corp.,* CCH para 62,700 (CA-2, June 1979). For yet another explanation applicable to some cases, see Howard P. Marvel, "Exclusive Dealing," *Journal of Law and Economics* (April 1982): 1–25.

15. Thompson, *Franchise Operations,* p. 59. See also Oliver Williamson, "Assessing Vertical Market Restrictions" *University of Pennsylvania Law Review* (April 1979): 960–966, and William S. Comanor and H. E. Frech III, "The Competitive Effects of Vertical Agreements?", *American Economic Review* (June 1985) pp. 539–546.

16. Gerald Brock, "Vertical Restraints in Industrial Gases," in *Impact Evaluations of Federal Trade Commission Vertical Restraints Cases,* ed. R. N. Lafferty, R. H. Lande, and J. B. Kirkwood, Bureau of Economics, Federal Trade Commission (1984), pp. 400–401.

17. *Business Week,* December 7, 1987, p. 65.

18. *Los Angeles Times,* 15 December 1985, Part IV, p. 9.

19. *Standard Oil of California and Standard Stations, Inc.* v. *U. S.* 337 U. S. 293 (1949).

20. *Fuchs Sugar, op. cit.;* Thompson, *Franchise Operations,* Chap. 4; A. R. Oxenfelt, *Marketing Practices in the TV Set Industry* (New York: Columbia University Press, 1964), p. 123. This is perhaps especially true under the "Guidelines," given their leniency. For a critical review of the "Guidelines," see Alan A. Fisher, Frederick I. Johnson, and Robert H. Lande, "Do the D.J. Vertical Restraints Guidelines Provide Guidance?" *Antitrust Bulletin* (Fall 1987): 609–642.

21. Thompson, *Franchise Operations,* Chap. 7.

22. Cited by Barbara Katz, "Competition in the Soft Drink Industry," *Antitrust Bulletin* (Summer 1979): 280.

23. *U. S.* v. *White Motor Co.,* 372 U.S. 253 (1963).

24. *U. S.* v. *Arnold Schwinn & Co.,* 388 U.S. 365 (1967).

25. *Continental TV, Inc., et al.* v. *GTE Sylvania Inc.,* 433 U. S. 36 (1977).

26. Thomas R. Overstreet, Jr., *Resale Price Maintenance: Economic Theories and Empirical Evidence* (Federal Trade Commission, Bureau of Economics, 1983), especially pages 6–7, 114–115, 151–155.

27. For another overview, see William S. Comanor, "The Two Economics of Vertical Restraints," *Review of Industrial Organization* (Summer 1990): 99–126.

28. See S. C. Hollander's summary in B. S. Yamey, ed., *Resale Price Maintenance* (Chicago: Aldine, 1966), pp. 67–100; Leonard Weiss, *Case Studies in American Industry,* 3rd ed. (New York: Wiley, 1980), pp. 282–288; J. F. Pickering, "The Abolition of Resale Price Maintenance in Great Britain," *Oxford Economic Papers* (March 1975): 120–146.

29. Ward Bowman, "Resale Price Maintenance–A Monopoly Problem," *Journal of Business* (July 1952): 141–155.

30. In general see Robert L. Steiner, "The Nature of Vertical Restraints," *Antitrust Bulletin* (Spring 1985): 143–197. In particular see the articles by Sharon Oster and Timothy Greening in *Impact Evaluations of Federal Trade Commission Vertical Restraint Cases* (FTC (1984): 48–180.

31. Roger D. Blair and David L. Kaserman, *Antitrust Economics* (Homewood, IL: Irwin, 1985), pp. 349–353.

32. *Wall Street Journal,* 11 April 1991, p. B1.

33. *Dr. Miles Medical Co.* v. *John D. Park & Sons Co.,* 220 U. S. 373 (1911).

34. *United States* v. *Colgate & Co.,* 250 U. S. 300 (1919).

35. *Russell Stover Candies, Inc.* v. *FTC,* 718 F.2d 256 (1983).

36. Steiner, "Vertical Restraints," p. 193. See also Victor Goldberg, "Enforcing Resale Price Maintenance: The FTC Investigation of Lenox," *American Business Law Journal* (Summer 1980): 225–256.

37. *Monsanto Co.* v. *Spray-Rite Service Co.,* 104 S. Ct. 1464 (1984); *Business Electronics Corp.* v. *Sharp Electronics Corp.,* 108 S. Ct. 1515 (1988).

38. For detailed instructions to manufacturers see Mary J. Sheffet and Debra L. Scammon, "Resale Price Maintenance: Is It Safe to Suggest Retail Prices?" *Journal of Marketing* (Fall 1985): 82–96.

39. *Wall Street Journal,* 3 May 1988; see also *Wall Street Journal,* 27 February 1991, p. B1.

Chapter 11

Multinational Corporations

The multinational corporate enterprise represents the contemporary stage of development of the national corporate enterprise, which in its turn developed from the local corporate enterprise, which in its turn evolved from the noncorporate local enterprise.
— *Harry G. Johnson*

Mammoth American oil companies are famous for their international expanse. Their production facilities and marketing outlets blanket the globe. Exxon, for example, operates in more than 100 countries. Much the same could be said of most major U. S. companies. IBM's foreign operations accounted for 60 percent of its sales in 1990. Gillette and Coca-Cola had equally impressive fractions from foreign sales in 1990— 65 percent and 54 percent, respectively.

Foreign corporations also stretch transnationally. In recent years many familiar American companies have been acquired by foreign firms— for example, Pillsbury, Columbia Pictures, CBS Records, Carnation, and Farmers Insurance. So many formerly American tire companies—Firestone, Armstrong, Uniroyal-Goodrich, and General Tire—have been bought out by foreigners that, except for Goodyear, this industry is now in foreign hands. Japanese acquisitions have become especially noteworthy, as indicated in the Appendix to this chapter.

Dating back centuries, multinationalism is by no means new, but it has grown at a fantastic rate of late. While U. S. companies have flowered in foreign lands, foreign companies have scampered into the United States. Big business has, in short, outgrown national boundaries.

This spread of multinationalism has created dozens of new policy issues. Many of these issues relate to antitrust policy because power is a basic problem with multinationalism—power transcending and evading the legal reach of individual nations. Before we take up specific policies, however, we must find answers to several preliminary questions. Hence, this chapter's outline is as follows:

I. Who are the multinationals?
II. How strong are they abroad?
III. Why do firms become multinational?
IV. What is *good* about multinationals?
V. What is *bad* about multinationals?
VI. What policies govern multinationals?[1]

211

I. Who Are the Multinationals?

A. U. S. Multinationals

Multinational corporations (MNCs) are distinguished by wholly owned foreign subsidiaries, partially owned foreign joint ventures, or patent and trademark licensing agreements abroad. If cosmopolitan enough, these corporations have far-flung research and development activities, multinational management organizations, and even global business strategies.

Those multinationals calling the United States home are also at home on lists of our leading corporations, such as the list in Table 5–3 in Chapter 5. Indeed, as of 1990, General Motors and Exxon were two of the largest industrial companies in the world, each with over $100 billion in global sales, an amount exceeding the gross national product of most countries. Ford Motors, Mobil, IBM, and GE also rank highly among multinational corporations. And in 1990 seven of the world's fifteen leading multinationals were based in the United States, these among them.[2]

B. Non-U. S. Multinationals

Whereas several hundred multinationals originate from the United States, several hundred more are based in other lands. Some of the largest of these are listed in Table 11–1. Notice that large economically powerful countries like Germany and Japan are the ones most typically called home by these non-American companies. For nearly all of the companies mentioned in Table 11-1, most of their revenues come from sales outside rather than inside their home country.

II. How Strong Are the Multinationals?

In aggregate terms, roughly 400 multinational enterprises produce perhaps as much as one-third of the free world's industrial output. Taken together, the largest 1,000 corporations in the world (virtually all of which are to some extent multinational) were worth $6.7 trillion in 1990.[3]

On a less aggregated basis, the eminence of multinationals is quite variable, but rough patterns are discernible. Variations along two dimensions are particularly revealing. One dimension is the state of economic development of the host country. That is, the share of industrial activity in the hands of multinational firms appears to be greater in poor countries than in rich countries. The other dimension is the level of technology involved in the product or production process: The share of industrial activity accounted for by multinationals appears to be greatest where relatively sophisticated technology is involved and least where the technology is relatively rudimentary.

Data for U. S. multinationals in 1970 illustrate these two dimensions taken together. At the high end, these firms could be credited with approximately 40 percent of the sales of such high technology wares as chemicals, electrical machinery, and transportation equipment in Brazil and Mexico. At the low end, these firms accounted for only about 3 percent of the combined sales of simple technology items like food, paper, textiles, and wood products in the advanced countries of France and West Germany. In between these extremes, U. S. multinationals garnered about 12 percent of simple technology sales in Brazil and Mexico and 12 percent of complex technology sales in France and West Germany.[4] There are exceptions to this pattern, but these exceptions often have obvious explanations. Over 50 percent of Canada's heavy industry and mining is owned by non-Canadian corporations, an unusually high proportion due largely to Canada's close proximity to the United States.[5] But exceptions haunt all generalizations.

A survey of 180 U. S. multinationals in Mexico during the mid-1970s revealed that 44 percent of them ranked first in their product line in Mexico and another 20 percent ranked second.

Table 11-1

Selected Multinational Corporations with High Portions of Total Sales Outside Their Home Country

Company	Home Country	1991 Sales ($ billions)	1991 Assets ($ billions)
Royal Dutch Shell	Britain/Netherlands	$103.8	$105.3
Toyota Motor	Japan	78.1	65.2
Daimler-Benz	Germany	57.3	49.8
Hitachi	Japan	56.1	60.6
Matsushita Electric	Japan	48.6	62.3
Siemens	Germany	44.9	41.8
Unilever	Britain/Netherlands	41.3	25.3
Nestlé	Switzerland	35.6	28.7
Honda	Japan	30.5	21.0
Philips Electric	Netherlands	30.2	29.1
Hoechst	Germany	28.5	23.5
Sony	Japan	26.6	32.7
Bayer	Germany	25.6	24.9
ICI	Britain	22.3	20.6

Source: Fortune, July 27, 1992, p. 179.

Similar results came from U. S. multinationals in Brazil, where 42 percent ranked first and 26 percent ranked second in their respective industries. Very large market shares went with these lofty positions. Twenty-five percent of the surveyed multinationals in Mexico and Brazil had market shares exceeding 50 percent. Another 25 percent of these firms enjoyed market shares in the 25 to 50 percent range.[6] In other words, multinationals are not merely big in *absolute* terms; they also tend to be big in *relative* terms, frequently dominating the markets in which they operate abroad, especially in less developed countries.

To say that multinational corporations typically capture hefty market shares in the less developed countries in which they operate is not the same as saying that multinationals devote most of their attention to the less developed countries. The vast bulk of multinational activity occurs within a circle made up of the developed countries of North America, Europe, and Japan. In 1979, 72 percent of U. S. direct foreign investment was located in what could be called developed countries. Less developed countries accounted for only 25 percent of these investments, an amount just slightly above the share accounted for by Canada alone (21 percent). Conversely, most subsidiaries of foreign multinationals in the United States are of European parentage, and those European parents favor affiliations in prosperous countries just as much as their U. S. brethren do.

III. Why Do Firms Become Multinationals?

The obvious motive for foreign investment is, in a word, profit. But such could be said of practically everything businesses do, so the question of motive deserves a more enlightening answer. That answer comes in several parts because there is no single explanation for all multinationalism, no solitary theory that can fit all the facts. Here we survey four of the main explanations—(1) resource extraction, (2) monopolistic advantages, (3) tariff jumping, and (4) comparative advantage.

A. Resource Extraction

Many multinational endeavors originate in efforts to secure raw materials that nature has placed in remote spots. Such was true for petroleum, many metal ores, and bananas, as is suggested by the very names of some of the oldest and largest multinational corporations—Standard Oil of New Jersey (Exxon), Rio Tinto Zinc, International Minerals & Chemical, and United Fruit.

A large chunk of Japan's rapidly growing direct foreign investment is grounded on this motive. As Terutomo Ozawa explains:

> This pattern of behavior could be expected of a country that lacked the natural resources yet emphasized the development of resource-consuming heavy and chemical industries. Here the economics is not a cost-pinching, short-term calculation but a security-primacy, long-term calculation. Japan's demand for and dependence on overseas resources have increased enormously.[7]

Much the same could be said, though perhaps less stridently, about Britain and the Netherlands, whose Royal–Dutch Shell, British Petro-leum, and Unilever faced dependence on foreign resources from their first stirrings.

B. Monopolistic Advantages

Foreign expansion for resource purposes tends to be vertical in the sense of backward integration toward raw materials. But much if not most present foreign expansion is actually horizontal, in the sense of, say, an auto firm producing autos abroad. A major explanation for this horizontal multinationalism draws on industrial organization theory for its insights.[8] In particular, it is observed that direct foreign investment frequently occurs in industries where monopolistic advantages prevail both at home and abroad. These advantages may be grounded in advanced technology (chemicals and computers, for example), potent product differentiation (as in the case of soft drinks and drugs), and economies of scale (as in autos). Many of these advantages are protected by industrial property rights at home and abroad—that is, patents, proprietary know-how, and trademarks. The basic idea is that these monopolistic advantages give the multinational enterprise an advantage over host country rivals, or at least give the multinational's foreign subsidiaries an equal chance in host country markets. Without such special advantages, the foreigner would be at a *dis*advantage because local firms would naturally tend to be more familiar with local market conditions, local laws, local customs, and other local mysteries important to business success. A nice illustration of this is provided by Tandy Corporation, whose Radio Shack store in Holland geared its first Christmas promotion to December 25, unaware that the Dutch customarily exchange holiday gifts on December 6, St. Nicholas Day. They badly missed the market.[9]

Statistical studies support the theory of direct foreign investment by finding high correlations between direct foreign investment on the one hand and four-firm concentration or advertising intensity or R & D expenditure on the other. In Mexico, for instance, foreign firms accounted for 100 percent of 1970 industry sales in transportation equipment, rubber, electrical equipment, and office equipment—all of which evince special advantages for member firms. In contrast, 1970 sales of foreign firms accounted for very small percentages in leather, textiles, and apparel—4.6 percent, 7.1 percent, and 4.0 percent, respectively.[10] Canadian experience further illustrates the importance of monopolistic advantages. To quote the conclusion of a Canadian study:

> Where the advantages are potent (heavy advertising and research and development, heavy use of sophisticated managerial personnel and nonproduction workers generally) domestic-controlled establishments shrink to a competitive fringe. Conversely, the multinational presence shrinks where these assets are unimportant or where being small, local, and flexible affords a positive advantage.[11]

C. Tariff Jumping

National tariff barriers have in the past promoted much direct foreign investment. For example, formation of the European Economic Community (EEC) in the late 1950s led to low tariffs on *intra*-European trade but to high tariffs against *non*-European suppliers. United States exporters to Europe were thereby handicapped. So, instead of building plants in the United States and exporting to Europe, these firms leaped the EEC's tariff wall during the 1960s by building plants inside the EEC. They then could supply the EEC market duty free. High tariffs in less developed countries have had a similar effect.

The importance of tariff jumping in the past is revealed in a questionnaire survey of 76 U. S. multinationals in 1971. When asked why they had invested directly in foreign markets, 25 of these firms, or roughly one-third, mentioned among their answers, "Unable to reach market from United States because of tariffs, transportation costs, or nationalistic purchasing policies." The only reason given more frequently

was "Maintain or increase market share locally," which likewise suggests a concern with overcoming the economic disadvantages of tariff and transportation costs that might inhibit the export of home productions.[12]

If a similar survey were conducted today these factors would probably receive much less emphasis because tariff barriers and transportation costs have fallen, at least among advanced countries and for most industries. The motive is still important, though, as newer barriers like "voluntary quotas" have replaced the old. All major Japanese auto companies now own assembly plants in the United States because the United States has attempted to protect its domestic firms by imposing voluntary quotas on Japanese imports.

D. Comparative Advantage

When semiconductor companies like Texas Instruments and National Semiconductor build factories in Asia or Mexico for the "off-shore" assembly of electrical products, or when Japanese textile manufacturers establish mills in Taiwan or South Korea, their motivation springs from factors not easily incorporated into the foregoing considerations. Host country resources are not uprooted. Monopolistic advantages are not being exploited to penetrate host country markets. Indeed, host country markets are not even the destination of the products produced, so tariff jumping is likewise not involved. The ultimate destination is either the multinational's home market or international trade generally.

What appears to propel many of these direct investments is comparative advantages in host countries, a notion derived from classical trade theory. A U. S. firm may decide to supply the European market by locating a plant in Singapore. A Japanese firm in the same industry may supply the United States from a plant in Hong Kong. In this way capital, technology, and managerial talent can be moved across national boundaries to exploit the comparative advantages the host countries have in cheap, semi-skilled labor or in other immobile inputs. The more this brand of multinationalism grows, the more truly international the multinational corporations become. The simple home-host axis of attention breaks down as, for instance, capital from the Eurocurrency market is used by a U. S. multinational to build an operation in India that will use raw materials from Africa and ship final goods all over the globe. Curiously, many corporations enter this particular mode of international dependency and mobility not because of any monopolistic *strengths* at home or abroad but because of *weaknesses* in competitive position. Their struggle for survival forces them to seek out and use comparative advantages wherever they might be.[13]

To summarize, several inducements encourage multinationalism. Backward integration into resource extraction, horizontal expansion to cash in on monopolistic advantages, tariff jumping to maintain or expand local market positions, and geographic diversification in pursuit of comparative-competitive advantages are apparently the main motives. There are others—such as the achievement of earnings stability through international diversification—but these need not detain us.

One further observation is worthy of pause, the observation that motives frequently work in combination, spurring multinational undertakings through multiforces.

IV. What Is Good About Multinationals?

Multinationalism is obviously good for the multinationals themselves, for otherwise they would stay at home. But the question of their benefits and costs to the world in general and to home and host countries in particular remains open. In fact, this broader question has ignited tremendous controversy, with arguments for and against multinationals multiplying with each passing year.[14] Given the immensity of this subject, we can do little more than outline the economic pros and cons as viewed by home and host countries, beginning first with the favorable prospects for home countries.

A. Arguments in Favor of MNCs: Home Country Perspective

1. BALANCE OF PAYMENTS

At first glance it might appear that a home country's balance of payments would suffer from multinationalism among its corporations because direct foreign investment implies a transfer of capital abroad. However, the balance of payments effects may be favorable to the home country because such investment eventually reaps returns in the form of interest, dividends, patent royalties, and other fees. Moreover, the capital for foreign expansion need not always come from home, given the alternative sources of Eurocurrency credit and offshore retained earnings. Finally, multinationals frequently export components for assembly abroad, which exports help the home country's balance of payments. Thus, many people contend that there is a plus here.

2. SECURE RAW MATERIALS

As suggested earlier, multinationalism may help a home country secure lines of raw material supplies.

3. PROMOTE TRADE AND MONETARY STABILITY

A study of U. S. multinationals concludes that they "contribute significantly to the effectiveness of international monetary arrangements, to the maintenance of liberal U. S. trade policies, and thus to these important national interests of the United States."[15]

B. Arguments Favoring Multinationals: Host Country Perspective

1. MOBILIZE HOST COUNTRY RESOURCES

A multinational's infusion of capital and managerial skill can mobilize host country resources, thereby boosting output and efficiency, expanding export sales, and improving the *host* country's balance of payments position. In other words, multinationals can provide the wherewithal to promote economic development and prosperity.

2. TRANSFER OF TECHNOLOGY

For less developed host countries, the multinationals can be a major source of new technology. Over 90 percent of the world's most advanced technology is in the hands of multinationals who may transfer it to less developed countries by direct foreign investment or licensing, thereby saving these countries the tremendous costs of developing that technology from scratch for themselves. Even developed host countries benefit because the international diffusion of new knowledge could similarly add to their productive capabilities and product modernity.

3. INCREASED COMPETITION

Competition in a host country would be stimulated by the new entry of a multinational. Local firm market power would lessen, and overall concentration in the host country market could fall.

It must be stressed that empirical testing of these potential benefits for home and host countries is very difficult because most claimed benefits rest on an assumption that there are no good alternative sources of these benefits except multinationals. If, for example, their capital were not made available, it is assumed that host country capital sources or foreign aid could not easily fill the gap. This presents a research problem in the sense that nobody really knows what might have been, given that it hasn't been. Still, some evidence solidly favors multinationalism.

V. What Is Bad About Multinationals?

The arguments against multinationals also divide along home and host country lines. It will be ob-vious that several such arguments directly contradict favorable ones given earlier in which cases both cannot be right, at least not as they apply to any one particular multinational project.

A. Arguments Against Multinationals: Home Perspective

1. WORSEN BALANCE OF PAYMENTS

Because multinationals often substitute capital outflows from home countries for exports, it has been argued that they worsen the home country's balance of payments.

2. EXPORTING JOBS

To the extent multinationals build factories abroad rather than at home they give the appearance of fostering employment abroad at the expense of employment at home. Moreover, it is argued that multinationalism weakens the bargaining power of labor because it gives corporations the option of moving production abroad if they do not wish to meet labor demands at home. As in other cases, the validity of these contentions varies from industry to industry, obscuring any general conclusion. Still, some jobs apparently are exported and some labor unions are weakened, although the numbers and degrees involved do not seem particularly large.[16]

3. MARKET POWER IN HOME MARKET

As we have seen, multinationalism is often grounded on monopolistic advantages in home countries. A reverse causality is also possible. That is, multinationalism itself may give a corporation certain advantages in its home market that purely domestic rivals cannot match. In particular, these advantages may stem from international vertical integration, the spreading of joint costs over many geographic markets, and cross-subsidization (which entails drawing on profits abroad to boost one's market position at home). Statistical search for the presence of such power enhancement at home has converted the possibility into probability.[17]

B. Arguments Against Multinationals: Hosts' Perspective

1. NET CAPITAL OUTFLOW

Rather than provide net capital inflows that finance industrial expansion in host countries, multinationals may contribute to a net capital outflow from host countries, or so it is sometimes argued. Indeed, much financing for multinational enterprises abroad is obtained locally through retained earnings and host country credit.[18] When coupled with claims that multinationals remit excess profits and royalties to home, the contention gains plausibility. And when coupled with certain assumptions, it is not without empirical support in at least some cases.[19]

2. TRANSFER PRICING

Aggravating the possibility of net capital outflows is the problem of transfer pricing. When a subsidiary abroad buys raw materials, technology, or services from its parent multinational company, it is charged an arbitrary intracompany price that might well be exhorbitant. For example, the multinational oil companies apparently overcharged their Canadian subsidiaries $3.2 billion on crude oil imported into Canada over the years 1958 to 1970.[20] Investigations in Colombia for the late 1960s disclosed that drug giant Hoffman-LaRoche was overcharging its subsidiary (as a percentage of world market prices) by 94 percent for Atelor, by 96 percent for Trimatoprium, by over 5,000 percent for Chlordiazepoxide, and by over 6,000 percent for Diazepam.[21] A major motive for this kind of behavior is taxes. By manipulating intracompany prices, multinationals can cause profits to show up in nations whose tax bite is least burdensome. Moreover, they can take profits out of a host country in a way that evades regulation.

Multinationals apparently use transfer pricing to avoid billions of dollars of U. S. tax obligations. In 1990 the Internal Revenue Service published data revealing that foreign-based companies sold $543 billion worth of goods and services in the United States during 1986 but claimed to have experienced net *losses* of $1.5 billion on that business. Losses limit one's tax obligation. By some estimates, foreign-based multinationals dodge as much as $20 billion in U. S. taxes every year through transactions like the one illustrated in Figure 11–1. In one of the most notable cases to date, Toyota settled with the IRS for $1 billion after being accused of overcharging its U. S. subsidiary for years on most cars, trucks, and parts shipped to the United States.[22]

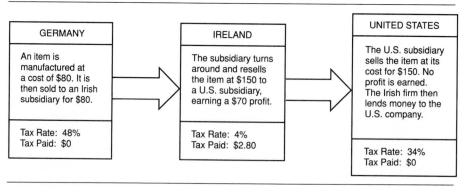

Figure 11–1

Transfer Pricing to Avoid U.S. Tax Obligations

Source: *Newsweek*, April 15, 1991, pp. 48–49

3. INAPPROPRIATE TECHNOLOGY

Indonesia's importation of modern farm equipment, ranging from mechanical rice hullers to tillers and tractors, eliminated several hundred thousand jobs during the 1970s. Moreover, it has been estimated that Indonesia's exports supported 60,000 fewer jobs in 1979 than in 1971 despite the fact that exports expanded eightfold with the aid of multinational oil and mineral companies.[23] These experiences and many like them nurture arguments that, however attractive a multinational's new technology might appear at superficial first sight, it is in the end often damaging to the interests of less developed countries. In particular, the technology too often tends to be labor-saving and capital-intensive—characteristics befitting the needs of the *advanced* countries where the technology originated, but *contrary* to the requirements of most *less developed* countries (which are so laden with labor as to have 680 million people needing work).[24]

4. DISTORTIONS OF DEMAND

Multinationalism grounded on monopolistic advantages in advertising, trademarks, and related product differentiation, like that of Coca-Cola, is often criticized for creating inappropriate tastes, especially in less developed countries.[25] A notorious example stems from the attempts of food manufacturers to expand their sales of infant formula at the expense of mother's milk in less developed countries. Breast-feeding is cheap and nutritious. Bottle feeding strains small budgets and often threatens babies' health.[26]

5. QUESTIONABLE PAYMENTS

During the late 1970s and early 1980s, more than 450 large U. S. corporations disclosed to the U. S. Securities and Exchange Commission that they had made more than $1 billion in economic and political payoffs to foreign heads of state, cabinet ministers, and other government officials. The bribes were paid to influence purchasing decisions, tax policies, and elections. Gulf Oil, for example, confessed to making secret payments of $4 million to the ruling party in South Korea. Exxon paid $59 million to Italian politicians over eight years to advance its "business objectives." United Brands was found to have bribed Honduran officials $2.5 million to win tax breaks. And in 1989 Goodyear pleaded guilty to having paid nearly $1 million in bribes to Kuwaiti officials to boost tire sales.[27] Despite explanations that in many cases this practice is customary in foreign countries, critics accuse multinationals of improperly, immorally, and illegally interfering in the official affairs of foreign host countries.

6. RESTRICTIVE BUSINESS TRADE PRACTICES

The massive size and economic power of major multinationals raises suspicions that they are all too frequently engaged in restrictive practices adversely affecting host countries—weak hosts in particular. Both horizontal and vertical restrictions have been found. Among horizontal offenses, monopolization is by no means unknown, but cartelization is surely the most commonly encountered.[28] The activities of the International Electrical Association (I.E.A.), an international cartel in heavy electrical equipment, illustrates the problem:

> The cartel comprises over 50 European and Japanese producers and covers sales in most of the markets of the non-Communist world outside the United States, Western Europe, and Japan (amounting to almost $2 billion annually). . . . These cartel arrangements directly harm importing countries because of the onerous mark-up on cartelized sales as well as common policies among members restricting technology transfers to non-producing countries. On the basis of data from one product section, it is estimated that successful collusive agreements may raise prices 15 to 25 percent above the competitive rate.[29]

Vertical restrictions arise in the distribution or licensing process. These include exclusive dealing, tying, and territorial allocations among foreign distributors. Evidence concerning restraints such as these comes from studies of contracts transferring technology from multinational corporations to producers in less developed countries. Table 11–2 summarizes the results of several such studies by the United Nations Conference on Trade and Development covering license agreements in India, the Philippines, and Spain. It may be seen that restrictions limiting the exports of licensees have been common. Tying provisions requiring licensees to purchase specified materials from the licensor or from other designated suppliers have been less frequent but common nevertheless. Still other restraints, such as minimum royalty payments, posttermination limitations, and restrictions on production methods appear very infrequently, but in certain individual instances they can be important.

In sum, multinationals cannot clearly qualify for supercitizenship awards. Abundant evidence of assorted evils is available to incite critics in home and host countries. Still, much of the adverse evidence is blunted by the same problem that affects favorable evidence and argument— namely, no one really knows what might have been. Moreover, the evils cannot obliterate the considerable benefits of much multinationalism. For example, despite the restrictive practices, transfer payments, and so on, there is good evidence that on balance multinational corporations help to boost the exports of developing poor countries above what they would be otherwise. Between 1966 and 1986 the exports of U. S.-owned subsidiaries in developing countries grew faster than did the exports of their host developing countries as a group, "so that their share of developing countries' exports of manufacturers increased from 3.9 to 7.2 percent over the period."

> The importance of United States affiliates as exporters was particularly notable in Latin America, where they increased their share of world exports by 60 percent between 1966 and 1986, while during the same period Latin America lost export shares. This suggests that without transnational corporations, Latin American export performance would have been worse than it was.[30]

It appears, then, that we have a mixed bag—some good and some bad—with the mix depending on the individual circumstances and particular issues.[31]

Table 11–2
Percentage of Contracts Studied Imposing Restrictions on Licensees, India, Philippines, and Spain

Type of Restriction	India (pre-1964)	India (1964–1969)	Philippines (1970)	Spain (1950–1973)
Global ban on exports	3.4%	0.9%	19.3%	44.4%
Partial ban on exports	40.0	46.2	13.0	25.9
Tied purchases	14.6	4.7	26.4	30.6
Minimum royalty restriction	5.2	1.2	5.1	N.A.[a]

[a]N.A. = not available.

Source: United Nations, Conference on Trade and Development, *Restrictive Business Practices* U.N. doc. TD/B/C.2/104/Rev. 1 (1971); *Major Issues Arising from the Transfer of Technology: A Case Study of Spain*, U.N. doc. TD/B/AC.11/17 (1974).

VI. What Policies Govern Multinationals?

Given that multinationals can be both praised and pilloried, they have provoked ambiguous policy responses. On the one hand, home and host governments have often tried to encourage them with tax inducements, loan guarantees, and insurance protection. On the other hand, multinationals have posed enough of a problem from time to time and place to place that home and host country policies of various sorts have been implemented to control or discourage them. Space limitations force us to focus on this latter type, a focus that is best divided into three categories (1) home country policies, (2) host country policies, and (3) international policies.

A. Home Country Control Policies

1. U. S. ANTITRUST

Restrictive business practices and monopolization by U. S. multinationals are to some extent checked by Sections 1 and 2 of the Sherman Act because that Act applies to "commerce . . . with foreign nations" as well as to "commerce among the several states." The same *per se* and *rule of reason* approaches are involved as discussed earlier in Chapters 6 and 7. However, the anticompetitive acts of multinationals can be checked only insofar as they may affect U. S. commerce, where "commerce" is interpreted to include (1) protection of the *American* consuming public, and (2) protection of *American* export and investment opportunities. Note: This does *not* mean that the reach of the Sherman Act is limited to conduct that takes place within our borders. When foreign acts have a substantial and foreseeable effect on U. S. commerce, they are subject to U. S. antitrust law regardless of where they occur.[32] Even the acts of foreign firms are covered.

The foreign reach of the Sherman Act is thus not purely elastic. If, for example, a cartel of multinationals has no direct or intended effect on U. S. consumers or U. S. export opportunities, then that cartel would be operating outside the scope of U. S. interests and law. Moreover, the jurisdictional reach of U. S. law has occasionally been abbreviated (a) by successfully argued defenses that the prohibited acts were *compelled* by foreign government laws or pressure,[33] and (b) by the limits of what is called "personal" jurisdiction, which refers to the fact that foreign firms who become defendants can often dodge court appearances, document disclosures, and enforcement penalties because they have nothing solid in the U. S. that authorities can get hold of, no assets in the United States to levy penalties or damages against.

One further gap in the law is the explicit legal exemption provided by the Webb-Pomerene Act (1918) for *export cartels* made up of domestic U. S. firms. This act permits U. S. producers who properly register their "association" with the FTC to fix prices on their exports, allocate world markets among their members, and collude in other ways that without this exemption would violate the Sherman Act. The Webb-Pomerene exemption does not go so far as to allow export associations (a) to restrain domestic U. S. trade, or (b) to restrain the export trade of any U. S. competitor of the association, or (c) enter into cartel arrangements with foreign producers. But it goes far enough that in the past about 4 percent of U. S. export trade has been in the hands of Webb associations.[34]

Apart from cartelization and monopolization, U. S. law may prohibit an international merger if the circumstances are right. In particular, both parties to the merger must be, according to the Clayton Act, "engaged in commerce," which by interpretation covers less ground than the "affects commerce" standard applied under the Sherman Act.[35] Moreover, there is the additional geographic limitation under Section 7 of the Clayton Act that the illegal merger must lessen competition in a *"section of the country,"* implying a relatively narrow scope for offensive competitive injury.

The foregoing outline of U. S. law in this area may be illuminated by brief reference to a few cases. Illegal monopolizing, merging, and cartelizing—each is illustrated.

A monopolization case brought against *United Fruit* (UF, now United Brands) during the 1950s illustrates application of Section 2 of the Sherman Act.[36] United Fruit was first organized by merger back in the days of massive horizontal combinations and William McKinley. Thereafter it accounted for 60 to 80 percent of all United States and Canadian banana imports until 1954, when charges of monopolization were filed against it. In North America, UF cultivated the image of "Chiquita Banana," but in Central America is became known as "el pulpo" (the octopus). Among other things, it controlled 81 percent of the combined banana exports of Colombia, Costa Rica, Guatemala, Honduras, and Panama during the early 1950s. At the same time, UF owned or controlled 56 percent of the mature banana acreage in these countries. All told, it controlled 2.7 million acres.

Against this background the Justice Department's accusation of 1954 seems plausible. The charges covered three broad areas: (1) general monopolization, (2) dominant control of land and transportation facilities, and (3) exclusionary and predatory practices. This last category reflects intent, and if the case had gone to trial this accusation would have been more fully documented or disproved. As it stands, the complaint merely alleges in rather broad terms such tactics as engrossing, refusal to sell, and flooding local markets. These charges must have had some foundation, however, for UF agreed in 1958 to a consent decree that, by usual standards, was rather strict. Besides prohibiting UF from engaging further in exclusionary or predatory practices, the decree required UF to create out of its own assets a new competitor capable of importing into the United States a million banana stems

per year—the rough equivalent of 35 percent of UF's imports in 1957. The divestiture brought Del Monte into the banana industry.

United States v. *Joseph Schlitz Brewing Company* (1966) illustrates application of Section 7 of the Clayton Act.[37] In 1964, when it was the second-largest brewer in the United States, Schlitz acquired a controlling interest in Labatt, a large Canadian brewer that in turn owned a U. S. subsidiary, General Brewing Corporation, whose beer sold well in western states. Thus, Schlitz gained control of its competitor, General, through its purchase of the foreigner Labatt. Moreover, the merger ended some direct competition between Schlitz and Labatt because Labatt was beginning to market its premium Labatt beer through the General Brewing sales organization. The court found that Labatt "had the desire, the intention and the resourcefulness to enter the United States markets and to make General Brewing a stronger competitor in those markets." Hence, Schlitz's foreign acquisition lessened actual and potential competition in the United States in violation of Section 7.

Worries about America's competitiveness abroad have grown in recent decades. *Hazeltine Research, Inc.* v. *Zenith Radio Corporation* (1969) is therefore interesting because it illustrates how foreign cartels may block U. S. exports. In this case Zenith's exports of radio and television equipment to Canada were hampered by a patent pool. Organized by Canadian G.E. and other large companies, the pool held key Canadian patents on this equipment and licensed those patents only to firms that manufactured their products in Canada. (Related pools controlled British and Australian markets.) According to the court:

> The Pool's campaign against importation of radio and television receivers from the United States is highly organized and effective. Patent agents, investigators, and agents of the conspiring companies as well as the Canadian manufacturers and distributors trade associations at the behest of the

Pool have systematically policed the market in order to locate and stop the sale of imported receivers and have immediately attacked by infringement suit or threat thereof any dealer found to be selling imported receivers.[38]

Although American courts could not dissolve the Canadian patent cartel, they could prevent the cartel from suing Zenith for patent infringement.

2. U. S. FOREIGN CORRUPT PRACTICES ACT

To meet the problem of questionable payments abroad, Congress passed the Foreign Corrupt Practices Act in 1977. Enforced by the Securities and Exchange Commission, this law threatens jolting fines and prison sentences for corporate officials caught paying bribes abroad. It also regulates corporate accounting practices to dry up secret slush funds because these funds were a major means of bribery in the past.

The law apparently had its intended effect. A General Accounting Office survey of major corporations revealed that officials of 76 percent of the responding companies thought the law had deterred bribery significantly. Nevertheless, the Reagan Administration tried to repeal the law on grounds that U. S. corporations were suffering losses because they could not compete equally with others who paid bribes. After hearings, Congress passed amendments in 1988 that weakened the law but did not trash it:

> The more important amendments provided that the government would have to show that the [offending] corporation "knew" or had "reason to know" that their foreign sales agent would use the payments made to him or her to make bribes. Gifts of a "reasonable" value and based on "local custom" to foreign officials are no longer illegal.[39]

Severe penalies for proven violations remained harsh.

3. U. S. CONTROLS ON TECHNOLOGY TRANSFERS

As in the case of international investments generally, the basic orientation of U. S. policy toward transfers of technology by its multinationals is one of neutrality, neither promoting nor discouraging such transfers. A major exception concerns technology of potential military significance. In cooperation with the Department of Defense, the Department of Commerce regulates the transfer of technology to preserve national security. All forms of transfer are covered, not just the export of machinery or equipment.

4. FOREIGN ANTITRUST POLICY

The home countries of major multinationals outside the United States—mainly in Europe and Japan—have antitrust policies that are generally much weaker than those of the United States. "In any country," Corwin Edwards once wrote, "the relation of business to government is deeply rooted in political, constitutional, and legal traditions, in traditions as to the structure and relation of economic classes, and in traditions of social and religious ethics."[40] As it turns out, the cultural heritage of no foreign country is equal to that of the United States when it comes to honoring competition. As a result, foreign multinationals confront no serious checks to their power or activities in their homelands. Whereas the United States has a per se rule banning cartels, foreign authorities tend to make a rule of reason approach, approving cartel activities that can be excused for promoting some perceived benefit such as boosting employment or exports. Whereas U. S. law may attack single-firm dominance because that dominance is in itself considered undesirable, foreign laws permit dominance and attack only serious abuses of that dominance.[41]

Where U. S. and foreign laws tend toward equality, they tend toward equal leniency. For example, export cartels win as much approval in Europe as they win in the United States under the Webb-Pomerene Act. Moreover, multinationals seem to be more active in those European export cartels than in U. S. export cartels. Data from what was formerly West Germany, for instance, reveals that multinationals participated in

70 percent of all German export cartels in 1977.[42] Because multinationals can belong to such cartels in more than one country, they may even be able to influence competition among such export groups.

Although foreign antitrust laws are in general less robust than those of the United States, they are gaining strength over time, and in some specific respects they now prove to be more stringent than the U. S. variety. In some ways, antitrust policy has become one of America's most notable exports.[43]

B. Host Country Control Policies

1. NATIONALIZATION AND DOMESTICATION

As noted, many foreign countries have antitrust policies. These policies apply to multinationals operating in those countries as foreigners, but they are not as important as other policies affecting multinationals. One such policy is *nationalization,* in which case the host country's government buys or otherwise captures the multinational's local assets and operations. Such nationalization occurred on a grand scale in the OPEC countries, who used their fantastic oil earnings to buy (through compensated seizure) those parts of Exxon, Mobil, Shell, and their fellow oil giants that were located within their borders. Dozens of billions of dollars in assets changed hands in the process. No less ambitious but much less massive was Malaysia's twenty-year plan to reduce foreign control of its industry from 60 percent to 30 percent by 1990.

Domestication also refers to local ownership policies, but private not government ownership. For many years after World War II, for instance, Japan strictly limited all direct investments, joint ventures, and licensing agreements to the point of denying foreign companies any more than a 49 percent equity interest in Japanese enterprises and insisting that at least half of any venture's directors and auditors be Japanese nationals. More recently, many less developed countries have accepted foreign enterprises on their soil on

condition that domestic ownership and management be phased in over time.

Perhaps the most interesting development in recent years respecting multinationals is that nationalization and domestication policies for control of foreign investment were abandoned or relaxed in many countries during the 1980s and early 1990s after such policies had spread rather widely only shortly before. For example, Canada embarked on a program of domestication and nationalization with passage of the Foreign Investment Review Act in 1981. Its main intent was to help Canadian companies purchase foreign-owned assets in Canada by guaranteeing private loans made for this purpose and to review new foreign-owned companies. Then in 1985 there was an about-face when the Foreign Investment Review Act was repealed and replaced by the Investment Canada Act. Thereafter, review of new foreign-owned businesses was eliminated except those relating to Canada's "cultural heritage or national identity." Acquisitions of Canadian corporations by foreigners were to be reviewed only if the assets acquired exceeded $5 million in value. Other countries recently relaxing foreign ownership restrictions include Australia, New Zealand, India, and Mexico.[44] Not only are foreign ownership restrictions disappearing; some countries are now trying to *encourage* foreign investment. Poland and other recently freed countries in Eastern Europe come most immediately to mind in this regard. (On the other hand, many people in the United States are growing wary of Japanese ownership of U. S. companies, as suggested in the Appendix of this chapter. Perhaps U. S. policy will, contrary to trends elsewhere, be changed to discourage further foreign takeovers.)

2. REGULATION OF TRANSFER PRICING

Numerous host countries, including the United States, have attempted to curb abuses of transfer pricing by applying a variety of customs, tax, and restrictive practices laws. The main problem in all these efforts is to determine how close a multinational's arbitrary intracompany price comes to an appropriate arm's length price, when in practice such arm's length prices are often, if not usually, unavailable.[45]

3.   REGULATION OF VERTICAL RESTRAINTS

Many governments, those in less developed countries especially, have tried to regulate vertical restraints by screening investment projects and licensing agreements to detect and root out offensive conduct. Mexico's law of 1972 covering technology agreements illustrates this approach, as indicated in the following official summary:

> Contracts shall not be approved when they refer to technology freely available in the country; when the price or counterservice is out of proportion to the technology acquired. . . ; when they restrict the research or technological development of the purchaser; when they permit the technology supplier to interfere in the management of the purchaser company or oblige it to use, on a permanent basis, the personnel appointed by the supplier; when they establish the obligation to purchase inputs from the supplier only or to sell the goods produced by the technology imported exclusively to the supplier company; when they prohibit or restrict the export of goods in a way contrary to the country's interest; when they limit the size of production or impose prices on domestic production or on exports of the purchaser; when they prohibit the use of complementary technology; when they oblige the importer to sign exclusive sales or representation contracts with the supplier company covering the national territory; when they establish excessively long terms of enforcement, which in no case may exceed a 10-year obligation on the importer company, or when they provide that claims arising from the interpretation or fulfilment of such contracts are to be submitted to the jurisdiction o foreign courts."[46]

An interesting variation on this theme is a code of similar rules established jointly in 1970 by members of the Andean Group (Bolivia, Chile, Colombia, Ecuador, Peru, and Venezuela). Although this code is common to these countries,

it is administered by the individual nations separately.

As with restrictions on direct ownerships, these regulations have been relaxed in recent years. Multinationals are increasingly regarded as beneficial.

C. International Policies

Many problems are associated with the home and host country policies that we have discussed.[47] None is more obvious than the problem of mismatched geographic scope. National laws are only national, whereas multinational corporations are multinational or, as some like to say, transnational. National governments, operating individually, have often found it difficult to get good information out of multinationals, let alone good behavior. Aside from the limits that local jurisdiction imposes, small countries are limited by their fear that hard-line policies would simply cause multinationals to shift their business to more receptive or more timid countries. Stated differently, countries cannot be very bold if, in pursuit of the benefits multinationals offer, they compete against each other to attract multinationals to their shores.

For these and other reasons there have been efforts to establish *international* measures for the control of multinational enterprises. In 1976 a set of "Guidelines for Multinational Enterprises" was negotiated by the Organization of Economic Co-operation and Development, or OECD, which is a loose-knit international organization of two dozen industrialized countries from North America and Europe plus some others like Japan. In 1980 a branch of the UN, the United Nations Conference on Trade and Development (UNCTAD), completed a ten-year effort to devise a code of conduct controlling restrictive business practices in international trade. UNCTAD also has a code of conduct for the transfer of technology. Finally, in 1986 the United Nations published a "Code of Conduct on Transnational Corporations" that covered environmental protection and human rights as well as more directly commercial matters.[48]

Although such codes and guidelines have enjoyed widespread official support *in principle,* the actual drafting of them has been a terribly complex process. The members of these international organizations bring widely divergent existing laws, economic interests, political ideologies, and regulatory outlooks to the negotiating table. It is not surprising, then, that the codes these organizations have so far produced tend to be softened with vague terminology and qualifying loopholes. Moreover, compliance with these codes is entirely voluntary.[49] The OECD's guidelines, for instance, cover such topics as information disclosure, competition, transfer pricing, employee relations, and technology transfer. On competition the guidelines state the following:

> Enterprises should. . . .
> 1. Refrain from actions which would adversely affect competition in the relevant market by abusing a dominant position of market power, by means of, for example,
>   a. anti-competitive acquisitions,
>   b. predatory behavior toward competitors,
>   c. unreasonable refusals to deal,
>   d. anti-competitive abuse of [patents],
>   e. discriminatory (i.e., unreasonably differentiated) pricing . . .
> 2. Allow purchasers, distributors and licensees freedom to resell, export, purchase and develop their operations consistent with law, trade conditions, the need for specialization and sound commercial practice;
> 3. Refrain from participating in or otherwise purposely strengthening the restrictive effects of international or domestic cartels or restrictive agreements which adversely affect or eliminate competition and which are not generally or specifically accepted under applicable national or international legislation . . .[50]

Understandably, the multinationals probably do not take these international efforts very seriously. The multinationals should nevertheless heed the words of Oscar Schachter, who likened these efforts to the efforts of a cross-eyed javelin thrower: "They hold only slight promise and they may even be laughable, but they bear close watching."[51]

Summary

Multinational corporations have been around a long time, but in the past four decades they have sprouted and spread more quickly and widely than ever before. Collectively, they now account for very big chunks of the free world's economic activity, and individually the largest among them—such as Exxon and IBM—are bigger even than most of the world's countries. From the viewpoint of the multinationals themselves, North America, Europe, and Japan constitute their prime markets, mainly because of the economic prosperity of those lands. From the viewpoint of host countries, however, the multinationals appear most awesome to the less developed countries because their economies tend to be much more dominated by multinationals than those of advanced countries.

Although the immense size of the multinationals stems partly from their transnational diversification, it also derives from their prominence in specific national markets. The large market shares of U. S. multinationals in Latin America speak tellingly to this effect, not to mention the supremacy of companies like IBM in Europe and elsewhere.

Four explanations for multinationalism are particularly pertinent to our inquiry. (1) Backward integration to extract distant resources motivated many of the older multinationals, particularly the oil companies. (2) Firms possessing monopolistic advantages at home often deploy those same advantages abroad to their good profit. These advantages include technological wizardry, marketing prowess, and economies of scale. (3) Foreign investment may substitute for exports when foreign tariffs inhibit those exports. (4) Comparative advantage also helps to explain some multinationalism.

Although multinationals frequently bring benefits to home and host countries alike, they also raise serious problems. Given our interest in policy, we have focused most intently on the negative side of the ledger, which lists such items as monopoly power, transfer pricing, restrictive business practices (both horizontal and vertical), inappropriate technology, and questionable payments.

Policies governing these problems may be pigeonholed by source. Among home countries, the United States is most important. Its limited international application of a relatively strict antitrust policy—covering cartels (other than export cartels), monopolization, and mergers among other things—is alone quite notable. Add to this the government's attempt to squash bribery and you have a peerless record. Among host countries, policies of nationalization and domestication are most notorious because they strike at the roots of multinationalism. Less widely publicized but often no less significant are host country attempts at conduct control—that is, regulations enforced through registration and review of agreements with foreign firms.

Finally, our review of international policies reveals a fledgling effort to curb the abuses of multinationals through moral suasion. Voluntary codes of conduct have emerged from diplomatic circles, codes formally endorsed by several international agencies—OECD, UNCTAD, and UN. Thus far, these efforts have delivered nary a jolt to the multinationals, but they bear watching.

Questions and Exercises for Chapter 11

1. As measured by share of national markets, multinationals thrive best under what conditions? When are they less prominent?
2. Among the several economic motives for multinationalism, which seem most anticompetitive for host country industry or worldwide industry and which seem most procompetitive? Explain.
3. Why, in light of the motives for multinationalism, are most of the biggest multinationals based in North America and Europe?
4. Refute the assertion that, from a social point of view, multinationals are economically undesirable, both at home and abroad.
5. Why might host countries be less than delighted hosts for multinationals?
6. What are the strengths and the weaknesses of U. S. antitrust policy in dealing with multinationals (from the U. S. viewpoint)?
7. What is the most potent policy weapon of host countries and why? Does use of this weapon incur any economic costs in the way of lost benefits?
8. Identify and explain the Foreign Corrupt Practices Act.
9. What international policy steps have been taken? What are their strengths and weaknesses?

Appendix to Chapter 11
(From the *Wall Street Journal,* 1990)

Like fast-growing kudzu vines, Japanese money is spreading across America, buying up tens of billions of dollars in Treasury bonds and sewage-treatment plants, skyscrapers and ski resorts, grain elevators and golf courses. Japanese investment in U. S. real estate has increased sevenfold since 1985, while investment in manufacturing leaped to $12 billion from $3 billion in the same period. The purchases have included high-profile "trophies," such as Columbia Pictures and a controlling interest in Rockefeller Center, and shows little sign of slowing. Unlike the short-lived, oil-fueled Arab investment boom of the 1970s, this one is driven by more fundamental causes. High savings rates in Japan have left the newly wealthy Japanese with huge quantities of money to spread around the globe. Low American savings rates, combined with huge budget deficits, have left the U. S. dependent on those funds. Moreover, the dollar's steep decline [relative to the yen] in the last five years has turned the U. S. into a bargain basement for the Japanese. . . .

This deluge of Japanese money heightens the economic uncertainties growing in America. For decades, Americans have been investing heartily overseas and assuring concerned foreigners that they would benefit from the investments. Now that the shoe is on the other foot, Americans don't like it at all. In a recent nationwide *Wall Street Journal*/NBC News poll, 60% of registered voters said the Japanese already invested "too much" in the United States. . . .

Economists tend to assume business people and investors around the globe are motivated by the same consideration of the bottom line. [If so, the Japanese invasion might be little cause for concern.] But some close observers of Japan insist the Japanese have developed a different, more threatening breed of capitalism—one driven as much by national goals as individual profit.

"The Japanese have a much stronger sense of 'we' and 'they' than Americans" and they are "importing their insularity into the U. S." says Ivan Hall, a professor at Gakushuin University in Tokyo. American employees of Japanese companies, for example, complain their opportunities for advancement are slim. And American companies say Japanese firms here favor suppliers from Japan over those in the U. S. In addition, some observers worry that Japanese companies work to keep knowledge-intensive, high-paying jobs at home while situating lower-skilled jobs in the U. S. The observers also fear that during a global downturn, the Japanese might shift the burden of unemployment to the U. S. and away from their own country. . . .

Do the Japanese play by different rules? When Michigan State University economist Mordechai Kreinin studied the Australian operations of 62 multinational companies—42 of them owned by U. S. or European interests, 20 by Japanese— his findings were stark. Factories owned by American companies, and to a slightly lesser extent European firms contained equipment made

in America, Japan and a variety of European countries, without a pronounced national pattern. By contrast, the "overwhelming preponderance" of the equipment used in Japanese-owned factories came from Japan, he wrote in *The World Economy,* a British journal.

"The Japanese are different," Mr. Kreinin says in an interview. "When an American or European company buys machinery to set up a plant, they take competitive bids. But the Japanese go directly to Japan." He attributes this partly to tradition, and partly to the so-called *keiretsu*—large, loosely organized groups of companies in Japan that own each other's stock and tend to buy from each other.

American construction companies are among those that have most keenly felt the impact of this tendency to buy Japanese. They complain that while American firms building facilities in Japan generally use Japanese prime contractors, Japanese companies here don't reciprocate; instead, they generally use Japanese contractors.

It's the same story in the auto-parts business. Even though Japanese auto makers now produce more than a million vehicles a year in the U. S., most of the parts still come from Japanese manufacturers. Japanese auto makers have repeatedly promised to buy U. S. parts, and some of them now have set numerical targets for U. S. purchases. So far, though, the targets are small and the progress slow.

All told, according to Norman Glickman and Douglas Woodward, authors of a recent book on foreign investment in the U. S., Japanese-affiliated companies in the U. S. imported $71.1 billion worth of goods in 1987 while exporting only $20.8 billion of goods. The difference—about $50 billion—was about the size of the U. S. trade deficit with Japan that year.

Mr. Kreinin's Australian study found that, in addition to preferring Japanese suppliers, Japanese multinationals are far more likely to rely on managers from home. Most Western operations he examined were managed entirely by Australians. Only one of the 20 Japanese operations was wholly Australian-run. Even when Australian managers were used, they were often shadowed by Japanese "advisers" who exercised the real power.

Japanese government statistics partially support his point. They show that 45% of the top officials and 85% of the chief executives of Japanese companies' overseas subsidiaries are Japanese. Only 20% of the top officials of foreign units in Japan are sent by the home office. . . .

As for their operations in the U. S., certainly some Japanese companies are trying to mollify their hosts. When Americans complained that Japanese operations in the U. S. didn't contribute much to local charities, Japan's government began mulling a tax break for overseas philanthropy. And when Americans complained that the Japanese hired too few minorities and were insensitive to the concerns of blacks, Keidanren, Japan's big business group, helped produce a Japanese-television version of "Eyes on the Prize," a PBS documentary on the civil-rights movement. . . .

However, in the end, it will take more than good public relations to assuage the concerns of Americans. To do that, Japanese companies would have to begin acting more like their European and American counterparts: More non-Japanese would have to be given prominent positions in management and more non-Japanese suppliers would have to be awarded business.[52]

Notes

1. An excellent book on most of the issues is Richard E. Caves, *Multinational Enterprise and Economic Analysis* (Cambridge, England: Cambridge University Press, 1982).

2. *Business Week,* July 16, 1990, p. 111.

3. Ibid.

4. U. S. Senate, Committee on Finance, *Implications of Multinational Firms for World Trade and Investment and for U. S. Trade and Labor* (Washington DC, 1973), pp. 735–746.

5. *Wall Street Journal,* 18 February 1981, p. 1.

6. Richard S. Newfarmer and Willard F. Mueller, *Multinational Corporations in Brazil and Mexico: Structural Sources of Economic and Noneconomic Power,* U. S. Senate, Subcommittee on Multinational Corporations, Committee on Foreign Relations (1975), pp. 83, 86, 132, 136.

7. Terutomo Ozawa, *Multinationalism, Japanese Style* (Princeton, NJ: Princeton University Press, 1979), pp. 22–24.

8. Stephen Hymer, *The International Operations of National Firms* (Cambridge, MA: MIT Press, 1976); Richard Caves, "International Corporations: The Industrial Economics of Foreign Investment," *Economica* (February 1971): 1–27.

9. "Radio Shack's Rough Trip," *Business Week,* May 30, 1977, p. 55. A Canadian firm sparked riots in Bangladesh in 1989 when the stylized drawing of its three-bells logo, which was printed on the inner sole of its sandals, resembled the Arabic characters for Allah. Muslims consider the sole of the foot a symbol of disrespect. *San Jose Mercury News,* 26 June 1989, p. 4A.

10. John M. Connor and Willard F. Mueller, "Manufacturing, Denationalization and Market Structure: Brazil, Mexico, and the United States," *Industrial Organization Review* (no. 2, 1978): 86–105.

11. R. E. Caves, M. E. Porter, A. M. Spence, and J. T. Scott, *Competition in The Open Economy* (Cambridge, MA: Harvard University Press, 1980), pp. 91–92. See also R. E. Caves, "Causes of Direct Foreign Investment," *Review of Economics and Statistics* (August 1974): 279–293.

12. J. Frank Gaston, "Why Industry Invests Abroad," in *The Multinational Corporation,* vol. 2 (U. S. Department of Commerce, 1973), pp. 6–10.

13. Ozawa, *Multinationalism,* pp. 54–75.

14. For sweeping reviews, one pro and one con, see Raymond Vernon, *Storm Over The Multinationals* (Cambridge, MA: Harvard University Press, 1977), and R. J. Barnet and R. E. Müller, *Global Reach* (New York: Simon and Schuster, 1974).

15. C. F. Bergsten, T. Horst, and T. H. Moran, *American Multinationals and American Interests* (Washington, DC: Brookings Institution, 1978), pp. 303–304.

16. Ibid., pp. 99–120.

17. Ibid., pp. 230–248. See also E. Pagoulatos and R. Sorensen "International Trade, International Investment, and Industrial Profitability of U. S. Manufacturing," *Southern Economic Journal* (January 1976): 425–434; and Mark Hirschey, "Market Power and Foreign Involvement," *Review of Economics & Statistics* (May 1982): 343–346.

18. Ronald Müller, "(More) on Multinationals: Poverty Is the Product," *Foreign Policy* 13 (1973–74): 85–88.

19. Thomas J. Biersteker, *Distortion or Development?* (Cambridge, MA: MIT Press, 1978), pp. 85–102; S. Lall and P. Streeten, *Foreign Investment, Transnationals and Developing Countries* (Boulder, CO: Westview Press, 1977).

20. Director of Investigation and Research, Combines Investigation Act, *The State of Competition in The Canadian Petroleum Industry* Vol. 1 (Ottawa, 1981), pp. 18–19, 61–70.

21. S. Lall, "The International Pharmaceutical Industry and Less-Developed Countries," *Oxford Bulletin of Economics and Statistics* (August 1974): 161.

22. *Newsweek,* April 15, 1991, pp. 48–49; *Business Week,* September 10, 1990, pp. 48–49. See also Alan Rugman and Lorraine Eden, eds., *Multinationals and Transfer Pricing* (Beckenham: Croom Helm, 1985).

23. *Wall Street Journal,* 25 September 1979, p. 1.

24. L. T. Wells, "Economic Man and Engineering Man: Choice of Technology in a Low Wage Country," *Public Policy* (Summer 1973): 39–42; L. J. White, "Appropriate Technology, X-Inefficiency and a Competitive Environment," *Quarterly Journal of Economics* (November 1976): 575–589; Frances Stewart, "Technology and Employment in LDCs," *World Development* (March 1974): 17–46.

25. G. K. Helleiner, "The Role of Multinational Corporations in the Less Developed Countries' Trade in Technology," *World Development* (April 1975): 161–189.

26. James E. Post, "Assessing the Nestlé Boycott," *California Management Review* (Winter 1985): 113–131. For examples of misrepresentation in drug promotion see Milton Silverman, *The Drugging of the Americas* (Berkeley: University of California Press, 1976).

27. Marshall B. Clinard, *Corporate Corruption: The Abuse of Power* (New York: Praeger, 1990), pp. 121–126; N. Jacoby, P. Nehemkis, and R. Eells, *Bribery and Extortion In World Business: A Study of Corporate Political Payments Abroad* (New York: Macmillan, 1977).

28. *Restrictive Business Practices,* U. N. doc. TD/B/C.2/104/Rev. 1 (1971); *Restrictive Business Practices,* U. N. doc. TD/B/390 (1973); Robert E. Smith, "Cartels and The Shield of Ignorance," *Journal of International Law and Economics* (June 1973): 53–83; and *Restrictive Business Practices of Multinational Enterprises* (Paris: OECD, 1977).

29. Barbara Epstein and Richard S. Newfarmer, *International Electrical Association: A Continuing Cartel,* Report for the Committee on Interstate and Foreign Commerce, U. S. House of Representatives (June 1980), p. 12.

30. Magnus Blomstrom, *Transnational Corporations and Manufacturing Exports from Developing Countries* (New York: United Nations, 1990), p. 57.

31. For similar conclusions see Bergsten, Horst, and Moran, *American Multinationals;* Biersteker, *Distortion or Development?;* Benjamin I. Cohen, *Multinational Firms and Asian Exports* (New Haven, CT: Yale University Press, 1975); I. A. Litvak and C. J. Maule, "Foreign Firms: Social Costs and Benefits in Developing Countries," *Public Policy* (Spring 1975): 167–187; Caves, *Multinational Enterprise.*

32. *U. S.* v. *Aluminum Company of America,* 148 F. 2d 416 (2d Cir. 1945); *Steele* v. *Bulova Watch Co.,* 344 U. S. 280 (1952); *Continental Ore Co.* v. *Union Carbide,* 370 U. S. 690 (1962). For a survey see Robert E. Smith,

"The Limited International Reach of U. S. Antitrust Policy," in *Issues after a Century of Federal Competition Policy,* ed. R. L. Wills, J. A. Caswell, and J. D. Culbertson (Lexington, MA: Lexington Books, 1987), pp. 147–165.

33. *American Banana* v. *United Fruit Company,* 213 U. S. 347 (1909); *Continental Ore* v. *Union Carbide,* 370 U. S. 690 (1962).

34. Federal Trade Commission, *Webb-Pomerene Associations: A 50-Year Review* (Washington, D. C., 1967), p. 35.

35. *U. S.* v. *American Building Maintenance Industries,* 422 U. S. 271 (1975).

36. There were Section 1 elements as well. *U. S.* v. *United Fruit Company,* CCH Trade Cases para. 68, 941 (1958). For details see U. N. doc TD/B/390, *op. cit.,* pp. 47–50.

37. *U. S.* v. *Jos. Schlitz,* 253 F. Supp. 129 (N.D. Cal. 1966); 385 U. S. 37 (1966).

38. *Hazeltine Research Inc.* v. *Zenith Radio Corp.,* 239 F. Supp. 51 (N.D. Ill. 1965); 395 U. S. S. Ct. 100 (1969).

39. Marshall B. Clinard, *Corporate Corruption: The Abuse of Power* (New York: Praeger, 1990), p. 127. The argument that inability to bribe has caused U. S. companies to lose exports may be questioned. As pointed out by N. C. Miller, many past bribes involved no exports whatever or involved U. S. companies competing against each other not against foreign competitors. "In fact," he reports, "there is no documentary evidence that U. S. companies have lost exports as a result of the 1977 law." *Wall Street Journal,* April 30, 1981, p. 22.

40. Corwin D. Edwards, *Trade Regulations Overseas* (Dobbs Ferry, NY: Oceana Publications, 1966), p. iii.

41. For a survey see *Comparative Summary of Legislations on Restrictive Business Practices* (Paris: Organization for Economic Co-Operation and Development, 1978).

42. Committee of Experts on Restrictive Business Practices, *Restrictive Business Practices of Multinational Enterprises* (Paris: OECD, 1977), p. 20.

43. For a survey, see Joel Davidow, "The Worldwide Influence of U. S. Antitrust Policy," *Antitrust Bulletin* (Fall 1990): 603–630.

44. Steven Globerman, "Determinants of Government Policies Towards Foreign Direct Investment," mimeo, 1986.

45. For a summary of policies see United Nations Conference on Trade and Development, *Dominant Positions of Market Power of Transnational Corporations: Use of The Transfer Pricing Mechanism,* U. N. doc. TD/B/C.2/167 (1978), pp. 28–36.

46. Government of Mexico, *Law on Transfer of Technology and The Use and Exploitation of Patents and Trademarks,* 1972, Foreword, p. 4.

47. See, e.g., D. F. Greer, "Control of Terms and Conditions for International Transfers of Technology to Developing Countries," in *Competition in International Business: Law and Policy on Restrictive Practices* (New York: Columbia University Press, 1981), pp. 41–83.

48. United Nations Centre on Transnational Corporations, *The United Nations Code of Conduct on Transnational Corporations* (New York: United Nations, 1986).

49. For discussions see Joel Davidow, "Multinationals, Host Governments and Regulation of Restrictive Business Practices," *Columbia Journal of World Business* (Summer 1980): 14–19; L. R. Primoff, "International Regulation of Multinational Corporations and Business—The United Nations Takes Aim," 11, *Journal of International Law and Economics* (1977): 287–324.

50. *International Investment and Multinational Enterprises* (Paris: OECD, 1984 revised edition), p. 19.

51. Address to Columbia Conference on Competition in International Business, Nov. 9, 1979.

52. Excerpts from Urban C. Lehner and Alan Murray, "Strained Alliance: 'Selling of America' to Japanese Touches Some Very Raw Nerves," *Wall Street Journal,* 19 June 1990, pp. A1 and A17.

PART III

Information Policy

Chapter 12

Product Standardization and Information Disclosure

The grocery store has become a Tower of Babel, and consumers need to be linguists, scientists and mind readers to understand the many labels they see.
— *Dr. Louis Sullivan,*
Secretary of Health and Human Services
(1990)

The 1990s opened with a deluge of health claims aimed at consumers. Sweet chocolate cupcakes were said to be "99% fat free, no cholesterol." Cookies were marketed as a good source of oat bran. Some products seemed to be self-contradictory—like low-salt pretzels and no-fat ice cream. There were also cooking oils with bright labels claiming "No Cholesterol."

However, most cooking oils *never* had any cholesterol and *never* will. At the same time, labels on many grocery products—especially processed foods such as luncheon meats, sauces, and soups—denied that they contained monosodiumglutamate (MSG), which can be threatening to some hypersensitive people. Although MSG was not added directly to these products, many of them contained hydrolyzed vegetable protein (HVP), an added ingredient made up partly of MSG. In 1990, U.S. companies added 45 million pounds of HVP to their food products. Meat and poultry processors could refer to it as "natural flavoring" on their labels if they wished.[1]

Because of government actions, food labels have improved greatly since 1990, but shoppers still lack full knowledge. Ignorance is a problem afflicting many other markets as well.

This chapter (1) examines this problem and its several consequences, and (2) reviews two broad classes of policy solutions that can be called *standardization* and *information disclosure*. These policies operate on the principle of revelation. They are supposed to *educate* consumers, to *aid* them in making comparisons, and to *reveal* relevant product characteristics.

Other policies besides standardization and disclosure relate to the problem of buyer knowledge. We should therefore distinguish between the policies of immediate concern and two other broad groups of policies by listing all three together:

1. Forced *standardization* and *disclosure* of information (for example, contents labeling and grade rating).

2. *Prohibitions* against unfair and deceptive practices (such as bans on misleading advertising).
3. Direct regulation of *product features* and *production processes* (such as safety).

Whereas (1) the disclosure policies of the present chapter are generally *pre*scriptive and positive, policies (2) governing deceptive practices, which are discussed in the next chapter, are generally *pro*scriptive and negative. They prohibit misleading conduct but they do not usually require sellers to reveal information or aid consumers. Policies (3) that directly regulate product quality, efficacy, and safety are covered in Chapters 20 and 21. Under them, businesses seem to be confronted with as many "thou shalts" as "thou shalt nots." In these cases, the government attempts to protect consumers from unsafe, impure, and ineffective products not by informing consumers of these dangers (although that is part of the policy) but by directly regulating product features and production processes. The consumer is, in other words, denied a free choice in these instances. This last approach is obviously the most severe of the policy options, and it is accordingly based on justifications that go well beyond buyer ignorance. The issue of safety, for instance, raises problems of external costs—thus its postponement to later chapters.

A policy that defies classification in any of the preceding categories is the issuance and enforcement of trademarks. In some ways, though, trademarks, are a part of the problem, not the solution, and so they are taken up in this chapter.

I. The Problem

A. Buyer Knowledge

Under the ideal circumstances of perfect competition, reviewed in Chapter 2, it was assumed that all buyers pursued their goal of welfare optimum with the aid of perfect knowledge. This implies that each buyer:

1. Is an expert buyer, readily able to appraise product quality objectively.
2. Has a well-defined set of stable preferences.
3. Is aware of all purchase alternatives and the terms offered by sellers.
4. Is able to calculate accurately the marginal gains and losses of choosing one combination of commodities over another to obtain the highest possible benefit for any given expenditure.

If all buyers met this description, it would be very difficult for sellers to sell them goods they did not really want, to exaggerate the quality of one brand over another, or to charge outrageous prices for goods more cheaply available elsewhere.

The key question is, then: *What determines buyer knowledge or the lack thereof?* The answer comes in two parts—**buyer character** and **product type.** For convenience we can divide all buyers into two broad groups: (1) professional business buyers and (2) household consumers. Products and services, on the other hand, may be divided into (1) search goods, (2) experience goods, and (3) credence goods.

Among buyers, business buyers come about as close to being highly knowledgeable and fully informed as one could expect. Indeed, professional purchasing agents of large firms specialize in buying such goods and services as raw materials, transportation, insurance, and office supplies. Moreover, they often have the assistance of engineers, scientists, financial wizards, and other experts who conduct tests, arrange credit, guide negotiations, and the like—all with an eye to maximizing profits. The most important reason for this expertise is the ability of professional buyers to spread the costs of obtaining their expertise over a large volume of purchases. Thus, the absolute total dollar costs of purchasing may be huge, but on a per-unit basis these costs will be small.

On the other hand, we have the typical householder, who by comparison is a 91-pound weakling. Although not a moron, he or she runs a small-scale operation. Of course, assistance from the spouse or helpmate may be offered, but it probably hinders as often as it helps in deciding which breakfast cereal is the most nutritious per dollar cost, which TV set is the most dependable, which laundry detergent gives the "whitest white," which bank offers the best loan terms, and so on.

Lest I overstate the ignorance of the typical household consumer, I hasten to add that product type also determines the degree to which the purchase decision is well informed. In the case of *search goods*—like fresh fruits and vegetables, raw meat, apparel, shoes, jewelry, and maybe furniture as well—the consumer can judge on the basis of fairly simple inspection *prior* to actual purchase whether a given article is wholesome, handsomely styled, properly fitting, and reasonably priced for the level of quality it represents. At least in these instances, the consumer typically acts in a relatively well-informed manner, being less sensitive to the blandishments of exhortative advertising, the attractiveness of package coloring, or the image conveyed by brand name.

In contrast, *experience goods* are those whose utility can be fully assessed only *after* purchase. To evaluate brands of bottled beer accurately, for example, consumers obviously have to buy alternative brands in order to experience their taste. And even after purchase, this experience with beer may not be so scientifically expressed as to be very informative. The same holds for detergents, automobiles, appliances, cake mixes, and related products. It is largely the presence of hidden qualities and inadequate experience that makes these goods more unknowable than search goods.

Finally, *credence goods* are those that cannot be fully evaluated through inspection, or normal use, or even simple study of general in-

formation. One's assessment of their value is either impossible or costly in relation to any additional information obtained. These goods include various drugs, cosmetics, medical devices, vitamin supplements, and auto oil additives whose performance is by nature rather "iffy." They may or may not work, depending on the circumstances, so you can never be certain if they really do work. Inevitably, consumers are particularly error prone when it comes to credence goods.

Of course, it is an oversimplification to categorize goods and services in this way. Goods and services most commonly comprise various blends of search, experience, and credence *qualities*. That is, search qualities are known before purchase, experience qualities become known costlessly after purchase, and credence qualities are expensive or impossible for individual consumers to judge even after purchase.[2]

From the foregoing we may derive a sneak preview of the purpose of standardization and disclosure policies: They should (1) make consumers more like professional buyers and (2) convert experience and credence qualities into search qualities. The freshness of milk, for example, is an experience quality unless plainly disclosed on the carton, in which case it then becomes a search quality. Educating consumers on the proper use of such disclosures gives them the powers of a professional.

Before delving into policy more deeply, however, we must first acknowledge more explicitly the adverse effects of buyer ignorance—(1) inefficiency, (2) imperfect competition, and (3) promotional waste. For this purpose, simplification has great pedagogical value, so in the following we often speak of search and experience *goods* rather than qualities. Moreover, we shall forgo further discussion of credence qualities.

B. Consequence 1: Consumer Inefficiency

Aside from the high frequency of consumer complaints, several empirical measures reveal substantial inefficiency due to inaccuracies in consumer buying behavior. Self-admission is one. When asked whether "advertising leads people to buy things they don't need or can't afford," 80 percent of all consumers surveyed said "yes."[3] Another measure is the degree to which price correlates with quality across brands within a given product class. If consumers were knowledgeable, low quality could sell only at low prices whereas high quality could justifiably command high prices. Thus, a high positive correlation (maximum possible being +1.0) between price and quality for a given product would indicate efficient buying behavior, whereas a low correlation (approaching zero or even turning negative) would signal something seriously amiss.

Every study of this type yet done has found surprisingly low correlations, with many products producing negative coefficients. Peter Riesz found an average correlation of only +.092 for forty packaged food products.[4] M. Friedman corroborated this result with an average correlation of +.09 for nine packaged food products.[5] R. T. Morris and C. S. Bronson's study of forty-eight diverse products (electric appliances, detergents, and tires included) produced a mean correlation of +.29.[6] Alfred Oxenfeldt's computation of correlations for thirty-five products in 1949 is old but particularly instructive because his sample included numerous search goods whereas the other studies were essentially confined to experience goods. Oxenfeldt's results for the eight products with highest correlation and the eight products with lowest correlation are presented in Table 12–1. Notice that those with highest correlations are all search goods, whereas seven of the eight

Table 12–1

Coefficients of Rank Correlation Between Brand Quality Score and Brand Price

Product	Number of Brands Tested	Coefficient of Rank Correlation
Top eight products		
Boys' shirts	8	0.82
Men's hats	30	0.76
Women's slips (knitted)	28	0.75
Mechanical pencils	26	0.71
Women's slips (other than knit)	67	0.70
Men's shoes	52	0.70
Diapers, gauze	11	0.57
Children's shoes	8	0.55
Bottom eight products		
Yellow, white, and spice mixes	9	−0.11
Mayonnaise	25	−0.13
Men's hosiery (wool)	9	−0.20
Vacuum cleaners	17	−0.26
Biscuit mixes	10	−0.46
Hot roll mixes	3	−0.50
Waffle mixes	3	−0.50
Gingerbread mixes	6	−0.81

Source: Alfred R. Oxenfeldt, "Consumer Knowledge: Its Measurement and Extent," *Review of Economics and Statistics* (October 1950), p. 310.

lowest could be considered experience goods (the possible exception being men's hosiery). This suggests that consumers are more adept at buying search goods than experience goods (something that correlates well with common sense).

A clearer notion of the monetary costs of consumer errors—and the monetary benefits achieved by their elimination—can be gained through brief theoretical consideration of demand curves. In essence, benefits arise from *error avoidance*—errors of commission and omission.[7]

An **error of commission** occurs when the buyer makes a purchase on the basis of an excessively favorable prepurchase assessment of the acquired good. In other words, the buyer gets not what he thinks he is getting but something less. The monetary loss of making such an error (or the gain from avoiding same) is illustrated in Figure 12–1 as the shaded area *ABC*. The demand curve *DACD* refers to what demand would

be like if the good were correctly evaluated, whereas *D'BD'* depicts an erroneously optimistic level of demand. The latter lies to the right of the former since the uninformed buyer wants to buy more at each possible price than he would if he were fully informed. Thus, given a fixed price equal to OP_0 (or constant marginal costs of supply indicated by P_0AB), the consumer buys an excess equal to the difference between Q_1 and Q_2, that is, $Q_1 - Q_2$. The amount he pays for this excess is the area Q_2ABQ_1, price times the excess quantity. However, the *true value* of the extra units amounts only to Q_2ACQ_1, or the trapezoid below *A* and *C*. Thus, the difference between dollar outlay Q_2ABQ_1 and true value Q_2ACQ_1 is *ABC*, the net loss.

Errors of omission are the opposite. They occur when the buyer buys *less* than he would with full knowledge. The monetary loss from making such an error is illustrated in Figure 12–2 by the area *GHE*. In this case the demand curve

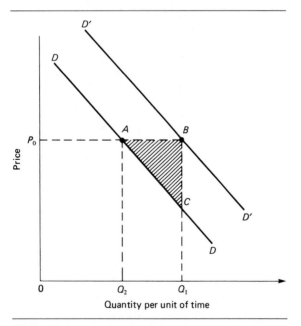

Figure 12–1
The Monetary Loss from an Error of Commission.

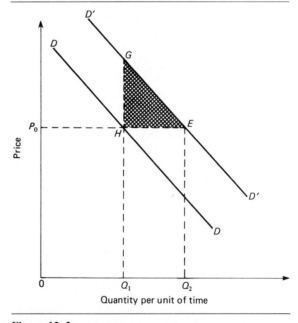

Figure 12–2
The Monetary Loss from an Error of Omission.

$D'GED'$ depicts what the demand would be like if the commodity were correctly evaluated, whereas DHD represents the erroneously pessimistic demand of buyers who underestimate the value of the product. Given a constant price P_0, a corrective movement from the poorly chosen amount Q_1 to the proper amount Q_2 requires an additional cash outlay equal to area Q_1HEQ_2. But the move yields a greater addition to total benefit, indicated by Q_1GEQ_2. Subtracting the added cost from this added benefit yields a *net* benefit of *HGE*, which in technical jargon is the amount of consumer's surplus the consumer misses out on when he errs in the direction of omission. It may now be seen that errors of omission lead to *under*allocations of resources to the particular products or brands, whereas errors of commission lead to *over*allocations to the chosen products or brands. Both forms of error are *mis*allocations, and they often represent opposite sides of the same coin. The more candy bars one eats, the less room he will have for fresh apples and carrots.

C. Consequence 2: Imperfect Competition

In the foregoing analysis, it was assumed that buyer knowledge would not affect overall price level. The eradication of errors may enhance competition among sellers, however, because they then find that their competitive efforts to reduce price or improve quality are rewarded by knowledgeably favorable consumer responses. That is, buyer ignorance reduces the ability of consumers to identify the best buy, and competition to provide best buys is therefore discouraged.

As regards knowledge of price, for instance, A. Maurizi and T. Kelly found that posting gasoline prices on signs big enough to be visible to passing motorists has a significant tendency to reduce gasoline prices below what they would otherwise be. Their 1970 comparison of New York City, where there was no price posting, and Los Angeles, where price posting was wide-spread, illustrates the point. Prices in New York would have been .73 cents per gallon lower for regular gas and 1.50 cents per gallon lower for premium gas (yielding a total saving of $25.4 million) if price posting in New York had been as extensive as it was in Los Angeles.[8] Moreover, Maurizi and Kelly estimate that posting by all gasoline stations on a nationwide basis would have saved consumers at least $525 million overall in 1975.

One obvious policy implication from this study of gasoline prices is that government should *not prohibit* private, voluntary dissemination of price information. The reason New York City had no gas price posting was because of just such a local prohibition. John Cady's analysis of prescription retail drug prices for the effect of state restrictions on retail drug price advertising confirms the point. Comparing retail prices of ten representative prescription drugs across states, he found that legal restrictions on price advertising *raised* prices an average of 4.3 percent, with the highest differential being 9.1 percent for one sampled product.[9]

More generally, casual observation tells us that competition to produce cigarettes with low tar and nicotine has been especially vigorous since consumer information on these factors has burgeoned through mandatory disclosure in ads. Similarly, the drive to improve gasoline mileage in cars cannot be totally unrelated to the public's recently improved information on mileage. Consumer knowledge also seems to reduce the adverse competitive impact of exhortative advertising. For *experience* goods like detergent, beer, soda pop, breakfast cereals, and the like, there is a strong positive correlation between monopoly profits and the intensity of advertising outlay. On the other hand, for *search* goods and services, such a positive relationship is either slight or nonexistent. Indeed, there is some evidence indicating that to the extent search qualities prevail, advertising tends to be *pro*competitive because of price advertising rather than *anti*competitive.[10]

D. Consequence 3: Waste and Misdirection

When buyers are *well informed*—because of either individual knowledge or search qualities in the products they buy—advertising tends to be more informative and less wastefully intensive than when buyers are poorly informed. As regards information content, for instance, anyone who has leafed through *Mining Magazine* or *Electrical Review* will conclude that advertising directed toward professional buyers is largely informative, revealing performance specifications, prices, guarantees, and the like. "Because the audience for such advertising is expert," Corwin Edwards explained, "the characteristic advertisement in such publications is of a kind that might persuade an expert: it provides information, avoids garbled treatment of facts, and addresses itself to the reader's intelligence."[11]

This obviously does not hold for most consumer-aimed advertising, which is replete with fear appeals, sexual enticements, worthless endorsements, meaningless jingles (like "Coke is the real thing"), puffery, and other trappings of exhortation and persuasion. Your own experience probably indicates there is a substantial variance across products and services in this respect. Where more search qualities are present, the advertising tends to be more informative. Grocery retailing, for instance, could be considered more of a search service than auto transmission repair, and the advertising of the former is much more informative. Confirming such casual observations from your own experience, scholarly studies indicate that advertisements for most apparel, footwear, household furnishings, and retailing are much more informative than advertisements for soft drinks, beer, cigarettes, detergents, prepared foods, and toiletries.[12]

A plausible explanation for this difference between search good and experience good advertising rests on the prepurchase evaluation that can be made of search goods. If the advertised properties of search goods stray too far from their actual properties, consumers are readily able to detect the discrepancies and penalize the promoters with refusals to buy. Advertisers of these products therefore feel constrained to use an informative approach.

As regards advertising intensity, producer search goods (bought by professional buyers) seem to have the lowest advertising to sales ratios of all products, averaging about 0.3 percent of sales. Consumer experience goods rest at the other end of the spectrum, with advertising intensities high enough—often 4 to 15 percent—to arouse suspicions that resources are sometimes wasted on the promotion of such products. Between these two extremes we find producer experience goods and consumer search goods with advertising-to-sales ratios averaging approximately 1 percent.[13]

We thus arrive at an interesting paradox: Advertising intensity and information content are *inversely* related. Generally speaking, the greater the dollar outlay relative to product sales, the lower is the information content of the advertising messages. Furthermore, in terms of adequate amounts and efficient applications of buyer knowledge, advertising is *least* informative where the need for information is greatest (consumer experience goods), whereas it is most informative where the need for information is least (producer search goods). This paradox makes it clear that the purpose of advertising is *not* to inform buyers; it is to gain sales by influencing buyers. It also points out the potential need for public information policies (insofar as their benefits exceed their costs, neither of which, unfortunately, are easily quantified).

II. Trademarks

The next question is: What policies can boost buyer knowledge and thereby curb the adverse consequences of ignorance? Incredible though it may seem in light of what has been said thus far, one such policy is the issuance and enforcement of **trademarks.** To see this more clearly, try imagining what the world would be like without trademarks. Without them how could *Consumer Reports* tell us in March 1981 that Panasonic microwave ovens were better than the Sunbeam brand? Or how could a friend advise us that Levi's trousers are a good buy? How could we be sure that, having been wholly satisfied with an Apple computer, we could ever get another one from the same manufacturer? How could we sue the Coca-Cola Company for damages if we found a dead mouse in one of its soda bottles? In other words, it can be argued that, to the extent consumers do learn from experience and to the extent they do learn to buy what they like (rather than merely like what they buy), trademarks can minimize *repeated* errors merely by identifying the producers of good, bad, or mediocre goods and services. Similarly, trademarks are necessary to spreading an individual's or a testing agency's specific knowledge to others. And, finally, in extreme cases of error, individual producers may be held legally as well as economically accountable for their share in any disaster. As Richard Caves and William Murphy have so aptly put it, "By offering the seller's good name as hostage, the trademark provides the buyer with cheap information and assurance about product quality."[14]

Despite these considerable social benefits, the trademark laws as they stand also involve *social costs.* Trademark policies are based on the assumption that trademarks serve primarily to identify the *origin* of goods and that the purposes of such identification are twofold.

1. Protection is furnished the seller from unfair competition through the infringement of his mark by an imitator or poacher.
2. Protection is furnished buyers who might be deceived into purchasing the goods of one seller in the belief that the goods are another's.[15]

Unfortunately, this emphasis on origin adds substantially to the social costs of the trademark system without contributing to its social benefits. Benefits derive from the *identification of a given level of quality,* not from the identification of a given origin. Identification of origin on an exclusive, perpetual, and carefully protected basis, as is now practiced, may serve *indirectly* to identify a given level of quality. But it also facilitates the creation of substantial market power, power that translates into social costs, power achieved by exhortative advertising and other means of questionable social worth.[16] As suggested earlier, the available evidence indicates that, when quality guarantees or quality identifications are established independently of trademarks (by professional buyers themselves, by government grade rating and standardization, by consumers search shopping for easily analyzable goods, and so on), monopoly power cannot be based on trademark differentiation and advertising, and burdensome social costs are avoided. The effects of the trademark system are therefore negative when (1) trademarks (and the persuasive advertising promoting them) provide the sole or major source of quality identification for the product *and* (2) grants of exclusive trademark use protect the goodwill (or monopoly) profits that attach to trademarks under such circumstances. Corrective policies could therefore be focused on one or both of the following objectives:

1. Permit trademarks to identify or guarantee quality but remove the rights of exclusivity and perpetuity currently awarded them.
2. Establish quality identifications and guarantees that are *independent* of the trademark system.

With respect to the first, nonexclusive trademark use, Edward Chamberlin once suggested a policy that would permit brand imitation as long as quality was maintained.[17] Such a policy would focus the law on identifying quality instead of origin, but this policy is rather radical and its adoption is unlikely.

With respect to the second possible focus of policy, quality identifications and guarantees that are independent of the trademark system, regulations abound. They merit the entire section that follows.

III. Standardization and Disclosure

As suggested by the heading "Standardization and Disclosure," information or identification policies other than trademarks may be divided into two categories.[18] And, as suggested by the items listed for each category, the ultimate purpose of these policies is to assist buyers in avoiding errors:

A. Standardization for easier price comparisons.
  1. Simplified quantity labeling.
  2. Uniform sizes.
  3. Price standardization (e.g., unit pricing).
  4. Warranty standards.
B. Quality disclosures.
  1. Ingredient disclosure.
  2. Open dating of perishables.
  3. Specific performance disclosures.
  4. Grade rating.

Standardization policies typically promote simplification or uniformity or both. The distinction between simplification and uniformity may be seen by an example. Suppose ten brick manufacturers were each making the same 50 kinds of brick. Since each producer offered a full range of 50 kinds, each firm's bricks would match those of the others and there would be perfect **uniformity** among sellers. With 50 varieties, however, the situation would not be simple. **Simplification** could be achieved if these firms agreed to cut down the number of their offerings to, say, 12 common types. This would yield a combination of simplification and uniformity—ten firms, each producing the same 12 kinds of brick. Alterna-

tively, simplification could be achieved at the expense of uniformity. If each of the ten brick makers cuts back his offerings to four *unique* items, with no one producing the same item, uniformity would disappear. The total, industry-wide variety, however, would have been simplified from 50 down to 40. As far as buyer errors are concerned, uniformity facilitates the comparison of different sellers' offerings, whereas simplification may help to keep buyers' minds from boggling.

Quality disclosures are quite different. They sharpen the buyer's awareness of "better" or "worse." For example, all mattress manufacturers may uniformly adhere to a few simple sizes—twin, double, queen, and king. But this says nothing about the range of quality (and some mattresses may feel as if they were made from 50 kinds of brick). Disclosure of ingredients might be helpful in this case, and grade rating would be even more helpful. Policies revealing ingredients and grades may thus be considered quality disclosures.

Before we take a detailed look at specific policies, one more preliminary point needs attention: Why must we rely on the government to elevate consumer knowledge in these ways? What is wrong with relying on free *private* enterprise? If information is a desirable good, ought not profit opportunities abound for anyone supplying information? The answer to all these questions is, in a word, *imperfections*. The nature of the commodity in question—information—is such that imperfections prevent its optimal provision by private enterprise.

One imperfection is particularly interesting. Buyers of information cannot be truly *well informed* about the information they want to buy. If they were, they would not then need to buy the information.[19] In other words, the seller of information cannot let potential buyers meticulously examine his product before sale lest he thereby give it away free. Buyers of information therefore do not know the value of the product they seek (information) until after they buy it. They are consequently vulnerable to errors of commission and omission. Only with objective, outside, nonmarket assistance can they overcome this handicap.

A. Standardization for Easy Price Comparisons

1. SIMPLIFIED QUANTITY LABELING

Try this little test on yourself. Which box of detergent is the best buy—25 "jumbo" ounces for 93 cents; 1½ pounds for 87 cents; or 25½ "full" ounces for 96 cents? Prior to the Fair Packaging and Labeling Act of 1966 (FPLA) grocery shoppers took, and failed, real-life tests like this more often than they probably care to remember. In 1965, for instance, a selected sample of thirty-three married women who were students or wives of students at Eastern Michigan University were asked to pick the most economical package for each of twenty supermarket products. Despite their above-average intelligence and their stimulated attention, these women typically spent 9.14 percent more on these groceries than they should have.[20] Small wonder they erred, what with the commingling of weight and fluid volumes for the same products; the use of meaningless adjectives, such as "jumbo" and "full"; the frequent appearance of fractional quantity units; and the designation of servings as "small," "medium," and "large," without any common standard of reference.

The Fair Packaging and Labeling act tidied things up a bit by providing the following:

1. The net quantity be stated in a uniform and prominent location on the package.
2. The net quantity be clearly expressed in a unit of measure appropriate to the product.
3. The net quantity of a serving must be stated if servings are mentioned.

This may not seem like much, but early and final versions of the FPLA were vigorously opposed by business interests. It took five years of congressional hearings and a persistent effort on the part of the late Senator Hart of Michigan to get the FPLA passed. Some opponents claimed that it was "a power grab based on the fallacious concepts that the consumer is Casper Milquetoast, business is Al Capone, and government is Superman."[21] Their opposition was based on what they apparently thought was a more accurate concept—the housewife as Superwoman. "We suggest," argued the editor of *Food Field Reporter,* "that the housewife . . . should be expected to take the time to divide fractionalized weights into fractionalized prices in order to determine the 'best buy.'"[22] Still others worried about what would happen to the Barbie doll: "Will the package have to say, in compliance with the act's rules, 'One doll, net,' on quantity, and then, on size, '34-21-34'?"[23] Despite such criticism, the FPLA seems to have worked fairly well. The Federal Trade Commission and Food and Drug Administration have encountered problems while enforcing the act but nothing insuperable. The problem of what to do with Barbie, for instance, was solved when the Federal Trade Commission declared that she was among the many commodities that were not covered by the act—toys, chinaware, books, souvenirs, and mouse traps, to name only a few.

2. UNIFORM PACKAGE SIZES

As already suggested, it would be easier for consumers to compare the price per unit of various brands and volumes if sellers adhered to a few common sizes of packaging. Senator Hart tried to have some compulsory rules for packaging uniformity or standardization written into the FPLA, but they were defeated by the opposition. Several *nonmandatory* standards have emerged from under the voluntary sections of the act. Dry cereals, for example, are supposed to be packaged in whole ounces only. These voluntary standards do not seem to be very helpful, however. For more stringent action, we must look to state and foreign laws. In the United States, several states have standardized the packaging of bread, butter, margarine, flour, corn meal, and milk.

Among foreign countries, Germany, France, England, and Canada have rather extensive mandatory standardization.[24] A few examples of Canadian policy are shown in Table 12–2.

Apart from easier price comparisons, packaging standardization discourages the practice of downsizing, which attracted some attention during the early 1990s. Downsizing occurs when a product's weight is quietly reduced while its price remains unchanged. In 1991, for example, Hershey's chocolate milk mix went from 16 ounces per can to 14.5 ounces per can (a 9 percent reduction) while the price remained at $1.89.[25] Although it is neither new nor illegal, downsizing is said to be deceptive by some consumer groups.

(Although U.S. policy grants wide latitude in package sizes, producers must by law abide by their stated quantities. Thus, 12 ounces of beer must be no less than 12 ounces. Enforcement seems necessary, and states police producers most vigorously. During 1983 West Virginia inspectors found that 23 percent of all items measured were short. This included "$3 million of chemicals, 180,000 gallons of milk, oceans of orange juice, warehouses full of beer and an eclectic list of other items.")[26]

3. PRICE STANDARDIZATION

Price standardization is an approach still more helpful to consumers than package uniformity and simplification. It may be found in two major forms—unit pricing and truth-in-lending (TIL). **Unit pricing** translates all package prices into a price per standard weight or measure, such as 25.3 cents per pound, or 71.4 cents per hundred count. Representing price in this way helps consumers compare prices without superhuman computations. Numerous studies have shown that unit pricing greatly reduces errors in price comparison. One such study found that with unit pricing people could pick the item of least cost 25 percent more often than without, and at the same time cut down their shopping time considerably.[27] Extensive national regulations of this type exist only in Germany and Switzerland. In the United States, eleven states have adopted unit-pricing regulations, led by Massachusetts in 1971.[28] Although United States laws thus have restricted application, many grocery stores have voluntarily adopted unit pricing.

Table 12–2
Selected Canadian Standardization Regulations

Product	Prescribed Weight or Volume
Jellies and jams	2½, 6, 9, 12, 24, or 48 ounces
Eggs	Multiples of 12
Frozen peas, corn, liver beans, and spinach	12 ounces or 2 pounds
Fruit and vegetable juices	5½, 6, 10, 14, 19, 28, 48, or 100 fluid ounces
Single-ply paper napkins	Multiples of 30 napkins
Liquid/lotion shampoos	Multiples of 25 milliliters between 25 and 250 milliliters;
	Multiples of 50 milliliters over 250 milliliters

Source: Package Standardization, Unit Pricing, Deceptive Packaging (Paris: Organization for Economic Co-operation and Development, 1975), pp. 31–35.

Of course, retailer adoption and actual consumer use of unit pricing are two different things. One survey estimated that only about 8.8 percent of observed purchases probably involved the use of unit pricing, and another study concluded that active use saves consumers only about 3 percent on their grocery bills. Multiplying these two estimates yields an estimated saving of no more than 0.264 percent on the cost of all purchases. Although this estimate is small, it nevertheless is greater than the costs borne by those retailers who have adopted unit pricing. Many consumer advocates therefore urge that federal legislation require nationwide unit pricing. They also urge that consumers be more thoroughly educated about its use.

Truth-in-lending (TIL) is one form of price standardization that since 1969 has been provided by United States government regulations.[29] However, the scope of these regulations is limited to consumer credit. Before adoption of TIL, numerous studies showed that only a few people knew how much they actually paid for credit. Two such studies in the 1950s, for instance, showed that 66 to 70 percent of consumers did not have even a vague idea of the annual *percentage rate,* let alone the dollar value, of interest they were paying on their *recent* installment purchases. They almost certainly did not know the interest rates charged by other credit suppliers, information that is necessary to comparative shopping. Why this vast ignorance? To make a long story short, there was no price standardization in the credit industry. One lender would use the add-on method; others would use a discount rate, or an annual percentage rate, or a monthly rate, or some combination of all three. Depending on the method, the price for the same amount of credit might be quoted as being 1 percent, 7 percent, 12.83 percent, or 16 percent. Indeed, some lenders would not quote *any* rate of charge. They would merely state the number and amount of the monthly payments required.

The purpose of the Truth-in-Lending Law is to let consumers know exactly what the price of credit is and to let them compare the prices of various lenders. Moreover, as argued by the late Senator Paul Douglas (a sponsor of the legislation): "The benefits of effective competition cannot be realized if the buyers (borrowers) do not have adequate knowledge of the alternatives which are available to them." To achieve these ends, the law requires disclosure of two fundamental aspects of credit prices:

1. The *finance charge,* which is the amount of money paid to obtain the credit.
2. The *annual percentage rate,* or APR, which provides a simple way of comparing credit prices regardless of the dollar amount charged or the length of time over which payments are made.

Several studies of awareness of credit cost subsequent to TIL have discovered significant improvement in debtor knowledge.

4.   WARRANTY STANDARDIZATION
The 1975 Magnuson-Moss Warranty–FTC Improvement Act contains a number of requirements for manufacturers regarding standards for written product warranties. For products priced above $15, manufacturers must now specify whether their warranty is full or limited, where:

1. A *full warranty* means that charges for repair or replacement during the warranty period are either minimal or nil.
2. A *limited warranty* limits the seller's obligations, placing more financial responsibility on the consumer.

Moreover, the law holds that the terms and conditions of a written warranty must be stated "in simple and readily understood language." This was in response to consumer complaints that only sober Philadelphia lawyers could understand the language of most product warranties.

Studies of the impact of this law indicate that its benefits may be limited. It appears, for instance, that only about 28 percent of all consumers actually read warranties before making their purchases, so warranty standardization would assist only a minority of consumers in comparative shopping.[30] Moreover, warranties are still very difficult to understand despite the law. Measuring language lucidity by the education level necessary to achieve understanding, one recent study of 125 warranties found that 34 percent of them were at the college graduate level and 44 percent more were at the some college level. Automobile warranties were found to be especially difficult, generating an average grade level score of 20.2.[31]

Notice, however, that the purposes of the Magnuson-Moss Act go well beyond warranty simplification. And in these other respects the act seems to have been more successful. For instance, there appears to have been some shift from limited to full warranties, and warranty coverage in terms of duration, scope, and remedies seems to have improved.[32] This bodes well for consumers because better warranties usually signal better product quality.[33] Also, the Magnuson-Moss Act requires manufacturers to provide the protection they promise in their warranties, and there is evidence that warranties have consequently become much better signals of quality. For example, a five-year auto warranty signals a more reliable car than a two-year warranty does. Several firms entering the market for television sets since 1976 have used their warranties as a means of supporting their reliability claims. On the whole, the policy seems to be a success.[34]

B. Quality Disclosures[35]

Critics of the policies ticked off heretofore correctly point out that they simply make price comparisons easier; they do not take into account differences in the *quality* of competing brands or products. Furthermore, some critics assert that these policies cause consumers to overemphasize price per unit and overlook quality per dollar spent. The latter argument is probably questionable. In any event, the general purpose of the following policies is to help buyers identify quality.

1. SIMPLE DISCLOSURE OF INGREDIENTS

The Wool Products Labeling Act of 1939, the Fur Products Labeling Act of 1951, and the Textile Fiber Products Identification Act of 1958 call for the disclosure of ingredients in fur and fiber products. All are enforced by the Federal Trade Commission. Under the first of these, almost all wool products must bear labels showing the percentage of the total fiber weight of virgin wool, reprocessed wool, and reused wool. Inclusion of any other fiber must also be identified by generic name (as opposed to trade name) if it exceeds 5 percent of the total. Similarly, the fur act requires fur product labels that disclose the true English name of the animal that grew the fur; the animal's home country if the fur is imported; and whether the fur is bleached, dyed, or otherwise artificially colored. Thus, rabbit cannot be passed off as "Baltic Lion," and sheared muskrat cannot be called "Hudson Seal"—not as long as the FTC's agents stay awake on the job.

Finally, the main purpose of the textile act is to reduce confusion that might be caused by the proliferation of manmade chemical fibers and their many trade names. The law requires labels revealing the *generic* names and percentages of all fibers that go into a fabric, except those that constitute less than 5 percent of the fabric. Thus, Dacron, which is a trade name, must be identified as polyester, its generic name. Over 700 other trade names must be identified as belonging to one of seventeen generic families specified by the FTC. To the extent consumers know the properties of these generic fibers in terms of washing, pressing, dying, and wearing them, the law helps. To the extent consumers do not know, it does not help.

Labeling regulations for the ingredients of food products has a shorter history. Since about 1972, the Food and Drug Administration has expanded its activity in labeling so that detailed disclosures of composition are now required on the labels of most food products. The disclosures include the following:

1. Ingredients such as whole wheat, oats, salt, and sugar.
2. Nutrition information, such as vitamins, minerals, protein, calories, fat, and carbohydrates.
3. Special information on foods intended for infants, nursing mothers, diabetics, and the allergic.

These disclosures are important because, among other benefits, a low-fat diet reduces the risk of heart disease and a low-sodium diet can help to prevent high blood pressure. Some experts estimate that about 15 percent to 20 percent of all shoppers "read labels assiduously and do the arithmetic needed to make sure they eat well."[36] Another 20 percent to 30 percent study labels "at least some of the time."[37] Hence, roughly 50 percent of the consuming public appears to benefit substantially by this information disclosure. This explains why, in recent years, the FDA has tried to extend information disclosure to fresh fruits and vegetables and the U.S. Department of Agriculture has taken steps to bring disclosure to all processed meats and poultry (like luncheon meats, canned chili, and hot dogs), which until 1991 were largely exempt.[38]

(Talk about ingredient disclosure: In 1991 a bill was introduced in Washington State's legislature that, if passed, would have required ticket agents, concert promoters, and musical artists to tell concertgoers about any prerecorded vocal tracks that might be used. The bill's sponsor, Representative Randy Tate, dubbed it the "Milli Vanilli billi," complaining that undisclosed lip syncing was all too common in "live" concerts.[39])

2. OPEN DATING

Freshness is obviously an important aspect of the quality of perishable food products. For many years food manufacturers dated their products for inventory control and retailer rotation. Until recently, however, these dates were disguised by codes not known to the public (and often not even known to grocery store managers or clerks). Thus, open dating is simply uncoded dating. As of 1985, federal law did not require open dating, but twenty-one states had some form of mandatory open dating, with dairy products being the prime target.[40] In addition, many grocery chains have voluntarily adopted it. One problem that remains to be resolved is standardization. "Sell-by" dating is customary, but a confusing variety of other dating methods are also used—"packing date," "expiration date," and so on.

Another form of open dating relates to autos. As of 1975, thirty-seven states had entered the snake pit of used car sales by prohibiting odometer tampering. Thereafter, the federal government also stepped in with passage of the Motor Vehicle Information and Cost Savings Act. This law requires a written, true-mileage disclosure statement at the time of sale for all self-propelled vehicles except those that are more than twenty-four years old or exceed 16,000 pounds. Moreover, the law prohibits disconnecting or resetting the odometer with intent to change the mileage reading or knowingly falsifying the written odometer statement.

In 1987 the Chrysler Corporation pleaded no contest to criminal charges that it had been selling cars as new that had been driven by company executives with disconnected odometers for as much as 400 miles. At least 32,750 cars were involved over a three-year period. The company agreed to pay fines of $16.4 million.[41]

3. SPECIFIC PERFORMANCE DISCLOSURES

Beginning with the 1977 models, all new cars sold in the United States have had labels disclosing the estimated number of miles they get per gallon of gas and an estimate of what yearly fuel cost would be if 15,000 miles were traveled per year. For example, the 1977 Volkswagen Rabbit Diesel, with a 90-cubic-inch engine, was reported to travel 44 miles per gallon and cost $188 in annual fuel expense. By contrast, the 1977 Dodge Royal Monaco with a 440-cubic-inch engine brandished a sticker saying that a standard year's travel in one of them would cost $886, since it averaged only 11 miles per gallon. The Federal Energy Act of 1975 requires these disclosures on the theory that they assist efficiency comparisons and in the hope that car buyers will react to these revelations by shying away from gas guzzlers.

The Federal Energy Act also requires that efficiency ratings appear on major home appliances like refrigerators, freezers, and dishwashers. Administered by the Federal Trade Commission through its rule-making procedures, this program is much more complex than is suggested by the simple energy labels adopted (see Figure 12–3 for a sample).[42] One particularly helpful feature of the label is that it places the appliance on a relative scale, so shoppers need not strain much in making comparisons of energy efficiency. Study of consumer response to this program indicates its favorable promise.[43] Of particular interest is the finding that consumers now give greater weight to energy efficiency, as indicated in Table 12–3. Table 12–3 also shows that as energy efficiency has risen in importance, brand names have fallen in importance.

Another illustration of specific performance disclosure is gasoline octane posting, which has been with us in one form or another since 1973 but only haphazardly enforced. The Federal Trade Commission, which has been the most vigorous advocate of octane posting, has argued that in the absence of octane posting, motorists would waste more than $300 million a year by purchasing gasoline with higher octane than they really need. Most people seem to think that higher octane produces greater power, but this is not true. Octane indicates only the antiknock properties of gasoline. The major petroleum

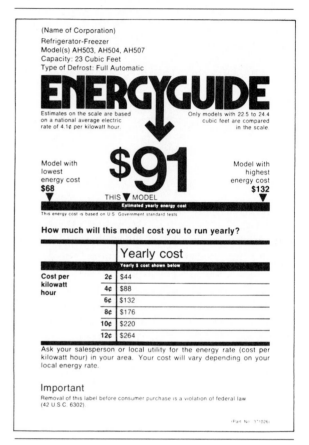

Figure 12–3
Appliance Energy Disclosure

companies have persistently opposed octane posting for fear that it would lead people to recognize that all brands of gasoline of a given octane rating are pretty much alike (which they are).[44]

4.　GRADE RATING
Disclosures of ingredients, freshness, dimensions, specific performance, and the like may guide buyers toward ideal purchasing patterns, but how close to the ideal can these raw data take them? Several recent studies have demonstrated formally what most students already know from informal experience—namely, the information-

Table 12–3
Consumer Rating of Attribute Importance Before and After Energy Labeling:
Refrigerators

Attribute	Percentage of Consumer Respondents Who Said the Attribute was Very Important to Their Choice	
	Before Energy Labeling	After Energy Labeling
Size	73.1	68.8
Price	52.5	58.6
Appearance/color	49.5	47.7
Yearly energy cost	34.6	43.9
Brand name	32.5	23.6

Source: Robert F. Dyer and Thomas J. Maronick, "An Evaluation of Consumer Awareness and Use of Energy Labels in the Purchase of Major Appliances," *Journal of Public Policy & Marketing* (vol. 7, 1988): 89.

processing capabilities of the human mind are quite limited. Indeed, some evidence even suggests that beyond a certain point additional information merely confuses and frustrates consumers. Thereafter, they no longer move toward their ideal decision, but *away* from it. Thus, grade rating is often recommended as a means of simplifying complex quality information into a simple a-b-c format.

The most active federal agency in this respect is the U.S. Department of Agriculture (USDA) whose agents grade meat, eggs, butter, poultry, grain, fruits, and vegetables. Beef, for example, is graded prime, choice, or good. This grading is not compulsory. Hence, large brand-name meat packers like Armour, Swift, and Morrell have elbow room to resist it. They prefer to promote the sale of beef under their own brand names whenever possible. Among the statistics that reflect resistance to grading, we find that during the 1950s only 27 percent of national packer beef was USDA graded, and all but one of the national brand-name packers advocated an end to federal grading. In contrast, the main supporters of the system have been independent

packers, retail food chains, independent retailers, and consumers. During 1955, for instance, 94 percent of all beef sold by retail food chains was USDA graded, and 85 percent of all chains surveyed said they favored compulsory grading or continuation of the present system. These and related data led W. F. Williams, E. K. Bowen, and F. C. Genovese to conclude:

1. Grade standards have tended to intensify competition.
2. Unbranded packers and wholesalers increased in numbers and volume of meat processed, whereas branded packers declined greatly in number.
3. The system has tended to increase the accuracy, ease, and effectiveness of prices in reflecting value differences at each stage in the marketing system for beef by assisting consumers in the expression of their preferences.[47]

The biggest problem with USDA grade ratings is its lack of standardization across products. Top-rated apples, peaches, chickens, and

Table 12–4
Summary of United States Standardization and Disclosure Policies

Policy	Enforcement Agencies[a]	Products Covered
A. Standardization		
1. Fair Packaging and Labeling Act (1966)	FTC, FDA	Grocery store items (e.g., foods and detergents)
2. Size uniformity and simplification	Various state authorities	Bread, margarine, flour, dairy products
3. Unit pricing	Various state authorities	Grocery store items
4. Truth in Lending Act (1969)	FTC, FRB	Consumer credit
5. Warranty standards	FTC	Durables over $15 with written warranty
B. Quality Disclosures		
1. Ingredient labeling:		
Wool Products Labeling Act (1939)	FTC	Wool products
Fur Product Labeling Act (1951)	FTC	Furs
Textile Fiber Identification Act (1958)	FTC	Textiles, apparel, etc.
Food, Drug and Cosmetic Act	FDA	Food products
2. Open dating of perishables	Various state authorities	Grocery perishables
3. Antitampering Odometer Law (1972)	NHTSA	Cars and trucks
4. Performance disclosures:		
Fuel efficiency	FEA, FTC	Autos, appliances
Octane rating	FTC, FEA	Gasoline
Tar and nicotine	FTC	Cigarettes
On time performance	ICC	Moving van services
5. Grade rating	USDA	Meat, eggs, butter, etc.
	NHTSA	Tires
	FDA	Sunscreens

[a]Key: FTC—Federal Trade Commission; FDA—Food and Drug Administration; FRB—Federal Reserve Board of Governors; NHTSA—National Highway Traffic Safety Administration; FEA—Federal Energy Administration; ICC—Interstate Commerce Commission; USDA—U.S. Department of Agriculture.

some other foods are variously awarded grades of No. 1, Extra No. 1, Fancy, and Grade A. For still other products, these grades would indicate second best.

Auto tires were the subject of an early demonstration of how grading could reduce buyers' erroneous reliance on brand names. Louis Bucklin found that without grading consumers tended to overestimate the value of heavily ad-vertised national brands of tires as compared to mildly promoted distributor and local brands but that with grade rating this bias tended to disappear.[48] Subsequent to that study and despite sharp objections by major tire manufacturers, a grade rating system was put into effect by the Department of Transportation in 1979 and 1980. Tires are now rated on the following three characteristics:

1. *Treadwear,* indicated by a numeral such as 200 or 400, with higher numerals indicating higher mileage.
2. *Traction,* where A, B, and C indicate good, fair, and poor traction on wet roads, respectively.
3. *Temperature,* where A indicates the coolest running tire, and B and C rank less well.

Tire manufacturers do their own testing and interpretation under the program, which has led to problems. In particular, the treadwear rating has been the most controversial. It was dropped by the Reagan Administration in 1983 at the urging of the big tire companies who argued that the ratings were unreliable. Michelin aided its cause by deliberately underrating its tires markedly. Why? "To show our disregard for the procedure," said a Michelin spokesman. "We think building up an image and brand acceptance is the way to go," he added. Two consumer groups filed suit to have the ratings reinstated, and a U.S. Court of Appeals decided that the Reagan Administration had been flouting the law by "arbitrarily and capriciously" suspending the treadwear grading rule indefinitely. In 1991, treadwear ratings were again being made.

Grade rating of sunscreens by the FDA reveals whether a sunscreen filters out only a very few ultraviolet-B rays (No. 1) or blocks virtually all of them (No. 29). Ultraviolet-B rays cause sunburn and some skin cancers. UV-A rays, which are of a longer wavelength, were once considered safe, but growing evidence shows they contribute to aging of the skin and to cataracts. Hence, the FDA has recently been working on standards for products that also protect against UV-A radiation.[50]

Summary

An economy without well-informed buyers would be like a university without students. Fortunately, buyers are not *always* ignorant, but they frequently are, depending on their expertise and the product in question. Experience and credence goods are especially troublesome, for they cannot be easily and fully assessed before purchase, as can search goods. When lapses occur, a number of adverse consequences may follow: (1) errors of commission and omission, (2) imperfect competition, and (3) wasteful and misdirected promotion arising from sellers' attempts to exploit this ignorance. Consumers often rely heavily on trademarks to guide their purchasing decisions because in a roundabout way trademarks often help to identify product quality. Even so, too heavy a reliance on trademarks and the advertising promoting them may contribute to erroneous purchasing behavior, in which case the owners of prominent trademarks gain at the expense of buyers.

Corrective policies have to focus on one or both of the following objectives: (1) Permit trademarks to identify quality, but remove the rights of ownership exclusivity and perpetuity that presently prevail. (2) Establish quality identifications independent of the trademark system. The first objective lies outside the realm of political possibility. The second has been furthered by two broad classes of policies—standardization (which includes simplified quantity labeling, uniform sizes, and unit pricing) and quality disclosures (which include ingredient labeling, open dating, performance disclosure, and grade rating) as outlined in Table 12–4.

Questions and Exercises for Chapter 12

1. Why are professional buyers generally more knowledgeable than consumers?
2. With the aid of a diagram, explain why errors of commission result in allocation inefficiency. (Hint: Is there any divergence between marginal social benefit and marginal social cost with such errors?)
3. With the aid of a diagram, explain why errors of omission result in allocation inefficiency.

4. Distinguish between search and experience goods in (a) characteristics, (b) implications for competition, and (c) nature and intensity of advertising.
5. What is the basic rationale behind standardization and disclosure policies?
6. Compare and contrast standardization versus quality disclosure.
7. After identifying unit pricing and truth-in-lending, explain why they are versions of price standardization.
8. What is the connection between search qualities and (a) open dating and (b) performance disclosure?
9. What has been the economic impact of grade rating in meat packing?

Appendix to Chapter 12: Voluntary Standards

Standards often do more than help buyers become informed. They can be used to ensure physical compatibility between related products made by different manufacturers and to assist in achieving economies of scale. When used for these purposes, standards are usually voluntary (the work of producers themselves) rather than mandatory (the work of the government). There are over 30,000 voluntary product standards now in effect in the United States.

Many standards also prevail in Europe . . . too many. The problem is that each country has its own standards, so for many products there is little standardization. Take electrical equipment, for instance. Philips, the large European electronics firm, "makes 29 different types of electrical outlets, 10 kinds of plugs, 12 kinds of cords, 3 kinds of television sets, 12 types of irons and 15 kinds of cake mixers." The number of "standard" European caps for lightbulbs is about 300. Such variety limits the scale of production runs and thereby prevents the full achievement of economies of scale. As the *The Wall Street Journal* reports:

> Varying standards force Philips to make a wider spectrum of goods than it wants to, driving up

production costs as economies of scale are lost. Wider variety necessitates higher inventories, meaning higher interest and storage costs. . . . Philips maintains that if Europe were truly a single market, appliances and customer electronics would be 7 percent to 10 percent cheaper, stimulating demand and adding to sales.[51]

The main reason European standards vary is that they protect local manufacturers. Indeed, these standards have become mandatory largely because of political pressures applied by local producers who want to be shielded from foreign rivals. Hence, we have yet another use for standards: They can be used to restrict competition.

Returning to the United States, it has been hypothesized that voluntary standards would be easier to devise in concentrated as opposed to unconcentrated industries. Greater concentration implies *fewer* firms, and fewness should aid in achieving the consensus that voluntary standards require. Moreover, greater concentration implies relatively *larger* firms, and large size would grant larger rewards from the net benefits that standards provide. Recent empirical evidence lends support to these views. The incidence of voluntary product standards seems to be positively associated with concentration in high technology industries.[52]

Notes

1. *Wall Street Journal,* 30 January 1990, p. B1.
2. For further discussion of these qualities, see R. H. Holton, "Consumer Behavior, Market Imperfections and Public Policy," in *Industrial Organization and Development,* ed. Markham and Papanek (Boston: Houghton Mifflin, 1970), pp. 102–115; Phillip Nelson "Information and Consumer Behavior," *Journal of Political Economy* (March/April 1970): 311–319; M. R. Darby and E. Karni, "Free Competition and the Optimal Amount of Fraud," *Journal of Law and Economics* (April 1973): 67–88.
3. R. A. Bauer and Stephen A. Greyser, *Advertising in America: The Consumer View* (Boston: Division of Research, Graduate School of Business Administration, Harvard University, 1968), p. 71. See also *Advertising Age* (26 July 1976), p. 20.
4. Peter C. Riesz, "Price-Quality Correlations for Packaged Food Products," *Journal of Consumer Affairs* (Winter 1979): 236–247.

5. Monroe Friedman, "Quality and Price Considerations in Rational Decision Making," *Journal of Consumer Affairs* (Summer 1967): 13–23.

6. R. T. Morris and C. S. Bronson, "The Chaos of Competition Indicated by Consumer Reports," *Journal of Marketing* (July 1969): 26–34. The mean correlation for fourteen products in Japan was −0.06. Yoshiko Yamada and Norleen Ackerman, "Price-Quality Correlations in the Japanese Market," *Journal of Consumer Affairs* (Winter 1984): 251–265.

7. The following draws heavily from S. Peltzman, "An Evaluation of Consumer Protection Legislation: The 1962 Drug Amendments," *Journal of Political Economy* (Sept./Oct. 1973): 1049–1091; T. McGuire, R. Nelson, and T. Spavins, "Comment on the Peltzman Paper," *Journal of Political Economy* (June 1975): 655–661; M. R. Darby and E. Karni, "Free Competition and the Optimal Amount of Fraud," *Journal of Law and Economics* (April 1973): 67–88; George Akerlof, "The Market for 'Lemons': Quality Uncertainty and the Market Mechanism," *Quarterly Journal of Economics* (August 1970): 488–500; and R. H. Nelson, "The Economics of Honest Trade Practices," *Journal of Industrial Economics* (June 1976): 281–293.

8. Alex Maurizi and Thom Kelly, *Prices and Consumer Information* (Washington, DC: American Enterprise Institute, 1978), p. 40. For other examples see D. Grant Devine and Bruce W. Marion, "The Influence of Consumer Price Information on Retail Pricing and Consumer Behavior," *American Journal of Agricultural Economics* (May 1979): 228–237; and Board of Governors of the Federal Reserve System, *Annual Percentage Rate Demonstration Project* (Submitted to U.S. Senate Committee on Banking, Housing, and Urban Affairs), 1987.

9. John F. Cady, "An Estimate of the Price Effects of Restrictions on Drug Price Advertising," *Economic Inquiry* (December 1976): 493–510.

10. See Douglas F. Greer, *Industrial Organization and Public Policy* 2nd ed. (New York: Macmillan, 1984), pp. 357–364.

11. C. D. Edwards, "Advertising and Competition," *Business Horizons* (February 1968): 60.

12. Bauer and Greyser, *Advertising in America*, pp. 296–297.

13. There are, of course, many other variables affecting interindustry differences in advertising intensity. See, e.g., M. M. Metwally, "Product Categories that Advertise Most," *Journal of Advertising Research* (February 1980): 25–31; L. W. Weiss, G. Pascoe, and S. Martin, "The Size of Selling Costs," *Review of Economics and Statistics* (November 1983): 668–672.

14. R. E. Caves and W. F. Murphy II, "Franchising: Firms, Markets, and Intangible Assets," *Southern Economic Journal* (April 1976): 572–586.

15. E. W. Kintner and J. L. Lahr, *An Intellectual Property Law Primer* (New York: Macmillan, 1975), p. 250.

16. Robert Feinberg, "Trademarks, Market Power, and Information," *Review of Industrial Organization* (vol. 2, no. 4, 1986): 376–385.

17. Edward H. Chamberlin, *The Theory of Monopolistic Competition*, 8th ed. (Cambridge, MA: Harvard University Press, 1962), p. 273; see also M. L. Greenhut, "Free Entry and the Trade Mark–Trade Name Product," *Southern Economic Journal* (October 1957): 170–181.

18. This division and much else in this section owe their origin to David Hemenway, *Industrywide Voluntary Product Standards* (Cambridge, MA: Ballinger, 1975). See also Paul A. David, "Some New Standards for the Economics of Standardization in the Information Age," in *Economic Policy and Technological Performance*, ed. P. Dasgupta and P. Stoneman (Cambridge: England: Cambridge University Press, 1987), pp. 206–239.

19. Kenneth Arrow, "Economic Welfare and the Allocation of Resources to Invention," in *The Rate and Direction of Inventive Activity: Economic and Social Factors* (New York: National Bureau of Economic Research, 1962).

20. M. P. Friedman, "Consumer Confusion in the Selection of Supermarket Products," *Journal of Applied Psychology* (December 1966): 529–534.

21. Michigan Chamber of Commerce, as quoted by R. L. Birmingham, "The Consumer as King: The Economics of Precarious Sovereignty," in *Consumerism*, ed. D. A. Aaker and G. S. Day (New York: Free Press, 1974), p. 186.

22. A. Q. Mowbray, *The Thumb on the Scale* (New York: Lippincott, 1967), p. 72.

23. *New York Times*, 8 June 1969.

24. Committee on Consumer Policy, *Package Standardization, Unit Pricing, Deceptive Packaging* (Paris: Organization for Economic Co-operation and Development, 1975).

25. Paul Farhi, "Sometimes Less is Less," *Washington Post*, National Weekly Edition, February 11–17, 1991, p. 23.

26. *Wall Street Journal*, 26 November 1984, pp. 1, 22.

27. For a summary of this and other studies see General Accounting Office, *Report to the Congress on Food Labeling: Goals, Shortcomings, and Proposed Changes* (#MWD–75–19) January 1975. This is the main source for this section.

28. *State Consumer Action: Summary '74*, Office of Consumer Affairs, Department of Health, Education, and Welfare [Pub. No. (OS) 75–116], pp. ix–x.

29. Material for this topic may be found in *Consumer Credit in the United States*, Report of the National Commission on Consumer Finance (Washington DC: U.S. Government Printing Office, 1972) Chapter 10; and *Technical Studies, Vol. I*, of the same commission, which includes papers by R. P. Shay, M. W. Schober, G. S. Day, and W. K. Brandt.

30. Federal Trade Commission, *Warranties Rules Consumer Baseline Study* (March 2, 1979), p. 129.

31. F. Kelly Shuptrine and Ellen M. Moore, "Even After the Magnuson-Moss Act of 1975, Warranties Are Not Easy to Understand," *Journal of Consumer Affairs* (Winter 1980): 394–404.

32. T. Schmitt, L. Kauter, and R. Miller, *Impact Report on the Magnuson-Moss Warranty Act* (Washington, DC: Federal Trade Commission, 1980).

33. J. L. Wiener, "Are Warranties Accurate Signals of Product Reliability?," *Journal of Consumer Research* (September 1985): 245–250.

34. Joshua Lyle Wiener, "An Evaluation of the Magnuson-Moss Warranty and Federal Trade Commission Improvement Act of 1975," *Journal of Public Policy and Marketing* (vol. 7, 1988): 65–82.

35. For another survey see John A. Miller, "Product Labeling and Government regulation," *Journal of Contemporary Business* (vol. 7, no. 4, 1979): 105–121.

36. Malcolm Gladwell, "You Are What You Read," *Washington Post, National Weekly Edition,* November 19–25, 1990, p. 38.

37. *Ibid.*

38. *Wall Street Journal,* 5 March 1991, p. B1; April 2, 1991, p. B3.

39. *San Jose Mercury News,* 15 February 1991, p. 5F.

40. Congress of the United States, Office of Technology Assessment, *Open Shelf-Life Dating of Food* (Washington, DC: August 1979). A study prompting Minnesota's law found that 44 percent of the baby formula being sold was over age and that since 64 percent of the store managers could not read a coded date, they could not rotate the stock.

41. *Wall Street Journal,* 15 December 1987, p. 22.

42. Federal Trade Commission, *Labeling and Advertising of Consumer Appliances* (February 1979).

43. D. L. McNeill and W. L. Wilkie, "Public Policy and Consumer Information: Impact of the New Energy Labels," *Journal of Consumer Research* (June 1979): 1–11.

44. See *Business Week* (May 31, 1976), p. 21, and F. C. Allvine and J. M. Patterson, *Competition Limited: The Marketing of Gasoline* (Bloomington, IN: Indiana University Press, 1972), pp. 24–25. It may be worth noting that the petroleum industry itself imposes extensive standards on its suppliers. According to the American Petroleum Institute: "All of our standards are written from the point of view of a consuming industry. . . . Our motive simply is to provide uniform performance requirements to the widest possible range of suppliers." Hemenway, *Product Standards,* p. 66.

45. Jacob Jacoby, "Perspectives on Information Overload" and N. K. Malhotra, "Reflections on the Information Overload Paradigm," both in *Journal of Consumer Research* (March 1984): 432–440, plus the citations therein.

46. J. R. Bettman, "Issues in Designing Consumer Information Environments," *Journal of Consumer Research* (December 1975): 169–177.

47. Willard F. Williams, E. K. Bowen, and F. C. Genovese, *Economic Effects of U.S. Grades for Beef,* U.S. Department of Agriculture Marketing Research Report No. 298 (Washington, DC, 1959), pp. vii, 158–180.

48. Louis P. Bucklin, "The Uniform Grading System for Tires: Its Effect upon Consumers and Industry Competition," *Antitrust Bulletin* (Winter 1974): 783–801.

49. *Wall Street Journal,* 3 February 1983, p. 50; April 25, 1984, p. 10; *San Jose Mercury News,* 3 February 1983, p. 6A.

50. *Business Week,* June 11, 1990, pp. 22–23.

51. *Wall Street Journal,* 7 August 1985, pp. 1, 16.

52. Albert N. Link, "Market Structure and Voluntary Product Standards," *Applied Economics* (vol. 15, 1983): 393–401. See also Sylvia Lane and Anastasios Papathanasis, "Certification and Industry Concentration Ratios," *Antitrust Bulletin* (Summer 1983): 381–395.

Chapter 13

Deceptive and Unfair Practices

It is a basic tenet of our economic system that information in the hands of consumers facilitates rational purchase decisions.
— *Federal Trade Commission*

A TV ad says that you can buy a Midas muffler for $18.95. Once you have it installed, however, you're charged $6.00 extra for clamps and hangers. Midas shops in California charged at least $24.95 on every $18.95 muffler sold in the mid-1980s, prompting state charges of deceptive advertising and $500,000 in fines.[1]

For seven years during the 1980s, Hertz Rent A Car charged customers and insurance companies higher prices for repairs to rental cars damaged by customers than it actually paid to have the repairs made, collecting more than $13 million in the process. Would you say this was unfair or deceptive?[2]

This chapter reviews state and federal policies governing deceptive and unfair practices. Federal policy centers on Section 5 of the Federal Trade Commission Act (as amended by the Wheeler-Lea Act of 1938), which states, "Unfair methods of competition in commerce, and unfair or deceptive acts or practices in commerce, are declared unlawful." Since passage of the FTC Act in 1914, more than 3,300 cases of deception have been prosecuted by the FTC.

Our survey of what is illegal is in five parts and focuses primarily on advertising: (1) the criteria applied to determine deception; (2) specific examples of advertising that have collided with the criteria; (3) FTC procedures; (4) remedies applied to clean up; and (5) miscellaneous unfair practices.

I. What Is Deception?

A. A Bit of History

Before the FTC Act, common law governed misrepresentation and deception. Successful prosecution was very difficult. The common law was rigged in favor of the con artist because conviction required a showing of *actual* deception in mind of an *injured* buyer and *deliberate* intent in the mind of the seller. Common law cases were consequently rare. Perhaps the only justification

255

for this approach was the fact that sellers could suffer harsh penalties if convicted.

The FTC Act, as amended by the Wheeler-Lea Act of 1938, changed all this. Thereafter none of these elements—actual deception, buyer injury, and deliberate intent—had to be proven for the FTC to reach a guilty verdict. Until recently the commission's decision hinged solely on whether or not a sales claim:

1. possessed the *capacity or tendency* to deceive
2. a *substantial number* of buyers
3. in some *material respect* regarding the purchase decision.

These three criteria for a violation were repeatedly endorsed by the courts for over forty-five years. Moreover, they also became the main standard for regulating deception at the state level, partly because many states enacted statutes almost identical to the Federal Trade Commission Act (often called "Little FTC Acts").

In 1983, however, there was a change, a retreat toward the old common law. President Reagan's conservative appointees to the FTC adopted a new and less stringent enforcement strategy. By it, Reagan's FTC considered a sales claim unlawful if the claim

1. was *likely* to deceive . . .
2. consumers *acting reasonably* in the circumstances . . .
3. and the result was *detrimental or injurious* to consumers.[3]

Our review of policy will take up the "old" FTC standard in some detail before turning to the "new" standard. Several advantages attend this approach. First, at the federal level, neither statutory language nor court interpretation has been altered substantially to adopt the new standard. The old standard persists. So far, only the FTC's enforcement practices have changed (e.g., case selection), and the commission appears to be returning to its old ways under the Bush Adminis-

tration. Second, at the state level, state attorneys general and state courts presently continue to apply the old standard. Indeed, state attorneys general have overwhelmingly rejected the new approach, so the old approach is being enforced, often with national consequences. Finally, there is the simple matter of learning. A full understanding of the new approach requires some background knowledge of the old approach.

In short, we begin with the old standard of (1) a *capacity or tendency* to deceive (2) a *substantial number* of consumers (3) in a *material* way. We next take up the new standard, which requires (1) a *likely* deception of (2) consumers acting *reasonably* (3) with *detrimental* results.

B. The Old Standard

Capacity or Tendency to Deceive. The old standard attacks acts or practices having a *capacity or tendency* to deceive.[4] Those acts or practices may be express or implied, oral or written, representations. They may omit pertinent facts. They may be in advertisements or in personal sales pitches.

Let's elaborate for advertising. Under this standard the law attacks the ad, not the advertiser. Proof of intent is not required. Likewise, proof of actual deception is not required. The commission or the court may examine an advertisement and determine on the basis of its own expertise whether there is a potential for deception. The commission need not poll consumers, or hear from complaining witnesses.[5] Even if suspected deceivers defend themselves by providing a parade of witnesses who say they have not been misled, the FTC can still find a violation.[6] (Despite the power of the FTC to rely on its own expertise under this old standard, it nevertheless supplemented its intuitive judgment with consumers' testimony, public opinion polls, and outside experts. Over the years 1970 to 1973 only 36 percent of all cases were decided solely on the basis of Commission expertise.[7])

Notice, too, the heavy emphasis on the word *deception* rather than something else—for example, instead of *falsehood* (an emphasis that is in the new standard as well). Innocent souls tend to think in simple terms: Truth should be legal, falsity illegal. This rule would be impractical, however, the controversies over truth being what they are. A better rule, the one actually applied by law, centers on the *deception* of potential buyers: "that which is not deceptive is legal, and that which is deceptive is illegal." This rule is different because falsity and deception are *not* necessarily the same. Although most false claims are deceptive, a claim may be false but not deceptive. Conversely, although most true claims are not deceptive, some true claims may be deceptive. These divergences arise because of the gap between any message's sender and its receiver. Whereas truth and falsity hinge on the literal content of the message sent, deception depends on what goes on in the minds of folks receiving the message—that is, the potential buyers.

Take, for example, the remarkable claim of potency made by "Newman's Own Virgin Lemonade" in 1989, which was that it restored virginity. (In a testimonial Whoopi Goldberg said, "Just seeing it being poured makes me feel virginal.") The claim was patently false, yet no one was deceived. So the FTC did not budge.

Examples of literal truth that actually deceive are equally easy to come by. In 1971 the FTC found deception in nonfalse television ads showing Hot Wheels and Johnny Lightning toy racers speeding over their tracks. To the TV viewer, the racers seemed to move like bullets, but this was merely a special effect that was achieved by filming the racers at close range from clever angles. The representation was technically accurate but nevertheless misleading.[8]

Many further examples relate to "half-true" advertisements that, although literally true, leave an overall impression that is quite incorrect. Profile Bread previously advertised that Profile was good for dieters because it had fewer calories per slice than other breads. This was true but only half true. The ads gave the impression that Profile was a low-calorie bread, with fewer calories per loaf. This was not true. Profile had fewer calories per slice only because it was *sliced thinner* than regular bread. Hence, the FTC and circuit court found deception.[9] (Profile was so bold as to claim that eating two slices before every meal would help weight loss.)

A Substantial Number of Deceived People. Given that deception lies in the mind of the observer rather than in the body of the advertisement, the next question is: Who among observers is to be protected? If one gullible person is misled, does that constitute illegal deception? What about 3 percent, or 15 percent, of the population? When reviewing a case in 1927, the Supreme Court held that Section 5 was "made to protect the trusting as well as the suspicious." Accordingly, the FTC and the appellate courts adopted a fairly stringent rule under the old standard, one that protected the ignorant, the unthinking, and the trusting as well as the suspicious and hard headed.[10] The authorities decided, for example, that a hair coloring could not claim that it colored hair permanently.

Still, the authorities did not go so far as to protect the "foolish or feeble minded." They permitted obvious spoofs, such as a rampaging bull that is released merely by uncorking a malt liquor (Schlitz). Moreover, the authorities permitted generous amounts of "puffery."

Thus, it could be said that the old standard asked only whether a *substantial number* of consumers had been misled. As two former FTC commissioners put it:

> The appropriate test has been variously stated as whether a "substantial segment," a "substantial percentage," "substantial numbers," or "some reasonably significant number" of consumers have been or could be misled.[11]

Materiality. According to the old standard, deceptions had to be *material*. That is, they would have to refer to price, performance, durability, or the like and thereby potentially affect the average purchase decision.

Here's an example drawn from a *Newsweek* article:

> Who *are* Frank Bartles and Ed Jaymes? To many consumers they are a folksy pair of aging entrepreneurs hawking their new Bartles & Jaymes wine cooler in humorous TV ads. Watching the bucolic duo as they sit on their sagging front porch and spin their tale . . . it's easy to get caught up in their quest for fame and fortune. . . .
>
> Frank and Ed tell the public why they got into the cooler business (Ed owns an orchard, Frank a vineyard), where they got the snazzy label (Ed ordered it by mail from France) or how they get their cooler to stores in major markets (in an old pickup truck). . . . In every ad, Frank pokes fun at big business, marketing, or advertising.[12]

The ads have been so convincing that "dozens of people wrote in offering financial help after watching an ad in which Frank urged viewers to buy more Bartles & Jaymes because Ed had to make a big balloon payment on the second mortgage he took out to start the company."[13] Yet, Bartles and Jaymes are fictitious characters. Their stories are tall tales. And their company is a dummy corporation actually owned and operated by the very largest wine producers in the country—Ernest and Julio Gallo, Inc. Why aren't these blatant misrepresentations challenged? They *are* deceptive, but the deceptions are apparently considered immaterial by enforcement authorities even though they are obviously material to Gallo's marketing efforts. The sales of Bartles & Jaymes coolers have been hotter than blazes.

To summarize the old standard, *an act or practice is deceptive if it has the capacity or tendency to mislead a substantial number of customers in a material way.*

C. The New Standard

When testifying before a congressional committee in 1984, James C. Miller, III, the main proponent of the new standard and chairman of the FTC at the time, said emphatically that "the Commission's [new] policy statement does not represent a departure, radical or otherwise, from precedent."[14] This is partly true because there appears to be considerable overlap between the old standard and the new one.

On the other hand, this defense of the FTC's new enforcement policy is a bit deceptive for several reasons. *First,* in 1982, a year before the FTC's action, Chairman Miller called on Congress to amend the FTC Act by rewriting it with the same language that appears in the new standards. Congress rejected the proposed amendment, but the mere fact that Miller sought a statutory change suggests that this new standard is really something new. And in defending his proposed amendment before Congress Mr. Miller identified numerous instances of deception under the "old" standard that would be allowed under the "new."

Second, most commentators on the new standards argue that they represent a substantial move toward greater leniency, a shift toward the common law standards that preceded the FTC Act.[15]

Finally and most important, after the FTC adopted the new standard in late 1983, the commission's enforcement efforts altered noticeably. For example, the FTC failed to act in the following instances:

- When the remarkable new sugar substitute NutraSweet became available, Coca-Cola advertised that Diet Coke was flavored "Now with NutraSweet," failing to mention that it also contained saccharin.
- The National Coffee Association promoted its caffeine-filled beverage with the message, "lets you calm yourself down."[16]

These claims have now been yanked from circulation under pressure from those still operating under the old standard—namely state enforcement agencies and some private review organizations. The FTC remains the main source of national enforcement, though, so its new policy deserves brief review.

Likelihood of Deception. Under the new standard, "likely to mislead" language replaces the "capacity or tendency" concept. The full implications of this substitution are not yet clear. However, it poses a more difficult burden of proof on plaintiffs and therefore a more lenient rule for advertisers. Proof that a claim is more likely to deceive than not would seem to require some showing of *actual deception*. And that is definitely not required by the "capacity or tendency" concept.

The Reasonable Consumer. Rather than protect a "substantial number" of consumers, the new policy protects those "*acting reasonably* in the circumstances." The rationale for this change is that, acting under the old standard, previous commissions squandered the taxpayers' money by prosecuting cases in which only a few consumers were likely to be misled. For example, the claim that a dye colored hair permanently should not have been attacked.

Critics of the new "reasonable consumer" criteria worry about trusting and unthinking souls. They also wonder about what could and could not be considered reasonable in today's age of exploding technology. Are people acting reasonably when they plunk down their money for the following?

- An electrical device emitting an ultrasonic sound (unhearable by humans) that allegedly irritates mice, fleas, roaches, and other pests, thereby driving them away.
- A pair of mail-order field binoculars said to have a fifty-mile range ("actually tell time on a clock a full mile away!") and priced at only $9.00.

- A set of tires that purportedly stop "25 percent quicker."
- Packets of common herbs, such as cayenne pepper, which are claimed to cure a wide variety of diseases, including cancer.

These examples come from actual cases of deception. And critics are concerned that advertisers may be able to evade the new standard simply by making their claims sufficiently preposterous that prosecutors would then not be able to prove that consumers were acting reasonably when they fell for the swindle.

Detrimental Results. In place of the materiality requirement of the old standard, the new standard substitutes the requirement that consumers suffer some *detriment*. In the words of former FTC Chairman Miller, "this means that consumers are likely to suffer injury," monetary or otherwise.

An example covered by the old standard but exempt from the new illustrates this change. Suppose that a retailer of stereo equipment advertises a going-out-of-business liquidation sale, offering name-brand receivers, speakers, and other audio equipment at alleged savings of 60 percent off "regular" prices. Suppose further that the "regular" prices are fictitiously inflated so that the "discount" prices are actually the same or even higher than the regular prices charged by more honest retailers. Still, folks flock to buy. The new standard ignores such scams, the reason being that consumers are not actually injured. If a consumer willingly pays the offered price to buy the product, he cannot rightfully complain. The fact that the difference between the "sale" price and the "regular" price is misrepresented is irrelevant. Willing payment by the consumer absolves the seller of wrongdoing, or so it is argued.

Critics of the injury test contend that honesty in the marketplace is desirable for its own sake. Moreover, they argue that exemptions such as this have adverse economic sideeffects because they force consumers to intensify their vigilance, to spend more time price shopping or product testing, and to develop greater doubts about the reliability of advertising generally.

In sum, the FTC's new standard of enforcement covers claims (1) *likely* to mislead (2) *reasonable* consumers (3) with *detrimental results*. This represents a retreat from the "old" standard that attacks claims having (1) the *capacity or tendency* to deceive (2) *substantial numbers* of consumers (3) in a *material way*. Still, there is a large overlap between the two standards.[17]

The annual number of FTC cases dropped dramatically under the new standard. However, the FTC's resources also dropped dramatically at the same time, so assessing the impact of the new standard is difficult. Workyears budgeted by Reagan's FTC for consumer protection fell about 40 percent "on the sometimes questionable premise that the marketplace ultimately will penalize purveyors of false and misleading claims."[18] Thus, the decline in enforcement might be attributed to financial changes as well as policy changes.

The significance of the new standard can be questioned for other reasons also. First, state attorneys general filled the vacuum left by the FTC. Texas challenged Kraft for calling Cheez-Whiz "real cheese." New York took action against Del Monte for claiming that its canned vegetables were "as nutritious as the vegetables you buy fresh and cook at home." And so on. One attorney general explained the flurry of state enforcement by saying that the FTC had become a "toothless watchdog asleep at the switch."[19] Second, early indications (in 1989, 1990, and 1991) suggested a possible return to the old standard and stepped-up enforcement by the FTC under President Bush. Big new cases have been filed. And the advertising industry itself is pressuring the FTC to restore vigorous enforcement out of fear that diverse state-by-state regulations will become chaotic.

Says Daniel Jaffe, spokesman for the Association of National Advertisers:

> We think it's totally counterproductive for the attorneys general to push the FTC aside in regulation. It's inevitable that they'll have inconsistent decisions.[20]

The main point is: The cases discussed in the following pages fit the old standard. Whether they would also meet the new standard is uncertain. Given the importance of the old standard to state enforcement activities and given the hints of rejuvenation at the FTC, however, we can deepen our understanding of deception with the following review of examples without misleading anyone in the process.

II. Examples of Deception

There is a rich variety of illegal deceptions. Unfortunately, we have space for only a few broad classes: (1) claims of composition, (2) claims of function or efficacy, (3) endorsements, and (4) mock-ups.[21]

A. Claims of Composition

The Fair Packaging and Labeling Act and similar acts governing textiles, furs, and woolens now regulate ingredient claims for many products. Those claims not so covered are subject of a host of FTC precedents under Section 5. Naked lies, such as calling pine wood walnut, are out. Many more slippery representations are now explicitly defined by the FTC. Here is a sampling:

- "Down" indicates feathers of any aquatic bird and therefore excludes chicken feathers.
- "Linoleum" designates a product composed of oxidized oil and gums mixed "intimately" with ground cork or wood flour.
- "Vanilla" unqualified describes only that which is obtained from the vanilla bean.

In 1983 the FTC decided against a leading advertising agency for its misleading promotion of a rubbing ointment used against arthritis pain. The product was called Aspercreme. Commercials on TV said, "Now, with amazing Aspercreme, you can get the strong relief of aspirin directly at the point of minor arthritis pain." Magazine ads said it "concentrates all the strong relief of aspirin directly at the point of pain." You would think that aspirin was the active ingredient in this product, wouldn't you? Well, it wasn't. It contained no aspirin whatever, so the name and the advertising were found to be illegal.[22] (My favorite example of a crooked name is that attached to Taiwan's best-selling cigarette—Long Life—which has 50 percent more tar than Marlboro does.[23])

B. Claims of Function or Efficacy

During the late 1960s, Firestone advertised that its "Super Sports Wide Oval" tires were

> built lower, wider. Nearly two inches wider than regular tires. To corner better, run cooler, stop 25% quicker.

When sued by the FTC, Firestone presented evidence that cars with these tires traveling 15 miles per hour *did* stop 25 percent more quickly than those with ordinary width tires. However, the tests were done on surfaces of very low friction that were equivalent in slickness to glare ice or waxed linoleum. Thus "Wide Ovals" might enable some poor soul who crashes through the end of his garage to stop short of the kitchen refrigerator, but slippery surfaces and slow speeds are obviously not typical of United States highway conditions. Hence, the FTC decided that Firestone's ads were deceptive.[24]

Deceptive claims of efficacy or function may even run afoul of the law when they are less explicit—when, that is, they enter the realm of innuendo and suggestion. A good example concerns Vivarin, a simple but costly tablet containing caffine and sugar in amounts roughly equivalent to those in half a cup of sweetened coffee. The offending ad, which ran in 1971, had a middle-aged woman speaking as if she had discovered a sure-fire aphrodisiac:

> One day it dawned on me that I was boring my husband to death. It wasn't that I didn't love Jim, but often by the time he came home at night I was feeling dull, tired and drowsy. [Then I began takin Vivarin.] All of a sudden Jim was coming home to a more exciting woman, me. We talked to each other a lot more. . . . And after dinner I was wide-awake enough to do a little more than just look at television. And the other day—it wasn't even my birthday—Jim sent me flowers with a note. The note began: "To my new wife. . . ."[25]

More recently, in 1990, Mobil Corporation was challenged by state authorities for claiming that its Hefty brand of plastic trash bags were degradable after burial in landfills. The implication was that environmentally conscientious consumers should prefer Hefty over other brands. However, the bags did not degrade rapidly enough to extend the life of municipal landfills or to make much of a positive contribution to the environment, so Mobil withdrew the claim under pressure.[26]

C. Endorsements

Mention of endorsements brings to mind athletes such as Joe Montana, Chris Evert, Jack Nicklaus, and Michael Jordan. These are certainly important people in advertising, and the FTC has several rules of thumb governing star testimonials. Thus, for example, an endorser must be a bona fide user of the product unless such would be clearly inappropriate (as was true when Joe Namath peddled pantyhose). Moreover, the commission urges that *ex*-users not be represented as current users, although this is obviously difficult to enforce.

Celebrity endorsements are not the only kind, or even the most important kind of endorsement.

There are "lay" endorsements, "expert" endorsements, "institutional" endorsements, "cartoon character" endorsements, and more, all of which have at one time or another reached the FTC's attention. The flavor of the commission's thinking in these and related matters may be tasted by quoting Section 255.3, Example 5, from the FTC's "Guides Concerning Use of Endorsements and Testimonials in Advertising":

> An association of professional athletes states in an advertisement that it has "selected" a particular brand of beverage as its "official breakfast drink." [The] association would be regarded as expert in the field of nutrition for purposes of this section, because consumers would expect it to rely upon the selection of nutritious foods as part of its business needs. Consequently, the association's endorsement must be based upon an expert evaluation of the nutritional value of the endorsed beverage [rather than upon the endorsement fee]. Furthermore, . . . use of the words "selected" and "official" in this endorsement imply that it was given only after direct comparisons had been performed among competing brands. Hence, the advertisement would be deceptive unless the association had in fact performed such comparisons . . . and the results . . . conform to the net impression created by the advertisement.[27]

D. Mock-ups

When filming TV commercials, technicians often substitute whipped potatoes for ice cream and wine for coffee. The real thing melts under the hot lights, or fades, or looks murky on TV screens. Such artificial alterations and substitutions for purposes of picture enhancement are called **mock-ups.** Although mock-ups are obviously innocuous (indeed, they may often reduce deception rather than produce it), advertisers have not confined their "doctoring" to innocent, nondeceptive, and prudent dimensions:

■ When Libby-Owens-Ford Glass Company wanted to demonstrate the superiority of its automobile safety glass, it smeared a competing brand with streaks of vaseline to create distortion, then photographed it at oblique camera angles to enhance the effect. The distortionless marvels of the company's own glass were "shown" by taking photographs with the windows rolled down.[28]

■ Volvo used TV ads in 1990 to depict its car, placed in a row with rival makes, being run over, topside, by a giant "monster" truck with huge tires. The Volvo's roof did not collapse as did the others, but the Volvo's roof was reinforced with lumber and steel that TV viewers could not see. Moreover, the other cars' roof-support pillars were cut to aid their collapse.[29]

In 1965, the Supreme Court voiced its opinion of such behavior in *Colgate-Palmolive Co.* v. *FTC.*[30] The TV commercial in question purported to show that Colgate's Rapid Shave shaving cream was potent enough to allow one to shave sandpaper with an ordinary blade razor. The ad's action and words went together: "apply . . . soak . . . and off in a stroke." But it was a hoax. What appeared to be sandpaper was actually loose grains of sand sprinkled on Plexiglas. And the soak was a two-second pause. Curious consumers who tried real sandpaper informed the FTC that it couldn't be done. So the commission asked Colgate to come clean. In its defense, Colgate claimed that you *could* shave sandpaper with very small grains of sand if it had been soaked for over an hour. It said the mock-up was necessary because sandpaper of such fine grain looked like plain paper on TV and the true soak could not be captured in a few seconds. Indeed, Colgate felt so adamant about defending its ad that it fought the FTC all the way to the Supreme Court. The key questions addressed by the Court were as follows:

1. Were undisclosed mock-ups of *mere appearance* acceptable? That is, could whipped potatoes stand in for ice cream? The court said yes.

2. Were undisclosed mock-ups demonstrating *un*true performance acceptable? That is, could Rapid Shave be "shown" shaving the ribs off a washboard? The court said no, clearly not.

3. Were undisclosed mock-ups demonstrating *true* performance acceptable? That is, assuming Rapid Shave *could* easily shave any sandpaper, was an undisclosed mock-up of this acceptable? The court again said no. When the appearance is *central* to the commercial and the clear implication is that we are seeing something real when in fact we are not, then the mock-up is illegal unless it is disclosed by saying "simulated" or something similar. Of course, if the real performance is possible and a real performance is shown, there is no problem.[31]

Absolute truth is thus not required. Inconsequential mock-ups for appearance's sake are permitted without an admission of fakery to the audience. Simulations are also allowed with disclosure. But mock-ups that materially deceive cannot be defended. Now, given your newly acquired knowledge of the law, let's test it. How would you react if you were an FTC Commissioner and you caught Campbell's Soup Company putting marbles in the bottom of its televised bowls of soup, thereby making the vegetables and other solid parts of the soup appear attractively and abundantly above the surface? Is this mere appearance? Or is it a material deception? (Your test is not a mock-up test. The case actually came up in 1970. For the FTC's answer see Note 31 at the end of the chapter.[32])

III. Federal Trade Commission Procedures

When attacking problems of deception (or other problems within its jurisdiction), the FTC may proceed in one of three ways: (1) complaint plus prosecution, (2) guides, or (3) trade regulation rules.[33]

A. Complaint Plus Prosecution

Complaint plus prosecution is a case-by-case approach in the sense that a particular ad or ad campaign is assailed. The complete chain of formal process is as follows: The advertiser is issued a complaint; his case is tried before an administrative law judge; the judge renders an initial decision; the initial decision is reviewed by the full FTC; the commission's decision may then be appealed by the respondent to federal courts of appeal on questions of law, perhaps even ending up (like the *Colgate-Palmolive* case) in the lap of the Supreme Court. This procedure may be cut short at the outset by consent settlement, in which instance a remedy is reached without formal trial. The consent decree binds the advertiser to the provisions of the decree.

B. Guides

Whereas such case-by-case proceedings are ad hoc, piecemeal, and particular, industry guides and trade regulation rules are broader, more general, and less judicial. Their more sweeping scope often improves the efficiency and efficacy of enforcement. Industry guides are distillations of case law, usually promulgated without formal hearings. They are issued to summarize and clarify case law for the benefit of the individuals regulated. These guides are nonbinding; they do not directly affect case-by-case procedure.

In short, industry guides are merely an expression of the FTC's view as to what is and what is not legal. There are guides for advertising fallout shelters, advertising shell homes, advertising fuel economy for new autos, advertising guarantees, and many others. We quoted one of them earlier: "Guides Concerning Use of Endorsements and Testimonials in Advertising."

Since the Reagan Administration's deregulation, the most noteworthy guides have been developed by the National Association of Attorneys General for state-level enforcement. Under their airline guidelines, for instance, airlines are supposed to point out when an advertised low fare applies to only one airport in a city. Moreover, any surcharges must be included in advertised prices, and restrictions on flight times and the like have to be prominently disclosed.[34]

C. Trade Regulation Rules

Trade rules are, in contrast to guides, much more serious. Like legislation, they embody the full force of law. Respondents may be prosecuted for violating the rule itself, rather than for violating the vague prohibitions of Section 5. Rules ease the burden of proof borne by the FTC's prosecuting attorneys because once a transgression is detected the respondent's only defense is to prove that the rule does not apply to his case. Because trade regulation rules carry so much force, the FTC formulates them by following an elaborate set of procedures:

> Rule-making proceedings consist of two parts—a preliminary private study conducted by the Commission and the final formulation of the rule with public participation. At the first stage, the Commission gathers through investigation, studies, and discussion information sufficient to support the rule, and then formulates a tentative version of the rule. Upon completion of these preliminary steps, a hearing is initiated: the procedures provide for notice of the proposed rule-making to be published in the Federal Register and for opportunity to be given to interested parties to participate in the hearing through submission of written data or views or oral argument. After due consideration has been given to all relevant matters of fact, law, policy and discretion . . . a rule or order is adopted by the Commission and published in the Federal Register.[35]

Since these rule-making procedures were first established in 1962, more than twenty rules have been enacted. Rules now govern door-to-door sales, grocery store stocking of sale merchandise, gasoline octane disclosure, mailorder merchandise, and warranty disclosure.[36]

The Magnuson-Moss Federal Trade Commission Improvement Act of 1975 greatly strengthened the FTC's authority to issue trade regulation rules. The FTC's efforts prior to 1975 were challenged by litigation, but Section 202 of the Act of 1975 gave the FTC express authority to devise rules defining specific acts or practices as unfair or deceptive. The first rule issued under the Act was the "Eyeglass Rule" of 1978, which among other things prohibits restraints on the advertising of optometrists. Such restraints (many imposed by state regulation) were found to *increase* the price of eyeglasses to consumers.[37]

On the other hand, the Federal Trade Commission Improvements Act of 1980 *weakened* FTC authority. And President Reagan's FTC, preferring a case-by-case approach, was very reluctant to use its rule-making authority and was eager to rescind old trade regulation rules.

IV. Remedies

The product of these and other procedures is a variety of remedies designed to quash current violations, discourage future violations, and, in rare instances, erase the ill effects of past violations. The remedies include cease and desist orders, affirmative disclosure, corrective advertising, advertising substantiation, and restitution.

A. Cease and Desist Orders

The traditional and in most instances the *only* remedy applied is an order to cease and desist. This order simply prohibits the offender from engaging further in practices that have been found unlawful or in closely similar practices. Thus, Firestone was ordered to stop advertising that its tires could stop 25 percent more quickly, and Colgate was ordered to cease "shaving" sand off Plexiglas amidst ballyhoo about sandpaper. By themselves, such orders are little more than slaps on the wrist. No penalties are levied. Penalties may be imposed only if the errant behavior persists *after* the order is issued. (Under the FTC Improvement Act of 1975, the commission may ask a federal court to impose civil penalties of up to $10,000 per day of violation against those who breach its cease and desist orders.) Because penalties do not apply to original violations, however, it is often argued that advertisers are not significantly deterred from dealing in deception.

In support of the argument, it has been estimated that *one-third* of the members of the Pharmaceutical Manufacturers Association have at one time or another engaged in illegally deceptive advertising. Moreover, recidivism is common. Once one deceptive campaign is stopped, another with different deceptions may be launched. Firestone's 25 percent quicker claim, for instance, was Firestone's third violation in fifteen years. These considerations illuminate a major advantage of relying more on the other, harsher remedies.

B. Affirmative Disclosure

The remedy of affirmative disclosure is especially appropriate for two particular kinds of deception—misrepresentation by silence and exaggerated claims of brand uniqueness. To check the problem of deceptive silence, an affirmative disclosure order prohibits the advertiser from making certain claims unless he discloses at the same time facts that are considered necessary to negate any deceptive inferences otherwise induced by silence. Perhaps the most familiar example of affirmative disclosure is the FTC's requirement that cigarette advertisers disclose the dangers inherent in smoking: "Warning: The Surgeon General Has Determined That Cigarette Smoking Is Dangerous to Your Health."

C. Corrective Advertising[39]

Whereas cease and desist orders may prevent the *continuance* of misleading claims into the future,

the purpose of corrective advertising is to wipe out any *lingering ill effects of* deception. What do we mean by lingering ill effects? There are several possibilities. From a purely economic point of view, deceptive advertising continues to generate sales even after it has stopped because of the "lagged effect" of advertising. As long as the ill-gotten gains in sales continue, the deception returns a profit and the deceiver's more truthful competitors suffer a disadvantage. Moreover, deceptive claims may be dangerous to consumer welfare when issues of health and safety are involved. If some folks continue to believe their tires stop 25 percent quicker, even after this claim is taken out of circulation, there is a problem of lingering ill effect. Accordingly, the typical corrective advertising order has had two parts:

1. Cease and desist making the deceptive claim.
2. Cease and desist *all* advertising of the product in question unless a specified portion of that advertising contains, for a specified period, a statement of the fact that prior claims were deceptive.

Until 1977, the legal status of corrective advertising was shaky. Appellate courts did not pass on its legality until the *Listerine* litigation. Listerine, which has been the nation's largest selling mouthwash (with about 40 percent of the market), was for decades promoted as a cold preventative as well. From 1938 to late 1972, Listerine labels declared that the stuff "KILLS GERMS BY MILLIONS ON CONTACT . . . For General Oral Hygiene, Bad Breath, Colds and resultant Sore Throats." Moreover, countless TV commercials showed mothers extolling the medicinal virtues of gargling with Listerine twice a day. "I think," they would crow, "we've cut down on colds, and those we do catch don't seem to last as long."

Although the makers of Listerine denied that their ads ever suggested that Listerine would prevent colds, millions of folks got that message.

The company's own polls showed that nearly two out of every three shoppers thought Listerine was a help for colds. Medical experts testifying at the FTC trial thought otherwise. Except for some temporary relief from sore throat irritation that could more easily be achieved by gargling with warm salt water, Listerine was, in the experts' eyes, worthless. Believing the experts and taking into account the prevalence of this deception, a unanimous commission ordered the company to include the following statement in a portion of its future ads: "Contrary to prior advertising, Listerine will not help prevent colds or sore throats or lessen their severity."

The *Listerine* case remains the high-water mark for this remedy. To my knowledge President Reagan's appointees to the FTC never imposed corrective advertising on any violator.

D. Advertising Substantiation[40]

In 1971 the FTC announced that from time to time it would thereafter drop a net into selected industries in hope of fishing out schools of deceptions. The net? . . . a requirement that advertisers in the target industries *substantiate* their current claims by submitting to the FTC, on demand, such tests, studies or other data concerning their advertising promises as they had in their possession *before* their claims were made.

The first substantiation orders were lowered on manufacturers of automobiles, air conditioners, electric shavers, and television sets. The resulting wave of submissions covered 282 claims made by 32 firms. FTC analysis of these 282 revealed some good news and some bad news. First, the good news: A majority of the claims were adequately substantiated. Next the bad news: "Serious questions" arose with respect to substantiation in about 30 percent of the responses. To quote some examples from the FTC Staff Report:

Automobiles: General Motors' advertising announced "101 advantages" designed to keep Chevrolet Chevelle from "becoming old before its time." As documentation for the claim General Motors listed such advantages as "full line of models," "Body by Fisher," and such safety items, already required by law, as "two front head restraints" and "back up light." . . .

Air Conditioners: Fedders, ordered to document its claim that its model ACL20E3DA alone had "extra cooling power," admitted that the claim was incorrect and stated that the claim would not be made in future advertising.[41]

Abetted by such discoveries as these, the program led to numerous formal complaints of violation. And in this light, ad substantiation might not strictly speaking be considered a remedy at all, for these formal proceedings resulted in the same kind of remedies as already mentioned—that is, cease and desist orders, corrective ads, and disclosures. Moreover, in 1984, Reagan's FTC relaxed the ad substantiation program considerably. Industry-wide rounds of requests were abandoned. Selection of claims to be challenged was based on the routine monitoring generally used for deception. Moreover, less demanding evidence sufficed for substantiation.

A recent empirical study of the impact of ad substantiation assessed the contents of magazine advertisements for four products—antiperspirants, pet foods, skin lotion, and prepared foods—in three separate years, one each for preregulation (1970), during regulation (1976), and subsequent Reagan relaxation (1984). Ad substantiation had a good impact when it was enforced. The number of factual claims made in advertisements fell during regulation (as would be expected), but the quality of the claims improved, being more inherently verifiable than before (e.g., Pepsi Cola now comes in a two-liter plastic bottle). After the Reagan relaxation, the advertising reverted to its old form, becoming "less and less informative and less reliable in substance and content."[42]

Despite the deregulation, the commission clings to the principle that advertisers are expected to have a "reasonable basis" for their claims *before* placing them in the media. Substantiation thus lives on in a limited way. And this could be considered a preventive remedy.

E. Restitution

The FTC Improvement Act of 1975 empowered the FTC to seek equitable relief for consumers through (1) recision or reformulation of contracts, (2) refund of money, or (3) payment of compensatory damages. If effectively used, such measures of restitution can reduce the economic incentive for behaving badly because they can extract the ill-gotten gains from offenders. They obviously can also help to make victims whole. Thus, for example, some of the FTC's largest awards of restitution to date have involved misrepresentation and fraud in land sales, one case yielding $8 million in refunds to more than 7,600 people who bought lots in Colorado.

Several limitations apply to restitution. For one, there is a three-year statute of limitations. For another, punitive damages are not allowed. Beyond these statutory limitations, there are some practical constraints that make this remedy most applicable to especially fraudulent and corrupt business practices.

Having reviewed remedies, you can now see that, with rare exceptions, such as those for corrective advertising and restitution, these remedies are innocuous. Advertisers dealing in deception suffer no penalties. Typically, they are simply told to cease and desist. Furthermore, by the time the FTC gets after them, they frequently want to change their ad campaigns anyway. This may sound too lenient, but it should be kept in mind that, at least in the past, proof of violation was fairly easy. Capacity or tendency plus substantial number and materiality could be considered pieces of cake for most prosecuting attorneys. Hence, although even the harshest of these remedies may seem light, it can be argued that none should be heavier if the burden of proof of misdeeds is also light. What is interesting is

that President Reagan's FTC adopted a heavier burden of proof ("likelihood," etc.) while simultaneously lightening up on the remedies.

V. Miscellaneous Unfair Practices

A. Consumer Protection

The FTC's enforcement of Section 5 extends considerably beyond advertising and deception. Misleading claims may be dispersed toe-to-toe just as easily as over the airwaves or on the printed page. Furthermore, our emphasis on deception should not obscure the fact that many practices are banned for being unfair, even if not deceptive. In the abstract, the FTC has said that "unfair" cannot be narrowly defined, that a number of factors would influence its judgment—such as, whether the questioned act or practice is immoral, unethical, oppressive, unscrupulous, or financially injurious to buyers. In the concrete, the FTC frowns on the following:

1. *Bait and switch,* in which the seller lures the buyer into the store with some kind of bait, like a sale price for a cheap model, then switches the buyer to something else.
2. *Merchandise substitution,* like the sale of 1990 model trucks as 1991 model trucks.
3. *High-pressure,* door-to-door sales without a three-day cooling-off period for buyer cancellation.
4. *Silent warranties,* that exist when a manufacturer follows a secret policy of extending warranties to some but not all customers.

The last of these arose when in the late 1970s the FTC accused auto makers of waging so-called secret warranty campaigns as a means of paying for repairs to troublesome cars on an individual basis (for individuals who were troublesome in their complaints), without formally notifying the general public. Ford's alleged campaign was especially massive, involving more than 6 million Ford cars and trucks produced between 1974 and 1978 that were susceptible to premature engine wear and cracked blocks. Under a consent order in 1980, Ford agreed to: (1) notify affected car owners by mail whenever it offers extended warranty coverage; (2) offer customers technical service bulletins describing in plain English the existence of any engine or transmission problems that could cost over $125 to repair; and (3) set up a toll-free 800 telephone number for owners to use in requesting service bulletins. The FTC action to end Ford's secrecy prior to this order reportedly saved consumers more than $30 million in repairs.[43]

Other FTC efforts to eradicate unfairnesses sparked stormy protests from the affected industries during the late 1970s. A proposed trade regulation rule to restrict advertising aimed at young children, particularly TV advertising of sugared cereals and candy, provoked shrill opposition from cereal and candy manufacturers, TV networks, grocers, and others in the business community. They derided the FTC for brazenly becoming a "National Nanny." They maintained that, as easy as it might be to sell candy to a baby (or, more accurately, to the baby's parents through the baby's prompted appeals), it was not unfair.

Equally controversial was a proposed rule regulating funeral parlors. After lengthy and costly study, the FTC's staff accumulated substantial evidence that funeral homes frequently if not regularly took financial advantage of bereaved survivors. They apparently did this by (1) refusing to provide adequate price information, (2) embalming without permission, (3) needlessly requiring a casket for cremation, (4) harrassing discount funeral homes, (5) misrepresenting local health requirements, (6) refusing to display inexpensive caskets, (7) disparaging customers who showed a concern for funeral costs (which average over $2,000), and by other means.[44]

Waging an intense lobbying campaign against the FTC, the commission's business foes succeeded in securing congressional passage of the Federal Trade Commission Improvements Act of 1980. The Senate version of this bill would have terminated the FTC's investigation of children's advertising, and the House bill would have killed the funeral proceedings. The final version did not go this far, but some shackles were imposed.

For example, the final bill trimmed the scope of any FTC rule regulating funeral home practices. The FTC's revised funeral industry merely:

- Requires the availability of price lists, including price quotations over the telephone.
- Prohibits funeral directors from saying that a deceased person must be embalmed (unless local law requires embalming).
- Prohibits claims that a casket is required for cremation.

This legislation of 1980 and the commission's new conservative complexion have resulted in retrenchment. The irony of this turn of events is that just a few years before the FTC Improvements Act of 1980 the FTC was being lambasted with criticism that it was *not* doing enough for consumer protection. Indeed, it was this criticism that eventually resulted in the proconsumerist FTC Improvements Act of 1975.

B. Businessperson Protection

While hostility was curbing FTC trade regulation rules protecting *consumers,* an important new rule protecting *business* people had clear sailing. This was the rule on "Disclosure Requirements and Prohibitions Concerning Franchising," which became effective in late 1979. The feverish growth of franchising during the 1960s and 1970s, especially in such fields as fast food, real estate, motels, hotels, hair salons, and rental services, resulted in total franchise sales of about $338 billion in 1980 from approximately 488,000 franchise establishments.[45] It also resulted in much fraud and misrepresentation by businessmen against other businessmen because many franchisors bilked franchisees.

Under the franchise system, one party (the franchisor) grants another party (the franchisee) the right to distribute or sell certain branded goods or services. In turn, the franchisee pays the franchisor for this privilege and agrees to operate the business according to the marketing plan of the franchisor. Duping prospective franchisees became commonplace during the 1960s and 1970s, prompting the attorney general of New York to complain that "franchising literally abounds with deceptive selling practices." These practices include franchisors'

> (1) misleading prospective franchisees about the potential profitability of their franchises, (2) refusing to show actual profit and loss statements to potential franchisees, (3) having "hidden charges" in the prices franchisees are charged for services and supplies, (4) using a celebrity's name to deceptively promote the franchise, (5) overpromising on their aids to franchisees, and (6) using high pressure tactics in closing the sale of a franchise.[46]

The FTC's trade regulation rule was patterned after sixteen state laws in existence at the time. It calls for the *disclosure* of such information as the business experience of the franchisor; the financial health of the franchisor; the total funds that must be paid to the franchisor; the recurring obligations of the franchisee; the rights of franchisees in contract terminations, cancellations, and renewals; and the restrictions franchisees face in purchasing supplies, selecting locations, and selling their goods and services. In addition, the rule *prohibits* the franchisor from making claims of potential earnings such as "make $50,000 profit" or "earn $70,000 per year" *unless* those claims are backed up by material facts sufficient to substantiate their accuracy, facts that are relevant to the prospective franchisee's business. Such supporting material must be disclosed to prospective franchisees before they commit themselves.[47]

Although the FTC's rule is perhaps too new to assess, study of the antecedent state laws sug-gests substantial improvement. Noting that Wisconsin's law reduced the apparent incidence of exaggerated prospective earnings from 37 to 15 percent, and noting other examples of heightened honesty in Wisconsin, S. D. Hunt and J. R. Nevin concluded, "The overall benefits of the full disclosure laws seem to outweigh their costs." On the other hand, a 1985 estimate by *Investor Alert* indicated that tens of thousands of individuals were bilked out of about $500 million annually in franchise and business opportunity frauds. Thus, the FTC can do only so much. According to a recent FTC survey of franchisees, 95 percent of them remembered getting the disclosure documents required by the trade regulation rule, but only 69 percent could remember taking the time to study them.[49] (Sometimes, doing one's homework pays.)

Summary

An opinion survey of 1,300 businesspersons who subscribed to the *Harvard Business Review* during the late 1980s yielded some interesting results. A substantial majority disagreed with the statement that in general, "advertisements present a true picture of the product advertised." This attitude helps to explain why approximately 90 percent of these businesspersons agreed that advertisers "should be forced to substantiate their claims."[50] If middle and top management executives feel this way, what are the rest of us to think about the need for policy in this area?

Section 5 of the Federal Trade Commission Act (as amended by the Wheeler-Lea Act of 1938) bans "Unfair methods of competition in commerce, and unfair or deceptive acts or practices in commerce . . ." The word *deceptive* is tricky. Truth and falsity are relevant but not conclusive, for true claims may deceive and false claims may not. Overall impressions in the buyer's mind count more than the literal meaning of claims.

Beyond this common thread, two standards of deception now prevail—an old standard used by the FTC, the courts, and state authorities for over forty-five years, and a new standard used in FTC enforcement since 1983. Under the old standard, practices are illegal if they (1) have the *capacity or tendency* to deceive (2) a *substantial number* of consumers (3) in a *material* way. The FTC's new standard bans practices that are (1) *likely* to mislead (2) consumers *acting reasonably* (3) to their *detriment or injury*. The old standard is more stringent because it protects the ignorant, the hasty, and the trusting as well as those acting reasonably.

Of the many specific types of deception that have collided with the old standard and might run afoul of the new, four were presented—those concerning (1) claims of composition, (2) claims of function or efficacy, (3) endorsements, and (4) mock-ups. A never-ending chain of cases under Section 5 has, over the years, outlined certain standards or rules in each of these areas. With respect to mock-ups, for instance, the Colgate Rapid Shave case is a particularly important link in the law. The Supreme Court reaffirmed what advertisers already believed—that undisclosed mock-ups of mere appearance were acceptable, and that undisclosed mock-ups demonstrating untrue performance were unacceptable. The court broke new ground by also ruling that undisclosed mock-ups demonstrating true performance were unacceptable insofar as the demonstration was central to the commercial. Ever since, the word *simulated* has appeared frequently on TV.

The FTC relies on three main procedures and four principal remedies to enforce the act. The procedures are (1) complaint plus prosecution, or consent decree, (2) advisory guides, and (3) compulsory trade regulation rules. The first is a case-by-case approach. The latter two are broader in scope, reaching entire industries or complete categories of deceptive acts.

The principal remedies are (1) cease and desist orders, (2) affirmative disclosure, (3) correc-tive advertising, (4) advertising substantiation, and (5) restitution. The first is the traditional mainstay. The other four are recent innovations that may be considered a little more stringent.

Finally, the FTC's zealous efforts to curb unfairness during the late 1970s sparked angry charges from industry that the FTC was being overbearingly unfair to business. The agency's staff was developing some of the most far-reaching proposals on record just at the time deregulation generally was coming into vogue. The result was the FTC Improvements Act of 1980 and, with the election of President Reagan, a decidedly more conservative group of commissioners. In addition to adopting a new standard of deception, this FTC (1) forsook trade regulation rules in favor of a case-by-case procedural approach, (2) dropped the corrective advertising remedy, and (3) weakened the ad substantiation program while still holding to the view that advertisers must have a reasonable basis for their claims before using them.

At the present time, it is uncertain how far President Bush's appointees to the FTC will go to restore the commission's old vigor and philosophy. Events hint of some restoration, but the commission has not yet explicitly renounced the new standard. In any case, state attorneys general, acting almost unanimously, have stepped in to fill the gap left by a reluctant FTC. They have launched many challenges to deception under their "Little FTC Acts," and they have formulated guides of proper conduct to coordinate their enforcement activities nationwide in industries with special problems, like the airline industry.

Questions and Exercises for Chapter 13

1. Distinguish between the policies of this chapter and those of the previous chapter in (a) purpose, (b) approach, and (c) nature of remedies.
2. The line between that which is legal and illegal is

drawn between that which is true and false. True or false? Explain.

3. Compare and contrast the old and the new standards of deception in (a) capacity or tendency versus likelihood and (b) substantial number versus reasonable consumers.

4. All claims that would cause injury would be material, but a claim could be material without causing injury. Explain.

5. How might deception occur in claims of efficacy? In endorsements?

6. Explain *Colgate–Palmolive* v. *FTC* in (a) facts, (b) issues, and (c) decision.

7. What is the main remedy in deceptive advertising cases? Why might this be an appropriate remedy if the standard of illegality is strict?

8. Compare and contrast guides and trade regulation rules in (a) purpose, (b) formulation procedure, and (c) legal clout.

9. Why might corrective advertising be an appropriate remedy? Inappropriate?

10. What is ad substantiation, and how has it changed over the years?

11. How can something be unfair but not deceptive? Illustrate with examples.

12. If some cost-benefit analysis happened to show that all the policies of this chapter were inefficient, would that mean that they should be ended? How would value judgments influence your answer? (You may refer back to Chapter 1.)

Notes

1. *San Jose Mercury News,* 1 July 1989, p. 1B.
2. *San Jose Mercury News,* 26 January 1988, p. 2A.
3. FTC enforcement policy letter October 14, 1983, reprinted in *Deception: FTC Oversight,* Hearings, U. S. Congress, House Subcommittee on Oversight and Investigations of the Committee on Energy and Commerce (March 26, 1984), pp. 184–185.
4. For an excellent brief explanation see Patricia P. Bailey and Michael Perschuk, "Analysis of the Law of Deception," reprinted in *Deception: FTC Oversight, op. cit.,* pp. 1040–1166.
5. *Montgomery Ward* v. *FTC,* 379 F. 2d 666 (7th Cir. 1967).
6. *Double Eagle Lubricants Inc.* v. *FTC,* 360 F. 2d 268 (10th Cir. 1965).
7. M. T. Brandt, and I. L. Preston, "The Federal Trade Commission's Use of Evidence to Determine Deception," *Journal of Marketing* (January 1977): 54–62.
8. Mattel, 79 FTC 667 (1971); Topper 79 FTC 681 (1971).
9. *National Bakers Services Inc.* v. *FTC,* 329 F. 2d 365 (7th Cir. 1964).
10. *Charles of the Ritz Dist. Corp.* v. *FTC,* 143 F. 2d 676 (2d Cir. 1944). See also Ira M. Millstein, "The Federal Trade Commission and False Advertising," *Columbia Law Review* (March 1964): 457–465.
11. Bailey and Perschuk, "Law of Deception," pp. 140–141.
12. *Newsweek,* August 5, 1985, p. 44.
13. Ibid.
14. *Deception: FTC Oversight, op. cit.,* p. 174.
15. See, e.g., *Deception: FTC Oversight, op. cit.;* L. D. Dahringer and D. R. Johnson, "The Federal Trade Commission Redefinition of Deception and Public Policy Implications: Let the Buyer Beware," *Journal of Consumer Affairs* (Winter 1984): 326–342. Indeed, while defending his proposed amendment, Miller himself said, "It tracks common law."
16. *Business Week,* December 2, 1985, pp. 136–140; *Washington Post National Weekly Edition,* July 1, 1985, p. 22.
17. For an argument of very little change see Gary T. Ford and John E. Calfee, "Recent Developments in FTC Policy on Deception," *Journal of Marketing* (July 1986): 82–103.
18. William J. Baer, "At the Turning Point: The Commission in 1978," *Journal of Public Policy and Marketing* (vol. 7, 1988): 19. On resources, see the article by Andrew J. Strenio, Jr., in the same journal.
19. *Wall Street Journal,* 17 April 1989, p. B6.
20. *Ibid.*
21. For more complete surveys, see E. W. Kintner, *A Primer on the Law of Deceptive Practices* (New York: Macmillan, 1971), and G. J. Alexander, *Honesty and Competition* (Syracuse, NY: Syracuse University Press, 1967).
22. *In the Matter of Ogilvy and Mather International, Inc.,* 101 F.T.C. 1 (1983). The ads also claimed Aspercreme was a "remarkable breakthrough," but its active ingredient had been in existence for nearly thirty years before the ad campaign.
23. *Forbes,* December 11, 1989, p. 92.
24. *Firestone Tire and Rubber Co.,* 81 FTC 398 (1972).
25. *Advertising of Proprietary Medicines,* Hearings, U. S. Senate, Subcommittee on Monopoly of the Select Committee on Small Business, 92nd Congress, First Session (1971), Part 1, pp. 24, 229.
26. *Wall Street Journal,* 28 June 1990, p. B4.
27. *Code of Federal Regulations,* Vol. 16, "Commercial Practices," p. 347.
28. Quoting from I. L. Preston, *The Great American Blow-Up* (Madison: University of Wisconsin Press, 1975), p. 235. The case is *Libby-Owens-Ford* v. *FTC,* 352 F 2d. 415 (6th Cir. 1965).

29. *Wall Street Journal,* 19 November 1990, p. B1.

30. *Colgate-Palmolive Co.,* v. *FTC,* 380 U. S. 374 (1965).

31. Preston, *op. cit.,* p. 238.

32. Consent settlement, *Campbell's Soup,* 77 FTC 664 (1970). The FTC thought this was deceptive. The July 11, 1985 issue of *The Wall Street Journal* gives us this update on food (p. 29):

While fewer ads are downright misleading these days, companies still fudge a lot. For example, maraschino-cherry syrup is painted on ham for appetite appeal. Some products are sprayed with glycerin to make them glisten. Cigarette smoke and humidifiers are used to simulate steam for baked goods. And plastic sometimes substitutes for ice. Director Lee Howard even vacuums individual corn flakes and applies a chemical fixative so that when they are poured from a box and collide in mid-air, little pieces don't break off.

33. Much of this and the next section is based on M. J. Trebilcock, A. Duggan, L. Robinson, H. Wilton-Siegel, and C. Massee. *A Study on Consumer Misleading and Unfair Trade Practices,* Vol. 1 (Ottawa: Information Canada, 1976). Chapter III; U. S. Congress, House, *Oversight Hearings into the Federal Trade Commission—Bureau of Consumer Protection, Hearings,* Committee on Government Operations, 94th Congress, Second Session (1976); and G. G. Udell and P. J. Fischer, "The FTC Improvement Act," *Journal of Marketing* (April 1977): 81–85.

34. *Wall Street Journal,* 14 December 1987, p. 25.

35. Trebilcock, et al., *Study on Trade Practices,* pp. 153–54.

36. Leaf through *Code of Federal Regulations,* Title 16.

37. In re FTC Trade Regulation Rule, Advertising of Ophthalmic Goods and Services, *Trade Regulation Rep.* No. 335 (June 1978). For background see Lee Benham, "The Effect of Advertising on the Price of Eyeglasses," *Journal of Law & Economics* (October 1972): 337–352.

38. R. Burack, "Introduction to the Handbook of Prescription Drugs," in *Consumerism,* ed. Aaker and Day (New York: Free Press, 1974), p. 257. The regulations referred to here are actually those of the FDA, not the FTC, but they are similar.

39. W. L. Wilkie, D. L. McNeill, and M. B. Mazis, "Marketing's 'Scarlet Letter:' The Theory and Practice of Corrective Advertising," *Journal of Marketing* (Spring 1984): 11–31.

40. This section draws on *Advertising 1972,* U.S. Senate, Committee on Commerce, 92nd Congress, Second Session (1972), pp. 336–483, and Dorothy Cohen, "The FTC's Advertising Substantiation Program," *Journal of Marketing* (Winter 1980): 26–35.

41. Reprinted in *Advertising 1972, op. cit.,* pp. 412–442. Many if not most of the questioned claims of the 1970s appear to represent "experience" qualities rather than "search" or "credence" qualities.

42. Harold H. Kassarjian, "Some Effects of Marketing and Advertising Regulation," in *Marketing and Advertising Regulation,* ed. P. E. Murphy and W. L. Wilkie (Notre Dame, IN: University of Notre Dame Press, 1990), pp. 263–277.

43. *Wall Street Journal,* 22 February 1980, p. 12.

44. *Funeral Industry Practices,* Final Staff Report to the Federal Trade Commission, June 1978. For lively accounts of the politics on these issues see Michael Pertschuk, *Revolt Against Regulation* (Berkeley: University of California Press, 1982); Susan Tolchin and Martin Tolchin, *Dismantling America: The Rush to Deregulate* (New York: Oxford University Press, 1983).

45. U.S. Department of Commerce, *Franchising in the Economy 1978–1980* (Government Printing Office, 1980), p. 1.

46. Shelby D. Hunt and John R. Nevin, "Full Disclosure Laws in Franchising: An Empirical Investigation," *Journal of Marketing* (April 1976): 54.

47. *Code of Federal Regulation,* Title 16, FTC, Part 436.

48. Hunt and Nevin, "Full Disclosure Laws," p. 62.

49. *San Jose Mercury News,* 19 January 1986, p. 1F (New York Times Wire Service).

50. Bonnie B. Reece and Stephen A. Greyser, "Executives' Attitudes toward Advertising Regulation: A Survey," in *Marketing and Advertising Regulation,* ed. P. E. Murphy and W. L. Wilkie (Notre Dame, IN: University of Notre Dame Press, 1990), pp. 255–262.

PART IV

Economic Regulation

Chapter 14

Introduction to Economic Regulation

Regulation is like growing old: we would rather not do it, but consider the alternative.
— *William G. Shepherd*

E conomic regulation is an industrial halfway house. Its residents are sheltered from all-out competition, yet they escape complete government control. Private firms own and operate enterprises, while government polices structure, conduct, and performance for purposes other than maintaining competition.

This chapter introduces Part IV by answering five questions:

   I. *What* is economic regulation?
   II. What *industries* have been so governed?
   III. *Why* has economic regulation occurred?
   IV. *Who* does the regulating?
   V. What are regulation's *basic problems?*

This chapter is thus an overview.[1]

I. What Is Economic Regulation?

Under free markets, the forces of supply and demand determine product price, product quality, firm profitability, entry, and exit. Antitrust and information policies do not greatly interfere because they operate at the periphery of markets. They remove imperfections to competition, not supplant it.

Under economic regulation, however, we find that price, product, profitability, entry, and exit are determined by *administrative processes* rather than by free-market forces. Such regulation originated centuries ago under Roman law. It then progressed in the Middle Ages to Church admonitions against charging anything other than a "just price." Growth continued in English common law, which established the notion that certain enterprises were "affected with a public interest." As Petersen wrote:

> certain occupations—such as baker, brewer, cab driver, ferryman, innkeeper, miller, smith, surgeon, and tailor—came to be viewed as closely connected with the well-being of society. Practitioners of these professions were not allowed to act solely in their self-interest, but were required to set prices and render service in a socially re-

sponsible manner. For example, an innkeeper whose establishment was far from the next resting spot was expected to refrain from exploiting his monopoly position and to keep rates at a reasonable level.[2]

This English common law tradition of obligation to serve at reasonable rates came to America with the colonists. Its problems came too—namely, the private plaintiff's heavy burden of proof and the common law's loose enforcement. Efforts to find substitute legal mechanisms eventually led to charters, franchises, and direct legislative control. These efforts had to conform to constitutional limitations on what the government could and could not do. So the evolution of regulation in the United States includes numerous opinions of the Supreme Court, chief arbiter of what is constitutional.

The most important case in this evolution was *Munn* v. *Illinois,* decided in 1877. *Munn* was the Supreme Court's first approval of the government's right to regulate private business that is "affected with a public interest."[3] The Illinois legislature had set a maximum price that Chicago warehouses could charge for grain storage. Warehouseman Munn challenged the constitutionality of this official price fixing but lost when the Supreme Court, looking to the common law for guidance, found:

> When private property is "affected with a public interest it ceases to be *juris priviti* only." . . . When, therefore, one devotes his property to the use in which the public has an interest, he, in effect, grants to the public an interest in that use and must submit to be controlled by the public for the common good to the extent of the interest he has thus created.[4]

After the legislature's maximum price law in *Munn* v. *Illinois,* the saga of economic regulation eventually branched and rebranched until it produced three broad characteristics that distinguish it from other forms of public policy toward business, three characteristics that provide the basis for the remaining portions of this section: (1) specific industry coverage, (2) the economic variables controlled, and (3) administration by commission.

Specific Industry Coverage. Unlike antitrust, which enjoys sweeping application, economic regulation singles out certain industries for attention, namely, those "affected with a public interest." This implies that some decision must be made as to what is and what is not in the public interest, a catchy phrase so vague as to include possibly everything except widget manufacturing. Electricity, natural gas, telephone service, and railroading have, along with a few other things, dominated the list of the elected. These industries display certain characteristics that tend to set them apart for this special treatment, characteristics we discuss shortly.

Economic Variables Controlled. Economic regulation entails administrative determination of one or more of the following variables:

1. Overall *price level* (or rate level) is a prime focus. Traditionally, this takes the form of *maximum* price level allowed, as suggested by *Munn,* but it also includes *minimum* price level allowed and even *specific* price setting. The basis for determining overall price level is typically producer's cost plus a "reasonable" rate of profit return, so price level regulation may also be called *profit level* regulation.

2. If regulated firms sold only one product or service to only one class of customer, then price level, once determined, would settle matters. But most firms' offerings and customers vary widely, as illustrated by the telephone company's residential versus business clientele. Accordingly, *price structure* is also regulated. That is, the price of one service relative to all others is often set, and the price of that service may further differ, depending on who is doing the buying and when.

3. Price regulation may be evaded by deliberate product deterioration, so *product quality* frequently becomes a part of economic regula-

tion. If so, regulators may judge whether service is "unjust, unsafe, improper, inadequate or insufficient," as when for instance utility commissions set standards for the voltage of electricity, the heating value of natural gas, and the accuracy of meters.

4. *Entry* is often controlled by licenses, exclusive franchises, or certificates of "convenience and necessity." Such doorkeeping was especially important in the past when transportation was more thoroughly regulated than it is now. Newcomers to common-carrier trucking and airline transport were kept off the roads and runways, lessening competition in many ways.

5. *Exit* control takes two forms. One is the obligation to serve individual paying patrons, an obligation that differs substantially from a nonregulated firm's right of refusal to sell. The second is regulatory control over abandonments, in which case the authorities may compel continued service to an entire class of customers or to a region that the firm would prefer to abandon. Exit from nonprofitable railroad service has been an especially hot issue for several decades now.

It must be stressed that economic regulation need not involve all these variables, or involve them to equal degrees. Entry into radio and TV broadcasting is tightly controlled, but pricing is not. Conversely, the field price of natural gas was tightly regulated during the 1960s and 1970s, but entry into field production was not. Of all the economic variables on the list, the one that is typically least attended to by officials is product quality. As Alfred Kahn explains:

> The reasons for this are fairly clear. Service standards are often much more difficult to specify by the promulgation of rules. Where they can be specified, they are often essentially uncontroversial. Where they cannot—and this is particularly the case when it comes to innovations, to the dynamic improvements of service—in a system in which the private companies do the managing and

government the supervision, there is no choice but to leave the initiative with the company itself.[5]

Thus, product quality tends to get short shrift in what follows as compared to price level, price structure, entry, and exit.

Administration by Commission. A final distinguishing characteristic of economic regulation relates to governmental mechanism—independent commissions dominate the scene. Indeed, it could be argued that commissions would not exist were it not for economic regulation. Reliance on city councils, state legislatures, franchise contracts, and other such mechanisms to do the job of continually manipulating and monitoring the many variables proved to be unsatisfactory as the country grew increasingly complex and dynamic. If done right, the job of economic regulation requires moderate expertise, persistent attentiveness, and considerable flexibility—qualities not usually found either in charters, which suffer the rigidities of contracts, or in legislative bodies, which suffer the distractions of other governmental duties. Thus, the job fell to commissions comprised of several members vested with fairly broad powers and subjected to judicial review.

In 1869 Massachusetts established the first state commission to regulate railroads, an innovation premised on the inability of cities to regulate the railroads effectively. In turn, the broad geographic expanse of the railroads proved to be too much for the states, so the first federal commission—the Interstate Commerce Commission—was created in 1887 to oversee the interstate activities of the railroads. Later, in 1907, electric power first came under state commission control in New York. Other states followed, but their geographic limitations again prompted an extension of federal authority with the founding of the Federal Power Commission.

Economic regulation is not strictly the preserve of commissions. Much energy regulation does not fit that mold. But as we shall see, commissions dominate.

II. What Industries Are Regulated?

A. Legal Background

After *Munn* v. *Illinois* authorized economic regulation as a constitutional government activity in 1877, the key legal question became "What industries so qualify?" The courts gave two answers—one for the period 1877–1934, another from 1934 to the present.

During the six and a half decades spanning 1877–1934, the Supreme Court took upon itself the job of sorting out those industries that could legally be regulated from those that could not. The court felt confident that it could distinguish industries "affected with a public interest" from others when statute laws were challenged. But the job became tangled in argument and opinion. No clear criteria presented themselves. Gas, electricity, water, and transport services qualified easily. Grain elevators, banks, and insurance companies likewise cleared but less assuredly. In contrast, sharply divided opinions of the Supreme Court kept food, apparel, and ice manufacturing from being regulated. You can appreciate the difficulties in such shorting by simply asking yourself: Why is insurance affected with a public interest and food is not?

Finally, in 1934, the Supreme Court quit trying to pick and choose among industrial candidates. *Nebbia* v. *New York* was the decision, and state regulation of the price of milk was the issue. A grocer named Nebbia violated the milk law but argued in his defense that the law was improper, that milk was not a business "affected with a public interest." The Supreme Court replied that it would no longer try to decide this sort of thing. It turned legislatures loose, saying that "a state is free to adopt *whatever* economic policy may reasonably be deemed public welfare." The only condition that "due process" required thereafter would be that the laws passed "have a reasonable relation to a proper legislative purpose and are neither arbitrary nor discriminatory."[6] Thus, ever since *Nebbia,* the government has been fairly free to regulate any industry it pleases.

B. The Roster of Industries

Despite this sweeping constitutional leeway, government has not run amok. The roster of the regulated, as shown in Table 14–1, is long but not endless. Indeed, several of the industries included on the list are no longer regulated at all or are in the midst of being *de*regulated—namely, trucking, airlines, railroading, crude oil, and natural gas production. Nevertheless, we discuss those with past regulation because their deregulation is either recent or incomplete and the industries are important. Moreover, many lessons are taught by the past regulatory experiences of those industries.

Although heavily regulated, banking, finance, insurance, and agriculture are not included here because of their various unique qualities.

C. Characteristics of Regulated Industries

Several characteristics of these industries set them apart from most others. First, they are usually considered **vital** industries. Food and clothing (and books) are equally vital yet unregulated, but transportation, communications, and energy are necessities not to be sneezed at.

Second, nearly all regulated industries sell **services** rather than commodities. The movement of goods from here to there is a service, as is a phone call or a kilowatt-hour of electricity. Unlike commodities, services cannot be stored. Their production and consumption coincide inseparably, like a coin's two sides. Most regulated industries must therefore maintain excess capacity to meet peak periods of consumption. In many cases they must also maintain direct connections by wire or pipe with their customers.

Third, most regulated industries are **capital intensive.** The guts of their operations are cables, turbine generators, switches, steel rails, and road

Table 14–1
Regulated or Recently Deregulated Industries in the United States, 1988

Industry	Gross National Product Amount (billions of $)	Percentage of 1988 GNP (percentage)
Electricity, gas, and sanitary services	$148.8	3.0%
Communications		
Telephone & telegraph	114.3	2.3
Radio & television broadcasting	15.0	0.3
Transportation		
Railroads	21.1	0.4
Trucking	69.6	1.4
Water	8.3	0.2
Airlines	37.1	0.8
Other	27.2	0.6
Crude oil and gas extraction	58.2	1.2
Total	$499.6	10.2%

Source: Survey of Current Business, January 1991, p. 33.

beds rather than mill hands, raw materials, or merchandise. This capital intensity can be measured by the value of assets relative to annual sales revenue. It is not unusual for assets to be 300 or 400 percent of annual sales revenue in regulated industries (airlines and trucking excepted). Three or four years of sales are then necessary to match asset value. In contrast, most asset values in manufacturing are much lower, averaging about 80 percent of annual sales receipts. Wholesale and retail trade figures are still less, at roughly 35 percent. Food stores have asset/sales ratios of merely 20 percent, so for them a single year's sales receipts cover assets five times over.

Finally, and perhaps most important, many regulated industries manifest **market failures** and **imperfections,** such as those mentioned earlier in Chapter 2. "Natural" monopoly heads the list, and others are explored subsequently.

III. Why Regulate?

There is no easy answer to the question of why regulation has come about. The industries regulated differ substantially despite their many common characteristics. The historical conditions surrounding the advent of regulation likewise differ from industry to industry. Moreover, the reasons regulation gets started for an industry need not be the same as the reasons for its continuation. As a result, scholarly opinions also differ, because each scholar approaches regulation from a different point of view (much like the proverbial blind men inspecting the elephant, one holding the tail, another an ear, and so forth).[7] In short, generalizations are hazardous.

One way to hazard our own generalizations would be to build on the discussions of Chapters 2 and 3. Chapter 2 suggests an *optimistic* or *public interest* explanation for regulation. That is, regulation may be viewed as a means of solving many of the free market's problems outlined in Table 2–2 on page 24, most notably the problems of natural monopoly (local telephone service, for example), common property resources (radio and TV broadcasting), instability (railroading), short-run protection for growth (airlines), and equity in income distribution (crude oil). To say this is an optimistic or public interest view implies the achievement of laudable, broadly based objectives. Widely held value judgments are supposedly served, even economic efficiency.

On the other hand, Chapter 3 suggests *pessimistic* or *private interest* explanations. Given that government action is often flawed by the shortcomings outlined in Table 3–4 on page 52, the public interest explanation could well be wrong. Economic regulation may originate and continue because of official ignorance, special interest effects, dynamic problems of delay and myopia, and even perhaps distributional inequity. The "capture" theory of regulation is one that is most commonly voiced along these lines. Regulatory commissions are said to be "captured" by the industries they regulate. The result is cartelization, with floors under prices and barriers against new entry, all for purposes of serving the private interest of those regulated at the expense of the public at large.[8] An even more cynical private interest theory holds that nobody but the bureaucrats who do the regulating really gain by regulation.

In truth, neither the optimist's public interest view nor the pessimist's private interest view can carry the full load of explaining economic regulation, broad though each of those views may be. Taken individually, each is too extreme to depict reality accurately. Yet each has too much validity to be discarded.

Various *blends* of these two views have therefore been offered by commentators. One blend argues that regulatory commissions go through a life cycle, the periods of which combine these explanations in varying degrees.

According to Marver Bernstein, for example, commissions (1) begin during a period of *gestation,* typified by a fervor for reform and a legislative mandate that reflects the public's needs; (2) progress into a *youthful* stage of halting policy and program development but zealous enforcement; (3) enter *maturity,* a time of lethargy and political isolation, during which "the commission finally becomes a captive of the regulated groups;" and (4) eventually end in *old age,* when the commission's primary mission becomes maintenance of the status quo for itself and its regulated industry.[9]

Another blend sees various explanations behind singular regulatory developments, such as the establishment of the Interstate Commerce Commission in 1887. Customers of the railroads supported regulation in hope of ending what they perceived as harsh price discrimination; the railroads themselves advocated regulation in hope of achieving cartelization; and so on. In this view, many diverse groups in combination sought to protect their interests through railroad regulation for many different reasons.[10]

Still other blends emphasize interindustry diversity. As Thomas McCraw has written:

> Neither "public interest" nor "capture," nor the two in combination adequately characterize the American experience with regulation over the last century. Sometimes regulation materialized with the support or even initiative of the industry involved (as with broadcasting), sometimes with the reluctant assent (as with the ICC), and sometimes against the rigid opposition (as with the Granger commissions and the SEC). Commissions often came into existence with broad popular support, sometimes amid obvious public apathy, but never in the face of mass-based, articulate opposition.[11]

The blend of explanations that seems most instructive to me centers on what may be called, for lack of a better word, "fairness."[12] Of course, the notion of fairness is slippery and ill-defined. What is fair to one group may be unfair to another.[13] What is fair in one era may be unfair in another. And attempts to achieve fairness often generate unfair side effects, as when, for example, as a result of airline regulation, those flying coach subsidized the luxury treatment of those flying first class. For all these reasons, I hesitate to use "fairness" to explain regulation's purposes, but a concept is needed that reflects diverse economic, political, and social values. And fairness, unfortunately, is it.[14]

Using fairness as our touchstone, then, Table 14–2 outlines the main purposes of regulation in terms of (A) fairness to buyers generally, (B) fairness to sellers generally, (C) fairness to certain *classes* of buyers as opposed to other buyers, (D)

Table 14–2
Outline of Answers to the Question Why Regulate?

A. FAIRNESS TO BUYERS GENERALLY
    1. *Problem:* natural monopoly
      Tools: maximum price level, exit control, product quality
      Examples: local electricity, local telephone service
    2. *Problem:* excessive "rent" or "windfall profit"
      Tools: maximum price level
      Examples: crude oil and natural gas production during the 1970s
B. FAIRNESS TO SELLERS GENERALLY
    1. *Problem:* destructive competition or instability
      Tools: minimum price level, entry control, product quality
      Examples: railroads, trucking, airlines
    2. *Problem:* common property resource, conservation
      Tools: entry and output control
      Examples: radio and TV broadcasting, crude oil 1930–1970
C. FAIRNESS AMONG DIFFERENT BUYERS
    1. *Problem:* "unfair" price discrimination
      Tools: price structure regulation
      Example: long-haul/short-haul in railroads
    2. *Problem:* need for cross-subsidy
      Tools: price structure regulation, entry and exit control
      Example: small-town air service, life-line energy rates
D. FAIRNESS AMONG DIFFERENT SELLERS
    1. *Problem:* diversified sellers versus specialized sellers (cream skimming)
      Tools: entry control, price structure regulation
      Example: AT&T versus long distance specialists
    2. *Problem:* new sellers versus old (intermodal rivalry)
      Tools: entry control, minimum prices, and price structure
      Examples: trucking versus railroads, cable TV versus broadcasting
E. FAIRNESS AS AN ADMINISTRATIVE PROCESS
    1. *Problem:* disruptive transitions
      Tools: all regulatory tools plus administrative delays
      Examples: railroad abandonments, energy shortages
    2. *Problem:* opportunities for complaints
      Tools: administrative procedures
      Examples: rate hearings

fairness to certain *classes* of sellers as opposed to others, and (E) fairness as an administrative process. The specific problems addressed— *whether real or imagined, logical or illogical*— are mentioned within each division, such as the classic problem of natural monopoly (A1) and the problem of price discrimination (C1). In addition, the regulatory tools referred to previously are distributed throughout Table 14–2 together with handy examples of the industries subjected to their use.

Before elaborating on Table 14–2, we should summarize the summary. Notice, for instance, that *maximum* price level control is the main tool of regulation aimed at fairness for buyers, whereas *minimum* price level control fosters fairness for sellers. When it comes to consideration of fairness *among* different buyers or sellers, price *structure* takes center stage because price structure reflects the rate one buyer pays as compared to that paid by another, or the rate one seller can charge as compared to what another charges. *Entry* limitations are protective of established sellers, so they are most important when the purpose of regulation is to achieve some notion of fairness for sellers, however unfair the results might be for buyers. Conversely, *exit* limitations tend to serve the interests of buyers, because sellers are then compelled to offer their services against their will. These generalities should not be lost in the thicket that follows.

A. Fairness to Buyers Generally

1. NATURAL MONOPOLY

In some situations, economic or technical conditions permit only one efficient supplier, which leads to "natural monopoly." Generally speaking, natural monopoly occurs when there is a *subadditivity of costs*. This happens when *one firm can produce the relevant output more cheaply than can two or more firms.*[15] Most commonly, this subadditivity (and therefore natural monopoly) is associated with substantial *economies of scale* relative to demand. That is, *cost per unit of output declines continuously as scale of operations increases*. This is shown in Figure 14–1, where, throughout the range of quantity demanded, long-run average and marginal costs fall for a single firm. Two firms could supply the market's requirements at high price P_2 but only at lofty unit costs. A competitive duel between two such firms could be won handily by the largest rival because greater size brings lower cost, enabling the larger firm to price below its competitor's cost. At price P_1 in Figure 14–1, a sole survivor could meet *all* market demand at a point where the unit cost curve is still falling as a function of output. There is, then, room for only one efficient enterprise, the monopoly power of which could be exploited to raise price to P_2.

Among regulated industries, costs decline as scale increases for local water, electric power, gas, telephone, and cable TV. The technology of transmission and the physical fact of direct connection are the main causes of this cost effect. Cables, pipelines, and other conduits have transmission capacities that grow *more* than proportionately to size or material makeup. As a consequence, the least expensive way to transmit electricity, gas, water, or telephone com-

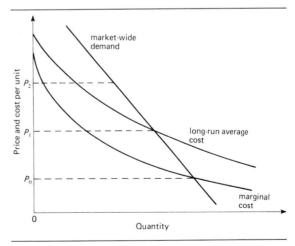

Figure 14–1
Decreasing Cost Industry

munications is typically through large lines. Furthermore, local distribution of these services requires direct connection to customers. Competition would therefore entail redundant line duplications, something obviously inefficient and wasteful—not to say damned inconvenient, ugly, and disruptive, given the excessive ditch digging, pipe laying, and wire hanging in which competition would entangle us.

The main tool of regulation in these instances is maximum price level control. Monopoly is permitted, even encouraged. But to prevent excess profits, price is held down to a level covering no more than cost plus a "fair" profit. For example, regulation of electric utilities was first initiated in New York in 1907 after it was discovered that the New York Gas and Electric Light Company sold current to residential consumers at an average price of 8.04 cents per kilowatt hour, with some paying as much as 15 cents, while the cost of production was only 3.66 cents.[17] Obligations to serve and quality surveillance accompany regulation of price level.

Viewed in terms of Figure 14–1, the objective is to hold price down to P_1, below monopoly price level P_2. Moving beyond simple fairness, efficiency could be served by a price set equal to marginal cost, as indicated by P_0. While such a single price yields insufficient revenues to cover total costs, a multipart price structure could be devised to achieve the same efficiency yet cover total costs.

2. WINDFALL PROFIT

Regulation of maximum price level has been applied outside the natural monopoly context to limit windfall profits. Figure 14–2 simplifies the issue by assuming that supply of the product is fixed at quantity Q. If demand is D_1, the free-market price would be P_1 and total revenue for sellers would be price times quantity, or area OP_1AQ. In economic jargon this revenue is called *rent* because quantity Q would be available even if price were zero. The supply of land, for instance, does not vary with price, thereby

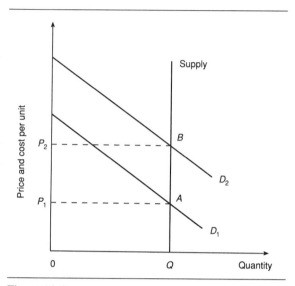

Figure 14–2
Windfall Profit Problem

providing a classic example. If demand increased to D_2, price would jump to P_2, increasing owner rental income by the added amount P_1P_2BA.

Although these rents gladden the hearts and fill the pocketbooks of sellers, those on the demand side may think the rents are unfair because they are windfalls rather than rewards for increased productive efforts. Regulation of maximum price level might seem to be the answer, and indeed this explains a major motive behind the price regulation of crude oil and natural gas production during the 1970s.

When the Organization of Petroleum Exporting Countries (OPEC) lifted the price of foreign oil by fantastic amounts in 1973 and later years, demand shifted to domestic energy sources and hiked the value of domestic oil and gas immensely. By one estimate, the capitalized value of the increased domestic rents amounted to a whopping $800 billion.[18] So the question became: Who gets this? Consumers or energy resource owners? The case for fairness to consumers held out the image of poor old folks in cold New England paying their last pennies to the rich oil and gas barons of Texas and Oklahoma. This image was convincing enough to prompt temporary price controls, which because of the shortages they caused may have been unfair to consumers denied supplies. Policy has since been modified to release price level from bondage.

B. Fairness to Sellers Generally

1. DESTRUCTIVE COMPETITION OR INSTABILITY

Certain characteristics of many regulated industries—their ponderous capital intensity and susceptibility to excess capacity in particular—expose them to dangers of "destructive" competition. At least that is what some defenders of regulation contend. Excess capacity is said to induce reckless price cutting. And heavy capital intensity translates into high fixed costs as a proportion of total cost. Once prices start to fall, they can plummet deeply before bottoming at average variable cost. The argument concludes, therefore, that such industries will be plagued by price wars financially destructive to producers and disruptive for consumers.

Notice that this argument cannot rationalize regulation in natural monopoly markets because natural monopolies, once established, face no competition. Notice, too, that the argument is designed to justify *minimum* price regulation, not *maximum* price regulation (as in the case of natural monopolies). Once a price floor is in place, entry restrictions are needed to prevent its collapse. Hence, this is an argument that has been invoked to justify minimum price and entry regulation in transportation.

Historically, sharp competition did precede the advent of transportation regulation. The railroads experienced price wars in the nineteenth century, and the railroads hoped that regulation would stem that price competition. During the Great Depression, severe competition plagued trucking and airlines, ushering in regulation of those carriers. Nevertheless, these historical circumstances were unique. Overbuilding hampered nineteenth-century railroading. And macroeco-

nomic policy now shields us from further depressions. Under normal circumstances, the argument of destructive competition has very limited application.

2. COMMON PROPERTY RESOURCE

A second rationale that fits the mold of fairness to sellers is best illustrated with reference to radio and television broadcasting. The radio spectrum used by broadcasters is a common property resource in the sense that no one really owns it and anyone could use it. But it is also a limited resource, with a limited number of bandwidths or channels. If broadcasters were granted free and unrestricted entry, they could flood the air waves, interfering with each other and garbling the reception of listeners and viewers. They could destroy a common asset. Accordingly, access to the spectrum is limited by licensing. Broadcasters, however, are not subject to price or profit control, only to entry restrictions. The arbitrary selection of licensees now in force is supposed to favor those broadcasters who best serve the public interest, but it is not clear that it actually does.

Another example of regulation based on conservation is crude oil from 1933–1973. As is explained later, oil reservoirs became common property resources under the rule of capture. State commissions therefore regulated production through well spacing and prorationing.

C. Fairness Among Different Buyers

1. "UNFAIR" PRICE DISCRIMINATION

The clamor for railroad regulation arose more from price discrimination than anything else. Indeed, the Interstate Commerce Act of 1887 made no explicit provision for the ICC to fix maximum overall rate levels. Instead, the act directed that rates approved by the commission be "just and reasonable" in structure.

As shown in Figure 9–1 on page 182 of Chapter 9, price discrimination can occur when different buyers have different elasticities of demand.

These differences typically arise in regulated industries for two main reasons—(1) big buyers often have higher elasticities than do small buyers because big buyers have opportunities for self-supply or monopsony power; (2) some buyers may be able to choose from among a number of sellers offering close substitutes, in which case these buyers' demand appears elastic to sellers, whereas other buyers have only one source of supply, something that lowers elasticity as seen by the seller. In both cases, low elasticity invites a high price; high elasticity, a low price.

In railroading, circa 1880, large shippers were able to extract lower rates than small shippers were. Moreover, some routes experienced intense competition while others were served by only one railroad. As a result, towns without rail competition were charged higher rates than those blessed with two or more railroads. Indeed, in many instances, prices on noncompetitive *short hauls* exceeded those on competitive *long hauls,* despite one's common-sense expectation that

rates should rise rather than fall with distance. This was considered unfair, not to mention potentially inefficient.

2.   NEED FOR CROSS-SUBSIDY

Just as regulation can *prevent* unfair price discrimination, it can also *impose* what some might consider "fair" price discrimination. In other words, regulators have occasionally held prices to certain buyers *up,* well above cost, so that the resulting excess profits could then be used to keep prices to other buyers *down,* well below cost.[19]

This *cross-subsidy* has usually benefited small towns at the expense of big cities because small towns tend to have "weak" demands and high unit costs whereas big cities have robust demands and low unit costs. The analogy on college campuses is the cross-subsidy from money-making sports such as football and basketball to money-losing sports such as fencing and gymnastics. Figure 14–3 illustrates this, assuming con-

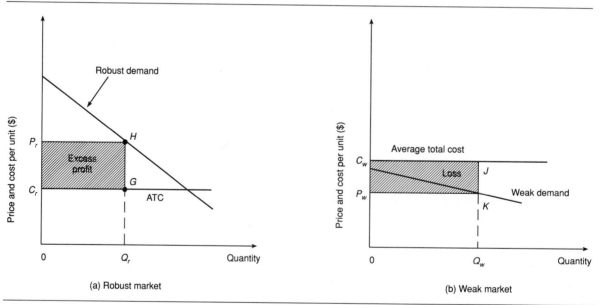

Figure 14–3
Cross-subsidy from Robust Market to Weak Market

stant costs per unit. Part (a) of the figure represents the robust market, with its strong demand and relatively low average total cost per unit (OC_r). Part (b) depicts the weak market, with its relatively feeble demand and higher cost per unit (OC_r). A regulated price of P_r in the robust market would generate excess profits, indicated by area P_rHGC_r (because total revenue would be OP_rHQ, and total cost would be OC_rGQ_r). These excess profits could then be used to cover the losses occurring in the weak market, indicated by area C_wJKP_w.

Before the Civil Aeronautics Board (CAB) was terminated in 1985, unprofitable airline service to small communities was subsidized by using profits from the heavily traveled trunkline routes between major cities. Similarly, the ICC has in the past required railroads to provide red-ink service on branch lines to country hamlets and to cover the losses using black-ink earnings on busier routes. Critics of such cross-subsidization argue that if subsidies are deemed desirable, they should not be achieved by such hidden redistributions. Rather, they should for reasons of efficiency come directly from government coffers.

D. Fairness Among Different Sellers

1. DIVERSIFIED SELLERS VS. SPECIALIZED SELLERS

When cross-subsidization is viewed from the sellers' side instead of the buyers' side, special problems arise that have been exploited to justify regulation. In particular, cross-subsidization opens opportunities for *cream skimming*. That is, the high profits on the creamy robust segments of the business (highly traveled routes, for instance) attract the entry of firms wanting to provide *only* the highly profitable service (leaving the unprofitable business to the regulated firm). In telecommunications, for example, new private-line microwave companies entered high-density long-distance service between major cit-

ies and ignored the less profitable, low-density connections between small cities. Regulated firms offering diversified services thus plead for protection from new entrants who specialize in lucrative segments, arguing that if such regulatory protection is denied, cross-subsidization will have to cease as competition eats up the excess profits that provide the subsidy. Regulated firms also plead for protection by arguing that they generate "economies of scope," that is, efficiencies from diversified as opposed to specialized service offerings.

2. NEW SELLERS VERSUS OLD SELLERS

In some cases regulation has been imposed on new industries because they competed against old industries already subject to regulation. The ICC regulation of trucking, for example, resulted when trucks became potent competitors of the railroads. The railroads lobbied strenuously for truck regulation during the 1920s and 1930s. Truckers resisted until the Great Depression changed their minds about the desirability of federal protection. Regulation followed despite the fact that, economically speaking, truck regulation makes little or no sense.

To cite another example, the advent of cable television threatened over-the-air broadcasters who were regulated by the Federal Communications Commission. Although spectrum scarcity may properly justify the regulation of over-the-air broadcasting, it cannot justify similar regulation of cable broadcasting. Nevertheless, the FCC restricted the growth of cable TV during the 1950s, 1960s, and 1970s to protect the over-the-air broadcasters.

E. Fairness As an Administrative Process

The essence of economic regulation is simply this: *Administrative procedures* replace the free market forces of demand and supply. Thus, a final possible explanation for regulation might well be this: People prefer administrative procedures to market forces, at least in some instances, *not* because they believe that administrative procedures can improve on the free market in obtaining good economic performance, but because they believe that the procedure *itself* is somehow fairer. As Bruce Owen and Ronald Braeutigam say, "It is the procedure as much as the ultimate outcome that matters. Or rather, the procedure *is* the outcome."[20]

1. TO TEMPER DISRUPTIVE TRANSITIONS

Features of economic regulation that might further procedural fairness are the delay inherent in regulation and due process for buyers. Given that peoples' lives are often built around particular configurations of utility and transportation services (where they live, size of home, type of heating, and so forth), it may well be true that they place some value on the delays that regulation entails. Rail passenger services therefore linger long after they are economically obsolete, and low-priced natural gas is made available long after its value has skyrocketed. Stated differently, the world is risky, and regulation may reduce risks by delaying disruptive changes. Changes are necessary for efficiency, though, which also delays efficient adjustments.

2. OPPORTUNITY TO VOICE COMPLAINTS

Another feature of the administrative process is that it provides a forum in which buyers and sellers can express their views. The voices of sellers may often drown out those of buyers, but regulation may nevertheless gain much public support for this procedural reason. As Donald Dewey puts it:

> [First] we expect group therapy—a release of tension and frustrations. . . . Fortunately, plenty of angry people in this world would rather testify at a public hearing—preferably before a TV camera—than blow up buildings or beat their kids.
>
> Second, we expect regulation to protect us from the kind of sharp commercial practice that is generally impossible in competitive industries. . . . The Penn Central Railroad will never

refund a nickel for a breakdown in service unless it is compelled to do so by a Utility Commission.

Third, we expect regulation to mitigate some of the consequences of the bureaucratization that comes with great size. To say the obvious, in any organization mistakes are made, and the larger the organization, the more difficult it is to pinpoint the responsibility for error. A complaint to a regulatory body is one way that the consumer has a striking back.[21]

One problem with placing value on the administrative process is that it requires administrators. The interests of those administrators may not coincide with the interests of either buyers or sellers.

IV. Who Regulates?

This brings us to the question of who does the regulating. The vast bulk of regulatory power rests with independent regulatory commissions. They are neither legislative, judicial, nor administrative. Rather, their duties run the gamut of governmental classifications. They make rules and thereby legislate; they hold hearings or adversary proceedings and thereafter adjudicate; they enforce regulatory laws and thereby administer.

A. Jurisdiction

Although commission duties are thus typically broad, their scope of jurisdiction is often narrow. One major division of jurisdiction concerns geography. State regulatory commissions govern *intra*state commerce, whereas federal agencies oversee *inter*state commerce. Product or service determines a second division. Many commissions regulate only one type of utility or a limited class of utilities. As shown in the top half of Table 14–3, which lists the main federal commissions, the Interstate Commerce Commission regulates interstate land transportation (and some waterway carriers); the Federal Energy Regulatory Commission regulates interstate transmis-

Table 14–3
The Main Federal Commissions and Selected State Commissions (Circa 1990)

Commission (and year of origin)	Number of Members	Number of Staff Members	Jurisdiction
Federal Commissions			
Interstate Commerce Commission (1887)	5	619	Railroads; some water shipping and trucking (with powers diminishing sharply)
Federal Energy Regulatory Commission (formerly the Federal Power Commission, 1934)	5	1,500	Electric power; some gas and pipelines
Federal Communications Commission (1934)	5	1,839	Telephone; television; radio; telegraph
Civil Aeronautics Board (1938–1985)	5	Now zero	Airlines (until its end in 1985)
Selected State Commissions			
California (1912)	5	1,100	Electric gas, telephone, railroads, buses, docks, water carriers, and more.
Colorado (1913)	3	98	Electric, gas, telephone, telegraph, water, buses, taxis, railroads.
Florida (1887)	5	377	Electric gas, telephone, telegraph, water, sewer, buses, trucks, railroads, and more.
Illinois (1913)	7	450	Electric, gas, telephone, water, buses, railroads, and more.
Massachusetts (1885)	3	111	Electric, gas, telephone, railroads, buses, trucks, taxis, water.
Pennsylvania (1908)	5	614	Electric, gas, telephone, telegraph, water, sewer, docks, airlines, buses, taxis, railroads, and more.

Source: National Association of Regulatory Commissioners, *1989 Annual Report on Utility and Carrier Regulation* (1990); Kenneth Chilton and Melinda Warren, *Regulation's Rebound* (St. Louis, MO: Center for the Study of American Business, Washington University, 1990).

sion and the wholesale price of electricity, and the rates and routes of natural gas pipelines; the Federal Communications Commission licenses broadcasters and regulates long-distance telephone rates and levels of service; and the now-defunct Civil Aeronautics Board had jurisdiction over all interstate air passenger service until 1985.

State commissions are less narrowly specialized. With varying scope, their main concerns are *local* gas, electric, telephone, water, and transit utilities (see the bottom half of Table 14–3). State or federal, the U. S. Supreme court summarized the commission concept when it said that these agencies were "created with the avowed purpose of lodging functions in a body specifically competent to deal with them by reason of information, experience and careful study of the business and economic conditions of the industry affected."[22]

B. Commission Structure and Personnel

Commission panels usually consist of three to seven members appointed to fixed terms by either the president (for federal posts) or the governor (for state posts, although several states elect commissioners). Appointments usually must be approved by legislative bodies, the U. S. Senate in the case of federal commissions. With but few exceptions, the commissioners so selected do not fit the ideal image of objective experts. They tend to be lawyers and businessmen whose sympathies often lie with the industry they regulate, or obscure politicians (still wet behind the ears and climbing, or washed up and on the way out).

Commissioners are aided by staffs of civil servants that are comprised mainly of accountants, engineers, lawyers, and economists. Many critics of regulation contend that commissions cannot do an adequate job because both staffers and commissioners are underpaid and overworked. The companies they regulate can afford good personnel in plenitude. Hence, control of corporate giants with this feeble machinery has been called herding elephants with flyswatters.[23]

In any event, a skeletal example of this machinery is in Figure 14–4, the organization chart for the Public Service Commission of Kentucky.

C. Procedures

Important regulatory decisions are made by quasi-judicial proceedings much like those in ordinary courts of law. Company attorneys are pitted against commission staff attorneys or outside "intervenor" attorneys. As Leonard Weiss and Allyn Strickland explain:

> Cases may be initiated by the staff and/or affected firms. The full commission may hear a case, but more commonly it is heard by a trial examiner. . . . The trial examiner is a lawyer appointed by the commission to hear evidence presented by the staff, the affected firms, and any intervenors admitted to the proceedings. . . .

> The hearing is similar to a court proceeding with prepared testimony, cross-examination of witnesses, and the usual rules of procedure. The participants complete the case by submitting briefs, which summarize their arguments, the relevant evidence, and appropriate precedents. The trial examiner then prepares a proposed decision, which he turns over to the commission. The commission reviews the case record and reaches its own decision, which may or may not be the same as the trial examiner's. Commission decisions are reached by majority vote [and] may be appealed on questions of law or procedure to the courts.[24]

This list of procedures may create the illusion that commissions are truly independent, but that is only an illusion. Many commentators argue that commissions tend to be more responsive to corporate than to consumer interests. Commission appointment and funding are controlled by politicians in the legislative and executive branches of government. In turn, these politicians are frequently beholden to the regulated firms, their trade associations, and their unions for political support of various kinds (including campaign contributions, of course).

Aside from political appointments, there is the crucial matter of information flow. According to political scientist W. T. Gormley, Jr., "If regulated industries dominate the regulatory process, it is through the control of information, not personnel." Gormley continues as follows:

> [Information] inputs—in the form of legal briefs, statistical compilations, feasibility studies, and customer surveys—come primarily from regulated industries, which spend enormous amounts of money on formal presentations in regulatory proceedings. . . . Regulated industry officials also frequently communicate informally with regulatory officials. A Common Cause study of federal regulatory commissioners' office contacts revealed that 46% of such contacts were with regulated industry representatives, while only 4% were with representatives of public interest groups or individual citizens (the remaining contacts were with members of the press, congressional officials, foreign visitors, and others).[25]

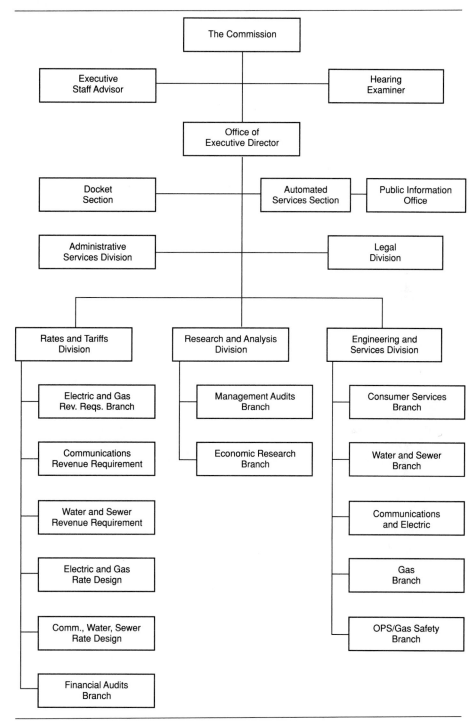

Figure 14–4
Organization Chart of the Public Service Commission of Kentucky

On the other hand, commissioners are by no means the puppets of those regulated. Public interests do get attention. The dire financial straits some public utilities currently face suggest that commissions can be less beholden to regulated firms than the foregoing characterization implies.

It is probably a symptom of the importance attached to independence that commissions occasionally recruit from academia on the assumption that professors are, on the whole, genuine experts and persons of integrity. Many such appointments have been particularly successful, notably those of Professors Alfred Kahn and Nicholas Johnson, two of regulation's brightest stars. Some commissioners serve outstandingly.

V. Basic Problems

Regulation has received much bad press of late, as suggested most dramatically by the trend toward *de*regulation in airlines, trucking, and railroads. Problems of personnel and procedures do not deserve all the blame for regulation's shortcomings. There are several basic problems of concept and execution. Although these problems can be fully appreciated only after studying the details of following chapters, this introduction to the topic would be incomplete without brief mention of the main problems.

First, many legislative mandates under which commissions work are vague or misguided because the purposes of regulation are often vague and misguided—especially those purposes concerning destructive competition and cross-subsidy.

Second, the task of regulation is inherently difficult. There is no regulatory cookbook with recipes for every occasion, no utility childcare guide. There are a few principles, plus plenty of questions lacking pat answers.

A third problem is what James McKie calls the "tar-baby" effect.[26] Each swipe regulators take at some supposed sin seems to ensnare reg-

ulators in ever deeper difficulties. The innocent and well-meaning souls who first devised regulation imagined it to be a rather simple matter. What could be easier, they must have asked, than restricting a natural monopolist's profit to some just percentage? Yet it is not so easy. Taking a punch at profit may mean a bulge in costs; striking at excess cost may hurt quality; close control of quality entails sticky details demanding nearly one bureaucrat for every hard hat; and so on. Pretty soon regulators are attempting to cover everything from plant purchases to billing frequencies, and in the process they get covered with tar.

Fourth and finally, regulation is generally a poor substitute for competition (even though it may be a lesser-of-two-evils substitute for unregulated natural monopoly). No one has expressed this sentiment better than Clair Wilcox:

> Regulation, at best, is a pallid substitute for competition. It cannot prescribe quality, force efficiency, or require innovation, because such action would invade the sphere of management. But when it leaves these matters to the discretion of industry, it denies consumers the protection that competition would afford. Regulation cannot set prices below an industry's costs however excessive they may be. Competition does so, and the high-cost company is compelled to discover means whereby its costs can be reduced. Regulation does not enlarge consumption by setting prices at the lowest level consistent with a fair return. Competition has this effect. Regulation fails to encourage performance in the public interest by offering rewards and penalties. Competition offers both.[27]

In short, free-market competition should be preferred wherever and whenever it can be secured.

Competition has grown with the trend toward deregulation. Surveying the future of regulation in the 1990s, Alfred Kahn writes that "the major issues of regulatory policy these days in the public utility area . . . [concern] how to accommodate traditional regulation to the increasing intrusion of competition."[28] Among the leading examples of that intrusion, Kahn mentions the following:

- The deregulation of certain wholesale bulk power sales, where the Federal Energy Regulatory Commission (FERC) has satisfied itself that the transactions were at arms' length and untainted by monopoly or monopsony power.
- The requirement by an increasing number of state utility commissions that local electric companies obtain their additional power requirements via competitive bids.
- The total deregulation of telephone equipment, which is now highly competitive.
- The burgeoning of private communications networks to such a point that more business phones are now linked in the first instance to their own switches than to those of the local telephone company.[29]

This is not to say that public utility regulation will soon be trashed. It remains strong for local electricity, gas, telephone, and water systems because buyers still demand protection from monopolies. According to one observer, "Nothing has changed except, perhaps, the industries classified as natural monopolies: Where the classification endures, so does public utility regulation."[30]

Summary

Under economic regulation, administrative processes rather than free-market forces of demand and supply determine price, product, profitability, entry, and exit. The seeds of this policy were sown in English common law and took root in the United States after *Munn* v. *Illinois* was decided in 1877. This case established the constitutionality of such regulation for industries "affected with a public interest."

For over sixty years after *Munn* the Supreme Court attempted to judge on a case-by-case basis which industries qualified for regulatory treatment. However, from *Nebbia* v. *New York* in 1934 to the present the court has given legislators a fairly free hand. As a result, we have an impressive list of important industries subjected to economic regulation—chief among them being electric power, natural gas, telephones, radio and TV broadcasting, railroads, and (until recently) airlines, trucks, and crude oil. Except for the last ones mentioned, these industries tend to be more capital intensive than others. Moreover, they provide vital services, often reaching consumers directly through pipes, wires, and conduits. Finally, they tend to manifest market imperfections and failures.

As outlined in Table 14–2, economic regulation is grounded on several rationales, all of which may be expressed in terms of fairness. (A) Fairness to buyers is of primary concern in dealing with natural monopoly or windfall profits (instances prompting maximum price level control). (B) Fairness to sellers is invoked to warrant treatment of two problems—destructive competition and common property resources. (C) Fairness among different buyers motivates regulation of price structure to end unfair price discrimination or to impose cross-subsidies. (D) Fairness among different sellers is the focus of regulation when diversified sellers are pitted against specialized "cream skimmers" and when new sellers vie against older regulated sellers. Entry control and price structure are the key tools for these cases. (E) Finally, regulation may be favored by some who perceive greater fairness in administrative processes than in free-market forces.

Who does the regulating? Commissions, primarily, which have been called the fourth branch of government because they combine legislative, judicial, and executive powers. The jurisdiction of state commissions tends to be broad in industry coverage but narrow in geographic coverage. The jurisdiction of federal commissions follows an opposite form, with industry coverage tending to be narrow but geographic reach extending na-

Table 14–4
Summary of Chapters on Economic Regulation

Chapter	Industry	Explanation	Major Focus of Regulation	Commission
15	Local electricity and gas	Natural monopoly	Price ceiling (profit level), and price structure	State utility commissions
16	Telecommunications	Natural monopoly, cross-subsidy	Price ceiling (profit level), price structure, entry and access	FCC and state commissions
17	Broadcast communications	Common property resource	Entry licensing	FCC
18	Transportation	Price discrimination, cross-subsidy, stability	Entry, exit, price structure, price floor	ICC, CAB
19	Crude oil and natural gas production	Stability, conservation, windfall profit	Price level (floor and ceiling)	Federal Energy Regulatory Commission and state agencies

tionwide to encompass interstate commerce. In structure, the commissions are headed by a panel of several members and supported by a staff of legal, technical, and economic civil servants. Though purportedly independent, these commissions are political creatures with political sensitivities. They respond to pressures from both consumers and companies, but the latter are often said to know the best pressure points.

Some of regulation's basic problems may be seen from this general survey. Two are most important. One is the problem of questionable rationale in many instances. The other is that competition has no really close substitute. The remaining chapters of Part IV, as outlined in Table 14–4, elucidate.

Questions and Exercises for Chapter 14

1. What characteristics of economic regulation distinguish it from antitrust policy?

2. What, legally and economically, sets regulated industries apart from other industries?

3. Why does either a purely *public interest* explanation or a purely *private interest* explanation for regulation seem inadequate?

4. Use a diagram (derived from Figure 14–1) to explain the natural monopoly problem (with inefficiency and excess profit).

5. Compare and contrast unfair price discrimination and the need for cross-subsidy as explanations for regulation.

6. Some people say oil and gas windfalls are no different from homeowner windfalls on house values, and therefore should be of no concern to public policy. Discuss, giving consideration to such factors as (a) dispersion of ownership, (b) production versus consumption, and (c) fairness, or equity.

7. What are the likely economic consequences of trying to secure fairness for sellers?

8. Compare state and federal commissions.

9. Why is it often said, as in the opening quotation from Shepherd, that regulation is unattractive and even evil (but not as bad as the alternatives)?

10. Why is competition preferable to regulation?

(Consult the first part of Chapter 5 to help your answer here.)

Notes

1. For more detailed overviews, see Alfred E. Kahn, *The Economics of Regulation* (New York: Wiley, 1970); Sanford V. Berg and John Tschirhart, *Natural Monopoly Regulation* (Cambridge, England: Cambridge University Press, 1988); K. Nowotny, D. B. Smith, and H. M. Trebing, eds., *Public Utility Regulation* (Boston: Kluwer Academic Publishers, 1989).

2. H. C. Petersen, *Business and Government* (New York: Harper & Row, 1981), p. 182.

3. *Munn v. Illinois*, 94 U. S. 113 (1877).

4. *Ibid.*

5. Kahn, *Economics of Regulation*, p. 22.

6. *Nebbia v. New York*, 291 U. S. 502 (1934).

7. For a lengthy review see Barry M. Mitnick, *The Political Economy of Regulation* (New York: Columbia University Press, 1980).

8. George J. Stigler, "The Theory of Economic Regulation" *Bell Journal of Economics* (Spring 1971): 3–26; Gabriel Kolko, *Railroads and Regulation, 1877–1916* (Princeton, NJ: Princeton University Press, 1965).

9. M. Bernstein, *Regulating Business by Independent Commission* (Princeton, NJ: Princeton University Press, 1955), pp. 74–102.

10. Mitnick, *Political Economy,* pp. 173–191. For an empirical demonstration see D. L. Kaserman, L. R. Kavanaugh, and R. C. Tepel, "To Which Fiddle Does the Regulator Dance? Some Empirical Evidence," *Review of Industrial Organization* (vol. 1, no. 4): 246–258.

11. Thomas K. McCraw, "Regulation in America," *Business History Review* (Summer 1975): 179–180.

12. For related views see Bruce Owen and Ronald Brauetigam, *The Regulation Game* (Cambridge, MA: Ballinger, 1978); Ann Friedlander and Richard de Neufville, "The Political Rationality of Federal Transportation Policy," in *Research in Law and Economics,* Vol. 1, ed. R. O. Zerbe, Jr. (Greenwich, CT: JAI Press, 1979), pp. 97–114; Donald Dewey, "Regulatory Reform," in *Regulation in Further Perspective,* ed. W. Shepherd and T. Gies (Cambridge, MA: Ballinger, 1974), pp. 27–40; Theodore E. Keeler, "Theories of Regulation and the Deregulation Movement," *Public Choice* (vol. 44, no. 1, 1984): 103–144.

13. Many examples may be found in Roger Noll and Bruce Owen, *The Political Economy of Deregulation* (Washington DC: American Enterprise Institute, 1983).

14. Crew and Kleindorfer would probably agree. They conclude that "the intellectual heritage of the legal system on economic issues, and therefore the regulatory apparatus, owes almost everything to notions of justice or fairness and almost nothing to notions of efficiency." Michael A. Crew and Paul R. Kleindorfer, *The Economics of Public Utility Regulation* (Cambridge: MA: MIT Press, 1986), pp. 27–28. See also E. E. Zajac, *Fairness or Efficiency* (Cambridge, MA: Ballinger, 1978).

15. William J. Baumol, "On the Proper Cost Tests for Natural Monopoly in a Multiproduct Industry," *American Economic Review* (vol. 67, 1977): 808–822.

16. For actual case histories see Neil W. Hamilton and Peter R. Hamilton, "Duopoly in the Distribution of Electricity," *Antitrust Bulletin* (Summer 1983): 281–309.

17. Douglas Anderson, "State Regulation of Electric Utilities," in *The Politics of Regulation,* ed. J. Q. Wilson (New York: Basic Books, 1980), p. 14.

18. Robert Stobaugh and Daniel Yergin, *Energy Future* (New York: Random House, 1979), p. 217.

19. R. A. Posner, "Taxation by Regulation," *Bell Journal of Economics* (Spring 1971): 22–50.

20. Owen and Braeutigam, *Regulation Game,* p. 26. See also M. C. O'Leary and D. B. Smith, "The Contributions of Economic Theory to the Regulatory Process," in *Public Utility Regulation,* ed. K. Nowotny, D. B. Smith, and Harry M. Trebing (Boston: Kluwer, 1989), pp. 223–238.

21. Dewey, "Regulatory Reform," pp. 35–37.

22. *Federal Trade Commission* v. *R. F. Keppel and Bros. Inc.,* 291 U. S. 304, 314 (1934).

23. B. C. Moore, Jr., "AT&T: The Phony Monopoly," in *Monopoly Makers,* ed. M. J. Green (New York: Grossman, 1973), p. 82.

24. L. Weiss and A. Strickland, *Regulation: A Case Approach* (New York: McGraw-Hill, 1976), pp. 8–9.

25. William T. Gormley, Jr., *The Politics of Public Utility Regulation* (Pittsburgh: University of Pittsburgh Press: 1983), pp. 31–32.

26. James W. McKie, "Regulation and the Free Market: The Problem of Boundaries," *Bell Journal of Economics* (Spring, 1970): 6–26.

27. Clair Wilcox, *Public Policies Toward Business* (Homewood, IL: Irwin, 1966), p. 476.

28. Alfred E. Kahn, "Deregulation: Looking Backward and Looking Forward," *Yale Journal on Regulation* (Summer 1990): 327–328.

29. *Ibid.*

30. Kenneth Nowotny, "The Economics of Public Utility Regulation: An Overview," in Nowotny, Smith, and Trebing *op. cit.,* p. 18. For another opinion that much endures see Douglas N. Jones, "Regulatory Concepts, Propositions, and Doctrines: Casualties and Survivors," *Journal of Economic Issues* (December 1988): 1089–1108.

Chapter 15

Electric and Gas Utility Regulation

A public utility commissioner today is about as popular as a baseball umpire. At best, he is taken for granted; at worse, he is an object of scorn and derision.
— *William T. Gormley, Jr.*

Public utility regulation was a dull subject when things went smoothly. During the 1940s, 1950s, and 1960s the price of electricity declined more than 50 percent relative to prices generally. Electricity output grew briskly at about 7 percent per year. Machinery hummed. Much the same could be said of natural gas.

But the 1970s and 1980s brought drastic changes. Electric and gas prices skyrocketed because of the industry's especially heavy dependence on two inputs whose costs soared—fuel and capital. Blackouts hit the eastern states. Three Mile Island threatened nuclear disaster and brought financial disaster. Utility consumers and owners everywhere organized armies of lobbyists for battle. And the turmoil has persisted.

The preceding chapter outlined the *what, why,* and *who* of electric and gas utility regulation (as well as regulation of other industries):

- *What* . . . mainly price level and price structure regulation plus, to a lesser degree, product quality, entry, and exit.
- *Why* . . . natural monopoly and price discrimination.
- *Who* . . . independent commissions—state public utilities commissions for intrastate sales, the Federal Energy Regulatory Commission for interstate sales.

After a brief description of the industry in Section I, this chapter delves into two further questions: *How* is utility price regulation actually accomplished? *How well* has it served the interests of society? Sections II and III answer the "how" question with discussions of price level and price structure regulation. You will recall that *price level* refers to *overall* revenues, costs, and returns, whereas *price structure* refers to the *specific prices* charged to specific customers for specific services at specific times. Section IV addresses the "how well" question by reviewing empirical studies of the impact of regulation and by surveying current problems. Space limitations force us to neglect other issues, such as product quality.

I. Industry Description

More than 2,700 billion kilowatt-hours (kwh) of electricity power the United States every year. Approximately 80 percent of it comes from several hundred private, investor-owned companies. The balance comes from government facilities. The federal government accounts for about 10 percent of all electricity generated in the United States (the Tennessee Valley Authority and the Bonneville Power Administration being the most famous sources of this current). State and local governments and cooperatives also account for 10 percent.

As illustrated in Figure 15–1, the typical investor-owned utility (IOU) is vertically integrated to span all three of the industry's three main stages—generation, transmission, and distribution. **Generation** comes first, mostly at large plants burning fossil fuels but also at nuclear and hydroelectric facilities. The electric power of many integrated IOUs is supplemented by several outside sources, which are shown three ways in Figure 15–1:

- PURPA qualified facilities are industrial plants or others that generate electricity in excess of their own needs. Under the Public Utility Regulatory Policy Act of 1978, investor-owned utilities must buy electricity from cogenerators who meet certain qualifying standards.
- Independent producers who are in the business of generating electricity and who are not subject to rate-of-return regulations.
- Some IOUs buy some of their power from other IOUs that have sufficient excess generating capacity to make contract commitments.

Transmission is the second stage. Most important in this regard is power transmission from the utility's remote generators to its customers in population centers. A utility's purchase of juice from other generators also entails transmission (sometimes over great distances, as when power comes from Canadian hydro facilities). When a

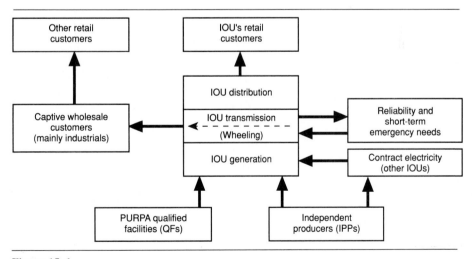

Figure 15–1
An Integrated Inverster Owned Utility (IOU) and Its Relationship With Suppliers and Buyers.

Source: Derived from Paul L. Jaskow, "Regulatory Failure, Regulatory Reform, and Structural Change in the Electric Power Industry," *Brookings Papers on Economic Activity: Microeconomics 1989* (1989), p. 146.

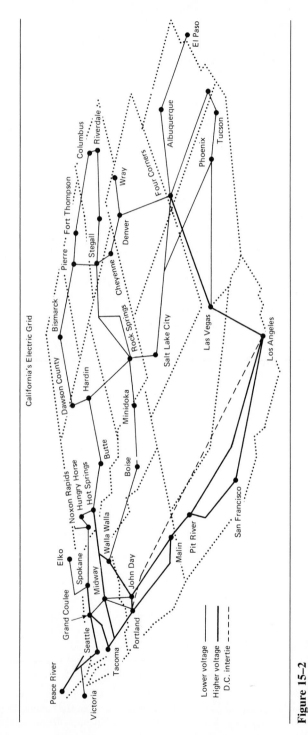

California's Electric Grid

Peace River
Victoria
Elko
Grand Coulee
Spokane
Seattle
Midway
Tacoma
John Day
Portland
Noxon Rapids
Hungry Horse
Hot Springs
Walla Walla
Butte
Boise
Minidoka
Malin
Pit River
San Francisco
Bismarck
Dawson County
Hardin
Pierre
Fort Thompson
Stegall
Columbus
Riverdale
Wray
Denver
Cheyenne
Rock Springs
Salt Lake City
Las Vegas
Los Angeles
Four Corners
Albuquerque
Phoenix
Tucson
El Paso

Lower voltage ————
Higher voltage ▬▬▬▬
D.C. intertie ‒ ‒ ‒ ‒

Figure 15–2
California's Electric Grid

utility's transmission lines are used by independent buyers and sellers, the utility is acting as an intermediary, "wheeling" electricity from another generator of the power to that generator's wholesale customers. Many transmissions of power between IOUs are short-term purchases and sales of electricity for purposes of coordination or emergency. Every major utility in the United States is linked to other utilities by a grid system, as illustrated in Figure 15–2 for California's electric utility companies. Plant failures and seasonal shortages may be covered by transfers of electricity from distant suppliers who have surpluses.

Finally, **distribution** to homes, office buildings, grocery stores, and other end users concludes the process. Electricity that is not retailed in this manner is sold wholesale. Wholesale purchasers are mainly industrial buyers, but many city and town governments own electrical distribution systems and they also buy at wholesale.

Regulation covers all segments of the industry. State regulatory commissions are primarily concerned with the retail and wholesale portions of the industry depicted at the top and left-hand side of Figure 15–1. In contrast, the Federal Energy Regulatory Commission focuses its attention on interstate transactions involving contract sales between IOUs, wheeling arrangements, and the like.

Natural gas also goes through a three-stage journey. *Production* in the field entails discovery and extraction. *Transportation* to cities and towns occurs by pipeline. *Distribution* to ultimate users employs extensive local pipeline networks. Utility regulation as defined in this chapter applies to only the last two of these stages.

II. Price Level Regulation

A. Objectives and Overview

There are any number of objectives that *could* guide price level regulation. Among the more obvious possibilities are speedy growth in service, conservation of energy, or optimal allocation of resources in the strict economic sense. For one reason or another, however, none of these is the main objective applied in practice. The main objective is to allow the utility sufficient revenues to pay its full costs plus a fair return on the fair value of its capital. Stated differently, *the main objective is to strike a reasonable balance between the interests of the consumers* (who should not be gouged by monopoly exploitation) *and the interests of the utility investors and operators* (who should not be ripped off by overzealous commissions or who, in more legalistic language, should not be deprived of their property without due process of law). As a Connecticut commissioner once put it, "We're the buffer between the company and the consumer. If you're the buffer, you're going to get buffeted."[1]

This effort is captured in a simple equation:

$$TR = OE + CD + VA \cdot r$$

where

> *TR* is total revenue
> *OE* is operating expenses (including taxes)
> *CD* is current depreciation
> *VA* is value of assets (less accumulated depreciation)
> *r* is rate of return

Notice that, on the right-hand side, operating expenses, *OE*, and current depreciation, *CD*, are both *annual dollar flows*. Capital, or asset value, *VA,* is not a dollar flow. It is the asset value of the utility firm at a *given point in time*, also called the **rate base**. However, once this capital value is multiplied by the allowed rate of return (such as 0.10, for 10 percent per year), the result *is* an annual dollar flow. The basic problem of price level regulation is to see to it that the annual flow of total revenue covers the annual flow of full cost, including depreciation, plus a fair or reasonable return on asset value, no more and no less. Generally speaking, the owners or operators would like to see more, which means that their interests lie with *high* estimates of the elements on the right-hand side. Consumers, on the other hand, would like to see less because their interests are generally served by *low* figures for these elements. It is the job of the commission to balance these conflicting interests—to determine that operating expenses, current depreciation, capital value, and rate of return may be neither too high nor too low, and then to permit a price level that generates the necessary total revenue. If prices are pressed too low, service could suffer and the firm could go bankrupt, injuring everyone involved.

A first step in estimating these elements is the selection of a test year from which data are derived. The last twelve months for which data are available have usually served commissions in the past. With rapid inflation, however, such data quickly grow old. So some commissions now accept data based on projections for a *future* test year. Such future data are by nature more speculative than historic, but the price level to be set is for future periods, so a future test year has the advantage of placing prices and costs in the same time frame.

Now, to appreciate how regulators determine permitted total revenue *(TR)*, each item of price level decision making must be discussed. We begin with operating expenses *(OE)*, and continue with current depreciation *(CD)*, rate base *(VA)*, and rate of return *r*.

B. Operating Expenses *(OE)*

Operating expenses are to some degree the easiest of all items for a commission to determine. They include such things as fuel costs (for coal, oil, gas, and uranium), workers' wages, managers' salaries, materials expense, advertising, and taxes. Of these, fuel, wages, and taxes are by far the largest components. Together, all operating expenses typically absorb about 70 percent and 90 percent of electric and gas operating revenue, respectively, as shown in Figure 15–3, which is based on data from fifteen major states in 1989.

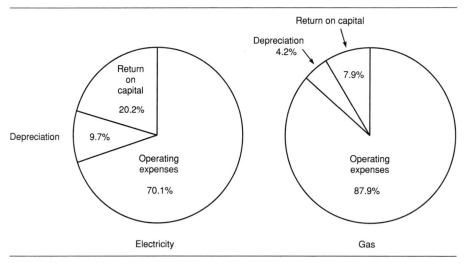

Figure 15–3
Use of Revenues for Electric and Gas Utilities in 15 States, 1989

Source: National Association of Regulatory Utility Commissioners, *1989 Annual Report on Utility and Carrier Regulation* (Washington DC, 1990), pp. 717, 747

These expenses are relatively easy to determine because few such expenses can be padded or fudged. Taxes, for example, are beyond the utility's control and therefore unquestioned. Similarly, the costs of fuel are usually shaped in open markets, and workers' wages are often settled by collective bargaining, so these too are rarely questioned by commissions.

Still, there are snarls, and we should discuss several of them.

Affiliate Dealings. When a utility owns the company from which it buys, or when both the utility and the supplier are jointly owned by the same holding company, arms-length bargaining no longer prevails and the utility may try to evade profit regulation by paying exorbitant prices on the purchases it makes from these affiliated suppliers. As of 1980, for example, thirty-seven electric utilities owned coal mines, with the result that more than 12 percent of all utility coal came from "captive" sources rather than open-market suppliers. An audit of these captive dealings disclosed that in the late 1970s American Electric Power Co. and Duquesne Light Co. had paid their mining subsidiaries about 30 percent above the going market price for coal. Thus, some major companies may be using their coal operations to reap profits otherwise denied in the rate-making process.[2]

Automatic Pass-Throughs. When the cost of oil and other fuels began soaring during the 1970s, utilities felt pinched because the slow regulatory process caused their utility prices to lag behind their fuel costs. To meet this problem most commissions began granting utilities the opportunity to pass higher fuel costs on to their customers immediately. The amounts involved in such automatic pass-throughs have been enormous. The problem is that automatic pass-throughs remove incentives for shrewd purchasing and open up opportunities for abuse.[3] As a result, some commissions have tried *partial* pass-throughs, which grant immediate and unchecked price increases for only a large fraction of the cost increase.

Wages and Salaries. Given the monopoly power of utilities and the nature of regulation, it has often been argued that wages and salaries of utility employees would tend to be excessive because increases could be passed on to consumers fairly easily. In fact, empirical evidence does not bear this out. Utility workers' wages do not seem too far out of line with those of comparable workers elsewhere.[4] And utility executives apparently earn considerably less, about 60 percent less according to one estimate, than executives at comparable manufacturing firms.[5] Of course, the problem is determining what is comparable. In the past, managing utilities was thought to be a relatively "easy" job, but the turbulence of recent times may well have changed that.

Judgment Calls on Minor Expenses. The problems continue as commissioners move down the list of expenses into minor categories. How much should be allowed for advertising? Does a monopolist need to advertise at all? What about public relations advertising, which tells us that Giant Electric is doing everything possible to clean up the environment but that smokestack scrubbers ought to be scrubbed? Does the tab for these ads belong to consumers or investors? How much should be allowed for executive expense accounts, executive jets, and executive travel? Should the gasoline expenses of corporate Cadillacs be approved when economical Toyotas would do? And what about the costs of company lawyers and accountants who represent the utility before the commission? Should consumers or investors pay the company's costs of coping with regulation?

Commissions' answers to these and similar questions vary widely, as you might guess. (An interesting tidbit regarding operating expenses is the fact that Florida and Arizona utilities have occasionally burned government confiscated marijuana in their power plants as free fuel.[6] The cost savings to electricity consumers have been small because the tonnages involved have not been especially great and the heat-generating capacity of marijuana is much less than that of coal. Mari-

---

Thumbnail Sketch 3: Federal Energy
Regulatory Commission

Established: 1977 (taking over for the Federal Power Commission, which was established in 1920).

Purpose: To regulate interstate aspects of the electric power and natural gas industries.

Legislative Authority: Federal Water Power Act of 1920; Federal Power Act of 1935; Natural Gas Act of 1930; Energy Policy and Conservation Act of 1975; Department of Energy Organization Act of 1977; Public Utility Regulatory Policy Act of 1978; and other legislation.

Regulatory Activity: Regulates rates charged for interstate transmission and sale of electricity and gas and oil pipeline services. Governs interconnections, mergers, and security issues of electric utilities. Licenses hydroelectric projects.

Organization: The FERC is an independent agency within but separate from the Department of Energy. Its five members are appointed by the president, and its staff divisions include the Office of Pipeline and Producer Regulation and the Office of Electric Power Regulation.

Budget: 1991 estimate, $123 million.

Staff: 1991 estimate, 1500.

---

juana contains 8,600 BTUs per pound compared to coal's 12,500 BTUs, so one ton of marijuana yields about 2,000 kilowatt-hours of electricity. Although the utilities have burned the marijuana free, its street value would be in the hundreds of millions of dollars. Fortunately or unfortunately, depending on how you look at it, the fumes do not affect people downwind from the plants because the marijuana is pulverized and mixed with coal before being burned.)

C. Current Depreciation *(CD)*

Current depreciation is an important item of cost because most utilities tend to be capital intensive. As shown in Figure 15–3, current depreciation of electric utilities amounts to about 10 percent of total sales, well over twice the level for all manufacturing.

No one disputes the necessity of including depreciation as a cost. In one sense, depreciation accounts for the using up of capital assets through wear and tear or obsolescence. In another sense, depreciation may be thought of as a payment to capital investors, much as wages, salaries, and materials expenses are payments to other input suppliers. This means that, of the elements in the summary equation, *both* current depreciation *and* capital value times rate of return go to the investors. As Alfred Kahn explains, "The return to capital . . . has two parts: the return *of* the money capital invested over the estimated economic life of the investment and the return (interest and profit) *on* the portion of the investment that remains outstanding."[7]

Although no one disputes depreciation's inclusion as a cost, its computation is often more controversial than the computation of operating expenses. First, the allowance for depreciation is quite different from operating expenses. Whereas operating expenses entail *actual money outlays*, depreciation does not. It is an *imputed cost*. The portion of total revenues depreciation "permits the company to earn does not, as is the case with normal operating expenses, go out in payments to outside parties—suppliers of raw materials, workers and so on."[8] It goes instead to investors.

Second, since current depreciation is an imputation, there are no hard rules for its reckoning. The actual figure arrived at for any asset in any one year depends on three things: (1) the depreciation base, (2) the asset's estimated life span, and (3) the method of write-off during its life. Each element is judgmental; each is therefore open to dispute.

The depreciation base is the original cost of the asset less any salvage value at life's end. Although original cost is straightforward, salvage value is a matter of estimate. Life span, too, is a matter of estimate. A short life with no assumed salvage value would tend to favor investors over consumers because it would lead to large, early write-offs. Conversely, a long life with high salvage value favors consumers because it leads to small annual write-offs.

As for possible write-off methods, they are too numerous and too complex to summarize here. The most common are called straight line, sinking fund, and retirement reserve. The major source of difference among them is whether the depreciation base is spread *evenly* or *un*evenly over the estimated life span. Most commissions use the straight line method, which has an even spread.

D. Capital Value or Rate Base (*VA*)

The most controversial part of price level regulation concerns asset value times rate of return (or rate base × percentage return) because this is the computation that determines profit. The Supreme Court's legal guide to commissions is about as solid as natural gas. Specific estimates or formulas are not so important, says the court. It's the end result that counts. The end result must be "just and reasonable." What is "just and reasonable"? Earnings "which enable the company to operate successfully, to maintain its financial integrity, to attract capital, and to compensate its investors for the risks assumed . . . even though they [the earnings] might produce only a meager return."[9]

This nebulous guide gives commissions great leeway in determining both capital value and rate of return. As regards **capital value,** there is a wide range of choice concerning (1) accounting devices, and (2) what is counted as real investment.

1.   **ACCOUNTING DEVICES**

At least four methods for computing the rate base have been adopted or proposed:

1.   *Original cost* values assets at their "actual," or "book," cost.
2.   *Reproduction cost* is the estimated cost of buying, building, and installing the same equipment at today's prices.
3.   *Replacement cost* is the estimated cost of replacing the present plant and equipment, much of which may be outdated, with the most efficient and reliable technology available, in amounts sufficient to supply the same service.
4.   *Mixed method,* or fair value, which is some combination, or rough averaging, of items 1 through 3.

Subtractions for *accumulated* depreciation must be made under any of the options, which expands the horizon for judgment still further.

As suggested by Table 15–1's sample data, most state commissions and the Federal Energy Regulatory Commission apply the original cost approach, which is followed in popularity by fair value. Replacement cost is shunned by all. The pros and cons of these techniques are endlessly debated.

It should be obvious that original cost is the easiest of all methods to estimate (a fact that partly explains its great popularity). The replacement cost approach is undoubtedly the most difficult because it amounts to little more than a

Table 15–1
Method of Rate-Base Valuation and Rate of Return Allowed by Selected State
Commissions, 1989

State	Rate-Base Valuation	Electric Return (percentage)	Gas Return (percentage)
Alaska	Original cost	11.85%	13.67%
Arizona	Fair value	8.46	6.48
California	Original cost	10.96	10.75
Colorado	Original cost	10.21	10.21
Florida	Original cost	10.40	10.03
Georgia	Original cost	10.80	11.44
Illinois	Original cost	11.46	12.07
Indiana	Fair value	9.97	10.19
Louisiana	Original cost	11.07	12.00
Maryland	Fair value	10.01	10.01
Michigan	Original cost	9.63	8.93
Missouri	Fair value	9.94	11.46
New Hampshire	Original cost	14.94	10.82
New Jersey	Other	10.65	11.80
New York	Original cost	8.96	10.00
North Carolina	Original cost	10.45	11.44
Oregon	Original cost	11.14	11.49
Pennsylvania	Original cost	11.18	10.86
Texas	Fair value	10.90	5.97
Washington	Other	10.22	11.95
Wyoming	Original cost	10.63	11.26

Source: National Association of Regulatory Utility Commissioners, *1989 Annual Report on Utility and Carrier Regulation* (Washington DC, 1990), pp. 445–446, 481.

playground for opinion. Reproduction cost lies somewhere in between.

The different methods produce different estimates of the rate base, *VA,* with original cost being the lowest during times of inflation. But *VA* is multiplied by *r* to determine ultimate return, so commissions might in practice make up for a low *VA* by allowing a high *r,* or vice versa. In fact, some evidence indicates just such an effect, so there is apparently no substantial difference in *realized* earnings of firms regulated by original cost, fair value, and reproduction cost jurisictions.[10]

2. ASSET INCLUSION

Regardless of accounting technique, there remains the equally important question of what is to be included in the rate base. Buildings, cables, trucks, dams, generators, switches, and the like obviously qualify. But what about the $2 billion nuclear power plant completed only a year ago but now shut down because geologists have just discovered an earthquake fault within a half mile of it? Who ought to pay for it? If the dead plant is included in the rate base, consumers will howl. If excluded, it will hurt investors. How would you decide as a commissioner? Related questions arise when the construction costs of reactors skyrocket and when the reactors are not needed because demand is less than forecast. Tens of billions of dollars have gone into nuclear plants that have been cancelled before completion and into cost overruns on completed plants. Inclusion is thus a major issue.

A basic tool regulators use to tackle this issue is the "prudence test." This test compares the cost of the actual investment and the cost of the alternative that a prudent person would have chosen, including in the rate base only prudent amounts. In principle, this test should allow for failures as well as successes. If utilities are granted *no more* than a fair return on *successful* prudent investments, they should be granted *no less* than a fair return on *unsuccessful* prudent investments. As Alfred E. Kahn explains:

> If [investors] can earn the cost of capital only on the successes and not on the failures, it follows that they will earn less than the cost of capital on all their dollars, taken together. And investors won't play that game once they understand that those are going to be the rules.[11]

Moreover, the only sensible way to apply the prudence test is to look at the circumstances prevailing *when the investment commitments were made*, not to look at them through the eyes of hindsight. To quote Kahn again, "Prudency . . . on the basis of hindsight, and only for the *failures,* is to play a regulatory game of heads-the-consumer-wins, tails-the-investor-loses: In effect it expropriates stockholder dollars."[12]

Following the prudence test without hindsight, much of the nuclear damage tab can properly be billed to ratepayers. Many of the problem plants were contracted for during the early 1970s

when oil and coal prices were soaring wildly and when the demand for electricity was growing at 7 percent per year. At 7 percent growth, a utility must double its productive capacity every ten years, and the lag time for nuclear plant completion is about ten years. In short, nukes looked good. Hence, many if not most plants that are a great pain today looked very promising when first planned, and were therefore "prudent."

On the other hand, utilities and their investors cannot be completely exonerated. Ample evidence points to massive imprudence by way of bad management because management "horror stories" abound. As summarized by *Forbes*:

> How could an experienced contractor like Bechtel have prepared the Midland plant site so poorly that the diesel generator building began settling excessively? How could Bechtel have installed the reactor backwards at San Onofre? How could Brown & Root have got the reactor supports 45 degrees out of whack at Comanche Peak? How could experienced operators pour defective concrete at Marble Hill and the South Texas project? . . . How could design control have been so lax that PG&E used the wrong drawings in calculating seismic response for the steel in the Diablo Canyon containment building?
>
> The [Nuclear Regulatory Commission] has a partial answer. "In some cases," an NRC study concluded, "no one was managing the project, the project had inertia, but no guidance and direction." . . . [An] Office of Technology Assessment study last spring came to the same conclusion: "Inadequate management has been one of the major causes of construction cost overruns and erratic operation."[13]

Therefore, when utilities have requested price increases of up to 50 percent in order to cover the costs of their nuclear projects, commissions have often reacted reasonably in granting only part of the request. During the last half of the 1980s, over $13 billion in plant construction costs were disallowed. This was approximately 10 percent of the average cost of all new plants under review during that time.[14] In a few specific cases, such as Public Service Company of New Hampshire, bankruptcy has been the result of disallowance.[15]

Aside from inclusion questions concerning solid plant and equipment, there is the further question of what to do about *intangible* assets. Would you as a commissioner permit the cost of patents, franchise papers, licenses, and purchase options to enter the rate base? Many commissions do permit them—to some extent.

E. Percentage Rate of Return (*r*)

Utility investors own utility bonds, preferred stock, and common stock. Keeping these investors contented is important because they supply funds for plant and equipment. And given the capital intensity of utilities, these funds are truly immense, accounting for as much as one-quarter to one-half of all new securities issued by nonfinancial corporations in a given year. If the allowed rate of return is too low, utilities may be unable to finance their facilities because the securities will not be attractive to investors. If the rate of return is too high, then consumers will pay needlessly high prices.

The percentage rate of return referred to in the regulatory equation, *r,* is actually a *weighted average* rate, averaged over the several securities just mentioned—bonds, preferred stocks, and common stocks. Thus *r* is determined by a two-step process: (1) determination of the individual security rates of return and (2) computation of the average.

1. INDIVIDUAL RATES

Although there are many methods of determining the individual rates of return, the most commonly used by commissions is *cost of capital.* The cost of bonds is taken to be the interest rate that contractually must be paid, a rate that for new bond issues must be comparable to the interest rates on new bonds of comparable risk in the capital market. Risk scoring is determined by rating services like Moody's and Standard & Poor's. In December 1980, for example, the interest on AAA bonds was 13.75 percent and on more risky BAA bonds it was 16 percent. In turn, regulatory climate influences these ratings, with generous commissions being considered favorable to utilities, or low risk, and stingy commissions being considered unfavorable to utilities, or high risk.[16] For an overall interest rate on various bond issues, the commission merely divides the annual dollar flow of interest obligations by the value of the outstanding bonded debt.

The cost of capital for preferred stocks is similarly determined. Preferred stocks earn a fixed dividend much like the fixed interest earnings of bonds. This dividend runs at a higher percentage rate than bond interest, however, because preferred stocks are a bit more risky than bonds. In the event of default, the claims of bond holders are met before the claims of preferred stock holders. Thus, the cost of preferred stock capital is higher than the cost of bond capital but less than of common stock capital.

Common stock capital (or equity capital) is the most risky and most difficult to cost because dividends on common stock are not fixed. Indeed, hard times may prevent dividend payments altogether, as happened when New York's massive Consolidated Edison skipped a dividend payment in 1974 (a first for the venerable company and a shock for all utility investors). In other words, the "cost" here is the rate that will be permitted *if* it can be earned. The problem is made all the more difficult by the fact that there is no simple, universally agreed on method for determining the cost of equity capital. Economic experts testifying in the same rate case come up with widely differing estimates—14%, 11%, 12.5%, and so on.

Perhaps the best way to appreciate this problem is to imagine yourself as the typical investor whose capital the utility is trying to attract. What rate of return would the company have to pay (and the commission have to approve) to get you to bite? If you are shrewd, that rate would depend on at least the following: (1) the rate you could earn if you put your money elsewhere, (2) the risk of the utility's stock, and (3) the leniency of the commission in other matters, such as the computation of the rate base.

R. L. Hagerman and B. T. Ratchford conducted an empirical analysis of factors influencing officially allowed rates of return on electric utility equity capital and found that these considerations apparently do influence commissions:

- Allowed rates rose as AAA corporate bond rates rose, indicating official awareness of investor options elsewhere.
- Allowed rates were higher for utilities with high debt/equity ratios, a measure of risk.
- Allowed rates were higher for utilities whose rate base was determined by the original cost method as compared to the fair value method, indicating that commissions make up for a low *VA* by allowing a higher *r*.[17]

2. COMPUTING AVERAGE RATE *r*

Once the cost of each component of capital is determined, the weighted average cost of capital is computed to estimate *r* in the equation on page 297. The weights come from the utility's capital structure. Say, for example, that the utility's capital is 50% bonded debt, 10% preferred stock, and 40% common equity capital. Suppose, further, that the estimated cost of capital for each is 9%, 11%, and 15%, respectively. Then the weighted average rate of return will be computed by multiplication and addition:

Bonds (50% at 9%)	$0.5 \times 0.09 = 0.045$
Preferred stock (10% at 11%)	$0.1 \times 0.11 = 0.011$
Common stock (40% at 15%)	$0.4 \times 0.15 = \underline{0.060}$
Weighted average (*r*)	0.116 or 11.6%

Moving from the hypothetical to the real, Table 15–1 reports overall rates of return allowed by a sample of commissions in 1989. Again, it must be stressed that these *allowed* rates do not necessarily correspond to rates actually *realized* by the companies, especially when it comes to equity capital. Nationally, for instance, the average al-

lowed return on equity was 10.3 percent in 1981, but the average realized return was only 9.1%.[18]

F. Conclusion: Translating *TR* into Price Level

One of the reasons realized rates may differ from allowed rates is that price level does not follow directly from the foregoing computations. Estimates of *OE, CD,* and *VA · r* yield an estimate of the target total revenue *(TR)* needed to cover these outlays, but they do not tell the commission exactly what *price level* will generate the needed total revenue.

Simply stated, *realized* total revenue will be price times quantity, that is, *TR = P × Q* (as 100 sandwiches at $2 each would fetch you $200 if you ran a lunch counter). This suggests an easy translation: If total revenue needs to be 10 percent higher to cover costs, then price needs to be 10 percent higher, too. Although commissions often act in this way, it is incorrect for them to assume a zero elasticity of demand. That is, they assume that the 10 percent higher price level will not reduce quantity at all.

In fact, demand is such that quantity does change with price, muddling the linkage between price level and total revenues. What is more, the resulting changes in quantity may alter the costs that justified the target total revenues in the first place, adding further complications. Thus, price level regulation is anything but precise. Allowables and realizations differ. About the only really solid answer a rate case provides relates to direction. If costs are rising, or realized return is less than allowed return, price level should move up. If opposites hold, price level should move down.

III. Price Structure Regulation

A. Introduction and Overview

Until recently the issue of price structure took a back seat to the issue of price level. Once price level was determined, commissions would usually let utilities devise their own price structure. Rapidly rising price levels and growing criticism from consumers and economists have buried this benign neglect. Now, price structure commands a big chunk of official attention.

According to judicial and legislative instructions, commissions may permit prices that jump around with time, place, type of buyer, and size of transaction. However, the jumps cannot be "unduly discriminatory." The differences in prices charged various classes of service must be "just and reasonable." In carrying out this vague mandate, commissions have permitted prices to vary with *cost of service* and *value of service*.

Cost of Service.   Prices based on the cost-of-service principle would, as the name implies, fully reflect the costs associated with a particular service or product. Stated differently, profit markups would not vary; all price/cost ratios would be the same across customers.

This is an easy principle to follow when costs can be broken down customer by customer. The cost of a meter, for instance, can be directly assigned to the customer using it. But this is a difficult principle to follow when there are *common costs* that cannot be directly assigned. For example, an electric utility's coal plant generates power for both residential and industrial buyers. How, then, is the capital cost of the plant to be assigned to homes versus factories?

Coping with these considerations has created two branches of the cost-of-service approach. One branch uses *fully distributed* costs to guide price setting. This method begins by assigning clearly identifiable costs to the particular customers responsible for those costs, then adds common (nonidentifiable) costs for different customers according to some arbitrary distribution formula. Physical proportions of output provide one such formula, in which case residential customers would be assigned 40 percent of the common costs if they accounted for 40 percent of the electricity output, industrial customers would be assigned 30 percent of the common costs if they bought 30 percent of the electricity, and so on.

The other branch of the cost-of-service approach uses *marginal cost* as the basis for pricing. Simply stated, marginal cost is the additional cost of producing additional units of output. Simply measured, marginal cost corresponds to clearly assignable costs and ignores common costs, but this is *too* simple and misleading. In fact, marginal costs vary widely depending on (a) the volume of additional units of output considered and (b) the time perspective assumed (i.e., short run or long run). The result is that arbitrary formulas or assumptions enter the estimation of marginal costs just as much as they enter the estimation of fully distributed costs, a result that leads to heated debate over which method is better.[19] In practice, utility regulators have stuck pretty close to the fully distributed cost method, but marginal cost pricing is making large inroads, as we shall see.

Value of Service.   When costs do not guide pricing, elasticities of demand often do. Customers with a low elasticity can be hit with a high price; those with a high elasticity require a low price if their patronage is to be held (as suggested in our earlier discussion of price discrimination at the beginning of Chapter 9). The term *value of service* derives from the idea that differing elasticities signal differing values to customers.

Because value-of-service pricing constitutes price discrimination, it may seem unfair. It can be argued, however, that under certain regulatory circumstances such pricing is desirable because it promotes static economic efficiency, that is, optimal allocation of resources. The theoretical ideal for efficiency would require that all prices match their marginal cost, but as we have just seen, prices matching marginal costs may not be high enough to cover undistributed common costs. Without coverage of all costs, the utility would go bankrupt. Thus, a second best formula furthering efficiency has been developed by economists, a formula that makes use of demand elasticities to get prices high enough to cover overall costs. Simply stated, this formula says that welfare is best served when prices exceed marginal cost to a degree that varies *inversely* with elasticity of demand. For customers with high elasticity, price should be close to marginal cost. For customers with low elasticity, price should be higher relative to marginal cost.

Figure 15–4 illustrates these so-called *Ramsey prices* (after economist Frank Ramsey).[20] A constant marginal cost of 4 cents per kilowatt-hour (kwh) is depicted for simplicity. Assuming two classes of customers—(1) residential buyers with a relatively low elasticity of demand and (2) industrial buyers with a relatively high elasticity of demand—price for the former would be higher than for the latter such that:

$$\left(\frac{P_r - MC_r}{P_r}\right) E_r = \left(\frac{P_i - MC_i}{P_i}\right) E_i$$

where

P_r is price to residential buyers
MC_r is marginal cost to residential buyers

P_i is price to industrial buyers
MC_i is marginal cost to industrial buyers
E_r is elasticity for residential buyers
E_i is elasticity for industrial buyers

Because prices to residential and industrial buyers are 10 cents per kilowatt-hour and 6 cents per kilowatt-hour in Figure 15–4, we then have

$$\left(\frac{10¢ - 4¢}{10¢}\right) E_r = \left(\frac{6¢ - 4¢}{6¢}\right) E_i$$

or

$$0.60\ E_r = 0.33\ E_i$$

This result implies that E_i is 80 percent larger than E_r, which is the case. Elasticity at point R in Figure 15–4 is 1.33. At point I it's 2.40.

No commission has the precise information needed to impose Ramsey prices. Even if the information were available, commissioners might not follow the formula, given their other value judgments besides efficiency. In any case, empirical studies reveal that the prices actually ap-

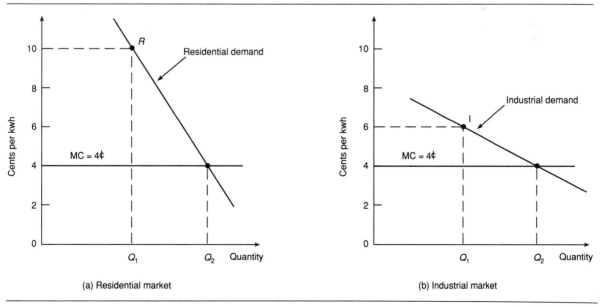

Figure 15–4
Ramsey Prices for Residential and Industrial Buyers of Electricity

proved by commissions usually deviate from Ramsey prices, but they occasionally reflect the spirit of Ramsey prices.[21]

Applications of the cost-of-service and value-of-service principles may be seen in the following three-part review of actual price structures. Three characteristics of purchases stand out—(1) who buys, (2) how much, and (3) when.

B. Who Buys? Customer Classes

Electric and gas utilities serve three broad classes of ultimate customer:

- Residential—about one-third of the energy.
- Commercial (e.g., banks and stores)—roughly one-fifth of the energy.
- Industrial (e.g., steel plants)—over two-fifths of the energy.

As shown by the first row of Table 15–2, which reports average prices for each class in 1988, residential and commercial buyers pay considerably more on average than industrial buyers do, and residential buyers pay the highest prices of all.

There are two rationales for this pattern. First, from a cost-of-service perspective, industrial buyers may be cheaper to supply, given their fewness, their great volumes per customer, and their willingness to provide some of the utility equipment needed at their factories. Second, from a value-of-service perspective, these prices apparently reflect differences in elasticity of demand. The quantity demanded by residential customers tends to be relatively *un*responsive to changes in price, yielding elasticity estimates for electricity in the neighborhood of 1. Their ability to substitute other sources of energy or to supply their own needs is rather limited. At the other end of the spectrum, industrial customers are quite responsive to changes in price because they enjoy greater options for substitute energy sources and self-supply. Accordingly, estimates of their elasticity of demand for electricity range higher at around 2. In between, commercial customers generally have fewer options than industrial buyers but more options than residential buyers, so their elasticity of demand is probably somewhere between 1 and 2. Indeed, by one estimate it is 1.36.[22]

To what extent can the observed price differences be explained by value of service as opposed to cost of service? To answer this question, we would need accurate estimates of just how much costs actually differ by customer classes to see whether the price variations correspond closely to the cost variations. If prices and costs moved together so that price/cost

---

Table 15–2
Price Discrimination by Class of Customer

	Residential	Commercial	Industrial
1. *Average price, 1988 (cents per kwh)*	7.79¢	7.15¢	4.80¢
2. *Price-cost margins (P-MC)/P*			
2a. Hayashi et al.	0.430	0.407	0.327
2b. Nelson et al.	0.108	0.155	0.249
2c. Thompson et al.	0.322	0.122	0.507

Sources: U.S. Department of Commerce, *Statistical Abstract of the United States 1990*, p. 572; P. L. Hayashi, M. Sevier, and J. M. Trapani, "Pricing Efficiency under Rate-of-Return Regulation: Some Empirical Evidence for the Electric Utility Industry," *Southern Economic Journal* (January 1985): 776–792; Jon P. Nelson and Mark J. Roberts, "Ramsey Numbers and the Role of Competing Interest Groups," *Quarterly Review of Economics and Business* (Autumn 1989): 21–42; Gerbert G. Thompson, Jr., David R. Kamerschen, and Albert L. Danielson, "Efficiency in Nuclear Power Pricing," *Review of Industrial Organization* (vol. 5, no. 2, 1990): 13–27.

ratios were the same for all buyers, then cost-of-service pricing would prevail and price discrimination based on value of service would be absent, despite the elasticity differences. Rows 2a through 2c of Table 15–2 reveal the jumble of research results in this area. Estimated price/cost margins, (P-MC)/P, vary substantially across classes, so cost-of-service pricing is *not* typical. Yet, value-of-service pricing does not show through the research either. By one set of estimates, that of Hayashi et al., margins accord with value-of-service principles, being highest for residential buyers (inelastic) and lowest for industrial buyers (elastic). However, Nelson et al. find a pattern that is exactly the reverse—with industrial buyers paying the highest markups and residential buyers paying the lowest. Finally, Thompson et al. land between with an estimate that *commercial* buyers pay the lowest markup of the three classes. The results vary widely because of differing data, time periods, model specifications, and the like. Further research is obviously needed.[23]

C. How Much is Bought? Quantity Structures

When Thomas Edison first wired New York City over 100 years ago, he had not yet invented meters, so he charged his customers a fixed price regardless of the quantity they purchased. A remnant of that practice remains today in that some utilities levy a fixed monthly customer charge that is independent of quantity consumed. The advent of metering brought a variety of price structures keyed to quantity as well as to customer class, however.

The main possibilities for quantity structures are indicated in the three panels of Figure 15–5. The first of these, the *flat rate* of panel 15–5(a), imposes a charge per unit of use that remains the same over all units. In terms of one's monthly bill, a doubling of consumption doubles the amount due.

Although commonly used after meters first became available, the flat rate was replaced by the *declining block rate* structure of panel 15–5(b) for most utilities during most of this century. Price per unit is constant within stated blocks of units, blocks such as 0–500 kwh, 501–1000 kwh, 1001–2000 kwh, and so on. The unit price falls in each successive block until the final open-ended block. In terms of one's monthly bill, a doubling of consumption here would likely result in *less* than a doubling of the total amount due. For obvious reasons, this structure has occasionally been dubbed "promotional pricing" because it encourages large-quantity consumption. To the extent economies of scale cause utility costs per unit to fall with added output, such a structure

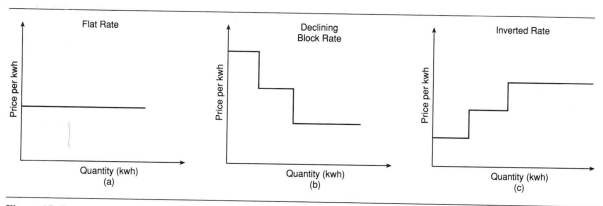

Figure 15–5
Alternate Price Structures as a Function of Quantity Purchased

has cost-of-service justifications. To the extent customers take care of necessities like lighting first and luxuries like air conditioning second, this structure may also conform to value-of-service principles because the high-priced blocks would be associated with inelastic (necessary) demands and the low-priced blocks would be associated with elastic (luxury) demands.

Recently, however, these rationales for declining block rates have been called into question. Economies of scale in electricity, for instance, are not nearly as pronounced as they once were. They still occur at the distribution stage, but they no longer occur for most electricity generation because output in most locales has grown to the point at which an efficient thermal plant is small in comparison to total output and because present technologies grant fewer advantages to greater generating size.[24] As regards demand, it is now argued that energy use should no longer be promoted, especially not for luxury purposes, because of environmental considerations.

Folks wanting to curb energy use for conservation or environmental reasons advocate adoption of *inverted rate* structures, as illustrated in panel 15–5(c). In this case unit price *rises* in successive blocks rather than falls, with the result that a monthly bill would rise at an increasing rate as added energy is consumed. Less than half of the states have tried inverted rates, and some of these have used them for only a few utility companies. For obvious reasons, inverted rates are not very popular among consumers, so flat rates and block rates remain most common.[25]

A variant of the inverted rate structure that has recently been tried in several states is the *lifeline* rate. The first 300 kilowatt-hours per month or thereabouts are priced at a below-cost price per unit, with price per unit thereafter rising into a flat or inverted rate structure. The purpose of the lifeline design is to help poor people pay for a subsistence quantity of electricity or gas. This is only a recent pricing innovation propelled by soaring costs of energy and concerns for equity.

Figure 15–2's panels depict quantity in kilowatt-hours. There is an additional measure of quantity in electricity consumption, however, that is particularly important in the quantity rate structures facing industrial buyers. This second measure of quantity does not gauge the amount of current consumed *over* a given period, as does the kilowatt-hour. Rather, it measures the *instantaneous* rate of consumption at a particular point in time as expressed in *kilowatts* (not kilowatt-*hours*). Given that an electric utility must have the capacity to meet this instantaneous demand as well as duration demand, the cost of maintaining that capacity should be borne by the customers responsible for it. This is the rationale behind the *demand,* or *kilowatt, charge* imposed on industrial buyers above and beyond the regular kilowatt-*hour* quantity charges. Demand charges often follow block rate designs, such as $4.00 per kilowatt for the first 100 kilowatts, $3.80 per kilowatt for the next 300 kilowatts, and $3.20 for all additional kilowatts.

The traditional method of pricing industrial buyers thus involves two elements—(1) a kilowatt-hour price and (2) a kilowatt price. Hence, the name two-part tariff (or Hopkinson tariff, after its originator). There is a key problem with the kilowatt price, however. Its rationale and measurement do not coincide. Its rationale is to pin the utility's peak capacity costs on those responsible. But its measurement refers solely to the peaks of *individual* industrial buyers at *anytime*, not to the *utility's* system-wide peak, which may or may not occur at the same time as an individual buyers' peak. In other words, the traditional kilowatt, or demand, charge is not really peak-load pricing at all because it does not vary with time of day or season of the year because use of utility capacity varies. Such timing has now been introduced into price structures (in addition to class and quantity distinctions), revolutionizing electric and gas pricing.

D. When? Peak-Load Pricing

Figure 15–6 illustrates the timing of electricity use in Omaha. The hourly timing over the day is typical of utilities everywhere, with use reaching a peak in late afternoon and falling into a gully at night. The solid line for summer lies above the dashed line for winter, disclosing that Omaha is in a region of the country where *summer peaking* prevails. This is typical where hot summers boost air conditioning demand appreciably. In New England and certain other areas *winter peaking* occurs because electricity is needed more against the winter than against the summer. (Gas peaking centers on winter everywhere, because space heating is one of gas's greatest blessings.)

For many decades people have had to pay more to telephone long distance during weekday daylight hours than to phone during nights and weekends. Traditionally, such *peak load pricing* has not been practiced by electric and gas utilities, but now there is a definite trend toward time-of-day and season-of-year price structures. In 1977, for instance, Wisconsin Power & Light Company began charging commercial customers 2.03 cents per kilowatt-hour between 8 A.M. and 10 P.M. and just 1.01 cents per kilowatt-hour at other times. Now over 50 percent of all retail power sold in Wisconsin is subject to peak-load pricing, and nearly all states provide for such pricing to some degree.

Charging peak users more than off-peak users serves many purposes:

- It improves a utility's capacity use, or load factor, which is the ratio of average demand over the year to peak demand, by discouraging peak demand while encouraging off-peak demand.
- In turn, better capacity use reduces cost. Long-run average cost per kwh may be as much as 13 percent lower for a load factor of 0.8 as compared to a load factor of 0.5.
- Peak-load pricing tends to slow the growth in

peak demand, reducing the need for capital outlays by utilities.
- It can reduce a utility's oil and gas use, thereby promoting conservation.
- It serves the principle of cost-of-service pricing.

To summarize before elaborating, higher prices during peak periods make sense because the costs of providing peak service are greater than those of providing off-peak service, as much as three to five times greater.[28]

One such cost is plant and equipment. Because a utility must have on hand capacity to satisfy total peak demand, capacity costs can be blamed mainly on those users who tap into the utility during peak hours. As for off-peak customers, *the plant and equipment are already there for the peak,* so capacity costs of serving them do not apply, although off-peak users do create costs for fuel and other variable inputs. Indeed, even fuel costs per unit tend to vary with time of demand because utilities usually fire up their least efficient, high-cost plants only during peak periods. The differences between plants can be substantial. In 1973, for instance, a major eastern electric company experienced fuel costs of 3.3 mills/kwh in its most efficient plant and 9.51 mills/kwh in its least efficient plant.[29] (Notice that these cost experiences do not contradict the economies of scale mentioned earlier. These are *short-run* cost comparisons, not long-run scalar comparisons. Moreover, they apply to generation, not distribution.)

Figure 15–7 shows peak and off-peak demands set against the short-run marginal cost curve of a hypothetical utility. If a uniform price of P_2 were charged to both peak and off-peak demands, capacity would have to equal OQ_2, which is peak quantity demanded at P_2. Off-peak demand would be OQ_0 given price P_2. Since OQ_2 greatly exceeds OQ_0, it is easy to see that peak demand would be responsible for making it necessary for the plant to produce OQ_2 (even if off-peak demand were nonexistent). Moreover, a

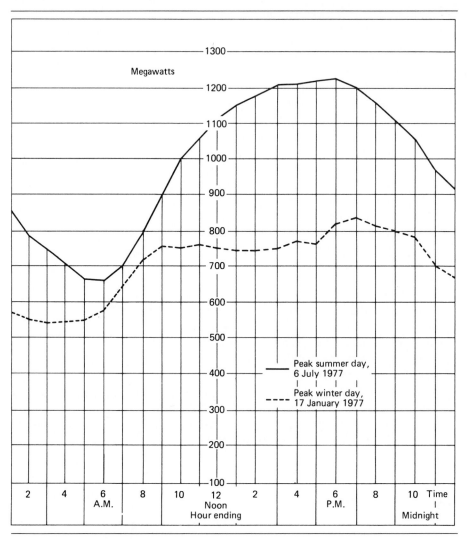

Figure 15–6
Omaha Public Power District, Typical Hourly Consumption of Electricity

Source: Harry Trebing (ed.), *Assessing New Pricing Concepts in Public Utilities* (East Lansing: Division of Research, Graduate School of Business Administration, Michigan State University, 1978), p. 278

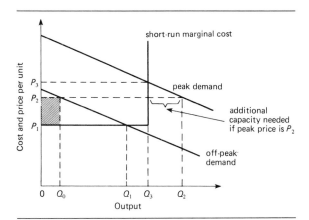

Figure 15–7
Peak-load Pricing

uniform price of P_2 would cause inefficient plant use because there would be tremendous excess capacity during off-peak periods. In short, such a uniform price is *too low* for peak demand (producing a state of overbuilding) and *too high* for off-peak demand (causing off-peak underuse). Indeed, off-peak demand to some extent subsidizes peak demand. The shaded area in Figure 15–4 indicates the amount by which off-peak revenues exceed off-peak costs.

With a more sensible rate structure, peak customers would be charged P_3 and off-peak customers would be charged P_1. At P_3, peak demand would be curtailed to OQ_3, eliminating the need for capacity over the Q_3 to Q_2 range. (It has been estimated that $13 *billion* of electric utility capital spending would have been avoided over the years 1977 to 1985 if all United States electric companies had used such peak-load pricing.[30] Conversely, off-peak demand would expand to OQ_1 under a reduced price of P_1. Off-peak excess capacity would be cut appreciably, thereby achieving more efficient plant use. Price for off-peak demand could not fall below P_1, however, without falling below marginal cost. And it is

only fair and economically proper that off-peak users pay those marginal costs.

One problem with time-of-day peak-load pricing is that manufacturing workers' lives can be seriously disrupted if their employers step up nighttime operations to save millions in energy costs. Workers moved to graveyard shifts because of peak-load pricing have complained of strained marriages, stunted social calendars, and injured health.[31]

E. Summary of Price Structure

When you take the many foregoing factors into account, you see that price structures vary substantially from state to state and utility to utility. Moreover, the price for any one utility can be quite complex, with price schedules filling several pages of fine print. Still, you can appreciate the essence of the matter by perusing Table 15–3, which shows excerpts from the 1991 price schedules of one of the country's largest utilities, Pacific Gas and Electric Company of California.

The residential customer schedule shown includes a fixed monthly fee of $5.00 together with quantity charges that combine inverted block and seasonal peak-load pricing. The inverted block effect is achieved by successively higher unit charges across two tiers, first 10.92¢ per kwh and then 13.68¢ per kwh. The seasonal peak-load effect is achieved by shortening the kwh range of the first tier in the summer months (May to October) as compared to the winter months (November to April). Thus, the price of 500 kwh would be $58.74 in the winter and $62.06 in the summer.

Under the schedule in Table 15–3 for small industrial customers, time-of-day peaks applied as well as seasonal peaks. The highest energy charge was 27.77¢ per kwh, which applied between noon and 6:00 P.M. on summer weekdays. The lowest energy charge was only a small fraction of that, 5.55¢ per kwh, which applied during winter nights, weekends, and holidays.

Table 15–3
Excepts From Pacific Gas and Electric Company's Electricity Price Structure, 1991

Residential Service Per Month (Territory Q)		
	Winter Months	*Summer Months*
Fixed Fee (monthly minimum)	$5.00	$5.00
Quantity Charge	kwh range	kwh range
Tier I 10.92 ¢ per kwh	0–350	0–230
Tier II 13.68 ¢ per kwh	350 & over	230 & over

Industrial Service Per Meter Per Month (Time of use)		
	Winter Months	*Summer Months*
Fixed Fee (monthly minimum)	$14.95	$14.95
Energy Charge		
Peak	—	27.77¢
Partial-Peak	7.41¢	13.88¢
Off-Peak	5.55¢	7.22¢
Summer Periods		
Peak: Noon–6:00 P.M., Monday to Friday.		
Partial-Peak: 8:30 A.M. to noon and 6:00 P.M. to 9:30 P.M., Monday to Friday		
Off-Peak: 9:30 P.M. to 8:30 A.M., weekends and holidays		

Source: Pacific Gas & Electric Company.

IV. Evaluation: Plaudits and Problems

A. Plaudits

How well has public utility regulation worked? Has it kept prices at reasonable levels, prevented unfair price discrimination, and promoted adequate service? Pat answers are not possible. Some commentators castigate utility regulation. Others applaud it. Some state commissions seem to do a good job. Others falter. More conclusive answers might be reached if we could compare utilities with and without regulation. But opportunities for such comparisons are curbed by the fact that virtually *all* investor-owned utilities in the United States are regulated.

Still, several studies have attempted to reach general conclusions about regulation's effects. Confined mainly to the question of price level, the best of these studies suggest that electric and gas prices are on average probably lower as a result of regulation's check on monopoly power. How much lower is not clear, maybe 5 to 10 percent.

Two main methods have been used to reach this conclusion. One compares utility prices with and without regulation under the limited circumstances in which such comparison is possible, such as the early history of utility regulation when some states had regulation and others did not.[32] The other and more imaginative approach uses assumptions from economic theory and data from real-world observations to calculate estimates of what profit-maximizing utility prices would be like in the absence of regulation. These fictitious unregulated prices are then compared to real regulated prices to measure regulation's impact. One of the most thorough studies of this sort yields favorable results for regulation.[33]

This generally laudatory verdict for utility regulation cannot be stretched to support all other areas of economic regulation. As we shall see, regulation of transportation has apparently caused price levels to rise rather than fall. Moreover, it must be stressed that utility regulation is not without its serious problems. Measured by criteria other than price level, regulation may well warrant low grades.[34] Quality of service, though, is generally good.

B. Problems and Prospects

Some of the problems are of long standing. Two of these—incentives and input efficiency—begin this concluding section of woe. Other problems have more recent origins. Two of these—conservation and wholesale competition—round out the analysis.

1. INCENTIVES

It would be nice if commissions could reward utilities that operate efficiently and progressively and penalize those that perform poorly. Competition contains such incentives, but no tidy incentive techniques have been devised for regulation. Traditionally, the only source of incentive has been regulatory lag. Earnings that rise inordinately from efficiency remain with the firm until regulators act to reduce rate levels, but they act only after a long lag. Conversely, earnings that fall with inefficiency must be borne by the firm until requests for rate increases are answered, which likewise entails some lag. The lag imperfectly and temporarily rewards goodness and punishes badness.

Recently, some commissions have become more deliberate in their attempts to instill proper incentives. For example, a big problem with nuclear power plants is that improper maintenance and operation result in costly shutdowns. As a consequence, more than a dozen commissions now reward utilities if they operate their plants above a target rate of use and penalize them for excessive idleness. Arkansas Power and Light Company, for instance, gets to retain fuel savings for operating Arkansas Nuclear One above 75

percent capacity and, conversely, must absorb the extra cost of operating the plant at less than 70 percent of full capacity. Other incentive programs cover construction costs, fuel purchases, and conservation efforts.[35]

2. INPUT EFFICIENCY

Some regulatory theorists argue that profit regulation contains some particularly unfavorable incentives. Because profit is keyed to the rate base, *there is an incentive to expand the rate base* (to substitute capital for labor) beyond the point that would be optimal in the absence of regulation.[36] Just how serious this so-called Averch-Johnson effect actually is no one can say. Empirical tests of the hypothesis have been mixed, half confirming and half refuting it.[37] Even if the effect does exist, it may not be as bad as it might seem. Although in *static* terms the bias favoring capital over other inputs may lift costs undesirably, the *dynamic* result may be *lower* costs through *improved technological progress,* given that most technological change tends to favor capital intensity.[38]

3. CONSERVATION

Given our intermittent energy crises and the serious pollution problems associated with energy, many utilities are turning to conservation. Less consumption means less need for power plants, less hassle.

The main impetus toward conservation has thus far come from government. As already noted, many declining block rate schedules have been scrapped in favor of flat or inverted rates, and peak-load pricing has become commonplace. State commissions were nudged in these and related directions when the federal government passed the Public Utility Regulatory Policies Act in 1978. The act encouraged these price structure reforms to promote increased conservation of electric energy and increased efficiency in plant use.[39] Moving beyond rate reform, a number of state commissions have pushed utilities into additional conservation programs to provide customers (1) free energy audits, (2) convenient financing for added home insulation, and (3) load management inducements. Less commonly but more intriguingly, a number of commissions have launched efforts to encourage solar power and cogeneration, both of which tend to put utilities out of the energy business.

The Public Utilities Regulatory Policies Act of 1978 (PURPA) requires utilities to buy surplus power from *cogenerators,* which are businesses that produce their own energy—like a sunflower seed processor that burns sunflower hulls to generate electricity or a cannery that burns peach pits. These energy suppliers were identified earlier in Figure 15–1 as PURPA-qualified facilities.

An especially big breakthrough for conservation occurred in 1990, when regulators in Rhode Island, New Hampshire, California, and several other states adopted new rules that allowed electric utilities to profit from their conservation efforts. Previously, conservation efforts were not financially rewarded:

> The problem, says John W. Rowe, New England electric's chief executive "was that we didn't see how we could afford to spend much money on something that both added costs and lowered revenues. . . ." [So] "there was no way we could make money on [conservation programs]. The rat has to smell the cheese."[40]

The cheese that commissions are now beginning to offer utilities is a return on conservation investments similar to the return they earn on regular investments. Hence, these utilities can now help customers to buy high-efficiency light bulbs, refrigerators, and electric motors, and then share in the savings by charging higher prices.

4.　INDEPENDENT POWER PRODUCERS

The PURPA-qualified facilities broke new ground because they sold electricity without being subjected to the rate-of-return regulation that governed regular utilities. They were the thin edge of a wedge that is now growing with the entry of independent power producers who likewise operate free of traditional regulatory restraints (see Figure 15–1). Projects are no longer limited to cogenerators who burn peach pits or to tiny wind-power operators. Independent power production is becoming big business, now running into many billions of dollars annually, and growing. Whereas nonutility power producers (including PURPA qualifiers) accounted for approximately 5 percent of America's electric generating capacity in 1990, that percentage is expected to jump to 12 percent by the year 2000, largely because independent power producers are expected to add 60,000 megawatts of capacity during the 1990s compared to the added 86,000 megawatts coming from regular utilities.[41]

Interestingly, some big utility companies are beginning to get into the unregulated power business themselves, petitioning the Federal Energy Regulatory Commission for permission to sell wholesale power to other utilities at negotiated market prices rather than at traditional regulated rates. Others own subsidiaries that are constructing facilities.

The upshot is this: A growing segment of the wholesale market is creating a free market in electricity. To the extent this free market sets the pattern for the future, regulated utility operations will be increasingly confined to the transmission and distribution stages (which retain natural-monopoly characteristics). Regulated utilities will become middlemen, as grocery stores are for breakfast cereal and detergent.

Summary

Investor-owned electric and gas utilities are subject to economic regulation in the classic sense. Regulation of price centers on finding numbers for the equation:

$$TR = OE + CD + VA \cdot r$$

When regulated properly, the price level generates sufficient total revenues *TR* to cover operating expenses *OE* and current depreciation *CD* plus a fair return *r* on the value of the utility's assets *VA*. Doing a halfway decent job of this is not impossible, but almost. Commissions act as arbitrators or buffers between the interests of customers and companies.

Operating expenses are usually rather easy to monitor because they typically entail payments to outsiders. Fuel, wages, and taxes account for the lion's share. Still, there are troubles. Payments to affiliated firms for coal or other inputs are not payments to outsiders, raising opportunities for evasion. Rapidly escalating fuel costs have forced the adoption of automatic pass-throughs, which likewise may open loopholes. Smaller portions of the expense budget call for judgment calls, and so on.

Current depreciation represents the return *of* the investors' capital. Wear and tear, obsolescence, and other factors warrant this expense, which in the case of utilities looms especially large. The estimate of annual depreciation for any asset depends on (1) the depreciation base, (2) estimated life span, and (3) method of write-off. Of the methods, commissions favor straight line.

The rate base *VA* is usually estimated by the original cost approach, but fair value and reproduction cost approaches have sufficient merit to capture advocates, both official and unofficial. The added question of what can be included in the rate base has provoked barbed debate. Cost overruns on nuclear plants and unneeded nuclear plant capacity have been especially troublesome lately. Many billions of dollars have been kept out of rate bases because many nuclear plants failed to pass the prudence test.

The tail of the price level equation—rate of return *r*—wags many a rate case. This is a composite, or weighted, average of the returns granted on bonds, preferred stock, and common stock. The cost of each of these securities is sought, a fairly easy job for the first two, much less easy for the last. Alternate earnings, risk, and a blend of other factors influence the outcome.

Once price level is settled, price structure needs attention, a need of swelling intensity lately. Two principles summarize the possibilities—(1) cost of service, and (2) value of service. They often yield similar price structures, but they need not. They vie for application in three main contexts—(1) who's buying, (2) how much, and (3) when. As for who, efficient Ramsey prices would have residential and commercial buyers paying higher price/cost ratios than industrial buyers pay to reflect value-of-service pricing, but the evidence is mixed. As for how much, price patterns vary as widely as the options available—fixed charge, flat rate, declining block rate, and inverted rate. Cost of service and value of service both enter here. As for when, peak-load pricing is an old idea whose time has come. Firmly grounded on cost-of-service principles, such pricing serves several laudable objectives.

Finally, our overall evaluation has pluses and minuses. On the plus side, empirical studies of price-level impact suggest that, on balance, utility regulation is an improvement over unregulated monopoly, at least for consumers. On the minus side, two problems with regulation have long been recognized—the lack of adequate incentives and the bias toward capital intensity. Two other problems have just recently grown in importance—the need for conservatism and the question of how to handle nonregulated generators of electricity.

Questions and Exercises for Chapter 15

1. Rearrange the equation on page 297 so that *r* is the unknown on the left-hand side. Why might utility regulation be considered an exercise in determining *r* instead of *TR?*
2. Identify the problem of affiliate dealings. What policy solutions would you propose?

3. Why is current depreciation (a) large, (b) necessary, and (c) a source of controversy?

4. How is r determined? Why might r and the actual rate of return differ?

5. Compare and contrast value-of-service pricing and cost-of-service pricing.

6. What are the two branches of cost-of-service pricing? Which is intended to further economic efficiency and why?

7. What is the purpose of Ramsey pricing? How does this compare with the purpose of ordinary price discrimination (see page 182) and cross subsidy (see page 284)?

8. Compare declining block rates and inverted rates in (a) definition, (b) consumption incentive, (c) purpose, and (d) frequency of use by commissions.

9. What are the advantages of peak-load pricing?

10. Explain why the kilowatt (demand) charge in the industrial two-part tariff is not really peak-load pricing.

11. What is good about regulatory lag? What is bad about it?

12. Why is incentive a problem when it comes to conservation?

Notes

1. *Wall Street Journal*, 23 May 1978, p. 40. See also M. C. O'Leary and D. B. Smith, "The Contribution of Economic Theory to the Regulatory Process," in *Public Utility Regulation*, ed. K. Nowotny, D. B. Smith, and H. M. Trebing (Boston: Kluwer, 1989), p. 224.

2. "Captive Customers?," *Wall Street Journal*, 10 May 1979, pp. 1, 21.

3. For examples see "Reining in Utilities," *Wall Street Journal*, 13 January 1976, pp. 1, 27. David Kaserman and Richard Tepel estimate that fossil fuel costs would be 10% lower without automatic pass-through. "The Impact of the Automatic Adjustment Clause on Fuel Purchase . . ." *Southern Economic Journal* (January 1982): 687–699.

4. Wallace Hendricks, "The Effect of Regulation on Collective Bargaining in Electric Utilities," *Bell Journal of Economics* (Autumn 1975): 451–465.

5. *Wall Street Journal*, 18 May 1981, p. 25.

6. *Wall Street Journal*, 3 September 1982, p. 19.

7. A. E. Kahn, *The Economics of Regulation*, vol. 1 (New York: Wiley, 1970), p. 32.

8. *Ibid.*

9. *Federal Power Commission* v. *Hope Natural Gas Co.*, 320 U.S. 591 (1944).

10. Randy A. Nelson and Walter J. Primeaux, Jr., "Rate Base Valuation Procedures and the Behavior of Regulated Firms," *Review of Economics and Business* (Winter 1984): 72–81. On the other hand, see H. C. Peterson, "The Effect of 'Fair Value' Rate Base Valuation on Electric Utility Regulation," *Journal of Finance* (December 1976): 1487–1490.

11. Alfred E. Kahn, "Who Should Pay for Power-Plant Duds?," *Wall Street Journal*, 15 August 1985, p. 26.

12. *Ibid.*

13. James Cook, "Nuclear Follies," *Forbes* (February 11, 1985), pp. 82–100.

14. *Wall Street Journal*, 3 November 1989, p. A5C.

15. For discussion of the legal implications, see A. L. Kolbe and W. B. Tye, "The *Duquesne* Opinion: How Much "Hope" is there for Investors in Regulated Firms?" and comment thereon by S. F. Williams and A. P. Buchmann in *Yale Journal on Regulation* (Winter 1991): 113–120.

16. Peter Navarro, "Electric Utility Regulation and National Energy Policy," *Regulation* (Jan/Feb, 1981): 20–27.

17. Robert L. Hagerman and Brian T. Ratchford, "Some Determinants of Allowed Rates of Return on Equity to Electric Utilities," *Bell Journal of Economics* (Spring 1978): 46–55.

18. Geoffrey S. Rothwell and Kelly A. Eastman, "A Note on Allowed and Realized Rates of Return of the U.S. Electric Utility Industry," *Journal of Industrial Economics* (September 1987): 105–110.

19. See, e.g., Harry M. Trebing, ed., *Issues in Public Utility Regulation* (East Lansing: Division of Research, Graduate School of Business Administration, Michigan State University, 1979), pp. 197–266; and J. R. Malko and P. R. Swensen, "Pricing and the Electric Utility Industry," in *Public Utility Regulation*, ed. K. Nowotny, D. B. Smith, and H. M. Trebing (Boston: Kluwer, 1989), pp. 45–47.

20. F. P. Ramsey, "A Contribution to the Theory of Taxation," *Economic Journal* (March 1927): 27–61. The modern version is in W. J. Baumol and O. F. Bradford, "Optimal Departures from Marginal Cost Pricing," *American Economic Review* (June 1970): 265–283.

21. Robert A. Meyer and Hayne E. Leland, "The Effectiveness of Price Regulation," *Review of Economics and Statistics* (November 1980): 555–556; Randy A. Nelson, "An Empirical Test of the Ramsey Theory . . . ," *Economic Inquiry* (April 1982): 277–290; Jon P. Nelson and Mark J. Roberts, "Ramsey Numbers and the Role of Competing Interest Groups in Electric Utility Regulation," *Quarterly Review of Economics and Business* (Autumn 1989): pp. 21–42.

22. For a survey of elasticity estimates, see L. D. Taylor, "The Demand for Electricity: A Survey," *Bell Journal of Economics* (Spring 1975): 74–110. For recent estimates, see the sources of Table 15–2.

23. P. L. Hayashi, M. Sevier, and J. M. Trapani, "Pricing Efficiency Under Rate-of-Return Regulation: Some Empirical Evidence for the Electric Utility Industry," *Southern Economic Journal* (January 1985): 776–792; J. P. Nelson and M. J. Roberts, "Ramsey Numbers and the

Role of Competing Interest Groups," *Quarterly Review of Economics and Business* (Autumn 1989): 21–42; G. G. Thompson, Jr., D. R. Kamerschen, and A. L. Danielson, "Efficiency in Nuclear Power Pricing," *Review of Industrial Organization* (vol. 5, no. 2, 1990): 13–27. For other studies reflecting on this issue, see Walter Primeaux and Randy A. Nelson, "An Examination of Price Discrimination and Internal Subsidization by Electric Utilities," *Southern Economic Journal* (July 1980): 84–99; John T. Wenders, "Economic Efficiency and Income Distribution in the Electric Utility Industry," *Southern Economic Journal* (April 1986): 1056–1067.

24. John F. Steward, "Plant Size, Plant Factor, and the Shape of the Average Cost Function in Electric Power Generation," *Bell Journal of Economics* (Autumn 1979): 549–565.

25. For a summary of rate structure practices across states, see the *Annual Report on Utility and Carrier Regulation* published by the National Association of Regulatory Utility commissioners.

26. For a thorough and advanced discussion see Michael A. Crew and Paul R. Kleindorfer, *Public Utility Economics* (New York: St. Martin's Press, 1979). For a theoretical and empirical review see Sanford V. Berg, ed., *Innovative Electric Rates* (Lexington, MA: Lexington Books, 1983).

27. For example, if a utility runs at 300 megawatts on the average but demand gets up to 400 megawatts sometime during the year, its load factor is 300/400 or 75%.

28. Charles R. Scherer, "Estimating Peak and Off-Peak Marginal Costs for an Electric Power System," *Bell Journal of Economics* (Autumn 1976): 575–601.

29. E. Berlin, C. J. Cicchetti, and W. J. Gillen, *Perspective on Power* (Cambridge, MA: Ballinger, 1975), p. 35.

30. *Wall Street Journal*, 12 August 1977, p. 1.

31. "Blues in the Night," *Wall Street Journal*, October 18, 1977, pp. 1, 19; and "Shifting the Load," *WSJ*, August 12, 1977, pp. 1, 23.

32. The leading study of this kind is G. J. Stigler and C. Friedland, "What Can the Regulators Regulate? The Case of Electricity," *Journal of Law and Economics* (October 1962): 1–16. They interpreted their data very pessi-mistically, leading subsequent analysts to conclusions more favorable to regulation. See, e.g., William Comanor, "Should Natural Monopolies Be Regulated?" *Stanford Law Review* (February 1970): 510–518, and H. C. Petersen, *Business and Government* (New York: Harper & Row, 1981), pp. 237–239. See also, R. Jackson, "Regulation and Electric Utility Rate Levels," *Land Economics* (August 1969): 372–376; and R. A. Nelson and W. J. Primeaux, Jr., "An Examination of the Relationship Between Technical Change and Regulatory Effectiveness," *Applied Economics* (June 1987): 773–788.

33. Robert A. Meyer and Hayne E. Leland, "The Effectiveness of Price Regulation," *Review of Economics and Statistics* (November 1980): 555–566.

34. For a review, see Paul L. Joskow and Nancy L. Rose, "The Effects of Economic Regulation," in *Handbook of Industrial Organization*, vol. 2, ed. R. Schmalensee and R. Willig (Amsterdam: North-Holland Press, 1989), pp.1450–1506.

35. John H. Landon, "Incentive Regulation in the Electric Utility Industry," National Economic Research Associates (mimeo), 1990.

36. Harvey Averch and Leland L. Johnson, "Behavior of the Firm under Regulatory Constraint," *American Economic Review* (December 1962): 1052–1069; Stanislaw H. Wellisz, "Regulation of Natural Gas Pipeline Companies: An Economic Analysis," *Journal of Political Economy* (February 1963): 30–43.

37. See L. L. Johnson's survey, "The Averch-Johnson Hypothesis after Ten Years," in *Regulation in Further Perspective*, ed. Shepherd and Gies (Cambridge, MA: Ballinger, 1974), pp. 67–78; plus Charles W. Smithson, "The Degree of Regulation and the Monopoly Firm," *Southern Economic Journal* (January 1978): 568–580; and Robert W. Spann, "Rate of Return Regulation," *Bell Journal of Economics* (Spring 1974): 38–52.

38. Kahn, *Economics of Regulation*, vol. II, pp. 106–107.

39. Paul L. Joskow, "Public Utility Regulatory Policy Act of 1978: Electric Utility Rate Reform," *Natural Resources Journal* (October 1979): 787–809.

40. *Wall Street Journal*, 5 November 1990, p. B1.

41. *Forbes*, March 18, 1991, pp. 82–83.

Chapter 16
Tele-communications

With one stunning decision, American Telephone & Telegraph Co. has placed a mammoth bet on the future—by turning its back on its past.
— James A. White
(January 1982)

The story of telecommunications divides into B. J. and A. J.—Before January and After January. On January 8, 1982, AT&T and the Justice Department announced the most historic antitrust settlement of all time. To end a monopolization suit halfway through trial and to break the shackles of a previous 1956 consent decree, AT&T agreed to divest its twenty-two local operating companies worth $87 billion in assets. AT&T would remain immense—retaining its Long Lines Department, Western Electric, and Bell Laboratories, altogether worth $49 billion in 1981—but the colossus planned to split. It happened on January 1, 1984.

AT&T's consent to wholesale dismemberment was a radical break with its past. For years, AT&T spent millions to advertise "The System is the Solution." And on announcement of the *dis*solution, AT&T president William Ellinghaus admitted, "I've been in the Bell system for 41 years and was raised with the idea that we should provide universal and end-to-end service. It's hard to pull away from that."[1]

What was AT&T like in the past? What pressures caused it to agree to division? What are the economic consequences for the future? Where does regulation fit in all this? These are the central questions of this chapter. To answer them we expand on the following outline:

   I. TECHNICAL, STRUCTURAL, AND HISTORICAL BACKGROUND
      A. Technical Background: Equipment and Connections
      B. Structural Background: Telecommunications Before and After January
      C. Historical Background: The Bell System Before January
  II. THE LOCAL OPERATING COMPANIES (STATE REGULATION)
      A. Before January
      B. After January
 III. AT&T (FCC REGULATION AND DEREGULATION)
      A. Before January: Price Level and Structure

B. After January: Competition
IV. RECENT DEVELOPMENTS
   A. Price Caps
   B. Baby Bell Ambitions
   C. New Technologies

Aside from the B. J.–A. J. distinction, another runs throughout the discussion, namely, the economic distinction between that which is naturally monopolistic (warranting regulation) and that which is potentially competitive (warranting no regulation). AT&T built its power by blending *both* types of business and by using regulation as a shield against interlopers in potentially competitive areas. AT&T therefore thought nothing of signing an antitrust consent decree in 1956 that confined it to regulated lines of business. However, as pictured in Figure 16–1 the boundary line between regulated-monopoly businesses and nonregulated-nonmonopoly businesses shifted during the ensuing years as new technologies (like microwave) and new regulatory decisions (like

Carterphone and *MCI*) gave outsiders the capability of competing against the Bell System in such areas as terminal equipment and long-distance service. The Bell System thus began to feel pinched—on the one side by new competitors and on the other side by the 1956 consent decree. Pressed still further by a government antitrust suit filed in 1974, AT&T agreed to a structural split reflecting the boundary of 1982 in exchange for an end to the 1956 decree and the 1974 suit. As AT&T Chairman Charles Brown explained it:

> The 1956 consent decree provided what we would say is a fence. The unspoken but assumed corollary to that was that the fence would stay there. But unilaterally the fence was opened with a hole (allowing competitors to sell telephones and provide long-distance service) where everybody could get in, but we couldn't get out.[2]

Because the split was achieved by AT&T's withdrawal from regulated local telephone service,

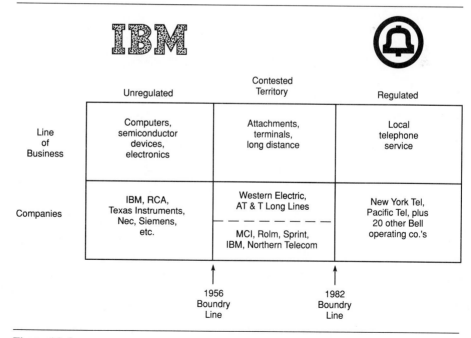

Figure 16–1
Summary of Telecommunications Developments and AT&T's Split

AT&T now continues to compete in the contested territory of Figure 16–1. And what is perhaps even more important, it has expanded into wholly unregulated lines of business like computers, thereby providing competition for firms like IBM.

I. Technical, Structural, and Historical Background

A. Technical Background: Equipment and Connections

Four main elements make up the telecommunications system, as shown in Figure 16–2. (1) *Terminal equipment* is the most visible part because it includes the 185 million telephones we use every day. Also included are private branch exchanges, or PBXs, which serve as switchboards for hotels, offices, and countless other businesses. Indeed, terminals now run the gamut from FAX machines to computers, sending and receiving everything from pictures to data. (2) A *local loop* connects terminals to the rest of the system. (3) In turn, the local loops meet at a hub known as the *central switch,* where a local call is routed from one local loop to another. Although there are now thousands of such switching facilities, there were none when telephony first started. Callers had to have direct wire connections to those on the receiving end. (4) Long-distance calls are switched into *long lines* for transmission to another central switch and further relay. Copper cables comprised these long lines until the advent of microwave and satellite communications, which now dominate the long-distance field along with fiber optic lines.

A major exception to this four-part pattern is private line service, for which there are about 30,000 business customers. Private lines bypass the central switch even for long-distance communications because all the equipment and circuitry are fully dedicated to private line customers.

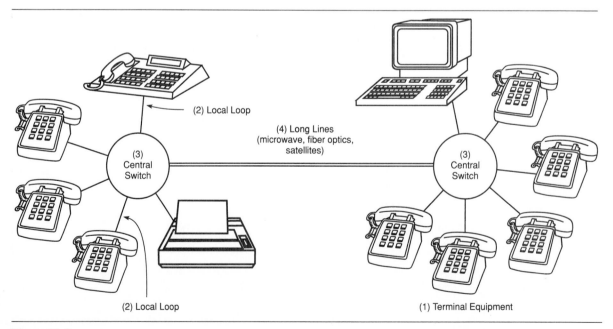

Figure 16–2
The Telecommunications Network

Television networks, banks, airlines, and other heavy users each spend tens of millions of dollars a year for such services. And "lines" is largely a misnomer, given the surge in microwave stations and satellites.

Looked at differently, the system is a combination of services and equipment. Services like local and long-distance calling ring up over $130 billion in sales every year. Telephone sets, PBXs, switching gear, satellites, and other equipment account for another $30 billion in sales each year.

Local loops and their associated central switch generate sufficient economies of scale to create a natural monopoly in services at the local level. Complete connection to two competing local companies would call for two local loops for each customer plus two central switches, with higher multiples for more rivals and with higher costs to boot.

Long-line technologies also have costs per unit of service that fall with added scale, but these cost reductions end at scales that are small relative to the large volumes of business flowing between major cities. For example, dozens of separate microwave systems could efficiently link New York and Chicago.[3] So monopoly is *not* natural for long lines. The same could be said with even greater force about telecommunica-tions equipment manufacturing, which has cost characteristics much like those of electronics manufacturing generally. Thus, there are serious limits to arguments invoking natural monopoly to justify regulation of this industry, limits that become especially important later in our discussion of competitive developments in long lines and equipment.

B. Structural Background: Telecommunications Before and After January

1. THE BELL SYSTEM

On January 8, 1982, the Bell System was a collection of diverse companies headed by AT&T. As shown in Figure 16–3, AT&T enjoyed controlling stock ownership of twenty-two separate local operating companies, whose main duty was regulated local telephone service and whose diverse geographic names divulge that the system resembled a quilted spread, with patches varying in size coast to coast. These local operating companies were spun off on January 1, 1984. They are now controlled by seven regional holding companies, as shown in Figure 16–4—Pacific Telesis, U. S. West, Southwestern Bell, Ameritech, Bell South, Bell Atlantic, and NYNEX.

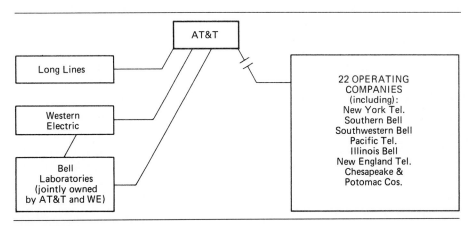

Figure 16–3
The Bell System Divestiture (Effective Date, January 1, 1984)

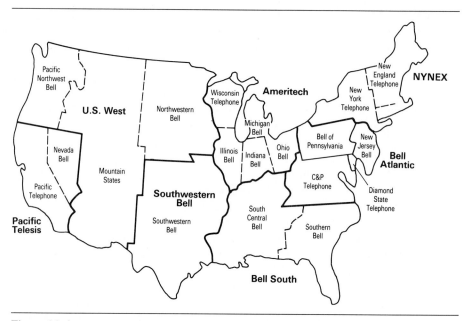

Figure 16–4
The Bell System: Old and New

These seven and their local operating affiliates can be called Bell Operating Companies, or BOCs.

The mechanics of the divestiture were amazing. People owning old AT&T stock suddenly became owners of eight companies—a new AT&T plus the seven spin-offs. Printing 655 million new stock certificates cost $2 million. The administrative expenses associated with reorganization ran upward of $300 million. The jobs of nearly 1 million employees were shuffled among the companies, and two years of preparations passed between the consent decree (1–8–82) and the official divestiture (1–1–84). Still, despite the immense planning, snafus abounded. Thousands of equipment installations and private-line hookups were untended for months. Horror stories filled the newspapers. And cries of crisis were heard throughout the land. Fortunately, the havoc has passed.[4]

The Bell Operating Companies now offer some long-distance services, but these are confined to short-range geographic zones called Local Access and Transport Areas, or LATAs. (There are 161 LATAs in the United States, some covering an entire state. Those for the region of Pacific Telesis are shown in Figure 16–5.) The *intra*-LATA long-distance service provided by all the Bell Operating Companies is a hefty chunk of the entire long-distance business in the United States. In revenue, it is about 20 percent of the grand total. However, the greatest volume of long-distance business by far is that occurring *between* LATAs. This *inter*-LATA long-distance service, which includes all interstate long-distance service, is what most people think of when they hear long-distance service mentioned. Hence, for the rest of this chapter we simplify "long distance" to mean inter-LATA long distance unless otherwise indicated.

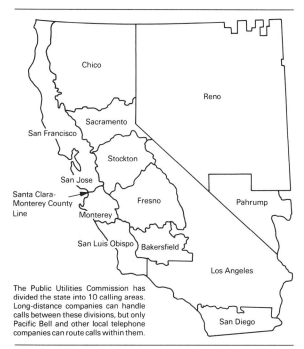

Figure 16–5
Local Access and Transport Areas, or LATAs, in California and Nevada, the States served by Pacific Telesis.

It is this long-distance market that gives the new AT&T, the company remaining after divestiture, its most massive source of revenues. The organization chart of Figure 16–6 indicates as much. There it may be seen that AT&T now is divided into two broad segments—AT&T Communications and AT&T Technologies. The former provides long-distance services and is in many ways the most interesting. Its heart is located in Bedminster, New Jersey, a command post of sorts with massive computers, monitors, and a 14-by-10 foot surveillance board that tracks the performance of AT&T's major switching centers. The long-distance network itself was built over the span of 100 years. It is, as one observer says, "unmatched by any of its competitors for

sophistication and ubiquity. With 932 million circuit miles of coaxial cable, microwave, satellite, and fiber optic routes connected to 167 switches that route telephone calls, the network is AT&T's biggest asset in its drive to dominate the emerging information industry."[5]

The second broad division, AT&T Technologies, is further subdivided into several branches covering research, equipment manufacturing, sales, and service, among other things. Western Electric, AT&T's old manufacturing arm, is now nothing more than a trade name. Its dozens of plants and its 170,000 employees have been spread among new branches—AT&T Network Systems and AT&T Technology Systems in particular. The one branch that most closely resembles its old self is AT&T Bell Laboratories. Some consider Bell Labs the crown jewel of AT&T's entire operations. World renowned for their research prowess, Bell Lab scientists and engineers can boast of many marvelous inventions. Their achievements have earned numerous Nobel prizes.

2. INDEPENDENTS

Although certainly formidable, AT&T and the Bell Operating Companies share the telecommunications industry with others, some of long standing. So-called *independent telephone companies* hold the local service monopolies in many areas (such that old AT&T never accounted for 100 percent but only about 82 percent of all telephones nationally). The largest of the independents is General Telephone & Electronics, or GTE. With 16 million telephone subscribers and over 160,000 employees, GTE is quite formidable. It owns equipment manufacturing and research facilities. Still, GTE is quite small compared to AT&T. By size and financial weight, it is more closely comparable to Bell South or to one of the other Bell Operating Companies than it is to AT&T.

Aside from independents grounded on regulated local utility service, the industry is now

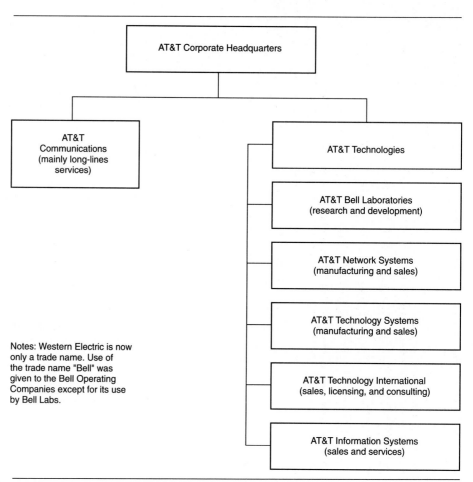

Figure 16–6
AT&T's Structure after the Divestiture

populated by two other groups: (1) those supplying long-distance service, like MCI and Sprint, and (2) equipment suppliers like Northern Telecom and Rolm. Many of these suppliers are newcomers to the industry who have, during the past two decades, crawled through the "fence" formerly protecting AT&T from competition in long-distance services and terminal equipment. Others in these groups, like GTE, are companies of long standing who have filled various niches in the industry but are now branching out to challenge AT&T in these big markets. Indeed, with further growth in competition in these areas, there may come a day when the *only* area of telecommunications needing continued regulation is local utility operations controlling local loops and central switches. Signs of this future make sense out of the split between AT&T and the operating companies.

The major long-distance service companies are shown in Table 16–1. MCI ranks a distant second to AT&T, with only about one-seventh of

Table 16–1
Leading Companies in Long-Distance Service, 1990

Company	Sales, 1990 ($ Billions)	Industry Share (Percentage)
AT&T	$34.6	70.4%
MCI	7.5	15.4
Sprint	5.2	10.6
Telecom	1.0	1.9
Others	0.6	1.2
Total	$48.9ᵃ	100.0%

ᵃExcludes $27.5 billion in payments to local phone companies to access to their networks.

Source: Wall Street Journal, 31 July 1990, p. A7.

the market. Although small compared to AT&T, this colorful firm played a major role in bringing competition to long distance. Sprint ranks third behind AT&T and MCI. These three together account for over 98 percent of all long-distance service.

Among equipment companies, more than fifty now compete with AT&T. Although AT&T probably retains over 50 percent of the overall business, its market share in some specific fields, like PBXs, has now dropped below 30 percent (down from above 80 percent before January 1984). Northern Telecom, which has been Canada's largest telecommunications company, is among the leaders in equipment. Rolm, NEC, Rockwell, and Siemens are also notable players in this field.

In sum, telecommunications were in the past heavily dominated by AT&T in every area of service and equipment. Now, since the divestiture of AT&T's twenty-two local operating companies, the industry has become clearly divided into three major parts: (1) local operating companies subject to state commission regulation, the largest of such companies being former AT&T subsidiaries now held by seven huge Bell Operating Companies, (2) national long-distance service companies lacking ownership connection with the local operating companies, and (3) equipment suppliers who sell gadgetry and gear of all kinds to the service companies (both local and long-distance) and to the folks who use the services (including you and me). AT&T continues to have considerable power in these latter two areas, but the immense advantages it formerly enjoyed as a *fully integrated system* have withered. Just what those advantages were and how they were used can be seen in the history that follows. History, in other words, suggests to us that competition in long-distance service and equipment could never have reached its full potential so long as AT&T remained intact.

C. Historical Background: AT&T Before January

Four periods highlight the history of AT&T before January 1982 and January 1984—(1) monopoly by patent, (2) open competition, (3) monopoly by regulation, and (4) partial deregulation.[6]

1. MONOPOLY BY PATENT, 1876–1894

Patent number 174,465 may be the most valuable patent of all time. Awarded to Alexander Graham Bell more than 100 years ago, it was the foundation of the Bell Telephone Company, predecessor to AT&T. From its roots in New England, the business spread briskly despite the fact that early telephone users had to string their own connecting wires. To encourage expansion with little capital commitment, the Bell Telephone Company entered into arrangements similar to modern franchises, licensing local telephone companies who paid for their rights by giving the Bell Company large blocks of stock ownership. In this manner of business lay the seeds of the holding company arrangement that ended with divestiture. The original patent and its exploitation through franchising proved to be extremely profitable, returning 46 percent annually.

Anticipating that these handsome profits would attract new entry on expiration of the original patent, the Bell System pressed several strategies during this period to perpetuate its power later:

- *Further Patenting:* The company's research effort produced 900 added patents by the expiration of the original patent in 1894.
- *Long Lines:* In 1885 a long-lines subsidiary was born. It was named American Telephone & Telegraph and was premised on the idea that a national telephone system would have a distinct advantage over a collection of isolated independent local companies.
- *Equipment Self-Supply:* Dropping the original policy of buying from independent equipment manufacturers, the Bell System acquired Western Electric and entered into an agreement that Bell would buy only from WE and WE would sell only to Bell.

2. COMPETITION, 1894–1913

Despite these several efforts, massive entry did occur after 1894 because of the rich profit potential and because the Bell System had failed to follow one additional strategy that would have cemented its power—namely, extensive geographic spread of local telephone service. The Bell System had ignored many small cities. They were therefore open to invasion by independent telephone companies.

The competition of newcomers led to sharply reduced prices and an explosive expansion of telephone coverage. What is more, the independents introduced many significant innovations, including the dial telephone.[7] By 1902 Bell's national market share slipped to just over 50 percent.

The Bell System stifled the competition by buying up many independents and denying others connection to its long-distance lines. These efforts eventually diminished under threat of antitrust prosecution, but not so far as to prevent Bell from being in a position to increase its market share to 79 percent by 1932.

3. MONOPOLY BY REGULATION, 1913–1956

Another prong in Bell's attack on competition was its promotion of regulation. In the early days, Bell vigorously opposed regulation, but fear of antitrust action, concern over the possibility of government ownership as in Europe, and appreciation that regulation could offer protection against competitors brought a change of heart. Desire for regulation was not limited to Bell. Many independents favored it, too, as did many in the general populace. Where monopoly prevailed, there were the typical dreads. Where competition prevailed, there was displeasure with the problems of multiple wiring and a lack of interconnection among systems.

In 1907 only a handful of states had commissions regulating the industry, and federal control did not exist. Regulation grew rapidly at both levels, however, during the next thirty years. And at both state and federal levels the Bell System was able to win favorable treatment at little cost to itself. Effective regulation was hampered by fractured jurisdictional reach and by Bell's policy of purchasing hardware from its unregulated equipment subsidiary, Western Electric. In short, regulation apparently served Bell's interests more than the public's for many years. As Gerald Brock says, "It gave the Bell system a powerful weapon to exclude competitors and justification for seeking a monopoly, as well as reducing chances of outright nationalization or serious antitrust action."[8]

Indeed, regulation provided AT&T with a screen that deflected antitrust action during the 1950s, action aimed at the divestiture of Western Electric. AT&T won the right to keep Western Electric by signing a consent decree in 1956 that restricted AT&T to regulated lines of business. At the time, it appeared that AT&T got something for nothing, and critics complained that the government had caved in to political pressures applied by AT&T. Yet, in the end, as we have seen, the burden of this 1956 decree proved to be too great for AT&T. Freedom from it motivated

AT&T's 1982 agreement to divest the operating companies.

4. PARTIAL DEREGULATION, 1956–1982

Two areas where regulation became particularly protective were long lines and terminal equipment. As we have seen, these areas now face considerable competition. Deregulation contributed to this competition even before divestiture. The steps toward deregulation were the "holes in the fence" that grew to irritate AT&T.

In *long lines* AT&T encountered competition before January when a series of regulatory and court decisions opened the field to new competitors. Because long lines were regulated by the Federal Communications Commission (FCC), the FCC was the key agency in this story of early competition, a story highlighted by the "Above 890 Decision" of 1959 and the "MCI Cases" of the 1960s and 1970s.

Above 890 Decision (1959). Prompted by two North Dakota television stations requesting permission to build microwave facilities for their own use, the FCC began a broad review of its microwave policy in late 1956.[9] Over 200 parties participated in the hearings. Those opposed to freer use of the spectrum above 890 megacycles were led by AT&T, whose main arguments were technical and economic. On the technical front, AT&T argued that multiplication of microwave facilities would foul up existing facilities with interference, causing "irreparable harm to the telephone company's ability to provide a basic nationwide communication service."[10] On the economic front, AT&T argued that entrants would engage in cream-skimming. They would enter only lucrative, high-volume markets between major cities, thereby ending AT&T's high profits there and ending the source of AT&T's subsidy to unprofitable markets in the hinterlands and in basic phone service. Tragedy would ensue, said AT&T, as this would "increase the cost of communications to the Nation's economy as a whole [and] would cast an added burden upon the individual and the small businessman who would continue to rely on common carriers.[11]

Those favoring freer use of the microwaves rebutted these points, but we need not delve into their counterarguments. The FCC found in their favor in 1959 with its landmark "Above 890" decision.[12] Yet the dire consequences predicted by AT&T did not follow. Although major, the decision was really quite limited. It merely opened the way for *private* (self use) microwave systems where space was available. It did not authorize new common carrier systems that could sell services to the public.

The MCI Case (1969, 1971). The regulatory barrier against *common carrier* microwave service lasted another ten years. It was finally knocked down at the instigation of pint-sized Microwave Communications, Inc. (MCI). MCI requested common carrier status from the FCC in 1963, proposing to build a microwave system between Chicago and St. Louis that would compete with AT&T by offering privately *leased* lines (capable of conveying voice, data, and facsimile), *at half AT&T's price*. Aside from the problem of winning common carrier status, MCI also faced the problem of securing interconnection with AT&T's local telephone companies. Interconnection was important because MCI's potential customers were relatively small communications users who needed local connections to reach MCI's long-distance lines.

AT&T vigorously opposed MCI's license before the FCC. AT&T argued once again that the scheme was technically foreboding. AT&T argued once again that this would be cream-skimming, with costly consequences for subsidized markets. Moreover, AT&T argued that MCI was incompetent, unqualified, and financially unfit to provide such a service. Finally, AT&T argued that authorization would be meaningless because AT&T would refuse local interconnection to MCI.

The legal battle reached partial resolution in 1969 when the FCC decided in favor of MCI.[13] A flood of similar applications followed, prompting the FCC to issue its "specialized Common Carrier Decision" in 1971, which announced a general policy in favor of competition and approved interconnection to effectuate the policy. Later, during the late 1970s and early 1980s, MCI widened its offerings to include dial-up service (again winning out over the protests of AT&T).

The story in *terminal equipment* is similar. We now think nothing of plugging a telephone into a wall outlet, just as we plug a TV set into our electric system, but for decades people could not do so. *All* attachments to the telecommunications system had to be supplied by AT&T. For an extreme example, AT&T persuaded North Carolina's Utility Commission to outlaw plastic phone-book covers that were not furnished by AT&T. Until recently, telephones could not be purchased from AT&T or anyone else. They were *rented* from AT&T, which owned them. (Out of 185 million phones now in the United States, more than 40 million of them are still leased from AT&T at rates ranging from $2.50 to $5.50 per month.) The evolution toward competition in terminal equipment before the January divestiture is highlighted by two cases—*Hush-A-Phone* (1956) and *Carterphone* (1968).

Hush-A-Phone (1956). The Hush-A-Phone was a cuplike device that snapped onto a telephone's mouthpiece. The effect it achieved was the same as if a caller cupped his or her hands between mouth and mouthpiece, namely, the muffling of background noise and privacy for what was said. AT&T railed against Hush-A-Phone, claiming that it distorted the speaker's voice a bit and questioning whether there was any real demand for the product.

The FCC sided with AT&T, but a federal appeals court sanely reversed the commission and favored Hush-A-Phone.[14] The court noted that users of Hush-A-Phone could only harm themselves (if indeed any harm was done), and do so in a way that they could easily duplicate with their hands. As for the absence of demand, well

over 100,000 Hush-A-Phones had been sold before AT&T's assault, and that was in any case a problem for Hush-A-Phone's manufacturer not for AT&T or the FCC. In short, the Hush-A-Phone case set the important precedent that some public harm must be shown in order to thwart an attachment.

Carterphone (1968). Shortly after *Hush-A-Phone* was decided, a tiny electronics company began selling what was called a Carterphone. This device contained a cradle that would hold an ordinary telephone handset. Without direct wire connection, the Carterphone could transmit a telephone voice into a radio broadcast for reception on mobile radios. By this means someone could call a radio dispatcher by telephone and talk over the mobile radio network.

In arguing against Carterphone, AT&T suggested a number of ways that the Carterphone might harm the telephone system but offered no evidence or example of any actual harm. The FCC therefore had little difficulty in finding against AT&T in 1968 (after lengthy legal skirmishing). This opened the door to competition a bit further.

There followed a series of FCC decisions during the 1970s that further liberalized the equipment. The PBXs were among the first devices to see competition. Then the market for telephones became competitive after the FCC decided in 1980 that people could buy their telephones from any supplier meeting minimum technical standards.

In sum, *even before* the breakup of AT&T in January 1984, the market for telecommunications equipment was moving in the direction of open competition.

This survey of the history of AT&T before divestiture illustrates how the corporation held on to its power for most of the twentieth century and also how that power began to erode before the divestiture of January 1984. We turn next to surveys of the regulation of price level and price structure at local and long-distance levels. These surveys also entail some history.

II. Local Operating Companies (State Regulation)

A. Before January: Price Level and Price Structure

1. PRICE LEVEL

The basic monthly charge for residential phone service varies substantially from place to place—$14.82 in Arlington, Virginia, and $16.15 in Bethesda, Maryland, to take examples from 1991 for two cities located near each other. A main reason for this variety is that *intra*state phone operations are regulated by state commissions. As in the case of electric and gas utilities, overall price levels for local service have in the past been set to generate total revenues that covered operating expenses and current depreciation plus a fair rate of return on an appropriately valued rate base (asset value). Thus, most of the issues that were discussed in connection with electric and gas utilities apply here as well.

For example, the method of rate-base valuation (original cost, fair value, etc.) adopted by a state commission for electric and gas utilities has applied to local telephone companies as well. Allowed rates of return likewise tend to move together, as may be seen by comparing the following figures for telephones with those in Table 15–1 on page 302 for electricity and gas: Alaska 11.17 percent, Arizona 10.38 percent, California 11.50 percent, and Colorado 11.67 percent.

For another example, a few state commissions introduced new procedural techniques for phone regulation designed to cope with the problem of rapidly inflating costs. The Michigan Public Service Commission granted permission in 1980 to Michigan Bell to increase its rates automatically for over three years depending on increases in the government's consumer price index.[15]

Still, since early times, telephone service had one major uniqueness. *Two* price levels were at issue, one level for *local calling,* which was regulated by state authorities, and one level for interstate *long-distance calling,* which was regulated by federal authorities. Given that the local operating companies' terminal equipment and central switches were used for *both* kinds of service, a thorny question arose: What portion of these assets should be used as the *rate base* in computing the price level of *local calling,* and what portion should be added to long lines assets for a *rate base* from which the *interstate* price level could be computed? A landmark Supreme Court case in 1930 held that the interstate rate base must include *some* portion of local exchange costs because local equipment is used for long-distance calls as well as for local calls.[16] The question of how much this should amount to touched off a lengthy feud between state and federal authorities. *Resolution of the dispute led long-distance prices to be quite high relative to true cost, yielding a subsidy for local phone service (including even the local service provided by independent phone companies connected to AT&T's long lines).*

2. PRICE STRUCTURE

In 1877 the first telephones were leased at $40 per year for business use and $20 per year for personal use. Thus, from the very start and still today, local price structure reflected value of service as well as cost of service. The traditional practice of charging business customers more than residential customers has some basis in costs because business users tend to place especially heavy demands on the system. But businesses also have demands that are *less elastic* than those of residential customers, paving the way for price discrimination. Just how much price discrimination has actually occurred is impossible to tell because major portions of total costs are common costs that cannot easily be delineated by service and by customer. Indeed, the difficulty of estimating costs is itself a prime reason that cost-of-service pricing has traditionally been neglected in the local service industry.

In addition to the business-residential price

differential, another differential has been customary that distinguishes between basic and nonbasic service. *Basic service* amounts to mere access to the system, as achieved by a single telephone and use of a local loop. *Nonbasic service* is everything beyond, including data transmission and long-distance toll calls. For as long as anyone can remember, promotion of basic service has been a guiding philosophy of both AT&T and government regulators. Hence, the price of basic service has been kept low relative to nonbasic services, so low as to entail subsidy. A major portion of this basic versus nonbasic differential was mentioned earlier, namely, the high price of long-distance service versus the low price of local service.

The amount of the subsidy for basic service is subject to sharp dispute because cost allocations are, at bottom, largely arbitrary. According to AT&T, however, the subsidy was quite substantial in the past. As indicated by AT&T's data for 1975 in Figure 16–7, the average monthly price for basic local service was only $9.00, but the total cost of that basic service was $16.15. This implies a subsidy of $7.15 from other, nonbasic services. (Notice that this is not value-of-service pricing because it is not based on a high elasticity for basic service and a low elasticity on nonbasic service. The actual elasticities are probably the reverse. It is instead *cross-subsidization*.)

Past divergence in prices and costs can be further seen in the fact that, with few exceptions, local service prices were not keyed to time of day, frequency, duration of call, and distance. Change is on the way, however. Such pricing for local service has now been introduced, partly as a result of the breakup.

Change is also reflected in one form of cost-of-service pricing introduced before the breakup—charging for directory assistance calls that were formerly free. When free to customers, such calls yielded some interesting statistics. In New York, for instance, the 1971 cost of directory assistance was $82.2 million for 500 million

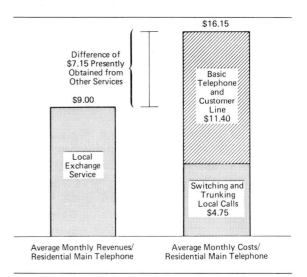

Figure 16–7
AT&T's 1975 Residential Cost Study

Source: Lawrence Garfinkel, "Network Access Pricing," in H. Trebing (ed.), *Issues in Public Utility Regulation* (East Lansing: Division of Research Graduate School of Business Administration, Michigan State University, 1979), p. 155.

calls, or about 16.5 cents per call. Nearly 80 percent of these assistance calls asked for local numbers, and 78 percent of these numbers were in fact listed in the local directory. Furthermore, and of particular interest, over 90 percent of all directory assistance calls came from only 30 percent of the customers, while half of all customers made no such calls during the period studied.[17] This means that when directory assistance calls are free, the service is abused and overused by a few customers who are subsidized by the rest. Now almost all states have approved charges for directory assistance. The typical approach is to permit five free calls per month, then charge 20 to 30 cents for each additional call. Such charges have cut directory assistance calling by half, saving more than $60 million in costs annually nationwide. The impact of cost-of-service pricing can be substantial.

B. After January: Price Level and Price Structure

1. LOCAL PRICE CONTROLS

What has happened to local service price levels and structures since the big break up? Let's take overall *levels* first. From 1982 to 1990 local phone charges rose, on average, roughly 40%, a pace of increase exceeding inflation generally.[18]

Why the whopping jump? There are three main reasons. The first is the breakup of AT&T. Once the local operating companies were severed from AT&T and established as independent entities, they could no longer count on the massive subsidies they formerly received from AT&T's interstate long-distance service. In 1981 those subsidies amounted to roughly $7 billion, or 35 percent of all interstate long-distance revenues.

The second reason is "bypass." It can be argued that these subsidies for local services would have ended even without the breakup of AT&T because the extra-high long-distance prices of the past could not last. They could not last because they were causing intensive long-distance users like big businesses to bypass the system, that is, to set up their own end-to-end long-distance connections free of any reliance on AT&T's long lines. Advances in technology have helped the bypassers. Using satellites, land-based microwave stations, and other technologies, they can set up their own long-distance communications systems if their requirements are great enough.[19]

The third reason for skyrocketing local price levels concerns depreciation. As a monopoly, the Bell System depreciated its equipment over periods of up to forty years. That slow depreciation kept local rates down, but it left the Bell Operating Companies holding a total of $26 billion in undepreciated equipment at the time of divestiture. After divestiture, the Bell Operating Companies pressed for much more rapid depreciation. The accelerated depreciation was said to

be necessary because rapid technological change was aging the equipment by obsolescence more rapidly than would occur simply by physical wear and tear. The accelerated depreciation raised expenses, however, thereby raising prices in the short run.

In sum, three main factors have elevated local price levels markedly—divestiture, bypass, and depreciation. What has been the reaction of local customers? Three cheers? Hardly. Protests have sprung up and petitions have circulated.[20] Consumer activists claim that the higher local price levels force many people, especially the poor, to give up their telephones.

For these and other reasons, there has been a rampage of regulatory change in the way state commissions treat local telephone companies. Figure 16–8 tries to summarize events as of 1991, but the chaotic conditions defy easy summary. One state, Nebraska, has reduced regulation to near nothingness. Two others, Iowa and Arizona, have deregulated some services completely while retaining regulation over others. A majority of states, twenty-seven in all, are experimenting with new approaches such as the "price cap" regulation that the FCC now applies to long-distance service (which we discuss shortly). Eleven states retain traditional regulation modified slightly by some reforms, and eight states had made no attempt to change at all as of 1991. It will be interesting to see whether the year 2000 brings clarity and consistency out of this confusion.

2. LOCAL PRICE STRUCTURES

This brings us to present-day local price *structures*. The economic consequences of higher local rate levels are so serious that local operating companies and state public utility commissions have recently been altering rate structures to help ease the burden. The traditional approach of charging a uniform flat monthly rate of, say, $15 to all the residential customers of a local operating company, regardless of intensity of use, is

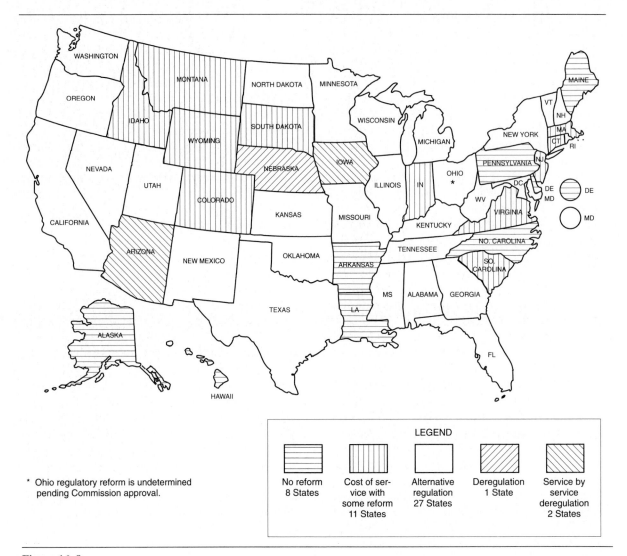

* Ohio regulatory reform is undetermined
  pending Commission approval.

LEGEND

| No reform 8 States | Cost of service with some reform 11 States | Alternative regulation 27 States | Deregulation 1 State | Service by service deregulation 2 States |

Figure 16–8
Alternative Approaches to Local Telephone Regulation, 1991

Source: William D. Thompson and Raymond A. Nuñez, "The Status of State Telephone Regulatory Reform: A Fifty-State Review," *NRRI Quarterly Bulletin* (March 1991), p. 37

giving way to two innovations—(1) local measured service and (2) lifeline service.

Local measured service adopts the approach of long-distance toll service. It calculates the number of calls placed each month, and the price of each call is based on its length, time of day,

and distance called. Depending on the design of local measured service, it can reduce phone bills for those who call sparingly. A six-month experiment in Vermont, for instance, found that compared to unlimited local calls under the old flat rate, timing calls resulted in lower bills for 75 percent of the residential users. Besides Vermont, forty-six other states were offering local measured services of various kinds in 1990. Almost all were voluntary programs offering customers a choice between the old flat rate and the new measured service. Thus far, a minority of customers have opted for local measured service, but that minority is growing.

Lifeline service gives low-cost, low-usage local service to the poor. California pioneered lifeline service in 1968. At this writing, California households with annual incomes of less than $14,300 can purchase 60 local calls each month for a low monthly fee of $2.23. Now all but seven states have some kind of program for customers with low incomes.

Notice the conflict between considerations of *efficiency* and *equity* here. It can be argued that, for sake of *efficiency,* local price *levels* should rise dramatically to better reflect the true costs of offering local services, costs that have in the past been hidden by massive subsidies. However, elevating price levels batter the poor. Hence, efficiency may undermine equity. Accordingly, it has been argued that for the sake of *equity* regulators should stem the overall rise and alter price *structures* to soften the blow to the disadvantaged. However, to the extent customers are protected in the name of equity, such a step could be costly because of inefficiency.

In sum, recent events at the local operating level could be considered, by and large, to be the bad news of our story in telecommunications. Is there any good news? Indeed, there is. It is found in our following discussion of the two remaining main segments of the industry—long-distance service and equipment.

III. AT&T (FCC Regulation and Deregulation)

Moving from the local operating companies to AT&T proper and the FCC, we find several interesting nuances: Long-distance price *structures* have always had more cost-of-service characteristics. And yet the artificially high overall *level* of prices has stirred competition and charges of cream skimming. Finally, competition in the long-distance and equipment markets has taken over for regulation.

A. Before January: Long-Distance Price Level and Price Structure

1. LONG-DISTANCE PRICE LEVEL

Several factors combined to make long-distance price levels relatively high in the past. One has already been noted—the shift of much of the local rate base to the long-distance rate base, thereby elevating the cost of long-distance service. Another factor was listless FCC regulation. For example, after the FCC completed a formal examination of AT&T's interstate rate base in 1935–1939, more than three decades passed before another thorough investigation of the rate base was attempted.

Finally, the FCC's allowed rate of return on AT&T's long-distance business tended to be generous. For example, the FCC took inflation into account to raise the allowed rate of return from 8.74 percent in 1975 to 12.75 percent in 1981.[21]

Despite the foregoing factors, long-distance rate levels had a long record of decline relative to consumer prices generally. Technological improvements and, most recently, intensifying competition have left their marks.

2. LONG-DISTANCE PRICE STRUCTURE

Prices that vary with time of day, frequency, duration of call, and distance have long been a feature of long-distance dial-up service. Such cost-of-service pricing has been possible in part because the equipment for monitoring long-distance calling has been around a long while.

Varying price by time, or peak-load pricing, is especially noteworthy because its application in long-distance telecommunications preceded its application in electricity and gas by many decades, yet its rationale is precisely the same. Telephone companies must have the capacity to meet the demand of their customers, but that de-

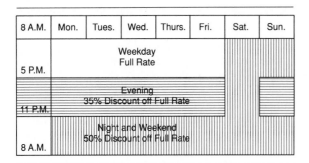

Figure 16–9
Long-Distance Time of Day Discounts, AT&T, 1991

mand varies substantially with the earth's rotation. The hourly cycle of long-distance telephone demand follows a pattern pretty much like the hourly cycle of electricity demand shown earlier in Figure 15–6 (page 312), with daylight business hours holding the loftiest levels. Long-distance calling also follows a daily cycle, with fewer calls being made on the typical Saturday or Sunday as compared to weekday calls. Both the hourly and daily cycles are reflected in peak-load pricing schedules that give discounts for evening, night, and weekend calling as illustrated in Figure 16–9 (which approximates AT&T's basic schedule in 1991 and is very similar to AT&T's schedule before divestiture).

B. After January: Competition in Long Distance and Equipment

For several years after the breakup of AT&T, polls reported that a majority of people thought the big divestiture was a mistake.[22] By 1990, however, public opinion had shifted to the point at which a solid majority favored the changes brought by the breakup.[23] These diverse reactions illustrate two points.

First, the divestiture imposed considerable costs, so many people had good reason to hold negative opinions. Table 16–2 presents a brief scorecard. Among the minuses, there have been higher prices for local service, greater confusion over terminal equipment selection and service, more rapid depreciation of local operating company equipment, and more confusion over telephone bills. As we have seen, the divestiture alone cannot be blamed for all these developments because deregulation in equipment and long distance were contributing to them well before the divestiture. Still, people see the divestiture as the one single, big event.

Second, and on the other hand, divestiture and deregulation taken together have produced huge benefits as well as costs. These benefits are listed as pluses on the right side of Table 16–2. Their order corresponds roughly to that of the minuses. Given the favorable shift in public opinion over time, it appears that these pluses are gaining ever greater appreciation with the populace. We can cover them under headings of "long-distance service" and "terminal equipment."

1. LONG-DISTANCE SERVICE

The divestiture decree bolstered the trend launched by deregulation. It required that the divested local operating companies provide equal access to all inter-LATA long-distance companies—AT&T, MCI, Sprint, and the rest. This in turn meant that long-distance customers would eventually have equal access to the long-distance companies.

The most notable consequence of this new competition in long distance was a substantial reduction in prices. MCI and Sprint led the way with prices that were 20 to 30 percent below those of AT&T in 1983 and 1984. By 1990 long-distance prices had fallen overall by about 40 percent following divestiture. (In late 1991, however, prices had stopped falling, and there were signs that they might begin to rise. A major reason was that tight oligopoly was developing, with only three firms in the market. Most of the many new entrants of the mid-1980s have now left the market, and because of losses Sprint may eventually depart as well, leaving a duopoly.)

Table 16–2
Scorecard on Deregulation and Divestiture

Minuses	*Pluses*
1. Higher local service prices (raising questions of equity)	1. Lower long-distance prices (furthering allocation efficiency)
2. Greater confusion over terminal equipment selection and service (reducing technical efficiency)	2. Equipment cost savings for both customers and phone companies (boosting technical efficiency)
3. More rapid depreciation of local operating company equipment (raising customer prices in the short run)	3. More rapid innovation in equipment and services (promoting progress)
4. More confusion over telephone bills and loss of regulatory oversight where monopoly power may remain.	4. Greater number of options for customers (giving a more competitive structure), and less government regulation.

Apart from lower prices, the long-distance business gained services of better quality and greater diversity. Regarding quality, AT&T accelerated its plans to adopt fiber optic cable when MCI and Sprint invested aggressively to achieve complete fiber optic systems. Regarding diversity, AT&T previously offered just a few service options. "Now," according to *Fortune,* "the big long-distance carriers can provide over 100 options to customers—everything from exotic conference hookups to international data transmission. Major corporations are now able to tailor their communications networks to specific needs, knowing they can count on suppliers eager to compete for their business."[24]

2.   TELECOMMUNICATIONS EQUIPMENT

As implied by Figure 16–10, competition has been much keener in the equipment sectors of the industry. A host of new rivals have successfully challenged AT&T. And the benefits of deregulation and divestiture are correspondingly greater—as measured by both prices and product improvements. In the first two years following divestiture, business equipment prices fell an esti-mated 20 to 25 percent.[25] Prices of home phones took even steeper tumbles. During one period of especially intense competition, some home phones were going for as little as $5 apiece!

What is more, the new competition has sparked dazzling advances in technology. Whereas terminal equipment used to be typified by drab, heavy, dial telephones that came in only one color (black), the market is now alive with models featuring Mickey Mouse, Garfield, automatic dialing, memory redialing, and countless other innovations. In office equipment, PBXs now seem to do everything except empty trash baskets. Inside local operating companies, new digital switches route voice and data communications over telephone lines by convering sound into digital pulses. Before digital switches were introduced in the United States by Northern Telecom, telephone companies used less efficient analog switches, which relayed communications in electronic waves. In short, the equipment innovations brought by new competition have been almost revolutionary. According to *Business Week,* deregulation and divestiture make sense mainly for this one reason, "The payoff in new technology is worth the pain of transition."[26]

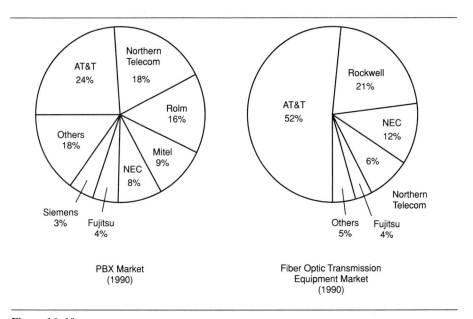

Figure 16–10
Where AT&T Stands in Two Major Equipment Markets, 1990

Source: *The Wall Street Journal,* April 18, 1990, p. B1; *Business Week,* February 25, 1991, p. 89

IV. Recent Developments

Three interesting new developments characterize the 1990s—price-cap regulation, diversification of the Bell Operating Companies, and technological changes that have undermined the natural monopoly of the local central switches.

A. Price-Cap Regulation

In 1989 the Federal Communications Commission voted to end the limits on AT&T's profits, as imposed by traditional rate-of-return regulation. Instead, the FCC adopted caps on long-distance prices. This approach has since been adopted by some state commissions for local and intra-LATA long-distance prices, and it is an approach that might spread even further to natural gas and electricity. A key to the application of price caps to AT&T's long-distance service was the new competition provided by MCI and Sprint. For AT&T, price caps can be thought of

as a temporary step on the trail to complete deregulation.

Price-cap regulation of AT&T has three main features:

1. Division of long-distance services into three "baskets"—one for 800 service, one for services primarily used by big businesses, and one for services primarily used by consumers and small businesses.
2. Acceptance of existing price levels in each basket as a base from which to calculate future price changes.
3. Allowing the weighted average price level for each basket to change, subject to a ceiling, or cap, that matches the percentage increases in the GNP price index, minus a 3 percent annual productivity adjustment (to reflect the estimated greater productivity gain in telecommunications as compared to other industries).

For example, if in a given year the GNP price index rises by 4 percent, the average level of AT&T 800 services could rise 1 percent after deducting the 3 percent productivity factor from the price index. Within that basket, prices of some services could rise 5 percent and others fall 7 percent, and still others remain unchanged so long as the overall weighted average did not increase by more than the 1 percent allowed by the formula. The formula (GNP price index minus 3%) is a rough way to account for cost changes over time.

Proponents of price cap regulation claim that it has several advantages over traditional rate-of-return regulation. First, it gives AT&T much greater flexibility in pricing its services, at least within each basket. Second, by breaking the direct connection between prices and costs, the price cap approach allows AT&T to keep profit increases that come from large improvements in efficiency, thereby giving AT&T greater incentive to cut costs. Third, by simplifying the regulatory process, the new approach is said to reduce the administrative burden of regulatory enforcement.

On the other hand, price cap regulation is not without its problems.[27] For one thing, price caps merely limit price *changes,* using old regulated prices as the bases from which the changes are made. Because regulated prices continue to be relied on, prices caps embody many of the same weaknesses as traditional regulation does. In addition, the added flexibility gives AT&T greater leeway to cross-subsidize from one service to another among those services within a given basket. Finally, the incentives for cost savings could also create incentives to reduce the quality of service. Whereas under traditional regulation there may have been some tendency for AT&T to "gold-plate" with excessive capital investment, there may be an opposite tilt as a result of price caps.

Whether price cap regulation turns out to be good or bad on balance remains to be seen. To assess it, the FCC has promised periodic review.

B. Freeing the Baby Bells

The court order implementing the divestiture of the Bell Operating Companies (and their formation into seven regional holding companies) placed important limits on what the Baby Bells could and could not do. In particular, they were permitted to supply local phone service within their regions, sell telephone equipment manufactured by others, and publish Yellow Pages for their regions. The Baby Bells were banned, however, from manufacturing equipment, producing information services (such as home shopping, weather, and sports news), and offering interstate long-distance telephone services. The idea behind these limits, which were supervised by the federal judge who presided over the breakup, is the same idea that propelled the breakup in the first place. Markets like equipment manufacturing are best controlled by competition, not regulation. Therefore, regulated monopolies like the Baby Bells should be kept out of them.

During the early 1990s, the Baby Bells have campaigned vehemently to be freed from these constraints. They have pooled millions of dollars to advertise messages like, "Stop Putting America On Hold," and "If You Like Being No. 2, You'll Love America's Telecommunications Policy." The Baby Bells have lobbied Congress to pass favorable legislation. And so on.

At this writing (in 1991) opposition to unleashing the Baby Bells is robust. It includes AT&T and MCI, who would have to compete with the Baby Bells if they were set free. The main problem with liberalization, according to the critics, is that the Baby Bells could take advantage of their monopolies in local services to make unwarranted gains in these other markets. As has been said:

> They could overcharge captive customers for local service and use the inflated profits to subsidize entry into new businesses, thus at once gouging consumers and stifling competitors. Another worry is that the [Baby] Bells could use their control over the local network to thwart competitors

who rely on phone connections to deliver services to customers.[28]

There is some basis for these worries because the Baby Bells have already behaved illegally toward these markets.[29] Yet by the time you read this, Congress or the courts may have caved in to the Baby Bells.

C. New Technologies

New technologies are undermining the natural monopoly each local operating company enjoys from its central switch control. The most obvious instance of this is the cellular phone, which requires no direct wire connections, making it ideal for cars, trains, and other mobile uses. Although cellular phone service is presently much more expensive than regular service, further technological breakthroughs will make it more competitive.

In addition, there are the following facts:

- Cable television companies are installing fiber optics that can transmit phone calls as well as video programs.
- Business firms are bypassing central switches by establishing private systems of their own, especially to link up to AT&T or MCI for long-distance calling.
- The FCC is exploring the possibility of assigning radio spectrum space to "personal communications networks," which would provide a form of cellular service much more cheaply.

These and other novelties are projected to displace no more than maybe 5 percent of all central switch business by the year 2000. Still, they herald the possibility of a new age when local phone service could be as competitive as long-distance service is now.[30] Modern technology often works miracles.

Summary

Government policy in telecommunications has been complex and confusing. On the one hand, it has encouraged monopoly power with patents and regulatory restrictions. On the other hand, it has encouraged competition with antitrust actions and regulatory relaxations. The reasons for this turmoil are several: (1) Economically, some parts of the industry are conducive to natural monopoly (local loops and central switches), whereas other parts can be served by competition (long lines and equipment). (2) Historically, technology has changed, so policy that may have been proper for one era has grown obsolete for another. (3) Politically, AT&T has seen its influence swell and contract. (4) Structurally, AT&T has in the past been fully integrated, a condition that arguably may have been based on genuine efficiencies, yet a condition that permitted AT&T to follow such anticompetitive strategies as refusing interconnection to local networks and denying attachments.

Our survey of this convoluted terrain began with an anatomical outline of telecommunications. Its main parts are: (1) terminal equipment, (2) local loops, (3) central switches, and (4) long lines. An alternative organization of the industry divides it into three broad economic sectors—(1) local phone service, (2) long-distance service, and (3) equipment. However the industry is characterized, AT&T in the past monopolized all segments of it except for some small pockets occupied by rather weak independents. Before January 1984, AT&T's local operating companies monopolized local service, its Long Lines Division monopolized long-distance service, and its Western Electric subsidiary monopolized equipment manufacturing. Now, After January, the local operating companies have been divested into seven regional Bell Operating Companies, long-distance companies besides AT&T have equal access to customers through connection to the newly independent local operating companies, and the equipment market has been invaded by many viable rivals like Northern Telecom and Rolm. Indeed, the Before January–After January distinction is a bit too crude. Deregulation launched competition in long distance and ter-

---

Thumbnail Sketch 4: Federal Communications Commission

Established: 1934

Purpose: To regulate interstate and foreign communications by telephone, television, radio, cable, and wire.

Legislative Authority: Communications Act of 1934; Communications Satellite Act of 1962.

Regulatory Activity: Regulates rates, practices, and service offerings of telephone, telegraph, radio, and satellite communications. It also allocates radio frequency bands and licenses and regulates radio and TV broadcasters.

Organization: The FCC is an independent federal commission of five members serving seven-year terms. Its major divisions include the Common Carrier Bureau, Mass Media Bureau, and Office of Engineering and Technology.

Budget: 1991 Estimate, $118 million.

Staff: 1991 Estimate, 1839.

---

minal equipment a few years before the January break up. In the case of long distance, the economies of scale that could justify regulation evaporated with technological change. In the case of equipment, they never existed.

Competition in long-distance service first became possible with the advent of microwave technology in the late 1940s and became even more possible with the development of satellite communications. Now more than a dozen companies offer a variety of long-distance services to the public as common carriers. This happy state of affairs came about slowly, however, because AT&T was able to delay new entry by employing several tactics: (1) securing regulatory restrictions, (2) denying interconnection, and (3) predatory pricing. Thus, competitive inroads had to grow by stages. Freedom to private, self-supply systems came with the "Above 890 Decision" in 1959. Competition in common-carrier offerings of private leased lines emerged after MCI won clearance in 1969 and others won clearance through the FCC's Specialized Common Carrier Decision in 1971. Finally, the immense dial-up market opened up in 1978.

Terminal equipment went through similar stages, beginning with items that could hardly be considered attachments at all (Hush-A-Phone and Carterphone) and progressing to the point of permitting all "plug-ins" that meet technical standards. Indeed, after 1982, terminal equipment was deregulated, with AT&T selling to customers in competition with others.

The January 1982–1984 breakup cemented these trends by doing the following:

- Divesting AT&T of its local operating companies.
- Giving long-distance companies equal access in connecting to the local operating companies.
- Giving the local operating companies the right to sell or lease terminal equipment in competition with other suppliers.

AT&T consented because the decree repealed a restrictive 1956 decree and gave AT&T its Long Lines Division, Western Electric, and Bell Labs (which have since been reorganized).

As regards *price levels,* continued regulation of the traditional kind governs local phone service in many states. These state commissions set price levels for intrastate (or intra-LATA) operations in ways quite similar to those concerning energy utilities. A major difference has been the below-cost price levels made possible by massive subsidies from extra high prices on nonbasic services, long distance in particular. Deregulation and divestiture have caused those subsidies to diminish. Local service price levels have therefore been ascending whereas those for long-distance service have been descending. This has prompted many states to drop traditional regulation.

As regards *price structures,* local service prices have in the past been notable for their value-of-service orientation plus heavy doses of cross-subsidization. Since 1980, however, there has been a trend toward cost-of-service pricing. Before January 1984 charges for directory assistance became commonplace. After January, local measured service began to spread as a means of coping with rising local price levels. On the other hand, a new area of cross-subsidization has taken root in the form of lifeline prices to help the poor. In long-distance service, cost-of-service pricing has been more evident. Peak-load pricing is the prime example.

Whereas recent developments in pricing have been controversial for their mix of benefits and costs (their disharmony in efficiency and equity), events in equipment have been unambiguously good. Deregulation and divestiture introduced keen competition, which in turn has pressed prices lower and quickened the pace of technological change. AT&T is no longer a lumbering monopolist in this area. It must be progressive to keep up with the likes of Northern Telecom and Rolm.

Finally, the 1990s bring several new developments. First, AT&T's long-distance prices no longer dance to the tune of rate-of-return regulation. Price caps now apply. Second, the Baby Bell operating companies are fighting feverishly to escape the restraints on their product manufacturing, information services, and long-distance service that were placed on them by the divestiture decree. Last, the natural monopolies of the Baby Bells are slowly becoming less and less natural as technological wonders open up the possibility of competition in local calling. Perhaps twentieth-century style regulation will become obsolete in the twenty-first century.

Questions and Exercises for Chapter 16

1. Describe the structure of AT&T and its component parts before and after divestiture.
2. Why did AT&T agree to divest its local operating companies?
3. What characteristics that are important to economic policy distinguish local telephone service from long-distance service and equipment?
4. AT&T used (a) regulation, (b) denial of access, and (c) price cutting to keep potential competitors at bay (Before January). Explain each strategy with the aid of an example.
5. Price levels in local service and long distance were in the past greatly influenced by cross-subsidy. What was the nature of this cross-subsidy, its extent, and its consequences for the pricing of new long-distance entrants in comparison to AT&T?
6. Compare and contrast the trends in price levels for local and long-distance service.
7. Compare and contrast the trends in price structures for local and long-distance service.
8. Deregulation and divestiture had substantially different effects on equipment. What were they? (Hint: Distinguish terminal equipment from other types.)
9. Which market has the most promising prospects for future competition, that for long-distance service or equipment? Explain your choice.

Notes

1. *Newsweek,* January 18, 1982, p. 59.
2. *Wall Street Journal,* 11 January 1982, p. 4. See also his statement in *Disconnecting Bell,* ed. H. M. Shooshan (New York: Pergamon, 1984), pp. 1–7.
3. Leonard Waverman, "The Regulation of Intercity Telecommunications," in *Promoting Competition in Regulated Markets,* ed. A. Phillips (Washington, DC: Brookings Institution, 1975), pp. 201–239.
4. *Wall Street Journal,* 13 December 1983, p. 29; January 13, 1984, p. 23; June 18, 1984, p. 1; *Time,* November 21, 1983, pp. 60–75.
5. Janet Guyon, "A Switch in Time," *Wall Street Journal,* 24 February 1986, p. 8D.
6. For an excellent overview, see Gerald W. Brock, *The Telecommunications Industry: The Dynamics of Market Structure* (Cambridge, MA: Harvard University Press, 1981). For a popular account, John Brooks, *Telephone: The First Hundred Years* (New York: Harper & Row, 1975).

7. R. Gabel, "The Early Competitive Era in Tele-communications, 1893–1920," *Law and Contemporary Problems* (Spring 1969): 340–359.

8. Brock, *Telecommunications Industry,* p. 161.

9. Alfred E. Kahn, *The Economics of Regulation,* Vol. II (New York: Wiley, 1971), pp. 129–132.

10. Brock, *Telecommunications Industry,* p. 203, quoting from the FCC report.

11. Ibid., from the FCC report.

12. *Allocation of Microwave Frequencies Above 890 Mc.,* 27 FCC 359 (1959).

13. *In the Matter of Microwave Communications Inc.,* 18 FCC 953 (1969).

14. *Hush-A-Phone Corporation* v. *U. S. and FCC,* 238 F.2d 266 (1956).

15. *Wall Street Journal,* 3 April 1980, p. 33.

16. *Smith* v. *Illinois Bell Telephone Company,* 282 U. S. 133 (1930).

17. Richard Stannard, "The Impact of Imposing Directory Assistance Charges," in *Assessing New Pricing Concepts in Public Utilities,* ed. H. Trebing (East Lansing: Division of Research Graduate School of Business Administration, Michigan State University, 1978), p. 92.

18. For a review of price trends see Robert W. Crandall, *After the Breakup* (Washington, D.C.: Brookings, 1991), pp. 54–62.

19. Leland L. Johnson, "Why Local Rates are Rising," *Regulation* (July/August 1983): 32.

20. *Wall Street Journal,* 27 September 1985, p. 1.

21. This last overall rate includes a return on common stock of 17%. Moreover, the last increase came on the heels of a liberalization in the treatment of current depreciation. The faster depreciation boosted AT&T's annual take by about $324 million. *Wall Street Journal,* 7 November 1980, p. 4.

22. *Business Week,* February 17, 1986, p. 90.

23. *Fortune,* January 2, 1989, p. 83.

24. *Ibid.,* p. 83.

25. *Wall Street Journal,* 24 February 1986, p. 40D.

26. *Business Week,* December 3, 1984, p. 86. For a detailed demonstration that AT&T's monopoly slowed technological change and that competition is favorable, see Kenneth Flamm, "Technological Advance and Costs: Commuters versus Communications," in *Changing the Rules,* ed. R. W. Crandall and K. Flamm (Washington, DC: Brookings Institution, 1989), pp. 13–61.

27. Leland L. Johnson, "Price Caps in Telecommunications Regulatory Reform," Rand Corporation, January 1989 (N-2894-MF/RC); Harry M. Trebing, "Telecommunications Regulation—The Continuing Dilemma," in *Public Utility Regulation,* ed. K. Nowotny, David B. Smith, and H. M. Trebing (Boston: Kluwer, 1989), pp. 93–130.

28. *Business Week,* March 12, 1990, p. 119.

29. *Wall Street Journal,* 9 January 1990, p. A1; *Business Week,* March 12, 1990, pp. 118–128; *Business Week,* March 4, 1991, pp. 22–24.

30. *Forbes,* March 18, 1991, pp. 118–124; *Business Week,* March 25, 1991, pp. 96–101.

Chapter 17
Broadcast Communications

While we make our media, our media make us.
— *Erik Barnouw*

The average television set is on nearly seven hours a day. Youngsters grow up spending more time in front of the TV than in the classroom. Oldsters watch TV more than thirty-two hours a week. Thus, TV has a tremendous influence on our lives.[1] In turn, the Federal Communications Commission influences TV because it regulates broadcast communications.

The story of this regulation is told in four episodes, which may be summarized in *TV Guide* fashion:

I. *Technical Background:* The radio spectrum has limits that raise havoc when exploited by the free market.

II. *Cast of Characters:* The TV industry has more actors than a miniseries. Local stations, networks, advertisers, program producers, regulators, and cable companies all play major parts.

III. *FCC Regulations:* The "cops," operating under broad legislative mandate, license broadcasters and urge good behavior.

IV. *Main Issues:* Often protecting established interests from innovative "robbers," the FCC encounters big problems—(1) network power, (2) cable TV, and (3) syndication rights.

Although TV is our main focus, radio broadcasting often enters the picture as TV's forerunner and fellow traveler.

I. Technical Background

In November 1920, radio station KDKA went on the air in Pittsburgh, giving birth to the broadcast industry. Hundreds of radio stations followed within the next few years. The main money behind these early stations came not from advertisers but from manufacturers of radio sets—like RCA and Westinghouse—who wanted to boost the sale of sets.

Unfortunately, the radio spectrum is a limited resource, with a limited number of wavelengths. This explosion of broadcasters crowded the dial. Interference ensued. Tuning one's set demanded exceptional skill. And early regulatory efforts were consequently "much like those of a lone traffic policeman trying to untangle a mass of stalled vehicles in a rush-hour traffic jam."[2]

The first such effort was the Radio Act of 1927, which established a Federal Radio Commission to organize the spectrum and license access to it. This law set two precedents that continue to this day. First, no licensee could *own* the channel assigned to it.[3] Second, each channel was supposed to be used for "the public interest, convenience, and necessity," a vague guide whose details had to be worked out.

The duties of the radio commission were later transferred to the Federal Communications Commission, created by the Communications Act of 1934. The resulting organization of the radio spectrum as it stands today is indicated by Table 17–1, which summarizes the spectrum's divisions and their assigned uses.

The television portion of the spectrum (not counting cable TV, which is not broadcast) has a total of sixty-eight channels—VHF channels 2 through 13, and UHF channels 14 through 69.

The number of possible stations using these channels is much larger, however. A broadcast signal can travel only a limited distance depending on the power of its transmission. As a consequence, broadcasters in different geographic areas can use the same channel. Through control of geographic separation, the total number of VHF station assignments in the United States approaches 700 and the total number of UHF station assignments is double that. These station assignments merely represent possibilities, however, because some station assignments go unused, especially UHF assignments. Moreover, many of the assignments are reserved for noncommercial uses such as educational TV.

Table 17–1 also hints at the wide range of other spectrum concerns. In 1982, for example, a debate raged over channel spacing on the AM radio dial. The question was whether the spacing should be reduced from 10 kilohertz to 9, the number used elsewhere in the world. At a more mundane level, the FCC must approve any device that broadcasts radio signals, even though those signals travel only a few feet. This includes things like "Sonic Scrub," a device that cleans false teeth placed in water by sending out ultrasonic waves that agitate the water to loosen de-

Table 17–1
Selected Radio Frequency Allocations

Megahertz (MH_z)		Frequency	Allocation
.003–	0.03	Very Low	Navigation; Sonar
.03 –	0.3	Low	Navigation
.3 –	3.0	Medium	AM radio; amateur
3.0 –	30.0	High	Amateur; short-wave; government
30.0 –	300.0	Very High	VHF television; FM radio; gadgets
300.0 –	3,000.0	Ultra High	UHF television; radar; CB; cellular
3,000.0 –	30,000.0	Super High	Satellite; microwave

Source: U.S. Congress, Senate Committee on Commerce, Science and Transportation, Subcommittee on Communications, *Amendments to the Communications Act of 1934*, Hearings, 96th Cong. 1st Sess. (1979), Part 1, pocket chart.

bris on the dentures. More commonly, it includes cordless phones and garage-door openers.[4]

In addition to VHF and UHF broadcasting, there are two more ways television signals can be carried into one's home—by satellite and by cable. These are important alternatives because they are not as limited in channel capacity as VHF and UHF broadcasting. Direct home reception from satellite is now too new to be of interest to us here. Cable, however, is booming, so it deserves close attention.

With cable, TV signals are piped into one's home by a wire connected to a local grid. The grid can pick up those signals from a variety of sources—local live production, tape replay, local over-the-air broadcast, distant transmission via satellite, and distant transmission via ground-based microwave. Because local wire carriage does not use the radio spectrum, cable has escaped much of the FCC's regulation of VHF and UHF broadcasting. Still, the FCC asserts some authority over cable.

II. The Cast of Characters

Regulation of the television industry cannot be understood without an understanding of the industry's participants and their roles—the viewers, advertisers, local stations, networks, program producers, cable companies, and regulators.[5] While you survey these parties, keep two things in mind. First, it is helpful to distinguish four crucial functions performed by these parties—(1) program *production*, (2) program *packaging*, (3) program *delivery* to home sets, and (4) the *funding* of production, packaging, and delivery. Some participants perform more than one of these functions, but there is substantial specialization. Second, keep Figure 17–1 in mind because it puts each party in place. The left side of Figure 17–1 depicts the Old System, which prevailed largely undisturbed from the mid-1940s to the mid-1970s. The right side incorporates the addition of cable, which has introduced a New System. Because

the New System represents an addition to the Old and is not yet dominant, we focus chiefly on the Old System until arriving at consideration of the cable companies.

A. Viewers and Advertisers

Over 97 percent of all households have television sets. As measured by viewing time per week, the people most fascinated by TV tend to be relatively uneducated, old, and of low income. The rest of us watch less often but nevertheless to a degree that in some ways astounds. The average viewing time for all individuals taken together is around *twenty-eight hours per week*.[6]

This audience is the *ultimate* source of funding for all commercial TV. This is true even of the Old System, where advertisers are the ones actually writing the checks and viewers watch "free." The viewers pay indirectly through their purchase of the advertisers' products. The advertisers are, in turn, the *proximate* source of funds for program production, packaging, and delivery. Spending on television advertising accounts for roughly 20 percent of all advertising and now runs well over $20 billion annually. In short, the orientation of the Old System is one in which the audience is "sold" to advertisers. Stations and networks compete for audiences whose attention is then marketed to marketers.

The monetary contributions of viewers are more direct when they are served by cable. Basic cable service is purchased for a hook-up charge and a monthly fee of about $18. To the extent that this basic service provides VHF and UHF broadcasts by wire (and presumably better reception), the fee essentially covers the added costs of delivery by cable. Program production and other costs are still paid by advertisers as in the Old System. Basic cable often includes other advertiser-supported channels such as ESPN, TNT, and CNN. Pay cable service provides *additional* pay TV channels such as Home Box Office to cable viewers at an additional fixed monthly fee. Thus, in the case of pay TV, the audience *directly* funds

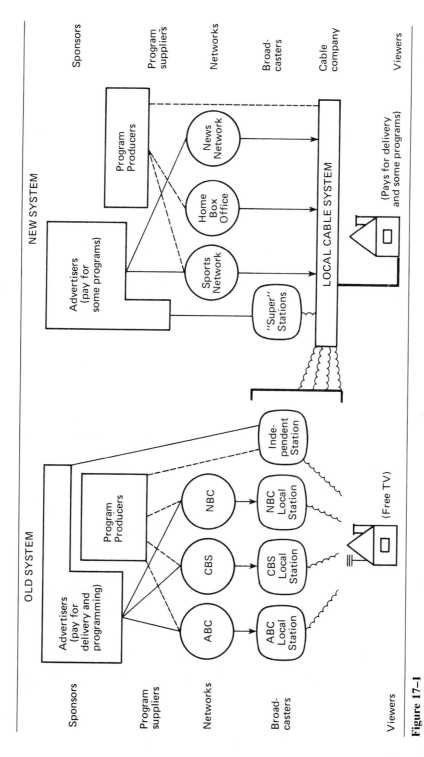

Figure 17-1
Outline of TV Industry Participants and Their Relationships

Table 17–2
The Financial Roles of Viewers and Advertisers in Commercial TV

Type of System	Cost of Program Production/Packaging	Cost of Delivery
VHF-UHF Broadcasting	Advertiser pays	Advertiser pays
Basic Cable	Advertiser pays	Viewer pays
Pay Cable	Viewer pays (all or part)	Viewer pays

all or most of the costs of program production, packaging, and delivery, thereby avoiding the advertising interruptions that occur so often on "free" TV. For the most part, programs are sold to the audience, whereas under the Old System the audience is sold to advertisers. In some cases viewers can be charged on a program-by-program basis. Table 17–2 summarizes these relationships and roles.

Statistics can also summarize the story: VHF and UHF broadcasting are received by 100 percent of all TV homes (either directly or by cable). Of these homes, 90 percent could receive cable if they chose to because the necessary wiring is in place. However, only about 60 percent of all homes subscribe to basic cable, and roughly 35 percent pay extra to watch premium cable networks. The special sporting events and rock concerts of pay-per-view TV attract viewers from about 10 percent of all TV households.

B. Local Broadcast Stations

The chief task of broadcast stations is to deliver programs to viewers. Some programming is produced by stations (local news in particular), but most programming is fed to the broadcasters by the networks or supplied by independent program producers and syndicators.

Of the 907 commercial stations reporting to the FCC in 1985, over 600 were affiliated with networks.[7] Affiliation entails a contractual agreement between station and network requiring the station to carry a minimum amount of network programs. Stations are compensated for carrying network programs when the networks pass on a portion of their advertising revenues to the stations. This compensation varies from station to station and depends on the amount of network programming a station carries. Overall, each network spends about $150 million to compensate its affiliates.[8] In addition, a portion of the time set aside for commercials in network programming is given to stations for them to sell to advertisers.

Outside the largest local markets like New York City and Los Angeles, no more than three commercial stations dominate local broadcasting. These three tend to occupy the VHF band and enjoy network affiliation. Stated differently, nonaffiliated VHF independents are a rare breed found mainly in places like New York, Los Angeles, Chicago, and San Francisco. The implication is that, from the individual viewer's point of view, television broadcasting is a highly concentrated business.

Even from a national vantage point broadcasting is more highly concentrated than would be suggested by the fact that there are more than 900 broadcast stations. Each of the three networks *owns* at least five of its affiliate stations located in prime markets (the FCC allows no more than twelve). And most of the main remaining stations are clustered by chain ownership. Metromedia, Westinghouse, and Storer are prominent among these chains.[9]

C. Networks

ABC, CBS, and NBC produce programs, package programs produced by others, and perform some delivery services. As regards *program production,* the networks can be credited for world news, most daytime programming, and most athletic coverage. In contrast, the situation comedies, detective stories, miniseries, movies, and dramas familiar to all prime-time evening viewers are not produced by the networks. Rather, they are purchased from independent program producers and *packaged* in the network schedule. Thus ABC, CBS, and NBC have traditionally performed a middleman function, producing or buying programs, packaging them into a schedule, and then selling pieces of the package to national advertisers along with the air time of their affiliate stations. Figure 17–1's Old System depicts this situation by sandwiching the networks between the advertisers and program producers on the top and the local broadcast stations on the bottom. Networks may thus be likened to merchandise wholesalers who bridge the gap between manufacturers and retailers.

Simple economics explains the existence of networks. Programs that are too expensive to produce locally can be produced nationally with affiliate stations sharing the cost. With each network affiliate showing a program and sharing the cost, the cost per station is lower than it would be if each station produced its own programs. Of course, numerous stations could deal with program suppliers outside the network context, and indeed to some extent they do. But even in this case networking offers efficiencies:

> One reason is that the negotiations over the price of programs are simpler and less costly, if a single agent, such as a network, represents two hundred or more stations than if each station negotiates separately. Another reason is that networks can solve the complicated problem of scheduling programs for all affiliates, rather than have each attack the scheduling problem separately.[10]

Although these factors explain networking, they do not explain the dominance of there being only three networks, a problem we turn to shortly.

Aside from their production and packaging activities, the major networks also perform some *delivery* services. First, each of them owns broadcast stations. These stations are located in the nation's largest cities, with the result that 25 percent of the population lives in markets served by one or more of these owned affiliates. Second, the networks bear the costs of delivering programs to local stations on microwave relay, cable, and satellite. Their long-distance delivery systems accommodate live national programming such as the Super Bowl.

D. Program Producers

The logos flashed on the screen at the end of most prime-time entertainment programs give their independent origins. Hollywood film companies are prominent among these program producers, but there are also dozens of others such as MTM Productions, that have been successful. Independent producers not only supply networks with programs; they also supply them to independent, nonaffiliated stations.

Nonnetwork programming is in part the preserve of syndicators who purchase programs from independent producers for subsequent resale to stations or to advertisers who place the programs with stations. In addition, many of the larger stations deal directly with independent producers. Much of the programming in this nonnetwork market is original, but a great deal of it is simply reruns of former network series.

E. Cable Companies

Cable television, the linchpin of the New System depicted in Figure 17–1, has grown rapidly. Cable's revenues from both subscribers and advertisers were almost $18 billion in 1990.[11]

Cable started during the 1950s merely as an amendment to the delivery system of broadcast television. Small communities not served by local stations and too distant to pick up clear signals from big-city stations were wired to large and lofty antennas that could catch those signals for the entire community. Cable also helped to improve reception in urban areas where tall buildings or hills created the "fuzzies." From this start based on *picture clarity,* cable grew because of an additional advantage over conventional broadcast delivery, namely, immense *channel capacity.* Although early cable systems carried only twelve channels, later systems were built to carry up to 100. This vast capacity offered the opportunity of great program diversity and viewer choice.

As suggested in Figure 17–1, cable TV has now matured into a complex system of its own, such that more than half of all TV homes receive at least twenty-five channels. At the base of the system are the cable companies responsible for wire delivery. Cable franchises are awarded to these companies for particular areas by local governments. These franchises are usually exclusive, thereby creating local monopolies. Local governments charge the cable companies franchise fees for the right to operate; the local governments may therefore benefit from these monopoly franchises. This monopoly status also led local governments to regulate the prices charged to subscribers to cable TV, but that regulation temporarily ended during the 1980s when the deregulation-minded Reagan Administration won legislation freeing most cable companies from price constraints. The prices of these monopolies soared thereafter, prompting a partial return to regulation in 1991. In mid-1991, the price for basic cable service to about one-third of all subscribers was regulated by local government authorities.[12] (We return to this issue of local cable system regulation later.)

As shown in Figure 17–1, some cable channels are devoted to the Old System's over-the-air

signals. Additional programming is supplied by nonnetwork "superstations," the most famous of which is Ted Turner's WTBS of Atlanta, beamed by satellite to more than 10 million cable subscribers in forty-eight states. Turner also pioneered with CNN in 1980, a cable news network. Other specialized cable networks offer an alluring variety of programming—sports, movies, music videos, "black" entertainment, and so on. Some of these are strictly pay TV, like Home Box Office and Showtime. Others accept advertising. Several of the cable networks are subsidiaries of cable companies, so these companies are not limited to delivery systems. (Time-Warner Inc., for instance, owns Home Box Office.) Moreover, ABC and CBS have also jumped into the act.[13] The proliferation of networks is certainly cable's greatest contribution to home entertainment.

F. The Federal Communications Commission

Operating from the sidelines is the FCC. A thumbnail sketch of the agency was given earlier, so further identification is not needed here. As for the FCC's regulatory activities in broadcasting, a special section is warranted.

III. FCC Regulation

Table 17–3 outlines the focus and purpose of FCC television regulation. Because the regulation differs markedly from the regulation of utilities, the table includes an outline of what is *not* regulated.

A. Access to the Spectrum

As we have seen, spectrum overcrowding was the main illness the FCC was created to remedy, and licensing was the medicine prescribed. No one may own or operate a broadcast station with-

Table 17–3
Focus and Purpose of FCC Regulation in Brief

What *IS* regulated by the FCC:	Purpose:
Access of broadcasters to the radio spectrum.	To keep signals clear; localism.
Ownership structure, locally and nationally.	To achieve diversity of ownership; localism.
Quantity of program types.	To serve the public interest; inform.
Miscellaneous: payola; employment balance.	To keep all operations fair.
WHAT *IS NOT* regulated by the FCC:	Rationale:
Prices and profits of stations, networks, or program producers.	They are not common carriers.
Prices and profits of cable companies.	Jurisdiction rests with local authorities.
Program content (although obscene and indecent materials are regulated).	Protected by the First Amendment.

out a license designating frequency assignment, call letters, operating power, and sign-on/sign-off times. In this connection the commission does not license local cable TV systems because they do not transmit over the air.

Given the limited nature of spectrum openings, the FCC is often forced to choose one of a number of applicants for the same frequency. This choice could be based on competitive bidding with the proceeds going into the public's coffers or to support educational TV, but it is not. It could be based on lottery, but it is not (although this is legally possible for new, low-power VHF "drop-in" stations). Rather, the choice is based on arbitrary judgment following a number of criteria: (1) diversification of ownership of media, (2) integration of ownership and management, (3) proposed programming service, (4) past broadcasting record on other frequency assignments, (5) efficient use of the frequency, and (6) character.[14]

Moreover, these licenses terminate automatically every five years. Renewal is customary but not necessarily automatic. Renewal is based on continued compliance with "public interest" criteria such as those just listed and with the presence or absence of rival applicants challenging the renewal. Licenses, many of which are extremely valuable, may be yanked by the FCC to punish wayward licensees. Indeed, this power is the commission's greatest enforcement weapon, a weapon that may be used to gain compliance with any of the regulations outlined in Table 17–3.

Stiff though this may sound, experience indicates that unchallenged renewal applicants are rarely scrutinized closely and that challenged applicants rarely lose out to challengers. As a former FCC commissioner rather cynically put it: "In general . . . licensees may violate FCC rules with impunity so long as they do not misrepresent facts to the Commission."[15]

A mildly amusing measure of this general laxity in wielding the licensing weapon is the surprise and outrage expressed in the business press whenever the commission acts so boldly as to actually terminate someone's license. A case in point was the reaction greeting the FCC's 1980 decision to strip RKO General Inc. of three prime television licenses. RKO was found to have lied to the commission. Moreover, its parent company, General Tire, was found to have pressured companies to advertise on RKO stations and made "questionable" payments abroad that were thought to be bribes. The *Wall Street Journal* editorially blasted the FCC for its harshness, mockingly calling it the Federal Character Commission.[16]

It must be stressed that only broadcast stations are licensed—not networks, program producers, or others. If the FCC wants to influence the behavior of these others, it must do so indirectly through its control of station licensing.

B. Ownership Structure

The commission restricts the number of broadcasting stations that any one individual or company may own to a total of twelve TV stations, twelve AM, and twelve FM radio stations. Moreover, a given individual or company cannot own more than one station of the same kind in the same place, precluding the possibility that two of your local TV stations are jointly owned.

Further ownership restrictions curb ownerships across media. Local newspapers and local TV stations are by and large kept separate. ABC, CBS, and NBC could not in the past own local cable companies, although nothing has prevented them from cable networking. Telephone companies cannot own cable systems in areas where they hold the local telephone franchise.[17]

The purpose behind these rules if fairly obvious. They promote a diversity and decentralization of ownership in an area crucial to the maintenance of democracy—namely, mass communications. As the FCC once said, "The premise is that a democratic society cannot function without the clash of divergent views."[18]

There has been substantial deregulation. The current limit of *twelve* stations each for TV, AM, and FM, is an increase over the old limit of *seven*. The Reagan Administration won this expansion of limits after heated debate with opponents and after a compromise that limited the twelve TV stations to serving no more than 25 percent of the national population. A massive wave of mergers followed the change. One of the largest of these mergers—that between ABC and Capital Cities—bumped into the 25 percent population ceiling even as the ink on the new rules was drying.

C. Quantity of Program Types

Deregulation under Reagan's appointees to the FCC went much further. In the past, the FCC insisted that licensees engage in some minimum amount of public service or merit programming. In particular, commercial television stations were required to show on their applications for renewal that they had provided a minimum of 5 percent local, 5 percent informational, and 10 percent nonentertainment programming (e.g., news, documentaries, political discussions, and religious programs). In addition, each station was supposed to ascertain and serve its community's programming "tastes, needs, and desires." The main rationale behind these old rules was that democracy requires a well-informed citizenry. And use the public's scarce radio spectrum should serve that public aim.

These regulations have been greatly relaxed. Quotas for merit programming no longer apply. Service to the local community's tastes, needs, and desires is no longer scrutinized. Why these changes? According to the FCC, they are warranted by the changing competition facing broadcasters—competition from cable TV in particular. This new competition, it is argued, forces broadcasters to provide merit programming and to meet the needs of the community. There is an ideological element as well, however. Mark Fowler, the FCC's conservative chairman under Reagan, saw "regulation as a kind of evil empire."[19]

Because of the Children's Television Act, passed in 1990, the FCC has reversed this deregulation trend, at least for children's programming. The act requires stations to carry educational and informational programs for children. Moreover, it limits advertisements during children's programs to 10.5 minutes an hour during weekends and 12 minutes an hour on weekdays.[20]

D. Miscellaneous Regulations

A number of regulations carry hopes of furthering various kinds of fairness. For one example, the FCC promotes equal employment opportunity in broadcasting. For another, the FCC attempts to curb payola—that is, undisclosed payments which are made to get material on the air. Payola is most commonly associated with disc jockeys who take bribes to play certain records. But it extends to television with its abundant opportunities to plug products. Payments as such are not banned because they support commercial broadcasting. It is, rather, *undisclosed* payments that rub the wrong way.[21]

E. What Is Not Regulated

1. PRICES AND PROFITS

No segment of the broadcast industry is subject to FCC regulation of prices or profits. Broadcasters are not considered common carriers or public utilities (nor are they treated like cable systems).

While noting this general absence of a public utility approach, it is interesting to observe that the main thrust of FCC policy is, if anything, to *boost* broadcasting profits rather than cap them. In particular:

- The FCC restricts entry by licensing access to the spectrum.
- The FCC created a few prime channels in each locality by its geographic spacing of VHF broadcasters and its mishandling of the UHF band.

- The FCC delayed the development of competing technologies with large channel capacities, cable especially.
- The FCC charges no more than a nominal fee for its licenses, thereby *giving* to licensees the use of valuable public properties (i.e., scarce channel assignments).

The result of these policies is, in brief, monopoly "rent"—that is, excessively high profit from restricted competition. The economics of this were explained earlier in Figure 14–2 on page 282 of Chapter 14, although in this case the government is *creating* rather than curbing those "rents."

The numbers demonstrating this circumstance are amazing. In 1975 the annual rate of pretax return on tangible capital invested for all VHF television stations was about 67 percent. In large cities where large audiences attract large advertising outlays, pretax profits regularly exceed 100 percent of tangible investment and sometimes exceed 200 percent.[22]

When sold to new owners, prime stations go for prices many times the cost of their physical assets, a phenomenon explained by the fact that the intangible license rights are worth millions of dollars. During the late 1980s and early 1990s stations typically sold for $10 to $40 million, and more than half of their value was for the licenses alone.[23]

You might reasonably ask, "Does the commission know what it is doing? Does it realize it's creating monopoly profits?" The answer is, "Yes, it does." But at least in the past, it has rationalized its protective policies on grounds of *cross-subsidization*. That is, the FCC acted on the belief that unprofitable merit programming (like religious shows) was financed by these excess profits. In other words, there was an implicit exchange between the FCC and the industry: The FCC limited competition among broadcasters in exchange for a commitment from broadcasters to use the resulting excess profits to finance unprofitable programs that were assumed to be of great social value.

Unfortunately, experts studying this exchange conclude that it was a very bad bargain, that broadcasters (and networks) came out far ahead in the deal at the expense of the public. In particular, it has been found that: (1) much merit programming, the evening news included, is not unprofitable; (2) that which is unprofitable is not so unprofitable as to justify the enormous excess profits earned; and (3) licensing limitation has virtually no effect whatever on program composition because most of these merit programs would apparently be aired regardless.[24]

Now that the FCC has greatly relaxed its requirements for merit programming, the attempt at cross-subsidy no longer prevails. Broadcasters can earn excess profits from their scarce licenses without the public service obligations of the past.

2. PROGRAM CONTENT

The FCC *cannot censor* program content. It is prohibited from doing so by the First Amendment's protection of free speech and by the Communications Act of 1934.

This is not to say, however, that the FCC has no influence whatever on content. In pursuit of audience ratings, the television industry has frequently served up abundant sex, violence, and other offensive fare. And from time to time the FCC has engaged in government by raised eyebrow, mildly pressuring the industry to clean up.

Bolstering the FCC's scowl is Section 1464 of the U.S. Criminal Code (Title 18), which bars the broadcast of obscene and indecent material. This deviation from free-speech policy is partly due to the accessibility of TV and radio to children. Although the obscenity provision has been vigorously enforced for decades, keeping obscenities off the air, indecency has been allowed in a limited way. Something indecent is less abhorrent than something obscene. Although indecencies are "patently offensive under contemporary community standards," they are more or less legal between the late-night hours from 10:00 P.M. to 6:00 A.M., when most children supposedly aren't watching television (or listening to radio). In 1988 the FCC went beyond this to impose a twenty-four-hour ban, but that regulation was overturned by the federal courts in 1991 when it was decided that a complete ban would be too offensive to the First Amendment.[25]

IV. Main Issues: Case Studies

Digging beneath this list of FCC powers to see how they have been employed in addressing specific issues, we find a recurrent theme, namely, the FCC has on balance tended to protect the industry's established interests against the intrusion of new competitive elements. This happened in (1) the FCC's allocation of VHF and UHF to television, a policy that solidified the power of ABC, NBC, and CBS against competitive networks, and (2) the FCC's deregulation of local cable systems in the mid-1980s. We also discuss (3) syndication rights, a controversial exception to this pattern.

A. Network Power and Spectrum Allocations

In 1980, roughly 90 percent of the television industry's viewers, revenues, and profits were accounted for by the three leading networks and their affiliate stations. Indeed, the three networks and the stations they owned accounted for more than half of the revenue of the industry. These national statistics disguise the fact that in most local markets the networks and their affiliates had virtually 100 percent of the business.

By the early 1990s ABC, CBS, and NBC had slipped badly. The rise of cable TV, the new entry of many independent broadcast stations, and the success of the Fox network combined to reduce the audience and advertising that the Big Three once enjoyed. Still, despite the considerable new competition, the networks have retained dominance over the medium. In 1990, for instance, ABC, CBS, and NBC attracted 65 percent of the prime time audience. Most cable shows could boast no more than 0.5 percent or 1.0 percent ratings. Hence, in 1990 the networks were attracting three to ten times the audience of any single competitor. And advertisers had to act accordingly: "The networks are still the single largest available audience in the strongest vehicle in the strongest medium. A major advertiser cannot not use them."[26]

Why do ABC, CBS, and NBC rule the video roost? The FCC has been a main factor, especially in its past pursuit of two related policies: (1) use of VHF for television, and (2) preservation of localism in apportioning the VHF band. Use of the VHF band began in the 1940s, when television was just getting started and when the leading equipment manufacturer of the day, RCA, was promoting VHF technology. The FCC approved thirteen VHF channels despite its recognition at the time that there would be "insufficient spectrum space . . . to make possible a truly nationwide competitive system."[27] If these VHF channels had been allocated to high-powered *regional* broadcasters, the total number of broadcasters nationally would have been limited to fewer than 100 or so, but the number of channels received by any individual viewer could have been six or more. Here is where localism came in, however. Rejecting the idea of having regional broadcasters, the FCC opted *to maximize the number of local broadcasters.* This meant that the total number of VHF stations in the country could be fairly large, but because of interference problems in their use of only a dozen channels, most localities could get no more than three VHF stations. Accordingly, the FCC dispersed VHF assignments across the country in such a way that *70 percent of all viewers could get no more than three commercial VHF stations over the air* (without cable). It is not surprising, then, that there are no more than three major broadcast networks.

At various times the FCC tried to rectify this situation but only half-heartedly and never effec-

tively. Protection of the established VHF stations and the three networks seems to have precluded vigorous remedy. In 1952, for instance, the FCC allocated the UHF space to television, multiplying local channel capacity considerably. But by that time the VHF system had become entrenched, and technical problems made UHF inferior to VHF, further hampering its success. A number of policy measures followed, all with the intent of bolstering UHF broadcasting. Television sets were by law required to have UHF tuning capacity, for example. But none of the steps taken was bold enough to endanger the toes of the established VHF interests.

Hand in hand with its feeble efforts to encourage UHF competition, the commission tried to lessen the networks' power by regulating the networks' contract relations with affiliate stations and independent program producers. Among other things, these FCC rules have prevented networks from contracting for exclusive station affiliations or sharing in the off-network rerun revenues of programs produced by independent producers. But these contract regulations did not increase the number of broadcast networks or the number of competing outlets available to viewers. All they did was increase the number of sources supplying programs to the industry and alter programming a bit.[28]

In short, the Commission has followed ambivalent policies concerning network power. It has tried to check that power with policies on ownership, contracts, and UHF development. Conversely, it has acted in ways that have nurtured that power. On balance, the latter effect has prevailed.

B. Cable Television

With its massive channel capacity and high-quality picture, cable television offers lush opportunities for achieving competition in program fare. Before the arrival of cable TV, the Big Three networks copied each others' programs in their attempt to attract mass audiences. The result was a lack of program diversity. Now, with many channels, a cable network's appeal to limited audiences—such as sports buffs or newshounds—has become profitable. Program diversity has consequently blossomed with competition among the cable networks.

However, all is not well in cable land. The local delivery of cable programs, controlled by the companies owning the wiring and other assets of local cable systems, is typically a monopoly, with all of monopoly's attendant problems. The vast majority of these cable monopolies receive the official approval of local governments because they are granted exclusive franchises. Competing cable systems cannot then operate. Thousands of these exclusive franchises comprise the dominant form of market structure in cable systems, but there have been several dozen local jurisdictions (about forty in 1991) where direct competition between cable systems has been allowed and even encouraged. These competitive situations usually involve no more than two rivals, but the duopolistic competition can be intense.

The policy of granting exclusive franchises for cable systems has stimulated several controversies. First, in the early days of cable, much debate centered on the question of whether or not these local delivery systems were natural monopolies. Many jurisdictions assumed that they were natural monopolies, so official selection of one company over others to obtain the monopoly franchise became a means by which local governments could extract commitments from cable companies to serve the public interest in various ways. In light of the many instances where duopolistic rivalry prevails, the assumption of natural monopoly has to be questioned.[29]

A second controversy began in 1986. Before 1986, municipal governments and other local authorities could regulate the monthly prices that cable companies charged their subscribers. The cable companies were, in other words, treated like electric utilities, which made sense given the

exclusive franchises that preserved their monopolies. After 1986, however, these local price regulations were outlawed by Congress and the Reagan Administration's FCC. Deregulation was in vogue at the time, and official Washington believed the cable industry's lobbyists who argued that cable systems would be held in competitive check by over-the-air broadcasters and by the luxury nature of their services. Hence, in the late 1980s there was a conflict of local and federal policies that created the worst of all possible worlds. *Municipal franchising established local monopolies while at the same time federal law banned price regulation of those monopolies.*

Controversy ensued when cable subscription prices soared, increasing 61 percent on average between 1986 and mid-1991.[30] More than half of the increase can be attributed to monopoly power.[31] The enlarged excess profits of the cable companies showed up in the market value of the cable companies when those companies were bought and sold (just as the monopoly profits of TV broadcast stations show up when their ownership changes hands). Before the cable deregulation law was enacted, buyers of cable systems were paying less than $1,000 per subscriber, on average. After deregulation in 1989, the price of cable companies had more than doubled to $2,600 per subscriber on average. Why did the $2,600 suggest that those persons owning cable systems enjoyed monopoly "rents"? *The $2,600 was three to four times more than the amount necessary to build a cable system from scratch.*[32] The extra amount reflects the value of the municipality's exclusive franchise absent price regulation, just as the extra amount typically paid for a TV broadcasting station reflects the value of the FCC license.

By 1990, the source of the soaring prices to subscribers became all the more evident in comparisons of monopolistic and duopolistic cable systems:

According to a survey of 52 markets by *Consumers' Research* magazine, prices for basic cable in competitive markets were about 18 percent lower than those in comparably sized, non-competitive markets ($14.23 per month in competitive markets vs. $17.32 in monopoly markets). Further, competitive markets offered more channels, lowering the per-channel price by about 30 percent.[33]

Consumers protested the price hikes, and pressure intensified for the *re*regulation of prices or the elimination of exclusive franchises to allow competition. In mid-1991 the Federal Communications Commission voted five to one to reinstate local price regulation. However, because of industry objections, the FCC's rule achieved only partial reregulation because many cable systems and nonbasic services were exempted. Under the 1991 ruling, the basic services of cable systems are subject to price regulation by municipal officials except when the cable systems compete with six or more over-the-air TV stations or with a multichannel video service, such as wireless cable or satellite services. According to the FCC, this means that renewed price regulation will cover only about 35 percent of all cable viewers in the United States. The other 65 percent live in exempt markets where the presence of at least six over-the-air broadcasters is assumed to provide enough competition that regulation need not apply to them. Hence, the reregulation has serious limits, and as of late 1991 consumer advocates remained upset enough to press for still further reregulation. More competition by way of easier entry would be another option. In any case, the controversy rages on.

(The FCC exempted nonbasic services because by law its jurisdiction covers only basic cable service. Anticipating that reregulation would be coming, many cable companies shifted channels out of their basic package into nonbasic offerings to dodge the reach of reregulation. USA Network, CNN, and ESPN were among the channels reclassified in 1990.[34])

C. Syndication Rights

During the late 1980s and early 1990s, when audiences stopped watching ABC, CBS, and NBC in droves, the Big Three networks urged repeal of some of the old FCC regulations that limited their market power. They focused on syndication rights in particular. The reason was clear. The syndication market was worth over $5 billion worldwide annually, the richest part of the TV industry.

The central issue was simple. Who could own television programs for purposes of *rerun* telecasting? Before 1970, shows like "Hawaii Five-O" and "I Love Lucy" were owned and controlled by the networks, which reaped profits when they were first telecast and then again later when they were rerun by local TV stations. After 1970, the networks were denied these syndication rights in an attempt to clip their power and stimulate competition in program production. The regulation had these effects. The number of independent program production companies grew from 30 in 1975 to 123 in 1990. The major Hollywood motion picture studios, like Paramount and Warner Brothers, also jumped into the act. And in 1990 the eight largest motion picture studios accounted for over 60 percent of the $3.4 billion in revenues generated by the domestic syndication of TV programs.[35] Popular TV shows can be especially lucrative in syndication. Reruns of "The Cosby Show" were worth $4.4 million per episode in 1991.[36]

A sharp ten-year battle erupted between the TV networks and the Hollywood studios during the 1980s and early 1990. The networks wanted the return of the syndication rights. The studios wanted to retain the rights. They battled over the votes of FCC commissioners. A crucial vote by the FCC in 1991 temporarily settled the issue by formulating a compromise. For the domestic market, the networks were allowed syndication rights but only for shows they produced completely in-house (free of ties with independent producers or Hollywood studios). To limit the quantity of shows the networks could acquire under this rule, new regulations limited the number of in-house productions to no more than 40 percent of the prime time schedule. Together with the usual risks and time lags associated with this business, these remaining restrictions were serious enough that it will probably be years before the networks have domestic rights to a significant number of hit shows.

For foreign distribution, the 1991 ruling allowed networks to acquire the syndication rights to any show they aired. This sounds generous for the networks, but conditions were attached that limit the networks' leeway here as well. Once a network first agrees to air a movie or a series, it must wait thirty days before offering the producer a foreign distribution deal. The delay lessens the chances that the networks will be able to acquire foreign syndication rights from studio producers.

As with all compromises, the FCC's 1991 ruling left both sides of the debate somewhat disappointed. At this writing (late 1991), the ruling seems ripe for appeal to the high court. Moreover, the networks and the studios will undoubtedly wage their battle in the halls of Congress, each side seeking favorable legislation. Owning syndication rights is like owning broadcast licenses or exclusive cable system franchises. Massive "rents" are involved, and the rent-seeking activity will continue. Like an afternoon soap opera, this story will go on and on.

Summary

Federal Communications Commission regulation of broadcasting is grounded on a genuine physical phenomenon—the limits of the radio spectrum relative to the demands for its use. This hiatus between nature's skimpiness and man's enthusiasm is bridged by two principles originating in early policy: (1) spectrum spaces are licensed, and (2) they are to be used for "the public interest, convenience, and necessity."

The FCC's allocation of space to television now includes twelve VHF channels and fifty-six UHF channels. Cable television is a nonbroadcast medium.

The television industry is home to a diversity of participants—viewers, advertisers, local stations, networks, program producers, cable companies, and regulators. Funding of the industry comes from viewers, either indirectly through the purchase of advertised goods (as prevailed in the Old System of Figure 17–1) or directly through pay TV (now a part of the New System). Despite the rise of pay TV, advertiser-supported TV still dominates, even in cable. Local broadcast stations are the heart of the traditional delivery system. Most stations are affiliated with one of the three major networks, which produce programs, package these and other programs into a schedule, and perform some delivery services. In the main, ABC, CBS, and NBC may be thought of as middlemen, bridging the gap between national advertisers and independent program producers on the one hand, and stations and viewers on the other. The independent program producers supply programs to networks (prime-time "entertainment" especially) and to local stations and syndicators as well. The cable companies offer wire delivery, which has the advantages of clear signals and large channel capacity. Their technology yields some characteristics of natural monopoly at the local level, so they are franchised by local government. Cable programming now includes the offerings of many cable networks, some of which are pay networks.

FCC regulation centers chiefly on the broadcast stations, because they are the ones actually using the radio spectrum. They are tethered by renewable licenses that are issued on various arbitrary "public interest" criteria. In addition, the FCC enforces certain ownership limitations designed to achieve diversity and localism. Program content is not expressly regulated, although in the past program types were limited with minimum merit programming a condition for license perpetuation.

In exercising their regulatory authority, the FCC and the local municipalities have tended to protect the industry's established interests and to stifle competition. The FCC helped to establish the power of ABC, CBS, and NBC when the commission decided on limited VHF allocations and localism. This meant that 70 percent of the populace could get no more than three VHF commercial channels. Local municipalities have restricted competition in cable systems by granting exclusive franchises rather than encouraging entry. The problem of local cable monopoly was compounded when federal authorities, including President Reagan's FCC, outlawed price regulation by the municipal authorities. This created unregulated, legally sanctioned monopolies. The rents created by this combination of federal and local policy were reflected in skyrocketing consumer prices and in escalating values for the exclusive franchises of the cable companies. The FCC has since authorized reregulation of subscription prices for basic cable services to homes lacking copious over-the-air alternatives (about 35 percent of the viewing populace).

Finally, syndication rights have been the focus of a battle between the networks (which air programs) and the Hollywood studios (which produce programs). Billions of dollars of rents are again involved. These rights were denied to the networks in 1970 when the FCC was attempting to curb the networks' power. When the networks began to lose power in the 1980s, they sought to regain those rights, which in the interim fell to the producing studios. A compromise prevails in the early 1990s that limits the networks and benefits the studios. The battle rages on, however, because the stakes are huge.

Questions and Exercises for Chapter 17

1. What is the rationale for FCC regulation of broadcasters?
2. Compare and contrast the roles of the following industry participants: (a) broadcast networks, (b) cable networks, (c) local broadcast stations, and (d) local cable companies.
3. Why are there only three main broadcast networks but many cable networks?
4. Explain ownership regulation in purpose and approach.
5. What have been the economic consequences of the prevailing method of licensing?
6. Many people have proposed selection of licensees on the basis of competitive bidding. Why?
7. The FCC does not regulate price and profit; yet cross-subsidization has been a rationale of past FCC regulation of "merit" programming. Explain and assess.
8. What economic forces lie behind the creation of networks?
9. Why do only three networks dominate the industry? Why has their power diminished in recent years?
10. You could buy a local cable company in 1984 for roughly $1,000 per subscriber. In 1989 the price had climbed to about $2,600 per subscriber. Why?
11. Syndication rights have something in common with FCC licenses and exclusive franchises for cable systems. Explain what that commonality is.
12. What changes in syndication rights occurred in 1970 and 1991? How did the change in 1970 affect competition in program production? How did changes in network power support the 1991 ruling?

Notes

1. G. Comstock, S. Chaffee, N. Katzman, M. McCombs, and D. Roberts, *Television and Human Behavior* (New York: Columbia University Press, 1978).

2. *Federal Regulation and Regulatory Reform*, Report by the Subcommittee on Oversight and Investigations of the Committee on Interstate and Foreign Commerce, U.S. Congress, House, 94th Cong., 2nd Session (1976), p. 250.

3. Some have argued that the sale (or giveaway) of spectrum spaces would eliminate the need for regulation. The idea is that spectrum ownership would, through economic incentives, lead to the best use of this scarce resource. See R. H. Coase, "The Federal Communications Commission," *Journal of Law and Economics* (October 1959): 1–40. For a brief critique of this view, see W. H. Melody, "Radio Spectrum Allocation: Role of the Market," *American Economic Review* (May 1980): 393–397.

4. *Business Week,* July 23, 1990, pp. 48–53.

5. James Rosse and James Dertouzos, "Economic Issues in Mass Communication Industries," *Proceedings of the Symposium on Media Concentration* (Washington, DC: Federal Trade Commission, 1978), pp. 87–110; Harvey J. Levin, *Fact and Fancy in Television Regulation* (New York: Russell Sage Foundation, 1980), pp. 25–47.

6. Comstock et al., *Television and Human Behavior,* p. 94.

7. *Business Week,* February 18, 1985, p. 38.

8. *Wall Street Journal,* 31 May 1989, p. B1.

9. Rosse and Dertouzos, "Economic Issues," p. 102.

10. Roger Noll, "Television and Competition," *Proceedings of the Symposium on Media Concentration,* p. 245.

11. *Wall Street Journal,* 19 March 1990, p. B1.

12. *Wall Street Journal,* 14 June 1991, p. B1.

13. Though prevented from stringing cable by regulations, the networks are free to offer cable programming.

14. The most important criteria seem to be followed. Margaret F. Barton, "Conditional Logit Analysis of FCC Decision Making," *Bell Journal of Economics* (Autumn 1979): 399–411.

15. Nicholas Johnson and John Dystel, "A Day in the Life: The Federal Communication Commission," *Yale Law Journal* (July 1973): 1605.

16. *Wall Street Journal,* 1 February 1980, p. 16; 24 June 1981, p. 28. A main argument was that other delinquents had not been so punished, but of course that is precisely the point here. See also *Fortune,* April 21, 1980, pp. 128–136.

17. For a survey see *Proceedings of the Symposium on Media Concentration,* Vol. II, pp. 378–428, 472–497.

18. FCC, Second Report and Order in Docket No. 18110, January 31, 1975, par. 111, as quoted by Levin, *Fact and Fancy,* p. 165.

19. *Business Week,* August 5, 1985, p. 51.

20. *Wall Street Journal,* 9 November 1990, p. B6.

21. R. H. Coase, "Payola in Radio and Television Broadcasting," *Journal of Law & Economics* (October 1979): 269–328.

22. Levin, *Fact and Fancy,* pp. 111–120. See also Paul W. MacAvoy, *Deregulation of Cable Television* (Washington, DC: American Enterprise Institute, 1977), p. 35. As Robert Crandall points out, television performers *also* gain monopoly revenues from FCC policies: "Actors often earn $100,000 per hour of filming in a continuing series and local newsmen may earn as much as $100,000 per year—prices greatly in excess of their earnings potentials elsewhere. These large salaries are greatly enhanced by the lack of channel choice in television." "Regulation of Television Broadcasting," *Regulation* (January/February, 1978): 39.

23. *Business Week,* July 23, 1990, p. 49; *Wall Street Journal,* 7 May 1991, p. B1.

24. Levin, *Fact and Fancy,* pp. 137–156; Crandall, "Regulation of TV Broadcasting," pp. 34–39. Another complaint is that merit programming lacks merit. Like entertainment programming, it dances to the tune of audience ratings. The alleged result is distorted news, noncontroversial documentaries, and assorted pap. Erik Barnouw, *The Sponsor* (New York: Oxford University Press, 1978), pp. 123–147.

25. *Wall Street Journal,* 20 May 1991, p. C15.

26. Bill Saporito, "TV's Toughest Year Is Just a Preview," *Fortune,* November 19, 1990, pp. 95–114. See also *Business Week,* June 18, 1990, pp. 26–28, which shows that the networks have been able to raise their prices to advertisers substantially despite the drop in audience share.

27. FCC Final Report, May 25, 1945, FCC Docket No. 6651, pp. 99–100.

28. Stanley M. Besen and Thomas G. Krattenmaker, "Regulating Network Television," *Regulation* (May/June 1981): 27–34.

29. Thomas W. Hazlett, "Duopolistic Competition in Cable Television: Implications for Public Policy," *Yale Journal on Regulation* (Winter 1990): 65–119.

30. *Business Week,* August 12, 1991, p. 67.

31. Robert Rubinovitz, "Market Power and Price Increases for Basic Cable Service Since Deregulation," U.S. Department of Justice, Antitrust Division, Discussion Paper, August 6, 1991.

32. Michael Kinsley, "Remote Control," *The New Republic,* April 23, 1990, p. 4.

33. John Merline, "Wired for Monopoly," *Washington Post National Weekly Edition,* June 3–9, 1991, p. 24. See also Hazlett, "Duopolistic Competition," p. 90, for a summary of other studies.

34. *Wall Street Journal,* 25 January 1991, p. B1.

35. *Wall Street Journal,* 10 April 1991, pp. A1 and A8.

36. *Newsweek,* April 22, 1991, p. 44.

Chapter 18

Transportation

During regulation, if you had operating rights and you could get out of bed in the morning, you could stay in business. But without operating rights, you've got to be efficient.
— John B. Curcio
President of Mack Truck, Inc.

The Civil Aeronautics Board expired on December 31, 1984. Its demise made history. Never before had a major regulatory agency been terminated. Ceremony being appropriate for closing the agency's headquarters, a U. S. Marine bugler played "Evening Colors" while a government executive lifted the CAB's official seal off the wall for donation to the Smithsonian Institution.

Whereas regulation is the main theme of previous chapters, *de*regulation is the main theme of this one. Whereas market imperfections and failures are stressed in previous chapters, *government* imperfections and failures are the stuffings of this one.

Over 100 years ago railroading became the first industry to be regulated by the federal government. That regulation was good at the outset, but its persistence, its growth, and its spread to other areas of transportation were bad. The error was recognized by many economists four decades ago, but only at the close of the 1970s did the government begin to back off.

Matters of industry identification are settled in Section I. Section II outlines the basic economics of the industry. Sections III and IV explain the origins and nature of transport regulation. The adverse effects of this regulation are covered in Section V, followed in Section VI by a rundown of deregulation and its effects.

I. Industry Identification

Of transportation's various modes, railroads have a central place. When federal regulation began in 1887, railroads virtually monopolized intercity freight traffic. Waterways provided some competition but only on certain routes. As Table 18–1 shows, the dominance of the railroads has dwindled markedly with the growth of trucking and oil pipelines. Railroads are also distinguished by the fact that, until the 1980s, *all* rail freight was federally regulated. Federal regulation never covered more than 45 percent of truck freight, 85

Table 18–1
Intercity Freight Traffic by Type of Transport (Percent of Total Ton-Miles)
(in percentages)

Year	Railroads	Trucks	Oil Pipelines	Inland Waterways	Airways
1940	61.3%	10.0%	9.5%	19.1%	0.00%
1950	56.2	16.3	12.1	15.4	0.03
1960	44.1	21.8	17.4	16.7	0.07
1970	39.7	21.3	22.3	16.5	0.17
1980	37.5	22.3	23.6	16.4	0.19
1988	37.0	25.0	21.9	15.5	0.33

Source: Transportation Association of America, *Transportation Facts and Trends* (July 1979): 8; *Statistical Abstract of the United States*, 1990, p. 597.

percent of oil pipeline volume, and 20 percent of inland waterway traffic.

Private automobiles account for the lion's share of intercity passenger traffic, roughly 81 percent. The remaining 19 percent is handled by formerly regulated modes—airways, buses, and railroads. By far the largest of these is the airways, which account for over 17 percent of all passenger-miles traveled.

II. The Basic Economics of Transportation

A. Demand Side

The demand for transportation services is essentially a *derived* demand. That is, transportation is not sought as an end in itself. Its demand derives from the demand for *other* goods and services that rely on transportation for their distribution. The demand for electricity creates a demand for coal, which in turn creates a demand for the shipment of coal from mines to power plants. The demand for Hawaiian vacations creates a demand for passenger travel from the mainland to Hawaii. And so forth.

This derivation of transportation demand heavily influences price elasticities of demand. For one thing, price elasticity varies substantially, depending on the ultimate end served. If, for example, transportation cost is a large portion of the final cost of a product—as it is for steel—then the price elasticity of demand for transportation is likely to be relatively high as compared to cases in which the transportation cost is a very small portion of the final cost of the product—as it is for semiconductor devices. In passenger transport, vacationers have a relatively high price elasticity of demand for air travel as compared to businesspeople (see Figure 18–1).

Demand for a specific mode of transport, say railroads, is influenced by more than the price of that mode. It is also influenced by the price of alternative modes—trucks, barges, pipelines, and so on. This gives rise to *intermodal* competition as distinct from *intra*modal competition. It is important to note that intermodal competition is likewise influenced by numerous *nonprice* factors, the most significant of which are speed of service, flexibility, reliability, and susceptibility of freight to damage. Nonprice factors determine the total costs borne by shippers and travelers.

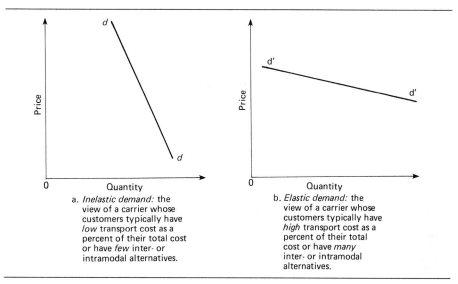

Figure 18–1
Differing Elasticities of Demand in Transportation

For example, slow movement of freight raises the shipper's cost of inventory. And slow movement of people raises the traveler's cost of time in transit. (Both confirm the old saying, "time is money.") Indeed, in some cases, speed is of the essence, as when a spare machine part is *air* freighted to minimize the time a crippled machine is shut down, idling workers and stopping production. In short, transportation entails much more than getting item X from point A to point B for price Y. It is a multidimensional service, and demand varies across the modes accordingly.

This helps to explain why, as shown in Table 18–1, the share of freight volume going to trucks and airplanes has been rising for four decades despite the fact that on average the price of truck and air service is much higher than that of railroad service. As compared to the railroads, average revenue per ton-mile has been nearly *five* times greater for trucks and over *fifteen* times greater for airplanes.[1]

When translating the demand for a given mode into demand facing a given carrier, *intra-*modal competition intervenes importantly. A monopolist in railroading would have a demand matching the demand for rail services, as influenced by int*er*modal substitutes. However, a railroad that vied with five other railroads would face demand that could switch to other railroads as well as to other modes. It follows that both intramodal and intermodal competition may be present. When both arise, the elasticity of demand, *as viewed by a carrier,* can be quite high, something that, absent collusion, prompts price competition and efficiency. (See Figure 18–1).

These observations apply mainly to specific routes, because shippers' demands are route specific. There are, in other words, a dozen major railroads, thousands of interstate truckers, and more than six airlines in the United States today, implying substantial intramodal competition in each case. But these are nationwide numbers, and they need not imply intramodal competition between say, Eugene, Oregon, and Ithaca, New York. With this observation we bump squarely into supply side considerations.

B. Supply Side

Three supply side elements deserve special attention—(1) concentration, (2) condition of entry, and (3) costs.

As suggested by the fairly large number of transportation firms, *concentration* in transportation is quite low when all modes are combined nationally. Generalizations are more difficult to come by, however, when the scope of the market is narrowed to more relevant dimensions of specific routes and, when appropriate, specific modes for specific services. Narrowing yields many submarkets, and the only safe generalization for them is that concentration tends to be lower (and the number of competitors higher), the heavier the volume of traffic. For example, concentration in air passenger service is lower between Chicago and Los Angeles than it is between Omaha and Santa Fe. Likewise, the number of trucking companies serving the Baltimore-Boston route is considerably larger than the number for those serving the Boise-Butte route.

As for the *condition of entry,* in the absence of regulation trucking is by far the easiest of the modes to enter. It is even easy as compared to other lines of business such as manufacturing. No special skills are required. The capital costs of buying a truck are paltry. Use of the highways is freely "leased" through the payment of road taxes. And so on. Airline entry is more difficult, given the higher costs of initial equipment (whether leased or purchased), the greater scarcity of skilled personnel, and the difficulty of obtaining airport berth assignments at many major airports. Established air carriers can also deter new entrants by responding aggressively. The difficulty of airline entry can be seen statistically: Of seventeen airlines formed between 1979 and 1985, the best years for entry to occur, only three remain, and they are pipsqueaks.

Compared to the easy entry of trucking and this rather difficult entry of airlines, entry for railroads and pipelines is much more difficult. Roadbeds for these modes are not publicly provided, necessitating their development from scratch and thereby requiring immense capital outlays for rights of way and construction. Moreover, railroads and pipelines display some characteristics of natural monopoly on lightly traveled routes, further hampering the prospects of new entrants.

A summary of transportation entry conditions goes something like this:

- Trucking (truck-load segment)—easy
- Airlines—moderately difficult to difficult
- Railroad (mainline)—extremely difficult
- Pipelines (interstate)—extremely difficult

Some theorists claim that carriers in one geographic region can expand to enter routes in other geographic regions with perfect ease. They say that markets for trucking and airlines are especially "contestable" in this manner. The theory has failed empirical tests however, so we shall skip it.[2]

Conditions concerning both concentration and entry are in part determined by the behavior of transportation *costs.* Costs may vary importantly along three dimensions: (1) the scale of a firm's operation, (2) distance, and (3) type of freight.

The first of these, *scale,* is particularly important in determining intramodal concentration and entry. Scale may be measured either by *overall firm size* or by *route density.* Size is self-evident. Density refers to the volume of traffic moving between two points, as indicated, say, by ton-miles per mile of road. Studies show that for railroads and pipelines costs generally fall with added scale as measured by firm size and route density, the latter especially. Diagrammatically, this is illustrated in Figure 18–2(a). Numerically, this is illustrated by 1973 estimates of railroad costs that fall from 3 cents to 1 cent per ton-mile as density increases from 1 to 6 million ton-miles per mile of railroad.[3] Table 18–2 gives numbers for pipelines. Thus, economies of scale are to some degree present in rail and pipeline operations, leading to intramodal natural monopoly

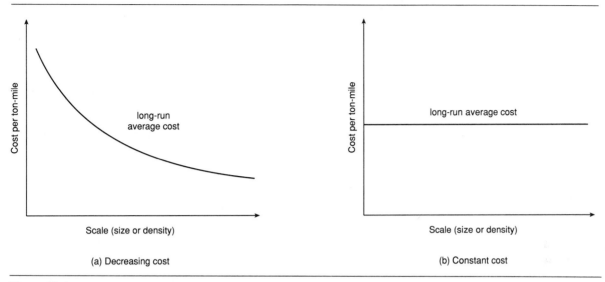

Figure 18–2
Unit Cost as a Function of Scale of Operations (Overall Firm Size or Route Density)

where traffic volume is thin and to natural oligopoly where traffic volume is fat enough to support several carriers. In contrast, there are no appreciable economies of scale in trucking, implying

Table 18–2
The Relationship Between Pipeline Diameter, Pipe Costs, and Flow Capacity

Diameter (inches)	Pipe Cost Factor	Capacity Factor
4	1.0	1
8	1.9	6
12	2.4	15
16	3.5	28
20	4.3	48

This says, for example, that 20-inch-diameter piping costs 4.3 times as much as 4-inch-diameter piping, yet has a capacity *48 times* that of 4-inch piping. The main reason for this is that capacity depends on cross section area, and the area of a circle is *pi* times the radius *squared*.

Source: George S. Wolbert, Jr., *U.S. Oil Pipelines* (Washington, DC: American Petroleum Institute, 1979), p. 99.

constant cost behavior such as depicted in Figure 18–2(b).[4] Airlines are somewhere between railroads and trucking because airline costs fall a bit with overall firm size and traffic density but not enough to justify natural monopoloy except on the most lightly traveled routes (and these tend to be short hops that have good bus and auto options as alternatives).[5]

As regards the influence of *distance* and *type of freight,* they are crucial in determining intermodal relative costs. Table 18–3 summarizes the situation.[6] In distance, the lowest-cost carriers for long-haul traffic tend to be railroads, pipelines, barges, and (for passengers) airlines. The lowest-cost carriers for short-haul traffic tend to be trucks for freight and buses for passengers.

A chief element influencing these tendencies for distance is the level of terminal costs as compared to line-haul costs. Terminal costs are the costs of sorting and loading freight, ticketing passengers, and the like. In total, these costs are fixed in that they do not vary with distance. Line-haul costs are the costs of actually moving a load from one place to another—that is, the cost of

Table 18–3
Low Cost Carriers As Classified by Distance and Type of Freight

	Type of Freight			
Distance	Bulk Liquid	Bulk Dry	High Value Commodities[a]	Passenger Service
Short haul	truck, railroad	truck, railroad	truck	bus
Long haul	pipeline, barge	railroad, barge	truck, rail, air	airline

[a]Mainly manufactured goods.

fuel, labor, equipment depreciation, and the like. In total, these costs are variable in that they rise with distance. When translated into *per-unit* terms, such as cost per ton-mile, terminal costs fall sharply with distance whereas line-haul costs do not. This means that modes with relatively high fixed terminal costs and low line-haul costs, like railroads and airlines, are relatively efficient on long hauls. But modes with relatively low fixed terminal costs and high line-haul costs, like trucks and buses, are relatively efficient on short hauls.[7]

Commodity type is equally important. Large shipments of bulk liquids, like crude oil and gasoline, are most cheaply moved by pipeline or barge. Large shipments of dry bulk commodities, like coal, iron ore, and wheat, are most cheaply moved by train or barge. Highly valued (and fragile) manufactured goods, like computers and glassware, are most cheaply shipped by truck. Further examples may be derived from Table 18–4, which shows how the freight of several commodity classes is distributed among the various modes. Railroads dominate the first three com-

Table 18–4
Percentage Distribution of Freight Ton-Miles by Mode for Selected Commodity Groups, 1965 (in percentages)

Commodity	Railroads	Trucks	Pipeline	Water	Air
Agriculture	53.3%	27.4%	0.0%	19.1%	0.2%
Coal mining	79.6	3.0	0.0	17.4	0.0
Chemicals	67.9	15.1	0.0	16.9	0.1
Iron ore	23.7	0.7	0.0	75.6	0.0
Petroleum & products	2.3	3.6	49.5	44.6	0.0
Textiles and apparel	21.1	77.8	0.0	0.2	0.9
Industrial machinery	30.6	62.2	0.0	6.1	1.1
Scientific instruments	8.2	87.3	0.0	0.8	3.7

Source: Paul O. Roberts and James T. Kneafsey, "Traffic Diversion and Energy Use Implications of Surface Transport Reform," in MacAvoy and Snow (eds.), *Regulation of Entry and Pricing in Truck Transportation* (Washington, DC: American Enterprise Institute, 1977), pp. 166–167.

modity classes; trucks the last three; pipelines and water carriers cover the middle two.

C. Summary of Economics

Taken alone, these several economic features of transportation cannot explain or justify economic regulation of the industry. The derived demand is commonplace. The low to moderate concentration and less than horrendous barriers to entry in trucking signal good opportunities for intramodal competition. The intramodal prospects for competition in airlines, railroading, and pipelines are less abundant, but in*ter*modal competition frequently makes up for this. Indeed, it is these economic considerations that have prompted economists to question the wisdom of transportation regulation and that spearheaded the drive toward deregulation.

Still, there are economic features, which, when combined with historic circumstances, help to explain if not justify the fact of past regulation. Elasticities of demand vary widely across shippers and commodities. Coupled with varying competitive conditions, they pave the way to stark discriminations in price, discriminations that could arouse shippers to press for regulation. Furthermore, the competitive forces may have been at certain places and times *too* great, causing the carriers themselves to cry out for regulatory protection. These and other possibilities are discussed next.

III. The History and Purposes of Regulation

It must be stressed that in its heyday from 1920 to 1975 transportation regulation was quite different from public utility regulation. Whereas the main purpose of utility regulation was to *substitute* for nonexistent competition, a main purpose of transportation regulation became the *suppression* or *supplementation* of competition through cartelization. Whereas a main focus of utility regulation was maximum price *level*, a main focus of transportation regulation was price *structure*. Movement beyond these broad generalizations entails details of history.

A. History of Transportation Regulation

In 1887 there were 149,214 miles of railroad track in the United States, about 325 percent more mileage than had existed just twenty-two years earlier. These statistics suggest two things. First, railroads were far and away the dominant means of transportation of the day. They bound the country together. And on routes not also served by water carriers, this prominence brought with it prospects of substantial monopoly power. Second, however, the rapid expansion of railroads meant that on some routes railroads competed vigorously with each other, even where water competition was absent. This mixture of monopoly and competition in an area where buyers themselves represented a mixture of varying demand elasticities led to sharp price discrimination among shippers, localities, and commodities. Prices were high for small-lot shippers, for isolated communities with no alternative means of transport, and for high-valued commodities. Conversely, prices were low for big shippers, for communities served by water or competing railroads, and for low-value commodities.

This discrimination became glaringly obvious in the many instances when long hauls were charged less than short hauls. The long haul between New York City and Chicago, for example, had numerous railroads competing on price. But each railroad took a different route between New York and Chicago, meaning that many short-haul communities along the way, such as Scranton and Akron, were served by only one railroad. With low-priced competitive long hauls and high-priced monopolistic short hauls, prices frequently seemed out of whack. The resulting outcry for regulation was bolstered by the surging populist sentiments of the day, for it was one

---

Thumbnail Sketch 5: Interstate Commerce Commission

Established: 1887 (making it the granddaddy of federal commissions)

Purpose: To regulate interstate surface and water transportation by railroads, trucks, (except agricultural and private trucking), buses, water carriers (except bulk freight), and pipelines carrying commodities other than oil, water, and natural gas.

Legislative Authority: Act to Regulate Commerce, 1887; Transportation Acts of 1920, 1940, and 1942; Motor Carrier Act of 1935; Railroad Revitalization and Regulatory Reform Act of 1976; Staggers Rail Act of 1980; and Motor Carrier Act of 1980 (the last two of which brought deregulation).

Regulatory Activity: Regulated (1) numbers of firms with entry and exit authority, and (2) price levels and structure. It rules on mergers and consolidations. Its powers have diminished, however, since 1980.

Organization: Five-member independent commission. Presidential appointments. Numerous divisions.

Budget: 1991 estimate, $44 million.

Staff: 1991 estimate, 644.

---

further grievance of the little folks against the big.

The long-haul and water-carrier competition did more than produce price discrimination. It produced intermittent price warfare and rate instability, which led some railroads to support regulation in hope of curbing "destructive" competition.[8] Whatever contribution this motive may have had at the outset, the objective of stabilization was not fully served until 1920, when minimum price regulation was introduced. The Act to Regulate Commerce of 1887 established the Interstate Commerce Commission (ICC) and gave it the power to stem price discrimination but nothing more. The act required that railroad rates be "just and reasonable," specifically outlawing "undue" discrimination between persons, companies, or communities and banning higher prices for short hauls than for long hauls along the same tracks.

Despite popular support for the act of 1887, it was quickly chopped down by the Supreme Court in a series of opinions instigated by the railroads.[9] To restore the ICC's lost powers, Congress passed a series of subsequent laws ad-

dressed to the specific problems motivating the original legislation. Especially noteworthy was the Mann-Elkins Act of 1910, which struck at long- and short-haul discrimination.

Shortly after this shoring up was completed, Congress took significant additional steps toward regulation with its Transportation Act of 1920. In a word, this act *cartelized* the industry. It gave the ICC power to set minimum rates, which, when coupled with earlier authority to set maximum rates, gave the ICC power to fix specific rates. The act of 1920 also authorized the elimination of competition through "pooling" and the joint use of terminals. Control over abandonments of service was introduced at this time as well.

These steps to protect the railroads from intramodal competition were grounded on the belief that the railroads had fallen on hard times. Reprehensible buccaneering had given way to financial floundering. Yet, however bad things may have been for the railroads in 1920, they grew considerably worse thereafter with the rise of trucking and the arrival of the Great Depression. The pinch from trucking caused the rail-

---

Thumbnail Sketch 6: Civil Aeronautics Board (now gone)

Established: 1940 (expired December 31, 1984)

Purpose: Originally, to regulate interstate air travel (passenger and freight). Later, to proceed with deregulation in orderly fasion.

Legislative Authority: Civil Aeronautics Act of 1938; Federal Aviation Act of 1958; Airline Deregulation Act of 1978.

Regulatory Activity: Control of entry and prices until scheduled deregulation occurred. Representation in international aviation.

Organization: An independent agency headed by a five-member commission appointed by the president. Bureaus for Consumer Protection and Economic Analysis.

Budget and staff: Now zero.

---

roads to begin lobbying for truck regulation in 1925. Passage of the necessary legislation was delayed ten years until the hardships of the Great Depression had fostered broader, nonrailroad support for the idea that cartel-like regulation of trucking was a good policy. This broader support for the Motor Carrier Act of 1935 came from the Interstate Commerce Commission, many state regulatory commissions, bus operators, and a few of the largest trucking companies. Those opposed to this expansion of ICC authority included a majority of the truckers and numerous organized shippers. The forces of opposition succeeded in keeping large chunks of trucking free from regulation—private (noncommon-carrier) and agricultural trucking in particular. Still, the act of 1935 treated common-carrier truckers as if they were railroads. Further protection for the railroads was provided when in 1940 water carriers were partially placed under ICC jurisdiction.

For a short time during the 1930s, the ICC also had a hand in regulating domestic airlines. Given their infancy at the time, the airlines were heavily dependent on government airmail contracts for solvency. When snags disrupted the airlines' bidding for this business, they fell dangerously close to bankruptcy. Events led to passage of the Civil Aeronautics Act of 1938, which transferred regulatory authority to the newly cre-

ated Civil Aeronautics Board (CAB) and thereby brought about official cartelization of the airways. Given the dire circumstances of the airlines at the time, it could be argued that the main purpose of this new branch of regulation was to prevent destructive competition. A collateral motive, however, was promotion. The act of 1938 provided subsidies to nurture the airlines in hope that they would grow strong enough to give "adequate, economical, and efficient service" on a nationwide scale, something helpful to the military, the postal service, and the country at large. Finally, a concern for airline safety also played a part. If pressed too hard by competition, airlines might try to cut costs by neglecting maintenance, hiring untrained personnel, and following other hazardous strategies. Although the CAB initially controlled safety, that duty passed to the Federal Aviation Administration (FAA) in 1958. Among other things, the FAA operates air traffic control centers, certifies the competence of pilots, and supervises the manufacture, operation, and maintenance of aircraft (duties unaffected by deregulation).

This pattern of multimode regulation that developed during the 1930s endured until the deregulation movement of the late 1970s. In railroading, deregulation began timidly with the Railroad Revitalization & Regulatory Reform Act of 1976. It was later expanded by the Staggers Rail Act of 1980. In airlines, the CAB itself began deregulation in 1977 by giving fresh interpretations to its then existing authority. Those liberalized interpretations were formally affirmed by Congress in the Airline Deregulation Act of 1978. Congress then lessened government control of the trucking industry by passing the Motor Carrier Act of 1980. Oil pipelines experienced no deregulation, but control of them passed from the ICC to the Federal Energy Regulatory Commission in 1977.

B. The Purposes of Regulation

When the history of regulation is stripped of its many dates and cumbersome legislative titles, we find an outline of several purposes served by regulation. As suggested earlier in Chapter 14, these purposes may be categorized as various sorts of fairness.

1. FAIRNESS TO SELLERS GENERALLY
The protective nature of much regulation was no accident. Railroads and airlines won the sympathy of Congress by arguing that regulation was needed (a) to prevent the instability caused by destructive competition and (b) to promote the growth and solvency of their industries.

2. FAIRNESS AMONG DIFFERENT BUYERS
(a) Prevention of price discrimination was the main purpose of the ICC Act of 1887 and a subsidiary purpose of much regulation that followed. (b) Regulation has also been defended as a means of cross-subsidization—that is, using the profits of high-density routes to subsidize the losses of low-density routes.

3. FAIRNESS AMONG DIFFERENT SELLERS
If railroads were regulated, it was only fair that common-carrier trucks and water carriers likewise be regulated. At least, that was the rationale of many officials in the 1930s.

4. FAIRNESS AS AN ADMINISTRATIVE PROCESS
History teaches that the market can be a harsh and volatile decision-making process. Some saw in regulation a slower, more benign method. This rationale is especially pertinent to abandonments of service.

However accurate this list of specifics may be, the sweep of surrounding economic circumstances adds to our understanding. It should be stressed, for instance, that the crisis conditions of the Great Depression contributed substantially to the flurry of protectionist regulatory activity of the 1930s. Notice, too, that deregulation proceeded in the 1970s almost as quickly as regulation was introduced in the 1930s. The inflationary crisis of the 1970s impelled a search for ways to quell prices through enhanced competition.

IV. The Nature of Regulation

Generalizations about the nature of transportation regulation are possible because the main modes faced very similar controls before deregulation. Two exceptions should be noted, however. First, pipelines have been treated very much like public utilities, and since we discussed utility regulation earlier in Chapter 15, we can now drop pipelines from further consideration. Second, several major segments of transportation have never been subject to appreciable regulation. Most notable among these exempt segments are private (shipper owned) trucking, agricultural commodity trucking, and intrastate airline services in California and Texas. These exemptions are notable because, previous to federal deregulation, they gave economists information on the way the industry might work without regulation.

These exceptions aside, transport regulation focused most intently on two economic variables—(A) the number of firms, and (B) prices. Safety has also been regulated, but we concentrate on these two economic variables.

A. The Number of Firms

Control of the number of firms extended to control of both entry and exit. *Entry* restrictions protected existing firms and were thereby looked on as a means of preventing destructive competition or promoting solvency and growth. *Exit* restrictions furthered the causes of cross-subsidization and procedural fairness, because they prevented or delayed withdrawals of unprofitable service.

Entry Control.   Entry restrictions applied to all modes but were most important in common-carrier trucking and airlines because these have been this century's most rapidly growing modes. To serve the public, a carrier first had to obtain a certificate of "public convenience and necessity," that is, a license to operate. Moreover, the certificates issued by the ICC and CAB were not for entry generally. They were, rather, quite narrowly restrictive. In trucking, for instance, a typical certificate approved carriage of certain commodities only between certain points, over only exactly specified routes. Given the many possible combinations of commodities, communities, and highways, it is no surprise that ICC grants of trucking authority numbered nearly 100,000 during the 1960s and 1970s. Similarly, airline certificates specified the city pairs, or routes, that an airline could serve. Given the narrow authority represented by these certificates of convenience and necessity, or operating rights, firms of a given mode could not compete with other authorized firms except insofar as their authorizations overlapped.

If operating rights had been dispensed freely to anyone wanting to enter, rights would have posed no significant barrier to entry, but this was not the case. When truck and airline regulations were first introduced in 1935 and 1938, existing carriers were issued certificates for their then existing services. They were thus "grandfathered" in. Thereafter, new approvals were tightly controlled, so new applicants confronted high hurdles. An applicant could not be assured certification even on evidence that it would provide better service at lower prices than existing carriers. The essential criterion was merely whether existing carriers could handle the freight or passenger

load. And existing carriers routinely argued that they could handle the load.

The fact that airline entry was restricted is illustrated by the experience of "trunk" carriers (i.e., carriers specializing in high-density, long-haul markets). For four decades after its birth in 1938, the CAB allowed *no* new trunk carrier entry despite tremendous growth in the industry over the period and despite entry applications from over 80 firms.[10]

In trucking, the severity of the entry restrictions was indicated by the problem of "gypsy" truckers who operated without ICC approval. Numbering in the thousands, they included truckers who normally carried exempt agricultural commodities and regulated truckers who went beyond the narrow limits of their operating rights. The ICC studied the problem in 1963 and estimated that regulated carriers lost $500 million to $1 billion to illegal truckers that year alone. The problem was serious enough for the regulated truckers to take vigilante action, financing their own efforts to capture the gypsies and turn them over to the ICC for prosecution.[11]

Exit Control.   Carrier exit has been controlled by regulation of route *abandonments* and firm *mergers*. This authority has been especially noteworthy for railroads, which, unlike the airlines and truckers, have faced long-term malaise, with stagnant demand, tepid profits, and occasional bankruptcies. From the end of World War II until recently, the railroad industry earned a rate of return in the 1 to 3 percent range, far below transportation and industry generally. Eastern railroads were especially hard pressed, experiencing deficits every year from 1975 through 1980.[12]

From its inception until 1976, the ICC approved the abandonment of nearly 70,000 miles of railroad tracks. The abandonments were granted only after deliberate delay because the ICC believed that low-density deficit routes should be subsidized by high-density profitable routes. In 1974, for instance, 20 percent of the country's railroad mileage was so little used as to account for only 2 percent of the total freight traffic.[13] Since the Railroad Revitalization & Regulatory Reform Act of 1976, abandonments have been much easier to obtain.

Exit by merger occurs when formerly independent carriers combine. The power of the ICC and the CAB to approve such actions further typified regulation. Broad considerations of national defense and efficiency produced lenient standards. Indeed, the ICC has encouraged railroad mergers rather than discouraged them. Exhibit A of this lenient attitude is the ICC's approval of the New York Central and Pennsylvania Railroad merger in the late 1960s, a merger that ended in massive disaster when the combination quickly tumbled into bankruptcy.

B. Price Regulation

1. PRICE LEVEL AND PROFIT

In theory, price level regulation in transportation was supposed to match that in public utilities. In practice, however, this was never the case.[14] Whereas public utilities are essentially monopolies in their local spheres of influence and can therefore be treated individually by regulatory commissions, transportation is populated by many firms that must be treated in groups. This clustering of numerous firms in transportation prevented the ICC and the CAB from determining "just and reasonable" price levels on the basis of a "fair" rate of return on individual company investment. Instead, price levels were determined from broad averages that included data from a number of companies within a given mode. Various factors other than fair return on investment were therefore used in assessing the need for price changes, the most important factor being the ratio of operating costs to total revenues.

The specific company clusters that drew up price proposals and represented the carriers' interests before the ICC and CAB were called *rate bureaus*. Rate bureaus were, in effect, regional cartels of truckers or railroads or airlines, as the case may be. Their power to establish price levels by joint agreement, subject to commission approval, was exempt from antitrust prosecution. This approach produced uniformity of prices among carriers of a given mode but widely differing individual rates of return on investment (given the individual carriers' differences in costs).

Price level regulation was thus inconsistent across carriers, and the main problem seems to have been that rate of return regulation is not appropriate when competition would otherwise regulate. In fact, average realized rates of return from the 1950s through the 1970s tended to be very low for railroads, rather high for trucks, and only moderate for airlines.

2. PRICE STRUCTURE

Two generalizations about price structure regulation in transportation are particularly pertinent. *First,* value-of-service pricing usually won out over cost-of-service pricing. This meant that price discrimination was quite common even though *prevention* of price discrimination was a major purpose of regulation in the first place.

The earliest and most notorious example of authorized value-of-service pricing was used by the railroads. Low-value agricultural commodities and raw materials were shipped at prices much lower than those charged to high-value manufactured goods. These rate disparities favored western farmers and miners, thereby furthering social objectives prevalent at the turn of the century. These disparities also followed disparities in elasticities of demand because low-valued bulk freight tended to have a higher price elasticity for rail transit than did high-valued manufactured goods. Competition with water carriers was keener in bulk commodities as compared to manufactured goods. Moreover, transportation costs have always been a higher portion of the total costs of bulk commodities as compared to manufactured goods.

A serious problem with this railroad structure was that it persisted long after the rise of truck competition had made it obsolete. Truck competition sharply reduced the railroads' monopoly power over the transit of manufactured goods, thereby raising the price elasticity of demand as viewed by the railroads. Nevertheless, the ICC prevented the railroads from raising their bulk prices and lowering their manufactured-goods prices. As a consequence, trucks grabbed ever larger lumps of the traffic of high-valued manufactures over time, leaving railroads to contend with low-priced, low-valued bulk freight like sand, gravel, and field crops.[15]

Value-of-service pricing also appeared *within* given commodity classes. Intermodal competition sometimes had this effect, as illustrated by comparing the 1963 rail rate on phosphate rock shipped from Bartow, Florida, to Montgomery, Alabama, with the rate on an identical distance from Bartow, Florida, to Pensacola, Florida. The former, without water competition, was $6.33 per ton. The latter, with water competition, was $4.25 per ton.[16] Similarly, some differences in airfares could be considered value-of-service pricing within a given commodity class. Thus, vacation fliers, as disclosed by length of stay or presence of a spouse, would often be charged less than business fliers were.

This is not to say that price discrimination under regulation was bad. As one economist put it, "Price discrimination is probably a necessary aspect of the transportation industry."[17] Indeed, defenders of regulation argued that price discrimination to achieve cross-subsidization was good.

Our *second* observation on price structure is simply that, when cost-of-service pricing *was* used by regulators, the costs that guided prices were usually average total (or "fully distributed") costs rather than marginal costs. Neglect of marginal cost considerations caused the ICC and CAB to disallow price discounts for off-peak periods and backhauls. Peak versus off-peak price differentials would have made economic sense for reasons explored earlier on pages 311–313. Even more important in transportation is the problem of empty backhauls. A truck shipping

beer from St. Louis to San Francisco, for example, might be empty going back to St. Louis. The marginal cost of shipping wine on the return trip would be very low given that the truck must return anyway. This could justify a low backhaul price for wine on this carrier going from California to Missouri. But the ICC consistently denied such low backhaul prices because they would have introduced "too much" competition into transportation. The result was that empty backhauls remained empty because the price structure was too rigid.

V. The Consequences of Regulation

A. An Overview: Prices

When first applied to railroads, regulation yielded greater benefits than costs, but it must be remembered that last century's economic conditions did not last.[18] As the railroads lost their monopoly power, regulation became less and less appropriate. Nearly all studies of transportation regulation in the twentieth century show the reverse—that the costs greatly exceeded the benefits.

A summary index of regulation's adverse consequences is a comparison of price level with and without regulation. Economic estimates of price level effect in trucking and airlines are possible because portions of these modes escaped regulation. In the mid-1950s, for example, fresh and frozen poultry and frozen fruits and vegetables were switched from regulated to exempt commodities in trucking. The U. S. Department of Agriculture conducted a before-and-after study of freight rates and service quality. Rates fell 33 percent on poultry and 19 percent on fruits and vegetables, and service quality apparently improved.[19] Other estimates based on regulated versus nonregulated comparisons at a given time suggest that deregulation would have reduced truck rates by 6.7 percent.[20]

In the air, travel within California and Texas could not be controlled by the CAB. A comparison of *intra*state air fares and *inter*state regulated air fares in 1975 is shown in Table 18–5. It does not take a pilot's keen eyes to see that, for routes of similar length and paired-city size, the unregulated *intra*state fares were far lower. More elaborate analyses of airline economics show regulation boosting prices 15 to 30 percent.[21]

When these percentages for trucking and airlines are translated into dollar amounts, the result is striking. Regulation of them cost several billion dollars per year in the mid-1970s.

Estimates of the costs of railroad regulation are less solid, given the lack of nonregulated sectors. Some estimates are quite high, with double-digit percentages and several billions in annual dollar amounts.[22] Other estimates are rather low, running no more than a few tenths of a percentage point and a few millions of dollars annually.[23] (Indeed, for reasons to be explained shortly, *de*regulation of railroads *increased* some rail prices.) In any event, the numbers cannot be used to defend past railroad regulation.

The next question is: Why did transportation regulation generally raise price levels? There are two answers: It raised *profits* in some instances. Furthermore, and more important, it raised *costs*

Table 18–5
Comparison Between Interstate and Intrastate Air Fares, 1975

City Pair	Miles	Fare ($)
Los Angeles—San Francisco	338	18.75
Chicago—Minneapolis	339	38.89
New York—Pittsburgh	335	37.96
Los Angeles—San Diego	109	10.10
Portland—Seattle	129	22.22
Dallas—Houston	239	13.89[a]
Las Vegas—Los Angeles	236	28.70
Chicago—St. Louis	258	29.63

[a]This is the night and weekend rate. Day-time week-day rate was $23.15.

Source: Civil Aeronautics Board Practices and Procedures, Report of the Subcommittee on Administrative Practice and Procedure, U.S. Senate (1975), p. 41.

of operation in many instances. Thus, our catalog of regulation's adverse effects must move from the summary index provided by price levels to the specifics of profits and costs.

B. Profits and Monopoly Power

A detailed study of trucking in the Rocky Mountain area showed that about one-fourth of the towns in that nine-state area were served by no more than one common-carrier trucker in 1972. Similarly, interviews of New Orleans retailers disclosed that, for more than half of their shipments, no more than two motor carriers were authorized to serve them.[24]

These examples imply that the ICC's entry restrictions in trucking artificially created instances of monopoly power. Confirmation is found in the high value of many truckers' certificates of convenience and necessity, or operating rights. ICC data on transactions in operating rights during 1967 to 1971 show that forty-three operating rights sold for a total of $3,844,100.[25] These rights had value only because they were tickets of admission to monopoly earnings. With stiff competition, they would have been worthless. Indeed, *de*regulation had exactly this effect. In 1980 many major truckers wrote off the lost value of their acquired operating rights—Consolidated Freightways lost $32.1 million, Yellow Freight $34.8 million, and Roadway Express $26.8 million.[26]

The relatively low to moderate overall profits in railroading and airlines during the past half century indicate that these modes gained less monopoly power from regulation than did trucking. Still, there may have been pockets of artificial power on specific routes. And such power as there was may have led to higher costs rather than higher profits.

C. Costs and Inefficiency

Regulation escalated costs by creating three kinds of inefficiency—(1) intramodal inefficiency,

(2) intermodal inefficiency, and (3) dynamic inefficiency.

Intramodal inefficiency occurs when there is substantial excess capacity for traffic that would move by a given mode in any event. For example, excess capacity arose from airline regulation when the airlines did not compete on price but competed instead by scheduling more flights on their routes, by offering spacious seating, and by offering sumptuous meals that required galley space (further reducing airplane seating capacity). The effect of overscheduling can be measured by the average load factor, that is, the percentage of total seats flown that were actually occupied by paying passengers. During the late 1950s and early 1960s the load factor for regulated trunk airlines was only 59 percent, whereas the load factor for unregulated California airlines was 71 percent.[27] Translating regulation's lower load factor into dollars and cents, it may have cost as much as 10 percent more per passenger-mile.[28] Shucking seats to make room for first class passengers and kitchen galleys may have boosted costs per passenger-mile by a similar magnitude. (In more concrete terms, it takes over $30,000 to fully fuel a Boeing 747. The fewer the people on board, the higher the cost per person.)

Intramodal inefficiency in trucking and railroading arose from regulation's bans on backhaul discounts and peak-load pricing. Moreover, about 30 percent of the ICC's operating rights in trucking were limited to one-way authority, thereby aggravating the problem of empty backhauls. For these and other reasons, regulation may be partially blamed for the fact that during the 1950s and 1960s, trucks operated at less than 50 percent and railroads less than 76 percent of capacity, resulting in costs in the billions.[29]

Intermodal inefficiency occurs when freight and passengers are misallocated among modes, that is, they are not moved by the most efficient, cheapest means. Regulation can have this effect when it distorts prices relative to costs. For example, thirty tons of machinery might move

1,000 miles most efficiently by train. If the train rate exceeds the truck rate, however, trucks will likely get the business regardless of resource costs.

Misallocation was never very serious in short hauls, where trucks rightly carried virtually everything. Nor was it much of a problem on really heavy, long-haul loads because trains always dominated there. Between these extreme conditions, it appears that regulation overpriced rail service, thereby causing more freight to move by truck than was economically warranted. Estimates of the costs of this and related misallocations of ground freight range from zero to $500 million annually.[30] Though less than the cost of excess capacity, these costs were probably not trivial.

Dynamic inefficiency refers to instances when regulation impeded progress, reducing productivity and raising costs. The ICC displayed special ineptitude when it delayed railroad innovations that could have cut costs and taken traffic away from other modes. In the early 1960s, for instance, Southern Railway tried to introduce "Big John" cars for bulk grain shipments. Twice as large as conventional boxcars yet considerably lighter in weight, the aluminum "Big Johns" would have permitted Southern to cut its rate by 60 percent. When put before the ICC, however, these new lower rates were denied because the ICC wanted to protect trucking. It took four years and an appeal to the Supreme Court to overcome the ICC's opposition.[31] Another example of obstructionism occurred when the ICC delayed for five years the introduction of unit coal trains in the East.[32]

D. Consequences of Regulation: Benefits?

In fairness, we should say that this century's transportation regulation was not totally lacking in benefits. Still, these benefits were probably minor in comparison to the costs, or they were questionable benefits. Let's quickly consider three claimed benefits—(1) cross-subsidy, (2) service quality, and (3) stability.

Empirical studies of cross-subsidies in trucking and airlines have shown that, in fact, the subsidies were slight. Trucks and airlines had greater flexibility in route selection than the cross-subsidy argument assumed, and they apparently exercised their flexibility to evade many loss situations.[33] In the case of railroads, cross-subsidies were clearly present and often large. Yet in this case it can be argued (as in all cases) that subsidies, if believed necessary, are most efficient when openly and directly paid from public funds rather than buried in the price structure of businesses.

In service quality, regulation admittedly maintained good quality. Indeed, in the case of airlines, regulation spurred increased frequency of flights, spacious seating, and other nonprice amenities. But the rigidities of regulation fixed quality at a given level, barring a *range* of qualities from "cheap" to "luxury" that customers might have liked. John Snow explained this by analogy. The regulatory system, he wrote,

> operates as if all restaurants were required to charge five dollars for a meal. This would result in an excellent choice of five-dollar meals. But the person who wanted a ten-dollar meal or a one-dollar meal would be out of luck.[34]

Finally, in furthering stability, regulation can take but small credit. The instabilities prompting regulation are now largely a thing of the past. And the economic characteristics of trucking and airlines are simply not the type that would normally provoke destructive competition. In short, a thumping of the benefits barrel yields a hollow ring.

VI. Deregulation

A. The Airlines

Under the leadership of Chairman Alfred E. Kahn, the CAB began deregulating the airlines in 1977. The CAB's relaxation of entry restrictions and fare restraints was endorsed by Congress with passage of the Airine Deregulation Act of 1978. Under the act, existing airlines could more freely expand or abandon their operating rights, and new airlines could more easily enter. As one CAB aide put it, the agency would hand out new routes "like confetti." The act also introduced price flexibility. Eventually, all CAB control of routes and pricing ended in 1983, and the CAB itself was abolished. The upshot is that we now have more experience with airline deregulation than with truck or railroad deregulation.

What has this experience shown? Were the adversities of regulation wiped out by deregulation? The answers are mixed. At the outset, during the first several years of airline deregulation from 1978 to about 1984, competition burst on the scene with abundant new entries, falling concentration, reduced prices, fresh varieties of service, and other developments that made deregulation look very good indeed. But reversals followed. A combination of anticompetitive practices by the major airlines and lax antitrust enforcement by the Reagan Administration led to significant exits through merger and bankruptcy, higher concentration, higher prices, and curtailed services.

Many people have been so upset by these reversals of the late 1980s and early 1990s that they have called for *reregulation* of airlines. Congressional hearings have considered the matter, but as of 1991 nothing has been done. Reregulation seems unlikely for several reasons. First, although now diluted, the benefits of deregulation remain considerable. Second, those with a stake in deregulation have political clout. Finally, the blame for the reversals lies not so much with deregulation as with poor antitrust enforcement. Reregulation may not be the solution so much as rejuvenated antitrust.

Let's survey the positive and negative swings of (1) entry-exit, (2) concentration, (3) prices, (4) services, and (5) efficiency.[35]

1. ENTRY

Just after deregulation air carriers that previously specialized in intrastate service—like Southwest Airlines in Texas—branched out into interstate markets. In addition, more than a dozen brand-new airlines took flight—People Express, Midway, Muse, and Jet America among them. By mid-1984 the expanding intrastates and brand-new carriers accounted for nearly 11 percent of all domestic air-passenger service. Additional entry was experienced in many city-pair markets when most of the major established carriers expanded their route structures. Eastern Airlines, for instance, opened transcontinental service to San Francisco and Los Angeles. As a result of all these various forms of entry, roughly half of all city-pair markets experienced an increase in the number of carriers between 1976 and 1983.[36]

However, after 1984 the story switches from one of births to one of deaths. By 1992 all but a couple of the new airlines had failed. Almost all the regional airlines that were expanding geographically in the late 1970s and early 1980s have now been acquired by major national carriers. PSA, Air Cal, Ozark, Republic, and Piedmont are among those that have disappeared in this manner. Topping off the recent trend toward fewer numbers, several major airlines fell on hard times—Pan Am, Eastern, Braniff, and Continental especially. As a consequence, they met with bankruptcy, liquidation, or dismemberment.

2. CONCENTRATION

The pattern for market concentration corresponds to that suggested by entry. Concentration at first fell following deregulation. The share of total domestic air traffic accounted for by the largest eight carriers fell from 80.4 percent in 1978 to 74.1 percent in 1983.[37] However, by 1990 national eight-firm concentration had rebounded to 91.9 percent and was rising. United, American, Delta, and Northwest now hold the top spots.

Current dominance is most clearly seen at the local and regional level. All major airlines have organized into hub-and-spoke systems. As a consequence, air travel into and out of most hub cities is dominated by just one or two airlines that control as much as 80 to 90 percent of the hub city's air traffic—Delta in Atlanta and Cincinnati, American in Dallas–Ft. Worth and Chicago, United in Chicago and Denver, Northwest in Minneapolis and Detroit, and so on. This in turn has led to a situation in which many city-pair markets, such as Detroit-Washington and Pittsburgh-Philadelphia, are now controlled by only one or two airlines.

Public policy, or lack of it, contributed to this trend. The Reagan Administration's laissez-faire ideology led to relaxed antitrust enforcement during the 1980s. Airline mergers consequently multiplied. Northwest and Republic, American and Air Cal, TWA and Ozark—these were among them.

Strategic behavior by the major carriers also contributed to the demise of the smaller airlines and growing concentration. For example, American Airlines and United Airlines own computer reservation systems, "Sabre" and "Apollo," that they lease to travel agents. These systems display the flight schedules and price information that travel agents use to book flights for passengers. During the mid-1980s, "Sabre" and "Apollo" accounted for over 80 percent of the lease business, giving American Airlines and United great leverage. They programmed these computer systems to display their own flight and airfare data to travel agents and customers ahead of the data for rival airlines. The resulting biases in these systems added to the market shares of American and United at the expense of their rivals.[38]

3. PRICES

Air fares temporarily fell because of the fresh competition that came with new entry and reduced concentration just after deregulation. As the established major airlines spread to new geographic markets, they promoted their new services with fantastic price reductions. Eastern Airlines, for example, promoted its entry into transcontinental markets with $99 fares between California and New York, forcing rivals to offer $99 bargains as well, at least temporarily. Most of the expanding intrastate carriers and new up-starts went even further once they took off. They did not limit their price cutting to temporary promotions or restricted discounts. The most successful among the upstarts and regionals adopted low prices as a general strategy. And those low prices were 40 to 50 percent off prevailing fares. The majors matched these fares when necessary to preserve their markets, so by 1983 overall air-fares were way below what they would have been with continued regulation.

Qualifications in geography and time are needed here, however. The huge price reductions did not reach all passengers, and they did not last. First, *geography:* The explosion of competition did not reach all routes. A sample of over 140 city-pairs reveals that, in general, fares fell substantially from 1976 to 1983 on routes linking *large* metropolitan areas (as follows in real terms):

- Long haul −8.7%
- Medium haul −12.1%
- Short haul −14.5%

On the other hand, routes linking *small* cities fared less well over the same period—prices *rising* 53.1 percent on medium-haul routes and 13.2 percent on short-haul routes.[39]

The sinking fares in big-city markets and the hefty hikes in small-city markets present an unsurprising pattern. Under CAB regulations, prices for big-city markets were deliberately held aloft in order to *cross-subsidize* relatively low prices for small-city markets. Ending the cross-subsidy thus hurt some travelers. In addition, the big-city markets were among those most heavily invaded by the cut-rate entrants.

The second qualification is *time.* As exits accumulated and concentration increased, real prices stopped falling between 1986 and 1988. Af-

ter 1988 they began to rise.[40] For example, following Eastern Airline's liquidation in early 1991, the major carriers that had competed with Eastern immediately raised their fares. United raised its cheapest round-trip Chicago-Miami fare almost double from $198 to $379.[41] Similarly, a statistical analysis of the price impact of airline mergers found that the union of Northwest and Republic increased fares out of Minneapolis-St. Paul by about 5.6 percent overall, and that the merger of TWA and Ozark increased fares on flights out of St. Louis by about 1.5 percent.[42]

Because Minneapolis and St. Louis are hub cities, these findings suggest that hub cities may have experienced the greatest anticompetitive effects from the trend toward concentration. In fact, a comparison of 1988 fares for fifteen hub cities with fares for nonhub cities found that a flight from a hub city would typically cost 27 percent more than otherwise.[43] Table 18–6 corroborates this finding with data from 1989. Adjusting for distance and other factors, Table 18–6 shows the prices for hub flights relative to prices for nonhub flights, first for the dominant carriers at each of the hubs listed and second for the other carriers at the hubs. Since nearly all the percentages are greater than 100, hub fares were generally higher. Moreover, Table 18–6 shows that your flight out of a hub city would cost much more if you flew with the hub's dominant carrier than if you flew with one of the hub's other airlines.

Portions of the price benefits of airline deregulation thus seem to have vanished. The adverse trend is likely to continue because the concentration trend is likely to continue. Just how far it will go is uncertain. In 1991, however, on balance air fares were probably lower than they would have been without deregulation, maybe 15 percent lower, which roughly translates into a $5 billion annual savings for air passengers.[44]

4. SERVICES
The deregulation record for services is likewise a positive-negative mix. To begin with the positive

Table 18–6
Comparison of Prices at Dominated Hubs to All Other Routes (1989)

Airport	Dominant Airline	Dominant Airline's Hub Prices as a Percentage of Its Prices Elsewhere	Other Airlines' Prices Relative to Elsewhere (in percentages)
Chicago	United	124%	117%
Dallas/Ft. Worth	American	134	114
Atlanta	Delta	145	97
Minneapolis	Northwest	129	117
Pittsburgh	USAir	128	110
Houston	Continental	123	107
St. Louis	TWA	113	91

Source: Severin Borenstein, "Dissipating the Airline Deregulation Dividend," *Cato Review of Business and Government* (Fall 1990): 71.

side, much of the early price cutting hinged on lower costs, and service curtailments were one way to cut costs. Most of the new entrants offered no-frills service—without food, without baggage forwarding, and so on. On average, the number of flight attendants per passenger decreased 16 percent between 1976 and 1983. All this was good because it increased the *range* of service offerings above what it had been with regulation. Travelers with limited budgets could get limited services. Travelers eager to pay more could easily get more by paying premium fares—first class or business class in particular. Moreover, a major element of service is the convenience of frequent departures. Flight departures increased 9.2 percent from 1977 to 1983, yielding large benefits in the years immediately following deregulation.

On the negative side, there appears to have been some deterioration in quality that has not been offset by price reductions. To the extent that planes are more crowded, ticket lines are longer, and seats are narrower without a corresponding reward in lower fares, one can say that service has suffered. This seems to have been the case ever since concentration has been on the

rise. In particular, detailed study of the TWA-Ozark and Northwest-Republic mergers reveals that while prices were increasing after these mergers, the merged companies were also reducing their available capacities in their respective hub cities—down 11.4 percent by TWA-Ozark in St. Louis and down 7.6 percent by Northwest-Republic in Minneapolis–St. Paul.[45]

5. EFFICIENCY

At first, efficiency improved with deregulation. Productivity growth accelerated from 2.8 percent per year before deregulation to 5.1 percent per year after.[46] Capacity utilization (the load factor) also rose. In short, output went up relative to input.

Since 1985, with the rise in concentration and curbed competition, this favorable trend has reversed somewhat. At this writing (1991) the net results still seem positive, though, especially in light of the fact that prices appear to be lower than they would have been with continued regulation.

SUMMARY

Overall, then, pluses and minuses followed airline deregulation. The pluses were especially apparent during the first six years following de-regulation when travel options grew, prices fell, the range of services broadened, and productivity improved. Since 1985, minuses have detracted from these pluses as exits accumulated and concentration increased. Whether on balance the pluses exceed the minuses is an open question. Some travelers and some cities have gained. Others have lost. Overall, the pluses may prevail. One thing is certain. The recent trend toward concentration in the industry cannot be blamed entirely on deregulation and the CAB's demise. The blame rests largely with lax antitrust enforcement.

B. Trucking Deregulation

Following the lead of the CAB, the ICC began easing its regulation of trucking without new legislation. Even before President Carter signed the Motor Carrier Act of 1980, competition shook the industry.

The Motor Carrier Act of 1980 did not abolish all regulation of interstate trucking, but it relaxed controls substantially over entry, price setting, operating authority, and carrier commodity restrictions. It is now much easier for trucking companies to enter markets or to expand their routes. Truckers can also decrease or increase their rates as much as 10 percent annually without ICC approval, and even more with approval (which has been easy).

The gains of this deregulation have been substantial. To understand those gains, we must first distinguish between truck-load (TL) and less-than-truckload (LTL) sectors. Truck load (TL) carriers handle sufficient volumes of freight for any one shipper that they can fill their trucks at the shipper's location. In contrast, LTL carriers, like Roadway and Consolidated, serve relatively small-volume shippers. LTL carriers need terminals to collect, consolidate, and then redispatch shipments. Some degree of centralized operation is thus necessary for LTL trucking companies. There are no economies of scale for

TL carriers. There are some economies of scale for LTL carriers.

1. ENTRY

Figure 18–3 shows the impact of deregulation on new entry and the total number of licensed motor carriers. Entry toddled along at about 550 new carriers per year during 1976–1977. Administrative relaxation then boosted the rate of entry a bit in 1978–1979. Finally, entry ballooned after the Motor Carrier Act of 1980, reaching almost 5,000 in 1982, about ten times the rate of new entry five years earlier. Deregulation thus drew newcomers to the business the way good chili draws big-rig drivers to a truck stop.

In turn, ballooning entry lifted the total number of licensed carriers considerably. That pop-

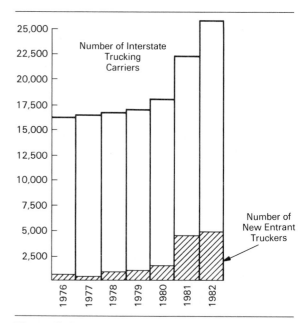

Figure 18–3
Entry and the Number of Interstate Motor Carriers, 1976–1982

Source: Thomas G. Moore, "Rail and Trucking Deregulation," in L. W. Weiss and M. W. Klass (eds.) *Regulatory Reform* (Boston: Little, Brown & Co., 1986) p. 31.

ulace numbered about 16,600 during the years 1976 to 1978. It then rose to 25,722 in 1982. (The upward steps in total numbers do not match the entries because exits were occurring as well as entries.) Virtually all the increases relate to TL carriers. There has been relatively little entry and expansion for TLT carriers because economic barriers to entry are greater for the TLT sector.[47]

2. CONCENTRATION

Comprehensive data are not available on TL carriers, but the huge increase in their numbers suggests that TL concentration has probably fallen since deregulation.

In contrast, concentration has increased among LTL truckers, at least on a national level. National four-firm concentration rose from 23 percent in 1978 to 42 percent in 1987. Eight-firm concentration jumped from 31 to 55 percent over the same period.[48]

Although a bit ominous, these LTL numbers are rather low when compared to those for airlines. Moreover, it is not clear whether they also reflect regional and local trends, which would typically be the levels of greater relevance to most LTL shippers. Hence, we need not push the panic button.

3. PRICING

A great many of the new carriers entering the market have been low-cost nonunion carriers—about 11,500 of them between 1978 and 1985 alone. This rattled the industry. In 1985 hourly labor costs of nonunion truckers were 30 percent lower than those of union truckers.[49] Coupled with greater freedom in setting rates and other factors, this sank prices dramatically. As summarized by Kenneth Labich, writing in 1985:

> Under the deregulation act, the industry continues to establish a bewildering array of rates through nine major rate bureaus run by trucking companies. The published rates, though, are now like sticker prices on cars—the starting point for wheeling and dealing. Since 1980 truckers have

been offering deep discounts—18% to 20% on average, and sometimes up to 40%.[50]

The biggest price cuts occurred among TL carriers as opposed to LTL carriers (-25 percent versus -15 percent from 1977 to 1982). The reason for this is that entry for nonunion truckers has been easiest in the truckload trade. Less-than-truckload service requires heavy investment in shipment terminals, warehouses, and the like.

Need we add that the downward price pressures have squeezed most of the excess profits out of the industry? The value of operating rights has fallen to zero, a drop worth an estimated $5.1 billion.[51] Moreover, the benefits in price reductions do not seem to have diminished with time— a contrast with airlines that occurs because trucking is inherently more competitive than airlines. Recent estimates of the benefits to shippers put the annual savings at about $7.1 billion (in 1982 dollars).[52]

To a large extent the lower prices have come out of trucking wages, which after deregulation declined relative to wages in other sectors. Before deregulation, trucking wages were comparatively high—about 25 percent higher than manufacturing wages. By 1987, trucking wages were about equal to manufacturing wages. Thus, deregulation cut the market power of the Teamsters Union as well as the market power of incumbent trucking companies.[53]

4. SERVICES

"Before 1980, any trucking company that used the word marketing was just learning how to spell it." So said the president of Yellow Freight. Now, the word "marketing" denotes improved services in trucking as well as lower pricing. Table 18–7 summarizes the results of a survey of over seventy major shippers in 1986. Their opinions on seven dimensions of quality revealed that, for the most part, service either improved or stayed about the same after the Motor Carrier Act of 1980. In the "overall" rating, only 14 per-

Table 18–7
Quality of Service after Motor Carrier Act of 1980

	Percentage of Shippers Saying Service		
	Improved	Unchanged	Worse
Quality of trucks	24	68	8
Promptness of service	47	46	7
Availability of service	73	17	10
Reliability	37	52	11
Adjustment of claims	18	63	19
Need for supervision	14	69	17
Willingness to serve off-line points	34	42	24
Overall	35%	51%	14%

Source: Thomas Gale Moore, "Rail and Trucking Deregulation," in *Regulatory Reform*, ed. L. W. Weiss and M. W. Klass (Boston: Little, Brown & Co., 1986), p. 35.

cent of the respondents thought quality of service had become worse.[54]

Better service does more than prompt smiles. Its economic effects run deep:

Shippers say that because they now can rely on increasingly efficient carriers to supply consistent, speedy service, they can reduce inventories significantly. Lever Brothers Co. and FMC Corp. have closed warehouses; now, they move some goods directly to customers. Partly because of more efficient transportation, U.S. companies have reduced inventory levels over the past five years by 20%, or $100 billion, from what they otherwise would have been, says Robert Delaney, the vice president for strategic planning at Leaseway Transportation Corp. in Cleveland.[55]

5. EFFICIENCY

The greater efficiency of truckers contributes to the combination of lower prices and improved service. With deregulation, empty backhauls are no longer empty. Outbound, it may be canned tuna on the truck. Inbound, machine tools might be the load. Terminal procedures are also changing to direct trucks to their most efficiently located loading and unloading dock, not just some

of the time but all the time. Furthermore, onboard computerized devices now monitor drivers, detailing truck speeds on different sections of highway, where and how long the driver stops, and how efficiently he shifts gears. Proper speeds and shifting practices can save up to 10 percent, or an average of about $3,000, in annual fuel expenses per truck. (And fuel accounts for as much as 20 percent of a trucker's total costs.) Deregulation has also encouraged carriers to acquire more fuel-efficient trucks: "One new model from Kenworth, for example, can get up to nine miles per gallon hauling an average-size 65,000-pound rig vs. about five miles per gallon for most older trucks on the road."[56]

The one area in which improved efficiency cannot be claimed is that of information costs. Without the standard regulated rates charged by all carriers and without the close similarities in their services, shippers must actively search for their best deals. They must also negotiate. A measure of the newly created search costs is the explosion in the number of transport brokers who are hired by shippers to find out about carrier prices, availabilities, and contract terms.

(The brokers act much as travel agents do for travelers.) There were 5,908 brokers in 1988, up from only 952 six years before. Although the added search costs associated with deregulation amount to several billion dollars annually, they are not large enough to negate the many positive efficiencies and lower prices associated with deregulation.[57]

SUMMARY

Unlike airlines, deregulation of motor carrier freight seems to have been unambiguously beneficial for society. This is especially true of the truckload segment of the industry because it is inherently more competitive than the LTL segment. Entry boomed after legal restraints on newcomers were lifted in 1980. (Concentration increased in LTL trucking but not to the point of being a problem.) Prices fell while service improved. Continued competition will pay future dividends to shippers and society. Deregulation of motor freight has recently swept Canada and Europe as well as the United States, and it is interesting that the results of deregulation abroad approach those in the United States.[58]

C. Railroad Deregulation

Railroad deregulation differs from airline and truck deregulation in three major particulars. First, *impetus*. Whereas the airlines and truckers stoutly resisted deregulation, the railroads heartily advocated deregulation. Second, *purpose*. Whereas the prime purpose in deregulating airlines and trucking was to increase competition, the prime purpose in deregulating the railroads was to increase rail profits. Indeed, this divergence of purpose explains the divergence in impetus. The railroads' low profits, bankruptcy, casualties, and declining share of the nation's traffic volume made them look like an endangered species. Third, *methods*. Whereas in airlines and trucking the main methods were downside price flexibility and easier entry, in railroads the main methods were *upside* price flexibility and easier *exit* (via merger and abandonments). These would not win railroads a greater traffic share, but they would lift profit prospects substantially.

In 1976 Congress passed the Railroad Revitalization & Regulatory Reform (the 4Rs) Act. Its 120 pages amounted to an immense CARE package, with such items of relief as (1) a promise of $1.6 billion in government subsidies, (2) new procedures to expedite merger approvals, (3) easier abandonment of low-density, money-losing branch lines, and (4) greater pricing freedom where railroads lacked "market dominance." In short, the act was a mix of more and less regulation.

Although promising on paper, the 4R act of 1976 was *interpreted* by the ICC in ways that brought little change. Indeed, the industry's profits tumbled rather than trebled. In pricing freedom, for instance, the qualifying phrase "market dominance" became a Catch-22. As interpreted, it permitted the railroads freedom to raise rates on *only* the 50 percent of their business where they in fact could not raise rates, where, that is, they lacked "market dominance" because they faced vigorous competition from trucks, water carriers, and pipelines.

Thus, the purpose of the ensuing Staggers Rail Act of 1980 was, in a sense, to do things right the second time around. The Staggers act authorized further subsidies and easier abandonments. Moreover, it allowed railroads to boost rates freely until they reached 160 percent of variable costs, a percentage that would gradually increase to 180 percent in 1984. On top of this, rates could be raised additional amounts without ICC approval to offset inflationary cost increases.

To implement this new flexibility, the ICC uses Ramsey pricing. Ramsey pricing allows railroads to raise prices well above cost on cargo having a low price elasticity of demand (like coal, with little intermodal competition), whereas it reduces price down toward marginal cost on cargo having a high price elasticity of demand (mainly manufactured goods with attractive trucking options). To prevent rates on inelastic ("captive") freight from rising too high, the ICC uses stand-alone costs to set price ceilings above which rail rates are not allowed to go. The standalone cost for coal shipments, for example, would be the cost that would be incurred if the system were designed to haul coal only. There are serious problems with Ramsey prices capped by stand-alone costs, but this current policy is arguably better than the old regulation.[59]

1. EXITS

The railroad acts of 1976 and 1980 can be credited with abandonments totaling tens of thousands of miles of track.[60] The mileage of large, Class 1 railroads fell from 192,000 miles in 1975 to 130,000 miles in 1990, a drop of 32 percent. Once inefficient, low-density tracks were dropped, railroad profits climbed toward healthy levels for the first time in decades. Return on investment jumped from around 1.5 percent in the late 1970s to more than 6 percent in the 1980s, and still more in the 1990s.

An interesting point, however, is that many miles of track abandoned by the Class I railroads ended up in the hands of small short-line railroads. These short-line railroads specialize in feeding freight to the larger long-line railroads from shippers some distance from the main tracks (a rather labor-intensive side of the business). Their costs are lower than those of the Class 1 long-line carriers because, for the most part, they are nonunion—(1) paying much lower wage rates, (2) using more flexible work rules, and (3) employing smaller work crews (without firemen on diesel locomotives, for instance).[61]

2. PRICING AND SERVICE

Generalizations on pricing and service are difficult in the case of railroads. Observations on service, for instance, follow from the foregoing. Where abandonments have occurred without independent replacement or local government sub-sidy, service can be judged to be poorer now. On the other hand, service has apparently improved in many areas, partly spurred by truck competition. As regards pricing, some prices have fallen, especially those pressed down by truck competition. Other prices have risen.

The most controversial price increases have been those for hauling coal. These increases have been huge because of Ramsey pricing where demand is price inelastic (given the lack of significant truck competition for coal). A few statistics help to explain the controversy. Over 70 percent of all U.S. coal production is shipped by rail, and coal constitutes roughly 40 percent of all rail cargo by weight. These numbers will increase as low-sulfur coal from the West is increasingly shipped to electric power plants in the East to replace the high-sulfur coal that has been such a serious pollution problem. Thus, coal cargo has become enormously profitable for the railroads, generating net earnings at nearly twice the rate that it generates gross revenues.[62] (Concentration here is also high. In the West, Burlington Northern alone accounted for over 65 percent of 1984's coal traffic. In the East, CSX has dominated, accounting for over 50 percent of the eastern coal traffic in 1984.)

Despite the price increases of a few bulk commodities like coal, price reductions elsewhere have produced an overall drop in average rail rates since deregulation. By one estimate, shippers were saving $3.5 to $5 billion annually by 1986 (after adjusting for commodity composition, length of haul, and fuel prices).[63]

3. EFFICIENCY AND LABOR COSTS

Greater efficiency helped to achieve this reduction in rail prices, as in airlines and trucking. For example, in 1981 the ICC deregulated piggyback service (carrying loaded truck trailers on flat-cars). The resulting gains in efficiency led to price reductions and a 50 percent increase in piggyback traffic in just three years.

More recently deregulation allowed rapid adoption of "double stackers," the railroads' latest weapon against trucking. Two 48-foot containers are stacked on a railroad car built like an elongated bathtub on wheels. The bottom container fits into the well of the car to ride only a few inches above the rails, cutting wind resistance for the top load and providing a smoother ride than piggyback trains do. Train capacity is nearly doubled and rail costs are cut 25 percent. Sending a container from Chicago to Los Angeles in 1991 cost a shipper $1,200 by rail versus about $1,800 by truck, a 50 percent differential that was winning cargo away from trucks in amounts not known before.[64]

Because intramodal competition is less intense for railroads than for airlines or trucks, labor costs have been a special problem for railroads even after deregulation. In 1991, the average unionized railroad employee earned $56,000 a year, including fringe benefits, which exceeded the average amount earned by college professors, professional rodeo cowboys, and nearly everyone else except investment bankers, doctors, and a few others. The $56,000 was nearly twice the $30,000 earned by the typical truck driver. Moreover, antiquated work rules require that more railroad workers be hired than is necessary to operate trains. For example, the industry has 22,000 brakemen whom it no longer needs because tracks are now switched automatically instead of manually. By one estimate the excess labor required by outdated work rules costs the railroads about $2 billion annually (in 1991 dollars).[65] Railroads will not reach their full competitive potential vis-à-vis trucks until their labor costs become more competitive.

PROBLEMS

Along with the controversies over coal prices and labor costs, there is a problem with high market concentration. "Most rail markets today," Theodore Keeler remarks, "contain no more than three firms, and many contain only one or two."[66] In the West as a whole, three railroads accounted for roughly 80 percent of all rail traffic during 1984.[67] In the East, the top three garnered

over 70 percent of the freight.[68] This is the result of much merging in recent years, and it means that further merging could reduce many markets to duopoly or monopoly status. To some extent, intermodal competition with trucks takes some of the punch out of these statistics. But a warning still seems warranted, just as it was in the case of airlines. Further merging could weaken the fresh competition secured by deregulation. Thus, deregulation should not include antitrust exemption.

Summary

Among transportation's several modes, trucks and airlines have been this century's sprinters. Railroads and inland waterways, the old mainstays, together still account for half of all freight volume, but the railroads have been troubled.

These developments indicate a certain degree of intermodal competition, as determined in large part by the industry's economics. Aside from price, demands for transportation are based on nonprice factors such as speed and reliability. Indeed, speed alone explains much of the success of trucks and airlines. On the supply side, we find that costs vary across modes, but they vary in such a way as to give certain modes advantages in certain traffic, such as railroads in large, long-haul, dry-bulk shipments and trucks in relatively small, short-haul, high-value shipments. These conditions inhibit intermodal competition in some services, but this lack is often made up for by opportunities for intramodal competition. The economics of trucking and airlines are particularly conducive to intramodal competition. Concentration in relevant markets for these modes need not be more than low to moderate. Entry into trucking is fairly easy. Costs are rather constant with scale for both trucking and airlines, implying no natural monopoly.

Regulation of the transportation industry sprang from a combination of economic conditions and historic circumstances. A mixture of monopoly power and competition in railroading produced stark price discrimination, prompting establishment of the ICC in 1887 to provide fairness *among* buyers. Fairness *to sellers* later motivated the cartelizing features of the Transportation Act of 1920, which followed a stressful time for the railroads. That stress deepened with the onslaught of trucking and the Great Depression, occasioning the spread of cartel-like regulation to a large portion of trucking in hopes of furthering fairness *among sellers*. Airlines were also brought under the umbrella at this time, for promotional and safety reasons as well as for fairness to sellers. Along the way, a restrictive policy toward railroad abandonments developed, illustrating fairness as an administrative process.

Regulation controlled entry, exit, and prices. *Entry* was artificially curbed by limited issuance of narrowly drawn operating rights. The effect was especially adverse in trucking and airlines, the growth sectors. *Exit* was controlled by surveillance of route abandonments and mergers. Railroads, the declining sector, hurt most from that policy. With respect to *prices,* levels of price followed no rational formula, for clustering in cartel-like rate bureaus stood in the way. Price structures mainly followed value-of-service rather than cost-of-service patterns. One adverse result was an inordinate shift of business from railroads to trucks during the first two-thirds of this century. Another was an absence of back-haul discounts and peak-load pricing.

The consequences of this regulation were higher prices in trucking and airlines due to higher profits and higher costs. The higher costs could be pinned on intramodal, intermodal, and dynamic inefficiencies. In railroads, the price effects of regulation are less clear. Low profits signaled low prices, but inefficiency may have caused high costs.

Deregulation of airlines and trucking vastly increased competition: (1) Entry burgeoned, mainly from low-cost nonunion carriers. (2) Prices have fallen far below what they would have been otherwise, and price structures now

better reflect costs (e.g., tumbling especially steeply for high-density routes and otherwise empty backhauls). (3) Service has for the most part improved, with better truck marketing, and wider varieties all around. (4) Efficiency has risen with gains in productivity.

The main purpose for deregulating railroads was, in contrast, to boost profits, which has been achieved. (1) Exits via abandonments have rescued the Class 1 railroads from high-cost, money-losing tracks. (2) Price flexibility has on balance lowered freight rates, but price increases on certain key commodities like coal have lifted profits. (3) Efficiency has been enhanced.

The one dark cloud is the rising intramodal concentration in areas where intermodal competition may be weak—namely, airlines and railroads. Further merging in these areas should be subjected to vigilant antitrust policy to preserve the competitive achievements of deregulation. The adverse effects of concentration in airlines are growing, which is especially apparent in higher prices and poorer service.

Questions and Exercises for Chapter 18

1. What is the relevance and importance of differing elasticities of demand in explaining (a) the origin of railroad regulation, and (b) the changes in rail prices after deregulation?
2. Use this chapter's early discussion of railroad costs to explain its later assertions that an easier abandonments policy should improve railroad profitability.
3. Compare and contrast railroad and truck costs in (a) long-haul versus short-haul and (b) speed.
4. Compare and contrast the origins of railroad and trucking regulation in (a) historical circumstances, (b) sources of lobbying support, and (c) economic rationales.
5. How and why did price regulation of transportation differ from price regulation of electric utilities?
6. What are the differences and similarities between value-of-service pricing and cross-subsidization?

7. Distinguish intramodal, intermodal, and dynamic inefficiencies.

8. Why was entry regulation important in trucking and airlines but unimportant in railroading?

9. What clues do we have that entry regulations in trucking and airlines were in fact restrictive? (Use evidence from regulation *and* deregulation periods.)

10. Compare and contrast deregulation in trucking and railroading with respect to (a) impetus, (b) purpose, (c) methods, and (d) economic consequences.

11. What have been the economic consequences of airline deregulation?

12. Should deregulation include antitrust "deregulation"? Why, or why not?

Notes

1. Transportation Association of America, *Transportation Facts and Trends* (July 1979): 7.

2. Thomas Gale Moore, "U.S. Airline Deregulation," *Journal of Law and Economics* (April 1986): 1–28. See also Samuel H. Baker and James B. Pratt, "Experience as a Barrier to Contestability in Airline Markets," *Review of Economics and Statistics* (May 1989): 352–356; and G. D. Call and T. E. Keeler, "Airline Deregulation Fares and Market Behavior: Some Empirical Evidence," in *Analytical Studies in Transport Economics*, ed. A. Daugherty (New York: Cambridge University Press, 1985). More generally see William G. Shepherd, "Contestability v. Competition," *American Economic Review* (September 1984): 572–587.

3. Robert G. Harris, "Economics of Traffic Density in the Rail Freight Industry," *Bell Journal of Economics* (Autumn 1977): 556–564. On pipelines see Leslie Cookenboo, Jr., *Crude Oil Pipelines* (Cambridge, MA: Harvard University Press, 1955).

4. Richard H. Spady and Ann F. Friedlaender, "Hedonic Cost Functions for the Regulated Trucking Industry," *Bell Journal of Economics* (Spring 1978): 159–179.

5. Richard E. Caves, *Air Transport and Its Regulators* (Cambridge, MA: Harvard University Press, 1962), pp. 55–83; Theodore E. Keeler, "Domestic Trunk Airline Regulation: An Economic Evaluation," in *Study on Federal Regulation*, Appendix to volume VI, Committee on Governmental Affairs, U. S. Senate, 96th Congress, 1st Session. (1978), pp. 107–109. For an overall survey on costs, see Ronald R. Braeutigam, "Regulatory Reform: Lessons for Natural Gas Pipelines," *Contemporary Policy Issues* (April 1990): 122–141.

6. Sources include Ann F. Friedlaender, *The Dilemma of Freight Transport Regulation* (Washington, DC: Brookings Institution, 1969), John R. Meyer and others,

The Economics of Competition in the Transportation Industries (Cambridge, MA: Harvard University Press, 1959), and T. H. Oum, "A Cross Section Study of Freight Transport Demand and Rail-Truck Competition in Canada," *Bell Journal of Economics* (Autumn, 1979): 463–482.

7. Transportation Association of America, *Facts and Trends*, pp. 14–15.

8. Paul W. MacAvoy, *The Economic Effects of Regulation: The Trunk-Line Railroad Cartels and the Interstate Commerce Commission Before 1900* (Cambridge, MA: MIT Press, 1965).

9. *Counselman v. Hitchcock*, 142 U. S. 547 (1892): *Interstate Commerce Commission v. Cincinnati, New Orleans and Texas Pacific Railway Co.*, 167 U. S. 479 (1897); *ICC v. Alabama Midland Railway Co.*, 168 U. S. 144 (1897).

10. William A. Jordan, *Airline Regulation in America* (Baltimore: Johns Hopkins University Press, 1970), pp. 14–33.

11. *Business Week*, April 23, 1979, pp. 142–144.

12. Association of American Railroads, *Yearbook of Railroad Facts* (Washington, DC: 1980), p. 20.

13. P. W. MacAvoy and J. W. Snow, eds., *Railroad Revitalization and Regulatory Reform* (Washington, DC: American Enterprise Institute, 1977), pp. 157–159.

14. See e.g., James R. Nelson, "Abstract of Regulation of Overland Movements of Freight," *Study on Federal Regulation*, Appendix to Vol. VI, U. S. Senate, Committee on Governmental Affairs, 96th Congress, 1st Session (1978), pp. 3–72; Caves, *Air Transport*, pp. 140–155.

15. MacAvoy and Snow, *Railroad Revitalization*, p. 103.

16. Friedlaender, *Freight Transport Regulation*, p. 62.

17. Ibid., p. 63.

18. Richard O. Zerbe, Jr., "The Costs and Benefits of Early Regulation of the Railroads," *Bell Journal of Economics* (Spring 1980): 343–350.

19. P. W. MacAvoy and J. W. Snow, eds., *Regulation of Entry and Pricing in Truck Transportation* (Washington, DC: American Enterprise Institute, 1977), pp. 8–9.

20. James Sloss, "Regulation of Motor Freight Transportation: A Quantitative Evaluation of Policy," *Bell Journal of Economics* (Autumn 1970): 327–366.

21. Keeler, "Domestic Trunk Airline Regulation," p. 119.

22. Anne F. Friedlaender, "The Social Costs of Regulating the Railroads," *American Economic Review* (May 1971): 226–234; Thomas G. Moore, "Deregulating Surface Transportation," in *Promoting Competition in Regulated Markets*, ed. A. Phillips (Washington, DC: Brookings Institution, 1975), pp. 55–98; and Douglas Caves, Laurits Christensen, and Joseph Swanson, "The High Cost of Regulating U. S. Railroads," *Regulation* (Jan./Feb. 1981): 41–46.

23. Nelson, "Abstract of Regulation," Kenneth D. Boyer, "Minimum Rate Regulation, Modal Split Sensitivities, and the Railroad Problem," *Journal of Political Economy* (June 1977): 493–512; Richard C. Levin, "Allocation in Surface Freight Transportation: Does Rate Regulation Matter?" *Bell Journal of Economics* (Spring 1978): 18–45.

24. MacAvoy and Snow, *Regulation of Entry and Pricing*, p. 21.

25. Milton Kafoglis, "A Paradox of Regulated Trucking," *Regulation* (Sept./Oct. 1977): 27–32.

26. *Wall Street Journal*, 26 September 1980, p. 20; 23 October 1980, p. 4. As a spokesman for Yellow Freight explained it, "The value attributable to restricted entry has been eliminated resulting in the decision to write off the investments." See also Michael W. Pustay, "Regulatory Reform and the Allocation of Wealth: An Empirical Analysis," *Quarterly Review of Economics and Business* (Spring 1983): 19–28.

27. Jordan, *Airline Regulation*, p. 203.

28. *Civil Aeronautics Board Practices and Procedures*, Report, U. S. Senate, Committee on the Judiciary, Subcommittee on Administrative Practice and Procedure, 94th Congress, 1st Session (1975), pp. 54–57.

29. Friedlaender, *Freight Transport Regulation*, pp. 84–88.

30. MacAvoy and Snow, *Regulation of Entry and Pricing*, p. 104.

31. *Arrow Transportation Co. v. Cincinnati, New Orleans and Texas Pacific Railway Co.*, 379 U. S. 642 (1965).

32. Paul W. MacAvoy and James Sloss, *Regulation of Transport Innovation: The ICC and Unit Coal Trains to the East Coast* (New York: Random House, 1967).

33. *Civil Aeronautics Board Practices . . . , op. cit.*, pp. 63–70; Clinton V. Oster, Jr., "The Impact of Deregulation On Service To Small Communities," *Journal of Contemporary Business* (vol. 9, no. 2): 103–121; Denis A. Breen and Benjamin J. Allen, "Common Carrier Obligations and the Provision of Motor Carrier Service to Small Rural Communities," *Quarterly Review of Economics and Business* (Winter 1980): 86–106.

34. MacAvoy and Snow, *Regulation of Transport Innovation*, p. 11.

35. Elizabeth E. Bailey, David R. Graham, and Daniel P. Kaplan, *Deregulating the Airlines* (Cambridge, MA: MIT Press, 1985); Daniel P. Kaplan, "The Changing Airline Industry," in *Regulatory Reform*, ed. L. W. Weiss and M. W. Klass (Boston: Little, Brown, 1986), pp. 40–77; Thomas G. Moore, "U.S. Airline Deregulation," *Journal of Law & Economics* (April 1986): 1–28; Alfred E. Kahn, "Surprises of Airline Deregulation," *American Economic Review* (May 1988): 316–322; William G. Shepherd, "The Airline Industry," in *The Structure of American Industry*, ed. Walter Adams, 8th ed. (New York: Macmillan, 1990).

36. Moore, *op. cit.*

37. Shepherd, "Airline Industry," p. 223.

38. *Ibid.*, p. 226.

39. Moore, "U.S. Airline Deregulation."

40. *Wall Street Journal*, 19 April 1990, p. B1 (a summary of several studies).

41. *Wall Street Journal*, 23 January 1991, p. B1.

42. Gregory Werden, Andrew S. Joskow, and Richard L. Johnson, "The Effects of Mergers on Economic Performance: Two Case Studies from the Airline Industry"; U.S. Department of Justice, Antitrust Division, Working Paper (October 2, 1989).

43. *Wall Street Journal*, 19 April 1990, p. B1 (referring to a GAO report).

44. Steven A. Morrison and Clifford Winston, "The Dynamics of Airline Pricing and Competition," *American Economic Review* (May 1990): 389–393.

45. Severin Borenstein, "Airline Mergers, Airport Dominance, and Market Power," *American Economic Review* (May 1990): 400–404.

46. Douglas W. Caves, Laurits R. Christensen, and Michael W. Tretheway, "Productivity Performance of U.S. Trunk and Local Service Airlines," *Economic Inquiry* (July 1983): 312–324.

47. Robert W. Kling, "Deregulation and Structural Change in the LTL Motor Freight Industry," *Transportation Journal* (Spring 1990): 47–53.

48. *Ibid.*

49. *Business Week*, January 21, 1985, pp. 90–91.

50. Kenneth Labich, "Blessings by the Truckload," *Fortune*, November 11, 1985, p. 138.

51. Michael W. Pustay, "Regulatory Reform and the Allocation of Wealth: An Empirical Analysis," *Quarterly Review of Economics and Business* (Spring 1983): 19–28.

52. C. Winston, T. Corsi, C. Grimm, and C. Evans, *The Economic Effects of Surface Freight Deregulation* (Washington, DC: Brookings Institution, 1990).

53. Organization for Economic Cooperation and Development, *Competition Policy and the Deregulation of Road Transport* (Paris: OECD, 1990), p. 55.

54. See also Richard Beilock and James Freeman, "Florida Motor Carrier Deregulation," *American Journal of Agricultural Economics* (February 1984): 91–98.

55. *Wall Street Journal*, 18 December 1985, p. 16.

56. Labich, "Blessings by the Truckload," p. 142.

57. W. Bruce Allen, "Deregulation and Information Costs," *Transportation Journal* (Winter 1990): 58–67.

58. OECD, *Competition Policy*, pp. 41–61.

59. William B. Tye, *The Transition to Deregulation: Developing Economic Standards for Public Policies* (New York: Quorum Books, 1991).

60. Theodore E. Keeler, *Railroads, Freight, and Public Policy* (Washington, DC: Brookings Institution, 1983), pp. 105–107.

61. Gary Slutsker, "Working on the Railroads," *Forbes*, March 24, 1986, pp. 126–130.

62. James Cook, "Profits over Principle," *Forbes*, March 25, 1985, p. 149; Shawn Tully, "Comeback Ahead for Railroads," *Fortune*, June 17, 1991, pp. 107–113.

63. C. C. Barnekov and A. N. Kleit, "The Costs of Railroad Regulation: A Further Analysis," Federal Trade Commission, Bureau of Economics, Working Paper No. 164, May 1988.

64. *Fortune*, June 17, 1991, pp. 107–113; *Wall Street Journal*, 28 July 1989, p. A 3B.

65. *Fortune*, June 17, 1991, p. 107.

66. Keeler, "Domestic Trunk Airline Regulation," p. 127.

67. Burlington Northern, Santa Fe–Southern Pacific, and Union Pacific.

68. CSX, Norfolk Southern, and Conrail. *Forbes*, March 25, 1985, p. 154.

Chapter 19

Energy: Petroleum

We want to build an energy future that's based on a range of diverse sources so that never again will this nation's energy well-being be swayed by events in any single foreign country.
— *President George Bush, 1991*
(Defending his energy policy proposals by acknowledging that oil motivated the war against Iraq)

I. Introduction

In August 1990 Iraq invaded Kuwait. Lacking oil from these countries, oil traders bid up the price of oil from $18 to $40 a barrel. The top line of Figure 19–1 (for nominal price) shows this increase with a huge spike over 1990. Prices at gas pumps also jumped—roughly 18 cents a gallon. The Bush Administration responded by sending 400,000 American combat troops to Saudi Arabia, together with planes, ships, and other war materials. Britain, France, and other countries contributed to the cause. Antiwar protesters cried "No Blood for Oil."

Japan resisted involvement. This surprised many people because, unlike the United States, Japan lacks domestic oil reserves and was at the time relying on Middle Eastern oil for 70 percent of its supplies. Yet the remarks of Kazuaki Harada, chief economist at Sanwa Bank's research institute, reflect Japan's attitude at the time:

> The Japanese economy is in very good shape, but I am worried about the American economy. The negative impact from rising oil prices is much more serious for the U. S. than Japan.[1]

Fortunately for the United States, oil prices fell almost as rapidly as they had risen (see Figure 19–1 again). Saudi Arabia and several other leading oil producers brought this about when they expanded their oil production by over 4 million barrels a day to compensate for the lost Iraqi and Kuwaiti supplies. Finally, in early 1991, the United States and its allies bombed the Iraqis out of Kuwait. The war was brief, but it cost the United States several hundred lives and several tens of billions of dollars.

As reflected in Figure 19–1, this was only one of many times that oil prices have jumped around. This was likewise not the first instance of supply volatility. Hence, one purpose of this chapter is to explain instability in the oil market. We glance back to the early 1900s when the

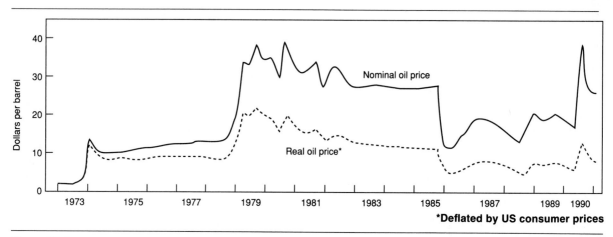

Figure 19–1
World Price of Oil, 1973–1991 (Saudi Arabian light until the end of 1982, North Sea Brent oil thereafter)

Source: *The Economist,* January 12, 1991, p. 67

United States enjoyed especially abundant oil supplies and then consider more recent times when the United States has imported half its needs. A second purpose of this chapter is to explore the policies that have governed the industry. Price floors were common when domestic oil was abundant. Price ceilings have appeared during shortages. Faced with recent shortages, the government has also tried to boost supplies in various ways. Conservation policies have also attracted considerable attention lately, so they will be covered. Indeed, as we shall see, conservation is the key to understanding the blasé attitude of the Japanese during the Persian Gulf crisis of 1990–1991. By conserving, the Japanese have curbed their demand for oil so greatly that they do not panic during disruption in supply.

The importance of oil to the U. S. economy is easy to state. Oil accounts for roughly half of all energy consumption, the remainder being divided among natural gas, coal, and other sources. The ability of free markets to arrange the production and distribution of oil is, for an economist, just as easy to state, at least in theory. Consumer demand and producer supply are guided by prices determined by the interaction of

supply and demand. It does not matter that oil is extracted from the earth or that it is an exhaustible resource that will be valued by future generations as well as our own. Many economists argue that the laws of demand and supply can, with little modification, be relied on to yield good results for all concerned.

Economic theory notwithstanding, oil has until recently been subjected to more regulation than have most industries. The story of that regulation is worth telling because of its immense impact, its interesting origins, its unique features, and its continuing attractiveness to many who would like this regulation renewed. In telling the story, we focus mainly on price regulation rather than on conservation. Moreover, the prices of interest here are "wellhead," or "field" prices. Prices at later stages of the production-distribution process have been regulated, but we ignore those regulations.

Our story has three main parts, as follows:

1. *Petroleum Before 1971:* Echoing the experience in transportation regulation, *price support* and stability were the main objectives of the regulation of crude oil from 1934 to 1971.

Domestic oil was abundant. And state governments were the main regulators.

2. *Petroleum During the 1970s:* The pre-1971
   abundance gave way to post-1971 shortage, a
   shortage that helped OPEC raise foreign oil
   prices repeatedly and astronomically. The
   federal government took the regulatory reins,
   imposing *price ceilings* on domestic oil during
   the 1970s.

3. *Conservation:* Following the shortages of the
   1970s, conservation has gained favor. Oil
   abundance during the 1980s caused some relaxation in this regard, but the Persian Gulf
   crisis of 1990-1991 revived interest in energy
   efficiency.

II. Price Regulation: Overview

When discussing the price floors and ceilings of
the first two parts of the story of regulation of the
price of oil, we touch on (1) regulation's main
purposes, (2) its major *characteristics,* (3) its
good and bad economic *effects,* and (4) *deregulation.*

In every respect, these price regulations
were complicated. The reasons they were complicated are themselves complicated. For one
thing, a multitude of goals were claimed for these
regulations, including equity, efficiency, stability,
and national defense. For another, the regulations varied to fit a vast array of suppliers—some
big, some little; some vertically integrated, some
not; and so on. Conversely, the regulations
twisted and turned to accommodate the diversity
of oil buyers and end users. Some buyers are major oil companies; others are small independents.
Some ultimate buyers (such as teenage Saturday
night "cruisers") have frivolous energy needs;
others (such as hospitals and farmers) have critical needs. Ultimate end uses range from jet fuel
to naphtha, asphalt to fuel oil.

We simplify. Our first simplifications are
found in the two panels of Figure 19–2, which
diagrammatically summarizes the price *floor* regulation of oil (1934–1971) and the price *ceiling*
regulation (1971–1981). Assuming pure competition, the supply curves labeled S have a positive
slope, indicating that additional supplies entail
additional costs.[2] The demand curves, D, display

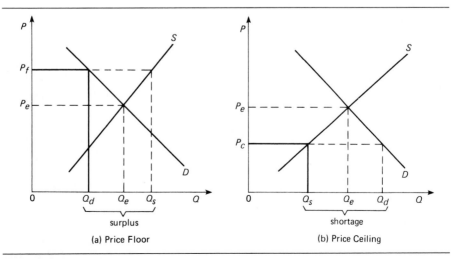

Figure 19–2
Price Regulation of Oil

the usual negative slope. Equilibrium is achieved in each instance by prices and quantities corresponding to the intersection of demand and supply, that is, P_e and Q_e.

To have any impact, a price floor would have to be *above* equilibrium price, as P_f is above P_e in Figure 19–2(a). At price P_f the quantity suppliers wish to offer, Q_s, exceeds the quantity buyers demand, Q_d, creating a surplus, $Q_s - Q_d$. This surplus would normally tend to drive price down toward P_e, expanding demand and contracting supply to eliminate the surplus. Thus, to enforce the price floor at P_f, supply must be artificially constrained not to exceed Q_d. This constraint was achieved in oil regulation prior to 1971 by restrictions on domestic output, so-called prorationing, and by quotas on imports from abroad.

Conversely, to have any impact, a price ceiling would have to be *below* equilibrium price, as P_c is below P_e in Figure 19–2(b). At price P_c the quantity suppliers offer is Q_s whereas quantity demanded is Q_d. Because demand exceeds supply, there is a shortage of $Q_d - Q_s$. Given that price is not allowed to ration quantity among buyers, nonprice mechanisms must allot existing supply and shift the demand curve back. After 1971 rationing was achieved by long lines at gas stations and official allocations. A 55-mph speed limit encouraged conservation.

Two key criteria for assessing the effect of these price regulations are *efficiency* and *equity*. Price floors and price ceilings are both *inefficient* because they lead to misallocations of resources. They result in too little being produced and consumed relative to the optimal amount Q_e. In technical jargon, Q_d in the floor case of 19–2 (a) and Q_s in the ceiling case of 19–2 (b) are outputs where marginal benefits (as indicated by the demand curve) exceed the marginal costs (as indicated by the supply curve). Society gains from added output until the marginal benefits match the added costs, as they do at Q_e. This, it must be noted, is only the most obvious form of inefficiency. Oil regulations also created production

inefficiencies because of the particular form they have taken. To enforce the pre-1971 oil price floor, for example, the output of low-cost, efficient oil wells tended to be more heavily restricted than the output of high-cost, inefficient wells. Given that price interference in oil has always produced inefficiency, it should be obvious that these regulations were never proposed as a means of advancing efficiency. Rather, inefficiency has always been their major social cost, with alleged benefits coming from other value judgment criteria such as equity or stability or conservation.

As regards *equity*, price floors favor sellers at the expense of buyers, whereas price ceilings favor buyers at the expense of sellers. The "equity" of price controls thus depends on the relative prosperity of buyers and sellers. If, as many believe, owners of oil properties are generally more wealthy than are oil consumers, the generalization most easily drawn in light of existing value judgments is that favoritism to producers is *inequitable* and favoritism to consumers is equitable. The oil price floor could thus be considered inequitable and the oil price ceilings could be considered equitable. Still, there are serious complications. As regards the alleged equity of price ceilings, for example, we must note the inequity suffered by those whose supplies are cut or totally denied by nonprice rationing.

Further complications in judging equity are best left to the discussion following. That discussion also acknowledges other policy objectives that have rationalized these regulations, stability in particular.

III. Oil Price Supports Before 1971

A. Purposes

Before 1934, the price of domestic crude oil was highly unstable.[3] That instability can be blamed on a combination of four main characteristics: (1) inelastic supply in the short run due to heavy sunk costs plus a "law of capture," (2) inelastic demand in the short run, (3) sharp shifts in the supply curve due to erratic results from oil exploration, and (4) shifts in the demand curve due to cyclical swings in general business activity. Given the inelasticity conditions, prices had to fall abysmally low to choke off supply or stimulate demand. Conversely, prices had to climb quite high to curb demand or boost output significantly. Although inelasticity alone is no problem, the added presence of shifts in demand and supply meant that prices were frequently called on to perform these difficult feats.

Things came to a head in the early 1930s. Discovery of the immense East Texas Field in 1930 and the country's simultaneous slide into depression combined to drive the price of oil down to amazingly low levels, even as low as 10 cents a barrel. As just suggested, this kind of instability may be attributed in part to the "law of capture." Under the "law of capture" crude oil belongs to whomever gets it out first. Couple this law with (1) fragmented property ownership over a given oil reservoir, (2) the fluid nature of the stuff, plus (3) standard profit-maximizing behavior, and you have a mad rush to drain the reservoir. The goal of each owner was simply (and crudely): "Get it out while the getting's good." Aside from instability, the results were:

- Appalling *physical waste,* because of reckless damage to the reservoir's natural drive pressures.
- Enormous *economic waste,* because of extraction and consumption of crude oil when its value was low and because of excessive investment in drilling and rigging.
- Shameful *environmental damage,* both because of the ugliness of oil rig forests and the pollution of streams and soils from oil run-off.

Stability and conservation thus justified the oil price supports in the early 1930s. An added purpose became apparent with time and with higher prices, namely, protection and prosperity for politically powerful oil producers.

B. Characteristics of the Regulation

Price support was achieved by official cartelization. That cartelization rested on a combination of state and federal policies.

1. STATE CONTROLS

Control of oil well output was achieved by *demand prorationing.* The basic idea was to stabilize price by reducing output as demand fell and expanding output as demand rose. Moreover, a generally restrictive hold on output lifted price above what it would have been on average. First instituted by state authorities in Oklahoma and Texas, demand prorationing later spread to Louisiana, Kansas, and New Mexico, thereby including the states most bountifully blessed with oil.

Operation of the system is illustrated in Figure 19–3. In essence, supply was restricted or expanded to whatever level was necessary for price to be at or above the "administered price" level. The supply curve looked like an L lying down. This configuration meant that supply was perfectly price elastic up to full capacity use (at the corner of the L). Not all wells were subject to regulation, the main exemptions being "discovery" wells and inefficient "strippers," the latter being wells physically incapable of producing more than a few barrels a day. Moreover, state authorities had no control over imports into the United States. Hence, exempt and import supplies were subtracted from projected demand before determining the output allowed from the regulated wells. In short, the fraction of allowed capacity use was reckoned monthly by the following formula:

fraction of capacity use for
regulated wells

$$= \frac{\text{demand} - (\text{exempts} + \text{imports})}{\text{total capacity of regulated wells}}$$

Thus, with decreased demand, or increased imports, or greater exempt output, state authorities

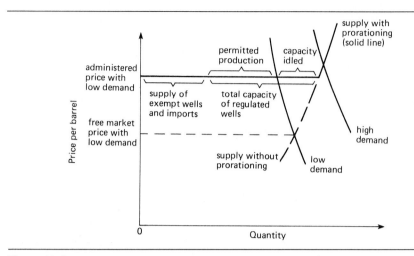

Figure 19–3
Restriction of Supply Under Demand Prorationing, Lifting Prices to "Administered
Level" Above Free Market Level

would reduce the "allowable" for regulated wells from, say, 90 percent to 80 percent capacity use. Competitive drilling under the law of capture was limited indirectly but not completely through additional regulations defining total capacity for each producer.

2. FEDERAL CONTROLS
The U. S. Bureau of Mines helped the states by providing the monthly estimates of oil demand used in the foregoing formula. More important, though, three federal measures backed up state prorationing: (1) The Connally "Hot" Oil Act of 1935 prevented the interstate shipment of crude oil produced in excess of state prorationing allowables. (2) The Interstate Oil Compact Commission Act, also of 1935, provided a forum for the prorationing agencies of producing states. They could thereby collude and coordinate their supply control efforts. (3) Mandatory import quotas came later beginning in 1959.

During the early years of prorationing, restrictions on imports were not needed. The United States enjoyed an abundance of oil, giving its oil a low price relative to foreign oil. In-

deed, as late as 1949, the U. S. accounted for 36 percent of the world's known reserves and 55 percent of its production. Thereafter, however, U. S. fortunes flagged, with the result that, during the 1950s, domestic oil came to be priced above foreign oil, in part because the domestic price was artificially supported (as described previously).

Low-priced imports gushed into the United States, playing havoc with prorationing. In 1958, for instance, regulated wells in Texas were held to only 33 percent capacity use, down from 100 percent in 1948. Continued price support thus depended on quotas against imports, which quotas were imposed on grounds of "national defense."

C. Effects of the Price Support System

The system had the effect of redistributing real income out of consumers' pockets into producers' pockets. The import quotas, for instance, elevated the price of oil to the point of costing consumers $7 to $8 billion a year extra. Not all of these billions took the form of excess profits for producers, however, because the regulations also raised producers' costs. In particular, there was substantial excess capacity and the most efficient wells were the ones most tightly constrained. These bloated costs amounted to approximately $2 billion a year. Finally, there were still further costs associated with the welfare loss of misallocated resources.

In short, the program was both inequitable and inefficient. Its main good was price stability (albeit at an artificially high level).

D. Deregulation

Defacto deregulation of the price support system followed the first serious signs of our oil depletion in 1969. Ominously, United States' productive capacity began a continuing decline while demand swelled to record levels. Prorationing allowables were pegged at 100 percent in 1972 and have remained there since. Import quotas were discontinued in 1973, as imports became the only means of meeting our voracious demands. The perceived problem shifted from a free-market price that was too low to one that was too high.

IV. Oil Price Ceilings After 1971[4]

A. Purposes of Ceilings: Stability and Equity

For a while, stability continued to serve as a major justification for oil price regulation. But as suggested by the shift from price floors to price ceilings, the nature of the stability problem changed dramatically. Whereas before 1971 the alleged problem was the *downside* instability associated with abundance and depression, after 1971 the problem became the *upside* instability associated with domestic shortage and price inflation.

Price ceilings were first introduced in 1971 as part of President Nixon's broader policy to curb inflation by wage-price controls. Thus, at the outset, oil was not singled out for special treatment but instead included in a general clampdown. Later, when oil did receive special attention, a major purpose of the price ceilings remained inflation control, or aggregate economic stability.

The shortages that made oil a threat to overall inflation were due to a number of factors besides the onset of diminishing U. S. productive capacity. The winter of 1969–1970 was the coldest in thirty years, putting a burden on fuel oil supply. Air-pollution standards shifted demand from dirty coal to relatively clean oil and gas. And so on.

The inflation threat went from bad to worse in 1973. That year the Organization of Petroleum Exporting Countries (OPEC) began a quick spurt of price hikes that quadrupled the cost of imports just when our dependence on imports had reached addictive proportions. As previously mentioned, our dire straits had forced the abandonment of import quotas and 100 percent capacity use in prorationing states. Moreover, European consumption reached an all-time high, putting OPEC in a particularly strong position. Then in October 1973, war erupted between Israel and the Arabs. A partial oil embargo followed, lifting the auction prices of crude oil as high as $17 a barrel, way above the existing $3 posted price (i.e., contract price). With a hop and a skip, OPEC lifted the posted price. Hopping first to $5.11, then skipping to $11.65 within a few months' time, OPEC shocked the United States and the world. Thereafter, OPEC escalated price by 5 to 10 percent annually until 1979, when it doubled the price from $14 to $28 a barrel.

Events of 1973–1974 raised an old problem besides inflation—the problem of equity. If the price of domestic oil were allowed to rise freely to match the price of oil imported from OPEC, there would have been a massive transfer of income from domestic oil consumers to domestic oil producers. The potential transfer has been variously estimated, but the order of magnitude is in any case huge—roughly $10 to $20 billion per year.[5]

Concern for inflation, stability, and equity mobilized political forces, swamping economic arguments that the free market should be allowed to work. Economically, the free market's soaring price would have curbed consumption (allocating oil to those most willing and able to pay for it) and would have provided incentive for increased domestic output (in the long run if not the short run). Most of President Nixon's top decision-makers—William Simon, Herbert Stein, and Roy Ash—were among those most ardently fond of the free market. Yet they were willing to betray their beliefs when confronted with (1) announcements of rapidly rising oil company profits, (2) embarrassing disclosures that Nixon's 1972 campaign had been financed in large part by the oil industry, (3) public and congressional suspicions that the shortage had been contrived by the major oil companies, and, of course, (4) public and congressional fears that the free market would brutalize poor consumers and aggravate inflation.[6] The acts emerging from these concerns were temporary but important.

B. Characteristics of the Policy

1. PRICE CEILINGS

Just before the embargo of 1973, the federal government's wage-price control policy evolved to the point of establishing a two-tier price system for crude oil. "Old" oil that was already flowing in 1972 was subjected to a low ceiling, and "new" oil from newly opened wells were free of any price ceiling. The idea was that the flow of old oil would continue at the lower price and that any price increases on that oil would give producers windfalls. However, new oil needed higher free-market prices because new oil cost more to find and produce than old oil. Without the incentive of higher prices, producers would not produce new oil nor would they invest in exploration. If viewed in terms of Figure 19–2(b), P_c would be the price of old oil and P_e would be the price of new oil.

There followed a complex series of legislative acts:

- 1973—Emergency Petroleum Allocation Act
- 1974—Federal Energy Administration Act
- 1975—Energy Policy and Conservation Act
- 1976—Energy Conservation and Production Act

Among other things, these acts created the Federal Energy Administration (FEA), authorized oil price controls after the expiration of the wage-price program, and provided for administrative allocations of oil and oil products. The FEA's implementation of the price ceiling provisions eventually led to a three-tier system of crude oil pricing fashioned on the two-tier model. In 1977, for example, old oil was $5.19 a barrel, new oil was $11.22 a barrel, and third-tier oil made up of stripper well output and imports was freely priced at $13.59, the "world" price.[7]

Figure 19–4 gives a simplified view incorporating only two prices—a control price for domestic crude labeled $P_{control}$ and an import price labeled P_{OPEC} indicates that the United States could purchase any amount at $14.50 per barrel. The upward slope of the domestic supply curve labeled S indicates that additional domestic production requires ever higher prices. In the absence of price control, the price of imports, P_{OPEC}, would determine market price, and the supply curve combining domestic and foreign sources would trace a schedule indicated by $KDBJI$. Demand intersects that supply schedule at point J, so total free-market supply would equal Q_D, with $Q_D - Q_s$ coming from imports. In this free-market case, domestic suppliers receive total revenues of $OABQ_s$. Their costs of production are the area under the supply curve, $OKBQ_s$. Thus their producers' surplus, or rent, is KAB, most of which could be considered windfall.

A price ceiling on domestic oil of $9.50 transfers some of this rent, or windfall, to consumers because they then pay a lower average price for oil. At $P_{control}$ of $9.50, domestic producers sup-

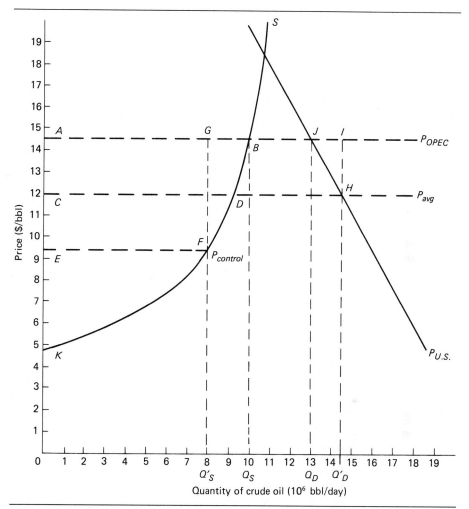

Figure 19–4
The Effect of a Price Ceiling on Crude Oil

Source: J. M. Griffin and H. B. Steele, *Energy Economics and Policy* (New York: Academic Press, 1980), p. 247.

ply Q'_S, earning total revenues equal to $OEFQ'_s$ of which only EFK is rent. Imports amounting to $Q'_D - Q'_S$ then meet the additional demand. At price P_{OPEC} the total amount spent on imports is $Q'_S GIQ'_D$. Combining this expenditure with the amount spent on domestic oil, $OEFQ'_S$, yields an overall amount spent of $OEFGIQ'_D$. If this total

dollar expenditure is divided by quantity Q'_D, the result is average price P_{avg}, which is what indicated to us the amount that would be imported to reach controlled equilibrium at point H.

The total dollar gain to consumers from price control is equal to area $AGFE$, because that is the *difference* between the amount they pay for Q'_D

oil *absent* control, namely $OAIQ'_D$, and the amount they pay *with* control, namely $OEFGIQ'_D$. The producers' loss from control is *ABFE*, which is slightly greater than the consumers' gain of *AGFE*. (It is slightly greater because *FGB* is an efficiency loss due to misallocation. Area *JIH* is also an efficiency loss.)

Notice that imports were greater with controls $(Q'_D - Q'_S)$ than without controls $(Q_D - Q_S)$. Thus, one adverse impact of the program was that it increased rather than decreased our dependency on OPEC oil. This added demand on OPEC many have helped OPEC maintain a price above what it would have been otherwise.

2. ENTITLEMENTS

A big problem with a two- or three-tier system can now be recognized. Refiners who buy crude oil for processing into consumer products compete with each other when selling refined products. If the prices refiners paid for their crude oil varied widely across tiers, then those having access to low-priced crude would have a tremendous competitive advantage over those getting high-priced crude. Thus, to equalize the price of crude oil to refiners, an elaborate scheme was devised called *the entitlements program.*

The basic idea was that a refiner had to have an "entitlement" to use a barrel of low-priced domestic oil. These entitlements were distributed among refiners on the basis of precontrol crude purchases. Moreover, the entitlement tickets were marketable to avoid the physical transfer of old oil in exchange for new oil. Those refiners having access to an above-average percentage of low-priced old oil had to buy entitlements from those refiners heavily reliant on high-priced new oil. The price of purchasing an entitlement reflected the cost difference in old and new oil. The market in entitlements, therefore, had the effect of equalizing the cost of crude oil to all refiners.

3. ALLOCATION REGULATIONS

Once price no longer rationed supplies among those demanding oil, various allocation regulations had to do the job. These were many and varied. Indeed, the entitlements program was a form of administrative rationing in which the entitlements functioned as ration tickets. A more obvious form of administrative allocation was the supplier/purchaser rule, under which a supplier of crude or refined products had to continue to supply his past purchasers with what was called "base-period volume." The vertical buy-sell relationships of the production-distribution process were, as a consequence, largely frozen, putting a chill on competition. A seller could not seek out the highest bidder for all his sales because he had to stand ready to supply past buyers minimal amounts.

Another level of allocation regulations handled ultimate end users by classifying them into four priority groups. At the very top priority, were those who were allowed all their fuel requirements without restraint—the Department of Defense, farmers, and medical and nursing facilities. At bottom priority were those who received no assured allocation whatever.

To summarize, the regulations President Nixon imposed in 1973 during the Arab oil embargo and OPEC price escalations were intended to promote domestic price stability and income equity. They applied to both crude oil and refined products but hit crude the hardest with first a two-tier then a three-tier price formula. Entitlements were needed to equalize the price of crude to refiners. Additional allocation controls tended to lock refiners and retailers into their historical relationships.

C. Effects of Oil Price Ceilings

The major effects of the control program, both good and bad, were premiered in Figure 19–4. On the good side, controls served the causes of macro stability and equity when the price of oil was held below what it would have been otherwise. Quantification of these effects is difficult, but in raw totals macro inflation may have been a few percentage points less and oil producers may have lost $13 billion to consumers annually during the mid-1970s. It must be acknowledged, however, that these are gross estimates that by argument, assumption, and analysis may vary considerably. Some economists would argue, for instance, that inflation is solely a monetary problem best controlled by monetary policy. As for equity in income distribution, conservative assumptions can be used to argue that the gains were "worth" no more than about $1.4 to $1.9 billion per year.[8]

On the bad side, the artificially low prices seem to have increased consumption and reduced domestic production compared to what they would have been. The consumption effect is easiest to appreciate. The price elasticity of demand for oil is roughly -0.5, which means that a 1 percent increase in the price of oil reduces the quantity demanded about 0.5 percent. With controls, the average price consumers paid was below the free-market price. If average price was as much as 10 percent lower, then consumption was roughly 5 percent too high.

The reduced production effect is more difficult to appraise because new oil was granted a high price to encourage its discovery and production. That price may not have been high enough, however, because the *cost* of new oil soared during the 1970s. Drilling costs per foot of well, for instance, rose 50 percent in constant dollars.[9] This resulted as the search for oil moved to more hostile environments. By 1980 skilled drillers in the Arctic were earning $90,000 a year (even young ones with no more than a high-school education), and unskilled people who aided the Arctic drillers by cooking and cleaning made $40,000 per year.[10] As for the low price on old oil, it too may have curbed production. The output of old oil can be boosted, or its rate of decline can be curbed, by the application of secondary recovery techniques such as steam injection. But these techniques are very expensive, and they will not be used unless oil's price is high enough to cover the high cost and a normal profit.

In technical jargon, there was a misallocation of resources because of these consumption and production effects. Consumers did not pay a price high enough to reflect accurately the economic value of a marginal, or additional, barrel of oil (regardless of whether that marginal barrel came from inside or outside the United States). The overall cost of inefficiency has been estimated to have been somewhere between $0.5 and $3.5 billion annually.[11] Thus, a liberal estimate of inefficiency's cost could exceed a conservative estimate of equity's benefit, yielding a negative verdict with respect to the control program's net value. (Such comparisons of inefficiency costs and equity benefits are awkward because those who pay the inefficiency costs may not be the same folks as those who receive the equity benefits. Theoretically, however, elimination of inefficiency's costs would provide savings that could be transferred to those who, in the process, lose their equity benefits.)

E. Summary on Oil Price Ceilings

In retrospect, the switch from price floors to price ceilings was a temporary policy reaction. Given the abrupt switch from oil abundance to oil scarcity, and given the severity of the ensuing problems of stability and equity, the ceilings are understandable if not justifiable. Awesome political pressures favored ceilings and nonprice rationing, pressures that even staunch friends of the free market could not rebuff. Although the controls did serve the ends of stability and equity, they created inefficiencies. Domestic scarcity fostered control, but control aggravated that scarcity. Decontrol has since dissipated the inefficiencies, and new taxes were introduced to handle the problem of equity. As for macro instability, oil's contribution to the problem was temporary, so it is appropriate that for this purpose, too, the controls were temporary.

Figure 19–5 summarizes the story in constant, 1980 dollars. After OPEC lifted the price of imported oil in 1973–1974, the price of domestic oil was held down by controls. After decontrol began in 1979, the domestic price drifted up

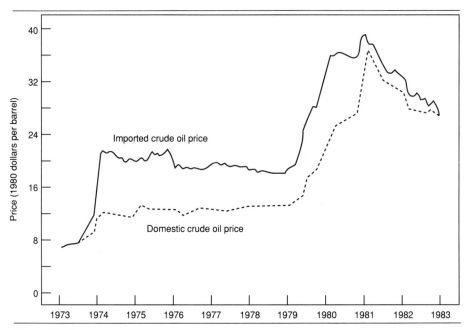

Figure 19–5

Source: U. S. Department of Energy, Monthly Energy Review; William H. Hogan, "Energy Policy; in P. R. Portney (ed.), *Natural Resources and the Environment* (Washington, D. C.: Urban Institute, 1984), p. 88

to meet the import price even as the import price skyrocketed further.

V. Conservation

A. Introduction

Three major considerations now darken America's energy future (and the world's as well):

- **Availability:** The United States is pumping itself dry. United States production is down from what it was in 1970, and it will continue to fall unless there is some technological breakthrough in the secondary recovery of oil from old wells. We therefore resort to imports. In 1990, just before the Persian Gulf War, 50 percent of U. S. consumption came from

abroad. Moreover, 25 percent came from the Persian Gulf region. That dependency is frightening. Table 19–1 shows why imports imply Middle Eastern entanglement. In 1991, the Middle East accounted for *two-thirds* of the world's proved oil reserves. Projections into the next century give the Middle East still more dominance. Because wars, revolutions, and other disruptions occur there regularly, the risks run high.

- **Environmental Problems:** Fossil fuel combustion, including coal as well as oil, causes more air pollution than anything else—85 percent of sulfur dioxide emissions and 95 percent of nitrogen dioxide emissions, for instance. The annual costs of the resulting crop losses and adverse health effects menace us. Crop losses range from $2.5 billion to $7.5 billion annually.

Table 19–1
Estimated Proved Oil Reserves, 1991

	Billions of Barrels	Percentage of World Total
U.S. and Canada	32.0	3.2%
Latin America	121.1	12.1
Asia-Pacific	50.2	5.0
Western Europe	14.4	1.4
USSR and East Europe	58.9	5.9
Africa	59.9	6.0
Middle East	662.6	66.4
	999.1	100.0%

Source: *Oil & Gas Journal*, December 31, 1990: 44–45.

Health damages fall between $12 billion and $80 billion annually.[12]

- **SocioPolitical Problems:** Efforts to increase domestic oil production target sensitive areas such as Alaska's Arctic National Wildlife Refuge and California's offshore continental shelf. Attempts to shift to nonfossil fuels trigger touchy problems as well. Nuclear power does not cause air pollution, but it inflicts other hazards. Because of the accident at Three Mile Island, because no state is eager to accept a site for nuclear waste disposal, and because of huge cost overruns on plant construction, the nuclear power industry has been slumping badly. Nearly 100 planned nuclear plants have been cancelled or indefinitely deferred, and since 1978 there have been no new orders for reactors.[13] These and related difficulties can be called sociopolitical problems because value judgments heavily affect them.

What can be done to brighten the future? Of all the options, one stands out—*conservation*. The marvel of conservation is that it solves many problems simultaneously. It reduces our dependence on risky foreign supplies. It improves the environment. It saves us from plunging reck-

lessly into unattractive alternatives. Moreover, it is surprisingly inexpensive. As J. P. Holdren, professor of energy and resources at the University of California-Berkeley, says: "Energy efficiency is the cleanest, cheapest, fastest way to improve the energy picture."[14]

In 1991 Congress considered nearly eighty bills intended to encourage conservation. Among other things, they proposed new minimums on automobile gas mileage, new standards for appliances and industrial motors, new regulations for office building and home construction, and higher taxes on gasoline. We take up tax policies first and general regulations second, concluding with brief surveys of President Bush's 1991 energy proposals and Japan's achievements.

B. Tax Policy

Raising taxes on energy consumption appeals to economists. Higher taxes would encourage conservation through the price mechanism rather than through regulatory commands. Higher prices would induce people to do the right thing rather than coerce them. Moreover, in situations like this, price signals usually operate with greater efficiency than bureaucratic edicts do. They may be more equitable as well.

Specifically, higher taxes would mean higher prices for gasoline, heating oil, boiler fuel, and so on. In turn, these higher prices would curb consumption, as already proven by events following the oil price increases of the 1970s referred to earlier in Figure 19–1. Before the early 1970s, low and falling energy prices encouraged energy consumption, especially oil and natural gas. As suggested by Figure 19–6, total energy consumption per dollar of gross national product was the same in 1972 as in 1950. Oil and natural gas consumption per dollar of the GNP was 33 percent higher in 1972 than in 1950.

After 1972, the price of oil jumped first to $12 a barrel from its previous $3 a barrel, and then it jumped again during the late 1980s, ending up close to $40 a barrel (in nominal terms). The con-

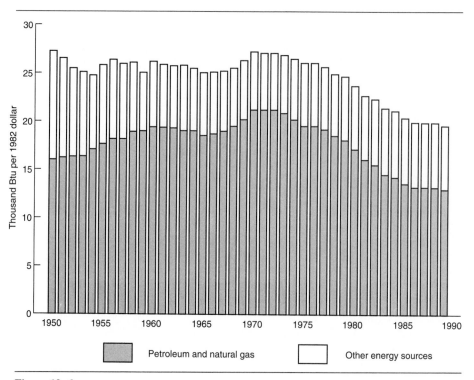

Figure 19–6

U.S. Energy Consumption per Dollar of Gross National Product, 1950–1989

Source: U.S. Department of Energy, Energy Information Administration, *Annual Energy Review 1989*, Table 8, p. 25. DOE/EIA/0384(89), Washington DC, 1990

sequences for energy consumption appear in Figure 19–6. From 1972 to 1985, relative energy consumption fell sharply. All the drop resulted from savings on oil and natural gas. Consumption of these in 1985, relative to the GNP, was 37 percent below 1972 levels. Much of this gain was owing to one source: Automobile fuel efficiency went from an average 13.4 miles per gallon in 1972 to 18.2 MPG in 1985, a 36 percent improvement.

Gains in energy efficiency stopped after 1985, however, as indicated by the level height of the bars in Figure 19–6 after 1985. Look back to Figure 19–1, and you will see the influence of the price of oil in this reversal. Price fell sharply after 1985, from almost $30 a barrel down to $14 a barrel in current dollars. After adjusting for inflation

to arrive at real prices, we see that a barrel of oil could be purchased in 1986 for little more than a barrel of oil back in 1972, before the price escalations of the 1970s. Prices, therefore, were no longer promoting energy conservation during the late 1980s, quite the opposite. And oil imports in 1990 were 50 percent of total consumption.

The time-series patterns of Figures 19–1 and 19–6 are corroborated by the cross-section evidence of Figure 19–7. In the United States, gasoline is priced remarkably lower than in any other major western country. During 1988, it was $0.95 a gallon, as shown in Figure 19–7. Italy, Denmark, and Japan are at the other end of the scale, with 1988 prices ranging from $3.47 per gallon in Japan to $3.90 in Italy. Comparing these countries with the United States and taking into

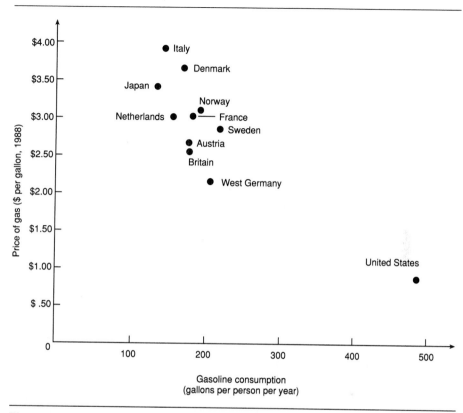

Figure 19–7
Price and Consumption of Gasoline by Country, 1988

Source: World Resources Institute, as reported in *The Wall Street Journal,* January 30, 1991, p. 1A.

account those in between like France and Britain, it is obvious that a higher price per gallon is associated with a lower level of consumption per capita. (Technically, the long-run price elasticity of demand for gasoline is in the neighborhood of −0.6 to −0.8).

Why do gasoline prices vary so widely internationally? *Taxes.* During the time of Figure 19–7's prices, federal, state, and local taxes on gasoline in the United States were a piddling $0.32 a gallon (on average). Gasoline taxes in Italy, Denmark, and Japan were, in contrast, astronomical–$2.17, $1.83, and $1.00 per gallon, respectively–and those countries have the highest

prices shown in Figure 19–7. French and British taxes were also quite high at $2.00 and $1.56. No foreign country listed in Figure 19–7 had a tax below $1.00 per gallon.[15] Thus, even if gasoline taxes in the United States were tripled, gas would still be cheap by world standards.

The basic economic rationale favoring higher gasoline taxes in the United States is not simply greater energy conservation as such. It is the fact that, at present, people do not see the true social costs of gasoline posted on the pump. The price they pay does not reflect the costs of crop losses, ill health, materials corrosion, and other adverse environmental impacts, or the costs of the Gulf

War and our military readiness to fight again for oil. All of these many costs taken together run well over $100 billion annually. Without seeing all the costs associated with gasoline consumption, people consume a lot more than can be justified economically. The result is economic inefficiency as well as energy inefficiency. (Economic efficiency would improve even if the revenues gained by additional gasoline taxes were offset by reductions in other taxes, reductions that would benefit people across income categories in a manner similar to the way the added gasoline tax would hit different income groups. For example, gasoline taxes are regressive in about the same way that Social Security payroll taxes are regressive. So the latter could be cut if the former were increased, yielding no positive net revenue, something that would make a gasoline tax increase more attractive politically.)

Other kinds of energy taxes could encourage energy conservation as well. Apart from taxes on other kinds of fuel, such as coal, there is now a federal tax directly on new cars. First levied in 1980, this "gas guzzler" tax rises as the fuel efficiency of the car falls. In 1986, for instance, the tax on a car getting 21.5 to 22.5 MPG was $500, whereas the tax on a car getting less than 12.5 MPG was $3,850.

C. Regulations (Nonprice Policies)

The biggest problem with substantially higher gasoline taxes in the United States is political infeasibility. The typical senator or congressman believes that pushing for such a tax increase, however wise it might be economically, is political suicide. Lacking the courage to provide needed leadership (and also hesitant to impose short-run costs to secure long-run gains), politicians prefer to pass measures that boost supply rather than trim demand. And when it comes to trimming demand, their preferred approach is usually one that is obscure, hidden, oblique— one that appears costless but isn't. This explains the attraction of direct regulation.

Since 1975, for instance, the federal government has tried to legislate improved automobile gas mileage by imposing corporate average fuel economy standards (called CAFE). These standards specify the minimum miles per gallon that an auto company's new cars must achieve each year, as an average of the company's new car fleet. Based on EPA's city-highway rating, the gas mileage minimum started at 18 miles per gallon for 1978, then escalated to 27.5 miles per gallon in 1990. When the legislation was passed in 1975, new cars averaged 15.8 miles per gallon. In 1990, they averaged 28.2 miles per gallon, an impressive 78.5 percent improvement in fuel efficiency in just fifteen years. Advocates of these regulations credit the gains to the CAFE standards and urge that they be raised further to 40 miles per gallon by the year 2000. In fact, most of the gains in new fleet fuel efficiency came during the years up to 1986 when gasoline prices were rising as a result of the oil price hikes we surveyed earlier. Hence, price increases can be credited with these gains as much as regulation, maybe more. Analysis shows that it is difficult to estimate the exact contributions of each factor.[16]

Whatever impact the CAFE standards may have had, regulation of this sort is inferior to a high gasoline tax for one compelling reason—human behavior. Buying a car with good gas mileage is one thing. Driving it is another. And without a higher price at the gas pump, motorists have less incentive to drive fewer miles, to carpool, to avoid jackrabbit starts, and to keep their cars properly tuned. In other words, a higher tax would affect our daily habits as well as our choice of a new car, whereas CAFE regulations influence only the latter. As already suggested, the most attractive feature of the CAFE approach is its political feasibility, not its economic trenchancy.

This is not to say that direct regulation has no place whatever in attempts to encourage conservation. People sometimes ignore price inducements because of inadequate information. In these instances, information regulations can be helpful. For example, federal rules require that EPA estimated gas mileage be disclosed on each new car's window sticker, together with a conversion of that mileage into an estimated annual cost for fuel. Likewise, energy efficiency labels must appear on large new household appliances like refrigerators and air conditioners.

Furthermore, information sometimes has little impact on people, partly because of the complexity of energy efficiency investments and partly because of inexplicable myopia. Assume, for example, that refrigerator A would reduce your electricity bill $10 a month compared to refrigerator B. If the purchase price of refrigerator

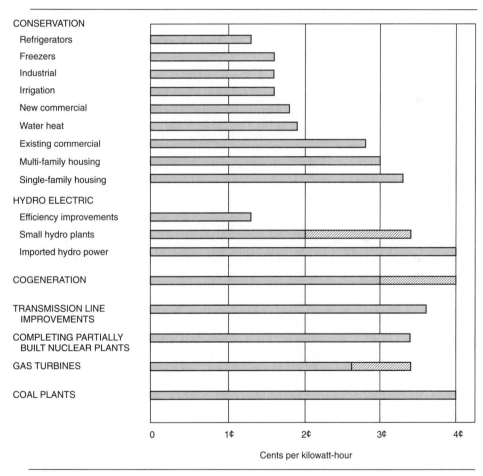

Figure 19–8
Comparative Costs of Obtaining Electric Energy: Conservation Versus Generation, Including Both Direct Costs and External Costs (Cross-Hatching Indicates a Range of Estimates)

Source: Bonneville Power Administration, as reported by Harold M. Hubbard, "The Real Cost of Energy," *Scientific American,* April 1991, p. 40

A was $100 higher than that of B, would you buy A or B? The economically correct decision is A because the extra $100 you pay at the outset is earned back in less than a year. The rate of return on this efficiency investment is therefore well over 100 percent annually, which is a good deal by any standard. Yet millions of people would choose B, forgoing this good return. Evidence shows that by their purchasing behavior, people *typically* turn down returns of 100 percent and even 200 percent on energy efficient appliances.[17]

Figure 19–8 puts the problem in a different perspective, one that illustrates the broader economic inefficiencies resulting from market imperfections of this kind. Figure 19–8 shows the costs of obtaining electric energy when various kinds of conservation are used (when the costs incurred are actually for energy savings) and by generating more electricity in various ways (e.g., by using gas turbines and coal). The estimated costs, in cents per kilowatt-hour, include *all* of society's costs in each case—the external costs of environmental damage as well as the costs of mining, transporting, and processing fuel. Notice that most of the conservation measures, especially those for home appliances, cost between 1¢ kwh and 2¢ kwh. However, the costs of generating new electricity are generally twice as high, in the range of 3¢ kwh to 4¢ kwh. To the extent that free-market behavior incorrectly shuns conservation and encourages new generation, regulations may be helpful.

There may thus be more behind the National Energy Conservation Act of 1987 than political expediency. Under this legislation, the Department of Energy developed minimum efficiency standards for major household appliances, including refrigerators, freezers, water heaters, air conditioners, and furnaces. The 1990 standards boosted the purchase prices of many new appliances while cutting their operating costs. The average payback period has been estimated to be about two years. Hence, the energy efficiencies from these regulations appear to be economically worthwhile. The estimated savings for con-

sumers will accumulate to $40 billion by 2015.[18] (Regulations for home construction and office buildings also appear to be cost-effective for much the same reason.)

D. President Bush's 1991 Energy Policy Proposal

Because a crisis is often necessary to spur historic new policies, the Persian Gulf War of 1991 seemed to many observers to be a time of opportunity as well as tragedy. They saw the war as a chance to focus on energy problems, that of oil in particular. In that context, President Bush offered his energy policy proposals of 1991, which the administration had already been working on for two years.

Given the war and the two years of preparation, these proposals were surprisingly thin. The president called for the following:

- Opening new off-shore areas and Alaska's Arctic National Wildlife Refuge to oil drilling.
- Relaxing licensing procedures for nuclear power plants.
- Reducing regulations on oil and natural gas pipelines.
- Spending more on research for new energy technologies, including electric cars.
- Converting fleet vehicles that are refueled at central locations (such as UPS delivery trucks) to nongasoline fuels like natural gas, propane, and methanol.

The lack of any major conservation provisions was deliberate. Energy Secretary James Watkins, a key architect of the plan, said the Bush Administration had a "basic philosophical disagreement" with people who called for higher energy taxes and added conservation regulations to reduce our foreign dependence on oil. Such measures, he said, "would reduce the nation's standard of living and economic competitiveness."[19]

The title of *Business Week's* article on the president's proposals summarized the critical reaction—"Wimping Out on Energy?"[20] A member of Congress called the plan "a back to the '50s" strategy to promote oil drilling. And within a few months the National Academy of Sciences urged immediate acceptance of an aggressive energy-conservation program that included the following:

- Tax incentives to achieve a 30 percent increase in auto fuel efficiency.
- Tougher new standards for household appliances.
- Use of small new fluorescent bulbs to cut 50 percent off the power used for lighting.
- More efficient motors to cut industrial energy use by 30 percent.[21]

The National Academy was especially concerned about one environmental issue in particular— global warming resulting from the "greenhouse effect" of fossil fuel emissions. A heated debate is now raging over conservation.

E. Japan's Energy Program

To claim, as the Bush Administration did, that significant conservation would "reduce the nation's standard of living and economic competitiveness" seems disingenuous. Evidence such as that presented in Figure 19–8 suggests that conservation may be less burdensome economically than all-out efforts aimed at new energy production. Moreover, several countries enjoying levels of economic well-being equal to ours get by with much less energy consumption per capita than we do. Energy use per dollar of gross national product is significantly lower in several advanced countries abroad, the most conspicuous one being Japan, which is arguably the most energy-efficient country in the world:

> Since 1973 it [Japan] has relentlessly implemented conservation policies that have paid off. During the first Arab embargo, oil provided nearly 80 percent of Japan's energy. By 1986, that had fallen to just 56 percent. Today [1991], Japan's economy produces 81 percent more real output for the same amount of energy than it did in 1973. It uses about

30 percent less energy, relatively, to fuel its houses, cars, appliances, and buildings than the United States. Its edge in manufacturing plants is even bigger. . . . *Overall, the Japanese economy is twice as energy efficient as America's.*[22]

Japanese consumers respond to tax-enhanced prices (note Figure 19–7, again). As regards industry, where the Japanese have an especially outstanding record, a long-range program of government regulation has been at work. The Ministry of International Trade and Industry (MITI) has efficiency targets for some 5,000 factories. Each factory has one to ten energy engineers who monitor energy use, check compliance, and report to MITI regularly. According to *The Wall Street Journal,* "One clear lesson to learn from Japan is that forcing core industries to become more energy-efficient is one thing that government *can* do well."[23]

We have thus come full circle. We can now see why the Japanese resisted involvement in the Persian Gulf War, why they were more worried about America than themselves. Japan's conservation policies yield energy independence (as well as other rewards like environmental improvement).

Summary

Economic policies governing oil divide into three periods: (1) price floor regulation from 1934 to 1971, (2) price ceiling regulation from 1971 to 1981, and (3) measures to encourage conservation beginning in about 1975 with passage of the Energy Policy and Conservation Act, which among other things authorized the CAFE standards for automobile efficiency.

Oil Price Floors: Stability and conservation were the chief targets of oil price supports, supplemented by goals of protection and prosperity for domestic oil producers. History seemed to verify the need for such regulation when discovery of the immense East Texas Field and the

Great Depression conspired to cause prices to plummet. The law of capture also contributed.

Official cartelization characterized these regulations. Prices were supported and stabilized by supply curtailments that fluctuated with demand. This prorationing was the work of state officials who were supported by several federal measures, the most important of which was an import quota. The program brought stability and aided producers but did so very inefficiently and at great cost to consumers. In the end, the program fizzled out because the key condition underlying it—domestic oil abundance—evaporated during the late 1960s.

Oil Price Ceilings: As the United States and the rest of the industrialized world grew increasingly dependent on OPEC oil during the early 1970s, OPEC exploited that dependence with huge price increases. The consequences were inflationary shock for consumers and massive windfall profits for producers. Thus, in the name of stability and equity, the federal government instituted price ceilings on domestic production, ceilings that were a natural outgrowth of the general wage-price control policy existing at the time. The Federal Energy Administration was the main agency involved.

Different prices for old and new oil were deemed appropriate on the theory that they would prevent windfalls on old oil while encouraging production of new oil. Moreover, allocation became an administrative chore once price no longer did the rationing.

Although the causes of stability and equity were served, there were large costs in inefficiency. Domestic production may have suffered. And consumption most certainly ballooned, something that aggravated our dependency on imports. These burdens were temporary, however, because the program was, as intended, temporary. Decontrol reduced the inefficiencies by slowing the decline in domestic production and curbing consumption. The problem of equity has been turned over to a windfall profits tax. And the derailment of OPEC has caused oil prices

to plunge toward preregulation levels (in real terms).

Conservation: The higher prices of the 1970s and early 1980s reduced oil consumption relative to gross national product. Conservation of various kinds led the way. For example, the corporate average fuel economy (CAFE) standards that were imposed on automobiles were a step. Minimum standards for household appliances were also put in place. Although direct regulations are sometimes warranted by market imperfections that seem resistant to correction any other way, direct regulations have their problems, especially those regulations aimed at consumers (rather than industrialists). Price changes, such as those that would follow hefty increases in gasoline taxes, seem to be a much superior way of achieving conservation. Price worked in this manner up through the mid-1980s. The cross-section data of Figure 19–7 further indicate the efficacy of higher prices. A key benefit of the price approach is its daily pressure on human behavior. Price changes spur habit changes.

The Persian Gulf War caused President Bush's 1991 energy plan to seem insufficient to many critics. Its call for added production instead of added conservation was especially curious—and controversial. The great advantage of conservation is that it achieves numerous ends all at once. It reduces our dependence on risky Persian Gulf supplies as our domestic production dwindles. It serves to improve the environment. It also relieves us, at least partially, of the necessity to compromise some highly prized values, thereby easing several sociopolitical problems. Japan's success at conservation through government policy offers a good case study of the possibilities. Still, it looks as if nothing momentous will come out of Washington unless the next crisis is much worse than the last. With real oil prices falling during the late 1980s and early 1990s, consumers (who are also voters) seem to be languishing in the grip of complacency. In the long run this may prove unfortunate.

Questions and Exercises for Chapter 19

1. Explain with the aid of diagrams why a price floor might be considered equitable to producers but a price ceiling equitable to consumers.
2. Is the allocation inefficiency associated with a price floor the same or different from the allocation inefficiency associated with a price ceiling? Explain.
3. Explain how the allowable production capacity under prorationing would be affected by (a) a drop in demand, (b) an increase in exempt production, and (c) a drop in imported oil.
4. Compare and contrast the stability rationales of the 1930s and 1970s.
5. What parallels and differences do you see in prorationing on the one hand and entitlements plus supply allocations on the other? Discuss in the context of Figure 19–2.
6. Compare and contrast two-tier price controls with *no* controls plus a windfall profits tax in (a) efficiency and (b) equity.
7. Why did the oil price controls of the 1970s increase consumption, and what supply source filled the demand?
8. Why, despite good intentions of aiding consumers with a price ceiling, might many consumers be harmed rather than helped by it?
9. Why are policies that encourage conservation considered more desirable than policies that encourage additional domestic oil production or nuclear power?
10. In *theory,* why would we expect an increase in gasoline taxes to encourage conservation? In *practice,* what empirical evidence supports the theory?
11. What are CAFE standards? Why might they be good policy? Why might they be bad policy?
12. Why do consumer behavior and Japanese experience suggest that direct regulation may sometimes be desirable for conservation?

Notes

1. *Wall Street Journal,* 8 August 1990, p. A7.
2. The assumption of pure competition is perhaps the biggest oversimplification in this analysis. At best, "workable" competition prevails, and some industry experts argue that noncompetitive oligopoly typifies oil and gas production in the U. S., primarily because of the dominance of such major firms as Exxon, Texaco, Mobil, Shell, and Chevron, but also because of extensive joint venture activity in the industry. See, e.g., John W. Wilson, Testimony, *The Natural Gas Industry,* Part I, U. S. Senate, Committee on the Judiciary, Subcommittee on Antitrust and Monopoly (1973), pp. 456–504.
3. Main sources for this section are M. G. de Chazeau and A. E. Kahn, *Integration and Competition in the Petroleum Industry* (New Haven: Yale University Press, 1959); Walter Measday, "The Petroleum Industry," in *The Structure of American Industry,* ed. W. Adams (New York: Macmillan, 1977); S. L. McDonald, *Petroleum Conservation in the United States* (Baltimore: Johns Hopkins Press, 1971); Cabinet Task Force on Oil Import Control, *The Oil Import Question* (Washington, DC: 1970).
4. Main sources for this section include Craufurd D. Goodwin, ed., *Energy Policy in Perspective* (Washington, DC: Brookings Institution, 1981), especially the chapters by de Marchi, Cochrane, and Yager; Paul W. MacAvoy (ed.), *Federal Energy Administration Regulation* (Washington, DC: American Enterprise Institute, 1977); W. David Montgomery, "A Case Study of Regulatory Programs of the Federal Energy Administration," in *Study on Federal Regulation,* Appendix to Vol. VI, U. S. Senate, Committee on Governmental Affairs (December 1978), and J. M. Griffin and H. B. Steele, *Energy Economics and Policy* (New York: Academic Press, 1980).
5. Griffin and Steele, *Energy Economics,* p. 248. See also Joseph P. Kalt, *The Economics and Politics of Oil Price Regulation* (Cambridge, MA: MIT Press, 1981), pp. 213–221.
6. See, e.g., de Marchi, in Goodwin, *Energy Policy,* pp. 425–468.
7. *The Energy Fact Book,* U. S. House, Subcommittee on Energy and Power of the Committee on Interstate and Foreign Commerce (Nov. 1980), p. 266.
8. K. J. Arrow and J. P. Kalt, "Why Oil Prices Should Be Decontrolled," *Regulation* (Sept./Oct. 1979): 13–17.
9. *Energy Fact Book,* p. 346.
10. *Wall Street Journal,* 14 April 1981, pp. 1, 15.
11. Arrow and Kalt, "Why Oil Prices Should Be Controlled," and Montgomery, "Case Study of Regulatory Programs."
12. Harold M. Hubbard, "The Real Cost of Energy," *Scientific American* (April 1991): 38–39.
13. Marshall Yates, "Nuclear Energy: A Failed Promise or a Promising Future?" *Public Utilities Fortnightly* (November 22, 1990): 12–13.
14. *Business Week,* September 16, 1991, p. 91.
15. Timothy Taylor, "Despite Rising Prices, It's Time to Raise Gas Taxes," *San Jose Mercury News,* September 2, 1990, p. 7C.
16. R. W. Crandall, H. K. Gruenspecht, T. E. Keeler, and L. B. Lave, *Regulating the Automobile* (Washington, DC: Brookings Institution, 1986), pp. 117–140.
17. Paul C. Stern, "Blind Spots in Policy Analysis:

What Economics Doesn't Say About Energy Use," *Journal of Policy Analysis and Management* (vol. 5, no. 2, 1986): 200–227.

18. J. E. McMahon et al., "Impacts of U. S. Appliance Energy Performance Standards on Consumers, Manufacturers, Electric Utilities, and the Environment," *Government, Non-Profit, and Private Programs,* Vol, 7 of *Proceedings from the ACEEE 1990 Summer Study on Energy Efficiency* (Washington, DC: American Council for an Energy Efficient Economy, August 1990), pp. 7.107–7.116.

19. *Wall Street Journal,* 21 February 1991, p. A3.

20. *Business Week,* February 25, 1991, p. 30.

21. *San Jose Mercury News,* 11 April 1991, p. 10A.

For other critiques of the Bush proposal, see Eric Hirst, "Boosting U.S. Energy Efficiency Through Federal Action," *Environment* (vol. 33, no. 2, March 1991): 7–11, 32–36; Gregg Easterbrook, "Waste of Energy," *New Republic,* March 18, 1991, pp. 26–31; "Energy and the Environment," *The Economist,* August 31, 1991, pp. 1–30; and "Conservation Power," *Business Week,* September 16, 1991, pp. 86–92.

22. *Newsweek,* January 21, 1991, p. 25 (emphasis added); see also *Wall Street Journal,* 8 August 1990, p. A7.

23. C. Chandler and M. W. Brauchli, "Oil Security," *Wall Street Journal,* 10 September 1990, p. 1A.

PART V

Social Regulation

Chapter 20

Safety, Health, and Pollution Regulation: An Overview

I like life better than figs.
— William Shakespeare

Regulations concerning safety, health, and pollution date back to ancient times. Their appearance in the United States originated in the last century with state and local laws. Regulation spread to the federal level with the Tea Importation Act of 1897 and the Food and Drug Act of 1906. Further developments followed but none as earthshaking as the explosion of social regulations in the 1960s and 1970s. That outburst had its heroes (e.g., Ralph Nader) and spectacular events (e.g., Earth Day 1970), but most important it produced reams of new legislation with titles such as the following:

- 1966—Highway Safety Act
- 1970—Clean Air Act Amendments
- 1970—Occupational Safety and Health Act
- 1972—Consumer Product Safety Act
- 1972—Water Pollution Control Act Amendments

The powers of old agencies were expanded and new agencies were created.

The words *safety, health,* and *pollution* all relate to harmful risks, but they convey different meanings. *Safety* often refers only to protection against violent accidents, such as auto crashes or workplace injuries. *Health* usually indicates security against risk of disease, infirmity, or death as might result, for example, from exposure to carcinogenic gases or tainted food. *Pollution* refers to assaults on the environment generally. Its scope of reference thus includes amenity losses, property damage, and injury to nonhuman creatures as well as threats to human safety (as when smog reduces pilot visibility) and threats to human health (as when carbon monoxide emissions trigger angina attacks). To simplify matters we often use safety and health interchangeably but let pollution stand alone in this discussion.

Three subsequent chapters discuss the details of regulation in three areas:

- Chapter 21. Consumer safety and health, as enforced by the Food & Drug Administration (FDA), National Highway Traffic Safety Administration (NHTSA), and Consumer Product Safety Commission (CPSC).

- Chapter 22. Labor safety and health, as enforced by the Occupational Safety and Health Administration (OSHA).
- Chapter 23. Environmental protection, as enforced by the Environmental Protection Agency (EPA).

This chapter introduces these others with several preliminaries. First, we must recognize that the free market is capable of handling harmful risk to some degree. Second, we identify problems with the free market's provision of safety and environmental protection. The main message is that, for various reasons, the free market provides *too little* safety and environmental protection. Third, we specify policy ideals as derived from benefit-cost analysis. Finally, we outline the main policy method currently used to correct the market's failures—a method broadly referred to as "regulation" or "command and control" but more revealingly described as "standard setting and enforcement." Standards set the aim of policy and divide the critics. Some say the standards are too lenient. Others claim the standards are too harsh, providing *too much* safety and environmental protection. Enforcement methods also attract controversy, so they too attract our attention.

I. Free-Market Provision of Safety and Environmental Cleanliness

Setting aside all considerations of morality and equity, the market can handle the problem of risk under ideal circumstances. The two main circumstances that must hold are (1) that *the risk be known* to those in danger, and (2) that *the risk be voluntarily accepted.* When risks are known and voluntarily accepted, a properly functioning free market will make adjustments in prices and quantities such that, given people's tastes and preferences, the right amounts of risk and risk prevention will be provided.

A. Safety

Because people other than Shakespeare "Like life better than figs," they typically shy away from risky, unsafe products and occupations (thereby voluntarily acting on their knowledge). However, a moment's reflection reveals that people do *not* demand absolute safety. They willingly accept the risk of dreadful injury, disease, and even death, as indicated by all sorts of everyday behavior—smoking, driving without seat belts, hang gliding, whatever. People are especially willing to accept risks when they are fully informed about the potential costs of hazards and they are compensated for them monetarily either by low prices for hazardous products or higher wages for hazardous employment, as compared with safer alternatives.

The free market's handling of risk that is both known and voluntarily accepted is illustrated in Figure 20–1, which assumes perfect competition. In part (a) of Figure 20–1, dealing with **consumer products,** two versions of the same product, one safe and one risky, generate two different demands, D_{safe} and D_{risky}. Demand for the risky version is less than demand for the safe version because of risk aversion. Nevertheless, the market could accommodate both demands by compensating those who choose the risky version with a lower price P_r, as compared to the price of the safer alternative, P_s.

In part (b) of Figure 20–1, illustrating the **labor market,** workers would not offer their labor services in the risky job except at a higher wage rate than the safer alternative, with the result that labor supply S_{risky} lies above supply curve S_{safe}. Given the demand for labor, D, equilibrium wage for risky work would be W_r, which is higher than that for safe work, W_s. Empirical research supports this theory with estimates that wage premiums are indeed paid for high-risk occupations. The estimates suggest that annually, and on av-

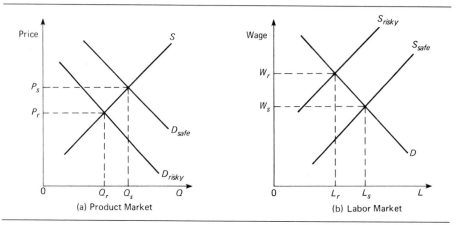

Figure 20–1
Free-Market Adjustment for Risk

erage, each added death per 1,000 workers is associated with about $2,200 in added wages per worker.[1] (Two qualifications apply, however. First, this average hides an immense range of estimates, some of which have been zero. Second, the ideal conditions assumed by theory do not hold in the real world, so the estimates may be shaky.[2])

Under ideal theoretical circumstances, the market does more than take risk into account; it provides the optimal amount of risk, given people's preferences. The ideal market is, in other words, *efficient*.[3] In the case of *labor safety,* the wage premium for risky work acts as an inducement for the employer to provide some job safety. An employer willingly incurs costs for safety because that safety lowers the risk premium he must pay to attract workers. The added costs of added safety are accepted as long as they are offset by greater wage savings, which wage reductions measure the benefits of the added safety to workers. Once the added costs of safety exceed the wage-saving benefits, risk reduction stops.

In sum, the efficiency of the ideal market lies in its nice balance of risk and safety. There is neither too much risk (too little safety) nor too much safety (too little risk), as measured by economic benefits and costs.

B. Pollution

Economic theory can crank out similar conclusions for the problem of pollution. Unfortunately, an explanation of this is more difficult than the explanation for safety, so we can do no more here than briefly state some generalities.

First, it must be appreciated that pollution abatement entails costs as well as benefits. Cleaning up the environment requires manpower, materials, and machinery—resources that could be used to produce other goods and services. Thus, getting *perfectly* clean is not necessarily desirable. Stated differently, cleanliness is not so much a technical problem as it is an economic problem. Technically, the air in Los Angeles could be purified immediately if all autos were abandoned and factories were closed, but the economic costs of these measures apparently exceed the benefits of clean air because people have not carried them out.

Second, it has been argued that, under ideal circumstances, the free market could handle pollution because those who demand cleanliness (call them pollutees) could pay polluters not to pollute. Pollutees would be willing to pay amounts reflecting the benefits they gain from cleanliness. And polluters would be willing to clean up as long as their cleaning costs were less than the payments they received from pollutees. Put on a personal level, you would be willing to pay your neighbor not to dump his trash on your property, a payment your neighbor accepts insofar as his costs of cleanliness are compensated.

Third, the ideal market principles just outlined can yield efficient results for pollution. That is, clean up occurs as long as benefits exceed costs. Once costs exceed benefits, however, no further cleanliness is provided because pollutees will not cover the polluters' costs of abatement. It can even be argued that a reversal of property rights, such that the polluters would then have to pay the pollutees for permission to pollute, would also yield efficient results. This is the Coase Theorem, named for its inventor, Ronald Coase.[4] He was the first to argue that in theory economic efficiency is unaffected by the assignment of property rights, an argument often used to denounce government intervention. This argument has very limited applicability, however.[5] The mix of cleanliness and dirtiness experienced by society *is* affected by property assignments even if efficiency is not, so an efficient world could be a terribly dirty one. Moreover, the theorem's assumptions lack realism. In fact, as suggested by the very limited applicability of the example of your neighbor's trash, the theory of the free markets' handling of pollution seems irrelevant. It is, in short, more a fantasy than a theory.

II. Shortcomings in the Market: Rationales for Government Intervention

Upon leaving the pleasant world of theory and entering the harsh world of reality, we find market imperfections and failures that may warrant government intervention. In particular, the two key conditions for free-market proficiency—(1) full knowledge of risks, and (2) voluntary exposure to risk—often do not hold. Without them, the market yields inefficient results, namely, too much risk. Moreover, aside from concerns for economic efficiency, society often seems to think that the free market's results are too risky in light of certain *non*economic value judgments—morality and equity in particular. Thus, we review four reasons for government policy—(1) morality, (2) equity, (3) ignorance, and (4) externalities causing involuntary risk exposure. Each is covered as it pertains first to safety and health and then to pollution.

A. Safety and Health: Market Shortcomings

1. MORALITY

Economic theory assumes that optimal allocation of resources and consumer sovereignty are society's supreme values, the ultimate criteria by which to judge good and bad. As we have seen repeatedly, however, folks often given higher rank to other considerations, especially in matters of life and death, where notions of morality frequently overwhelm economic criteria. This seems to be a major explanation for many safety regulations that do nothing but protect individuals from themselves. Motorcycle helmet laws and the provision of elaborate barriers to prevent people from jumping off bridges are examples.[6] Regarding occupational safety and health, Representative Phillip Burton once expressed the belief that all American workers have the *"inalienable right* to earn their living free from the ravages of job-caused death, disease, and injury."[7] Whether all American workers would like to see the prices of all products rise as a consequence of such a risk-free environment is another issue. Apparently some would reject economic trade-offs here as legitimate.

2. EQUITY

The free market handles risk by pricing risky products lower and risky jobs higher than safer alternatives. This means that the distribution of risk is tilted unfavorably against low-income people because they are pushed by force of frail financial circumstances into buying riskier products and working in riskier jobs. Risk acceptance in the ideal free market is more than merely a matter of taste; it is also a matter of income distribution. And the results may be considered inequitable.

Equity may even be a problem when income distribution is irrelevant. All meat eaters benefit, for example, when cattlemen use diethylstilbestrol (DES) to boost the livestock industry's productivity and thereby lower beef prices 3 percent or so. However, the use of DES also raises the risk of cancer to consumers, a risk that horribly collects its due from only a relatively few families despite the widespread benefits bestowed in the bargain. Millions gain a little benefit and run a little risk, but only a few are actually forced to pay the dreadful costs of contracting cancer. Many folks might think that these are serious mismatches of getting and deserving, that the imbalances are unfair or inequitable to the few unlucky souls who encounter the Grim Reaper earlier than expected.

3. IGNORANCE

The foregoing value judgments might be dismissed as maudlin or irrelevant. However, the problem of ignorance is not so easily dismissed. Even though press, TV, radio, and government agencies pour out massive amounts of information concerning product hazards, the public remains uninformed. Test yourself. As one who is above average in attentiveness and intelligence, how much do you know about diethylstilbestrol, Red Dye No. 2, saccharin, and zirconium, to name just a few substances given ample press coverage. Could you compute the marginal cost of added risk from using products laced with these chemicals? Are you even aware of which products formerly contained them? Probably not. Do you know your chances of surviving an auto crash with your seat belt on rather than off? Would you feel safe drinking milk containing traces of genetically engineered bovine somatotropin, which boosts a cow's milk output 10 percent?

If one assumes that the experts know the risks, there is in other words still the problem of *informing* consumers and workers. As A. Nichols and R. Zeckhauser point out, "This information must be available, transmitted to the affected parties, and understood."[8] Yet the free market often falls short on all three counts. Those with most of the information—namely producers and employers—have little incentive to make such information available because it could damage their marketing or hiring prospects.[9] Once available, transmission of information becomes a problem because of imperfections in the markets for information. Buyers of information are necessarily uninformed, and sellers' incentives suffer from piracy of their information by word of mouth. Finally, there is a problem of understanding once the problems of availability and transmission are whipped. People have difficulty processing information about complex technical matters, about small probabilities, and about myriads of things, all of which characterize consumer and worker safety and health.

Going beyond risk, there is the additional problem of uncertainty. **Risk** simply refers to a situation in which sufficient statistical evidence exists to allow experts to predict the probability that a particular event will occur. Thus, experts tell us that failure to wear seat belts more than doubles the frequency of death in auto accidents. Similarly, fatal blood clots strike women who use "The Pill" at a rate of about 30/1,000,000, whereas nonusers run a considerably lower risk of 5/1,000,000. As with the flip of a coin, the outcome in any particular instance of auto wreck or "Pill" use is unknown, but its *probability* is known.

In contrast, **uncertainty** is a black abyss. The statistical *probabilities are unknown* as well as the particular outcomes. Thus, experts may be able to establish a causal link between a hazard and bodily harm, but the linkage may elude numerical expression of risk:

> Giving mice a massive exposure to a chemical and observing that in a short period of time the mice develop cancer establishes that a substance is carcinogenic. It does not establish the extent to which the carcinogenic effect depends on dosage, the type of tissue exposed, the method of exposure, and the other features of environment in which the dosage was administered. One may conclude that the experimental results make it more likely that the same substance in dosages comparable to human exposure levels causes human cancer, but the extent to which the likelihood has been increased is not even roughly quantifiable.[10]

Uncertainty not only baffles consumers. It also befuddles experts, as indicated by the endless string of health and safety experts who appear before Congress every year with testimony that takes the form of "Well, on the one hand . . . but then, on the other hand. . . ." Senator Muskie expressed everyone's frustration with this when, after listening to a lot of "one hand . . . other hand" testimony, he quipped, "What I need is some one-armed scientists."

N. W. Cornell, R. G. Noll, and B. Weingast argue that uncertainty engenders a political demand for public controls more stringent than would otherwise be justified. They argue in particular that we should "minimax regret" by adopting "strategies that avoid the worst logically possible outcomes, thereby minimizing the maximum possible loss, no matter what the likelihood that the maximum loss will actually occur."[11]

4.   INVOLUNTARY RISK EXPOSURE, OR EXTERNALITIES

All the foregoing considerations relate to risks to which individuals expose *themselves* in the course of consumption or employment. Morality, equity, and ignorance may thus persuade some folks that government regulation is needed to protect people from *voluntary* exposure to hazard. But there is an added flaw in the market system, namely, externalities, or adverse third-party effects, which impose risks on people *in*voluntarily.

For an example from consumer product safety, Hot Rod Charlie may willingly buy and drive a cheap car with faulty brakes and flimsy tires (perhaps even reveling in its risky prospects), but the car poses a hazard to *other* people traveling the same roads as Charlie. (Surprise inspections of big-rig trucks in the San Francisco Bay area in 1989 discovered that 29 percent of the trucks had mechanical problems dangerous enough to ban them from service temporarily, faulty brakes being the most common problem.[12])

Aside from the *physical* externalities just alluded to, there is the further problem of *financial* externalities. The *costs* of these accidents and illnesses are not always confined to the individual consumer or worker but are also inflicted on society at large. As A. Nichols and R. Zeckhauser explain with respect to occupational safety and health:

> The family of a worker killed on the job, for example, is likely to qualify for survivor benefits under Social Security. More generally, the whole medical care system is laced with subsidies, so that when a worker seeks medical care, a substantial portion of the cost is borne by taxpayers as a whole. The retired worker who develops cancer as a result of earlier occupational exposure to a carcinogenic chemical, for example, is likely to have his medical bills paid by Medicare.[13]

In short, whenever there are physical or financial externalities, the uninhibited market system tends to yield too much risk because transacting parties do not confront the full gravity of their acts.

B. Pollution: Market Shortcomings

The foregoing topic titles may be recycled to outline the market's ineptitude in handling pollution.

1. MORALITY

It can be argued that the market system cannot adequately protect the environment because the market system serves only *human* interests. The well-being of grizzly bears, brown pelicans, and redwood trees is thus given no account whatever by the market except insofar as that well-being can be marketed to humans. Yet by the ethics of many environmentalists, nature's creatures ought to be protected by further rights that only the legal system can provide. Lest this notion seem utterly bizarre, it may be recalled that once upon a time slaves were, like redwoods, subhuman market merchandise unprotected by today's ethics and laws. Moreover, it has been argued before the Supreme Court that trees and rivers should have legal "standing," just as other inanimate objects (ships and corporations) already have "standing."[14]

2. EQUITY

Although the hazards and costs of pollution are not distributed equally among society's members, the main problem of equity in this context is not one of present-day distribution. Rather, it is a problem of equity and fairness to future generations who obviously lose as species of flora and fauna are exterminated, as lakes are killed by eutrophication, and as soils are contaminated by toxic wastes. To be sure, the market takes the future into account (otherwise no buildings would ever be erected). But the future is "discounted," with the result that the present generation is favored at the expense of future generations. In the eyes of many environmentalists, "the standard technique of 'discounting' the future with a negative exponential function lays

waste to the real future."[15] The implication is, then, that the market slights future generations in the limited extent to which environmental resources are preserved.[16]

3. IGNORANCE

To what extent is acid rain caused by sulfur dioxide emissions from coal-fired electric power plants? How far can the sulfur dioxide be carried by the weather? Is the atmosphere's rising carbon dioxide content causing a dangerous greenhouse effect? The answers to these and countless other environmental questions are unknown, illustrating that the problem of ignorance has scope beyond product and occupational safety and health.

4. EXTERNALITIES OR INVOLUNTARY RISK

To economists, the free market's main flaw in causing pollution is externalities. As explained earlier on pages 00 and 00, the problem arises because producers do not themselves pay the costs of disposing of their wastes cleanly. Rather, they impose these costs on *others* by fouling air, water, and land with their filth. Because these costs are external to the firm, they are called *external costs*. Such external costs arise from consumption as well as production, illustrated best perhaps by automobile pollution or pop bottle litter. The free market gives polluters a free ride via externalities. And just as you would take advantage of free rides in an amusement park, so too polluters take advantage of their free ride. The result is more pollution than economically warranted—misallocation.

Lest you doubt that pollution actually creates external costs, stop and reflect. Think of the added laundry bills borne by people living around smoky steel mills. Think of crop damage, houses being painted every five years instead of ten, days of labor lost to bronchitis or early death, medical expenses, dead fish, and so on. Tens of billions of dollars are involved annually.

The problem of externalities can be viewed as resulting from poorly defined property rights.

Neighbors solve their weekly trash problem by respecting each others' property rights. But no one owns our clean air or water, they are *common property resources*. As a result, there is no price placed on them, no market mechanism to limit and ration their use efficiently. As Larry Ruff puts it:

> Clean air, clean water, wilderness areas, and the earth's ozone layer are resources that provide nature and human society with a whole array of indispensable services, supporting recreation, industry, agriculture, health, and the very life-sustaining processes of the earth. When human society makes few demands on these resources, the supply is adequate for all. But as human numbers, concentrations, and activities grow, these demands begin to compete and interfere with one another, subjecting the environmental resources to more demands than they can meet. For most valuable resources, such conflicts are mediated by supply and demand in a market. *But for most of the resources affected by pollution, no natural markets exist and the market failure is total.*[17]

If we ask not why pollution occurs but why pollution, once out there, is not cleaned up by market processes, we have still another way of looking at the problem. Clean air and water are *public goods,* provision of which, like national defense, benefits all simultaneously. As pointed out previously on pages 28–29, collective, governmental action is often necessary to provide such public goods.

III. The Goal of Government Intervention: Efficiency?

A. Benefit-Cost Analysis

Considering the foregoing analysis, there are several possible goals for government intervention in these areas of safety, health, and pollution. In the past, ill-defined goals relating to morality, equity, and health generally held sway. Preambles to legislation have touted such aims as "fishable, swimmable rivers" and employee protection against "material impairment of health or functional capacity" without substantial regard for the costs of control.

However, after the heavy costs of control became apparent with more than a decade of implementation efforts, goals shifted somewhat toward efficiency as guided by benefit-cost analysis, especially after Ronald Reagan became president. His Executive Order 12291 of February 1981 directed regulatory agencies in the executive branch (like EPA and OSHA) to demonstrate, to the extent permitted by statutory laws, that the potential benefits of their major regulatory proposals outweigh the potential costs. As we shall see, some agency statutes can be construed as prohibiting benefit-cost analysis, so Order 12291 was less earthshaking than it might appear. Still, it was a major change over former procedures.

The basic economics of this objective are sketched in Figure 20–2, which refers to pollution but could equally well refer to safety and health with an appropriate change of labels. The horizontal axis ranges between two origins, one representing perfect dirtiness, the other perfect cleanliness. Society must obviously be at some point on that axis. At any such point, the marginal cost of pollution and the marginal cost of pollution abatement are measured vertically. For example, at dirty origin O, The marginal cost of pollution is very high while the marginal cost of abatement is zero. With market failure and no government intervention, society ends up somewhere close to the dirty origin. Moving from dirtiness toward cleanliness under the press of government policy, the marginal cost of pollution falls and the marginal cost of abatement rises. How far toward cleanliness should we go? If we went all the way to O^*, the marginal costs of abatement would be very high relative to the reduction in pollution costs obtained. The efficient solution thus falls short of perfect cleanliness; it

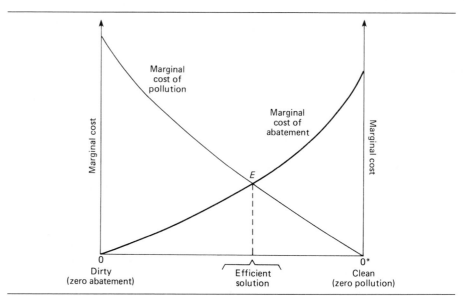

Figure 20–2
Efficiency in Pollution Abatement

occurs when the marginal cost of abatement equals the marginal cost of pollution.

In terms of benefit-cost, the *benefits* of abatement are the *reduced costs* of pollution, whereas the *costs* are the *increased costs* of abatement. The negatively sloped curve thus depicts the benefits, and the positively sloped curve depicts the costs. Efficiency occurs where they cross at *E*. Indeed, *if* there were an ideal market for environmental cleanliness, the negatively sloped curve would reflect demand for cleanliness and the positively sloped curve would reflect supply. Their intersection at *E* would be the equilibrium and efficient solution. To the left of that point not enough cleanliness is provided; to the right too much is.[18]

Conceptually, if Figure 20–2 were referring to safety, the *O* origin could reflect extreme danger; the *O** origin could depict perfect safety. The negatively sloped curve would then depict the marginal cost of risk, and the positively sloped curve would then represent the marginal cost of risk reduction. Accordingly, the benefits

and costs of moving toward safety would meet at efficient solution *E*.

However attractive this efficiency objective might be, there are serious hurdles to its practical application. Certainly the most sensational of these practical problems is the problem of finding a dollar value for the human lives saved by safety, health, and pollution control. Some people believe that putting a dollar value on human lives is impossible or morally repugnant. Others, mainly economists, reply that dollar values are placed on human lives all the time—either explicitly or implicitly, usually implicitly, when communities buy expensive fleets of ambulances, when the Air Force spends $4 million per life saved to equip fighter jets with ejection seats, when the government spends billions on highway guard rails, and so on. Moreover, economists are quick to point out that the valuation of *specific* lives is not necessary. Rather, the exercise entails evaluating "statistical" lives—say, for example, the 2,000 anonymous people saved annually by better auto brakes, not knowing whether John Smith and Suzy Jones are actually among those saved next year.

Still, even on the economists' own turf, practical difficulties remain. There is no consensus among economists on what the dollar value of a life is or on what method should be employed to find out. The most popular method translates the wage premium that workers receive for risky employment into a dollar value per life saved (on the theory that this premium reflects the amount people are willing to receive in exchange for risk exposure). There are conceptual problems with this method, however, and its estimates vary widely from zero to $9,000,000 per life saved (in 1988 dollars). Perhaps the most reasonable range is $1 million to $3 million with an average of about $2 million, but no one knows for sure.[19]

Less sensational but no less troublesome to the practical application of benefit-cost analysis are the many other areas in which unknowns intrude.[20] Indeed, placing a dollar value on lives, injuries, or amenity losses is only the last step in a sequence of several steps necessary to estimate the benefit of some safety or pollution abatement device. For example, the dollar benefit from catalytic mufflers on cars depends on the following:

1. The degree to which auto *emissions* are actually curbed, taking into account driving conditions and other factors.
2. The impact of reduced emissions on *ambient air* conditions, taking into account interactions with other pollutants and weather patterns.
3. The relationship between improved ambient air conditions and *physical effects* such as human death and illness, crop loss, property damage, aesthetic losses, and so on.
4. The *dollar value* one places on those physical improvements, including the dollar value of human lives.

With judgment and estimation entering at each step, the results are wide-ranging. It is not surprising, then, that estimates of the annual eco-

nomic benefits for *all* air pollution control in the late 1980s range from $10 billion to $104.3 billion.[21]

The problem of step 3 in the foregoing sequence is one example of a larger problem that hampers risk assessment generally. Other examples abound: What are the benefits of protecting workers from vinyl chloride? What are the benefits of protecting consumers against pesticide residues left on fruits and vegetables? These benefits depend on the harm caused by a lack of protection—that is, the harm done by exposure to these chemicals. This harm is often estimated by experimental studies of animals, rats in particular. But using rats instead of people, as is necessary, creates a problem. Exposing rats to the small doses that hundreds of millions of people would normally encounter in their daily lives would require that hundreds of millions of rats be tested, something that is prohibitively costly. For this reason, relatively few rats, several hundred for instance, are typically exposed to rather large doses of the suspected chemical to detect the potential harm of normal doses.

How is the inference from large experimental doses to small normal doses made? This is a critical question. The possibilities are illustrated in Figure 20–3 as the "Yardstick," the "Street Lamp," and the "Hockey Stick."

Projecting from the harm done by high, experimental doses (in the upper right-hand corner of each box) to the lesser harm likely done by low, actual doses (in the lower left-hand corner) is usually done by the yardstick approach of part (a) in Figure 20–3, where a linear dose-response relationship is assumed to hold, one that is straight like a yardstick. For example, if 100 rats are fed one bowl of the suspect chemical each day and 40 of them get cancer, it is assumed that half of that number, 20, would get cancer from half a bowl a day; that one-quarter of that number, or 10, would get cancer from one-quarter a bowl a day, and so on. Converting the rat results to humans would follow, so that beginning with zero exposure, it would be assumed that hu-

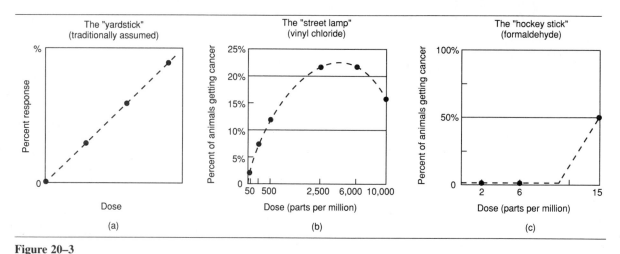

Figure 20–3

Possible Dose–Response Relationships When Translating Large-Dose Animal Studies into Human Risks

Source: Malcolm Gladwell, "Risk-Assessment Techniques Throw Researchers A Curve," *The Washington Post*, National Weekly Edition (April 2–8, 1990), p. 39.

man risk would rise linearly with ever greater exposure.

In fact, the linear assumption could be wrong, as illustrated in parts (b) and (c) of Figure 20–3. These alternatives derive from detailed studies of vinyl chloride and formaldehyde. As indicated in part (b), vinyl chloride is in fact *more* dangerous in small doses than would be implied by the yardstick's linear assumption. The incidence of cancer at first rises *more* than proportionally with increases in dosage, and then it levels off at extremely high doses. The resulting dose-response relationship looks like a street lamp. If policy decisions assume the linear relationship of the yardstick when in fact this curved relationship holds, then the risk of small and intermediate doses will be underestimated, perhaps substantially underestimated. Policy might then be too lenient. People could be at considerable risk when they thought policy was protecting them.

Figure 20–3 (c) illustrates the opposite possibility, which is true for formaldehyde. In this case, the dose-response relationship looks like a hockey stick, with the risk of cancer increasing only slightly or not at all until a high dose is reached, whereupon the risk rises rapidly. Here the customary linear extrapolation of risk from experimental high doses would again be wrong but in the opposite direction. The yardstick approach would be assuming risk for small and intermediate doses when in fact there would be essentially no risk at all. Policy based on the customary linear approach of Figure 20–3(a) would then be overly protective and perhaps overly costly as well.

Sometimes policy breaks from the customary yardstick approach when, in fact, the linear assumption of the yardstick is accurate. Error again arises, but differently. For example, the air quality standards for criteria pollutants are set by law at *threshold* levels, as would be suggested by a hockey-stick relationship. For instance, sulfur oxides at any level below 80 micrograms per cubic meter of air annually are acceptable under the law. Ever greater concentrations above that threshold are assumed to be ever more harmful. Evidence is accumulating that, to the contrary, the harm caused by these air pollutants follows the more linear relationship of Figure 20–3(a), so this threshold may be too lenient in allowing pollution below threshold levels.

In any case, the main point should be clear. It is difficult to estimate accurately the benefits of risk reduction. It is, in fact, often impossible. When physical risks are known, it is often difficult to place dollar values on those physical effects, as is true when human lives are saved. When the physical dangers themselves are unclear, as they are when we must extrapolate human risks from animal experiments, then the effort to estimate benefits becomes all the more uncertain. Little wonder, then, that benefit estimates cover an enormous range, like the $10 billion to $104.3 billion for air pollution benefits mentioned earlier.

Estimates for the *cost* side of the benefit-cost calculus are often more solid than the benefit side. Still those numbers also jump rather wildly about. Depending on whom you read, for instance, the costs of auto safety regulations in 1978 were $430 or $368 or $250 per car.[22]

To some, the practical infirmities of benefit-cost analysis are totally incapacitating. After considering the matter at length, a congressional committee concluded, "The limitations on the usefulness of benefit/cost analysis in the context of health, safety, and environmental regulatory decision making are so severe that they militate against its use altogether."[23] Economists, on the other hand, tend to be more optimistic. And as a last resort many of them contend that there is simply no other alternative to responsible decision making:

> The use of benefit-cost analysis to aid regulatory decisions should be compared not with an ideal but with the practical alternative. Reckless issuance of regulations in disregard of the costs will damage the public interest if the benefits to health and safety are too small to justify the costs.[24]

B. Cost Effectiveness

When placing dollar values on benefits is either impossible or undesirable, efficiency can still be served by following principles of *cost effectiveness*. The basic idea is to get the greatest amount of goodness per dollar spent. There are two ways of achieving this end depending on whether it is the dollar cost or unvalued goodness which is fixed: (1) If the total dollar cost is set at some maximum amount available, then the objective is to save the greatest number of lives (or some similar unvalued result) with that given cost. (2) If on the other hand, the unvalued objective is set at, say, a reduction of 10,000 traffic fatalities per year, then the objective is to achieve this result with the least cost possible.

Safety, health, and pollution regulations usually take the second of these forms, namely, standard setting for physical results. Thus, we can illustrate cost effectiveness for this kind of situation with a simple hypothetical example of cost minimization. Assume that Congress has set an objective of eliminating 10 million tons of sulfur dioxide from our atmosphere. Consultation with engineers and economists reveals six methods (or sources) of sulfur dioxide reduction, with total maximum reduction and total cost for each method as indicated in Table 20–1. The question is, then: Which method, or combination of methods, should be employed to achieve the 10 million tons reduction at least cost? The answer is: Begin with least-cost method A (which costs $100 per ton removed and eliminates 3 million tons), and then use successively higher cost methods or fractions thereof (D, and half of F) until the target of 10 million tons is reached. Total cost by this approach will be $2,000 million (A = $300m, D = $800m, ½F = $900m), which is much lower than any other possible combination of methods. (For example, B and F together would cost $4,200m.) The moral of the example is that low cost-per-unit techniques should be used first and most intensively.

Shifting from the hypothetical to the actual, Table 20–2 ranks selected highway safety measures by decreasing cost effectiveness, assuming a ten-year time horizon for both fatalities forestalled and costs incurred. Efficiency would require that we move down the list, adopting safety measures until meeting some specific objective in total lives saved, or, if cost is the constraint, until our total cost limit is reached. Of course *nonefficiency considerations may interfere. Manda-*

Table 20–1

Cost and Quantity Data for Finding Efficient Program to Reduce Sulfur Dioxide Emissions

(1) Method (Source)	(2) Total Reduction Possible by Method	(3) Total Cost with Full Application	(4) Cost per Ton of Reduction Col. (3)/Col. (2)
A	3 million tons	$ 300 million	$100
B	4 million tons	$2,400 million	$600
C	2 million tons	$ 800 million	$400
D	4 million tons	$ 800 million	$200
E	1 million tons	$ 500 million	$500
F	6 million tons	$1,800 million	$300

tory safety belt laws, the first measure on the list, may be rejected because it interferes with personal freedom, for example.

Such other considerations help to explain why many, if not most, government measures in the area of safety, health, and pollution are *not* actually cost effective. This is especially true if we look at the government as a whole and compare agencies and programs. Some agencies and programs enjoy immense popular and political support even though their payoffs in lives saved or other benefits may be relatively slight. Conversely, other agencies and programs may be overly neglected. Compare, for instance, the fol-

Table 20–2

Ranking of Highway Safety Measures by Decreasing Cost Effectiveness in 1976 Dollars Per Fatality Forestalled—10-Year Total

Safety Measure	Fatalities Forestalled	Total Cost ($ Millions)	Dollars Per Fatality Forestalled
Mandatory seat belt usage	89,000	$ 45.0	$ 506
55-mph speed limit	31,900	676.0	21,200
Regulatory road signs	3,670	125.0	34,000
Guard rails	3,160	108.0	34,100
Motorcycle rider helmets	1,150	61.2	53,300
Breakaway sign and lighting supports	3,250	379.0	116,000
Median barriers	529	121.0	228,000
Periodic auto inspections	1,840	3,890.0	2,120,000
Paved or stabilized shoulders	928	5,380.0	5,800,000

Source: National Transportation Policy Study Commission, *National Transportation Policies* (Washington, DC, June 1979), p. 413.

lowing numbers for radon gas (which seeps into homes) and asbestos (which is a hazard in schools and offices because of its former use in soundproofing and insulation). As of 1991, the U. S. government was spending $3,000 million annually to clean up asbestos that was blamed for causing as many as 30 deaths per year. At the same time, only $100 million a year was being spent to improve protection against radon, which was responsible for as many as 20,000 deaths per year (from lung cancer).[25] The estimated cost per life lost in each case reveals an immense difference.

asbestos: $100,000,000 per lost life

radon: $5,000 per lost life

It would seem, then, that we would be much better off if we spent less on asbestos and more on radon. The greater economic efficiency that would result would mean many more lives saved. Hence, efficiency *is* desirable. It repays our pursuit.

C. Efficiency in Policy Design

Whereas full-blown benefit-cost analysis mainly addresses the question of *how much* risk reduction do we want, cost effectiveness mainly addresses the question of *what tool* is best to achieve a given goal of risk reduction. Policy tools are essentially of four types: (1) direct regulation, (2) information improvement, (3) taxation, and (4) subsidy. Each policy has its strengths and weaknesses, hence efficiency is best served if the policy selected fits the problem.

Direct regulation is control by decree. The government enacts laws forbidding DDT, limiting auto emissions to "x" grams per mile, prohibiting sharp-edged toys, reducing factory noise, and so on. This is the major method of U. S. government intervention in these areas of safety, health, and pollution, and we discuss it at length later. The main point here is that regulation is not always the most efficient policy option available. It entails extensive meddling in the private affairs of businesses and people. It requires an army of government snoopers for enforcement. It rarely achieves its aims by least-cost means. Indeed, its general neglect of economic considerations can result in adverse side effects. For example, forcing safety features on autos may reduce auto fatalities, but they may also increase the price of autos to the point of inducing poor people to ride motorcycles, which are considerably more dangerous than autos.

Information improvement entails the same kind of activities as discussed earlier in Chapter 12. To the extent a safety problem can be corrected by information disclosure, this policy is undoubtedly superior to direct regulation. It is more efficient not only because it entails less government apparatus and less private and public resource expenditure but also because it permits greater flexibility on the part of those who face risks. An example is provided by saccharin, an artificial sweetener. In 1977, the Food and Drug Administration took steps to ban saccharin as a food additive after Canadian scientists found that it caused cancer in laboratory rats. Opponents of the ban argued that without saccharin people would consume more sugar, thereby aggravating such health risks as obesity, heart disease, and arthritis, Public outcry and subsequent congressional action forced the FDA to retreat. Warning labels took the place of prohibition.

The **taxation** approach includes a number of policy tools that might be called *market simulators*. The basic idea is to change behavior for the better by monetary inducements such as the market provides. Taxation of pollution offers the greatest opportunities in this respect, as we shall see. But the approach could be extended to include taxation of workplace injuries or the sale of limited pollution rights. Because this approach works by market principles, the results are usually more efficient than those obtained through direct regulation. Yet taxation and related methods can be employed when mere information improvement is either inappropriate or insufficient to the task.

Subsidies have been used in a very limited way in safety and health, but they have seen moderate action in the fight against pollution. Whereas taxes *goad,* subsidies *entice.* The government pays polluters to install abatement equipment or to clean up. Aside from government aid to purge the nation of its most hazardous toxic waste disposal sites, most federal subsidies have financed municipal sewage treatment facilities. A main problem with subsidies aimed at private industry is that, unlike direct regulation or taxation, subsidies yield abatement without product price increases, so the costs of abatement are disguised. Consumers do not confront the true social costs of production, including the costs of cleanliness. As a result, consumers are not encouraged to shift their purchases from high-pollution products to low-pollution products. Society's misallocation of resources may therefore persist under the subsidy approach.

In the chapters that follow we say very little about information improvement and subsidies. Taxation receives substantial attention because of its attractive properties. Occupying center stage is direct regulation, so we conclude this introductory chapter with an overview of safety, health, and pollution regulation.

IV. Regulation: an Overview

A. Historical and Institutional Contexts

To understand further why economic principles are often slighted in these matters, you must recognize that current policies did not derive from economic theorizing of the type imposed on you to this point. Almost without exception these policies emerged from historical and institutional backgrounds that contained three elements.[26] First, they were usually part of a broader reform movement—the Progressive movement of 1900–1912, the New Deal of FDR, the Great Society of LBJ, and so on. Second, influential journalists and idealistic writers contributed with scathing attacks on the status quo. Upton Sinclair *(The Jungle),* Rachel Carson *(Silent Spring),* and Ralph Nader *(Unsafe at Any Speed)* occupy prominent places in the pantheon of literate crusaders. Finally, and most important, the policies represent responses to specific tragedies or general conditions of crisis. Killer smogs, highway death tolls of epidemic proportions, blinding eyelash cosmetics, and grotesquely deformed babies propel the history of regulation in these areas.

Moving beyond the question of why the government got involved at all to the question of why regulation became the chosen instrument of that involvement, two observations are warranted. First, government tends to be dominated by lawyers, not economists or businesspeople. This is true of the executive branch as well as the legislative and judicial branches of government, so when a perceived problem arises, the legalistic, regulatory response comes natural to those in power. Second, many precedents for the regulatory approach were laid with reliance on regulations to handle public utilities, telecommunications, broadcast communications, and so on. Thus, imagine yourself in the shoes of an attorney turned United States senator, say, twenty years ago. You perceive a problem of hazardous products or annoying pollution and wonder: "What the hell can be done about it?" Creating a regulatory agency on which to dump the problem might seem a good idea.

The remaining question is what duties and powers should be invested in the agency to solve the problem? The question is treacherous because, hypothetically, the bad answers outnumber the good. And historically we have had our share of bad answers. Weak and halting efforts at food and drug regulation date back to 1906. Water pollution legislation goes back to the Refuse Act of 1899, but that law was not enforced until 1970. Legislators apparently learned from these bad experiences, for there has evolved a distinct pattern of fairly effective regulatory activities common to the several agencies operating in this area of safety, health, and pollution.

These regulatory activities are outlined in Table 20–3 together with the purpose of each, examples of each, and some rough indications of where each activity takes place. At first glance this looks confusing. The table's cluttered appearance seems to indicate only red tape and bureaucratic hassle, but there is method to the muddiness. Notice first that virtually all major regulatory activities fall into one of three broad categories: (1) standard setting, (2) enforcement, and (3) research. Broadly speaking, **standards** are necessary so that everyone involved—both regulators and regulated—know what they are *supposed to be doing* to attain good performance. In turn, **enforcement** of these standards is necessary to assure that the regulated *actually do* what they are supposed to. Finally, **research** is necessary to *evaluate* the agency's standards and enforcement programs. This last category includes follow-

Table 20–3
Outline of the Major Activities that Regulation Entails

Activity	Purpose	Examples	Locale of Activity
Standard setting			
Broad standards	To set goals and limits for regulators	"Safe" products; "swimmable" rivers	Set by Congress in legislative mandates
Narrow standards	To set goals and limits for firms and products regulated	Lead level in paint not to exceed 0.5%; dual braking systems in all autos	Usually set by agency after study and hearings
Enforcement for compliance			
Certification or permit	To approve of regulated firms' intentions and give guidance or premarket clearance	Engine design "X" approved; effluent permit granted	Laboratory; agency offices
Sample testing	To monitor regulated firms' activities on regular basis	Antibiotics batch tested for purity; smokestack emissions measured	Assembly line; plant floor; sewage outfalls; stacks
Field surveillance (optional)	To double check compliance and catch "mistakes"	Annual inspection of autos; investigate consumer complaints	Highway; retail stores; repair shops; homes
Remedies	To bring violators into line	Seize contaminated canned goods, force recall of autos; fine violators	Warehouses; stores; courtrooms; agency offices
Research			
Technical research	To explore new possibilities	Build experimental "safety" cars; test new monitoring devices	Laboratories
General surveillance	To assess program operation and discover new problems	Collect data on accidents; measure air quality	Hospital emergency rooms; highway patrol offices; weather stations; river banks, etc.

through to help assure that the regulat*ors* are doing what they ought to be doing (and not overlooking something important). Research also embraces the search for new ways of achieving old objectives. Discussion of the specific activities listed under each broad category illuminates these assertions.

B. Standard Setting

There are typically two kinds of standards—broad and narrow. **Broad standards** are vague, generalized concepts of what is desirable. Because they are typically set by Congress and because they are found in the legislation establishing regulatory agencies or amending established agency powers, broad standards may be viewed as the goals and limits governing the regulat*ors, not* the regulat*ed*. Thus, for example, the Consumer Product Safety Act says vaguely that one goal of the Consumer Product Safety Commission is "to protect the public against unreasonable risks of injury associated with consumer products." And the Federal Water Pollution Control Act of 1972 calls for "recreation in and on the water . . . by July 1, 1983." The purpose of broad standards is not limited to issuing mandates; it extends to giving time schedules and future goals.

Broad standards may be considered the regulators' standards for another reason. Namely, no private company or citizen can be prosecuted for violating these broad standards because they are *too* vague and *too* ill-defined to guide the actions of those who are regulated. For enforcement and prosection **narrow standards** are necessary. These are very specific; some so much so that they fill thousands of pages in the *Code of Federal Regulations*. A simple example given in Table 20–3 is the 0.5 percent lead standard for paint, one purpose of which is to prevent lead poisoning in toddlers who may innocently choose to cut their teeth on the window sill. These narrow standards are usually developed by the regulatory agencies themselves, not Con-

gress, although certain particularly earthshaking standards may be subject to congressional approval. Congress delegates this authority for a simple reason: specific, narrow standards tend to be highly technical and complex, involving tens of thousands of products, countless producers, hundreds of different problems, and other large dimensions of perplexity. Moreover, the *procedures* required to develop narrow standards are tangled snarls, involving notifications, hearings, conferences, and so on—in short, many things for which Congress has no capacity.

Narrow standards may be of two types: (1) performance standards or (2) design standards. **Performance standards** merely specify some specific level of performance—for example, for auto pollutants, no more than 3.4 grams of carbon monoxide emitted per mile traveled. This approach leaves it up to the regulated firm to devise some means of meeting the performance standard, and many different engine designs or exhaust control devices meet this example of auto regulation. In contrast, a **design standard** specifies the *particular designs* that are acceptable. This alternative approach is much less flexible but equally possible and frequently used.

C. Enforcement of Compliance

Certification and Permits. Once narrow standards are set, the next step is to get folks to abide by them. Implementation typically requires four distinct activities. The first, as outlined in Table 20–3, is certification, or the issuance of permits. The purpose of certification is to approve the regulated firms' intentions, to give guidance *before* massive investments in plant and equipment are made and *before* any harm is done. An example is the FDA's clearance of new drugs. All new drugs have to be certified as being in compliance with standards of safety and efficacy before they can be marketed.

Sometimes certification is undertaken not so much for the benefit of consumers as it is for the benefit of regulated firms. An example of this is

EPA's certification of engine designs that meet emission performance standards *prior* to actual production of those engines. Imagine the billions of dollars an auto company could lose if it invested in production facilities for an engine that it thought would meet standards only to find out later that in the view of the EPA the engine did not. When performance standards are involved, certification is particularly important.

Sample Testing or Monitoring. The second major enforcement activity is sample testing. In a word, this is monitoring. Once standards are set and certification (if any) is completed, there remains the question of what is actually going on at the factory. Do the goods coming off the assembly line comply with standards? Is the plant's sewage pure enough to be dumped into the local river? Are gases and particulates escaping in volumes greater than those specified by permit? Are foods and drugs manufactured in surroundings that are clean? The only way these questions can be answered is by extensive on-the-spot sampling, testing, inspecting, scouting, and detecting. Of course, an army of enforcement personnel is required for this task, more than 20,000 or so snoopers for all the agencies under review here. Budgetary limits hold the number down, so great reliance is placed on spot checking and small sampling.

Field Surveillance. An activity that is only sometimes used (and is therefore optional) is field surveillance, the third step outlined in Table 20–3. This may be considered a process of double checking or backup monitoring. When consumer products are under scrutiny (instead of, or in addition to, production processes), sample testing at production sites often is not enough to assure compliance. Because only sample testing is involved, some goods that are not up to snuff will reach retail shelves and showrooms. There may also be a problem of post-production tampering, wherein safety devices or pollution control devices are removed by retailers or consumers or employers to gain better gas mileage, greater convenience, lower operating costs, or some

other advantage. As a result, field surveillance is necessary to (1) detect substandard goods that have slipped through sample testing and (2) assure continued compliance. Field surveillance involves observation and sample purchasing at the retail level. In the case of autos, it may include the annual inspection of autos in use. Finally, and perhaps even more important, field surveillance also entails (3) the receipt and investigation of consumer and employee complaints. Swift action may be necessary even where formal standards are absent.

Remedies. Of all enforcement activities, the imposition of remedies is most readily understandable. Some remedies might be considered light penalties, such as seizure of the offending goods, closure of production plants, and compulsory product recalls. Yet these are not necessarily light at all. They can be expensively onerous in terms of lost inventories, idle plants, and replacement parts. Going one level higher in the echelon of remedies, fines and imprisonment are used under certain circumstances. The purpose served by granting regulators these various armaments should be obvious. They provide incentive. They motivate compliance.

D. Research

Major research activities may be divided into two groups. Those listed first in Table 20–3 are *scientific or technical*. Regulatory agencies conduct in-house research, or fund private research, to discover new and safer product designs, to devise improved testing equipment, to explore the relationship between poor air quality and human health, and so on. These activities are worthwhile for at least two reasons: (1) without official assumption or funding these areas of research are likely to be slighted, and (2) they enable regulators to keep abreast of technological developments, thereby improving the quality of regulatory effort. Indeed, this research often indicates where standards should be modified, abandoned, or imposed.

A second type of research may be called *general surveillance*. The forms of surveillance discussed earlier under compliance were "over the shoulder" types of surveillance. Their objective is to spot specific violations of specific standards. Although general surveillance may turn up specific violations, that is not the primary function. Rather, its purpose is to "keep the eyes peeled," a cliché connoting a general awareness of what is going on. Perhaps the best example of this is the National Electronic Injury Surveillance System maintained by the Consumer Product Safety Commission. This system connects the commission to over 100 hospital emergency rooms scattered throughout the country. The hospitals report a daily flow of information concerning product-related injuries and fatalities, thereby enabling the CPSC to maintain an up-to-the-minute vigilance over its area of concern.

Of the several regulatory activities neglected by the preceding review, perhaps none is more important than consumer education. As we have seen earlier, information disclosure can often correct the market's faults, and all the agencies of interest here have education programs. We do not discuss these programs here, however.

Note on Tort Liability. Besides regulation, matters of safety are also governed by tort liability law. However, as Steven Shavell explains, tort liability is a lawyer's ambulance at the base of the cliff whereas regulation is society's fence at the top:

> Liability in tort and the regulation of safety represent two very different approaches for controlling activities that create risks of harm to others. Tort liability is private in nature and works not by social command but rather indirectly, through the deterrent effect of damage actions that may be brought once harm occurs. Standards, prohibitions, and other forms of safety regulation, in contrast, are public in character and modify behavior in an immediate way through requirements that are imposed before, or at least independently of, the actual occurrence of harm.[27]

Each approach has its strengths and weaknesses, so each has its proper place when judged by efficiency. Moreover, Shavell argues that observed, real-world applications of each follow those strengths and weaknesses fairly well. Hence, if you chop down a tree and it falls on your sunbathing neighbor, tort liability applies. If, however, you operate a mushroom cannery, the cleanliness of your plant is subject to regulation. We focus on regulation because of its broader relevance to business and society.

Summary

Insofar as efficiency is our only concern, economic theory postulates that ideal markets produce ideal results when it comes to problems of safety, health, and pollution. These results do not entail zero risk because people willingly accept some risk, and the costs of achieving zero risk would be huge. Rather, the ideal market compensates those who accept risks with appropriately lower prices on risky products or higher wages for risky occupations. The ideal market also provides environmental protection. Risk reduction proceeds in all these ideal cases until the added benefits match the added costs.

The theory is useful because it suggests that real-world markets may not be complete failures and because it indicates efficient (benefit-cost) solutions. But the real world does not conform to theory's ideals. In particular, noneconomic value judgments such as (1) morality and (2) equity may cause people to call on the government even when the market is efficient. To many environmentalists and consumer advocates, efficiency is neither moral nor equitable. Moreover, there is the added problem that real-world markets are not efficient because people frequently (3) do not know about risks or (4) face risks involuntarily.

Of these last two justifications for government intervention, ignorance is probably most pertinent to consumer and worker safety and health. When experts know of risks, the information must be made available, transmitted to those affected, and understood, but this chain is often broken. Moreover, uncertainty often prevails, in which case the risk probabilities are unknown even to the experts.

Government action for safety and health can also be grounded on involuntary risk exposure, but this is most pertinent to pollution, where externalities run rife. Polluters use common property resources to dispose of their wastes, thereby inflicting costs on others. The result is too much pollution.

If efficiency were the goal of government intervention, benefit-cost analysis would determine how much safety, health, and environmental cleanliness should be provided. Steps in the direction of these noble aims would be desirable as long as the benefits from each step exceeded or equalled the costs. Unfortunately, benefit-cost analysis is very difficult to apply in practice. Benefit estimation is especially tough. Aside from difficulties in placing dollar values on such things as human lives, the linkages between government standards and physical effects often elude accurate estimation. A key problem in this respect is that estimates of risks must often rely on animal experiments and simplified dose-response assumptions. Because the cost side of the calculus is typically more fathomable, and because regulation usually sets physical standards, cost-effectiveness often proves useful. When evaluated by cost-effectiveness, information improvement and taxation generally rank higher than direct regulation and subsidies among policy tools.

Notwithstanding its considerable drawbacks, direct regulation dominates U. S. policy in these areas. This approach evolved to the point at which by 1970 three broad activities typified regulation in these areas—standard setting, enforcement, and research. Each of these activities divides into several subactivities, which have been summarized in Table 20–3.

Questions and Exercises for Chapter 20

1. Explain *how* and *how well* the free market can provide an optimal degree of worker safety under ideal circumstances.
2. Compare and contrast *risk* and *uncertainty* in the context of knowledge. Which is more readily capable of rationalizing government intervention?
3. Explain why each of the following might warrant policy attention: (a) airplane noise, (b) pesticide spraying on farms: (c) gladiator battles; (d) baby crib hazards.
4. Why was information improvement not mentioned as a possible policy in the case of pollution?
5. Why might cost-effectiveness be especially appropriate (as opposed to full-blown cost-benefit) when a risk reduction objective is set by criteria of morality?
6. What would you need to know to estimate the benefits of reducing water pollution from a paper mill?
7. Check your understanding of Table 20–1 by (a) eliminating Method F from consideration and then (b) finding the cost-effective means of reducing 10 million tons of sulfur dioxide.
8. Compare and contrast broad and narrow standards.
9. Outline the elements of enforcement, explaining the rationale for each element.
10. Regulation is regulation. Why, then, would research have any role?
11. What is the purpose and focus of these social regulations in terms of market structure, conduct, and performance?
12. Is it possible for someone to accept an existing environmental standard but argue for a tax as the means of enforcement using cost-effectiveness in support? Explain.

Notes

1. Ted R. Miller, "The Plausible Range for the Value of Life," *Journal of Forensic Economics* (vol. 3., no. 3, 1990): 17–39.

2. J. Paul Leigh, "Compensating Wages for Job-Related Death: The Opposing Arguments," *Journal of Economic Issues* (September 1989): 823–842.

3. W. Y. Oi, "The Economics of Product Safety," *Bell Journal of Economics* (Spring 1973): 3–28; T. R. Saving, "Welfare Aspects of Mandated Quality," in R. F. Lanzillotti, ed., *Economic Effects of Government-Mandated Costs* (Gainesville: University Presses of Florida, 1978), pp. 157–185.

4. R. H. Coase, "The Problem of Social Cost," *Journal of Law and Economics* (October 1960): 1–44.

5. John J. Donohue, III, "Law and Economics: The Road Not Taken," *Law & Society Review* (Vol. 22, No. 5, 1988): 903–926.

6. Tibor Scitovsky, *The Joyless Economy* (New York: Oxford University Press, 1976), Chapter 10.

7. Quoted by A. Nichols and R. Zeckhauser, "OSHA after a Decade: A Time for Reason," in L. W. Weiss and M. W. Klass, eds., *Case Studies in Regulation: Revolution and Reform* (Boston: Little, Brown, 1981), p. 212. (emphasis added).

8. Ibid., p. 207. On information see also Steven Kelman, "Regulation and Paternalism," in T. R. Machan and M. B. Johnson, eds., *Rights and Regulation* (San Francisco: Pacific Institute, 1983), pp. 217–248.

9. Even though, *by law,* companies must report worker injuries, harmful drug side effects, and other such adversities, they occasionally do not. See, for example, *Wall Street Journal* 2 December 1986, p. 1; 22 October 1991, p. A6; 10 December 1990, p. B4; 16 July 1990, p. A3.

10. N. W. Cornell, R. G. Noll, and B. Weingast, "Safety Regulation," in *Setting National Priorities* ed. Owen and Schultze (Washington DC: Brookings Institution, 1976), p. 468. See also Edmund A. C. Crouch and Richard Wilson, *Risk/Benefit Analysis* (Cambridge: Ballinger, 1982).

11. Cornell, Noll, and Weingast, "Safety Regulation," p. 469.

12. *San Jose Mercury News,* 17 February 1989, p. 2B. This result was said to be "pretty standard" for the state of California.

13. Nichols and Zeckhauser, "OSHA After a Decade," p. 208.

14. For more on this see, e.g., Aldo Leopold, *A Sand County Almanac* (New York: Oxford University Press, 1949), pp. 201–226; Christopher D. Stone, *Should Trees Have Standing?* (Los Angeles; William Kaufmann, Inc., 1974); and almost any issue of the scholarly journal *Environmental Ethics.*

15. Garrett Hardin, "Dr. Pangloss Meets Cassandra," *New Republic* (October 28, 1981), p. 34.

16. Talbot Page, *Conservation and Economic Efficiency* (Baltimore: Johns Hopkins University Press, 1977). See also R. C. D'Arge, W. D. Schulze, and D. S. Brookshire, "Carbon Dioxide and Intergenerational Choice," *American Economic Review* (May 1982): 251–256.

17. Larry E. Ruff, "Federal Environmental Regulation," in Weiss and Klass, *Case Studies in Regulation,* p. 236. (Emphasis added.)

18. An alternative way to appreciate the efficient solution is possible when one states the overall objective thus: to minimize the total cost of waste disposal, that is, to minimize the *sum* of total pollution cost and total abatement cost. At point O in Figure 20–2, total disposal costs are entirely in the form of total pollution costs, namely the entire area under the marginal cost of pollution curve. Conversely, at point O^*, the total cost is all abatement cost, equal to the entire area under the marginal cost of abatement curve. At the efficient solution the total cost of waste disposal is the area of the triangle OEO^*, which combines some cost of abatement (the left side area) with some cost of pollution (the right side area).

19. The basic computation is as follows: If statistical estimates reveal an annual wage premium of $500 for each added death per annum per thousand workers, then 1,000 workers must be paid $500 each for accepting the risk of that one death. $1,000 \times \$500 = \$500,000$, the value of that "statistical" life. W. Kip Viscusi, *Regulating Consumer Product Safety,* (Washington, DC: American Enterprise Institute, 1984), pp. 26–30; Daniel Seligman, "How Much Money Is Your Life Worth?", *Fortune* (March 3, 1986), pp. 25–27. For a useful survey see Miller, "Plausible Range."

20. This is especially true on the benefit side. For a brief survey see Nicholas Ashford et al., *The Benefits of Environmental, Health and Safety Regulation,* U. S. Senate, Committee on Governmental Affairs (March 1980). For details in one area, see A. M. Freeman III, *The Benefits of Environmental Improvement* (Baltimore: Johns Hopkins University Press, 1979).

21. Robert W. Hahn and John A. Hird, "The Costs and Benefits of Regulation: Review and Synthesis," *Yale Journal or Regulation* (Winter 1991): p. 273.

22. National Highway Traffic Safety Administration "The Contributions of Automobile Regulation" (Washington, DC, 1978), pp. 8–11.

23. U. S. Congress, House, Subcommittee on Oversight and Investigations of the Committee on Interstate and Foreign Commerce, *Federal Regulation and Regulatory Reform,* 94th Congress, 2d Session (1976), p. 515.

24. M. J. Bailey, *Reducing Risks to Life* (Washington, DC: American Enterprise Institute, 1980), p. 21.

25. Jeremy Main, "The Big Cleanup Gets It Wrong," *Fortune* (May 20, 1991), p. 100.

26. Mark Nadel, *The Politics of Consumer Protection* (Indianapolis: Bobbs-Merrill, 1971).

27. Steven Shavell, "Liability for Harm Versus Regulation of Safety," *Journal of Legal Studies* (June 1984): 357.

Chapter 21

Consumer Product Safety: FDA, NHTSA, and CPSC

By the time they have finished breakfast, most people have come into contact with twenty or thirty products that we regulate.

— *Dr. Alexander M. Schmidt*
(former commissioner of the Food and Drug Administration)

In 1989 Great Britain reported nearly 30,000 cases of salmonella, including sixty-one deaths. In 1981 there were almost 700 deaths in Spain from contaminated vegetable oil. Thousands of Spaniards survived after injesting the oil, but they now suffer paralysis, bone deformations, and neurological disorders. Thanks to the U.S. Food and Drug Administration, we enjoy more protection against these kinds of hazards than residents of most other countries do. Still, risks abound. Food-borne pathologic microorganisms kill an estimated 9,000 Americans every year, for instance.[1] Apart from food hazards, tens of thousands of people perish annually from the side effects of pharmaceuticals, auto crashes, and home accidents.

Thus, hundreds of thousands of consumer products are regulated for safety—from your bowl of breakfast cereal to the tires on your car. The best way to approach this mountain of regulation is to take each major agency in turn: (I) the Food and Drug Administration, (II) the National Highway Traffic Safety Administration, and (III) the Consumer Product Safety Commission. Our discussion of each is divided into three parts: (A) standards, (B) enforcement activities, and (C) chief controversies. One major regulatory activity mentioned in the previous chapter that cannot be covered here is research.

I. The Food and Drug Administration

A. Standards: Broad and Narrow

The FDA's origins date back to 1906, making it the granddaddy of these agencies. Major modifications in the FDA's powers occurred in 1938, 1958, 1962, and 1976. In jurisdiction, the agency's scope of authority goes well beyond the foods and drugs of its title to include cosmetics and medical devices. Within each of these four divisions, official attention spans a bewildering variety of products. Take drugs, for example;

433

there are over 35,000 prescription-drug products and over 120,000 over-the-counter formulations, such as aspirin, that are subject to FDA vigilance.[2]

Although safety is the FDA's primary concern, the agency devises and enforces standards tangential to safety—standards for product purity, product efficacy, and production cleanliness. These broad standards do not apply equally to all products under FDA jurisdiction. So a summary cross-tabulation between the four product classes and four broad standards is provided in Table 21–1. Authority is indicated by the dates the FDA was given duties in these respects. A listing of more than one date indicates strengthening of the law by amendment.

Thus, it may be seen that standards of safety and clean production processes now apply to all four product groups. Rigorous and complete standards of purity apply only to food and drugs. And standards of efficacy apply only to drugs and medical devices.

Why the differences in standard coverage? A partial answer is found in the preceding chapter. That is, the inadequacies of the free-market system do not strike all products equally, and government regulation of these qualities is not equally appropriate to all commodities. (How, for example, could you regulate the efficacy of cosmetics?) A still more complete answer hinges on a more complete understanding of what is meant by safety, purity, production cleanliness, and efficacy, which brings us to narrow standards.

1. SAFETY

In general, the FDA's narrow standards for safety in *drugs and medical devices* tend to be *relative*. They weigh risks against benefits, permitting substantial risks when the potential benefits are also great. For a hypothetical example, a drug that is known to kill ten out of every 100 patients who ingest it may nevertheless be approved for sale if it is fairly successful in curing malignancies that are otherwise incurable. Unfortunately, there are no simple criteria for drawing the line in benefit-risk trade-offs because it is not always simply a matter of life and death.[3] Is substantial risk of death tolerable in exchange for such benefits as pain relief or paralysis reduction? These are obviously judgment calls. Indeed, no drug is free of risk. All have potential side effects, so crude judgments are inevitable. (Seven percent of all hospital admissions relate to drug-induced problems. Even seemingly innocent products like Anacin and Tylenol can have possibly serious side effects for some people—kidney damage, for example.)

Although seriously hazardous substances are permitted if the benefits they bestow are truly great, such substances are carefully controlled as prescription drugs. Prescription drugs can be dispensed only by a licensed physician, dentist, veterinarian, or pharmacist. Nonprescription drugs,

Table 21–1
FDA's Broad Standards and Product Jurisdiction, by Date of Congressional Mandate

Broad Standard	Food	Drugs	Cosmetics	Medical Devices
Safety	1906, 1958	1906, 1938, 1962	1938	1938, 1976
Purity	1906, 1938	1906	(partially)	(partially)
Production cleanliness	1938	1938, 1966	1938	1938
Efficacy	—	1962	—	1976

or over-the-counter medicines, are generally regarded as safe for the consumer to select and use when he or she follows the required directions and warnings. (The contrast is illustrated by the many acne medications that are sold over the counter and Accutane, a prescription drug that cures a type of scarring acne but that should not be taken by pregnant women. It has caused birth defects in at least 100 and perhaps as many as 1,000 babies since its introduction in 1982.)

Safety standards for *foods* and *cosmetics* tend to be more nearly absolute. No risk at all is permitted, but there are enough exceptions to make this less than a general rule. The most clearly absolute standard in this area is the 1958 Delaney amendment to the Food, Drug, and Cosmetic Act, which states that "no additive shall be deemed to be safe . . . if it is found, after tests which are appropriate for the evaluation of the safety of food additives, to induce cancer in man or animal." In short, the Delaney clause reflects a congressional decision that *no* risk is warranted for carcinogenic food additives. Thus, when it was discovered in 1969 that the artificial sweetener cyclamate caused cancer in laboratory animals, the FDA had no choice but to ban it. Saccharin became the only remaining artificial sweetener, but that too was found to be carcinogenic in laboratory animals, and in 1977 the FDA banned saccharin as a general food additive. Public protest over the proposed saccharin ban caused Congress to grant an exception, permitting saccharin as an additive if accompanied by a warning label.

When a food ingredient is *not* an additive and when the risk involved is *not* cancer, relative standards then apply, opening the door for many more "exceptions." For example, a known carcinogen, aflatoxin, occurs naturally in peanuts. Also, environmental pollution puts mercury in fish, and mercury attacks the human nervous system. If a no-risk standard were applied to aflatoxin and mercury, we would have virtually no peanut or fish products. Permitted levels of these

substances and others like them are judged "safe enough" but not completely safe.

A cosmetic is considered "safe" when, *under normal use,* it is not hazardous. A nail polish could thus be "safe" even if drinking it would polish you off. Even when normal use is slightly hazardous (as with hair dyes), cosmetics are permitted *if* they carry clear warning of their dangers.

2. PURITY

Purity is not the same thing as safety, although the two often overlap. Pure strychnine is anything but safe. Conversely, watered down milk may be perfectly safe but it is hardly pure. Given the basic difference between purity and safety, it is possible to have *relative* standards of safety while imposing *absolute* standards of purity. And the FDA does have fairly absolute standards of purity for foods and drugs.

The standards concern two main types of purity—composition (or strength) and contamination. Thus, for drug **composition** and **potency** the major official compendiums of specific standards are the *United States Pharmacopeia* and the *National Formulary,* which together cover some 2,000 drug forms. By these standards, for example, a 5-grain aspirin tablet must contain 5 grains of aspirin (and all other drugs so regulated must meet their standards) within a tolerance of plus-or-minus 5 percent. Similarly, many foods are identified as to quality of contents to prevent watering down. Tomato paste, for instance, must contain not less than 25 percent salt-free tomato solids. Such standards of composition apply only to foods and drugs.

Contamination standards prohibit filthy, putrid, or decomposed products, be they foods, drugs, cosmetics, or medical devices. Thus, for example, the FDA claims that it does not permit any variations from "absolute cleanliness or soundness in foods."

The Act does not authorize "tolerances" for filth or decomposition in foods. It states that a food is adulterated if it consists *in whole or in part* of a filthy, putrid, or decomposed substrate.[4]

In practice, however, the standards are only reasonably absolute, since foreign matter is permitted "below the irreducible minimum after all precautions humanly possible have been taken to prevent contamination." This leniency is illustrated by standards governing tomato canning:

> In judging whether tomato products have been properly prepared to eliminate rot and decay, the Food and Drug Administration uses the Howard mold-count test, and refuses admission to import shipments and takes action against domestic shipments if mold filaments are present in more than 40% of the microscopic fields in the case of puree, paste, more than 30% in the case of catsup, or sauce, or more than 20% in the case of tomato juice.[5]

Lest the percentages that escape bother you, be confident that FDA standards for food purity usually go well beyond the point of assured safety.

3. PRODUCTION CLEANLINESS

Standards governing production cleanliness underscore this last statement. In fact, the mere processing of a food under insanitary conditions that may contaminate the food renders such food adulterated under the law:

> The maintenance of sanitary conditions requires extermination and exclusion of rodents, inspection and sorting of raw materials to eliminate the insect-infested and decomposed portions, fumigation, quick handling and proper storage to prevent insect development or contamination, the use of clean equipment, control of possible sources of sewage pollution, and supervision of personnel who prepare foods so that acts of misconduct may not defile the products they handle.[6]

The FDA provides details in *Current Good Manufacturing Practice Regulations,* which cover even such matters as building design, lighting, and ventilation. Similar standards apply to drugs, cosmetics, and medical devices.

(All this may sound comforting, but keep in mind that standards and enforcement are quite different. As with highway speed limits, compliance is sometimes short of the statute.)

4. EFFICACY

The issue of efficacy is in many ways similar to the issue of deceptive advertising. In both cases

---

Thumbnail Sketch 7: Food and Drug Administration

Established: 1931 (formerly Bureau of Chemistry in Agriculture Dept.).

Purpose: To protect the public against unsafe, impure, and ineffective drugs and medical devices, and to regulate hazards in foods, cosmetics, and radiation devices.

Legislative Authority: Food and Drug Act of 1906; Food, Drug, and Cosmetic Act of 1938 as amended in 1958 (food additives), 1960 (color additives), 1962 (drug efficacy), and 1976 (medical devices); Radiation Control for Health & Safety Act of 1968; Orphan Drug Act of 1983; New Drug Act of 1987.

Regulatory Activity: (1) Sets standards for safety, purity, production cleanliness, efficacy, and labeling of the products under its jurisdiction, (2) Enforces those standards with pre-market review and certification, sample testing, surveillance, and remedy imposition. Conducts research.

Organization: A division of the Department of Health and Human Services, headed by a commissioner.

Budget: 1991 estimate: $742 million.

Staff: 1991 estimate: 8,396.

the key question is whether the product performs as claimed. However, the FDA's regulation of efficacy differs markedly from ordinary curbs against deception. As we saw in Chapter 13, the FTC's fight against deception sweeps the mass media clean of most false and misleading *claims,* but it leaves even the most worthless deceptively promoted *products* on store shelves. No attempt is made by the FTC to sweep shelves clear of worthless junk. No attempt is made to restrict the use of deceptively promoted products to applications for which they are effective. Whereas regulation of sheer deception entails none of these measures, regulation of efficacy entails them all. A drug is *banned* if "there is a lack of substantial evidence that the drug will have the effect it purports or is represented to have under the condition of use prescribed, recommended, or suggested . . ."[7]

Justification for an efficacy standard rests in part on safety. Given that all drugs are to some degree poisonous, an ineffective drug would impose risk for no benefit. Risk also arises if ineffective therapies supplant effective therapies.

Because the efficacy standard was added by Congress only in 1962, drugs on the market before 1962 had to be reviewed for efficacy by the FDA. The review produced some interesting statistics. Of the first 512 over-the-counter drug products evaluated, seventy-five percent proved worthless.[8] The review also included prescription medicines. Although doctors are supposed to be knowledgeable about these things, many prescription drugs likewise lacked evidence of effectiveness. All told, the FDA's effectiveness review resulted in the removal of more than 6,000 drug products (or brands) from the market.[9]

B. FDA Enforcement

1. CERTIFICATION

The 1962 Drug Amendments also imposed standards of efficacy on new, post-1962 drugs. Enforcement of the standard for new drugs involved FDA premarket clearance or certification based on research materials supplied by the drug companies to the FDA. Safety, too, must be demonstrated, but of all aspects of premarket clearance, efficacy has stirred the greatest controversy, a controversy that we take up shortly.

Certification in other areas of FDA authority is somewhat of a hodgepodge. Medical devices are treated like drugs, with premarket clearance for safety and efficacy. Food additives are, in general, divided by a 1958 amendment into old additives generally recognized as safe and new additives that must be approved for safety before use. In cosmetics, prior approval for safety is not required, so enforcement is an ex-post affair.

2. SAMPLE TESTING AND FIELD SURVEILLANCE

During 1991 FDA agents inspected 18,609 establishments, ranging from food warehouses to cosmetic production plants. During the same year FDA technicians analyzed 18,346 samples of food and cosmetics, 6,024 samples of human drugs, 1,801 samples of animal drugs and feeds, and 991 samples of medical devices. But these are only *domestic* numbers. In addition, the FDA made 48,354 wharf inspections and analyzed 42,200 samples of imported products.[10]

Hidden beneath these numbers are some truly heroic efforts. Consider, for example, the case of Mr. Albert Weber, an FDA chemist with rare talents who was honored with a front-page *Wall Street Journal* article, cleverly written by Jonathan Kwitny. Some excerpts follow:

> Who knows what evil lurks in the hearts of mackerel? Albert Weber's nose knows.
>
> For, while a nose is a nose is a nose in most cases, Mr. Weber's proboscis stands between this country and one heck of a stomachache. Mr. Weber is the recognized dean of organoleptic analysts—food sniffers. He is one of some two dozen Food and Drug Administration chemists around the country who use their beaks instead of their beakers to check the heathfulness of suspect foods for which there aren't any convenient chemical tests. Mostly, that's rotten fish. Mr. Weber is the only one who does this work full time.
>
> His sizable snout has been compared to Namath's arm, Heifetz's hands and Einstein's brain. His judgments are accepted almost as law in court

cases involving hundreds of thousands of dollars in rejected foodstuffs. . . .

In the 32 years since [he started smelling fish], Mr. Weber hasn't grown to like his work any better. "How can you when you have to smell that stink all day?" he asks. But he has made adjustments. He will not allow friends to see him at work. He drives home alone. His wife stays out until after he has had a chance to shower and change. But the FDA needs him, and he says loyalty keeps him on the job. . . .

He smells about 4,000 fish or shrimp in a day and rates them Class I (good commercial), Class II (slightly decomposed) or Class III (advanced decomposed—or, as popularly known, "Phew-Yew!"). Some samples, he says, are "beyond Class III—you have to smell those at arm's length." Often in such cases he says he can tell by looking from across the room that a sample is bad. But visual opinions won't stand up in court if a food dealer challenges the FDA's rejection. Mr. Weber has to smell everything that comes his way.

Usually he breaks the skin of the fish or shrimp with his thumbnails and quickly sticks his nose into the crevice for a sniff. "As a rule, one sniff will do, but on the border line, maybe four. If you can't make up your mind by four sniffs, you shouldn't be doing this work," he says.[11]

By the way, the FDA must rule a shipment acceptable if the portion sampled contains no more than 20 percent Class II or 5 percent Class III. Thus, some fish and shrimp of the "Phew-Yew" variety get through. This, and similar standards, some critics claim, is too lenient. Likewise, some critics of the FDA contend that its inspectors do not canvas plants often enough or thoroughly enough. Accordingly, they would like to see *more* FDA regulation, not less. For example, in 1971 the General Accounting Office, a watchdog agency of Congress, checked up on FDA surveillance by inspecting a representative sample of ninety-seven food plants. The General Accounting Office found that "39, or about 40%, were operating under insanitary conditions."[12] More recently, the General Accounting Office found improvement. In 1985 only 7 percent of all processing plants sampled were insanitary. Still, the FDA could apparently use more people of Mr. Weber's caliber. With about 90,000 plants, mills, and other establishments needing surveillance, the FDA has huge enforcement responsibilities. (Note: The Department of Agriculture is responsible for meat and poultry plant inspections.)

3. REMEDIES

Table 21–2 reveals that constant vigilance is indeed necessary. Serious problems occur more often than most of us would like to think, and

Table 21–2
Summary of FDA Remedial Actions During Fiscal Year 1991

Program	Recalls	Seizures	Prosecutions	Injunctions
Food and cosmetics	566	66	2	5
Human drugs	651	60	27	11
Biologics	423	2	2	0
Medical devices and radiologics	1,127	36	9	3
Animal drugs and feeds	91	4	3	2
Total FDA Actions	2,858	168	43	21

Source: Food and Drug Administration, *FDA Quarterly Activities Report*, 4th Quarter/Fiscal Year 1991 (Washington, DC: Department of Health and Human Services, 1991), pp. 33–34.

they usually end in recalls. The year reported in Table 21–2 was not unusual. To overcome the drabness of these statistics, some recent and especially serious cases can be cited:

■ In 1987, Beech-Nut Nutrition Corporation, the nation's second-largest manufacturer of baby food, pleaded guilty on 215 felony counts. For five years the company had sold millions of containers of sugar water and flavoring that were labeled "100 percent" apple juice for babies. Beech-Nut paid $2.04 million in fines and court costs, a record amount.[13]

■ Cordis Corporation, the world's third-largest manufacturer of implanted heart pacemakers, produced and sold thousands of pacemakers during the 1980s that it knew were defective. Many failed. The company pleaded guilty to twenty-five criminal violations.[14]

■ In 1989 one of the nation's leading drug manufacturers, Eli Lilly & Company, temporarily closed its Indianapolis plant because of severe quality control problems. Certain production runs of ten different drugs were recalled in connection with the closure.[15]

■ At least forty-seven persons died in the Los Angeles area in 1985 when a certain soft cheese was contaminated with a bacterium known as *Listeria monocytogenes*. Since that time, the FDA has found *Listeria* contamination in more than 500 dairy products, including ice cream and milk as well as cheese.[16]

The laissez-faire ideology of the Reagan Administration adversely influenced enforcement. During the Reagan years, food and drug inspections fell nearly 40 percent. Overall, the number of FDA personnel declined 9 percent. Leadership faltered when over a six-year period thirty-six of sixty-four top career management positions were left vacant for periods ranging from four months to five years. Because of budget cuts, FDA equipment and facilities became dilapidated and obsolete.[17] At the same time, public needs rose. The AIDS epidemic hit. Food imports were up. (Only 2 percent of the shipments of imported food of 1982 were tested by the FDA, and 40 percent of these did not meet FDA standards.)[18] What had been regarded as a world-class regulatory agency thus began to attract derision and doubt. Reflecting a more positive attitude toward regulation, the Bush Administration reversed this trend.

C. Major Controversies

Still another way to view and evaluate the FDA is through the controversies it ignites. Two controversies stand out—one concerning new drug certification, the other concerning risky food additives.

1. REVIEW AND APPROVAL OF NEW DRUGS

In 1962, the Food, Drug, and Cosmetic Act was amended to raise the hurdles a new drug must clear before being marketed. The changes were prompted by thalidomide, a tranquilizer developed in Germany in 1957 that was approved for use in several European countries with tragic consequences. Women who had taken the drug during pregnancy gave birth to horribly deformed babies, about 8,000 in all. The toll in the United States was held to only a few because the drug was circulated here only for research when the FDA delayed granting its approval for general marketing on suspicion that it was unsafe. Premarket safety clearance had been part of U.S. law since 1938, but because of this tragedy two new stringencies were added to the standards for premarket clearance. First, the 1962 law required firms to provide scientific evidence of a new drug's *efficacy* as well as its safety. Second, the *research process* itself became subject to regulation to protect humans serving as research subjects.

Since the 1970s new drug development has followed a four-step sequence—pre-clinical R&D, clinical R&D, new drug application (NDA) review, and postmarketing surveillance. Figure 21–1 illustrates these steps, distinguishing the time

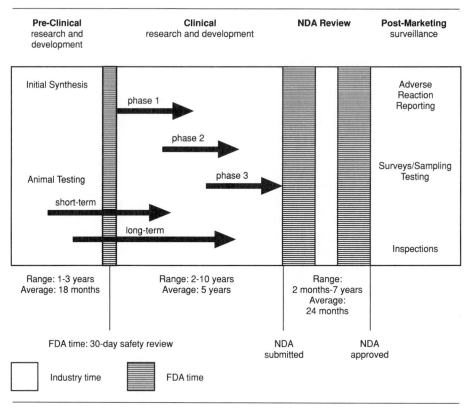

Figure 21–1
New Drug Development Sequence, 1970s–1990s (Average Time from Initial Synthesis to NDA Approval: 8.5 Years)

Source: *FDA Consumer,* November 1987, p. 5

taken by the drug companies and the FDA to accomplish each step.

The main *benefits* of the 1962 amendment are greater assurances of efficacy and safety. But these standards lengthened the time between discovery and marketing considerably, so that, as indicated in Figure 21–1, the normal trip from laboratory to pharmacy shelf takes about nine years, two or three times the previous duration. Thus, the *costs* of the 1962 amendment, aside from the R&D and administrative costs, are the lives lost and suffering endured while the marketing of beneficial new drugs is delayed (or perhaps never permitted at all). There is, in short, an ominous trade-off, or dilemma. *"Simply put,"*

to use the words of Upjohn's president, Dr. William Hubbard, Jr., *"do benefits of increased certainty about the drug arising from delay outweigh the benefits that might have arisen from its use during the delay?"*[19] Given the large element of judgment needed to answer this question, the FDA is in a no-win situation. Any movement along the trade-off incites critics and defenders.[20]

Critics of the FDA point first to the substantial drop in new drug introductions that followed the 1962 amendments, as shown in Figure 21–2. Between 1945 and 1962 an average of 39 new chemical entities were approved by the FDA each year. Thereafter, from 1963 to 1985 an average of just 18 new chemical entities were

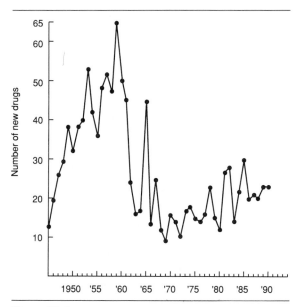

Figure 21–2
FDA New Drug Approvals by Year, 1945–1990

Sources: 1945–1979: Larry L. Deutsch,
"Pharmaceuticals: The Critical Role of Innovation,"
Industry Studies, ed. by Larry L. Deutsch (Englewood
Cliffs, NJ: Prentice-Hall, forthcoming); 1980–1990: FDA.

cleared each year, a tremendous drop of 54 percent. The critics concede that some decline was to be expected, given that ineffective drugs would no longer be approved. But the critics also have a long list of complaints associated with this trend:

- Drug development costs have soared to more than $100 million per drug.

- The higher costs of drug R&D hurt small firms severely and boosted the four largest firms' share of innovation output from 24 percent in the late 1950s to 48.7 percent from 1967 to 1971.

- Most important, critics claim that American medical care has deteriorated, that the array of effective new drugs available to American patients has been needlessly and injuriously restricted as compared to new drugs available in foreign countries. Chymopapain, metaproterenol, and propranolol are among the dozens of

cures suffering "bureaucratic lag"—that is, they were available abroad long before they were here.[21]

Defenders of FDA regulations concede that the number of new drug introductions has taken a nose dive, but they argue that the post-1962 regulations cannot be blamed for all of the decline. They claim that research *opportunities* withered as the new mines opened by breakthrough discoveries during the 1940s and 1950s petered out. In support of this claim, defenders point out that new drug introductions began to decline *before* the 1962 amendments took hold, and that new drug introductions have declined in Germany, France, England, and other advanced countries as well as in the United States despite no comparable changes in their laws.[22] Moreover, the FDA's defenders deny that United States medical care has suffered substantially under efficacy regulation. They contend that the decline in introductions is mainly accounted for by elimination of drugs representing little or no important therapeutic gain.[23] The disproportionately greater loss of trivial drugs is understandable, they say, because rising costs of new drug development would tend to cripple the profit prospects of trivial drugs before crippling the profit prospects of important drugs, given that trivial drugs ordinarily have weaker profit potential to begin with.

As for the problem of extended time lags, the FDA's defenders admit to delays. They contend, however, that drugs in the research stage can be obtained through "compassionate approval" procedures, and that the FDA can move quickly, as it did for the AIDS drug AZT.[24]

Exactly where the truth lies between the objections and rebuttals is uncertain. In any event, there were two interesting developments in the early 1980s. *First,* as if admitting to excessive past delay, the FDA modified its procedures in 1981 and 1984 to gain greater speed.[25] The 1984 rules, for instance, cut six months off the last stage of the approval process and for the first time allowed a drug company to submit clinical studies done in foreign countries to support claims of safety and efficacy. *Second,* as Figure 21–2 indicates, the trend in new drug approvals is now on the rise. Whether this turnabout can be credited to the regulatory changes of the early 1980s is uncertain. Those changes do save some time and costs but not by whopping amounts. More credit for the rise in new drugs might be given to several newly found research frontiers, such as those based on gene splicing. According to one expert, speaking in 1991, "We're witnessing a major upheaval in the pharmaceutical industry, driven by the biological sciences."[26]

In 1991 the FDA announced plans to obtain even greater speed in the approval process for new drugs. The stated object was to reduce the time to about six years, a 30 to 40 percent drop. Perhaps by the time you read this these plans will be in effect.[27]

Some critics of the FDA go so far as to urge repeal of the 1962 amendments. This seems unlikely, however. The nasty trade-off remains. Hasty approval of new drugs is dangerous simply because new drugs can be dangerous, as was illustrated in two unfortunate cases of the late 1970s and early 1980s. Dozens of deaths were linked to two new drugs—Oraflex and Selacryn—shortly after they were placed on the market. Neither drug was a medical breakthrough. Safer substitutes were available for both. (One was a pain killer and the other treated high blood pressure.) Hence, there was little to redeem their deadly side effects. Compounding these tragedies, the manufacturers of these drugs did not report the deaths to the FDA in a timely manner, thereby delaying removal of the products from the market. Criminal prosecutions ensued.[28]

2. FOOD ADDITIVES

In 1990 the FDA banned Red Dye No. 3, a food coloring that, among other things, gave the cherries in canned fruit cocktail their red hue but which also caused cancer in rats. Food industry lobbyists angrily objected. They admitted that there might be some cancer risk in Red Dye No. 3, but stressed that it was a tiny risk. Laboratory rats developed tumors only when the dye was 4 percent of their total diet. To match this level to exposure, people would have to eat 13,898 servings of fruit cocktail per day for seventy years. Defenders of the ban rebutted by saying that this was just a *color* additive of virtually no benefit whatever. To this the industry replied that food color matters. It makes food appetizing. Without Red Dye No. 3, cocktail cherries would be brown.[29]

The main bone of contention in food additives concerns the Delaney clause, which sets a no-risk standard for carcinogenic food additives.[30] Critics contend that such an absolute no-risk standard is *foolish* when carcinogens abound. Moreover, it is *inconsistent* with the relative benefit-risk standard adopted for aflatoxin, mercury, and other harmful substances that enter the food supply naturally or inadvertently. Moreover, critics favor a benefit-risk or benefit-cost approach as a matter of *principle,* not just of consistency. They point out that food additives often have tremendous benefits—extending product shelf life, preventing food-borne disease (like botulism), providing convenience, improving nutrition, and enhancing appeal through taste and color. For a concrete example, it has been estimated that bread without additives would cost 17 percent *more* than bread made with additives, mainly because of the increased distribution and selling costs that greater perishability would entail. As for the risks, advocates of a benefit-risk approach cite numbers such as those presented in Table 21–3 to argue that the risks associated with cancerous substances in food are no greater, and in many cases much smaller, than the risks people willingly face daily. (In fact, recent estimates indicate that 98 percent of the cancer risk we encounter in food is not a result of additives of the kind controlled by the Delaney clause, but of the kinds of food we eat—for example, fat has been linked to several kinds of tumors—or to nat-

Table 21–3
Annual Risk of Death for Individual Participants or Those Subject to Exposure (Mid-1970s)

Activity	Risk	
Drinking 1 diet soda/day (saccharin)	1 in	100,000
Eating 4 tablespoons peanut butter/day (aflatoxin)	1 in	25,000
Drinking Miami or New Orleans water	1 in	800,000
Smoking (all bad effects)	1 in	300
Taking contraceptive pills	1 in	50,000
Power boating	1 in	5,900
Motor vehicle travel	1 in	4,500
Home accidents	1 in	83,000
Breathing (air pollution)	1 in	6,700
Getting hit by lightning	1 in	2,500,000

Source: P. B. Hutt, "Unresolved Issues in the Conflict Between Individual Freedom and Government Control of Food Safety," *Food Safety: Where Are We?*, U.S. Senate, Committee on Agriculture, Nutrition, and Forestry (July 1979), pp. 296–297.

urally occurring substances in food—for example, aflatoxin in corn and peanuts, or urethane in alcohol.[31]

Defenders of the Delaney clause rebut, first, by making the factual observation that, contrary to popular misconception, not all additives tested prove to be cancerous. Second, they claim that a distinction between risks that are natural or inevitable on the one hand, and those that are deliberately introduced into food on the other, is a meaningful distinction to make for policy purposes because the latter are *manageable* risks. Third, defenders say that a benefit-risk approach is fraught with too many uncertainties and dangers to be acceptable. "Any program," they say, "that assumes the ability to identify, quantify, and evaluate risks present in food will lead to serious damage to individual members of the pop-

ulation."[32] Finally, and not altogether consistent with the foregoing, defenders claim that there is enough flexibility in the present system to handle special cases, as when Congress exempted saccharin in response to public protest.

Scientific advances aggravate the debate. It is now possible to detect the presence of very minute quantities of a substance—like one part per billion. Such very minute quantities might pose very minute risks of cancer—say, less risk than the risk of being hit by lightning. If additives contain such substances, should they be banned as unsafe, or should they be considered safe because the risks are so tiny as to be virtually nil, or, in legal terms, *de minimus*?

In recent years, the FDA has been saying that *de minimus* risk is acceptable. It has argued that a one-in-a-million risk of cancer is "essentially negligible" and therefore not worth worrying about. (Notice that the only risk in Table 21–3 that is worse than this is getting hit by lightning.) For this reason, the FDA has been very slow to ban some substances that pose no more than slight risk. Indeed, Red Dye No. 3 was banned only because the FDA was forced into action after four lawsuits by the Public Citizen Health Research Group. It thus appears that relaxed standards in this area must depend on Congress, not the FDA. A literal reading of the Delaney clause apparently leaves the FDA no room to maneuver. The Bush Administration urged Congress to adopt a negligible risk test, but as of 1992 the law remained unchanged.

One thing that complicates policy in this area is that people are not always consistent in their fear of risks, so it is difficult for experts to act on behalf of consumers in such situations. People seem to accept risks they are familiar with, like skiing and airline travel, or that they have control over, like smoking. On the other hand, they seem to think that risks are more important and unacceptable if exposure to them affects children, is involuntary, seems unfair, appears to be unnecessary, or could result in a dread condition.[33] Thus, the debate goes on.

II. The National Highway Traffic Safety Administration

A. Standards

1. BROAD STANDARDS

The compelling need for the strong automobile safety legislation . . . lies embodied in these statistics: 1.6 million dead since the coming of the automobile; over 50,000 to die this year. And, unless the accelerating spiral of death is arrested, 100,000 Americans will die as a result of their cars in 1975.[34]

With these words Congress justified its establishment of the National Highway Traffic Safety Administration (NHTSA) in 1966. Congress could have abolished automobiles or (as in the early days in England) required each moving auto to be preceded by a pedestrian carrying a red flag. But these policies defy practical consideration. So, instead, Congress ordered NHTSA to devise and enforce specific standards in furtherance of motor vehicle safety. Such are the vague, broad standards guiding NHTSA policy.

2. NARROW STANDARDS

On getting the green light in 1966, the NHTSA got quickly into high gear. The agency, which is housed in the Department of Transportation, issued twenty-nine specific equipment standards in its first four years. Since that time NHTSA has more or less coasted, issuing fewer and fewer new standards each year while concentrating on enforcing and modifying its old standards.

A simple list of the equipment covered—such as tires, windshields, child restraints, steering columns, brakes, and motorcycle helmets—reveals nothing more systematic than the jumbled contents of an average private garage. Nevertheless, all standards have one prime criterion: They must meet "the need for motor vehicle safety." Moreover, all standards may be classified, analyzed, and organized in three groups.[35]

100 Series, Precrash Standards. These standards improve the capacity of drivers to *avoid* crashes and reduce the capacity of cars to *cause* crashes. Examples include No. 101, which requires that clearly identified, well-illuminated essential controls be within easy reach of a driver restrained by safety belts; No. 105, which requires split braking systems, incorporating emergency features capable of stopping the car under certain specified conditions; and No. 109, which requires that tires meet minimum standards of quality, endurance, and high-speed performance.

200 Series, Crash Standards. These standards are aimed at protecting auto occupants and highway pedestrians *during* a crash. Their implementation softens blows, holds riders snug, and cuts down on flying debris. Examples include No. 202, which requires head restraints hindering "whiplash"; No. 203, which requires padded, collapsible steering systems; No. 205, which requires shatterproof glass; and No. 206, which requires especially strong and reliable door latches.

300 Series, Postcrash Standards. The purpose of these standards is to keep injuries and losses to a minimum in the period *after* a crash has occurred. Few such standards have been issued—for example, No. 301, which tries to minimize fire hazards by specifying certain features of fuel tanks, fuel tank filler pipes, and fuel tank connections; and No. 302, which requires that flame-resistant materials be used in auto interiors.

In addition to these equipment standards, a number of nonequipment standards govern manufacturing and distributing practices. The most important of these concern product identification and record keeping. They enable manufacturers and retailers to track down purchasers of autos, tires, motorcycles, and other equipment long after purchase in the event a recall is necessary.

B. Enforcement

1. CERTIFICATION

The NHTSA's certification efforts are minor in comparison to its other enforcement activities. For the most part, manufacturers accept the re-

---

Thumbnail Sketch 8: National Highway Traffic Safety Administration

---

Established: 1966 (called the National Highway Safety Agency 1966–1970).

Purpose: Administers federal programs designed to increase motor vehicle safety (and fuel economy).

Legislative Authority: National Traffic and Motor Vehicle Safety Act of 1966; Highway Safety Acts of 1966 and 1970; Energy Policy and Conservation Act of 1975.

Regulatory Activity: Sets and enforces mandatory standards for the safety of motor vehicles and related equipment (such as motorcycle helmets). Regulate fuel economy. Conducts research.

Organization: A division of the Department of Transportation, headed by an administrator.

Budget: 1991 estimate: $175 million.

Staff: 1991 estimate: 595.

---

sponsibility of testing old and new equipment to check compliance with the standards. If satisfied, the manufacturers then certify to the NHTSA (and often to buyers via stickers) that the products meet standards.

2. TESTING AND SURVEILLANCE

Each year NHTSA selects over 100 motor vehicle models for several hundred tests to check compliance with standards. This represents a very small sample compared to the 400 different models of the 10 million vehicles produced. But compliance testing involves over 4,000 separate items of equipment on these vehicles, including door locks, seat belts, brake systems, and lights.[36]

Field surveillance includes the agency's toll-free Auto Safety Hotline, which allows consumers to contact NHTSA directly to register safety-related complaints or obtain information. The hotline averages 500 to 600 calls per day. Folks contacting manufacturers instead of NHTSA may rest assured that the manufacturers themselves must notify the agency of their knowledge of hazards. If these and other sources of information reveal disturbing signs, NHTSA launches a defects investigation. Over 200 such investigations occur in a typical year.

3. REMEDIES

The NHTSA has a number of remedies at its disposal. Of these, recalls are by far the most familiar and most commonly used. The majority of recall campaigns are initiated voluntarily by manufacturers (under threat of compulsory recall). Moreover, recalls have resulted in some of the most astounding statistics passing through these pages. Between NHTSA's founding in 1966 and early 1980, approximately 83.7 million vehicles were recalled for safety defects in 2,942 separate campaigns.[37] Because 155.8 million cars were sold in the United States during that time, this suggests that one out of every two cars was recalled! But some cars were recalled more than once, so it is not literally true that 50 percent of all cars leaving the showroom proved faulty. For example, Ford recalled Escort and Lynx *eight* times shortly after their introduction to fix safety and other defects (despite touting these cars as "the highest quality products in Ford history").[38]

C. Controversies

1. RESULTS OF REGULATION

The estimated costs of mandated safety features vary from a few hundred to many hundreds of dollars per car. Given these costs, and given that our own necks are at stake, more than idle curiosity compels us to ask about the benefits these standards bestow. Have they made any difference? Some observers claim that they haven't, arguing that as cars get safer people drive more recklessly.[39] Others claim otherwise.[39] NHTSA, for instance, claims that its efforts "have saved more than 55,000 lives between 1966 and 1978, and . . . this figure will amount to 150,000 by 1987."[40] Where, then, does the answer lie?

In my opinion the best studies reveal substantial gains.[41] The results of one such study are shown in Figure 21–3.[42] It compares occupant fatalities per 100,000 cars in Maryland from 1972 to 1975 across three classes of cars: (1) unregulated models, (2) belt-equipped 1964 to 1967 models, and (3) post-NHTSA-era models from 1968 to 1975. Comparing the last category with the first reveals an overall 39 percent reduction in fatality rates. Figure 21–3 also shows the impact of the 55 miles per hour speed limit of 1974 and 1975. It is estimated that this speed limit saved about 4,500 lives per year nationwide.

A 1986 study sponsored by the Brookings Institution estimated that:

> Had automobiles been as unsafe in 1981 as in 1965 . . . total fatalities would have been 18,000 to 22,000 above their actual 1981 level. The estimate of lives saved per year is about 30% of the total deaths that would have been predicted without safer automobiles.[43]

If we value the *benefits* of these avoided fatalities at $1 million apiece, and if we accept the Brookings estimate that the *costs* of safety run $671 to $981 per car, then we have the following benefit-cost estimates for auto safety regulation in *billions* of 1981 dollars:[44]

	Benefits	*Costs*
Optimistic estimate	$35.1	$ 7.0
Pessimistic estimate	$19.5	$10.3

Once it is recognized that still more benefits can be credited to auto safety (e.g., reduced legal and

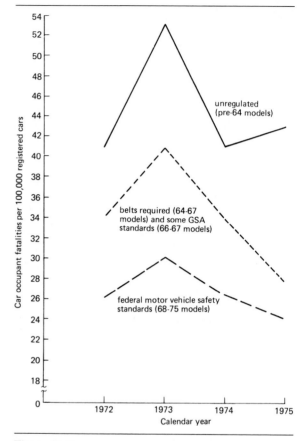

Figure 21–3
Car Occupant Fatalities per 100,000 Registered Cars, by Type of New-Car Safety Regulations, Maryland, 1972–1975

Source: *Federal Regulation and Regulatory Reform,* Subcommittee on Oversight and Investigations of the Committee on Interstate and Foreign Commerce, U.S. House of Representatives, 94th Congress, 2nd session (1976), p. 170.

court costs, property loss, and insurance administration), then it seems safe to conclude that, overall, the benefits of safer passenger cars are probably much greater than the costs are.

2. PASSIVE RESTRAINTS
Of all proposed safety standards, none has kindled sharper dispute than the "passive restraint"

standard. It was promulgated by the Carter Administration in 1977 but was rescinded by the Reagan Administration in 1981, just before its actual implementation. Then, in 1983, a unanimous Supreme Court rebuffed the Reagan revocation, saying that the administration acted in an "arbitrary and capricious" manner.

An ordinary seat belt is an "active restraint" because people must actively buckle it. In contrast, "passive restraints" work automatically—air bags and automatic belts being the chief examples. The urge to require passive restraints arose because people do not actively buckle up. No more than about 15 to 20 percent of all auto travelers voluntarily use seat belts. If lap and shoulder belts were used 100 percent, an estimated 16,000 lives would be saved each year.

After the Supreme Court rebuffed the Reagan Administration's rejection of passive restraints, the Reagan Administration did not convert. Responding to strong opposition from the auto industry, the administration continued to avoid a passive restraint standard by launching several efforts to boost use of seat belts. In particular, states were urged to pass mandatory laws requiring the use of seat belts, promising that passive restraints would not be required if two-thirds of the U.S. population became covered by this coercion. Many states adopted mandatory use laws, with fines as high as $50 for an offense. And many people started using their seat belts for the first time, boosting use rates in states with mandatory laws to about 40 percent. But this was not enough. By 1989, the passive restraint rule became a certainty. Of the two options for meeting the new rule—airbags and automatic seat belts—airbags became the popular choice. The main impetus came from Chrysler Corporation Chairman Lee Iacocca. After many years of vigorous opposition to air bags, Iacocca decided to have them installed as standard equipment on all U.S.-made Chrysler cars beginning in 1990. This action put pressure on the other auto companies to do the same. It seems likely that well over half of all cars produced in the United Staes, perhaps 80 percent, will have air bags by mid-1994. Indeed, air bags may eventually be required by law. Estimated to save approximately 10,000 lives annually, air bags add $400 to $1,000 to the cost of producing a car.

A favorable benefit-cost computation for passive restraints supported official approval of passive restraints in 1977.[45] Opponents of the standard were neither passive nor restrained, however, and they won delays with some interesting arguments. First, there were some technical problems, such as the tendency of air bags to inflate inadvertently. Second, there was a problem of equity. The few who *do* buckle up their safety belts would be forced to pay heavy costs just so those who chose *not* to wear safety belts could be automatically protected. Is this fair? Finally, there is an issue of individual freedom here. Why force passive restraints on people? No adverse third party effects are present as long as "active" belts are available to all passengers who want to wear them. Shouldn't freedom outweigh benefit-cost efficiency? The issues are fascinating.

III. The Consumer Product Safety Commission

A. Standards

1. BROAD STANDARDS

Created on October 27, 1972, the CPSC is the youngest of the three agencies reviewed here. The legislation establishing the CPSC states that its primary purpose is "to protect the public against unreasonable risks of injury associated with consumer products." To this end, the CPSC administers five laws:

1. The Consumer Product Safety Act
2. The Federal Hazardous Substances Act
3. The Flammable Fabrics Act
4. The Poison Prevention Packaging Act
5. The Refrigerator Safety Act

Thumbnail Sketch 9: The Consumer Product Safety Commission

Established: 1972

Purpose: To protect the public against unreasonable risks of injury from consumer products; to promote public awareness of common hazards; and to promote research into the causes of product-related deaths and injuries.

Legislative Authority: The Consumer Product Safety Act, Federal Hazardous Substances Act, Flammable Fabrics Act, and Poison Prevention Act.

Regulatory Activity: (1) Establishes some mandatory consumer product standards and assists in the development of voluntary standards. (2) Bans certain products. (3) Requires manufacturers to report product defects or dangers. (4) Collects information on product-related injuries.

Organization: An independent regulatory agency headed by a chairman and four commissioners.

Budget: 1991 estimate: $37 million.

Staff: 1991 estimate: 525.

The last four of these preceded the CPSC's creation and were therefore formerly administered by other agencies, such as the FDA and the FTC. The overall significance of these regulations may be measured in round numbers as follows:

> An estimated 20 million consumers are injured each year through the use of consumer products, of which 110,000 are permanently disabled and 30,000 are killed. The Commission also estimates that there are more than 10,000 different consumer products and more than 2.5 million manufacturers, importers, packagers, distributors, and retailers who are subject to Commission regulations.[46]

The only consumer products not included under the CPSC's umbrella are those covered by other agencies: foods, drugs, cosmetics, medical devices, firearms, pesticides, motor vehicles, aircraft, and boats.

2. NARROW STANDARDS

Most mothers do not know it, but 2,375 inches is a very important measure to them. Before 1973 about 150 babies died annually in a rather bizarre fashion. When playfully dangling their feet between two slats of their cribs, these babies slipped out—their hips and torso following their feet toward the floor. However, their naturally large heads would not clear the slats, causing the babies to strangle or hang to death. The industry's crib slat spacing of 3.5 inches was clearly too great, but what spacing was proper? Formal research into the question led to studies of babies' buttocks, because buttock bulk could protect babies from passing beyond the threshold of danger. Of particular interest was the anterior-posterior measurement of baby buttocks when compressed between two slats by the downward force of a baby's weight. It was concluded that slat spacing of 2.375 inches would protect 95 percent of all infants from self-strangulation. Hence, the commission's standard for baby cribs reads in part: "The distance between components (such as slats, spindles, crib rods and corner posts) shall not be greater than 6 centimeters (2⅜ inches) at any point."[47]

This was one of the first and easiest to formulate of all the commission's narrow standards. As Steven Kelman comments:

> The CPSC's crib safety standard represents something like an ideal case of product safety regulation, displaying all the potential advantages of

such regulation and none of the pitfalls. The decision to intervene in the marketplace with mandatory rules involved a hazard of which most consumers are totally ignorant, and the risks of which are assumed involuntarily by an infant unable to protect itself. The cost of making the product safe was minimal. The safety change did not reduce the utility or attractiveness of the product, and the likelihood that the standard would indeed reduce injury and death was extremely high.[48]

Were all CPSC standards as ideal as this, the commission would be one big continuous picnic. Unfortunately, that is not the case. Most standards relate to complex problems and may take years to formulate. For this reason the CPSC relies mainly upon voluntary standards as opposed to mandatory standards. Whereas mandatory standards are developed by the CPSC itself, voluntary standards are developed by industry groups acting under the guidance and prodding of the CPSC, which retains rights of final approval. Use of voluntary procedures saves the CPSC's resources, broadens its scope, and improves the chances of self-enforced industry compliance. Still, the voluntary procedure offers no panacea. Proposed ladder standards consumed tens of thousands of manhours, reams of paper, and hundreds of thousands of dollars belonging to both industry and government.

Given the difficulties of standard formulation and given the thousands of products subject to CPSC jurisdiction, the commission has set some vague priorities to guide its endeavors. The main criteria have been (1) frequency and severity of injuries, (2) causality of injuries, and (3) chronic illness and future injuries. Product data concerning these criteria are obtained through an information-gathering network that connects the CPSC to hospital emergency rooms.

In the late 1970s and early 1980s the commission began to weigh its standards by benefit-cost criteria. It defended its power mower rules, for example, by saying that they would benefit consumers $211 million in avoiding injury expenses while costing $190 million annually in equipment and implementation. This benefit-cost orientation was a radical change for an agency of this type, but heavy pressure by agency critics brought it about.

In round numbers, the CPSC has several dozen standards on the books, half of which are bans of various types. In addition, the agency enforces nearly 100 special packaging and labeling regulations.[49]

B. Enforcement

1. CERTIFICATION

The CPSC's certification activities are, like those of NHTSA's, minimal. Section 14 of the Consumer Product Safety Act puts the onus on manufacturers to certify that their products meet CPSC standards. Any certification testing procedures not explicitly set by standards may be set by the commission.

2. SAMPLE TESTING AND FIELD SURVEILLANCE

Each year the CPSC conducts several thousand inspections and sample collections. Compliance is also monitored by: (a) the agency's National Electronic Injury Surveillance System, which feeds data from a large sample of hospital emergency rooms to the CPSC on a regular basis; (b) its review of death certificates in cases where a consumer product may have been at fault; (c) a consumer hotline; and (d) reports from manufacturers who learn of hazards in their products.

3. REMEDIES

When establishing the CPSC, Congress gave the agency a wide variety of remedial weapons, including product seizures, recalls, injunctions, cease and desist orders, and civil and criminal penalties. The agency's most potent weapon is the recall. During 1990–1991, the CPSC obtained recalls affecting more than 59 million products that created hazards or that fell short of standards. Among the products involved (and their problems) were automatic coffeemakers (fire hazard), ceiling fans (falling on people), exercise devices (spring breakage), toys (choking hazard), and water coolers containing lead (lead poisoning).[50]

C. Controversy

The greatest controversy surrounding the CPSC is whether the agency itself should continue to live, and, if so, what powers it should retain. When created, the CPSC's life span was regulated by a "sunset" provision, which automatically killed the agency after a fixed duration unless Congress deliberately revived it. In 1981, when the agency's budget and continued existence were up for review, the Reagan Administration called on Congress to kill the CPSC, or if not kill it at least cut its budget and powers considerably. Backing the administration was an army of business lobbyists representing the National Association of Manufacturers, the National Mass Retailing Institute, the Toy Manufacturers of America, and others who felt oppressed by the commission. The commission had, according to its critics, grown overzealous, unreasonable, incompetent, unnecessary, and redundant.[51]

As a result, the agency's budget and staff were slashed by 50 percent during the 1980s. Moreover, President Reagan appointed commissioners who, in accord with Reagan's wishes, did very little. The CPSC became, as one observer put it, "an invisible agency."[52]

Since 1990, however, the CPSC has rebounded. Its budget and staff are no longer falling. Its activity level has jumped. Much of the rebound may be attributed to a revived concern for hazards affecting children (a concern that was instrumental in getting the commission started in the first place). Infant beanbag pillows caused the suffocation deaths of sixteen babies from 1987 to 1989 and were on their way to causing fifteen to twenty deaths per year when they were recalled in 1990. Also, an estimated 450 children were killed and another 160,000 seriously injured by all-terrain vehicles before the vehicles came under CPSC control. Foot-long metal lawn darts

that were tossed into children as well as into targets, and toys that choked babies despite compliance with old CPSC standards—these and many other problems involving children gave the agency new life in the early 1990s.[53] Indeed, the Consumer Product Safety Improvement Act of 1990 strengthened the agency rather than weakened it.[54]

Among its overall achievements, the commission claims to have reduced children's poisonings by 80 percent, electrocution deaths of all people by 55 percent, and injuries from power lawnmowers by 38 percent. Now that the agency seems safe from the hazards of the Reagan years, it can continue its work.

Summary

Until fairly recently in our history the government was largely reactive rather than preventative in the area of consumer safety. As former Commissioner Statler of the CPSC once put it, government was "the ambulance at the bottom of the cliff instead of the fence atop."[55] Even the original Food and Drug Act of 1906 was reactive, because it made no provision for premarket safety certification. Beginning in 1938, however, this changed. After 107 people died from Elixir Sulfanilamide, Congress gave the FDA power to build a preventative safety fence for drugs, a fence that has since been extended to protect against hazards in consumer goods generally.

The FDA imposes standards for safety, purity, production cleanliness, and efficacy in foods, drugs, cosmetics, and medical devices. Safety standards for drugs and medical devices tend to be relative. That is, the greater the benefits, the higher the risks that will be permitted. Safety standards for foods and cosmetics tend to be more absolute, as illustrated most sharply by the Delaney clause banning carcinogenic food additives. Leeway is allowed, however, for other hazards that would be very costly to remove completely. Such partial relativity extends beyond safety standards to include purity, production cleanliness, and efficacy.

The FDA's enforcement activities include premarket certification, sample testing, and plant inspections. Given the many thousands of products and plants involved, the task is immense. Among remedies, recalls are the mainstay, backed up by seizures and even the possibility of criminal penalties.

Stormy controversies have raged over the 1962 drug amendments and the Delaney clause. The premarket hurdles of the 1962 amendments yield benefits of assured safety and efficacy, but they do so at the cost of considerable delay in getting new drugs to market (not to mention other costs like higher R&D expenses). Critics pooh-pooh the benefits and stress the costs while defenders of the policy have an opposite placement of emphasis. A kind of compromise has occurred, with expedited procedures granted to new breakthrough drugs, and modified review regulations. The Delaney dispute has produced compromise in the form of a saccharin exemption and attempts by the FDA to approve *de minimus* risks.

The National Highway Traffic Safety Administration implements vague broad standards with over 50 narrow standards. These set design and performance specifications from bumper to bumper. Compliance is checked by agency testing and by surveillance systems of various kinds. Certainly the most graphic measure of the agency's impact lies in its recalls, which constitute the chief remedy. By early 1980, 83.7 million vehicles had been recalled for hazards in 2,942 campaigns.

Just how much NHTSA has preserved life and limb is subject to dispute, but the best evidence shows a significant impact, especially from the agency's early standards. Among specific proposed standards, by far the most controversial was the passive restraint standard issued in 1977, rescinded in 1981, and reissued in 1984 for full achievement in 1991. Although defensible on benefit-cost grounds (only because people shun safety belts), the standard poses problems of technical inconvenience, economic inequity, and interference with personal freedom.

The Consumer Product Safety Commission was established "to protect the public against unreasonable risks of injury associated with consumer products." Probably the best narrow standards evolving from this mandate relate to child safety—toys, baby cribs, and protective caps on containers of toxic substances. Another plus is the agency's increased reliance on benefit-cost analysis in standard formulation.

After a timid start, the CPSC's enforcement effort grew some teeth in the late 1970s and early 1980s. Annual tallies of recalled products mounted into the tens of millions of units. Partly because of this increasing bite, opposition to the agency billowed as business interests increasingly lobbied for the agency's demise or curtailment. The agency survived, but just barely. Its recent revival is based partly on a renewed concern for hazards threatening children.

Questions and Exercises for Chapter 21

1. Compare and contrast the narrow safety standards for drugs and for foods. Why do they differ?
2. Why are there no efficacy standards for food and cosmetics?
3. Why is the FDA in a no-win situation on the issue of premarket clearance of drugs? Do you think less stringent premarket study coupled with closer postmarket surveillance would be a good compromise? How would this shift the focus of enforcement among the categories of Table 20–3 of the last chapter?
4. Explain how value judgments might influence one's opinion on the issue of food additives.
5. Where, among enforcement activities, has the NHTSA placed its greatest effort? What defenses and criticisms might be made of this approach?

6. What value judgments would influence your assessment of auto passive restraint policy?

7. Why has the CPSC's baby crib standard been uncontroversial?

8. Pick a pro or con position on continuation of the CPSC and argue your case.

Notes

1. T. Roberts and E. van Ravensway, "The Economics of Food Safety," *National Food Review* (vol. 12, no. 3, issue 3, 1989): U. S. Department of Agriculture Economic Research Service, pp. 1–8.

2. *The Economist,* August 12, 1989, p. 61.

3. Statement of Commissioner Schmidt, *Reforming Federal Drug Regulation* (Washington, DC: American Enterprise Institute, 1976), p. 26–27.

4. Food and Drug Administration, *Requirements of the United States Food, Drug and Cosmetic Act* (1972), p. 6.

5. Ibid., p. 12. On meat regulations see Kenneth J. Meier, *Regulation* (New York: St. Martin's Press, 1985), pp. 93–94).

6. FDA, *Requirements . . . of ACt,* p. 5.

7. Federal Food, Drug, and Cosmetic Act, Section 505(d).

8. *FDA Consumer,* December 1987–January 1988, p. 12.

9. *FDA Annual Report 1975,* p. 36; 1976, p. 33. See also Sidney Wolfe and C. Coley, *Pills That Don't Work* (New York: Farrar, Straus, & Giroux, 1981), according to which, 607 ineffective drugs remained on the market in 1979, costing consumers $1.1 billion annually.

10. *FDA Quarterly Activities Report, Fourth Quarter/ Fiscal Year 1991* (Washington, DC: Department of Health and Human Services, FDA), pp. 32–33.

11. *Wall Street Journal,* 7 October 1975, p. 1.

12. *Dimensions of Insanitary Conditions in the Food Manufacturing Industry,* Report of the Comptroller General of the United States, B–164031 (2), April 18, 1972, p. 2.

13. Vern Modeland, "Juiceless Baby Juice Leads to Full-Strength Justice," *FDA Consumer* (June 1988): 14–17; *Wall Street Journal,* 31 March 1989, p. B8.

14. Morton Mintz, "A Snail's Pace on Pace Makers," *Washington Post, National Weekly Edition,* Aug. 28–Sept. 3, 1989, p. 33.

15. *Wall Street Journal,* 6 November 1989, p. B4.

16. Frank E. Young, "FDA: The Cop on the Beat," *FDA Consumer,* April 1988, p. 6.

17. Walter Williams, "Cutting Off Our Nose In Spite of Our Needs," *Washington Post National Weekly Edition,* October 22–28, 1990, p. 26.

18. *Wall Street Journal,* 29 September 1989, p. C9.

19. W. N. Hubbard, Jr., in *Reforming Federal Drug Regulation,* supra note 3, p. 13.

20. For good summaries see Denise Grady, "Bottleneck at the FDA," *Discover* (November 1981): 52–56; and Larry L. Duetsch, "Pharmaceuticals: The Critical Role of Innovation," in *Industry Studies,* ed. Larry Deutsch (Englewood Cliffs: Prentice Hall, forthcoming 1993).

21. See e.g., Sam Peltzman, "An Evaluation of Consumer Protection Legislation: The 1962 Drug Amendments," *Journal of Political Economy* (September 1973): 1049–91; H. G. Grabowski and J. M. Vernon, "Consumer Protection Regulation in Ethical Drugs," *American Economic Review* (February 1977): 359–364; H. G. Grabowsky, *Drug Regulation and Innovation* (Washington, DC: American Enterprise Institute, 1976): William Wardell, "More Regulation or Better Therapies?" *Regulation* (September/October 1979): 25–33.

22. It is interesting that West Germany finally did institute new regulations in 1978 despite the negative experience of the U. S. you see in Figure 21–2. These regulations are less stringent than those here, however, which may explain why, in 1984, a West German physician's magazine reported that "There isn't a month without a pharmaceutical scandal. . . . Preparations have been pulled off the market for safety reasons." *Wall Street Journal,* 31 May 1984, p. 31. On the slower rate of new product introductions worldwide, see Henry G. Grabowski, "An Analysis of U. S. International Competitiveness Pharmaceuticals," *Managerial and Decision Economics,* Special Issue (Spring 1989).

23. During 1950–1962 roughly 70 percent of all newly approved drugs could be judged of "little or no gain." During 1962–1972, roughly 40 percent could be so classified. *Examination of the Pharmaceutical Industry 1973–1974,* Part 7, Hearings before the Subcommittee on Health of the Committee on Labor and Public Welfare, U. S. Senate, 93rd Congress, 2nd Session (1974), p. 3050.

24. AZT was approved in March 1987 after a total drug development time of only two years. *FDA Consumer,* November 1987, p. 5.

25. *Wall Street Journal,* 12 August 1981, p. 25; 16 September 1981, p. 25; 16 September 1981, p. 8; 12 December 1984, p. 18.

26. *Fortune,* August 12, 1991, p. 79.

27. *Wall Street Journal,* 11 November 1991, p. A14.

28. The offenders were big drug companies—Eli Lilly (Oraflex) and Smithkline Beckman (Selacryn). For details see *Deficiencies in FDA's Regulation of the New Drug "Oraflex",* Report by the Committee on Government Operations, U. S. Congress, House, 1983; *Wall Street Journal,* 13 December 1984, p. 5; *Washington Post National Weekly Edition,* January 14, 1985, p. 32. More generally, a GAO study released in 1990 reviewed all 198 drugs that were approved from 1976 to 1985, looking for unanticipated side effects. Of those, 102 drugs were found to have side effects harmful enough to warrant withdrawal from the market or major changes in labels to warn of the hazards. The FDA criticized the study whereas others endorsed it. *San Jose Mercury News,* 27 May 1990, p. 26A.

29. *Wall Street Journal,* 30 January 1990, p. B4.

30. Extended coverage of the debate may be found in *Food Safety: Where Are We?* U. S. Senate, Committee on Agriculture, Nutrition, and Forestry (July 1979); and Richard A. Merrill, "FDA's Implementation of the Delaney Clause," *Yale Journal on Regulation* (Winter 1988): 1–88.

31. *San Jose Mercury News,* 20 February 1990, p. 12A: Ken Flieger, "How Safe Is Safe?" *FDA Consumer,* September 1988, pp. 16–17.

32. *Food Safety: Where Are We?* p. 366.

33. William W. Lowrance, *Of Acceptable Risk: Science and the Determination of Safety,* as summarized by Carol S. Kramer, "Food Safety: The Consumer Side of the Environmental Issue," Discussion Paper FAP90-06, Resources for the Future, 1990, p. 12. See also Michael Specter, "Fear of Frying," *The Washington Post National Weekly Edition,* May 15–21, 1989, p. 9.

34. Senate Report No. 1301, 89th Congress, Second Session (1966), pp. 1–2.

35. For a more detailed and more interesting excursion through these standards, look into the *Code of Federal Regulations* Title 49.

36. NHTSA, *Motor Vehicle Safety,* 1979, p. 45.

37. Ibid., p. 46.

38. *Wall Street Journal,* 25 August 1981, p. 22.

39. Sam Peltzman, "The Effects of Automobile Safety Regulation," *Journal of Political Economy* (July/Aug., 1975): 667–725. The basic assumption is that people have a fairly fixed preference for risk and therefore increase driving "intensity" as the inherent risk of autos falls. This contrasts with the assumption underlying regulation which is that there is a fairly fixed driving "intensity" and that safety features thereby reduce overall risk. Query: Does the fact that accidents rise markedly in rainy weather, during holiday periods, and on certain obviously hazardous stretches of road indicate fixed risk preference or fixed driving intensity in varying risk situations?

40. NHTSA, *Traffic Safety '78,* p. 6.

41. For a critique of Peltzman see Leon S. Robertson, "A Critical Analysis of Peltzman's, 'The Effects of Automobile Safety Regulation,'" *Journal of Economic Issues* (September 1977): 587–600. See also T. J. Zlatoper, "Factors Affecting Motor Vehicle Deaths in the USA: Some Cross-Sectional Evidence," *Applied Economics* (June 1987): pp. 753–761.

42. U. S. House, Committee on Interstate and Foreign Commerce, Subcommittee on Oversight and Investigations, *Federal Regulation and Regulatory Reform,* 94th Congress, 2nd Session (1976), p. 170.

43. Robert W. Crandall, Howard K. Gruenspecht, Theodore E. Keeler, and Lester B. Lave, *Regulating the Automobile* (Washington, DC: Brookings Institution, 1986), p. 69.

44. Ibid., p. 77.

45. Secretary of Transportation, *Public Notice Concerning Motor Vehicle Occupant Crash Protection,* June 9, 1976.

46. *Better Enforcement of Safety Requirements Needed By the Consumer Product Safety Commission,* Report by the Comptroller General of the United States (GAO), HRD-76-148 (July 26, 1976), p. 1.

47. *Federal Code of Regulations,* Title 16, Chapter II, Section 1508, 4, p. 174.

48. Steven Kelman, "Regulation by the Numbers—A Report on the Consumer Product Safety Commission," *Public Interest* (Summer 1974), p. 86. Kudos may also go to CPSC's poison prevention packaging standards, which are *performance* rather than design standards. They are phrased in terms of how *difficult* it is for a large sample of children between the ages of 12 and 51 months to open containers and how *easy* it is for adults to open these same containers. They require: "(1) Child-resistant effectiveness of not less than 85 percent without demonstration and not less than 80 percent after a demonstration of the proper means of opening. . . . (2) Adult-use effectiveness of not less than 90 percent . . ." where the adults are "age 18 to 45 years inclusive, with no overt physical or mental handicaps." CFR Title 16, Chapter II, p. 330–331.

49. Consumer Product Safety Commission, *Annual Report 1981,* Part II, pp. 176–190.

50. U. S. Consumer Product Safety Commission, "Accomplishments in 1990–1991,"mimeo. A major problem with CPSC's recalls (and those of NHTSA as well) is that quite frequently, relatively few of the offending products are ever actually replaced or repaired. A CPSC 1978 study revealed that in 36 recall campaigns involving nearly 2½ million small electrical appliances, an average of only 12 percent of the items were repaired or replaced. This understates the success rate because the 12 percent makes no allowance for products retired from service or repaired independently of the campaigns. Still, the rate is low, apparently because of (a) inadequate publicity, (b) inadequate consumer incentive, and (c) a "numbness" to hazards brought on by so many recalls. *Consumer Reports* (January 1981), pp. 45–48.

51. For a recent critique see W. Kip Viscusi, *Regulating Consumer Product Safety* (Washington, DC: American Enterprise Institute, 1984).

52. Kenneth J. Meier, *Regulation: Politics, Bureaucracy, and Economics* (New York: St. Martin's Press, 1985), p. 106. See also *Washington Post National Weekly Edition,* December 24, 1984, p. 33.

53. *Newsweek,* April 18, 1988, pp. 47–48; *San Jose Mercury News,* 20 April 1990, p. 12A.

54. Warren Brown, "Defects in Consumer Protection," *Washington Post National Weekly Edition,* May 27–June 2, 1991, p. 32.

55. *Wall Street Journal,* 30 April 1981, p. 48.

Chapter 22

Labor Safety and Health: OSHA

*[S]ince the Occupational Safety
and Health Act was enacted, its
implementation has aroused very deep
felt reactions of all sorts. On the one
hand, it has been praised by workers
as a program that has provided the
protections needed to make workers
safe. On the other hand, it has been
denounced by employers as creating a
petty bureaucracy whose inspectors are
asked to enforce ridiculous regulations
and harass employers for minor
infractions.*
— *Senator Alan Cranston*

In 1989 a chemical plant exploded in Pasadena, Texas, killing 23 workers, injuring 124 others, and tosing metal debris as far as six miles away. Less violent dangers also threaten workers. Experts estimate, for instance, that by the end of this century as many as 200,000 deaths in the United States will have been caused by asbestos-related diseases.

In 1970 Congress overwhelmingly approved the Occupational Safety and Health Act in hope of cutting workplace casualties. At the time, job-related accidents were producing 15,000 deaths and 2.2 million disabling injuries annually, and job-related health hazards were causing perhaps as many as 100,000 deaths and 400,000 new cases of occupational disease each year. The good intentions behind the OSH Act still win everybody's blessing. But the Occupational Safety and Health Administration (OSHA), which implements the act, has become one of the most controversial agencies in Washington.

Business organizations like the Chamber of Commerce and the National Association of Manufacturers applaud the idea of reduced worker risk but vilify OSHA for the following:

- Perpetrating misguided, "Mickey Mouse" standards not related to safety and health.
- Arbitrary and inconsistent enforcement actions, often amounting to harassment.
- A lack of results, a complete failure to reduce death, injury, and disease despite enormous compliance costs.[1]

Unionized labor stands staunchly in defense, saying that the OSH Act "is a sound law; it is an effective law, and it is a law which is absolutely essential to the future well-being of American workers and their families."[2] Yet even these friends of OSHA voice qualms, complaining that standards are too lax, that inspection personnel are too sparse, that delays in enforcement are all too common.

Our review of OSHA covers standards first and enforcement activities second, followed by discussions of controversies and proposals for reform. A distinction between safety (against accidents like falls) and health (against diseases like cancer) is maintained throughout.

By way of preliminary clarification, be aware that states can set up their own programs of workers protection which, if approved by OSHA, receive federal funding and supplant federal authority. Moreover, OSHA effects do not detract from workman's compensation programs, which compensate victims and their families for job-related casualties while at the same time protecting employers from costly negligence suits. The OSHA approach attempts to prevent loss in the first place rather than smooth its aftermath.

I. Standards

A. Broad Standards

Congress stated OSHA's goal in general terms: "to assure so far as possible every working man and woman in the Nation safe and healthy working conditions."[3] To guide OSHA in determining what is safe and healthy, the OSH Act goes on to say that OSHA can impose standards "reasonably necessary or appropriate to provide safe or healthful employment and places of employment." For toxic substances, the act calls for protection "to the extent feasible," which is a bit more specific than the "reasonably necessary" language applicable to all risks, but not much.[4] These vague, broad standards have touched off intense legal battles, as we shall see.

B. Narrow Standards

To assist OSHA's launching, Congress ordered OSHA to adopt existing "national consensus standards." These were voluntary safety and health standards developed prior to the OSH Act by industry trade associations or research organizations such as the National Fire Protection Association. When arguing against the establishment of OSHA, business lobbyists claimed these consensus standards made government intervention unnecessary. So, assuming they were sound, OSHA's first director adopted thousands of them hastily. Unfortunately, these consensus standards were riddled with obsolete, inane, irrelevant, and even stupid provisions, leading OSHA into a concern for such things as the shape of toilet seats and the presence of hooks on restroom walls. The resulting ridicule heaped on OSHA lingers to this day, even though OSHA purged these standards of over 900 faulty provisions in 1978.

Two characteristics further marred OSHA's early standards, characteristics that to some extent remain. First, the standards were dominated by *design* standards rather than *performance* standards (in part because of their consensus origins). That is, they were specification-oriented rather than performance-oriented. Ladders had to have rungs one inch thick rather than support a capacity of 500 pounds. There are advantages to design standards, such as ease of inspection enforcement and clarity for compliance. But there are also disadvantages, such as interference with safety innovations, a frequent failure to achieve the desired result, and greater expense as compared to cheaper but equally safe alternatives. Starting with the Carter Administration, OSHA moved to rectify this bias by converting many of its design standards into performance standards.

The second further failing of OSHA's early standards was their emphasis on *safety* to the neglect of *health*. One of the major justifications for regulating worker protection is workers' ignorance of hazards, and the ignorance problem arises most starkly in connection with health, not safety. If a forklift truck lacks a driver's canopy to catch falling objects, or if a section of guard rail is missing from a catwalk 100 feet above a plant floor, the hazard is readily apparent to workers. But what about those who handle betanaphthylamine, or those who breathe small

---

Thumbnail Sketch 10: Occupational Safety and Health Administration

---

Established: 1970

Purpose: To develop and enforce workplace safety and health standards.

Legislative Authority: Occupational Safety and Health Act of 1970.

Regulatory Activity: Sets and enforces safety and health standards; engages in liaison, education, and consultation activities with employers, employees, and trade associations. OSHA's decisions are subject to review by the Occupational Safety and Health Review Commission (OSHRC). The National Institute for Occupational Safety and Health (NIOSH) conducts research and recommends standards to OSHA.

Organization: A division of the Department of Labor headed by an Assistant Secretary of Labor. (OSHRC is an independent commission, and NIOSH is housed in the Health and Human Services Department.)

Budget: 1991 estimate: $286 million.

Staff: 1991 estimate: 2,478.

---

amounts of vinyl chloride gas when manufacturing plastic pipe? The danger is less apparent, and the unhealthy consequences may emerge only after considerable delay.

The seriousness of health problems can be illustrated by a few startling statistics. Occupational diseases take an estimated 100,000 lives per year. Just one substance can be devastating. Many thousands of workers were excessively exposed to asbestos during the 1940s through 1960s, before its carcinogenic properties were known. That exposure now accounts for up to 10,000 cancers each year and will continue to do so for the next 20 years.

Respectable standard setting for health was delayed for nearly two decades, partly because of President Reagan's ideological opposition to the agency, partly because of persistent legal challenges by businesses, and partly because of the inherent difficulties in assessing health risks. During OSHA's first eighteen years, it completed only twenty-four substance-specific health regulations. In contrast, the National Cancer Institute had by that time identified 110 workplace chemicals that were confirmed or suspected carcinogens. Other authorities were urging new or

improved standards for 300 chemicals.[5] Finally, in 1989, OSHA set and strengthened standards on 376 toxic chemicals in the workplace, significantly reducing the risks experienced by an estimated 21 million workers.[6] The substances now covered include benzene, perchloroethylene, lead, formaldehyde, mercury, acrylonitrile, and cotton dust.

Reinvigorated under the Bush Administration, OSHA has recently turned its attention to some new and especially alarming hazards. Hospital orderlies are often pricked with needles hidden in trash. Paramedics get splattered with blood. Four million other health-care workers experience similar exposure to AIDS and other blood-borne diseases. Although AIDS is the most publicized risk, more than 200 health-care workers die every year from hepatitis B or its complications. In 1990 OSHA proposed new standards that for the first time curbed biological hazards in the workplace.

Table 22–1 summarizes several OSHA standards by year of issue, by safety or health classification, by risk level, and by estimated cost of compliance in millions of dollars per life saved. The costs obviously cover a wide range—added

Table 22–1
Risks and Cost-Effectiveness of Selected OSHA Regulations, by Cost Per Premature
Death Averted (1990 Dollars)

Regulation	Year Issued	Health (H) or Safety (S)	Mortality Risk per Million Exposed	Cost per Death Averted (million of $)
Underground construction standard	1989	S	38,700	$ 0.1
Standards for servicing auto wheels	1984	S	630	0.4
Concrete & masonry construction standards	1988	S	630	0.6
Crane and suspended platform standards	1988	S	81,000	0.7
Trenching & excavation standards	1989	S	14,310	1.5
Grain dust explosion standards	1987	S	9,450	2.8
Benzene occupational exposure standards	1987	H	39,600	8.9
Ethylene oxide exposure standards	1984	H	1,980	20.5
Acrylonitrile exposure standards	1978	H	42,300	51.5
Lockout/tagout when servicing machinery	1989	S	4	70.9
Arsenic exposure standards	1978	H	14,800	106.9

Source: The Council on Environmental Quality, *Environmental Quality*, 21st Annual Report (Washington, DC: U.S. Government Printing Office, 1991), pp. 282–283.

safety in underground construction work being achieved very cheaply compared to reducing health risks from arsenic exposure, for example.

OSHA may set a permanent standard for safety or health on its own initiative, in response to the appeals of employees or employers, or in response to the recommendations of the National Institute for Occupational Safety and Health (NIOSH), which was also established by the OSH Act.

Regardless of where a standard's impetus originates, the procedures for developing standards are, as in the case of NHTSA, CPSC, and other such agencies, quite complex and protracted. Notices, hearings, and even judicial appeals are involved. The first appellate authority to rule on questions concerning OSHA's standards is the Occupational Safety and Health Review Commission (OSHRC), which is an independent agency comprised of three commissioners appointed by the president.[7] After OSHRC, which was established by the OSH Act for the express purpose of reviewing OSHA decisions, appeals may be pursued in the federal courts. The Supreme Court's rulings on standards for benzene and cotton dust occupy us later.

II. Enforcement

Like those of police parking patrols, OSHA's enforcement activities center on inspections and citations. Consultations with employers and education programs for employees also play a part. Certification and permit activities, so prominent in activities of the FDA and the EPA, play no part at all.

A. Inspections

Robert Stewart Smith once quipped that "the typical establishment will see an OSHA inspector about as often as we see Halley's comet."[8] There is much truth in this. In 1991 there were 1,200 OSHA inspectors for roughly 6 million workplaces in the United States. As a result, the agency could typically visit no more than about 2 percent of the workplaces. The Texas chemical plant mentioned at the outset had not received a comprehensive safety examination for fourteen years before its explosion in 1989. In the twenty-three states where OSHA standards are enforced by state authorities, the record seems especially lax. In 1991, for example, twenty-five workers in a North Carolina poultry processing plant died in a fire when locked exit doors blocked their escape. North Carolina had only twenty-seven inspectors at the time to watch over 180,000 employers—that is, only one inspector for every 7,000 employers. It is not surprising, then, that the poultry plant had never been inspected in its eleven years of operation.[9]

To the limited extent they do occur, OSHA inspections are of four kinds: programmed inspections, accident investigations, employee complaints, and abatement follow-ups:

1. *Programmed inspections,* by far the largest in number, are scheduled on the basis of sample selection. The sample is not random, because every OSHA administration has made an effort to target its inspections on high-hazard industries such as construction, logging, longshoring, and metal fabricating. Early administrations were less successful in this effort than recent administrations, partly because data deficiencies hampered target sampling. Inspections of small fruitcake bakeries with forty years of totally harmless operation were not uncommon. Rather than risk the wrath of such businesses, the Reagan Administration drew its focus more narrowly than any previous administration by announcing a sweeping exemption for nearly three-fourths of all U.S. manufacturing companies.[10]

2. *Accident investigations* are inspections triggered by fatalities and catastrophies. Some states also respond to reports of amputations, permanent disfigurements, and lengthy hospitalizations.

3. *Employee complaints* also trigger unscheduled inspections. Given that workers are OSHA's main constituency, unionized workers especially, it is not surprising that in times past OSHA responded eagerly to employee complaints. OSHA has grown circumspect about complaint investigations, however, inspecting only where hazards appear serious while handling other complaints by mail or telephone.

4. Finally, OSHA conducts *follow-up inspections* in situations where citations for serious, willful, or repeated violations have been issued, or where a court has issued a restraining order in an imminent danger situation. Follow-up inspections for nonserious violations are rare.

To round out this statistical survey, notice that most inspections are for safety rather than health, revealing a continuing tilt in favor of safety.

B. Citations and Other Remedies

In recent years slightly more than half of all inspected workplaces have been found in compliance. Citations greeted the violations of the remainder, multiple citations in instances of multiple offenses.

Monetary penalties put bite in these citations, varying in average severity from several thousand dollars for "willful" violations to several hundred dollars for "serious" or "repeat" violations to only a few dollars for "nonserious" offenses.

Just as parking tickets stimulate people's frustration and irritation, so too OSHA's citations have often proved annoying, provoking charges of harassment and worse. For example, small businessman Irvin Dawson attracted some press attention when in 1974 he closed his Cleveland business for one day to protest "the loss of rights of [American] citizenry under the so-called OSHA." An OSHA inspector had cited him for such nonserious violations as the following:

- Failing to post a copy of the act (which he never received).
- Failure to maintain a separate OSHA folder even though he had all necessary records.
- The presence of an "insufficiently" guarded fan, which was dust-covered, its cord wrapped around the base, without brushes, and obviously not in use.[11]

Because of reform, these kinds of cases now seem rare. Indeed, under the Reagan Administration, opposite tendencies held sway. There were numerous instances of alarming hazards drawing only minor fines. For example:

> On July 23, 1984, a Unocal Corp. refinery in Lemont, Ill., erupted in an immense fireball, rocking the ground for 50 miles. The accident killed 17 and injured 17. In proposing fines totaling $31,000, OSHA cited the company for improper inspection and maintenance of pressure vessels and lack of

training for fire-brigade members, among other things.[12]

Only recently, under the Bush Administration, have fines risen to notable magnitudes. In November 1991, OSHA fined Angus Chemical Company $10 million after eight workers were killed in a fertilizer plant explosion. This set a new record for fines, the previous record having been established only two months earlier when OSHA fined Citgo $5.8 million in connection with an oil refinery fire that killed six workers.[13] In 1990 OSHA fined employers $63 million stemming from 99,225 violations serious enough to threaten injury or death.

Fines are not the only remedy. OSHA's equivalent of a recall is the *imminent danger* citation, which applies when there is reasonable certainty that the hazard threatens death or serious physical injury before it can be corrected by normal procedures. If the employer fails to rectify the violation immediately, OSHA can go to the nearest federal district court for legal action.

Firms taking offense at being accused of offenses can appeal to the Occupational Safety and Health Review Commission (OSHRC). Past appeals, which run into the thousands, reveal that employers can be just as "nitpicky" as OSHA. For example, violators have argued that their citations should be invalidated on grounds that nonemployees had notified OSHA of the discovered dangers and that a roof needed no railing because it was not, strictly speaking, an "open-sided floor or platform."[14] Many cases get into the federal courts.

C. New Directions in Enforcement

To encourage voluntary compliance and cooperation, OSHA has developed a number of programs that make it seem less like a club-wielding policeman. These programs include maintaining liaison activities, providing technical services and information, consulting with employees, and operating a wide variety of training programs for employers and employees. Consulting, for instance, includes on-site visits by *non*enforcement personnel to (1) survey workplaces, (2) inform employers of hazards, and (3) suggest corrective measures. Consultations are of greatest benefit to small businesses lacking the wherewith-all to hire in-house safety and health experts or to buy the services of private consulting firms. The highly technical nature of many OSHA regulations necessitates expert interpretation, and OSHA consultation can inexpensively provide that expert interpretation for those who want to comply without also risking citations and penalties.[15]

An innovative break from normal enforcement procedures is the labor-management committee. Representatives of both labor and management form in-plant committees to formulate safety and health programs, respond to worker complaints, conduct monthly inspections, and see to it that hazards are eliminated. OSHA approval of a committee program wins exemption for that plant from OSHA's normal inspection-citation procedures.

III. Key Controversies

A. Benefit-Cost Analysis

1. THE ISSUE

The OSH Act's history reveals no recognition by Congress or by those testifying before Congress that there is a trade-off between benefit and cost—that is, that added benefit from risk reduction requires added cost. As John Mendeloff summarized his review of the record:

> The most striking characteristic of the testimony and the congressional commentary was their idealism and their silence on the costs of regulation. In the whole legislative history, I found only two brief statements by Republican conservatives that point out that intervention can do more harm than good. In contrast, the idea that even one injury or

fatality is too many is frequently repeated, along with assertions about the infinite value of human life.[16]

In the end, Congress gave only implicit recognition to the problem of cost by vaguely saying in the act that standards need to go no further than "reasonably necessary" and "to the extent feasible." OSHA interpreted these qualifiers to mean that, in general, *costs need not* be weighed against benefits. Costs would be considered relevant only when they were so high as to seriously jeopardize the financial condition of the industry or its companies—when, that is, plant doors would be closed and workers would lose their jobs. OSHA's refusal to weigh benefits and costs was repeatedly challenged by business, but the issue was not resolved until the Supreme Court ruled in OSHA's favor in *American Textile Manufacturers Institute* v. *Raymond Donovan, Secretary of Labor* (1981).[17]

To prepare the ground for our discussion of this important case, we must first explore some of the reasons behind Congress's and OSHA's aversion to benefit-cost analysis (though under Reagan and Bush, OSHA has relied more on benefit-cost).

2. COST ESTIMATION

Rough estimates put the annual cost of health and safety regulation somewhere around $8 billion.[18] This can be no more than a very rough guess because the cost of specific individual standards is itself typically speculative. The classic example concerns vinyl chloride, which causes a fatal form of liver cancer. In 1974, after discovering the problem, OSHA proposed a standard that would reduce the allowable level of vinyl chloride gas exposure from 500 parts per million parts of air to 1 part per million (ppm). Industry studies predicted that the strict standard would shut down all polyvinyl chloride plants and severely cripple the entire plastics industry, costing the economy $65 to $90 *billion* in lost GNP and eliminating between 1.7 and 2.2 million jobs.

OSHA did not flinch and imposed the 1 ppm standard anyway.

What happened then? It turned out that the total cost did not exceed $250 million, few workers actually lost their jobs, and the product's price rose only about 6 percent.[19] These costs were substantial, but they were hardly as bad as the industry's dire projections.

The example indicates the practical difficulty of projecting a proposed standard's costs. Those who have the best data—industry members—also have an incentive to exaggerate costs. Even when costs are not deliberately exaggerated, they may be inflated from a failure to account for technological change. In the case of vinyl chloride, for example, the industry's credibility was never questioned. Technological developments after the standard was set saved the day, the standard, and the industry. In short, it was a "technology-forcing" standard that happened to pay off. Its great success has undoubtedly fed OSHA's past doubts about relying heavily on benefit-cost analysis.

OSHA's rather casual attitude toward costs in the past is further explained by its bias favoring engineering controls and opposing personal protective equipment. Guarding workers against excessive noise, toxic fumes, and other health hazards can often be achieved much more cheaply by means of earmuffs, respirators, and other personal protective equipment than by insulating partitions, ventilation systems, and other engineering alterations to production processes. Yet OSHA has shown partiality for engineering controls on grounds that "personal protective equipment can be as effective as engineering controls only if it is carefully implemented (for example, to assure proper fit and maintenance.)"[20] Critics of the agency poohpooh this rationalization, pointing instead to political and idealogical reasons, such as workers' general dislike for respirators and earmuffs plus union opposition. Moreover, economists argue that physical effectiveness alone is not the issue

but, rather, *cost-effectiveness*. And judged by cost-effectiveness, personal protective equipment should receive the favorable bias, not engineering controls. For example, one study estimates that the total cost of achieving an industrial noise limit of 85 decibels by personal protective gear would be $2.4 billion, considerably less than the $19.4 billion cost of engineering controls.[21]

Business interests, it need hardly be said, favor personal gear, countering labor's position and putting OSHA in a bind. OSHA's solution has been a compromise. Its health standards have mandated engineering controls "to the extent feasible," thereby appeasing its labor constituents. At the same time, however, OSHA has eased industry's burden by allowing very gradual implementation of those controls. Its lead standard allows a phase-in over ten years. And its cotton dust standard had a four-year grace period.

3. BENEFITS

Even though the vinyl chloride standard proved to be economically feasible, its costs were nevertheless high relative to the risk reduction—$9 million per life likely to be saved, by one estimate.[22] This means that, *by implication*, OSHA has put an extremely high value on human life when considering benefits. (See Table 22–1 again.) Many economists critically point out that OSHA's implicit values greatly exceed the values estimated by economists and used by other agencies, such as the EPA and the FAA. Business interests criticize OSHA without specifying their benefit values.[23]

Rather than criticize OSHA's high implicit values, John Mendeloff asks "why?" and then comes up with some interesting answers:

■ Workers are not perceived as choosing their risks as freely as consumers choose theirs because of occupational and geographic immobilities. Thus, what is appropriate for other agencies may not be appropriate for OSHA.

- Spending great amounts to save identifiable victims, such as workers trapped in a coal mine cave-in, is commonplace. Quite often the potential victims of occupational hazards are in a small, identifiable group.
- Unionized labor is OSHA's chief client, and labor leaders give tremendous weight to protection. Thus, for political reasons, OSHA's benefit values are high.[24]

As a matter of *principle,* then, OSHA tends to treasure *any* perceived benefits. Probing further, we find that in the past OSHA has resisted explicit benefit computation as a *practical* matter also. As former labor secretary Ray Marshall once said, "Uncertainty involved in assessing the health benefits of regulations renders precise cost-benefit analysis difficult."[25] Indeed, OSHA used "uncertainty" to excuse itself from reckoning even the nonmonetary benefits of its benzene standard, and the result was a major Supreme Court case (*American Petroleum Institute* v. *Marshall*).

Benzene is used to make solvents, pesticides, detergents, and other petrochemical products. High exposure, well above 10 parts per million parts of air, has been associated with leukemia. In 1977, OSHA ordered a sharp reduction in exposure limit from the old 10 ppm standard to a new 1 ppm standard without evidence that the old 10 ppm was in fact unsafe. The petroleum industry challenged the new standard's benefits, arguing in federal court that it would prevent, at most, only one case of leukemia every 15 to 38 years. OSHA defended itself by arguing that the evidence was "too imprecise" to establish risk below the old 10 ppm standard. It was enough to know, said OSHA, that benzene caused leukemia at high levels of exposure, because that established the absence of a "safe level" below which exposure would be assuredly risk-free.[26]

The Supreme Court's 1980 judgment of the benzene case is itself somewhat uncertain because five of the nine justices wrote opinions. Nevertheless, the court struck down the strict new benzene standard largely because it was based more on speculation than on scientific fact.[27] Justice Stevens, writing for four members of the court, said that OSHA failed in issuing the benzene standard to establish that it was "reasonably necessary and appropriate" to remedy a "significant risk." OSHA had not obtained any "empirical evidence" or "opinion testimony" that "exposure to benzene at or below the 10 ppm level had ever in fact caused leukemia." As a result of this case, then, OSHA could no longer blithely *assume* that, once a substance has been shown to cause cancer at some (high) level of exposure, it can require employers to reduce exposure to the lowest "feasible" level. Benefits must be based on actual estimates, not on assumptions.

As a result of the benzene case, OSHA developed a capability in risk analysis—the study of health risks and ways to reduce hazards. Then, in the late 1980s, OSHA revived its efforts to establish a 1 ppm standard for benzene when new evidence showed that the established 10 ppm standard was indeed not safe enough. At 10 ppm, workers ran risks of leukemia and bone cancer that were three and four times greater than the risks facing workers not exposed to benzene.[28]

4. BENEFITS AND COSTS TOGETHER

Although the Supreme Court ruled in the benzene case that benefits could not be merely assumed, it did not go so far as to say that benefits must be weighed against costs. That issue was addressed in *American Textile Manufacturers Institute* v. *Donovan,* the landmark "cotton dust" case of 1981.[29] Approximately 800,000 textile workers are exposed to cotton dust, which causes byssinosis, or "brown lung," a disease that produces breathlessness, chronic cough, and occasionally death. OSHA's standard set a ceiling of 0.2 milligrams of dust per cubic meter of air. The standard's benefits and costs were hotly disputed by OSHA and the textile industry. OSHA claimed that brown lung afflicted 20 percent of the textile workers, whereas the industry said the proportion was only 2 percent. OSHA estimated the cost of compliance to be $656.5 million, whereas the industry's estimate was $2 billion, or three times as much. The key issue before the court, however, was not whose numbers were correct. Rather, it was whether benefits had to be weighed against costs to establish a health standard's validity. OSHA said "no." Industry urged "yes."

The Supreme Court decided "no." After noting that Congress can expressly call for benefit-cost analysis when it wants to (as it has for dams and other water projects), the court went on to point out that the OSH Act is devoid of benefit-cost language. Moreover, the court felt that requiring a benefit-cost test for workplace health standards "would inevitably" lead to less protection and would violate the law. By using the word "feasible," which means "capable of being done," Congress "defined the basic relationship between costs and benefits by placing the 'benefit' of worker health above all other considerations save those making attainment of this 'benefit' unachievable." Thus, the court, like OSHA, defined feasibility in technical rather than economic terms.

Notice that the court did not say that benefit-cost could not be used—only that it need not be used. Thus, OSHA could use benefit-cost analysis if it wanted to, but such was not absolutely necessary. During the Reagan and Bush Administration, the agency did after all turn to greater use of benefit-cost.

B. Effects of OSHA

Another hot controversy centers on the question of whether OSHA has in fact made any headway in reducing job-related casualties. Business spokespeople argue that "the available data on workplace injuries suggest that OSHA activities have not brought about demonstrable reductions in the incidence of injuries and illnesses in the workplace."[30] Union spokesmen argue otherwise, saying:

> Fatalities have decreased 10% during the program's history; that means the lives of thousands of workers have been saved. Similarly, thousands of workers have been spared serious injuries with a 15% overall decline in total injuries during the program's history.[31]

Academic researchers are also divided, but their work merits closer attention. The problem with raw data on injury and illness rates, such as those just alluded to, is that injuries and illnesses are affected by many factors other than OSHA. These other factors are especially important in assessing trends in job-related illnesses as opposed to injuries. Illnesses like cancer are caused by such nonoccupational factors as smoking, air pollution, and food impurities. Thus, for example, it is often impossible to tell whether an asbestos worker's lung cancer is job-related or not, and correspondingly whether a decline in lung cancer among asbestos workers is due to reduced exposures on the job or improved conditions among other possible causes. Good studies of OSHA's impact would take these other factors into account to isolate the role of regulation. Academic studies typically attempt to do this through multiple-regression analysis. Unfortunately, such analysis has been conducted only for the safety side of OSHA's efforts. For health, there is too much muddling by other factors and too many impurities in the available data to permit a retrospective estimate of OSHA's impact on illness. Moreover, health analysis is severely hampered by the fact that occupational illness often strikes only after *accumulated* exposure and a *long lag*. Liver cancer of the type caused by vinyl chloride, for instance has a latency period of ten to thirty years.

What, then, do academic studies of OSHA's safety performance show? They show little if any aggregate impact, looking at overall injury rates at industry-wide levels. In an early study, Robert S. Smith analyzed pre- and post-OSHA injury rates across industries to see if those industries receiving OSHA's special attention improved relative to those not targeted by OSHA. There was no significant difference.[32] John Mendeloff constructed a statistical model of factors causing temporal variations in aggregate U.S. injury rates *prior* to OSHA (including such factors as percentage of males in the workforce 18 to 24 years of age, a factor that increases injuries because these fellows tend to be careless or inexperienced). He then checked to see if observed injury rates *after* OSHA were in fact lower than could be accounted for by these other, non-OSHA factors, and he found that they were not.[33] William Curington shifted the focus from the *frequency* with which injuries occur to the *severity* of injuries. Yet his findings were similar. OSHA apparently has had no significant impact on the overall severity of workplace injuries.[34]

The only studies that show significant reductions in the frequency and severity of injuries in association with OSHA's efforts are those using disaggregated data—that is, data on specific types of injuries or data on specific plants inspected by OSHA. Mendeloff, for instance, applied his before-and-after technique to check the trend in injuries when workers were caught in or between machinery. These injuries, he argued, were of the type most likely to be affected by OSHA standards. Using data from California, Mendeloff found that post-OSHA injury rates were as much as 30 percent lower than they would have been otherwise.[35] Because these caught-in-between injuries account for fewer than 10 percent of all injuries, extrapolation of these and related results to an aggregate level led Mendeloff to some small but not negligible numbers:

> Perhaps the total effect of OSHA on the manufacturing rate has been to reduce it by 3 to 5%. For the construction industry the range might be sim-

ilar, but for most sectors the effects would almost certainly be smaller. . . . For the entire private sector, the reduction might be on the order of 2 to 3%—approximately 40,000 to 60,000 out of the two million disabling injuries that occur nationally each year.[36]

Robert S. Smith undertook a different disaggregated study, looking at the impact of OSHA's 1973–1974 inspections on the injury experience of specific industrial plants. He found a statistically significant 16 percent reduction in injury rates for the 1973 inspections and a nonsignificant reduction of 5 percent for 1974.[37]

A major problem with all these studies concerns the accuracy of the data they rely on. During the late 1980s, it was discovered that numerous companies—many of them large and famous like Chrysler, General Dynamics, and Scott Paper—were willfully underreporting injuries and illnesses.[38] A team of researchers from the University of California at Davis discovered in 1987 that only 60 percent of all work-related injuries and illnesses suffered at semiconductor manufacturing plants were being reported to OSHA. The 40 percent that were omitted were mostly minor injuries like acid burns on fingers, but the revelation was rather startling nonetheless.[39] This extensive underreporting of injuries implies that statistical analyses of OSHA's impact may be underestimating OSHA's influence.

Let's set aside this problem of underreporting for the moment, however. Let's assume that the disaggregated studies are reasonably accurate, that OSHA has indeed had a favorable impact but the impact is so minimal as to fuel critics' charges that "OSHA has not affected injury rates significantly in either a statistical or a practical sense."[40] It is natural, then, that we ask, "Why are the results so small?" And a search for answers reveals many reasons why OSHA *should not be expected* to have much of an impact on overall injury rates.

First, and most important, a large proportion of injuries are apparently caused by human error or human recklessness instead of faulty tools, unguarded machinery, or other environmental factors controllable by standards. Another large proportion is caused by some interaction of human and environmental factors. Exactly what these proportions are is difficult to determine. An official of the National Safety Council estimated on the basis of workman's compensation cases that 19 percent of occupational accidents are caused solely by human factors, 63 percent are caused by some combination of human and environmental factors, and only 18 percent are caused wholly by environmental elements.[41]

A second reason for doubting that OSHA, at best, could not generate dramatic results is that many hazards arise from temporary circumstances—such as wet floors or trash-blocked aisles, which precipitate falls. Given the intermittence and in many plants the nonexistence of OSHA's inspections, such hazards are resistant to the OSHA approach. Taking this temporary element and the human element together, President Carter's Interagency Task Force on Workplace Safety and Health concluded that no more than "perhaps 25% of injuries are preventable by enforcement of present OSHA standards."[42]

A third and rather obvious possible reason for OSHA's ineffectiveness is that compliance may have been lax until recently. The penalties levied have been piddling in all but a few instances, averaging just a few dollars per violation. Moreover, inspections have been, from the typical employer's view, rare, if not as rare as Halley's comet. (When enforcement fell sharply during the Reagan Administration, work-related injuries and illnesses rose. Some observers say

---

Table 22–2
Projected Benefits of Selected Occupational Health Regulations

Regulation	Benefits	Comments
Asbestos (Settle)	630 to 2,563 deaths avoided per year (United States) from asbestosis and cancer. Social cost of disease avoided is $164 to $652 million per year.	Benefits do not occur until many years after imposition of regulation. Estimate includes medical costs plus cost to workers from lost life expectancy.
Vinyl Chloride (Ashford, Zolt et al.)	Approximately 2,000 deaths from all types of cancer avoided in the period 1976–2000 as a result of OSHA vinyl chloride standard.	Takes into account worker mobility, job tenure, exposure variations.
Cotton dust (Research Triangle Institute)	Imposition of exposure limit of 0.2 mg/m^3 would avoid 1,749 cases of byssinosis per year initially. Eventually, imposition of 0.2 mg standard would result in decrease in total number of cases of byssinosis by 21,674.	Using the number of cases of byssinosis (brown lung) may be misleading, because it fails to differentiate between the different grades and severities of the disease.

Source: R. Settle, "Benefits and Costs of the Federal Asbestos Standard," U. S. Department of Labor, 1975; N. A. Ashford, E. M. Zolt et al., "Evaluating Chemical Regulations," U. S. Council on Environmental Quality, 1979; Research Triangle Institute, "Inflationary Impact Statement: Cotton Dust," U. S. Department of Labor, OSHA, 1979; all as reported by Center for Policy Alternatives at the Massachusetts Institute of Technology, *Benefits of Environmental, Health, and Safety Regulation*, U. S. Senate, Committee on Governmental Affairs (1980), p. 32.

these developments are causally related, but it is not clear that they are.[43])

In sum, the OSHA approach to injuries is inherently handicapped. Large aggregate results from it are simply not to be expected. This negative conclusion is probably less appropriate for *health* standards, given that human error and transient conditions probably contribute less to illness than to injury. Exposure limits backed by monitoring might have more potency here, once again underscoring the fact that OSHA's strong suit is really in health rather than safety. Unfortunately, full verification of these optimistic presumptions for health is impossible, given the grave difficulties in conducting retrospective tests of OSHA's impact on illness noted earlier. However, estimates of the prospective impact of health standards are available. Table 22–2 outlines forecast estimates of the benefits associated with three health standards mentioned previously, those for asbestos, vinyl chloride, and cotton dust.

Although to this point we have measured OSHA's impact in terms of injury, illness, and death rates, it is important to note in closing that these merely summarize benefits taking many alternative forms, some easily quantifiable, others not. A reduction in workplace casualties reduces workmen's compensation liabilities, disability and other income maintenance costs, medical expenses, and health insurance. Moreover, curbing casualties increases worker productivity by improving worker health, shrinking absenteeism, and diminishing worker turnover. Intangible benefits include lessened pain and suffering for workers and their families. Thus, even if OSHA's success is limited, the ramifications of that success might be considerable.[44]

IV. Policy Improvements

In light of what has been said, the goal of proposed policy changes should be sharper reductions in workplace casualties or greater economic efficiency or both. Proposed changes fitting this description can be divided into two classes, depending on how the main problems with past policy are perceived.

The *first* class of proposed changes might be called reforms in the *execution* of the present approach. Examples of previous changes along this line include (1) the abolition of over 900 "consensus" standards that were ridiculously obsolete, petty, and irrelevant, (2) the trend toward targeting inspections on industries and plants with the worst casualty records, and (3) OSHA's shift of emphasis away from safety toward health. These reforms never questioned the standards-inspection-penalty approach of direct regulation in concept or principle. Rather, they represented improvements in the execution of that approach. Critics urge further such changes, three of which we review: (1) greater use of cost-effectiveness in designing standards; (2) greater reliance on benefit-cost analysis in designing standards; and (3) a shift to more cooperative enforcement.

The *second* broad class of proposed changes covers those that do question the standards-inspection-penalty approach of direct regulation. These might be called *conceptual* changes because they assume that the present approach is inherently flawed. They imply abandonment of the present concept and urge movement toward rather radically different policies, such as an injury tax.

A. Changes in Execution of the Present Approach

1. COST EFFECTIVENESS
If a thousand lives can be saved by either method A or method B, but method A is much cheaper, then why not use method A? This is the essence of cost effectiveness. And this is essentially the query of economists when they question the wisdom of design standards and engineering controls. OSHA has acknowledged the faults of

design standards and has made an effort to replace many of them with performance standards, but OSHA's critics contend that the agency could do more. As for engineering controls, OSHA has rarely wavered from its insistence that engineering controls are preferable to personal protective equipment despite the fact that engineering controls are typically many times more costly and sometimes less protective of workers. Thus, a very commonly recommended change is that OSHA forsake its infatuation with engineering controls and adopt a more flexible stance toward personal protective equipment.

2. BENEFIT-COST ANALYSIS

The Supreme Court's "cotton dust" opinion said that OSHA *need not* weigh benefits against costs in formulating standards. The court did not go so far as to say that OSHA *could not* do so. Thus, a change toward greater reliance on benefit-cost was made by the Reagan Administration after Executive Order 12291 instructed that each regulation's benefits should exceed its costs. The trend toward benefit-cost assessment of proposed policies continued with the Bush Administration.

Unfortunately, benefit-cost still has serious problems in this context, as may be illustrated by the cotton-dust case. After the Supreme Court upheld the Carter Administration's standard, saying that benefit-cost need not be conducted, the Reagan White House ordered a benefit-cost review of the standard, apparently hoping to find grounds for its relaxation or termination.[45] In the end, the White House urged that the engineering controls be scrapped and replaced by respirators and close monitoring of workers' health. OSHA, however, in an unusual move, rebuffed the White House and retained the engineering control standard, largely because, by that time in 1983, 80 percent of the affected textile plants had *already* installed the necessary equipment. Actual experience with the controls showed that they were much less costly than the industry alleged in its

estimates challenging the rule in court ($182 million instead of $2 billion). Indeed, by that time, the industry itself opposed repeal of the engineering standard because it improved productivity and made the employees happier.[46]

In other words, the Reagan Administration did not use benefit-cost as an objective tool of analysis but as a pretext to abolish or relax regulations. Reagan's OSHA followed what *Business Week* called a "see no evil" policy.[47] Hence, when we note that still greater reliance on benefit-cost analysis might benefit the agency, we hasten to add that this tool ought to be used responsibly. Also, benefit-cost studies need not be followed slavishly, given the importance of noneconomic values in this area.

3. COOPERATIVE ENFORCEMENT

OSHA's critics doubt that a marked reduction in occupational casualties will ever occur without a marked reduction in the animosity business displays toward OSHA and its labor constituency. To this end, a number of recommended changes have been offered in hope of securing warm yet effective cooperation among all concerned. One major previous change, for instance, brought in-plant government-business consultations. Proposed changes, such as complete elimination of "first instance" penalties and less reliance on general duty clause citations, amount to little more than relaxed enforcement. But some prospective strides toward cooperation have merit and may help to quell what the National Association of Manufacturers calls a "rebellion" against "OSHA's impudence and imprudence."[48]

B. Changes in Concept: Diminishing Direct Regulation

When choosing its method of intervention, Congress gave no consideration to any approach other than the enforcement of standards. Thousands of occupational safety and health standards were already used to some degree by industry—the so-called consensus standards in particular, voluntarily developed and deployed. Moreover, the idea of *enforcing* standards had previously been tried for federal contractors and for a few industries receiving special congressional attention, coal mining in particular. Thus, the precedents were there. The standard-enforcement approach fit experience and ideology. Legislators and lobbyists alike consequently ignored other options.

1. INFORMATION AND EDUCATION

One other option that received last-minute recognition and secondary inclusion was the information and education option. Given that the main source of market failure in this area is the workers' ignorance of hazards, the provision of more information and training to workers would greatly help and would lessen the need for an elaborate standards-enforcement effort. As workers learn about hazards, they can demand higher, risk-adjusted wages or press for elimination of the risk, or adopt strategies to avoid it. Indeed, the OSH Act's provisions to keep workers informed and trained resulted from the efforts of Ralph Nader's staff, "whose skepticism toward both union and government bureaucrats led it to favor strengthening workers' capabilities to protect themselves."[49]

Current government efforts in this area exist. In the past these programs have been miniscule, however. Still more could be done.

2. INJURY TAXES

Rather than set standards and police them, the government could induce employers to reduce casualties by taxing injuries. The higher the tax, the greater the incentive to reduce injuries. Robert S. Smith, for example, estimates from 1970 data that an injury tax of $2,000 per injury would reduce the manufacturing injury rate an average of about 8.2 percent, whereas an injury tax of $4,000 would curb injuries about 16.3 percent.[50] The basic idea is that employers would improve safety to avoid these levies as long as the added

cost of such improvement was less than the cost of the prospective taxes.

In theory, there are a number of advantages to the tax approach as opposed to the standards-enforcement approach.

- *Ease of Administration:* Regular and detailed inspections of workplaces would no longer be necessary (although accident and complaint inspections could continue). Firms would have to report injuries to the "tax" authorities, but such reporting is already in place for workman's compensation and OSHA.

- *Sweep of Incentive:* The current approach cannot reach the 75 percent or so injuries caused by human factors or temporary conditions. A tax on *all* injuries would induce employers and employees to work on the *whole range* of factors causing injuries, not just the physical conditions specified by standards. We could expect closer attention to work practices, employee training, and safety-related personnel policies.

- *Prices Reflecting Social Costs:* If for technical reasons the injury tax had *no* effect on the injury rate of a high-risk industry, it would still be beneficial. The cost of the tax would raise the product's price, which in turn would shift consumer demand toward goods produced by safer means.

- *Cost Effectiveness:* With a tax, it is left up to the employers (and employees) to determine the best way to curtail injuries. Such flexibility will yield a variety of methods among different firms and industries, as employers seek out what for them are the most efficient ways of gaining safety. If, in other words, a tax achieved the same level of safety as the present standards, it would probably do so more cheaply than the present standards.

- *Innovation:* The inflexibilities of standards tend to stifle safety innovations. Thus, another possible advantage of an injury tax is that it would not block any avenues of technological change.[51]

The tax approach is not without its weaknesses. For one thing, it would not work well for illnesses because of the difficulty in linking specific cases of illness to workplace conditions and because of the long latency periods of many illnesses. A tax not on illnesses but on toxic emissions themselves might be possible, but then many of the advantages mentioned earlier would be lost. Emission fees are quite an attractive approach for curbing pollution generally, but they seem less attractive in the workplace, given that personal protective equipment could make emissions per se somewhat irrelevant.

Among other weaknesses of the tax approach, certainly the most crucial are political. No support for the tax approach comes from businessmen, labor leaders, or politicians. Businessmen apparently fear that their total cost burden (abatement costs plus tax costs) would be greater under a tax approach than at present. Labor leaders would probably lose some of the powers they presently enjoy as OSHA's prime political supporter. Moreover, as Mendeloff points out, "By allowing employers to choose the methods for reducing injuries, the injury tax could lead to difficult problems for unions: replacing or firing workers with bad accident records; stricter discipline for violation of safety rules; requiring workers to wear safety shoes or safety glasses."[52] As for politicians, they are unlikely to move unless pushed by either businessmen or labor leaders. Moreover, the injury tax is so passive and automatic in comparison to the active and deliberate standards-enforcement approach that it gives appearances of being a "license to maim," an image that might be exploited by the enemies of any politician who advocated an injury tax. Finally and most fundamentally:

> One should not expect the Congressional decision-making process to accord with the analytic ideal of reviewing policy options to see which rank highest in achieving specific objectives. Politicians are more interested in finding issues that

meet their political needs than in finding policies that meet analytic needs.[53]

Thus, there is perhaps a governmental failure in coping with this market failure. Dramatic departure from the OSHA approach, however attractive the injury tax might be to economists, does not appear in the offing.

Summary

A poster popular among western state industrialists depicts "The Cowboy after OSHA"—he wears a hard hat and goggles; his horse sports a safety net to guard riders against falls, and a box beneath the horse's rear catches slippery emissions. It's a wonder that labor unions have not retaliated with a poster of "Mr. Blue-Collar Before OSHA"—his blue collar is not visible beneath the full-body cast.

OSHA is, in short, a controversial government agency. With good intentions acceptable to everyone, Congress set forth vague broad standards urging safe and healthy working conditions "so far as possible" and "to the extent feasible." OSHA's implementation has usually generated narrow standards that were more "technically" than "economically" possible or feasible, thereby ignoring cost-effectiveness or benefit-cost justifications. OSHA's early standards were particularly ill-conceived because they were (1) drawn largely from consensus standards, (2) design-oriented instead of performance-oriented, and (3) focused on safety rather than health. Time has brought improvements.

Enforcement of these standards centers on inspections and citations, the results of which are subject to review by the Occupational Safety and Health Review Commission, an independent agency created by the OSH Act. Scheduled inspections are most numerous, with sampling targeted on the riskiest firms and industries. Accident investigations are prompted by very serious mishaps. Employee complaints trigger still another class of inspections. And follow-up inspections check on the remedial efforts of employers. Citations result from detected violations, with penalties ranging from pocket change to moderately ponderous amounts.

Responding to past criticism, OSHA has shifted its enforcement efforts toward consultation, education, and cooperation. Many critics remain dissatisfied, however, some saying more should be done in this direction, others saying less.

Two key controversies hit OSHA—(1) the question of whether benefit-cost analysis should guide standard development, and (2) the question of whether OSHA has actually reduced workplace casualties. Opposition to benefit-cost analysis stems from allegiance to value judgments other than economic efficiency and from skepticism that the practical difficulties of benefit-cost estimation can ever be overcome. Advocacy of benefit-cost elevates economic efficiency above other value judgments and discounts the practical difficulties. Looking at the word *feasibility* in the OSH Act, the Supreme Court decided in the cotton-dust case that health standards *need not* pass a benefit-cost test. Safety standards presumably escape as well. Still, there has been a shift toward benefit-cost.

By nature, health casualties defy easy measurement, and most safety mishaps have causes beyond OSHA's reach. Tests of OSHA's impact thus breed controversy. At best, OSHA has had slight overall impact on safety, most of the improvement coming from injury categories sensitive to the standards approach.

What improvements might be made without abandoning the standards approach? Advocates espouse (1) greater reliance on cost-effectiveness, especially as it relates to personal protective equipment in lieu of engineering controls; (2) benefit-cost tests for all standards; and (3) a shift toward "cooperative" enforcement. What of different methods? Information and education efforts could be considerably expanded. And if

Congress wanted to be really daring (yet rational), it could pass an injury tax.

Questions and Exercises for Chapter 22

1. Compare and contrast safety versus health in (a) OSHA's emphasis, (b) strength of regulatory rationale, and (c) appropriateness for a tax.
2. Compare the engineering approach versus protective equipment approach in (a) OSHA's emphasis, and (b) typical cost-effectiveness.
3. What controversies surround OSHA's inspections?
4. How has OSHA assessed the benefits of its proposed regulations?
5. Explain the relevance and importance of the cotton-dust case in (a) facts, (b) issues, and (c) results.
6. What has been the impact of OSHA in actually increasing safety?
7. Why is the OSHA approach limited in what it can be expected to achieve?
8. Is there room for improvement within the present OSHA framework? Explain.
9. What are the advantages of an injury tax? Disadvantages?

Notes

1. U. S. Senate, Committee on Labor and Human Resources, *Oversight on the Administration of the Occupational Safety and Health Act,* Hearings (1980), Vol. 1, pp. 766–805, Vol. 2, pp. 1271–1309. See also Cathy Trost, "Occupational Hazard," *Wall Street Journal,* 22 April 1988, p. 25R.
2. Statement of Steelworkers President, Lloyd McBride, ibid., p. 700.
3. Occupational Safety and Health Act, Section 2(b).
4. Ibid., Section 6(b)(5).
5. S. A. Shapiro and Thomas O. McGarity, "Reorienting OSHA: Regulatory Alternatives and Legislative Reform," *Yale Journal on Regulation* (Winter 1989): 1–3.
6. *Wall Street Journal,* 16 January 1989, p. C16.
7. Nicholas A. Ashford, *Crisis in the Workplace: Occupational Disease and Injury* (Cambridge, MA: MIT Press, 1976), pp. 144–145, 167–173.
8. Robert S. Smith, *The Occupational Safety and Health Act* (Washington, DC: American Enterprise Institute, 1976), p. 62.

9. *Business Week*, September 23, 1991, p. 42.

10. *Wall Street Journal*, 24 September 1981, p. 17.

11. As related by Murray L. Weidenbaum in *Business, Government, and the Public*, 2nd ed. (Englewood Cliffs, NJ: Prentice-Hall, 1981), pp. 82–83.

12. *Wall Street Journal*, 18 March 1986, p. 18.

13. *Washington Post*, November 1, 1991, p. A19.

14. *The President's Report on Occupational Safety and Health* (1974), pp. 95–97.

15. Though not included in the OSH Act, on-site consultation began in 1975 after amendment. The program was greatly expanded under the Carter Administration.

16. John Mendeloff, *Regulating Safety: An Economic and Political Analysis of Occupational Safety and Health Policy* (Cambridge, MA: MIT Press, 1979), p. 20.

17. *American Textile Manufacturers Institute, Inc. v. R. J. Donovan Sec. of Labor*, 69 L Ed 2d 185 (1981).

18. Estimates by Robert Crandall and Edward Denison, as cited by R. W. Hahn and J. A. Hird, "The Costs and Benefits of Regulation: Review and Synthesis," *Yale Journal of Regulation* (Winter 1991): 233–278.

19. For accounts of the story see David D. Doniger, *The Law and Policy of Toxic Substances Control: A Case Study of Vinyl Chloride* (Baltimore: Johns Hopkins University Press, 1978); and H. R. Northrup, R. L. Rowan, and C. R. Perry, *The Impact of OSHA* (Philadelphia: Industrial Research Unit, University of Pennsylvania, 1978), pp. 291–418.

20. Mendeloff, *Regulating Safety*, p. 163.

21. John F. Morrall, III, "Exposure to Occupational Noise," in *Benefit-Cost Analyses of Social Regulation*, ed. (Washington, DC): American Enterprise Institute, 1979), pp. 33–58.

22. Northrup, Rowan, and Perry, *Impact of OSHA*, pp. 390–405.

23. As of 1986, OSHA assumed a value of $2 million to $5 million. *Fortune* (March 3, 1986), p. 27.

24. Mendeloff, *Regulating Safety*, pp. 71–79.

25. U.S. Senate, *Oversight* Hearings, p. 1016.

26. *Wall Street Journal*, 9 January 1980, p. 42.

27. *Ray Marshall, Sec. of Labor v. American Petroleum Institute*, 65 L Ed 2d 1010 (1980).

28. *Wall Street Journal*, 2 September 1987, p. 14. More recently, in 1989, the Environmental Protection Agency issued regulations on benzene to protect people living near industrial plants.

29. *American Textile Manufacturers Institute, Inc. v. R. J. Donovan, Sec. of Labor*, 69 L Ed 2d 185 (1981).

30. U.S. Senate, *Oversight*, Hearings, Vol. 1, p. 779.

31. Ibid., Vol. 2, p. 1215.

32. Robert Stewart Smith, *The Occupational Safety and Health Act: Its Goals and Its Achievements* (Washington, DC: American Enterprise Institute, 1976).

33. Mendeloff, *Regulating Safety*, 102–105.

34. William P. Curington, "Safety Regulation and Workplace Injuries," *Southern Economic Journal* (July 1986): 51–72.

35. Mendeloff, *Regulating Safety*, p. 111.

36. Ibid., p. 117.

37. Robert Stewart Smith, "The Impact of OSHA Inspections on Manufacturing Injury Rates," *Journal of Human Resources* (Spring 1979): 145–170.

38. *Wall Street Journal*, 2 February 1987, p. 44; 22 July 1987, p. 4; 30 July 1987, p. 10; 28 September 1987, p. 12; 15 January 1988, p. 8.

39. *San Jose Mercury News*, 16 October, 1987, pp. 1B–2B.

40. Albert Nichols and Richard Zeckhauser, "OSHA after a Decade: A Time for Reason," in Weiss and Klass, eds., *Case Studies in Regulation: Revolution and Reform* (Boston: Little, Brown, 1981), p. 217.

41. Ibid., p. 215.

42. U.S. Senate, *Oversight* Hearings, p. 3.

43. *Wall Street Journal*, 5 July 1990, p. B1.

44. An optimistic and upper bound extrapolation of the Smith and Mendeloff estimates yields an annual benefit of $4.6 billion. See the last source of Table 22–1.

45. *Wall Street Journal*, 10 February 1982, p. 30.

46. *Wall Street Journal*, 20 May 1983, p. 4. See also *Washington Post National Weekly Edition*, May 28, 1984, pp. 31–32. Embarrassment contributed to White House defeat. "As part of their argument, budget office officials cited an industry-commissioned study that they said concluded that respirators and close monitoring of workers' health would be sufficient . . . The officials' argument was undercut when the author of the study . . . disputed drawing such a conclusion."

47. *Business Week*, April 14, 1986, p. 45. See also George C. Eads and Michael Fix, *Relief or Reform?* (Washington, DC: Urban Institute Press, 1984), pp. 194–197.

48. U.S. Senate, *Oversight* Hearings, p. 803.

49. Mendeloff, *Regulating Safety*, p. 25.

50. Robert S. Smith, "The Feasibility of an 'Injury Tax' Approach to Occupational Safety," *Law and Contemporary Problems* (Summer-Autumn 1974): 741.

51. Nichols and Zeckhauser, "OSHA after a Decade," pp. 228–229.

52. Mendeloff, *Regulating Safety*, p. 29.

53. Ibid., p. 156.

Chapter 23

Environmental Protection

There is no such thing as a free lunch in nature.
— *Barry Commoner*

Throughout this book we have encountered the old economic axiom, "There is no such thing as a free lunch." When discussing the market's ability to allocate scarce resources, we found that more steel for cars meant less for railroads. When studying control of cotton dust, we learned that worker health could be bought only at the expense of hundreds of millions of dollars in resources that could have been used elsewhere, for hospitals or schools perhaps. The economic world is thus a Rubik's cube: Getting one red square in place simultaneously displaces blue, green, and yellow squares.

In nature there is likewise no such thing as a free lunch. Nature's laws of conservation of mass and energy tell us that we never really "consume" anything. When we use minerals, fuels, and other materials, we merely change their form, extract their services, and push them around a bit. When ultimately discarded as trash, sewage, exhaust, or other waste, they remain in our environment. Natural dissipation and chemical conversion make some of these wastes harmless. Others, however, become costly hazards. Twenty people died and 6,000 others became seriously ill when in 1948 the industrial town of Donora, Pennsylvania, was blanketed by thick smog laced with sulfur dioxide. In England a smog attack killed 300 Londoners in December 1962. One's waste can thus become another's woe.

It is the task of environmental policy to contend with the fact that there is *no free lunch either in nature or economics*. What goes up, must come down, often hitting us. And procuring protection diverts economic resources from other things worth billions of dollars.

Our review of environmental policy answers four questions:

   I. What is pollution?
  II. What has been done about it?
 III. What is the impact of current policy?
 IV. What policy improvements might be made?

I. What Is Pollution?

Our environment—the air, water, and land around us—serves us in three ways. First, it provides a *habitat,* that is, life-support surroundings. Destruction of our habitat or the habitat of other creatures is not merely inconvenient; it is deadly. Second, the environment provides natural *resources* useful for the production of goods and services. Clean air, for instance, is a handy source of oxygen for combustion and a convenient place to dispose of combustion wastes. River water quenches thirst, yields fish, floats transport, powers electric generators, and irrigates crops. Minerals like coal and oil give energy. And so on. Third, environmental *amenities* make life pleasant. Swimming, boating, fishing, skiing, hiking, picnicking, and sight-seeing—the list of nature's pleasant offerings is copious.

In a physical sense, pollution occurs whenever man alters the environment. In an economic sense, *pollution occurs when one use of the environment diminishes other service capabilities of value to mankind.* Typically, resource exploitation injures habitat and amenity properties, as when use of the atmosphere as an exhaust repository creates smog that kills people, hides picturesque mountains, and blots out beautiful sunsets. However, pollution also occurs when one resource use hurts another resource use. Chemical waste disposal competes with commercial fishing, and strip-mining interferes with farming. Furthermore, amenity uses may even produce pollution, as when thoughtless picnickers litter the landscape with beer cans and pop bottles, diminishing the pleasure of other picnickers. Pollution is, in short, a problem of scarce environmental capacities relative to man's demands. Misuse is equivalent to misallocation. *There is too much pollution when the environment is used too much for waste disposal relative to cleaner endeavors.*

A. Air Pollutants

The wastes dumped into the air are certainly the most obvious because they impair breathing, burn eyes, cloud visibility, and worse. The main chemicals at fault and their total annual emission tonnage from 1970–1989 are given in Table 23–1.

- *Total Suspended Particulates* (TSP): In addition to soot and dust, particulates are composed of organic compounds containing metals, sulfur, and nitrogen. Industrial processes and fuel combustion in stationary sources are the main sources of particulates, which lessen visibility and cause respiratory ailments.
- *Sulfur Dioxide* (SO_2): Coal and oil combustion in stationary sources like electric power plants are the main sources of sulfur dioxide, which in high concentrations is associated with acute and chronic respiratory disease. Moreover, SO_2 reacts in the atmosphere to form sulfuric acid, thereby contributing to the infamous acid rain.
- *Nitrogen Dioxide* (NO_2): This stuff plays a major role in the atmospheric reactions that produce smog. Its effects on health remain uncertain except that high-level exposure can cause pulmonary edema. Motor vehicles and electric generating plants are the chief sources.
- *Hydrocarbons* (HC): Hydrocarbons are vapors of gasoline, chemical solvents, and various burned fuels. Atmospheric reactions convert them into *ozone,* which as everyone in Southern California knows, severely irritates mucous membranes, hampers breathing, and aggravates the symptoms of people suffering asthma and other ailments.
- *Carbon Monoxide* (CO): Primarily a product of auto and truck exhaust, and a favorite means of dispatch for many suicides, carbon monoxide can concentrate in urban air to the point of affecting mental function, visual acuity, and alertness among normal people. Suf-

Table 23–1
National Air Pollution Emission Estimates, 1970 to 1989 (million metric tons per year)

Year	TSP[a]	SO_2	NO_2	HC	CO	LEAD
1970	18.5	28.3	18.1	27.5	101.4	203.8
1975	10.6	25.6	19.2	22.8	84.1	147.0
1977	9.1	26.9	20.9	24.2	81.8	141.2
1979	8.9	24.8	21.6	22.4	81.7	108.7
1981	8.0	22.6	20.9	21.3	77.4	56.4
1983	7.1	20.7	19.3	20.3	74.5	46.4
1985	7.3	21.1	19.8	20.2	69.5	20.9
1987	7.0	20.7	19.4	19.4	64.2	8.0
1989	7.2	21.1	19.9	18.5	60.9	7.2
Percentage change 1970–1989	−61%	−25%	+10%	−33%	−40%	−96%

[a]See text for explanations of abbreviations.

Source: The Council on Environmental Quality, *Environmental Quality, 21st Annual Report* (Washington, DC: 1991), pp. 320–322.

ferers of anemia, emphysema, and other lung diseases suffer more.

■ *Lead:* Antiknock gasoline additives were the major source of lead before regulatory reduction. Breathing lead causes heart and neurological damage. (Four tons of lead enter the atmosphere of Mexico City every day, doubling the proportion of children with IQs below 80 from 9 percent of the population, which is normal, to 20 percent, which indicates excessive mental retardation.[1])

Less pervasive but in many ways more hazardous than these pollutants are numerous toxic substances like mercury, beryllium, vinyl chloride, and asbestos. Fortunately, their hazards are localized. Airborne asbestos fibers, for instance, can congregate around asbestos mills, freshly demolished buildings, and mining areas. Overall, 2.4 billion pounds of toxic chemicals were discharged into U. S. air in 1987.

Most recently, and most insidiously, we have two worldwide problems—the greenhouse effect and depletion of ozone by chlorofluorocarbons (CFCs). As carbon dioxide and other by-products of fuel combustion accumulate in the atmosphere, an ever larger portion of the sun's radiation that would normally bounce back into space is trapped, causing the earth's atmosphere to heat up. The higher atmospheric temperatures will soon cause alarming changes such as higher ocean levels (as the polar ice caps melt) and regions of perpetual drought. Chlorofluorocarbons (CFCs) are a family of chemicals used widely in refrigerators, air conditioners, and in manufacturing plastic foams, semiconductor devices, sterilants, and many other items. The CFCs contribute to the greenhouse effect. Even more harmfully, their gases drift up to the highest levels of the earth's atmosphere where they destroy the ozone layer that screens out the sun's dangerous ultraviolet rays. These rays cause skin cancer, eye ailments, and other serious health problems as well as environmental damage to crops and fish. The greenhouse effect and the ozone shield's depletion will continue well into the next century regardless of what policies might be enacted today. Immense amounts of petroleum and coal will continue to be burned, contributing to the greenhouse effect. And CFCs have lifespans lasting many decades, so that those already released will continue to wreak havoc for generations.[2]

B. Water Pollution

Ground water and surface water are both susceptible to a wide variety of pollutants. For our purposes we classify these pollutants as either *degradable* or *nondegradable*. Once in the water, degradable pollutants change through chemical and biological processes. They are, in short, subject to nature's self-cleansing capabilities as long as they do not concentrate to the point of overwhelming those capabilities. Domestic sewage (like wildlife sewage) is among these degradable wastes along with the organic waste materials of food canneries, paper mills, and oil refineries.

Bacterial degradation of organic waste consumes the oxygen dissolved in water, so a common measure of these pollutants is biochemical oxygen demand (or BOD). As organic waste discharges increase, BOD increases. Conversely, an increase in BOD *reduces* the dissolved oxygen in water. Dissolved oxygen is therefore a measure of water quality important to fish as well as to humans. Low levels of dissolved oxygen ruin fish habitat.

Nondegradable pollutants do not change in the water, or change only very slowly. Mercury, lead, cadmium, PCBs, and DDT persist in nature long after emission. They can be directly poisonous or more deviously dangerous. Some, like DDT, can concentrate in animals highly placed in nature's food chain, harming their reproductive capacities or doing other damage. Some nondegradable pollutants are so persistent that they even elude water purification processes, as illustrated by the fact that drinking water derived from the Mississippi River has been linked to cancer fatalities in Louisiana.[3]

"Point" sources of water pollution, such as factory effluent pipes and municipal sewage outfalls, are what most people think of when they consider sources of surface water pollution. However, "nonpoint" sources, such as stormwater runoff, cropland erosion, and pasture runoff, are more important sources of pollution for many water bodies. Figure 23–1 shows estimates that blame nonpoint sources for 65 percent of the pollution of 370,000 stream miles in the United States. Unfortunately, nonpoint sources pose especially difficult problems for policy control.

Many sources of ground-water pollution likewise elude public policy because they are hidden below ground. Septic tanks, underground storage tanks, landfills, and abandoned disposal sites for hazardous waste rank high on the list of contributors to ground-water pollution, and these sources number in the multimillions. Some abandoned hazardous waste sites, like Love Canal, are famous for their filth.[4]

Progress against water pollution has been slower than the progress suggested in Table 23–1 for air pollution, but modest headway is detectable. Rather than run through the numbers for BOD, suspended solids, phosphorus, and the many other water pollutants, we can glance at the time pattern for oil spills in and around U. S. waters in Figure 23–2. The trend of pollution over the past two decades has been erratic and less pronounced than would have been desirable, but it seems to be going downward nevertheless. Much the same could be said of many other water pollutants. The fact that there is still a long way to go, however, is revealed in one statistic: In 1985 roughly 40 percent of the nation's shellfish beds were closed to harvesting for some or all of the year because of contamination.

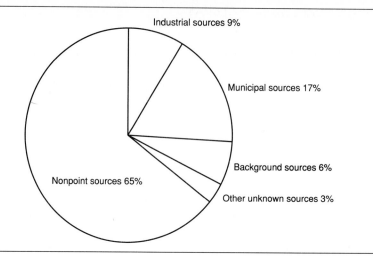

Figure 23–1

Major Causes of Stream Pollution

Source: U.S. Environmental Protection Agency, *Environmental Progress and Challenges: EPA's Update* (Washington DC: Environmental Protection Agency, August 1988), p. 46

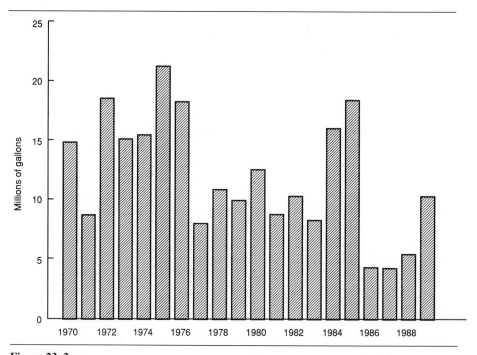

Figure 23–2

Oil Spills in and Around U.S. Waters, 1979–1989. (1989 data are for Exxon Valdez Oil Spill Only)

Source: Council on Environmental Quality, *Environmental Quality, 21st Annual Report* 1991, p. 307

C. Land Pollution

Unsound hazardous waste disposal also pollutes the land because it reduces the capacity of the land to render environmental services. Moreover, millions of tons of solid wastes—ranging from highway litter to scrapped automobiles and appliances—have their adverse effects as well. Aside from dumping, the earth's surface is marred by strip mining, highway construction, off-road vehicle recreation, and other acts of gouging, tearing, grading, and paving. The damage is not limited to the amenity losses suffered by hikers, campers, and sightseers. Agriculture and forestry can also be dented.

D. Why Does Pollution Occur?

We need not repeat the discussions on pages 26 to 29 of Chapter 2 and pages 418 and 419 of Chapter 20, which give explanations of why pollution occurs. It can be helpful, however, to quickly recollect three concepts that lie at the heart of the matter: (1) **External costs** arise when individuals or firms or government facilities impose costs on others by emitting wastes burdening others. Polluters naturally reduce their own costs of waste disposal if they can by shifting the costs to others. (2) **Common property resources,** like the air, are open to exploitation by everybody. Each individual's use diminishes the usefulness of the property to others, but individuals do not confront these costs because they are not obliged to compensate others. The result is an overuse of common property resources. (3) **Public goods** are, for our purposes, goods jointly consumed. The mere *existence* of species, the *opportunity* to visit national parks, and the *cleanliness* of air and water are public goods whose free-market provision is seriously hampered by the free-rider problem. Free riding is a plausible strategy in the case of public goods because, for the free rider, paying and receiving are severed. Unlike private goods, where paying and receiving are inextricably linked, people might pay for a public good yet not receive it, or they might *not* pay and actually get it.

There is, in short, too much pollution from a free-market system because the polluters do not have to pay. The intent of policy should be, then, to make polluters pay. (The free-market's response is illustrated in Mexico City, where beginning in 1991 one could obtain 90 seconds of oxygen for $1.70 in oxygen booths like telephone booths.)

II. What Has Been Done About Pollution?

There are many possible approaches to environmental policy—moral suasion, direct regulation, subsidies, and taxation among them.[5] Practically all have been tried at one time or another here and abroad. Our experience with moral suasion, for instance, includes publicity campaigns featuring cartoon characters who urge us not to be "litter bugs" or chirp "give a hoot, don't pollute." Although some ardent environmentalists have faith that the rest of us can someday be converted to their staunch ethical views and clean behavior, moral suasion has had little impact to date. It works best only during crises (like serious smog attacks) and among souls attuned to nature's wonders (backpackers, for instance). William Baumol and Wallace Oates thus have a right to be skeptical when they say, "Unfortunately, if greater moral commitment is the prerequisite for a better environment, it may wait indefinitely. As in the case of the Victorian gentleman who refused to remove his clothing to save a drowning person, morality may be preserved even though the cause is lost."[6]

The approach tried most persistently in the United States has been direct regulation, despite the fact that regulations before about 1970 were abysmal failures.[7] Why the failures? Key elements of the overall regulatory strategy outlined earlier in Table 20–3 on page 427 were always left

---

Thumbnail Sketch 11: The Environmental Protection Agency

Established: 1970

Purpose: To protect and improve the physical environment.

Legislative Authority: Clean Air Act and Amendments of 1970, 1977, and 1990; Water Pollution Control Act Amendments of 1972, 1977; Federal Insecticide, Fungicide and Rodenticide Act of 1972; Noise Control Act of 1972; Safe Drinking Water Act of 1974; Toxic Substances Control Act of 1976; Resource Conservation and Recovery Act of 1976 and Amendment of 1986; Comprehensive Environmental Response Compensation, and Liability Act of 1980; Hazardous and Solid Waste Amendments of 1984; Medical Waste Tracking Act of 1988.

Regulatory Activity: In league with state and local governments, the EPA controls pollution through standard setting, enforcement, and research in six areas: air, water, solid waste, toxic substances, radiation, and noise.

Organization: An independent agency, located in the executive branch, headed by a presidentially appointed administrator.

Budget: 1991 estimate: $3984 million.

Staff: 1991 estimate: 16,223.

---

out of those earlier efforts. The Refuse Act of 1899 required a permit for the discharge of refuse into navigable waters, but standards were never set to guide permit provisions and enforcement was absent until 1970. Air and water legislation of the late 1940s and early 1950s authorized research but little else. Slight progress was made in the 1960s when Congress provided broad ambient standards. Without narrow standards limiting the *emissions of specific sources,* however, enforcement to achieve those broad ambient standards proved impossible. As the environmental movement reached its pinnacle in 1970, these futile federal efforts became the butt of scathing criticism and even ridicule.[8]

Government finally "got tough," greatly modifying its half-baked earlier efforts with the Clean Air Amendments of 1970 and the 1972 Water Pollution Act Amendments. As subsequently further amended in 1977, 1988, and 1990, these amendments remain the basis of present policy, supplemented by the Toxic Substances Control Act of 1976, the Resource Conservation and Recovery Act of 1976, the Noise Control Act

of 1972, the Safe Drinking Water Act of 1974, and other regulations. How could Congress be confident that these new regulatory efforts would succeed when earlier efforts failed? They were more comprehensive, less riddled with gaps. They incorporated all the major elements of Table 20–3: standards, enforcement, and research. Still, critics have not been so confident, as we shall see.

Printing these measures would make a fat book over 400 pages long, so our survey must be condensed. We cover air, water, and toxic substances and outline standards and enforcement for each.

One last preliminary: During the 1980s, the Reagan Administration tried to reverse these regulatory developments. It proposed legislation that would have crippled the Clean Air Act. It slashed the EPA's enforcement budget. It appointed incompetent administrators. And so on. Yet for all its efforts, the Reagan Administration had little lasting impact. Much of our review, therefore, refers back to the 1970s, as if time had stood still during the 1980s. A major reason the Reaganites failed was that their anti-environmental actions provoked a robust proenvironmental reaction among the populace. For example, between 1983 and 1989, membership in the Sierra Club, the Audubon Society, the National Wildlife Federation, and the Wilderness Society soared threefold from 1,702,000 to 7,199,000.[9]

A. Air Pollution Regulation

1. BROAD STANDARDS FOR AIR

In 1970 Congress acted, it said "to protect and enhance the quality of the Nation's air resources so as to promote the public health and welfare and the productive capacity of its population." This vague pronouncement might seem sufficient for a broad standard, but Congress elaborated with specifics. It called for the attainment by 1975 of a set of national "primary ambient-air quality standards" and later attainment of "secondary" ambient standards. The primary ambient standards were to be set by the Environmental Protection Agency (EPA) so as to protect human health, whereas the secondary standards were intended to protect against all other damage (to property, animals, vegetation, materials, visibil-

ity, and aesthetics). The EPA responded with an early version of these standards in 1971 for so-called "criteria" pollutants. Now modified, these standards set maximum ambient thresholds for particulate matter, sulfur oxides, carbon monoxide, nitrogen dioxide, ozone, hydrocarbons, and lead, some of which are given in Table 23–2 for 1989.

Three characteristics of these broad standards for criteria pollutants deserve special notice. *First,* they are ambient standards, *not emission* standards. They specify air quality thresholds. They do not place emission limits on particular polluters, a task that is left to narrow standards and the issuance of permits under those narrow standards. The distinction is underscored by the fact that Congress took a different approach for "hazardous air pollutants," which (by its broad standard) "may reasonably be anticipated to result in an increase in mortality or an increase in serious irreversible, or incapacitating reversible, illness." Ambient standards would not do for these horrors, so Congress directed the EPA to identify such hazardous air pollutants" and set *emission* standards providing

Table 23–2
Selected National Ambient Air Quality Standards (NAAQS) for Criteria Pollutants
(Maximum Levels in Effect in 1989)

Pollutant	Averaging Time	Primary Standard (micrograms per cubic meter of air)	Secondary Standard (micrograms per cubic meter of air)
Particulates	Annual (average)	50	50
	24 hours[a]	150	150
Sulfur oxides	Annual (average)	80	—
	24 hours[a]	365	—
	3 hours[a]	—	1,300
Ozone	1 hour	235	235
Lead	3 months	1.5	1.5

[a]Not to be exceeded more than once a year.

Source: Paul R. Portney, "Air Pollution Policy," in *Public Policies for Environmental Protection,* ed. Paul R. Portney (Washington, DC: Resources for the Future, 1990), pp. 34–35.

"an ample margin of safety to protect public health." Asbestos, beryllium, mercury, vinyl chloride, and several other noxious substances have received such attention.

Second, the ambient air standards for regular, criteria pollutants are based on a *threshold* concept, implying an absence of adverse effect from pollution levels below the specified threshold. Exposure-effect function *A* in Figure 23–3 illustrates this threshold concept. Greater exposure to air pollution (moving to the right horizontally) does not cause higher mortality (vertical movement) until after a threshold is crossed. This is contrasted to the *continuous* exposure-effect function labeled *B,* which shows adverse effects starting with very low pollution exposure. Since passage of the 1970 Clean Air Act Amendments, growing evidence suggests that the continuous function is the best picture of reality. Retention of the threshold concept has therefore elicited sharp criticism, especially from those who advocate a larger place for benefit-cost analysis in setting standards. They say that the continuous function implies *zero* pollution if the act's "health and welfare" objective is to be honored. But because zero pollution could be obtained only at horrendous cost (closing down Los Angeles, for instance), critics contend that we must weigh benefits and costs along the continuum indicated by the empirical evidence.[10]

The *third* thing to notice about the national ambient air quality standards is that they are *national,* not regional or local. This uniformity produced a tricky problem. Areas not meeting standards would obviously have to cut back emissions to comply with the thresholds, but what about the many areas that already enjoyed air quality *better* than the standards? Would their air be allowed to deteriorate to the level of the national standards? What would this mean for national parks like the Grand Canyon where visibility is especially important?

Prompted by environmentalists, Congress amended the Act in 1977 to meet this problem, with the result that, in practice, *special* broad ambient standards now apply to "attainment" areas to "prevent significant deterioration." Congress directed that attainment areas be subdivided into three classes:

Class I. Crucial areas such as national parks where virtually *no* deterioration would be permitted (only about 1 percent of U. S. land area).

Class II. Areas where moderate deterioration would be permitted (most of the United States).

Class III. Areas which could deteriorate to the point of equalling threshold standards.

An interesting irony in this approach is that it creates a contradiction in policy because the resulting gradations imply a *continuous* exposure-effect function contrary to the *threshold* exposure-effect originally assumed. Either the threshold concept is right, and these gradations in ambient standards are wrong, or the threshold concept is wrong and these gradients are right (and indeed further gradations should be adopted). Some critics maintain that benefit-cost gradations should be developed that vary by region because bene-

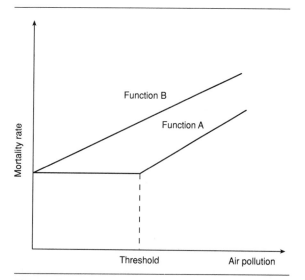

Figure 23–3
Threshold (A) and No-Threshold (B) Exposure-Effect Functions

fits and costs vary by region.[11] Such would serve consistency but add complexity.[12]

2. NARROW STANDARDS FOR AIR

Narrow standards for the criteria pollutants are outlined in Table 23–3. Because their purpose is to restrict *emissions* from specific sources, these standards fall into two main divisions: (A) Stationary sources, like factories and electric power plants, and (B) mobile sources like autos, trucks, and buses. Stationary sources are further subdivided by area, by old versus new source, and by state versus EPA formulation. State environmental protection agencies have major responsibilities under the Clean Air Act because they must formulate plans, set narrow standards, and enforce those standards with permits and surveillance, all to achieve the broad ambient air standards mentioned earlier. To guide the states in setting their narrow standards the law offers technical catch-phrases like "reasonably available control measures" and "lowest achievable emission rate," which standards are the most stringent among all the stationary standards because they apply to old and new sources in nonattainment areas (see A.1.a and A.1.b. in Table 23–3). The EPA sets some stationary standards itself, however, under its authority to set New Source Performance Standards for certain new sources, most notably new electric generating plants that burn coal. Thus, states share new source authority with the EPA, and the states' new source standards in nonattainment areas (A.1.b.) are quite similar to the EPA's New Source Performance Standards despite differences in the guideline language.

More concretely, the typical narrow standard calls for a certain percentage of abatement as guided by technological possibilities, ambient air conditions, and other considerations. For exam-

---

Table 23–3
Narrow Emissions Standards under the Clean Air Act, by Source and Area

A. STATIONARY SOURCES (LIKE POWER PLANTS)
    1. *Nonattainment Areas: State Standards*
        a. Old Sources—"reasonably available control measures."
        b. New Sources—"lowest achievable emission rate" plus an offset with old sources, cost considered.
    2. *Attainment Areas: State Standards*
        a. Old Sources—no alteration needed unless source is "modified," in which case it becomes "new."
        b. New Sources—"major" sources must adopt "best available control technology for maximum degree of pollution reduction achievable, taking into account cost."
    3. *EPA New Source Performance Standards*
        For certain new source categories, the "best technological system of continuous emissions reduction that has been adequately demonstrated, considering costs and other environmental impacts."
B. MOBILE SOURCES (VEHICLES)
    Differ by type of vehicle and model year. The 1990 Amendments to the Clean Air Act provide the following standards for autos, to be phased in over the 1994 to 1996 model years:

Carbon monoxide	3.40 grams per mile
Hydrocarbons	0.025 grams per mile
Nitrogen oxides	0.40 grams per mile

ple, in areas of New York, New Jersey, and Connecticut that do not meet the ambient ozone standard, controls call for 40 to 50 percent reductions in the hydrocarbons emitted by 15 categories stationary sources.

This percentage reduction approach reached a peak of sorts when Congress itself set narrow standards for automobiles in the 1970 Clean Air Act Amendments. Those original standards called for 90 percent reductions in hydrocarbons, carbon monoxide, and nitrogen oxide emissions below the levels of 1970–1971 model cars. The 90 percent curtailments were to be reached by 1976, but economic difficulties and technical troubles caused Congress to bow repeatedly to industry demands for postponements and revisions. The standards set by the 1990 amendments and shown at the bottom of Table 23–3 thus approximate 90 percent reductions for carbon monoxide and nitrogen oxide. Successful abatement has been more readily achieved for hydrocarbons, so the standard for hydrocarbons in Table 23–3 is a 99 percent reduction from 1971.[13]

Consideration of economic cost has influenced narrow standard setting, either implicitly or explicitly. Implicit consideration of cost motivated the repeated postponement of auto emission deadlines, for instance. Honda and Volvo were able to produce virtually pollution-free cars by the mid-1970s, signifying the *technical* feasibility of the early deadlines. But American manufacturers could not shoulder the costs of converting to these technologies and shrunken car sizes, so they won delays by threatening shutdowns. Implicit consideration of cost is also allowed by the word *reasonably,* which qualifies narrow standards for old stationary sources in nonattainment areas (category A.1.a. in Table 23–3). Explicit consideration of cost is provided for in all other narrow standards, as study of Table 23–3 reveals.

3.   ENFORCEMENT FOR AIR

Enforcement entails (1) certification or permit at least for new sources, mobile and stationary, (2) monitoring, and (3) remedies. In the case of au-

tos, *certification* carries the main burden. Manufacturers deliver prototype vehicles to the EPA for certification, and these vehicles must meet the emission standards for their model year before any others like them can be marketed. The analogous process for stationary sources is *permitting,* authority for which is divided among all three levels of government. Before a new petroleum refinery can be built, for example, its owners must obtain a pollution permit that sets emission limits and grants operating clearance.

Monitoring of mobile sources entails assembly-line testing and on-the-road testing to assure that compliance carries beyond the prototype stage. Implementation of assembly-line testing was long delayed because of bureaucratic infighting and manufacturer footdragging, but now about 20,000 autos are sampled annually before shipment to buyers. On-the-road testing is needed as well as assembly-line auditing because poor maintenance or tampering can neutralize or damage the control equipment. Indeed, cars are supposed to meet standards for their first 50,000 miles. After stumbling over more delays than those for assembly-line testing, on-the-road testing has become a major environmental program. By the end of 1985, twenty-nine states had inspection programs. Major cities with severe pollution problems—like Los Angeles, New York, and Denver—get the greatest attention. Hence, all told, about 46 million vehicles, or 29 percent of the total U. S. fleet, are subject to emissions inspection annually or biennially.[14]

As for stationary sources, the EPA inspects or monitors only about 10 percent of the major sources annually, so it must rely on state and local authorities to cover most emitters. A wide range of surveillance activities is involved— stack tests, source inspections, and opacity readings among them. In some cases, fuel samples are analyzed for sulfur content because such is the chief source of sulfur dioxide.

Remedies include auto recalls, civil fines, and in serious cases even criminal penalties. The least burdensome and most common of remedies is the "notice of violation," which amounts to little more than a warning ticket and which in the late 1980s numbered 2,000 or so annually (counting both EPA and state citations). Civil and criminal legal actions are more serious but less frequent, numbering in the high hundreds each year (again combining EPA and state efforts.)[15]

Of course, the compliance of emission sources must be translated into improvements in ambient air conditions to be successful. The substantial reductions in emissions shown earlier in Table 23–1 suggest that we can now breathe easier than before, but emissions and ambient conditions are not necessarily the same thing, given the weather and other factors. Hence, Figure 23–

4 shows the average ambient concentrations of the criteria air pollutants from 1976 through 1988, compared to the broad standard for each (NAAQS as indicated by the dashed line). Dramatic improvement is evident in a few instances, and at least some improvement is shown for all pollutants. Only ozone had an average that remained above standard in 1988.

There is a catch here, however. Figure 23–4 reports *average* performance for the entire nation (as measured at several hundred sites around the country). Just as a person can drown in a lake with an average depth of one foot, the ambient air in specific locales, like Los Angeles, remains

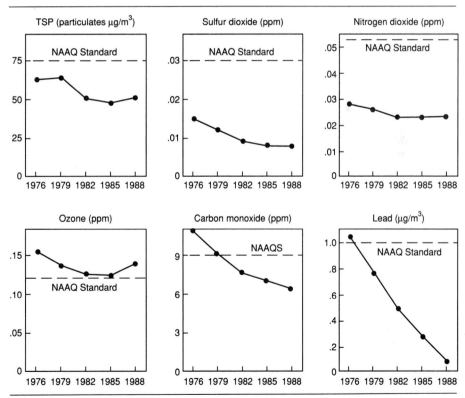

Figure 23–4
National Average Ambient Concentrations of Criteria Air Pollution, 1977–1988

Source: Council on Environmental Quality, *Environmental Quality, 21st Annual Report,* 1991, p. 323

Table 23–4
Nonattainment Areas in Counties or Parts of Counties, January 1989

Criteria Air Pollutant	Number of Counties or Parts of Counties Having Nonattainment Areas
Total suspended particulates (TSP)	317
Sulfur dioxide (SO$_2$)	67
Nitrogen dioxide (NO$_2$)	4
Ozone (O$_3$)	341
Carbon monoxide (CO)	123
Total number of U.S. counties	529

Source: Paul R. Portney, "Air Pollution Policy," in *Public Policies for Environmental Protection,* ed. Paul R. Portney (Washington, DC: Resources for the Future, 1991), p. 45.

pretty bad. Accordingly, Table 23–4 reports the number of counties or parts of counties having nonattainment areas in January 1989. The story told by Table 23–4 is dirtier than that told by Figure 23–4. Locally, there was substantial nonattainment for ozone, suspended particulates, and carbon monoxide. In 1989, therefore, an estimated 133 million Americans were still exposed occasionally to dangerous levels of smog and 78 million faced health-threatening levels of carbon monoxide.

The respectably good record on emissions compliance is thus somewhat illusory. Take autos, for example. The penalty for noncompliance has been a fine of $10,000 per "dirty" car. No such fine has ever been paid (although there have been some recalls). This suggests a record of good compliance. The record was made possible in large part, however, by regular relaxation of the deadlines for meeting various standards. Fines of $10,000 per car would have effectively closed down the auto industry, something unthinkable. Compliance was therefore partly contrived.

B. Water Pollution Regulation

1. BROAD STANDARDS FOR WATER

The 1972 Water Pollution Amendments state that their goal is "to restore and maintain the chemical, physical, and biological integrity of the Nation's waters." More specifically, the 1972 Act called for an amazing feat when it urged ". . . that the discharge of pollutants into the navigable waters be *eliminated* by 1985." The elimination of all discharges was to be preceded by attainment of two interim broad standards, both of which were technically oriented but tempered slightly by cost considerations:

- 1977 was the deadline for achieving the *Best Practicable Control Technology* (BPT) in industry and secondary treatment for municipal sewage.
- 1983 was the deadline for achieving the *Best Available Control Technology* (BAT) in industry and best practicable technology for municipal systems. "Fishable and swimmable" waters were the ambient goal here.

The 1977 deadline saw only 81 percent of all major industrial dischargers and 58 percent of all municipal dischargers in compliance.[16] There were several reasons for the substantial failure, one of which was unrealistic stringency in the 1977 BPT standards. It then dawned on Congress that complete elimination of discharges by 1985 was likewise an unrealistic objective, so late in 1977 Congress amended the 1972 act, postponing the BPT standards until 1979 for polluters deemed to have made a good-faith effort to meet the old 1977 deadline and substantially altering the best available control technology standards (BAT). Three classes of pollutants were given different deadlines and different definitions of BAT:

1. Most stringent was a 1984 BAT standard without qualification for toxic pollutants like mercury, arsenic, and zinc.
2. A 1984 BAT standard tempered by "reasonableness" of control cost was set for "conventional" pollutants like human waste and organic debris (BOD).
3. Least stringent was a call for controls by 1987 on "unconventional" pollutants such as ammonia and commercial solvents.

Lest these relaxations give the appearance of a sell-out to industrial and municipal lobbyists, notice that total elimination of all discharges would not only have been *extremely* costly (running into the hundreds of billions of dollars), it would *not* have assured fishable-swimmable waters because these strict standards would have applied only to *point* sources of pollutants, like factories and sewage plants. They would not reach *nonpoint* sources of pollution such as urban storm runoff or agricultural runoff. As we have seen, nonpoint sources account for hefty portions of several pollutant discharges—suspended solids 92 percent, fecal coliforms 98 percent, and total phosphates 53 percent. Complete control of point sources would have still left many water bodies degraded.

The main point to recognize in these standards is their technological orientation. They hinge on "what can be done with available technology, rather than what should be done to achieve ambient water quality standards, to balance benefits and costs, or to satisfy any other criteria. Since production processes, quantities and composition of waste loads, and treatment technologies vary substantially across industries, separate discharge standards must be developed for the different categories of industry."[17]

2. **NARROW STANDARDS FOR WATER**
Emission levels for tens of thousands of specific point sources have been derived from the broad BPT and BAT standards. For example, the majority of effluent limitations under BPT have taken the form of a maximum allowable discharge quantity of a specific pollutant per unit of production—say, two pounds of suspended solids per 1,000 pounds of product. The allowables are usually expressed in averages for 30 days with a 24-hour maximum. And the specific pollutants controlled vary from industry to industry, but just about all include BOD and suspended solids.[18]

3. **ENFORCEMENT FOR WATER**
These discharge limits for specific pollutants are incorporated into source-by-source *permits* that also establish schedules for upgrading controls to meet such limits. They require monitoring and periodic reports on compliance. Roughly 67,000 permits have been issued, as *every* public or private facility that discharges wastes directly into U. S. waters is required to obtain a permit.

The EPA focuses most of its *monitoring* activities on major permit holders, roughly 12 percent of the total. Definition of "major" is based chiefly on effluent volume, so this 12 percent of permit holders accounts for well over 50 percent by volume of all discharges. Small dischargers qualify for major status and close surveillance if their effluent is particularly toxic.

One of the best studies of water pollution compliance to date was conducted by the U. S. General Accounting Office (GAO) during 1980–1982. A total of 257 industrial facilities were sampled in six states, and 79 percent of them were not in compliance with their discharge permits. Moreover, 16 percent were in *significant* noncompliance.[19] Hence, as of the early 1980s, there was a compliance problem.

Perhaps compliance will be better by the year 2000. State and federal authorities have stepped up their *remedial* efforts in recent years, issuing over 3,000 administrative orders each year and instigating judicial action on 500 to 600 other cases annually. Criminal penalties are becoming more common, too, with a growing number of jailings and a growing volume of fines.[20]

What effect have these efforts had on observed water quality? Do these efforts translate into fishable and swimmable waters or better readings or dissolved oxygen? The trend is mixed. There have been dramatic improvements in some areas. Others have experienced declines. Overall, on average, there appear to have been modestly positive gains.[21] Considering that things would now be much worse if nothing had been done, some success can be claimed.

C. Toxic Substances Regulation

Aside from toxic air and water pollutants, the EPA has substantial additional authority to regulate toxic substances. This authority may be conveniently divided into two broad areas of responsibility—(1) control of hazardous *products,* or components of products, and (2) control of hazardous *wastes* other than those directly entering the air or water.[22]

1. HAZARDOUS PRODUCTS OR COMPONENTS
Hazardous products include, most prominently, pesticides, which are subject to EPA control by authority of the Federal Insecticide, Fungicide, and Rodenticide Act (1947, as amended in 1972 and 1978). Hazardous components of products include a wide variety of chemical substances used as insulators, refrigerants, aerosol propellants, and what not. These chemical components and many hazardous substances serving as final products are subject to EPA regulation under the Toxic Substances Control Act of 1976. The EPA must share its authority in these realms with the FDA, CPSC, and OSHA, something which lends confusion to the matter.

Broad standards to guide the EPA in this area have never been clearly enunciated by Congress, but they can be inferred from the statutory language defining toxic or hazardous substances.

The basic idea is to protect people and the environment from "unreasonable" risks of injury, ill health, or destruction while at the same time giving due consideration to the economic cost of doing so. Narrow standards defy such simple summary because they vary case by case, because the hazards vary from cancer to genetic alteration to species annihilation to destruction of the upper atmosphere. The specific activities the EPA pursues to fend off "unreasonable" risks are fairly easy to summarize, however, because they mirror those of the Food and Drug Administration discussed earlier:

- *Burden of Proof:* The EPA may require the manufacturers of hazardous substances to prove through appropriate tests that those substances are "reasonably" safe for their intended uses. In all other areas, the EPA bears the burden of showing harm before acting.
- *Premarket Notification and Registration:* The EPA must be notified of new pesticides and new chemical concoctions *prior* to their manufacture and marketing. As a corollary, the EPA maintains an inventory of all pesticides and hazardous substances with information on their properties, structures, and uses. The EPA's initial inventory of commercial chemicals subject to the Toxic Substances Control Act listed 43,000 unique formulations reported by almost 7,400 manufacturers and importers.
- *Regulatory Options:* The restrictions the EPA can impose range widely from rather mild labeling requirements to partial or complete prohibitions. The EPA has, for instance, banned the use of DDT on crops and prohibited the manufacture or use of chlorofluorocarbons as aerosol spray propellants.
- *Remedies:* Seizures and recalls are weapons in the EPA's arsenal of remedies, along with others mentioned previously.

2. HAZARDOUS WASTES
Hazardous wastes come from hospitals, research facilities, and government installations, but in-

dustry is their most prolific source. Besides toxicity, the hazards of concern are inflammability, corrosivity, and reactivity (e.g., spontaneous explosion). The tragedy of Love Canal tipped everyone off to the problem, and subsequent study has revealed that over 260 million metric tons of such wastes are generated annually in the United States. As of 1980 approximately 90 percent of them were being disposed of in environmentally dangerous ways—by improper burning, by deposit in unsecured landfills, and by illegal "midnight dumping."

The Resource Conservation and Recovery Act of 1976 requires safe disposal of hazardous wastes. The EPA's regulations under the act define hazardous wastes and establish a "cradle-to-grave" management system to track the movement of wastes from point of generation to point of proper disposal. The system includes standards for generators of hazardous wastes, standards for transporters, and standards and permits for owners and operators of facilities that store, treat, or dispose of hazardous wastes.

Unfortunately, the Resource Conservation and Recovery Act of 1976 could *not* effectively reach *past* transgressions, such as those who had caused the problem at Love Canal. It was, to some extent, only closing the barn door after the horse had left. To address the problem of *uncontrolled* hazardous sites, Congress passed the Comprehensive Environmental Response, Compensation, and Liability Act in 1980, often called the "Superfund Bill." Under this act, the EPA can require that sites be cleaned up by the "responsible parties" who created the hazard. If no one is able or willing to clean up the site quickly enough, the EPA itself may proceed, financed by the $1.6 billion superfund, a special fund built on taxes on petroleum and chemical production. The following are among the major steps implementing the law:

■ Identification of all uncontrolled hazardous sites in the United States. Over 27,000 have been found.

■ Once identified, these sites are assessed to determine the seriousness of the hazard. As of 1989, 1,077 sites had been placed on the National Priorities List for being especially dangerous (and the EPA estimates that, eventually, some 2,000 sites will be so rated).

■ For these especially dangerous sites, cleanup actions follow—either quick removal actions or longer-term remedial work, depending on the urgency of the risk.

Congress took still further steps in this area by passing the Hazardous and Solid Waste Amendments of 1984. Ground water is the act's major concern, because ground water supplies roughly 50 percent of the nation's drinking water and 20 percent of all water used, and yet this same ground water has been severely contaminated in many spots—Miami, Atlantic City, and San Jose among them. The 1984 amendments try to protect ground water from further contamination by, among other things, setting new technical standards for underground tanks that store petroleum and chemical products and for land disposal facilities (e.g., double liners and ground-water monitoring).

As regards remedies for toxics, jail sentences have become increasingly common for offenders. Before 1984, the EPA had not sent even one felon to the slammer. In 1991, jail sentences totalled over 500 months for all federal environmental laws, and most of these sentences related to toxics violations. Criminal fines have likewise burgeoned in federal court actions, rising from near zero in 1984 to about $14 million in 1991. Interestingly, there is a trade-off here. Executives of large corporations tend to escape jail, being penalized instead by heavy corporate fines. In contrast, the executives of small corporations typically end up behind bars, even when their company's offenses are comparable to those of large corporations. Apparently judges don't feel as comfortable sending *Fortune 500* executives to jail as they do the less powerful.[23]

III. What Is the Impact of Policy? Costs and Benefits

A. The Costs of Abatement

A typical car carries $800 worth of pollution control equipment. That may not sound like much, but the manufacture and sale of roughly 10 million autos a year converts that few hundred dollars into $8 billion, demonstrating that the costs of pollution abatement equipment can be towering. Moreover, such capital cost are only part of the story; additional abatement outlays go for operation and maintenance—that is fuel, labor, repair, and the like.

Figure 23–5 shows that abatement, regulation, and research costs that resulted from pollution control in the United States during 1988 were about $86 billion. Only $4.5 billion of this went to pay the costs of governmental activities

and research. The vast bulk of it went to pay the costs of abatement equipment, engineering personnel, and the like, with roughly equal expenditures going to protect the water, air, and land from abuse. Projections out to the year 2000 show overall expenditures reaching $160 billion annually, assuming full implementation of all regulations presently on the books. To put these figures in perspective, it may be noted that 1988's total of $86 billion was about 2 percent of the GNP. The projected total of $160 billion in the year 2000 is estimated to run a bit more—at about 2.8 percent of the GNP. These are, in other words, hefty sums, amounting to hundreds of dollars per person annually.

Unfortunately, there are still further possible costs or adverse economic impacts not reflected in Figure 23–5. *Inflation* may be aggravated when the costs of abatement show up in higher product prices. *Productivity growth* may be cut as invest-

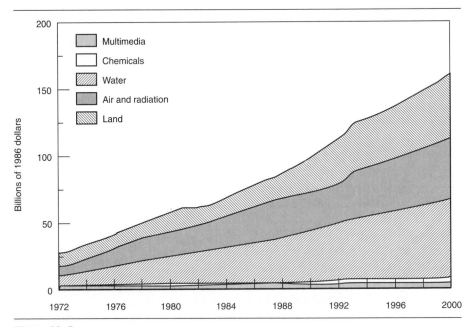

Figure 23–5

Total Annualized Costs of U.S. Pollution Control, by Media, Asuming Full Implementation of Regulations After 1991, 1972–2000

Source: Council on Environmental Quality, *Environmental Quality, 21st Annual Report,* 1991, p. 53

ment resources are diverted from plant and equipment that would produce goods and services into capital expenditures for pollution abatement hardware. *Unemployment* may rise at the local level because of plant closings and at the national level because of adverse macroeconomic effects. *Foreign trade balances* might tilt against us as the heavy costs of abatement put our domestic producers at a disadvantage vis-à-vis their foreign competitors, many of whom may face more lenient regulations or may have their abatement costs covered by government subsidies.

Estimates of these additional impacts are very tough to calculate. At the macroeconomic level there are many more factors influencing inflation, productivity growth, unemployment, and export-import performance than pollution abatement efforts. Nevertheless, estimates incorporating these sundry other influences show that the macroeconomic impacts of pollution control are very slight—fractions of percentage points up and down, here and there.[24] The main reason macroeconomic impacts are muted is that, although large in absolute dollar terms, the costs are small as a percentage of the GNP.

B. The Benefits of Abatement

The benefits of pollution abatement are much harder to estimate than are the costs of abatement, largely because those benefits take the form of *reduced pollution damage and avoidance costs,* costs which by the very nature of the pollution problem are not solidly registered in any marketplace but are instead external costs. Reduced *damage* costs include (1) reduced cost of ill health (hospital and medical bills, job absenteeism, pain, suffering, and early death), (2) lessened crop damage, (3) diminished deterioration of materials like rubber and paint, (4) reduced cleaning expenses, (5) enhanced aesthetic enjoyment of vistas, parks, or everyday neighborhoods, and so on. Reduced pollution *avoidance* costs include (1) less travel expense to reach fishable-swimmable waters, (2) reduced commuting time and cost as cleaner city centers

attract dwellers, and (3) curbed use of air conditioners. Stated differently, economists define the benefits of environmental regulation as the total amount people would be willing to pay for pollution control. And that amount should correspond to the curtailments in pollution costs associated with abatement.

The benefits of abatement are so difficult to determine that estimates are usually expressed as a *range* of possible values rather than any one value in particular. Moreover, comprehensive estimates of the overall benefits of air or water pollution abatement tend to be especially difficult because of the wide diversity of positive effects associated with abatement. For example, control of water pollution yields benefits for recreation, biological diversity, aesthetic appeal, commercial fishing, human health, and industrial efficiency, among other things. Table 23–5, meager though it may be, thus presents the sketchy evidence that is available regarding comprehensive benefits from abatement. The estimate for air pollution indicates annual abatement benefits in 1981 somewhere in the range between $22.7 billion and $62.1 billion. By far the largest chunk of these benefits—well over half of the total—were a result of improved health. The estimates for

Table 23–5

Estimated Annual Benefits from Air Pollution Control (1981) and Potential Benefits from Water Pollution Control (1985), in Billions of Dollars

	Range of Estimates	*Reasonable Point*
Air Pollution Control Benefits (1981)	$22.7—$62.1	N.A.[a]
Water Pollution Control Benefits (1985)	$ 5.7—$27.7	$14.0

[a]N.A. = not available.

Source: Paul R. Portney, "Air Pollution Policy," and A. Myrick Freeman III, "Water Pollution Policy," in *Public Policies for Environmental Protection*, ed. Paul R. Portney (Washington, DC: Resources for the Future, 1990), pp. 60, 123.

water pollution abatement are much smaller—in the $5.7 billion to $27.7 billion range. A point estimate for air is lacking, but for water it is $14.0 billion.

It is tempting to compare these benefit estimates to the cost estimates of the previous section to see if these benefits exceed the costs. Unfortunately, these benefit estimates are too speculative to allow anything other than very rough comparisons. Moreover, any such comparisons must be qualified by the fact that these are *total* dollar values rather than *marginal* dollar values. Thus, if total benefits exceed total costs, there is some indication of good policy. We cannot know exactly how good it is, however, because we have no knowledge of marginal values, and marginal costs can exceed marginal benefits even if total costs are less than total benefits.

This said, rough comparisons put air pollution abatement policy in a good light while creating economic doubts for water policy. The total social cost of air pollution regulations in 1981 were about $25 billion according, to the data of Figure 23–5. This cost falls in the lower end of the air abatement benefits estimated for Table 23–5, so it is almost certain that total benefits exceeded total costs for air policy. The total social cost of water pollution regulations in 1984 were about $27 billion, according to the data of Figure 23–5, which matches the upper end of the range of water benefits in Table 23–5 and is nearly twice the point estimate of $14 billion. Hence, it is almost certain that the total costs of water abatement exceeded the total benefits.

Table 23–6 further illustrates the economic attractions of air pollution regulation and also demonstrates the refinement that is sometimes possible when one looks at the impact of a specific policy rather than at the uncertain jumble we encounter when looking at comprehensive totals (like those of Table 23–5). Since 1973, the EPA has phased out lead in gasoline, which reduces lead in the atmosphere, which in turn reduces mental retardation among children, curbs hypertension in adults, and yields other gains.

Table 23–6
Annualized Benefits and Costs of Lead Regulation, Assuming Partial Misfueling, 1985 and 1992 (millions of 1984 dollars)

	1985	1992
Benefits		
Children's health effects	$232	$372
Adult blood pressure	1,790	4,872
Other (e.g., fuel economy)	142	1,207
Total benefits	2,164	6,451
Costs		
Total costs (refining unleaded gasoline)	100	458
Net (Benefits − Costs)	2,064	5,993

Source: Paul R. Portney, "Air Pollution Policy," in *Public Policies for Environmental Protection*, ed. Paul R. Portney (Washington, DC: Resources for the Future, 1990), p. 64.

Hence, the benefits of this reduction include the cost savings of less compensatory education for children and fewer dollars for the medical treatment of heart attacks and strokes. In a comparison, the costs of eliminating lead from gasoline are only a tiny fraction of the benefits. The bottom line of Table 23–6 therefore shows a very large net benefit for society.

In sum, benefits appear to exceed the costs of many environmental regulations. As we see in the next section, however, the record in this regard could be improved. The benefits currently obtained by policy could be achieved at much less than the current costs if policy followed more closely the principles of cost-effectiveness. One way to achieve greater cost-effectiveness would be to rely more heavily on economic incentives for enforcement.

IV. Policy Alternatives: Economic Incentives

A. Problems with the Present Approach

As we have seen, the present standards-enforcement approach is technologically and bureaucratically oriented. It has produced some desirable results, but it suffers many deficiencies, including the following.

1. TECHNICAL KNOWLEDGE

Technology-based standard setting, if done properly, requires that bureaucrats understand production and abatement technologies as well as or better than industry insiders. What are "best practicable" and "best available" technologies? What is the "lowest achievable emission rate"? Can autos with internal combustion engines really be expected to emit no more than 3.4 grams of carbon monoxide per mile?

If only a few pollutants, polluters, and industries were involved, this depth-of-knowledge problem would be trifling, but there are dozens of pollutants emitted by countless polluters in thousands of industries. Once consideration of control costs is included in the standard setting, as often called for by legislation and practicality, the knowledge problem is compounded. Little wonder, then, that the EPA, with its staff numbering over 15,000, is far and away the single largest federal agency reviewed in this book.

2. ARBITRARY DECISIONS

The statutory qualifiers guiding EPA decision making—"practical," "feasible," "available," and "reasonable"—call for judgments, *arbitrary* judgments. In turn, polluters can and do challenge these judgments in federal courts. Shortly after BPT water standards were developed, for instance, 250 of them were challenged, bogging the program down for years. Distinguishing between sources stirs similar conflicts. When, for example, does a modification to a production process transform an "old" source into a "new" source under the Clean Air Act? Does a new boiler do it? Or conversion from coal to residual fuel oil? Or expanded output?

3. BENEFIT-COST

Why require autos in Fargo, North Dakota, to be as pollution-free as those in Los Angeles? The $800 cost per car is the same, but the benefits

gained are worth nickels in Fargo while probably exceeding $800 in Los Angeles. A "two-car" policy of strict controls in major metropolitan areas and relaxed controls elsewhere would attain most of the benefits of reducing auto emissions without saddling residents of clean-air areas with heavy costs. Opportunities for benefit-cost strategies such as this abound but go neglected by the EPA.

4. COST-EFFECTIVENESS OR EFFICIENCY

We can discard the foregoing criticism if we assume that the benefits of abatement are too elusive to justify adoption of full-fledged benefit-cost criteria (with both benefits and costs variable in monetary terms). However, once we accept EPA's ambient environmental standards as given (for their nonmonetized desirabilities), we can still criticize current policy for not being cost-effective. The same degree of abatement presently achieved could, in other words, be achieved at less cost to society. Although data do not exist to estimate the total cost savings for all programs nationally, some studies suggest cost savings for certain regions and pollutants to be over 80 percent. Possible savings of 30 to 35 percent, which have been found for water policy nationally, are perhaps more realistic but no less impressive.[25]

The main reason the standard-enforcement approach lacks cost-effectiveness is that it usually requires all polluters of a given class to abate by more-or-less *equal* percentages, ignoring the fact that the cost of abatement varies substantially by source. If sources with low-cost abatement could be curbed more than sources with high-cost abatement, then a given level of abatement could be achieved most cheaply.

Table 23–7 illustrates the point. The hypothetical data are the same as those used in Table 20–1 on page 424, and the problem is the same: How can we eliminate 10 million tons of sulfur dioxide pollution? The most efficient way, as we saw when discussing Table 20–1, is to use that source or method with the *lowest cost per unit* of

Table 23–7
Cost of 50 Percent Abatement by All Sources of SO_2 Using Data from Table 20–1

(1) Source of Pollution	(2) Emissions in Millions of Tons	(3) 50% Reduction, Each Source	(4) Cost in Millions of Dollars
A	3 m	0.5 × 3 m = 1.5 m	1.5 m × $100 = $ 150 m
B	4 m	0.5 × 4 m = 2.0 m	2.0 m × $600 = $1,200 m
C	2 m	0.5 × 2 m = 1.0 m	1.0 m × $400 = $ 400 m
D	4 m	0.5 × 4 m = 2.0 m	2.0 m × $200 = $ 400 m
E	1 m	0.5 × 1 m = 0.5 m	0.5 m × $500 = $ 250 m
F	6 m	0.5 × 6 m = 3.0 m	3.0 m × $300 = $ 900 m
Totals	20 m	0.5 × 20 m = 10 m	$3,300 m

abatement first (source A), second lowest cost next (source D), and so on, until the 10-million-ton target is reached. Total cost by this approach would be $2,000 million. Notice that some sources of pollution (A and D) are required to abate *completely,* another to abate only *partially* (½ F), and the remainder *not at all* (B, C, and E).

Alternatively, we could achieve the 10-million-ton target by calling for 50 percent abatement by each source. As shown in column (2) of Table 23–7, all sources together emit 20 million tons. So 50 percent abatement by each would hit the ten-ton target. The tonnage reduction of each source is then given in column (3) of Table 23–7 (1.5 m for A, for instance). And the total cost of each source's abatement effort is given in column (4), where the tonnage reduction is multiplied by the abatement cost per ton of reduction (as computed earlier in column (4) of Table 20–1). Adding the costs of all sources yields a total cost for this 50 percent across-the-board cutback of $3,300 million. This total cost is *65 percent higher* than the $2,000 million cost of relying on low-cost abatement more heavily than on high-cost abatement. Yet the achievement is the same at 10 million tons of SO_2 abatement.

5. INCENTIVE TO ABATE

Compliance delays and failures such as those mentioned earlier suggest that many polluters find it cheaper to challenge regulations in court, to violate established standards, and to wheedle and waffle in negotiating with the EPA as long as they can. The EPA has now elevated fines to eradicate the gains of noncompliance. Even if we assume that this particular problem of incentives is now solved, there still remains another. All a polluter need do is meet his standard. There is *no* incentive to do better and abate more if the opportunity avails itself through newly discovered low-cost technologies.

6. INNOVATION

The standard-enforcement approach can be faulted also for not encouraging innovation in control technologies. As A. V. Kneese and C. L. Schultze put it:

> Auto emission controls pay no attention to the potentialities of new engine developments. The law that stipulates water effluent limits based on the "best available technology economically achievable" discourages innovation because that would put firms in the ironic position of handing the regulatory authorities the means of imposing on

them new and more costly standards of pollution control.[26]

Other problems with the standards-enforcement approach could be mentioned, but the foregoing are the main ones.[27] To correct or alleviate most if not all these deficiencies, economists advocate a shift toward policies embodying economic incentives, including marketable permits and effluent taxes. These alternatives are not panaceas. They too have faults, and, indeed, many economists believe they are inappropriate for controlling highly toxic pollutants, whose environmental dangers are so serious as to warrant tight regulation and virtually 100 percent abatement. Still, policies imposing economic incentives could supplant the vast bulk of standards-enforcement regulation, Congress willing.

B. Bubbles and Offsets: First Steps

To introduce our discussion of such policies we can acknowledge two steps in the desired direction already taken by the EPA. In 1979 its **bubble** policy was introduced. Whereas before the EPA had regulated discharges stack by stack, calling for near-equal percentage emission cutbacks at each physical source, the bubble policy now places an imaginary bubble over an entire plant, allowing the plant to meet its overall emission standards by putting extra controls on discharge points that have low control costs and relaxing controls on discharge points that have high control costs. Because plant managers make the decision as to where in the plant's abatement will be greatest, the plant's overall abatement cost is minimized without the EPA having to acquire detailed knowledge of technology and expense. The large potential cost savings from the plant by plant bubble approach are illustrated in a study of fifty-two Du Pont plants having a total of 548 sources of hydrocarbon emissions. Source-by-source reduction of 85 percent of the emissions cost $105.7 million annually (in 1975 dollars). In contrast, the same 85 percent reduction on a plant-by-plant basis would have cost only $42.6 million, a remarkable 63.1 percent saving.[28]

By the late 1980s, there were 132 federal- and state-sanctioned bubbles. The estimated cost savings from these bubbles exceeded $435 million (in comparison to the costs of traditional air pollution regulations). As an extra bonus, many of these bubbles were achieving greater emission reductions than required by the original regulations while the rest were yielding equivalent reductions.[29]

Even before bubbles became fashionable, **offsets** were being tried, as provided under the 1977 Clean Air Act Amendments. Offsets arose because without them, industrial growth in nonattainment areas would have been completely shackled, for growth would have brought new sources of pollution where pollution already exceeded ambient standards (see item A.1.b. in Table 23–3 for reference). The idea of the offset is to permit a new source to pollute insofar as that new source offsets the new pollution by getting old sources in the area to reduce their pollution commensurately. In one case under the program, a cement company wanting to build in New Braunfels, Texas, entered into an agreement to pay for the installation of dust collectors at another local company. In another instance the Times Mirror Company was able to expand greatly a paper mill near Portland, Oregon, after purchasing the right to emit about 150 tons of extra hydrocarbons into the air annually, which tonnage was previously emitted by local dry cleaning and wood-coating establishments. The purchase price? About $50,000.[30] By 1985 over 2,500 such offset transactions had occurred.

Why would new sources want to pay others to abate instead of abating themselves? Because it would be cheaper that way. Why would an old source agree to abate? Because the compensation received would cover the cost of abatement and maybe more. It is the combination of these questions and answers that reveals the social cost savings in the offset approach. Overall, abatement remains unchanged or increases because the low-cost abaters are induced to carry the abatement burden for high-cost abaters.

C. Marketable Pollution Permits

Many economists urge that the bubble and offset policies be expanded until full-fledged **markets for pollution rights** are established to protect both air and water.[31] Imagine, for instance, that total allowable emissions of sulfur dioxide in the northern Ohio area would be set at, say, 100,000 tons annually. One hundred permits of 1,000 tons each could then be auctioned off to the highest bidders among those who want to pollute. Those facing relatively high abatement costs would bid high for permits because they would rather pay to pollute than pay to abate. Those facing relatively low abatement costs would bid low because for them rights to pollute would not be worth much, given their relative ease of abating. Low-cost abaters would thus abate more than high-cost abaters for a cost-effective result. The General Accounting Office estimated in 1981 that a "viable market in air pollution rights" could cut pollution control costs *at least* 40%.[32] That would be nearly $9 billion off the cost in 1979. Substantial savings for water could be expected as well.

There are, aside from cost-effectiveness, a number of other good qualities that recommend marketable pollution permits. Implementation of this approach would probably be much simpler than the standards-enforcement approach, for the knowledge required of the regulators would be greatly reduced, and fewer arbitrary judgments subject to court challenge would have to be made. There would be, in a word, less *meddling* in the affairs of businesspeople, because they would then assume most of the burden of deciding the where, the who, and the how of abatement. Another bonus of this approach is that it would encourage rather than stifle innovations in abatement technology. Abaters would not be wedded to specific technologies, and they would be constantly on the lookout for new ways to abate at lower costs.

One potential drawback to marketable permits is that they give the appearance of being *inequitable*. The standards-enforcement approach tends to call for equal percentage curtailments from all sources, which sounds fair. By comparison, marketable permits would cause low-cost abaters to abate more and allow high-cost abaters to abate less, giving low-cost abaters a greater share of the overall financial burden than before. Whether or not this is in fact unfair, however, depends on one's definition of fairness. With standards-enforcement the physical percentages tend toward equality, but the financial burden falls heaviest on the high-cost abaters. (Check column (4) of Table 23–7 again.) With marketable permits, the physical percentages diverge substantially, but the financial burden is spread more evenly because the share of low-cost abaters rises and that of high-cost abaters falls. Value judgments differ among people, but most folks might find this latter result more fair than the former. Notice, too, that with permits the costs are not merely more evenly distributed; they are, through efficiency, *lower overall,* which seems fairer to society as a whole. Finally, staunch environmentalists might even find fairness in this approach. They could enter the bidding to keep some permits out of the hands of polluters, thereby reducing the level of pollution even below EPA-authorized levels.

Spurred by these several attractive features of marketable permits, Congress passed such a system for sulfur dioxide abatement at electric power plants. This 1990 measure is so important that it warrants an appendix to this chapter.

D. Effluent Taxes

Effluent taxes (or emission fees) work on the same principle as marketable pollution permits do. The main difference in concept is that, whereas the permit approach sets the *quantity* of pollution allowed and lets the market determine the price of pollution rights, the tax approach sets the *price* polluters must pay to pollute and lets the ultimate quantity of pollution be determined by abatement costs relative to the tax. Any quantity of abatement achieved by marketable permits could be realized through a tax by raising the tax on pollution high enough to discourage an equal amount of pollution.

Figure 23–6 illustrates the tax approach with familiar data taken from Tables 20–1 and 23–7. The cost of abatement rises by steps: Source A at $100 per ton of SO_2 removed; source D at $200 per ton; and so on. With a tax on SO_2 emissions, each source would have to decide whether to pollute and pay the tax or abate and avoid the tax. Cost minimization determines the choice. If the tax were, say, $250 per ton of SO_2 emitted, sources A and D, whose abatement costs are $100 and $200 per ton, would find it in their interest to abate and avoid the tax, with the result that 7 million tons of SO_2 would be removed from the air. Remaining sources accounting for 13 million tons would choose to pollute and pay, because their costs per ton of abatement exceed the $250 tax per ton. (Their total tax bill would be $250 × 13 million = $3,250 million, but their total abatement bill would be $5,500 million.) Raising the tax to $450 per ton would, however, induce abatement from sources F and C as well as A and D because $450 exceeds their abatement costs of $300 and $400, respectively. With A, D, F, and C abating, 15 million tons of SO_2 would be removed from the air. It follows that still higher taxes would bring still greater abatement.

Development of taxes requires (1) selection of a *basis* for each tax, such as the tonnage of SO_2, the poundage of BOD, or the volume of hydrocarbons, (2) methods of *monitoring* the flow of pollutants under the selected bases, and (3) specification of the tax *rate*. According to economic ideals, the tax rate should correspond to the marginal costs of pollution, for it would then generate a degree of abatement at which the marginal cost of pollution would just match the marginal cost of abatement (as shown earlier in Figure 20–2 on page 420). In reality, this cannot be done because we do not know the marginal costs of pollution with accuracy. The implication of the ideal is, however, that tax rates would be highest where pollution is most concentrated, where the pollutant is most harmful, and where the greatest number of people are threatened.

Given the great conceptual similarity between emission taxes and marketable permits, it is hardly surprising that the qualities of the two approaches are similar. The tax requires no more than a modicum of technical knowledge and relatively few arbitrary decisions on the part of government officials, qualities that minimize intrusion into the affairs of businesses. The tax is cost-effective because low-cost abaters curb their pollution more than high-cost abaters do. The tax imposes economic incentives to innovate new and cheaper abatement technologies. Finally, the equity implications are similar, too.

Permits and taxes do differ, however. Theoretically, the marketable permit approach might be superior to a tax on grounds that the quantity of abatement achieved is more certain in advance of program implementation. The permit approach is also more insulated against inflation, for tax rates would have to be raised

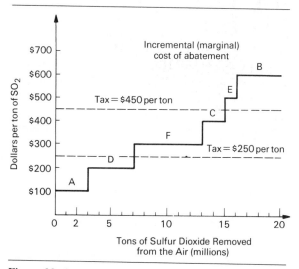

Figure 23–6
Effluent Tax Approach to Abatement

with inflation to maintain a constant degree of abatement.[33]

Among the tax's advantages, the tax presses polluters to abate more and more as innovation reduces the cost of abatement. Figure 23–7 illustrates this for a single polluter. Two curves for the marginal cost of abatement are shown—one for old, high-cost technology, MC_{old}, the other for new, low-cost technology, MC_{new}. (Both rise with greater abatement, which is more realistic than the constant abatement cost per polluter assumed earlier.) At the tax rate indicated, cost minimization would cause the firm to abate to point *J (M)* under the old technology and to point *K (N)* under the new technology. The reason for this is that the total cost of abatement plus tax is reduced from area *OJLO** to area *OKLO** by such "good" behavior.[34] Notice that these savings also induce greater innovation in abatement methods than otherwise.

The tax approach has won adoption in Euro-

pean efforts to control water pollution, especially in Germany, Italy, France, and the Netherlands. It has been used against aircraft noise, pesticides, and other nuisances as well.[35]

Proposals for emission taxes in the United States have generally been rebuffed, however, primarily for political reasons. There is a small "feedstock" charge on chemicals and petroleum feedstocks to finance the costs of cleaning up hazardous waste sites. There is also a CFC tax. These fees are typically so small, however, that they do not affect behavior appreciably. The closest thing to a large-scale pollution tax presently in force in the United States is the mandatory deposit on beverage containers that 10 states currently impose. Oregon's "Bottle Bill" of 1971 introduced the idea by imposing a mandatory refundable deposit of 5 cents on standard beer and soda pop containers plus a larger deposit on unique containers. The purpose of the program was to encourage the use and reuse of reusable containers to cut down on solid waste, reduce litter, and save energy. By all accounts the program has been resoundingly successful on all counts. Yet stiff opposition by beverage industry interests and container manufacturers has prevented the spread of this policy to the national level or even beyond the 10 states currently in the unlittered lot.[36]

In short, the tax approach represents more than the ivory-towered theorizing of economists. It has been tried both here and abroad in various ways that illuminate its promise. That promise has only begun to be tapped, and it is hoped that experiments with it will be greatly expanded in the future.

Summary

What is pollution? It occurs when one use of the environment, waste disposal in particular, diminishes other environmental service capabilities of value—habitat and amenity services especially.

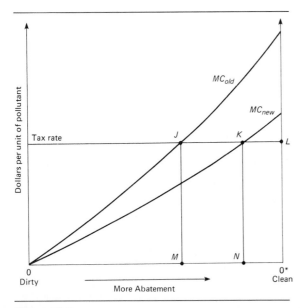

Figure 23–7
Incentive to Abate Further Under a Tax, Given an Innovation

The waste substances of greatest damage to the air are particulates, sulfur dioxide, nitrogen oxides, hydrocarbons, lead, and carbon monoxide. Water pollutants are more varied, ranging from simply BOD to highly toxic metals. Land pollutants include solid wastes and toxic chemicals. Many pollutants can be neutralized by the environment's dissipation and purification processes, suggesting that 100 percent abatement of all pollutants is neither necessary nor desirable. On the other hand, complacency is not warranted either, for even the most innocent of pollutants can become injurious through concentration.

What has been done about pollution? The U. S. strategy has been direct control through the development of elaborate emission standards and their enforcement. The standards have been technologically based, tempered slightly by cost considerations. The result is that emitters of a given class are typically pressed to curb their discharges by some fairly common percentage figure, like 60 percent. In turn, enforcement follows a bureaucratic-legalistic course entailing (1) certifications or permits, (2) monitoring, and (3) remedies of assorted types and severity.

Broad standards for ambient *air* conditions incorporate a threshold concept at primary and secondary levels presumed to be protective of humans first and other things second. Modified to prevent substantial deterioration in relatively clean areas, these broad standards have been translated into narrow emission standards that vary by mobility and age of emitting source, by enforcement agency, and by attainment status (see Table 23–3). Enforcement effort has yielded a level of compliance distorted upward by shifting standards and incomplete monitoring, with the result that ambient standards in many areas have not been achieved.

Broad *water* standards originally aimed to completely eliminate point-source discharges by 1985. Best practicable (BPT) and best available (BAT) technologies were steps along the way. Stumbling on the very first step (BPT in 1977),

officials revamped policy to postpone BPT standards for some, modify BAT standards for all, and drop the idea that emissions be eliminated. Narrow standards under these guidelines set emission limits for specific sources, as enforced by 67,000 permits, extensive monitoring, and threatened penalties.

Toxic substances, both as products and wastes, have grabbed the attention of the EPA. Regulations are tighter here than elsewhere, incorporating such features as a burden of proof of safety on proponents of new chemical substances and cradle-to-grave control of hazardous wastes.

What is the impact of these policies? For one thing, they perpetrate costs now running more than $100 billion annually. Though indeed large, these costs are a tiny fraction of the GNP, so macroeconomic impacts on unemployment, inflation, productivity growth, and trade balances tend to be slight.

The benefits of pollution control can be measured, at least theoretically, by the amount pollution costs are reduced, which should broadly correspond to people's willingness to pay for a cleaner environment. Practical difficulties reduce measurement to guesswork, but that guesswork has succeeded in demonstrating that abatement is worth scores of billions of dollars a year in improved health, broadened recreation opportunities, reduced property damage, and so on.

What policy improvements could be made? Greater reliance on instruments imposing economic incentives—that is, marketable pollution permits and emission taxes—would seem to be wise. They have the advantage of (1) requiring less technical knowledge, (2) minimizing bureaucratic meddling, (3) promoting cost-effectiveness or efficiency, and (4) accommodating and even encouraging innovation in abatement technology. Their cost-effectiveness is a particularly attractive point; studies indicate that immense cost savings, 80 percent in some cases, could be realized without compromising environmental ideals.

These alternatives have their own drawbacks, and they therefore should not take over the entire burden of policy. What seems best is a mix of instruments, including even moral suasion in the mix. The standards-enforcement approach seems particularly well suited to handling the problem of toxic substances, which in many instances must be banned. Marketable permits and emission taxes seem most appropriate for emissions that are generated regularly and that are fairly easily monitored—BOD and SO_2, for example.

Questions and Exercises for Chapter 23

1. The *economic* definition of pollution differs from the *physical* definition. How does the economic definition relate to optimal allocation of resources? How does "scarcity" influence problem assessment here?
2. What has been the trend in air and water pollutants?
3. Why is it important to distinguish between pollutants in their severity and persistence?
4. Why do present regulations embody the entire range of regulatory activities—broad and narrow standards, permits, certification, and so forth?
5. Characterize the broad standards for "criteria" air pollutants.
6. To what extent have costs been taken into account, either systematically or haphazardly, in developing and amending air and water standards?
7. Compare and contrast hazardous substance control with water pollution control of conventional pollutants.
8. What types of costs arise from abatement? Benefits?
9. Identify bubbles and offsets, explaining how they help lessen regulatory costs.
10. Compare and contrast the regulatory approach with the marketable permits approach.
11. What is similar about marketable permits and effluent taxes? What is different?

Appendix to Chapter 23

The Clean Air Act Amendments of 1990 retained a command and control philosophy. They also used the primary and secondary National Ambient Air Quality Standards for overall air quality, as described in the text. So much is "old hat." The 1990 amendments were revolutionary, however. They called for a 50 percent reduction in sulfur dioxide emissions and provided an innovative enforcement mechanism. Marketable permits will be relied on in a big way for the first time.

The amendments are complex, bringing abatement in two phases according to whether a given coal-burning power plant is among the 110 largest (with a 1995 compliance deadline) or among all the others (with a year 2000 deadline). The basic idea is simple, though. A ceiling of 8.9 million tons of SO_2 emissions has been set (a broad standard of sorts). This allowed amount will be allocated to coal-fired power plants in the form of annual allowances that match each plant's emission limits (narrow standards). Thus, if ABC plant has emission limits of, say, 200 tons annually, it will be given 200 allowances. If the company owning the plant can reduce SO_2 emissions *below* its allowable level, it will have allowances (one ton of extra SO_2 abatement per year equalling one allowance) that it can save for future use, trade with another polluter, or sell to another polluter. Conversely, a company that operates *above* its allowable level will have to purchase enough allowances from others to cover its excess emissions. Any emissions not covered by allowances will result in a fine of $2,000 per ton of emission, which is a rather steep fine. Hence, it is expected that firms with excess emissions will either shut down or purchase the necessary permits rather than remain in violation.

There will thus be a market in SO_2 allowances, with some companies selling them (those who abate more than the standard) and some companies buying (those who abate less than the standard). To enforce the program, to make certain that each polluter has an allowance for each ton of SO_2 emitted, all controlled utilities must be equipped with a continuous emission monitoring (CEM) system. Just as your bank must keep track of every penny in your checking account, CEM technology has to keep track of every ton of SO_2 emitted from controlled power plants. The CEM equipment must be installed in the largest utilities by November 15, 1993 and in the other utilities by January 1, 1995.

Congress and the EPA hope that the market for allowances will achieve three ends:

1. Incentives for sources to choose least-cost control options (cost-effectiveness).
2. Incentives to reduce emissions below allowable levels.
3. Flexibility.[37]

Cost-effectiveness gets a boost because those with low costs of abatement will abate more (in order to sell their allowances), whereas those facing high costs of abatement will abate less (preferring instead to buy allowances). The incentive to reduce emissions below allowable levels comes about because it is profitable not to pollute under the system insofar as a company can abate at a cost that falls below the price that allowances will have in the marketplace. The price of these allowances by some estimates is expected to run as high as $1,100 per ton of SO_2. Finally, flexibility is encouraged in two ways. On a large scale, companies will have the flexibility to abate more or less than their standards (to become sellers or buyers of allowances). On a small scale, companies will have enhanced flexibility in choosing technologies and strategies to abate, thereby becoming internally cost-effective. Their strategies could include the following:

- Substituting one SO_2 source for another.
- Pooling emission reduction requirements across two or more affected units.

- Crafting compliance strategies that take advantage of limited time extensions that will be available.[38]

Notes

1. *Washington Post National Weekly Edition* (December 12–18, 1988), p. 9.

2. *The Economist,* March 11, 1989, pp. 87–88; *Wall Street Journal,* 28 March 1988, p. 6.

3. T. Page, R. H. Harris, and S. S. Epstein, "Drinking Water and Cancer Mortality in Louisiana," *Science* (July 2, 1977): 55–57.

4. After abandonment by the Hooker Chemical and Plastics Company, which had used Love Canal as a dumping site from 1947 to 1953, several hundred homes and an elementary school were constructed in the area, which is in Niagara Falls, NY. After residents complained of abnormal numbers of miscarriages, birth defects, cancer, and a variety of other illnesses, the area was checked by health authorities who found what they called a "grave and imminent peril." Contaminated ground water was seeping into basements and rising to the surface. The air contained pollution 5,000 times maximum safe levels. More than 260 families had to be evacuated and the area quarantined. Damage suits topped $3 billion.

5. For a review see William J. Baumol and Wallace E. Oates, *Economics, Environmental Policy and the Quality of Life* (Englewood Cliffs, NJ: Prentice Hall, 1979), pp. 217–366, or Tom Tietenberg, *Environmental and Natural Resource Economics,* 2nd ed. Glenview, IL: Scott, Foresman, 1988).

6. Baumol and Oates, *Economics . . . Quality of Life,* p. 5.

7. Allen V. Kneese and Charles L. Schultze, *Pollution, Prices, and Public Policy* (Washington, DC: Brookings Institution, 1975), pp. 30–50.

8. David Zwick and Mary Benstock, *Water Wasteland* (New York: Grossman, 1971), and John Esposito, *Vanishing Air* (New York: Grossman, 1970).

9. Walter A. Rosenbaum, *Environmental Politics and Policy,* 2nd ed. (Washington, DC: Congressional Quarterly Press, 1991), pp. 23–26. On the stability of policy see Paul R. Portney, ed., *Public Policies for Environmental Protection* (Washington, DC: Resources for the Future, 1990).

10. A. Myrick Freeman III. "Air and Water Pollution Policy," in *Current Issues in U. S. Environmental Policy,* ed. P. R. Portney (Baltimore: Johns Hopkins University Press, 1978), pp. 31–34.

11. David Harrison, Jr. and Paul R. Portney, "Making Ready for the Clean Air Act," *Regulation* (March/April 1981): 24–31.

12. Advocates of benefit-cost qualify their endorsement. For example, Paul Portney, co-author of the article cited in note 11, says the "science" of valuing environmental benefits and costs is still "far short" of being able to make comparisons between benefits and costs in a precise way. Hence, "the balancing approach is best left in a qualitative or judgmental form." Portney, "EPA and . . . Regulation," p. 15.

13. Because 1970–1971 cars were already under control as compared to earlier cars, the 90 percent initial reduction was actually more than 90 percent when compared to pre-1968 uncontrolled cars.

14. Council on Environmental Quality, *Environmental Quality 1984* (Washington, DC, 1985), p. 65.

15. Council on Environmental Quality, *Environmental Quality 20th Annual Report* (Washington, DC, 1990), pp. 154–157.

16. Council on Environmental Quality, *Environmental Quality 1978* (Washington, DC, 1978), pp. 108–110.

17. A. Myrick Freeman III, "Water Pollution Policy," in *Public Policies for Environmental Protection*, ed. P. R. Portney, p. 106.

18. Two contrasting cases illustrate the point: Canning industry pollutants are BOD, suspended solids, fecal coliform, pH, oil and grease. Inorganic chemical industry pollutants include these (except fecal coliform) and also ammonia, fluoride, sulfite, sulfide, cyanide, bromide, arsenic, barium, cadmium, chromium, copper, iron, lead, manganese, and other metals.

19. General Accounting Office, "Waste Water Discharges Are Not Complying With EPA Control Permits" (Washington, DC: 1983), pp. 7–10.

20. Council on Environmental Quality, *Environmental Quality, 20th Annual Report* (Washington, DC, 1990), pp. 156–159.

21. Freeman, "Water Pollution Policy," pp. 114–120.

22. For other summaries, see the articles by Roger C. Dower and Michael Shapiro in *Public Policies for Environmental Protection*, ed. Paul R. Portney (Washington, DC: Resources for the Future, 1990), pp. 151–241.

23. *Wall Street Journal*, 9 December 1991, p. B1.

24. Portney, "EPA and . . . Regulation," pp. 10–11. As regards foreign comparisons, it may be noted that by many indicators Japan, our main rival, has made greater environmental improvements than we have. See Organization for Economic Co-operation and Development, *Environmental Indicators, A Preliminary Set* (Paris: OECD, 1991). Moreover, tough standards trigger innovation in the area of abatement technology, which can then be marketed abroad. See, e.g., Michael E. Porter, "America's Green Strategy," *Scientific American* (April 1991), p. 168.

25. For a survey see Tom H. Tietenberg, "Economic Instruments for Environmental Regulation," *Oxford Review of Economic Policy* (Spring 1990): 17–31. Fraas and Munley analyze the cost of technologies that EPA accepted and rejected when developing BAT standards for water abatement. They find that by giving greater weight to cost effectiveness, EPA "could have reduced the cost of BAT-level treatment requirements by one-third and, at the same time, achieved some small additional pollution reduction." Arthur G. Fraas and Vincent G. Munley, "Economic Objectives within a Bureaucratic Decision Process," *Journal of Environmental Economics and Management* (vol. 17, 1989): 45.

26. Kneese and Schultze, *Pollution . . . and Public Policy,* pp. 82–83.

27. For a full discussion see Baumol and Oates, *Economics and . . . Quality of Life,* pp. 230–245, 323–366.

28. M. T. Maloney and Bruce Yandle, "Bubbles and Efficiency," *Regulation* (May/June 1980): 49–52.

29. Robert W. Hahn and Gordon L. Hester, "Where Did All the Markets Go? An Analysis of EPA's Emissions Trading Program," *Yale Journal on Regulation* (Winter 1989): 109–153.

30. For further examples see National Commission on Air Quality, *To Breathe Clean Air* (Washington, DC, 1981), pp. 136–137.

31. The idea originated with J. H. Dales, *Pollution, Property, and Prices* (Toronto: University of Toronto Press, 1968).

32. *Wall Street Journal*, 18 June 1981, p. 25.

33. Baumol and Oates, *Economies and . . . Quality of Life,* pp. 250–253.

34. To break this down, at the J solution total abatement cost will be the area under the marginal cost of abatement curve, OJM, and the total tax bill will be the tax rate MJ times the amount of pollution MO^*, which is area $MJLO^*$. Both together are total combined cost area $OJLO^*$. At the K solution, total abatement cost is area OKN, and the tax bill is area $NKLO^*$. The combined total is then area $OKLO^*$.

35. Organization for Economic Co-operation and Development, *Economic Instruments for Environmental Protection* (Paris: OECD, 1989), pp. 33–73.

36. W. Kent Moore and David L. Scott, "Beverage Container Deposit Laws: A Survey of the Issues and Results," *Journal of Consumer Affairs* (Summer 1983): 57–80. California is not discussed by Moore and Scott.

37. Carl S. Paretto and Sam K. Bae, "A Market-based Approach to Pollution Control," *Public Utilities Fortnightly* (May 1, 1991): 26–30.

38. Ibid.

PART VI

Miscellaneous Policies

Chapter 24
Patents and R&D Funding

Chapter 25
Promotion and Protection Policies

Chapter 26
Equal Employment Opportunity

Chapter 24

Patents and
R&D Funding

*The patent system added the fuel of
interest to the fire of genius.*
— Abe Lincoln

From the first squawky telephone to the latest supersonic airplane, technological change has done more than anything else to shape our modern economy and everyday life. Innovation spurs growth, boosts productivity, lifts profits, lengthens lives, generates jobs, and enriches experiences. Nearly half of all this century's gains in real income can be attributed to technological progress. The lion's share of the products we now use and take for granted simply did not exist only four generations ago—television, frozen food, zippers, computers, air conditioning, penicillin, nylon, refrigerators, synthetic detergents, Frisbees, and so on.

Two government policies promoting technical progress are the concern of this chapter—patents and R&D funding. To be sure, invention and innovation would exist without these policies. The wheel is evidence of that. But there would be considerably less invention and innovation. Thus, the main purpose of these policies is to stimulate more technical progress than the free market would provide.

Our discussion of patents answers such questions as: What is a patent? What can be patented? Why have patents? What are the benefits and costs of patents? Our discussion of government funding of research and development covers two basic questions: What amounts of money are involved? Why is such funding needed?[1]

I. The Patent System: Nature and Scope

A. Background

A patent is a **monopoly right** to make and sell some product, or use some process, that is governmentally granted for a limited number of years as a reward for invention. The character and duration of this right differs from country to country. United States law grants "for the terms of seventeen years [from the patent's date] . . .

the right to exclude others from making, using, or selling the invention throughout the United States."[2] The right is a form of private property that can be bought and sold, traded, given away, and leased or licensed for the use of others (who pay a "royalty" for the privilege). The invention covered can even go unused if the owner wishes. Moreover, although only individuals can be awarded patents, corporate employees typically "assign" their patents to their employers, and independent inventors often sell or license their patents to others for commercial application.

Regardless of ultimate ownership, roughly half of all patents go unused because the inventions they cover are too far ahead of their time, too costly to develop relative to the potential profit, or too unsettling to the ultimate owner's old way of doing things. Many go unused because close substitutes for the invention are available. Thus, the monopoly granted may be only a measly one.

Indeed, more than 4 million patents have been issued since inception of the system. Of late, the annual flow tops 70,000. If these figures are not big enough to suggest to you that many if not most patented inventions are rather pedestrian, consider the following: an electric fork that winds spaghetti, an alarm clock that hits you on the head, and a diaper for parakeets. (Emerson once said, "Build a better mousetrap and the world will beat a path to your door." People still believe that. About 3,300 mousetrap patents have been granted since 1838, when the first one was issued.)[3]

Fortunately, enforcement of any patent is left up to the patent holder. Accused infringers must be hauled into court by patentees. The original Bell telephone patents, for instance, were enforced with more than 600 infringement suits initiated by Bell interests. What is more, the patent office does not have final say as to what constitutes a valid patent. The federal courts have final say. So, once in court, an infringer almost always defends himself against a patentee's attack by

claiming the patent is invalid. This defense is by no means futile because court judges generally hold more stringent standards of patentability than the patent office. Approximately 20 percent of all patents coming under court review are declared invalid and unenforceable. The chief cause for rejection is a lack of "inventiveness."[4] The remaining reasons for invalidation can be understood only after an explanation of what can and cannot be patented.

B. Patentability

According to statute law, "Whoever invents or discovers any new and useful process, machine, manufacture, or composition of matter, or any new and useful improvement thereof, may obtain a patent therefor." Embedded in the language are four criteria for patentability: (1) inventiveness, (2) novelty, (3) utility, and (4) subject matter.

To cross the threshold of **inventiveness,** the discovery must be "nonobvious" at the time "to a person having ordinary skill in the art." There must, in other words, be some creativity. Just how much creativity is required and how much creativity went into any claimed invention are often difficult to judge. The uncertainties in the "nonobvious" standard are, in fact, almost vague and various enough to call for discriminating creativity on the part of patent examiners. To restate the problem more concretely, do you think the following should qualify? Putting a rubber erasure on the end of a pencil? Making doorknobs of clay rather than metal or wood? Devising a motorized golf bag cart? All three were in fact awarded patents, but when tested in court, two were found wanting. Given the nature of the problem, it is hard to disagree with Judge Learned Hand, who once grumbled that the test of invention was little more than a vague and fugitive "phantom."[5]

As for **novelty,** the invention must not be previously known or used. This standard is fairly straightforward, but it takes patent examiners a long time to review past patents and published scientific papers in search of duplication. Of all standards, **utility** is certainly the least demanding. As the extravagant examples given earlier and Figure 24–1 illustrate, many approved inventions are empty of all but the most fantastic applications.

Because patentable **subject matter** is limited to mechanical, electrical, or chemical processes and compositions, much is excluded. Discovery of fundamental laws of nature, such as $E = mc^2$, may not be patented, however brilliant or useful their discovery may be. The same holds for mathematical formulas, managerial strategies, teaching methods, and the like. Products of nature are likewise unpatentable, although this rule has exceptions.

In 1980 the Supreme Court made headlines by deciding that manmade living organisms could be patented. The organism at issue was a new bacterium capable of "eating" crude oil, making it useful in cleaning up oil spills. The decision had broad implications because it opened the door for patents on all kinds of newly created creatures. In 1988 a patent was granted for a genetically engineered mouse (to be used in tests of carcinogenic substances). Genetically altered cattle, swine, and chickens are now in the works. These developments have sparked controversy because to some people they gave birth to a Brave New World. One overwrought group claimed that such patenting "lays the groundwork for corporations to own the processes of life in the centuries to come."[6]

Controversy also surrounds patents for computer software.[7] Prompted by some suggestive Supreme Court opinions and a rise in applications for software patents, the Patent and Trademark Office stated in 1989 that mathematical algorithms are, as such, not patentable (because they are like laws of nature) but that *applications* of mathematical algorithms, as found in software, may be patented as new processes. IBM and Apple have pursued this extension of patentability. Other software developers have not. To obtain a patent, the details of a software program must be made public, something unattractive to many software innovators. Moreover, a patent can take three years to obtain and cost as much as $20,000 in legal fees. Because software can be copyrighted as well as patented, many software developers prefer the copyright alternative. (Software copyrights are less protective than patents, but they are cheaper to obtain and longer lasting.)

Figure 24–1
The Twidd, a device that facilitates thumb twiddling, won patent No. 4,227,342 in 1979. The patent states: "To those twiddlers who lack sufficient coordination, not only is the repose and peace of mind which thumb twiddling normally brings not available, but the inability to carry out the twiddling successfully, including inadvertent bumping of the thumbs, . . . causes additional frustration." *(Wall Street Journal,* January 19, 1983, p. 25)

C. Obtaining a Patent

The rules and regulations of patentability give the appearance of an imposing thicket, blocking all but a privileged few, but of the more than 100,00 patent applications filed annually, 65 percent or so gain patent office approval. Applicants are aided not only by lenient standards of invention and utility but also by an army of clever, well-heeled patent attorneys. Indeed, these attorneys are often more crucial to obtaining a patent than an invention is.[8]

The point is driven home by citing patent 549,160, which a patent attorney obtained for himself in 1895, and which covered what later proved to be the wonder machine of our modern age—the automobile. According to legend, George Selden stole ideas from genuine auto engineers and bluffed his way far enough along to see his auto patent earn $5.8 million in royalties and gain the approval of a U. S. District Court. The only person willing and able to challenge the validity of Selden's patent was Henry Ford, who eventually won his case in circuit court.[9]

II. Two Case Studies

At its best, the patent system stimulates progress, rewards deserving inventors and innovators, and arouses competition. At its worst, it fosters opposite tendencies. Each extreme may be vividly depicted by a case history.

A. United States Gypsum and Wallboard

There is nothing especially clever about wallboard, looking at it with today's familiarity. It is plaster sandwiched between two sheets of paper. At the turn of the century, all wallboard was produced with open edges that exposed the plaster filler. Exposure caused the edges to chip and crumble when bumped in transit. The obvious remedy for this problem—paper covering for the edges as well as the body of the wallboard—was hit on in 1912 and won for its discoverer, one Utzman, patent 1,034,746. This patent covered the process of closing the edges of wallboard by folding the bottom cover sheet over the edge and then affixing the top cover sheet.

Realizing its great value, United States Gypsum Corporation (called U. S. Gypsum), the leading wallboard producer of the day, acquired the Utzman patent and then used it as a springboard to four decades of industry dominance.[10] On the face of it, the odds against U. S. Gypsum's conquest were rather large, for it was based on a brittle springboard. Aside from the fact that the Utzman patent lasted only seventeen years, competitors could easily "invent around" it by closing wallboard edges in other, equally obvious ways. The top cover sheet could fold toward the bottom, the two cover sheets could *both* fold to overlap the edge, the two cover sheets could be imbedded in the center of the plaster edge, a separate sheet could cap the edge, and so on. U. S. Gypsum, however, was able to control the competition these options offered its smaller rivals by tenaciously suing for infringement at every fold. After thus "softening" up its competitors, U. S. Gypsum bought their renegade patents.

In exchange for the cooperation of its rivals, U. S. Gypsum licensed them to use its accumulated patents through agreements that fixed the prices all parties charged for their wallboard. While building these arrangements, U. S. Gypsum seems to have avoided court and favored nontrial settlements as often as possible, perhaps out of fear that its patents would be found invalid if ever truly tested. In other words, competitors were sufficiently strong and U. S. Gypsum's patents were sufficiently weak that the company could not monopolize the trade. At best, it attained a 57 percent market share. Even so, U. S. Gypsum was resourceful enough to construct a network of license agreements that effectively cartelized the industry. "According to the plans we have," an optimistic executive said at one point, "we figure that there is a possibility of us holding the price steady on wallboard for the next fourteen or fifteen years which means much to the industry."[11] How much it meant is measured by the fact that in 1928, U. S. Gypsum reportedly earned a profit of $11.09 per 1,000 square feet of wallboard over the manufacturing cost of $10.50.

Subsequent patents on wallboard became the basis of subsequent cartelization, but the cartel's life was cut short by action of the Antitrust Division of the Department of Justice. Attacked for violating the Sherman Act, the cartel was dissolved after the Supreme Court decided in 1947 that "regardless of motive, the Sherman Act bars patent exploitation of the kind that was here attempted."[12]

B. Chester Carlson and Xerox

Born to the wife of an itinerant barber and raised in poverty, Chester Carlson invented xerography.[13] Various family tragedies compelled Carlson to work unceasingly from age 12 to support his family and his education. His dire boyhood circumstances induced dreams of escape. In his own words,

> At this stage in my life, I was entranced by the accounts I read of the work and successes of independent inventors and of the rewards they were able to secure through the patents on their inventions. I, too, might do this, I thought; and this contemplation gave stimulus and direction to my life.[14]

After working his way through to a physics degree at the California Institute of Technology, Carlson accepted a research position at Bell Telephone Laboratories in 1930, a position made temporary by the Great Depression. Although plagued by financial difficulties during the Depression, he found a job in the patent department of another company. His tasks there impressed on him the need for quick, inexpensive copies of drawings and documents. Thus it was that in 1935 Carlson began a spare-time search for a copy machine. Although he was working full time and attending law school at night (in hope of becoming a patent attorney!), his research and experimentation were extensive, leading eventually to his key idea of combining electrostatics and photoconductive materials. The first successful demonstration of Carlson's ideas took place in a room behind a beauty parlor in Astoria, Long Island, on October 22, 1938. He used a crude device to copy the message "10–22–38 Astoria."

Four patents awarded to Carlson between 1940 and 1944 covered his basic concepts. During the same years, he tried to find a firm that would develop his invention for commercial use, but he encountered a stream of rejections, including those of twenty large firms—IBM, Remington Rand, and Eastman Kodak among them. The project was finally picked up for experimentation by Battelle Memorial Institute, a nonprofit research outfit, which thereby gained partial rights to any future earnings on the patents. Battelle devised a number of major patentable improvements, including use of a selenium plate, which allowed copies to be made on ordinary as opposed to chemically coated paper. Battelle did not have the resources to manufacture and market the machine, however.

Quest for a commercial innovator led to another round of rejections from big companies, whereupon, in 1946, the task was undertaken by Haloid Company, a small firm earning an annual net income of only $101,000. Motivated by partial rights to potential earnings and led by a bright, enthusiastic fellow named Joseph Wilson, Haloid pushed the project to fruition. Among the landmarks on the long road that followed were (1) the first marketing of an industrial-use copier in 1950; (2) a change of company name from Haloid to Xerox; (3) first profit earnings in 1953; (4) development by 1957 of a prototype office copier, the cost of which nearly bankrupted the company; and (5) commercial introduction of the famous 914 console copier in 1959, more than twenty years after Carlson began his initial experiments.

All told, over $20 million was spent on the development of xerography before 1959. It is doubtful whether such a large financial commitment would ever have been made by the people who made it without patent protection. Besides Carlson's first four patents, the project generated well over 100 improvement patents for various machine designs, selenium drums, paper-feeding devices, copy counters, powder dispensers, and so on. The significance of patents to Xerox is summarized by Joseph Wilson:

> We have become an almost classic case for those who believe the [patent] system was designed to permit small, weak companies to become healthy. During the early years of xerography we were investing almost as much in research as we were realizing in profit. Unless the first faltering efforts had been protected from imitators, the business itself probably would have foundered, thus obliterating opportunities for jobs for thousands throughout the world.[15]

(Carlson, Battelle and Wilson were each eventually rewarded with eight-digit earnings.)

III. Why Patents?

The Xerox story implies several justifications for the patent system that now ought to be openly stated. At bottom, support rests on three legs: "natural law" property, "exchange for secrets," and "incentives."

A. Natural Law

The natural law thesis asserts that inventors have a natural property right to their own idea. "It would be a gross immorality in the law," John Stuart Mill argued, "to set everybody free to use a person's work without his consent and without giving him an equivalent."[16] Although this view appeals to our sense of fairness, it is not without its practical problems. For one thing, it implicitly assumes that invention is the work of a single, identifiable mind, or at most a few minds. Today, however, invention is usually the product of a faceless corporate team, and any resulting patent rights rest with the corporation, not with the deserving inventors, individual or otherwise. Of course, corporations may fund the research and thereby accept the risks, so the property argument could be extended to corporate research on grounds of "just" compensation.

This extension does not square with the fact that corporations doing research for the U. S. Department of Defense get exclusive patent rights on their defense work without bearing any financial risk. The property rationale is further undermined by the fact that patents protect only a few classes of ideas. If one is seriously concerned about the fair treatment of thinkers, why forsake those who push back the frontiers of knowledge in areas excluded from patent eligibility—such as pure science, mathematics, economics, and business administration? Is the inventor of parakeet diapers more deserving than the inventor of double-entry bookkeeping?

B. Exchange for Secrets

Patent law requires that inventors disclose their invention to the public. Without patent protection, it is a pretty safe bet that inventors would try to rely on secrecy more than they now do to protect their ideas from theft. Thus the exchange-for-secrets rationale "presumes a bargain between inventor and society, the former surrendering the possession of secret knowledge in exchange for the protection of a temporary exclusivity in its industrial use."[17] Widespread public knowledge is assumed to be more beneficial than secret knowledge because openness fertilizes technological advance. One discovery may trigger dozens of others among many inventors. And, although the initial discovery cannot be used freely for seventeen years, secrecy might prevent full diffusion of its application for an even longer duration.

Just how well society comes out in the bargain is impossible to say. The benefits of openness and the costs of temporary monopoly defy accurate estimation, especially the former. About all that can be said with confidence is that abolition of the patent system would cause the burial of *some* knowledge currently revealed in patent applications.[18]

C. Incentive

The justification most solidly illustrated by the story of Xerox, and the justification most supportive of the patent system, is that it provides incentive to invent and innovate. This rationale rests on two propositions: first, that more invention and innovation than would occur in the absence of some special inducement are desirable, and second, that giving out patents is the best method of providing such special inducement. In other words, discoveries would surely occur without patents, but it is believed that their unearthing will be appreciably hastened, or that more of them will be obtained, if the vast profit potential exclusive patents provide is used to lure inventors and innovators into action.

There can be no doubt that many inventions and innovations depend on patents for their existence or early arrival. Stories of people like Chester Carlson tell us that garrets and garages shelter thousands of inventors so inspired. As for innovation, which is the commercial application of an invention rather than the invention itself, evidence shows patents providing further incentive. A good test of this incentive would compare the commercial development of inventions *with* and *without* patent protection. The inventions that emerge from government-funded research and development yield data for such a test because those doing the research sometimes get exclusive patent rights and sometimes not. (When not, the patent is publicly available to anyone.) These data show that commercial development of inventions (i.e., innovation) is two or three times more common *with* exclusive patent protection than without.[19] Results like these prompted a change in policy in 1980. Amendments to patent law now allow universities and small businesses to patent all technology developed with federal funds.

Still, the incentive thesis needs qualification at two levels. First, social benefits of cost savings and added consumer surplus may be rightly credited to the patent system for fathering "patent-dependent" inventions and innovations, but patent protection of these discoveries also creates social costs. These costs are the usual ones associated with monopoly—such as higher prices than otherwise. When these costs are deducted from the social benefits provided by these patent-dependent discoveries, the *net result* is considerably smaller than that suggested by brash talk of the gross benefits. This qualification of the incentive thesis is nevertheless not very serious because theory can demonstrate that the social benefits of these patent-dependent discoveries nearly always exceed those social costs to yield a positive net social benefit.[20] (See Appendix to this chapter.)

The second and higher-level qualification is critical, however. We may comfortably assume that patent-dependent inventions and innovations are always, on balance, beneficial, but we *cannot* jump from there to conclude that the *patent system itself* is, on balance, always beneficial. Inability to make this leap weakens the incentive thesis. Thus, a more thorough discussion of the patent system's costs and benefits is needed.

IV. Benefits and Costs of Patents

If the net social benefits of patent-dependent discoveries and developments were all that counted, the value of patent systems could not be questioned. However, patents, are extended to *all* inventions that meet the legal qualifications, including inventions that are *not* dependent on the patent system for their existence. Whatever social benefits may be claimed for these *non*patent-dependent inventions, they cannot be attributed to the patent system for the simple reason that their existence does not hinge on patent protection. Patent protection for these nondependent inventions does create social costs, however—costs of the monopoly kind. So in such cases there will *always be net social costs* from patents. Given that (1) patent dependency always yields net social benefits, and (2) *non*patent dependency of patented inventions always yields net social costs, economists have devised the following criterion for judging the value of the patent system. As stated by F. M. Scherer, one "must weigh the *net* benefits associated with inventions which would not have been available without patent protection against the *net* social losses associated with patented inventions that would be introduced even if no patent rights were offered."[21]

Unfortunately, balance scales capable of this weighing have not yet been invented (patentable or otherwise). Some have even said the task is and always will be impossible because there is no sure way of telling whether a given invention is, or is not, patent dependent. Still, the major considerations that would guide educated guesswork on the issue have been sketched, and they include the following.

A. Tallies of Patent Dependency

Rough approximations have occasionally been made about the number of patent-dependent versus nonpatent-dependent inventions on the assumption that, if the former number falls considerably short of the latter, the net benefits of the former are also likely to fall short of the net costs of the latter. For example, these two figures have been crudely estimated by classifying discoveries of individual inventors (and perhaps those of small firms too) in the patent-dependent group and relegating those of corporations (or *large* corporations) into the nonpatent-dependent group. Questionnaire surveys of patentees rather consistently reveal that, in general, individual inventors rely heavily on patent protection to sustain their efforts, whereas most corporations claim that patents are neither the chief goal nor principal determinant of their innovative efforts.[22]

By this broad measure it would appear that *non*patent-dependent inventions easily outnumber patent-dependent inventions by a ratio some-

where in the neighborhood of 3 or 4 to 1. However, the very rough nature of this approximation is underscored by substantial differences of patent dependency across industries. Edwin Mansfield asked the R&D directors of 100 U. S. corporations what proportion of their 1981–1983 inventions could be considered patent dependent—that is, would not have been developed but for the protection patents gave them. Table 24–1 reports his findings. Of the twelve industry groups, four appear to count very little on patents, their executives replying with a zero rate of patent dependency. In fact, the only industries reporting notably large proportions were pharmaceuticals, chemicals, and petroleum.

Patent dependency has also been examined by study of situations in which patents have not been available. Neither Switzerland nor the Netherlands had patent systems during the latter

Table 24–1

The Estimated Percentage of Patent-Dependent Inventions in Twelve Industry Groups, 1981–1983

Industry Group	Percentage of Inventions Whose Existence Depends on Patent Protection
Pharmaceuticals	60%
Other chemicals	38
Petroleum	25
Machinery	17
Fabricated metal products	12
Electrical equipment	11
Primary metals	1
Instruments	1
Office equipment	0
Motor vehicles	0
Rubber products	0
Textiles	0

Source: Edwin Mansfield, "Patents and Innovation: An Empirical Study," *Management Science* (February 1986), p. 175.

half of the nineteenth century and the first decade of this century. Yet the absence of patents failed to petrify industry in either.[23]

If, on the whole, patents are no more forceful in stimulating invention and innovation than is indicated by these items of evidence, obviously there must be other sources of incentive, other factors propelling progress. In the first place, to the extent *secrecy* can be maintained, it provides protection in lieu of patent protection. Second, many companies engage in progressive activities to remain *competitive* or to gain competitive leadership. Introduction of new products or product improvements is a form of product differentiation, much like advertising. Natural lags, including temporary secrecy and retooling requirements, prevent immediate imitation of these efforts, gaining prestige and customer loyalty for the innovators. Third, even when imitation is not substantially delayed, innovative investments are not always or even usually flushed down the drain by the price competition of imitators. High concentration, stiff barriers to entry, first mover advantages, and similar sources of *market power other than patents* furnish a basis for post-imitation price discipline in many industries. Finally, even when R&D does not on average pay its own way, it may nevertheless persist. Like gamblers, inventors and innovators often have distorted visions. They tend to see the Chester Carlsons more clearly than the Feckless Floyd failures. They *overrate their chances* of winning the spectacular treasures, and, as a consequence, they often subsidize their R&D efforts from unrelated earnings.

Table 24–2 contains interesting data reflecting on this issue. A team of economists at Yale University surveyed 650 high-level R&D managers representing 130 different lines of business to get their judgments about the effectiveness of different methods of protecting their innovations. Their judgments were expressed on a scale of 1 (not effective at all) to 7 (very effective for protection). The averages of the responses for the

Table 24–2
Effectiveness of Alternative Means of Protecting the Competitive Advantages of New or Improved Processes and Products (1 = not effective, 7 = very effective)

Method of Appropriation	Overall Average Responses	
	Processes	*Products*
Patents to prevent duplication	3.52	4.33
Patents to secure royalties	3.31	3.75
Secrecy	4.31	3.57
Lead time	5.11	5.41
Moving quickly down the learning curve	5.02	5.09
Sales or service efforts	4.55	5.59

Source: R. C. Levin, A. K. Klevorick, R. R. Nelson, and S. G. Winter, "Appropriating the Returns for Industrial Research and Development," *Brookings Papers on Economic Activity,* No. 3 (1987), p. 794.

six alternative methods shown in Table 24–2 turn out to be rather remarkable. Respondents rated patents the least effective means of protecting process innovations, scoring them lower than secrecy, lead time (first mover advantages), learning and experience (another form of first mover advantage), and marketing hustle. Patents were ranked a little better for product innovations, but they still trailed all other methods except secrecy. Breaking down the responses by individual industry yielded results consistent with those of Table 24–1. Those in the pharmaceutical and chemical industries judged patents to be the most important method of protecting the potential profits appropriated from their innovations.

Notice that most of these nonpatent protections probably apply most strongly to medium-sized or large firms. Secrecy cannot be maintained by a small individual inventor who must go around displaying his or her ideas in hope of finding a firm that will commercialize them. A small company cannot gain much of a jump on its rivals if its brand name is less entrenched and its distribution channels are shallower than those of its larger rivals. A small company likewise tends to be less diversified than its larger foes, so it may have fewer opportunities to subsidize its R&D during periods of financial drought. Perhaps these considerations explain why individual inventors and small firms profess greater reliance on the patent system and claim a keener interest in its perpetuation than do big firms. (This does not necessarily mean that the patent system is, on balance, procompetitive. The story of U. S. Gypsum should dispel hasty conclusions of that kind.)

To summarize, various empirical tallies of patent dependency indicate that the system provides life support for only a minority of inventions and innovations, a minority whose origins are of usually humble size. This minority wins credit for the system. But since patents are also showered indiscriminately on the nonpatent-dependent majority of inventions, it would appear from tally-type evidence that the net costs of the majority exceed the net benefits of the minority, and the system should therefore be reformed or abolished. However, we must hold off the executioners, at least momentarily.

B. The Economic Significance of Patent-Dependent Inventions

Although the weight of numbers suggests that the patent system is economically unfit, that measure may be misleading. It has been estimated that relatively few patented inventions account for most of the economic value of all patented inventions. According to the numbers of Pakes and Simpson, more than half the value of all patents accrues to between 5 and 10 percent of the patents.[24] What if the relatively few inventions that are patent dependent include the relatively few inventions that are truly revolutionary, whereas, at the same time, the relatively numerous nonpatent-dependent inventions include only simple improvements or inanities? It has been argued that, to some extent, there is a direct relationship between the economic significance of inventions and their patent dependency. F. M. Scherer speaks for this view:

> It is conceivable that without a patent system some of the most spectacular technical contributions—those which effect a genuine revolution in production or consumption patterns—might be lost or (more plausibly) seriously delayed. . . . Such innovations may lie off the beaten paths of industrial technology, where no firm or group of firms has a natural advantage, and the innovator may be forced to develop completely new marketing channels and production facilities to exploit them. They may entail greater technological and market uncertainties, higher development costs, and longer inception-to-commercialization lags than the vast bulk of all industrial innovation. Entrepreneurs may be willing to accept their challenge only under highly favorable circumstances—notably, when it is anticipated that if success is achieved, it can be exploited to the fullest through the exercise of exclusive patent rights.

> That such cases exist is virtually certain. Black and white television and the development of Chester Carlson's xerographic concepts are probable examples.[25]

Undoubtedly it is this possibility, coupled with notions of "natural law" property, that persuades politicians to keep the patent system intact. At a bare minimum, such crude *qualitative* accounting raises serious doubts about the accuracy of negative conclusions derived from simple *quantitative* tallies.

C. The Social Cost of Nondependent Inventions

The qualifications cannot end there, however, not in fairness to those critical of patents, anyway. Just as the net benefits of dependent cases need qualification, so too the net costs of granting patents in nondependent cases need amplification—an exercise that tips the balance back in the negative direction, especially where revolutionary innovations of this nondependent stripe are concerned.

First, granting monopoly rights over knowledge that is not dependent on patents artificially restricts use of that knowledge below what is socially optimal. The marginal cost of using technical knowledge is zero in the sense that knowledge can be used over and over and over again, by one person or many, without even the slightest danger of exhaustion through wear and tear. No one is compelled to get less of it when anyone else gets more. Ideally, therefore, technology should be *freely* available to all potential users because the "pure" marginal cost of its dissemination and application is zero. But the grant of monopoly leads to exclusions, either directly or by the extraction of a royalty price that exceeds zero.[26]

A second social cost, one stemming from that just mentioned, is a blocking effect. Potential inventors who might like to use a patented invention to further their research in different or related fields may be blocked from doing so, in which case the patent would not be fostering progress but inhibiting it.

Third, if a patent is extended to a firm with a pre-existing monopoly position, then suppression of the patented invention is possible under certain circumstances.[27]

(These first three points were dramatically illustrated in May 1989 when some of the nation's top computer scientists took to the streets to picket against the prospect that basic computer software would become patented. They claimed that patenting would stifle creativity because it would raise costs of litigation, restrict the use of new ideas, and so on. Their picket signs said, "Innovation Not Litigation" and "No Writs for Bits."[28] The problem arises because much software relies on the same building blocks. "It would be the same if you could patent a four-note musical sequence," says the vice-president of WordPerfect Corporation. "Any time you write a song, you have to make sure you don't infringe. You have to spend more time researching than writing."[29])

Fourth, patents give rise to monopoly powers and restrictive practices that go well beyond those inherent in patents themselves.

It is at this last point that patent policy collides with antitrust policy. Pure and simple patent monopoly escapes antitrust attack for obvious reasons. As seen earlier in the story of U. S. Gypsum, however, patents may be cleverly accumulated and manipulated to construct fortresses of monopoly power or networks of price-fixing agreements. The line between proper use and malevolent abuse of patent rights is difficult to draw, but the antitrust authorities and federal courts have over time made the attempt. As a result, the following practices, among others, have been declared illegal:

- *Restrictive Licensing.* If a number of patent licensees are restricted to charging prices specified by the patent holder, or if a number of licensees collude to allocate markets using patent licenses to formalize their agreement, violation is likely, as in the *Gypsum* case.[30]
- *Cross-licensing.* Two or more patent holders may exchange rights of access to each other's patents, something which is often desirable in light of the fact that several firms may contribute to the technology of a single item, such as a TV set. However, patent "pools" that exclude others, or fix prices, or otherwise restrain trade are illegal.[31]
- *Acquisition of Patents.* Monopoly power built on the acquisition of many patents (as opposed to relying on one's own inventiveness) may be attacked under Section 7 of the Clayton Act.[32]
- *Tying.* Tying the sale of an unpatented product (like salt) to a patented product (a salt-dispensing machine used in food processing) is virtually per se illegal.[33]

In brief, antitrust policy permits patent holders to earn their legitimate reward for invention, a reward that may be monopolistically plump, but patent rights cannot be stretched beyond legitimate rights. Tight interpretation of legitimacy has held down the social costs of the patent system but not to the point of quieting cries for reform.

V. Proposals for Reform

A. Proposals to Weaken the System

Ideology and evidence lead few folks to advocate complete abolition of the U. S. patent system. The natural law property thesis rests on strongly held value judgments unrelated to economic benefits and costs. There is also enough incentive provided by the system to produce some social benefits. Whether these benefits exceed the social costs is, as we have seen, uncertain, but the benefits are large enough that abolition of the system might give the appearance of throwing the baby out with the bath water. Hence, critics who want the system weakened usually advocate reform, not abolition.

One of the most obvious improvements that could be made in the system is the elimination of improvident patent grants. The test of inventiveness could be tightened substantially.

A number of other proposed changes would lessen the monopoly power of patents. These include such things as shorter patent life and compulsory licensing. Reducing patent life below seventeen years would reduce monopoly's duration. Compulsory licensing would simply require patent holders to license their patents to all who wanted to use them at a "reasonable" royalty fee. This would reduce monopoly power because it would end the exclusiveness that patents presently bestow. Empirical studies of compulsory licensing indicate that it would also substantially deflate the system's incentives but by less than abolition would.

B. Changes That Strengthen the System

As the U. S. economy grew sluggish in the late 1970s, our technological superiority was called increasingly into question. This spurred proposals to *strengthen* the patent system rather than weaken it. The result was a new patent law in December 1980. The law gives small businesses and universities exclusive patent rights to products invented with federal research funding.

Another provision of the new law reduced the likelihood that courts would declare patents invalid. Unlike before, the Patent Office can now recheck on the validity of a challenged patent. The results of the recheck, if favorable to the patent, solidify its validity. Moreover, all appeals in U. S. patent-infringement suits now go to the Court of Appeals for the Federal Circuit, a court of last resort for patent cases. This new court has been upholding patents 80 percent of the time versus the 30 percent under the previous system.

(Getting caught for patent infringement can be costly. In early 1986, Kodak's instant-photography cameras and film were judged to be in violation of Polaroid's patents. Kodak had to cease production and grant refunds on all instant cameras already sold—moves that cost it an estimated $800 million. In addition, Kodak had to pay damages to Polaroid, which amounted to nearly $1 billion.[34])

Finally, recent legislation strengthens drug-related patents. The change, in effect, lengthens the life of patents covering products that must receive Food and Drug Administration approval prior to marketing. The problem addressed was the lengthy time it takes the Food and Drug Administration to approve new products—ten years in many cases. Thus new product "X" might be patented shortly after invention in 1980 but not sold until after 1990. With the patent expiring in 1997, there would be only seven years of legal monopoly in the market instead of the seventeen accorded products not needing premarket clearance. The intent of the new legislation, then, is to extend patent life by the amount of time the product is under premarket regulatory review.[35]

All in all, these several changes indicate the prevailing mood of recent years. Rather than tear down the patent system, there has been a substantial movement to build it up, to grant more protection to inventors.[36]

VI. Federal Funding of R&D

A. Trends

The federal government has seated itself at the dining table of technology, supped gluttonously, and has begun picking up the tab. Back in 1940 federal expenditures on R&D amounted to no more than $74.1 million, which was 0.8 percent of the total federal budget and barely 0.07 percent of the GNP. A further mark of that era is the fact that federal spending on *agricultural* R&D

exceeded *defense* R&D spending. World War II, the cold war, the space race, and the war in Vietnam changed all that. By the mid-1960s federal R&D spending had soared to exceed $14 *billion*, which relative to total federal spending of all kinds topped 12 percent, and compared to the GNP exceeded 2 percent. Defense R&D spending exploded to forty-one times the size of agriculture outlays.[37]

The contribution this jump in federal R&D funding made to overall R&D may be seen in Figure 24–2, which shows total outlays in constant (1982) dollars over the period 1955 to 1989. Between 1955 and 1965, federal funding tripled in real terms. Private expenditures, although also growing in real terms, slipped as a percentage of the total to 35 percent in 1965.

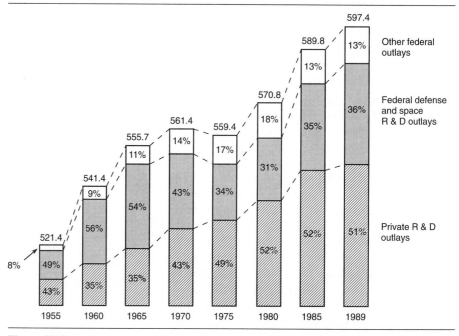

Figure 24–2
Trend in private and federal R&D outlays, constant dollars (1982).

Source: U.S. Department of Commerce, *Statistical Abstract of the United States,* 1981 (Washington, D.C.: U.S. Government Printing Office, 1981), p. 598; National Science Board, *Science and Engineering Indicators,* 1989 (Washington, D.C.: NSB, 1989).

Table 24–3
Federal R&D Funding by Function: 1979 and 1989

Function	Amount (millions of dollars)		As a % of Total	
	1979	1989	1979	1989
National defense	$13,791	$40,574	48.9%	65.6%
Health	3,401	7,724	12.1	12.5
Energy	3,461	2,427	12.3	3.9
Space	3,136	4,589	11.1	7.4
General science	1,119	2,379	4.0	3.8
Natural resources	1,010	1,208	3.6	2.0
Transportation	798	1,019	2.8	1.6
Agriculture	552	910	2.0	1.5
Other	941	993	3.3	1.6
Total	$28,208	$61,823	100.0%	100.0%

Source: U.S. Department of Commerce, *Statistical Abstract of the United States, 1986* (Washington, DC: U.S. Government Printing Office, 1986), p. 579: National Science Board, *Science and Engineering Indicators, 1989* (Washington, D.C.: NSB, 1989), p. 285.

Between 1965 and 1980, federal real outlays remained fairly constant except for a slight drop in 1975. Then, during the 1980s federal expenditures skyrocketed, mainly because of a jump in spending for defense R&D. Defense R&D nearly doubled during the Reagan Administration, rising from $16.5 billion in 1980 to $30.0 billion in 1988 (in 1982 constant dollars). Private R&D spending likewise rose during the 1980s, so the combination of increases in defense and private R&D during the 1980s make that decade stand out in Figure 24–2. By 1989 total spending was $97.4 billion in 1982 dollars (or nearly $125 billion in current dollars), with about equal shares being spent by government and industry. Figure 24–2 also shows that defense and space were big beneficiaries of the spurt in federal outlays from 1955 to 1965. Defense and space, especially space, then experienced a real and relative decline in support between 1965 and 1975.

More recent and more detailed trends in the composition of federal expenditures are depicted in Table 24–3. The most notable change is again the enormous increase for defense, going from $13.7 billion in 1979 to $40.6 billion in 1989.

As a percentage of the federal total, defense jumps from 48.9 percent to 65.6 percent during the same years. Among the items moving in the opposite direction, energy deserves special mention. It slid in absolute dollars and in percentage share over the Reagan era. (Yet its slide put it back to where it was in 1973.) Natural resources, transportation, and agriculture all fell in percentage share although they experienced current dollar increases.

B. The Reasons for Federal Funding

Why has the government opened its purse so widely to these pursuits? Why has the distribution of money moved around so much? What guides Washington in these matters? There are no really solid answers because noneconomic value judgments play a crucial role in the decision making. Which will reduce the threat of death more—a billion dollars spent for a new military weapon or for a cure for cancer? Which will do more to relieve the energy crisis by the year 2000—a billion dollars spent on nuclear or on solar power? No one knows for sure; speculation reigns amid the inherent uncertainties. Hence, value judgments are inescapable, and these shift under the press of political, social, international, and technical developments.

Still, there are a few broad economic foundations for this effort.[38] To begin with, most federal R&D is allocated to areas where the federal government stands as the sole or chief consumer of the ultimate product. National defense and space are the most obvious instances. Because the federal government has prime responsibility for provision of these public goods (a responsibility recognized by even the most miserly conservatives), it is strongly felt that the government should also take responsibility for technological advance in these areas, the advances themselves being public goods.

Other R&D programs are grounded on the belief that private incentives are lacking. That is, the social benefits of advancement greatly exceed the benefits that can be privately captured, or if they can be captured, such would be undesirable. Research in basic science, health, environmental protection, and crime prevention probably fit this justification.

Still other programs can be defended as offsets to market imperfections of somewhat different sorts. Single R&D projects in such areas as nuclear power and urban mass transportation couple costs of billions of dollars with risks of ominous magnitudes, so much so that even our largest and most courageous private companies are scared to undertake them without government support. The necessity for government R&D funding in agriculture, housing, construc-

tion, and coal is often defended because these industries tend to be populated by firms too small and too scattered to shoulder the burdens of even medium-sized R&D projects.

In recent years yet another justification for government R&D funding has gained attention—namely, funding to improve our international competitiveness. Figure 24–3 shows that the United States' share of many key world markets has fallen sharply. Between 1978 and 1988, the United States accounted for declining shares in cars, machine tools, computer hard disks, DRAMs, and customized semiconductor chips. Much the same can be said of biotechnology, pharmaceuticals, robotics, supercomputers, and consumer electronics. Japan, Germany, South Korea, France, and others have grown relative to the United States in many areas that might be considered important to our industrial well-being. At the same time, many foreign governments have directed their R&D funding toward commercial industrial development to improve their international competitiveness.

Table 24–4 thus shows some interesting contrasts as well as offering a potential explanation for the rise of foreign countries vis-à-vis the United States in many world markets. The first column shows that the United States has in the past led all other countries in its governmental financing of R&D. In 1988, 32.7 percent of all U. S. business R&D was funded by the federal government, a level of effort much above that of, say, Germany (12.1 percent) or Japan (1.7 percent). On the other hand, in the second column, the United States ranked way below all other countries in the percentage of government R&D that was aimed specifically at industrial development (as opposed to military prowess, basic research, and other nonindustrial ends). Some small countries, like Ireland, Denmark, and Finland, seem especially concerned about their international competitiveness as reflected in these measures of industrial emphasis.

Because of an ideological aversion to anything that could be called an "industrial policy,"

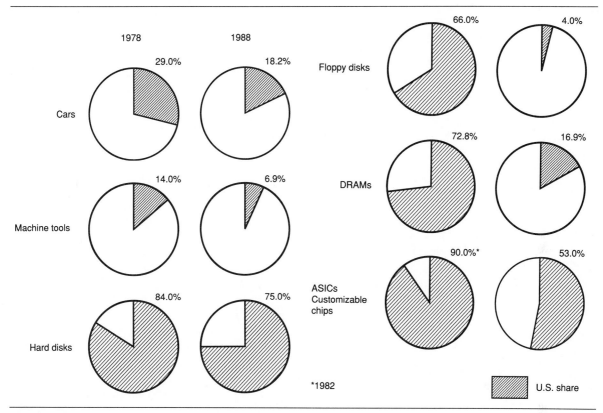

Figure 24–3
U.S. Share of World Markets in Six Key Industries, 1978–1988.

Source: *Fortune,* January 1, 1990, p. 74; Dataquest Integrated Circuit Engineering, National Machine Tool Builders Association, Disk/Trend Report, Automobile International.

the Reagan and Bush Administrations opposed federal R&D funding for industrial purposes until 1991, when the Bush Administration suddenly woke up to the issue. In that year the White House began pushing programs that would subsidize the development of supercomputers, electric cars, biotechnology, high-speed trains, high-definition television, computer software, and selected other commercial technologies. According to the *Wall Street Journal,* "The change in the White House . . . reflects pressure from business groups and Congress to increase funding for commercial technologies, and concern that the U. S. is losing trade battles with Japan and Europe."[39] A shift away from defense R&D can

of course also be justified by the reduced military threats facing the United States since the fall of the USSR.

Two interesting economic findings in this connection are the following. First, the payoffs to federal sponsorship of nondefense projects are sometimes immense. For example, the rate of return to federal investment in softwood plywood research has been estimated to be in the range of 200 to 700 percent.[40] Second, federal funding does not seem to cause private funding to fall below what it would be otherwise. Rather, there is complementarity. By one estimate of the average impact, in the early 1980s every $1.00 of government contract R&D performed in industry in-

Table 24–4
Comparison of the United States and Other Countries in Percentage of Business R&D Financed by Government and Percentage of Government R&D Funding Aimed at Industrial Development, 1988

Country	Percentage of Business R&D Funded by Government	Percentage of Government R&D Aimed at Industrial Development
United States	32.7	0.2
France	21.3	12.8
United Kingdom	19.4	8.0
Netherlands	14.5	23.2
Ireland	13.8	34.9
Spain	13.7	20.7
Germany	12.1	14.0
Canada	11.8	13.8
Denmark	11.8	17.8
Australia	5.6	9.5
Finland	4.6	28.2
Japan	1.7	4.8

Source: Organization for Economic Co-operation and Development, *Industrial Policy in OECD Countries, Annual Review 1990* (Paris: OECD, 1990), pp. 111, 114.

duced about $0.27 of private R&D expenditure.[41]

Summary

The U. S. government's promotion of technical progress dates from the days of the Founding Fathers. Patents originate in the Constitution, which authorizes legislation to "promote the progress of science and useful arts, by securing for limited times to authors and inventors the exclusive right to their respective writings and discoveries." Under present law, patents last seventeen years and cover discoveries that pass fairly lenient standards of inventiveness, novelty, and utility. Admissible subject matter is essentially limited to mechanical and chemical products or processes, thereby excluding fundamental laws of nature and other worthwhile dis-

coveries. Lately, however, new life forms and software programs have received coverage.

At its best, the patent system stimulates progress, rewards deserving inventors and innovators, and arouses competition by nourishing small firms. The history of Xerox illustrates these beneficent effects. On the other hand, deserving and getting do not always coincide under the system, with the result that patents protect discoveries that would be available anyway. Moreover, patents often provide hooks on which to hang restrictive practices, and they occasionally even stifle technical progress.

The main justifications for the patent system are "natural law" property, "exchange for secrets," and "incentives." Each has appeal; each has problems. As the law presently stands, too much is arbitrarily excluded to make the natural law argument natural, and society gets in on too few of the secrets it bargains for. That patent incentives pull some discoveries from the nether world cannot be doubted, but this effect is easily exaggerated.

Ideally, a benefit-cost analysis would compare the net benefits of patent-dependent inventions with the net costs of extending patents to nonpatent-dependent inventions. Unfortunately, data deficiencies permit no more than speculation on this score. What little evidence is available indicates that net benefits have the best chance of exceeding net costs on those patents that are extended to individual inventors and small firms. Chemicals and pharmaceuticals might also enjoy favorable balances. These findings have led reformists to call for changes in the system.

Federal funding of R&D has grown from little more than a teenager's weekly allowance to amounts in excess of $60 billion. In recent decades, defense and space R&D have been emphasized at the expense of civilian R&D, but the dissolution of the Soviet Union will perhaps reverse this in the 1990s. Noneconomic value judgments play a particularly prominent role in this policy area.

Questions and Exercises for Chapter 24

1. In each case, why wouldn't the following be patentable? (a) a vampire protection kit, (b) the discovery of a cure for inflation, (c) the shoe.
2. Why was U. S. Gypsum attacked under the antitrust laws when its monopoly power was based on patents?
3. Identify and assess the natural law property rationale for patents.
4. Which rationale for patents most convincingly supports the award of exclusive patents from government financed R&D?
5. Conceptually, how would one conduct a benefit-cost analysis of the patent system?
6. What evidence indicates that the number of patent-dependent inventions is actually quite small?
7. Why does the story of Xerox support the patent system despite the fact that patent-dependent in-

ventions seem to be a rather small fraction of all patented inventions?
8. What policies bolster the incentive effect of patents?
9. Why might federal funding of R&D be warranted?

Appendix to Chapter 24: The Economic Benefits of Cost-Reducing Inventions

When patents bring forth new *products,* the net social benefits are easy to imagine because new products yield new consumer surpluses even when priced at monopoly levels. Less intuitively plausible are the net benefits associated with *production process* innovations, when no new product is involved and when the monopoly control granted by the patent can convert a purely competitive industry into a monopoly. Figures 24–4 (a) and (b) illustrate the two possibilities in this regard.

If, as in Figure 24–4 (a), production costs per unit drop substantially from C_1 under pure competition to C_2 under monopoly, then buyers will gain an immediate benefit from the invention—namely, a price reduction from P_1 to P_2, which increases quantity from Q_1 to Q_2. Under pure competition, price equals marginal cost, as P_1 equals C_1 in Figure 24–4 (where marginal cost is assumed constant and therefore also equal to average cost). When cost falls from C_1 to C_2 because of the invention, price will not fall as much because patent monopoly prevails as well as cost C_2, and the monopolist's price, P_2, will be above C_2. Still the price reduction increases consumers' surplus from AEP_1 to ABP_2.

Aside from the price reduction, society also gains by the fact that, after the invention, fewer resources are used to produce Q_1, a savings represented by the area JP_1EH. Although most of these savings are pocketed by the monopolist in the form of excess profits, they are nevertheless genuine and the monopolist is, after all, a member of society, not a Martian. Once the patent expires, the industry could return to a purely

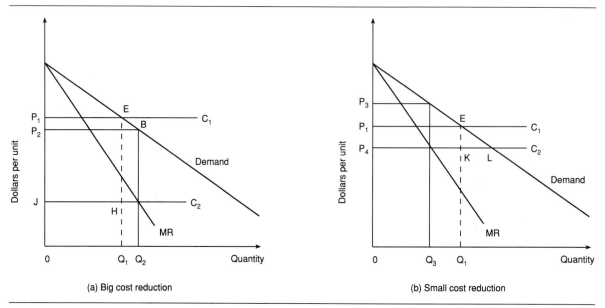

Figure 24–4
The Economic Effects of Patent-Dependent Cost-Reducing Inventions

competitive structure (assuming favorable conditions), at which time price will drop to C_2 and all gains then pass to buyers (consumers).

The cost reduction in panel (b) of Figure 24–4 is smaller, C_1 to C_3. Indeed, it is small enough to suggest that, with conversion to monopoly, price could actually rise from P_1 to P_3, given that marginal revenue MR equals marginal cost C_3 at quantity Q_3, which is less than Q_1. However, the monopolist's price cannot rise above P_1 because the pure competitors can sell at P_1, and they would be encouraged to do so at any price above P_1. Thus, in this case price is likely to remain at P_1, implying no immediate gain for buyers. All the immediate social gains take the form of reduced resource use in the production of Q_1, a reduction represented by area P_1EKP_4. These savings go to the monopolist (still a member of society). If pure competition returns after expiration of the patent, buyers then reap the benefits when price falls to P_4 from P_1. The gain in consumer surplus then equals P_4P_1EL, because triangle ELK is added to the cost savings of P_1EKP_4 just mentioned. Thus, in this case, too, a patent-dependent invention yields net social benefits even though the patent creates a seventeen-year monopoly.[42]

Notes

1. For a more extensive survey see Erich Kaufer, *The Economics of the Patent System* (Chur, Switzerland: Harwood Academic Publishers, 1989).
2. U.S.C. Section 154 (1970).
3. Penny Ward Moser, "Dreams, Schemes, and 3,300 Better Mousetraps," *Discover* (December 1985): 72.
4. Stacy V. Jones, *The Patent Office* (New York: Praeger, 1971), pp. 43–44.
5. *Harries* v. *Air King Prods. Co.*, 183 F. 2d 158, 162 (2d Cir. 1950).
6. *Wall Street Journal*, 17 June 1980, p. 3; 31 December 1980, pp. 1, 8; 13 April 1988, p. 32; *New Republic*, May 23 1988, pp. 7–9; *Forbes*, June 25, 1990, pp. 138–139.
7. Stanley M. Besen and Leo J. Raskind, "An Introduction to the Law and Economics of Intellectual Property," *Journal of Economic Perspectives* (Winter 1991): 3–27.

8. Specific evidence is provided by F. M. Scherer, "Firm Size, Market Structure, Opportunity, and the Output of Patented Inventions," *American Economic Review* (December 1965): 1111, note 20. See also Corwin D. Edwards, *Maintaining Competition* (New York: McGraw-Hill, 1964 edition), p. 218.

9. Jones, *Patent Office,* pp. 77–79; Irene Till, "The Legal Monopoly," in *The Monopoly Makers,* ed. M.J. Green (New York: Grossman, 1973), pp. 293–294.

10. This section is based primarily on *United States v. United States Gypsum Co.* 333 U. S. 366 (1947); and Clair Wilcox, *Competition and Monopoly in American Industry,* Monograph No. 21 of the Temporary National Economic Committee, U. S. Congress (1940), pp. 161–163.

11. *U. S.* v. *U. S. Gypsum, op. cit.,* 374.

12. Ibid., p. 393.

13. This section is based on J. Jewkes, D. Sawers, and R. Stillerman, *The Sources of Invention* (New York: Norton, 1969), pp. 321–323; D. V. DeSimone, Testimony, *Economic Concentration,* Part 3, U. S. Senate Subcommittee on Antitrust and Monopoly, (1965), pp. 1108–1111; E. A. Blackstone, "The Copying-Machine Industry: Innovations, Patents, and Pricing," *Antitrust Law & Economics Review* (Fall 1972): 105–122; and F. M. Scherer, *The Economic Effects of Compulsory Patent Licensing* (New York: New York University Graduate School of Business Administration, 1977), p. 9.

14. DeSimone "Testimony."

15. DeSimone, Testimony, U. S. Senate, p. 1111.

16. Cited by Floyd L. Vaughan, *The United States Patent System* (Norman: University of Oklahoma Press, 1956), p. 27.

17. Fritz Machlup, *An Economic Review of the Patent System,* Study No. 15, U. S. Senate, Subcommittee on Patents, Trademarks, and Copyrights, 85th Congress, Second Session (1958), p. 21.

18. C. T. Taylor and Z. A. Silberston, *The Economic Impact of the Patent System* (Cambridge, UK: Cambridge University Press, 1973), p. 352.

19. U. S. House of Representatives, Subcommittee on Domestic and International Scientific Planning and Analysis, *Background Materials on Government Patent Policies,* Vol. II, 94th Congress, 2nd Session (1976), p. 97.

20. For a review, see Scherer, "Firm Size," (1977), pp. 25–34.

21. F. M. Scherer, *Industrial Market Structure and Economic Performance* (Chicago: Rand McNally, 1970), p. 384.

22. For a survey of the surveys, see Scherer, "Firm Size," pp. 50–56.

23. Eric Schiff, *Industrialization without Patents* (Princeton, NJ: Princeton University Press, 1971).

24. Ariel Pakes and Margaret Simpson, "Patent Renewal Data," *Brookings Papers on Economic Activity* (Microeconomics, 1989): 331–401.

25. Scherer, *Industrial Market Structure,* p. 388.

26. Wassily Leontief, "On Assignment of Patent Rights on Inventions Made Under Government Research Contracts," *Harvard Law Review* (January 1964): 492–497.

27. For a review of suppression cases, see Vaughan, *United States Patent System,* pp. 227–260.

28. *San Jose Mercury News,* 25 May 1989, p. F1. See also *Wall Street Journal,* 14 March 1989, p. B1.

29. *San Jose Mercury News,* 6 March 1989, p.1A.

30. *U. S.* v. *United States Gypsum Co.* 333 U. S. 364 (1948); *U. S.* v. *Masonite Corp.,* 316 U. S. 265 (1942); *Newburgh Moire Co.* v. *Superiors Moire Co.,* 237 F.2d 283 (3d Cir. 1956).

31. *U. S.* v. *Line Material Co.,* 333 U. S. 287 (1948); *U. S.* v. *Singer Manufacturing Co.,* 374 U. S. 174 (1963).

32. *U. S.* v. *Lever Bros. Co.,* 216 F. Supp. 887 (S.D.N.Y. 1963); *Kobe, Inc.* v. *Dempsey Pump Co.,* 198 F.2d 416 (10th Cir. 1952).

33. *International Salt Co.* v. *U. S.,* 332 U. S. 392 (1947).

34. *Fortune,* March 3, 1986, pp. 34–39; *Wall Street Journal,* 17 May 1988, p. 33 and 17 October 1989, p. B10; and *Business Week,* October 29, 1940, p. 39.

35. *Business Week,* February 16, 1981, p. 29.

36. *Business Week,* May 22, 1989, pp. 78–89; and *Fortune,* June 23, 1986, pp. 57–63.

37. National Science Foundation, *Federal Funds for Research, Development, and Other Scientific Activities* (NSF 77–301, 1977), p. 4; and Edwin Mansfield, *The Economics of Technical Change* (New York: Norton, 1968), p. 163.

38. For details see Mansfield, *Economics of Technical Change,* pp. 186–187; *Priorities and Efficiency in Federal Research and Development,* A Compendium of Papers, Subcommittee on Priorities and Economy in Government of the Joint Economic Committee, U. S. Congress, 94th Congress, Second Session (1976); John E. Tilton, *U. S. Energy R&D Policy* (Washington, DC: Resources for the Future, 1974); Paul Horwitz, "Direct Government Funding of Research and Development," in *Technological Innovation for a Dynamic Economy,* C. T. Hill and J. M. Utterback (New York: Pergamon Press, 1979), pp. 255–291; and Albert N. Link and George Tassey, *Strategies for Technology-based Competition* (Lexington, MA: Lexington Books, 1987), pp. 69–101.

39. *Wall Street Journal,* 13 May 1991, p. A16.

40. Barry J. Seldon, "A Nonresidual Estimation of Welfare Gains from Research," *Southern Economic Journal* (July 1987): 64–80. See also *Wall Street Journal,* 2 October 1991, p. B2.

41. David M. Levy and Nestor E. Terleckyj, "Effects of Government R&D on Private R&D Investment and Productivity," *Bell Journal of Economics,* (Autumn 1983): pp. 551–561.

42. For further discussion, see Dan Usher, "The Welfare Economics of Invention," *Economica* (August 1964): 279–287; William D. Nordhaus, *Invention, Growth, and Welfare* (Cambridge, MA: MIT Press, 1969); F. M. Scherer, *Industrial Market Structure and Economic Performance,* 2nd ed. (Chicago: Rand McNally, 1980), pp. 442–444.

Chapter 25

Promotion and Protection Policies

The Japanese have a strategy of world conquest. They have finished their job in the U.S. Now they're about to devour Europe.
— *Edith Cresson,*
France's Prime Minister (1991)

On December 18, 1991, General Motors announced that it was going to close twenty-one factories and cut 74,000 jobs.[1] The news hit hard. A recession was tormenting the country at the time. Moreover, GM had already closed sixteen plants and trimmed 36,345 jobs over the four years preceding this announcement. Ford and Chrysler were also hurting.

In contrast, Japanese automakers were doing fine. Their imports were selling well, and during the 1980s and early 1990s they built ten auto plants in the United States while GM, Ford, and Chrysler were closing theirs. In 1991, 31 percent of all cars sold in the United States carried Japanese nameplates, and almost half of these were produced in the United States. This explains how a University of Michigan professor could say, "There's no question that there will be a U.S. automobile industry. It's just that the owners will be [Japanese]."[2] This also explains why Michigan's Senator Riegle reacted to GM's December 1991 announcement with alarm. "This is very much an economic Pearl Harbor," he cried. "Something has got to be done about it."[3]

As if the auto story was not shocking enough, many other U.S. industries have also been slipping, as Figure 25–1 demonstrates. The share of U.S. sales coming from U.S. factories dropped sharply over the decade of the 1980s in computers, telephone equipment, semiconductors, machine tools, and so on. The number of U.S. production workers employed in the industries shown in Figure 25–1 fell 23 percent over the decade from 1.93 million to 1.49 million. Accordingly, *Business Week* published a special report questioning America in its title, *Can You Compete?*[4] Worried that we would all end up flipping hamburgers at McDonalds, people shouted for the "Reindustrialization of America." Pundits proclaimed that the economic malaise could be replaced by prosperity by the year 2000 if only business, labor, and government committed themselves to the task, and if the last of these groups—government—instituted bold new policies for promoting and protecting American in-

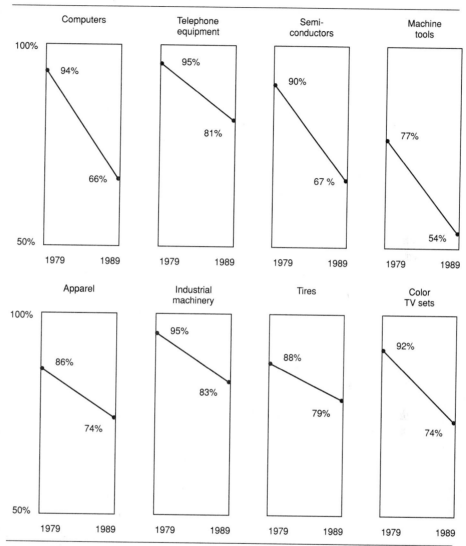

Figure 25–1
U.S. Factories' Share of U.S. Markets in 1979 and 1989

Source: *Fortune,* September 24, 1990, p. 64; Department of Commerce, Ward's Automotive Yearbook, Semiconductor Industries Association, Electronic Industries Association, National Machine Builders Association. Reprinted with permission.

dustries. Fresh subsidies for high-tech sectors were called for. New barriers against Japanese imports were pushed. An "industrial policy" was said by some to be our salvation.

The adjectives "fresh" and "new" suggest that policies of promotion and protection have been around a long time. And, indeed, they have been. Thus, with an eye on what might happen in the future simply out of frustration, this chapter surveys promotion and protection policies of the past and present. Our survey is a lengthy one because the variety of such policies is bewildering. U.S. shipping lines are aided by a law requiring that all Alaskan oil be moved by American tankers. Cotton, wool, apple, and potato interests are served by advertising campaigns financed from special taxes. Books and magazines enjoy unusually low postal rates. And so on.

Here we focus on four major classes of such policies, each of which may be illustrated by the experiences of important industries:

I. Direct Subsidies: Transportation and Energy
II. Loans and Loan Guarantees: The Chrysler Bailout
III. Import Protection: Steel and Autos
IV. Price Supports: Agriculture

When you review these policies of promotion and protection, you will notice that the reasons for such policies range widely. National defense, income equity, stability, efficiency, conservation, progress, economic growth, national prestige—the list of alleged benefits is so long that one wonders how a pennant for the hapless Chicago Cubs misses mention. Although some of these laudable purposes are indeed served by policies of promotion and protection, the plain fact is that much if not most of the motivation is simply special interest politics, whereby a few are able to benefit at the expense of the many. Because the few who benefit usually benefit a great deal per capita or per firm, they press their political representatives hard with lobbying efforts and campaign funding. Because the many who pay higher taxes or higher prices pay relatively little per capita or per firm, their countervailing pressures are weak and diffuse by comparison. Thus, one reason special interest politics can succeed is a *disparity* in the concentration of benefits relative to costs. A second reason is *logrolling*, which is simply the exchange of political favors. This explains how minorities can gain at the expense of the majority. For example, Detroit's representatives in Congress vote for federal tobacco subsi-

dies benefiting rural Southerners because those representing rural Southerners vote loan guarantees for Chrysler Corporation. Little wonder, then, that presidents, with broadly based political constituencies, have time and again proposed the abolition or substantial curtailment of special favors, only to be rebuffed by Congress.

I. Direct Subsidies

A. Theory

Nearly every economist has his or her own definition of subsidies. According to one, they are "Government programs that modify the operation of the market mechanism or of the tax laws for limited sectors of the economy or limited groups of the population."[5] According to another, subsidies work "through the private market, by altering certain market prices" in order to "induce someone to increase or decrease his purchases, or his production, or use of some particular thing or group of things."[6]

Such general definitions typically have two features in common. First, they stress that subsidies merely *modify markets* rather than totally supplant them. This excludes from the realm of subsidies government activities like equipping an army, floating a navy, or issuing currency. Second, they specify the *limited scope* of subsidies, thereby stressing sectoral favoritism. This excludes such broad or common benefits as investment tax credits and Social Security.

At this level of generality, every policy reviewed in this chapter could be considered a subsidy. But the *mechanisms* by which these subsidies operate, and their immediate *impact* on the marketplace differ enough to allow categorized treatment. The **direct subsidies** of this section include, in ascending order of government involvement, the following:

1. *Tax breaks* for favored goods and services, such as the tax deferral exporters receive under the DISC program.

2. *Direct payments* to producers or consumers to help cover the costs of producing or consuming certain favored commodities or services. An example is the federal government's funding of railroad passenger service through Amtrak.
3. *Government ownership and operation* of certain kinds, such as government ownership and operation of the Synthetic Fuels Corporation, which in the past promoted synfuels development. Much government ownership is not for purposes of subsidy (it is, for instance, an alternative to regulation in the field of public utilities). But much of it clearly is.

The impact of such direct subsidies on the favored markets may be seen in Figure 25–2. Assuming pure competition for simplicity, S_1 represents supply without subsidy and embodies all per-unit costs of producing various quantities of the commodity in question, including tax costs and a normal return to investors. Free-market price and quantity will then be P_1 and Q_1, where S_1 intersects demand. A subsidy has the effect of lowering cost per unit, thereby shifting the supply curve down from S_1 to S_2. The vertical distance between S_1 and S_2 is the amount of subsidy per unit, and any given quantity, say Q_1, will be supplied at an equivalently lower price. The subsidy thus lowers the price charged to buyers below that necessary to cover full unit cost. Given Figure 25–2's demand, the result is a lower price of P_2 (despite real unit costs at C), and a larger quantity at Q_2. For a concrete example from Amtrak in 1981, the typical rail passenger paid $25 for a trip, but Amtrak's cost of supplying that trip was $60. Subtracting $25 from $60, we see that the average subsidy was $35 per passenger.[7]

Recognizing that a direct subsidy increases quantity above the free-market level, we can note that such subsidies may serve legitimate economic purposes. If the free-market result is for

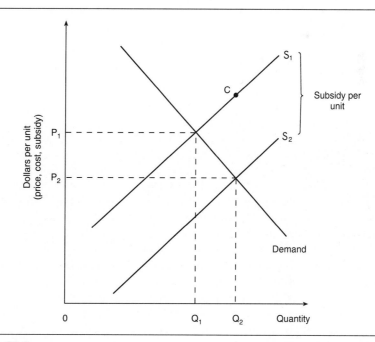

Figure 25–2
The Impact of Direct Subsidies

some reason flawed, so that too little quantity is provided, then a subsidy would be warranted insofar as the benefits of the added quantity exceed the costs of the added quantity. If, for example, railroad passenger travel yielded such external benefits as reduced pollution, curbed fuel consumption, and less highway congestion as compared to auto travel, it might well be that a subsidy for Amtrak of $35 per average passenger is warranted. Still, these external benefits would have to be worth at least $35 per passenger to be warranted by economic efficiency criteria. In other words, we who do not ride trains should be willing to pay some of the costs of those who do *to the extent* that we benefit by their train travel.

I should hasten to add, however, that relatively few subsidies probably serve such laudable purposes, and among these few the subsidy magnitudes are not as finely determined as economists would like. During the first twenty years after its inception in 1971, for instance, Amtrak gobbled up more than $500 million per year, on average, in government subsidies. Yet Amtrak's external benefits have been valued at less than $25 million per year. Estimated benefits to Amtrak passengers themselves have been great enough to justify the subsidies supporting Amtrak's operations in the northeast corridor linking Boston, New York, Philadelphia, and Washington, D.C., plus a few other heavily travelled routes, like Los Angeles to San Diego. On the other hand, positive net benefits have not been found for low-density, long-haul routes like Chicago to San Francisco.[8] (Facing these facts, Presidents Carter, Reagan, and Bush all tried to cut Amtrak subsidies and to some extent they succeeded. In 1981 operating subsidies were $720 million, which covered more than 50 percent of the company's operating costs. By 1992 operating subsidies had fallen to $321 million, offsetting less than 30 percent of the operating costs. Despite these curbs, a substantial increase in ridership has helped move Amtrak toward profitable independence. Annual passenger miles were

close to 4.5 billion in 1981 and greater than 6.0 billion in 1991, a 30 percent jump. W. Graham Claytor, Jr., now a legend in railroad circles, deserves more credit for Amtrak's recent success than anyone else. At age 70, he was appointed chief executive of Amtrak in 1982. First attracted to railroading when locomotives still burned coal and eventually elevated to the presidency of Southern Railway, Mr. Claytor is at this writing in early 1992 pushing 80 years and still rolling under a full head of steam.[9])

B. Direct Subsidies in Practice: International Comparisons

The United States subsidizes industries at a very low rate compared to the subsidies made by other countries to their industries. Figure 25–3 illustrates this fact for the 1980s, dividing direct subsidies into two broad categories. First, the "national accounts" data, reflected by the solid dots in Figure 25–3, include only cash subsidies. They exclude tax concessions, soft loans, and government participation in ownership. These cash subsidies amounted to only about 0.5 percent in the United States as a percentage of gross domestic product during the 1980s. They were twice as large in Japan and many times larger in European countries—reaching 6 percent in Ireland and 7 percent in Sweden. The second category, which is added to the first for most countries in Figure 25–3, covers tax concessions and other noncash direct subsidies, as estimated by the European Commission (only for the European countries). The average rate for these other subsidies from 1981 to 1986 was a hefty 8.6 percent of the value of output, which is two to three times greater than the average amounts for cash subsidies. Italy's noncash subsidies reached about 16 percent of the value of total output during the period, topping the other countries by a huge margin and making Italy the most heavily subsidized country on the chart.[10] Incidentally, a major reason why cash subsidies are small rela-

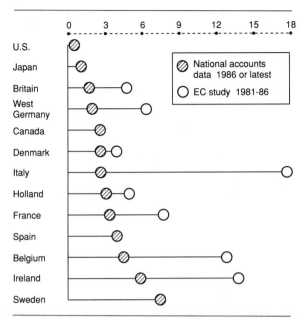

Figure 25–3
Government Subsidies to Industry as a Percent of
Total Output Value, 1980s Data.

Source: *The Economist,* February 24, 1990, p. 71.
Reprinted with permission.

tive to other subsidies is public awareness. Cash
subsidies are more readily detectable, and therefore more open to political attack, than subtle
subsidies.

C. Direct Subsidies in Practice:
U.S. Transportation and Energy

Historically, the U.S. government has probably
poured more direct subsidies into transportation
and energy than any other sectors of the economy save perhaps education. Beginning with last
century's railroad land grants and continuing
with this century's airline subsidies, nuclear
power assistance, and much more, the total figure, if ever computed, would surely be in the
hundreds of billions of dollars. Our brief review
of recent subsidies for these two sectors divides

into three parts: (1) tax breaks, (2) direct payments, and (3) government ownership.

1. TAX BREAKS

The tax system can be manipulated to grant subsidies by lowering the tax liability of favored
firms or individuals who, by virtue of their special identity or behavior, thereby benefit relative
to others. Stanley S. Surrey explains that these
tax subsidies substitute for direct government expenditures, so they could also be called tax
expenditures.

> The Federal Income tax system consists of really
> two parts: one part comprises the structural pro-
> visions necessary to implement the income tax on
> individual and corporate net income; the second
> part comprises a system of tax expenditures
> under which governmental financial assistance
> programs are carried out through special tax pro-
> visions rather than through direct government ex-
> penditures. The second system is simply grafted
> on to the structure of the income tax proper; it has
> no basic relation to that structure and is not nec-
> essary to its operation. Instead, the system of tax
> expenditures provides a vast subsidy apparatus
> that uses the mechanisms of the income tax as the
> method of paying the subsidies.[11]

These subsidies take a variety of forms, including exclusions from income, deductions from
income, preferential rates of tax, and deferrals of
tax. One example of recent energy subsidies is
the so-called tax credit, which permits the tax
payer to treat a portion of the purchase price of
energy-related equipment as if it were a tax payment. The Energy Tax Act of 1978 offered tax
credits to individuals equalling 15 percent but not
more than $300 of the cost of outfitting their
homes with energy-saving items like insulation,
storm windows and doors, weather stripping,
and clock thermostats. Solar credits were larger,
and related credits were showered on businesses.
In 1980 these several tax credits were extended
and expanded to the point of saving consumers
an estimated $600 million and businesses an es-

timated $5 billion during the years following. Now they have ended.

The purpose behind these and related tilts in the tax system is to curb energy consumption or redirect it toward new and cleaner energy sources such as solar and wind power. Because the combustion of oil and coal is presently the single largest contributor to air pollution, such objectives seem sound. The subsidies encourage behavior having substantial external benefits. In addition, conservation and conversion enhance our security against the interruption of oil imports and benefit future generations with less costly energy supplies than otherwise.

2. DIRECT CASH PAYMENTS

Estimates of the federal government's direct cash subsidies to the nuclear power industry vary widely depending on where one draws the line. If one counts spending on early military reactors that provided the technological basis for later commercial reactors, plus government outlays for research on nuclear waste disposal, plus the cut-rate prices the government charges private parties for enriching uranium fuel, then the total subsidy from 1950 through 1980 came to a whopping $37 billion. If, on the other hand, one excludes all forms of support other than money spent directly on civilian reactors, then the government's contribution amounted to "only" $12.8 billion.[12]

In transportation, Amtrak's subsidies could be considered direct payments because Amtrak is technically a private, not a government, corporation. Another railroad heavily dependent on federal largesse is Conrail. Not to be confused with Amtrak, Conrail is primarily a freight railroad that operates about 13,700 miles of track in sixteen eastern and midwestern states. Created by Congress in 1976 out of the remains of six bankrupt railroads, the largest of which was the Penn Central, Conrail issued common stock to the estates of the bankrupt precursor railroads and gained debt and preferred stock financing from the federal government. Most of the gov-

ernment's multibillion dollar subsidy to date is actually in the form of loans. But prospects for the repayment of those loans plus interest are so dim as to warrant their classification as direct subsidies.

Ocean shipping has likewise a hand in the government's purse. Until the Reagan Administration submarined them in 1981, subsidies for ship building ran $100 million per year. In addition, subsidies over $300 million annually help to cover operating costs.[13]

3. GOVERNMENT OWNERSHIP

Figure 25–4 inventories the extent of government ownership in twelve countries as of 1984. The figure reveals one of the most striking features of government ownership of business, at least in the past—namely, its pervasiveness in energy and transportation sectors. Aside from postal service and telecommunications, government ownership has been concentrated in such industries as electricity, gas, oil production, coal, railways, and airlines.

The reasons for this are *not* all related to subsidies. Government ownership is, for one thing, an alternative to price and profit regulation in dealing with natural monopolies (and this helps to explain the prevalence of nationalization in electricity and gas). Still, many of the reasons for this pattern *are* related to subsidies, given that government-owned companies can succeed without earning profits. Here are several examples:

- *First,* many governments use public enterprises as a way to bolster employment in depressed industries, and transportation and energy are often considered key industries to national defense and national self-sufficiency.
- *Second,* undertakings in energy and transportation often entail massive capital commitments or very risky prospects, two features that tend to discourage private investment and give pretexts for government ownership.
- *Third,* subsidies to energy and transportation through the device of government ownership

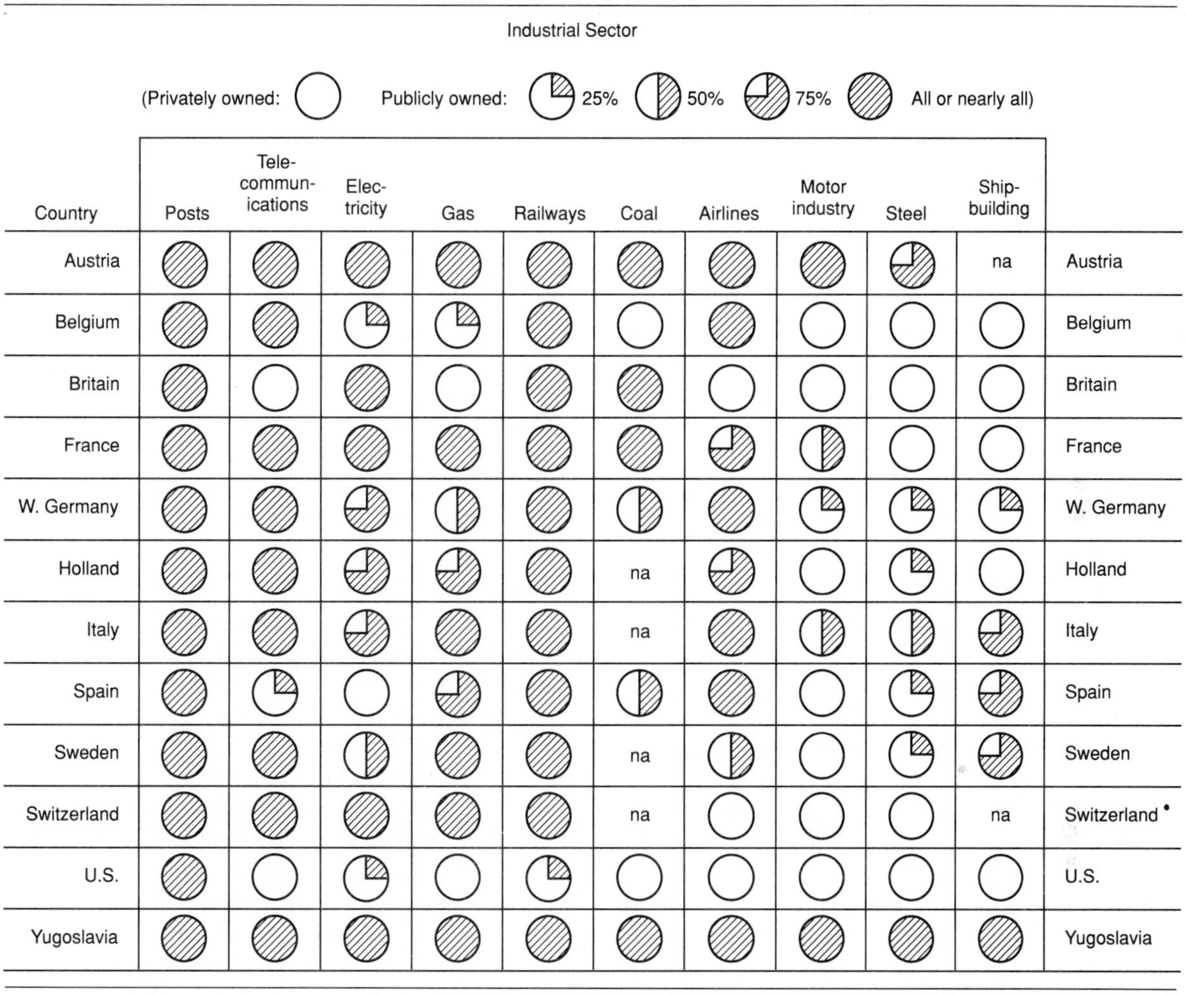

Industrial Sector

(Privately owned: ◯   Publicly owned: ◔ 25%   ◐ 50%   ◕ 75%   ⬤ All or nearly all)

Country	Posts	Telecommunications	Electricity	Gas	Railways	Coal	Airlines	Motor industry	Steel	Shipbuilding	Country
Austria	all	all	all	all	all	all	all	all	75%	na	Austria
Belgium	all	all	25%	25%	all	—	all	—	—	—	Belgium
Britain	all	—	all	—	all	all	—	—	—	—	Britain
France	all	all	all	all	all	all	75%	50%	—	—	France
W. Germany	all	all	75%	50%	all	50%	all	75%	25%	25%	W. Germany
Holland	all	all	75%	75%	all	na	75%	—	25%	—	Holland
Italy	all	75%	all	all	all	na	all	50%	50%	75%	Italy
Spain	all	25%	—	75%	all	50%	all	—	25%	75%	Spain
Sweden	all	all	50%	all	all	na	50%	—	25%	75%	Sweden
Switzerland	all	all	all	all	all	na	—	—	—	na	Switzerland •
U.S.	all	—	25%	—	25%	—	—	—	—	—	U.S.
Yugoslavia	all	all	all	all	all	all	all	all	all	all	Yugoslavia

Figure 25–4
Scope of Government Ownership in Selected Sectors in Selected Countries, 1984

Note: The proportions shown are often approximate.
*n.a. = Not available.
Source: William G. Shepherd, *Public Policies Toward Business,* 8th Ed. (Homewood, IL: Irwin, 1991), p. 394

can be used to subsidize certain *consumers* of energy and transportation, be they other industries or common folk. (Here ownership is a subsidy for achieving other subsidies.)[14]

Notice that the data in Figure 25–4 are for 1984. Since then, government ownership has be-

come extremely unpopular. "Privatization," as it is called, has replaced government ownership to a degree unimaginable only a few years ago. This trend is especially true of the communist countries that formerly comprised Eastern Europe and the Soviet Union (as represented by Yugoslavia in Figure 25–4). Under communism, virtually all industrial businesses were nationalized. Converting to capitalism has required massive sell-offs of auto companies, food processors, shoe manufacturers, and countless other state enterprises. Although privatization has been (and will continue to be) especially dramatic in the formerly communist countries, it has been under way even longer in Western Europe and South America. A leader of the movement was Margaret Thatcher's government in Great Britain, which, beginning in 1980, privatized firms in aerospace, petroleum, automobiles, highway freight transportation, telecommunications, radiochemicals, and several other sectors.[15] Latin American trends are illustrated by Mexico, which has recently privatized telecommunications, banks, mines, and communally owned farmlands.[16]

Why the immense surge in sell-offs? Empirical studies comparing the economic performance of publicly owned and privately owned enterprises reveal that state-owned enterprises typically lag behind their privately owned counterparts in production efficiency.[17] Sluggish employees, obsolescent facilities, and lax managements frequently characterize government ownership. These conditions go a long way toward explaining the rising popularity of privatization.

Still, a major caveat must accompany this explanation for privatization. The inefficiency commonly associated with government ownership may *not* be due to government ownership, at least not in many instances. Rather, the inefficency may be caused by another factor that frequently accompanies government ownership—namely, monopoly power. Research discloses that state-owned enterprises usually perform well when they face competition. Research, as we saw in earlier chapters, also discloses that privately owned firms can be quite *in*efficient when they do not face competition. Hence, to the extent monopoly is the problem rather than public ownership, privatization will improve economic performance only if it is accompanied by increased competi-

tion as well.[18] (This is an immense problem for the privatization of what previously were Soviet Union enterprises because the Soviet Union deliberately centralized each industry's production into only one or a few plants. This precluded competition under communism, and it is hampering the creation of competition in postcommunist countries.)

As suggested in Figure 25–4, government ownership never seriously took hold in the United States. Sweeping privatization here is therefore not possible. Even so, there is an interesting recent case of abandoned government ownership, a case originally grounded on subsidy—the Synthetic Fuels Corporation (SFC).

In 1980 Congress established the U.S. Synthetic Fuels Corporation (SFC), a subsidized government enterprise the express mission of which was to subsidize the commercial development of "synfuels"—that is, oil from shale rock and gas and other fuels from coal. Originally authorized to spend $20 billion over its first five years and to seek as much as $68 billion more in future years, the Synthetic Fuels Corporation launched an entirely new industry with its nose in the federal trough. The original objective was to foster the production of the equivalent of 2 million barrels of oil a day by 1992, about 10 percent of expected oil consumption.

However, this objective proved to be more volatile than a gasoline torch. In 1985 Congress cut SFC's funding to zero, and in 1986 the corporation closed its doors.[19] The U.S. Synthetic Fuels Corporation fizzled badly. With imported oil priced at $12 a barrel in 1986, and SFC's subsidies climbing as high as $60 to $90 a barrel, it began to look utterly ridiculous. Still, at the time of its founding in 1980, world oil was priced well over $30 a barrel and climbing. Also the United States was (and still is) very rich in coal. Hence, it seemed at the time like a good way to become less dependent on imported oil.[20]

II. Loans and Loan Guarantees

A. Theory

Government credit programs loom immensely. Uncle Sam's loans and loan guarantees resemble direct subsidies because they reduce costs to recipients and thereby influence the market in the fashion of Figure 25–1. Here, however, the cost savings are hidden. Government **direct loans** are simply loans granted by the government itself, usually at interest rates much below those of private lenders. The loans issued under government **loan guarantees** are the loans of private lenders such as banks, but the government guarantees that the loans plus interest will be paid off even if the borrower defaults. In this case, the main cost savings to borrowers is again a reduced interest rate because the guarantee reduces the private lender's risk. In short, defaults under any of these programs leave the government holding the bag.

Because the borrowers benefiting from government loans and loan guarantees *are* expected to repay, it may appear that these forms of subsidy are costless to taxpayers except for the occasional defaults and administrative burdens. But this is not true. These particular costs comprise only one class of government costs that may be called *ultimate fiscal costs*. Another class of government costs emerges from the fact that these credit activities raise the government's cost of borrowing, and indeed the government is a very big borrower. These may be called *initial fiscal costs*. Finally, there are nongovernmental *economic costs* that arise because government loans and loan guarantees divert credit away from nonsubsidized borrowers. Murry Weidenbaum explains these classes of costs in reverse order:

1. *The economic cost.* Since they do little if anything to increase the total supply of investment funds in the economy, government credit programs take credit away from other potential borrowers. These unsubsidized borrowers might have produced more for society than the recipients of the government-supported credit. This can be the situation when the presence of federal credit encourages individuals or organizations to incur expenditures that they would forgo in the absence of the federal subsidy.

2. *The initial fiscal cost.* To the extent that government credit programs increase the total size of government-related credit, they cause an increase in the interest rates that are paid in order to channel these funds away from the private sector. Some increase, therefore, results in the interest rates paid on the public debt, which is a direct cost to the taxpayer.

3. *The ultimate fiscal cost.* When defaults occur on the part of the borrowers whose credit is guaranteed by the federal government, the Treasury winds up bearing the ultimate cost of the credit. In such cases, the government credit programs become a form of backdoor spending whereby federal expenditures are incurred in the absence of direct appropriations for the purpose.[21]

Thus, government credit programs permit subsidized borrowers to elbow out unsubsidized borrowers, producing hidden costs as well as visible administrative costs. The social benefits associated with this effort are the benefits gained from channeling more credit—and ultimately more real economic resources—into beneficial activities such as education, pollution control, transportation, and energy conservation.

B. The Scope of Federal Credit Activities

Figure 25–5 shows the towering growth of federal credit programs over the 1970s and 1980s. Beginning at just under 220 billion in total credit obligations outstanding in 1972, the total jumped 60 percent during the Carter Administration and then jumped 60 percent again during Reagan's reign. At the end of 1989, total credit obligations

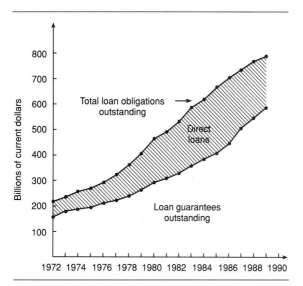

Figure 25–5
Growth of Total Federal Credit Outstanding,
1972–1989

Source: *Statistical Abstract of the United States, 1990*
(Washington, D.C.), p. 316; *Statistical Abstract of the
United States, 1981* (Washington, D.C.), p. 252.

outstanding were approaching $800 billion. Loan
guarantees have clearly surged the most.

Direct loans are issued by two kinds of agencies. *On-budget agencies* are subject to traditional budget control. These include:

- The Small Business Administration, which makes loans to small businesses for expansion.[22]
- The Economic Development Administration, which makes loans to businesses for commercial expansion or survival in economically distressed areas.
- The Export-Import Bank, which finances export sales, especially sales of durable goods like aircraft and computers.

Off-budget agencies include the U.S. Railway Association, which makes loans to Conrail, and the Rural Electrification and Telephone Revolving Fund, which supports public utilities in rural areas.

C. The Chrysler Bailout

In total dollar volume, the industry benefiting most from federal credit programs is housing. The Federal Housing Administration, or FHA, is the most familiar part of this effort (with outstanding loan guarantees of $347 billion in 1990). Nevertheless, one single loan guarantee of only $1.5 billion has attracted more attention in recent years than all housing credit subsidies combined—Chrysler's loan guarantee of 1980.

Chrysler's trouble began in 1973 when OPEC quadrupled the price of oil. This hurt the entire U.S. auto industry because it sparked a deep recession, and it caused auto buyers to shift from gas-guzzling American cars to fuel-efficient compact imports (see Figure 25–6). This hurt Chrysler more than it did GM and Ford, and forced it to cut capital spending and staff to a degree that sapped its strength against later difficulties.

In 1978 Chrysler suffered a $205 million loss. The following year its problems worsened when once again gasoline prices jumped, causing the public to switch further to small cars. Simultaneously, another recession hit the industry (see Figure 25–6). Chrysler's subcompacts sold well in 1979, but its losses tumbled past the billion mark. Appeals to the federal government brought help. Scary visions aroused by the prospects of Chrysler's going under were enough to jolt politicians of every stripe and stature. After all, with over $100 billion in annual sales and over 800,000 employees, the domestic auto industry is immensely important to the economy. Chrysler's 140,000 employees in 1979 were backed up by hundreds of thousands more in independent firms supplying parts, selling cars, and the like. Washington apparently could not turn its back on these hordes just before the 1980 elections.

Hence, Congress approved a $1.5 billion loan guarantee scheme to be administered by a special Loan Guarantee Board. The law establishing the board required that Chrysler match every

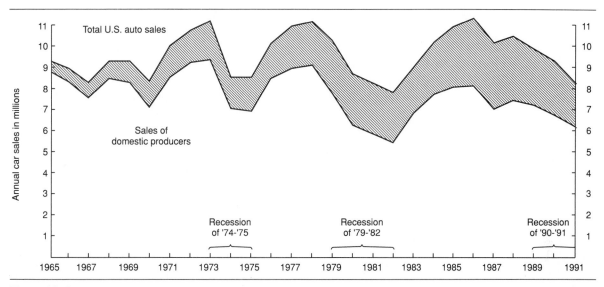

Figure 25–6
U.S. Retail Auto Sales: Domestic and Imports

Source: Automotive News, Wards Automotive, Wall Street Journal, and Motor Vehicle Manufacturers Association.

chunk of loan-guarantee money with equivalent dollar-for-dollar concessions from other sources, namely, discounts from Chrysler's parts suppliers, reduced wages from employees, and partial forgiveness of debt obligations from Chrysler's existing creditors. Moreover, the law required that Chrysler formulate a plan of survival—firing workers, closing plants, and developing new products—to satisfy the Loan Guarantee Board that Chrysler would be a "going concern" in the auto business after December 31, 1983.

Chrysler succeeded in satisfying the demands of the board, but just barely. As shown in Figure 25–6, 1980, 1981, and 1982 proved to be very bad years for the domestic industry. Chrysler increased its market share slightly in 1981 to 8.6 percent, but the general state of the industry's depression pushed its losses past the billion-dollar mark for the third year in a row, and 1982 didn't help either. Then suddenly, like a bolt from the blue, Chrysler got just what it needed— a huge wave of auto sales generally. Riding that

wave, Chrysler's profits jumped fantastically to 51.3 percent and 72.0 percent of stockholders' equity in 1983 and 1984—the best profit rates in the entire industry. Chrysler paid off its government loans way before schedule. And Lee Iacocca, Chrysler's chief throughout the battle, became a national hero.[23]

The story is stirring, but the main question for us here is whether the government should stand ready to catch stumbling corporate giants before they crash to the ground. Big rescue operations for Lockheed and Seatrain preceded Chrysler's. And some influential people advocate the establishment of a governmentally-sponsored Reconstruction Finance Corporation that would bail out faltering companies on a routine basis. The question is thus a serious one.

The case *in favor* of such bailouts is fairly self-evident: (1) Big failures can have ripple effects, causing panic in financial markets and puncturing business confidence. (2) Bailouts need be no more than temporary, provided they have appropriate controls and incentives. (3) The government's cost of permitting failure–that is, the resulting costs of unemployment compensation, welfare, and the like—exceed the government's cost of rescuing big beleaguered companies. And (4) the government may be at fault for the trouble.

On the other hand, the case *against* big bailouts is less obvious, so we should linger over the arguments. First, there are the appreciable costs of any federal credit program noted earlier. Initial and ultimate fiscal costs must be borne. And then additional economic costs are important in this context. As big distressed companies receive guaranteed loans at less than the going market rate, they have an incentive to borrow more than they otherwise might. It can be argued that the pool of loanable funds remaining for healthy companies is thereby reduced and the interest rates charged to healthy borrowers increased. Helping the weak at the expense of the strong weakens the economy.

Second, it is argued that bailouts adversely affect business incentives. "The possibility of bankruptcy is a necessary incentive for efficiency," explains Murry Weidenbaum. "I don't think big companies should be bailed out. After all, it's a profit-and-loss system."[24] In other words, waste, mismanagement, and inefficiency should be penalized lest they infect corporate boardrooms with sloth. Labor incentives would also be distorted by bailouts, for unions would then not face the unemployment consequences of outrageous wage demands.[25]

Third, bailouts favor big companies over small ones. Total corporate bankruptcies exceeded 25,000 the same year Congress approved Chrysler's bailout. In fact, corporate bankruptcies exceeded 25,000 annually during the entire last half of the 1970s. But Congress flinches only for the big ones, and all but a few bankruptcies involve relatively small firms. (In autos, Chrysler may be contrasted with Studebaker-Packard, which was allowed to fold. Because small firms account for most of the economy's new jobs and

a surprisingly large share of all technological innovations, a bias against small companies in favor of the big ones seems unwise. It might, moreover, encourage needless big-business growth.

Fourth and finally, bailouts may not be needed because the economic trauma of big business failures is not, in the end, as horrid as it may seem. In particular, bankruptcy is *not* necessarily the same thing as liquidation. It may involve nothing more than a restructuring of the liabilities and net worth of the stricken company. To be sure, creditors and owners lose in the process, but the company's plants do not crumble into a heap. Nor do all the jobs vanish overnight.[26] Penn Central, for example, went through bankruptcy and the trains still run (albeit in the case of Penn Central's trains they are now run by subsidized Conrail).

As harsh as this may sound, it must be remembered that the economy regularly experiences tremendous volatility and turnover. Change is constant. Little of it should be prevented because most of it is probably for the best. By one estimate, each area in the United States loses an average of 50 percent of its job base every five years. New jobs replace the old ones to bring stability or growth to most areas.[27]

In short, business people, the public, and influential politicians may look aghast at big corporate failures, but it is not clear that huge safety nets should be strung up. The problem might warrant indirect policies, such as tighter treatment of large conglomerate mergers. But, in general, big bailouts seem unwise. If careful scrutiny were brought to bear on the myriad other federal credit programs, many of them might also lose their economic appeal. Still, *political* appeal seems to be what counts here. We should therefore not be surprised to see federal credit operations above $600 billion continuing in the future, with ample slices of the pie serving purposes other than such laudable ones as external benefits and national defense.

(Chrysler Update: In January 1992, Chrysler again faced disaster. A severe recession ripped the industry in 1990–1991, as indicated in Figure 25–6. Its cars lagged a bit behind the other auto companies in style, and Chrysler lost almost $1 billion in 1991, a rupture of red ink reminiscent of 1979 and 1980. Chrysler has several new models coming out later in 1992 that could, if popular, save the company. However, if they do not sell well, it could be "curtains" because it seemed doubtful that a bailout for Chrysler would recur. In recent years, the federal government has committed hundreds of billions of taxpayers' money to bailouts of banks and savings and loans. Although these obligations stem from deposit insurance programs (and from crooks) rather than from loans or loan guarantees, the principle is the same. In these banking cases, the government has been caught by committing its good name to assure the soundness of someone else's liability. Congress (and the public) could thus be souring on bailouts. If so, and if Chrysler continues to stumble, the best the company could hope for would be a takeover by a stronger company.)

III. Import Protection

A. Theory

In May 1981, Japan's minister of international trade and industry announced that Japan would limit auto shipments to the United States to 1.68 million cars during the ensuing year, down 7 percent from the previous year. Restraint was promised for later years as well. Detroit cheered.

Why would Japan want to restrict its exports? Was it stupidly shooting itself in the foot? No, Japan wasn't shooting itself in the foot so much as choosing its poison, for it acted under threats from the U.S. government. If Japan had not curbed auto exports "voluntarily," Congress and the president would have probably slapped still harsher limits on Japanese auto sales through an import quota or tariff.[28] This type of "protection racket" has become quite common in recent years—affecting TV sets, textiles, steel,

baseball mitts, bicycles, and other commodities as well as autos—because genuine quotas and tariffs are all too real.

1. THE CASE FOR FREE TRADE: COMPARATIVE ADVANTAGE

Although economists are notorious for their differences of opinion, they nearly all agree that free trade is generally good. This goodness can be viewed in the abstract or in the concrete, but it is a goodness for society at large, the overall economy.

In the abstract, free traders cite the theory of **comparative advantage.** Without trade, we in the United States could consume only what we produce. If we wanted to consume bananas, we would have to produce them. If we wanted to consume coffee, we would have to produce coffee. And so on for all the thousands of things that fracture our personal budgets. Given resource scarcity and technological realities, this tight connection between domestic consumption and domestic production would mean that obtaining some of the things we enjoy could prove very costly. Producing our own bananas, for instance, would take abundant land, labor, and capital away from apples, peaches, and oranges, squeezing our consumption of those delicious fruits. Our welfare would, in other words, be bounded by our limited domestic production capabilities.

With free trade, these bounds are broken. Our *consumption* possibilities reach beyond our domestic *production* possibilities. We can consume what *other* countries produce as well as what we produce. Of course, we must give up in trade some of the goods we produce in order to get the goods other countries produce, just as without trade we would have to give up oranges and get more bananas. But *the terms of trade internationally are better than the terms of production exchange domestically because of the principle of comparative advantage.* The quantity of, say, oranges we would have to give up in exports to get a certain quantity of bananas imported would be *less* than the quantity of oranges we would have to give up in curtailed domestic production to get the same quantity of bananas domestically. Bananas simply cost less through international trade than they do through domestic production. National productive endowments differ, and our comparative advantage lies in oranges whereas Ecuador's lies in bananas. More broadly but more realistically, international trade patterns reveal a U.S. comparative advantage in (1) capital equipment goods like airplanes and machinery, (2) high technology goods like computers, and (3) certain agricultural commodities like wheat and soybeans.

2. THE CASE AGAINST FREE TRADE: COMPARATIVE ADVANTAGE QUALIFIED

The theory of comparative advantage stood alone for nearly two centuries as the main explanation for international trade and the major defense for free trade. The theory had some problems, but none were serious, not until recently when two major problems emerged—one empirical and one theoretical. The result is that free trade has been called into question in some situations.

Empirically, much in the real world does not support the theory of comparative advantage. The theory presumes, in particular, a static world of near-perfect competition, when in fact we live in a *dynamic world* characterized by *imperfect competition*. One feature of dynamics, for instance, is the fact that costs can change over time as a result of added (accumulated) output, just as the per-unit cost of producing 747 airplanes falls as Boeing produces more 747s. This is called *learning-by-doing*. Another feature of dynamics is the technological change that over time is yielded by R&D investments. As far as imperfect competition is concerned, we know from past chapters that many firms enjoy monopoly power, that many buyers are poorly informed, and so on.

Given real-world conditions that diverge from the assumptions behind the theory of comparative advantage, we might then expect to find trade flows deviating from those predicted by the theory. And, indeed, deviations abound. Of particular interest are the many instances when we both export *and* import the *same commodity*. We export and import semiconductors, textile machinery, industrial furnaces, and motion pictures, to name a few examples. In the classical theory of comparative advantage, this cannot happen. Comparative advantage cannot explain how, say, oranges might move both ways across our borders. What is happening then?

A major real-world "imperfection" is product differentiation, which helps to explain those instances of intraindustry trade that are illustrated by motion pictures. Although both are movies, U.S. science fiction spectaculars are different from British dramas, so each finds a market in both the United States and Britain. Other real-world complications center on dynamics and technological change. In the best empirical study of this issue to date, Scherer and Huh find that across industries, "Intra-industry trade was greater [over 1965–1985], the more important learning by doing is, the more R&D-intensive the industry was, the more relevant academic engineering research (but not basic scientific research) was, and the less individualized products were to specific customers' needs."[29]

Given these several empirical problems, it is no surprise that new theories of trade now challenge the old theory of comparative advantage and its free-trade policy prescription. Theorists Paul Krugman, James Brander, and Barbara Spencer, among others, have spearheaded the effort.[30] They have shown that, under certain conditions (which could be considered more realistic than those supporting comparative advantage), official tampering with trade can be economically beneficial. In particular, the new theories explore what is called *strategic trade policy*. Because learning-by-doing, innovation, monopoly position, and other such elements (rather than comparative advantage) are driving much trade, strategic trade theory views countries and industries as if they were game pieces on a chessboard. These "pieces" can be moved to strategically advantageous positions by discouraging imports or sub- sidizing exports, or both. For example, in the past Japan never produced jet airliners that ri- valed Boeing's. Furthermore, it seems doubtful that with free trade Japan could ever do so be- cause Boeing would always be at least one step ahead of the Japanese in low-cost capability. Be- cause of learning-by-doing, Boeing's lengthy past experience with production gives it cost efficien- cies that newcomers have difficulty matching. Thus, to develop a commercial jet aircraft indus- try, Japan could protect its producers from Boeing imports, subsidize JAL purchases of Jap- anese aircraft, and thereby boost Japanese pro- duction to give Japanese aircraft companies the experience they need to lower their costs of pro- duction toward those of Boeing. The push would provide a running start. Indeed, Airbus Industrie of Europe, which now ranks second only to Boeing in worldwide commercial aircraft produc- tion, exists only because of just such policies. (Air- bus subsidies from the governments of Britain, France, Germany, and Spain totalled about $10 billion over 1970–1990.[31])

Economists have thus demonstrated that in theory barriers to imports, or subsidies for ex- ports, or some combination of these interven- tions can yield economic gains to a country exceeding the gains of free trade under certain cir- cumstances. Strategic trade policy could there- fore occasionally be superior to free trade policy.

3. THE AMENDED CASE FOR FREE TRADE: COMPETITION

Although it is important, strategic trade policy suffers from the following several shortcomings:

1. One nation's use of strategic trade policy might provoke protectionist responses among its trade partners, touching off a trade war of retaliation and counterretaliation. If so, all na- tions would then be worse off.
2. Good information on costs and technologies is necessary to implement a strategic trade pol- icy successfully. Governments usually lack this information.

3. The theoretical gains from strategic trade pol- icies are typically quite small. Hence, policy errors, even tiny ones, could prevent the re- alization of net gains.
4. The interventions that strategic trade policies might justify will typically benefit some peo- ple and hurt others. There is thus a danger that strategic pretexts could result in exces- sive or misguided intervention that is, in fact, grounded on nothing more than redistribution inequities.

The upshot is that strategic trade theory does not destroy the principle of free trade as a general policy ideal. It merely weakens the notion that comparative advantage can always justify an in- dividual nation's free trade policy. Paul Krug- man, a leading strategic trade theorist, concludes the matter more neatly:

> It is possible, then, both to believe that compara- tive advantage is an incomplete model of trade and to believe that free trade is nevertheless the right policy. In fact, this is the position taken by most of the new trade theorists themselves.[32]

What then might justify free trade? Why do we see vast free trade areas now being formed in Europe, North America, and elsewhere? *Com- petition* is a one-word explanation. The basic idea of comparative advantage is that we can buy some goods more cheaply abroad than at home. (And despite complications this idea retains a great deal of truth.) Regarding competition, the basic idea is that free trade provides rivals for domestic suppliers and thereby permits pur- chasers to buy more cheaply *at home* (as well as abroad) than otherwise. Import competition con- strains domestic pricing. Conversely, to the ex- tent that tariffs and quotas repress imports, they therefore also boost domestic monopoly power.

Table 25–1 illustrates. The dollar price of a 1989, European-made, Peugot 205 automobile is reported for two European countries that in 1989 blocked Japanese imports (Britain and France) and two European countries that openly al-

Table 25–1
Price Impact of Trade Competition for a Peugeot 205
Auto (Pretax 1989)

Country	Pretax Price 1989 (in U.S. dollars)	
No Japanese Competition (*Quota Countries*)		
Britain	$10,241	
France	8,536	
Average		$9,388
Japanese Competition (*Nonquota Countries*)		
Belgium	$ 7,858	
Denmark	5,831	
Average		$6,844

Source: Fortune, December 17, 1990, p. 134; BEUC–The
European Consumers' Organization.

lowed Japanese imports (Belgium and Denmark).
Prices were clearly higher in the former than in
the latter—an average of $9,388 versus $6,844.
Japanese import competition thus reduced the
price of the European car 27 percent. Expanding
on these data leads to an estimated annual savings of $33 billion for European car buyers if im-
port competition had been freely allowed.

What is more, the benefits of import competition often go beyond price. To return to
America, accumulated evidence indicates that
over the past thirty years foreign auto producers
have been, on the whole, more innovative and
more quality conscious as well as more price
competitive than domestic American producers.
Who led the way with disk brakes, fuel efficiency, diesel engines, compact styling, and better "fits and finishes"? Was it Detroit? The
growth of auto imports shown in Figure 25–6,
from 6.1 percent of the U.S. market in 1965 to
31.1 percent in 1987, suggests the answer. Toyota, Honda, Mazda, and their brethren have
checked the market power of GM, Ford, and
Chrysler, preventing what otherwise would be
tight-knit oligopoly and pushing the domestic Big
Three toward better overall performance.[33]

Unfortunately, it *is* possible for foreign countries to exploit strategic opportunities (as suggested earlier) and thereby compete "unfairly"
with our industries to the extent that we follow
free trade. For example:

> If Japan and Europe do subsidize or otherwise
> promote some of the industries that compete with
> American firms, America does lose. In the imper-
> fectly competitive world that the new trade theory
> is concerned with, it can lose in a big way.[34]

Given this situation, America could respond by
introducing exceptions to its free trade efforts,
and understandably so. Protective tariffs or
counteracting subsidies would be difficult to resist politically even if, on the whole, they were
costly to the United States. A major justification
for such actions is this: Retaliatory intervention
against foreign interventions can often cause
those foreign interventions to be dropped. Thus,
our short-run intervention could, in the long run,
move everyone toward the global ideal of free
trade. (Two steps forward after one step back.)

To summarize, free trade is **always** the best
policy from a **global** perspective because of comparative advantage and competition. Free trade
is **usually** the best policy from an **individual nation's** perspective, but not always. Strategic interventions by some nations (whether wise or
not) may provoke understandable retaliatory interventions by other nations who suffer as a consequence. The general presumption in favor of
free trade is next illustrated by a look at the typical consequences of protection.

4. THE BASIC ECONOMICS OF TARIFFS AND QUOTAS

If we assume a standardized final product like
textiles, produced under competitive conditions
at home and displaying perfectly elastic supply
in the world market, the impact of import restraints is easily understood with the aid of Figure 25–7 where S_d represents the domestic supply
curve, and D_d the domestic demand curve. S_f indicates that foreign supply is perfectly elastic at

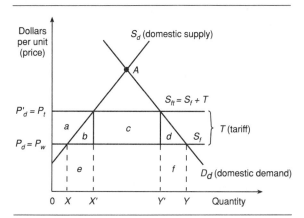

Figure 25–7
The Effects of Tariffs and Quotas

world price P_w; that is, as much or as little can be purchased at price P_w as desired. With free trade, domestic price would equal the world price, $P_d = P_w$, and the supply curve confronting domestic consumers would be, first, the low-cost portion of S_d below $P_d = P_w$ in the lower left-hand corner plus, second, the portion of foreign supply S_f spanning quantity range XY. Thus, with free trade, consumers are charged price P_w and they buy OX from domestic producers plus imports of XY from foreign producers for a total consumption of OY.

Tariffs. A tariff of T per unit would be like a tax on imports, lifting the price of imports above the world price P_w to P_t. This tariff-inflated price P_t then establishes a new domestic price P'_d above the old domestic price P_d. The consequences of this tariff for quantity are that domestic consumption *falls* from OY to OY' while domestic production *rises* from OX to OX'. Imports are thus pinched back by the tariff from XY under free trade to $X'Y'$. Clearly, if the tariff were still higher, imports would be pinched further until in the end they could be reduced to zero at the intersection of S_d and D_d, point A.

Recalling that multiplication of a dollar-per-unit value times the number of units yields a total dollar result, we know that the economic effects of the tariff can be divided into four parts corresponding to areas a, b, c, and d in Figure 25–7, as follows:

a. The redistribution effect.
b. The loss-due-to-production effect.
c. The tariff revenue effect.
d. The loss-due-to-consumption effect.

Taken together $(a + b + c + d)$ these areas comprise a total loss to consumers corresponding to their lost consumers' surplus. Area a is called the redistribution effect because it is a transfer from consumers to domestic producers. The move from quantity X and price P_d to quantity X' and price P'_d increases the total revenue of domestic producers by amount $a + b + e$. Portion $b + e$ represents increased domestic costs of production, so a is added rent or windfall profit to producers.

Area b, the loss-due-to-production effect, depicts that portion of total added production cost, $b + e$, which is rather senseless. Quantity XX' could either be imported at total cost e, or produced domestically at higher total cost $e + b$. The difference, b, shows a sacrifice in production efficiency from the tariff, a violation of the principle of comparative advantage.

Area c is the total revenue the government gains from the tariff. Multiplying imported quantity $X'Y'$ by tariff rate T yields area c. Notice that if the tariff were so high as to cause zero imports, there would be no tariff revenue at all.

Finally, area d, the loss-due-to-consumption effect, is the lost consumers' surplus associated with the decline in consumption from Y to Y'. This is analogous to the loss in consumers' surplus resulting from monopoly pricing (or, conversely, the efficiency gain associated with elimination of monopoly) depicted many chapters ago in Figure 3–2 on page 46.

In short, two of the four areas, a and c, amount to *transfers* or *redistributions* from domestic consumers to others—to domestic producers in the case of a and to government in the case of *c*. The two remaining areas, *b* and *d*, represent *efficiency* or *welfare losses*. They amount to consumer losses not recouped by others in society.

Quotas.   A quota works not on price directly, as does a tariff, but on *quantity*. A quota on steel, for instance, might say that no more than 10 million tons of steel can be imported annually. Because the effects of a quota resemble those on a tariff, Figure 25–7 can depict a quota if we imagine that the quantity of imports legally allowed is X' Y', down from the free-trade volume of XY. Supply thus restricted, domestic price is again bumped up to P'_d, which is above the old domestic price P_d and above the continuing world price P_w. As a consequence, consumers lose combined area $a + b + c + d$, as under a tariff.

Of this total loss, areas *a*, *b*, and *d* entail losses comparable to those experienced under a tariff, namely, *(a)* a redistribution effect, *(b)* a loss-due-to-production effect, and *(d)* a loss-due-to-consumption effect. The main difference between a tariff and a quota lies in the fact that under a quota, area *c* does *not* represent tariff revenue. Area *c* might go to domestic firms in the business of importing who buy at world price P_w and sell at domestic price P'_a. Area *c* might be captured by the domestic government if import licenses for the amount X' Y' are auctioned off to high bidders. It might go to foreign suppliers granted quota "allotments," which suppliers then price discriminate by charging up to P'_d while charging everyone else the world market price P_w. In other words, the disposition of *c* depends on how the quota is administered. Indeed, it could be some mix of these possibilities.

Voluntary Restraint Agreements (or VRAs)   Since the first half of this century, when ardent protectionism produced lofty tariff rates averaging 40, 50, and even 60 percent, tariffs have fallen substantially here and abroad. Levered down by several rounds of multinational negotiations, average tariff rates now lie in the neighborhood of

5 percent.[35] This liberalism fostered a stupendous sixfold increase in the volume of international trade between 1948 and 1978. However, partly in reaction to these swelling trade flows, a movement toward "new protectionism" has been building since 1973. In Europe, new protectionism has fostered an outbreak of regular quotas. In the United States, new protectionism has spawned a variety of voluntary export restraints, or VRAs.

As illustrated by our introductory story on Japanese autos, *voluntary export restraints* are similar to quotas in that they constitute quantitative restrictions. They differ from regular quotas, however, because they are not imposed unilaterally by the *importing* country against those in the outside world. Rather, they are "voluntarily" agreed to by selected *exporting* countries, usually in the belief that such self-restraint will forestall importing countries from imposing stiff tariffs or quotas. In economic impact, voluntary export restraints differ from quotas primarily by what happens to area *c* in Figure 25–7. Whereas the destination of those *c* revenues can vary under regular quotas, it ends up in the exporting country under voluntary export restraints because the exporting country is the one administering the restraint. Indeed, the enticement offered by area *c*'s scarcity rents encourages exporters to cooperate with importers. They "volunteer," in other words, in part because they are "bought off."

These voluntary export restraints can be informal, as in the case of Japanese autos, or they can be formal, as in the case of textiles. A so-called Multifiber Agreement has governed the world textile trade since 1977. During the 1980s, the accord set guidelines holding exports of major Asian producers to the United States and European Common Market at a growth rate not to exceed 2 percent per year.[36]

Antidumping Provisions.   Voluntary export restraints, quotas, and tariffs are sometimes used as weapons against "dumping." The Trade Act

Amendments of 1974 were important for developing a new, rather protective definition of dumping. Under the old Antidumping Act of 1921, it was unlawful for foreigners to dump products on the U.S. market at prices less than the *prices they charged at home*. Under the 1974 amendments it became unlawful for foreigners to dump products in the United States at prices less than their *cost of production, including overhead costs of at least 10 percent of direct costs, plus an 8 percent profit margin*. This new standard placed a higher floor under import prices than before. If, for example, steel prices in Japan are pressed down by recession to the point of yielding zero profit, the Japanese could not sell in the United States except at prices *higher* than at home. The consequences of illegal dumping are in any case the same as under the old law. If it can be shown (1) that products are in fact being dumped in the United States at unfair prices, and (2) that this injures domestic producers, then punitive protective action may ensue. The Commerce Department and the United States International Trade Commission share responsibility for determining the facts and imposing antidumping duties against foreign goods, a responsibility that can be met only by following complex procedures.

Cost Estimates. If the total dollar cost to U.S. consumers caused by tariffs, quotas, and voluntary export restraints were ever added up, the annual number would probably exceed $50 billion.[37] We do not really know what the sum is because estimation of areas *a, b, c,* and *d* in Figure 25–7 is difficult for even *one* product, let alone *all* the products affected by import restrictions. Nevertheless, Table 25–2 is suggestive. It gives the estimated annual total consumer cost of restraints on four products, broken down by the designations of Figure 25–7 (*a, b, c,* and *d*). The totals, which are for a year in the mid-1980s, range from $31.2 billion for textiles and apparel down to $1.1 billion for sugar. Steel and autos fall in between at $6.7 billion and $5.8 billion, respectively. Most of the cost in each case is due to the redistribution effect (*a*).

Table 25–2
The Economic Impact of Import Restrictions on Four Products, Mid-1980s
(Millions of Dollars)

Economic Cost to Consumers	Textiles & Apparel	Steel	Auto	Sugar
Redistribution effect, *a* (subsidy to producers)	$22,000	$3,800	$2,600	$ 550
Loss due to inefficiency *b* & *d*	4,850	330	200	130
Tariff revenue effect or quota scarcity rent, *c*	4,335	2,560	2,990	415
Total consumer cost[a] (*a* + *b* + *c* + *d*)	31,185	6,690	5,790	1,095

[a]Calculated by adding over the separate costs, although these differ slightly from the figures stated by Hufbauer et al.

Source: Gary C. Hufbauer, Diane T. Berliner, Kimberly A. Elliott, *Trade Protection in the United States: 31 Case Studies* (Washington, DC: Institute for International Economics, 1986), pp. 14–15.

Comparing the total consumer costs to the estimated number of jobs saved by the restraints in each of these industries yield some interesting numbers. The costs per job were huge—$42,000 for textiles and apparel, $750,000 for steel, $105,000 for autos, and $60,000 for sugar. (Note: Workers do not receive all this money. This is what consumers pay overall per job saved, with some going to inefficiency, some going to foreigners in rents, and so on.)

B. Import Protection in Steel

1. ECONOMIC BACKGROUND[38]

The American steel industry's battle against imports is rooted in the 1960s, when imports leaped from 4.7 percent of domestic consumption in 1960 to 16.7 percent in 1968. Imports dipped a bit in the mid-1970s, reaching a low of 12.4 percent in 1973; but they rebounded thereafter, crossing the 20 percent mark in 1981 and the 25 percent mark in 1985.

Since 1985 American steel's fortunes have reversed dramatically, with imports falling to 17 percent of domestic consumption in 1990. Two changes explain the drop. First, the yen/dollar exchange rate plunged by half after 1985, so each American dollar would thereafter buy only half as many Japanese yen and only half as much Japanese steel as before (all else equal). The dollar plunged relative to other currencies as well, so imported steel in general became more costly than American steel after 1985. Second, the U.S. industry has become more efficient and cost-competitive in many steel products because of the rise of the so-called minimills, which now account for about 25 percent of all U.S. output. Using electric furnaces and relatively large loadings of scrap, these minimills produced a ton of cold rolled sheet steel for $335 in 1990, a cost roughly 25 percent lower than the costs of either the Japanese or U.S. integrated firms.[39] The heavy import competition of the 1970s and 1980s encouraged minimills because for many steel products these mills are superefficient.

Looking back, we find the main explanation for the booming imports of the 1970s and 1980s also lies in comparative costs, but then America's costs were relatively higher than Japan's and minimills were not yet established. The single most important reason for America's relatively higher domestic costs at that time can be found in one component. In 1976 U.S. labor costs were nearly $160 per ton, whereas Japanese labor costs were only $60 per ton. The difference, $100, was roughly equal to the ultimate price difference per ton at the time.[40] Lagging productivity can elevate per-unit costs like this. The problem, however, was extremely high steelworker wages in the United States, not poor productivity. In the 1970s and 1980s, steelworker hourly earnings were 30 to 70 percent above U.S. average hourly earnings. High by domestic standards, U.S. steelworker earnings were also high by international standards, despite the fact that foreign steel workers were also pretty well paid. Such were the consequences, in large part, of a strong steelworkers' union in the United States. Indeed, steadily declining employment in steel since 1966 should have prompted wage moderation, not the skyward momentum actually observed.

2. PROTECTIONIST POLICY

Steelworker pay envelopes might have thinned instead of fattened if the U.S. government had been less protective of the industry. The protection came in three phases.

Phase I, 1969–1974. In 1969 voluntary export restraints were added to the existing tariff on steel of about 6 percent. These early voluntary restraints set import quotas of Japanese and European steel, allowing domestic steel production to be about 10 percent higher than it would have been otherwise.

Phase II, 1978–1982. Booming economic conditions abroad kept foreign producers busy during the mid-1970s, but they returned to the U.S. market during the late 1970s. Protection then took a new form—"trigger prices"—which set a floor under import prices. Officially announced by the U.S. government periodically, trigger prices were based on Japanese costs of production plus freight to America. For example, $422.95 per ton was the trigger price for the second quarter of 1981. These prices were *minimum* price targets for all foreigners, not just the Japanese, because products priced below the trigger level would trigger expedited antidumping investigations. With few exceptions, foreign exporters kept above trigger levels, so U.S. prices rose.

Phase III, 1982–1992. Suffering badly from the severe 1982 recession and from increasing imports, the steel industry then pressed for more protection than the trigger prices were giving. After scrapping the trigger price mechanism, the Reagan Administration extracted voluntary export quotas from 1982 to 1985, first from the European Community and then from many others, including Japan, South Korea, Brazil, and Argentina.[41] These voluntary restraint agreements remained in place and were renewed by the Bush Administration through March 1992, but they became superfluous from 1988 to 1992 because the tumbling value of the dollar's international exchange rate lowered imports to 17 percent of U.S. consumption—well below the 20 percent target of the voluntary quotas.[42]

Summary on Steel. The U.S. industry became vulnerable to outside competition in the 1970s because it lacked internal competition, as later admitted by Walter F. Williams, CEO of Bethlehem Steel, when he spoke to *Business Week* in 1989:

> With a near-monopoly on the U.S. market, domestic producers dictated to customers what steel to buy and charged premium prices. At Bethlehem, there were perks aplenty—limos, jets, and company-supported country clubs. Complacency bred poor quality and service. "We thought nobody could touch us," says Williams.[43]

The three phases of protection cushioned the competitive impact of the imports, raising domestic producer prices above what they would

have been without protection—5 percent in Phase I, 1 to 6 percent in Phase II, and 12 percent in Phase III (before 1988).[44] Imports remained forceful enough to improve domestic efficiency, however. To quote CEO Walter Williams again, "We woke up almost too late. The shock will prevent us from becoming complacent."[45]

In January 1992, it appeared that steel's twenty years of protection were about to end. Apart from the lower value of the dollar, which eased the import pressure "naturally," there was another reason to expect future freedom for imports. A growing number of domestic users of steel did not like paying inflated prices for their steel inputs. Manufacturers of automobiles, farm machinery, appliances, and many other products need low-cost steel inputs to remain competitive against foreign producers. In other words, quotas against steel imports may save steel industry jobs, but they also have the bad side effect of snuffing out other jobs as other industries' production costs rise. By one estimate, the mid-1980s quotas saved 17,000 steel industry jobs but cost 52,400 jobs in other industries.[46] While lobbying against the renewal of steel's voluntary restraint agreement in 1989, executives of Caterpillar Inc. took to wearing buttons that said, "Steel VRAs Steal Jobs."[47]

C. Import Protection in Autos

Japan's share of total U.S. auto sales jumped from 9.3 percent in 1976 to 21.2 percent in 1980, a huge increase—over twofold—in just four years. Why? The Japanese could produce a car at much less cost than Americans could—a whopping $2,000 less in 1980. Moreover, Japanese cars were vastly superior in every measure of quality—repair record, fit and finish, durability, fuel efficiency, and so on.

The "voluntary" restraint agreement extracted from the Japanese in 1981 limited auto shipments to the United States to 1.68 million cars per year, which curbed Japanese imports substantially. During the early 1980s, the prices of imported cars were as a consequence 8 to 15 percent higher than otherwise and the prices of domestic autos were roughly 5 to 10 percent higher than othewise.[48]

The voluntary restraint agreement was renewed in 1986 at a more lenient level, allowing 2.3 million cars per year instead of 1.68 million. This implied that there would be a renewed surge of Japanese imports during the late 1980s, but such was not the case. As a percentage of the U.S. market, Japanese imports ended the decade of the 1980s in about the same position as they began, running close to 20 percent. And in 1992 the Japanese lowered their VRA to 1.65 million cars with little effect.

Import pressure eased during the late 1980s for several reasons. First, the value of the dollar fell relative to the yen, raising the imported prices of Toyotas, Hondas, and the rest. Second, the U.S. automakers responded by improving their production efficiencies and product quality. The combination of these factors lowered the cost disadvantage of U.S. producers dramatically from $2,000 per car in 1980 to about $500 per car in 1990.[49]

Finally, and most interestingly, the Japanese began producing cars in the United States at "transplants." As indicated in Figure 25–8, Japanese imports actually fell slightly from 18.6 percent in 1987 to 17.0 percent in 1991. However, during the same years, Japanese cars produced in the United States nearly tripled in share, rising from 4.7 percent to 13.7 percent. Thus, in the end, the pressure of Japanese imports eased to the point at which a VAR of 2.3 million cars were superfluous because imports were only 1.7 million. But Japanese nameplate cars accounted for a larger percentage of the U.S. market than ever before—totalling more than 30 percent in 1991. (More of the new Hondas on American highways now come from Ohio than anywhere else!) Thus, in 1991, U.S. auto interests were shouting for steep cuts in the volume of cars imported from Japan *and more*—an overall ceiling on the Japanese companies' share of the U.S. car market.[50]

It turns out that Japanese transplants are almost as efficient as their counterparts in Japan. Also, their cars are essentially equal in quality. How can this be? Do the Japanese rely on robots everywhere? Do they have fanatical workers drawing poverty wages? Table 25–3 suggests that the answer lies in better management. A team of MIT professors who studied Japanese methods call it "lean manufacturing."[51] The chief characteristics of this approach are teamwork, close communication among workers, elimination of waste, efficient use of resources, and continual improvement. Table 25–3 indicates, for instance, that both here and abroad relatively little Japanese assembly space is used for repairs and that the vast majority of the workforce is organized into teams. Workers in Japanese plants, including U.S. transplants, can stop the production line at any time to fix problems. This reduces assembly defects substantially, yet does not hurt productivity (especially not in Japan, where luxury cars are built with fewer manhours, nineteen, than a famous European company spends repairing its expensive sedans after finishing assembly). The overall result in 1989–1990 was that a car could be built in a transplant for $200 less than one built in Japan and delivered to the United States.[52] Little wonder that the Japanese are building transplants in the United States while the American companies are closing their own plants. Little wonder, also, that import protection did not protect the American companies in the long run.

During the 1950s through 1960s, GM, Ford, and Chrysler dominated the U.S. industry. Lolling in monopoly power, they did not compete on price, durability, fuel economy, service, or such. They received a rude awakening, however, just like steel.

What, then, is the best policy? After analyzing the auto situation in depth, Robert Crandall concluded, "In the end, it is new competition,

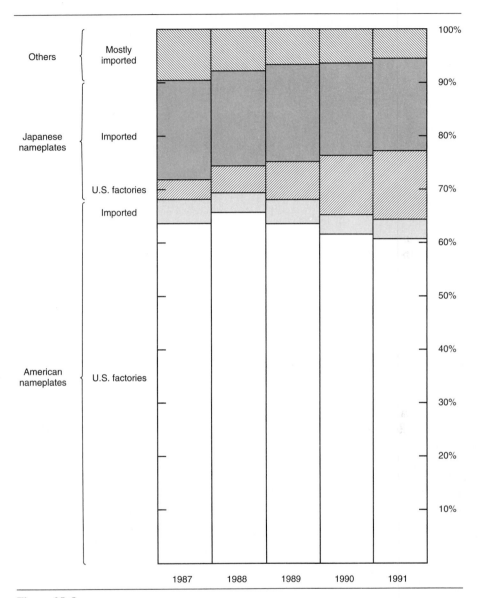

Figure 25–8
Origins of the Cars Carrying American and Japanese Nameplates.

Source: *The Wall Street Journal*, January 6, 1989, p. C9; January 5, 1990, p. A2; January 7, 1992, p. B6.

Table 25–3

Comparison of Japanese, American, and European Auto Companies on Selected Key Statistics (Averages over Plants, 1989)

Indicator	Japanese in Japan	Japanese in USA	Americans in USA	European Producers
Productivity (labor hours per vehicle)	16.8	21.2	25.1	36.2
Assembly defects per 100 vehicles	60	65	82	97
Repair area (percentage of assembly space)	4.1	4.9	12.9	14.4
Percentage of workforce in a team	69.3	71.3	17.3	0.6
Percentage of Absenteeism	5.0	4.8	11.7	12.1

Source: The Economist, August 20, 1991, p. 65 (based on MIT and J. D. Power & Associates data).

not the restriction of competition, that will revitalize the U.S. automobile industry."[53] (Note: This complements our earlier findings regarding privatization.)

Summary on Import Protection

Import restrictions serve as a major protectionist instrument—costly to consumers and society as a whole but coveted dearly by special interests. Such protection is difficult to defend economically, yet it persists. Tariffs declined substantially after World War II, only to be partially replaced by quantitative restrictions and a newly tightened definition of illegal dumping. Such have been the shelters provided to American steel and automobile companies. Their predicament arose when they grew lethargic from too much monopoly power (or, more accurately, oligopoly power). The protections have cost U.S. consumers billions of dollars in the past and have saved relatively few American jobs. Steel's restraints now lack bite because of the dollar's decline and the minimills' rise. Autos' restraints no

longer have bite because the world's best producers now run transplants on American soil.[54]

IV. Price Supports: Agriculture

The U.S. Department of Agriculture has one bureaucrat for every twenty-five American farms. They administer a dazzling array of promotion and protection programs for our largest industry (whose crop, livestock, and dairy sales exceed $170 billion annually). There are loans and loan guarantees for equipment, feed, seed, housing, electrical power, telephone service, emergencies, flood prevention, conservation, and even youth programs. There are direct subsidies for irrigation water, agricultural research, and marketing information. Tariffs and quotas fend off imports of meat, sugar, peanuts, and dairy products. Tax beaks abound.

Of special interest to us are **price supports** and **direct income payments,** two policies of old lineage differing from those of preceding sections. We proceed by first outlining the problems these policies are supposed to cure. An explanation of the operation of these policies comes next, followed in conclusion by an evaluation.

A. Agriculture's Problems[55]

Today's agricultural policy started sixty years ago during the Great Depression. Little wonder, then, that the main farm problems addressed by policy—instability and poverty—cast especially dark shadows in those days, which are the source of many of the following statistics.

1. INSTABILITY

Over time, farm prices and incomes trace a silhouette that looks like a mountain range. Ups and downs in corn prices produced a wild coefficient of annual variation of 28 percent from 1910 to 1949. Over the months of 1981, cotton prices plummeted from $0.87 cents to $0.57 cents a pound. From a broader perspective, the net income of all farmers gyrated from $18.7 billion to $33.3 billion and back to $18.7 during the mid-1970s.

What causes this instability? It is a combination of what may be called internal and external conditions. The *internal conditions* determine the *shape* of agriculture's demand and supply curves plus *location* on those curves. The *external conditions* produce *shifts* of demand and supply. Taken alone, neither the internal nor external conditions exert jolting influences, but taken together they can knock farmers around.

In particular, there are four internal conditions:

1. *Pure Competition:* With a very large number of producers, easy entry, and standardized products, agriculture can be characterized as purely competitive. There are, for instance, over 80,000 cotton farmers in the United States. And Grade AA white eggs are the same no matter whose chickens lay them.
2. *Gestation Period:* The time span between crop planting and harvesting or between livestock birth and maturity creates a lag between farm inputs and outputs. Cows, for example, have only one calf each year, and the calf isn't ready for market until it's almost two years old. Rough guesses about future market conditions consequently guide today's decisions, which in turn determine next season's output.
3. *Inelastic Demand:* A 10 percent drop in the price of corn stimulates only a 2 percent increase in quantity demanded. Quantity demanded is also unresponsive to price changes for wheat, milk, and other basic farm commodities because of their necessity to consumers. (Inelasticity also stems from the fact that, on average, farmers get only $0.40 of the consumer's dollar after transportation and processing.)
4. *Inelastic Supply:* Large swings in price likewise fail to generate large changes in quantities supplied, especially in the short run. Once a crop is planted, near-term supply is fairly fixed. Once buildings and equipment are designed for dairy farming, they cannot easily be converted to orchard operations. The same is true for other outputs.

To oversimplify, condition (1) denies farmers any monopolistic control over their prices or quantities, so prices and quantities tend toward equilibrium at the intersection of demand and supply. Gestation condition (2) means that movement from one equilibrium to another may not be smooth. Inelasticity conditions (3) and (4) make demand and supply curves very steep, implying that price must rise or fall markedly to close gaps in demand and supply.

Figure 25–9 partially illustrates the consequences for instability. Competition pushes price toward equilibrium points like E, E', or E^*. With inelastic supply shifting from S_1 to S_2 and back to S_1 against inelastic demand curve D_i, price lurches from P_1 to P_2, creating a choppy price pattern over time. In contrast, the same to and fro shifting of supply against elastic demand D_e generates a smoother price pattern over time because price fluctuates between P_1 and P_3 instead of P_1 and P_2.

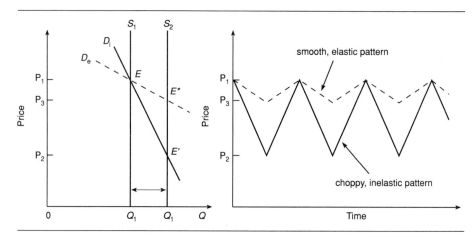

Figure 25–9
Price Instability in Agriculture

If supply stood still at S_1 in Figure 25–9, and if demand curve D_i remained stable, there would be no movement away from E. *External conditions* thus contribute to instability by causing *shifts* in supply and demand:

1. *Supply Side:* Capricious weather, crop diseases, and injurious pestilence shift supply about. Freezes in January 1982 damaged Florida's pole bean crop, lifting the price from $12 to $20 a bushel within a week. Conversely, especially good weather in 1979 boosted California's artichoke output 40 percent, driving the price down to $4 a carton from $10 the year before.

2. *Demand Side:* Domestic demand shifts with the general business cycle. Foreign demand for U.S. crops varies with the success or failure of crops abroad. Now, with about one out of every three acres of U.S. farm land producing for exports, swings in export demand pack a wallop.

Agreeing that the combination of these external and internal conditions causes sharp disturbances, you may nevertheless wonder, "Why is any government intervention needed? Aren't other industries also unstable?" To be sure they are, so our discussion should acknowledge the fact that agriculture is more unstable than most industries. Moreover, when stabilization policies were first formulated during the Great Depression, one-quarter of the population was rural, giving farmers powerful political clout. Finally, it can be argued that stability, if achieved by policy, promotes farm efficiency and productivity. Without stability, farmers would try to protect themselves by investing in nonproductive cash reserves rather than productive buildings, machinery, and equipment. Without stability, farmers would also tend to hedge their bets through diversified farming even though specialized farming has proved to be more efficient.

2. **POVERTY**

Were stability the only problem, agricultural policies could be aimed solely at price or income stabilization, but they haven't been. They have also been aimed at price and income *elevation* and *maintenance*. The reason may be seen in a few statistics that fertilized the roots of present policy. In 1939, income per capita of the farm population averaged only 37 percent of nonfarm income. Two decades later farm folk were only half as well off as city folk. A large part of the problem lay in chronic output abundance, which tended to depress farm prices and incomes. Rapid productivity growth pushed crop supply curves to the right faster than demand shifted with expanding population and personal income. Cotton yield per acre, for instance, leaped from 191 to 524 pounds between the mid-1930s and mid-1960s. More broadly, whereas one farmer formerly produced food and fiber for nine other people, he or she now produces enough for fifty-five others.[56] Hybrid seeds, pesticides, fertilizers, and modern farm equipment have, in short, wrought production miracles that may have contributed to economic woes.

Still, one must raise caution flags. These numbers misleadingly suggest that all farmers suffer downtrodden fates when in fact their earnings vary widely. Some face poverty, but many enjoy riches. Moreover, their fortunes as a class have improved dramatically in recent decades. Guided by the old disparity of nonfarm over farm income, farmworker population shrank from 11 to 3 million between 1940 and 1988. The migration from country to city simultaneously reduced the income disparity. And the late 1980s were fairly prosperous for farmers. Taking into account the income that farm families earned off the farm as well as on the farm, plus government subsidies, the average farm household income was $34,246 in 1986. This was 11 percent *higher* than the $30,759 average of all American households.[57] The suggestion of farm prosperity must be qualified by two facts, however: (1) Farm income alone, not counting off-farm sources, is below the average for all households. (2) Farm income remains highly variable, so it can be quite depressed at times, as indeed it was in the early 1980s. (In 1981, the ratio of farm to nonfarm income was 76 percent.)

Note: Agricultural policy is thus grounded, at least loosely, on two important economic problems—instability and neediness. These problems, however, are incomplete explanations for policy. In fact, their seriousness has greatly eased over time. Political and sociological explanations should therefore also be acknowledged. Because of movies, TV depictions, family origins, history, and other factors, there is a myth that farmers are especially deserving of assistance. It is a matter of equity or fairness as opposed to efficiency, and notions of equity or fairness in this case do not necessarily correspond to such economic measures as income. In the 1700s and 1800s

> the agrarian myth vested Jefferson's hardworking yeoman with a legendary superiority stemming from the prevailing Protestant ethic of hard work as a measure of moral worth. Farmers were perceived as being free of the moral depravity of urban life, they protected democratic values, and yet they suffered economic exploitation at the hands of others. As the general threads of this belief system persist into the 1990s, a nation in which farm families account for only 2 percent of its population continues to hold beliefs that strongly support family farming and the work of people who are still seen as committed to citizenship, to individual freedom, to hard work, and to moral virtue, yet who remain underappreciated and underrewarded.[58]

In short, much farm policy makes no economic sense. It rests on this myth.

B. Government Policy

If simple stability were the sole objective of government policy, official intervention would not attempt to influence average price, only the *amplitude* of prices' peaks and valleys. Government might do this, for instance, with an "ever-normal granary," buying up part of bumper crops when price is low, storing the purchases, and then selling out of storage when crops are poor and prices are high. The buying would lift the low prices above what they would otherwise be, and the selling would hold the high prices down below what they would otherwise be. Price fluctuations would thus be reduced while the average price level remained untouched.

The idea is an old one, dating back to ancient China. And in theory it is a good one. In practice, however, there are problems—such as inappropriateness for perishable crops like lettuce and uncertainty in knowing exactly when to buy and sell. In any case, this is *not* the concept guiding U.S. policy because stability has not been our sole objective. Aims of income elevation and maintenance were grafted onto stability, so *price supports,* supplemented by *direct income payments,* have been the focus of U.S. policy. In turn, this focus has necessitated various *supply restrictions*.

Figure 25–10 summarizes farm support from 1949 to 1988. The top potion of Figure 25–10 traces government payments as a percentage of total farm income. (as shown on the right scale). Notice that the late 1980s display record high involvement. In 1987, 30 percent of all farm income came from the federal government. President Reagan could not buck the myth or contend with farm-state Republican senators like Robert Dole and Jesse Helms. The 1960s and early 1970s also weighed heavily on taxpayers.

The bottom portion of Figure 25–10 depicts a rough measure of the farmers' well-being. It shows the ratio of two price indexes—an index of prices received for crops divided by an index of prices paid by farmers for their production inputs (e.g., fertilizer and equipment). The base for both indexes is 1949 ($=100$), so the starting ratio in 1949 is 1.00 (100/100 on the left scale). If crop prices fell relative to input prices, farm incomes suffered. The ratio registers this by likewise falling. If, conversely, crop prices rose relative to input prices, the ratio rose and farm incomes likewise elevated. Thus, it may be seen that government payments as a percentage of total farm income tended to move inversely with this ratio of price indexes measuring farmers' well-being. There is a systematic connection here. The gov-

ernment's payments have been particularly immense when the need, as measured by farm price conditions, has been particularly great. In fact, as we see next, most farm aid is *not* keyed to the incomes of farmers as such but to the *prices* of their crops.

1. PRICE SUPPORTS

Rather than be guided by estimated average equilibrium prices, as would be fitting for the operation of an ever-normal granary, Congress and the Department of Agriculture have used various standards of *fairness* in setting levels of price support. From the 1930s to the early 1970s the standard was **parity.** This standard assumed that farmers received fair prices for their crops relative to their costs from 1910–1914, when farming was particularly prosperous. This fairness eroded over ensuing years when prices farmers *received* for their crops did not rise as much as prices they *paid* for fuel, machinery, clothing, and other things. Hence, the idea was to support farm prices near parity by lifting them in step with other prices. To illustrate by hypothetical example, the parity price for corn would now be $5 a bushel if in 1910–1914 corn was priced at $1 a bushel and since that time the prices farmers paid had gone up fivefold. Price support at parity would then require that the government guarantee $5 a bushel to corn farmers. The absurdity of pegging everything to 1910–1914 caught up with the farm program during the 1950s, forcing the government to introduce large departures from the parity standard. Now fairness is largely determined by simple reference to present costs of production (somewhat in the fashion of public utility pricing), although the Department of Agriculture still publishes parity prices for farm commodities, and support prices for a few products are still expressed as percentages of parity.

The mechanics of the price support program are essentially as follows. Before harvest, the Secretary of Agriculture announces a price support level for each of the covered crops—mainly

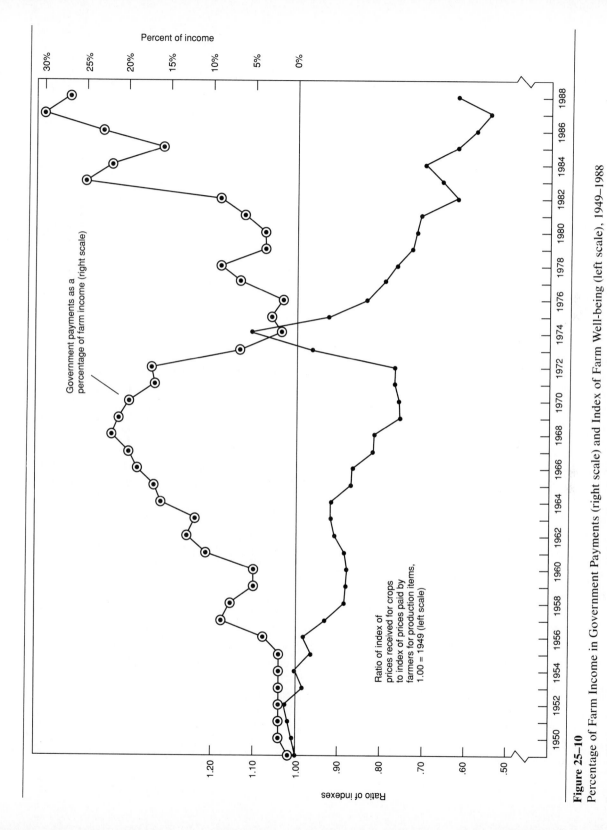

Figure 25–10

Percentage of Farm Income in Government Payments (right scale) and Index of Farm Well-being (left scale), 1949–1988

Source: *Economic Report of the President, 1991*, p. 398; David Rapp, *How the U.S. Got into Agriculture* (Washington, D.C.: Congressional Quarterly, Inc. 1988), p. 14.

cotton, wheat, rice, feed grains, soybeans, peanuts, and tobacco (less than half of all farm marketings). If after harvest the market price is low, farmers can store their output, borrowing from the government's Commodity Credit Corporation (CCC) amounts equal to the value of the goods when priced at support level. If market price later rises *above* support level, farmers can then sell their goods on the market and repay the loans from the proceeds, keeping for themselves the difference between market and support price. If market price remains *below* support level, the loan may be paid in full by turning the goods over to the government.

The simple economics of the system are illustrated in Figure 25–11 for cotton. Free-market price would be $0.50 a pound, as determined by the interaction of supply and demand. Corresponding quantity would be 7 billion pounds. Setting support price at $0.80 a pound would dislodge the market from this equilibrium, with free-market demand taking no more than 5 billion pounds. If supply were not artificially restricted, the government would then have to buy up (collect in loan payments) all output in excess of 5 billion pounds, which in this case, 3.2 billion pounds, is the difference between 8.2 and 5. At support price of $0.80 a pound, that would cost the government $2.56 billion. This subsidy would show up on the government's budget books, and come out of taxpayers' pockets. In addition there is a hidden subsidy paid by consumers through a higher market price, $1.5 billion in this case, which is the price difference, $0.30, times 5 billion pounds.

To flesh this example out with some real numbers, from 1984 to 1987 taxpayers paid farmers about $13.8 billion annually while consumers paid $7.8 billion more annually in higher prices. The total cost of the subsidy thus exceeded $20 billion yearly.[59]

2. DIRECT INCOME PAYMENTS

Rather than go through all the rigmarole of CCC loans, surplus purchases, and the rest (which is actually so confusing as to leave even farmers perplexed), the government could of course just pay farmers the difference between market price and some supposedly "fair" price.[60] In Figure 25–11, for instance, the government could simply pay farmers $0.30 a pound on no more than 7 billion pounds (distributed proportionately among cotton farmers according to past output). If market price fell below $0.50, the payments could expand accordingly. In comparison to price supports, such direct income payments would result in lower, market-clearing prices. In turn, lower market-clearing prices would yield many favorable effects. They would eliminate:

- Consumer-paid subsidies, thereby benefiting the poor, who spend a larger portion of their income on food than the rich.
- Government purchases of surpluses.
- The need for import restrictions (which have protected crops like sugar and peanuts, whose support price is usually above world market price).

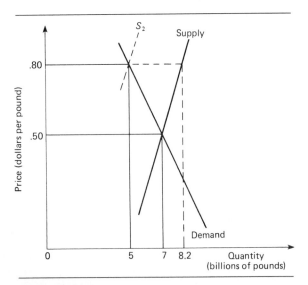

Figure 25–11
Price Support for Cotton

One drawback with direct payments is that tax-payers would have to pay more to keep farmers equally well off once the consumers' burden was reduced by lower prices. But that taxpayer burden would not be greater than the *combined* taxpayer-plus-consumer burden of price supports.

Another drawback to direct income payments is that, despite their economic advantages, they have been opposed by farmland's politicians. With price supports, the consumer's part of the subsidy is hidden. With direct payments, the entire subsidy is in the federal budget for all to see—embarrassingly so. Although perennially proposed from the late 1940s on, direct payments were always shunned by Congress until the Food and Agriculture Act of 1977, which finally introduced direct payments for wheat, cotton, and feed grains. Still, price supports were not abandoned for these crops. Instead, support pices (i.e., loan prices) were lowered below what they would have been, and direct payments were made to cover the difference between these lower loan prices and higher "target" prices. For example, the loan price for wheat in 1988 was $2.21 a bushel (guaranteed by CCC loan to participating farmers) and the target price was higher at $4.23 a bushel (guaranteed by direct payments for a portion of the crop of participating farmers). Thus, if market price fell to, say, $2.00 a bushel, participating farmers could get $2.21 through price support loans plus $2.02 ($4.23 − $2.21) in direct payments for the quantity of their output so covered.[61]

Direct payments now comprise a major addition to the loan programs for wheat, cotton, rice, and some other crops. Nearly $10 billion was paid directly in 1987, an amount exceeding CCC outlays. (Not all direct payments are in cash, by the way. Since 1986, the Department of Agriculture has switched some subsidies to payments in kind (PIKs). Under the PIK program, certificates are issued to farmers in certain dollar amounts (e.g., $10,000) that can then be redeemed for commodities from the government's massive inventories of wheat, rice, feed grains, or milk—commodities collected under the CCC price support program.[62] In this way the government sheds some surpluses. In the next section, we cover policies that try to prevent surpluses in the first place.)

3. SUPPLY RESTRICTIONS

Depending on how high support prices are set and what market conditions prevail, the surpluses CCC might acquire could be quite high.[63] During the 1980s some surpluses approached amounts that could supply all of America's needs for a full year. Ploys to dispose of such surpluses have proliferated over the years—crop destruction, foreign aid, domestic welfare grants, PIKs, and school lunch larding, some of which are still with us. In 1981 the government handed out roughly $2 billion in surplus milk products, much of it in low-priced sales abroad. (And we accuse others of dumping!)

Of course the best attack against the problem of surpluses (aside from abolishing price supports above equilibrium levels) is supply constraint. Figure 25–11 shows that the surplus of 3.2 billion pounds (8.2 − 5) would vanish if the supply curve could be held back to S_2. This is the essential idea behind various official production restraints that have from time to time graced agricultural policy:

- *Permanent acreage allotments* restrict planting to a fixed number of plots having official permits. More common forty years ago than now, this technique is still used for tobacco and peanuts.
- *Land set-asides* induce grain farmers to restrict planting by offering rewards of price supports (and/or direct income payments) to those who participate. Farmers are given a choice—they either reduce their acreage in the support crop (by percentages that vary yearly) and receive protection, or strike out on their own, plant all they want, and forgo government guarantees.

■ *Marketing agreements* are encouraged by federal laws for some dairymen, orchard owners, and vegetable farmers. These organizations may require their members to withhold or destroy some of their crop. These restrictions need not be associated with specific official price supports, although they elevate price indirectly.

Some idea of the magnitude of past supply restraints can be kindled if America's *total* crop acreage of 350 million acres is mentally compared to some annual figures on set-asides and other acreage reductions. In each of the years 1962, 1966, 1972, 1987, and 1988 more than *60 million* acres were withheld from production, a land area bigger than Nebraska.[64] Set-asides fell toward zero in 1980–1981 because of high export demand and other factors. But they bounced back to record highs above 75 million acres in 1987 and 1988. Do you notice any irony in a subsidy program that discourages rather than encourages output?

C. A Critique of Farm Policy

Many critics of U.S. farm policy favor *some* protection for farmers against temporary downside economic and natural disasters. Hendrik Houthakker of Harvard, for instance, advocates "a distress-loan rate set at very low support levels to temper the extreme variations in crop prices that make it so hard for farmers to plan their capital expenditures and thus to increase their efficiency."[65] As practiced, however, farm policy has been less of a safety net and more of a dole (a "rip-off," Houthakker has said). Among the program's most obvious flaws, we find the following.

1. OBSOLESCENCE
However wise price supports may have been during the Great Depression (or even the 1950s and 1960s), they seem less appropriate today. Farm incomes *were* abnormally low. Output *was*

perhaps overly abundant. But now, after an out-migration of farm population and other developments, farm incomes are on average quite respectable and output is eagerly bought by the world's hungry. Our exports zoomed from $7 billion in 1970 to over $40 billion in 1981 and 1990. Yet another measure of changing conditions is the growing animosity farmers themselves express toward traditional farm policy. The American Farm Bureau Federation (AFBF), a very large lobbying group, urges abandonment of production restraints and calls for lower price support levels. "If market prices are low," says AFBF's Mike Durando, "it should be a signal to farmers that too much wheat is being grown. The government is interfering with that signal system."[66]

2. INEQUITY
Although farm poverty has served as an ostensible reason for farm subsidies, the fact is that the richest farmers hog the bulk of the benefits. In 1987, for example, 26 percent of the farms receiving direct payments had marketings over $100,000, and they received 58 percent of the payments, an average of $30,492 per farm.[67] Knowing that farm subsidies are linked to prices and output rather than income directly, you should not be surprised by this. Don Paarlberg, former Assistant Secretary of Agriculture isn't. He says the subsidies "put nickels and dimes into the pockets of some farmers and wads of dollars into the pockets of others."[68]

3. DISTORTIONS
When cotton is overpriced by government supports, synthetic fibers like nylon, rayon, and polyester capture large slices of the textile trade for no good economic reason. When peanut acreage is held down by allotments to boost prices, competing oil seeds like soybeans and sunflower seeds get an artificial stimulus to sprout, grow, and cover the vegetable oil market. When government subsidies are capitalized in higher land prices, and when the subsidies en-

courage capital-intensive farming (as they have), they might well make farming *more* risky, not less risky. Fluctuations in price now seem to cause greater fluctuations in net income than in earlier times.

These several distortions and many others arise from the farm program simply because that program pushes, pulls, props, and depresses the free market in unnatural ways. Resources are therefore misallocated; inefficiency ensues.[69]

4.   ENVIRONMENTAL PROBLEMS

The research council of the National Academy of Sciences estimates that agriculture causes water pollution damages that might be as high as $16 billion annually. The council blames farm policy, at least in part, because acreage restrictions encourage chemical-intensive farming on the land that remains in production. Moreover, the price-support programs discourage crop rotation, which permits the use of nitrogen-fixing plants as an alternative to heavy doses of synthetic fertilizers.[70]

5.   CONTRADICTIONS

On the one hand government busily tries to restrict agriculture outputs with acreage allotments, land set-asides, and the like. On the other hand, government finances water projects, agricultural research, farmer education, and other means of increasing farm output. One odd result from such inconsistent policies is that something like *two-fifths* of all land made farmable by government-subsidized water projects is planted in price-support crops.[71]

Would the agriculture industry collapse if the government's heaviest props were buried? Probably not. Many sectors of the industry succeed without props. Moreover, the private sector has devices for dealing with the uncertainty and risk that accompany instability. Many farmers now produce under contracts to food processors at fixed prices. (This is the way tomato farmers in New Jersey supply Campbell's Soup, for instance.) Hedging in commodity futures markets

is also possible. A farmer can therefore secure a set price for his crop by selling futures at a guaranteed price before planting.[72] Finally, plowing under the heaviest subsidies need not imply total government withdrawal. Distress-loan rates (or direct payments) set at very low price levels need not produce the problems we have discussed. International arrangements could be made to smooth export fluctuations. The collection an dissemination of agricultural statistics could continue and even grow, providing farmers with better market information and assuaging uncertainty.

What are the chances for major reform? Smaller than a soy bean, it seems. To be sure, minor reforms occur occasionally—as when in 1990 Congress set a limit of $100,000 on the annual amount of direct payments going to any one farmer. But *major* reform seems doubtful, which is why articles appear entitled, "Why Is Agricultural Policy So Difficult to Reform?"[73]

The agrarian myth mentioned earlier explains much of the inertia. Another big influence is the fact that these kinds of policies prevail worldwide. Agriculture is perhaps *the* most heavily subsidized and protected industry of them all. As Table 25–4 indicates, for instance, 66 percent of the income of Japanese farmers can be attributed to protection and subsidy. Correspondingly, Japanese consumers pay 35 percent more for food than they would otherwise. Other countries are not as heavily involved as Japan, but agricultural markets are not "free markets" in any of the free-market economies of Table 25–4. Thus, because "everybody does it," major reforms may appear radical to our citizenry and unfair to our farmers. It has been estimated that U.S. farmers would lose about $26 billion a year if official supports were removed here while those abroad remained in place. Because of the magnitude and prevalence of supports, U.S. farmers would also lose if supports were removed everywhere abroad as well as in the United States, but the losses would then be

Table 25–4
Agricultural Producer and Consumer Subsidy Equivalents by Country or Region,
1986–1987

Country	Producer Benefit as a Percentage of Producer Income	Consumer Cost as a Percentage of Consumer Expenditure
Japan	66%	− 35%
European Community	33	− 17
Other Western Europe	47	− 20
Canada	27	− 15
United States	26	− 8
Australia	12	0
New Zealand	10	0

Source: Vernon O. Roningen and Praveen M. Dixit, *How Level is the Playing Field? An Economic Analysis of Agricultural Policy Reforms in Industrial Market Economies* (Washington, DC: U.S.D.A., Economic Research Service, Report 239, 1989), p. 4.

much less, about 40 percent less.[74] (The disparity in farmers' losses under unilateral versus multilateral liberalization holds for every country. Hence, farmers in each nation resist unilateral liberalization and the "everybody does it" argument thrives. Multilateral liberalization would cost farmers in the countries of Table 25–4 an estimated $65 billion annually, so they resist that, too. But consumers and taxpayers would gain over $100 billion annually from multilateral liberalization, so it would generate large *net* benefits to industrial market societies.[75] If rooted in competition, free markets bear fruit.)

Summary

At this point you may be tempted to turn Winston Churchill's famous words around and murmur to yourself, "Never has so much been done for so few by so many." Taxpayers and consumers, as we have seen, support favored business groups and activities through a wide assortment of promotion and protection policies.

By broad division these interferences with free markets include (1) direct subsidies, (2) loans and loan guarantees, (3) import protection, and (4) agricultural price supports.

1. *Direct subsidies* include tax breaks, direct payments, and government ownership and operation of certain kinds. The basic idea is to have taxpayers pay some of the costs of selected goods and services. With costs reduced, prices for these goods and services are likewise trimmed, encouraging greater output and consumption than otherwise (whether justified by such laudable reasons as external benefits or not).

Tax breaks work by lowering taxes on pet sectors and activities (thereby increasing the tax burdens of others). Energy tax credits have been particularly popular. In contrast, direct payments amount to expenditure handouts. Energy has been blessed here, too, particularly nuclear energy. Transportation, especially railroad and ocean transportation, have also benefited by huge direct payments. Finally, much government ownership embodies subsidization. Our biggest recent example in the United States is the Synthetic Fuels Corporation, which acted as a banker, broker, and buyer for private synfuel companies. The SFC's conceptual grounding was undermined by critics, and its existence by plunging oil prices.

2. *Loans* grant government credit at reduced interest rates. *Loan guarantees* provide borrowers with low-interest private funds secured by government backing. The economic effects of these credit instruments are similar to direct subsidies, although the costs to the Treasury and society are less apparent. Economic costs arise when credit is diverted from worthy nonsubsidized borrowers to less worthy subsidized borrowers. Initial fiscal costs impose burdens for financing the public debt. Ultimate fiscal costs include default losses. Chrysler's loan guarantee and the S&L bailout illustrate the many pros and cons involved here.

3. *Import protection*—whether it be achieved by tariffs, quotas, or voluntary restraint agreements (VRAs)—benefits domestic producers at the expense of society at large. Because free trade promotes international comparative advantage and competitive discipline, the costs of import protection to consumers can be quite large—tens of billions of dollars annually once all inefficiency and transfer effects are taken into account. Recent official protection for steel began in 1969 when steel's 6 percent tariff was supplemented by VRAs extracted from Japanese and European producers. Those restraints ended in 1974, but a new definition of dumping shifted protection to trigger pricing, followed by voluntary quotas. Lately, American steel has gained from a fall in the dollar and a rise in efficient minimills. A VRA for Japanese autos has also been in place to protect America's high-cost, low-quality producers. By building transplants on U.S. soil, the Japanese sidestepped the quota, garnering over 30 percent of all U.S. sales in 1991. The competition from foreign plants and transplants has forced the American producers to improve.

4. *Price supports* in agriculture grew out of the Great Depression, when instability and poverty pummelled the industry. Instability remains a problem but not poverty. Nevertheless, price supports at income-boosting levels persist. The basic idea is to lift selected crop prices with guaranteed price floors, implemented by surplus purchases, land set-asides, and other methods of keeping supplies off the market. The alternative technique of direct income payments allows market prices to fall, yielding substantial benefits over price supports. Direct payments are used for a few crops as a supplement to price supports. Some government intervention seems warranted by the instability problem but only a bushel and a peck. Liberalization would yield large net benefits.

Questions and Exercises for Chapter 25

1. Referring to broad definitions of subsidy, the text says that "every policy reviewed in this chapter could be considered a subsidy." Explain.
2. How would external benefits be drawn in Figure 25–2 to justify the subsidy depicted? Explain your result.
3. Why are tax breaks subsidies?
4. In what ways are direct payments and government ownership alike? In what ways different?
5. Compare and contrast Amtrak and synfuels subsidies in (a) methods, (b) amounts, (c) rationales, and (d) success or failure.
6. Why has privatization become popular? Does it guarantee net gains? Does this trend portend the removal of government from agriculture? Why or why not?
7. What are the economic costs of government loan and loan guarantees?
8. Argue your preferred case on the Chrysler bailout, pro or con.
9. Why do economists favor free trade?
10. What is strategic trade policy? What are its attractions? Drawbacks?
11. Double the tariff in Figure 25–7 and indicate in your own diagram the resulting (a) redistribution effect, (b) loss-due-to-production effect, (c) the tar-

iff revenue effect, and (d) loss-due-to-consumption effect.

12. What made the American steel and auto industries vulnerable to imports?

13. What have been the consequences of import protection in (a) steel and (b) autos?

14. Explain the causes of instability in agriculture?

15. Compare and contrast price supports as shown in Figure 25–11 with direct subsidies shown in Figure 25–2. Why the differences?

16. Why are direct payments an improvement over price supports as a method of government intervention in agriculture? What has been American policy regarding direct payments?

17. Evaluate U.S. farm policy in comparison to a policy of very low, safety-net support.

Notes

1. *Wall Street Journal,* 19 December 1991, p. A3.

2. *Wall Street Journal,* 16 February 1990, p. A1.

3. *Wall Street Journal,* 20 December 1991, p. A2.

4. *Business Week,* December 17, 1990, pp. 60–93.

5. Hendrik S. Houthakker, Testimony, *The Economics of Federal Subsidy Programs,* Hearings, U.S. Congress, Joint Economic Committee, 92nd Congress, 1st Session (1972), p. 14.

6. Carl S. Shoup, *Testimony,* ibid., p. 5.

7. *Wall Street Journal,* 25 June 1981, p. 48. Average subsidy on the Washington-Cincinnati run was much higher at $137 a ticket, so high that it would have been cheaper for the government to close that line and buy airline tickets for the rail travelers affected.

8. Steven A. Morrison, "The Value of Amtrak," *Journal of Law and Economics* (October 1990): 361–382.

9. *Wall Street Journal,* 5 April 1990, pp. A1, A15; 1 May 1991, p. 1B; *Washington Post National Weekly Edition,* May 6–12, 1991, p. 20.

10. Other estimates corroborate this and raise the ranking of Japan and Britain. See Gary C. Hufbauer and Joanna S. Erb, *Subsidies in International Trade* (Washington, DC: Institute for International Studies, 1984), pp. 3–7.

11. S. S. Surrey, "Tax Subsidies as a Device for Implementing Government Policy," *The Economics of Federal Subsidy Programs,* U.S. Congress Joint Economic Committee, 92nd Congress, 1st Session (1972), p. 49.

12. *Wall Street Journal,* 12 March 1981, p. 10.

13. *Washington Post National Weekly Edition,* May 20, 1985, p. 32; August 19, 1985, pp. 6–8. After shipbuilding subsidies ended in the United States, the number of U.S. shipbuilders fell from fifty-seven in 1982 to fourteen in 1990. Those remaining survive on Navy orders. Only one commercial order was given to a U.S. shipyard between 1985 and 1990. *Business Week,* July 9, 1990, p. 58.

14. Kenneth D. Walters and R. Joseph Monsen, "State-Owned Business Abroad: New Competitive Threat," *Harvard Business Review* (March–April 1979): 160–170.

15. Richard E. Caves "Lessons from Privatization in Britain," *Journal of Economic Behavior and Organization* (March 1990): 145–169.

16. *Wall Street Journal,* 20 January 1992, p. A10.

17. For surveys, see John Vickers and George Yarrow, *Privatization: An Economic Analysis* (Cambridge, MA: MIT Press, 1988); and Simon Domberger and John Piggot, "Privatization Policies and Public Enterprise," *Economic Record* (June 1986): 145–162.

18. This point is stressed by J. A. Kay and D. S. Thompson in "Privatization: A Policy in Search of a Rationale," *Economic Journal* (March 1986): 18–32.

19. *Washington Post National Weekly Edition,* May 5, 1986, p. 32.

20. On the other hand, a better way to curb oil imports would have been to tax them and allow domestic prices of oil and gas to rise freely—thereby simultaneously discouraging energy consumption, encouraging conventional domestic energy production, and indirectly encouraging nonconventional synfuels production to the extent warranted by the higher prices. See, e.g., Paul L. Joskow and Robert S. Pindyck, "Synthetic Fuels: Should the Government Subsidize Nonconventional Energy Supplies?," *Regulation* (September/October 1979): 19–23.

21. Murray L. Weidenbaum, *Business, Government, and the Public* (Englewood Cliffs, NJ: Prentice-Hall, 1981), p. 194.

22. The Small Business Administration originated in 1953 as an outgrowth of a Korean war program that funneled military supply contracts to small business. With loans of only $17 billion in 1988, it does not have the capacity to help more than a handful of the country's 10 million small businesses. But support for small business seems to benefit society greatly. It is a striking fact that most new employment in our economy comes not from the big GMs or GEs but from small businesses. A massive study by D. L. Birch of MIT shows that, during the 1970s, small firms (with 20 or fewer employees) generated *two-thirds* of all new jobs in the United States. This was due partly to a shift in the economy toward services, away from manufactures, but it was also due to entrepreneurial spunk. D. L. Birch, "The Job Generation Process," in *Conglomerate Mergers—Their Effects on Small Business and Local Communities, Hearings,* U.S. Congress, House, Subcommittee on Antitrust of the Committee on Small Business, 96th Congress, 2nd Session (1980), pp. 649–671.

23. For details see Robert Reich and John Donohue, *New Deals: The Chrysler Revival and the American System* (New York: Time Books, 1985).

24. *Business Week,* March 24, 1980, p. 104.

25. A major reason auto imports were battering the United States producers during the 1970s is that domestic cars were priced about $1,500 above comparable import models, and $700 to $800 of that price disadvantage was due to higher auto worker wage rates here than abroad. This was not because of higher wages generally in the

United States, as U.S. autoworkers earned high wages even by American standards. Their average wage was 46 percent above the all-manufacturing average in 1979, up from 29 percent in 1960. For more see "Japan's Edge in Auto Costs," *Business Week,* September 14, 1981, pp. 92, 97; "Why Detroit Still Can't Get Going," *Business Week,* November 9, 1981, pp. 106–110; Office of Technology Assessment, *U.S. Industrial Competitiveness: A Comparison of Steel, Electronics, and Automobiles* (Washington DC: U.S. Congress, 1981), pp. 58–60.

26. For an analysis of bankruptcy, see Philip B. Nelson, *Corporation in Crisis: Behavioral Observations for Bankruptcy Policy* (New York: Praeger Publishers, 1981).

27. D. L. Birch, "Job Generation," p. 230.

28. *Wall Street Journal,* 22 April 1981, p. 2; 4 May 1981, pp. 3, 8; *Fortune,* May 4, 1981, pp. 156–164.

29. F. M. Scherer and Keun Huh, "The Determinants of U.S. Intra-Industry Trade," Bureau of the Census, Center for Economic Studies, Discussion Paper CES 90–13, December 1990.

30. See, e.g., Elhanan Helpman and Paul Krugman, *Market Structure and Foreign Trade: Increasing Returns, Imperfect Competition, and the International Economy* (Cambridge, MA: MIT Press, 1985).

31. *Forbes,* July 23, 1990, p. 41.

32. See, e.g., Paul R. Krugman, "Is Free Trade Passé?" *Journal of Economic Perspectives* (Fall 1987): 131–144.

33. For details see Lawrence J. White, *The Automobile Industry Since 1945* (Cambridge, MA: Harvard University Press, 1971); and U.S. Congress, House, Subcommittee on Trade of the Committee on Ways and Means, *Auto Situation: 1980* (Washington, DC: 1980).

34. *The Economist,* September 22, 1990, "Survey of World Trade," p. 25.

35. A. V. Deardorff and R. M. Stern, *An Economic Analysis of the Effects of the Tokyo Round of Multilateral Trade Negotiations,* U.S. Senate, Committee on Finance, Subcommittee on International Trade (June 1979), pp. 41–44.

36. *Wall Street Journal,* 23 December 1981, p. 19.

37. Gary C. Hufbauer and Howard F. Rosen, *Trade Policy for Troubled Industries* (Washington, DC: Institute for International Economics, 1986), p. 5.

38. In general see Walter Adams and Hans Mueller, "The Steel Industry," in Walter Adams, ed., *The Structure of American Industry* (New York: Macmillan, 1986), pp. 74–125; Donald F. Barnett and Louis Schorsch, *Steel: Upheaval in a Basic Industry* (Cambridge, MA: Ballinger, 1983); and Robert W. Crandall, *The U.S. Steel Industry in Recurrent Crisis* (Washington, DC: Brookings Institution, 1981).

39. Donald F. Barnett and Robert W. Crandall, "The American Steel Industry," in *Industry Studies,* ed. Larry L. Duetsch (Englewood Cliffs, NJ: Prentice Hall, forthcoming).

40. U.S. Congress, Office of Technology Assessment, *Technology and Steel Industry Competitiveness* (Washington, DC: 1980), p. 135.

41. Adams and Mueller, "Steel Industry," p. 97.

42. *Wall Street Journal,* 13 December 1989, P. A2; 14 June 1989, p. A16.

43. *Business Week,* June 5, 1989, p. 109.

44. G. C. Hufbauer, D. T. Berliner, and K. A. Elliott, *Trade Protection in the United States: 31 Case Studies* (Washington, DC: Institute for International Economics, 1986), pp. 154–178.

45. *Business Week,* June 5, 1989, p. 109.

46. *Fortune,* May 8, 1989, p. 107.

47. *Wall Street Journal,* 14 June 1989, p. A16.

48. Hufbauer, Berliner, and Elliott, *Trade Protection,* pp. 256–257; and Robert W. Crandall, "The Effects of U.S. Trade Protection for Autos and Steel," *Brookings Papers on Economic Activity* (No. 1, 1987), pp. 271–288.

49. *Wall Street Journal,* 16 February 1990, p. A6.

50. *Wall Street Journal,* 14 January 1991, p. B1.

51. J. P. Womack, D. T. Jones, and D. Roos, *The Machine That Changed the World* (Rawson Associates, 1990). For a review see Alex Taylor, III, "New Lessons from Japan's Carmakers," *Fortune,* October 22, 1990, pp. 165–168.

52. David Wong, "The U.S. Auto Industry in the 1990s," *Business Review* (Federal Reserve Bank of Philadelphia) July–August 1990, p. 17.

53. Robert W. Crandall, "The Effects of U.S. Trade Protection . . . ," *op. cit.,* p. 288.

54. For longer summaries see Robert Z. Lawrence and Robert E. Litan, "The Protectionist Prescription: Errors in Diagnosis and Cure," *Brookings Papers on Economic Activity* (No. 1, 1987), pp. 289–310; and *Economic Report of the President,* 1991, Chapter 7.

55. Basic references include Dale E. Hathaway, *Government and Agriculture: Economic Policy in a Democratic Society* (New York: Macmillan, 1963); Leonard W. Weiss, *Case Studies in American Industry* (New York: John Wiley & Sons, 1980), pp. 21–89; Bruce L. Gardner, *The Governing of Agriculture* (Lawrence: The Regents Press of Kansas, 1981); and David Rapp, *How the U.S. Got Into Agriculture* (Washington, D.C.: Congressional Quarterly, Inc., 1988).

56. This does not take account of our large net exports which would probably boost the number past 60. For statistics such as these see any basic annual, such as the *Economic Report of the President,* or *Statistical Abstract of the United States.*

57. *Statistical Abstract of the United States, 1990,* p. 648. For elaboration see Bruce L. Gardner, "Changing Economic Perspectives on the Farm Problem," *Journal of Economic Literature* (March 1992), pp. 62–101.

58. James T. Bonnen and William P. Browne, "Why Is Agricultural Policy So Difficult to Reform?", in *The Political Economy of U.S. Agriculture,* ed. C. S. Kramer (Washington, DC: Resources for the Future, 1989), p. 12.

59. Estimate of William Lin as cited by Bruce Gardner, "Changing Economic Perspectives on the Farm Problem," *Journal of Economic Literature* (March 1992), p. 89.

60. See Terri Minsky, "Farmers' Confusion on Corn Reserve Plan Could Lead to Problems at Harvest Time," *Wall Street Journal,* 25 September 1980, p. 38.

61. For details see U.S. Department of Agriculture, Economic Research Service, *The Basic Mechanisms of U.S. Farm Policy,* (Publication No. 1479), January 1990.

62. Ibid.; and Rapp, *How the U.S. Got Into Agriculture,* pp. 131–147.

63. For details, see Robert Green and Harry Baumes, "Supply Control Programs for Agriculture," in *Agriculture-Food Policy Review* (Washington, DC: U.S.D.A., Economic Research Service, Report 620, 1989), pp. 143–168.

64. *Ibid.,* pp. 154–155.

65. *Business Week,* April 18, 1977, p. 111.

66. *Fortune,* October 19, 1981, p. 129.

67. *Statistical Abstract, 1990,* p. 649. See also Robert D. Reinsel, "The Distribution of Direct Payments, 1986," in *Agriculture-Food Policy Review* (Washington, DC: U.S.D.A., Economic Research Service, Report 620, 1989), pp. 205–225.

68. *Business Week,* February 11, 1980, p. 58.

69. For an interesting detailed example of distortion, see *Wall Street Journal,* 10 April 1978, p. 28.

70. *Wall Street Journal,* 8 September 1989, p. B7D. See also *Business Week,* June 4, 1990, pp. 140–144.

71. *New Republic,* September 22, 1979, p. 6; *San Jose Mercury News,* 9 March 1988, p. 4A.

72. For more on private mechanisms, see Bruce Gardner, *The Governing of Agriculture* (Lawrence: Regents Press of Kansas, 1981).

73. J. T. Bonnen and W. P. Browne, "Why is Agricultural Policy So Difficult to Reform?" in *The Political Economy of U.S. Agriculture,* ed. C. S. Kramer (Washington, DC, Resources for the Future, 1989), pp. 7–33.

74. Vernon O. Roningen and Praveen M. Dixit, *How Level Is the Playing Field? An Economic Analysis of Agricultural Policy Reforms in Industrial Market Economies* (Washington, DC: U.S.D.A., Economic Research Service, Report 239, 1989), p. 30.

75. *Ibid.,* p. 28. An exception is notable, though. The farmers of Australia and New Zealand would actually gain by multilateral liberalization because they have a comparative advantage in agriculture and they presently rely on little government support.

Chapter 26
Equal Employment Opportunity

We hold these truths to be self-evident,
that all men are created equal . . .
— The Declaration of Independence

Equality, in a vague, abstract sense, has always been a main value in America. Equality in specific, concrete areas, however, has evolved in America only by fits and starts. Freedom for slaves and voting rights for women emerged slowly. Equality in the marketplace has yet to be fully realized, but momentum has been building. Markets for housing, consumer credit, hotel accommodations, and several other goods and services have won the focus of antidiscrimination policies.

Here we consider policies concerning equality in labor markets. Broadly stated, their aim is to secure for minorities equal opportunity regarding employment, wages, fringe benefits, promotion, and work conditions. By legal definition, the minorities so protected now actually comprise a majority of the population—all females, all blacks, all those of Spanish, Asian, Pacific Island, or American Indian ancestry, all those handicapped, all "old" workers between ages 40 and 64, and members of religious and ethnic groups such as Jews, Catholics, Greeks, and Slavs. Before discussing policy, however, we review evidence of the problem addressed by these policies. After discussing the problem and the policies, we evaluate the policies, paying particular attention to affirmative action programs.

I. The Problem of Discrimination

A. Earnings Differentials

Race. On average, blacks earn lower incomes than do whites, and women earn less than do men. These discrepancies have been around a long time—decades, even centuries.

Figure 26–1 illustrates the black/white discrepancy for male income earners over the period from 1963 to 1987. In 1963 working black men earned 25 percent less than working white men did. In 1987 the deficit was 19 percent.

How much of this discrepancy, past and present, can be attributed to racial discrimination

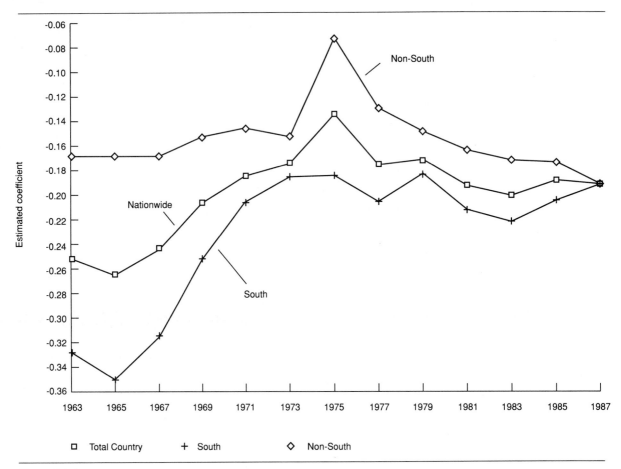

Figure 26–1
Estimated Percentage Black Male Deficit in (hourly wage) Relative to White Males

Source: John J. Donohue III and James Heckman, "Continuous Versus Episodic Change: The Economic Status of Blacks," *Journal of Economic Literature* (December 1991), p. 1610.

in labor markets? Certainly not all of it. Factors other than race influence workers' pay, and blacks and whites differ in these other factors as well as in race. Earnings tend to be lower in southern states as compared to northern and western states (30 percent lower when white Southerners are compared with other whites). Because blacks are disproportionately numerous in the South, part of the overall black-white discrepancy can therefore be explained by geography.

Earnings also rise with education, reflecting returns to investment in "human capital" (economists' jargon for developed or refined productive skills and knowledge). This is shown in Table 26–1, which reports median earnings of year-round, full-time workers by race, sex, and education in 1990. White male college graduates earned $41,089. This was 55 percent more than earned by white males who ended their education after completing high school and 106 percent more than earned by drop outs. Education pays

Table 26–1
Median Earnings of Year-Round, Full-Time Workers, by Race, Sex, and Education, 1990

Race and Sex	Less than High School	Four Years of High School	Four Years or More of College
Earnings			
White male	$19,905	$26,506	$41,089
White female	12,748	16,906	27,435
Black male	16,195	20,283	31,383
Black female	12,359	16,439	26,725
Ratios			
Black men to white men	0.81	0.77	0.76
White women to white men	0.64	0.64	0.67
Black women to white women	0.97	0.97	0.97
Black women to black men	0.76	0.81	0.85

Source: Claudette E. Bennett, *Black Population in the United States: March 1990 and 1989*, Current Population Reports, Series P–20, No. 448 (Washington, DC: U.S. Bureau of the Census, August 1991), p. 3.

off for blacks, too. Because whites complete high school and college with greater frequency than blacks do, education differences, like geographic differences, cause earnings differentials between blacks and whites. Thus, in general, to the extent blacks and whites differ in these and other pertinent respects, their earnings likewise differ, just as the earnings of various whites differ in these respects.

Once these elements are taken into account, however, the effects of labor market discrimination remain glaring. Figure 26–1 shows a past deficit in the South as well as elsewhere, indeed a bigger one than elsewhere. Table 26–1 shows that regardless of educational attainment, black men earned substantially lower median incomes in 1990 than white men did. In fact, the black/white ratio of earnings among men falls with higher educational achievements—0.81 to 0.77 to 0.76. Just how much labor market discrimination contributes to the overall black deficit is difficult to say, but the contribution seems substantial. A recent study of 1980 data estimated that *half* the deficit could be attributed to labor market dis-

crimination, with the balance resulting from education, geography, work experience, marital status, and other factors.[1] Earlier studies estimated that *one-fourth* of the earnings differential could be pinned on labor market discrimination, with the rest being attributable to, among other things, geography, work experience, and education (including the quality of education as well as quantity—that is, differences in school facilities and teacher competence).[2]

Notice that these estimates of one-fourth to one-half refer only to *prevailing labor market discrimination*. They take no account of *past* labor market discrimination against blacks, or *education discrimination*. Thus, the estimates of one-fourth to one-half may understate the economic impact of racial discrimination in general. *Past* labor market discrimination will adversely affect the skill levels and experience of today's black workers, so estimates that assign some of the pay gap to these factors will be less damning of discrimination than they would be otherwise. The same applies to *education discrimination*. Regarding the quality of education, blacks have been disadvantaged because of segregation and schools of poor quality, especially before the 1970s. Regarding years of schooling, blacks could not be expected to stay in school as long as whites if the economic rewards blacks gained from added schooling were severely crimped by labor market discrimination. This differential in payoffs is suggested in Table 26–1 by the growing deficit for black males as their education level rises. In short, then, racial discrimination of various kinds—education discrimination, past labor market discrimination, and prevailing labor market discrimination—might account for a bulky part of the black/white earnings gap.[3] The distinction between *past* discrimination and *prevailing labor market* discrimination is especially useful for our later discussion of policy.

Sex. Table 26–1 discloses a huge pay gap between men and women as well. White women, with a high school education or less, working year-round and full-time, earned only 64 percent of what similarly situated men earned in 1990. College-educated white females earned only 67 cents for every dollar going to their male counterparts. Indeed, the gap gives white and black women *with college degrees* about the same annual earnings as men with no more education than high school—$27,435 and $26,725 for white and black females, respectively, versus $26,506 for male high school graduates.

Because males and females share the same classrooms while growing up, these discrepancies cannot be accounted for by divergent qualities of education, or for that matter by differences in geographic distribution. Some of the pay differential between sexes can be attributed to educational attainments but not as much as one might think. (In 1990 more men, both black and white, had completed college than women, but more women had completed high school than men.[4]) Some of the earnings discrepancies between the sexes can also be blamed on the fact that women often interrupt their careers to raise children, limit their choice of work opportunities to obtain flexible hours, and otherwise meet home responsibilities in ways harmful to their incomes. But only *some*. Accounting for all such factors does not eliminate the earnings differential.

Table 26–2 demonstrates this with data from 1987. Women *without* children experience a much smaller wage gap than women *with* children, so home attachments explain much of the female deficit (e.g., 0.863 versus 0.627). Once age, region, schooling, industry, occupational skill, and other factors are also taken into account, the deficit drops further until, according to these data, females earn 90.7 cents for every dollar of male income. This leaves nearly 10 percentage points, or something on the order of *one–fourth* of the total gap, to be blamed on sex discrimination.

As before, though, we must qualify this estimate. Like the black/white pay deficit, it can be argued that this one-fourth gender gap is an underestimate of discrimination's impact. For example, men stay a longer time in a present job than women do, and this fact is often used as a variable to explain away part of the pay gap. However, discrimination that lowers pay and lowers promotion opportunities for women likewise lowers their incentives for staying in any particular job. When men and women are paid the same, they quit with the same frequency.[5] We may thus speculate that, overall, the experience

Table 26–2

Female-to-Male Hourly Earnings Ratios (1987, White Workers, Ages 20–44)

	With Children	Without Children
Standardized for age and region only	0.627	0.863
Standardized for age, region, schooling, industry, occupational-skill level, and labor force turnover	0.720	0.907

Source: June O'Neill, "Women and Wages," *The American Enterprise* (November/December 1990): 32.

for women might be similar to that for blacks. Discrimination might cause more than *one-fourth* of the gender pay gap. Its impact might approach *one-half* under an expansive interpretation of the data.[6]

B. Specific Kinds of Labor Market Discrimination

Average annual earnings of comparable blacks and whites or comparable females and males can diverge because of (1) hourly *wage rate differences* paid by a given employer, (2) *employment disparities* in hires, layoffs, overtime opportunities, promotions, and job assignments, and (3) *occupational discrimination* such as that which shunts women into nursing instead of full-fledged doctoring. In other words, labor market discrimination takes forms other than the blatant wage rate discrimination that would occur if an employer paid two equally experienced people, working elbow to elbow in exactly the same job, different wage rates. Although there was a time (in 1927) when a New York apparel manufacturer seeking laborers could unabashedly advertise "White Workers $24; Colored Workers $20," that has not been the case for quite a while.[7]

Employment Discrimination. Employment discrimination shows up in unemployment statistics. Nonwhite males consistently experience unemployment rates twice as high as those for white males of comparable age. This, along with the pay gap, discourages blacks from seeking work with the same dedication as whites do, so it has the side effect of lowering black participation in the labor force.[8] When the unemployment effect and labor force participation effect combine, the result is seen in Table 26–3. Table 26–3 reports the percentage of men with *zero* annual earnings from 1939 to 1984 by race. Blacks have always fared worse than whites in these statistics. Notice also that the discrepancy is growing over time. For 20 to 24-year-olds, the black/white ratio jumps from 1.2 in 1939 to 2.0 in 1969 and then to 3.1 in 1984. A major reason for this

Table 26–3
Percentages of Men with Zero Annual Earnings (Unemployed or Not in the Labor Force), 1939–1984

Ages:	20–24	25–54
1939		
Blacks	32	28
Whites	27	25
1949		
Blacks	20	11
Whites	16	7
1959		
Blacks	14	8
Whites	8	5
1969		
Blacks	16	8
Whites	8	4
1979		
Blacks	23	16
Whites	7	5
1984		
Blacks	28	16
Whites	9	5

Source: Gerald D. Jaynes, "The Labor Market Status of Black Americans: 1939–1985," *Journal of Economic Perspectives* (Fall 1990): 21.

change is that, in absolute terms, the incidence of zero earnings among blacks has again headed up toward depression levels after several decades of decline.

Direct confirmation of hiring discrimination comes from a study made by the Urban Institute that sent matched pairs of black and white men to compete for the same jobs in Chicago and Washington, D.C., in 1990. Twenty male college students of conventional appearance—10 white and 10 black—were selected and trained to yield 10 pairs of job seekers similar in mannerisms, language, personality, physique, and interview style. Biographies were created maintaining the similarity of each pair. In all, 576 hiring audits occurred. Each had two men applying in turn for an entry-level job appearing in newspaper want ads, the men being so similar that systematic differences in treatment by employers could be attributed only to race. The good news, as summarized in Table 26–4, was that 73 percent of the audits measured no discrimination. (Unmeasured discrimination is discussed later.) The bad news was that 20 percent of the time the white applicant advanced further than the black in obtaining an application, getting an interview, and in other respects. The black applicant advanced further than the white in 7 percent of the audits. In 15 percent of the audits, the white was offered a job, but his equally qualified black partner was not. The reverse occurred 5 percent of the time. "In sum," the report concludes, "if equally qualified black and white candidates are in competition for a job, when differential treatment occurs, it is three times more likely to favor the white applicant than to favor the black."[9] The study goes on to note that "the reported measures of differential treatment focus on outcomes of the hiring process, and no not include instances of discouraging treatment (negative comments, longer

waits for scheduled appointments, cursory interviews), which were experienced by black applicants in as many as half the audits."

Occupation Discrimination.   Figure 26–2 discloses occupation discrepancies. These disparities, often caused by cultural traditions as well as more overt forms of discrimination, cause women to become clerical workers, secretaries, flight attendants, elementary school teachers, and toilers in other relatively low-paid callings. Blacks still face particularly severe difficulties breaking into the executive ranks of major corporations. Those who do reach high corporate levels tend to be public relations or personnel directors—visible but not exactly venerable positions.[10] Indeed, this observation leads to another, namely, that blacks who do gain access to the better occupations usually end up in the lowest and least desirable jobs *within* each occupation group:

> Within the professional, technical, and managerial class, for example, white workers tend to be lawyers, doctors, engineers, and social scientists. Black workers, on the other hand, are more likely to be funeral directors, welfare workers, and teachers. . . . [Among] clerical workers are grouped both white insurance adjusters and black postal clerks, among salesworkers both white stockbrokers and black newsboys.[11]

Much the same could be said of occupational discrimination against women. Men, for example, make up only a small fraction of elementary school teachers. Yet a disproportionate number of elementary school principals are men.[12]

C. Economic Costs of Discrimination

If we assume, for sake of simplicity, that the labor market could be divided into two similar parts, A and B, then the impact of occupational and employment discrimination can be illustrated in Figure 26–3. Without discrimination, it is assumed that workers could shift between market A and market B fairly freely, with the result

Table 26–4

Results of Urban Institute Audit Study of Employment Discrimination, 1990

Test of Discrepancy	Percentage of All Audits Completed
Who advanced further in *the application process?*	
White favored	20
Black favored	7
Equal treatment	73
Who actually got *a job offer?*	
White favored	15
Black favored	5

Source: M. A. Turner, M. Fox, and R. J. Struyk, *Opportunities Denied, Opportunities Diminished: Discrimination in Hiring* (Washington, DC: Urban Institute Press, Report 91-9, 1991).

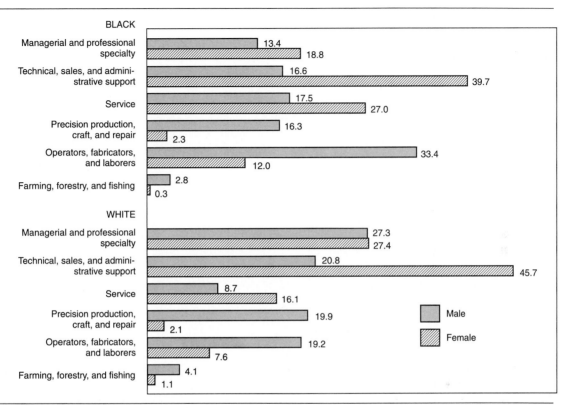

Figure 26–2
Occupational Distribution of the Employed Civilian Labor Force, by Sex and Race: March 1990

Source: Claudette E. Bennett, *The Black Population in the United States: March 1990 and 1989* (Washington, D.C.: U.S. Bureau of the Census, Series P-20, No. 448, August 1991), p. 14.

that labor supply S_A and labor supply S_B would intersect their respective labor demand curves in such a way as to yield the same equilibrium wage in both markets, namely W_E. Wage equality prevails because any difference in wage between markets A and B would cause labor to shift from the low wage sector to the high sector, restoring the original equality.

Once discrimination is introduced, barring blacks from market A, this tendency toward wage equality disappears. Barring blacks from A shifts supply in that market to S'_A. As blacks drift into market B, supply there shifts outward to S'_B. With available labor quantities reduced in A and

expanded in B, equilibrium wage rates diverge to W_A on the high side and W_B on the low side. The obvious implication is that whites in market A gain by the discrimination. Less obvious is the fact that many other whites lose because of the discrimination, in particular, those who work in markets like B, which are open to blacks. While some whites gain and some lose, all blacks lose. Such theorizing can encompass sex biases also.

Aside from microeconomic consequences like these, there are aggregate efficiency losses reducing the nation's output of goods and services. Unemployed, underemployed, and inappropriately employed minority people cannot

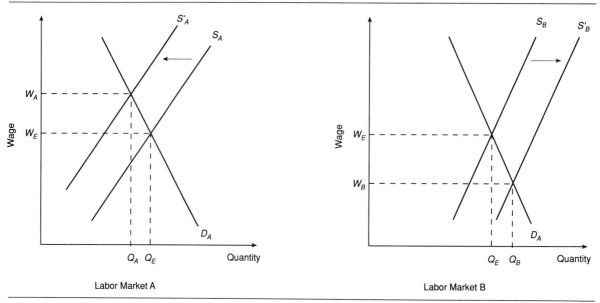

Figure 26–3
The Impact of Occupational Discrimination

produce to their full potential. Denying them the opportunity to perform in jobs best suited to their talents, devotions, and interests deprives society of the full potential fruits of their labors. Putting some round numbers on the nation's economic loss due to racial discrimination, the President's Council of Economic Advisors estimated in 1966 that it was $27 billion annually. That is, if the unemployment rate and average productivity of blacks were equal to those of whites at the time, total production of our economy would have been $27 billion greater than it was.[13]

Labor market discrimination has lessened in some respects since the 1960s, in part because of equal opportunity policies.

II. Equal Opportunity Policies

Federal government antidiscrimination policies are enunciated in a variety of laws and directives, including the Fifth and Fourteenth Amendments to the Constitution and the Pregnancy Discrimi-

nation Act of 1978. Space limitations force us to discriminate against peripheral issues. Our focus is therefore confined to three broad areas: (A) equal employment opportunity *generally*, (B) more stringent policies concerning *government contractors*, and (C) *affirmative action*, which in some configurations is an extreme and controversial form of enforcement common to both areas A and B.

A. Equal Employment Opportunity Generally

Prompted by massive demonstrations and violent riots, the Civil Rights Act was enacted in 1964. Under Title VII of the Act, firms, unions, apprenticeship programs, and employment agencies are prohibited from discriminating against any individual on the basis of race, color, sex, or national origin. The terms of employment so covered include hiring, training, paying, promoting, and firing workers. The 1964 act was expanded by the Equal Employment Opportunity Act of

1972, which amended Title VII. Further amendments passed in 1991. As thus amended, the act applies to all employers with fifteen or more employees, including educational institutions, plus state and local governments.

The Equal Employment Opportunity Commission (EEOC) enforces Title VII, as amended. An independent agency composed of five commissioners, EEOC conducts its enforcement through the following procedures:

1. *Complaint:* Any person, organization, or agency may file a written charge of discrimination.
2. *Informal Investigation:* Informal investigation determines the EEOC's jurisdiction and the seriousness of the charges.
3. *Conciliation:* The EEOC urges the opposing parties to reach voluntary accommodation. If the charges carry weight, conciliation usually entails a promise from the employer to stop discriminating, to take some "affirmative action," and to pay back-wages or other compensation to the claimant.
4. *Suit:* If attempts at reconciliation prove futile, the EEOC can conduct a detailed formal investigation and file suit against the respondent party in federal court.

5. *Remedies:* Court-imposed remedies can be quite severe, including affirmative action of various kinds and back pay.[14]

Besides handling individuals' complaints, 120,000 of which were in backlog at one time, the EEOC may investigate and prosecute cases of systematic discrimination. These are allegations of patterns of employment discrimination throughout an entire company or industry. The most famous of these cases involved American Telephone and Telegraph. In the early 1970s the EEOC accused AT&T and its operating companies of systematic job discrimination against blacks and Spanish-Americans. As for women, AT&T was allegedly "the largest oppressor of women workers in the United States." Telephone operators, at the time 99.9 percent female, suffered "virtually intolerable" working conditions including "authoritarian" work rules and limited opportunities for advancement. AT&T, whose workforce was 13 percent racial minority and 55 percent female, denied the charges but agreed to two consent decrees in 1973 and 1974, the likes of which were momentous. Back pay and salary adjustments for thousands of employees came to $68 million. AT&T also agreed to pursue ambitious percentage goals to put women

---

Thumbnail Sketch 12: Equal Employment Opportunity Commission

Established: 1964

Purpose: To enforce Title VII of the 1964 Civil Rights Act banning discrimination based on race, sex, color, religion, or national origin in hiring, firing, promotion, wages, and all other conditions of employment.

Legislative Authority: Title VII of the Civil Rights Act of 1964; Age Discrimination in Employment Act of 1967; Equal Employment Opportunity Act of 1972; the Pregnancy Discrimination Act of 1978; and the Civil Rights Act of 1991.

Regulatory Activity: The commission (1) investigates charges of discrimination, (2) presses suits in federal court, (3) develops guidelines on employment discrimination.

Organization: An independent agency headed by a five-member commission. The president appoints commissioners with Senate approval.

Budget: 1991 estimate: $196 million.

Staff: 1991 estimate: 3,250.

and minorities into craft jobs and managerial posts (and to attract men into operator and clerical jobs).[15] Since then, "Virtually every decision that's made of a personnel nature has an EEO consideration in it," according to AT&T's director of equal employment and affirmative action, Don Liebers.[16]

The EEOC also has authority to issue regulatory guidelines. Though not legally binding, these guidelines signal the agency's position in future litigation and thereby carry some force in business circles. Recent guidelines address such issues as religious accommodation (arranging time off for those observing non-Christian holi-

Table 26–5
Deciphering the Civil Rights Act of 1991[a]

What the Supreme Court Said	*What the Act Does*
Wards Cove Packing Co. v. *Atonio*, 1989 The court made it the responsibility of an employee to show that an employer used practices adversely affecting women and minorities without any "business necessity."	The act returns the burden of proof to employers, forcing them to justify practices adversely affecting women and minorities. It says employers must show that their employment practices are "job-related . . . and consistent with business necessity," codifying these standards for the first time. It also requires plaintiffs in discrimination cases to specify the hiring or promotion method they consider to have a "disparate impact" on the work force.
Patterson v. *McLean Credit Union*, 1989 The court limited the coverage of a key race discrimination statute to hiring, not discrimination after the person started working. Some 200 claims of harassment on the job, discriminatory firing, or other job bias were dismissed in the first eight months following the ruling.	The act makes it clear that all phases of employment discrimination are covered by law.
Price Waterhouse v. *Hopkins*, 1989 The court said an employer could avoid liability, even if there was proof of intentional discrimination, as long as there was another motive for the challenged job action.	The act makes intentional discrimination unlawful in every case.
Lorance v. *AT&T*, 1989 The court said women who were laid off as the result of an allegedly discriminatory seniority rule should have objected at the time the rule was made, rather than at the time they lost their jobs.	The act lets those harmed by seniority systems challenge them at the time they are actually affected.

[a]The Civil Rights Act was passed to counter several controversial Supreme Court decisions.
Source: The Washington Post, October 31, 1991.

days) and sexual harassment (the problem of male superiors forcing their lustful intentions on female underlings, or vice versa). The EEOC's guidelines on sexual harassment, for instance, say that conduct that "unreasonably" interferes with someone's work performance or breeds "an intimidating, hostile or offensive work environment" is unlawful. This vague language seems to extend the definition of sexual harassment beyond the realms of hiring, promotion, and pay, which federal courts have recognized and attacked. Thus, critics contend that these guidelines "invite an avalanche of questionable charges" concerning "vague, subjective encounters between coworkers" amounting to little more than "innocent flirtation."[17] (As yet there has been no avalanche.)

Enforcement of the Civil Rights Act slowed under the conservative ideology of the Reagan Administration.[18] It slowed further in 1989 when the Supreme Court, freshly stocked with conservative justices, decided a number of civil rights cases in a manner that weakened the law substantially. Table 26–5 summarizes them. All have now been negated by the Civil Rights Act of 1991, which was passed in response to the Supreme Court's decisions.

Wards Cove Packing Company v. *Atonio* tops the list in significance. Before the Supreme Court's decision in this case, people who felt wronged could sue their employer, claiming that some hiring practice, such as an aptitude test, had an adverse "disparate impact" on a protected group even though there may have been no discriminatory intent by the employer. Once adverse disparate impact was proven (by a showing, for instance, that few members of the protected group could pass the test), then the burden of proof shifted to the employer to show that the practice (i.e., the exam) was job related. In *Wards Cove* the Supreme Court put the entire burden of proof on the plaintiff—proof that the practice was *not* job-related as well as proof of its adverse disparate impact. Thus, the 1991 Civil Rights Act restored the earlier interpretation.

Now, if a plaintiff proves the disparate impact of a practice, the burden of proof again shifts to the employer to show that the allegedly discriminatory practice is "job-related" for the position in question and consistent with "business necessity." Failure of the employer to do so implies a violation. Under *Wards Cove* and the other 1989 decisions, employers had the advantage over plaintiffs. Now the legal leverage has shifted back toward its earlier fulcrum.

B. Policy Toward Government Contractors

In 1980, Firestone Tire & Rubber Company received word from Washington that it could no longer sell goods and services to the federal government. The potential cost to Firestone? About $40 million annually. The reason for purging Firestone from the roster of government contractors? A dispute over affirmative action at one of its Texas plants.[19]

Legal authority for such action against federal contractors rests not on Title VII of the Civil Rights Act but on Executive Order #11246, promulgated by President Johnson in 1965 and adhered to by subsequent presidents. Like Title VII, the order prohibits discrimination by race, color, religion, and national origin. Unlike Title VII, this order is enforced by the Office of Federal Contract Compliance (OFCC), a division of the Department of Labor, which has set standards for federal contractors above and beyond those of Title VII:

> It requires (1) an analysis of all major job classifications and an explanation of why minorities may be underutilized; (2) the establishment of goals, targets, and affirmative action commitments designed to relieve any shortcoming identified; and (3) the development and supply of data to government organizations.[20]

The specifics of these standards reached severely detailed dimensions before the Reagan Administration relaxed them in 1981. The number of affirmative action steps required of construction contractors was, for example, reduced from six-teen to nine. Various paperwork and reporting requirements were scrapped or trimmed. And goals for minority hiring were made less stringent. Still, the standards exceed those of EEOC under Title VII.

The importance of this niche in the law should not be overlooked. Most enterprises of any significant size are federal contractors. Those with contracts worth at least $50,000 are supposed to take affirmative action to hire and promote women and minorities (although those with fewer than 250 employees and contract business of less than $1 million are exempt from preparing any *written* affirmative action plans). The regulations cover 30 million workers.

C. Affirmative Action

When one individual has a *right,* others must perform duties to honor that right. You have, for example, a right to peacefully assemble with others, a right that permits you to go to a movie theater. Others are duty bound not to detain you. However, getting into the theater is merely a "liberty," for if the theater is full, no one is obligated to give you his or her seat.

Similarly, the original idea behind the Civil Rights Act was to give minorities and women the "right" to *equal opportunity,* not the "right" to a job. The duty of employers thereafter was to give no consideration to race, color, and so on. Employers were not obliged to give women and minorities jobs or to promote them. As Senator Hubert Humphrey, a champion of civil rights, explained during Senate debate on the bill:

> Nothing in Title VII . . . tells any employer whom he may hire. What the bill does . . . is simply to make it an illegal practice to use race as a factor in denying employment. It provides that men and women shall be employed on the basis of their qualifications, not as Catholic citizens, not as Jewish citizens, not as colored citizens, but as citizens of the United States.[21]

Obvious exceptions were allowed. Kosher butchers must, for instance, meet certain reasonable religious criteria, but the gist is clear. Employment procedures could no longer consider groups of people, only *individuals*. And since this was merely a procedural change, there was no guarantee that results would change (that workforce composition would actually change), only that *opportunities* would improve for the disadvantaged.

Problems arose, however, in interpreting what was meant by "equal opportunity," problems associated with the fact that prevailing labor market discrimination accounted for only a fraction of observed group discrepancies. As we have seen, *educational discrimination* and *past labor market discrimination* played major roles. Thus, one question to arise was this: To what extent could an employer demand of his job applicants aptitude tests, work experience, or educational prerequisites? Could a night club owner refuse to hire go-go dancers lacking two or more years of college? Could restaurant managers require passing grades on spelling tests of those seeking jobs as waitresses and cooks? In 1971, the Supreme Court ruled in *Griggs* v. *Duke Power* that seemingly "neutral" requirements for hiring, job placement, or promotion could not be used if they had a "disparate impact" on protected groups unless such requirements could be shown to have a "demonstrable relationship to successful performance" on the job.[22] This is what the 1991 Civil Rights Act confirmed after the *Wards Cove* hiatus.

Affirmative action also evolved. This entails preferential treatment for minorities and women instead of strict neutrality. In its most innocent guise, this might mean deliberate selection of the black person when choosing between a black and a white of precisely equal qualifications (rather than, say, flipping a coin). Slightly more intense affirmative action occurs when employers make special efforts to recruit minorities and women or to help them acquire training. Posting job vacancy notices in black schools or black churches that were previously ignored illustrates these possibilities. On yet a higher plateau of affirmative action, employers set goals and timetables against which to measure their efforts. Such goals might specify certain percentages of minorities and women in various job classifications, but they need not be considered mandatory. Finally, affirmative action came to include quota systems, which assign slots in hiring, training, or promoting minorities and women in some fixed proportion to the slots assigned to unprotected job candidates, white males in particular. Proportions for either goals or quotas are usually based on some estimates of the proportions prevailing in locally available work forces. And the art of designing goal or quota systems has developed into an elaborate, complex science, now thought worthy of sophisticated statistical techniques that we cannot discuss here.[23]

The main problem with affirmative action goals and quotas is that they move away from *individual opportunity* toward *group results,* thereby fostering if not exactly promoting "reverse" discrimination. When Congress passed the Civil Rights Act of 1964, it stressed that nondiscrimination should not be interpreted as requiring any employer "to grant preferential treatment to any individual or to any group" on the basis of any statistical "imbalances" in its work force. Yet the Equal Employment Opportunity Commission and the Office of Federal Contract Compliance have in the past required employers to adopt specific goals and quotas to erase statistical imbalances. Strictly speaking, these official efforts have been confined to government contractors and to instances of proven past illegal discrimination. The courts have upheld these remedies insofar as they were merely "goals" or, if genuine quotas, were "necessary correctives for the employer's past discrimination." Nevertheless, such affirmative action has stirred bitter controversy.

Of all the affirmative action cases to reach the Supreme Court, none has been more controversial than the *Weber* case of 1979, which held that *employers and unions could establish voluntary programs incorporating quotas even when there was no evidence of past discrimination by the employer.*[24] The employer in question was Kaiser, whose Gramercy, Louisiana, plant had a labor force of craft workers (electricians, machinists, and so on) that was only 2 percent black, a considerably smaller number than the 39 percent black composition of the Gramercy area labor force generally. During the 1970s, Kaiser tried to recruit *already trained* black craftsmen but found very few. Escalating its efforts, Kaiser, in agreement with the local union, set up an in-plant training program that would admit one black for every one white until the percentage of black craft workers equalled 39 percent (a goal that would take an estimated thirty years to realize). Black and white applicants were selected according to seniority within their respective racial groups. Thus, it came to pass in 1974 that Brian Weber, a white man, was repeatedly turned down for craft training even though he had more seniority than several successful black candidates.

Weber sued, challenging the 50 percent minority quota under Title VII of the Civil Rights Act. A Supreme Court majority of five decided against Weber, however, Justice Brennan's opinion stressed three things:

1. *The voluntary and temporary nature of the program.* ". . . since the Kaiser-USWA plan was adopted voluntarily, we are not concerned with what Title VII requires or with what a court might order to remedy a past proven violation of the act." Although Congress did say that government could not "*require* any employer . . . to grant preferential treatment . . . on account of a de facto racial imbalance in the employer's work force," Congress never said that voluntary preferential treatment was *impermissible.* "The natural inference is that Congress chose not to forbid all voluntary race-conscious affirmative action."

2. *The problem of historic disadvantage:* "The purposes of the [Kaiser] plan mirror those of the statute. Both were designed to break down old patterns of racial segregation and hierarchy. Both were structured to 'open employment opportunities for Negroes in occupations which have been traditionally closed to them.'"

3. *Legislative intent:* "The prohibition of racial discrimination . . . of Title VII [a literal reading of which Weber relies upon] must . . . be read against the background of the legislative history of Title VII and the historical context from which the Act arose. Examination of those sources makes clear that an interpretation of the sections that forbade all race-conscious affirmative action would 'bring about an end completely at variance with the purpose of the statute' and must be rejected."

Chief Justice Burger and Justice Rehnquist dissented. Burger accused the majority of rewriting Title VII "to achieve what it regards as a desirable result." Rehnquist vigorously complained that the majority's holding was a "tour de force reminiscent not of jurists . . . but of escape artists, such as Houdini. . . . Quite simply, Kaiser's racially discriminatory admission quota is flatly prohibited by the plain language of Title VII."

Thus, the arguments written in the *Weber* opinion, pro and con, reflect the arguments surrounding affirmative action in the press, in Congress, in scholarly papers, and, indeed, in the workplace.[25] Those *favoring* strong affirmative action tend to stress fairness in results set against a backdrop of regrettable history:

> [It] is fundamental that civil rights without economic rights are mere shadows.
> —*Judge Charles R. Weiner*[26]

The courts have acknowledged that it is simply not enough to say, at this point in time, "all persons should have equal opportunity;" given the fact that discrimination against women and minorities was a matter of national policy and common practice, that in essence racism has been as much a part of our history in this country as the Declaration of Independence.
> —*Congresswoman Shirley Chisholm*[27]

> [There are reasons] to believe that our society operates so as to pass on from one generation to the next that racial inequality originally engendered by historical discrimination. [So we should not] expect the continued application of racially *neutral* procedures to lead eventually to an outcome no longer reflective of our history of discrimination.
> —*Professor Glenn C. Loury*[28]

In contrast, those who *oppose* affirmative action stress fairness in procedures and impracticalities:

> Under the present bureaucratic formulation, affirmative action is, in reality, affirmative discrimination.
> —*Senator Jesse Helms*[29]

> What gives our government the right to decide which group is the most deserving of special treatment? And how do they make these decisions? Obviously, blacks have suffered in the past. . . . But how does one decide that blacks need more special consideration than Jews, . . . or the Italians, the Irish, or the Chinese?
> —*Senator S. I. Hayakawa*[30]

> No one can really know what the "results" of a truly nondiscriminatory employment policy would be for any particular employer: workers do not distribute themselves among firms in a perfectly random manner, and there is no reason to suppose that job qualifications (education, experience, talent, proven integrity, or ambition) are distributed in precise, statistically even proportions across every ethnic group at every level of employment.
> —*Professor Jeremy Rabkin*[31]

Recently, some minority people have come to oppose affirmative action, or at least to feel ambivalent about it, saying:

> [It] has opened doors that would have remained shut, forced companies to look to employment groups they had ignored, and decreased racism by

Table 26–6
Responses of 202 CEOs of Fortune 500 and Service 500 Companies (1989)

Question: Which of the following statements comes closest to describing your own company's affirmative action activities?

Answer:

We have affirmative action goals but no numerical quotas.	54%
We have specific quotas for hiring and promoting.	18%
We hire and promote on merit and talent alone.	14%
Other.	14%

Source: Fortune, March 13, 1989, p. 88.

prodding workplace integration. But it has also brought unwelcome baggage: assumptions that minorities were hired only because of race, and what may be unwarranted skepticism about their abilities. This makes some minorities fear that even promotions and accomplishments they earn by working harder than their peers won't be respected.[32]

Supreme Court Justice Clarence Thomas (who was EEOC chairman under Reagan) distinguishes himself as a black who opposes affirmative action. Indeed, Justice Thomas illustrates that the composition of the Supreme Court has changed to the point where a case like *Weber* might now be decided differently.

Although the court's composition has changed and affirmative action has been weakened by the Reagan and Bush Administrations, affirmative action remains popular with many corporate executives. An opinion poll taken by *Fortune* and CNN News proves revealing. Table 26–6 reports the responses of 202 CEOs of Fortune 500 and Service 500 companies to a key question in the poll—namely, what are the affirmative action activities of your company? Almost three-quarters of the respondents, 72 percent, said they used goals or quotas, mostly the former.

Why this support for something so controversial? When asked to characterize the results of affirmative action programs in private U. S. enterprises, 68 percent of the *Fortune*/CNN respondents rated them as "good," "very good," or "outstanding." Another 29 percent thought the results were "fair." Only 3 percent gave responses of "poor" or "not sure."[33] An earlier *Fortune* poll disclosed that CEOs liked affirmative action because it improved employee morale, enlarged pools from which to hire workers, and (according to some people in management) improved productivity.[34] (Notice that, with goals instead of quotas, businesses need not feel pushed. Businesses apparently achieve their goals only about 10 percent of the time.[35])

III. Evaluation

The precise impact of equal employment opportunity policies is impossible to measure. If one looks at individual cases one can find evidence of substantial progress. For example, a 1979 study of the changes wrought in AT&T as a result of its 1973 consent decree reveals, among other things, that:

- Women increased their share of all management jobs from 22.4 to 28.5 percent.
- Blacks held 12 percent of Bell system jobs in 1979, up from 10.6 percent in 1973.
- Hispanic employment went from 2.5 to 3.9 percent.[36]

More qualitatively, a spokesman for a Bell Operating Company has said that, before the consent decree, "We were not using all the talent available." But under the decree, the company discovered that its minority and female workers were a "gold mine" for high-quality managers.[37]

On the other hand, evidence from specific cases is not always good. Murray Weidenbaum cites possibilities in St. Louis to suggest that affirmative action could have perverse effects:

> A company could avoid the entire problem [of Title VII] by locating its new plants in largely white communities, making it more difficult for minority group applicants to obtain jobs. In such an event, the EEOC's actions would hurt the very people it is trying to help.[38]

Aggregate data more reflective of the overall picture indicate progress in some respects but continued problems in others. According to the numbers in Table 26–7, the pay gap between white males and others has been falling over the past several decades. Most striking are the significant gains shown for black women, whose earnings have previously been lower than for any group reported. Notice, however, that Table 26–

7 compares only the *earnings* of those *who actually have jobs*. Those without jobs are ignored. And as we saw earlier in Table 26–3, there is a growing gap between black and white men when it comes to having any job at all.

If we set aside the bad news and concentrate on the good news in the aggregate statistics, we must next confront the question of whether government policy has contributed to the good news. The answer emits complexities because the progress we observe in Table 26–7 could be caused by factors other than the Civil Rights Act and its amendments. In fact, some analysts argue that the law has had no effect whatever, that the observed changes can be attributed to trends set in motion before the Civil Rights Act appeared in 1964.

Granted the presence of enough mixed evidence to preclude universal agreement, a preponderance of solid evidence indicates that, on the whole, the Civil Rights Act has made a positive contribution to equal opportunity. Look back at Figure 26–1, for instance. The black male pay deficit was greatest in the southern states before 1964 and civil rights enforcement concentrated on the South. Correspondingly, almost all the reduction in the nationwide average deficit since 1964 stems from a reduction of the racial pay gap in the South. This evidence undermines claims that pre-1964 trends should be credited instead of the Civil Rights Act. The pre-1964 trend toward racial equality in earnings was caused largely to black migration from the South, where wages were relatively low, to the North, where wages were relatively high. This black outmigration slowed toward zero after 1965.[39]

Apart from helping to reduce the pay gap between the races, the Civil Rights Act has several other achievements that are worth summarizing:

Table 26–7
Median Earning Ratios of Year-Round, Full-Time Workers, by Race and Sex, 1969 to 1989

Race and Sex	1969	1979	1989
Ratios			
Black men to White men	0.67	0.73	0.72
White women to White men	0.58	0.59	0.66
Black women to White women	0.79	0.93	0.92
Black women to Black men	0.68	0.74	0.85

Source: Claudette E. Bennett, *Black Population in the United States: March 1990 and 1989*, Current Population Reports, Series P-20, No. 448 (Washington, DC: U. S. Bureau of the Census, August 1991), p. 11.

1. Equal employment opportunity policy, affirmative action in particular, has raised the occupational level of nonwhite males, something that partially explains the reduced pay deficit of nonwhite males.

2. Affirmative action policy for government con-tractors increased the employment of blacks and women at contractor establishments when that policy was enforced during the 1960s and 1970s. During the Reagan and Bush Adminis-trations, when enforcement dropped mark-edly, the rate of employment improvement for blacks and women likewise fell substantially.
3. The largest gains from policy have been by black women, as reflected in the general earn-ings statistics of Table 26–7. Under the affir-mative action programs of federal contractor firms, black women have enjoyed especially rapid advancement.
4. On the whole, white women have experienced no more than negligible benefits from the pol-icy. White women have gained in their share of employment in the economy as a whole and also in relative income earnings. But these changes cannot be credited to equal employ-ment opportunity policy except only ten-uously and marginally.[40]

Thus, overall, the policy has had a positive impact. Discrimination has abated. The exact magnitudes in earnings, employment, and occu-pation remain somewhat uncertain, but they seem positive and substantial on balance. In-deed, the changes have been large enough to give those who oppose affirmative action a new ar-gument—namely, that affirmative action is no longer needed, that reverse discrimination now outweighs regular discrimination. Solid evidence contradicts this contention (see, e.g., Table 26–4 again), but the argument's mere existence seems complementary of the policy. It also points out the possibility that, however effective these pol-icies have been in the past, they may not be ef-fective in the future.

Summary

Abundant data from decades past indicate sub-stantial labor market discrimination against mi-norities and women. As recently as 1990, the median earnings of year-round, full-time black and female workers were 28 and 34 percent be-low those of comparable white males. These pay gaps are partially explained by regional varia-tions, education attainments, and the like. Yet once these factors are accounted for, gaps still remain—gaps attributable to prevailing labor market discrimination, past labor market dis-crimination, and past education discrimination—gaps at least one-quarter the size of the original unadjusted pay gaps.

Labor market discrimination can take three forms: (1) wage rate differences among fellow employees, (2) employment bias in terms of hir-ing, firing, layoffs, overtime, promotion, and the like, and (3) occupational discrimination. The first of these is easily detected and remedied, so it has not been much of a problem for quite a while. The latter two are more subtle and persis-tent, so it is not surprising that current policy fo-cuses most heavily on them. Direct evidence of employment discrimination has been obtained from audits in which matched pairs of white and black males compete for the same jobs.

Title VII of the 1964 Civil Rights Act, as amended in 1972, crowns federal policy in this area. It prohibits all labor market discrimination based on race, color, sex, or national origin. The Equal Employment Opportunity Commission, which enforces Title VII, can right individual or systematic wrongs by force of moral suasion or court action. Government contractors face ad-ditional and more stringent standards under Executive Order #11246, which is implemented by the Office of Federal Contract Compliance in the Department of Labor.

Of all enforcement techniques employed by these agencies, none has sparked more contro-versy than affirmative action goals and quotas. Courts have found goals legal as long as they re-main mere "goals" (even if diligently pursued). Quotas were for a long time limited to instances of proven past illegal discrimination, and there-fore could not be required of employers gener-ally. Quotas voluntarily and temporarily used to correct racial imbalance were approved in the *Weber* case, prompting outcries of reverse discrimination and worse. Still, *Weber* has lost its punch. Quotas remain a rarity compared to other forms of affirmative action and pure merit (Table 26–6).

Debate over affirmative action is likely to continue. Presidents Reagan and Bush abandoned the pursuit of quotas and goals. The Supreme Court made proof of discrimination more difficult in 1989, which also deflated equal opportunity efforts. On the other hand, Congress repaired the court's damage, and major businesses still seem supportive of affirmative action other than quotas.

The economic lot of minorities and women has recently improved substantially in many respects. Improvements in education and other factors have propelled much of this change. Policy also deserves substantial credit regarding nonwhites (male and female). White females, in general, have been helped no more than marginally.

Questions and Exercises for Chapter 26

1. To what extent can disparities in income earnings be attributed to employment discrimination? Explain.
2. How is employment discrimination manifested?
3. How is occupation discrimination manifested?
4. What are the equity and efficiency implications of employment discrimination?
5. What written authority makes employment discrimination illegal generally? Government contractor discrimination?
6. Identify EEOC and OFCC in (a) scope of authority, (b) procedures, and (c) remedies.
7. Given three types of discrimination influencing earnings disparities—educational, *past* labor market, and *prevailing* labor market discrimination—which is (are) the main concern of equal opportunity in the narrow, procedural sense? Which is (are) addressed by affirmative action?

8. Can you identify differing value judgments on the two sides of the affirmative action debate? Or differing definitions and priorities among value judgments?
9. What has been the trend in minority and sexual disparities over time? Why has the contribution of policy been disputed?
10. What has been the contribution of policy?
11. Compare and contrast the *Weber* and *Wards Cove* cases.

Notes

1. Jeremiah Cotton, "On the Discrimination of Wage Differentials," *Review of Economics and Statistics* (May 1988): pp. 236–243.

2. Bradley R. Shiller, *The Economics of Poverty and Discrimination* (Englewood Cliffs, NJ: Prentice Hall, 1973), pp. 125–126.

3. *Ibid.*, p. 126. For more on racial discrimination and earnings, see the collection of papers in *Journal of Economic Perspectives* (Fall 1990): 3–84; and Gerald D. Jaynes and Robin M. Williams, eds., *A Common Destiny: Blacks and American Society* (Washington, DC: National Academy Press, 1989). A few conservative commentators deny that discrimination is significant. Thomas Sowell, for instance, contends, "Not only history but also economics argues against the widespread assumption that group income differences are largely a function of discrimination, rather than human capital differences for differences in age, geographic distribution and other factors." *Wall Street Journal*, 4 December 1980, p. 22.

4. Claudette E. Bennett, *Black Population in the United States: March 1990 and 1989* (Washington, DC: U.S. Census Bureau, Series P-20, No. 448, August 1991), p. 31.

5. Barbara R. Bergmann, "Does the Market for Women's Labor Need Fixing?" *Journal of Economic Perspectives* (Winter 1989): 43–60.

6. Hilda Kahne, "Economic Perspectives on the Roles of Women in the American Economy," *Journal of Economic Literature* (December 1975): 1259–1261; Mary Corcoran, "The Structure of Female Wages," *American Economic Review* (May 1978): 165–170.

7. Orley Ashenfelter, "Changes in Labor Market Discrimination Over Time," *Journal of Human Resources* (Fall 1970): 403–430.

8. Bennett, *Black Population*, p. 22.

9. M. A. Turner, M. Fix, and R. J. Struyk, *Opportunities Denied, Opportunities Diminished: Discrimination in Hiring* (Washington, DC: Urban Institute Press, Report 91-9, 1991), p. 32. Similar results were found for an audit matching Hispanics and Anglos—H. Cross *et al.*, *Employer Hiring Practices: Differential Treatment of Hispanic and*

Anglo Job Seekers (Washington, DC: Urban Institute, 1990).

10. *Wall Street Journal,* 9 July 1980, pp. 1, 23.

11. Shiller, *Economics of Poverty,* p. 129.

12. *Wall Street Journal,* 25 February 1981, p. 25. See also Bergmann, "Women's Labor Needs," pp. 46–52. Of course, sexism can operate against men who want to become secretaries, nurses, and flight attendants, as well as against women who want to become truck drivers, lawyers, and engineers.

13. *Economic Report of the President 1966* (Washington, DC: 1966), p. 10. For an updated estimate of $37.6 billion in 1978 see C. C. Ciccone and J. D. Fisk, "An Estimate of the Loss in Potential Gross National Product . . . ," in U. S. Congress, Joint Economic Committee, *The Cost of Racial Discrimination,* Hearings, 96th Cong., 1st Sess., (1980), pp. 2–5.

14. For details, see e.g., *Federal Regulatory Directory, 1979–80.* (Washington, DC: Congressional Quarterly, Inc., 1979), pp. 182–185; *Promises and Perceptions: Federal Efforts to Eliminate Discrimination,* U. S. Commission on Civil Rights (1981), pp. 17–28; or David P. Twomey, *A Concise Guide to Employment Law: EEO & OSHA* (Cincinnati, OH: South-Western Publishing, 1986).

15. Lester A. Sobel (ed.), *Quotas & Affirmative Action* (New York: Facts On File, 1980), pp. 84–87.

16. Carol Loomis, "AT&T in the Throes of 'Equal Employment,' " *Fortune,* January 15, 1979, p. 56.

17. Joann Lublin, "Guidelines-Happy at the EEOC?" *Wall Street Journal,* 28 August 1980, p. 16.

18. Susan C. Faludi, "Women Lost Ground in the 1980s," *Wall Street Journal,* 18 October 1991, p. B4.

19. *Wall Street Journal,* 22 July 1980, p. 28.

20. G. F. Bloom and H. R. Northrup, *Economics of Labor Relations* (Homewood, IL: Irwin, 1977), p. 712. For details see *Promises . . . ,* pp. 5–16.

21. Quoted in Sobel, p. 2.

22. *Griggs* v. *Duke Power Company,* 401 U. S. 424 (1971).

23. For an entire book of techniques, see Harold P. Hayes, *Realism in EEO* (New York: John Wiley & Sons, 1980).

24. *Kaiser Aluminum & Chemical Corp.* v. *Weber,* 443 U. S. 193 (1979).

25. For accessible yet articulate pro and con commentaries on *Weber* by two noted legal scholars see Ronald Dworkin, "How to Read the Civil Rights Act," *New York Review of Books,* December 20, 1979, pp. 37–43; Bernard Meltzer, "The Weber Case: Double Talk and Double Standards," *Regulation* (September/October, 1979), pp. 34–43.

26. Quoted in Sobel, *Quotas and Affirmative Action,* p. 20.

27. Ibid., p. 5.

28. Glenn C. Loury, "Is Equal Opportunity Enough?" *American Economic Review* (May 1981): 124. (Emphasis added). See also U. S. Commission on Civil Rights, *Affirmative Action in the 1980s: Dismantling the Process of Discrimination* (1981).

29. Sobel, *Quotas and Affirmative Action,* p. 3.

30. Ibid., p. 6.

31. Jeremy Rabkin, "The Stroke of a Pen," *Regulation* (May/June, 1981): p. 16.

32. *Wall Street Journal,* 27 June 1989, p. 1A.

33. Alan Farnham, "Holding Firm on Affirmative Action," *Fortune,* March 13, 1989, p. 87.

34. Anne B. Fisher, "Businessmen Like to Hire by the Number," *Fortune,* September 16, 1985, pp. 26–30.

35. *Newsweek,* December 30, 1985, p. 67. See also Jonathan S. Leonard, "Women and Affirmative Action," *Journal of Economic Perspectives* (Winter 1989): 69–71.

36. Sobel, *Quotas and Affirmative Action,* p. 87.

37. *Washington Post National Weekly Edition,* August 27, 1984, p. 23.

38. Murray L. Weidenbaum, *Business, Government, and the Public* (Englewood Cliffs, NJ: Prentice Hall, 1981), p. 148.

39. John J. Donohue III and James Heckman, "Continuous Versus Episodic Change: The Economic Status of Blacks," *Journal of Economic Literature* (December 1991): 1603–1643. See also the papers in *Journal of Economic Perspectives* (Fall 1990): 3–84.

40. Leonard, "Women and Affirmative Action," pp. 61–75. On Britain see A. Zabalza and Z. Tzannatos, "The Effect of Britain's Antidiscriminatory Legislation on Relative Pay and Employment," *Economic Journal* (September 1985): 679–699.

List of Abbreviations Used

AT&T	American Telephone & Telegraph Company
BAT	best available technology
BOC	Bell operating company
BPT	best practical technology
CAB	Civil Aeronautics Board
CCC	Commodity Credit Corporation
CPSC	Consumer Product Safety Commission
EEC	European Economic Community
EEOC	Equal Employment Opportunity Commission
EPA	Environmental Protection Agency
FCC	Federal Communications Commission
FDA	Food and Drug Administration
FERC	Federal Energy Regulatory Commission
FPC	Federal Power Commission (FERC predecessor)
FPLA	Fair Packaging and Labeling Act
FTC	Federal Trade Commission
GAO	General Accounting Office
GTE	General Telephone & Electronics, Inc.
IBM	International Business Machines, Inc.
ICC	Interstate Commerce Commission
LATA	Local Access and Transport Area
MCI	Microwave Communications Incorporated
NHTSA	National Highway Traffic Safety Administration
NIOSH	National Institute for Occupational Safety and Health
NRA	National Recovery Administration

OECD	Organization for Economic Cooperation and Development
OMB	Office of Management and Budget
OPEC	Organization of Petroleum Exporting Countries
OSHA	Occupational Safety and Health Administration
OSHRC	Occupational Safety and Health Review Commission
PBX	private branch exchange
PCM	plug compatible peripheral manufacturer
R&D	research and development
RFC	Reconstruction Finance Corporation
SEC	Securities and Exchange Commission
SFC	Synthetic Fuels Corporation
TIL	truth-in-lending
UHF	ultra high frequency
UN	United Nations
UNCTAD	United Nations Conference on Trade and Development
VHF	very high frequency

Glossary

aggregate concentration The total economic activity, very broadly defined, accounted for by leading firms, e.g., percent of corporate assets controlled by the top 200 corporations.

allocation efficiency The ideal levels of output for goods and services, or ideal *mix* of outputs. Also known as Pareto optimality when coupled with technical efficiency.

averaged fixed cost Total fixed costs divided by quantity.

average variable cost Total variable cost divided by quantity.

average total cost The sum of average fixed and average variable cost. Also the total cost divided by quantity.

Bell operating company The telecommunications companies that provide local and intra-LATA telephone service, including most importantly the seven regional companies formed after the breakup of AT&T.

benefit-cost analysis Policy assessment that weighs the monetary benefits against the monetary costs, derived from the notion of allocation efficiency or Pareto optimality.

broad standards Vague, generalized concepts of what are desirable targets for safety, health, and environmental regulation, although some broad standards, like the ambient air standards for air pollution, are rather specific.

cartel An agreement among sellers not to compete in some way, usually by fixing price or allocating territories.

certification Legal approval of a firm's actions—for trucking goods, selling a certain drug, and the like.

collusive conduct Tacit or explicit agreement among competitors not to compete (on price or some other variable of potential rivalry).

common carrier Providing service to others (as opposed to own use) at a price, without the usual rights of refusal to sell.

common property resource A resource open to anyone's use.

comparative advantage If two nations (or regions) have different opportunity costs of producing a good, then the nation with the lower opportunity cost has a comparative advantage in that good.

concentration ratio Share of market sales accounted for by the top four, eight, or some other absolute number of firms in the market.

conduct (in markets) The strategies or behavior of firms in a market regarding prices, promotion, output, and the like.

conglomerate firms Firms that operate in diverse markets, e.g., banking, insurance, and auto rentals.

conglomerate merger The merger of two or more firms from different, unrelated markets.

consent decree Legally binding out-of-court settlement of a civil prosecution.

consumer sovereignty The notion that people's preferences are stable and they should be fully respected.

consumers' surplus The amount consumers would be willing to pay for some good *less* the amount they actually pay. Example: You might be willing to pay $4 for a McDonald's Big Mac, and if it were that expensive, that is what you would actually pay. However, they sell for less. The difference is "consumers' surplus."

cost effectiveness Minimizing the cost of achieving some set goal (whose benefits may not be measurable). Alternatively, maximizing the benefit achieved from the expenditure of some fixed cost (which may be fixed by budget limits).

cost-of-service pricing Prices that fully reflect the costs associated with providing a particular service or product. The "costs" may be marginal costs or average total costs.

cream skimming Supplying an especially profitable market while ignoring other, related, but less profitable (even unprofitable) markets. It often arises because of cross-subsidy.

credence goods Those that cannot be evaluated through inspection or normal use.

cross elasticity of demand The percentage change in the quantity of one product divided by the percentage change in price of another product.

cross-subsidy Raising price on one good or service, thereby earning excess profits that are used to reduce price below cost on another good or service.

demand Quantity of a product that would be purchased at various possible prices during some period. Can refer to market-wide demand or individual firm demand.

direct loans Loans granted by the government, usually at interest rates much below those of private lenders.

direct subsidy Tax breaks, direct payments , or government ownership and operation to promote certain business interests.

economic profit Profit in excess of "normal" profit, i.e., above the opportunity cost of capital.

economic regulation Regulation covering traditional economic matters, e.g., antitrust and public utility regulation.

economies of scale Technical efficiencies associated

with large-scale operations that lower the cost per unit of a product or service.

elasticity of demand Percentage change in quantity demanded divided by percentage change in price. "Elastic" if greater than one. "Inelastic" if less than one.

entry barriers Advantages that firms already in a market have over potential new-entrant firms.

equity The issue of who gets the goods and services produced. As an ideal, not clearly defined.

error of commission Purchasing more of a product or brand than would occur with full knowledge.

error of omission Purchasing less of a product or brand than would occur with full knowledge.

exclusionary conduct Actions that may exclude rivals from a market or substantially weaken them.

exclusive dealing A seller prohibits his buyers from buying goods from the seller's rivals.

experience goods Those that the buyer can evaluate only after purchase, through experience.

external benefits Benefits experienced by people outside the market, e.g., the benefits of education to nonstudents.

external costs Costs imposed on people outside the market, e.g., the costs of pollution.

field surveillance Backup to monitoring that includes investigation of consumer complaints and annual inspection of cars on the road.

fixed costs Those that, in terms of total dollars, do not vary with output, e.g., property taxes.

functional discounts Price discounts based on type of buyer, e.g., wholesale buyer versus retail buyer.

government The process within a group for making and enforcing decisions.

health regulation Protection against risk of disease.

Herfindahl-Hirschman Index (H-Index) The sum of the squares of market shares. Pure monopoly would be 10,000.

horizontal merger The merger of two or more firms in the same market.

imperative ethic Judging actions or rules to be morally right or wrong in and of themselves, regardless of their consequences or end effects.

imperfect competition Market conditions fall short of

the perfectly competitive ideal because of monopoly power, collusive behavior, or lack of full knowledge.

institution Selected elements of a scheme of values mobilized to accomplish a particular purpose or function.

intermodal competition Competition between modes of transport—e.g., trucks, railroads, airlines, etc.

intramodal competition Competition between carriers of a certain mode—e.g., competition between trucking companies.

lifeline rate An especially low price for a limited quantity of public utility service in order to assist poor households.

load factor A measure of capacity utilization. The amount actually supplied as a percentage of the amount that could be supplied at full use.

loan guarantees Loans of private lenders that are guaranteed by the government against risks of default.

local loop the line connecting telecommunications terminal equipment to a central switch.

long lines Long distance telecommunications connections, now primarily comprised of microwave, satellites, and fiber optic cables.

marginal cost The added cost due to the additional output of one more unit.

marginal revenue The change in total revenue due to the sale of one more unit of output.

marginal social benefit Added benefit to society of producing one more unit of output, including any external benefits.

marginal social cost Added cost to society of producing one more unit of a product, including any external costs.

market An organized process by which buyers and sellers exchange goods and services for money.

market failures Instances when the market fails to achieve efficiency even in cases of perfect competition, e.g., external costs.

market imperfections Deviations from perfect competition, such as fewness of firms, barriers to entry, and misformation.

monitoring Sample testing, inspecting, and related efforts to check compliance with social regulations.

monopoly (pure) Market with one firm, blocked entry, and no close substitutes.

monopoly power Power to control price and exclude competitors, at least to some degree.

multinational corporations Those with wholly owned foreign subsidiaries, partially owned foreign joint ventures, or patent and trademark licensing arrangements abroad.

narrow standards Specific standards of design or performance that apply to firms for purposes of social regulation.

natural monopoly Monopoly caused by technical necessity, e.g., large economies of scale relative to demand.

nolo contendere Out-of-court settlement of a criminal prosecution which is not an admission of guilt.

normal profit Profit which matches the investors' opportunity cost of capital, i.e., that which is sufficient to keep capital committed to a firm.

oligopoly Market with a few firms and difficult entry, where the product may be either differentiated (e.g., soda pop) or standardized (e.g., alumimum ingots).

original cost Determining the rate base by using the "actual" or "book" cost of assets.

Pareto optimality A situation where no one can be made better off without making someone else worse off. Also allocation efficiency coupled with technical efficiency.

patent Legal grant of monopoly over the use of an invention for 17 years.

perfect competition A market with a very large number of small, knowledgeable buyers and sellers, easy entry, and homogeneous product.

performance (of markets) The achievements or end results of the market process, particularly as they apply to the basic questions raised by scarcity, namely, what, how, who, and what's new (the ideal answers being allocation efficiency, technical efficiency, equity, and brisk progress).

permit Legal approval of a firm's actions, e.g., the permit to build an oil refinery at a certain location.

per se rule Proof of violation only requires proof that the offending conduct actually occurred. The reasonableness of the situation or surrounding circumstances or effects are irrelevant.

predatory practices Aggressive behavior causing deliberate short-run losses (e.g., deep price cutting) in order to make long-run gain once rivals are driven from the field, or disciplined, or deterred from entry.

price ceiling A legally set maximum price.

price discrimination A seller sells the same commodity or service at more than one price. (More broadly, variations in price/cost ratios.)

price floor A legally set minimum price.

price level regulation Regulation of the overall level of a firm's prices, allowing enough total revenue to cover costs and a "fair" rate of profit.

price structure regulation Regulation of the prices charged to different buyers, for different quantities, at different times, etc.

private line service Telecommunications service dedicated to a single user.

product differentiation Nonprice variations across brands (or firms) of a given product, usually due to advertising, style, trademark, and the like.

public goods Goods collectively consumed with zero marginal cost to supply an additional consumer.

quality disclosure Contents labeling, grade rating, and other measures designed to reveal product quality.

quantity discounts Price discounts based on the quantity purchased at one time.

quota A physical limit on the quantity of goods that may be imported.

rate base The value of the assets of a regulated public utility, which is multiplied by a percentage rate of return to calculate the interest and profit allowed to the utility.

remedies Enforcement activity that sets penalties or attempts to alter behavior, e.g., recalls, fines, divestitures, plant closures, and so forth.

replacement cost The estimated cost of replacing a utility's assets with modern plant and equipment at current prices.

reproduction cost The estimated cost of building a utility's rate base at current prices.

resale price maintenance A manufacturer or other supplier sets the price that their distributors (retailers) must charge, usually minimum resale prices.

risk A probability of hazard to safety, health, or environmental quality.

rule of reason Extensive analysis of such things as circumstances, consequences, and motives in order to judge guilt.

safety regulation Protection against violent accidents, such as auto crashes or workplace accidents. More generally, risk regulation.

search goods Those that the buyer can evaluate prior to purchase.

social regulation Regulation of health, safety, equal employment opportunity, and other such "social" matters.

standardization Policies that promote product simplification or uniformity in order to aid interbrand comparisons.

structure (of markets) Variables such as the number of firms, market shares, condition of entry, and the degree of product differentiation, which are fairly stable over time and influence market conduct and performance.

subsidy Government payment, tax break, or modification of the market mechanism for the benefit of limited sectors of the economy.

supply The quantities offered for sale at various possible prices during some period.

tariff A levy (like a tax) on the importation of goods.

technical efficiency Production at lowest possible cost. Ideal answer to the How? question.

teleological ethic Judgment of right or wrong based on the end results or ultimate nonmoral consequences produced by an act or policy.

territorial price discrimination Lower prices in one territory as compared to others.

territorial restrictions A manufacturer gives distributors exclusive territories or assigned locations.

tying A seller sells one line of goods only if the buyer purchases others also.

value-of-service pricing Varying prices according to the "value" of the service to the buyer as measured by elasticity of demand, i.e., low elasticity is charged a high price while high elasticity gets a low price.

values (or value judgments) Generalized concepts of what is desirable, e.g., efficiency, equity, and freedom.

variable costs Those that, in terms of total dollars, rise with added output, e.g., materials and fuel costs.

vertical integration Operation at more than one stage

of the production-distribution process, e.g., an auto company that makes its own steel.

vertical merger The merger of two firms in a buyer/supplier relationship.

volume discounts Price discounts based on the volume purchased over some time period.

workable competition Structural conditions that are as decentralized and open as technology might permit, plus conduct that is vigorously competitive. The "ideal," given the impossibility of perfect competition.

X-inefficiency Technical inefficiency (high cost production) due to lassitude, slack, mismanagement, inertia, and the like.

Name Index

Case Index

Subject Index